Mc Graw Hill connect™

Student Quick Tips

Use this Student Quick Tips guide for a quick and easy start with McGraw-Hill Connect. You'll get valuable tips on registering, doing assignments, and accessing resources, as well as information about the support center hours.

Getting Started

TIP: To get started in Connect, you will need the following:

- Your instructor's Connect Web Address

  Sample of Connect Web Address:

  http://www.mcgrawhillconnect.com/class/instructorname_section_name

- Connect Access Code

TIP: If you do not have an access code or have not yet secured your tuition funds, you can click "Free Trial" during registration. This trial will provide temporary Connect access (typically three weeks) and will remind you to purchase online access before the end of your trial.

Registration and Sign In

1. Go to the Connect Web Address provided by your instructor
2. Click on **Register Now**
3. Enter your email address

TIP: If you already have a McGraw-Hill account, you will be asked for your password and will not be required to create a new account.

4. Enter a registration code or choose **Buy Online** to purchase access online

McGraw Hill connect™

(Continued: **Registration and Sign In**)

5. Follow the on-screen directions

TIP: Please choose your Security Question and Answer carefully. We will ask you for this information if you forget your password.

6. When registration is complete, click on **Go to Connect Now**
7. You are now ready to use **Connect**

Trouble Logging In?

- Ensure you are using the same email address you used during registration
- If you have forgotten your password, click on the "Forgot Password?" link at your Instructor's Connect Course Web Address
- When logged into Connect, you can update your account information (e.g. email address, password, and security question/answer) by clicking on the *"My Account"* link located at the top-right corner

Home (Assignments)

TIP: If you are unable to begin an assignment, verify the following:

- The assignment is available (start and due dates)
- That you have not exceeded the maximum number of attempts
- That you have not achieved a score of 100%
- If your assignment contains questions that require manual grading, you will not be able to begin your next attempt until your instructor has graded those questions

(Continued: **Home Assignments**)

TIP: Based on the assignment policy settings established by your Instructor, you may encounter the following limitations when working on your assignment(s):

- Ability to Print Assignment
- Timed assignments – once you begin a "*timed assignment*," the timer will not stop by design

TIP: "*Save & Exit*" vs. "*Submit*" button

- If you are unable to complete your assignment in one sitting, utilize the "*Save & Exit*" button to save your work and complete it at a later time
- Once you have completed your assignment, utilize the "*Submit*" button in order for your assignment to be graded

Library

TIP: The *Library* section of your Connect account provides shortcuts to various resources.

- If you purchased ConnectPlus, you will see an *eBook* link, which can also be accessed from the section information widget of the *Home* tab
- *Recorded Lectures* can be accessed if your instructor is using *Tegrity Campus* to capture lectures. You may also access recorded lectures when taking an assignment by clicking on the projector icon in the navigation bar
- Many McGraw-Hill textbooks offer additional resources such as narrated slides and additional problems, which are accessible through the *Student Resources* link

Reports

TIP: Once you submit your assignment, you can view your available results in the *Reports* tab.

- If you see a dash (-) as your score, your instructor has either delayed or restricted your ability to see the assignment feedback
- Your instructor has the ability to limit the amount of information (e.g. questions, answers, scores) you can view for each submitted assignment

Need More Help?

CONTACT US ONLINE

Visit us at:

www.mcgrawhillconnect.com/support

Browse our support materials including tutorial videos and our searchable Connect knowledge base. If you cannot find an answer to your question, click on "Contact Us" button to send us an email.

GIVE US A CALL

Call us at:

1-800-331-5094

Our live support is available:

Mon-Thurs:	8 am – 11 pm CT
Friday:	8 am – 6 pm CT
Sunday:	6 pm – 11 pm CT

Financial and Managerial Accounting

5th edition

INFORMATION FOR DECISIONS

John J. Wild

University of Wisconsin at Madison

Ken W. Shaw

University of Missouri at Columbia

Barbara Chiappetta

Nassau Community College

ACC 212

NORTHERN VIRGINIA COMMUNITY COLLEGE

Volume 2

Mc Graw Hill Education

1 2 3 4 5 6 7 8 9 0 BRP BRP 17 16 15 14

ISBN-13: 978-1-259-33495-5
ISBN-10: 1-259-33495-3

Learning Solutions Consultant: Dave Fleming
Project Manager: Nina Meyer

Adapting to the Needs of Today's Students

Financial and Managerial Accounting, 5e

Enhancements in technology have changed the spectrum of how we live and learn in the world today. Being able to download and work with learning tools on smart phones, tablets, or laptop computers empowers students to drive their own learning by putting increasingly intelligent technology into their hands.

No two students are alike, and whether the goal is to become an accountant or a businessperson or simply to be an informed consumer of accounting information, *Financial and Managerial Accounting (FinMan)* has helped generations of students succeed by giving them support in the form of leading-edge accounting content that engages students, paired with state-of-the-art technology that elevates their understanding of key accounting principles.

With *FinMan* on your side, you'll be provided with **engaging content** in a **motivating style** to help students see the relevance of accounting. Students are motivated when reading materials that are clear and pertinent. *FinMan* excels at engaging students. Its chapter-opening vignettes showcase dynamic, successful entrepreneurial individuals and companies guaranteed to **interest and excite students, and highlights the usefulness of accounting to those business owners**. This edition's featured companies—**Polaris, Arctic Cat, KTM,** and **Piaggio**—captivate students with their products and annual reports, which are a pathway for learning financial statements. Further, this book's coverage of the accounting cycle fundamentals is widely praised for its clarity and effectiveness.

FinMan also delivers innovative technology to help student performance. ***Connect Accounting*** provides students with instant grading and feedback for assignments that are completed online. With our new **Intelligent Response Technology,** we are taking our accounting content to the next level, delivering assessment material in a **more intuitive, less restrictive** format that adapts to the needs of today's students.

Our new content features:

- **a general journal interface** that looks and feels more like that found in practice.
- **an auto-calculation** feature that allows students to focus on concepts rather than rote tasks.
- **a smart (auto-fill) drop-down design**.

The end result is content that better prepares students for the real world. *Connect Accounting* also includes digitally based, interactive adaptive learning tools that provide an opportunity to engage students more effectively by offering varied instructional methods and more personalized learning paths that build on different learning styles, interests, and abilities, allowing students to work at their own pace.

McGraw-Hill LearnSmart™ is an intelligent learning system that uses a series of adaptive questions to pinpoint each student's knowledge gaps. LearnSmart then provides an optimal learning path for each student, so that they spend less time in areas they already know and more time in areas they don't. The result is LearnSmart's adaptive learning path that helps students retain more knowledge, learn faster, and study more efficiently.

Our **Interactive Presentations** teach each chapter's core learning objectives in a rich multimedia format, bringing the content to life. Your students will come to class prepared when you assign Interactive Presentations. Students can also review the Interactive Presentations as they study.

Guided Examples provide students with narrated, animated, step-by-step walkthroughs of algorithmic versions of assigned exercises. Students appreciate the Guided Examples because they can help students learn accounting and complete assignments when outside of class.

Connect Plus Accounting integrates a media-rich online version of the textbook with *Connect Accounting*.

> "This is an excellent book that is well-written and contains excellent illustrations. It has the best online supplements of any of the texts that I have reviewed. . . . This is an excellent book that I would recommend to all of my colleagues."
>
> **— KAREN CRISONINO, County College of Morris**

About the Authors

JOHN J. WILD is a distinguished professor of accounting at the University of Wisconsin at Madison. He previously held appointments at Michigan State University and the University of Manchester in England. He received his BBA, MS, and PhD from the University of Wisconsin.

Professor Wild teaches accounting courses at both the undergraduate and graduate levels. He has received numerous teaching honors, including the Mabel W. Chipman Excellence-in-Teaching Award, the departmental Excellence-in-Teaching Award, and the Teaching Excellence Award from the 2003 and 2005 business graduates at the University of Wisconsin. He also received the Beta Alpha Psi and Roland F. Salmonson Excellence-in-Teaching Award from Michigan State University. Professor Wild has received several research honors and is a past KPMG Peat Marwick National Fellow and is a recipient of fellowships from the American Accounting Association and the Ernst and Young Foundation.

Professor Wild is an active member of the American Accounting Association and its sections. He has served on several committees of these organizations, including the Outstanding Accounting Educator Award, Wildman Award, National Program Advisory, Publications, and Research Committees. Professor Wild is author of *Fundamental Accounting Principles, Financial Accounting, Managerial Accounting,* and *College Accounting*, each published by McGraw-Hill/Irwin. His research articles on accounting and analysis appear in *The Accounting Review, Journal of Accounting Research, Journal of Accounting and Economics, Contemporary Accounting Research, Journal of Accounting, Auditing and Finance, Journal of Accounting and Public Policy*, and other journals. He is past associate editor of *Contemporary Accounting Research* and has served on several editorial boards including *The Accounting Review*.

In his leisure time, Professor Wild enjoys hiking, sports, travel, people, and spending time with family and friends.

KEN W. SHAW is an associate professor of accounting and the Deloitte Professor of Accounting at the University of Missouri. He previously was on the faculty at the University of Maryland at College Park. He received an accounting degree from Bradley University and an MBA and PhD from the University of Wisconsin. He is a Certified Public Accountant with work experience in public accounting.

Professor Shaw teaches financial accounting at the undergraduate and graduate levels. He received the Williams-Keepers LLC Teaching Excellence award in 2007, was voted the "Most Influential Professor" by three School of Accountancy graduating classes, and is a two-time recipient of the O'Brien Excellence in Teaching Award. He is the advisor to his School's chapter of the Association of Certified Fraud Examiners.

Professor Shaw is an active member of the American Accounting Association and its sections. He has served on many committees of these organizations and presented his research papers at national and regional meetings. Professor Shaw's research appears in the *Journal of Accounting Research; Contemporary Accounting Research; Journal of Financial and Quantitative Analysis; Journal of the American Taxation Association; Strategic Management Journal; Journal of Accounting, Auditing, and Finance; Journal of Financial Research*; and other journals. He has served on the editorial boards of *Issues in Accounting Education and the Journal of Business Research*. Professor Shaw is co-author of *Fundamental Accounting Principles, Managerial Accounting,* and *College Accounting*, published by McGraw-Hill.

In his leisure time, Professor Shaw enjoys tennis, cycling, music, and coaching his children's sports teams.

BARBARA CHIAPPETTA received her BBA in Accountancy and MS in Education from Hofstra University and is a tenured full professor at Nassau Community College. For the past two decades, she has been an active executive board member of the Teachers of Accounting at Two-Year Colleges (TACTYC), serving 10 years as vice president and as president from 1993 through 1999. As an active member of the American Accounting Association, she has served on the Northeast Regional Steering Committee, chaired the Curriculum Revision Committee of the Two-Year Section, and participated in numerous national committees. Professor Chiappetta has been inducted into the American Accounting Association Hall of Fame for the Northeast Region. She had also received the Nassau Community College dean of instruction's Faculty Distinguished Achievement Award. Professor Chiappetta was honored with the State University of New York Chancellor's Award for Teaching Excellence in 1997. As a confirmed believer in the benefits of the active learning pedagogy, Professor Chiappetta has authored Student Learning Tools, an active learning workbook for a first-year accounting course, published by McGraw-Hill/Irwin.

In her leisure time, Professor Chiappetta enjoys tennis and participates on a U.S.T.A. team. She also enjoys the challenge of bridge. Her husband, Robert, is an entrepreneur in the leisure sport industry. She has two sons—Michael, a lawyer, specializing in intellectual property law in New York, and David, a composer, pursuing a career in music for film in Los Angeles.

Dear Colleagues/Friends,

As we roll out the new edition of *Financial and Managerial Accounting,* we thank each of you who provided suggestions to improve our textbook. As teachers, we know how important it is to select the right book for our course. This new edition reflects the advice and wisdom of many dedicated reviewers, symposium and workshop participants, students, and instructors. Our book consistently rates number one in customer loyalty because of you. Together, we have created the most readable, concise, current, accurate, and innovative accounting book available today.

Throughout the writing process, we steered this book in the manner you directed. Reviewers, instructors, and students say this book's enhanced presentation, graphics, and technology cater to different learning styles and helps students better understand accounting. *Connect Plus Accounting* offers new features to improve student learning and to assist instructor teaching and grading. You and your students will find all these tools easy to apply.

We owe the success of this book to you and other instructors who graciously took time to help us focus on the changing demands of today's students and their learning needs. We feel fortunate to have witnessed our profession's extraordinary devotion to teaching. Your feedback and suggestions are reflected in everything we write. Please accept our heartfelt thanks for your dedication in helping today's students learn, understand, and appreciate accounting.

With kindest regards,

John J. Wild *Ken W. Shaw* *Barbara Chiappetta*

McGraw-Hill connect plus+ | ACCOUNTING

Adapting to the Needs of

McGraw-Hill *Connect Plus Accounting* is a complete online assignment, learning, and textbook assessment solution that connects your students with the tools and resources needed to achieve success through faster learning, more efficient studying, and higher retention of knowledge. Key features found in *Connect Plus Accounting* include:

Intelligent Response Technology Intelligent Response Technology is *Connect Accounting's* new student interface for end-of-chapter assessment content. Intelligent Response Technology provides a general journal application that looks and feels more like what you would find in a general ledger software package, improves answer acceptance to reduce student frustration with formatting issues (such as rounding), and, for select questions, provides an expanded table that guides students through the process of solving the problem.

"I like that this system was formatted like real-world accounting is."

—**Student, Rose State College**

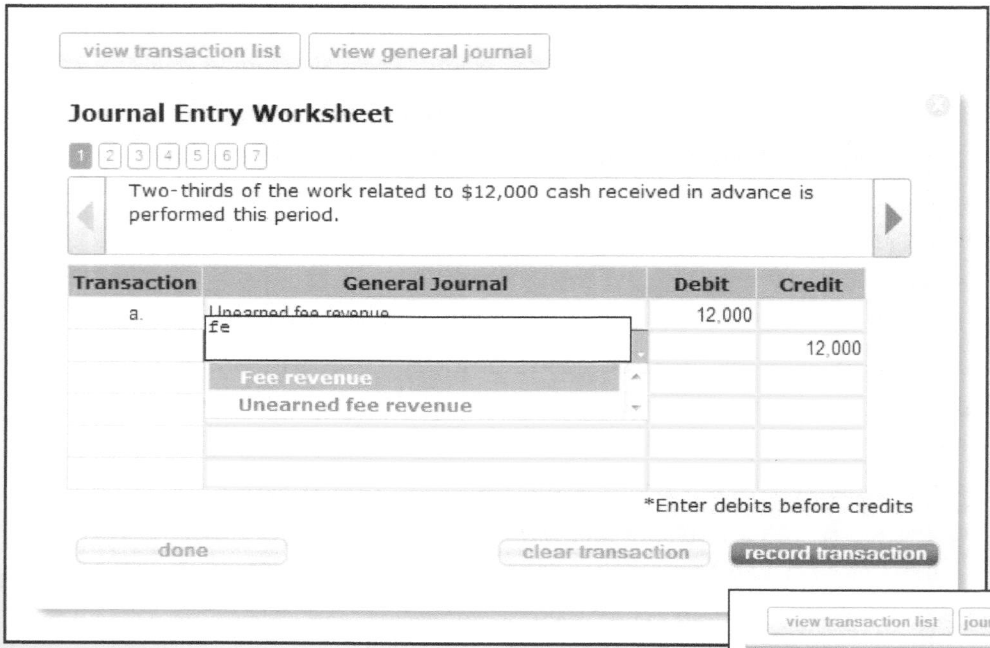

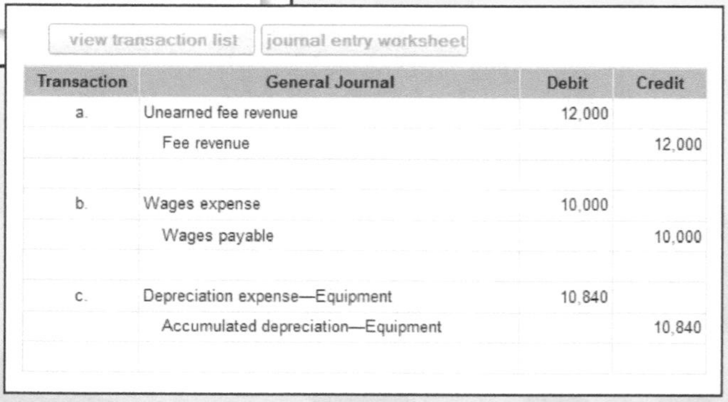

"I love how the general journal was set up. It felt like what I would be filling out if I had an accounting job."

—**Student, Chabot Community College**

Today's Students!

1. Complete the table to determine the cost assigned to ending inventory and cost of goods sold using specific identification.

Specific Identification

Available for Sale				Cost of Goods Sold			Ending Inventory		
Date	Activity	Units	Unit Cost	Units Sold	Unit Cost	COGS	Ending Inventory-Units	Cost Per Unit	Ending Inventory-Cost
Mar. 1	Beginning Inventory	150							
Mar. 20	Purchase	220							
Mar. 30	Purchase	90							
		460				$ 0			$ 0

contact MH Publishing | check my work | View Hint #1 | references | ebook & resources

BIZKID COMPANY
Income Statement
For Year Ended August 31, 2011

Sales	✓		$ 218,880 ✓
Less: Sales discounts	✓	$ 3,349 ✓	
Less: Sales returns and allowances	✓	14,446 ✓	17,795
Net sales	✓		201,085
Cost of goods sold	✓		85,312 ✓
Gross profit	✓		115,773
Expenses			
Selling expenses			
Sales salaries expense	✓	29,987 ✓	
Rent expense-selling space	✓	10,287 ✓	
Store supplies expense	✓	2,627 ✓	
Advertising expense	✓	18,605 ✓	
Total selling expenses			61,506
General and administrative expenses			
Accounts payable	✗	876 ✓	
Accum-depreciation - store equipment	✗	9,785 ✗	
Total general and administrative expenses			10,661
Total expenses			72,167

BIZKID COMPANY
Income Statement
For Year Ended August 31, 2011

Sales		$ 218,880
Less: Sales discounts	$ 3,349	
Less: Sales returns and allowances	14,446	17,795
Net sales		201,085
Cost of goods sold		85,312
Gross profit		115,773
Expenses		
Selling expenses		
Sales salaries expense	29,987	
Rent expense-selling space	10,287	
Store supplies expense	2,627	
Advertising expense	18,605	
Total selling expenses		61,506
General and administrative expenses		
Office salaries expense	876	
Rent expense-office space	2,627	
cf		3,503
Cost of goods sold		65,009
Office salaries expense		
Office supplies expense		
Rent expense office space		

ask your instructor a question | report a content issue | check my work | references

Connect Accounting helps students learn more efficiently by providing feedback and practice material when they need it, where they need it. *Connect* grades homework automatically and gives immediate feedback on any questions students may have missed.

"This system has improved the journal entry and T-account set-up processes to more accurately resemble the way it is done in class."

—Student, Tallahassee Community College

Adapting to the Needs of

Interactive Presentations *Connect Accounting's* Interactive Presentations teach each chapter's core learning objectives and concepts through an engaging, hands-on presentation, bringing the text content to life. Interactive Presentations harness the full power of technology to truly engage and appeal to all learning styles. Interactive Presentations are ideal in all class formats—online, face-to-face, or hybrid.

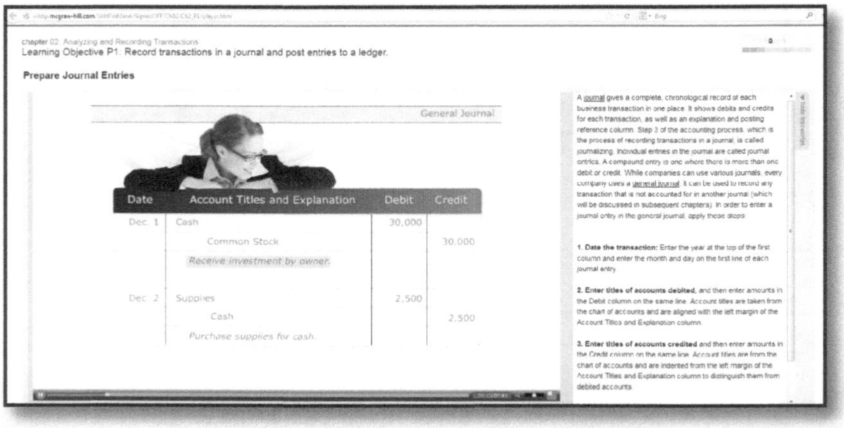

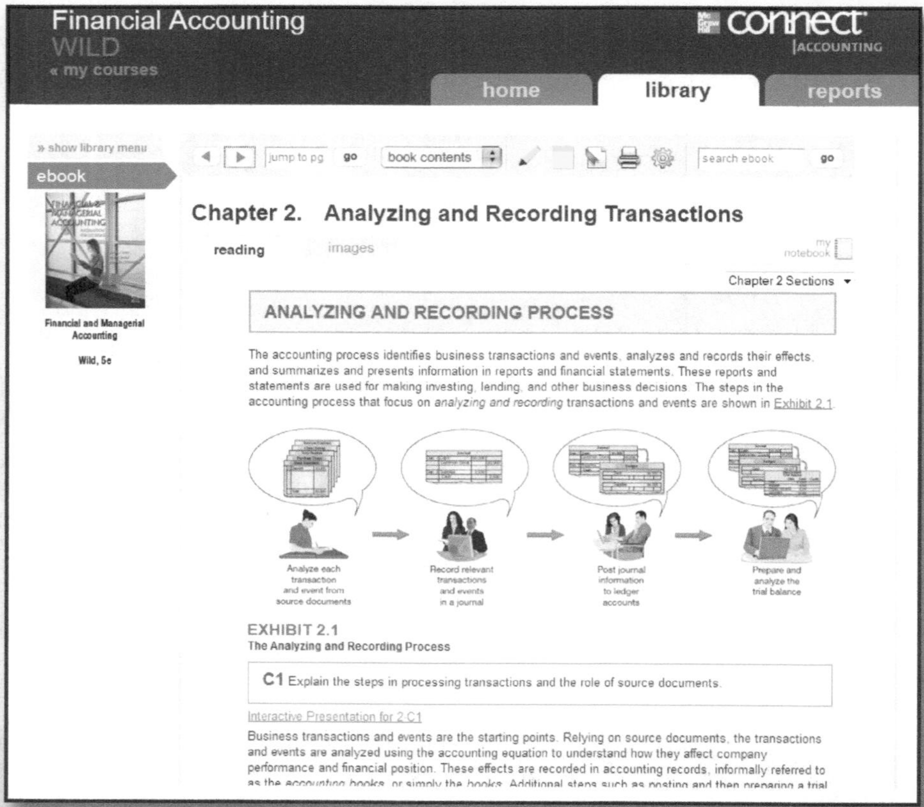

Integrated eBooks *Connect Plus* includes a media-rich eBook. With it, you can share your notes with your students, and they can insert their own notes, highlight the text, search for specific information, and review their materials. Using an eBook with *Connect* gives your students a complete digital solution that allows them to access their materials from any computer. And over time, as more and more students use mobile devices, our eBooks will even enable them to learn on the go.

Today's Students!

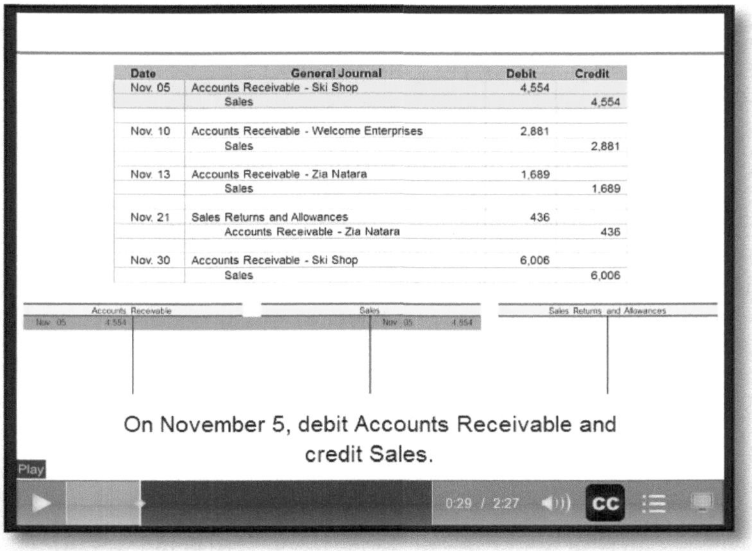

Guided Examples Guided Examples provide narrated, animated, and step-by-step walkthroughs of algorithmic versions of assigned exercises in *Connect Accounting*, allowing the student to identify, review, or reinforce the concepts and activities covered in class. Guided Examples provide immediate feedback and focus on the areas where students need the most guidance.

LearnSmart No two students are alike. McGraw-Hill LearnSmart™ is an intelligent learning system that uses a series of adaptive questions to pinpoint each student's knowledge gaps. LearnSmart then provides an optimal learning path for each student, so that they spend less time in areas they already know and more time in areas they don't. The result is that LearnSmart's adaptive learning path helps students retain more knowledge, learn faster, and study more efficiently.

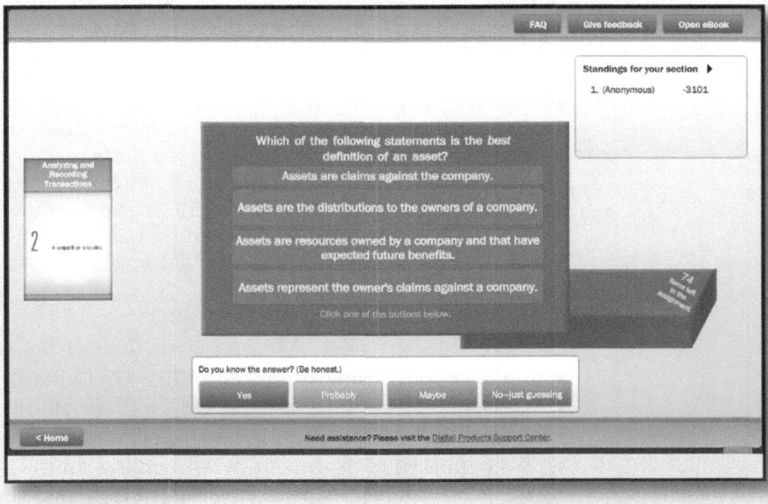

Student Resource Library The *Connect Accounting* Student Study Center gives access to additional resources such as recorded lectures, online practice materials, an eBook, and more.

Adapting to the Needs of

Alternate Chapter Options

This edition of *Financial and Managerial Accounting* features five alternate chapters that can be substituted for the traditional chapters through McGraw-Hill Learning Solutions or Create. These chapters provide alternate methods of teaching and learning chapter material and are fully supported in *Connect.* Alternate chapters available include:

- Chapter 5 - "Inventories and Cost of Sales" featuring the *periodic inventory method*
- Chapter 10 - "Long-Term Liabilities" featuring the *effective interest method*
- Chapter 12 - "Reporting on the Statement of Cash Flows" featuring the *direct method*
- Chapter 16 - "Process Cost Accounting" featuring the *First-In, First-Out method*
- Chapter 20 - "Master Budgets and Planning" featuring manufacturing budgets

Contact your publisher's representative or learning solutions specialist for more information.

McGraw-Hill connect® plus+ | ACCOUNTING

McGraw-Hill's solutions are proven to improve student performance. With *Connect Accounting*, students can access a wealth of engaging resources to help them study more effectively and perform at a higher level on homework and exams. *Connect Accounting* also allows instructors to assign McGraw-Hill's world class content and assess student performance.

The integrated solutions for *Financial and Managerial Accounting* have been specifically designed to help you achieve your course goals of improving student readiness, enhancing student engagement, and increasing their comprehension of content. McGraw-Hill's adaptive learning component, LearnSmart, provides assignable modules that help students master chapter core content and come to class more prepared. In addition, Interactive Presentations deliver learning objectives in an interactive environment, giving students access to course-critical content anytime, anywhere. Known for its engaging style, the *FinMan* solution employs the use of current companies, LearnSmart, and our instant feedback on practice problems to help students engage with our materials, comprehend the content, and achieve higher outcomes in the course.

Simple Assignment Management and Smart Grading

With *Connect Plus Accounting,* creating assignments is easier than ever, so you can spend more time teaching and less time managing. *Connect Accounting* enables you to:

- Create and deliver assignments easily with select end-of-chapter questions and test bank items.
- Go paperless with the eBook and online submission and grading of student assignments.
- Have assignments scored automatically, giving students immediate feedback on their work and side-by-side comparisons with correct answers.
- Reinforce classroom concepts with practice tests and instant quizzes.

Today's Instructors

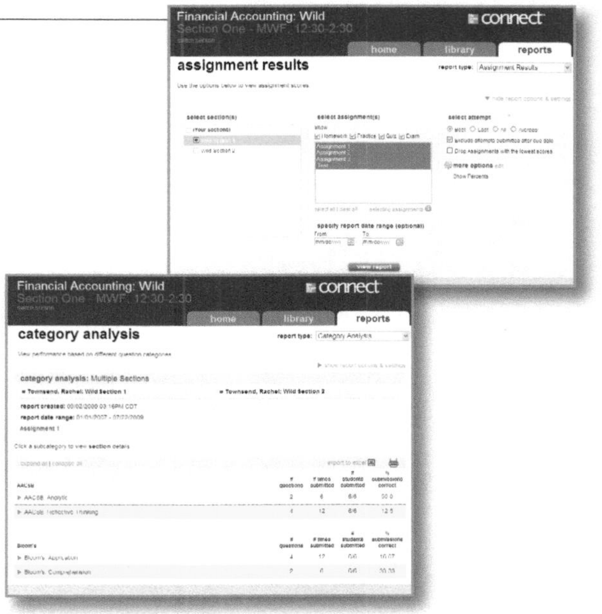

Student Reporting

Connect Accounting keeps instructors informed about how each student, section, and class is performing, allowing for more productive use of lecture and office hours. The reporting function enables you to:

- View scored work immediately and track individual or group performance with assignment and grade reports.
- Access an instant view of student or class performance relative to learning objectives.
- Collect data and generate reports required by many accreditation organizations, such as AACSB and AICPA.
- Identify low-performance students with the "At Risk" student report.

Instructor Library

The *Connect Accounting* Instructor Library is your repository for additional resources to improve student engagement in and out of class. You can select and use any asset that enhances your lecture. The *Connect Accounting* Instructor Library includes: access to the eBook version of the text, PowerPoint files, Solutions Manual, Instructor Resource Manual, and Test Bank.

Tegrity: Lectures 24/7

Make your classes available anytime, anywhere. With simple one-click recording, instructors can record lectures, presentations, and step-by-step problem solutions with Tegrity. Using Tegrity with *Connect Accounting*, instructors can post recordings directly to *Connect* for student viewing. Students can also search for a word or phrase and be taken to the exact place in your lecture that they need to review.

To learn more about Tegrity watch a two-minute Flash demo at **http://tegritycampus.mhhe.com**.

McGraw-Hill Customer Experience Group Contact Information

At McGraw-Hill, we understand that getting the most from new technology can be challenging. That's why our services don't stop after you purchase our products. You can e-mail our Product Specialists 24 hours a day to get product training online. Or you can search our knowledge bank of Frequently Asked Questions on our support Website. For Customer Support, call 800-331-5094 or visit **www.mhhe.com/support**. One of our Technical Support Analysts will be able to assist you in a timely fashion.

How Can Text-Related Web Resources Enrich My Course?

Online Learning Center (OLC)

We offer an Online Learning Center (OLC) that follows *Financial and Managerial Accounting* chapter by chapter. It doesn't require any building or maintenance on your part. It's ready to go the moment you and your students type in the URL:
www.mhhe.com/wildFINMAN5e

As students study and learn from *Financial and Managerial Accounting*, they can visit the Student Edition of the OLC Website to work with a multitude of helpful tools:

- Generic Template Working Papers
- Chapter Learning Objectives
- Interactive Chapter Quizzes
- PowerPoint® Presentations
- Excel Template Assignments

A secured Instructor Edition stores essential course materials to save you prep time before class. Everything you need to run a lively classroom and an efficient course is included. All resources available to students, plus . . .

- Instructor's Resource Manual
- Solutions Manual
- Solutions to Excel Template Assignments
- Test Bank
- Solutions to Sage 50 Complete Accounting and QuickBooks templates

The OLC Website also serves as a doorway to other technology solutions, like course management systems.

Online Course Management

McGraw-Hill Higher Education and Blackboard have teamed up. What does this mean for you?

1. Single sign-on. Now you and your students can access McGraw-Hill's *Connect*™ and Create™ right from within your Blackboard course—all with one single sign-on.

2. Deep integration of content and tools. You get single sign-on with *Connect* and Create, you also get integration of McGraw-Hill content and content engines right in Blackboard. Whether you're choosing a book for your course or building *Connect* assignments, all the tools you need are right where you want them—inside Blackboard.

3. One grade book. Keeping several grade books and manually synchronizing grades in Blackboard is no longer necessary. When a student completes an integrated *Connect* assignment, the grade for that assignment automatically (and instantly) feeds your Blackboard grade center.

4. A solution for everyone. Whether your institution is already using Blackboard or you just want to try Blackboard on your own, we have a solution for you. McGraw-Hill and Blackboard can now offer you easy access to industry-leading technology and content, whether your campus hosts it, or we do. Be sure to ask your local McGraw-Hill representative for details.

McGraw-Hill Campus™

McGraw-Hill Campus™ is a new one-stop teaching and learning experience available to users of any learning management system. This complimentary integration allows faculty and students to enjoy single sign-on (SSO) access to all McGraw-Hill Higher Education materials and synchronized grade-book with our award-winning McGraw-Hill Connect platform. McGraw-Hill Campus provides faculty with instant access to all McGraw-Hill Higher Education teaching materials (eTextbooks, test banks, PowerPoint slides, animations and learning objects, and so on), allowing them to browse, search, and use any instructor ancillary content in our vast library at no additional cost to instructor or students. Students enjoy SSO access to a variety of free (quizzes, flash cards, narrated presentations, and so on) and subscription-based products (McGraw-Hill *Connect*). With this integration enabled, faculty and students will never need to create another account to access McGraw-Hill products and services. For more information on McGraw-Hill Campus please visit our website at **www.mhcampus.com**.

CourseSmart

CourseSmart is a new way to find and buy eTextbooks. CourseSmart has the largest selection of eTextbooks available anywhere, offering thousands of the most commonly adopted textbooks from a wide variety of higher education publishers. CourseSmart eTextbooks are available in one standard online reader with full text search, notes, highlighting, and email tools for sharing between classmates. Visit **www.CourseSmart.com** for more information on ordering.

How Can Adaptive Online Learning Improve Student Performance?

ALEKS® Significantly Increase Student Success and Retention

"After I adopted ALEKS for my Principles of Accounting course, I got fewer and shorter lines for my office hours, and the class average jumped 10-15 percent overall. It's a win-win situation."

—**Professor Fatma Cebenoyan, Hunter College, NY**

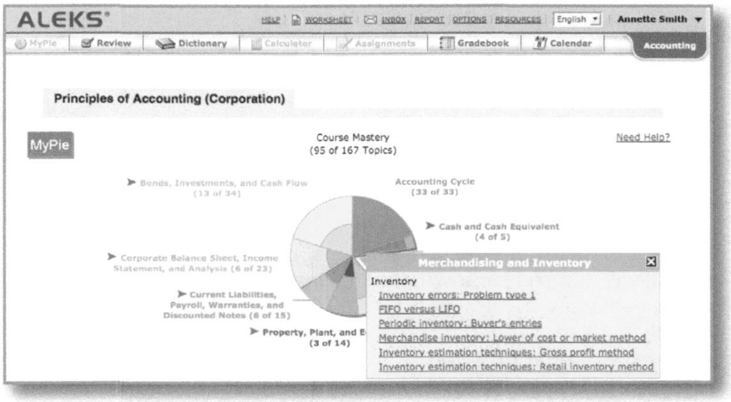

ALEKS: A Superior, Student-Friendly Accounting Experience:

- **Artificial Intelligence** Fills Individual Student Knowledge Gaps
- **Cycle of Learning & Assessment** Increases Learning Momentum & Engages Students
- **Adaptive, Open-Response Environment** Avoids Multiple-Choice Questions
- **Customizable Curriculum** Aligns with Your Course Syllabi and Textbooks
- **Dynamic, Automated Reports** Monitor Detailed Student & Class Progress

To learn more, visit: **www.aleks.com/highered/business**

ALEKS is a registered trademark of ALEKS Corporation.

Innovative Textbook Features

Using Accounting for Decisions

Whether we prepare, analyze, or apply accounting information, one skill remains essential: decision-making. To help develop good decision-making habits and to illustrate the relevance of accounting, our book uses a unique pedagogical framework we call the Decision Center. This framework is comprised of a variety of approaches and subject areas, giving students insight into every aspect of business decision-making; see three examples to the right and one below. Answers to Decision Maker and Ethics boxes are at the end of each chapter.

Decision Insight

Women Entrepreneurs The Center for Women's Business Research reports that women-owned businesses, such as Nom Nom Truck, are growing and that they:

- Total approximately 11 million and employ nearly 20 million workers.
- Generate $2.5 trillion in annual sales and tend to embrace technology.
- Are philanthropic—70% of owners volunteer at least once per month.
- Are more likely funded by individual investors (73%) than venture firms (15%). ■

Decision Ethics

Payables Manager As a new accounts payable manager, you are being trained by the outgoing manager. She explains that the system prepares checks for amounts net of favorable cash discounts, and the checks are dated the last day of the discount period. She also tells you that checks are not mailed until five days later, adding that "the company gets free use of cash for an extra five days, and our department looks better. When a supplier complains, we blame the computer system and the mailroom." Do you continue this payment policy? ■ [Answer—p. 208]

Decision Maker

Entrepreneur You purchase a batch of products on terms of 3/10, n/90, but your company has limited cash and you must borrow funds at an 11% annual rate if you are to pay within the discount period. Is it to your advantage to take the purchase discount? Explain. ■ [Answer—p. 208]

Total Asset Turnover **Decision Analysis**

A company's assets are important in determining its ability to generate sales and earn income. Managers devote much attention to deciding what assets a company acquires, how much it invests in assets, and how to use assets most efficiently and effectively. One important measure of a company's ability to use its assets is **total asset turnover,** defined in Exhibit 8.18.

A1 Compute total asset turnover and apply it to analyze a company's use of assets.

$$\textbf{Total asset turnover} = \frac{\textbf{Net sales}}{\textbf{Average total assets}}$$

EXHIBIT 8.18
Total Asset Turnover

The numerator reflects the net amounts earned from the sale of products and services. The denominator reflects the average total resources devoted to operating the company and generating sales.

CAP Model

The Conceptual/Analytical/Procedural (CAP) Model allows courses to be specially designed to meet your teaching needs or those of a diverse faculty. This model identifies learning objectives, textual materials, assignments, and test items by C, A, or P, allowing different instructors to teach from the same materials, yet easily customize their courses toward a conceptual, analytical, or procedural approach (or a combination thereof) based on personal preferences.

Learning Objectives

CONCEPTUAL

C1 Explain the steps in processing transactions and the role of source documents. (p. 50)

C2 Describe an account and its use in recording transactions. (p. 51)

C3 Describe a ledger and a chart of accounts. (p. 54)

C4 Define *debits* and *credits* and explain double-entry accounting. (p. 55)

ANALYTICAL

A1 Analyze the impact of transactions on accounts and financial statements. (p. 59)

A2 Compute the debt ratio and describe its use in analyzing financial condition. (p. 69)

PROCEDURAL

P1 Record transactions in a journal and post entries to a ledger. (p. 56)

P2 Prepare and explain the use of a trial balance. (p. 65)

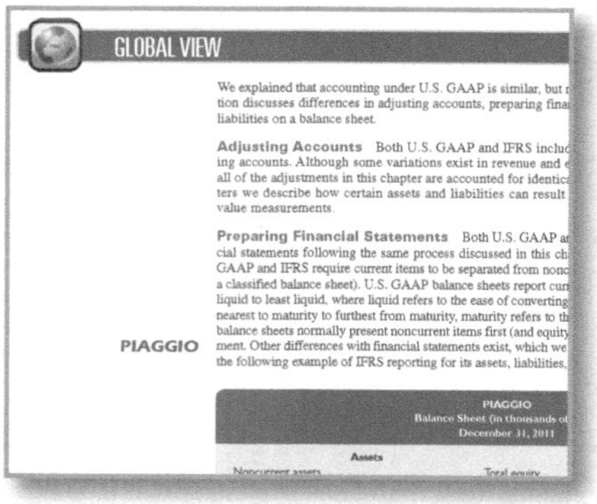

Global View

This section explains international accounting practices relating to the material covered in that chapter. This section is purposefully located at the end of each chapter so that each instructor can decide what emphasis, if at all, is to be assigned to it. The aim of this Global View section is to describe accounting practices and to identify the similarities and differences in international accounting practices versus that in the United States. As we move toward global convergence in accounting practices, and as we witness the likely conversion of U.S. GAAP to IFRS, the importance of student familiarity with international accounting grows. This innovative section helps us begin down that path of learning and teaching global accounting practices.

"We are very impressed with the text itself. The updated look, colors, illustrations, . . . the inclusion of IFRS information will help the transition in the future—which is a good thing. We have the flexibility to pick and choose for now with the way you have laid out the information."

—**Bob Urell, Irvine Valley College**

Bring Accounting To Life

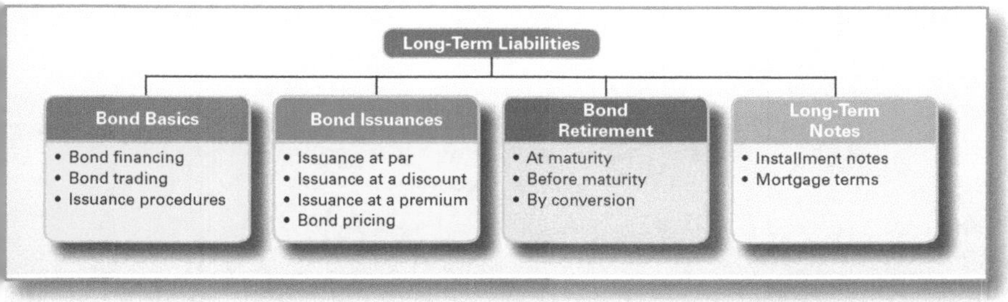

Chapter Preview With Flowchart

This feature provides a handy textual/visual guide at the start of every chapter. Students can now begin their reading with a clear understanding of what they will learn and when, allowing them to stay more focused and organized along the way.

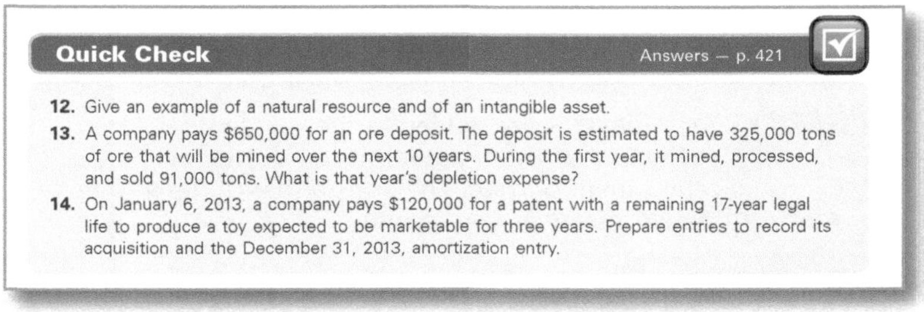

Quick Check Answers — p. 421

12. Give an example of a natural resource and of an intangible asset.
13. A company pays $650,000 for an ore deposit. The deposit is estimated to have 325,000 tons of ore that will be mined over the next 10 years. During the first year, it mined, processed, and sold 91,000 tons. What is that year's depletion expense?
14. On January 6, 2013, a company pays $120,000 for a patent with a remaining 17-year legal life to produce a toy expected to be marketable for three years. Prepare entries to record its acquisition and the December 31, 2013, amortization entry.

Quick Check

These short question/answer features reinforce the material immediately preceding them. They allow the reader to pause and reflect on the topics described, then receive immediate feedback before going on to new topics. Answers are provided at the end of each chapter.

"I like the layout of the text and the readability. The illustrations and comics in the book make the text seem less intimidating and boring for students. The PowerPoint slides are easy to understand and use, the pictorials are great, and the text has great coverage of accounting material. The addition of IFRS information and the updates to the opening stories are great. I like that the decision insights are about businesses the students can relate to (i.e., Facebook, women start-up businesses, etc)."

—Jeannie Liu, Chaffey College

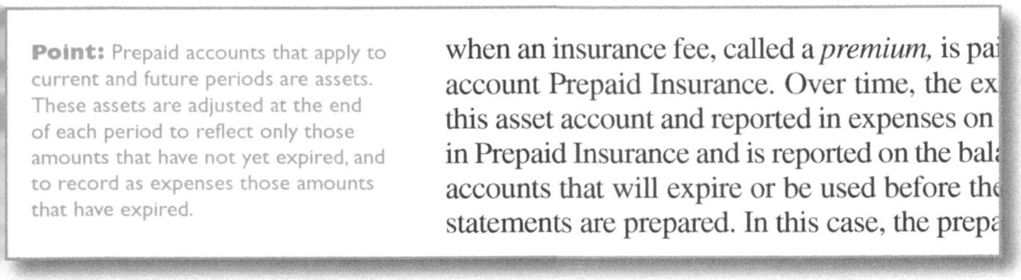

Point: Prepaid accounts that apply to current and future periods are assets. These assets are adjusted at the end of each period to reflect only those amounts that have not yet expired, and to record as expenses those amounts that have expired.

when an insurance fee, called a *premium,* is pai
account Prepaid Insurance. Over time, the ex
this asset account and reported in expenses on
in Prepaid Insurance and is reported on the bal
accounts that will expire or be used before th
statements are prepared. In this case, the prepa

Marginal Student Annotations

These annotations provide students with additional hints, tips, and examples to help them more fully understand the concepts and retain what they have learned. The annotations also include notes on global implications of accounting and further examples.

Outstanding Assignment Material

Once a student has finished reading the chapter, how well he or she retains the material can depend greatly on the questions, exercises, and problems that reinforce it. This book leads the way in comprehensive, accurate assignments.

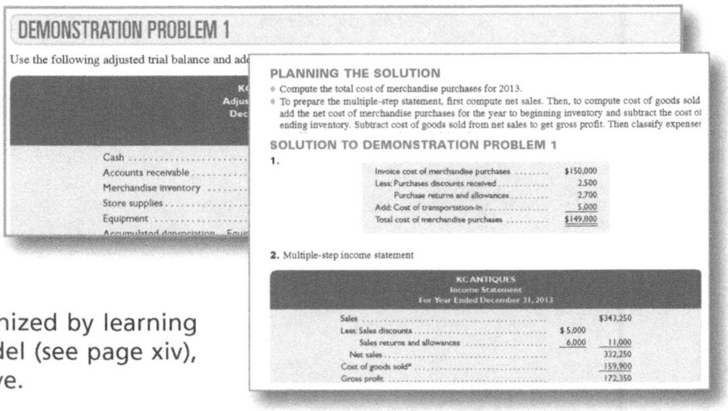

DEMONSTRATION PROBLEM 1

Use the following adjusted trial balance and add

Cash
Accounts receivable
Merchandise inventory
Store supplies
Equipment

PLANNING THE SOLUTION

- Compute the total cost of merchandise purchases for 2013.
- To prepare the multiple-step statement, first compute net sales. Then, to compute cost of goods sold add the net cost of merchandise purchases for the year to beginning inventory and subtract the cost of ending inventory. Subtract cost of goods sold from net sales to get gross profit. Then classify expenses

SOLUTION TO DEMONSTRATION PROBLEM 1

1.

Invoice cost of merchandise purchases		$150,000
Less: Purchases discounts received		2,500
Purchase returns and allowances		2,700
Add: Cost of transportation-in		5,000
Total cost of merchandise purchases		$149,800

2. Multiple-step income statement

KC ANTIQUES
Income Statement
For Year Ended December 31, 2013

Sales		$343,250
Less: Sales discounts	$ 5,000	
Sales returns and allowances	6,000	11,000
Net sales		332,250
Cost of goods sold*		159,900
Gross profit		172,350

Demonstration Problems present both a problem and a complete solution, allowing students to review the entire problem-solving process and achieve success.

Chapter Summaries provide students with a review organized by learning objectives. Chapter Summaries are a component of the CAP model (see page xiv), which recaps each conceptual, analytical, and procedural objective.

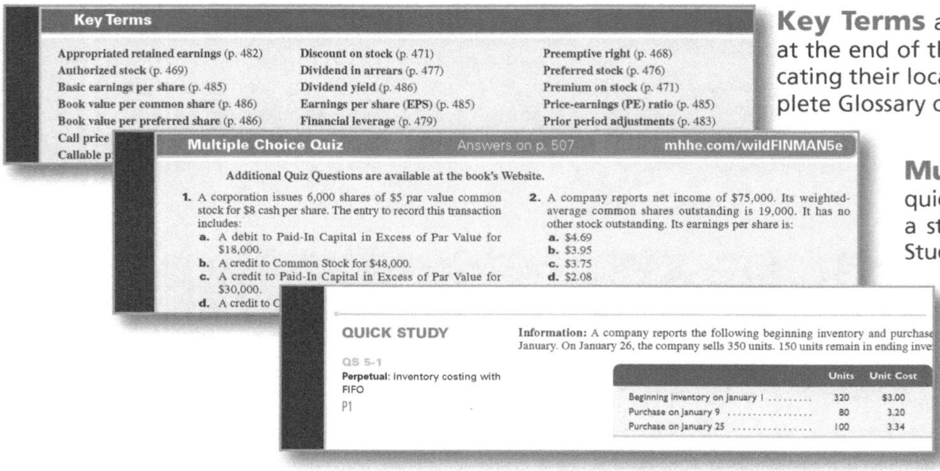

Key Terms

Appropriated retained earnings (p. 482)
Authorized stock (p. 469)
Basic earnings per share (p. 485)
Book value per common share (p. 486)
Book value per preferred share (p. 486)
Call price
Callable p
Discount on stock (p. 471)
Dividend in arrears (p. 477)
Dividend yield (p. 486)
Earnings per share (EPS) (p. 485)
Financial leverage (p. 479)
Preemptive right (p. 468)
Preferred stock (p. 476)
Premium on stock (p. 471)
Price-earnings (PE) ratio (p. 485)
Prior period adjustments (p. 483)

Multiple Choice Quiz — Answers on p. 507 — mhhe.com/wildFINMAN5e

Additional Quiz Questions are available at the book's Website.

1. A corporation issues 6,000 shares of $5 par value common stock for $8 cash per share. The entry to record this transaction includes:
   a. A debit to Paid-In Capital in Excess of Par Value for $18,000.
   b. A credit to Common Stock for $48,000.
   c. A credit to Paid-In Capital in Excess of Par Value for $30,000.
   d. A credit to C
2. A company reports net income of $75,000. Its weighted-average common shares outstanding is 19,000. It has no other stock outstanding. Its earnings per share is:
   a. $4.69
   b. $3.95
   c. $3.75
   d. $2.08

QUICK STUDY

QS 5-1
Perpetual: Inventory costing with FIFO
P1

Information: A company reports the following beginning inventory and purchase January. On January 26, the company sells 350 units. 150 units remain in ending inve

	Units	Unit Cost
Beginning inventory on January 1	320	$3.00
Purchase on January 9	80	3.20
Purchase on January 25	100	3.34

Key Terms are bolded in the text and repeated at the end of the chapter with page numbers indicating their location. The book also includes a complete Glossary of Key Terms.

Multiple Choice Quiz questions quickly test chapter knowledge before a student moves on to complete Quick Studies, Exercises, and Problems.

Quick Study assignments are short exercises that often focus on one learning objective. Most are included in *Connect Accounting*. There are usually 8-10 Quick Study assignments per chapter.

Exercises are one of this book's many strengths and a competitive advantage. There are about 10-15 per chapter and most are included in *Connect Accounting*.

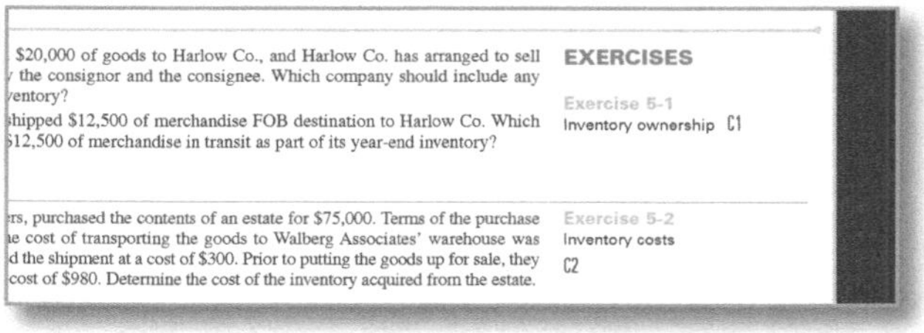

EXERCISES

Exercise 5-1
Inventory ownership C1

$20,000 of goods to Harlow Co., and Harlow Co. has arranged to sell the consignor and the consignee. Which company should include any entory?
hipped $12,500 of merchandise FOB destination to Harlow Co. Which 12,500 of merchandise in transit as part of its year-end inventory?

Exercise 5-2
Inventory costs
C2

rs, purchased the contents of an estate for $75,000. Terms of the purchase e cost of transporting the goods to Walberg Associates' warehouse was d the shipment at a cost of $300. Prior to putting the goods up for sale, they cost of $980. Determine the cost of the inventory acquired from the estate.

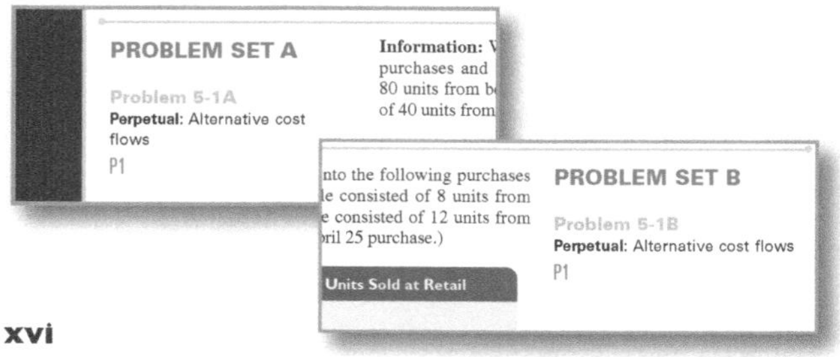

PROBLEM SET A

Problem 5-1A
Perpetual: Alternative cost flows
P1

Information: V
purchases and
80 units from b
of 40 units from

PROBLEM SET B

Problem 5-1B
Perpetual: Alternative cost flows
P1

nto the following purchases
e consisted of 8 units from
e consisted of 12 units from
ril 25 purchase.)

Units Sold at Retail

Problem Sets A & B are proven problems that can be assigned as homework or for in-class projects. All problems are coded according to the CAP model (see page xiv), and Set A is included in *Connect Accounting*.

Helps Students Master Key Concepts

Beyond the Numbers exercises ask students to use accounting figures and understand their meaning. Students also learn how accounting applies to a variety of business situations. These creative and fun exercises are all new or updated, and are divided into sections:

- Reporting in Action
- Comparative Analysis
- Ethics Challenge
- Communicating in Practice
- Taking It To The Net
- Teamwork in Action
- Hitting the Road
- Entrepreneurial Decision
- Global Decision

Beyond the Numbers

REPORTING IN ACTION
A1
Polaris

BTN 12-1 Refer to Polaris' financial statements in Appendix A to answer the following.

1. Is Polaris' statement of cash flows prepared under the direct method or the indirect method? How do you know?
2. For each year 2011, 2010, and 2009, is the amount of cash provided by operating activities more or less than the cash paid for dividends?
3. What is the largest amount in reconciling the difference between net income and cash flow from operating activities in 2011? In 2010? In 2009?
4. Identify the largest cash inflow and outflow for investing *and* for financing activities in 2012 and in 2010.

Fast Forward

5. Obtain Polaris' financial statements for a year ending after December 31, 2011, from either its Website (Polaris.com) or the SEC's database (www.sec.gov). Since December 31, 2011, what are Polaris'

SERIAL PROBLEM
Success Systems
A1 P1 P2
Sage 50 QB

(This serial problem started in Chapter 1 and continues through most of the chapters. If the Chapter 1 segment was not completed, the problem can begin at this point. It is helpful, but not necessary, to use the Working Papers that accompany this book.)

SP 2 On October 1, 2013, Adria Lopez launched a computer services company called **Success Systems,** which provides consulting services, computer system installations, and custom program development. Adria adopts the calendar year for reporting purposes and expects to prepare the company's first set of financial statements on December 31, 2013. The company's initial chart of accounts follows.

Account	No.	Account	No.
Cash	101	A. Lopez, Capital	301
Accounts Receivable	106	A. Lopez, Withdrawals	302
Computer Supplies	126	Computer Services Revenue	403
Prepaid Insurance	128	Wages Expense	623
Prepaid Rent	131	Advertising Expense	655
Office Equipment	163	Mileage Expense	676
Computer Equipment	167	Miscellaneous Expenses	677
Accounts Payable	201	Repairs Expense—Computer	684

Serial Problem uses a continuous running case study to illustrate chapter concepts in a familiar context. The Serial Problem can be followed continuously from the first chapter or picked up at any later point in the book; enough information is provided to ensure students can get right to work.

"The serial problems are excellent.... I like the continuation of the same problem to the next chapters if applicable. I use the Quick Studies as practice problems. . . . Students have commented that this really works for them if they work (these questions) before attempting the assigned exercises and problems. I also like the discussion (questions) and make this an assignment. You have done an outstanding job presenting accounting to our students."

—Jerri Tittle, Rose State College

The End of the Chapter Is Only the Beginning Our valuable and proven assignments aren't just confined to the book. From problems that require technological solutions to materials found exclusively online, this book's end-of-chapter material is fully integrated with its technology package.

connect ACCOUNTING

- Quick Studies, Exercises, and Problems available in *Connect* are marked with an icon.

mhhe.com/wildFINMAN5e

- Problems supported with Microsoft Excel template assignments are marked with an icon.

Sage 50 Complete Accounting

QB

- Problems supported by the Sage 50 Complete Accounting or Quickbooks are marked with an icon.
- Assignments that focus on global accounting practices and companies are often identified with an icon.

Enhancements in This Edition

This edition's revisions are driven by instructors and students. General revisions to the entire book follow (including chapter-by-chapter revisions):

- Revised and updated assignments throughout
- Updated ratio/tool analysis and data for each chapter
- New material on International Financial Reporting Standards (IFRS) in most chapters, including global examples
- New and revised entrepreneurial examples and elements
- Revised serial problem through nearly all chapters
- New art program, visual info-graphics, and text layout
- New Polaris (maker of ATVs, snowmobiles, motorcycles, and electric vehicles) annual report with comparisons to competitors, including Arctic Cat, KTM (IFRS), and Piaggio (IFRS) with new assignments
- Updated graphics added to each chapter's analysis section
- New technology content integrated and referenced in the book
- Updated Global View section in each chapter
- New innovative assignments sprinkled throughout the book

Chapter 1

Twitter NEW opener with new entrepreneurial assignment
Streamlined and reorganized discussion of the users of accounting information
Updated salary information and new margin notes on the value of education
New presentation on the 'fraud triangle' and its relevance to accounting and internal control
New discussion on the joint role of the FASB and IASB in standard setting
Revised layout for accounting principles and assumptions
New information on the Dodd-Frank act and its relevance to accounting
New survey data from executives on the impact of fraud in the economic downturn
New world map on the adoption of IFRS or a variant of IFRS across countries
New company (Dell) for the return on assets section of Decision Analysis

Chapter 2

Nom Nom Truck NEW opener with new entrepreneurial assignment
Reorganized discussion and presentation of assets, liabilities, and equity accounts
Revised description of journalizing and posting of transactions
New headings on each general journal for this chapter's major illustration introducing our unique four-step transaction analysis
Revised global view and new Piaggio's (abbreviated) balance sheet
Updated debt ratio discussion using recent Skechers's information

Chapter 3

ash&dans NEW opener with new entrepreneurial assignment
New layout for the types of adjustments
New example of unearned revenues using USA Today
Enhanced and emphasized the innovative three-step process for adjusting accounts
Updated IFRS and FASB revenue recognition convergence
Added six new Quick Studies to directly apply the three-step adjustment process
Expanded explanation of temporary and permanent accounts
Revised visual display of four-step closing process
Enhanced display of general ledger for ease in learning

Chapter 4

Faithful Fish NEW opener with new entrepreneurial assignment
Enhanced exhibit on transportation costs and FOB terms, with inclusion of entries
New discussion of online ordering, tracking numbers, RFID, and FOB
Revised the two-step explanation of recording merchandise sales
New discussion on the importance and risks of accounting for sales returns
Revised visual display of a sales invoice
Revised discussion of merchandising purchases and sales
New Volkswagen example of IFRS income statement

Chapter 5

Feverish Ice Cream NEW opener with new entrepreneurial assignment
Enhanced exhibit that visually shows cost flows from inventory to financial statements, with superior info-graphics
Added new discussion on inventory controls
New explanatory boxes added to selected exhibits as learning aids
Expanded assignments covering perpetual and periodic inventory measurement
New material on IFRS and inventory methods

Chapter 6

CHEESEBOY NEW opener with new entrepreneurial assignment
New discussion of payroll controls
Expanded presentation of 'Hacker's Guide'
New discussion of the lock box and its purpose
New data on sources of fraud complaints
New evidence on methods to override controls
New visual on document to bond (insure) an employee
New example of MLB controls, or lack thereof

Chapter 7

Under Armour NEW opener with new entrepreneurial assignment
Added explanation of credit card sales
New discussion of mobile payment systems using mini-card-readers and iPads
New illustration comparing bad debts recognition under the allowance method versus the direct write-off method
Revised exhibit on aging of accounts receivable, including all detailed accounts
New illustration on why the banker's rule is commonly applied

Chapter 8

BizChair.com NEW opener with new entrepreneurial assignment
New learning boxes added to selected exhibits identifying salvage value
New explanation on how asset purchases occurring on different days of the month are commonly processed
New example of extraordinary repairs applied to the stealth bomber
New notes added to emphasize that depreciation is cost allocation, and not valuation
New explanation on how drugmakers fight patent expirations
New information on the Mickey Mouse Protection Act for intangibles
New goodwill example using Google's purchase of YouTube

Chapter 9

SmartIT Staffing NEW opener with new entrepreneurial assignment
Revised unearned revenues example based on Rihanna ticket sales
Added explanation on the role of sellers as tax collection 'agents' for the government
New information on franchise costs and how they are accounted for
Added select formulas to enhance the exhibit on payroll deductions
Updated payroll rates to 2012 with discussion on likely adjustments for 2013 and 2014
Added discussion on maximum withholding allowances claimed
New discussion on IRS actions against companies that fail to pay employment taxes
New evidence on payroll fraud, its median loss, and time taken to uncover such frauds

Chapter 10

barley & birch NEW opener with new entrepreneurial assignment
New explanation on why debt (credit) financing is less costly than equity financing
New margin graphics (four) illustrating how a debt's carrying value is periodically adjusted until it equals maturity value at the end of its life
New margin boxes on calculator functions to compute the price of bonds
New explanation of what is investment grade debt
New discussion on the role of unreported liabilities and the 2008-2009 financial crisis
Reference to changes in lease accounting
New discussion of collateral and its role in debt financing
New separate appendix learning objectives on amortizing a discount or a premium using effective interest

Chapter 11

Groupon NEW opener with new entrepreneurial assignment
New discussion of Facebook's IPO and the role of accounting information
New reference to corporate governance
New reference to state laws and where companies incorporate
New examples using Target for stock quotes and Google for stock splits
New discussion of fraudulent information dissemination and stock prices
Updated the global view on equity accounting

For Better Learning

Chapter 12

TOMS NEW opener with new entrepreneurial assignment
Revised graphics to better illustrate cash inflows and outflows for operating, investing, and financing activities
Revised graphic to better reflect cash and cash equivalents
Added discussion on the use of T-accounts for reconstructing transactions impacting cash
New margin clarification for computing free cash flow
New discussion on the potential for IASB and FASB to issue guidance for the statement of cash flow that would require the direct method... stay tuned

Chapter 13

Motley Fool REVISED opener with new entrepreneurial assignment
New companies—Polaris, Arctic Cat, KTM and Piaggio—data throughout the chapter, exhibits, and illustrations
New boxed discussion on the role of financial statement analysis to fight and prevent fraud
Enhanced horizontal, vertical, ratio analysis using new companies and industry data
Streamlined global view section

Chapter 14

Back to the Roots NEW opener with new entrepreneurial assignment
New analytical learning objective
Updated ACFE statistics on fraud costs
New exhibit and discussion on fraud occurrence and average fraud loss by industry
Revised discussion of direct and indirect costs and related exhibit for added clarity
New summary of cost classifications and associated managerial decisions
New Decision Analysis to focus on raw materials inventory turnover and days' sales in raw materials inventory
Moved discussion of types of manufacturing costs to appear before presentation of manufacturer's financial statements
Expanded discussion of financial statements for service companies
New end of chapter assignments on raw materials inventory management and cost classification for service companies
Moved cycle time discussion to Chapter 23

Chapter 15

Astor and Black NEW opener with new entrepreneurial assignment
Reorganized discussion of job order costing for service companies
New discussion of accounting for nonmanufacturing costs and their role in pricing decisions
Added new journal entries for indirect materials and indirect labor for improved learning

Chapter 16

Three Twins Ice Cream NEW opener with new entrepreneurial assignment
Revised comparison of job order and process costing systems
New comparison of reports produced from job order and process costing systems
Added details for accounts used in the entry to record sales in process costing
Added new process costing assignments
Revisions to two learning objectives

Chapter 17

Belgium Brewing Company NEW opener with new entrepreneurial assignment
New section on activity-based costing for service providers
Enhanced discussions and exhibits on overhead allocation methods
New Decision Insight on the use of activity-based costing for business decisions
New section on the costs of quality
Added several new assignments for better learning

Chapter 18

Leather Head Sports NEW opener with new entrepreneurial assignment
New graphics on relations between per-unit fixed and variable costs and volume
Revised discussion of per-unit fixed and variable costs
Moved discussion of margin of safety to section on break-even
Revised discussion of assumptions in CVP analysis
Enhanced the formatting and layout of several key exhibits
New discussion and examples of using the contribution margin income statement to perform sensitivity analyses and compute sales needed for target income
Revised data for estimating cost behavior
New discussion on the use of RFID tags to control inventory costs and for error-reduction

Chapter 19

Samanta Shoes REVISED opener with entrepreneurial assignment
New Global View with reference to McDonald's international operations
Revised section on limitations of variable costing
New discussion of absorption costing and IFRS
Revised several exhibits for better learning
Enhanced examples of absorption and variable costing and their differences
Added new assignments for better learning

Chapter 20

Freshii NEW opener with new entrepreneurial assignment
New discussion on incentive compensation and budgeting
Expanded global view on foreign currency exchange rates and budgeting
Updated discussion on Apple's cash cushion
Added new end of chapter assignments

Chapter 21

Folsom Custom Skis NEW opener with new entrepreneurial assignment
New discussion on budgeting for service providers
Revised several exhibits for learning clarity
Revised discussion of predicting activity levels
New enhanced exhibit on framework for understanding total overhead variance, including formulas
Revised discussion of controllable and volume variances

Chapter 22

United By Blue NEW opener with new entrepreneurial assignment
Revised discussion linking direct and indirect expenses to controllable and uncontrollable costs
Highlighted four-step process to prepare departmental income statements
Moved discussion and illustration of profit margin and investment turnover to main body of chapter
Added discussion on cycle time and cycle efficiency
New exhibit on how to prepare departmental performance reports
Edited discussion of example on preparing departmental performance reports
New discussion on issues in computing return on (assets) investment and residual income
New discussion on the link between executive compensation and company performance
Updated global view on division reporting and its explanation for added clarity

Chapter 23

Charlie's Brownies NEW opener with new entrepreneurial assignment
New discussion on outsourcing of information and technology services
Simplified discussions and exhibits for several examples of managerial decisions
Streamlining of selected explanations

Chapter 24

Gamer Grub REVISED opener with new entrepreneurial assignment
Updated graphic on industry cost of capital estimates
New presentation on payback periods for health care providers
New discussion on link between CEO compensation and IRR
Simplified computation of the accounting rate of return
New example showing calculation of net present value with salvage value
New exhibit showing formula for computing average investment
Enhanced graphics on NPV and IRR decision rules

Appendix C

myYearbook (MeetMe Inc.) NEW opener with new entrepreneurial assignment
New discussion of the two optional presentations for comprehensive income per FASB guidance in 2012
Revised discussion of accounting for securities
New reference to Greek debt in the context of international operations

Appendix D

New examples of LLPs and their prevalence among professional services
New discussion of the potential for multiple drawing accounts in practice
Revised and streamlined three-step process to liquidate a partnership

Appendix E

Expanded discussion and examples of hackers and internal controls
New pneumonic tool for system principles
Enhanced exhibit on system components
New discussion on voice recognition controls
New discussion on cloud computing, its implications to accounting, and its risks
New references to XBRL, Great Plains, and QuickBooks in accounting
Updated discussion and examples for ERP

Instructor Supplements

Instructor's Resource CD-ROM

ISBN13: 9780077598624
ISBN10: 0077598628

This is your all-in-one resource. It allows you to create custom presentations from your own materials or from the following text-specific materials provided in the CD's asset library:

- **Instructor's Resource Manual**
  Written by April Mohr, Jefferson Community and Technical College, SW.
  This manual contains (for each chapter) a Lecture Outline, a chart linking all assignment materials to Learning Objectives, and additional visuals with transparency masters.
- **Solutions Manual**
  Written by John J. Wild, Ken W. Shaw, and Anita Kroll, University of Wisconsin–Madison.
- **Test Bank**
  Revised by Laurie Hays, Western Michigan University.
- **PowerPoint® Presentations**
  Prepared by Anna Boulware, St. Charles Community College.
  Presentations allow for revision of lecture slides, and includes a viewer, allowing screens to be shown with or without the software.

Student Supplements

Working Papers

Vol. 1, Chapters 1-13
ISBN13: 9780077598709
ISBN10: 0077598709

Vol. 2, Chapters 12-24
ISBN13: 9780077598723
ISBN10: 0077598725

Written by John J. Wild.

Connect Accounting with LearnSmart Two Semester Access Code Card

ISBN13: 9780077598594
ISBN10: 0077598598

Connect Plus Accounting with LearnSmart Two Semester Access Code Card

ISBN13: 9780077598617
ISBN10: 007759861x

Carol Yacht's Sage 50 Complete Accounting 2013 Student Guide and Templates

ISBN13: 9780077796860
ISBN10: 0077796861

Prepared by Carol Yacht.

To better prepare students for accounting in the real world, selected end-of-chapter material in the text is tied to Sage 50 Complete Accounting 2013 software (formerly Peachtree). The accompanying student guide provides a step-by-step walkthrough for students on how to complete the problem in the software.

QuickBooks Pro 2013 Student Guide and Templates

ISBN13: 9780077598686
ISBN10: 0077598687

Prepared by Carol Yacht.

To better prepare students for accounting in the real world, selected end-of-chapter material in the text is tied to QuickBooks software. The accompanying student guide provides a step-by-step walkthrough for students on how to complete the problem in the software.

Assurance of Learning Ready

Many educational institutions today are focused on the notion of assurance of learning, an important element of some accreditation standards. *Financial and Managerial Accounting* is designed specifically to support your assurance of learning initiatives with a simple, yet powerful solution. Each test bank question for *Financial and Managerial Accounting* maps to a specific chapter learning objective listed in the text. You can use our test bank software, EZ Test Online or *Connect Accounting* to easily query for learning objectives that directly relate to the learning objectives for your course. You can then use the reporting features of EZ Test to aggregate student results in similar fashion, making the collection and presentation of assurance of learning data simple and easy.

> "Connect certainly offers so much for the students and at the same time helps the professors. The professors can offer more learning opportunities to the students without intensive time investment."
>
> **—Constance Hylton, George Mason University**

AACSB Statement

The McGraw-Hill Companies is a proud corporate member of AACSB International. Understanding the importance and value of AACSB accreditation, *Financial and Managerial Accounting* recognizes the curricula guidelines detailed in the AACSB standards for business accreditation by connecting selected questions in the test bank to the six general knowledge and skill guidelines in the AACSB standards. The statements contained in *Financial and Managerial Accounting* are provided only as a guide for the users of this textbook. The AACSB leaves content coverage and assessment within the purview of individual schools, the mission of the school, and the faculty. While *Financial and Managerial Accounting* and the teaching package make no claim of any specific AACSB qualification or evaluation, we have within *Financial and Managerial Accounting* labeled select questions according to the six general knowledge and skills areas.

Acknowledgments

John J. Wild, Ken W. Shaw, Barbara Chiappetta, and McGraw-Hill/Irwin would like to recognize the following instructors for their valuable feedback and involvement in the development of *Financial and Managerial Accounting,* 5e. We are thankful for their suggestions, counsel, and encouragement.

Khaled Abdou, Penn State University - Berks
Anne Marie Anderson, Raritan Valley Community College
Elaine Anes, Heald College -Fresno
Jerome Apple, University of Akron
Thomas Arcuri, Florida State University
Jack Aschkenazi, American Intercontinental University
Sidney Askew, Borough of Manhattan Community College
Lawrence Awopetu, University of Arkansas -Pine Bluff
Jon Backman, Spartanburg Community College
Charles Baird, University of Wisconsin-Stout
Richard Barnhart, Grand Rapids Community College
Judy Benish, Fox Valley Tech College
Patricia Bentley, Keiser University
Jaswinder Bhangal, Chabot College
Sandra Bitenc, University of Texas at Arlington
Susan Blizzard, San Antonio College
Marvin Blye, Wor-Wic Community College
Patrick Borja, Citrus College
Anna Boulware, St. Charles Community College
Gary Bower, Community College of Rhode Island-Flanagan
Billy Brewster, University of Texas at Arlington
Leslee Brock, Southwest Mississippi Community College
Gregory Brookins, Santa Monica College
Regina Brown, Eastfield College
Marci Butterfield, University of Utah
Roy Carson, Anne Arundel Community College
Deborah Carter, Coahoma Community College
Roberto Castaneda, DeVry University Online
Amy Chataginer, Mississippi Gulf Coast Community College
Gerald Childs, Waukesha County Technical College
Colleen Chung, Miami Dade College- Kendall
Shifei Chung, Rowan University
Robert Churchman, Harding University
Marilyn Ciolino, Delgado Community College
Thomas Clement, University of North Dakota
Oyinka Coakley, Broward College
Susan Cockrell, Birmingham-Southern College
Lisa Cole, Johnson County Community College
Robbie R. Coleman, Northeast Mississippi Community College
Jackie Conrecode, Florida Gulf Coast University
Debora Constable, Georgia Perimeter College
Cheryl Corke, Genesse Community College
James Cosby, John Tyler Community College
Ken Couvillion, Delta College
Karen Crisonino, County College of Morris
Loretta Darche, Southwest Florida College
Judy Daulton, Piedmont Technical College
Dorothy Davis, University of Louisiana-Monroe
Stan Davis, University of Tennessee at Chattanooga
Walter DeAguero, Saddleback College
Mike Deschamps, MiraCosta College
Pamela Donahue, Northern Essex Community College
Steve Doster, Shawnee State University
Larry Dragosavac, Edison Community College
Samuel Duah, Bowie State University
Robert Dunlevy, Montgomery County Community College
Ron Dustin, Fresno City College
Jerrilyn Eisenhauer, Tulsa Community College-Southeast
Ronald Elders, Virginia College
Terry Elliott, Morehead State University
Albert Fisher, College of Southern Nevada
Annette Fisher, Glendale Community College

David Flannery, Bryant and Stratton College
Hollie Floberg, Tennessee Wesleyan College
Linda Flowers, Houston Community College
Jeannie Folk, College of DuPage
Rebecca Foote, Middle Tennessee State University
Paul Franklin, Kaplan University
Tim Garvey, Westwood College
Barbara Gershman, Northern Virginia Community College-Woodbridge
Mike Glasscock, Amarillo College
Diane Glowacki, Tarrant County College
Ernesto Gonzalez, Florida National College
Gloria Grayless, Sam Houston State University
Ann Gregory, South Plains College
Rameshwar Gupta, Jackson State University
Pat Halliday, Santa Monica College
Keith Hallmark, Calhoun Community College
Rebecca Hancock, El Paso Community College-Valley Verde
Mechelle Harris, Bossier Parish Community College
Tracey Hawkins, University of Cincinnati-Clermont College
Thomas Hayes, University of Arkansas-Ft. Smith
Laurie Hays, Western Michigan University
Rita Hays, Southwestern Oklahoma State University
Roger Hehman, University of Cincinnati-Clermont College
Cheri Hernandez, Des Moines Area Community College
Margaret Hicks, Howard University
Melanie Hicks, Liberty University
James Higgins, Holy Family University
Patricia Holmes, Des Moines Area Community College
Barbara Hopkins, Northern Virginia Community College-Manassas
Wade Hopkins, Heald College
Les Hubbard, Solano College
Deborah Hudson, Gaston College
James Hurst, National College
Constance Hylton, George Mason University
Christine Irujo, Westfield State University
Todd Jensen, Sierra College
Fred Jex, Macomb Community College
Gina M. Jones, Aims Community College
Jeff Jones, College of Southern Nevada
Rita Jones, Columbus State University
Sandra Jordan, Florida State College at Jacksonville
Dmitriy Kalyagin, Chabot College
Thomas Kam, Hawaii Pacific University
Naomi Karolinski, Monroe Community College
Shirly A. Kleiner, Johnson County Community College
Tamara Kowalczyk, Appalachian State University
Anita Kroll, University of Wisconsin-Madison
David Krug, Johnson County Community College
Christopher Kwak, DeAnza College
Jeanette Landin, Empire College
Beth Lasky, Delgado Community College
David Laurel, South Texas College
Charles Lewis, Houston Community College
Danny Litt, University of California Los Angeles
Jeannie Liu, Chaffey College
James L. Lock, Northern Virginia Community College
Debra Luna, El Paso Community College
Amado Mabul, Heald College
Lori Major, Luzerne County Community College
Jennifer Malfitano, Delaware County Community College
Maria Mari, Miami Dade College-Kendall
Thomas S. Marsh, Northern Virginia Community College-Annandale
Karen Martinson, University of Wisconsin-Stout
Brenda Mattison, Tri-County Technical College
Stacie Mayes, Rose State College
Donald McWilliams, Jackson State University
Jeanine Metzler, Northampton Community College
Theresa Michalow, Moraine Valley Community College
Kathleen Michele Francois, WECA – Madison

Julie Miller, Chippewa Valley Tech College
Tim Miller, El Camino College
John Minchin, California Southern University
Edna C. Mitchell, Polk State College
Jill Mitchell, Northern Virginia Community College
Angela Mott, Northeast Mississippi Community College
Timothy Murphy, Diablo Valley College
Kathleen O'Donnell, Onondaga Community College
Ahmed Omar, Burlington County College
Margaret Parilo, Cosumnes River College
Paige Paulsen, Salt Lake Community College
Yvonne Phang, Borough of Manhattan Community College
Gary Pieroni, Diablo Valley College
James Racic, Lakeland Community College
David Ravetch, University of California Los Angeles
Ruthie Reynolds, Howard University
Cecile Roberti, Community College of Rhode Island
Patrick Rogan, Cosumnes River College
Paul Rogers, Community College of Beaver County
Helen Roybark, Radford University
Alphonse Ruggiero, Suffolk County Community College
Arjan Sadhwani, South University
Kin Kin Sandhu, Heald College
Marcia Sandvold, Des Moines Area Community College
Richard Sarkisian, Camden County College
Gary Schader, Kean University
Tracy Schmeltzer, Wayne Community College
Debbie Schmidt, Cerritos College
Darlene Schnuck, Waukesha County Technical College
Elizabeth Serapin, Columbia Southern University
Geeta Shankhar, University of Dayton
Regina Shea, Community College of Baltimore County—Essex
James Shelton, Liberty University
Jay Siegel, Union County College
Jaye Simpson, Tarrant County College
Gerald Singh, New York City College of Technology
Erik Slayter, California Polytechnic State University San Luis Obispo
Lois Slutsky, Broward College-South
Gerald Smith, University of Northern Iowa
Kathleen Sobieralski, University of Maryland University College
Charles Spector, State University of New York at Oswego
Diane Stark, Phoenix College
Thomas Starks, Heald College
Carolyn L. Strauch, Crowder College
Latazia Stuart, Fortis University Online
David Sulzen, Ferrum College
Dominique Svarc, William Rainey Harper College
Linda Sweeney, Sam Houston State University
Margaret Tanner, University of Arkansas—Ft. Smith
Ulysses Taylor, Fayetteville State University
Anthony Teng, Saddleback College
Paula Thomas, Middle Tennessee State University
Teresa Thompson, Chaffey Community College
Leslie Thysell, John Tyler Community College
Jerri Tittle, Rose State College
Melanie Torborg, Globe University
Shafi Ullah, Broward College
Bob Urell, Irvine Valley College
Adam Vitalis, University of Wisconsin-Madison
Patricia Walczak, Lansing Community College
Terri Walsh, Seminole State College-Oviedo
Shunda Ware, Atlanta Technical College
Dave Welch, Franklin University
Jean Wells-Jessup, Howard University
Christopher Widmer, Tidewater Community College
Andrew Williams, Edmonds Community College
Gayle Williams, Sacramento City College
Kenneth L. Wild, University of London
Jonathan M. Wild, University of Wisconsin
John Woodward, Polk State College
Wanda Wong, Chabot College
Patricia Worsham, Norco College, Riverside Community College
Lynnette Yerbury, Salt Lake Community College
Judy Zander, Grossmont College
Mary Zenner, College of Lake County
Jane Zlojutro, Northwestern Michigan College

The authors extend a special thank you to our contributing and technology supplement authors:

Contributing Authors: Jo Lynne Koehn, University of Central Missouri; Anita Kroll, University of Wisconsin; Kathleen O'Donnell, Onondaga Community College

Accuracy Checkers: Dave Krug, Johnson County Community College; Albert Fisher, College of Southern Nevada; Judy Zander, Grossmont College; Ann McCarthy, Eastern Carolina University; Mark McCarthy, East Carolina University; and Helen Roybark, Radford University

LearnSmart Authors: April Mohr, Jefferson Community and Technical College, SW; Anna Boulware, St. Charles Community College; Brenda Mattison, Tri County Technical College; and Dominique Svarc, William Rainey Harper College

Online Quizzes: Constance Hylton, George Mason University

Interactive Presentations: Jeannie Folk, College of DuPage

PowerPoint: Anna Boulware, St. Charles Community College

Instructor Resource Manual: April Mohr, Jefferson Community and Technical College, SW

Test Bank: Laurie Hays, Western Michigan University

QuickBooks and **Sage 50 Complete Accounting:** Carol Yacht

Excel Templates: Jack Terry

"This textbook does address many learning styles and at the same time allows for many teaching styles ... our faculty have been very pleased with the continued revisions and supplements. From paper working papers ... to continually improved homework sites and e-books. I'm a 'Wild' fan!"

—Rita Hays, Southwestern Oklahoma State University

In addition to the helpful and generous colleagues listed above, we thank the entire McGraw-Hill/Irwin *Financial and Managerial Accounting,* 5e team, including Tim Vertovec, Steve Schuetz, Christina Sanders, Aaron Downey of Matrix Productions, Lori Koetters, Matthew Baldwin, Carol Bielski, Patricia Plumb, Jeremy Cheshareck, Ron Nelms, Xin Lin, Julie Hankins, and Brian Nacik. We also thank the great marketing and sales support staff, including Michelle Heaster and Kathleen Klehr. Many talented educators and professionals worked hard to create the supplements for this book, and for their efforts we're grateful. Finally, many more people we either did not meet or whose efforts we did not personally witness nevertheless helped to make this book everything that it is, and we thank them all.

John J. Wild *Ken W. Shaw* *Barbara Chiappetta*

Brief Contents

* Appendices D&E are available on the book's Website, **mhhe.com/wildFINMAN5e**, and as print copy from a McGraw-Hill representative.

Contents

* Appendices D&E are available on the book's Website, **mhhe.com/wildFINMAN5e**, and as print copy from a McGraw-Hill representative.

Financial and Managerial Accounting

INFORMATION FOR DECISIONS

Managerial Accounting Concepts and Principles

14

A Look Back

Chapter 13 described the analysis and interpretation of financial statement information. We applied horizontal, vertical, and ratio analyses to better understand company performance and financial condition.

A Look at This Chapter

We begin our study of managerial accounting by explaining its purpose and describing its major characteristics. We also discuss cost concepts and describe how they help managers gather and organize information for making decisions. The reporting of manufacturing activities is also discussed.

A Look Ahead

The remaining chapters discuss the types of decisions managers must make and how managerial accounting helps with those decisions. The first of these chapters, Chapter 15, considers how we measure costs assigned to certain types of projects.

Learning Objectives

CONCEPTUAL

C1 Explain the purpose and nature of, and the role of ethics in, managerial accounting. (p. 610)

C2 Describe accounting concepts useful in classifying costs. (p. 614)

C3 Define product and period costs and explain how they impact financial statements. (p. 616)

C4 Explain how balance sheets and income statements for manufacturing and merchandising companies differ. (p. 619)

C5 Explain manufacturing activities and the flow of manufacturing costs. (p. 622)

C6 Describe trends in managerial accounting. (p. 625)

ANALYTICAL

A1 Assess raw materials inventory management using raw materials inventory turnover and days' sales in raw materials inventory. (p. 628)

PROCEDURAL

P1 Compute cost of goods sold for a manufacturer. (p. 620)

P2 Prepare a manufacturing statement and explain its purpose and links to financial statements. (p. 623)

Decision Insight

Fun-guys

"We didn't even know what a good mushroom tasted like."
—**NIKHIL ARORA** (on right)

OAKLAND, CA—Nearing college graduation, Alex Velez and Nikhil Arora spurned the glamor of investment banking for a more down-to-earth calling: urban mushroom farming using coffee grounds. Complete strangers, each was intrigued by the idea of turning waste into food (and wages). "We both fell in love with the idea of using coffee waste and started doing research and brainstorming," says Nikhil. After researching mushroom-growing techniques and determining there was a demand for their product, the duo wrote up a business plan, set up a managerial accounting system, and began farming. The result is **Back to the Roots (backtotheroots.com),** a socially conscious company with estimated 2012 revenues of over $5 million.

The company's production process begins with several thousand pounds of used coffee grounds that local coffee shops would typically discard. The company's second key raw material, mushroom seeds, is then added to the coffee grounds. The passage of time and moisture combine with the coffee grounds and mushroom seeds to yield delicious mushrooms in as little as 10 days. Then, the used coffee grounds and mushroom roots are packaged and sold as mulch for landscaping. This simple, sustainable production process "starts with waste and creates delicious food and fertile mulch," explains Alex.

Alex and Nikhil stress that college is the best time to start a new business. Risk is low, and "if the owners are passionate and have a good plan, someone will provide financing to get the business going," says Nikhil. In Back to the Roots' case, $5,000 of start-up financing was provided by a contest for social innovation sponsored by their college. In addition to passion and seed money, the owners stress that understanding basic managerial principles, product and period costs, manufacturing statements, and cost flow is critical. Managerial accounting information enables the owners to monitor and control costs and make good decisions. An understanding of costs and a keen eye for demand led the owners to ask, as Alex explains, "whether we could take this one step more and enable people to grow mushrooms at home." The company now sells Grow-Your-Own Mushroom Gardens for home use.

Alex and Nikhil believe that entrepreneurs fill a void by creating a niche. While financial success depends on monitoring and controlling operations to best meet customers' needs, the owners measure success by more than just profits. "For 2011, we collected and diverted over 1 million pounds of coffee grounds from landfill and enabled families to grow over 250,000 pounds of fresh food. In 2012, we've already been collecting 40,000 lbs. per week," exclaims Nikhil. Now, Alex and Nikhil hope to continue to grow their business, while staying focused on sustainability, healthy communities, and green development. Insists Nikhil, "our goal is to show people that you can create a successful company and create a positive impact in the community."

[Sources: *Back to the Roots* Website, January 2013; *Bloomberg Business Week,* http://images.businessweek.com/ss/09/10/1009_entrepreneurs_25_and_under/4.htm; *Whole Foods Market Blog,* August 20, 2011; *White House Champions of Change* blog, August 8, 2011, posted by Ari Matusiak.]

Chapter Preview

Managerial accounting, like financial accounting, provides information to help users make better decisions. However, managerial accounting and financial accounting differ in important ways, which this chapter explains. This chapter also compares the accounting and reporting practices used by manufacturing and merchandising companies. A merchandising company sells products without changing their condition. A manufacturing company buys raw materials and turns them into finished products for sale to customers. A third type of company earns revenues by providing services rather than products. The skills, tools, and techniques developed for measuring a manufacturing company's activities apply to service companies as well. The chapter concludes by explaining the flow of manufacturing activities and preparing the manufacturing statement.

Managerial Accounting Concepts and Principles

Managerial Accounting Basics
- Purpose of managerial accounting
- Nature of managerial accounting
- Managerial decisions
- Fraud and ethics in managerial accounting

Managerial Cost Concepts
- Types of cost classifications
- Identification of cost classifications
- Cost concepts for service companies

Reporting Manufacturing Activities
- Manufacturer costs
- Balance sheet
- Income statement
- Flow of activities
- Manufacturing statement
- Managerial accounting trends

MANAGERIAL ACCOUNTING BASICS

Managerial accounting is an activity that provides financial and nonfinancial information to an organization's managers and other internal decision makers. This section explains the purpose of managerial accounting (also called *management accounting*) and compares it with financial accounting. The main purpose of the financial accounting system is to prepare general-purpose financial statements. That information is incomplete for internal decision makers who manage organizations.

Purpose of Managerial Accounting

C1 Explain the purpose and nature of, and the role of ethics in, managerial accounting.

The purpose of both managerial accounting and financial accounting is providing useful information to decision makers. They do this by collecting, managing, and reporting information in demand by their users. Both areas of accounting also share the common practice of reporting monetary information, although managerial accounting usually includes the reporting of more nonmonetary information. They even report some of the same information. For instance, a company's financial statements contain information useful for both its managers (insiders) and other persons interested in the company (outsiders).

The remainder of this book looks carefully at managerial accounting information, how to gather it, and how managers use it. We consider the concepts and procedures used to determine the costs of products and services as well as topics such as budgeting, break-even analysis, product costing, profit planning, and cost analysis. Information about the costs of products and services is important for many decisions that managers make. These decisions include predicting the future costs of a product or service. Predicted costs are used in product pricing, profitability analysis, and in deciding whether to make or buy a product or component. More generally, much of managerial accounting involves gathering information about costs for planning and control decisions.

Point: Nonfinancial information, also called nonmonetary information, includes customer and employee satisfaction data, the percentage of on-time deliveries, and product defect rates.

Point: Costs are important to managers because they impact both the financial position and profitability of a business. Managerial accounting assists in analysis, planning, and control of costs.

Planning is the process of setting goals and making plans to achieve them. Companies formulate long-term strategic plans that usually span a 5- to 10-year horizon and then refine them with medium-term and short-term plans. Strategic plans usually set a firm's long-term direction by developing a road map based on opportunities such as new products, new markets, and capital investments. A strategic plan's goals and objectives are broadly defined given its long-term orientation. Medium- and short-term plans are more operational in nature. They translate the strategic plan into actions. These plans are more concrete and consist of better defined objectives and goals. A short-term plan often covers a one-year period that, when translated in monetary terms, is known as a budget.

Control is the process of monitoring planning decisions and evaluating an organization's activities and employees. It includes the measurement and evaluation of actions, processes, and outcomes. Feedback provided by the control function allows managers to revise their plans. Measurement of actions and processes also allows managers to take corrective actions to avoid undesirable outcomes. For example, managers periodically compare actual results with planned results. Exhibit 14.1 portrays the important management functions of planning and control.

EXHIBIT 14.1

Planning and Control (including monitoring and feedback)

Managers use information to plan and control business activities. In later chapters, we explain how managers also use this information to direct and improve business operations.

Nature of Managerial Accounting

Managerial accounting has its own special characteristics. To understand these characteristics, we compare managerial accounting to financial accounting; they differ in at least seven important ways. These differences are summarized in Exhibit 14.2. This section discusses each of these characteristics.

EXHIBIT 14.2

Key Differences between Managerial Accounting and Financial Accounting

	Financial Accounting	Managerial Accounting
1. Users and decision makers	Investors, creditors, and other users external to the organization	Managers, employees, and decision makers internal to the organization
2. Purpose of information	Assist external users in making investment, credit, and other decisions	Assist managers in making planning and control decisions
3. Flexibility of practice	Structured and often controlled by GAAP	Relatively flexible (no GAAP constraints)
4. Timeliness of information	Often available only after an audit is complete	Available quickly without the need to wait for an audit
5. Time dimension	Focus on historical information with some predictions	Many projections and estimates; historical information also presented
6. Focus of information	Emphasis on whole organization	Emphasis on an organization's projects, processes, and subdivisions
7. Nature of information	Monetary information	Mostly monetary; but also nonmonetary information

Users and Decision Makers Companies accumulate, process, and report financial accounting and managerial accounting information for different groups of decision makers. Financial accounting information is provided primarily to external users including investors, creditors, analysts, and regulators. External users rarely have a major role in managing a company's daily activities. Managerial accounting information is provided primarily to internal users who are responsible for making and implementing decisions about a company's business activities.

Point: It is desirable to accumulate certain information for management reports in a database separate from financial accounting records.

Purpose of Information Investors, creditors, and other external users of financial accounting information must often decide whether to invest in or lend to a company. If they have already done so, they must decide whether to continue owning the company or carrying the loan. Internal decision makers must plan a company's future. They seek to take advantage of opportunities or to overcome obstacles. They also try to control activities and ensure their effective and efficient implementation. Managerial accounting information helps these internal users make both planning and control decisions.

Flexibility of Practice External users compare companies by using financial reports and need protection against false or misleading information. Accordingly, financial accounting relies on accepted principles that are enforced through an extensive set of rules and guidelines, or GAAP. Internal users need managerial accounting information for planning and controlling their company's activities rather than for external comparisons. They require different types of information depending on the activity. This makes standardizing managerial accounting systems across companies difficult. Instead, managerial accounting systems are flexible. The design of a company's managerial accounting system depends largely on the nature of the business and the arrangement of its internal operations. Managers can decide for themselves what information they want and how they want it reported. Even within a single company, different managers often design their own systems to meet their special needs. The important question a manager must ask is whether the information being collected and reported is useful for planning, decision making, and control purposes.

Point: The *Institute of Management Accountants* issues statements that govern the practice of managerial accounting. Accountants who pass a qualifying exam are awarded the CMA.

Timeliness of Information Formal financial statements reporting past transactions and events are not immediately available to outside parties. Independent certified public accountants often must *audit* a company's financial statements before it provides them to external users. Thus, because audits often take several weeks to complete, financial reports to outsiders usually are not available until well after the period-end. However, managers can quickly obtain managerial accounting information. External auditors need not review it. Estimates and projections are acceptable. To get information quickly, managers often accept less precision in reports. As an example, an early internal report to management prepared right after the year-end could report net income for the year between $4.2 and $4.8 million. An audited income statement could later show net income for the year at $4.6 million. The internal report is not precise, but its information can be more useful because it is available earlier.

Internal auditing plays an important role in managerial accounting. Internal auditors evaluate the flow of information not only inside but also outside the company. Managers are responsible for preventing and detecting fraudulent activities in their companies.

Point: Financial statements are usually issued several weeks after the period-end. GAAP requires the reporting of important events that occur while the statements are being prepared. These events are called *subsequent events.*

Point: Independent auditors test the integrity of managerial accounting records when they are used in preparing financial statements.

Time Dimension To protect external users from false expectations, financial reports deal primarily with results of both past activities and current conditions. While some predictions such as service lives and salvage values of plant assets are necessary, financial accounting avoids predictions whenever possible. Managerial accounting regularly includes predictions of conditions and events. As an example, one important managerial accounting report is a budget, which predicts revenues, expenses, and other items. If managerial accounting reports were restricted to the past and present, managers would be less able to plan activities and less effective in managing and evaluating current activities.

EXHIBIT 14.3

Focus of External Reports

Reports to external users focus on company as a whole

Focus of Information Companies often organize into divisions and departments, but investors rarely can buy shares in one division or department. Nor do creditors lend money to a company's single division or department. Instead, they own shares in or make loans to the entire company. Financial accounting focuses primarily on a company as a whole as depicted in Exhibit 14.3. The focus of managerial accounting is different. While top-level managers are responsible for managing the whole company, most other managers are responsible for much smaller sets of activities. These middle-level and lower-level managers need managerial accounting reports dealing with specific activities, projects, and subdivisions for which they are responsible. For instance, division sales managers are directly responsible only for the results achieved in their divisions. Accordingly, division sales managers need information about results achieved in their own divisions to improve their performance. This information includes the level of success achieved by each individual, product, or department in each division of the whole company as depicted in Exhibit 14.4.

EXHIBIT 14.4

Focus of Internal Reports

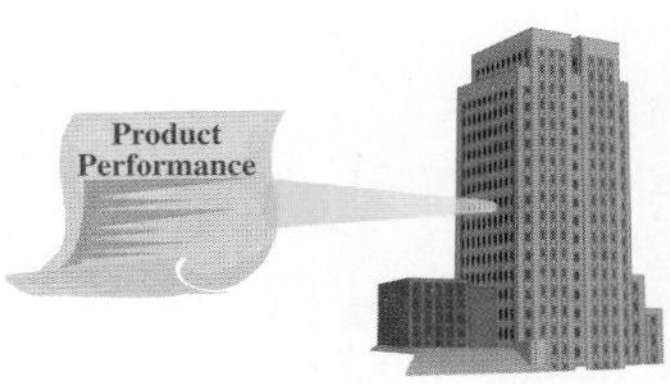

Reports to internal users focus on company units and divisions, along with the company as a whole

Nature of Information Both financial and managerial accounting systems report monetary information. Managerial accounting systems also report considerable nonmonetary information. Monetary information is an important part of managerial decisions, and nonmonetary information plays a crucial role, especially when monetary effects are difficult to measure. Common examples of nonmonetary information are the quality and delivery criteria of purchasing decisions.

Decision Ethics

Production Manager You invite three friends to a restaurant. When the dinner check arrives, David, a self-employed entrepreneur, picks it up saying, "Here, let me pay. I'll deduct it as a business expense on my tax return." Denise, a salesperson, takes the check from David's hand and says, "I'll put this on my company's credit card. It won't cost us anything." Derek, a factory manager for a company, laughs and says, "Neither of you understands. I'll put this on my company's credit card and call it overhead on a cost-plus contract my company has with a client." (*A cost-plus contract means the company receives its costs plus a percent of those costs.*) Adds Derek, "That way, my company pays for dinner *and* makes a profit." Who should pay the bill? Why? ■ [Answer—p. 633]

Managerial Decision Making

The previous section emphasized differences between financial and managerial accounting, but they are not entirely separate. Similar information is useful to both external and internal users. For instance, information about costs of manufacturing products is useful to all users in making decisions. Also, both financial and managerial accounting affect peoples' actions. For example, **Trek**'s design of a sales compensation plan affects the behavior of its salesforce when selling its manufactured bikes. It also must estimate the dual effects of promotion and sales compensation plans on buying patterns of customers. These estimates impact the equipment purchase decisions for manufacturing and can affect the supplier selection criteria established by purchasing. Thus, financial and managerial accounting systems do more than measure; they also affect people's decisions and actions.

Fraud and Ethics in Managerial Accounting

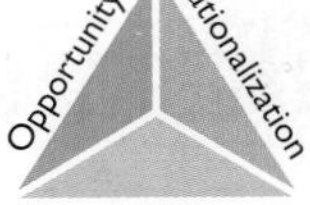

Fraud, and the role of ethics in reducing fraud, are important factors in running business operations. Fraud involves the use of one's job for personal gain through the deliberate misuse of the employer's assets. Examples include theft of the employer's cash or other assets, overstating reimbursable expenses, payroll schemes, and financial statement fraud. Three factors must exist for a person to commit fraud: opportunity, pressure, and rationalization. This is known as the *fraud triangle*. Fraud affects all business and it is costly: A 2010 *Report to the Nation* from the Association of Certified Fraud Examiners (ACFE) estimates the average U.S. business loses 5% of its annual revenues to fraud. This report also shows that the frequency and average loss from fraud vary by industry; the mining industry has a relatively small number of frauds but a high ($1 million) average loss per fraud. The banking industry has the highest number (16.6%) of the total frauds reported in the current ACFE report.

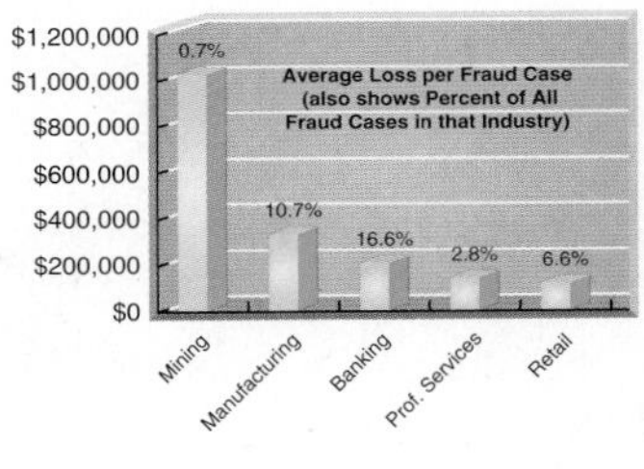

The most common type of fraud, where employees steal or misuse the employer's resources, results in an average loss of $135,000 per occurrence. For example, in a billing fraud, an employee sets up a bogus supplier. The employee then prepares bills from the supplier and pays these bills from the employer's checking account. The employee cashes the checks sent to the bogus supplier and uses them for his or her own personal benefit.

More generally, although there are many types of fraud schemes, all fraud:

- Is done to provide direct or indirect benefit to the employee.
- Violates the employee's obligations to the employer.
- Costs the employer money or loss of other assets.
- Is hidden from the employer.

Implications for Managerial Accounting Fraud increases a business's costs. Left undetected, these inflated costs can result in poor pricing decisions, an improper product mix, and faulty performance evaluations. Management can develop accounting systems to closely track costs and identify deviations from expected amounts. In addition, managers rely on an **internal control system** to monitor and control business activities. An internal control system is the policies and procedures managers use to:

- Urge adherence to company policies.
- Promote efficient operations.
- Ensure reliable accounting.
- Protect assets.

Combating fraud and other dilemmas requires ethics in accounting. **Ethics** are beliefs that distinguish right from wrong. They are accepted standards of good and bad behavior. Identifying the ethical path can be difficult. The preferred path is a course of action that avoids casting doubt on one's decisions.

Point: The IMA also issues the Certified Management Accountant (CMA) and the Certified Financial Manager (CFM) certifications. Employees with the CMA or CFM certifications typically earn higher salaries than those without.

Point: The **Sarbanes-Oxley Act** requires each issuer of securities to disclose whether it has adopted a code of ethics for its senior officers and the content of that code.

The **Institute of Management Accountants** (IMA), the professional association for management accountants, has issued a code of ethics to help accountants involved in solving ethical dilemmas. The IMA's Statement of Ethical Professional Practice requires that management accountants be competent, maintain confidentiality, act with integrity, and communicate information in a fair and credible manner.

The IMA provides a "road map" for resolving ethical conflicts. It suggests that an employee follow the company's policies on how to resolve such conflicts. If the conflict remains unresolved, an employee should contact the next level of management (such as the immediate supervisor) who is not involved in the ethical conflict.

Quick Check Answers — p. 634

1. Managerial accounting produces information (*a*) to meet internal users' needs, (*b*) to meet a user's specific needs, (*c*) often focusing on the future, or (*d*) all of these.
2. What is the difference between the intended users of financial and managerial accounting?
3. Do generally accepted accounting principles (GAAP) control and dictate managerial accounting?

MANAGERIAL COST CONCEPTS

C2 Describe accounting concepts useful in classifying costs.

An organization incurs many different types of costs that are classified differently, depending on management needs (different costs for different purposes). We can classify costs on the basis of their (1) behavior, (2) traceability, (3) controllability, (4) relevance, and (5) function. This section explains each concept for assigning costs to products and services.

Types of Cost Classifications

Classification by Behavior At a basic level, a cost can be classified as fixed or variable. A **fixed cost** does not change with changes in the volume of activity (within a range of activity known as an activity's *relevant range*). For example, straight-line depreciation on equipment is a fixed cost. A **variable cost** changes in proportion to changes in the volume of activity. Sales commissions computed as a percent of sales revenue are variable costs. Additional examples of fixed and variable costs for a bike manufacturer are provided in Exhibit 14.5. When cost items are combined, total cost can be fixed, variable, or mixed. *Mixed* refers to a combination of fixed and variable costs. Equipment rental often includes a fixed cost for some minimum amount and a variable cost based on amount of usage. Classification of costs by behavior is helpful in cost-volume-profit analyses and short-term decision making. We discuss these in Chapters 18 and 23.

EXHIBIT 14.5

Fixed and Variable Costs

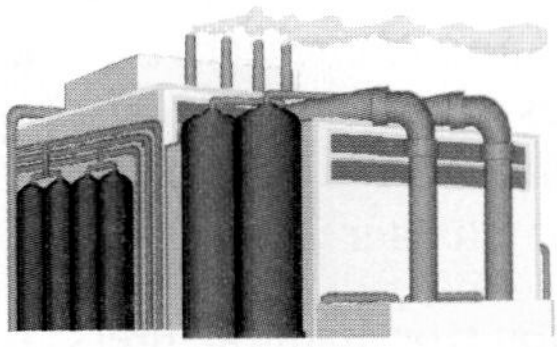

Fixed Cost: Rent for Rocky Mountain Bikes' building is $22,000, and it doesn't change with the number of bikes produced.

Variable Cost: Cost of bicycle tires is variable with the number of bikes produced—this cost is $15 per pair.

Classification by Traceability A cost is often traced to a **cost object,** which is a product, process, department, or customer to which costs are assigned. **Direct costs** are those traceable to a single cost object. For example, if a product is a cost object, its material and labor costs are usually directly traceable. Direct costs for a bicycle, when it is the cost object, include raw materials such as wheels, brakes, chains, and wages and benefits of employees who work directly on making bikes. **Indirect costs** are those that cannot be easily and cost–beneficially traced to a single cost object. An example of an indirect cost is a maintenance department that benefits two or more departments. Salaries of Rocky Mountain Bikes' maintenance department employees are considered indirect if the cost object is bicycles. However, these salaries are direct if the cost object is the maintenance department. Exhibit 14.6 identifies examples of both direct and indirect costs for the maintenance department, when the maintenance department is considered the cost object. Classification of costs by traceability is useful for cost allocation. This is discussed in Chapter 22.

EXHIBIT 14.6

Direct and Indirect Costs of a Maintenance Department

Direct Costs (to a Maintenance Department)

- Salaries of maintenance department employees
- Equipment purchased by maintenance department
- Materials purchased by maintenance department
- Maintenance department equipment depreciation

Indirect Costs (to a Maintenance Department)

- Factory accounting
- Factory administration
- Factory rent
- Factory manager's salary
- Factory light and heat
- Factory internal audit
- Factory intranet
- Insurance on factory

Decision Maker

Entrepreneur You wish to trace as many of your assembly department's direct costs as possible. You can trace 90% of them in an economical manner. To trace the other 10%, you need sophisticated and costly accounting software. Do you purchase this software? ■ [Answer—p. 633]

Classification by Controllability A cost can be defined as **controllable** or **not controllable.** Whether a cost is controllable or not depends on the employee's responsibilities, as shown in Exhibit 14.7. This is referred to as *hierarchical levels* in management, or *pecking order.* For example, investments in machinery are controllable by upper-level managers but not lower-level managers. Many daily operating expenses such as overtime often are controllable by lower-level managers. Classification of costs by controllability is especially useful for assigning responsibility to and evaluating managers.

EXHIBIT 14.7

Controllability of Costs

Senior Manager
Controls costs of investments in land, buildings, and equipment.

Supervisor
Controls daily expenses such as supplies, maintenance, and overtime.

Classification by Relevance A cost can be classified by relevance by identifying it as either a sunk cost or an out-of-pocket cost. A **sunk cost** has already been incurred and cannot be avoided or changed. It is irrelevant to future decisions. One example is the cost of a company's office equipment previously purchased. An **out-of-pocket cost** requires a future outlay of cash and is relevant for decision making. Future purchases of equipment involve out-of-pocket costs. A discussion of relevant costs must also consider opportunity costs. An **opportunity cost** is the potential benefit lost by choosing a specific action from two or more alternatives. One example is a student giving up wages from a job to attend evening classes. Consideration of opportunity cost is important when, for example, an insurance company must decide whether to outsource its payroll function or maintain it internally. This is discussed in Chapter 23.

Point: Opportunity costs are not recorded by the accounting system.

C3 Define product and period costs and explain how they impact financial statements.

Classification by Function Another cost classification (for manufacturers) is capitalization as inventory or to expense as incurred. Costs capitalized as inventory are called **product costs,** which refer to expenditures necessary and integral to finished products. They include direct materials, direct labor, and indirect manufacturing costs called *overhead costs*. Product costs pertain to activities carried out to manufacture the product. Costs expensed are called **period costs,** which refer to expenditures identified more with a time period than with finished products. They include selling and general administrative expenses. Period costs pertain to activities that are not part of the manufacturing process. A distinction between product and period costs is important because period costs are expensed in the income statement and product costs are assigned to inventory on the balance sheet until that inventory is sold. An ability to understand and identify product costs and period costs is crucial to using and interpreting a *manufacturing statement* described later in this chapter.

Exhibit 14.8 shows the different effects of product and period costs. Period costs flow directly to the current income statement as expenses. They are not reported as assets. Product costs are first assigned to inventory. Their final treatment depends on when inventory is sold or disposed of. Product costs assigned to finished goods that are sold in year 2013 are reported on the 2013 income statement as part of cost of goods sold. Product costs assigned to unsold inventory are carried forward on the balance sheet at the end of year 2013. If this inventory is sold in year 2014, product costs assigned to it are reported as part of cost of goods sold in that year's income statement.

Point: Only costs of production and purchases are classed as product costs.

Point: Product costs are either in the income statement as part of cost of goods sold or in the balance sheet as inventory. Period costs appear only on the income statement under operating expenses. See Exhibit 14.8.

The difference between period and product costs explains why the year 2013 income statement does not report operating expenses related to either factory workers' wages or depreciation on factory buildings and equipment. Instead, both costs are combined with the cost of raw materials to compute the product cost of finished goods. A portion of these manufacturing costs

EXHIBIT 14.8

Period and Product Costs in Financial Statements

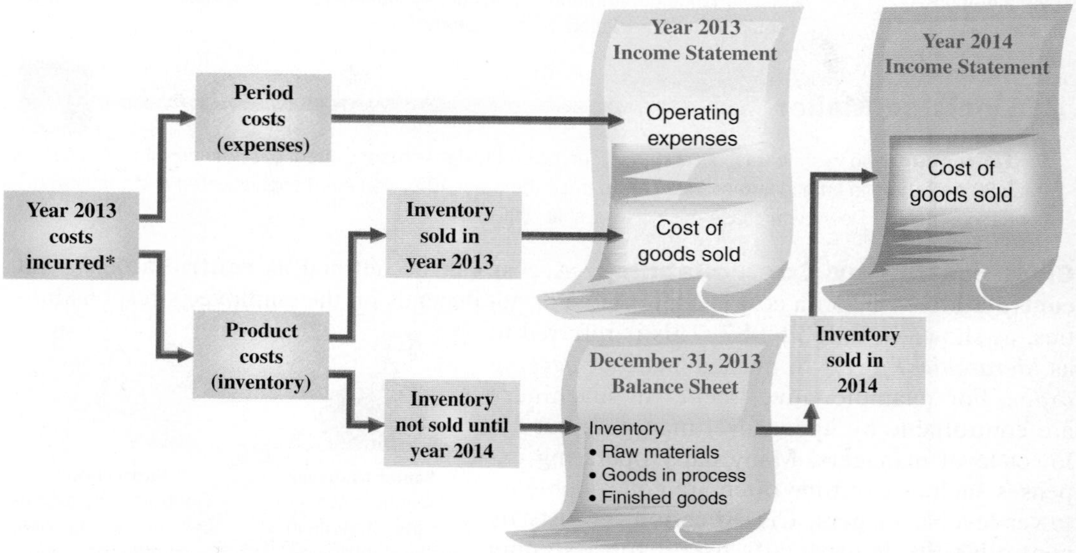

* This diagram excludes costs to acquire assets other than inventory.

(related to the goods sold) is reported in the year 2013 income statement as part of cost of goods sold. The other portion is reported on the balance sheet at the end of that year as part of inventory. The portion assigned to inventory could be included in any or all of raw materials, goods in process, or finished goods inventories.

Point: For a team approach to identifying period and product costs, see *Teamwork in Action* in the *Beyond the Numbers* section.

Exhibit 14.9 summarizes typical managerial decisions for various cost classifications.

EXHIBIT 14.9

Summary of Cost Classifications and Example Managerial Decisions

Costs Classified By	Example Managerial Decision
Behavior (variable or fixed)	How many units must we sell to break even? What will profit be if we raise the selling price? Should we add a new line of business?
Traceability (direct or indirect)	How well did our departments perform?
Controllability (controllable or not)	How well did our division managers perform?
Relevance (sunk, out-of-pocket, opportunity)	Should we make or buy a product? Should we keep or replace equipment?

Decision Maker

Purchase Manager You are evaluating two potential suppliers of seats for the manufacturing of motorcycles. One supplier (A) quotes a $145 price per seat and ensures 100% quality standards and on-time delivery. The second supplier (B) quotes a $115 price per seat but does not give any written assurances on quality or delivery. You decide to contract with the second supplier (B), saving $30 per seat. Does this decision have opportunity costs? ■ [Answer—p. 634]

Identification of Cost Classifications

It is important to understand that a cost can be classified using any one (or combination) of the five different means described here. To do this we must understand costs and operations. Specifically, for the five classifications, we must be able to identify the *activity* for behavior, *cost object* for traceability, *management hierarchical level* for controllability, *opportunity cost* for relevance, and *benefit period* for function. Factory rent, for instance, can be classified as a product cost; it is fixed with respect to number of units produced, it is indirect with respect to the product, and it is not controllable by a production supervisor. Potential multiple classifications are shown in Exhibit 14.10 using different cost items incurred in manufacturing mountain bikes. The finished bike is the cost object. Proper allocation of these costs and the managerial decisions based on cost data depend on a correct cost classification.

EXHIBIT 14.10

Examples of Multiple Cost Classifications

Cost Item	By Behavior	By Traceability	By Function
Bicycle tires	Variable	Direct	Product
Wages of assembly worker*	Variable	Direct	Product
Advertising	Fixed	Indirect	Period
Production manager's salary	Fixed	Indirect	Product
Office depreciation	Fixed	Indirect	Period

* Although an assembly worker's wages are classified as variable costs, their actual behavior depends on how workers are paid and whether their wages are based on a union contract (such as piece rate or monthly wages).

Cost Concepts for Service Companies

The cost concepts described are generally applicable to service organizations. For example, consider **Southwest Airlines**. Its cost of beverages for passengers is a variable cost based on number of passengers. The cost of leasing an aircraft is fixed with respect to number of passengers. We can also trace a flight crew's salary to a specific flight whereas we likely cannot trace wages for the ground crew to a specific flight. Classification by function (such as product

Point: All expenses of service companies are period costs because these companies do not have inventory.

Service Costs

- Beverages and snacks
- Cleaning fees
- Pilot and copilot salaries
- Attendant salaries
- Fuel and oil costs
- Travel agent fees
- Ground crew salaries

versus period costs) is not relevant to service companies because services are not inventoried. Instead, costs incurred by a service firm are expensed in the reporting period when incurred.

Managers in service companies must understand and apply cost concepts. They seek and rely on accurate cost estimates for many decisions. For example, an airline manager must often decide between canceling or rerouting flights. The manager must also be able to estimate costs saved by canceling a flight versus rerouting. Knowledge of fixed costs is equally important. We explain more about the cost requirements for these and other managerial decisions in Chapter 23.

Quick Check Answers — p. 634

4. Which type of cost behavior increases total costs when volume of activity increases?
5. How could traceability of costs improve managerial decisions?

REPORTING MANUFACTURING ACTIVITIES

Companies with manufacturing activities differ from both merchandising and service companies. The main difference between merchandising and manufacturing companies is that merchandisers buy goods ready for sale while manufacturers produce goods from materials and labor. **Payless** is an example of a merchandising company. It buys and sells shoes without physically changing them. **Adidas** is primarily a manufacturer of shoes, apparel, and accessories. It purchases materials such as leather, cloth, dye, plastic, rubber, glue, and laces and then uses employees' labor to convert these materials to products. **Southwest Airlines** is a service company that transports people and items.

Manufacturer's Costs

Direct Materials **Direct materials** are tangible components of a finished product. **Direct material costs** are the expenditures for direct materials that are separately and readily traced through the manufacturing process to finished goods. Examples of direct materials in manufacturing a mountain bike include its tires, seat, frame, pedals, brakes, cables, gears, and handlebars. The chart in the margin shows that direct materials generally make up about 45% of manufacturing costs in today's products, but this amount varies across industries and companies.

Typical Manufacturing Costs in Today's Products

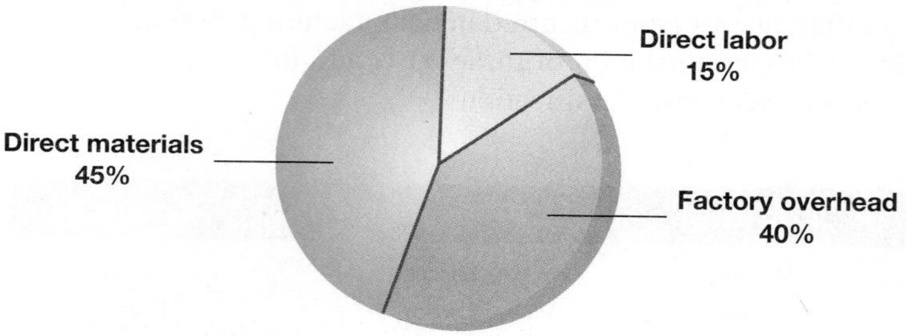

Direct Labor **Direct labor** refers to the efforts of employees who physically convert materials to finished product. **Direct labor costs** are the wages and salaries for direct labor that are separately and readily traced through the manufacturing process to finished goods. Examples of direct labor in manufacturing a mountain bike include operators directly involved in converting raw materials into finished products (welding, painting, forming) and assembly workers who attach materials such as tires, seats, pedals, and brakes to the bike frames. Costs of other workers on the assembly line who assist direct laborers are classified as **indirect labor costs. Indirect labor** refers to manufacturing workers' efforts not linked to specific units or batches of the product.

Point: Indirect labor costs are part of factory overhead.

Factory Overhead **Factory overhead** consists of all manufacturing costs that are not direct materials or direct labor. **Factory overhead costs** cannot be separately or readily traced to finished goods. These costs include indirect materials and indirect labor, costs not directly traceable to the product. Overtime paid to direct laborers is also included in overhead because overtime

Point: Factory overhead is also called *manufacturing overhead.*

is due to delays, interruptions, or constraints not necessarily identifiable to a specific product or batches of product. Factory overhead costs also include maintenance of the mountain bike factory, supervision of its employees, repairing manufacturing equipment, factory utilities (water, gas, electricity), production manager's salary, factory rent, depreciation on factory buildings and equipment, factory insurance, property taxes on factory buildings and equipment, and factory accounting and legal services. Factory overhead does *not* include selling and administrative expenses because they are not incurred in manufacturing products. These expenses are called *period costs* and are recorded as expenses on the income statement when incurred.

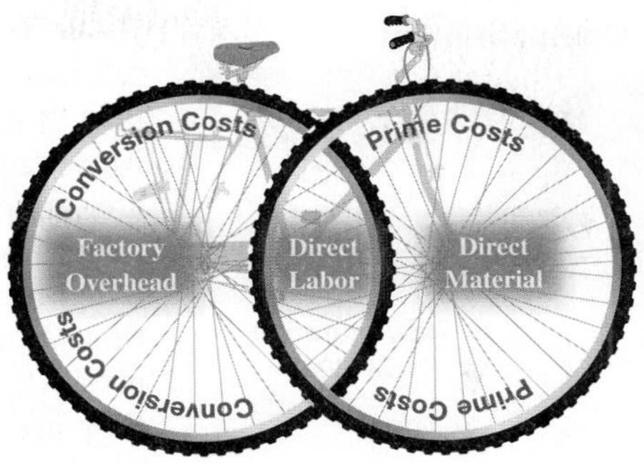

EXHIBIT 14.11

Prime and Conversion Costs and Their Makeup

Prime costs = Direct materials + Direct labor.
Conversion costs = Direct labor + Factory overhead.

Prime and Conversion Costs Direct material costs and direct labor costs are also called **prime costs**—expenditures directly associated with the manufacture of finished goods. Direct labor costs and overhead costs are called **conversion costs**—expenditures incurred in the process of converting raw materials to finished goods. Direct labor costs are considered both prime costs and conversion costs. Exhibit 14.11 conveys the relation between prime and conversion costs and their components of direct material, direct labor, and factory overhead.

Since manufacturing activities differ from both selling merchandise and providing services, the financial statements differ slightly between these companies. This section considers some of these differences and compares them to accounting for a merchandising or service company. First we use the cost classification concept of traceability to discuss a manufacturer's costs.

Manufacturer's Balance Sheet

C4 Explain how balance sheets and income statements for manufacturing and merchandising companies differ.

Manufacturers carry several unique assets and usually have three inventories instead of the single inventory that merchandisers carry. Exhibit 14.12 shows three different inventories in the current asset section of the balance sheet for Rocky Mountain Bikes, a manufacturer. The three inventories are raw materials, goods in process, and finished goods.

EXHIBIT 14.12

Balance Sheet for a Manufacturer

ROCKY MOUNTAIN BIKES
Balance Sheet
December 31, 2013

Assets		**Liabilities and Equity**	
Current assets		Current liabilities	
Cash	$ 11,000	Accounts payable	$ 14,000
Accounts receivable, net	30,150	Wages payable	540
Raw materials inventory	**9,000**	Interest payable	2,000
Goods in process inventory	**7,500**	Income taxes payable	32,600
Finished goods inventory	**10,300**	Total current liabilities	49,140
Factory supplies	350		
Prepaid insurance	300		
Total current assets	68,600	Long-term liabilities	
Plant assets		Long-term notes payable	50,000
Small tools, net	1,100	Total liabilities	99,140
Delivery equipment, net	5,000		
Office equipment, net	1,300		
Factory machinery, net	65,500	Stockholders' equity	
Factory building, net	86,700	Common stock, $1.2 par	24,000
Land	9,500	Paid-in capital	76,000
Total plant assets, net	169,100	Retained earnings	49,760
Intangible assets (patents), net	11,200	Total stockholders' equity	149,760
Total assets	$248,900	Total liabilities and equity	$248,900

Inventories of Rocky Mountain Bikes

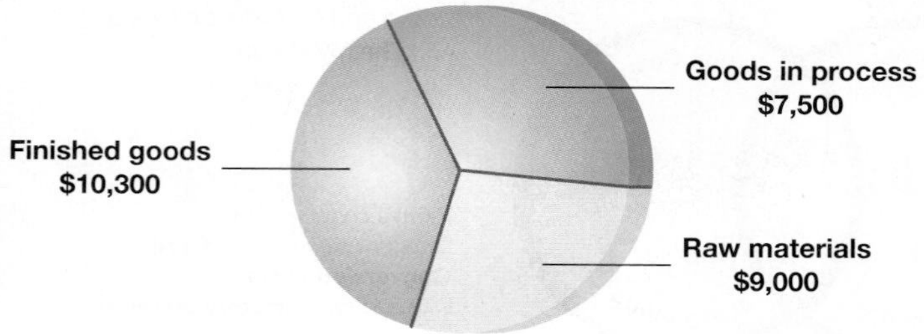

Point: Reducing the size of inventories saves storage costs and frees money for other uses.

Raw Materials Inventory **Raw materials inventory** refers to the goods a company acquires to use in making products. It uses raw materials in two ways: directly and indirectly. Most raw materials physically become part of a product and are identified with specific units or batches of a product. Raw materials used directly in a product are called *direct materials*. Other materials used to support production processes are sometimes not as clearly identified with specific units or batches of product. These materials are called **indirect materials** because they are not clearly identified with specific product units or batches. Items used as indirect materials often appear on a balance sheet as factory supplies or are included in raw materials. Some direct materials are classified as indirect materials when their costs are low (insignificant). Examples include screws and nuts used in assembling mountain bikes and staples and glue used in manufacturing shoes. Using the *materiality principle,* individually tracing the costs of each of these materials and classifying them separately as direct materials does not make much economic sense. For instance, keeping detailed records of the amount of glue used to manufacture one shoe is not cost beneficial.

Goods in Process Inventory Another inventory held by manufacturers is **goods in process inventory,** also called *work in process inventory.* It consists of products in the process of being manufactured but not yet complete. The amount of goods in process inventory depends on the type of production process. If the time required to produce a unit of product is short, the goods in process inventory is likely small; but if weeks or months are needed to produce a unit, the goods in process inventory is usually larger.

Finished Goods Inventory A third inventory owned by a manufacturer is **finished goods inventory,** which consists of completed products ready for sale. This inventory is similar to merchandise inventory owned by a merchandising company. Manufacturers also often own unique plant assets such as small tools, factory buildings, factory equipment, and patents to manufacture products. The balance sheet in Exhibit 14.12 shows that Rocky Mountain Bikes owns all of these assets. Some manufacturers invest millions or even billions of dollars in production facilities and patents. **Briggs & Stratton**'s recent balance sheet shows about $1 billion net investment in land, buildings, machinery, and equipment, much of which involves production facilities. It manufactures more racing engines than any other company in the world.

Balance Sheets for Merchandising and Service Companies The current assets section of the balance sheet will look different for merchandising and service companies as compared to manufacturing companies. A merchandiser will report only merchandise inventory rather than the three types of inventory reported by a manufacturer. A service company's balance sheet does not have any inventory held for sale.

Manufacturer's Income Statement

P1 Compute cost of goods sold for a manufacturer.

The main difference between the income statement of a manufacturer and that of a merchandiser involves the items making up cost of goods sold. Exhibit 14.13 compares the components of cost of goods sold for a manufacturer and a merchandiser. A merchandiser adds cost of goods purchased to beginning merchandise inventory and then subtracts ending merchandise inventory to get cost of goods sold. A manufacturer adds cost of goods manufactured to beginning finished goods inventory and then subtracts ending finished goods inventory to get cost of goods sold.

A merchandiser often uses the term *merchandise* inventory; a manufacturer often uses the term *finished goods* inventory. A manufacturer's inventories of raw materials and goods in process are not included in finished goods because they are not available for sale. A manufacturer also shows cost of goods *manufactured* instead of cost of goods *purchased.* This difference

EXHIBIT 14.13

Cost of Goods Sold Computation

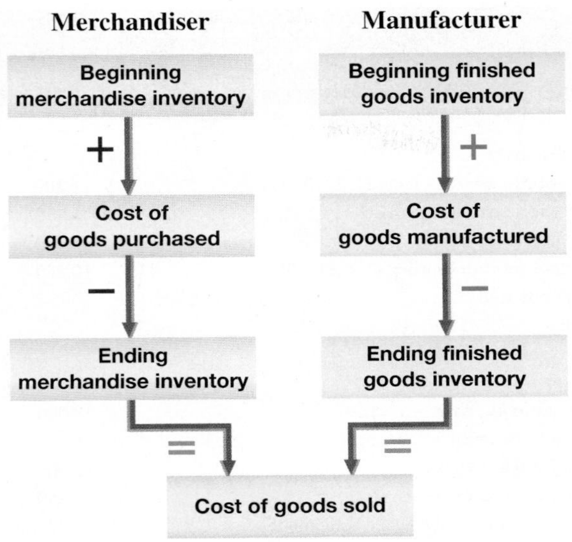

occurs because a manufacturer produces its goods instead of purchasing them ready for sale. We show later in this chapter how to derive cost of goods manufactured from the manufacturing statement.

The Cost of Goods Sold sections for both a merchandiser (Tele-Mart) and a manufacturer (Rocky Mountain Bikes) are shown in Exhibit 14.14 to highlight these differences. The remaining income statement sections are similar.

EXHIBIT 14.14

Cost of Goods Sold for a Merchandiser and Manufacturer

Merchandising (Tele-Mart) Company		Manufacturing (Rocky Mtn. Bikes) Company	
Cost of goods sold		Cost of goods sold	
Beginning *merchandise* inventory	$ 14,200	**Beginning *finished goods* inventory**	$ 11,200
Cost of merchandise *purchased*	234,150	**Cost of goods *manufactured****	170,500
Goods available for sale	248,350	Goods available for sale	181,700
Less ending *merchandise* inventory	12,100	**Less ending *finished goods* inventory**	10,300
Cost of goods sold	$236,250	Cost of goods sold	$171,400

* Cost of goods manufactured is reported in the income statement of Exhibit 14.15.

Although the cost of goods sold computations are similar, the numbers in these computations reflect different activities. A merchandiser's cost of goods purchased is the cost of buying products to be sold. A manufacturer's cost of goods manufactured is the sum of direct materials, direct labor, and factory overhead costs incurred in producing products. Next we show a manufacturer's income statement.

Reporting Performance Exhibit 14.15 shows the income statement for Rocky Mountain Bikes. Its operating expenses include sales salaries, office salaries, and depreciation of delivery and office equipment. Operating expenses do not include manufacturing costs such as factory workers' wages and depreciation of production equipment and the factory buildings. These manufacturing costs are reported as part of cost of goods manufactured and included in cost of goods sold. We explained why and how this is done in the section "Classification by Function."

Point: Manufacturers treat costs such as depreciation and rent as product costs if they are related to manufacturing.

Income Statement for Service Company Since a service provider does not make or buy inventory to be sold, it does not report cost of goods manufactured or cost of goods sold. Instead, its operating expenses include all of the costs it incurred in providing its service. Southwest Airlines reports large operating expenses for employee pay and benefits, fuel and oil, and depreciation.

EXHIBIT 14.15

Income Statement for a Manufacturer

ROCKY MOUNTAIN BIKES
Income Statement
For Year Ended December 31, 2013

Sales		$310,000
Cost of goods sold		
Finished goods inventory, Dec. 31, 2012	$ 11,200	
Cost of goods manufactured	**170,500**	
Goods available for sale	181,700	
Less finished goods inventory, Dec. 31, 2013	10,300	
Cost of goods sold		171,400
Gross profit		138,600
Operating expenses		
Selling expenses		
Sales salaries expense	18,000	
Advertising expense	5,500	
Delivery wages expense	12,000	
Shipping supplies expense	250	
Insurance expense—Delivery equipment	300	
Depreciation expense—Delivery equipment	2,100	
Total selling expenses		38,150
General and administrative expenses		
Office salaries expense	15,700	
Miscellaneous expense	200	
Bad debts expense	1,550	
Office supplies expense	100	
Depreciation expense—Office equipment	200	
Interest expense	4,000	
Total general and administrative expenses		21,750
Total operating expenses		59,900
Income before income taxes		78,700
Income taxes expense		32,600
Net income		$ 46,100

Quick Check Answers — p. 634

6. What are the three types of inventory on a manufacturing company's balance sheet?
7. How does cost of goods sold differ for merchandising versus manufacturing companies?

Flow of Manufacturing Activities

C5 Explain manufacturing activities and the flow of manufacturing costs.

To understand manufacturing and its reports, we must first understand the flow of manufacturing activities and costs. Exhibit 14.16 shows the flow of manufacturing activities for a manufacturer. This exhibit has three important sections: *materials activity, production activity,* and *sales activity.* We explain each activity in this section.

Point: Knowledge of managerial accounting provides us a means of measuring manufacturing costs and is a sound foundation for studying advanced business topics.

Materials Activity The far left side of Exhibit 14.16 shows the flow of raw materials. Manufacturers usually start a period with some beginning raw materials inventory carried over from the previous period. The company then acquires additional raw materials in the current period. Adding these purchases to beginning inventory gives total raw materials available for use in production. These raw materials are then either used in production in the current period or remain in inventory at the end of the period for use in future periods.

Production Activity The middle section of Exhibit 14.16 describes production activity. Four factors come together in production: beginning goods in process inventory, direct materials,

EXHIBIT 14.16

Activities and Cost Flows in Manufacturing

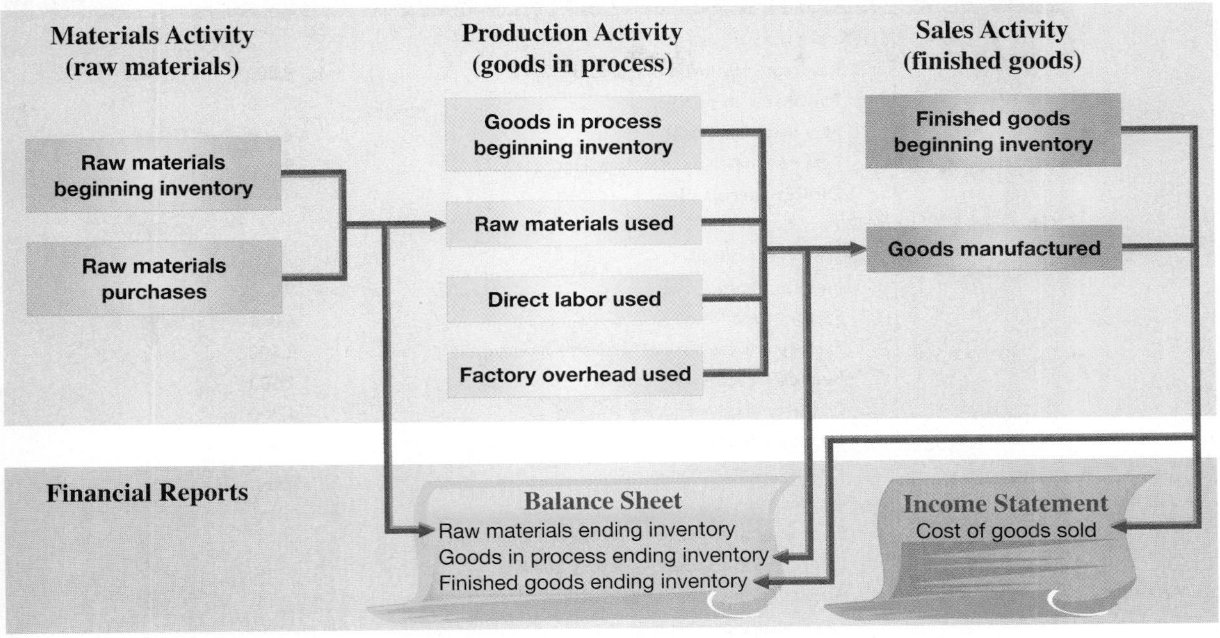

direct labor, and overhead. Beginning goods in process inventory consists of partly assembled products from the previous period. Production activity results in products that are either finished or remain unfinished. The cost of finished products makes up the cost of goods manufactured for the current period. Unfinished products are identified as ending goods in process inventory. The cost of unfinished products consists of direct materials, direct labor, and factory overhead, and is reported on the current period's balance sheet. The costs of both finished goods manufactured and goods in process are *product costs.*

Sales Activity The company's sales activity is portrayed in the far right side of Exhibit 14.16. Newly completed units are combined with beginning finished goods inventory to make up total finished goods available for sale in the current period. The cost of finished products sold is reported on the income statement as cost of goods sold. The cost of products not sold is reported on the current period's balance sheet as ending finished goods inventory.

Manufacturing Statement

P2 Prepare a manufacturing statement and explain its purpose and links to financial statements.

A company's manufacturing activities are described in a **manufacturing statement,** also called the *schedule of manufacturing activities* or the *schedule of cost of goods manufactured.* The manufacturing statement summarizes the types and amounts of costs incurred in a company's manufacturing process. Exhibit 14.17 shows the manufacturing statement for Rocky Mountain Bikes. The statement is divided into four parts: *direct materials, direct labor, overhead,* and *computation of cost of goods manufactured.* We describe each of these parts in this section.

① The manufacturing statement begins by computing direct materials used. We start by adding beginning raw materials inventory of $8,000 to the current period's purchases of $86,500. This yields $94,500 of total raw materials available for use. A physical count of inventory shows $9,000 of ending raw materials inventory. This implies a total cost of raw materials used during the period of $85,500 ($94,500 total raw materials available for use − $9,000 ending inventory). (*Note:* All raw materials are direct materials for Rocky Mountain Bikes.)

② The second part of the manufacturing statement reports direct labor costs. Rocky Mountain Bikes had total direct labor costs of $60,000 for the period. This amount includes payroll taxes and fringe benefits.

Point: Direct material and direct labor costs increase with increases in production volume and are called *variable costs.* Overhead can be both variable and fixed. When overhead costs vary with production, they are called *variable overhead.* When overhead costs don't vary with production, they are called *fixed overhead.*

EXHIBIT 14.17

Manufacturing Statement

ROCKY MOUNTAIN BIKES
Manufacturing Statement
For Year Ended December 31, 2013

①	**Direct materials**		
	Raw materials inventory, Dec. 31, 2012	$ 8,000	
	Raw materials purchases	86,500	
	Raw materials available for use	94,500	
	Less raw materials inventory, Dec. 31, 2013	9,000	
	Direct materials used		$ 85,500
②	**Direct labor**		60,000
③	**Factory overhead**		
	Indirect labor	9,000	
	Factory supervision	6,000	
	Factory utilities	2,600	
	Repairs—Factory equipment	2,500	
	Property taxes—Factory building	1,900	
	Factory supplies used	600	
	Factory insurance expired	1,100	
	Depreciation expense—Small tools	200	
	Depreciation expense—Factory equipment	3,500	
	Depreciation expense—Factory building	1,800	
	Amortization expense—Patents	800	
	Total factory overhead		30,000
④	Total manufacturing costs		175,500
	Add goods in process inventory, Dec. 31, 2012		2,500
	Total cost of goods in process		178,000
	Less goods in process inventory, Dec. 31, 2013		7,500
	Cost of goods manufactured		$170,500

Point: Manufacturers sometimes report variable and fixed overhead separately in the manufacturing statement to provide more information to managers about cost behavior.

③ The third part of the manufacturing statement reports overhead costs. The statement lists each important factory overhead item and its cost. Total factory overhead cost for the period is $30,000. Some companies report only *total* factory overhead on the manufacturing statement and attach a separate schedule listing individual overhead costs.

④ The final section of the manufacturing statement computes and reports the *cost of goods manufactured.* (Total manufacturing costs for the period are $175,500 [$85,500 + $60,000 + $30,000], the sum of direct materials used and direct labor and overhead costs incurred.) This amount is first added to beginning goods in process inventory. This gives the total goods in process inventory of $178,000 ($175,500 + $2,500). We then compute the current period's cost of goods manufactured of $170,500 by taking the $178,000 total goods in process and subtracting the $7,500 cost of ending goods in process inventory that consists of direct materials, direct labor, and factory overhead. The cost of goods manufactured amount is also called *net cost of goods manufactured* or *cost of goods completed.* Exhibit 14.15 shows that this item and amount are listed in the Cost of Goods Sold section of Rocky Mountain Bikes' income statement and the balance sheet.

A managerial accounting system records costs and reports them in various reports that eventually determine financial statements. Exhibit 14.18 shows how overhead costs flow through the system: from an initial listing of specific costs, to a section of the manufacturing statement, to the reporting on the income statement and the balance sheet.

Management uses information in the manufacturing statement to plan and control the company's manufacturing activities. To provide timely information for decision making, the statement is often prepared monthly, weekly, or even daily. In anticipation of release of its much-hyped iPad, **Apple** grew its inventory of critical components, and its finished goods

EXHIBIT 14.18

Overhead Cost Flows across Accounting Reports

ROCKY MOUNTAIN BIKES
Factory Overhead Costs
For Year Ended December 31, 2013

direct labor	$ 9,000
upervision	6,000
ther overhead items*	15,000
otal overhead	$30,000

rhead items are listed in Exhibit 14.17.

ROCKY MOUNTAIN BIKES
Manufacturing Statement
For Year Ended December 31, 2013

Direct materials	$ 85,500
Direct labor	60,000
Factory overhead	30,000
Total manuf. costs	175,500
Beg. goods in process	2,500
Total goods in process	178,000
End. goods in process	(7,500)
Cost of goods manuf.	$170,500

ROCKY MOUNTAIN BIKES
Income Statement
For Year Ended December 31, 2013

Sales		$310,000
Cost of goods sold		
Beg. finished goods	11,200	
Cost of goods manuf.	170,500	
End. finished goods	(10,300)	
Cost of goods sold	171,400	
Gross profit	138,600	
Expenses	59,900	
Income taxes	32,600	
Net income	$ 46,100	

ROCKY MOUNTAIN BIKES
Balance Sheet–PARTIAL
December 31, 2013

Cash	$11,000
Accounts receivable, net	30,150
Raw materials inventory	9,000
Goods in process inventory	7,500
Finished goods inventory	10,300
Factory supplies	350
Prepaid insurance	300
Total current assets	$68,600

inventory. The manufacturing statement contains information useful to external users but is not a general-purpose financial statement. Companies rarely publish the manufacturing statement because managers view this information as proprietary and potentially harmful to them if released to competitors.

Quick Check Answers — p. 634

8. A manufacturing statement (*a*) computes cost of goods manufactured for the period, (*b*) computes cost of goods sold for the period, or (*c*) reports operating expenses incurred for the period.
9. Are companies required to report a manufacturing statement?
10. How are both beginning and ending goods in process inventories reported on a manufacturing statement?

Trends in Managerial Accounting

C6 Describe trends in managerial accounting.

The analytical tools and techniques of managerial accounting have always been useful, and their relevance and importance continue to increase. This is so because of changes in the business environment. This section describes some of these changes and their impact on managerial accounting.

Customer Orientation There is an increased emphasis on *customers* as the most important constituent of a business. Customers expect to derive a certain value for the money they spend to buy products and services. Specifically, they expect that their suppliers will offer them the right service (or product) at the right time and the right price. This implies that

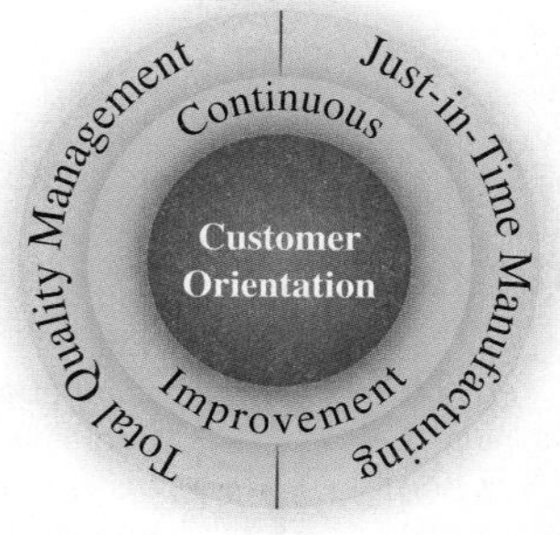

companies accept the notion of **customer orientation,** which means that employees understand the changing needs and wants of their customers and align their management and operating practices accordingly.

Global Economy Our *global economy* expands competitive boundaries and provides customers more choices. The global economy also produces changes in business activities. One notable case that reflects these changes in customer demand and global competition is auto manufacturing. The top three Japanese auto manufacturers (**Honda**, **Nissan**, and **Toyota**) once controlled more than 40% of the U.S. auto market. Customers perceived that Japanese auto manufacturers provided value not available from other manufacturers. Many European and North American auto manufacturers responded to this challenge and regained much of the lost market share.

E-Commerce People have become increasingly interconnected via smartphones, text messaging, and other electronic applications. Consumers thus expect and demand to be able to buy items electronically, whenever and wherever they want. Many businesses have enhanced their Websites to allow for online transactions. Online sales now make up over 7% of total retail sales.

Service Economy Businesses that provide services, such as telecommunications and health care, constitute an ever-growing part of our economy. In developed economies like the United States, service businesses typically account for over 60% to 70% of total economic activity.

Companies must be alert to these and other factors. Many companies have responded by adopting the **lean business model,** whose goal is to *eliminate waste* while "satisfying the customer" and "providing a positive return" to the company.

Lean Practices **Continuous improvement** rejects the notions of "good enough" or "acceptable" and challenges employees and managers to continuously experiment with new and improved business practices. This has led companies to adopt practices such as total quality management (TQM) and just-in-time (JIT) manufacturing. The philosophy underlying both practices is continuous improvement; the difference is in the focus.

Point: Goals of a TQM process include reduced waste, better inventory control, fewer defects, and continuous improvement. Just-in-time concepts have similar goals.

Total quality management focuses on quality improvement and applies this standard to all aspects of business activities. In doing so, managers and employees seek to uncover waste in business activities including accounting activities such as payroll and disbursements. To encourage an emphasis on quality, the U.S. Congress established the Malcolm Baldrige National Quality Award (MBNQA). Entrants must conduct a thorough analysis and evaluation of their business using guidelines from the Baldrige committee. **Ritz Carlton Hotel** is a recipient of the Baldrige award in the service category. The company applies a core set of values, collectively called *The Gold Standards,* to improve customer service.

Point: The time between buying raw materials and selling finished goods is called *throughput time*.

Just-in-time manufacturing is a system that acquires inventory and produces only when needed. An important aspect of JIT is that companies manufacture products only after they receive an order (a *demand-pull* system) and then deliver the customer's requirements on time. This means that processes must be aligned to eliminate any delays and inefficiencies including inferior inputs and outputs. Companies must also establish good relations and communications with their suppliers. On the downside, JIT is more susceptible to disruption than traditional systems. As one example, several **General Motors** plants were temporarily shut down due to a strike at an assembly division; the plants supplied components *just in time* to the assembly division.

"My boss wants us to appeal to a younger and hipper crowd. So, I'd like to get a tattoo that says-- 'Accounting rules!'"

Value Chain The **value chain** refers to the series of activities that add value to a company's products or services. Exhibit 14.19 illustrates a possible value chain for a retail cookie company. Companies can use lean practices to increase efficiency and profits.

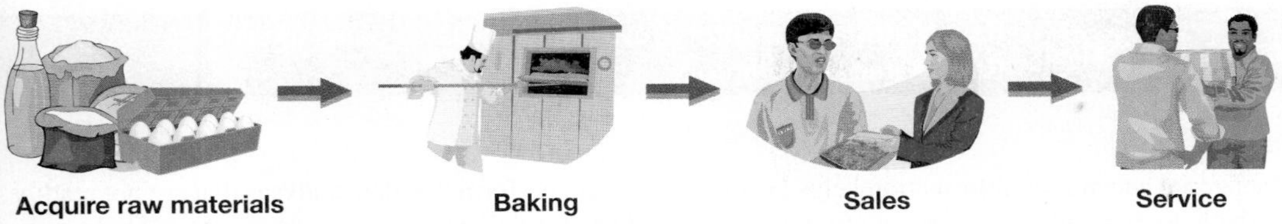

EXHIBIT 14.19

Typical Value Chain (Cookie Retailer)

Decision Insight

Global Lean **Toyota Motor Corporation** pioneered lean manufacturing, and it has since spread to other manufacturers throughout the world. The goals include improvements in quality, reliability, inventory turnover, productivity, exports, and—above all—sales and income. ■

Implications for Managerial Accounting Adopting the lean business model can be challenging because to foster its implementation, all systems and procedures that a company follows must be realigned. Managerial accounting has an important role to play by providing accurate cost and performance information. Companies must understand the nature and sources of cost and must develop systems that capture costs accurately. Developing such a system is important to measuring the "value" provided to customers. The price that customers pay for acquiring goods and services is an important determinant of value. In turn, the costs a company incurs are key determinants of price. All else being equal, the better a company is at controlling its costs, the better its performance.

Decision Insight

Balanced Scorecard The *balanced scorecard* aids continuous improvement by augmenting financial measures with information on the "drivers" (indicators) of future financial performance along four dimensions: (1) *financial*—profitability and risk, (2) *customer*—value creation and product and service differentiation, (3) *internal business processes*—business activities that create customer and owner satisfaction, and (4) *learning and growth*—organizational change, innovation, and growth. ■

GLOBAL VIEW

Managerial accounting is more flexible than financial accounting and does not follow a set of strict rules. However, many international businesses use the managerial accounting concepts and principles described in this chapter.

Customer Focus Nestlé, one of the world's leading nutrition and wellness companies, adopts a customer focus and strives to understand its customers' tastes. For example, Nestlé employees spent three days living with people in Lima, Peru, to understand their motivations, routines, buying habits, and everyday lives. This allowed Nestlé to adjust its products to suit local tastes.

Reporting Manufacturing Activities Nestlé must classify and report costs. In reporting inventory, Nestlé includes direct production costs, production overhead, and factory depreciation. A recent Nestlé annual report shows the following:

(in millions of Swiss francs)	Ending Inventory	Beginning Inventory
Raw materials, work in progress, and sundry supplies	3,243	3,175
Finished goods	4,182	4,741

Nestlé managers use this information, along with the more detailed information found in a manufacturing statement, to plan and control manufacturing activities.

Decision Analysis — Raw Materials Inventory Turnover and Days' Sales in Raw Materials Inventory

A1 Assess raw materials inventory management using raw materials inventory turnover and days' sales in raw materials inventory.

Managerial accounting information helps business managers perform detailed analyses that are not readily available to external users of accounting information. Inventory management is one example. Using publicly available financial statements, an external user can compute the *inventory turnover* ratio. However, a managerial accountant can go much further.

Raw Materials Inventory Turnover

A business manager can assess how effectively a company manages its *raw materials* inventory by computing the **raw materials inventory turnover ratio** as shown in Exhibit 14.20.

EXHIBIT 14.20

Raw Materials Inventory Turnover

Raw materials inventory turnover = Raw materials used/Average raw materials inventory

This ratio reveals how many times a company turns over (uses in production) its raw materials inventory during a period. Generally, a high ratio of raw materials inventory turnover is preferred, as long as raw materials inventory levels are adequate to meet demand. To illustrate, Rocky Mountain Bikes reports direct (raw) materials used of $85,500 for a year, with a beginning raw materials inventory of $8,000 and an ending raw materials inventory of $9,000 (see Exhibit 14.17). Raw materials inventory turnover for Rocky Mountain Bikes for that year is computed as in Exhibit 14.21.

EXHIBIT 14.21

Raw Materials Inventory Turnover Computed

Raw materials inventory turnover = $85,500/[($8,000 + $9,000)/2] = 10.06 (rounded).

Days' Sales in Raw Materials Inventory

To further assess raw materials inventory management, a manager can measure the adequacy of raw materials inventory to meet production demand. **Days' sales in raw materials inventory** reveals how much raw materials inventory is available in terms of the number of days' sales. It is a measure of how long it takes raw materials to be used in production. It is defined and computed for Rocky Mountain Bikes in Exhibit 14.22.

EXHIBIT 14.22

Days' Sales in Raw Materials Inventory Turnover

Days' sales in raw materials inventory = Ending raw materials inventory/Raw materials used × 365
= $9,000/$85,500 × 365 = 38.4 days (rounded)

This computation suggests that it will take 38 days for Rocky Mountain Bikes' raw materials inventory to be used in production. Assuming production needs can be met, companies usually prefer a *lower* number of days' sales in raw materials inventory. Just-in-time manufacturing techniques can be useful in lowering days' sales in raw materials inventory; for example, **Dell** keeps less than seven days of production needs in raw materials inventory for most of its computer components.

DEMONSTRATION PROBLEM 1: COST BEHAVIOR AND CLASSIFICATION

Understanding the classification and assignment of costs is important. Consider a company that manufactures computer chips. It incurs the following costs in manufacturing chips and in operating the company.

1. Plastic board used to mount the chip, $3.50 each.
2. Assembly worker pay of $15 per hour to attach chips to plastic board.
3. Salary for factory maintenance workers who maintain factory equipment.
4. Factory supervisor pay of $55,000 per year to supervise employees.
5. Real estate taxes paid on the factory, $14,500.
6. Real estate taxes paid on the company office, $6,000.
7. Depreciation costs on machinery used by workers, $30,000.
8. Salary paid to the chief financial officer, $95,000.
9. Advertising costs of $7,800 paid to promote products.

10. Salespersons' commissions of $0.50 for each assembled chip sold.

11. Management has the option to rent the manufacturing plant to six local hospitals to store medical records instead of producing and assembling chips.

Classify each cost in the following table according to the categories listed in the table header. A cost can be classified under more than one category. For example, the plastic board used to mount chips is classified as a direct material product cost and as a direct unit cost.

	Period Costs	Product Costs			Unit Cost Classification		Sunk Cost	Opportunity Cost
Cost	Selling and Administrative	Direct Material (Prime Cost)	Direct Labor (Prime and Conversion)	Factory Overhead (Conversion Cost)	Direct	Indirect		
1. Plastic board used to mount the chip, $3.50 each		✔			✔			

SOLUTION TO DEMONSTRATION PROBLEM 1

	Period Costs	Product Costs			Unit Cost Classification		Sunk Cost	Opportunity Cost
Cost*	Selling and Administrative	Direct Material (Prime Cost)	Direct Labor (Prime and Conversion)	Factory Overhead (Conversion Cost)	Direct	Indirect		
1.		✔			✔			
2.			✔		✔			
3.				✔		✔		
4.				✔		✔		
5.				✔		✔		
6.	✔							
7.				✔		✔	✔	
8.	✔							
9.	✔							
10.	✔							
11.								✔

* Costs 1 through 11 refer to the 11 cost items described at the beginning of the problem.

DEMONSTRATION PROBLEM 2: REPORTING FOR MANUFACTURERS

A manufacturing company's balance sheet and income statement differ from those for a merchandising or service company.

Required

1. Fill in the [BLANK] descriptors on the partial balance sheets for both the manufacturing company and the merchandising company. Explain why a different presentation is required.

Manufacturing Company

ADIDAS GROUP Partial Balance Sheet December 31, 2013	
Current assets	
Cash	$10,000
[BLANK]	8,000
[BLANK]	5,000
[BLANK]	7,000
Supplies	500
Prepaid insurance	500
Total current assets	$31,000

Merchandising Company

PAYLESS SHOE OUTLET Partial Balance Sheet December 31, 2013	
Current assets	
Cash	$ 5,000
[BLANK]	12,000
Supplies	500
Prepaid insurance	500
Total current assets	$18,000

2. Fill in the [BLANK] descriptors on the income statements for the manufacturing company and the merchandising company. Explain why a different presentation is required.

Manufacturing Company

ADIDAS GROUP Partial Income Statement For Year Ended December 31, 2013	
Sales	$200,000
Cost of goods sold	
Finished goods inventory, Dec. 31, 2012	10,000
[BLANK]	120,000
Goods available for sale	130,000
Finished goods inventory, Dec. 31, 2013	(7,000)
Cost of goods sold	123,000
Gross profit	$ 77,000

Merchandising Company

PAYLESS SHOE OUTLET Partial Income Statement For Year Ended December 31, 2013	
Sales	$190,000
Cost of goods sold	
Merchandise inventory, Dec. 31, 2012	8,000
[BLANK]	108,000
Goods available for sale	116,000
Merchandise inventory, Dec. 31, 2013	(12,000)
Cost of goods sold	104,000
Gross profit	$ 86,000

3. A manufacturer's cost of goods manufactured is the sum of (a) ______, (b) ______, and (c) ______ costs incurred in producing the product.

SOLUTION TO DEMONSTRATION PROBLEM 2

1. Inventories for a manufacturer and for a merchandiser.

Manufacturing Company

ADIDAS GROUP Partial Balance Sheet December 31, 2013	
Current assets	
Cash	$10,000
Raw materials inventory	8,000
Goods in process inventory	5,000
Finished goods inventory	7,000
Supplies	500
Prepaid insurance	500
Total current assets	$31,000

Merchandising Company

PAYLESS SHOE OUTLET Partial Balance Sheet December 31, 2013	
Current assets	
Cash	$ 5,000
Merchandise inventory	12,000
Supplies	500
Prepaid insurance	500
Total current assets	$18,000

Explanation: A manufacturing company must control and measure three types of inventories: raw materials, goods in process, and finished goods. In the sequence of making a product, the raw materials move into production—called *goods in process inventory*—and then to finished goods. All raw materials and goods in process inventory at the end of each accounting period are considered current assets. All unsold finished inventory is considered a current asset at the end of each accounting period. The merchandising company must control and measure only one type of inventory, purchased goods.

2. Cost of goods sold for a manufacturer and for a merchandiser.

Manufacturing Company

ADIDAS GROUP
Partial Income Statement
For Year Ended December 31, 2013

Sales		$200,000
Cost of goods sold		
Finished goods inventory, Dec. 31, 2012	10,000	
Cost of goods manufactured	120,000	
Goods available for sale	130,000	
Finished goods inventory, Dec. 31, 2013	(7,000)	
Cost of goods sold		123,000
Gross profit		$ 77,000

Merchandising Company

PAYLESS SHOE OUTLET
Partial Income Statement
For Year Ended December 31, 2013

Sales		$190,000
Cost of goods sold		
Merchandise inventory, Dec. 31, 2012	8,000	
Cost of purchases	108,000	
Goods available for sale	116,000	
Merchandise inventory, Dec. 31, 2013	(12,000)	
Cost of goods sold		104,000
Gross profit		$ 86,000

Explanation: Manufacturing and merchandising companies use different reporting terms. In particular, the terms *finished goods* and *cost of goods manufactured* are used to reflect the production of goods, yet the concepts and techniques of reporting cost of goods sold for a manufacturing company and merchandising company are similar.

3. A manufacturer's cost of goods manufactured is the sum of (a) *direct material,* (b) *direct labor,* and (c) *factory overhead* costs incurred in producing the product.

DEMONSTRATION PROBLEM 3: MANUFACTURING STATEMENT

The following account balances and other information are from SUNN Corporation's accounting records for year-end December 31, 2013. Use this information to prepare (1) a table listing factory overhead costs, (2) a manufacturing statement (show only the total factory overhead cost), and (3) an income statement.

Advertising expense	$ 85,000	Goods in process inventory, Dec. 31, 2012	$ 8,000
Amortization expense—Factory Patents	16,000	Goods in process inventory, Dec. 31, 2013	9,000
Bad debts expense	28,000	Income taxes	53,400
Depreciation expense—Office equipment	37,000	Indirect labor	26,000
Depreciation expense—Factory building	133,000	Interest expense	25,000
Depreciation expense—Factory equipment	78,000	Miscellaneous expense	55,000
Direct labor	250,000	Property taxes on factory equipment	14,000
Factory insurance expired	62,000	Raw materials inventory, Dec. 31, 2012	60,000
Factory supervision	74,000	Raw materials inventory, Dec. 31, 2013	78,000
Factory supplies used	21,000	Raw materials purchases	313,000
Factory utilities	115,000	Repairs expense—Factory equipment	31,000
Finished goods inventory, Dec. 31, 2012	15,000	Salaries expense	150,000
Finished goods inventory, Dec. 31, 2013	12,500	Sales	1,630,000

PLANNING THE SOLUTION

- Analyze the account balances and select those that are part of factory overhead costs.
- Arrange these costs in a table that lists factory overhead costs for the year.
- Analyze the remaining costs and select those related to production activity for the year; selected costs should include the materials and goods in process inventories and direct labor.

- Prepare a manufacturing statement for the year showing the calculation of the cost of materials used in production, the cost of direct labor, and the total factory overhead cost. When presenting overhead cost on this statement, report only total overhead cost from the table of overhead costs for the year. Show the costs of beginning and ending goods in process inventory to determine cost of goods manufactured.
- Organize the remaining revenue and expense items into the income statement for the year. Combine cost of goods manufactured from the manufacturing statement with the finished goods inventory amounts to compute cost of goods sold for the year.

SOLUTION TO DEMONSTRATION PROBLEM 3

SUNN CORPORATION
Factory Overhead Costs
For Year Ended December 31, 2013

Amortization expense—Factory patents	$ 16,000
Depreciation expense—Factory building	133,000
Depreciation expense—Factory equipment	78,000
Factory insurance expired	62,000
Factory supervision	74,000
Factory supplies used	21,000
Factory utilities	115,000
Indirect labor	26,000
Property taxes on factory equipment	14,000
Repairs expense—Factory equipment	31,000
Total factory overhead	$570,000

SUNN CORPORATION
Manufacturing Statement
For Year Ended December 31, 2013

Direct materials	
Raw materials inventory, Dec. 31, 2012	$ 60,000
Raw materials purchase	313,000
Raw materials available for use	373,000
Less raw materials inventory, Dec. 31, 2013	78,000
Direct materials used	295,000
Direct labor	250,000
Factory overhead	570,000
Total manufacturing costs	1,115,000
Goods in process inventory, Dec. 31, 2012	8,000
Total cost of goods in process	1,123,000
Less goods in process inventory, Dec. 31, 2013	9,000
Cost of goods manufactured	$1,114,000

SUNN CORPORATION
Income Statement
For Year Ended December 31, 2013

Sales		$1,630,000
Cost of goods sold		
Finished goods inventory, Dec. 31, 2012	$ 15,000	
Cost of goods manufactured	1,114,000	
Goods available for sale	1,129,000	
Less finished goods inventory, Dec. 31, 2013	12,500	
Cost of goods sold		1,116,500
Gross profit		513,500
Operating expenses		
Advertising expense	85,000	
Bad debts expense	28,000	
Depreciation expense—Office equipment	37,000	
Interest expense	25,000	
Miscellaneous expense	55,000	
Salaries expense	150,000	
Total operating expenses		380,000
Income before income taxes		133,500
Income taxes		53,400
Net income		$ 80,100

Summary

C1 Explain the purpose and nature of, and the role of ethics in, managerial accounting. The purpose of managerial accounting is to provide useful information to management and other internal decision makers. It does this by collecting, managing, and reporting both monetary and nonmonetary information in a manner useful to internal users. Major characteristics of managerial accounting include (1) focus on internal decision makers, (2) emphasis on planning and control, (3) flexibility, (4) timeliness, (5) reliance on forecasts and estimates, (6) focus on segments and projects, and (7) reporting both monetary and nonmonetary information. Ethics are beliefs that distinguish right from wrong. Ethics can be important in reducing fraud in business operations.

C2 Describe accounting concepts useful in classifying costs. We can classify costs on the basis of their (1) behavior—fixed vs. variable, (2) traceability—direct vs. indirect, (3) controllability—controllable vs. uncontrollable, (4) relevance—sunk vs. out of pocket, and (5) function—product vs. period. A cost can be classified in more than one way, depending on the purpose for which the cost is being determined. These classifications help us understand cost patterns, analyze performance, and plan operations.

C3 Define product and period costs and explain how they impact financial statements. Costs that are capitalized because they are expected to have future value are called *product costs;* costs that are expensed are called *period costs.* This classification is important because it affects the amount of costs expensed in the income statement and the amount of costs assigned to inventory on the balance sheet. Product costs are commonly made up of direct materials, direct labor, and overhead. Period costs include selling and administrative expenses.

C4 Explain how balance sheets and income statements for manufacturing and merchandising companies differ. The main difference is that manufacturers usually carry three inventories on their balance sheets—raw materials, goods in process, and finished goods—instead of one inventory that merchandisers carry. The main difference between income statements of manufacturers and merchandisers is the items making up cost of goods sold. A merchandiser adds beginning merchandise inventory to cost of goods purchased and then subtracts ending merchandise inventory to get cost of goods sold. A manufacturer adds beginning finished goods inventory to cost of goods manufactured and then subtracts ending finished goods inventory to get cost of goods sold.

C5 Explain manufacturing activities and the flow of manufacturing costs. Manufacturing activities consist of materials, production, and sales activities. The materials activity consists of the purchase and issuance of materials to production. The production activity consists of converting materials into finished goods. At this stage in the process, the materials, labor, and overhead costs have been incurred and the manufacturing statement is prepared. The sales activity consists of selling some or all of finished goods available for sale. At this stage, the cost of goods sold is determined.

C6 Describe trends in managerial accounting. Important trends in managerial accounting include an increased focus on satisfying customers, the impact of a global economy, and the growing presence of e-commerce and service-based businesses. The lean business model, designed to eliminate waste and satisfy customers, can be useful in responding to recent trends. Concepts such as total quality management, just-in-time production, and the value chain often aid in application of the lean business model.

A1 Assess raw materials inventory management using raw materials inventory turnover and days' sales in raw materials inventory. A high raw materials inventory turnover suggests a business is more effective in managing its raw materials inventory. We use days' sales in raw materials inventory to assess the likelihood of production being delayed due to inadequate levels of raw materials. We prefer a high raw materials inventory turnover ratio and a small number of days' sales in raw materials inventory, provided that raw materials inventory levels are adequate to keep production steady.

P1 Compute cost of goods sold for a manufacturer. A manufacturer adds beginning finished goods inventory to cost of goods manufactured and then subtracts ending finished goods inventory to get cost of goods sold.

P2 Prepare a manufacturing statement and explain its purpose and links to financial statements. The manufacturing statement reports computation of cost of goods manufactured for the period. It begins by showing the period's costs for direct materials, direct labor, and overhead and then adjusts these numbers for the beginning and ending inventories of the goods in process to yield cost of goods manufactured.

Guidance Answers to Decision Maker and Decision Ethics

Production Manager It appears that all three friends want to pay the bill with someone else's money. David is using money belonging to the tax authorities, Denise is taking money from her company, and Derek is defrauding the client. To prevent such practices, companies have internal audit mechanisms. Many companies also adopt ethical codes of conduct to help guide employees. We must recognize that some entertainment expenses are justifiable and even encouraged. For example, the tax law allows certain deductions for entertainment that have a business purpose. Corporate policies also sometimes allow and encourage reimbursable spending for social activities, and contracts can include entertainment as allowable costs. Nevertheless, without further details, payment for this bill should be made from personal accounts.

Entrepreneur Tracing all costs directly to cost objects is always desirable, but you need to be able to do so in an economically feasible manner. In this case, you are able to trace 90% of the assembly department's direct costs. It may not be economical to spend more money on a new software to trace the final 10% of costs. You need to make a cost–benefit trade-off. If the software offers benefits beyond tracing the remaining 10% of the assembly department's costs, your decision should consider this.

Purchase Manager Opportunity costs relate to the potential quality and delivery benefits given up by not choosing supplier (A). Selecting supplier (B) might involve future costs of poor-quality seats (inspection, repairs, and returns). Also, potential delivery delays could interrupt work and increase manufacturing costs. Your company could also incur sales losses if the product quality of supplier (B) is low. As purchase manager, you are responsible for these costs and must consider them in making your decision.

Guidance Answers to Quick Checks

1. *d*
2. Financial accounting information is intended for users external to an organization such as investors, creditors, and government authorities. Managerial accounting focuses on providing information to managers, officers, and other decision makers within the organization.
3. No, GAAP do not control the practice of managerial accounting. Unlike external users, the internal users need managerial accounting information for planning and controlling business activities rather than for external comparison. Different types of information are required, depending on the activity. Therefore it is difficult to standardize managerial accounting.
4. Variable costs increase when volume of activity increases.
5. By being able to trace costs to cost objects (say, to products and departments), managers better understand the total costs associated with a cost object. This is useful when managers consider making changes to the cost object (such as when dropping the product or expanding the department).
6. Raw materials inventory, goods in process inventory, and finished goods inventory.
7. The cost of goods sold for merchandising companies includes all costs of acquiring the merchandise; the cost of goods sold for manufacturing companies includes the three costs of manufacturing: direct materials, direct labor, and overhead.
8. *a*
9. No; companies rarely report a manufacturing statement.
10. Beginning goods in process inventory is added to total manufacturing costs to yield total goods in process. Ending goods in process inventory is subtracted from total goods in process to yield cost of goods manufactured for the period.

Key Terms

Continuous improvement (p. 626)
Control (p. 611)
Controllable or **not controllable cost** (p. 615)
Conversion costs (p. 619)
Cost object (p. 615)
Customer orientation (p. 626)
Days' sales in raw materials inventory (p. 628)
Direct costs (p. 615)
Direct labor (p. 618)
Direct labor costs (p. 618)
Direct materials (p. 618)
Direct material costs (p. 618)
Ethics (p. 614)
Factory overhead (p. 618)
Factory overhead costs (p. 618)
Finished goods inventory (p. 620)
Fixed cost (p. 614)
Goods in process inventory (p. 620)
Indirect costs (p. 615)
Indirect labor (p. 618)
Indirect labor costs (p. 618)
Indirect material (p. 620)
Institute of Management Accountants (IMA) (p. 614)
Internal control system (p. 614)
Just-in-time (JIT) manufacturing (p. 626)
Lean business model (p. 626)
Managerial accounting (p. 610)
Manufacturing statement (p. 623)
Opportunity cost (p. 616)
Out-of-pocket cost (p. 616)
Period costs (p. 616)
Planning (p. 610)
Prime costs (p. 619)
Product costs (p. 616)
Raw materials inventory (p. 620)
Raw materials inventory turnover ratio (p. 628)
Sunk cost (p. 616)
Total quality management (TQM) (p. 626)
Value chain (p. 626)
Variable cost (p. 614)

Multiple Choice Quiz

Answers on p. 651

mhhe.com/wildFINMAN5e

Additional Quiz Questions are available at the book's Website.

1. Continuous improvement
a. Is used to reduce inventory levels.
b. Is applicable only in service businesses.
c. Rejects the notion of "good enough."
d. Is used to reduce ordering costs.
e. Is applicable only in manufacturing businesses.

2. A direct cost is one that is
a. Variable with respect to the cost object.
b. Traceable to the cost object.
c. Fixed with respect to the cost object.
d. Allocated to the cost object.
e. A period cost.

3. Costs that are incurred as part of the manufacturing process, but are not clearly traceable to the specific unit of product or batches of product, are called
a. Period costs.
b. Factory overhead.
c. Sunk costs.
d. Opportunity costs.
e. Fixed costs.

4. The three major cost components of manufacturing a product are
a. Direct materials, direct labor, and factory overhead.
b. Period costs, product costs, and sunk costs.
c. Indirect labor, indirect materials, and fixed expenses.
d. Variable costs, fixed costs, and period costs.
e. Opportunity costs, sunk costs, and direct costs.

5. A company reports the following for the current year.

Finished goods inventory, beginning year	$6,000
Finished goods inventory, ending year	3,200
Cost of goods sold	7,500

Its cost of goods manufactured for the current year is
a. $1,500.
b. $1,700.
c. $7,500.
d. $2,800.
e. $4,700.

[I] Icon denotes assignments that involve decision making.

Discussion Questions

1. Describe the managerial accountant's role in business planning, control, and decision making.

2. Distinguish between managerial and financial accounting on
a. Users and decision makers. **b.** Purpose of information.
c. Flexibility of practice. **d.** Time dimension.
e. Focus of information. **f.** Nature of information.

3. [I] Identify the usual changes that a company must make when it adopts a customer orientation.

4. Distinguish between direct labor and indirect labor.

5. Distinguish between (*a*) factory overhead and (*b*) selling and administrative overhead.

6. Distinguish between direct material and indirect material.

7. What product cost is listed as both a prime cost and a conversion cost?

8. [I] Assume that we tour **Polaris**' factory where it makes its products. List three direct costs and three indirect costs that we are likely to see. **Polaris**

9. [I] Should we evaluate a manager's performance on the basis of controllable or noncontrollable costs? Why?

10. [I] Explain why knowledge of cost behavior is useful in product performance evaluation.

11. Explain why product costs are capitalized but period costs are expensed in the current accounting period.

12. [I] Explain how business activities and inventories for a manufacturing company, a merchandising company, and a service company differ.

13. [I] Why does managerial accounting often involve working with numerous predictions and estimates?

14. How do an income statement and a balance sheet for a manufacturing company and a merchandising company differ?

15. Besides inventories, what other assets often appear on manufacturers' balance sheets but not on merchandisers' balance sheets?

16. Why does a manufacturing company require three different inventory categories?

17. Manufacturing activities of a company are described in the ________. This statement summarizes the types and amounts of costs incurred in its manufacturing ________.

18. What are the three categories of manufacturing costs?

19. List several examples of factory overhead.

20. [I] List the four components of a manufacturing statement and provide specific examples of each for **Polaris**. **Polaris**

21. Prepare a proper title for the annual "manufacturing statement" of **Arctic Cat**. Does the date match the balance sheet or income statement? Why?

Arctic Cat

22. Describe the relations among the income statement, the manufacturing statement, and a detailed listing of factory overhead costs.

23. Define and describe two measures to assess raw materials inventory management.

24. Can management of a company such as **Polaris** use cycle time and cycle efficiency as useful measures of performance? Explain.

Polaris

25. Access **Dell**'s annual report (10-K) for the fiscal year ended February 3, 2012, at the SEC's EDGAR database (SEC.gov) or its Website (Dell.com). From its financial statement notes, identify the titles and amounts of its inventory components.

connect

QUICK STUDY

QS 14-1
Managerial accounting defined
C1

Managerial accounting (choose one)

1. Is directed at reporting aggregate data on the company as a whole.
2. Provides information that is widely available to all interested parties.
3. Must follow generally accepted accounting principles.
4. Provides information to aid management in planning and controlling business activities.

QS 14-2
Managerial accounting versus financial accounting
C1

Identify whether each description most likely applies to managerial or financial accounting.

1. ________ Its primary users are company managers.
2. ________ Its information is often available only after an audit is complete.
3. ________ Its primary focus is on the organization as a whole.
4. ________ Its principles and practices are very flexible.
5. ________ It is directed at external users in making investment, credit, and other decisions.

QS 14-3
Product and period costs
C3

Which of these statements is true regarding product and period costs?

1. Factory maintenance is a product cost and sales commission is a period cost.
2. Sales commission is a product cost and depreciation on factory equipment is a product cost.
3. Sales commission is a product cost and factory rent is a period cost.
4. Factory wages are a product cost and direct material is a period cost.

QS 14-4
Fixed and variable costs
C2

Which of these statements is true regarding fixed and variable costs?

1. Fixed costs stay the same and variable costs increase in total as activity volume increases.
2. Both fixed and variable costs increase as activity volume increases.
3. Both fixed and variable costs stay the same in total as activity volume increases.
4. Fixed costs increase and variable costs decrease in total as activity volume decreases.

QS 14-5
Direct and indirect costs
C2

Verdi Company produces sporting equipment, including leather footballs. Identify each of the following costs as direct or indirect if the cost object is a football produced by Verdi.

1. Electricity used in the production plant.
2. Labor used on the football production line.
3. Salary of manager who supervises the entire plant.
4. Depreciation on equipment used to produce footballs.
5. Leather used to produce footballs.

QS 14-6
Inventory reporting for manufacturers C4

Three inventory categories are reported on a manufacturing company's balance sheet: (a) raw materials, (b) goods in process, and (c) finished goods. Identify the usual order in which these inventory items are reported on the balance sheet.

1. (b)(c)(a) **2.** (c)(b)(a) **3.** (a)(b)(c) **4.** (b)(a)(c)

QS 14-7
Cost of goods sold
P1

Compute cost of goods sold for year 2013 using the following information.

Finished goods inventory, Dec. 31, 2012	$345,000
Goods in process inventory, Dec. 31, 2012	83,500
Goods in process inventory, Dec. 31, 2013	72,300
Cost of goods manufactured, year 2013	918,700
Finished goods inventory, Dec. 31, 2013	283,600

QS 14-8
Cost of goods sold P1

A company has year-end cost of goods manufactured of $4,000, beginning finished goods inventory of $500, and ending finished goods inventory of $750. Its cost of goods sold is

1. $4,250 **2.** $4,000 **3.** $3,750 **4.** $3,900

QS 14-9
Manufacturing flows identified
C5

Identify the usual sequence of manufacturing activities by filling in the blank (1, 2 or 3) corresponding to its order: ______ Production activities; ______ sales activities; ______ materials activities.

QS 14-10
Cost of goods manufactured
P2

Prepare the 2013 manufacturing statement for Briton Company using the following information.

Direct materials	$190,500
Direct labor	63,150
Factory overhead costs	24,000
Goods in process, Dec. 31, 2012	157,600
Goods in process, Dec. 31, 2013	142,750

QS 14-11
Lean business concepts
C6

Match each lean business concept with its best description by entering its letter in the blank.

1. ______ Just-in-time manufacturing
2. ______ Continuous improvements
3. ______ Customer orientation
4. ______ Total quality management

A. Focuses on quality throughout the production process.
B. Flexible product designs can be modified to accommodate customer choices.
C. Every manager and employee constantly looks for ways to improve company operations.
D. Inventory is acquired or produced only as needed.

QS 14-12
Direct materials used
C5

Nestlé reports beginning raw materials inventory of 3,243 and ending raw materials inventory of 3,904 (both numbers in millions of Swiss francs). If Nestlé purchased 16,200 (in millions of Swiss francs) of raw materials during the year, what is the amount of raw materials it used during the year?

QS 14-13
Raw materials inventory management A1

Refer to QS 14-12 and compute raw materials inventory turnover and the number of days' sales in raw materials inventory.

connect

EXERCISES

Exercise 14-1
Characteristics of financial accounting and managerial accounting

C1

In the following chart, compare financial accounting and managerial accounting by describing how each differs for the items listed. Be specific in your responses.

	Financial Accounting	Managerial Accounting
1. Time dimension	________	________
2. Users and decision makers	________	________
3. Timeliness of information	________	________
4. Purpose of information	________	________
5. Nature of information	________	________
6. Flexibility of practice	________	________
7. Focus of information	________	________

Exercise 14-2
Planning and control descriptions

C1

Complete the following statements by filling in the blanks.

1. ________ ________ usually covers a period of one year.

2. ________ is the process of monitoring planning decisions and evaluating an organization's activities and employees.

3. ________ is the process of setting goals and making plans to achieve them.

4. ________ ________ usually covers a period of 5 to 10 years.

Exercise 14-3
Sources of accounting information

C1

Both managerial accounting and financial accounting provide useful information to decision makers. Indicate in the following chart the most likely source of information for each business decision (a decision can require major input from both sources, in which case both can be marked).

Business Decision	Primary Information Source	
	Managerial	Financial
1. Determine amount of dividends to pay stockholders	____	____
2. Evaluate a purchasing department's performance	____	____
3. Report financial performance to board of directors	____	____
4. Estimate product cost for a new line of shoes	____	____
5. Plan the budget for next quarter	____	____
6. Measure profitability of all individual stores	____	____
7. Prepare financial reports according to GAAP	____	____
8. Determine location and size for a new plant	____	____

Exercise 14-4
Cost classifications C2

(1) Identify each of the five cost classifications discussed in the chapter. (2) List two purposes of identifying these separate cost classifications.

Exercise 14-5
Cost analysis and classification

C2

Listed here are product costs for the production of soccer balls. (1) Classify each cost (a) as either variable or fixed and (b) as either direct or indirect. (2) What pattern do you see regarding the relation between costs classified by behavior and costs classified by traceability?

Product Cost	Cost by Behavior		Cost by Traceability	
	Variable	Fixed	Direct	Indirect
1. Leather covers for soccer balls	____	____	____	____
2. Annual flat fee paid for office security	____	____	____	____
3. Coolants for machinery	____	____	____	____
4. Wages of assembly workers	____	____	____	____
5. Lace to hold leather together	____	____	____	____
6. Taxes on factory	____	____	____	____
7. Machinery depreciation	____	____	____	____

Exercise 14-6
Cost analysis and identification
C3

Georgia Pacific, a manufacturer, incurs the following costs. (1) Classify each cost as either a product or a period cost. If a product cost, identify it as direct materials, direct labor, or factory overhead, and then as a prime and/or conversion cost. (2) Classify each product cost as either a direct cost or an indirect cost using the product as the cost object.

	Product Cost						
	Prime		Conversion				
Cost	Direct Material	Direct Labor	Direct Labor	Overhead	Period Cost	Direct Cost	Indirect Cost
1. Factory utilities	____	____	____	____	____	____	____
2. Advertising	____	____	____	____	____	____	____
3. Amortization of patents on factory machine	____	____	____	____	____	____	____
4. State and federal income taxes	____	____	____	____	____	____	____
5. Office supplies used	____	____	____	____	____	____	____
6. Bad debts expense	____	____	____	____	____	____	____
7. Small tools used	____	____	____	____	____	____	____
8. Payroll taxes for production supervisor	____	____	____	____	____	____	____
9. Accident insurance on factory workers	____	____	____	____	____	____	____
10. Depreciation—Factory building	____	____	____	____	____	____	____
11. Wages to assembly workers	____	____	____	____	____	____	____
12. Direct materials used	____	____	____	____	____	____	____

Exercise 14-7
Balance sheet identification and preparation
C4

Current assets for two different companies at calendar year-end 2013 are listed here. One is a manufacturer, Salomon Skis Mfg., and the other, Sun Fresh Foods, is a grocery distribution company. (1) Identify which set of numbers relates to the manufacturer and which to the merchandiser. (2) Prepare the current asset section for each company from this information. Discuss why the current asset section for these two companies is different.

Account	Company 1	Company 2
Cash	$ 7,000	$ 5,000
Raw materials inventory	—	42,000
Merchandise inventory	45,000	—
Goods in process inventory	—	30,000
Finished goods inventory	—	50,000
Accounts receivable, net	62,000	75,000
Prepaid expenses	1,500	900

Exercise 14-8
Cost of goods manufactured and cost of goods sold computation
P1 P2

Using the following data, compute (1) the cost of goods manufactured and (2) the cost of goods sold for both Garcia Company and Culpepper Company.

	Garcia Company	Culpepper Company
Beginning finished goods inventory	$12,000	$16,450
Beginning goods in process inventory	14,500	19,950
Beginning raw materials inventory	7,250	9,000
Rental cost on factory equipment	27,000	22,750
Direct labor	19,000	35,000
Ending finished goods inventory	17,650	13,300
Ending goods in process inventory	22,000	16,000
Ending raw materials inventory	5,300	7,200
Factory utilities	9,000	12,000
Factory supplies used	8,200	3,200
General and administrative expenses	21,000	43,000
Indirect labor	1,250	7,660
Repairs—Factory equipment	4,780	1,500
Raw materials purchases	33,000	52,000
Sales salaries	50,000	46,000

Check Garcia COGS, $91,030

Exercise 14-9
Cost of goods sold computation
P1

Compute cost of goods sold for each of these two companies for the year ended December 31, 2013.

		Viking Retail	Log Homes Manufacturing
3	Beginning inventory		
4	Merchandise	$275,000	
5	Finished goods		$450,000
6	Cost of purchases	500,000	
7	Cost of goods manufactured		900,000
8	Ending inventory		
9	Merchandise	115,000	
10	Finished goods		375,000

Check Viking COGS, $660,000

Exercise 14-10
Cost flows in manufacturing
C5

The following chart shows how costs flow through a business as a product is manufactured. Some boxes in the flowchart show cost amounts. Compute the cost amounts for the boxes that contain question marks.

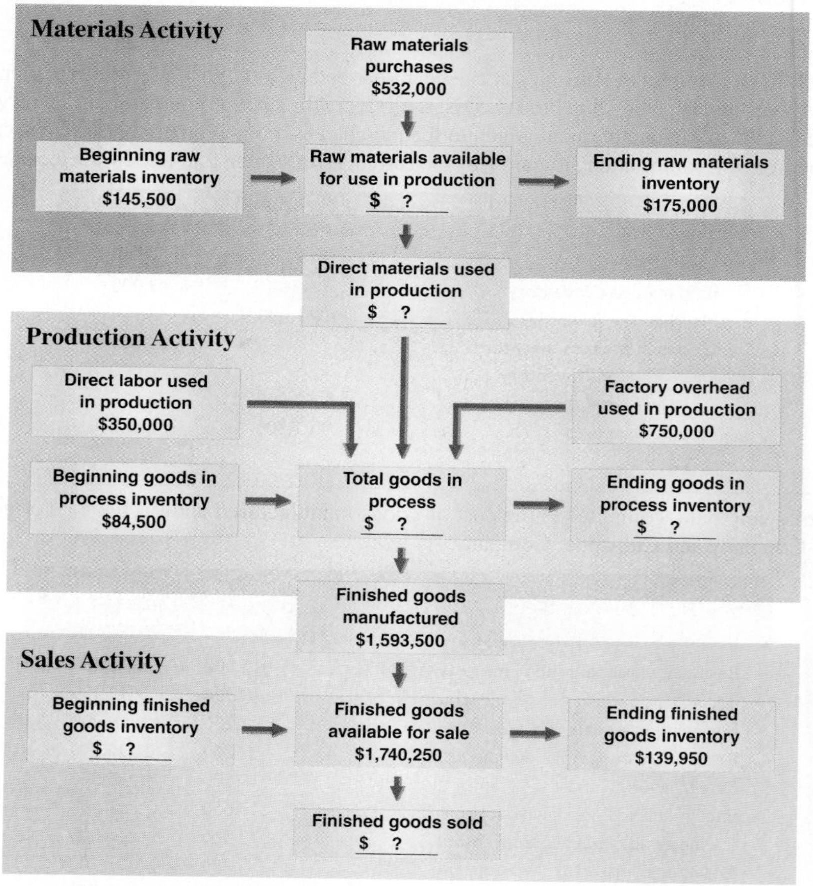

Exercise 14-11
Components of accounting reports
P2

For each of the following accounts for a manufacturing company, place a ✔ in the appropriate column indicating that it appears on the balance sheet, the income statement, the manufacturing statement, and/or a detailed listing of factory overhead costs. Assume that the income statement shows the calculation of cost of goods sold and the manufacturing statement shows only the total amount of factory overhead. (An account can appear on more than one report.)

	Account	Balance Sheet	Income Statement	Manufacturing Statement	Overhead Report
3	Accounts receivable				
4	Computer supplies used in office				
5	Beginning finished goods inventory				
6	Beginning goods in process inventory				
7	Beginning raw materials inventory				
8	Cash				
9	Depreciation expense—Factory building				
10	Depreciation expense—Factory equipment				
11	Depreciation expense—Office building				
12	Depreciation expense—Office equipment				
13	Direct labor				
14	Ending finished goods inventory				
15	Ending goods in process inventory				
16	Ending raw materials inventory				
17	Factory maintenance wages				
18	Computer supplies used in factory				
19	Income taxes				
20	Insurance on factory building				
21	Rent cost on office building				
22	Office supplies used				
23	Property taxes on factory building				
24	Raw materials purchases				
25	Sales				

Exercise 14-12
Manufacturing statement preparation
P2

Given the following selected account balances of Shanta Company, prepare its manufacturing statement for the year ended on December 31, 2013. Include a listing of the individual overhead account balances in this statement.

Sales	$1,250,000
Raw materials inventory, Dec. 31, 2012	37,000
Goods in process inventory, Dec. 31, 2012	53,900
Finished goods inventory, Dec. 31, 2012	62,750
Raw materials purchases	175,600
Direct labor	225,000
Factory computer supplies used	17,840
Indirect labor	47,000
Repairs—Factory equipment	5,250
Rent cost of factory building	57,000
Advertising expense	94,000
General and administrative expenses	129,300
Raw materials inventory, Dec. 31, 2013	42,700
Goods in process inventory, Dec. 31, 2013	41,500
Finished goods inventory, Dec. 31, 2013	67,300

Check Cost of goods manufactured, $534,390

Exercise 14-13
Income statement preparation
P2

Use the information in Exercise 14-12 to prepare an income statement for Shanta Company (a manufacturer). Assume that its cost of goods manufactured is $534,390.

Exercise 14-14
Management concepts
C6

Following are three separate events affecting the managerial accounting systems for different companies. Match the management concept(s) that the company is likely to adopt for the event identified. There is some overlap in the meaning of customer orientation and total quality management and, therefore, some responses can include more than one concept.

Event	Management Concept
______ 1. The company starts reporting measures such as the percent of defective products and the number of units scrapped.	a. Continuous improvement (CI)
______ 2. The company starts reporting measures on customer complaints and product returns from customers.	b. Total quality management (TQM)
______ 3. The company starts measuring inventory turnover and discontinues elaborate inventory records. Its new focus is to pull inventory through the system.	c. Just-in-time (JIT) system
	d. Customer orientation (CO)

Exercise 14-15
Customer orientation in practice
C6

Customer orientation means that a company's managers and employees respond to customers' changing wants and needs. A manufacturer of metal parts has created a customer satisfaction survey that it asks each of its customers to complete. The survey asks about the following factors: (A) product performance; (B) price; (C) lead time; (D) delivery. Each factor is to be rated as unsatisfactory, marginal, average, satisfactory, or very satisfied.

a. Match the competitive forces 1 through 4 to the factors on the survey. A factor can be matched to more than one competitive force.

Survey Factor	Competitive Force
A. Product performance	______ **1.** Time
B. Price	______ **2.** Quality
C. Lead time	______ **3.** Cost
D. Delivery	______ **4.** Flexibility of service

b. How can managers of this company use the information from this customer satisfaction survey to better meet competitive forces and satisfy their customers?

Exercise 14-16
Cost classifications for a service company
C2

Listed below are costs of providing an airline service. Classify each cost as (a) either variable or fixed and (b) as either direct or indirect. Consider the cost object to be a flight.

	Cost by Behavior		Cost by Traceability	
Cost	Variable	Fixed	Direct	Indirect
1. Advertising	___	___	___	___
2. Beverages and snacks	___	___	___	___
3. Regional vice-president salary	___	___	___	___
4. Depreciation on ground equipment	___	___	___	___
5. Fuel and oil used in planes	___	___	___	___
6. Flight attendant salaries	___	___	___	___
7. Pilot salaries	___	___	___	___
8. Ground crew wages	___	___	___	___
9. Travel agent salaries	___	___	___	___

connect

PROBLEM SET A

Problem 14-1A
Managerial accounting role
C1

This chapter explained the purpose of managerial accounting in the context of the current business environment. Review the *automobile* section of your local newspaper; the Sunday paper is often best. Review advertisements of sport-utility vehicles and identify the manufacturers that offer these products and the factors on which they compete.

Required

Discuss the potential contributions and responsibilities of the managerial accounting professional in helping an automobile manufacturer succeed. (*Hint:* Think about information and estimates that a managerial accountant might provide new entrants into the sport-utility market.)

Problem 14-2A
Opportunity cost estimation and application
C1 C2

Refer to *Decision Maker*, **Purchase Manager,** in this chapter. Assume that you are the motorcycle manufacturer's managerial accountant. The purchasing manager asks you about preparing an estimate of the related costs for buying motorcycle seats from supplier (B). She tells you this estimate is needed because unless dollar estimates are attached to nonfinancial factors, such as lost production time, her supervisor will not give it full attention. The manager also shows you the following information.

- Production output is 1,000 motorcycles per year based on 250 production days a year.
- Production time per day is 8 hours at a cost of $2,000 per hour to run the production line.
- Lost production time due to poor quality is 1%.
- Satisfied customers purchase, on average, three motorcycles during a lifetime.
- Satisfied customers recommend the product, on average, to 5 other people.
- Marketing predicts that using seat (B) will result in 5 lost customers per year from repeat business and referrals.
- Average gross profit per motorcycle is $3,000.

Required

Estimate the costs (including opportunity costs) of buying motorcycle seats from supplier (B). This problem requires that you think creatively and make reasonable estimates; thus there could be more than one correct answer. (*Hint:* Reread the answer to *Decision Maker* and compare the cost savings for buying from supplier [B] to the sum of lost customer revenue from repeat business and referrals and the cost of lost production time.)

Check Estimated cost of lost production time, $40,000

Problem 14-3A
Cost computation, classification, and analysis
C2 C3

Listed here are the total costs associated with the 2013 production of 1,000 drum sets manufactured by DrumBeat. The drum sets sell for $500 each.

	Cost by Behavior		Cost by Function	
Costs	Variable	Fixed	Product	Period
1. Plastic for casing—$17,000	$17,000	____	$17,000	____
2. Wages of assembly workers—$82,000	____	____	____	____
3. Property taxes on factory—$5,000	____	____	____	____
4. Accounting staff salaries—$35,000	____	____	____	____
5. Drum stands (1,000 stands outsourced)—$26,000	____	____	____	____
6. Rent cost of equipment for sales staff—$10,000	____	____	____	____
7. Upper management salaries—$125,000	____	____	____	____
8. Annual flat fee for maintenance service—$10,000	____	____	____	____
9. Sales commissions—$15 per unit	____	____	____	____
10. Machinery depreciation, straight-line—$40,000	____	____	____	____

Required

1. Classify each cost and its amount as (*a*) either variable or fixed and (*b*) either product or period. (The first cost is completed as an example.)
2. Compute the manufacturing cost per drum set.

Check (1) Total variable production cost, $125,000

Analysis Component

3. Assume that 1,200 drum sets are produced in the next year. What do you predict will be the total cost of plastic for the casings and the per unit cost of the plastic for the casings? Explain.
4. Assume that 1,200 drum sets are produced in the next year. What do you predict will be the total cost of property taxes and the per unit cost of the property taxes? Explain.

Problem 14-4A
Cost classification and explanation
C2 C3

Assume that you must make a presentation to the marketing staff explaining the difference between product and period costs. Your supervisor tells you the marketing staff would also like clarification regarding prime and conversion costs and an explanation of how these terms fit with product and period cost. You are told that many on the staff are unable to classify costs in their merchandising activities.

Required

Prepare a one-page memorandum to your supervisor outlining your presentation to the marketing staff.

Problem 14-5A
Ending inventory computation and evaluation
C4

Notaro's Boot Company makes specialty boots for the rodeo circuit. On December 31, 2012, the company had (*a*) 300 pairs of boots in finished goods inventory and (*b*) 1,200 heels at a cost of $8 each in raw materials inventory. During 2013, the company purchased 35,000 additional heels at $8 each and manufactured 16,600 pairs of boots.

Required

1. Determine the unit and dollar amounts of raw materials inventory in heels at December 31, 2013.

Check (1) Ending (heel) inventory, 3,000 units; $24,000

Analysis Component

2. Write a one-half page memorandum to the production manager explaining why a just-in-time inventory system for heels should be considered. Include the amount of working capital that can be reduced at December 31, 2013, if the ending heel raw material inventory is cut by half.

Problem 14-6A
Inventory computation and reporting
C4 P1

mhhe.com/wildFINMAN5e

Shown here are annual financial data at December 31, 2013, taken from two different companies.

	Sports World Retail	Sno-Board Manufacturing
Beginning inventory		
Merchandise	$200,000	
Finished goods		$500,000
Cost of purchases	300,000	
Cost of goods manufactured		875,000
Ending inventory		
Merchandise	175,000	
Finished goods		225,000

Required

1. Compute the cost of goods sold section of the income statement at December 31, 2013, for each company. Include the proper title and format in the solution.

Check (1) Sno-Board's cost of goods sold, $1,150,000

2. Write a half-page memorandum to your instructor (*a*) identifying the inventory accounts and (*b*) describing where each is reported on the income statement and balance sheet for both companies.

Problem 14-7A
Manufacturing and income statements; inventory analysis
P2 A1

The following calendar year-end information is taken from the December 31, 2013, adjusted trial balance and other records of DeLeon Company.

Advertising expense	$ 28,750	Direct labor	$ 675,480
Depreciation expense—Office equipment	7,250	Income taxes expense	233,725
Depreciation expense—Selling equipment	8,600	Indirect labor	56,875
Depreciation expense—Factory equipment	33,550	Miscellaneous production costs	8,425
Factory supervision	102,600	Office salaries expense	63,000
Factory supplies used	7,350	Raw materials purchases	925,000
Factory utilities	33,000	Rent expense—Office space	22,000
Inventories		Rent expense—Selling space	26,100
Raw materials, December 31, 2012	166,850	Rent expense—Factory building	76,800
Raw materials, December 31, 2013	182,000	Maintenance expense—Factory equipment	35,400
Goods in process, December 31, 2012	15,700	Sales	4,525,000
Goods in process, December 31, 2013	19,380	Sales discounts	62,500
Finished goods, December 31, 2012	167,350	Sales salaries expense	392,560
Finished goods, December 31, 2013	136,490		

Required

1. Prepare the company's 2013 manufacturing statement.

2. Prepare the company's 2013 income statement that reports separate categories for (*a*) selling expenses and (*b*) general and administrative expenses.

Check (1) Cost of goods manufactured, $1,935,650

Analysis Component

3. Compute the (*a*) inventory turnover, defined as cost of goods sold divided by average inventory, and (*b*) days' sales in inventory, defined as 365 times ending inventory divided by cost of goods sold, for both its raw materials inventory and its finished goods inventory. (To compute turnover and days' sales in inventory for raw materials, use raw materials used rather than cost of goods sold.) Discuss some possible reasons for differences between these ratios for the two types of inventories. Round answers to one decimal place.

Problem 14-8A
Lean business concepts
C6

Many fast-food restaurants compete on lean business concepts. Match each of the following activities at a fast-food restaurant with the lean business concept it strives to achieve. Some activities might relate to more than one lean business concept.

_______ **1.** Courteous employees
_______ **2.** Food produced to order
_______ **3.** Clean tables and floors
_______ **4.** Orders filled within three minutes
_______ **5.** Standardized food making processes
_______ **6.** New product development
_______ **7.** Customer satisfaction surveys
_______ **8.** Standardized menus from location to location
_______ **9.** Drive-through windows
_______ **10.** Continually changing menus

a. Just-in-time (JIT)
b. Continuous improvement (CI)
c. Total quality management (TQM)

PROBLEM SET B

Problem 14-1B
Managerial accounting role
C1

This chapter described the purpose of managerial accounting in the context of the current business environment. Review the *home electronics* section of your local newspaper; the Sunday paper is often best. Review advertisements of home electronics and identify the manufacturers that offer these products and the factors on which they compete.

Required

Discuss the potential contributions and responsibilities of the managerial accounting professional in helping a home electronics manufacturer succeed. (*Hint:* Think about information and estimates that a managerial accountant might provide new entrants into the home electronics market.)

Problem 14-2B
Opportunity cost estimation and application
C1 C2

Refer to *Decision Maker,* **Purchase Manager,** in this chapter. Assume that you are the motorcycle manufacturer's managerial accountant. The purchasing manager asks you about preparing an estimate of the related costs for buying motorcycle seats from supplier (B). She tells you this estimate is needed because unless dollar estimates are attached to nonfinancial factors such as lost production time, her supervisor will not give it full attention. The manager also shows you the following information.

- Production output is 1,000 motorcycles per year based on 250 production days a year.
- Production time per day is 8 hours at a cost of $500 per hour to run the production line.
- Lost production time due to poor quality is 1%.
- Satisfied customers purchase, on average, three motorcycles during a lifetime.
- Satisfied customers recommend the product, on average, to four other people.
- Marketing predicts that using seat (B) will result in four lost customers per year from repeat business and referrals.
- Average gross profit per motorcycle is $4,000.

Required

Check Cost of lost gross profit, $16,000

Estimate the costs (including opportunity costs) of buying motorcycle seats from supplier (B). This problem requires that you think creatively and make reasonable estimates; thus there could be more than one correct answer. (*Hint:* Reread the answer to *Decision Maker,* and compare the cost savings for buying from supplier [B] to the sum of lost customer revenue from repeat business and referrals and the cost of lost production time.)

Problem 14-3B
Cost computation, classification, and analysis
C2 C3

Listed here are the total costs associated with the 2013 production of 15,000 Blu-ray Discs (BDs) manufactured by Nextgen. The BDs sell for $18 each.

	Cost by Behavior		Cost by Function	
Costs	Variable	Fixed	Product	Period
1. Plastic for BDs—$1,500	$1,500		$1,500	
2. Wages of assembly workers—$30,000				
3. Cost of factory rent—$6,750				
4. Systems staff salaries—$15,000				
5. Labeling (12,000 outsourced)—$3,750				
6. Cost of office equipment rent—$1,050				
7. Upper management salaries—$120,000				
8. Annual fixed fee for cleaning service—$4,520				
9. Sales commissions—$0.50 per BD				
10. Machinery depreciation, straight-line—$18,000				

Required

1. Classify each cost and its amount as (*a*) either variable or fixed and (*b*) either product or period. (The first cost is completed as an example.)
2. Compute the manufacturing cost per BD.

Check (2) Total variable production cost, $35,250

Analysis Component

3. Assume that 10,000 BDs are produced in the next year. What do you predict will be the total cost of plastic for the BDs and the per unit cost of the plastic for the BDs? Explain.
4. Assume that 10,000 BDs are produced in the next year. What do you predict will be the total cost of factory rent and the per unit cost of the factory rent? Explain.

Problem 14-4B
Cost classification and explanation
C2 C3

Assume that you must make a presentation to a client explaining the difference between prime and conversion costs. The client makes and sells 200,000 cookies per week. The client tells you that her sales staff also would like a clarification regarding product and period costs. She tells you that most of the staff lack training in managerial accounting.

Required

Prepare a one-page memorandum to your client outlining your planned presentation to her sales staff.

Problem 14-5B
Ending inventory computation and evaluation
C4

Sharp Edges makes specialty skates for the ice skating circuit. On December 31, 2012, the company had (*a*) 1,500 skates in finished goods inventory and (*b*) 2,500 blades at a cost of $20 each in raw materials inventory. During 2013, Sharp Edges purchased 45,000 additional blades at $20 each and manufactured 20,750 pairs of skates.

Required

1. Determine the unit and dollar amounts of raw materials inventory in blades at December 31, 2013.

Check (1) Ending (blade) inventory, 6,000 units; $120,000

Analysis Component

2. Write a one-half page memorandum to the production manager explaining why a just-in-time inventory system for blades should be considered. Include the amount of working capital that can be reduced at December 31, 2013, if the ending blade raw materials inventory is cut in half.

Problem 14-6B
Inventory computation and reporting
C4 P1

Shown here are annual financial data at December 31, 2013, taken from two different companies.

	Badger (Retail)	Naima (Manufacturing)
Beginning inventory		
Merchandise	$100,000	
Finished goods		$300,000
Cost of purchases	250,000	
Cost of goods manufactured		586,000
Ending inventory		
Merchandise	150,000	
Finished goods		200,000

Required

1. Compute the cost of goods sold section of the income statement at December 31, 2013, for each company. Include the proper title and format in the solution.

2. Write a half-page memorandum to your instructor (*a*) identifying the inventory accounts and (*b*) identifying where each is reported on the income statement and balance sheet for both companies.

Check (1) Badger cost of goods sold, $200,000

Problem 14-7B
Manufacturing and income statements; analysis of inventories P2 A1

The following calendar year-end information is taken from the December 31, 2013, adjusted trial balance and other records of Elegant Furniture.

Advertising expense	$ 20,250	Direct labor	$ 562,500
Depreciation expense—Office equipment	8,440	Income taxes expense	136,700
Depreciation expense—Selling equipment	10,125	Indirect labor	59,000
Depreciation expense—Factory equipment	35,400	Miscellaneous production costs	8,440
Factory supervision	121,500	Office salaries expense	70,875
Factory supplies used	6,060	Raw materials purchases	894,375
Factory utilities	37,500	Rent expense—Office space	23,625
Inventories		Rent expense—Selling space	27,000
Raw materials, December 31, 2012	40,375	Rent expense—Factory building	93,500
Raw materials, December 31, 2013	70,430	Maintenance expense—Factory equipment	30,375
Goods in process, December 31, 2012	12,500	Sales	5,000,000
Goods in process, December 31, 2013	14,100	Sales discounts	57,375
Finished goods, December 31, 2012	177,200	Sales salaries expense	295,300
Finished goods, December 31, 2013	141,750		

Required

1. Prepare the company's 2013 manufacturing statement.

2. Prepare the company's 2013 income statement that reports separate categories for (*a*) selling expenses and (*b*) general and administrative expenses.

Check (1) Cost of goods manufactured, $1,816,995

Analysis Component

3. Compute the (*a*) inventory turnover, defined as cost of goods sold divided by average inventory, and (*b*) days' sales in inventory, defined as 365 times ending inventory divided by cost of goods sold, for both its raw materials inventory and its finished goods inventory. (To compute turnover and days' sales in inventory for raw materials, use raw materials used rather than cost of goods sold.) Discuss some possible reasons for differences between these ratios for the two types of inventories. Round answers to one decimal place.

Problem 14-8B
Lean business concepts
C6

Canon manufactures digital cameras and must compete on lean manufacturing concepts. Match each of the following activities that it engages in with the lean manufacturing concept it strives to achieve. (Some activities might relate to more than one lean manufacturing concept.)

_____ **1.** Manufacturing facilities are arranged to reduce move time and wait time.
_____ **2.** Canon conducts focus groups to determine new features that customers want in digital cameras.
_____ **3.** Canon monitors the market to determine what features its competitors are offering on digital cameras.
_____ **4.** Canon asks production workers for ideas to improve production.
_____ **5.** The manufacturing process is standardized and documented.
_____ **6.** Cameras are produced in small lots, and only to customer order.
_____ **7.** Lenses are received daily based on customer orders.
_____ **8.** Customers receive a satisfaction survey with each camera purchased.
_____ **9.** Orders received are filled within two business days.
_____ **10.** Canon works with suppliers to reduce inspection time of incoming materials.

a. Just-in-time (JIT)
b. Continuous improvement (CI)
c. Total quality management (TQM)

SERIAL PROBLEM

Success Systems
C2 C4 P2

(This serial problem begins in Chapter 1 and continues through most of the book. If previous chapter segments were not completed, the serial problem can begin at this point. It is helpful, but not necessary, to use the Working Papers that accompany the book.)

SP 14 Adria Lopez, owner of Success Systems, decides to diversify her business by also manufacturing computer workstation furniture.

Required

1. Classify the following manufacturing costs of Success Systems by behavior and traceability.

Product Costs	Cost by Behavior		Cost by Traceability	
	Variable	Fixed	Direct	Indirect
1. Monthly flat fee to clean workshop	____	____	____	____
2. Laminate coverings for desktops	____	____	____	____
3. Taxes on assembly workshop	____	____	____	____
4. Glue to assemble workstation component parts	____	____	____	____
5. Wages of desk assembler	____	____	____	____
6. Electricity for workshop	____	____	____	____
7. Depreciation on tools	____	____	____	____

2. Prepare a manufacturing statement for Success Systems for the month ended January 31, 2014. Assume the following manufacturing costs:
   Direct materials: $2,200
   Factory overhead: $490
   Direct labor: $900
   Beginning goods in process: none (December 31, 2013)
   Ending goods in process: $540 (January 31, 2014)
   Beginning finished goods inventory: none (December 31, 2013)
   Ending finished goods inventory: $350 (January 31, 2014)
3. Prepare the cost of goods sold section of a partial income statement for Success Systems for the month ended January 31, 2014.

Check (3) COGS, $2,700

Beyond the Numbers

REPORTING IN ACTION
C1
Polaris

BTN 14-1 Managerial accounting is more than recording, maintaining, and reporting financial results. Managerial accountants must provide managers with both financial and nonfinancial information including estimates, projections, and forecasts. An important estimate for **Polaris** is its reserve for warranty claims, and the company must provide shareholders information on these estimates.

Required

1. Access and read Polaris's "Product warranties" section of the "Organization and Significant Accounting Policies" footnote to its financial statements, from Appendix A. What is the warranty period for Polaris's products? How does management establish and adjust the warranty reserve? What are some of the effects if the company's actual results differ from its estimates?
2. What is the management accountant's role in determining those estimates?
3. What are some factors that could impact the warranty accrual in a given year?

Fast Forward

4. Access **Polaris**'s annual report for a fiscal year ending after December 31, 2011, from either its Website [Polaris.com] or the SEC's EDGAR database [www.SEC.gov]. Answer the questions in parts (1), (2), and (3) after reading the current "Organization and Significant Accounting Policies". Identify any major changes.

COMPARATIVE ANALYSIS
C2
Polaris
Arctic Cat

BTN 14-2 Both **Polaris** and **Arctic Cat** provide warranties on the products they sell. Accurate estimates of these future warranty claims are important. Access the annual report or 10-K for both Polaris (from Appendix A) and Arctic Cat. The Polaris report is for the year ended December 31, 2011, and the Arctic Cat report is for the year ended March 31, 2011.

Required

1. Read the "Product warranties" section of the "Organization and Significant Accounting Policies" footnote for Polaris. For each of the three years reported, compare the dollar amounts of the annual warranty expense and actual warranty claims paid. Is Polaris' warranty expense higher, lower, or about the same as its warranty claims paid?
2. Read the "Product Warranties" section of the "Summary of Significant Accounting Policies" footnote for Arctic Cat. For each of the three years reported, compare the dollar amounts of the annual warranty expense and actual warranty claims paid. Is Arctic Cat's warranty expense higher, lower, or about the same as its warranty claims paid?
3. Using the answers from parts (1) and (2), which company made more accurate estimates of warranty costs over the most recent three years?

ETHICS CHALLENGE
C1 C3

BTN 14-3 Assume that you are the managerial accountant at Infostore, a manufacturer of hard drives, CDs, and DVDs. Its reporting year-end is December 31. The chief financial officer is concerned about having enough cash to pay the expected income tax bill because of poor cash flow management. On November 15, the purchasing department purchased excess inventory of CD raw materials in anticipation of rapid growth of this product beginning in January. To decrease the company's tax liability, the chief financial officer tells you to record the purchase of this inventory as part of supplies and expense it in the current year; this would decrease the company's tax liability by increasing expenses.

Required

1. In which account should the purchase of CD raw materials be recorded?
2. How should you respond to this request by the chief financial officer?

COMMUNICATING IN PRACTICE

C6

BTN 14-4 Write a one-page memorandum to a prospective college student about salary expectations for graduates in business. Compare and contrast the expected salaries for accounting (including different subfields such as public, corporate, tax, audit, and so forth), marketing, management, and finance majors. Prepare a graph showing average starting salaries (and those for experienced professionals in those fields if available). To get this information, stop by your school's career services office; libraries also have this information. The Website JobStar.org (click on *Salary Info*) also can get you started.

TAKING IT TO THE NET

C1

BTN 14-5 Managerial accounting professionals follow a code of ethics. As a member of the Institute of Management Accountants, the managerial accountant must comply with Standards of Ethical Conduct.

Required

1. Identify, print, and read the *Statement of Ethical Professional Practice* posted at www.IMAnet.org. (Search using "statement of ethical professional practice and select the Ethics Center and Helpline link. Under Ethical Practices, select Learn More.")
2. What four overarching ethical principles underlie the IMA's statement?
3. Describe the courses of action the IMA recommends in resolving ethical conflicts.

TEAMWORK IN ACTION

C5 P2

BTN 14-6 The following calendar-year information is taken from the December 31, 2013, adjusted trial balance and other records of Dahlia Company.

Advertising expense	$ 19,125	Direct labor	$ 650,750
Depreciation expense—Office equipment	8,750	Indirect labor	60,000
Depreciation expense—Selling equipment	10,000	Miscellaneous production costs	8,500
Depreciation expense—Factory equipment	32,500	Office salaries expense	100,875
Factory supervision	122,500	Raw materials purchases	872,500
Factory supplies used	15,750	Rent expense—Office space	21,125
Factory utilities	36,250	Rent expense—Selling space	25,750
Inventories		Rent expense—Factory building	79,750
Raw materials, December 31, 2012	177,500	Maintenance expense—Factory equipment	27,875
Raw materials, December 31, 2013	168,125	Sales	3,275,000
Goods in process, December 31, 2012	15,875	Sales discounts	57,500
Goods in process, December 31, 2013	14,000	Sales salaries expense	286,250
Finished goods, December 31, 2012	164,375		
Finished goods, December 31, 2013	129,000		

Required

1. *Each* team member is to be responsible for computing **one** of the following amounts. You are not to duplicate your teammates' work. Get any necessary amounts from teammates. Each member is to explain the computation to the team in preparation for reporting to class.

a. Materials used.
b. Factory overhead.
c. Total manufacturing costs.
d. Total cost of goods in process.
e. Cost of goods manufactured.

2. Check your cost of goods manufactured with the instructor. If it is correct, proceed to part (3).
3. *Each* team member is to be responsible for computing **one** of the following amounts. You are not to duplicate your teammates' work. Get any necessary amounts from teammates. Each member is to explain the computation to the team in preparation for reporting to class.
   a. Net sales.
   b. Cost of goods sold.
   c. Gross profit.
   d. Total operating expenses.
   e. Net income or loss before taxes.

Point: Provide teams with transparencies and markers for presentation purposes.

BTN 14-7 Alex Velez and Nikhil Arora of **Back to the Roots** must understand manufacturing costs to effectively operate and succeed as a profitable and efficient business.

ENTREPRENEURIAL DECISION
C1 C2 C6

Required

1. What are the three main categories of manufacturing costs the owners must monitor and control? Provide examples of each.
2. What are four goals of a total quality management process? How can Back to the Roots use TQM to improve its business activities?

BTN 14-8 Visit your favorite fast-food restaurant. Observe its business operations.

HITTING THE ROAD
C1 C2

Required

1. Describe all business activities from the time a customer arrives to the time that customer departs.
2. List all costs you can identify with the separate activities described in part 1.
3. Classify each cost from part 2 as fixed or variable, and explain your classification.

BTN 14-9 Access **Piaggio**'s Website (www.piaggiogroup.com) and select "Governance" and then select "Company boards." Read the section dealing with the role of its board of directors.

GLOBAL DECISION
C1

PIAGGIO

Required

1. Identify the role of Piaggio's board of directors.
2. How would management accountants be involved in assisting the board of directors in carrying out their responsibilities? Explain.

ANSWERS TO MULTIPLE CHOICE QUIZ

1. c
2. b
3. b
4. a
5. Beginning finished goods + Cost of goods manufactured (COGM) − Ending finished goods = Cost of goods sold
   $6,000 + COGM − $3,200 = $7,500
   COGM = $4,700

Job Order Costing and Analysis

15

A Look Back

Chapter 14 introduced managerial accounting and explained basic cost concepts. We also described the lean business model and the reporting of manufacturing activities, including the manufacturing statement.

A Look at This Chapter

We begin this chapter by describing a cost accounting system. We then explain the procedures used to determine costs using a job order costing system. We conclude with a discussion of over- and underapplied overhead.

A Look Ahead

Chapter 16 focuses on measuring costs in process production companies. We explain process production, describe how to assign costs to processes, and compute and analyze cost per equivalent unit.

Learning Objectives

CONCEPTUAL

C1 Describe important features of job order production. (p. 654)

C2 Explain job cost sheets and how they are used in job order cost accounting. (p. 656)

ANALYTICAL

A1 Apply job order costing in pricing services. (p. 667)

PROCEDURAL

P1 Describe and record the flow of materials costs in job order cost accounting. (p. 658)

P2 Describe and record the flow of labor costs in job order cost accounting. (p. 660)

P3 Describe and record the flow of overhead costs in job order cost accounting. (p. 661)

P4 Determine adjustments for overapplied and underapplied factory overhead. (p. 666)

Decision Insight

Suit Yourself!

"Be fearless!"

—**DAVID SCHOTTENSTEIN**

COLUMBUS, OH—Watching Italian tailors hand-sew high-quality men's suits, David Schottenstein decided to start his own men's clothing store. David's aspirations were high: Sell custom-made mens' suits, hand-sewn and made from the finest fabrics, at prices up to 80 percent less than competitor's clothes. David recalls thinking, "If I have to crawl around on my hands and knees to measure people's inseams to get this business started, I'm going to do it." The result is **Astor and Black** **(AstorandBlack.com),** a startup international company with sales in 2010 of over $20 million.

David's employees travel to customers' homes, offices, and clubs around the world to do personal fittings. Customers select the fabrics, buttons, stitching, and other details, and then tailors hand-sew each suit to exact customer specifications. "I like to pick out my own stuff, and it's easier than going to a store," says Malcolm Jenkins, All-Pro NFL cornerback and owner of over 30 Astor and Black suits. David stresses that "customer service and satisfying each customer's individual needs" are what drive success.

David's business model is based on selling a higher volume of suits than competitors, but at lower margins per suit. This requires David to carefully monitor costs. Astor and Black, like other makers of custom products, uses a state-of-the-art job order cost accounting system to track costs. Such a system tracks the cost of materials, labor, and overhead for each suit, enabling David to make quick business decisions regarding costs and selling prices. Job order costing allows entrepreneurs like David to better isolate costs and avoid the run away costs often experienced by startups that fail to use such costing techniques. "We keep our fixed costs low by not stocking inventory," explains David, "and we use minimal office space as our sales mainly occur in customer's homes or offices."

David encourages young entrepreneurs to believe in themselves. "People have great ideas all the time but find all the [wrong] reasons not to do it. You have to be fearless," says David. In David's case, that fearlessness began with selling rare cigars and trading stocks as a teenager. "It was bizarre," says his father Tom. "He was a kid on a mission." With attention to detail and insights gained from job order costing information, David's business continues to expand, now offering women's suits and online tailoring, allowing customers to create a simulated version of the outfit they want. "Be brazen or you will be done on the day you start," says David.

[Sources: *Astor and Black* Website, January 2013; *Yourhiddenpotential.co.uk* Website, May 8, 2011; *The Columbus Dispatch*, June 22, 2008; *Forbes*, May 9, 2011; *Smart Business Online*, www.sbonline.com, June 2009.]

Chapter Preview

This chapter introduces a system for assigning costs to the flow of goods through a production process. We then describe the details of a *job order cost accounting system.* Job order costing is frequently used by manufacturers of custom products or providers of custom services. Manufacturers that use job order costing typically base it on a perpetual inventory system, which provides a continuous record of materials, goods in process, and finished goods inventories.

Job Order Costing and Analysis

Job Order Cost Accounting
- Cost accounting system
- Job order production
- Job order costing of services
- Events in job order costing
- Job cost sheet

Job Order Cost Flows and Reports
- Materials cost flows and documents
- Labor cost flows and documents
- Overhead cost flows and documents
- Summary of cost flows

Adjusting Factory Overhead
- Factory overhead T-account
- Underapplied or overapplied overhead

JOB ORDER COST ACCOUNTING

This section describes a cost accounting system and job order production and costing.

Cost Accounting System

Point: Cost accounting systems accumulate costs and then assign them to products and services.

An ever-increasing number of companies use a cost accounting system to generate timely and accurate inventory information. A **cost accounting system** records manufacturing activities using a *perpetual* inventory system, which continuously updates records for costs of materials, goods in process, and finished goods inventories. A cost accounting system also provides timely information about inventories and manufacturing costs per unit of product. This is especially helpful for managers' efforts to control costs and determine selling prices. (A **general accounting system** records manufacturing activities using a *periodic* inventory system. Some companies still use a general accounting system, but its use is declining as competitive forces and customer demands have increased pressures on companies to better manage inventories.)

C1 Describe important features of job order production.

The two basic types of cost accounting systems are *job order cost accounting* and *process cost accounting.* We describe job order cost accounting in this chapter. Process cost accounting is explained in the next chapter.

Job Order Production

Many companies produce products individually designed to meet the needs of a specific customer. Each customized product is manufactured separately and its production is called **job order production,** or *job order manufacturing* (also called *customized production,* which is the production of products in response to special orders). Examples of such products include synthetic football fields, special-order machines, a factory building, custom jewelry, wedding invitations, and artwork. The production activities for a customized product represent a **job.**

Boeing's aerospace division is one example of a job order production system. Its primary business is twofold: (1) design, develop, and integrate space carriers and (2) provide systems engineering and integration of Department of Defense (DoD) systems. Many of its orders are customized and produced through job order operations.

When a job involves producing more than one unit of a custom product, it is often called a **job lot.** Products produced as job lots could include benches for a church, imprinted T-shirts for a 10K race or company picnic, or advertising signs for a chain of stores. Although these orders involve more than one unit, the volume of production is typically low, such as 50 benches, 200 T-shirts, or 100 signs. Another feature of job order production is the diversity, often called *heterogeneity,* of the products produced. Namely, each customer order is likely to differ from another in some important respect. These variations can be minor or major.

Decision Insight

Custom Design Managers once saw companies as the center of a solar system orbited by suppliers and customers. Now the customer has become the center of the business universe. **Nike** allows custom orders over the Internet, enabling customers to select materials, colors, and to personalize their shoes with letters and numbers. Soon consumers may be able to personalize almost any product, from cellular phones to appliances to furniture. ■

Job Order Costing of Services

The principle of customization is equally applicable to both manufacturing *and* service companies. Most service companies meet customers' needs by performing a custom service for a specific customer. Examples of such services include an accountant auditing a client's financial statements, an interior designer remodeling an office, a wedding consultant planning and supervising a reception, and a lawyer defending a client. Whether the setting is manufacturing or services, job order operations involve meeting the needs of customers by producing or performing custom jobs. We show an example of job order costing for an advertising service in the Decision Analysis section of this chapter.

Events in Job Order Costing

The initial event in a normal job order operation is the receipt of a customer order for a custom product. This causes the company to begin work on a job. A less common case occurs when management decides to begin work on a job before it has a signed contract. This is referred to as *jobs produced on speculation.*

Step 1: **Predict the cost to complete the job.** This cost depends on the product design prepared by either the customer or the producer.

Step 2: **Negotiate price and decide whether to pursue the job.** Other than for government or other cost-plus contracts, the selling price is determined by market factors. Producers evaluate the market price, compare it to cost, and determine whether the profit on the job is reasonable. If the profit is not reasonable, the producer would determine a desired **target cost.**

Point: Some jobs are priced on a *cost-plus basis:* The customer pays the manufacturer for costs incurred on the job plus a negotiated amount or rate of profit.

Step 3: **Schedule production of the job.** This must meet the customer's needs and fit within the company's own production constraints. Preparation of this work schedule should consider workplace facilities including equipment, personnel, and supplies. Once this schedule is complete, the producer can place orders for raw materials. Production occurs as materials and labor are applied to the job.

An overview of job order production activity is shown in Exhibit 15.1. This exhibit shows the March production activity of Road Warriors, which installs security devices into cars and trucks. The company converts any vehicle by adding alarms, reinforced exterior, bulletproof glass, and bomb detectors. The company began by catering to high-profile celebrities, but it now caters to anyone who desires added security in a vehicle.

Job order production for Road Warriors requires materials, labor, and overhead costs. Recall that direct materials are goods used in manufacturing that are clearly identified with a particular job. Similarly, direct labor is effort devoted to a particular job. Overhead costs support production of more than one job. Common overhead items are depreciation on factory buildings and equipment, factory supplies, supervision, maintenance, cleaning, and utilities.

Exhibit 15.1 shows that materials, labor, and overhead are added to Jobs B15, B16, B17, B18, and B19, which were started during March. Special tires and bulletproof glass are added to Jobs B15 and B16, while Job B17 receives a reinforced exterior and bulletproof glass. Road Warriors completed Jobs B15, B16, and B17 in March and delivered Jobs B15 and B16 to

Point: Many professional examinations including the CPA and CMA exams require knowledge of job order and process cost accounting.

EXHIBIT 15.1

Job Order Production Activities

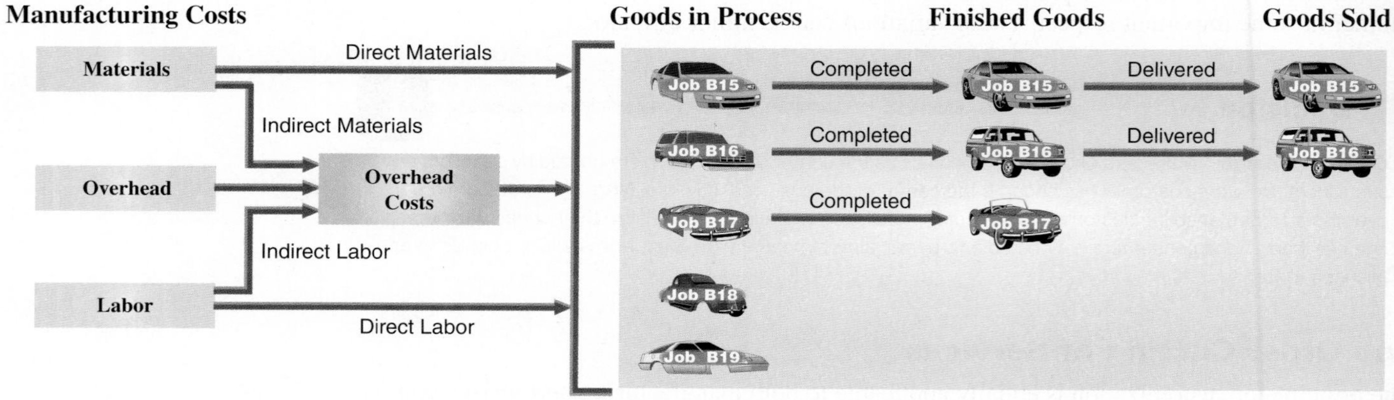

customers. At the end of March, Jobs B18 and B19 remain in goods in process inventory and Job B17 is in finished goods inventory. Both labor and materials costs are also separated into their direct and indirect components. Their indirect amounts are added to overhead. Total overhead cost is then allocated to the various jobs.

Decision Insight

Target Costing Many producers determine a target cost for their jobs. Target cost is determined as follows: Expected selling price − Desired profit = Target cost. If the projected target cost of the job as determined by job costing is too high, the producer can apply *value engineering,* which is a method of determining ways to reduce job cost until the target cost is met. ■

Job Cost Sheet

C2 Explain job cost sheets and how they are used in job order cost accounting.

General ledger accounts usually do not provide the accounting information that managers of job order cost operations need to plan and control production activities. This is so because the needed information often requires more detailed data. Such detailed data are usually stored in subsidiary records controlled by general ledger accounts. Subsidiary records store information about raw materials, overhead costs, jobs in process, finished goods, and other items. This section describes the use of these records.

A major aim of a **job order cost accounting system** is to determine the cost of producing each job or job lot. In the case of a job lot, the system also aims to compute the cost per unit. The accounting system must include separate records for each job to accomplish this, and it must capture information about costs incurred and charge these costs to each job.

A **job cost sheet** is a separate record maintained for each job. Exhibit 15.2 shows a job cost sheet for an alarm system that Road Warriors produced for a customer. This job cost sheet identifies the customer, the job number assigned, the product, and key dates. Costs incurred on the job are immediately recorded on this sheet. When each job is complete, the supervisor enters the date of completion, records any remarks, and signs the sheet. The job cost sheet in Exhibit 15.2 classifies costs as direct materials, direct labor, or overhead. It shows that a total of $600 in direct materials is added to Job B15 on four different dates. It also shows seven entries for direct labor costs that total $1,000. Road Warriors *allocates* (also termed *applies, assigns,* or *charges*) factory overhead costs of $1,600 to this job using an allocation rate of 160% of direct labor cost (160% × $1,000)—we discuss overhead allocation later in this chapter.

Point: Factory overhead consists of costs (other than direct materials and direct labor) that ensure the production activities are carried out.

Cost Flows: During Production While a job is being produced, its accumulated costs are kept in **Goods in Process Inventory.** The collection of job cost sheets for all jobs in process makes up a subsidiary ledger controlled by the Goods in Process Inventory account in the general ledger. Managers use job cost sheets to monitor costs incurred to date and to predict and control costs for each job.

EXHIBIT 15.2

Job Cost Sheet

Accounting System: Exhibit 15-2

File Edit Maintain Tasks Analysis Options Reports Window Help

Road Warriors, Los Angeles, California — **JOB COST SHEET**

Customer's Name Carroll Connor **Job No.** B15

Address 1542 High Point Dr. **City & State** Malibu, California

Job Description Level 1 Alarm System on Ford Expedition

Date promised March 15 **Date started** March 3 **Date completed** March 11

Direct Materials			Direct Labor			Overhead		
Date	Requisition	Cost	Date	Time Ticket	Cost	Date	Rate	Cost
3/3/2013	R-4698	100.00	3/3/2013	L-3393	120.00	3/11/2013	160% of Direct Labor Cost	1,600.00
3/7/2013	R-4705	225.00	3/4/2013	L-3422	150.00			
3/9/2013	R-4725	180.00	3/5/2013	L-3456	180.00			
3/10/2013	R-4777	95.00	3/8/2013	L-3479	60.00			
			3/9/2013	L-3501	90.00			
			3/10/2013	L-3535	240.00			
			3/11/2013	L-3559	160.00			
	Total	600.00		Total	1,000.00		Total	1,600.00

REMARKS: Completed job on March 11, and shipped to customer on March 15. Met all specifications and requirements.

SUMMARY:

Materials	600.00
Labor	1,000.00
Overhead	1,600.00
Total cost	3,200.00

Signed: *C. Luther, Supervisor*

Cost Flows: Job Completion When a job is finished, its job cost sheet is completed and moved from the jobs in process file to the finished jobs file. This latter file acts as a subsidiary ledger controlled by the **Finished Goods Inventory** account.

Cost Flows: Job Delivery When a finished job is delivered to a customer, the job cost sheet is moved to a permanent file supporting the total cost of goods sold. This permanent file contains records from both current and prior periods. When the job is finished, the company also prepares a journal entry that credits Sales and debits Cash (or Accounts Receivable).

Point: Documents (electronic and paper) are crucial in a job order system, and the job cost sheet is a cornerstone. Understanding it aids in grasping concepts of capitalizing product costs and product cost flow.

Decision Maker

Management Consultant One of your tasks is to control and manage costs for a consulting company. At the end of a recent month, you find that three consulting jobs were completed and two are 60% complete. Each unfinished job is estimated to cost $10,000 and to earn a revenue of $12,000. You are unsure how to recognize goods in process inventory and record costs and revenues. Do you recognize any inventory? If so, how much? How much revenue is recorded for unfinished jobs this month? ■ [Answer—p. 671]

Quick Check

Answers — p. 671

1. Which of these products is likely to involve job order production? (*a*) inexpensive watches, (*b*) racing bikes, (*c*) bottled soft drinks, or (*d*) athletic socks.
2. What is the difference between a job and a job lot?
3. Which of these statements is correct? (*a*) The collection of job cost sheets for unfinished jobs makes up a subsidiary ledger controlled by the Goods in Process Inventory account, (*b*) Job cost sheets are financial statements provided to investors, or (*c*) A separate job cost sheet is maintained in the general ledger for each job in process.
4. What three costs are normally accumulated on job cost sheets?

JOB ORDER COST FLOWS AND REPORTS

P1 Describe and record the flow of materials costs in job order cost accounting.

Materials Cost Flows and Documents

Materials

This section focuses on the flow of materials costs and the related documents in a job order cost accounting system. We begin analysis of the flow of materials costs by examining Exhibit 15.3. When materials are first received from suppliers, the employees count and inspect them and record the items' quantity and cost on a receiving report. The receiving report serves as the *source document* for recording materials received in both a materials ledger card and in the general ledger. In nearly all job order cost systems, **materials ledger cards** (or files) are perpetual records that are updated each time units are purchased and each time units are issued for use in production.

Point: Some companies certify certain suppliers based on the quality of their materials. Goods received from these suppliers are not always inspected by the purchaser to save costs.

To illustrate the purchase of materials, Road Warriors acquired $450 of wiring and related materials on March 4, 2013. This purchase is recorded as follows.

Assets = Liabilities + Equity
+450 +450

Mar. 4	Raw Materials Inventory—M-347	450	
	Accounts Payable		450
	To record purchase of materials for production.		

EXHIBIT 15.3

Materials Cost Flows through Subsidiary Records

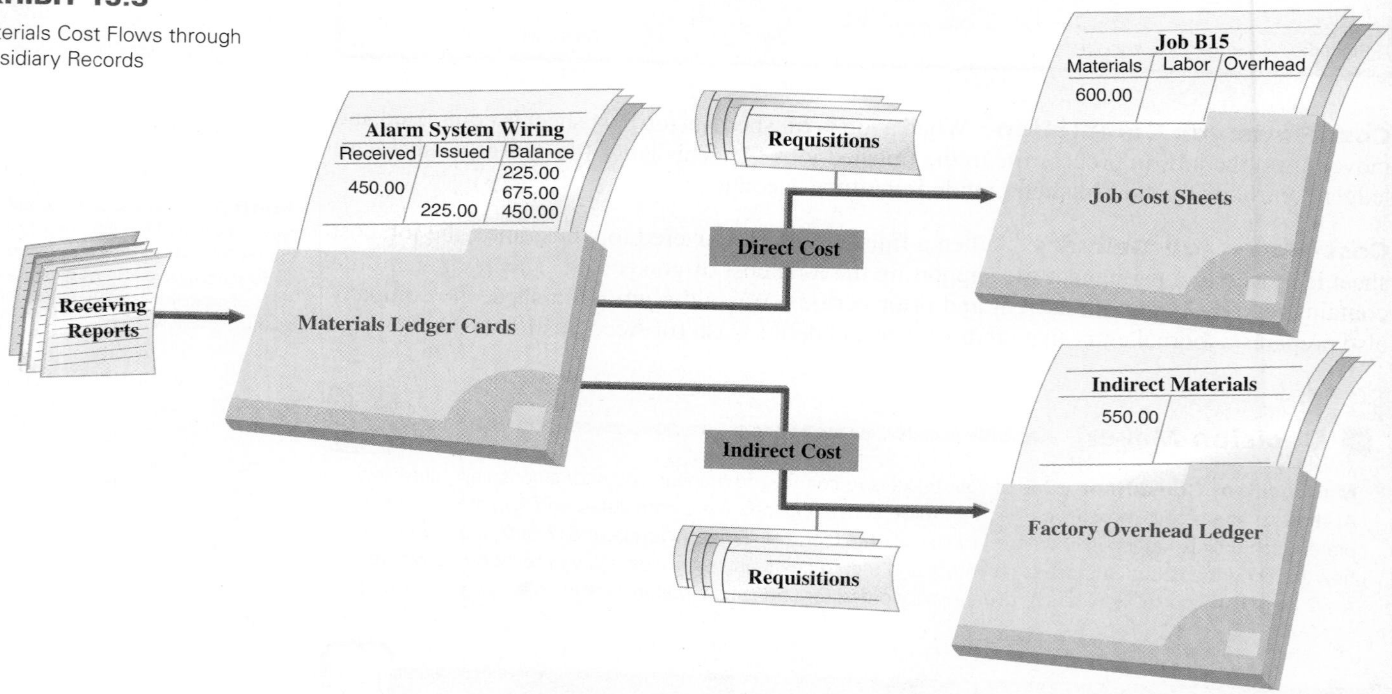

Exhibit 15.3 shows that materials can be requisitioned for use either on a specific job (direct materials) or as overhead (indirect materials). Cost of direct materials flows from the materials ledger card to the job cost sheet. The cost of indirect materials flows from the materials ledger card to the Indirect Materials account in the factory overhead ledger, which is a subsidiary ledger controlled by the Factory Overhead account in the general ledger.

Exhibit 15.4 shows a materials ledger card for material received and issued by Road Warriors. The card identifies the item as alarm system wiring and shows the item's stock number, its location in the storeroom, information about the maximum and minimum quantities that should be available, and the reorder quantity. For example, alarm system wiring is issued

EXHIBIT 15.4

Materials Ledger Card

MATERIALS LEDGER CARD

Road Warriors
Los Angeles, California

Item	Alarm system wiring	Stock No.	M–347	Location in Storeroom	Bin 137
Maximum quantity	5 units	Minimum quantity	1 unit	Quantity to reorder	2 units

	Received				Issued				Balance		
Date	Receiving Report Number	Units	Unit Price	Total Price	Requisition Number	Units	Unit Price	Total Price	Units	Unit Price	Total Price
									1	225.00	225.00
3/4/2013	C-7117	2	225.00	450.00					3	225.00	675.00
3/7/2013					R–4705	1	225.00	225.00	2	225.00	450.00

and recorded on March 7, 2013. The job cost sheet in Exhibit 15.2 showed that Job B15 used this wiring.

When materials are needed in production, a production manager prepares a **materials requisition** and sends it to the materials manager. The requisition shows the job number, the type of material, the quantity needed, and the signature of the manager authorized to make the requisition. Exhibit 15.5 shows the materials requisition for alarm system wiring for Job B15. To see how this requisition ties to the flow of costs, compare the information on the requisition with the March 7, 2013, data in Exhibits 15.2 and 15.4.

Point: Requisitions are often accumulated and recorded in one entry. The frequency of entries depends on the job, the industry, and management procedures.

EXHIBIT 15.5

Materials Requisition

MATERIALS REQUISITION No. R–4705

Road Warriors
Los Angeles, California

Job No. B15
Material Stock No. M–347
Date 3/7/2013
Material Description Alarm system wiring
Quantity Requested 1
Requested By *C. Luther*

Quantity Provided 1
Date Provided 3/7/2013
Filled By *M. Bateman*
Material Received By *C. Luther*
Remarks

The use of alarm system wiring on Job B15 yields the following entry (locate this cost item in the job cost sheet shown in Exhibit 15.2).

Mar. 7	Goods in Process Inventory—Job B15	225	
	Raw Materials Inventory—M-347		225
	To record use of material on Job B15.		

Assets = Liabilities + Equity
+225
−225

This entry is posted both to its general ledger accounts and to subsidiary records. Posting to subsidiary records includes a debit to a job cost sheet and a credit to a materials ledger card. (*Note:* An entry to record use of indirect materials is the same as that for direct materials *except* the debit is to Factory Overhead. In the subsidiary factory overhead ledger, this entry is posted to Indirect Materials.)

Point: Exhibit 15.12 shows this entry.

P2 Describe and record the flow of labor costs in job order cost accounting.

Labor

Labor Cost Flows and Documents

Exhibit 15.6 shows the flow of labor costs from clock cards and the Factory Payroll account to subsidiary records of the job order cost accounting system. Recall that costs in subsidiary records give detailed information needed to manage and control operations.

EXHIBIT 15.6

Labor Cost Flows through Subsidiary Records

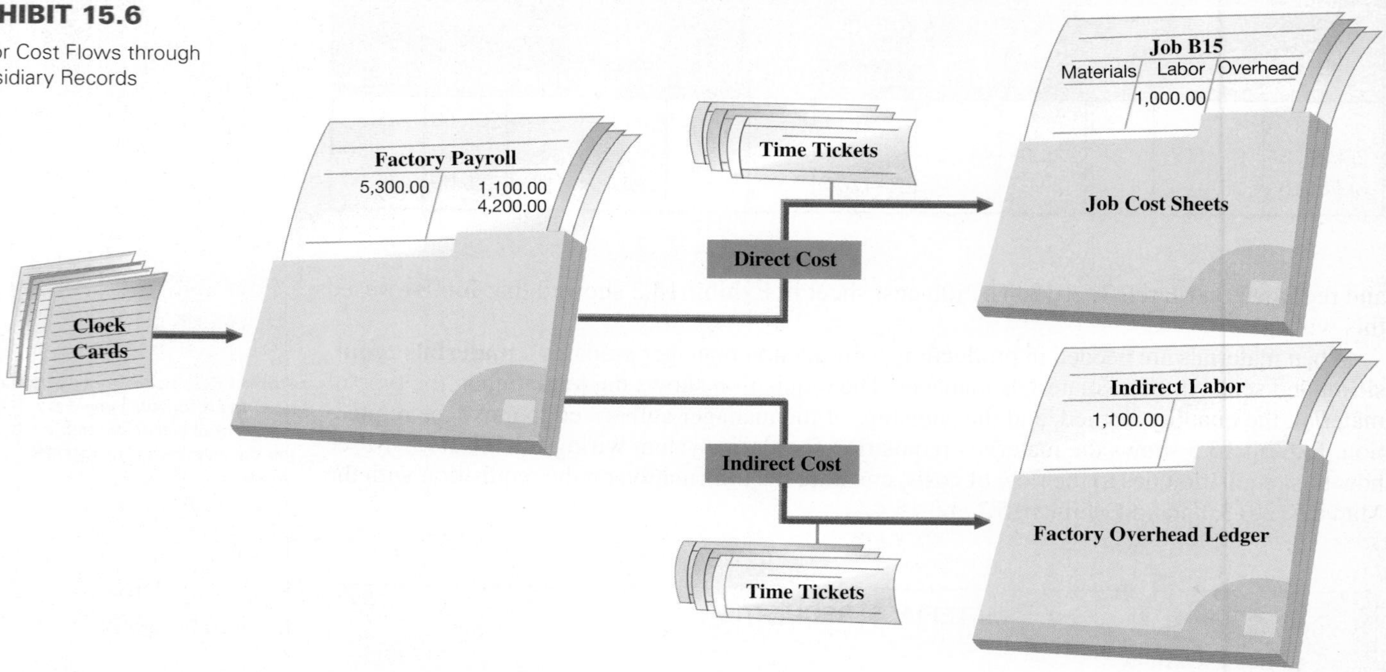

Point: In the accounting equation, we treat accounts such as Factory Payroll and Factory Overhead as temporary accounts, which hold various expenses until they are allocated to balance sheet or income statement accounts.

The flow of costs in Exhibit 15.6 begins with **clock cards.** Employees commonly use these cards to record the number of hours worked, and they serve as source documents for entries to record labor costs. Clock card data on the number of hours worked is used at the end of each pay period to determine total labor cost. This amount is then debited to the Factory Payroll account, a temporary account containing the total payroll cost (both direct and indirect). Payroll cost is later allocated to both specific jobs and overhead.

According to clock card data, workers earned $1,500 for the week ended March 5. Illustrating the flow of labor costs, the accrual and payment of these wages are recorded as follows.

Assets = Liabilities + Equity
−1,500 −1,500

Mar. 6	Factory Payroll	1,500	
	Cash		1,500
	To record the weekly payroll.		

Point: Many employee fraud schemes involve payroll, including overstated hours on clock cards.

To assign labor costs to specific jobs and to overhead, we must know how each employee's time is used and its costs. Source documents called **time tickets** usually capture these data. Employees regularly fill out time tickets to report how much time they spent on each job. An employee who works on several jobs during a day completes a separate time ticket for each job. Tickets are also prepared for time charged to overhead as indirect labor. A supervisor signs an employee's time ticket to confirm its accuracy.

Exhibit 15.7 shows a time ticket reporting the time a Road Warrior employee spent working on Job B15. The employee's supervisor signed the ticket to confirm its accuracy. The hourly rate and total labor cost are computed after the time ticket is turned in. To see the effect of this time ticket on the job cost sheet, look at the entry dated March 8, 2013, in Exhibit 15.2.

EXHIBIT 15.7

Time Ticket

ROAD WARRIORS
Road Warriors
Los Angeles, California

No. L–3479

TIME TICKET Date ..March 8.. 20 ..13..

Employee Name	Employee Number	Job No.
T. Zeller	3969	B15

TIME AND RATE INFORMATION:

Start Time	Finish Time	Elapsed Time	Hourly Rate
9:00	12:00	3.0	$20.00
Approved By ....C. Luther....		Total Cost	$60.00

Remarks
....

When time tickets report labor used on a specific job, this cost is recorded as direct labor. The following entry records the data from the time ticket in Exhibit 15.7.

Mar. 8	Goods in Process Inventory—Job B15	60	
	Factory Payroll		60
	To record direct labor used on Job B15.		

Assets = Liabilities + Equity
+60 +60

The debit in this entry is posted both to the general ledger account and to the appropriate job cost sheet. (*Note:* An entry to record indirect labor is the same as for direct labor *except* that it debits Factory Overhead and credits Factory Payroll. In the subsidiary factory overhead ledger, the debit in this entry is posted to the Indirect Labor account.)

Point: Exhibit 15.12 shows this entry.

Overhead Cost Flows and Documents

P3 Describe and record the flow of overhead costs in job order cost accounting.

Factory overhead (or simply overhead) cost flows are shown in Exhibit 15.8. Factory overhead includes all production costs other than direct materials and direct labor. Two sources of overhead costs are indirect materials and indirect labor. These costs are recorded from requisitions for indirect materials and time tickets for indirect labor. Two other sources of overhead are (1) vouchers authorizing payments for items such as supplies or utilities and (2) adjusting entries for costs such as depreciation on factory assets.

Overhead

Factory overhead usually includes many different costs and, thus, a separate account for each is often maintained in a subsidiary factory overhead ledger. This ledger is controlled by the Factory Overhead account in the general ledger. Factory Overhead is a temporary account that accumulates costs until they are allocated to jobs.

Point: Companies also incur *nonmanufacturing* costs, such as advertising, salesperson's salaries, and depreciation on assets not used in production. These types of costs are not considered overhead, but instead are treated as period costs and charged directly to the income statement. These period costs can be relevant to managers' pricing decisions.

Recording Overhead Recall that overhead costs are recorded with debits to the Factory Overhead account and with credits to other accounts such as Cash, Accounts Payable, and

EXHIBIT 15.8

Overhead Cost Flows through Subsidiary Records

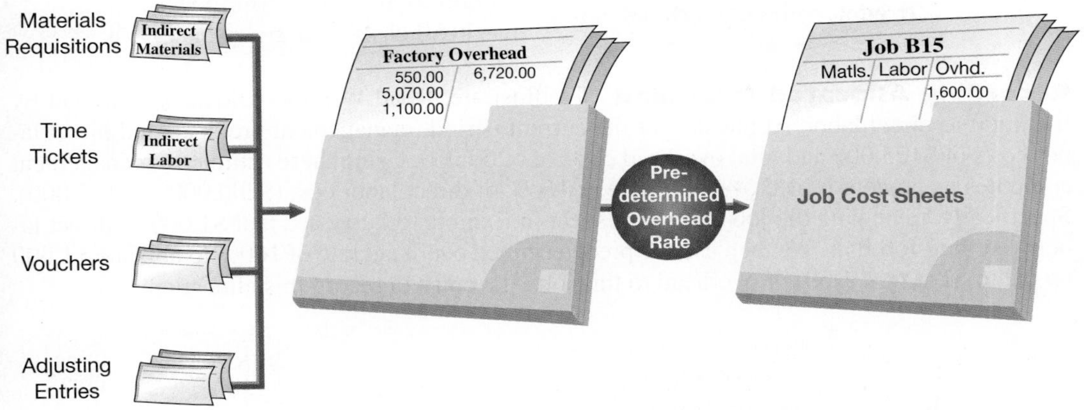

Accumulated Depreciation—Equipment. In the subsidiary factory overhead ledger, the debits are posted to their respective accounts such as Depreciation Expense—Equipment, Insurance Expense—Warehouse, or Amortization Expense—Patents.

To illustrate the recording of overhead, the following two entries reflect the depreciation of factory equipment and the accrual of utilities, respectively, for the week ended March 6.

Assets	= Liabilities	+ Equity
−600		−600

Assets	= Liabilities	+ Equity
	+250	−250

Mar. 6	Factory Overhead	600	
	Accumulated Depreciation—Equipment		600
	To record depreciation on factory equipment.		
Mar. 6	Factory Overhead	250	
	Utilities Payable		250
	To record the accrual of factory utilities.		

Entries to record indirect materials and indirect labor follow:

Factory Overhead	$	
Raw Materials Inventory		$
Factory Overhead	$	
Factory Payroll		$

In the subsidiary factory overhead ledger, these entries are posted to Indirect Materials and Indirect Labor, respectively.

Exhibit 15.8 shows that overhead costs flow from the Factory Overhead account to job cost sheets. Because overhead is made up of costs not directly associated with specific jobs or job lots, we cannot determine the dollar amount incurred on a specific job. We know, however, that overhead costs represent a necessary part of business activities. If a job cost is to include all costs needed to complete the job, some amount of overhead must be included. Given the difficulty in determining the overhead amount for a specific job, however, we allocate overhead to individual jobs in some reasonable manner.

Overhead Allocation Bases We generally allocate overhead by linking it to another factor used in production, such as direct labor or machine hours. The factor to which overhead costs are linked is known as the *allocation base.* A manager must think carefully about how many and which allocation bases to use. This managerial decision influences the accuracy with which overhead costs are allocated to individual jobs. In turn, the cost of individual jobs might impact a manager's decisions for pricing or performance evaluation. In Exhibit 15.2, overhead is expressed as 160% of direct labor. We then allocate overhead by multiplying 160% by the estimated amount of direct labor on the jobs.

Point: The predetermined overhead rate is computed at the start of the period and is used throughout the period to allocate overhead to jobs. Predetermined overhead rates can be estimated using mathematical equations, statistical analysis, or professional experience.

Overhead Allocation Rates We cannot wait until the end of a period to allocate overhead to jobs because perpetual inventory records are part of the job order costing system (demanding up-to-date costs). Instead, we must predict overhead in advance and assign it to jobs so that a job's total costs can be estimated prior to its completion. This estimated cost is useful for managers in many decisions including setting prices and identifying costs that are out of control. Being able to estimate overhead in advance requires a **predetermined overhead rate,** also called *predetermined overhead allocation* (or *application*) *rate.* This rate requires an estimate of total overhead cost and an allocation factor such as total direct labor cost before the start of the period. Exhibit 15.9 shows the usual formula for computing a predetermined overhead rate (estimates are commonly based on annual amounts). This rate is used during the period to allocate overhead to jobs. It is common for companies to use multiple activity (allocation) bases and multiple predetermined overhead rates for different types of products and services.

EXHIBIT 15.9

Predetermined Overhead Allocation Rate Formula

$$\textbf{Predetermined overhead rate} = \frac{\textbf{Estimated}}{\textbf{overhead costs}} \div \frac{\textbf{Estimated}}{\textbf{activity base}}$$

Recording Allocated Overhead To illustrate, Road Warriors allocates overhead by linking it to direct labor. At the start of the current period, management predicts total direct labor costs of $125,000 and total overhead costs of $200,000. Using these estimates, management computes its predetermined overhead rate as 160% of direct labor cost ($200,000 ÷ $125,000). Specifically, reviewing the job order cost sheet in Exhibit 15.2, we see that $1,000 of direct labor went into Job B15. We then use the predetermined overhead rate of 160% to allocate $1,600 (equal to $1,000 × 1.60) of overhead to this job. The entry to record this allocation is

Example: If management predicts total direct labor costs of $100,000 and total overhead costs of $200,000, what is its predetermined overhead rate? *Answer:* 200% of direct labor cost.

Assets	= Liabilities	+ Equity
+1,600		+1,600

Mar. 11	Goods in Process Inventory—Job B15	1,600	
	Factory Overhead		1,600
	To assign overhead to Job B15.		

Since the allocation rate for overhead is estimated at the start of a period, the total amount assigned to jobs during a period rarely equals the amount actually incurred. We explain how this difference is treated later in this chapter.

Decision Ethics

Web Consultant You are working on seven client engagements. Two clients reimburse your firm for actual costs plus a 10% markup. The other five pay a fixed fee for services. Your firm's costs include overhead allocated at $47 per labor hour. The managing partner of your firm instructs you to record as many labor hours as possible to the two markup engagements by transferring labor hours from the other five. What do you do? ■ [Answer—p. 671]

Summary of Cost Flows

We showed journal entries for charging Goods in Process Inventory (Job B15) with the cost of (1) direct materials requisitions, (2) direct labor time tickets, and (3) factory overhead. We made separate entries for each of these costs, but they are usually recorded in one entry. Specifically, materials requisitions are often collected for a day or a week and recorded with a single entry summarizing them. The same is done with labor time tickets. When summary entries are made, supporting schedules of the jobs charged and the types of materials used provide the basis for postings to subsidiary records.

Point: Study the flow of manufacturing costs through general ledger accounts and job cost sheets. Use Exhibit 15.11 as reinforcement.

To show all production cost flows for a period and their related entries, we again look at Road Warriors' activities. Exhibit 15.10 shows costs linked to all of Road Warriors' production activities for March. Road Warriors did not have any jobs in process at the beginning of March, but it did apply materials, labor, and overhead costs to five new jobs in March. Jobs B15 and B16 are completed and delivered to customers in March, Job B17 is completed but not delivered, and Jobs B18 and B19 are still in process. Exhibit 15.10 also shows purchases of raw materials for $2,750, labor costs incurred for $5,300, and overhead costs of $6,720.

EXHIBIT 15.10

Job Order Costs of All Production Activities

ROAD WARRIORS
Job Order Manufacturing Costs
For Month Ended March 31, 2013

			Overhead		Goods		Cost of
Explanation	Materials	Labor	Incurred	Allocated	in Process	Finished Goods	Goods Sold
Job B15	$ 600	$1,000		$1,600			$3,200
Job B16	300	800		1,280			2,380
Job B17	500	1,100		1,760		$3,360	
Job B18	150	700		1,120	$1,970		
Job B19	250	600		960	1,810		
Total job costs	1,800	4,200		$6,720	$3,780	$3,360	$5,580
Indirect materials	550		$ 550				
Indirect labor		1,100	1,100				
Other overhead			5,070				
Total costs used in production	2,350	$5,300	$6,720				
Ending materials inventory	1,400						
Materials available	3,750						
Less beginning materials inventory	(1,000)						
Materials purchased	$2,750						

The upper part of Exhibit 15.11 shows the flow of these costs through general ledger accounts and the end-of-month balances in key subsidiary records. Arrow lines are numbered to show the flows of costs for March. Each numbered cost flow reflects several entries made in March. The lower part of Exhibit 15.11 shows summarized job cost sheets and their status at the end of March. The sum of costs assigned to the jobs in process ($1,970 + $1,810) equals the

EXHIBIT 15.11

Job Order Cost Flows and Ending Job Cost Sheets

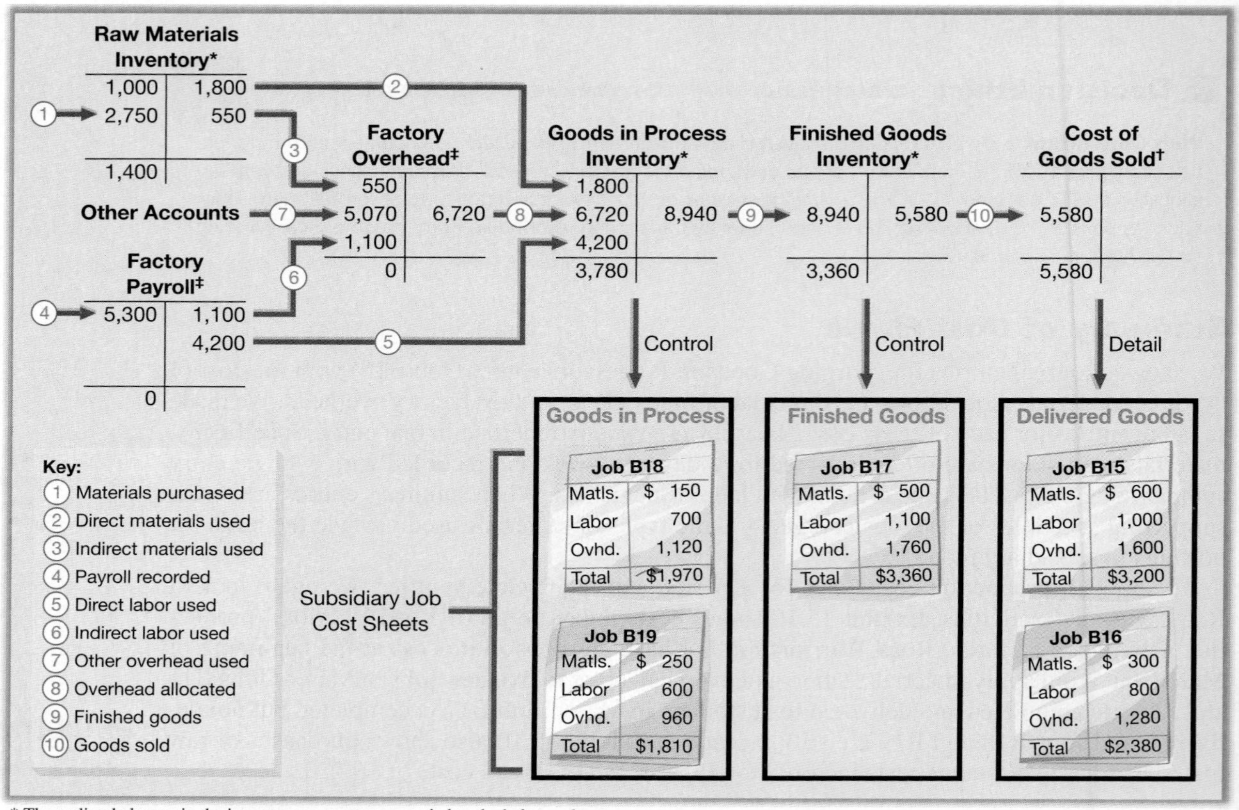

* The ending balances in the inventory accounts are carried to the balance sheet.
† The Cost of Goods Sold balance is carried to the income statement.
‡ Factory Payroll and Factory Overhead are considered temporary accounts; when these costs are allocated to jobs, the balances in these accounts are reduced.

$3,780 balance in Goods in Process Inventory shown in Exhibit 15.10. Also, costs assigned to Job B17 equal the $3,360 balance in Finished Goods Inventory. The sum of costs assigned to Jobs B15 and B16 ($3,200 + $2,380) equals the $5,580 balance in Cost of Goods Sold.

Exhibit 15.12 shows each cost flow with a single entry summarizing the actual individual entries made in March. Each entry is numbered to link with the arrow lines in Exhibit 15.11.

Decision Maker

Entrepreneur Competitors' prices on one of your product segments are lower than yours. Of the total product cost used in setting your prices, 53% is overhead allocated using direct labor hours. You believe that product costs are distorted and wonder whether there is a better way to allocate overhead and to set product price. What do you suggest? ■ [Answer—p. 671]

Quick Check

Answers — p. 671

5. In job order cost accounting, which account is debited in recording a raw materials requisition? (*a*) Raw Materials Inventory, (*b*) Raw Materials Purchases, (*c*) Goods in Process Inventory if for a job, or (*d*) Goods in Process Inventory if they are indirect materials.
6. What are four sources of information for recording costs in the Factory Overhead account?
7. Why does job order cost accounting require a predetermined overhead rate?
8. What events result in a debit to Factory Payroll? What events result in a credit?

EXHIBIT 15.12

Entries for Job Order Production Costs*

①	Raw Materials Inventory	2,750	
	Accounts Payable		2,750
	Acquired materials on credit for factory use.		
②	Goods in Process Inventory	1,800	
	Raw Materials Inventory		1,800
	To assign costs of direct materials used.		
③	Factory Overhead	550	
	Raw Materials Inventory		550
	To record use of indirect materials.		
④	Factory Payroll	5,300	
	Cash (and other accounts)		5,300
	To record salaries and wages of factory workers (including various payroll liabilities).		
⑤	Goods in Process Inventory	4,200	
	Factory Payroll		4,200
	To assign costs of direct labor used.		
⑥	Factory Overhead	1,100	
	Factory Payroll		1,100
	To record indirect labor costs as overhead.		
⑦	Factory Overhead	5,070	
	Cash (and other accounts)		5,070
	To record factory overhead costs such as insurance, utilities, rent, and depreciation.		
⑧	Goods in Process Inventory	6,720	
	Factory Overhead		6,720
	To apply overhead at 160% of direct labor.		
⑨	Finished Goods Inventory	8,940	
	Goods in Process Inventory		8,940
	To record completion of Jobs B15, B16, and B17.		
⑩	Cost of Goods Sold	5,580	
	Finished Goods Inventory		5,580
	To record sale of Jobs B15 and B16.		

* Exhibit 15.12 provides summary journal entries. *Actual* overhead is debited to Factory Overhead. *Allocated* overhead is credited to Factory Overhead.

ADJUSTING FACTORY OVERHEAD

Refer to the debits in the Factory Overhead account in Exhibit 15.11 (or Exhibit 15.12). The total cost of factory overhead incurred during March is $6,720 ($550 + $5,070 + $1,100). The $6,720 exactly equals the amount assigned to goods in process inventory (see ⑧). Therefore, the overhead incurred equals the overhead applied in March. The amount of overhead incurred rarely equals the amount of overhead applied, however, because estimates rarely equal the exact amounts actually incurred. This section explains what we do when too much or too little overhead is applied to jobs.

Factory Overhead T-Account

Exhibit 15.13 shows a Factory Overhead T-account. The company applies overhead using a predetermined rate estimated at the beginning of the period. At the end of the period, the company receives bills for its actual overhead costs.

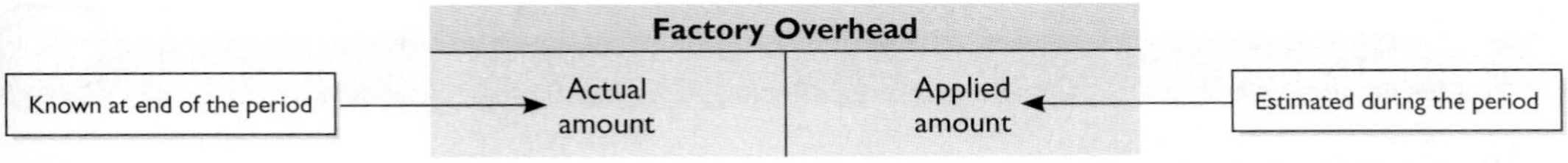

EXHIBIT 15.13

Factory Overhead T-account

Exhibit 15.14 shows what to do when actual overhead does not equal applied overhead. When less overhead is applied than is actually incurred, the remaining debit balance in the Factory Overhead account is called **underapplied overhead.** When the overhead applied in a period exceeds the overhead incurred, the resulting credit balance in the Factory Overhead account is called **overapplied overhead.** In either case, a journal entry is needed to adjust Factory Overhead and Cost of Goods Sold. Exhibit 15.14 summarizes this entry.

Overhead Costs	Factory Overhead Balance Is	Overhead Is	Journal Entry Required		
Actual > Applied	Debit	Underapplied	Cost of Goods Sold	#	
			Factory Overhead		#
Actual < Applied	Credit	Overapplied	Factory Overhead	#	
			Cost of Goods Sold		#

EXHIBIT 15.14

Adjusting Factory Overhead

Underapplied or Overapplied Overhead

P4 Determine adjustments for overapplied and underapplied factory overhead.

To illustrate, assume that Road Warriors actually incurred *other overhead costs* of $5,550 instead of the $5,070 shown in Exhibit 15.11. This yields an actual total overhead cost of $7,200 in March. Since the amount of overhead applied was only $6,720, the Factory Overhead account is left with a $480 debit balance as shown in the ledger account in Exhibit 15.15.

EXHIBIT 15.15

Underapplied Overhead in the Factory Overhead Ledger Account

Factory Overhead				Acct. No. 540
Date	**Explanation**	**Debit**	**Credit**	**Balance**
Mar. 31	Indirect materials cost	550		550 Dr.
31	Indirect labor cost	1,100		1,650 Dr.
31	Other overhead cost	5,550		7,200 Dr.
31	Overhead costs applied to jobs		6,720	480 Dr.

Example: If we do not adjust for underapplied overhead, will net income be overstated or understated? *Answer:* Overstated.

The $480 debit balance reflects manufacturing costs not assigned to jobs. This means that the balances in Goods in Process Inventory, Finished Goods Inventory, and Cost of Goods Sold do not include all production costs incurred. When the underapplied overhead amount is immaterial, it is allocated (closed) to the Cost of Goods Sold account with the following adjusting entry.

Mar. 31	Cost of Goods Sold	480	
	Factory Overhead		480
	To adjust for underapplied overhead costs.		

Assets = Liabilities + Equity
−480
+480

The $480 debit (increase) to Cost of Goods Sold reduces income by $480. (When the underapplied (or overapplied) overhead is material, the amount is normally allocated to the Cost of Goods Sold, Finished Goods Inventory, and Goods in Process Inventory accounts. This process is covered in advanced courses.)

We treat overapplied overhead at the end of the period in the same way we treat underapplied overhead, except that we debit Factory Overhead and credit Cost of Good Sold for the amount.

Decision Insight

Job Order Learning Many companies invest in their employees, and the demand for executive education is strong. Annual spending on training and education exceeds $20 billion. Annual revenues for providers of executive education continue to rise, with about 40% of revenues coming from custom programs designed for one or a select group of companies. ■

Quick Check

Answers — p. 672

9. In a job order cost accounting system, why does the Factory Overhead account usually have an overapplied or underapplied balance at period-end?
10. When the Factory Overhead account has a debit balance at period-end, does this reflect overapplied or underapplied overhead?

GLOBAL VIEW

Porsche AG manufactures high-performance cars. Each car is built according to individual customer specifications. Customers can use the Internet to place orders for their dream cars. Porsche employs just-in-time inventory techniques to ensure a flexible production process that can respond rapidly to customer orders. For a recent year, Porsche reported €33,781 million in costs of materials and €9,038 million in personnel costs, which helped generate €57,081 million in revenue.

Pricing for Services — Decision Analysis

A1 Apply job order costing in pricing services.

The chapter described job order costing mainly using a manufacturing setting. However, these concepts and procedures are applicable to a service setting. Consider AdWorld, an advertising agency that develops Web-based ads for small firms. Each of its customers has unique requirements, so costs for each individual job must be tracked separately.

AdWorld uses two types of labor: Web designers ($65 per hour) and computer staff ($50 per hour). It also incurs overhead costs that it assigns using two different predetermined overhead allocation rates: $125 per designer hour and $96 per staff hour. For each job, AdWorld must estimate the number of designer and staff hours needed. Then total costs pertaining to each job are determined using the procedures in the chapter. (*Note:* Most service firms have neither the category of materials cost nor inventory.)

To illustrate, a manufacturer of golf balls requested a quote from AdWorld for an advertising engagement. AdWorld estimates that the job will require 43 designer hours and 61 staff hours, with the following total estimated cost for this job.

Direct Labor		
Designers (43 hours × $65)	$ 2,795	
Staff (61 hours × $50)	3,050	
Total direct labor		$ 5,845
Overhead		
Designer related (43 hours × $125)	5,375	
Staff related (61 hours × $96)	5,856	
Total overhead		11,231
Total estimated job cost		$17,076

AdWorld can use this cost information to help determine the price quote for the job (see *Decision Maker,* **Sales Manager,** scenario in this chapter).

Another source of information that AdWorld must consider is the market, that is, how much competitors will quote for this job. Competitor information is often unavailable; therefore, AdWorld's managers must use estimates based on their assessment of the competitive environment.

Decision Maker

Sales Manager As AdWorld's sales manager, assume that you estimate costs pertaining to a proposed job as $17,076. Your normal pricing policy is to apply a markup of 18% from total costs. However, you learn that three other agencies are likely to bid for the same job, and that their quotes will range from $16,500 to $22,000. What price should you quote? What factors other than cost must you consider? ■ [Answer—p. 671]

DEMONSTRATION PROBLEM—JOB ORDER COSTING

The following information reflects Walczak Company's job order production activities for May.

Raw materials purchases	$16,000
Factory payroll cost	15,400
Overhead costs incurred	
Indirect materials	5,000
Indirect labor	3,500
Other factory overhead	9,500

Walczak's predetermined overhead rate is 150% of direct labor cost. Costs are allocated to the three jobs worked on during May as follows.

	Job 401	Job 402	Job 403
In-process balances on April 30			
Direct materials	$3,600		
Direct labor	1,700		
Applied overhead	2,550		
Costs during May			
Direct materials	3,550	$3,500	$1,400
Direct labor	5,100	6,000	800
Applied overhead	?	?	?
Status on May 31	**Finished (sold)**	**Finished (unsold)**	**In process**

Required

1. Determine the total cost of:

a. The April 30 inventory of jobs in process.

b. Materials used during May.

c. Labor used during May.

d. Factory overhead incurred and applied during May and the amount of any over- or underapplied overhead on May 31.

e. Each job as of May 31, the May 31 inventories of both goods in process and finished goods, and the goods sold during May.

2. Prepare summarized journal entries for the month to record:

a. Materials purchases (on credit), the factory payroll (paid with cash), indirect materials, indirect labor, and the other factory overhead (paid with cash).

b. Assignment of direct materials, direct labor, and overhead costs to the Goods in Process Inventory account. (Use separate debit entries for each job.)

c. Transfer of each completed job to the Finished Goods Inventory account.

d. Cost of goods sold.

e. Removal of any underapplied or overapplied overhead from the Factory Overhead account. (Assume the amount is not material.)

3. Prepare a manufacturing statement for May.

PLANNING THE SOLUTION

- Determine the cost of the April 30 goods in process inventory by totaling the materials, labor, and applied overhead costs for Job 401.
- Compute the cost of materials used and labor by totaling the amounts assigned to jobs and to overhead.
- Compute the total overhead incurred by summing the amounts for the three components. Compute the amount of applied overhead by multiplying the total direct labor cost by the predetermined overhead rate. Compute the underapplied or overapplied amount as the difference between the actual cost and the applied cost.
- Determine the total cost charged to each job by adding the costs incurred in April (if any) to the cost of materials, labor, and overhead applied during May.
- Group the costs of the jobs according to their completion status.
- Record the direct materials costs assigned to the three jobs, using a separate Goods in Process Inventory account for each job; do the same for the direct labor and the applied overhead.
- Transfer costs of Jobs 401 and 402 from Goods in Process Inventory to Finished Goods.
- Record the costs of Job 401 as cost of goods sold.
- Record the transfer of underapplied overhead from the Factory Overhead account to the Cost of Goods Sold account.
- On the manufacturing statement, remember to include the beginning and ending goods in process inventories and to deduct the underapplied overhead.

SOLUTION TO DEMONSTRATION PROBLEM

1. Total cost of

a. April 30 inventory of jobs in process (Job 401).

Direct materials	$3,600
Direct labor	1,700
Applied overhead	2,550
Total cost	$7,850

b. Materials used during May.

Direct materials	
Job 401	$ 3,550
Job 402	3,500
Job 403	1,400
Total direct materials	8,450
Indirect materials	5,000
Total materials used	$13,450

c. Labor used during May.

Direct labor	
Job 401	$ 5,100
Job 402	6,000
Job 403	800
Total direct labor	11,900
Indirect labor	3,500
Total labor used	$15,400

d. Factory overhead incurred in May.

Actual overhead	
Indirect materials	$ 5,000
Indirect labor	3,500
Other factory overhead	9,500
Total actual overhead	18,000
Overhead applied (150% × $11,900)	17,850
Underapplied overhead	$ 150

e. Total cost of each job.

	401	402	403
In-process costs from April			
Direct materials	$ 3,600		
Direct labor	1,700		
Applied overhead*	2,550		
Cost incurred in May			
Direct materials	3,550	$ 3,500	$1,400
Direct labor	5,100	6,000	800
Applied overhead*	7,650	9,000	1,200
Total costs	$24,150	$18,500	$3,400

* Equals 150% of the direct labor cost.

Total cost of the May 31 inventory of goods in process (Job 403) = $3,400

Total cost of the May 31 inventory of finished goods (Job 402) = $18,500

Total cost of goods sold during May (Job 401) = $24,150

2. Journal entries.

a.

Raw Materials Inventory	16,000	
Accounts Payable		16,000
To record materials purchases.		
Factory Payroll	15,400	
Cash		15,400
To record factory payroll.		
Factory Overhead	5,000	
Raw Materials Inventory		5,000
To record indirect materials.		
Factory Overhead	3,500	
Factory Payroll		3,500
To record indirect labor.		
Factory Overhead	9,500	
Cash		9,500
To record other factory overhead.		

b. Assignment of costs to Goods in Process Inventory.

Goods in Process Inventory (Job 401)	3,550	
Goods in Process Inventory (Job 402)	3,500	
Goods in Process Inventory (Job 403)	1,400	
Raw Materials Inventory		8,450
To assign direct materials to jobs.		
Goods in Process Inventory (Job 401)	5,100	
Goods in Process Inventory (Job 402)	6,000	
Goods in Process Inventory (Job 403)	800	
Factory Payroll		11,900
To assign direct labor to jobs.		
Goods in Process Inventory (Job 401)	7,650	
Goods in Process Inventory (Job 402)	9,000	
Goods in Process Inventory (Job 403)	1,200	
Factory Overhead		17,850
To apply overhead to jobs.		

c. Transfer of completed jobs to Finished Goods Inventory.

Finished Goods Inventory	42,650	
Goods in Process Inventory (Job 401)		24,150
Goods in Process Inventory (Job 402)		18,500
To record completion of jobs.		

d.

Cost of Goods Sold	24,150	
Finished Goods Inventory		24,150
To record sale of Job 401.		

e.

Cost of Goods Sold	150	
Factory Overhead		150
To assign underapplied overhead.		

3.

WALCZAK COMPANY
Manufacturing Statement
For Month Ended May 31

Direct materials		$ 8,450
Direct labor		11,900
Factory overhead		
Indirect materials	$5,000	
Indirect labor	3,500	
Other factory overhead	9,500	18,000
Total production costs		38,350
Add goods in process, April 30		7,850
Total cost of goods in process		46,200
Less goods in process, May 31		3,400
Less underapplied overhead		150
Cost of goods manufactured		$42,650

Note how underapplied overhead is reported. Overapplied overhead is similarly reported, but is added.

Summary

C1 Describe important features of job order production. Certain companies called *job order manufacturers* produce custom-made products for customers. These customized products are produced in response to a customer's orders. A job order manufacturer produces products that usually are different and, typically, produced in low volumes. The production systems of job order companies are flexible and are not highly standardized.

C2 Explain job cost sheets and how they are used in job order cost accounting. In a job order cost accounting system, the costs of producing each job are accumulated on a separate job cost sheet. Costs of direct materials, direct labor, and overhead are accumulated separately on the job cost sheet and then added to determine the total cost of a job. Job cost sheets for jobs in process, finished jobs, and jobs sold make up subsidiary records controlled by general ledger accounts.

A1 Apply job order costing in pricing services. Job order costing can usefully be applied to a service setting. The resulting job cost estimate can then be used to help determine a price for services.

P1 Describe and record the flow of materials costs in job order cost accounting. Costs of materials flow from receiving reports to materials ledger cards and then to either job cost sheets or the Indirect Materials account in the factory overhead ledger.

P2 Describe and record the flow of labor costs in job order cost accounting. Costs of labor flow from clock cards to the Factory Payroll account and then to either job cost sheets or the Indirect Labor account in the factory overhead ledger.

P3 Describe and record the flow of overhead costs in job order cost accounting. Overhead costs are accumulated in the Factory Overhead account that controls the subsidiary factory overhead ledger. Then, using a predetermined overhead rate, overhead costs are charged to jobs.

P4 Determine adjustments for overapplied and underapplied factory overhead. At the end of each period, the Factory Overhead account usually has a residual debit (underapplied overhead) or credit (overapplied overhead) balance. If the balance is not material, it is transferred to Cost of Goods Sold, but if it is material, it is allocated to Goods in Process Inventory, Finished Goods Inventory, and Cost of Goods Sold.

Guidance Answers to Decision Maker and Decision Ethics

Management Consultant Service companies (such as this consulting firm) do not recognize goods in process inventory or finished goods inventory—an important difference between service and manufacturing companies. For the two jobs that are 60% complete, you could recognize revenues and costs at 60% of the total expected amounts. This means you could recognize revenue of $7,200 (0.60 × $12,000) and costs of $6,000 (0.60 × $10,000), yielding net income of $1,200 from each job.

Web Consultant The partner has a monetary incentive to *manage* the numbers and assign more costs to the two cost-plus engagements. This also would reduce costs on the fixed-price engagements. To act in such a manner is unethical. As a professional and an honest person, it is your responsibility to engage in ethical behavior. You must not comply with the partner's instructions. If the partner insists you act in an unethical manner, you should report the matter to a higher authority in the organization.

Entrepreneur An inadequate cost system can distort product costs. You should review overhead costs in detail. Once you know the different cost elements in overhead, you can classify them into groups such as material related, labor related, or machine related. Other groups can also be formed (we discuss this in Chapter 22). Once you have classified overhead items into groups, you can better establish overhead allocation bases and use them to compute predetermined overhead rates. These multiple rates and bases can then be used to assign overhead costs to products. This will likely improve product pricing.

Sales Manager The price based on AdWorld's normal pricing policy is $20,150 ($17,076 × 1.18), which is within the price range offered by competitors. One option is to apply normal pricing policy and quote a price of $20,150. On the other hand, assessing the competition, particularly in terms of their service quality and other benefits they might offer, would be useful. Although price is an input customers use to select suppliers, factors such as quality and timeliness (responsiveness) of suppliers are important. Accordingly, your price can reflect such factors.

Guidance Answers to Quick Checks

1. *b*
2. A job is a special order for a custom product. A job lot consists of a quantity of identical, special-order items.
3. *a*
4. Three costs normally accumulated on a job cost sheet are direct materials, direct labor, and factory overhead.
5. *c*
6. Four sources of factory overhead are materials requisitions, time tickets, vouchers, and adjusting entries.
7. Since a job order cost accounting system uses perpetual inventory records, overhead costs must be assigned to jobs before the end of a period. This requires the use of a predetermined overhead rate.
8. Debits are recorded when wages and salaries of factory employees are paid or accrued. Credits are recorded when direct labor

costs are assigned to jobs and when indirect labor costs are transferred to the Factory Overhead account.

9. Overapplied or underapplied overhead usually exists at the end of a period because application of overhead is based on estimates of overhead and another variable such as direct labor. Estimates rarely equal actual amounts incurred.

10. A debit balance reflects underapplied factory overhead.

Key Terms

Clock card (p. 660)
Cost accounting system (p. 654)
Finished Goods Inventory (p. 657)
General accounting system (p. 654)
Goods in Process Inventory (p. 656)
Job (p. 654)
Job cost sheet (p. 656)
Job lot (p. 654)
Job order cost accounting system (p. 656)
Job order production (p. 654)
Materials ledger card (p. 658)
Materials requisition (p. 659)
Overapplied overhead (p. 665)
Predetermined overhead rate (p. 662)
Target cost (p. 655)
Time ticket (p. 660)
Underapplied overhead (p. 665)

Multiple Choice Quiz

Answers on p. 689

mhhe.com/wildFINMAN5e

Additional Quiz Questions are available at the book's Website.

1. A company's predetermined overhead allocation rate is 150% of its direct labor costs. How much overhead is applied to a job that requires total direct labor costs of $30,000?
a. $15,000
b. $30,000
c. $45,000
d. $60,000
e. $75,000

2. A company's cost accounting system uses direct labor costs to apply overhead to goods in process and finished goods inventories. Its production costs for the period are: direct materials, $45,000; direct labor, $35,000; and overhead applied, $38,500. What is its predetermined overhead allocation rate?
a. 10%
b. 110%
c. 86%
d. 91%
e. 117%

3. A company's ending inventory of finished goods has a total cost of $10,000 and consists of 500 units. If the overhead applied to these goods is $4,000, and the predetermined overhead rate is 80% of direct labor costs, how much direct materials cost was incurred in producing these 500 units?
a. $10,000
b. $ 6,000
c. $ 4,000
d. $ 5,000
e. $ 1,000

4. A company's Goods in Process Inventory T-account follows.

Goods in Process Inventory			
Beginning balance	9,000		
Direct materials	94,200		
Direct labor	59,200		
Overhead applied	31,600	?	Finished goods
Ending balance	17,800		

The cost of units transferred to Finished Goods inventory is
a. $193,000
b. $211,800
c. $185,000
d. $144,600
e. $176,200

5. At the end of its current year, a company learned that its overhead was underapplied by $1,500 and that this amount is not considered material. Based on this information, the company should
a. Close the $1,500 to Finished Goods Inventory.
b. Close the $1,500 to Cost of Goods Sold.
c. Carry the $1,500 to the next period.
d. Do nothing about the $1,500 because it is not material and it is likely that overhead will be overapplied by the same amount next year.
e. Carry the $1,500 to the Income Statement as "Other Expense."

Icon denotes assignments that involve decision making.

Discussion Questions

1. Why must a company estimate the amount of factory overhead assigned to individual jobs or job lots?

2. The chapter used a percent of labor cost to assign factory overhead to jobs. Identify another factor (or base) a company might reasonably use to assign overhead costs.

3. What information is recorded on a job cost sheet? How do management and employees use job cost sheets?
4. In a job order cost accounting system, what records serve as a subsidiary ledger for Goods in Process Inventory? For Finished Goods Inventory?
5. What journal entry is recorded when a materials manager receives a materials requisition and then issues materials (both direct and indirect) for use in the factory?
6. How does the materials requisition help safeguard a company's assets?
7. Polaris uses a "time ticket" for some employees. What is the difference between a clock card and a time ticket?
8. What events cause debits to be recorded in the Factory Overhead account? What events cause credits to be recorded in the Factory Overhead account?
9. Piaggio applies overhead to product costs. What account(s) is(are) used to eliminate overapplied or underapplied overhead from the Factory Overhead account, assuming the amount is not material?
10. Assume that Arctic Cat produces a batch of 1,000 snowmobile helmets. Does it account for this as 1,000 individual jobs or as a job lot? Explain (consider costs and benefits).
11. Why must a company prepare a predetermined overhead rate when using job order cost accounting?
12. How would a hospital apply job order costing? Explain.
13. Harley-Davidson manufactures 30 custom-made, luxury-model motorcycles. Does it account for these motorcycles as 30 individual jobs or as a job lot? Explain.
14. Assume Sprint will install and service a server to link all of a customer's employees' smartphones to a centralized company server, for an upfront flat price. How can Sprint use a job order costing system?

connect

QUICK STUDY

QS 15-1
Jobs and job lots C1

Determine which products are most likely to be manufactured as a job and which as a job lot.

1. Hats imprinted with company logo.
2. Little League trophies.
3. A hand-crafted table.
4. A 90-foot motor yacht.
5. Wedding dresses for a chain of stores.
6. A custom-designed home.

QS 15-2
Job cost sheets C2

List the three types of costs that are typically recorded on a job cost sheet. How can managers use job cost sheets?

QS 15-3
Job cost sheets C2

Clemens Cars' job cost sheet for job A40 shows that the cost to add security features to a car was $10,500. The car was delivered to the customer, who paid $14,900 in cash for the added features. What journal entries should Clemens record for the completion and delivery of job A40?

QS 15-4
Direct materials journal entries P1

During the current month, a company that uses a job order cost accounting system purchases $50,000 in raw materials for cash. It then uses $12,000 of raw materials indirectly as factory supplies and uses $32,000 of raw materials as direct materials. Prepare entries to record these three transactions.

QS 15-5
Direct labor journal entries P2

During the current month, a company that uses a job order cost accounting system incurred a monthly factory payroll of $180,000, paid in cash. Of this amount, $40,000 is classified as indirect labor and the remainder as direct. Prepare entries to record these transactions.

QS 15-6
Factory overhead journal entries P3

During the current month, a company that uses a job order cost accounting system incurred a monthly factory payroll of $175,000, paid in cash. Of this amount, $44,000 is classified as indirect labor and the remainder as direct for the production of Job 65A. Factory overhead is applied at 90% of direct labor. Prepare the entry to apply factory overhead to this job lot.

QS 15-7
Factory overhead rates P3

A company incurred the following manufacturing costs this period: direct labor, $468,000; direct materials, $354,000; and factory overhead, $117,000. Compute its overhead cost as a percent of (1) direct labor and (2) direct materials. Express your answers as percents, rounded to the nearest whole number.

QS 15-8
Entry for over- or underapplied overhead P4

A company's Factory Overhead T-account shows total debits of $624,000 and total credits of $646,000 at the end of a period. Prepare the journal entry to close the balance in the Factory Overhead account to Cost of Goods Sold.

QS 15-9
Entry for over- or underapplied overhead P4

A company allocates overhead at a rate of 150% of direct labor cost. Actual overhead cost for the current period is $950,000, and direct labor cost is $600,000. Prepare the entry to close over- or underapplied overhead to cost of goods sold.

QS 15-10
Predetermined overhead rate P3

At the beginning of a period a company predicts total direct materials costs of $900,000 and total overhead costs of $1,170,000. If the company uses direct materials costs as its activity base to allocate overhead, what is the predetermined overhead rate it should use during the period?

QS 15-11
Pricing services A1

An advertising agency is estimating costs for advertising a music festival. The job will require 200 direct labor hours at a cost of $50 per hour. Overhead costs are applied at a rate of $65 per direct labor hour. What is the total estimated cost for this job?

QS 15-12
Job order production C1

Refer to this chapter's Global View. **Porsche AG** is the manufacturer of the Porsche automobile line. Does Porsche produce in jobs or in job lots? Explain.

connect

EXERCISES

Exercise 15-1
Job order production C1

Match the terms below with their definitions.

1. Cost accounting system
2. Target cost
3. General accounting system
4. Job
5. Job order production
6. Job lot

a. Production of products in response to customer orders.
b. A system that records manufacturing costs using a periodic inventory system.
c. A system that records manufacturing costs using a perpetual inventory system.
d. The expected selling price of a job minus its desired profit.
e. Production of more than one unit of a custom product.
f. Production activities for a customized product.

Exercise 15-2
Job cost computation C2

The following information is from the materials requisitions and time tickets for Job 9-1005 completed by Great Bay Boats. The requisitions are identified by code numbers starting with the letter Q and the time tickets start with W. At the start of the year, management estimated that overhead cost would equal 110% of direct labor cost for each job. Determine the total cost on the job cost sheet for Job 9-1005.

Date	Document	Amount
7/1/2013	Q-4698	$1,250
7/1/2013	W-3393	600
7/5/2013	Q-4725	1,000
7/5/2013	W-3479	450
7/10/2013	W-3559	300

Exercise 15-3
Documents in job order cost accounting P1 P2 P3

The left column lists the titles of documents and accounts used in job order cost accounting. The right column presents short descriptions of the purposes of the documents. Match each document in the left column to its numbered description in the right column.

A. Time ticket
B. Materials ledger card
C. Factory Payroll account
D. Clock card
E. Materials requisition
F. Factory Overhead account
G. Voucher

______ **1.** Shows amount of time an employee works on a job.
______ **2.** Temporarily accumulates the cost of incurred overhead until the cost is assigned to specific jobs.
______ **3.** Temporarily accumulates incurred labor costs until they are assigned to specific jobs or to overhead.
______ **4.** Communicates the need for materials to complete a job.
______ **5.** Shows only total time an employee works each day.
______ **6.** Shows amount approved for payment of an overhead or other cost.
______ **7.** Perpetual inventory record of raw materials received, used, and available for use.

Exercise 15-4
Analysis of cost flows
C2 P1 P2 P3

As of the end of June, the job cost sheets at Racing Wheels, Inc., show the following total costs accumulated on three custom jobs.

	Job 102	Job 103	Job 104
Direct materials	$15,000	$33,000	$27,000
Direct labor	8,000	14,200	21,000
Overhead	4,000	7,100	10,500

Job 102 was started in production in May and the following costs were assigned to it in May: direct materials, $6,000; direct labor, $1,800; and overhead, $900. Jobs 103 and 104 are started in June. Overhead cost is applied with a predetermined rate based on direct labor cost. Jobs 102 and 103 are finished in June, and Job 104 is expected to be finished in July. No raw materials are used indirectly in June. Using this information, answer the following questions. (Assume this company's predetermined overhead rate did not change across these months).

1. What is the cost of the raw materials requisitioned in June for each of the three jobs?
2. How much direct labor cost is incurred during June for each of the three jobs?
3. What predetermined overhead rate is used during June?
4. How much total cost is transferred to finished goods during June?

Check (4) $81,300

Exercise 15-5
Overhead rate; costs assigned to jobs
P3

In December 2012, Shire Computer's management establishes the year 2013 predetermined overhead rate based on direct labor cost. The information used in setting this rate includes estimates that the company will incur $747,500 of overhead costs and $575,000 of direct labor cost in year 2013. During March 2013, Shire began and completed Job No. 13-56.

1. What is the predetermined overhead rate for year 2013?
2. Use the information on the following job cost sheet to determine the total cost of the job.

Check (2) $22,710

JOB COST SHEET

Customer's Name Keiser Co. **Job No.** 13-56

Job Description 5 plasma monitors—61 inch

	Direct Materials		Direct Labor		Overhead Costs Applied	
Date	**Requisition No.**	**Amount**	**Time-Ticket No.**	**Amount**	**Rate**	**Amount**
Mar. 8	4-129	$5,000	T-306	$ 700		
Mar. 11	4-142	7,020	T-432	1,250		
Mar. 18	4-167	3,330	T-456	1,250		
Totals						

Exercise 15-6
Analysis of costs assigned to goods in process
P3

Lorenzo Company uses a job order cost accounting system that charges overhead to jobs on the basis of direct material cost. At year-end, the Goods in Process Inventory account shows the following.

Accounting System
File Edit Maintain Tasks Analysis Options Reports Window Help

Goods in Process Inventory — Acct. No. 121

Date	Explanation	Debit	Credit	Balance
2013				
Dec. 31	Direct materials cost	1,500,000		1,500,000
31	Direct labor cost	300,000		1,800,000
31	Overhead costs	600,000		2,400,000
31	To finished goods		2,350,000	50,000

Sales Purchases General Ledger Payroll Inventory Company Analysis

1. Determine the overhead rate used (based on direct material cost).
2. Only one job remained in the goods in process inventory at December 31, 2013. Its direct materials cost is $30,000. How much direct labor cost and overhead cost are assigned to it?

Check (2) Direct labor cost, $8,000

Exercise 15-7
Cost flows in a job order cost system
P1 P2 P3 P4

The following information is available for Lock-Safe Company, which produces special-order security products and uses a job order cost accounting system.

	April 30	May 31
Inventories		
Raw materials	$43,000	$ 52,000
Goods in process	10,200	21,300
Finished goods	63,000	35,600
Activities and information for May		
Raw materials purchases (paid with cash)		210,000
Factory payroll (paid with cash)		345,000
Factory overhead		
Indirect materials		15,000
Indirect labor		80,000
Other overhead costs		120,000
Sales (received in cash)		1,400,000
Predetermined overhead rate based on direct labor cost		70%

Compute the following amounts for the month of May.

1. Cost of direct materials used.
2. Cost of direct labor used.
3. Cost of goods manufactured.
4. Cost of goods sold.*
5. Gross profit.
6. Overapplied or underapplied overhead.

*Do not consider any underapplied or overapplied overhead.

Check (3) $625,400

Exercise 15-8
Journal entries for materials
P1

Use information in Exercise 15-7 to prepare journal entries for the following events for the month of May.

1. Raw materials purchases for cash.
2. Direct materials usage.
3. Indirect materials usage.

Exercise 15-9
Journal entries for labor
P2

Use information in Exercise 15-7 to prepare journal entries for the following events for the month of May.

1. Factory payroll costs in cash.
2. Direct labor usage.
3. Indirect labor usage.

Exercise 15-10
Journal entries for overhead
P3

Use information in Exercise 15-7 to prepare journal entries for the following events for the month of May.

1. Factory overhead excluding indirect materials and indirect labor (record credit to Other Accounts).
2. Application of overhead to goods in process.

Exercise 15-11
Adjusting factory overhead P4

Refer to information in Exercise 15-7. Prepare the journal entry to allocate (close) overapplied or underapplied overhead to Cost of Goods Sold.

Exercise 15-12
Adjusting factory overhead
P4

Record the journal entry to close over- or underapplied factory overhead to Cost of Goods Sold for each of the independent cases below.

	Marsh Concert Promotions	Ellis Home Builders
Actual indirect materials costs	$22,000	$ 12,500
Actual indirect labor costs	46,000	46,500
Other overhead costs	17,000	47,000
Overhead applied	88,200	105,200

Exercise 15-13
Recording events in job order costing
P1 P2 P3 P4

Using Exhibit 15.12 as a guide, prepare summary journal entries to record the following transactions and events *a* through *h* for a company in its first month of operations.

a. Raw materials purchased on account, $90,000.
b. Direct materials used in production, $36,500. Indirect materials used in production, $19,200.
c. Paid cash for factory payroll, $50,000. Of this total, $38,000 is for direct labor and $12,000 is for indirect labor.
d. Paid cash for other actual overhead costs, $11,475.
e. Applied overhead at the rate of 125 percent of direct labor cost.

f. Transferred cost of jobs completed to finished goods, $56,800.
g. Sold jobs on account for $82,000. The jobs had a cost of $56,800.
h. Close underapplied or overapplied overhead to cost of goods sold.

Exercise 15-14
Factory overhead computed, applied, and adjusted
P3 P4

In December 2012, Infovision established its predetermined overhead rate for movies produced during year 2013 by using the following cost predictions: overhead costs, $1,680,000, and direct labor costs, $480,000. At year end 2013, the company's records show that actual overhead costs for the year are $1,652,000. Actual direct labor cost had been assigned to jobs as follows.

Movies completed and released	$425,000
Movies still in production	50,000
Total actual direct labor cost	$475,000

1. Determine the predetermined overhead rate for year 2013.
2. Set up a T-account for overhead and enter the overhead costs incurred and the amounts applied to movies during the year using the predetermined overhead rate.
3. Determine whether overhead is overapplied or underapplied (and the amount) during the year.
4. Prepare the adjusting entry to allocate any over- or underapplied overhead to Cost of Goods Sold.

Check (3) $10,500 overapplied

Exercise 15-15
Factory overhead computed, applied, and adjusted
P3 P4

In December 2012, Cardozo Company established its predetermined overhead rate for jobs produced during year 2013 by using the following cost predictions: overhead costs, $750,000, and direct labor costs, $625,000. At year end 2013, the company's records show that actual overhead costs for the year are $830,000. Actual direct labor cost had been assigned to jobs as follows.

Jobs completed and sold	$513,750
Jobs in finished goods inventory	102,750
Jobs in goods in process inventory	68,500
Total actual direct labor cost	$685,000

1. Determine the predetermined overhead rate for year 2013.
2. Set up a T-account for Factory Overhead and enter the overhead costs incurred and the amounts applied to jobs during the year using the predetermined overhead rate.
3. Determine whether overhead is overapplied or underapplied (and the amount) during the year.
4. Prepare the adjusting entry to allocate any over- or underapplied overhead to Cost of Goods Sold.

Check (3) $8,000 underapplied

Exercise 15-16
Overhead rate calculation, allocation, and analysis
P3

Sunrise Company applies factory overhead based on direct labor costs. The company incurred the following costs during 2013: direct materials costs, $650,000; direct labor costs, $3,000,000; and factory overhead costs applied, $1,800,000.

1. Determine the company's predetermined overhead rate for year 2013.
2. Assuming that the company's $71,000 ending Goods in Process Inventory account for year 2013 had $20,000 of direct labor costs, determine the inventory's direct materials costs.
3. Assuming that the company's $490,000 ending Finished Goods Inventory account for year 2013 had $250,000 of direct materials costs, determine the inventory's direct labor costs and its overhead costs.

Check (3) $90,000 overhead costs

Exercise 15-17
Costs allocated to ending inventories
P1 P2 P3

Deschamps Company's ending Goods in Process Inventory account consists of 5,000 units of partially completed product, and its Finished Goods Inventory account consists of 12,000 units of product. The factory manager determines that Goods in Process Inventory includes direct materials cost of $10 per unit and direct labor cost of $7 per unit. Finished goods are estimated to have $12 of direct materials cost per unit and $9 of direct labor cost per unit. The company established the predetermined overhead rate using the following predictions: estimated direct labor cost, $300,000, and estimated factory overhead, $375,000. The company allocates factory overhead to its goods in process and finished goods inventories based on direct labor cost. During the period, the company incurred these costs: direct materials, $535,000; direct labor, $290,000; and factory overhead applied, $362,500.

1. Determine the predetermined overhead rate.
2. Compute the total cost of the two ending inventories.
3. Compute cost of goods sold for the year (assume no beginning inventories and no underapplied or overapplied overhead).

Check (3) Cost of goods sold, $671,750

Exercise 15-18
Cost-based pricing
A1

Hansel Corporation has requested bids from several architects to design its new corporate headquarters. Frey Architects is one of the firms bidding on the job. Frey estimates that the job will require the following direct labor.

	Labor	Estimated Hours	Hourly Rate
2	Architects	150	$300
3	Staff	300	75
4	Clerical	500	20

Frey applies overhead to jobs at 175% of direct labor cost. Frey would like to earn at least $80,000 profit on the architectural job. Based on past experience and market research, it estimates that the competition will bid between $285,000 and $350,000 for the job.

Check (1) $213,125

1. What is Frey's estimated cost of the architectural job?
2. What bid would you suggest that Frey submit?

Exercise 15-19
Direct materials journal entries
P1

A recent balance sheet for **Porsche AG** shows beginning raw materials inventory of €83 million and ending raw materials inventory of €85 million. Assume the company purchased raw materials (on account) for €3,108 million during the year. (1) Prepare journal entries to record (a) the purchase of raw materials and (b) the use of raw materials in production. (2) What do you notice about the € amounts in your journal entries?

connect

PROBLEM SET A

Problem 15-1A
Production costs computed and recorded; reports prepared
C2 P1 P2 P3 P4

Sage 50 QB

Ciolino Co.'s March 31 inventory of raw materials is $80,000. Raw materials purchases in April are $500,000, and factory payroll cost in April is $363,000. Overhead costs incurred in April are: indirect materials, $50,000; indirect labor, $23,000; factory rent, $32,000; factory utilities, $19,000; and factory equipment depreciation, $51,000. The predetermined overhead rate is 50% of direct labor cost. Job 306 is sold for $635,000 cash in April. Costs of the three jobs worked on in April follow.

	Job 306	Job 307	Job 308
Balances on March 31			
Direct materials	$ 29,000	$ 35,000	
Direct labor	20,000	18,000	
Applied overhead	10,000	9,000	
Costs during April			
Direct materials	135,000	220,000	$100,000
Direct labor	85,000	150,000	105,000
Applied overhead	?	?	?
Status on April 30	Finished (sold)	Finished (unsold)	In process

Required

1. Determine the total of each production cost incurred for April (direct labor, direct materials, and applied overhead), and the total cost assigned to each job (including the balances from March 31).
2. Prepare journal entries for the month of April to record the following.
   a. Materials purchases (on credit), factory payroll (paid in cash), and actual overhead costs including indirect materials and indirect labor. (Factory rent and utilities are paid in cash.)
   b. Assignment of direct materials, direct labor, and applied overhead costs to the Goods in Process Inventory.
   c. Transfer of Jobs 306 and 307 to the Finished Goods Inventory.
   d. Cost of goods sold for Job 306.
   e. Revenue from the sale of Job 306.
   f. Assignment of any underapplied or overapplied overhead to the Cost of Goods Sold account. (The amount is not material.)

Check (2f) $5,000 underapplied

(3) Cost of goods manufactured, $828,500

3. Prepare a manufacturing statement for April (use a single line presentation for direct materials and show the details of overhead cost).
4. Compute gross profit for April. Show how to present the inventories on the April 30 balance sheet.

Analysis Component

5. The over- or underapplied overhead is closed to Cost of Goods Sold. Discuss how this adjustment impacts business decision making regarding individual jobs or batches of jobs.

Problem 15-2A
Source documents, journal entries, overhead, and financial reports
P1 P2 P3 P4

Sage 50

Farina Bay's computer system generated the following trial balance on December 31, 2013. The company's manager knows something is wrong with the trial balance because it does not show any balance for Goods in Process Inventory but does show balances for the Factory Payroll and Factory Overhead accounts.

	Debit	Credit
Cash	$102,000	
Accounts receivable	75,000	
Raw materials inventory	80,000	
Goods in process inventory	0	
Finished goods inventory	15,000	
Prepaid rent	3,000	
Accounts payable		$ 17,000
Notes payable		25,000
Common stock		50,000
Retained earnings		271,000
Sales		373,000
Cost of goods sold	218,000	
Factory payroll	68,000	
Factory overhead	115,000	
Operating expenses	60,000	
Totals	$736,000	$736,000

After examining various files, the manager identifies the following six source documents that need to be processed to bring the accounting records up to date.

Materials requisition 21-3010:	$10,200 direct materials to Job 402
Materials requisition 21-3011:	$18,600 direct materials to Job 404
Materials requisition 21-3012:	$5,600 indirect materials
Labor time ticket 6052:	$36,000 direct labor to Job 402
Labor time ticket 6053:	$23,800 direct labor to Job 404
Labor time ticket 6054:	$8,200 indirect labor

Jobs 402 and 404 are the only units in process at year-end. The predetermined overhead rate is 200% of direct labor cost.

Required

1. Use information on the six source documents to prepare journal entries to assign the following costs.
  a. Direct materials costs to Goods in Process Inventory.
  b. Direct labor costs to Goods in Process Inventory.
  c. Overhead costs to Goods in Process Inventory.
  d. Indirect materials costs to the Factory Overhead account.
  e. Indirect labor costs to the Factory Overhead account.

2. Determine the revised balance of the Factory Overhead account after making the entries in part 1. Determine whether there is any under- or overapplied overhead for the year. Prepare the adjusting entry to allocate any over- or underapplied overhead to Cost of Goods Sold, assuming the amount is not material.

Check (2) $9,200 underapplied overhead

3. Prepare a revised trial balance.

4. Prepare an income statement for year 2013 and a balance sheet as of December 31, 2013.

(3) T. B. totals, $736,000
(4) Net income, $85,800

Analysis Component

5. Assume that the $5,600 on materials requisition 21-3012 should have been direct materials charged to Job 404. Without providing specific calculations, describe the impact of this error on the income statement for 2013 and the balance sheet at December 31, 2013.

Problem 15-3A
Source documents, journal entries, and accounts in job order cost accounting

P1 P2 P3

Widmer Watercraft's predetermined overhead rate for year 2013 is 200% of direct labor. Information on the company's production activities during May 2013 follows.

a. Purchased raw materials on credit, $200,000.

b. Paid $126,000 cash for factory wages.

c. Paid $15,000 cash to a computer consultant to reprogram factory equipment.

d. Materials requisitions record use of the following materials for the month.

Job 136	$ 48,000
Job 137	32,000
Job 138	19,200
Job 139	22,400
Job 140	6,400
Total direct materials	128,000
Indirect materials	19,500
Total materials used	$147,500

e. Time tickets record use of the following labor for the month.

Job 136	$ 12,000
Job 137	10,500
Job 138	37,500
Job 139	39,000
Job 140	3,000
Total direct labor	102,000
Indirect labor	24,000
Total	$126,000

f. Applied overhead to Jobs 136, 138, and 139.

g. Transferred Jobs 136, 138, and 139 to Finished Goods.

h. Sold Jobs 136 and 138 on credit at a total price of $525,000.

i. The company incurred the following overhead costs during the month (credit Prepaid Insurance for expired factory insurance).

Depreciation of factory building	$68,000
Depreciation of factory equipment	36,500
Expired factory insurance	10,000
Accrued property taxes payable	35,000

j. Applied overhead at month-end to the Goods in Process (Jobs 137 and 140) using the predetermined overhead rate of 200% of direct labor cost.

Required

1. Prepare a job cost sheet for each job worked on during the month. Use the following simplified form.

Job No. ________	
Materials	$ ________
Labor	________
Overhead	________
Total cost	$ ________

Check (2f) Cr. Factory Overhead, $177,000

2. Prepare journal entries to record the events and transactions *a* through *j*.

3. Set up T-accounts for each of the following general ledger accounts, each of which started the month with a zero balance: Raw Materials Inventory; Goods in Process Inventory; Finished Goods Inventory;

Factory Payroll; Factory Overhead; Cost of Goods Sold. Then post the journal entries to these T-accounts and determine the balance of each account.

4. Prepare a report showing the total cost of each job in process and prove that the sum of their costs equals the Goods in Process Inventory account balance. Prepare similar reports for Finished Goods Inventory and Cost of Goods Sold.

Check (4) Finished Goods Inventory, $139,400

Problem 15-4A
Overhead allocation and adjustment using a predetermined overhead rate
P3 P4

mhhe.com/wildFINMAN5e

In December 2012, Yerbury Company's manager estimated next year's total direct labor cost assuming 50 persons working an average of 2,000 hours each at an average wage rate of $25 per hour. The manager also estimated the following manufacturing overhead costs for year 2013.

Indirect labor	$ 319,200
Factory supervision	240,000
Rent on factory building	140,000
Factory utilities	88,000
Factory insurance expired	68,000
Depreciation—Factory equipment	480,000
Repairs expense—Factory equipment	60,000
Factory supplies used	68,800
Miscellaneous production costs	36,000
Total estimated overhead costs	$1,500,000

At the end of 2013, records show the company incurred $1,520,000 of actual overhead costs. It completed and sold five jobs with the following direct labor costs: Job 201, $604,000; Job 202, $563,000; Job 203, $298,000; Job 204, $716,000; and Job 205, $314,000. In addition, Job 206 is in process at the end of 2013 and had been charged $17,000 for direct labor. No jobs were in process at the end of 2012. The company's predetermined overhead rate is based on direct labor cost.

Required

1. Determine the following.
   a. Predetermined overhead rate for year 2013.
   b. Total overhead cost applied to each of the six jobs during year 2013.
   c. Over- or underapplied overhead at year-end 2013.
2. Assuming that any over- or underapplied overhead is not material, prepare the adjusting entry to allocate any over- or underapplied overhead to Cost of Goods Sold at the end of year 2013.

Check (1c) 12,800 underapplied

(2) Cr. Factory Overhead $12,800

Problem 15-5A
Production transactions, subsidiary records, and source documents
P1 P2 P3 P4

Sager Company manufactures variations of its product, a technopress, in response to custom orders from its customers. On May 1, the company had no inventories of goods in process or finished goods but held the following raw materials.

Material M	200 units @ $250 =	$50,000
Material R	95 units @ 180 =	17,100
Paint	55 units @ 75 =	4,125
Total cost		$71,225

On May 4, the company began working on two technopresses: Job 102 for Worldwide Company and Job 103 for Reuben Company.

Required

Using Exhibit 15.2 as a guide, prepare job cost sheets for jobs 102 and 103. Using Exhibit 15.4 as a guide, prepare materials ledger cards for Material M, Material R, and paint. Enter the beginning raw materials inventory dollar amounts for each of these materials on their respective ledger cards. Then, follow the instructions in this list of activities.

a. Purchased raw materials on credit and recorded the following information from receiving reports and invoices.

Receiving Report No. 426, Material M, 250 units at $250 each.
Receiving Report No. 427, Material R, 90 units at $180 each.

Instructions: Record these purchases with a single journal entry. Enter the receiving report information on the materials ledger cards.

b. Requisitioned the following raw materials for production.

Requisition No. 35, for Job 102, 135 units of Material M.
Requisition No. 36, for Job 102, 72 units of Material R.
Requisition No. 37, for Job 103, 70 units of Material M.
Requisition No. 38, for Job 103, 38 units of Material R.
Requisition No. 39, for 15 units of paint.

Instructions: Enter amounts for direct materials requisitions on the materials ledger cards and the job cost sheets. Enter the indirect material amount on the materials ledger card. Do not record a journal entry at this time.

c. Received the following employee time tickets for work in May.

Time tickets Nos. 1 to 10 for direct labor on Job 102, $90,000.
Time tickets Nos. 11 to 30 for direct labor on Job 103, $65,000.
Time tickets Nos. 31 to 36 for equipment repairs, $19,250.

Instructions: Record direct labor from the time tickets on the job cost sheets. Do not record a journal entry at this time.

d. Paid cash for the following items during the month: factory payroll, $174,250, and miscellaneous overhead items, $102,000.

Instructions: Record these payments with journal entries.

e. Finished Job 102 and transferred it to the warehouse. The company assigns overhead to each job with a predetermined overhead rate equal to 80% of direct labor cost.

Instructions: Enter the allocated overhead on the cost sheet for Job 102, fill in the cost summary section of the cost sheet, and then mark the cost sheet "Finished." Prepare a journal entry to record the job's completion and its transfer to Finished Goods.

f. Delivered Job 102 and accepted the customer's promise to pay $400,000 within 30 days.

Instructions: Prepare journal entries to record the sale of Job 102 and the cost of goods sold.

g. Applied overhead to Job 103 based on the job's direct labor to date.

Instructions: Enter overhead on the job cost sheet but do not make a journal entry at this time.

Check (h) Dr. Goods in Process Inventory, $71,050

h. Recorded the total direct and indirect materials costs as reported on all the requisitions for the month.

Instructions: Prepare a journal entry to record these costs.

i. Recorded the total direct and indirect labor costs as reported on all time tickets for the month.

Instructions: Prepare a journal entry to record these costs.

Check Balance in Factory Overhead, $1,625 Cr., overapplied

j. Recorded the total overhead costs applied to jobs.

Instructions: Prepare a journal entry to record the allocation of these overhead costs.

k. Compute the balance in the Factory Overhead account as of the end of May.

PROBLEM SET B

Problem 15-1B
Production costs computed and recorded; reports prepared
C2 P1 P2 P3 P4

Tavella Co.'s August 31 inventory of raw materials is $150,000. Raw materials purchases in September are $400,000, and factory payroll cost in September is $232,000. Overhead costs incurred in September are: indirect materials, $30,000; indirect labor, $14,000; factory rent, $20,000; factory utilities, $12,000; and factory equipment depreciation, $30,000. The predetermined overhead rate is 50% of direct labor cost. Job 114 is sold for $380,000 cash in September. Costs for the three jobs worked on in September follow.

	Job 114	Job 115	Job 116
Balances on August 31			
Direct materials	$ 14,000	$ 18,000	
Direct labor	18,000	16,000	
Applied overhead	9,000	8,000	
Costs during September			
Direct materials	100,000	170,000	$ 80,000
Direct labor	30,000	68,000	120,000
Applied overhead	?	?	?
Status on September 30	Finished (sold)	Finished (unsold)	In process

Required

1. Determine the total of each production cost incurred for September (direct labor, direct materials, and applied overhead), and the total cost assigned to each job (including the balances from August 31).
2. Prepare journal entries for the month of September to record the following.
   a. Materials purchases (on credit), factory payroll (paid in cash), and actual overhead costs including indirect materials and indirect labor. (Factory rent and utilities are paid in cash.)
   b. Assignment of direct materials, direct labor, and applied overhead costs to Goods in Process Inventory.
   c. Transfer of Jobs 114 and 115 to the Finished Goods Inventory.
   d. Cost of Job 114 in the Cost of Goods Sold account.
   e. Revenue from the sale of Job 114.
   f. Assignment of any underapplied or overapplied overhead to the Cost of Goods Sold account. (The amount is not material.)
3. Prepare a manufacturing statement for September (use a single line presentation for direct materials and show the details of overhead cost).
4. Compute gross profit for September. Show how to present the inventories on the September 30 balance sheet.

Check (2f) $3,000 overapplied

(3) Cost of goods manufactured, $500,000

Analysis Component

5. The over- or underapplied overhead adjustment is closed to Cost of Goods Sold. Discuss how this adjustment impacts business decision making regarding individual jobs or batches of jobs.

Problem 15-2B
Source documents, journal entries, overhead, and financial reports

P1 P2 P3 P4

Swisher Company's computer system generated the following trial balance on December 31, 2013. The company's manager knows that the trial balance is wrong because it does not show any balance for Goods in Process Inventory but does show balances for the Factory Payroll and Factory Overhead accounts.

	Debit	Credit
Cash	$ 48,000	
Accounts receivable	42,000	
Raw materials inventory	26,000	
Goods in process inventory	0	
Finished goods inventory	9,000	
Prepaid rent	3,000	
Accounts payable		$ 10,500
Notes payable		13,500
Common stock		30,000
Retained earnings		87,000
Sales		180,000
Cost of goods sold	105,000	
Factory payroll	16,000	
Factory overhead	27,000	
Operating expenses	45,000	
Totals	$321,000	$321,000

After examining various files, the manager identifies the following six source documents that need to be processed to bring the accounting records up to date.

Materials requisition 94-231:	$4,600 direct materials to Job 603
Materials requisition 94-232:	$7,600 direct materials to Job 604
Materials requisition 94-233:	$2,100 indirect materials
Labor time ticket 765:	$5,000 direct labor to Job 603
Labor time ticket 766:	$8,000 direct labor to Job 604
Labor time ticket 777:	$3,000 indirect labor

Jobs 603 and 604 are the only units in process at year-end. The predetermined overhead rate is 200% of direct labor cost.

Required

1. Use information on the six source documents to prepare journal entries to assign the following costs.

a. Direct materials costs to Goods in Process Inventory.

b. Direct labor costs to Goods in Process Inventory.

c. Overhead costs to Goods in Process Inventory.

d. Indirect materials costs to the Factory Overhead account.

e. Indirect labor costs to the Factory Overhead account.

Check (2) $6,100 underapplied overhead

2. Determine the revised balance of the Factory Overhead account after making the entries in part 1. Determine whether there is under- or overapplied overhead for the year. Prepare the adjusting entry to allocate any over- or underapplied overhead to Cost of Goods Sold, assuming the amount is not material.

(3) T. B. totals, $321,000

3. Prepare a revised trial balance.

(4) Net income, $23,900

4. Prepare an income statement for year 2013 and a balance sheet as of December 31, 2013.

Analysis Component

5. Assume that the $2,100 indirect materials on materials requisition 94-233 should have been direct materials charged to Job 604. Without providing specific calculations, describe the impact of this error on the income statement for 2013 and the balance sheet at December 31, 2013.

Problem 15-3B
Source documents, journal entries, and accounts in job order cost accounting
P1 P2 P3

Prescott Company's predetermined overhead rate is 200% of direct labor. Information on the company's production activities during September 2013 follows.

a. Purchased raw materials on credit, $125,000.

b. Paid $84,000 cash for factory wages.

c. Paid $11,000 cash for miscellaneous factory overhead costs.

d. Materials requisitions record use of the following materials for the month.

Job 487	$30,000
Job 488	20,000
Job 489	12,000
Job 490	14,000
Job 491	4,000
Total direct materials	80,000
Indirect materials	12,000
Total materials used	$92,000

e. Time tickets record use of the following labor for the month.

Job 487	$ 8,000
Job 488	7,000
Job 489	25,000
Job 490	26,000
Job 491	2,000
Total direct labor	68,000
Indirect labor	16,000
Total	$84,000

f. Allocated overhead to Jobs 487, 489, and 490.

g. Transferred Jobs 487, 489, and 490 to Finished Goods.

h. Sold Jobs 487 and 489 on credit for a total price of $340,000.

i. The company incurred the following overhead costs during the month (credit Prepaid Insurance for expired factory insurance).

Depreciation of factory building	$37,000
Depreciation of factory equipment	21,000
Expired factory insurance	7,000
Accrued property taxes payable	31,000

j. Applied overhead at month-end to the Goods in Process (Jobs 488 and 491) using the predetermined overhead rate of 200% of direct labor cost.

Required

1. Prepare a job cost sheet for each job worked on in the month. Use the following simplified form.

Job No. ________	
Materials	$ ________
Labor	________
Overhead	________
Total cost	$ ________

2. Prepare journal entries to record the events and transactions *a* through *j*.

3. Set up T-accounts for each of the following general ledger accounts, each of which started the month with a zero balance: Raw Materials Inventory, Goods in Process Inventory, Finished Goods Inventory, Factory Payroll, Factory Overhead, Cost of Goods Sold. Then post the journal entries to these T-accounts and determine the balance of each account.

4. Prepare a report showing the total cost of each job in process and prove that the sum of their costs equals the Goods in Process Inventory account balance. Prepare similar reports for Finished Goods Inventory and Cost of Goods Sold.

Check (2f) Cr. Factory Overhead, $118,000

(3) Finished goods inventory, $92,000 bal.

Problem 15-4B
Overhead allocation and adjustment using a predetermined overhead rate
P3 P4

In December 2012, Pavelka Company's manager estimated next year's total direct labor cost assuming 50 persons working an average of 2,000 hours each at an average wage rate of $15 per hour. The manager also estimated the following manufacturing overhead costs for year 2013.

Indirect labor	$159,600
Factory supervision	120,000
Rent on factory building	70,000
Factory utilities	44,000
Factory insurance expired	34,000
Depreciation—Factory equipment	240,000
Repairs expense—Factory equipment	30,000
Factory supplies used	34,400
Miscellaneous production costs	18,000
Total estimated overhead costs	$750,000

At the end of 2013, records show the company incurred $725,000 of actual overhead costs. It completed and sold five jobs with the following direct labor costs: Job 625, $354,000; Job 626, $330,000; Job 627, $175,000; Job 628, $420,000; and Job 629, $184,000. In addition, Job 630 is in process at the end of 2013 and had been charged $10,000 for direct labor. No jobs were in process at the end of 2012. The company's predetermined overhead rate is based on direct labor cost.

Required

1. Determine the following.

a. Predetermined overhead rate for year 2013.

b. Total overhead cost applied to each of the six jobs during year 2013.

c. Over- or underapplied overhead at year-end 2013.

2. Assuming that any over- or underapplied overhead is not material, prepare the adjusting entry to allocate any over- or underapplied overhead to Cost of Goods Sold at the end of year 2013.

Check (1c) $11,500 overapplied

(2) Dr. Factory Overhead, $11,500

Problem 15-5B
Production transactions, subsidiary records, and source documents
P1 P2 P3 P4

King Company produces variations of its product, a megatron, in response to custom orders from its customers. On June 1, the company had no inventories of goods in process or finished goods but held the following raw materials.

Material M	120 units @ $200	=	$24,000
Material R	80 units @ 160	=	12,800
Paint	44 units @ 72	=	3,168
Total cost			$39,968

On June 3, the company began working on two megatrons: Job 450 for Encinita Company and Job 451 for Fargo, Inc.

Required

Using Exhibit 15.2 as a guide, prepare job cost sheets for jobs 20 and 21. Using Exhibit 15.4 as a guide, prepare materials ledger cards for Material M, Material R, and paint. Enter the beginning raw materials inventory dollar amounts for each of these materials on their respective ledger cards. Then, follow instructions in this list of activities.

a. Purchased raw materials on credit and recorded the following information from receiving reports and invoices.

Receiving Report No. 20, Material M, 150 units at $200 each.
Receiving Report No. 21, Material R, 70 units at $160 each.

Instructions: Record these purchases with a single journal entry. Enter the receiving report information on the materials ledger cards.

b. Requisitioned the following raw materials for production.

Requisition No. 223, for Job 450, 80 units of Material M.
Requisition No. 224, for Job 450, 60 units of Material R.
Requisition No. 225, for Job 451, 40 units of Material M.
Requisition No. 226, for Job 451, 30 units of Material R.
Requisition No. 227, for 12 units of paint.

Instructions: Enter amounts for direct materials requisitions on the materials ledger cards and the job cost sheets. Enter the indirect material amount on the materials ledger card. Do not record a journal entry at this time.

c. Received the following employee time tickets for work in June.

Time tickets Nos. 1 to 10 for direct labor on Job 450, $40,000.
Time tickets Nos. 11 to 20 for direct labor on Job 451, $32,000.
Time tickets Nos. 21 to 24 for equipment repairs, $12,000.

Instructions: Record direct labor from the time tickets on the job cost sheets. Do not record a journal entry at this time.

d. Paid cash for the following items during the month: factory payroll, $84,000, and miscellaneous overhead items, $36,800.

Instructions: Record these payments with journal entries.

e. Finished Job 450 and transferred it to the warehouse. The company assigns overhead to each job with a predetermined overhead rate equal to 70% of direct labor cost.

Instructions: Enter the allocated overhead on the cost sheet for Job 450, fill in the cost summary section of the cost sheet, and then mark the cost sheet "Finished." Prepare a journal entry to record the job's completion and its transfer to Finished Goods.

f. Delivered Job 450 and accepted the customer's promise to pay $290,000 within 30 days.

Instructions: Prepare journal entries to record the sale of Job 450 and the cost of goods sold.

g. Applied overhead cost to Job 451 based on the job's direct labor used to date.

Instructions: Enter overhead on the job cost sheet but do not make a journal entry at this time.

h. Recorded the total direct and indirect materials costs as reported on all the requisitions for the month.

Instructions: Prepare a journal entry to record these.

Check (h) Dr. Goods in Process Inventory, $38,400

i. Recorded the total direct and indirect labor costs as reported on all time tickets for the month.

Instructions: Prepare a journal entry to record these costs.

j. Recorded the total overhead costs applied to jobs.

Instructions: Prepare a journal entry to record the allocation of these overhead costs.

k. Compute the balance in the Factory Overhead account as of the end of June.

Check Balance in Factory Overhead, $736 Cr., overapplied

SERIAL PROBLEM

Success Systems

P1 P2 P3

(This serial problem began in Chapter 1 and continues through most of the book. If previous chapter segments were not completed, the serial problem can begin at this point. It is helpful, but not necessary, to use the Working Papers that accompany the book.)

SP 15 The computer workstation furniture manufacturing that Adria Lopez started in January is progressing well. As of the end of June, Success Systems' job cost sheets show the following total costs accumulated on three furniture jobs.

	Job 6.02	Job 6.03	Job 6.04
Direct materials	$1,500	$3,300	$2,700
Direct labor	800	1,420	2,100
Overhead	400	710	1,050

Job 6.02 was started in production in May, and these costs were assigned to it in May: direct materials, $600; direct labor, $180; and overhead, $90. Jobs 6.03 and 6.04 were started in June. Overhead cost is applied with a predetermined rate based on direct labor costs. Jobs 6.02 and 6.03 are finished in June, and Job 6.04 is expected to be finished in July. No raw materials are used indirectly in June. (Assume this company's predetermined overhead rate did not change over these months).

Required

1. What is the cost of the raw materials used in June for each of the three jobs and in total?
2. How much total direct labor cost is incurred in June?
3. What predetermined overhead rate is used in June?
4. How much cost is transferred to finished goods inventory in June?

Check (1) Total materials, $6,900

(3) 50%

Beyond the Numbers

REPORTING IN ACTION

C1

Polaris

BTN 15-1 Polaris' financial statements and notes in Appendix A provide evidence of growth potential in its sales.

Required

1. Identify at least two types of costs that will predictably increase as a percent of sales with growth in sales.
2. Explain why you believe the types of costs identified for part 1 will increase, and describe how you might assess Polaris' success with these costs. (*Hint:* You might consider the gross margin ratio.)

Fast Forward

3. Access Polaris' annual report for a fiscal year ending after December 31, 2011, from its Website [Polaris.com] or the SEC's EDGAR database [www.sec.gov]. Review and report its growth in sales along with its cost and income levels (including its gross margin ratio).

COMPARATIVE ANALYSIS

C1

Polaris

Arctic Cat

BTN 15-2 Manufacturers and merchandisers can apply just-in-time (JIT) to their inventory management. Both **Polaris** and **Arctic Cat** want to know the impact of a JIT inventory system for their operating cash flows. Review each company's statement of cash flows in Appendix A to answer the following.

Required

1. Identify the impact on operating cash flows (increase or decrease) for changes in inventory levels (increase or decrease) for both companies for each of the three most recent years.

2. What impact would a JIT inventory system have on both Polaris' and Arctic Cat's operating income? Link the answer to your response for part 1.

3. Would the move to a JIT system have a one-time or recurring impact on operating cash flow?

ETHICS CHALLENGE

P3

BTN 15-3 An accounting professional requires at least two skill sets. The first is to be technically competent. Knowing how to capture, manage, and report information is a necessary skill. Second, the ability to assess manager and employee actions and biases for accounting analysis is another skill. For instance, knowing how a person is compensated helps anticipate information biases. Draw on these skills and write a one-half page memo to the financial officer on the following practice of allocating overhead.

Background: Assume that your company sells portable housing to both general contractors and the government. It sells jobs to contractors on a bid basis. A contractor asks for three bids from different manufacturers. The combination of low bid and high quality wins the job. However, jobs sold to the government are bid on a cost-plus basis. This means price is determined by adding all costs plus a profit based on cost at a specified percent, such as 10%. You observe that the amount of overhead allocated to government jobs is higher than that allocated to contract jobs. These allocations concern you and motivate your memo.

Point: Students could compare responses and discuss differences in concerns with allocating overhead.

COMMUNICATING IN PRACTICE

C1 C2

BTN 15-4 Assume that you are preparing for a second interview with a manufacturing company. The company is impressed with your credentials but has indicated that it has several qualified applicants. You anticipate that in this second interview, you must show what you offer over other candidates. You learn the company currently uses a periodic inventory system and is not satisfied with the timeliness of its information and its inventory management. The company manufactures custom-order holiday decorations and display items. To show your abilities, you plan to recommend that it use a cost accounting system.

Required

In preparation for the interview, prepare notes outlining the following:

1. Your cost accounting system recommendation and why it is suitable for this company.

2. A general description of the documents that the proposed cost accounting system requires.

3. How the documents in part 2 facilitate the operation of the cost accounting system.

Point: Have students present a mock interview, one assuming the role of the president of the company and the other the applicant.

TAKING IT TO THE NET

C1

BTN 15-5 Many contractors work on custom jobs that require a job order costing system.

Required

Access the Website AMSI.com and click on *Construction Management Software,* and then on STARBUILDER. Prepare a one-page memorandum for the CEO of a construction company providing information about the job order costing software this company offers. Would you recommend that the company purchase this software?

TEAMWORK IN ACTION

C1

BTN 15-6 Consider the activities undertaken by a medical clinic in your area.

Required

1. Do you consider a job order cost accounting system appropriate for the clinic?
2. Identify as many factors as possible to lead you to conclude that it uses a job order system.

ENTREPRENEURIAL DECISION

C1 C2

BTN 15-7 Refer to the chapter opener regarding David Schottenstein and his company, Astor and Black. All successful businesses track their costs, and it is especially important for start-up businesses to monitor and control costs.

Required

1. Assume that Astor and Black uses a job order costing system. For the basic cost category of direct materials, explain how a job cost sheet for Astor and Black would differ from a job cost sheet for a service company.
2. For the basic cost categories of direct labor and overhead, provide examples of the types of costs that would fall into each category for Astor and Black.

HITTING THE ROAD

C2 P1 P2 P3

BTN 15-8 Job order cost accounting is frequently used by home builders.

Required

1. You (or your team) are to prepare a job cost sheet for a single-family home under construction. List four items of both direct materials and direct labor. Explain how you think overhead should be applied.
2. Contact a builder and compare your job cost sheet to this builder's job cost sheet. If possible, speak to that company's accountant. Write your findings in a short report.

GLOBAL DECISION

C1

KTM

PIAGGIO

BTN 15-9 KTM and Piaggio are competitors in the global marketplace. KTM's and Piaggio's financial statements are in Appendix A.

Required

1. Determine the change in KTM's and Piaggio's inventories for the most recent year reported. Then identify the impact on net resources generated by operating activities (increase or decrease) for the change in inventory level (increase or decrease) for KTM and Piaggio for that same year.
2. How would the move to a just-in-time (JIT) system likely impact future operating cash flows and operating income?
3. Would a move to a JIT system likely impact KTM more than it would Piaggio? Explain.

ANSWERS TO MULTIPLE CHOICE QUIZ

1. c; $30,000 × 150% = $45,000
2. b; $38,500/$35,000 = 110%
3. e; Direct materials + Direct labor + Overhead = Total cost;
   Direct materials + ($4,000/.80) + $4,000 = $10,000
   Direct materials = $1,000
4. e; $9,000 + $94,200 + $59,200 + $31,600 − Finished goods = $17,800
   Thus, finished goods = $176,200
5. b

16

Process Costing and Analysis

A Look Back

Chapter 14 introduced managerial accounting and described cost concepts and the reporting of manufacturing activities. Chapter 15 explained job order costing—an important cost accounting system for customized products and services.

A Look at This Chapter

This chapter focuses on how to measure and account for costs in process operations. We explain process production, describe how to assign costs to processes, and compute cost per equivalent unit for a process.

A Look Ahead

Chapter 17 introduces the activity-based costing (ABC) system, which provides managers with strategic cost information that is not readily available from other costing methods.

Learning Objectives

CONCEPTUAL

C1 Explain process operations and the way they differ from job order operations. (p. 692)

C2 Define and compute equivalent units and explain their use in process cost accounting. (p. 699)

C3 Describe accounting for production activity and preparation of a process cost summary using weighted average. (p. 700)

C4 *Appendix 16A*—Describe accounting for production activity and preparation of a process cost summary using FIFO. (p. 711)

ANALYTICAL

A1 Compare process cost accounting and job order cost accounting. (p. 695)

A2 Explain and illustrate a hybrid costing system. (p. 707)

PROCEDURAL

P1 Record the flow of direct materials costs in process cost accounting. (p. 696)

P2 Record the flow of direct labor costs in process cost accounting. (p. 697)

P3 Record the flow of factory overhead costs in process cost accounting. (p. 697)

P4 Record the transfer of completed goods to Finished Goods Inventory and Cost of Goods Sold. (p. 705)

Decision Insight

Sweet Success

"Anyone can do it!"

—NEAL GOTTLIEB

SAN FRANCISCO—After returning from a stint in the Peace Corps, Neal Gottlieb wanted to start the "most Earth-friendly business I could think of." Using the $70,000 he saved from delivering newspapers and other boyhood jobs, Neal started **Three Twins Ice Cream (ThreeTwinsIceCream.com),** a manufacturer and seller of organic ice cream. Business started slowly, with Neal as the lone employee in a single ice cream shop. "I made ice cream in the morning, ran the shop all day, then cleaned up and did paperwork at night," recalls Neal.

Working 166 straight days without a day off and recording gross sales of $49 on one cold, rainy Monday, Neal decided he had to expand into the wholesale ice cream business or abandon his dreams. Neal's gamble paid off—today Three Twins Ice Cream is certified organic in more ice cream flavors than any ice cream company in the world, and as Neal says, "I'm happy to say I don't mop floors anymore."

In addition to using only organic ingredients, Neal strives to make his entire operation Earth-friendly. "Everything we give the customer can be composted," explains Neal. Cups and spoons are made from pressed sugar cane, potatoes, and corn starch. His production strategy adds overhead costs; for example, spoons cost 4 cents each instead of 1 cent each for plastic spoons. Neal explains that "using organic ingredients isn't the cheapest option, but it's the best." With costly raw materials and overhead costs, Neal must be adept at interpreting product cost reports. Without good cost and production process controls, his income would quickly melt away.

With costly raw materials and overhead costs, Neal relies on process cost summary reports to enable him to monitor and control costs of materials, labor, and overhead in his production processes. Accurate costing is especially useful in companies like Neal's, where different products require different processes and costs. Traditional flavors like vanilla, chocolate, and strawberry can be made in large quantities in large production runs, while treats like Peanut Butter Confetti Crunch and The Chocolate Project are made in small quantities.

Neal's recipe is working. Three Twins recently built a 4,200 square foot manufacturing facility to expand its business and reduce costs. Neal's factory allows him to produce larger quantities of ice cream at lower cost because he now makes his own mix. "We used to pay $15 per gallon for our mix; we can now make mix for less than $7 per gallon," explains Neal. Neal responded to these cost savings by lowering his selling prices and saw demand for his products grow.

From humble beginnings, Three Twins' sales are growing at almost 100 percent per year. "We want to be a national brand," says Neal. "We believe we have the potential to find a huge market." Still, Neal advises would-be entrepreneurs to "enjoy what they do, work hard, and give back."

[Sources: *Three Twins Ice Cream Company* Website, January 2013; *Marin Independent Journal*, July 2010; sf.eater.com, April 2010; *North Bay Business* Journal, April 2010; *Napa Valley Register*, April 2007]

Chapter Preview

The type of product or service a company offers determines its cost accounting system. Job order costing is used to account for custom products and services that meet the demands of a particular customer. Not all products are manufactured in this way; many carry standard designs so that one unit is no different than any other unit. Such a system often produces large numbers of units on a continuous basis, all of which pass through similar processes. This chapter describes how to use a process cost accounting system to account for these types of products. It also explains how costs are accumulated for each process and then assigned to units passing through those processes. This information helps us understand and estimate the cost of each process as well as find ways to reduce costs and improve processes.

Process Costing and Analysis

Process Operations
- Comparing job order and process operations
- Organization of process operations
- GenX Company—an illustration

Process Cost Accounting
- Job order versus process cost systems
- Direct and indirect costs
- Accounting for materials costs
- Accounting for labor costs
- Accounting for factory overhead

Equivalent Units of Production (EUP)
- Accounting for goods in process
- Differences between EUP for materials, labor, and overhead

Process Costing Illustration
- Physical flow of units
- EUP
- Cost per EUP
- Cost reconciliation
- Process cost summary
- Transfers to finished goods and to cost of goods sold
- Trends in process operations

PROCESS OPERATIONS

C1 Explain process operations and the way they differ from job order operations.

Process operations, also called *process manufacturing* or *process production,* is the mass production of products in a continuous flow of steps. This means that products pass through a series of sequential processes. Petroleum refining is a common example of process operations. Crude oil passes through a series of steps before it is processed into different grades of petroleum. **Exxon Mobil**'s oil activities reflect a process operation. An important characteristic of process operations is the high level of standardization necessary if the system is to produce large volumes of products. Process operations also extend to services. Examples include mail sorting in large post offices and order processing in large mail-order firms such as **L.L. Bean**. The common feature in these service organizations is that operations are performed in a sequential manner using a series of standardized processes. Other companies using process operations include:

Company*	Product or Service	Company	Product or Service
Kellogg	Cereals	Heinz	Ketchup
Pfizer	Pharmaceuticals	Penn	Tennis balls
Proctor & Gamble	Household products	Hershey	Chocolate
Coca-Cola	Soft drinks	Jiffy Lube	Oil changes

*For virtual tours of process operations visit PennRacquet.com/factory.html (tennis balls) and Hersheys.com/ads-and-videos/how-we-make-chocolate.aspx (chocolate).

Each of these examples of products and services involves operations having a series of *processes,* or steps. Each process involves a different set of activities. A production operation that processes chemicals, for instance, might include the four steps shown in Exhibit 16.1. Understanding such processes for companies with process operations is crucial for measuring their costs. Increasingly, process operations use machines and automation to control product quality and reduce manufacturing costs.

EXHIBIT 16.1

Process Operations: Chemicals

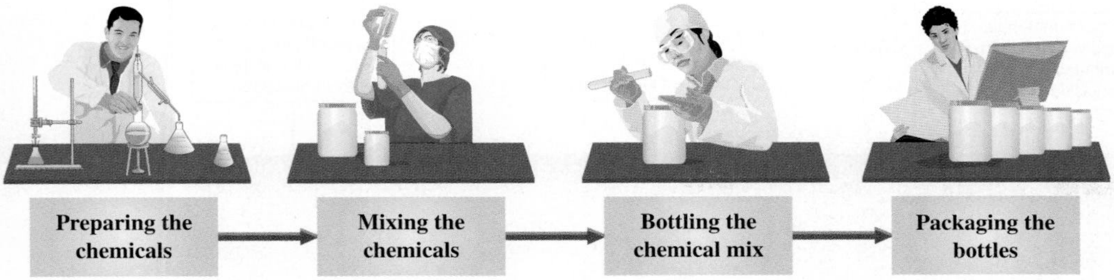

Comparing Job Order and Process Operations

Job order and process operations can be considered as two ends of a continuum. Important features of both systems are shown in Exhibit 16.2. We often describe job order and process operations with manufacturing examples, but both also apply to service companies. In a job order costing system, the measurement focus is on the individual job or batch. In a process costing system, the measurement focus is on the process itself and the standardized units produced.

EXHIBIT 16.2

Comparing Job Order and Process Operations

Job Order Operations

- Custom orders
- Heterogeneous products and services
- Low production volume
- High product flexibility
- Low to medium standardization

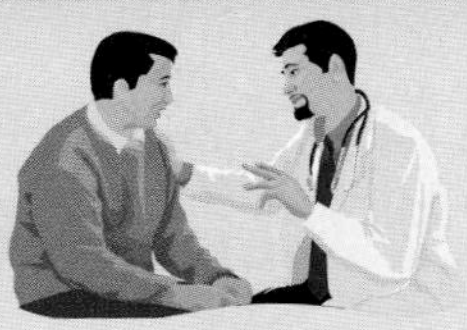

Process Operations

- Repetitive procedures
- Homogeneous products and services
- High production volume
- Low product flexibility
- High standardization

Organization of Process Operations

In a process operation, each process is identified as a separate *production department, workstation,* or *work center.* With the exception of the first process or department, each receives the output from the prior department as a partially processed product. Depending on the nature of the process, a company applies direct labor, overhead, and, perhaps, additional direct materials to move the product toward completion. Only the final process or department in the series produces finished goods ready for sale to customers.

Tracking costs for several related departments can seem complex. Yet because process costing procedures are applied to the activity of each department or process separately, we need to consider only one process at a time. This simplifies the procedures.

When the output of one department becomes an input to another department, as is the case in sequential processing, we simply transfer the costs associated with those units from the first department into the next. We repeat these steps from department to department until the final process is complete. At that point the accumulated costs are transferred with the product from Goods in Process Inventory to Finished Goods Inventory. The next section illustrates a company with a single process, but the methods illustrated apply to a multiprocess scenario as each department's costs are handled separately for each department.

Decision Insight

Processing Health Many service companies use process departments to perform specific tasks for consumers. Hospitals, for instance, have radiology and physical therapy facilities with special equipment and trained employees. When patients need services, they are processed through departments to receive prescribed care. Service companies need process cost accounting information as much as manufacturers to estimate costs of services, to plan future operations, to control costs, and to determine customer charges. ■

GenX Company—An Illustration

The GenX Company illustrates process operations. It produces Profen®, an over-the-counter pain reliever for athletes. GenX sells Profen to wholesale distributors, who in turn sell it to

EXHIBIT 16.3

Floor Plan of GenX's Factory

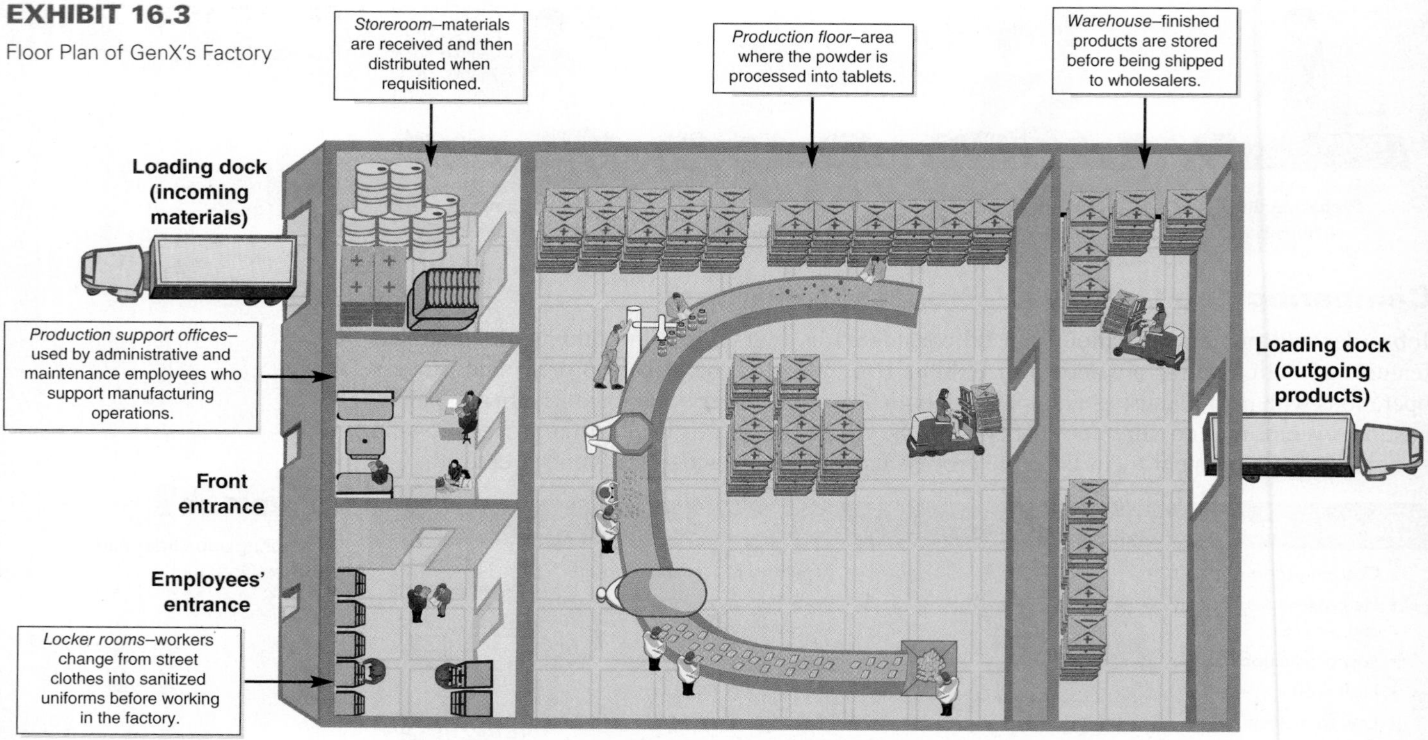

retailers. Profen is produced by mixing its active ingredient, Profelene, with flavorings and preservatives, molding it into Profen tablets, and packaging the tablets. Exhibit 16.3 shows a summary floor plan of the GenX factory, which has five areas.

Point: Electronic monitoring of operations is common in factories.

The first step in process manufacturing is to decide when to produce a product. Management determines the types and quantities of materials and labor needed and then schedules the work. Unlike a job order process, where production often begins only after receipt of a custom order, managers of companies with process operations often forecast the demand expected for their products. Based on these plans, production begins. The flowchart in Exhibit 16.4 shows the production steps for GenX. The following sections explain how GenX uses a process cost accounting system to compute these costs. Many of the explanations refer to this exhibit and its numbered cost flows ① through ⑩. (*Hint:* The amounts for the numbered cost flows in Exhibit 16.4 are summarized in Exhibit 16.21. Those amounts are explained in the following pages, but it can help to refer to Exhibit 16.21 as we proceed through the explanations.)

EXHIBIT 16.4

Process Operations and Costs: GenX

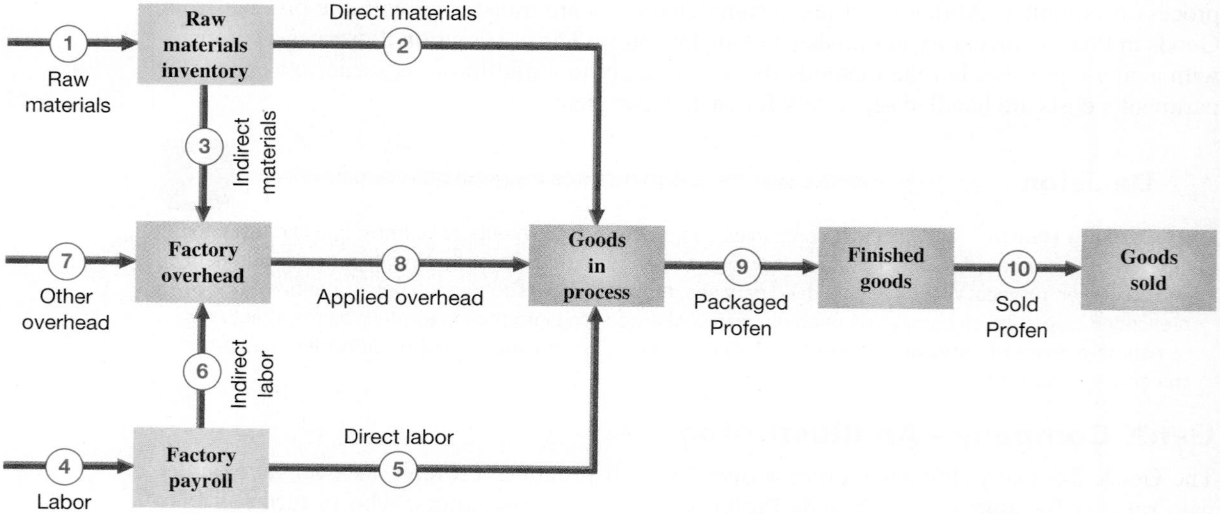

PROCESS COST ACCOUNTING

Comparing Job Order and Process Cost Accounting Systems

A1 Compare process cost accounting and job order cost accounting.

Process and job order operations are similar in that both combine materials, labor, and overhead in the process of producing products. They differ in how they are organized and managed. The measurement focus in a job order costing system is on the individual job or batch, whereas in a process costing system, it is on the individual process. Regardless of the measurement focus, we are ultimately interested in determining the cost per unit of product (or service) resulting from either system.

Both **job order cost accounting systems** and **process cost accounting systems** track direct materials, direct labor, and overhead costs. However, these two accounting systems differ in terms of measuring unit costs. A job order system measures cost per unit upon completion of a job, by dividing the total cost for that job by the number of units in that job. A process costing system measures unit costs at the end of a period (for example, a month) by dividing the total costs for that process by the number of units passing through that process to determine the cost per equivalent unit (defined later in the chapter). Differences in the way these two systems apply materials, labor, and overhead costs are highlighted in Exhibit 16.5.

Point: The cost object in a job order system is the specific job; the cost object in a process costing system is the process.

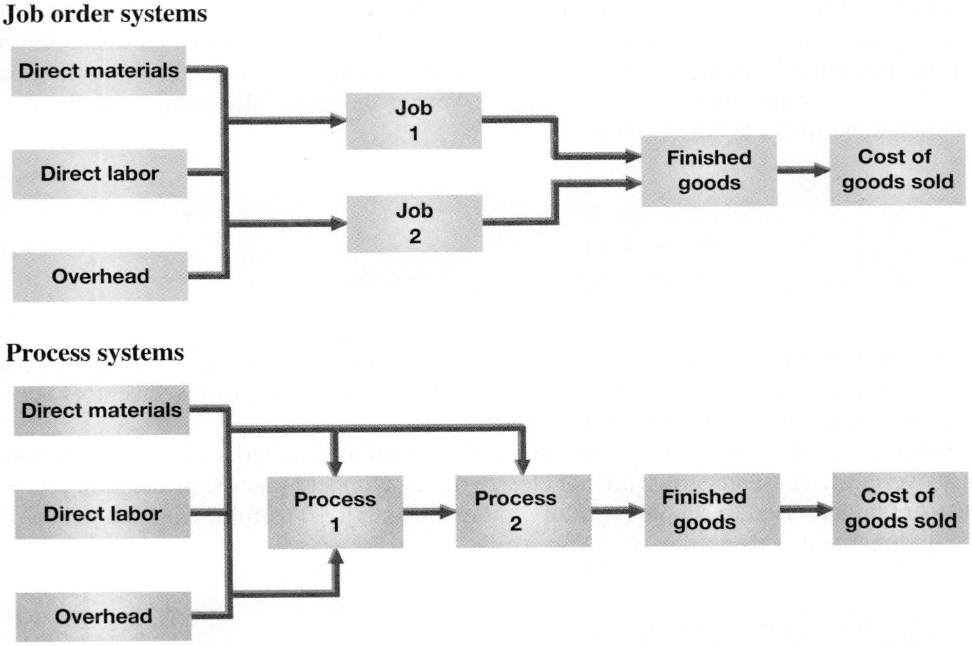

EXHIBIT 16.5

Comparing Job Order and Process Cost Accounting Systems

Direct and Indirect Costs

Like job order operations, process cost accounting systems use the concepts of direct and indirect costs. If a cost can be traced to the cost object, it is direct; if it cannot, it is indirect. Materials and labor that can be traced to specific processes are assigned to those processes as direct costs. Materials and labor that cannot be traced to a specific process are indirect costs and are assigned to overhead. Some costs classified as overhead in a job order system may be classified as direct costs in process cost accounting. For example, depreciation of a machine used entirely by one process is a direct cost of that process.

Decision Insight

JIT Boon to Process Operations Companies that adopt JIT manufacturing often organize their production system as a series of sequential processes. One survey found 60% of companies that converted to JIT used process operations; this compares to only 20% before converting to JIT. ■

P1 Record the flow of direct materials costs in process cost accounting.

Accounting for Materials Costs

In Exhibit 16.4, arrow line ① reflects the arrival of materials at GenX's factory. These materials include Profelene, flavorings, preservatives, and packaging. They also include supplies for the production support office. GenX uses a perpetual inventory system and makes all purchases on credit. The summary entry for receipts of raw materials in April follows (dates in journal entries numbered ① through ⑩ are omitted because they are summary entries, often reflecting two or more transactions or events).

Assets	=	Liabilities	+	Equity
+11,095		+11,095		

①	Raw Materials Inventory	11,095	
	Accounts Payable		11,095
	Acquired materials on credit for factory use.		

Arrow line ② in Exhibit 16.4 reflects the flow of direct materials to production, where they are used to produce Profen. Most direct materials are physically combined into the finished product; the remaining direct materials include those used and clearly linked with a specific process. The manager of a process usually obtains materials by submitting a *materials requisition* to the materials storeroom manager. In some situations, materials move continuously from raw materials inventory through the manufacturing process. **Pepsi Bottling**, for instance, uses a process in which inventory moves continuously through the system. In these cases, a **materials consumption report** summarizes the materials used by a department during a reporting period and replaces materials requisitions. The entry to record the use of direct materials by GenX's production department in April follows.

Assets	=	Liabilities	+	Equity
+9,900				
−9,900				

②	Goods in Process Inventory	9,900	
	Raw Materials Inventory		9,900
	To assign costs of direct materials used in production.		

This entry transfers costs from one asset account to another asset account. (When two or more production departments exist, a company uses two or more Goods in Process Inventory accounts to separately accumulate costs incurred by each.)

In Exhibit 16.4, the arrow line ③ reflects the flow of indirect materials from the storeroom to factory overhead. These materials are not clearly linked with any specific production process or department but are used to support overall production activity. The following entry records the cost of indirect materials used by GenX in April.

Example: What types of materials might the flow of arrow line ③ in Exhibit 16.4 reflect? *Answer:* Goggles, gloves, protective clothing, recordkeeping supplies, and cleaning supplies.

Assets	=	Liabilities	+	Equity
−1,195				−1,195

③	Factory Overhead	1,195	
	Raw Materials Inventory		1,195
	To record indirect materials used in April.		

After the entries for both direct and indirect materials are posted, the Raw Materials Inventory account appears as shown in Exhibit 16.6. The April 30 balance sheet reports the $4,000 Raw Materials Inventory account as a current asset.

EXHIBIT 16.6

Raw Materials Inventory

Raw Materials Inventory					Acct. No. 132
Date		**Explanation**	**Debit**	**Credit**	**Balance**
Mar.	31	Balance			4,000
Apr.	30	Materials purchases	11,095		15,095
	30	Direct materials usage		9,900	5,195
	30	Indirect materials usage		1,195	4,000

Accounting for Labor Costs

P2 Record the flow of direct labor costs in process cost accounting.

Exhibit 16.4 shows GenX factory payroll costs as reflected in arrow line ④. Total labor costs of $8,920 are paid in cash and are recorded in the Factory Payroll account.

④	Factory Payroll	8,920	
	Cash		8,920
	To record factory wages for April.		

Assets = Liabilities + Equity
−8,920 −8,920

Time reports from the production department and the production support office triggered this entry. (For simplicity, we do not separately identify withholdings and additional payroll taxes for employees.) In a process operation, the direct labor of a production department includes all labor used exclusively by that department. This is the case even if the labor is not applied to the product itself. If a production department in a process operation, for instance, has a full-time manager and a full-time maintenance worker, their salaries are direct labor costs of that process and are not factory overhead.

Arrow line ⑤ in Exhibit 16.4 shows GenX's use of direct labor in the production department. The following entry transfers April's direct labor costs from the Factory Payroll account to the Goods in Process Inventory account.

⑤	Goods in Process Inventory	5,700	
	Factory Payroll		5,700
	To assign costs of direct labor used in production.		

Assets = Liabilities + Equity
+5,700 +5,700

Arrow line ⑥ in Exhibit 16.4 reflects GenX's indirect labor costs. These employees provide clerical, maintenance, and other services that help produce Profen efficiently. For example, they order materials, deliver them to the factory floor, repair equipment, operate and program computers used in production, keep payroll and other production records, clean up, and move the finished goods to the warehouse. The following entry charges these indirect labor costs to factory overhead.

Point: A department's indirect labor cost might include an allocated portion of the salary of a manager who supervises two or more departments. Allocation of costs between departments is discussed in a later chapter.

⑥	Factory Overhead	3,220	
	Factory Payroll		3,220
	To record indirect labor as overhead.		

Assets = Liabilities + Equity
−3,220
+3,220

After these entries for both direct and indirect labor are posted, the Factory Payroll account appears as shown in Exhibit 16.7. The temporary Factory Payroll account is now closed to another temporary account, Factory Overhead, and is ready to receive entries for May. Next we show how to apply overhead to production and close the temporary Factory Overhead account.

EXHIBIT 16.7
Factory Payroll

Factory Payroll					Acct. No. 530
Date		Explanation	Debit	Credit	Balance
Mar.	31	Balance			0
Apr.	30	Total payroll for April	8,920		8,920
	30	Direct labor costs		5,700	3,220
	30	Indirect labor costs		3,220	0

Accounting for Factory Overhead

P3 Record the flow of factory overhead costs in process cost accounting.

Overhead costs other than indirect materials and indirect labor are reflected by arrow line ⑦ in Exhibit 16.4. These overhead items include the costs of insuring production assets, renting the factory building, using factory utilities, and depreciating equipment not directly related to a specific process. The following entry records overhead costs for April.

Assets	=	Liabilities	+	Equity
−180		+645		−2,425
−750				
−850				

		Debit	Credit
⑦	Factory Overhead	2,425	
	Prepaid Insurance		180
	Utilities Payable		645
	Cash		750
	Accumulated Depreciation—Factory Equipment		850
	To record overhead items incurred in April.		

After this entry is posted, the Factory Overhead account balance is $6,840, comprising indirect materials of $1,195, indirect labor of $3,220, and $2,425 of other overhead.

Arrow line ⑧ in Exhibit 16.4 reflects the application of factory overhead to production. Factory overhead is applied to processes by relating overhead cost to another variable such as direct labor hours or machine hours used. With increasing automation, companies with process operations are more likely to use machine hours to allocate overhead. In some situations, a single allocation basis such as direct labor hours (or a single rate for the entire plant) fails to provide useful allocations. As a result, management can use different rates for different production departments. Based on an analysis of its operations, GenX applies its April overhead at a rate of 120% of direct labor cost, as shown in Exhibit 16.8.

Point: The time it takes to process (cycle) products through a process is sometimes used to allocate costs.

EXHIBIT 16.8

Applying Factory Overhead (Production Department)

Overhead applied	=	**Direct labor cost**	×	**Predetermined rate**
$6,840	=	$5,700	×	120%

GenX records its applied overhead with the following entry.

Assets	=	Liabilities	+	Equity
+6,840				+6,840

		Debit	Credit
⑧	Goods in Process Inventory	6,840	
	Factory Overhead		6,840
	Allocated overhead costs to production at 120% of direct labor cost.		

After posting this entry, the Factory Overhead account appears as shown in Exhibit 16.9. For GenX, the amount of overhead applied equals the actual overhead incurred during April. In most cases, using a predetermined overhead rate leaves an overapplied or underapplied balance in the Factory Overhead account. At the end of the period, this overapplied or underapplied balance should be closed to the Cost of Goods Sold account, as described in the job order costing chapter.

EXHIBIT 16.9

Factory Overhead

Factory Overhead — **Acct. No. 540**

Date		Explanation	Debit	Credit	Balance
Mar.	31	Balance			0
Apr.	30	Indirect materials usage	1,195		1,195
	30	Indirect labor costs	3,220		4,415
	30	Other overhead costs	2,425		6,840
	30	Applied to production departments		6,840	0

Example: If applied overhead results in a $6,940 credit to the factory overhead account, does it yield an over- or underapplied overhead amount? *Answer:* $100 overapplied overhead

Decision Ethics

Budget Officer You are working to identify the direct and indirect costs of a new processing department that has several machines. This department's manager instructs you to classify a majority of the costs as indirect to take advantage of the direct labor-based overhead allocation method so it will be charged a lower amount of overhead (because of its small direct labor cost). This would penalize other departments with higher allocations. It also will cause the performance ratings of managers in these other departments to suffer. What action do you take? ■ [Answer—p. 716]

Quick Check Answers — p. 716

1. A process operation (*a*) is another name for a job order operation, (*b*) does not use the concepts of direct materials or direct labor, or (*c*) typically produces large quantities of homogeneous products or services.
2. Under what conditions is a process cost accounting system more suitable for measuring production costs than a job order cost accounting system?
3. When direct materials are assigned and used in production, the entry to record their use includes (*a*) a credit to Goods in Process Inventory, (*b*) a debit to Goods in Process Inventory, or (*c*) a debit to Raw Materials Inventory.
4. What are the three cost categories incurred by both job order and process operations?
5. How many Goods in Process Inventory accounts are needed in a process cost system?

EQUIVALENT UNITS OF PRODUCTION

C2 Define and compute equivalent units and explain their use in process cost accounting.

We explained how materials, labor, and overhead costs for a period are accumulated in the Goods in Process Inventory account, but we have not explained the arrow lines labeled ⑨ and ⑩ in Exhibit 16.4. These lines reflect the transfer of products from the production department to finished goods inventory, and from finished goods inventory to cost of goods sold. To determine the costs recorded for these flows, we must first determine the cost per unit of product and then apply this result to the number of units transferred.

Accounting for Goods in Process

If a process has *no beginning and no ending goods in process inventory,* the unit cost of goods transferred out of a process is computed as follows:

$$\frac{\textbf{Total cost assigned to the process (direct materials, direct labor, and overhead)}}{\textbf{Total number of units started and finished in the period}}$$

If a process has a beginning or ending inventory of partially processed units (or both), then the total cost assigned to the process must be allocated to all completed and incomplete units worked on during the period. Therefore, the denominator must measure the entire production activity of the process for the period, called **equivalent units of production** (or **EUP**), a phrase that refers to the number of units that could have been started *and* completed given the cost incurred during a period. This measure is then used to compute the cost per equivalent unit and to assign costs to finished goods and goods in process inventory.

To illustrate, assume that GenX adds (or introduces) 100 units into its process during a period. Suppose at the end of that period, the production supervisor determines that those 100 units are 60% of the way through the process. Therefore, equivalent units of production for that period total 60 EUP (100 units × 60%). This means that with the resources used to put 100 units 60% of the way through the process, GenX could have started and completed 60 whole units.

Point: For GenX, "units" might refer to individual Profen tablets. For a juice maker, units might refer to gallons.

Differences in Equivalent Units for Materials, Labor, and Overhead

In many processes, the equivalent units of production for direct materials are not the same with respect to direct labor and overhead. To illustrate, consider a five-step process operation shown in Exhibit 16.10.

EXHIBIT 16.10

An Illustrative Five-Step Process Operation

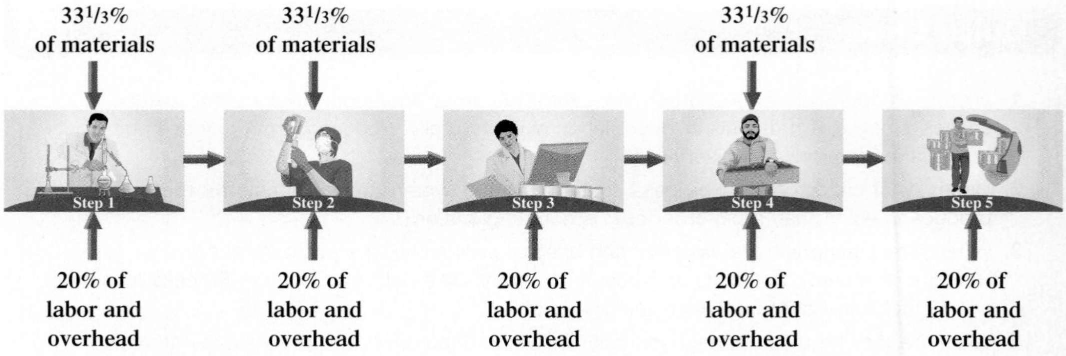

This exhibit shows that one-third of the direct material cost is added at each of three steps: 1, 2, and 4. One-fifth of the direct labor cost is added at each of the five steps. One-fifth of the overhead also is added at each step because overhead is applied as a percent of direct labor for this company.

When units finish step 1, they are one-third complete with respect to direct materials but only one-fifth complete with respect to direct labor and overhead. When they finish step 2, they are two-thirds complete with respect to direct materials but only two-fifths complete with respect to direct labor and overhead. When they finish step 3, they remain two-thirds complete with respect to materials but are now three-fifths complete with respect to labor and overhead. When they finish step 4, they are 100% complete with respect to materials (all direct materials have been added) but only four-fifths complete with respect to labor and overhead.

For example, if 300 units of product are started and processed through step 1 of Exhibit 16.10, they are said to be one-third complete *with respect to materials*. Expressed in terms of equivalent finished units, the processing of these 300 units is equal to finishing 100 EUP with respect to materials (300 units × 33⅓%). However, only one-fifth of direct labor and overhead has been applied to the 300 units at the end of step 1. This means that the equivalent units of production *with respect to labor and overhead* total 60 EUP (300 units × 20%).

Decision Insight

Process Services Customer interaction software is a hot item in customer service processes. Whether in insurance, delivery, or technology services, companies are finding that this software can turn their customer service process into an asset. How does it work? For starters, it cuts time spent on service calls because a customer describes a problem only once. It also yields a database of customer questions and complaints that gives insights into needed improvements. It recognizes incoming phone numbers and accesses previous interactions. ■

PROCESS COSTING ILLUSTRATION

C3 Describe accounting for production activity and preparation of a process cost summary using weighted average.

This section applies process costing concepts and procedures to GenX. **This illustration uses the weighted-average method for inventory costs. The FIFO method is illustrated in Appendix 16A.** (Assume a weighted-average cost flow for all computations and assignments in this chapter unless explicitly stated differently. When using a just-in-time inventory system, different inventory methods yield similar results because inventories are immaterial.)

Exhibit 16.11 shows selected information from the production department for the month of April. Accounting for a department's activity for a period includes four steps involving analysis of (1) physical flow, (2) equivalent units, (3) cost per equivalent unit, and (4) cost assignment and reconciliation. The next sections describe each step.

EXHIBIT 16.11

Production Data

Beginning goods in process inventory (March 31)	
Units of product	30,000 units
Percentage of completion—Direct materials	100%
Percentage of completion—Direct labor	65%
Direct materials costs	$ 3,300
Direct labor costs	$ 600
Factory overhead costs applied (120% of direct labor)	$ 720
Activities during the current period (April)	
Units started this period	90,000 units
Units transferred out (completed)	100,000 units
Direct materials costs	$ 9,900
Direct labor costs	$ 5,700
Factory overhead costs applied (120% of direct labor)	$ 6,840
Ending goods in process inventory (April 30)	
Units of product	20,000 units
Percentage of completion—Direct materials	100%
Percentage of completion—Direct labor	25%

Step 1: Determine the Physical Flow of Units

A *physical flow reconciliation* is a report that reconciles (1) the physical units started in a period with (2) the physical units completed in that period. A physical flow reconciliation for GenX is shown in Exhibit 16.12 for April.

EXHIBIT 16.12

Physical Flow Reconciliation

Units to Account For		Units Accounted For	
Beginning goods in process inventory	30,000 units	Units completed and transferred out	100,000 units
Units started this period	90,000 units	Ending goods in process inventory	20,000 units
Total units to account for	**120,000 units**	Total units accounted for	**120,000 units**

reconciled

The weighted-average method does not require us to separately track the units in beginning work in process from those units started this period. Instead, the units are treated as part of a large pool with an average cost per unit.

Step 2: Compute Equivalent Units of Production

The second step is to compute *equivalent units of production* for direct materials, direct labor, and factory overhead for April. Overhead is applied using direct labor as the allocation base for GenX. This also implies that equivalent units are the same for both labor and overhead.

GenX used its direct materials, direct labor, and overhead to make finished units of Profen and to begin processing some units that are not yet complete. We must convert the physical units measure to equivalent units based on how each input has been used. Equivalent units are computed by multiplying the number of physical units by the percentage of completion for each input—see Exhibit 16.13.

EXHIBIT 16.13

Equivalent Units of Production—Weighted Average

Equivalent Units of Production	Direct Materials	Direct Labor	Factory Overhead
Equivalent units completed and transferred out (100,000 × 100%)	100,000 EUP	100,000 EUP	100,000 EUP
Equivalent units for ending goods in process			
Direct materials (20,000 × 100%)	20,000		
Direct labor (20,000 × 25%)		5,000	
Factory overhead (20,000 × 25%)			5,000
Equivalent units of production	120,000 EUP	105,000 EUP	105,000 EUP

The first row of Exhibit 16.13 reflects units transferred out in April. The production department entirely completed its work on the 100,000 units transferred out. These units have 100% of the materials, labor, and overhead required, or 100,000 equivalent units of each input (100,000 × 100%).

The second row references the ending goods in process, and rows three, four, and five break it down by materials, labor, and overhead. For direct materials, the units in ending goods in process inventory (20,000 physical units) include all materials required, so there are 20,000 equivalent units (20,000 × 100%) of materials in the unfinished physical units. Regarding labor, the units in ending goods in process inventory include 25% of the labor required, which implies 5,000 equivalent units of labor (20,000 × 25%). These units are only 25% complete and labor is used uniformly through the process. Overhead is applied on the basis of direct labor for GenX, so equivalent units for overhead are computed identically to labor (20,000 × 25%).

The final row reflects the whole units of product that could have been manufactured with the amount of inputs used to create some complete and some incomplete units. For GenX, the amount of inputs used to produce 100,000 complete units and to start 20,000 additional units is equivalent to the amount of direct materials in 120,000 whole units, the amount of direct labor in 105,000 whole units, and the amount of overhead in 105,000 whole units.

Step 3: Compute the Cost per Equivalent Unit

Equivalent units of production for each product (from step 2) is used to compute the average cost per equivalent unit. Under the **weighted-average method,** the computation of EUP does not separate the units in beginning inventory from those started this period; similarly, this method combines the costs of beginning goods in process inventory with the costs incurred in the current period. This process is illustrated in Exhibit 16.14.

EXHIBIT 16.14

Cost per Equivalent Unit of Production—Weighted Average

Cost per Equivalent Unit of Production	Direct Materials	Direct Labor	Factory Overhead
Costs of beginning goods in process inventory	$ 3,300	$ 600	$ 720
Costs incurred this period	9,900	5,700	6,840
Total costs	$13,200	$6,300	$7,560
÷ Equivalent units of production (from Step 2)	120,000 EUP	105,000 EUP	105,000 EUP
= Cost per equivalent unit of production	$0.11 per EUP*	$0.06 per EUP†	$0.072 per EUP‡

*$13,200 ÷ 120,000 EUP †$6,300 ÷ 105,000 EUP ‡$7,560 ÷ 105,000 EUP

Point: Managers can examine changes in monthly costs per equivalent unit to help control the production process. When prices are set in a competitive market, managers can use process cost summary information to determine which costs should be cut to achieve a profit.

For direct materials, the cost averages $0.11 per EUP, computed as the sum of direct materials cost from beginning goods in process inventory ($3,300) and the direct materials cost incurred in April ($9,900), and this sum ($13,200) is then divided by the 120,000 EUP for materials (from step 2). The costs per equivalent unit for labor and overhead are similarly computed. Specifically, direct labor cost averages $0.06 per EUP, computed as the sum of labor cost in beginning goods in process inventory ($600) and the labor costs incurred in April ($5,700), and this sum ($6,300) divided by 105,000 EUP for labor. Overhead costs averages $0.072 per EUP, computed as the sum of overhead cost in the beginning goods in process inventory ($720) and the overhead costs applied in April ($6,840), and this sum ($7,560) divided by 105,000 EUP for overhead.

Step 4: Assign and Reconcile Costs

The EUP from step 2 and the cost per EUP from step 3 are used in step 4 to assign costs to (a) units that production completed and transferred to finished goods and (b) units that remain in process. This is illustrated in Exhibit 16.15.

EXHIBIT 16.15

Report of Costs Accounted For—Weighted Average

Cost of units completed and transferred out		
Direct materials (100,000 EUP × $0.11 per EUP)	$11,000	
Direct labor (100,000 EUP × $0.06 per EUP)	6,000	
Factory overhead (100,000 EUP × $0.072 per EUP)	7,200	
Cost of units completed this period		$ 24,200
Cost of ending goods in process inventory		
Direct materials (20,000 EUP × $0.11 per EUP)	2,200	
Direct labor (5,000 EUP × $0.06 per EUP)	300	
Factory overhead (5,000 EUP × $0.072 per EUP)	360	
Cost of ending goods in process inventory		2,860
Total costs accounted for		**$27,060**

Cost of Units Completed and Transferred The 100,000 units completed and transferred to finished goods inventory required 100,000 EUP of direct materials. Thus, we assign $11,000 (100,000 EUP × $0.11 per EUP) of direct materials cost to those units. Similarly, those units had received 100,000 EUP of direct labor and 100,000 EUP of factory overhead (recall Exhibit 16.13). Thus, we assign $6,000 (100,000 EUP × $0.06 per EUP) of direct labor and $7,200 (100,000 EUP × $0.072 per EUP) of overhead to those units. The total cost of the 100,000 completed and transferred units is $24,200 ($11,000 + $6,000 + $7,200) and their average cost per unit is $0.242 ($24,200 ÷ 100,000 units).

Cost of Units for Ending Goods in Process There are 20,000 incomplete units in goods in process inventory at period-end. For direct materials, those units have 20,000 EUP of material (from step 2) at a cost of $0.11 per EUP (from step 3), which yields the materials cost of goods in process inventory of $2,200 (20,000 EUP × $0.11 per EUP). For direct labor, the in-process units have 25% of the required labor, or 5,000 EUP (from step 2). Using the $0.06 labor cost per EUP (from step 3) we obtain the labor cost of goods in process inventory of $300 (5,000 EUP × $0.06 per EUP). For overhead, the in-process units reflect 5,000 EUP (from step 2). Using the $0.072 overhead cost per EUP (from step 3) we obtain overhead costs with in-process inventory of $360 (5,000 EUP × $0.072 per EUP). Total cost of goods in process inventory at period-end is $2,860 ($2,200 + $300 + $360).

As a check, management verifies that total costs assigned to those units completed and transferred plus the costs of those in process (from Exhibit 16.15) equal the costs incurred by production. Exhibit 16.16 shows the costs incurred by production this period. We then reconcile the *costs accounted for* in Exhibit 16.15 with the *costs to account for* in Exhibit 16.16.

EXHIBIT 16.16

Report of Costs to Account For—Weighted Average

Cost of beginning goods in process inventory		
Direct materials	$3,300	
Direct labor	600	
Factory overhead	720	$ 4,620
Cost incurred this period		
Direct materials	9,900	
Direct labor	5,700	
Factory overhead	6,840	22,440
Total costs to account for		**$27,060**

At GenX, the production department manager is responsible for $27,060 in costs: $4,620 that is assigned to the goods in process at the start of the period plus $22,440 of materials, labor, and overhead incurred in the period. At period-end, that manager must show where these costs are assigned. The manager for GenX reports that $2,860 are assigned to units in process and $24,200 are assigned to units completed (per Exhibit 16.15). The sum of these amounts equals $27,060. Thus, the total *costs to account for* equal the total *costs accounted for* (minor differences can sometimes occur from rounding).

Process Cost Summary An important managerial accounting report for a process cost accounting system is the **process cost summary** (also called *production report*), which is prepared separately for each process or production department. Three reasons for the summary are to (1) help department managers control and monitor their departments, (2) help factory managers evaluate department managers' performances, and (3) provide cost information for financial statements. A process cost summary achieves these purposes by describing the costs charged to each department, reporting the equivalent units of production achieved by each department, and determining the costs assigned to each department's output. For our purposes, it is prepared using a combination of Exhibits 16.13, 16.14, 16.15, and 16.16.

Point: The key report in a job order costing system is a job cost sheet, which reports manufacturing costs per job. A process cost summary reports manufacturing costs per equivalent unit of a process or department.

The process cost summary for GenX is shown in Exhibit 16.17. The report is divided into three sections. Section ① lists the total costs charged to the department, including direct materials, direct labor, and overhead costs incurred, as well as the cost of the beginning goods in process inventory. Section ② describes the equivalent units of production for the department. Equivalent units for materials, labor, and overhead are in separate columns. It also reports direct

EXHIBIT 16.17

Process Cost Summary

GenX COMPANY
Process Cost Summary (Weighted-Average Method)
For Month Ended April 30, 2013

① **Costs Charged to Production**

Costs of beginning goods in process		
Direct materials	$3,300	
Direct labor	600	
Factory overhead	720	$ 4,620
Costs incurred this period		
Direct materials	9,900	
Direct labor	5,700	
Factory overhead	6,840	22,440
Total costs to account for		$27,060

② **Unit Cost Information**

Units to account for:		Units accounted for:	
Beginning goods in process	30,000	Completed and transferred out	100,000
Units started this period	90,000	Ending goods in process	20,000
Total units to account for	120,000	Total units accounted for	120,000

Equivalent Units of Production (EUP)	**Direct Materials**	**Direct Labor**	**Factory Overhead**
Units completed and transferred out	100,000 EUP	100,000 EUP	100,000 EUP
Units of ending goods in process			
Direct materials (20,000 × 100%)	20,000		
Direct labor (20,000 × 25%)		5,000	
Factory overhead (20,000 × 25%)			5,000
Equivalent units of production	120,000 EUP	105,000 EUP	105,000 EUP

Cost per EUP	**Direct Materials**	**Direct Labor**	**Factory Overhead**
Costs of beginning goods in process	$ 3,300	$ 600	$ 720
Costs incurred this period	9,900	5,700	6,840
Total costs	$13,200	$6,300	$7,560
÷EUP	120,000 EUP	105,000 EUP	105,000 EUP
Cost per EUP	$0.11 per EUP	$0.06 per EUP	$0.072 per EUP

③ **Cost Assignment and Reconciliation**

Costs transferred out (cost of goods manufactured)		
Direct materials (100,000 EUP × $0.11 per EUP)	$11,000	
Direct labor (100,000 EUP × $0.06 per EUP)	6,000	
Factory overhead (100,000 EUP × $0.072 per EUP)	7,200	$ 24,200
Costs of ending goods in process		
Direct materials (20,000 EUP × $0.11 per EUP)	2,200	
Direct labor (5,000 EUP × $0.06 per EUP)	300	
Factory overhead (5,000 EUP × $0.072 per EUP)	360	2,860
Total costs accounted for		$27,060

reconciled

materials, direct labor, and overhead costs per equivalent unit. Section ③ allocates total costs among units worked on in the period. The $24,200 is the total cost of goods transferred out of the department, and the $2,860 is the cost of partially processed ending inventory units. The assigned costs are then added to show that the total $27,060 cost charged to the department in section ① is now assigned to the units in section ③.

Quick Check Answers — p. 716

6. Equivalent units are (*a*) a measure of a production department's productivity in using direct materials, direct labor, or overhead; (*b*) units of a product produced by a foreign competitor that are similar to units produced by a domestic company; or (*c*) generic units of a product similar to brand name units of a product.
7. Interpret the meaning of a department's equivalent units with respect to direct labor.
8. A department began the period with 8,000 units that were one-fourth complete with respect to direct labor. It completed 58,000 units, and ended with 6,000 units that were one-third complete with respect to direct labor. What were its direct labor equivalent units for the period using the weighted-average method?
9. A process cost summary for a department has three sections. What information is presented in each of them?

Transfers to Finished Goods Inventory and Cost of Goods Sold

P4 Record the transfer of completed goods to Finished Goods Inventory and Cost of Goods Sold.

Arrow line ⑨ in Exhibit 16.4 reflects the transfer of completed products from production to finished goods inventory. The process cost summary shows that the 100,000 units of finished Profen are assigned a cost of $24,200. The entry to record this transfer follows.

⑨	Finished Goods Inventory	24,200	
	Goods in Process Inventory		24,200
	To record transfer of completed units.		

Assets = Liabilities + Equity
+24,200
−24,200

The credit to Goods in Process Inventory reduces that asset balance to reflect that 100,000 units are no longer in production. The cost of these units has been transferred to Finished Goods Inventory, which is recognized as a $24,200 increase in this asset. After this entry is posted, there remains a balance of $2,860 in the Goods in Process Inventory account, which is the amount computed in Step 4 previously. The cost of units transferred from Goods in Process Inventory to Finished Goods Inventory is called the **cost of goods manufactured.** Exhibit 16.18 reveals the activities in the Goods in Process Inventory account for this period. The ending balance of this account equals the cost assigned to the partially completed units in section ③ of Exhibit 16.17.

EXHIBIT 16.18

Goods in Process Inventory

Goods in Process Inventory					Acct. No. 134
Date		Explanation	Debit	Credit	Balance
Mar.	31	Balance			4,620
Apr.	30	Direct materials usage	9,900		14,520
	30	Direct labor costs incurred	5,700		20,220
	30	Factory overhead applied	6,840		27,060
	30	Transfer completed product to warehouse		24,200	2,860

Arrow line ⑩ in Exhibit 16.4 reflects the sale of finished goods. Assume that GenX sold 106,000 units of Profen this period, and that its beginning inventory of finished goods consisted of 26,000 units with a cost of $6,292. Also assume that its ending finished goods inventory consists of 20,000 units at a cost of $4,840. Using this information, we can compute its cost of goods sold for April as shown in Exhibit 16.19.

Point: We omit the journal entry for sales, but it totals the number of units sold times price per unit. The Accounts Receivable (or Cash) account is debited and the Sales Revenue account is credited.

EXHIBIT 16.19
Cost of Goods Sold

Beginning finished goods inventory	$ 6,292
+ Cost of goods manufactured this period	24,200
= Cost of goods available for sale	$30,492
− Ending finished goods inventory	4,840
= Cost of goods sold	$25,652

The summary entry to record cost of goods sold for this period follows:

Assets	= Liabilities +	Equity
−25,652		−25,652

(10)	Cost of Goods Sold	25,652	
	Finished Goods Inventory		25,652
	To record cost of goods sold for April.		

The Finished Goods Inventory account now appears as shown in Exhibit 16.20.

EXHIBIT 16.20
Finished Goods Inventory

Finished Goods Inventory Acct. No. 135

Date		Explanation	Debit	Credit	Balance
Mar.	31	Balance			6,292
Apr.	30	Transfer in cost of goods manufactured	24,200		30,492
	30	Cost of goods sold		25,652	4,840

Summary of Cost Flows Exhibit 16.21 shows GenX's manufacturing cost flows for April. Each of these cost flows and the entries to record them have been explained. The flow of costs through the accounts reflects the flow of production activities and products.

EXHIBIT 16.21*
Cost Flows through GenX

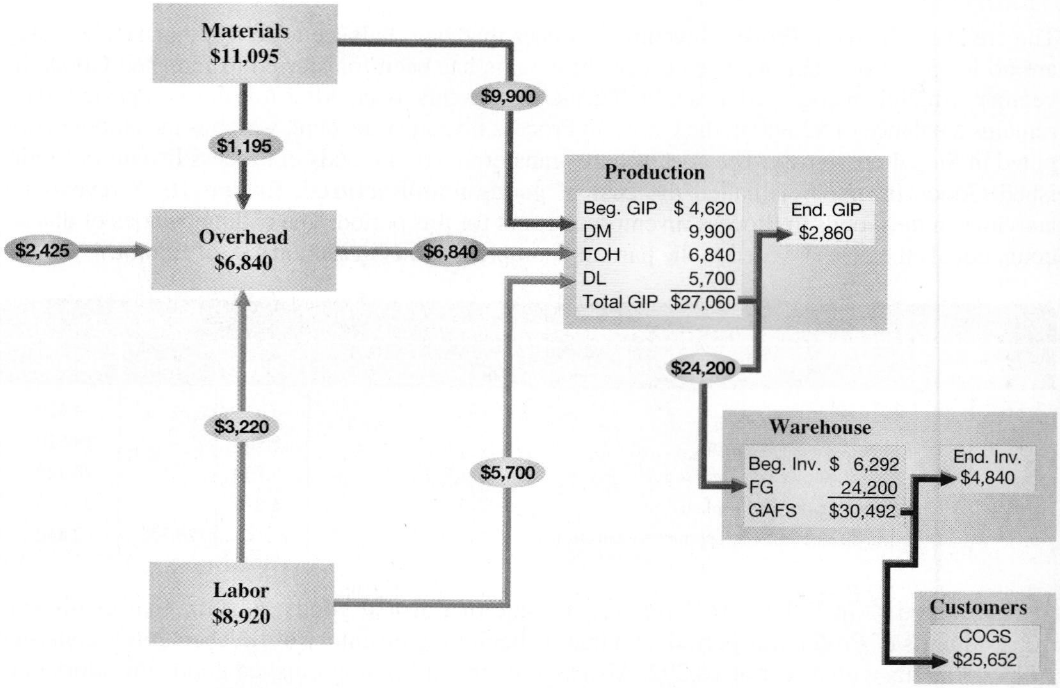

*Abbreviations: GIP (goods in process); DM (direct materials); DL (direct labor); FOH (factory overhead); FG (finished goods); GAFS (goods available for sale); COGS (cost of goods sold).

Trends in Process Operations

Some of the recent trends in process operations are discussed in the following paragraphs.

Process Design Management concerns with production efficiency can lead companies to entirely reorganize production processes. For example, instead of producing different types of computers in a series of departments, a separate work center for each computer can be established in one department. The process cost system is then changed to account for each work center's costs.

Just-in-Time Production Companies are increasingly adopting just-in-time techniques. With a just-in-time inventory system, inventory levels can be minimal. If raw materials are not ordered or received until needed, a Raw Materials Inventory account might be unnecessary. Instead, materials cost is immediately debited to the Goods in Process Inventory account. Similarly, a Finished Goods Inventory account may not be needed. Instead, cost of finished goods may be immediately debited to the Cost of Goods Sold account.

Automation Advances in technology increasingly enable companies to automate their production processes. This allows them to reduce direct labor costs. Reflecting this, some companies focus on **conversion costs per equivalent unit,** which is the combined costs of direct labor and factory overhead per equivalent unit.

Services Service-based businesses are increasingly prevalent. For routine, standardized services like oil changes and simple tax returns, computing costs based on the process is simpler and more useful than a cost per individual job.

Customer Orientation Focus on customer orientation also leads to improved processes. A manufacturer of control devices improved quality and reduced production time by forming teams to study processes and suggest improvements. An ice cream maker studied customer tastes to develop a more pleasing ice cream texture.

GLOBAL VIEW

As part of a series of global environmental goals, the international giant **Anheuser-Busch InBev** set targets to reduce its water usage. The company uses massive amounts of water in beer production and in its cleaning and cooling processes. To meet these goals, the company followed recent trends in process operations. These included extensive redesign of production processes and the use of advanced technology to increase efficiency at wastewater treatment plants. As a result water usage decreased by almost 37 percent in its global operations.

Hybrid Costing System — Decision Analysis

A2 Explain and illustrate a hybrid costing system.

This chapter explained the process costing system and contrasted it with the job order costing system. Many organizations use a *hybrid system* that contains features of both process and job order operations. A recent survey of manufacturers revealed that a majority use hybrid systems (also called *operation cost systems*).

To illustrate, consider a car manufacturer's assembly line. On one hand, the line resembles a process operation in that the assembly steps for each car are nearly identical. On the other hand, the specifications of most cars have several important differences. At the **Ford** Mustang plant, each car assembled on a given day can be different from the previous car and the next car. This means that the costs of materials (subassemblies or components) for each car can differ. Accordingly, while the conversion costs (direct labor and overhead) can be accounted for using a process costing system, the component costs (direct materials) are accounted for using a job order system (separately for each car or type of car).

A hybrid system of processes requires a *hybrid costing system* to properly cost products or services. In the Ford plant, the assembly costs per car are readily determined using process costing. The costs of additional components can then be added to the assembly costs to determine each car's total cost (as in job order costing). To illustrate, consider the following information for a daily assembly process at Ford.

Assembly process costs	
Direct materials	$10,600,000
Direct labor	$5,800,000
Factory overhead	$6,200,000
Number of cars assembled	1,000
Costs of three different types of steering wheels	$240, $330, $480
Costs of three different types of seats	$620, $840, $1,360

The assembly process costs $22,600 per car. Depending on the type of steering wheel and seats the customer requests, the cost of a car can range from $23,460 to $24,440 (a $980 difference).

Today companies are increasingly trying to standardize processes while attempting to meet individual customer needs. To the extent that differences among individual customers' requests are large, understanding the costs to satisfy those requests is important. Thus, monitoring and controlling both process and job order costs are important.

Decision Ethics

Entrepreneur You operate a process production company making similar products for three different customers. One customer demands 100% quality inspection of products at your location before shipping. The added costs of that inspection are spread across all customers, not just the one demanding it. If you charge the added costs to that customer, you could lose that customer and experience a loss. Moreover, your other two customers have agreed to pay 110% of full costs. What actions (if any) do you take? ■ [Answer—p. 716]

DEMONSTRATION PROBLEM

Pennsylvania Company produces a product that passes through a single production process. Then completed products are transferred to finished goods in its warehouse. Information related to its manufacturing activities for July follows.

Raw Materials	
Beginning inventory	$100,000
Raw materials purchased on credit	211,400
Direct materials used	(190,000)
Indirect materials used	(51,400)
Ending inventory	$ 70,000
Factory Payroll	
Direct labor incurred	$ 55,500
Indirect labor incurred	50,625
Total payroll (paid in cash)	$106,125
Factory Overhead	
Indirect materials used	$ 51,400
Indirect labor used	50,625
Other overhead costs	71,725
Total factory overhead incurred	$173,750
Factory Overhead Applied	
Overhead applied (200% of direct labor)	$111,000

Production Department	
Beginning goods in process inventory (units)	5,000
Percentage completed—Materials	100%
Percentage completed—Labor and overhead	60%
Beginning goods in process inventory (costs)	
Direct materials used	$ 20,000
Direct labor incurred	9,600
Overhead applied (200% of direct labor)	19,200
Total costs of beginning goods in process	$ 48,800
Units started this period	20,000
Units completed this period	17,000
Ending goods in process inventory (units)	8,000
Percentage completed—Materials	100%
Percentage completed—Labor and overhead	20%
Finished Goods Inventory	
Beginning finished goods inventory	$ 96,400
Cost transferred in from production	321,300
Cost of goods sold	(345,050)
Ending finished goods inventory	$ 72,650

Required

1. Prepare a physical flow reconciliation for July as illustrated in Exhibit 16.12.
2. Compute the equivalent units of production in July for direct materials, direct labor, and factory overhead.
3. Compute the costs per equivalent units of production in July for direct materials, direct labor, and factory overhead.
4. Prepare a report of costs accounted for and a report of costs to account for.
5. Prepare summary journal entries to record the transactions and events of July for (a) raw materials purchases, (b) direct materials usage, (c) indirect materials usage, (d) factory payroll costs, (e) direct labor usage, (f) indirect labor usage, (g) other overhead costs (credit Other Accounts), (h) application of overhead to production, (i) transfer of finished goods from production, and (j) the cost of goods sold.

PLANNING THE SOLUTION

- Track the physical flow to determine the number of units completed in July.
- Compute the equivalent unit of production for direct materials, direct labor, and factory overhead.
- Compute the costs per equivalent unit of production with respect to direct materials, direct labor, and overhead; and determine the cost per unit for each.
- Compute the total cost of the goods transferred to production by using the equivalent units and unit costs. Determine (a) the cost of the beginning in-process inventory, (b) the materials, labor, and overhead costs added to the beginning in-process inventory, and (c) the materials, labor, and overhead costs added to the units started and completed in the month.
- Determine the cost of goods sold using balances in finished goods and cost of units completed this period.
- Use the information to record the summary journal entries for July.

SOLUTION TO DEMONSTRATION PROBLEM

1. Physical flow reconciliation.

Units to Account For		Units Accounted For	
Beginning goods in process inventory	5,000 units	Units completed and transferred out	17,000 units
Units started this period	20,000 units	Ending goods in process inventory......	8,000 units
Total units to account for	**25,000 units**	Total units accounted for	**25,000 units**

reconciled

2. Equivalent units of production.

Equivalent Units of Production	Direct Materials	Direct Labor	Factory Overhead
Equivalent units completed and transferred out	17,000 EUP	17,000 EUP	17,000 EUP
Equivalent units in ending goods in process			
Direct materials (8,000 × 100%)	8,000		
Direct labor (8,000 × 20%)		1,600	
Factory overhead (8,000 × 20%)			1,600
Equivalent units of production	25,000 EUP	18,600 EUP	18,600 EUP

3. Costs per equivalent unit of production.

Costs per Equivalent Unit of Production	Direct Materials	Direct Labor	Factory Overhead
Costs of beginning goods in process	$ 20,000	$ 9,600	$ 19,200
Costs incurred this period	190,000	55,500	111,000*
Total costs	$210,000	$65,100	$130,200
÷ Equivalent units of production (from part 2) ..	25,000 EUP	18,600 EUP	18,600 EUP
= Costs per equivalent unit of production	$8.40 per EUP	$3.50 per EUP	$7.00 per EUP

*Factory overhead applied

4. Reports of costs accounted for and of costs to account for

Report of Costs Accounted For

Cost of units transferred out (cost of goods manufactured)		
Direct materials ($8.40 per EUP × 17,000 EUP)	$142,800	
Direct labor ($3.50 per EUP × 17,000 EUP)	59,500	
Factory overhead ($7.00 per EUP × 17,000 EUP)	119,000	
Cost of units completed this period		$ 321,300
Cost of ending goods in process inventory		
Direct materials ($8.40 per EUP × 8,000 EUP)	67,200	
Direct labor ($3.50 per EUP × 1,600 EUP)	5,600	
Factory overhead ($7.00 per EUP × 1,600 EUP)	11,200	
Cost of ending goods in process inventory		84,000
Total costs accounted for		**$405,300**

Report of Costs to Account For

Cost of beginning goods in process inventory		
Direct materials	$ 20,000	
Direct labor	9,600	
Factory overhead	19,200	$ 48,800
Cost incurred this period		
Direct materials	190,000	
Direct labor	55,500	
Factory overhead	111,000	356,500
Total costs to account for		**$405,300**

reconciled

5. Summary journal entries for the transactions and events in July.

a.	Raw Materials Inventory	211,400	
	Accounts Payable		211,400
	To record raw materials purchases.		
b.	Goods in Process Inventory	190,000	
	Raw Materials Inventory		190,000
	To record direct materials usage.		
c.	Factory Overhead	51,400	
	Raw Materials Inventory		51,400
	To record indirect materials usage.		
d.	Factory Payroll	106,125	
	Cash		106,125
	To record factory payroll costs.		
e.	Goods in Process Inventory	55,500	
	Factory Payroll		55,500
	To record direct labor usage.		
f.	Factory Overhead	50,625	
	Factory Payroll		50,625
	To record indirect labor usage.		
g.	Factory Overhead	71,725	
	Other Accounts		71,725
	To record other overhead costs.		
h.	Goods in Process Inventory	111,000	
	Factory Overhead		111,000
	To record application of overhead.		
i.	Finished Goods Inventory	321,300	
	Goods in Process Inventory		321,300
	To record transfer of finished goods from production.		
j.	Cost of Goods Sold	345,050	
	Finished Goods Inventory		345,050
	To record cost of goods sold.		

APPENDIX

FIFO Method of Process Costing

16A

C4 *Appendix 16A*—Describe accounting for production activity and preparation of a process cost summary using FIFO.

The **FIFO method** of process costing assigns costs to units assuming a first-in, first-out flow of product. The objectives, concepts, and journal entries (not amounts) are the same as for the weighted-average method, but computation of equivalent units of production and cost assignment are slightly different.

Exhibit 16A.11 shows selected information from GenX's production department for the month of April. Accounting for a department's activity for a period includes four steps: (1) determine physical flow, (2) compute equivalent units, (3) compute cost per equivalent unit, and (4) determine cost assignment and reconciliation. This appendix describes each of these steps using the FIFO method for process costing.

EXHIBIT 16A.11

Production Data

Beginning goods in process inventory (March 31)	
Units of product	30,000 units
Percentage of completion—Direct materials	100%
Percentage of completion—Direct labor	65%
Direct materials costs	$ 3,300
Direct labor costs	$ 600
Factory overhead costs applied (120% of direct labor)	$ 720
Activities during the current period (April)	
Units started this period	90,000 units
Units transferred out (completed)	100,000 units
Direct materials costs	$ 9,900
Direct labor costs	$ 5,700
Factory overhead costs applied (120% of direct labor)	$ 6,840
Ending goods in process inventory (April 30)	
Units of product	20,000 units
Percentage of completion—Direct materials	100%
Percentage of completion—Direct labor	25%

Step 1: Determine Physical Flow of Units A *physical flow reconciliation* is a report that reconciles (1) the physical units started in a period with (2) the physical units completed in that period. The physical flow reconciliation for GenX is shown in Exhibit 16A.12 for April.

EXHIBIT 16A.12

Physical Flow Reconciliation

Units to Account For		Units Accounted For	
Beginning goods in process inventory	30,000 units	Units completed and transferred out	100,000 units
Units started this period	90,000 units	Ending goods in process inventory	20,000 units
Total units to account for	**120,000 units**	Total units accounted for	**120,000 units**

reconciled

FIFO assumes that the 100,000 units transferred to finished goods during April include the 30,000 units from the beginning goods in process inventory. The remaining 70,000 units transferred out are from units started in April. Of the total 90,000 units started in April, 70,000 were completed, leaving 20,000 units unfinished at period-end.

Step 2: Compute Equivalent Units of Production—FIFO GenX used its direct materials, direct labor, and overhead both to make complete units of Profen and to start some units that are not yet complete. We need to convert the physical measure of units to equivalent units based on how much of each input has been used. We do this by multiplying the number of physical units by the percentage of processing applied to those units in the current period; this is done for each input (materials, labor, and overhead). The FIFO method accounts for cost flow in a sequential manner—earliest costs are the first to flow out. (This is different from the weighted-average method, which combines prior period costs—those in beginning Goods in Process Inventory—with costs incurred in the current period.)

Three distinct groups of units must be considered in determining the equivalent units of production under the FIFO method: (a) units in beginning Goods in Process Inventory that were completed this period, (b) units started *and* completed this period, and (c) units in ending Goods in Process Inventory. We must determine how much material, labor, and overhead are used for each of these unit groups. These computations are shown in Exhibit 16A.13. The remainder of this section explains these computations.

EXHIBIT 16A.13

Equivalent Units of Production—FIFO

Equivalent Units of Production	Direct Materials	Direct Labor	Factory Overhead
(a) Equivalent units to complete beginning goods in process			
Direct materials (30,000 × 0%)	0 EUP		
Direct labor (30,000 × 35%)		10,500 EUP	
Factory overhead (30,000 × 35%)			10,500 EUP
(b) Equivalent units started and completed*	70,000	70,000	70,000
(c) Equivalent units in ending goods in process			
Direct materials (20,000 × 100%)	20,000		
Direct labor (20,000 × 25%)		5,000	
Factory overhead (20,000 × 25%)			5,000
Equivalent units of production	90,000 EUP	85,500 EUP	85,500 EUP

*Units completed this period	100,000 units
Less units in beginning goods in process	30,000
Units started and completed this period	70,000 units

(a) Beginning Goods in Process Under FIFO, we assume that production first completes any units started in the prior period. There were 30,000 physical units in beginning goods in process inventory. Those units were 100% complete with respect to direct materials as of the end of the prior period. This means that no materials (0%) are needed in April to complete those 30,000 units. So the equivalent units of *materials* to complete beginning goods in process are zero (30,000 × 0%)—see first row under row "(a)" in Exhibit 16A.13. The units in process as of April 1 had already been through 65% of production prior to this period and need only go through the remaining 35% of production. The equivalent units of *labor* to complete the beginning goods in process are 10,500 (30,000 × 35%)—see the second row under row "(a)." This implies that the amount of labor required this period to complete the 30,000 units started in the prior period is the amount of labor needed to make 10,500 units, start-to-finish. Finally, overhead is applied based on direct labor costs, so GenX computes equivalent units for overhead as it would for direct labor.

(b) Units Started and Completed This Period After completing any beginning goods in process, FIFO assumes that production begins on newly started units. GenX began work on 90,000 new units this period. Of those units, 20,000 remain incomplete at period-end. This means that 70,000 of the units started in April were completed in April. These complete units have received 100% of materials, labor, and overhead. Exhibit 16A.13 reflects this by including 70,000 equivalent units (70,000 × 100%) of materials, labor, and overhead in its equivalent units of production—see row "(b)."

(c) Ending Goods in Process The 20,000 units started in April that GenX was not able to complete by period-end consumed materials, labor, and overhead. Specifically, those 20,000 units received 100% of materials and, therefore, the equivalent units of materials in ending goods in process inventory are 20,000 (20,000 × 100%)—see the first row under row "(c)." For labor and overhead, the units in ending goods in process were 25% complete in production. This means the equivalent units of labor and overhead for those units are 5,000 (20,000 × 25%) as GenX incurs labor and overhead costs uniformly throughout its production process. Finally, for each input (direct materials, direct labor, and factory overhead), the equivalent units for each of the unit groups (a), (b), and (c) are added to determine the total equivalent units of production with respect to each—see the final row in Exhibit 16A.13.

Step 3: Compute Cost per Equivalent Unit—FIFO To compute cost per equivalent unit, we take the product costs (for each of direct materials, direct labor, and factory overhead from Exhibit 16A.11) added in April and divide by the equivalent units of production from step 2. Exhibit 16A.14 illustrates these computations.

EXHIBIT 16A.14

Cost per Equivalent Unit of Production—FIFO

Cost per Equivalent Unit of Production	Direct Materials	Direct Labor	Factory Overhead
Costs incurred this period	$9,900	$5,700	$6,840
÷ Equivalent units of production (from Step 2)	90,000 EUP	85,500 EUP	85,500 EUP
Cost per equivalent unit of production	$0.11 per EUP	$0.067 per EUP	$0.08 per EUP

It is essential to compute costs per equivalent unit for *each* input because production inputs are added at different times in the process. The FIFO method computes the cost per equivalent unit based solely on this period's EUP and costs (unlike the weighted-average method, which adds in the costs of the beginning goods in process inventory).

Step 4: Assign and Reconcile Costs The equivalent units determined in step 2 and the cost per equivalent unit computed in step 3 are both used to assign costs (1) to units that the production department completed and transferred to finished goods and (2) to units that remain in process at period-end.

In Exhibit 16A.15, under the section for cost of units transferred out, we see that the cost of units completed in April includes the $4,620 cost carried over from March for work already applied to the 30,000 units that make up beginning Goods in Process Inventory, plus the $1,544 incurred in April to complete those units. This section also includes the $17,990 of cost assigned to the 70,000 units started and completed this period. Thus, the total cost of goods manufactured in April is $24,154 ($4,620 + $1,544 + $17,990). The average cost per unit for goods completed in April is $0.242 ($24,154 ÷ 100,000 completed units).

EXHIBIT 16A.15

Report of Costs Accounted For—FIFO

Cost of units transferred out (cost of goods manufactured)		
Cost of beginning goods in process inventory		$ 4,620
Cost to complete beginning goods in process		
Direct materials ($0.11 per EUP × 0 EUP)	$ 0	
Direct labor ($0.067 per EUP × 10,500 EUP)	704	
Factory overhead ($0.08 per EUP × 10,500 EUP)	840	1,544
Cost of units started and completed this period		
Direct materials ($0.11 per EUP × 70,000 EUP)	7,700	
Direct labor ($0.067 per EUP × 70,000 EUP)	4,690	
Factory overhead ($0.08 per EUP × 70,000 EUP)	5,600	17,990
Total cost of units finished this period		24,154
Cost of ending goods in process inventory		
Direct materials ($0.11 per EUP × 20,000 EUP)	2,200	
Direct labor ($0.067 per EUP × 5,000 EUP)	335	
Factory overhead ($0.08 per EUP × 5,000 EUP)	400	
Total cost of ending goods in process inventory		2,935
Total costs accounted for		**$27,089**

The computation for cost of ending goods in process inventory is in the lower part of Exhibit 16A.15. The cost of units in process includes materials, labor, and overhead costs corresponding to the percentage of these resources applied to those incomplete units in April. That cost of $2,935 ($2,200 + $335 + $400) also is the ending balance for the Goods in Process Inventory account.

Management verifies that the total costs assigned to units transferred out and units still in process equal the total costs incurred by production. We reconcile the costs accounted for (in Exhibit 16A.15) to the costs that production was charged for as shown in Exhibit 16A.16.

EXHIBIT 16A.16

Report of Costs to Account For—FIFO

Cost of beginning goods in process inventory		
Direct materials	$3,300	
Direct labor	600	
Factory overhead	720	$ 4,620
Costs incurred this period		
Direct materials	9,900	
Direct labor	5,700	
Factory overhead	6,840	22,440
Total costs to account for		**$27,060**

The production manager is responsible for $27,060 in costs: $4,620 that had been assigned to the department's Goods in Process Inventory as of April 1 plus $22,440 of materials, labor, and overhead costs the department incurred in April. At period-end, the manager must identify where those costs were assigned. The production manager can report that $24,154 of cost was assigned to units completed in April and $2,935 was assigned to units still in process at period-end. The sum of these amounts is $29 different from the $27,060 total costs incurred by production due to rounding in step 3—rounding errors are common and not a concern.

The final report is the process cost summary, which summarizes key information from Exhibits 16A.13, 16A.14, 16A.15, and 16A.16. Reasons for the summary are to (1) help managers control and monitor costs, (2) help upper management assess department manager performance, and (3) provide cost information for financial reporting. The process cost summary, using FIFO, for GenX is in Exhibit 16A.17. Section ① lists

EXHIBIT 16A.17

Process Cost Summary

GenX COMPANY
Process Cost Summary (FIFO Method)
For Month Ended April 30, 2013

① **Costs charged to production**

Costs of beginning goods in process inventory		
Direct materials	$3,300	
Direct labor	600	
Factory overhead	720	$ 4,620
Costs incurred this period		
Direct materials	9,900	
Direct labor	5,700	
Factory overhead	6,840	22,440
Total costs to account for		$27,060

② **Unit cost information**

Units to account for		Units accounted for	
Beginning goods in process	30,000	Transferred out	100,000
Units started this period	90,000	Ending goods in process	20,000
Total units to account for	120,000	Total units accounted for	120,000

Equivalent units of production	**Direct Materials**	**Direct Labor**	**Factory Overhead**
Equivalent units to complete beginning goods in process			
Direct materials (30,000 × 0%)	0 EUP		
Direct labor (30,000 × 35%)		10,500 EUP	
Factory overhead (30,000 × 35%)			10,500 EUP
Equivalent units started and completed	70,000	70,000	70,000
Equivalent units in ending goods in process			
Direct materials (20,000 × 100%)	20,000		
Direct labor (20,000 × 25%)		5,000	
Factory overhead (20,000 × 25%)			5000
Equivalent units of production	90,000 EUP	85,500 EUP	85,500 EUP

Cost per equivalent unit of production	**Direct Materials**	**Direct Labor**	**Factory Overhead**
Costs incurred this period	$9,900	$5,700	$6,840
÷ Equivalent units of production	90,000 EUP	85,500 EUP	85,500 EUP
Cost per equivalent unit of production	$0.11 per EUP	$0.067 per EUP	$0.08 per EUP

③ **Cost assignment and reconciliation**
(cost of units completed and transferred out)

Cost of beginning goods in process		$ 4,620
Cost to complete beginning goods in process		
Direct materials ($0.11 per EUP × 0 EUP)	$ 0	
Direct labor ($0.067 per EUP × 10,500 EUP)	704	
Factory overhead ($0.08 per EUP × 10,500 EUP)	840	1,544
Cost of units started and completed this period		
Direct materials ($0.11 per EUP × 70,000 EUP)	7,700	
Direct labor ($0.067 per EUP × 70,000 EUP)	4,690	
Factory overhead ($0.08 per EUP × 70,000 EUP)	5,600	17,990
Total cost of units finished this period		24,154
Cost of ending goods in process		
Direct materials ($0.11 per EUP × 20,000 EUP)	2,200	
Direct labor ($0.067 per EUP × 5,000 EUP)	335	
Factory overhead ($0.08 per EUP × 5,000 EUP)	400	
Total cost of ending goods in process		2,935
Total costs accounted for		$27,089*

reconciled

*$29 difference due to rounding

the total costs charged to the department, including direct materials, direct labor, and overhead costs incurred, as well as the cost of the beginning goods in process inventory. Section ⟨2⟩ describes the equivalent units of production for the department. Equivalent units for materials, labor, and overhead are in separate columns. It also reports direct materials, direct labor, and overhead costs per equivalent unit. Section ⟨3⟩ allocates total costs among units worked on in the period.

Decision Maker

Cost Manager As cost manager for an electronics manufacturer, you apply a process costing system using FIFO. Your company plans to adopt a just-in-time system and eliminate inventories. What is the impact of the use of FIFO (versus the weighted-average method) given these plans? ■ [Answer—p. 716]

Summary

C1 Explain process operations and the way they differ from job order operations. Process operations produce large quantities of similar products or services by passing them through a series of processes, or steps, in production. Like job order operations, they combine direct materials, direct labor, and overhead in the operations. Unlike job order operations that assign the responsibility for each job to a manager, process operations assign the responsibility for each *process* to a manager.

C2 Define and compute equivalent units and explain their use in process cost accounting. Equivalent units of production measure the activity of a process as the number of units that would be completed in a period if all effort had been applied to units that were started and finished. This measure of production activity is used to compute the cost per equivalent unit and to assign costs to finished goods and goods in process inventory. To compute equivalent units, determine the number of units that would have been finished if all materials (or labor or overhead) had been used to produce units that were started and completed during the period. The costs incurred by a process are divided by its equivalent units to yield cost per unit.

C3 Describe accounting for production activity and preparation of a process cost summary using weighted average. A process cost summary reports on the activities of a production process or department for a period. It describes the costs charged to the department, the equivalent units of production for the department, and the costs assigned to the output. The report aims to (1) help managers control their departments, (2) help factory managers evaluate department managers' performances, and (3) provide cost information for financial statements. A process cost summary includes the physical flow of units, equivalent units of production, costs per equivalent unit, and a cost reconciliation. It reports the units and costs to account for during the period and how they were accounted for during the period. In terms of units, the summary includes the beginning goods in process inventory and the units started during the month. These units are accounted for in terms of the goods completed and transferred out, and the ending goods in process inventory. With respect to costs, the summary includes materials, labor, and overhead costs assigned to the process during the period. It shows how these costs are assigned to goods completed and transferred out, and to ending goods in process inventory.

C4 *Appendix 16A*—Describe accounting for production activity and preparation of a process cost summary using FIFO. The FIFO method for process costing is applied and illustrated to (1) report the physical flow of units, (2) compute the equivalent units of production, (3) compute the cost per equivalent unit of production, and (4) assign and reconcile costs.

A1 Compare process cost accounting and job order cost accounting. Process and job order manufacturing operations are similar in that both combine materials, labor, and factory overhead to produce products or services. They differ in the way they are organized and managed. In job order operations, the job order cost accounting system assigns materials, labor, and overhead to specific jobs. In process operations, the process cost accounting system assigns materials, labor, and overhead to specific processes. The total costs associated with each process are then divided by the number of units passing through that process to get cost per equivalent unit. The costs per equivalent unit for all processes are added to determine the total cost per unit of a product or service.

A2 Explain and illustrate a hybrid costing system. A hybrid costing system contains features of both job order and process costing systems. Generally, certain direct materials are accounted for by individual products as in job order costing, but direct labor and overhead costs are accounted for similar to process costing.

P1 Record the flow of direct materials costs in process cost accounting. Materials purchased are debited to a Raw Materials Inventory account. As direct materials are issued to processes, they are separately accumulated in a Goods in Process Inventory account for that process.

P2 Record the flow of direct labor costs in process cost accounting. Direct labor costs are initially debited to the Factory Payroll account. The total amount in it is then assigned to the Goods in Process Inventory account pertaining to each process.

P3 Record the flow of factory overhead costs in process cost accounting. The different factory overhead items are first accumulated in the Factory Overhead account and are then allocated, using a predetermined overhead rate, to the different processes. The allocated amount is debited to the Goods in Process Inventory account pertaining to each process.

P4 Record the transfer of completed goods to Finished Goods Inventory and Cost of Goods Sold. As units complete the final process and are eventually sold, their accumulated cost is transferred to Finished Goods Inventory and finally to Cost of Goods Sold.

Guidance Answers to Decision Maker and Decision Ethics

Budget Officer By instructing you to classify a majority of costs as indirect, the manager is passing some of his department's costs to a common overhead pool that other departments will partially absorb. Since overhead costs are allocated on the basis of direct labor for this company and the new department has a relatively low direct labor cost, the new department will be assigned less overhead. Such action suggests unethical behavior by this manager. You must object to such reclassification. If this manager refuses to comply, you must inform someone in a more senior position.

Entrepreneur By spreading the added quality-related costs across three customers, the entrepreneur is probably trying to remain competitive with respect to the customer that demands the 100% quality inspection. Moreover, the entrepreneur is partly covering the added costs by recovering two-thirds of them from the other two customers who are paying 110% of total costs. This act likely breaches the trust placed by the two customers in this entrepreneur's application of its costing system. The costing system should be changed, and the entrepreneur should consider renegotiating the pricing and/or quality test agreement with this one customer (at the risk of losing this currently loss-producing customer).

Cost Manager Differences between the FIFO and weighted-average methods are greatest when large work in process inventories exist and when costs fluctuate. The method used if inventories are eliminated does not matter; both produce identical costs.

Guidance Answers to Quick Checks

1. *c*
2. When a company produces large quantities of similar products/services, a process cost system is often more suitable.
3. *b*
4. The costs are direct materials, direct labor, and overhead.
5. A goods in process inventory account is needed for *each* production department.
6. *a*
7. Equivalent units with respect to direct labor are the number of units that would have been produced if all labor had been used on units that were started and finished during the period.
8.

Units completed and transferred out	58,000 EUP
Units of ending goods in process	
Direct labor (6,000 × 1/3)	2,000 EUP
Units of production	60,000 EUP

9. The first section shows the costs charged to the department. The second section describes the equivalent units produced by the department. The third section shows the assignment of total costs to units worked on during the period.

Key Terms

Conversion costs per equivalent unit (p. 707)
Cost of goods manufactured (p. 705)
Equivalent units of production (EUP) (p. 699)
FIFO method (p. 711)
Job order cost accounting system (p. 695)
Materials consumption report (p. 696)
Process cost accounting system (p. 695)
Process cost summary (p. 704)
Process operations (p. 692)
Weighted-average method (p. 702)

Multiple Choice Quiz

Answers on p. 735 mhhe.com/wildFINMAN5e

Additional Quiz Questions are available at the book's Website.

1. Equivalent units of production are equal to
   a. Physical units that were completed this period from all effort being applied to them.
   b. The number of units introduced into the process this period.
   c. The number of finished units actually completed this period.
   d. The number of units that could have been started and completed given the cost incurred.
   e. The number of units in the process at the end of the period.
2. Recording the cost of raw materials purchased for use in a process costing system includes a
   a. Credit to Raw Materials Inventory.
   b. Debit to Goods in Process Inventory.
   c. Debit to Factory Overhead.
   d. Credit to Factory Overhead.
   e. Debit to Raw Materials Inventory.
3. The production department started the month with a beginning goods in process inventory of $20,000. During the month, it was assigned the following costs: direct materials, $152,000; direct labor, $45,000; overhead applied at the rate of 40% of direct labor cost. Inventory with a cost of $218,000 was transferred to finished goods. The ending balance of goods in process inventory is
   a. $330,000.
   b. $ 17,000.
   c. $220,000.
   d. $112,000.
   e. $118,000.

4. A company's beginning work in process inventory consists of 10,000 units that are 20% complete with respect to direct labor costs. A total of 40,000 units are completed this period. There are 15,000 units in goods in process, one-third complete for direct labor, at period-end. The equivalent units of production (EUP) with respect to direct labor at period-end, assuming the weighted-average method, are
- **a.** 45,000 EUP.
- **b.** 40,000 EUP.
- **c.** 5,000 EUP.
- **d.** 37,000 EUP.
- **e.** 43,000 EUP.

5. Assume the same information as in question 4. Also assume that beginning work in process had $6,000 in direct labor cost and that $84,000 in direct labor is added during this period. What is the cost per EUP for labor?
- **a.** $0.50 per EUP
- **b.** $1.87 per EUP
- **c.** $2.00 per EUP
- **d.** $2.10 per EUP
- **e.** $2.25 per EUP

A Superscript letter A denotes assignments based on Appendix 16A

Icon denotes assignments that involve decision making.

Discussion Questions

1. What is the main factor for a company in choosing between the job order costing and process costing accounting systems? Give two likely applications of each system.
2. The focus in a job order costing system is the job or batch. Identify the main focus in process costing.
3. Can services be delivered by means of process operations? Support your answer with an example.
4. Are the journal entries that match cost flows to product flows in process costing primarily the same or much different than those in job order costing? Explain.
5. Identify the control document for materials flow when a materials requisition slip is not used.
6. Explain in simple terms the notion of equivalent units of production (EUP). Why is it necessary to use EUP in process costing?
7. What are the two main inventory methods used in process costing? What are the differences between these methods?
8. Why is it possible for direct labor in process operations to include the labor of employees who do not work directly on products or services?
9. Assume that a company produces a single product by processing it first through a single production department. Direct labor costs flow through what accounts in this company's process cost system?
10. After all labor costs for a period are allocated, what balance should remain in the Factory Payroll account?
11. Is it possible to have under- or overapplied overhead costs in a process cost accounting system? Explain.
12. Explain why equivalent units of production for both direct labor and overhead can be the same as, and why they can be different from, equivalent units for direct materials.
13. Companies such as Piaggio apply process operations. List the four steps in accounting for production activity in a reporting period (for process operations).
14. Companies such as KTM commonly prepare a process cost summary. What purposes does a process cost summary serve?
15. Are there situations where Polaris can use process costing? Identify at least one and explain it.
16. Arctic Cat produces snowmobiles with a multiple process production line. Identify and list some of its production processing steps and departments.

PIAGGIO

KTM

Polaris

Arctic Cat

connect

QUICK STUDY

QS 16-1
Process vs. job order operations
C1

For each of the following products and services, indicate whether it is most likely produced in a process operation or in a job order operation.

1. Tennis courts
2. Apple juice
3. Vanilla ice cream
4. Luxury cars

QS 16-2
Recording costs of direct materials P1

Blanche's Boxes makes cardboard shipping cartons in a single operation. This period, Blanche purchased $62,000 in raw materials. Its production department requisitioned $50,000 of those materials for use in producing cartons. Prepare journal entries to record its (1) purchase of raw materials and (2) requisition of direct materials.

QS 16-3
Recording costs of direct labor
P2

Refer to the information in QS 16-2. Blanche's Boxes incurred $135,000 in factory payroll costs, of which $125,000 was direct labor. Prepare journal entries to record its (1) total factory payroll incurred and (2) direct labor used in production.

QS 16-4
Recording costs of factory overhead
P3

Refer to the information in QS 16-2 and QS 16-3. Blanche's Boxes requisitioned $9,000 of indirect materials from its raw materials and used $10,000 of indirect labor in its production of boxes. Also, it incurred $156,000 of other factory overhead costs. It applies factory overhead at the rate of 140% of direct labor costs. Prepare journal entries to record its (1) indirect materials requisitioned, (2) indirect labor used in production, (3) other factory overhead costs incurred, and (4) application of overhead to production.

QS 16-5
Recording transfer of costs to finished goods P4

Refer to the information in QS 16-2, QS 16-3, and QS 16-4. Blanche's Boxes completed 20,000 boxes costing $275,000 and transferred them to finished goods. Prepare its journal entry to record the transfer of the boxes from production to finished goods inventory.

QS 16-6
Weighted average: Computing equivalent units of production
C2

The following refers to units processed in Sunflower Printing's binding department in March. Compute the total equivalent units of production with respect to labor for March using the weighted-average inventory method.

	Units of Product	Percent of Labor Added
Beginning goods in process	150,000	80%
Goods started	310,000	100
Goods completed	340,000	100
Ending goods in process	120,000	25

QS 16-7
Computing EUP cost C2

The cost of beginning inventory plus the costs added during the period should equal the cost of units ____________________ plus the cost of ____________________.

QS 16-8
Hybrid costing A2

Explain how a car maintenance and repair garage might use a hybrid costing system.

QS 16-9^A
FIFO: Computing equivalent units C4

Refer to QS 16-6 and compute the total equivalent units of production with respect to labor for March using the FIFO inventory method.

QS 16-10
Steps in process costing
C3

Put the four steps in accounting for production activities in the order in which they would occur.

a. Determine physical flow of units
b. Compute the cost per equivalent unit
c. Compute equivalent units of production
d. Assign and reconcile costs

QS 16-11
Process cost summary C3

List the headings of the three major sections of a process cost summary. Refer to Exhibit 16.17.

QS 16-12
Process cost summary C3

Anheuser-Busch InBev is attempting to reduce its water usage. How could a company manager use a process cost summary to determine if the program to reduce water usage is successful?

QS 16-13
Process vs. job order costing
A1

Label each statement below as either true ("T") or false ("F").

1. The cost per equivalent unit is computed as the total costs of a process divided by the number of equivalent units passing through that process.
2. Service companies are not able to use process costing.
3. Costs per job are computed in both job order and process costing systems.
4. Job order and process operations both combine materials, labor, and overhead in producing products or services.

QS 16-14
Weighted average: Computing equivalent units of production
C2

The following refers to units processed by an ice cream maker in July. Compute the total equivalent units of production with respect to labor for July using the weighted-average inventory method.

	Gallons of Product	Percent of Labor Added
Beginning goods in process	320,000	25%
Goods started	620,000	100
Goods completed	680,000	100
Ending goods in process	240,000	75

QS 16-15A
FIFO: Computing equivalent units C4

Refer to QS 16-14 and compute the total equivalent units of production with respect to labor for July using the FIFO inventory method.

connect

EXERCISES

Exercise 16-1
Terminology in process cost accounting
C1 A1 P1 P2 P3

Match each of the following items A through G with the best numbered description of its purpose.

A. Factory Overhead account
B. Process cost summary
C. Equivalent units of production
D. Goods in Process Inventory account
E. Raw Materials Inventory account
F. Materials requisition
G. Finished Goods Inventory account

_______ 1. Notifies the materials manager to send materials to a production department.
_______ 2. Holds costs of indirect materials, indirect labor, and similar costs until assigned to production.
_______ 3. Holds costs of direct materials, direct labor, and applied overhead until products are transferred from production to finished goods (or another department).
_______ 4. Standardizes partially completed units into equivalent completed units.
_______ 5. Holds costs of finished products until sold to customers.
_______ 6. Describes the activity and output of a production department for a period.
_______ 7. Holds costs of materials until they are used in production or as factory overhead.

Exercise 16-2
Recording costs of materials
P1

Prepare journal entries to record the following production activities.

1. Purchased $80,000 of raw materials on credit.
2. Used $42,000 of direct materials in production.
3. Used $22,500 of indirect materials.

Exercise 16-3
Recording costs of labor
P2

Prepare journal entries to record the following production activities.

1. Incurred total labor cost of $95,000, which is paid in cash.
2. Used $75,000 of direct labor in production.
3. Used $20,000 of indirect labor.

Exercise 16-4
Recording overhead costs
P3

Refer to information in Exercise 16-3. Prepare journal entries to record the following production activities.

1. Paid overhead costs (other than indirect materials and indirect labor) of $38,750.
2. Applied overhead at 110% of direct labor costs.

Exercise 16-5
Recording cost of completed goods P4

Prepare journal entries to record the following production activities.

1. Transferred completed products with a cost of $135,600 to finished goods inventory.
2. Sold $315,000 of products on credit. Their cost is $175,000.

Exercise 16-6
Recording cost flows in a process cost system
P1 P2 P3 P4

Laffer Lumber produces bagged bark for use in landscaping. Production involves packaging bark chips in plastic bags in a bagging department. The following information describes production operations for October.

		Bagging Department
3	Direct materials used	$ 522,000
4	Direct labor used	$ 130,000
5	Predetermined overhead rate (based on direct labor)	175%
6	Goods transferred from bagging to finished goods	$(595,000)

The company's revenue for the month totaled $950,000 from credit sales, and its cost of goods sold for the month is $540,000. Prepare summary journal entries dated October 31 to record its October production activities for (1) direct material usage, (2) direct labor usage, (3) overhead allocation, (4) goods transfer from production to finished goods, and (5) credit sales.

Check (3) Cr. Factory Overhead, $227,500

Exercise 16-7
Interpretation of journal entries in process cost accounting
P1 P2 P3 P4

The following journal entries are recorded in Kiesha Co.'s process cost accounting system. Kiesha produces apparel and accessories. Overhead is applied to production based on direct labor cost for the period. Prepare a brief explanation (including any overhead rates applied) for each journal entry *a* through *j*.

a.	Raw Materials Inventory	52,000	
	Accounts Payable		52,000
b.	Goods in Process Inventory	42,000	
	Raw Materials Inventory		42,000
c.	Factory Payroll	26,000	
	Cash		26,000
d.	Goods in Process Inventory	32,000	
	Factory Payroll		32,000
e.	Factory Overhead	10,000	
	Cash		10,000
f.	Factory Overhead	10,000	
	Raw Materials Inventory		10,000

g.	Factory Overhead	6,000	
	Factory Payroll		6,000
h.	Goods in Process Inventory	33,600	
	Factory Overhead		33,600
i.	Finished Goods Inventory	88,000	
	Goods in Process Inventory		88,000
j.	Accounts Receivable	250,000	
	Sales		250,000
	Cost of Goods Sold	100,000	
	Finished Goods Inventory		100,000

Exercise 16-8
Weighted average: Computing equivalent units of production
C2

During April, the production department of a process manufacturing system completed a number of units of a product and transferred them to finished goods. Of these transferred units, 60,000 were in process in the production department at the beginning of April and 240,000 were started and completed in April. April's beginning inventory units were 60% complete with respect to materials and 40% complete with respect to labor. At the end of April, 82,000 additional units were in process in the production department and were 80% complete with respect to materials and 30% complete with respect to labor.

1. Compute the number of units transferred to finished goods.
2. Compute the number of equivalent units with respect to both materials used and labor used in the production department for April using the weighted-average method.

Check (2) EUP for materials, 365,600

Exercise 16-9
Weighted average: Costs assigned to output and inventories
C2 P4

The production department described in Exercise 16-8 had $850,000 of direct materials and $650,000 of direct labor cost charged to it during April. Also, its beginning inventory included $118,840 of direct materials cost and $47,890 of direct labor.

1. Compute the direct materials cost and the direct labor cost per equivalent unit for the department.
2. Using the weighted-average method, assign April's costs to the department's output—specifically, its units transferred to finished goods and its ending goods in process inventory.

Check (1) $2.65 per EUP of direct materials

Exercise 16-10A
FIFO: Computing equivalent units of production C4

Refer to the information in Exercise 16-8 to compute the number of equivalent units with respect to both materials used and labor used in the production department for April using the FIFO method.

Exercise 16-11A
FIFO: Costs assigned to output C4 P4

Refer to the information in Exercise 16-9 and complete its parts (1) and (2) using the FIFO method. (Round cost per equivalent unit to two decimal places.)

Exercise 16-12
Weighted average: Equivalent units computed C2

The production department in a process manufacturing system completed 80,000 units of product and transferred them to finished goods during a recent period. Of these units, 24,000 were in process at the beginning of the period. The other 56,000 units were started and completed during the period. At period-end, 16,000 units were in process. Compute the department's equivalent units of production with respect to direct materials under each of three separate assumptions:

1. All direct materials are added to products when processing begins.
2. Direct materials are added to products evenly throughout the process. Beginning goods in process inventory was 50% complete, and ending goods in process inventory was 75% complete.
3. One-half of direct materials is added to products when the process begins and the other half is added when the process is 75% complete as to direct labor. Beginning goods in process inventory is 40% complete as to direct labor, and ending goods in process inventory is 60% complete as to direct labor.

Check (3) EUP for materials, 88,000

Exercise 16-13A
FIFO: Equivalent units computed C4

Refer to the information in Exercise 16-12 and complete it for each of the three separate assumptions using the FIFO method for process costing.

Check (3) EUP for materials, 76,000

Exercise 16-14
Flowchart of costs for a process operation P1 P2 P3 P4

The following flowchart shows the August production activity of the Spalding Company. Use the amounts shown on the flowchart to compute the missing four numbers identified by blanks.

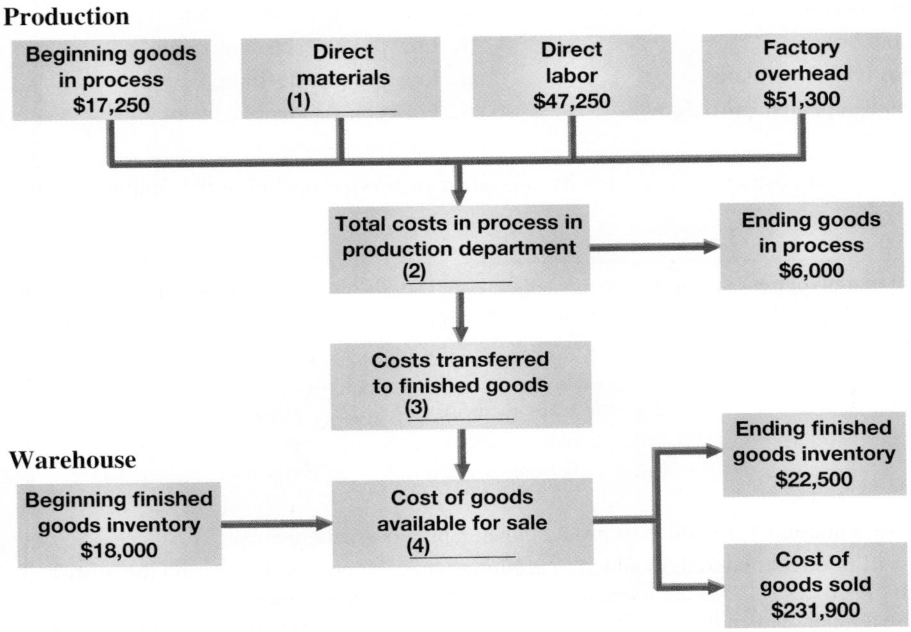

Exercise 16-15
Weighted average: Completing a process cost summary
C3

The following partially completed process cost summary describes the July production activities of Ashad Company. Its production output is sent to its warehouse for shipping. All direct materials are added to products when processing begins. Beginning goods in process inventory is 20% complete with respect to direct labor and overhead. Prepare its process cost summary using the weighted-average method.

Equivalent Units of Production	**Direct Materials**	**Direct Labor**	**Factory Overhead**
Units transferred out	32,000	32,000	32,000
Units of ending goods in process	2,500	1,500	1,500
Equivalent units of production	34,500	33,500	33,500

Costs per EUP	**Direct Materials**	**Direct Labor**	**Factory Overhead**
Costs of beginning goods in process	$ 18,550	$ 760	$ 1,520
Costs incurred this period	357,500	62,890	125,780
Total costs	$376,050	$63,650	$127,300

Units in beginning goods in process (all completed during July)	2,000
Units started this period	32,500
Units completed and transferred out	32,000
Units in ending goods in process	2,500

Exercise 16-16[A]
FIFO: Completing a process cost summary C3 C4

Refer to the information in Exercise 16-15. Prepare a process cost summary using the FIFO method. (Round cost per equivalent unit calculations to two decimal places.)

Exercise 16-17
Matching of product to cost accounting system
C1

For each of the following products and services, indicate whether it is most likely produced in a process operation or in a job order operation.

1. Beach towels
2. Bolts and nuts
3. Lawn chairs
4. Headphones
5. Designed patio
6. Door hardware
7. Cut flower arrangements
8. House paints
9. Concrete swimming pools
10. Custom tailored dresses
11. Grand pianos
12. Table lamps

Exercise 16-18
Compare process and job order operations
C1

Label each item *a* through *h* below as a feature of either a job order or process operation.

a. Heterogeneous products and services
b. Custom orders
c. Low production volume
d. Routine, repetitive procedures
e. Focus on individual batch
f. Low product standardization
g. Low product flexibility
h. Focus on standardized units

Exercise 16-19
Hybrid costing system A2

Explain a hybrid costing system. Identify a product or service operation that might well fit a hybrid costing system.

Exercise 16-20
Weighted average: Equivalent units computed
C2

ProChem manufactures aspirin in a process operation. Details on production activity follow. Compute the department's equivalent units of production with respect to direct materials under each of two separate assumptions.

Beginning goods in process	31,500
Goods started	189,500
Goods completed	191,500

1. All direct materials are added to products when processing begins.
2. One-half of direct materials is added to products when the process begins and the other half is added when the process is 75% complete as to direct labor. Beginning goods in process is 20% complete as to direct labor, and ending goods in process inventory is 45% complete as to direct labor.

Check (2) EUP for materials, 206,250

Exercise 16-21A
FIFO: Equivalent units computed C4

Refer to the information in Exercise 16-20 and complete it for each of the two separate assumptions using the FIFO method for process costing.

Check (2) EUP for materials, 190,500

Exercise 16-22
Weighted average: Process cost summary C3

Hi-Test Company uses the weighted-average method of process costing to assign production costs to its products. Information for September follows. Assume that all materials are added at the beginning of its production process, and that direct labor and factory overhead are added uniformly throughout the process.

Goods in process inventory, September 1 (2,000 units, 100% complete with respect to direct materials, 80% complete with respect to direct labor and overhead; includes $45,000 of direct material cost, $25,600 in direct labor cost, $30,720 overhead cost)	$101,320
Units started in April	28,000
Units completed and transferred to finished goods inventory	23,000
Goods in process inventory, September 30 (? units, 100% complete with respect to direct materials, 40% complete with respect to direct labor and overhead)	?
Costs incurred in September	
Direct materials	$375,000
Direct labor	$155,000
Overhead applied at 120% of direct labor cost	?

Required

Fill in the blanks labeled *a* through *uu* in the following process cost summary.

HI-TEST COMPANY
Process Cost Summary
For Month Ended September 30

Costs Charged to Production		
Costs of beginning goods in process		
Direct materials	$ 45,000	
Direct labor	25,600	
Factory overhead	30,720	$101,320
Costs incurred this period		
Direct materials	$375,000	
Direct labor	155,000	
Factory overhead	(a)____	(b)____
Total costs to account for		(c)____

Check (c) $817,320

Unit Cost Information

Units to account for		Units accounted for	
Beginning goods in process	2,000	Completed and transferred out	23,000
Units started this period	28,000	Ending goods in process	(d)____
Total units to account for	(e)____	Total units accounted for	(f)____

Equivalent Units of Production (EUP)				**Direct Materials**	**Direct Labor**	**Factory Overhead**
Units completed and transferred out				(g)____EUP	(h)____EUP	(i)____EUP
Units of ending goods in process						
Materials	(j)____	×	100%	(k)____EUP		
Direct labor	(l)____	×	40%		(m)____EUP	
Factory overhead	(n)____	×	40%			(o)____EUP
Equivalent units of production (EUP)				(p)____EUP	(q)____EUP	(r)____EUP

[continued on next page]

[continued from previous page]

Cost per EUP	Direct Materials	Direct Labor	Factory Overhead
Costs of beginning goods in process	$ 45,000	$ 25,600	$30,720
Costs incurred this period	375,000	155,000	(s)____
Total costs	$420,000	$180,600	(t)____
÷ EUP	(u)____	(v)____	(w)____
Cost per EUP	(x)____	(y)____	(z)____

Check (z) $8.40 per EUP

Cost Assignment and Reconciliation	Cost/EUP	×	EUP		
Costs transferred out					
Direct materials	(aa)____	×	(bb)____	(cc)____	
Direct labor	(dd)____	×	(ee)____	(ff)____	
Factory overhead	(gg)____	×	(hh)____	(ii)____	
Costs of goods completed and transferred out					(jj)____
Costs of ending goods in process					
Direct materials	(kk)____	×	(ll)____	(mm)____	
Direct labor	(nn)____	×	(oo)____	(pp)____	
Factory overhead	(qq)____	×	(rr)____	(ss)____	
Costs of ending goods in process					(tt)____
Total costs accounted for					(uu)____

connect

PROBLEM SET A

Problem 16-1A
Production cost flow and measurement; journal entries
P1 P2 P3 P4

Sage 50 QB

Sierra Company manufactures woven blankets and accounts for product costs using process costing. The following information is available regarding its May inventories.

	Beginning Inventory	Ending Inventory
Raw materials inventory	$ 60,000	$ 92,500
Goods in process inventory	435,000	515,000
Finished goods inventory	633,000	605,000

The following additional information describes the company's production activities for May.

Raw materials purchases (on credit)		$ 250,000
Factory payroll cost (paid in cash)		1,530,000
Other overhead cost (Other Accounts credited)		87,000
Materials used		
Direct		$ 157,500
Indirect		60,000
Labor used		
Direct		$ 780,000
Indirect		750,000
Overhead rate as a percent of direct labor		115%
Sales (on credit)		$2,500,000

Required

Check (1b) Cost of goods sold $1,782,500

1. Compute the cost of (a) products transferred from production to finished goods, and (b) goods sold.
2. Prepare summary journal entries dated May 31 to record the following production activities during May: (a) raw materials purchases, (b) direct materials usage, (c) indirect materials usage, (d) payroll costs, (e) direct labor costs, (f) indirect labor costs, (g) other overhead costs, (h) overhead applied, (i) goods transferred from production to finished goods, and (j) sale of finished goods.

Problem 16-2A
Weighted average: Cost per equivalent unit; costs assigned to products
C2 C3

mhhe.com/wildFINMAN5e

Victory Company uses weighted-average process costing to account for its production costs. Direct labor is added evenly throughout the process. Direct materials are added at the beginning of the process. During November, the company transferred 700,000 units of product to finished goods. At the end of November, the goods in process inventory consists of 180,000 units that are 30% complete with respect to labor. Beginning inventory had $420,000 of direct materials and $139,000 of direct labor cost. The direct material cost added in November is $2,220,000, and the direct labor cost added is $3,254,000.

Required

1. Determine the equivalent units of production with respect to (a) direct labor and (b) direct materials.
2. Compute both the direct labor cost and the direct materials cost per equivalent unit.
3. Compute both direct labor cost and direct materials cost assigned to (a) units completed and transferred out, and (b) ending goods in process inventory.

Check (2) Direct labor cost per equivalent unit, $4.50

(3b) $783,000

Analysis Component

4. The company sells and ships all units to customers as soon as they are completed. Assume that an error is made in determining the percentage of completion for units in ending inventory. Instead of being 30% complete with respect to labor, they are actually 60% complete. Write a one-page memo to the plant manager describing how this error affects its November financial statements.

Beginning goods in process consisted of 60,000 units that were 100% complete with respect to direct materials and 80% complete with respect to direct labor. Of the 700,000 units completed, 60,000 were from beginning goods in process and 640,000 units were started and completed during the period.

Problem 16-3A
Weighted average: Journalizing in process costing; equivalent units and costs
C2 P1 P2 P3

Sage 50 QB

Elliott Company produces large quantities of a standardized product. The following information is available for its production activities for March.

Raw materials		**Factory overhead incurred**	
Beginning inventory	$ 16,000	Indirect materials used	$ 70,000
Raw materials purchased (on credit)	250,000	Indirect labor used	45,000
Direct materials used	(168,000)	Other overhead costs	164,790
Indirect materials used	(70,000)	Total factory overhead incurred	$279,790
Ending inventory	$ 28,000		
		Factory overhead applied (140% of direct labor cost)	
Factory payroll		Total factory overhead applied	$279,790
Direct labor used	$199,850		
Indirect labor used	45,000		
Total payroll cost (paid in cash)	$244,850		

Additional information about units and costs of production activities follows.

Units		**Costs**		
Beginning goods in process inventory	2,000	Beginning goods in process inventory		
Started	20,000	Direct materials	$2,500	
Ending goods in process inventory	5,000	Direct labor	2,650	
		Factory overhead	3,710	$ 8,860
Status of ending goods in process inventory		Direct materials added		168,000
Materials—Percent complete	100%	Direct labor added		199,850
Labor and overhead—Percent complete	35%	Overhead applied (140% of direct labor)		279,790
		Total costs		$656,500
		Ending goods in process inventory		$ 84,110

During March, 10,000 units of finished goods are sold for $120 cash each. Cost information regarding finished goods follows.

Beginning finished goods inventory	$150,000
Cost transferred in	572,390
Cost of goods sold	(592,390)
Ending finished goods inventory	$130,000

Required

1. Prepare journal entries dated March 31 to record the following March activities: (a) purchase of raw materials, (b) direct materials usage, (c) indirect materials usage, (d) factory payroll costs, (e) direct labor costs used in production, (f) indirect labor costs, (g) other overhead costs—credit Other Accounts, (h) overhead applied, (i) goods transferred to finished goods, and (j) sale of finished goods.

2. Prepare a process cost summary report for this company, showing costs charged to production, units cost information, equivalent units of production, cost per EUP, and its cost assignment and reconciliation.

Check (2) Cost per equivalent unit: materials, $7.75; labor, $10.80; overhead, $15.12

Analysis Component

3. The company provides incentives to its department managers by paying monthly bonuses based on their success in controlling costs per equivalent unit of production. Assume that the production department underestimates the percentage of completion for units in ending inventory with the result that its equivalent units of production in ending inventory for March are understated. What impact does this error have on the March bonuses paid to the production managers? What impact, if any, does this error have on April bonuses?

Problem 16-4A
Weighted Average: Process cost summary; equivalent units
C2 C3 P4

mhhe.com/wildFINMAN5e

Fast Co. produces its product through a single processing department. Direct materials are added at the start of production, and direct labor and overhead are added evenly throughout the process. The company uses monthly reporting periods for its weighted-average process cost accounting system. Its Goods in Process Inventory account follows after entries for direct materials, direct labor, and overhead costs for October.

Goods in Process Inventory — Acct. No. 133

Date		Explanation	Debit	Credit	Balance
Oct.	1	Balance			335,930
	31	Direct materials	102,050		437,980
	31	Direct labor	408,200		846,180
	31	Applied overhead	244,920		1,091,100

Its beginning goods in process consisted of $59,450 of direct materials, $172,800 of direct labor, and $103,680 of factory overhead. During October, the company started 140,000 units and transferred 150,000 units to finished goods. At the end of the month, the goods in process inventory consisted of 20,000 units that were 80% complete with respect to direct labor and factory overhead.

Required

1. Prepare the company's process cost summary for October using the weighted-average method.

2. Prepare the journal entry dated October 31 to transfer the cost of the completed units to finished goods inventory.

Check (1) Costs transferred out to finished goods, $982,500

Problem 16-5A
Weighted average: Process cost summary, equivalent units, cost estimates
C2 C3 P4

Tamar Co. manufactures a single product in one department. All direct materials are added at the beginning of the manufacturing process. Direct labor and overhead are added evenly throughout the process. The company uses monthly reporting periods for its weighted-average process cost accounting. During May, the company completed and transferred 22,200 units of product to finished goods inventory. Its 3,000 units of beginning goods in process consisted of $19,800 of direct materials, $123,300 of direct labor, and $98,640 of factory overhead. It has 2,400 units (100% complete with respect to direct materials and 80% complete with respect to direct labor and overhead) in process at month-end. After entries to record direct materials, direct labor, and overhead for May, the company's Goods in Process Inventory account follows.

Goods in Process Inventory — Acct. No. 133

Date		Explanation	Debit	Credit	Balance
May	1	Balance			241,740
	31	Direct materials	496,800		738,540
	31	Direct labor	1,203,300		1,941,840
	31	Applied overhead	962,640		2,904,480

Required

1. Prepare the company's process cost summary for May using the weighted-average method.

2. Prepare the journal entry dated May 31 to transfer the cost of completed units to finished goods inventory.

Check (1) EUP for both labor and overhead, 24,120 EUP

(2) Cost transferred out to finished goods, $2,664,000

Analysis Components

3. The cost accounting process depends on numerous estimates.

a. Identify two major estimates that determine the cost per equivalent unit.

b. In what direction might you anticipate a bias from management for each estimate in part 3a (assume that management compensation is based on maintaining low inventory amounts)? Explain your answer.

Problem 16-6A[A]
FIFO: Process cost summary; equivalent units; cost estimates
C3 C4 P4

Refer to the data in Problem 16-5A. Assume that Tamar uses the FIFO method to account for its process costing system. The following additional information is available:

- Beginning goods in process consisted of 3,000 units that were 100% complete with respect to direct materials and 40% complete with respect to direct labor and overhead.
- Of the 22,200 units completed, 3,000 were from beginning goods in process. The remaining 19,200 were units started and completed during May.

Required

1. Prepare the company's process cost summary for May using FIFO.

2. Prepare the journal entry dated May 31 to transfer the cost of completed units to finished goods inventory.

Check (1) EUP for both labor and overhead, 22,920 EUP

(2) Cost transferred out to finished goods, $2,667,840

Problem 16-7A
FIFO: Costs per equivalent unit; costs assigned to products
C2 C4

During May, the production department of a process manufacturing system completed a number of units of a product and transferred them to finished goods. Of these transferred units, 37,500 were in process in the production department at the beginning of May and 150,000 were started and completed in May. May's beginning inventory units were 60% complete with respect to materials and 40% complete with respect to labor. At the end of May, 51,250 additional units were in process in the production department and were 60% complete with respect to materials and 20% complete with respect to labor. The production department had $505,035 of direct materials and $396,568 of direct labor cost charged to it during May. Its beginning inventory included $74,075 of direct materials cost and $28,493 of direct labor cost.

1. Compute the number of units transferred to finished goods.

2. Compute the number of equivalent units with respect to both materials used and labor used in the production department for May using the FIFO method.

3. Compute the direct materials cost and the direct labor cost per equivalent unit for the department.

4. Using the FIFO method, assign May's costs to the units transferred to finished goods and assign costs to its ending goods in process inventory.

Check (2) EUP for materials, 195,750

Problem 16-8A[A]
FIFO: Cost per equivalent unit; costs assigned to products
C2 C3 C4

Refer to the information in Problem 16-2A and complete its parts (1) through (4) using the FIFO method of process costing. Round cost per equivalent unit calculations to two decimal places.

Check (2) $4.61 direct labor cost per EUP; $2.71 direct materials cost per EUP

Problem 16-9A[A]
FIFO: Process cost summary, equivalent units, cost estimates
C2 C3 C4 P4

Dengo Co. manufactures a single product in one department. Direct labor and overhead are added evenly throughout the process, while direct materials are added at the beginning of the process. The company uses the FIFO method of process costing. During October, the company completed and transferred 22,200 units to finished goods inventory. Of the units completed, 3,000 were from beginning inventory and the remaining 19,200 were started and completed during the month. Beginning goods in process were 100% complete with respect to direct materials and 40% complete with respect to direct labor and overhead. The company has 2,400 units (100% complete with respect to direct materials and 80% complete with respect to direct labor and overhead) in process at month-end. Information on costs of beginning inventory and costs added during the month follows.

Cost	Raw Materials	Direct Labor	Overhead
Of beginning inventory	$ 9,900	$ 61,650	$ 49,320
Added during the month	248,400	601,650	481,320

Check (1) EUP for both labor and overhead, 22,920 EUP

(2) Cost transferred out to finished goods, $1,333,920

Required

1. Prepare the company's process cost summary for October using the FIFO method.

2. Prepare the journal entry dated October 31 to transfer the cost of completed units to finished good inventory.

Analysis Component

3. The company provides incentives to department managers by paying monthly bonuses based on their success in controlling costs per equivalent unit of production. Assume that the production department underestimates the percentage of completion for units in ending inventory with the result that its equivalent units of production for October are understated. What impact does this error have on the October bonuses paid to the production managers? What impact, if any, does this error have on November bonuses?

PROBLEM SET B

Problem 16-1B

Production cost flow and measurement; journal entries

P1 P2 P3 P4

Dream Toys Company manufactures video game consoles and accounts for product costs using process costing. The following information is available regarding its June inventories.

	Beginning Inventory	Ending Inventory
Raw materials inventory	$ 72,000	$110,000
Goods in process inventory	156,000	250,000
Finished goods inventory	160,000	198,000

The following additional information describes the company's production activities for June.

Raw materials purchases (on credit)	$200,000
Factory payroll cost (paid in cash)	400,000
Other overhead cost (Other Accounts credited)	170,500
Materials used	
Direct	$120,000
Indirect	42,000
Labor used	
Direct	$350,000
Indirect	50,000
Overhead rate as a percent of direct labor	75%
Sales (on credit)	$1,000,000

Check (1b) Cost of goods sold, $600,500

Required

1. Compute the cost of (a) products transferred from production to finished goods, and (b) goods sold.

2. Prepare journal entries dated June 30 to record the following production activities during June: (a) raw materials purchases, (b) direct materials usage, (c) indirect materials usage, (d) payroll costs, (e) direct labor costs, (f) indirect labor costs, (g) other overhead costs, (h) overhead applied, (i) goods transferred from production to finished goods, and (j) sale of finished goods.

Problem 16-2B

Weighted average: Cost per equivalent unit; costs assigned to products

C2 C3

Abraham Company uses process costing to account for its production costs. Direct labor is added evenly throughout the process. Direct materials are added at the beginning of the process. During September, the production department transferred 80,000 units of product to finished goods. Beginning goods in process consisted of 2,000 units that were 100% complete with respect to direct materials and 85% complete with respect to direct labor. Of the 40,000 units completed, 2,000 were from beginning goods in process and 78,000 units were started and completed during the period. Beginning goods in process had $58,000 of direct materials and $86,400 of direct labor cost. At the end of September, the goods in process inventory consists of 8,000 units that are 25% complete with respect to labor. The direct materials cost added in September is $712,000, and direct labor cost added is $1,980,000.

Required

1. Determine the equivalent units of production with respect to (a) direct labor and (b) direct materials.

2. Compute both the direct labor cost and the direct materials cost per equivalent unit.

3. Compute both direct labor cost and direct materials cost assigned to (a) units completed and transferred out, and (b) ending goods in process inventory.

Check (2) Direct labor cost per equivalent unit, $25.20

(3b) $120,400

Analysis Component

4. The company sells and ships all units to customers as soon as they are completed. Assume that an error is made in determining the percentage of completion for units in ending inventory. Instead of being 25% complete with respect to labor, they are actually 75% complete. Write a one-page memo to the plant manager describing how this error affects its September financial statements.

Problem 16-3B
Weighted Average: Journalizing in process costing; equivalent units and costs

C2 P1 P2 P3 P4

Oslo Company produces large quantities of a standardized product. The following information is available for its production activities for May.

Raw materials		**Factory overhead incurred**	
Beginning inventory	$ 32,000	Indirect materials used	$ 40,560
Raw materials purchased (on credit)	221,120	Indirect labor used	36,320
Direct materials used	(197,120)	Other overhead costs	34,432
Indirect materials used	(40,560)	Total factory overhead incurred	$111,312
Ending inventory	$ 15,440		
		Factory overhead applied (90% of direct labor cost)	
Factory payroll		Total factory overhead applied	$111,312
Direct labor used	$123,680		
Indirect labor used	36,320		
Total payroll cost (paid in cash)	$160,000		

Additional information about units and costs of production activities follows.

Units		**Costs**		
Beginning goods in process inventory	4,000	Beginning goods in process inventory		
Started	12,000	Direct materials	$2,880	
Ending goods in process inventory	3,000	Direct labor	2,820	
		Factory overhead	2,538	$ 8,238
Status of ending goods in process inventory		Direct materials added		197,120
Materials—Percent complete	100%	Direct labor added		123,680
Labor and overhead—Percent complete	25%	Overhead applied (90% of direct labor)		111,312
		Total costs		$440,350
		Ending goods in process inventory		$ 50,610

During May, 10,000 units of finished goods are sold for $120 cash each. Cost information regarding finished goods follows.

Beginning finished goods inventory	$148,400
Cost transferred in from production	389,740
Cost of goods sold	(474,540)
Ending finished goods inventory	$ 63,600

Required

1. Prepare journal entries dated May 31 to record the following May activities: (a) purchase of raw materials, (b) direct materials usage, (c) indirect materials usage, (d) factory payroll costs, (e) direct labor costs used in production, (f) indirect labor costs, (g) other overhead costs—credit Other Accounts, (h) overhead applied, (i) goods transferred to finished goods, and (j) sale of finished goods.

2. Prepare a process cost summary report for this company, showing costs charged to production, unit cost information, equivalent units of production, cost per EUP, and its cost assignment and reconciliation.

Check (2) Cost per equivalent unit: materials, $12.50; labor, $9.20; overhead, $8.28

Analysis Component

3. This company provides incentives to its department managers by paying monthly bonuses based on their success in controlling costs per equivalent unit of production. Assume that production overestimates the percentage of completion for units in ending inventory with the result that its equivalent units of production in ending inventory for May are overstated. What impact does this error have on bonuses paid to the managers of the production department? What impact, if any, does this error have on these managers' June bonuses?

Problem 16-4B
Weighted average: Process cost summary; equivalent units
C2 C3 P4

Braun Company produces its product through a single processing department. Direct materials are added at the beginning of the process. Direct labor and overhead are added to the product evenly throughout the process. The company uses monthly reporting periods for its weighted-average process cost accounting. Its Goods in Process Inventory account follows after entries for direct materials, direct labor, and overhead costs for November.

Goods in Process Inventory					Acct. No. 133
Date		**Explanation**	**Debit**	**Credit**	**Balance**
Nov.	1	Balance			21,300
	30	Direct materials	116,400		137,700
	30	Direct labor	426,800		564,500
	30	Applied overhead	640,200		1,204,700

The 7,500 units of beginning goods in process consisted of $6,800 of direct materials, $5,800 of direct labor, and $8,700 of factory overhead. During November, the company finished and transferred 100,000 units of its product to finished goods. At the end of the month, the goods in process inventory consisted of 12,000 units that were 100% complete with respect to direct materials and 25% complete with respect to direct labor and factory overhead.

Required

Check (1) Cost transferred out to finished goods, $1,160,000

1. Prepare the company's process cost summary for November using the weighted-average method.
2. Prepare the journal entry dated November 30 to transfer the cost of the completed units to finished goods inventory.

Problem 16-5B
Weighted average: Process cost summary; equivalent units; cost estimates
C2 C3 P4

Switch Co. manufactures a single product in one department. Direct labor and overhead are added evenly throughout the process. Direct materials are added as needed. The company uses monthly reporting periods for its weighted-average process cost accounting. During January, Switch completed and transferred 220,000 units of product to finished goods inventory. Its 10,000 units of beginning goods in process consisted of $7,500 of direct materials, $14,240 of direct labor, and $35,600 of factory overhead. 40,000 units (50% complete with respect to direct materials and 30% complete with respect to direct labor and overhead) are in process at month-end. After entries for direct materials, direct labor, and overhead for January, the company's Goods in Process Inventory account follows.

Goods in Process Inventory					Acct. No. 133
Date		**Explanation**	**Debit**	**Credit**	**Balance**
Jan.	1	Balance			57,340
	31	Direct materials	112,500		169,840
	31	Direct labor	176,000		345,840
	31	Applied overhead	440,000		785,840

Check (1) EUP for both labor and overhead, 232,000

(2) Cost transferred out to finished goods, $741,400

Required

1. Prepare the company's process cost summary for January using the weighted-average method.
2. Prepare the journal entry dated January 31 to transfer the cost of completed units to finished goods inventory.

Analysis Components

3. The cost accounting process depends on several estimates.
   a. Identify two major estimates that affect the cost per equivalent unit.
   b. In what direction might you anticipate a bias from management for each estimate in part 3a (assume that management compensation is based on maintaining low inventory amounts)? Explain your answer.

Problem 16-6B^A
FIFO: Process cost summary; equivalent units; cost estimates
C3 C4 P4

Refer to the information in Problem 16-5B. Assume that Switch uses the FIFO method to account for its process costing system. The following additional information is available.

- Beginning goods in process consists of 10,000 units that were 75% complete with respect to direct materials and 60% complete with respect to direct labor and overhead.
- Of the 220,000 units completed, 10,000 were from beginning goods in process; the remaining 210,000 were units started and completed during January.

Required

1. Prepare the company's process cost summary for January using FIFO. Round cost per EUP to one-tenth of a cent.
2. Prepare the journal entry dated January 31 to transfer the cost of completed units to finished goods inventory.

Check (1) Labor and overhead EUP, 226,000

(2) Cost transferred out, $743,554

Problem 16-7B
FIFO: Costs per equivalent unit; costs assigned to products
C2 C4

During May, the production department of a process manufacturing system completed a number of units of a product and transferred them to finished goods. Of these transferred units, 62,500 were in process in the production department at the beginning of May and 175,000 were started and completed in May. May's beginning inventory units were 40% complete with respect to materials and 80% complete with respect to labor. At the end of May, 76,250 additional units were in process in the production department and were 80% complete with respect to materials and 20% complete with respect to labor. The production department had $683,750 of direct materials and $446,050 of direct labor cost charged to it during May. Its beginning inventory included $99,075 of direct materials cost and $53,493 of direct labor cost.

1. Compute the number of units transferred to finished goods.
2. Compute the number of equivalent units with respect to both materials used and labor used in the production department for May using the FIFO method.
3. Compute the direct materials cost and the direct labor cost per equivalent unit for the department.
4. Using the FIFO method, assign May's costs to the units transferred to finished goods and assign costs to its ending goods in process inventory.

Check (2) EUP for materials, 273,500

Problem 16-8B^A
FIFO: Cost per equivalent unit; costs assigned to products
C2 C3 C4

Refer to the information in Problem 16-2B and complete its parts (1) through (4) using the FIFO method of process costing. Round cost per equivalent unit calculations to two decimal places.

Check (2) $24.66 direct labor cost per EUP; $8.28 direct materials cost per EUP

Problem 16-9B^A
FIFO: Process cost summary, equivalent units, cost estimates
C2 C3 C4 P4

Belda Co. manufactures a single product in one department. Direct labor and overhead are added evenly throughout the process. Direct materials are added as needed. The company uses the FIFO method of process costing. During March, the company completed and transferred 220,000 units to finished goods inventory. Of the units completed, 10,000 were from beginning inventory and the remaining 210,000 were started and completed during the month. Beginning goods in process were 75% complete with respect to direct materials and 60% complete with respect to direct labor and overhead. The company has 40,000 units (50% complete with respect to direct materials and 30% complete with respect to direct labor and overhead) in process at month-end. Information on costs of beginning inventory and costs added during the month follows.

Cost	Raw Materials	Direct Labor	Overhead
Of beginning inventory	$ 16,800	$ 27,920	$ 69,800
Added during the month.........	223,200	352,560	881,400

Required

Check (1) EUP for both labor and overhead, 226,000 EUP

(2) Cost transferred out to finished goods, $1,486,960

1. Prepare the company's process cost summary for March using the FIFO method.

2. Prepare the journal entry dated March 31 to transfer the cost of completed units to finished good inventory.

Analysis Component

3. The company provides incentives to department managers by paying monthly bonuses based on their success in controlling costs per equivalent unit of production. Assume that the production department overestimates the percentage of completion for units in ending inventory with the result that its equivalent units of production for March are overstated. What impact does this error have on bonuses paid to the managers of the production department? What impact, if any, does this error have on these managers' April bonuses?

SERIAL PROBLEM

Success Systems

C1 A1

(This serial problem began in Chapter 1 and continues through most of the book. If previous chapter segments were not completed, the serial problem can begin at this point.)

SP 16 The computer workstation furniture manufacturing that Adria Lopez started is progressing well. At this point, Adria is using a job order costing system to account for the production costs of this product line. Adria has heard about process costing and is wondering whether process costing might be a better method for her to keep track of and monitor her production costs.

Required

1. What are the features that distinguish job order costing from process costing?

2. Do you believe that Adria should continue to use job order costing or switch to process costing for her workstation furniture manufacturing? Explain.

COMPREHENSIVE PROBLEM

Major League Bat Company

Weighted average: Review of Chapters 2, 4, 14, 16

CP 16 Major League Bat Company manufactures baseball bats. In addition to its goods in process inventories, the company maintains inventories of raw materials and finished goods. It uses raw materials as direct materials in production and as indirect materials. Its factory payroll costs include direct labor for production and indirect labor. All materials are added at the beginning of the process, and direct labor and factory overhead are applied uniformly throughout the production process.

Required

You are to maintain records and produce measures of inventories to reflect the July events of this company. Set up the following general ledger accounts and enter the June 30 balances: Raw Materials Inventory, $25,000; Goods in Process Inventory, $8,135 ($2,660 of direct materials, $3,650 of direct labor, and $1,825 of overhead); Finished Goods Inventory, $110,000; Sales, $0; Cost of Goods Sold, $0; Factory Payroll, $0; and Factory Overhead, $0.

1. Prepare journal entries to record the following July transactions and events.

a. Purchased raw materials for $125,000 cash (the company uses a perpetual inventory system).

b. Used raw materials as follows: direct materials, $52,440; and indirect materials, $10,000.

c. Incurred factory payroll cost of $227,250 paid in cash (ignore taxes).

d. Assigned factory payroll costs as follows: direct labor, $202,250; and indirect labor, $25,000.

e. Incurred additional factory overhead costs of $80,000 paid in cash.

Check (1f) Cr. Factory Overhead, $101,125

f. Allocated factory overhead to production at 50% of direct labor costs.

2. Information about the July inventories follows. Use this information with that from part 1 to prepare a process cost summary, assuming the weighted-average method is used.

Check (2) EUP for overhead, 14,200

Units	
Beginning inventory	5,000 units
Started	14,000 units
Ending inventory	8,000 units
Beginning inventory	
Materials—Percent complete	100%
Labor and overhead—Percent complete	75%
Ending inventory	
Materials—Percent complete	100%
Labor and overhead—Percent complete	40%

3. Using the results from part 2 and the available information, make computations and prepare journal entries to record the following:

g. Total costs transferred to finished goods for July (label this entry g).

(3g) $271,150

h. Sale of finished goods costing $265,700 for $625,000 in cash (label this entry h).

4. Post entries from parts 1 and 3 to the ledger accounts set up at the beginning of the problem.

5. Compute the amount of gross profit from the sales in July. (*Note:* Add any underapplied overhead to, or deduct any overapplied overhead from, the cost of goods sold. Ignore the corresponding journal entry.)

Beyond the Numbers

REPORTING IN ACTION

C2

Polaris

BTN 16-1 Polaris reports in notes to its financial statements that, in addition to its products sold, it includes the following costs (among others) in cost of sales: customer shipping and handling expenses, warranty expenses, and depreciation expense on assets used in manufacturing.

Required

1. Why do you believe Polaris includes these costs in its cost of sales?

2. What effect does this cost accounting policy for its cost of sales have on Polaris' financial statements and any analysis of those statements? Explain.

Fast Forward

3. Access Polaris' financial statements for the years after December 31, 2011, from its Website (Polaris.com) or the SEC's EDGAR Website (sec.gov). Review its footnote relating to Organization and Significant Accounting Policies. Has Polaris' changed its policy with respect to what costs are included in the cost of sales? Explain.

COMPARATIVE ANALYSIS

C1

Polaris

Arctic Cat

BTN 16-2 Manufacturers such as Polaris and Arctic Cat usually work to maintain a high-quality and low-cost operation. One ratio routinely computed for this assessment is the cost of goods sold divided by total expenses. A decline in this ratio can mean that the company is spending too much on selling and administrative activities. An increase in this ratio beyond a reasonable level can mean that the company is not spending enough on selling activities. (Assume for this analysis that total expenses equal the cost of goods sold plus total operating expenses.)

Required

1. For Polaris and Arctic Cat refer to Appendix A and compute the ratios of cost of goods sold to total expenses for their two most recent fiscal years. (Record answers as percents, rounded to one decimal.)

2. Comment on the similarities or differences in the ratio results across both years between the companies.

ETHICS CHALLENGE

C1

BTN 16-3 Many accounting and accounting-related professionals are skilled in financial analysis, but most are not skilled in manufacturing. This is especially the case for process manufacturing environments (for example, a bottling plant or chemical factory). To provide professional accounting and financial services, one must understand the industry, product, and processes. We have an ethical responsibility to develop this understanding before offering services to clients in these areas.

Required

Write a one-page action plan, in memorandum format, discussing how you would obtain an understanding of key business processes of a company that hires you to provide financial services. The memorandum should specify an industry, a product, and one selected process and should draw on at least one reference, such as a professional journal or industry magazine.

COMMUNICATING IN PRACTICE

A1 C1 P1 P2

BTN 16-4 You hire a new assistant production manager whose prior experience is with a company that produced goods to order. Your company engages in continuous production of homogeneous products that go through various production processes. Your new assistant e-mails you questioning some cost classifications on an internal report—specifically why the costs of some materials that do not actually become part of the finished product, including some labor costs not directly associated with producing the product, are classified as direct costs. Respond to this concern via memorandum.

TAKING IT TO THE NET

C1

BTN 16-5 Many companies acquire software to help them monitor and control their costs and as an aid to their accounting systems. One company that supplies such software is **proDacapo** (prodacapo.com). There are many other such vendors. Access proDacapo's Website, click on "Prodacapo Process Management," and review the information displayed.

Required

How is process management software helpful to businesses? Explain with reference to costs, efficiency, and examples, if possible.

TEAMWORK IN ACTION

C1 P1 P2 P3 P4

BTN 16-6 The purpose of this team activity is to ensure that each team member understands process operations and the related accounting entries. Find the activities and flows identified in Exhibit 16.4 with numbers ①–⑩. Pick a member of the team to start by describing activity number ① in this exhibit, then verbalizing the related journal entry, and describing how the amounts in the entry are computed. The other members of the team are to agree or disagree; discussion is to continue until all members express understanding. Rotate to the next numbered activity and next team member until all activities and entries have been discussed. If at any point a team member is uncertain about an answer, the team member may pass and get back in the rotation when he or she can contribute to the team's discussion.

ENTREPRENEURIAL DECISION

C3 A2

BTN 16-7 This chapter's opener featured Neal Gottlieb and his company **Three Twins Ice Cream**.

Required

1. Neal recently built a large manufacturing facility. Explain how his company's process cost summary report would differ after his new manufacturing facility is operating.
2. How does holding raw materials inventories increase costs? If the items are not used in production, how can they impact profits? Explain.
3. Suppose Three Twins Ice Cream decides to allow customers to make their own unique ice cream flavors. Why might the company then use a hybrid costing system?

BTN 16-8 In process costing, the process is analyzed first and then a unit measure is computed in the form of equivalent units for direct materials, direct labor, overhead, and all three combined. The same analysis applies to both manufacturing and service processes.

HITTING THE ROAD
C2

Required

Visit your local **U.S. Mail** center. Look into the back room, and you will see several ongoing processes. Select one process, such as sorting, and list the costs associated with this process. Your list should include materials, labor, and overhead; be specific. Classify each cost as fixed or variable. At the bottom of your list, outline how overhead should be assigned to your identified process. The following format (with an example) is suggested.

Point: The class can compare and discuss the different processes studied and the answers provided.

Cost Description	Direct Material	Direct Labor	Overhead	Variable Cost	Fixed Cost
Manual sorting		X		X	
⋮					
Overhead allocation suggestions:					

BTN 16-9 **Piaggio**, **Polaris**, and **Arctic Cat** are competitors in the global marketplace. Selected data for Piaggio follow.

GLOBAL DECISION
C1

PIAGGIO
Polaris
Arctic Cat

(millions of euros)	Current Year	Prior Year
Cost of goods sold	€1,061.9	€1,023.1
Operating expenses	349.1	351.2
Total expenses	€1,411.0	€1,374.3

Required

1. Review the discussion of the importance of the cost of goods sold divided by total expenses ratio in BTN 16-2. Compute the cost of goods sold to total expenses ratio for Piaggio for the two years of data provided. (Record answers as percents, rounded to one decimal.)
2. Comment on the similarities or differences in the ratio results calculated in part *1* and in BTN 16-2 across years and companies. (Record answers as percents, rounded to one decimal.)

ANSWERS TO MULTIPLE CHOICE QUIZ

1. d
2. e
3. b; $20,000 + $152,000 + $45,000 + $18,000 − $218,000 = $17,000
4. a; 40,000 + (15,000 × 1/3) = 45,000 EUP
5. c; ($6,000 + $84,000) ÷ 45,000 EUP = $2 per EUP

17

Activity-Based Costing and Analysis

A Look Back

Chapters 15 and 16 described costing systems used by companies to accumulate product costing information for the reporting of inventories and cost of goods sold.

A Look at This Chapter

This chapter introduces the activity-based costing (ABC) system with the potential for greater accuracy of cost allocations. ABC provides managers with cost information for strategic decisions that is not readily available with other costing methods.

A Look Ahead

Chapter 18 discusses the importance of information on both costs and sales behavior for managers in performing cost-volume-profit (CVP) analysis, which is a valuable managerial tool.

Learning Objectives

CONCEPTUAL

C1 Distinguish between the plantwide overhead rate method, the departmental overhead rate method, and the activity-based costing method. (p. 738)

C2 Explain cost flows for activity-based costing. (p. 743)

C3 Describe the four types of activities that cause overhead costs. (p. 750)

ANALYTICAL

A1 Identify and assess advantages and disadvantages of the plantwide overhead and departmental overhead rate methods. (p. 743)

A2 Identify and assess advantages and disadvantages of activity-based costing. (p. 748)

PROCEDURAL

P1 Allocate overhead costs to products using the plantwide overhead rate method. (p. 739)

P2 Allocate overhead costs to products using the departmental overhead rate method. (p. 740)

P3 Allocate overhead costs to products using activity-based costing. (p. 744)

Decision Insight

Successful Brew

"It's just following your instincts, knowing the basics, and sticking with what's important."

—**KIM JORDAN**

FORT COLLINS, CO—Kim Jordan's entrepreneurial roots were anything but frothy. "For about eight months, we didn't pay ourselves," explains Kim. "We borrowed money from parents and made payroll . . . looking at the bills, we had to decide which to pay." From those meager beginnings, Kim created **New Belgium Brewing Company (NewBelgium.com),** which is committed to the Belgian brewing tradition of delicious beers with loads of character.

"We did have a set of values, a purpose, and some outcomes that we wanted to achieve," says Kim. "Four things were important to us: to produce world class Belgium-style beers, to promote beer culture, to be environmental stewards, and to have fun!" To achieve those goals, Kim set up an accounting system to measure, track, summarize, and report on operations. "It is important to have the ability to read financial statements, including product cost reports," insists Kim. With costly raw materials and overhead costs, understanding product cost reports helps Kim control her operations and make good decisions.

"There has to be execution," explains Kim. That focus on execution includes allocating overhead costs to different beers. In smaller businesses, a single plantwide overhead allocation rate is often sufficient. But as businesses grow and offer more diverse product lines, more sophisticated costing techniques are often needed. Activity-based costing (ABC) helps managers monitor and control overhead costs and ensure product quality. ABC is especially useful in companies like Kim's, where different products require different processes and varying levels of overhead. Traditional brews like Blue Paddle and Fat Tire can be made in large quantities in long production runs. Seasonal beers like Snow Day and Somersault, and specialty brews like Cocoa Mole Ale and Prickly Passion, are made in small batches. ABC helps in allocating overhead costs, such as product development, plant maintenance, and clean-up costs, to different products. "Our co-workers [all employees] get to see all of our financials!" Kim explains that this in turn helps shape the product cost reports for her business, including the control procedures applied in the brewery.

Kim's company is riding high with the right accounting systems and controls for long-run success. "Stasis is not an option," says Kim. "If we're all in the same place today that we were five years ago, that wouldn't be very interesting." Kim smiles and adds, "There's something wrong if making beer can't be fun!"

[Sources: *NewBelgium Website,* January 2013; *Entrepreneur,* November 2009; *50entrepreneurs.com,* March 2010; *CNNMoney.com,* June 2009; *Beverage World,* September 2009]

Chapter Preview

Prior chapters described costing systems used to assign costs to product units. This discussion emphasized the valuation of inventory and the cost of goods sold. Although the information from these prior costing systems conforms to generally accepted accounting principles (GAAP) for external reporting, it has limitations. This chapter introduces the activity-based costing (ABC) system, which is used by managers who desire more accurate product cost information.

Activity-Based Costing and Analysis

Assigning Overhead Costs

- Single plantwide overhead rate method
- Multiple departmental overhead rate method
- Activity-based costing rates and method

Applying Activity-Based Costing

- Step 1 Identify activities and their costs
- Step 2 Trace overhead costs to cost pools
- Step 3 Determine activity rates
- Step 4 Assign overhead costs to cost objects

Assessing Activity-Based Costing

- Advantages of activity-based costing
- Disadvantages of activity-based costing
- Activity-based costing for service providers
- Types of activities

ASSIGNING OVERHEAD COSTS

C1 Distinguish between the plantwide overhead rate method, the departmental overhead rate method, and the activity-based costing method.

Managerial activities such as product pricing, product mix decisions, and cost control depend on accurate product cost information. Distorted product cost information can result in poor decisions. Knowing accurate costs for producing, delivering, and servicing products helps managers set a price to cover product costs and yield a profit.

In competitive markets, price is established through the forces of supply and demand. In these situations, managers must understand product costs to assess whether the market price is high enough to justify the cost of entering the market. Disparities between market prices and producer costs give managers insight into their efficiency relative to competitors.

Product costs consist of direct materials, direct labor, and overhead (indirect costs). Since the physical components of a product (direct materials) and the work of making a product (direct labor) can be traced to units of output, the assignment of costs of these factors is usually straightforward. Overhead costs, however, are not directly related to production volume, and therefore cannot be traced to units of product in the same way that direct materials and direct labor can.

For example, we can trace the cost of putting tires on a car because we know there is a logical relation between the number of cars produced and the number of tires needed for each car. The cost to heat an automobile manufacturing factory, however, is not readily linked with the number of cars made. Consequently, we must use an allocation system to assign overhead costs such as utilities and factory maintenance. This chapter introduces three methods of overhead allocation: (1) the single plantwide overhead rate method, (2) the departmental overhead rate method, and (3) the activity-based costing method.

Point: Evidence suggests overhead costs have steadily increased while direct labor costs have steadily decreased as a percentage of total manufacturing costs over recent decades. This puts greater importance on accurate cost allocations.

Exhibit 17.1 summarizes some key features of these three alternative methods. Both the *plantwide overhead rate method* and the *departmental overhead rate method* use volume-based measures such as direct labor hours, direct labor dollars, or machine hours to allocate overhead costs to products. These methods differ in that the plantwide method uses a single rate for allocating overhead costs, and the departmental rate method uses at least two rates. The departmental method arguably provides more accurate cost allocations than the single rate allocations of the plantwide method. In contrast, *activity-based costing* focuses on activities and the costs of carrying out activities. Rates based on these activities are then used to assign overhead to products in proportion to the amount of activity required to produce them. Activity-based costing typically uses more overhead allocation rates than the plantwide and departmental methods.

EXHIBIT 17.1

Overhead Cost Allocation Methods

Method	Overhead Allocations Based on	Overhead Allocation Rates Based on
Plantwide rate	One rate	Volume-based measures such as direct labor hours or machine hours
Departmental rate	Two or more rates	Volume-based measures such as direct labor hours or machine hours
Activity-based costing	At least two (but often many) rates	Activities that drive costs, such as number of batches of product produced

Plantwide Overhead Rate Method

P1 Allocate overhead costs to products using the plantwide overhead rate method.

Cost Flows under Plantwide Overhead Rate Method The first method of allocating overhead costs to products is known as the *single plantwide overhead rate method,* or simply the *plantwide overhead rate method*. For this method, the target of the cost assignment, or **cost object,** is the unit of product—see Exhibit 17.2. The overhead rate is determined using volume-related measures such as direct labor hours, direct labor cost dollars, or machine hours, which are readily available in most manufacturing settings. In some industries, overhead costs are closely related to these volume-related measures. In such cases it is logical to use this method as a basis for assigning indirect manufacturing costs to products.

EXHIBIT 17.2

Plantwide Overhead Rate Method

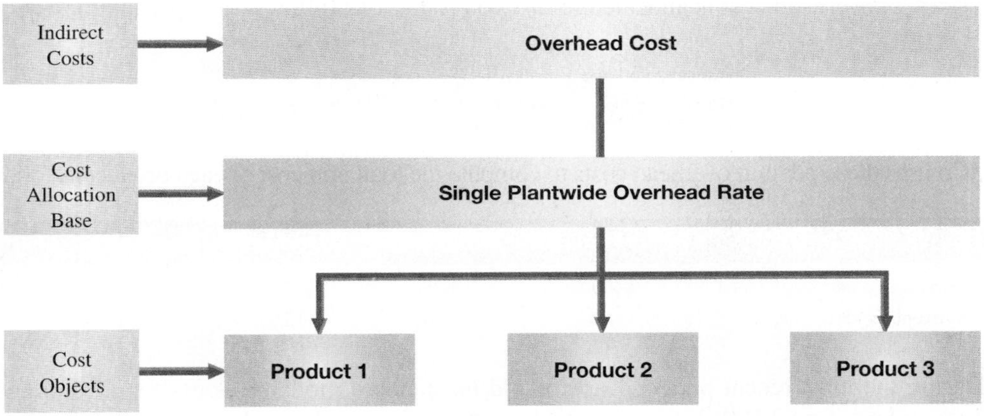

Applying the Plantwide Overhead Rate Method Under the single plantwide overhead rate method, total budgeted overhead costs are combined into one overhead cost pool. This cost pool is then divided by the chosen allocation base, such as total direct labor hours, to arrive at a single plantwide overhead rate. This rate then is applied to assign costs to all products based on the allocation base such as direct labor hours required to manufacture each product.

To illustrate, consider data from KartCo, a go-kart manufacturer that produces both standard and custom go-karts for amusement parks. The standard go-kart is a basic model sold primarily to amusement parks that service county and state fairs. Custom go-karts are produced for theme parks who want unique go-karts that coordinate with their respective themes.

Assume that KartCo applies the plantwide overhead rate method and uses direct labor hours (DLH) as its overhead allocation base. KartCo's budgeted DLH information is in Exhibit 17.3.

EXHIBIT 17.3

KartCo's Budgeted Direct Labor Hours

	Number of Units	Direct Labor Hours per Unit	Total Direct Labor Hours
Standard go-kart . . .	5,000	15	75,000
Custom go-kart	1,000	25	25,000
Total			100,000

KartCo's budgeted overhead cost information is in Exhibit 17.4. Its overhead cost consists of indirect labor and factory utilities.

EXHIBIT 17.4
KartCo's Budgeted Overhead Cost

Indirect labor cost	$4,000,000
Factory utilities	800,000
Total overhead cost	$4,800,000

The single plantwide overhead rate for KartCo is computed as follows.

$$\text{Plantwide overhead rate} = \text{Total budgeted overhead cost} \div \text{Total budgeted direct labor hours}$$
$$= \$4{,}800{,}000 \div 100{,}000 \text{ DLH}$$
$$= \$48 \text{ per DLH}$$

This plantwide overhead rate is then used to allocate overhead cost to products based on the number of direct labor hours required to produce each unit as follows.

Overhead allocated to each product unit = Plantwide overhead rate × DLH per unit

For KartCo, overhead cost is allocated to its two products as follows (on a per unit basis).

Standard go-kart:	$48 per DLH × 15 DLH = $ 720
Custom go-kart:	$48 per DLH × 25 DLH = $1,200

KartCo uses these per unit overhead costs to compute the total unit cost of each product as follows.

	Direct Materials	Direct Labor	Overhead	Total Cost per Unit
Standard go-kart	$400	$350	$ 720	$1,470
Custom go-kart	600	500	1,200	2,300

During the most recent period, KartCo sold its standard model go-karts for $2,000 and its custom go-karts for $3,500. A recent report from its marketing staff indicates that competitors are selling go-karts similar to KartCo's standard model for as low as $1,200. KartCo management believes it must be competitive, but management is concerned that meeting this lower price would result in a loss of $270 ($1,200 − $1,470) on each standard go-kart sold.

In the case of its custom go-kart, KartCo has been swamped with orders and is unable to meet demand. Accordingly, management is considering a change in strategy. Some discussion has ensued about dropping its standard model and concentrating on its custom model. Yet management recognizes that its pricing and cost decisions are influenced by its cost allocations. Thus, before making any strategic decisions, management has directed its cost analysts to further review production costs for both the standard and custom go-kart models. To pursue this analysis, the cost analysts first turned to the departmental rate method.

Departmental Overhead Rate Method

P2 Allocate overhead costs to products using the departmental overhead rate method.

Cost Flows under Departmental Overhead Rate Method Many companies have several departments that produce various products and consume overhead resources in substantially different ways. Under such circumstances, use of a single plantwide overhead rate can produce cost assignments that fail to accurately reflect the cost to manufacture a specific product. In these cases, use of multiple overhead rates can result in better overhead cost allocations and improve management decisions.

The *departmental overhead rate method* uses a different overhead rate for each production department. This is usually done through a two-stage assignment process, each with its different cost objects (target of cost assignment). In the first stage the departments are the cost objects and in the second stage the products are the cost objects (see Exhibit 17.5).

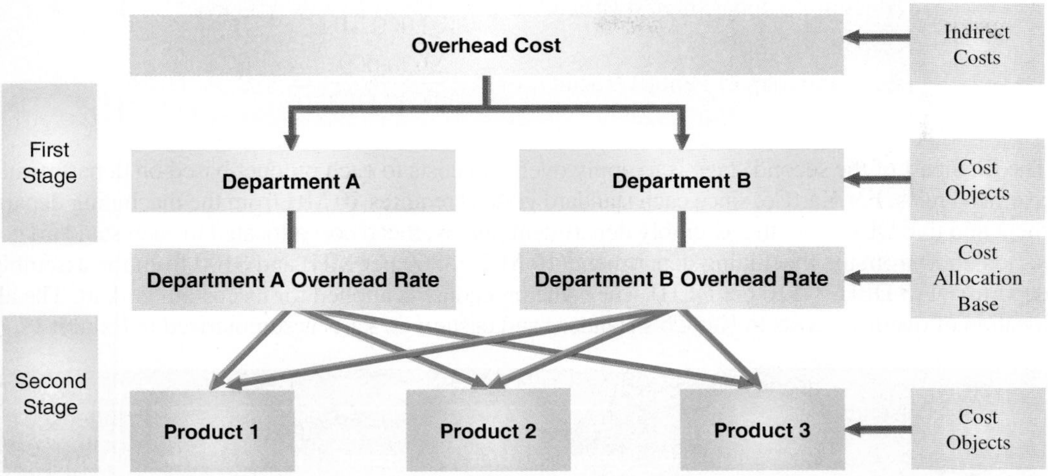

EXHIBIT 17.5

Departmental Overhead Rate Method

Exhibit 17.5 shows that under the departmental overhead rate method, overhead costs are first determined separately for each production department. Next, an overhead rate is computed for each production department to allocate the overhead costs of each department to products passing through that department. The departmental overhead rate method allows each department to have its own overhead rate and its own allocation base. For example, an assembly department can use direct labor hours to allocate its overhead cost while the machining department can use machine hours as its base.

Applying the Departmental Overhead Rate Method To illustrate the departmental overhead rate method, let's return to KartCo. KartCo has two production departments, the machining department and the assembly department. The first stage requires that KartCo assign its $4,800,000 overhead cost to its two production departments. KartCo determines from an analysis of its indirect labor and factory utilities that $4,200,000 of overhead costs are traceable to its machining department and the remaining $600,000 are traceable to its assembly department.

Point: In some cases it is difficult for companies to trace overhead costs to distinct departments as some overhead costs can be common to several departments. In these cases, companies must allocate overhead to departments applying reasonable allocation bases.

The second stage demands that after overhead costs are assigned to departments, each department determines an allocation base for its operations. For KartCo, the machining department uses machine hours (MH) as a base for allocating its overhead and the assembly department uses direct labor hours (DLH) as the base for allocating its overhead. Each machine is operated by a person, so that each machine hour also uses one direct labor hour. (With increased automation and the use of robots to perform manufacturing tasks, machine hours can differ from direct labor hours for many companies.) For this stage, the relevant information for KartCo's machining and assembly departments is in Exhibit 17.6.

EXHIBIT 17.6

Allocation Information for Machining and Assembly Departments

	Number of Units	Machining Department		Assembly Department	
		Hours per Unit	Total Hours	Hours per Unit	Total Hours
Standard go-kart	5,000	10 MH per unit	50,000 MH	5 DLH per unit	25,000 DLH
Custom go-kart	1,000	20 MH per unit	20,000 MH	5 DLH per unit	5,000 DLH
Totals			70,000 MH		30,000 DLH

Each department computes its own overhead rate using the following formula.

$$\text{Departmental overhead rate} = \frac{\text{Total departmental overhead cost}}{\text{Total units in departmental allocation base}}$$

For KartCo, its departmental overhead rates are computed as follows.

$$\text{Machining department overhead rate} = \frac{\$4{,}200{,}000}{70{,}000 \text{ MH}} = \$60 \text{ per MH}$$

$$\text{Assembly department overhead rate} = \frac{\$600{,}000}{30{,}000 \text{ DLH}} = \$20 \text{ per DLH}$$

The final part of the second stage is to apply overhead costs to each product based on departmental overhead rates. For KartCo, since each standard go-kart requires 10 MH from the machining department and five DLH from the assembly department, the overhead cost allocated to each standard go-kart is $600 from the machining department (10 MH × $60 per MH) and $100 from the assembly department (5 DLH × $20 per DLH). The same procedure is applied for its custom go-kart. The allocation of overhead costs to KartCo's standard and custom go-karts is summarized in Exhibit 17.7.

EXHIBIT 17.7

Overhead Allocation Using Departmental Overhead Rates

		Standard Go-Kart		Custom Go-Kart	
	Departmental Overhead Rate	Hours per Unit	Overhead Allocated	Hours per Unit	Overhead Allocated
Machining department	$60 per MH	10 MH per unit	$600	20 MH per unit	$1,200
Assembly department	$20 per DLH	5 DLH per unit	100	5 DLH per unit	100
Totals			$700		$1,300

Allocated overhead costs vary depending upon the allocation methods used. Exhibit 17.8 summarizes and compares the allocated overhead costs for standard and custom go-karts under the single plantwide overhead rate and the departmental overhead rate methods. The overhead cost allocated to each standard go-kart decreased from $720 under the plantwide overhead rate method to $700 under the departmental overhead rate method, whereas overhead cost allocated to each custom go-kart increased from $1,200 to $1,300. These differences occur because the custom go-kart requires more hours in the machining department (20 MH) than the standard go-kart requires (10 MH).

EXHIBIT 17.8

Comparison of Plantwide Overhead Rate and Departmental Overhead Rate Methods

Overhead per Unit Under:	Standard Go-Kart	Custom Go-Kart
Plantwide overhead rate method	$720	$1,200
Departmental overhead rate method.........	$700	$1,300

Compared to the plantwide overhead rate method, the departmental overhead rate method usually results in more accurate overhead allocations. When cost analysts are able to logically trace costs to cost objects, costing accuracy is improved. For KartCo, costs are traced to departments and then assigned to units based on how long they spend in each department. The single plantwide overhead rate of $48 per hour is a combination of the $60 per hour machining department rate and the $20 per hour assembly department rate.

For KartCo, using the multiple departmental overhead rate method yields the following total costs for its products.

	Direct Materials	Direct Labor	Overhead	Total Cost per Unit
Standard go-kart..........	$400	$350	$ 700	$1,450
Custom go-kart	600	500	1,300	2,400

These costs per unit under the departmental overhead rate method are different from those under the plantwide overhead rate method. Further, this information suggests that KartCo management seriously review future production for its standard go-kart product. Specifically, these cost data imply that KartCo cannot make a profit on its standard go-kart if it meets competitors' $1,200 price.

Assessing the Plantwide and Departmental Overhead Rate Methods The plantwide and departmental overhead rate methods have three key advantages: (1) They are based on readily available information, like direct labor hours. (2) They are easy to implement. (3) They are consistent with GAAP and can be used for external reporting needs. Both suffer from an important disadvantage, in that overhead costs are frequently too complex to be explained by one factor like direct labor hours or machine hours. Further, technological advances often lower direct labor costs as a percentage of total manufacturing costs. (In some companies, direct labor cost is such a small part of total cost that it is treated as overhead.)

A1 Identify and assess advantages and disadvantages of the plantwide overhead and departmental overhead rate methods.

The usefulness of overhead allocations based on the single plantwide overhead rate for managerial decisions depends on two critical assumptions: (1) overhead costs change with the allocation base (such as direct labor hours); and (2) all products use overhead costs in the same proportions.

The reasonableness of these assumptions varies. For companies that manufacture few products or whose operations are labor-intensive, the single plantwide method can yield reasonably useful information for managerial decisions. However, for companies with many different products or those with products that use overhead costs in very different ways, the assumptions of the single plantwide rate are not reasonable. When overhead costs, like machinery depreciation, bear little if any relation to direct labor hours used, allocating overhead cost using a single plantwide overhead rate based on direct labor hours can distort product cost and lead to poor managerial decisions. Despite such shortcomings, some companies continue to use the plantwide method for its simplicity.

The departmental overhead rate method is more refined than the plantwide overhead rate method, but it too has limitations that can distort product costs. The departmental overhead rate method assumes that different products are similar in volume, complexity, and batch size, and that departmental overhead costs are directly proportional to the department allocation base (such as direct labor hours and machine hours for KartCo). When products differ in batch size and complexity, they usually consume different amounts of overhead costs. This is likely the case for KartCo with its high-volume standard model and its low-volume custom model built to customer specifications. In addition, since the departmental overhead rate method still allocates overhead costs based on measures closely related to production volume, it also fails to accurately assign many overhead costs, like machine depreciation or utility costs, that are not driven by production volume.

The next section describes the activity-based costing method, which is designed to overcome some of the limitations of the plantwide and departmental overhead rate methods.

Decision Ethics

Department Manager Three department managers jointly decide to hire a consulting firm for advice on increasing departmental effectiveness and efficiency. The consulting firm spends 50% of its efforts on department "A" and 25% on each of the other two departments. The manager for department "A" suggests that the three departments equally share the consulting fee. As a manager of one of the other two departments, do you believe equal sharing is fair? ■ [Answer—p. 756]

Activity-Based Costing Rates and Method

Cost Flows under Activity-Based Costing Method **Activity-based costing (ABC)** attempts to more accurately assign overhead costs to the users of overhead by focusing on *activities*. The basic principle underlying activity-based costing is that an **activity,** which is a task, operation, or procedure, is what causes costs to be incurred. For example, cutting raw materials consumes labor and machine hours. Likewise, warehousing products consumes resources (costs) such as employee time for driving a forklift, the electricity to power the forklift, and the wear and tear on a forklift. Also, training employees drives costs such as fees or salaries paid to trainers and the training supplies required. Generally, all activities of an organization can be linked to use of resources. An **activity cost pool** is a collection of costs that are related to the same or similar activity. Pooling costs to determine an **activity overhead (pool) rate** for all costs incurred by the same activity reduces the number of cost assignments required.

C2 Explain cost flows for activity-based costing.

There are two basic stages to ABC as shown in Exhibit 17.9. The first stage of ABC cost assignment is to identify the activities (cost objects) involved in manufacturing products and match those activities with the costs they cause (drive). To reduce the total number of activities

EXHIBIT 17.9
Activity-Based Costing Method

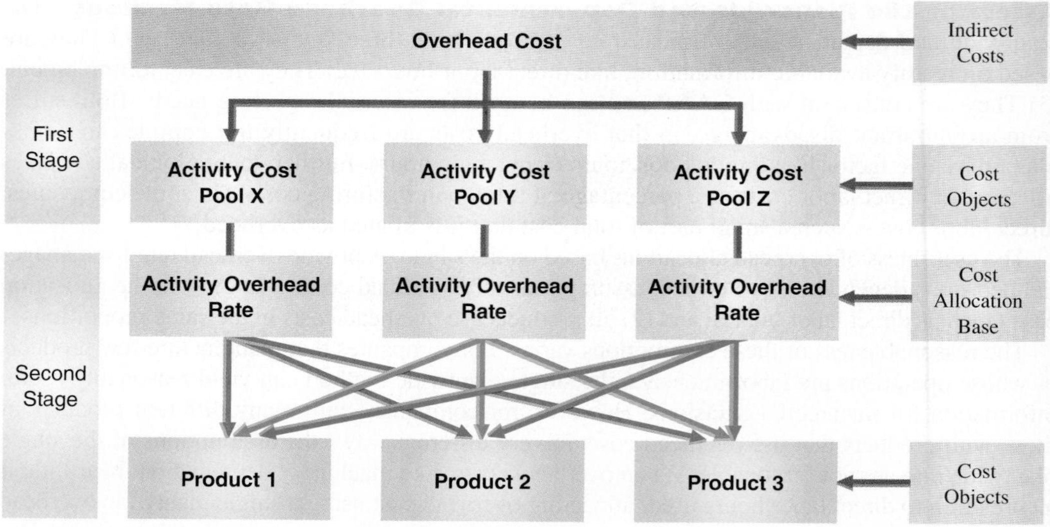

Point: Homogeneous means similar.

that must be assigned costs, the homogeneous activities (those caused by the same factor such as cutting metal) are grouped into activity cost *pools*. The second stage of ABC is to compute an activity rate for each cost pool and then use this rate to allocate overhead costs to products, which are the cost objects of this second stage. ABC is like the departmental method in that it uses more than one overhead rate. It differs from the departmental method in that it focuses on activities rather than departments.

Quick Check Answers — p. 757

1. Which method of cost assignment requires more than one overhead rate? (a) Plantwide overhead rate method (b) Departmental overhead rate method (c) ABC (d) Both *b* and *c*.
2. Which method of overhead costing is the most accurate when products use overhead costs in different proportions? (a) Departmental overhead rate method (b) Plantwide overhead rate method.
3. ABC assumes that costs are incurred because of what? (a) Management decisions (b) Activities (c) Financial transactions.

APPLYING ACTIVITY-BASED COSTING

Activity-based costing accumulates overhead costs into activity cost pools and then uses activity rates to allocate those costs to products. This involves four steps: (1) identify activities and the costs they cause; (2) group similar activities into activity cost pools; (3) determine an activity rate for each activity cost pool; and (4) allocate overhead costs to products using those activity rates. To illustrate, let's return to KartCo and apply steps 1 through 4.

Step 1: Identify Activities and the Costs They Cause

Step 1 in applying ABC is to identify activities and the costs they cause. This is commonly done through discussions with employees in production departments and through reviews of production activities. The more activities that ABC tracks, the more accurately overhead costs are assigned. However, tracking too many activities makes the system cumbersome and costly to maintain. Consequently, we try to reach a balance where it is often necessary to reduce the number of activities tracked by combining similar activities. An activity can also involve several related tasks. The aim of this first step is to understand actions performed in the organization that drive costs.

KartCo has total overhead cost of $4,800,000 consisting of $4,000,000 indirect labor costs and $800,000 factory utilities costs. Details gathered by KartCo about its overhead costs are shown in Exhibit 17.10. Column totals for indirect labor and factory utilities correspond to amounts in Exhibit 17.4. Activity-based costing provides more detail about the activities and the costs they cause than is provided from traditional costing methods.

P3 Allocate overhead costs to products using activity-based costing.

EXHIBIT 17.10

KartCo Overhead Cost Details

Activity	Indirect Labor	Factory Utilities	Total Overhead
Machine setup	$ 700,000	—	$ 700,000
Machine repair	1,300,000	—	1,300,000
Factory maintenance	800,000	—	800,000
Engineer salaries	1,200,000	—	1,200,000
Assembly line power	—	$600,000	600,000
Heating and lighting	—	200,000	200,000
Totals	$4,000,000	$800,000	$4,800,000

Decision Maker

Cost Analyst Your employer is exploring the possibility of implementing an activity-based costing system in the plant where you are newly assigned as a cost analyst. Your responsibilities are to identify manufacturing activities and link them to the costs they drive. You have never worked in this type of manufacturing operation and you are unsure about what activities are performed and their costs. What steps should you pursue to yield a quality report? ■ [Answer—p. 756]

Step 2: Trace Overhead Costs to Cost Pools

Step 2 in applying ABC is to assign activities and their overhead costs to cost pools. Overhead costs are commonly accumulated by each department in a traditional accounting system. Some of these overhead costs are traced directly to a specific activity cost pool. At KartCo, for example, the assembly department supervisor's salary is assigned to its design modification cost pool and its machine repair costs are traced to its setup cost pool. Companies try to trace as many overhead costs to specific activity cost pools as possible to improve costing accuracy.

Recall that a premise of ABC is that operations are a series of activities that cause costs to be incurred. Instead of combining costs from different activities into one plantwide pool or multiple departmental pools, ABC focuses on activities as the cost object in the first step of cost assignment. We are then able to *trace* costs to a cost object and then combine activities that are used by products in similar ways to reduce the number of cost allocations.

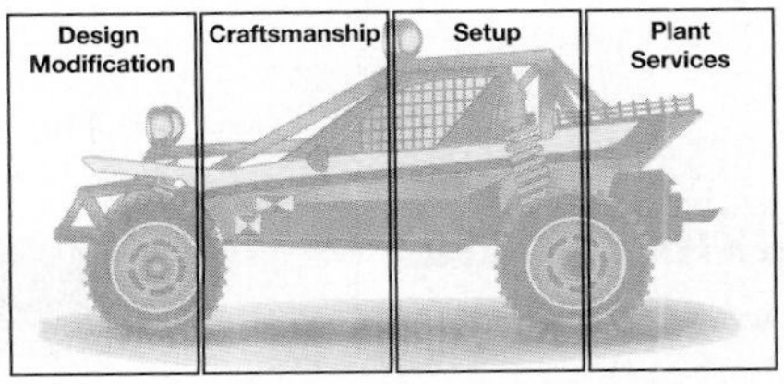

After a review and analysis of its activities, KartCo management assigns its overhead costs into its four activity cost pools as shown in Exhibit 17.11. To assign costs to pools, management looks for costs that are caused by the activities of that pool and activity level. It is crucial that activities in each cost pool be similar and reflect a similar activity level.

EXHIBIT 17.11

Assigning Overhead to Activity Cost Pools

Activity Pools	Activity Cost	Pool Cost
Craftsmanship		
Assembly line power	$ 600,000	$ 600,000
Setup		
Machine setup	700,000	
Machine repair	1,300,000	2,000,000
Design modification		
Engineer salaries	1,200,000	1,200,000
Plant services		
Factory maintenance	800,000	
Heating and lighting	200,000	1,000,000
Total overhead cost		$4,800,000

Exhibit 17.11 shows that $600,000 of overhead costs are assigned to the craftsmanship cost pool; $2,000,000 to the setup cost pool; $1,200,000 to the design-modification cost pool; and $1,000,000 to the plant services cost pool. This reduces the potential number of overhead rates from six (one for each of its six activities) to four (one for each activity pool).

Step 3: Determine Activity Rates

Step 3 is to compute activity rates used to assign overhead costs to final cost objects such as products. Proper determination of activity rates depends on (1) proper identification of the factor that drives the cost in each activity cost pool and (2) proper measures of activities.

The factor that drives cost, or **activity cost driver,** is that activity causing costs in the pool to be incurred. For KartCo's overhead, craftsmanship costs are mainly driven (caused) by assembling products, setup costs are driven by system repairs and retooling, design-modification costs are driven by new features, and plant service costs are driven by building occupancy. The activity cost driver, a measure of activity level, serves as the allocation base. KartCo uses the following activity drivers and expected activity levels for its activity pools.

Activity Pool	Activity Driver (# of)	Expected Activity Level
Craftsmanship	Direct labor hours	30,000 DLH
Setup	Batches	200 batches
Design modification.	Designs	10 design modifications
Plant services	Square feet	20,000 square feet

In general, cost pool activity rates are computed as:

Cost pool activity rate = Overhead costs assigned to pool ÷ Number of activities

For KartCo, the activity rate for the craftsmanship cost pool is computed as:

Craftsmanship cost pool activity rate = $600,000 ÷ 30,000 DLH = $20 per DLH

The activity rate computations for KartCo are summarized in Exhibit 17.12.

EXHIBIT 17.12

Activity Rates for KartCo

Activity Cost Pools	Activity Measure Chosen	Overhead Costs Assigned to Pool	÷	Number of Activities	=	Activity Rate
Craftsmanship	DLH	$ 600,000		30,000 DLH		$20 per DLH
Setup	Batches	2,000,000		200 batches		$10,000 per batch
Design modification	Number of designs	1,200,000		10 designs		$120,000 per design
Plant services	Square feet	1,000,000		20,000 sq. ft.		$50 per sq. ft.

Step 4: Assign Overhead Costs to Cost Objects

Step 4 is to assign overhead costs in each activity cost pool to final cost objects using activity rates. (This is referred to as the *second-stage assignment;* where steps 1 through 3 make up the *first-stage assignment.*) To accomplish this, overhead costs in each activity cost pool are allocated to product lines based on the level of activity for each product line. After costs in all cost pools are allocated, the costs for each product line are totaled and then divided by the number of units of that product line to arrive at overhead cost per product unit.

For KartCo, overhead costs in each pool are allocated to the standard go-karts and the custom go-karts using the activity rates from Exhibit 17.12. The activities used by each product line and the overhead costs allocated to standard and custom go-karts under ABC for KartCo are summarized in Exhibit 17.13. To illustrate, of the $600,000 of overhead costs in the craftsmanship cost pool, $500,000 is allocated to standard go-karts as follows.

Overhead from craftsmanship pool allocated to standard go-kart	**= Activities consumed**	**× Activity rate**	
	= 25,000 DLH	**× $20 per DLH**	**= $500,000**

We know that standard go-karts require 25,000 direct labor hours and the activity rate for craftsmanship is $20 per direct labor hour. Multiplying the number of direct labor hours by the activity rate yields the craftsmanship costs assigned to standard go-karts. Custom go-karts consumed 5,000 direct labor hours, so we assign $100,000 (5,000 DLH × $20 per DLH) to that product line. We similarly allocate overhead to setup, design modification, and plant services pools for each type of go-kart.

EXHIBIT 17.13

Overhead Allocated to Go-Karts for KartCo

	Standard Go-Karts			Custom Go-Karts		
	Activities Consumed	Activity Rate	Activity Cost Allocated	Activities Consumed	Activity Rate	Activity Cost Allocated
Craftsmanship	25,000 DLH	$20 per DLH	$ 500,000	5,000 DLH	$20 per DLH	$ 100,000
Setup	40 batches	$10,000 per batch	400,000	160 batches	$10,000 per batch	1,600,000
Design modification	0 designs	$120,000 per design	0	10 designs	$120,000 per design	1,200,000
Plant services	12,000 sq. ft.	$50 per sq. ft.	600,000	8,000 sq. ft.	$50 per sq. ft.	400,000
Total cost			$1,500,000			$3,300,000

In assigning overhead costs to products, KartCo assigned no design modification costs to standard go-karts because standard go-karts are sold as "off-the-shelf" items.

Overhead cost per unit is computed by dividing total overhead cost allocated to each product line by the number of product units. KartCo's overhead cost per unit for its standard and custom go-karts is computed and shown in Exhibit 17.14.

EXHIBIT 17.14

Overhead Cost per Unit for Go-Karts Using ABC

	(A) Total Overhead Cost Allocated	(B) Budgeted Units of Production	(A ÷ B) Overhead Cost per Unit
Standard go-kart	$1,500,000	5,000 units	$ 300 per unit
Custom go-kart	3,300,000	1,000 units	$3,300 per unit

Total cost per unit for KartCo using ABC for its two products follows.

	Direct Materials	Direct Labor	Overhead	Total Cost per Unit
Standard go-kart . . .	$400	$350	$ 300	$1,050
Custom go-kart	600	500	3,300	4,400

Assuming that ABC more accurately assigns costs, we now are able to help KartCo's management understand how its competitors can sell their standard models at $1,200 and why KartCo is flooded with orders for custom go-karts. Specifically, if the cost to produce a standard go-kart is $1,050, as shown above (and not $1,470 as computed using the plantwide rate or $1,450 computed using departmental rates), a profit of $150 ($1,200 − $1,050) occurs on each standard unit sold at the competitive $1,200 market price. Further, selling its custom go-kart at $3,500 is a mistake by KartCo management because it is losing $900 ($3,500 − $4,400) on each custom go-kart sold. That is, KartCo has underpriced its custom go-kart relative to its production costs and competitors' prices, which explains why the company has more custom orders than it can supply.

Point: Accurately assigning costs to products is key to setting many product prices. If product costs are inaccurate and result in prices that are too low, the company loses money on each item sold. Likewise, if product prices are improperly set too high, the company loses business to competitors. ABC can be used to more accurately set prices.

Overhead allocation per go-kart under the single plantwide rate method, multiple departmental rate method, and ABC is summarized in Exhibit 17.15. Overhead cost allocated to standard

EXHIBIT 17.15

Comparison of Overhead Allocations by Method

Overhead Cost Allocation Method	Overhead Cost per Go-Kart	
	Standard Go-Kart	Custom Go-Kart
Plantwide method	$720	$1,200
Departmental method	700	1,300
Activity-based costing	300	3,300

go-karts is much less under ABC than under either of the volume-based costing methods. One reason for this difference is the large design modification costs that were spread over all go-karts under both the plantwide rate and the departmental rate methods even though standard go-karts require no engineering modification. When ABC is used, overhead costs commonly shift from standardized, large-volume products to low-volume, customized specialty products that consume disproportionate resources.

Differences between ABC and Multiple Departmental Rates Using ABC differs from using multiple departmental rates in how overhead cost pools are identified and in how overhead cost in each pool is allocated. When using multiple departmental rates, each department is a cost pool, and overhead cost allocated to each department is assigned to products using a volume-based factor (such as direct labor hours or machine hours). This assumes that overhead costs in each department are directly proportional to the volume-based factor. ABC, on the other hand, recognizes that overhead costs are more complex. For example, purchasing costs might make up one activity cost pool (spanning more than one department) that would include activities such as the number of invoices. ABC emphasizes activities and costs of carrying out these activities. Under ABC, only costs related to the same activity are grouped into a cost pool. Therefore, ABC arguably better reflects the complex nature of overhead costs and how these costs are used in making products.

Decision Maker

Entrepreneur You are the entrepreneur of a start-up pharmaceutical company. You are assigning overhead to product units based on machine hours in the packaging area. Profits are slim due to increased competition. One of your larger overhead costs is $10,000 for cleaning and sterilization that occurs each time the packaging system is converted from one product to another. These overhead costs average $0.10 per product unit. Can you reduce cleaning and sterilizing costs by reducing the number of units produced? If not, what should you do to control these overhead costs? ■ [Answer—p. 757]

Quick Check

Answers — p. 757

4. What is a cost driver? Provide an example of a typical cost driver.
5. What is an activity driver? Provide an example of a typical activity driver.
6. Traditional volume-based costing methods tend to: (a) overstate the cost of low-volume products, (b) overstate the cost of high-volume products, or (c) both a and b.

ASSESSING ACTIVITY-BASED COSTING

A2 Identify and assess advantages and disadvantages of activity-based costing.

While activity-based costing improves the accuracy of overhead cost allocations to products, it too has limitations. This section describes the major advantages and disadvantages of activity-based costing.

Advantages of Activity-Based Costing

More Accurate Overhead Cost Allocation Companies have typically used either a plantwide overhead rate or multiple departmental overhead rates because these methods are more straightforward than ABC and are acceptable under GAAP for external reporting. Under these traditional systems, overhead costs are pooled in a few large pools and are spread uniformly across high- and low-volume products. With ABC, overhead costs are grouped into activity pools. There are usually more activity pools under ABC than cost pools under traditional costing, which usually increases costing accuracy. More important is that overhead costs in each ABC pool are caused by a single activity. This means that overhead costs in each activity pool are allocated to products based on the cost of resources consumed by a product (input) rather than on how many units are produced (output). In sum, overhead cost allocation under ABC is more accurate because (1) there are more cost pools, (2) costs in each pool are more similar, and (3) allocation is based on activities that cause overhead costs.

Point: ABC can allocate the selling and administrative costs expensed by GAAP to activities; such costs can include marketing costs, costs to process orders, and costs to process customer returns.

More Effective Overhead Cost Control In traditional costing, overhead costs are usually allocated to products based on either direct labor hours or machine hours. Such allocation typically leads management to focus attention on direct labor cost or machine hours. Yet, direct labor or machine hours are often not the cause of overhead costs and often not even linked with these volume-related measures. As we saw with KartCo, design modifications markedly affect its overhead costs. Consequently, a plantwide overhead rate or departmental overhead rate based on direct labor or machine hours can mislead managers, preventing effective control of overhead costs and leading to product mispricing. ABC, on the other hand, can be used to identify activities that can benefit from process improvement. ABC can also help managers effectively control overhead cost by focusing on processes or activities such as batching setups, order processing, and design modifications instead of focusing only on direct labor or machine hours. For KartCo, identification of large design-modification costs would allow managers to work on initiatives to improve this process. Besides controlling overhead costs, KartCo's better assignment of overhead costs (particularly design-modification costs) for its go-karts helps its managers make better production and pricing decisions.

Focus on Relevant Factors Basing cost assignment on activities is not limited to determining product costs, as illustrated by KartCo. ABC can be used to assign costs to any cost object that is of management interest. For instance, a marketing manager often wants to determine the profitability of various market segments. Activity-based costing can be used to accurately assign costs of shipping, advertising, order-taking, and customer service that are unrelated to sales and costs of products sold. Such an activity-based analysis can reveal to the marketing department some customers that are better left to the competition if they consume a larger amount of marketing resources than the gross profit generated by sales to those customers. Generally, ABC provides better customer profitability information by including all resources consumed to serve a customer. This allows managers to make better pricing decisions on custom orders and to better manage customers by focusing on those that are most profitable.

Better Management of Activities Being competitive requires that managers be able to use resources efficiently. Understanding how costs are incurred is a first step toward controlling costs. One important contribution of ABC is helping managers identify the causes of costs, that is, the activities driving them. **Activity-based management (ABM)** is an outgrowth of ABC that draws on the link between activities and cost incurrence for better management. Activity-based management can be useful in distinguishing **value-added activities,** which add value to a product, from *non-value-added activities,* which do not. For KartCo, its value-added activities include machining, assembly, and the costs of engineering design changes. Its non-value-added activity is machine repair. The way to control a cost requires changing how much of an activity is performed.

Decision Insight

The ABC's of Decisions Business managers must make long-term strategic decisions, day-to-day operating decisions, and decisions on the type of financing the business needs. Survey evidence suggests that managers find ABC more useful in making strategic, operating, and financing decisions than non-ABC methods. ■

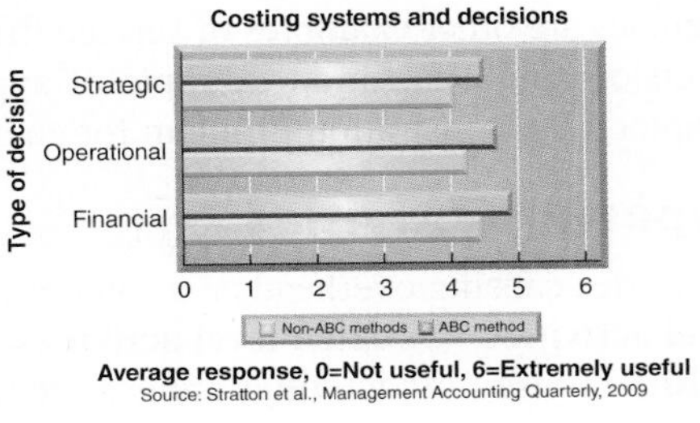

Costs of Quality A focus on the costs of activities, via ABC and ABM, lends itself to assessments of the **costs of quality.** These costs refer to costs resulting from manufacturing defective products or providing services that do not meet customer expectations. Exhibit 17.16 summarizes the typical costs of quality.

EXHIBIT 17.16

Types of Quality Costs

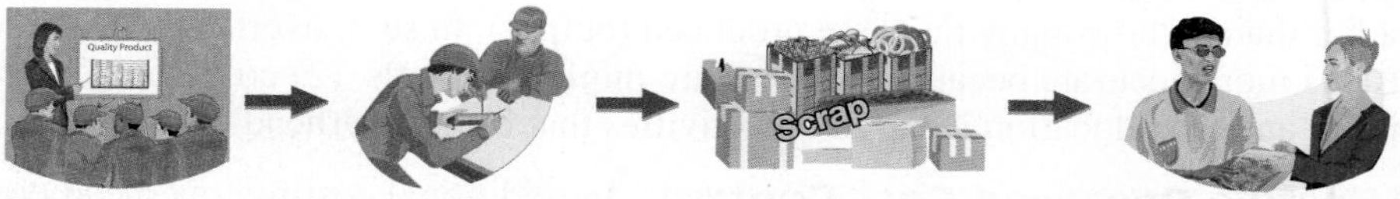

Prevention and appraisal costs are incurred before a good or service is provided to a customer. The purpose of these costs is to reduce the chance the customer is provided a defective good or service. Prevention activities focus on quality training and improvement programs to ensure quality is built into the product or service. Common appraisal costs include the costs of inspections to ensure that materials and supplies meet specifications and inspections of finished goods.

Internal failure costs are incurred after a company has manufactured a defective product but before that product has been delivered to a customer. Internal failure costs include the costs of reworking products, reinspecting reworked products, and scrap.

Finally, external failure costs are incurred after a customer has been provided a defective product or service. Examples of this type of costs include costs of warranty repairs and costs of recalling products. A focus on activities and quality costs can lead to higher quality and lower costs.

Disadvantages of Activity-Based Costing

Costs to Implement and Maintain ABC Designing and implementing an activity-based costing system requires management commitment and financial resources. For ABC to be effective, a thorough analysis of cost activities must be performed and appropriate cost pools must be determined. Collecting and analyzing cost data are expensive and so is maintaining an ABC system. While technology, such as bar coding, has made it possible for many companies to use ABC, it is still too costly for some. Managers must weigh the cost of implementing and maintaining an ABC system against the potential benefits of ABC in light of company circumstances.

Uncertainty with Decisions Remains As with all cost information, managers must interpret ABC data with caution in making managerial decisions. In the KartCo case, given the huge design-modification costs for custom go-karts determined under the ABC system, a manager might be tempted to decline some custom go-kart orders to save overhead costs. However, in the short run, some or all of the design-modification costs cannot be saved even if some custom go-kart orders are rejected. Managers must examine carefully the controllability of costs before making decisions.

ABC for Service Providers

While we showed how to use ABC in a manufacturing setting, ABC also applies to service providers. The only requirements for ABC are the existence of costs and demand for reliable cost information. A study found that ABC improves health care costing accuracy, enabling improved profitability analysis and decision making. Likewise, **First Tennessee National Corporation,** a bank, applied ABC and found that 30% of its certificate of deposit (CD) customers provided nearly 90% of its profits from CDs. Further, 30% of the bank's CD customers were actually losing money for the bank. The bank's management used ABC to correct the problem and increase profits. Laboratories performing medical tests, accounting and law offices, and advertising agencies are other examples of service firms that can benefit from ABC. (Refer to this chapter's Decision Analysis for an example of applying ABC to assess customer profitability and this chapter's Demonstration Problem for an example of applying ABC to a law firm.)

Types of Activities

C3 Describe the four types of activities that cause overhead costs.

Activities causing overhead cost can be separated into four levels of types of activities: (1) **unit level activities,** (2) **batch level activities,** (3) **product level activities,** and (4) **facility level activities.** These four activities are described as follows.

Activity Levels

Unit level activities are performed on each product unit. For example, the machining department needs electricity to power the machinery to produce each unit of product. Unit level costs tend to change with the number of units produced.

Batch level activities are performed only on each batch or group of units. For example, machine setup is needed only for each batch regardless of the units in that batch, and customer order processing must be performed for each order regardless of the number of units ordered. Batch level costs do not vary with the number of units, but instead with the number of batches.

Product level activities are performed on each product line and are not affected by either the numbers of units or batches. For example, product design is needed only for each product line. Product level costs do not vary with the number of units or batches produced.

Facility level activities are performed to sustain facility capacity as a whole and are not caused by any specific product. For example, rent and factory maintenance costs are incurred no matter what is being produced. Facility level costs do not vary with what is manufactured, how many batches are produced, or the output quantity.

In the KartCo example, the craftsmanship pool reflects unit level costs, the setup pool reflects batch level costs, the design-modification pool reflects product level costs, and plant services reflect facility level costs.

Additional examples of activities commonly found within each of the four activity levels are shown in the following table. This is not a complete list, but reviewing it can help in understanding this hierarchy of production activities. This list also includes common measures used to reflect the specific activity identified. Knowing this hierarchy can help us simplify and understand activity-based costing.

Activity Level	Examples of Activity	Activity Driver (Measure)
Unit level	Cutting parts	Machine hours
	Assembling components	Direct labor hours
	Printing checks	Number of checks
Batch level	Calibrating machines	Number of batches
	Receiving shipments	Number of orders
	Sampling product quality	Number of lots produced
Product level	Designing modifications	Change requests
	Organizing production	Engineering hours
	Controlling inventory	Parts per product
Facility level	Cleaning workplace	Square feet of floors*
	Providing electricity	Kilowatt hours*
	Providing personnel support	Number of employees*

* Facility level costs are not traceable to individual product lines, batches, or units. They are normally assigned to units using a unit-level driver such as direct labor hours or machine hours even though they are caused by another activity.

Quick Check Answers — p. 757

7. What are three advantages of ABC over traditional volume-based allocation methods?
8. What is the main advantage of traditional volume-based allocation methods compared to activity-based costing? How should a manager decide which method to use?

GLOBAL VIEW

Toyota Motor Corporation pioneered *lean manufacturing,* which focuses on eliminating waste while satisfying customers. Many lean manufacturers embrace **lean accounting,** which has two key components. First, the company applies lean thinking to eliminate waste in its accounting process. Second, instead of focusing on cost allocation methods such as activity-based costing, the company develops alternative performance measures that better reflect the benefits of manufacturing process changes. Examples include the percentage of products produced without defects, the percentage of ontime deliveries, and the level of sales per employee.

Decision Analysis — Customer Profitability

Are all customers equal? To help answer this, let's return to the KartCo case and assume that costs of providing customer support (such as delivery, installation, and warranty work) are related to the distance a technician must travel to provide services. Also assume that, as a result of applying activity-based costing, KartCo plans to sell its standard go-kart for $1,200 per unit. If the annual cost of customer services is expected to be $250,000 and the distance traveled by technicians is 100,000 miles annually, KartCo would want to link the cost of customer services with individual customers to make efficient marketing decisions.

Using these data, an activity rate of $2.50 per mile ($250,000/100,000 miles) is computed for assigning customer service costs to individual customers. For KartCo, it would compute a typical customer profitability report for one of its customers, Six Flags, as follows.

Customer Profitability Report—Six Flags

Sales (10 standard go-karts × $1,200)		$12,000
Less: Product costs		
Direct materials (10 go-karts × $400 per go-kart)	$4,000	
Direct labor (10 go-karts × $350 per go-kart)	3,500	
Overhead (10 go-karts × $300 per go-kart, Exhibit 17.14)	3,000	10,500
Product profit margin		1,500
Less: Customer service costs (200 miles × $2.50 per mile)		500
Customer profit margin		$ 1,000

Analysis indicates that a total profit margin of $1,000 is generated from this customer. The management of KartCo can see that if this customer requires service technicians to travel more than 600 miles ($1,500 ÷ $2.50 per mile), the sale of 10 standard go-karts to this customer would be unprofitable. ABC encourages management to consider all resources consumed to serve a customer, not just manufacturing costs that are the focus of traditional costing methods.

DEMONSTRATION PROBLEM

Silver Law Firm provides litigation and mediation services to a variety of clients. Attorneys keep track of the time they spend on each case, which is used to charge fees to clients at a rate of $300 per hour. A management advisor commented that activity-based costing might prove useful in evaluating the costs of its legal services, and the firm has decided to evaluate its fee structure by comparing ABC to its alternative cost allocations. The following data relate to a typical month at the firm. During a typical month the firm handles seven mediation cases and three litigation cases.

	Activity Driver	Total Amount	Consumption by Service Type: Litigation	Consumption by Service Type: Mediation	Activity Cost
Providing legal advice	Billable hours	200	75	125	$30,000
Overhead costs					
Internal support departments					
Preparing documents	Documents	30	16	14	$ 4,000
Occupying office space	Billable hours	200	75	125	1,200
Heating and lighting of office	Billable hours	200	75	125	350
External support departments					
Registering court documents	Documents	30	16	14	1,250
Retaining consultants (investigators, psychiatrists)	Court dates	6	5	1	10,000
Using contract services (couriers, security guards)	Court dates	6	5	1	5,000
Total overhead costs					$21,800

Required

1. Determine the cost of providing legal services to each type of case using activity-based costing (ABC).
2. Determine the cost of each type of case using a single plantwide rate for nonattorney costs based on billable hours.
3. Determine the cost of each type of case using multiple departmental overhead rates for the internal support department (based on number of documents) and external support department (based on billable hours).
4. Compare and discuss the costs assigned under each method for management decisions.

PLANNING THE SOLUTION

- Compute pool rates and assign costs to cases using ABC.
- Compute costs for the cases using the volume-based methods and discuss differences between these costs and the costs computed using ABC.

SOLUTION TO DEMONSTRATION PROBLEM

1. We need to set up activity pools and compute pool rates for ABC. All activities except "occupying office space" and "heating and lighting" are unit level (meaning they are traceable to the individual cases handled by the law firm). "Preparing documents" and "registering documents" are both driven by the number of documents associated with each case. We can therefore combine these activities and their costs into a single pool, which we call "clerical support." Similarly, "retaining consultants" and "using services" are related to the number of times the attorneys must go to court (court dates). We combine these activities and their costs into another activity cost pool labeled "litigation support." The costs associated with occupying office space and the heating and lighting are facility level activities and are not traceable to individual cases. Yet they are costs that must be covered by fees charged to clients. We assign these costs using a convenient base—in this example we use the number of billable hours, which attorneys record for each client. Providing legal advice is the direct labor for a law firm.

Activity Pool	Activity Cost	Pool Cost	Activity Driver	Pool Rate (Pool Cost ÷ Activity Driver)
Providing legal advice	$30,000	$30,000	200 billable hours	$150 per billable hour
Clerical support				
Preparing documents	4,000			
Registering documents	1,250	5,250	30 documents	$175 per document
Litigation support				
Retaining consultants	10,000			
Using services	5,000	15,000	6 court dates	$2,500 per court date
Facility costs				
Occupying office space	1,200			
Heating and lighting	350	1,550	200 billable hours	$7.75 per billable hour

We next determine the cost of providing each type of legal service as shown in the following table. Specifically, the pool rates from above are used to assign costs to each type of service provided by the law firm. Since litigation consumed 75 billable hours of attorney time, we assign $11,250 (75 billable hours × $150 per billable hour) of the cost of providing legal advice to this type of case. Mediation required 125 hours of attorney time, so $18,750 (125 billable hours × $150 per billable hour) of the cost to provide legal advice is assigned to mediation cases. Clerical support cost $175 per document, so the costs associated with activities in this cost pool are assigned to litigation cases (16 documents × $175 per document = $2,800) and mediation cases (14 documents × $175 per document = $2,450). The costs of activities in the litigation support and the facility cost pools are similarly assigned to the two case types.

We compute the total cost of litigation ($27,131.25) and mediation ($24,668.75) and divide these totals by the number of cases of each type to determine the average cost of each case type: $9,044 for litigation and $3,524 for mediation. This analysis shows that charging clients $300 per billable hour without regard to the type of case results in litigation clients being charged less than the cost to provide that service ($7,500 versus $9,044).

	Pool Rate	Litigation		Mediation	
Providing legal advice.	$150 per billable hour	75 hours	$11,250.00	125 hours	$18,750.00
Clerical support.	$175 per document	16 docs	2,800.00	14 docs	2,450.00
Litigation support	$2,500 per court date	5 court dates	12,500.00	1 court date	2,500.00
Facility costs	$7.75 per billable hour	75 hours	581.25	125 hours	968.75
Total cost			$27,131.25		$24,668.75
÷ Number of cases			3 cases		7 cases
Average cost per case			**$9,044**		**$3,524**
Average fee per case			**$7,500***		**$5,357†**

* (75 billable hours × $300 per hour) ÷ 3 cases
† (125 billable hours × $300 per hour) ÷ 7 cases

2. The cost of each type of case using a single plantwide rate for nonattorney costs (that is, all costs except for those related to providing legal advice) based on billable hours is as follows.

Total overhead cost/ Total billable hours = $21,800/200 billable hours = $109 per hour

We then determine the cost of providing each type of legal service as follows.

		Litigation		Mediation	
Providing legal advice	$150 per billable hour	75 hours	$11,250	125 hours	$18,750
Overhead (from part 2)	$109 per billable hour	75 hours	8,175	125 hours	13,625
Total cost			$19,425		$32,375
÷ Number of cases			3 cases		7 cases
Average cost per case			**$6,475**		**$4,625**
Average fee per case (from part 1)			**$7,500**		**$5,357**

3. The cost of each type of case using multiple departmental overhead rates for the internal support department (based on number of documents) and external support department (based on billable hours) is determined as follows.

		Departmental Cost	Base	Departmental Rate (Departmental Cost ÷ Base)
Internal support departments				
Preparing documents	$ 4,000			
Occupying office space	1,200			
Heating and lighting of office	350	$ 5,550	30 documents	$185 per document
External support departments				
Registering documents	1,250			
Retaining consultants	10,000			
Using contract services	5,000	16,250	200 billable hours	$81.25 per hour

The departmental overhead rates computed above are used to assign overhead costs to the two types of legal services. For the internal support department we use the overhead rate of $185 per document to assign $2,960 ($185 × 16 documents) to litigation and $2,590 ($185 × 14 documents) to mediation. For the external support department we use the overhead rate of $81.25 per hour to assign $6,093.75 ($81.25 × 75 hours) to litigation and $10,156.25 ($81.25 × 125 hours) to mediation. As shown below, the resulting average costs of litigation cases and mediation cases are $6,768 and $4,499, respectively. Using this method of cost assignment, it *appears* that the fee of $300 per billable hour is adequate to cover costs associated with each case.

		Litigation		Mediation	
Attorney fees	$150 per billable hour	75 hours	$11,250.00	125 hours	$18,750.00
Internal support	$185 per document	16 documents	2,960.00	14 documents	2,590.00
External support	$81.25 per hour	75 hours	6,093.75	125 hours	10,156.25
Total cost			$20,303.75		$31,496.25
÷ Number of cases			3 cases		7 cases
Average cost per case			**$6,768**		**$4,499**
Average fee per case (from part 1)			**$7,500**		**$5,357**

4. A comparison and discussion of the costs assigned under each method follows.

	Method of Assigning Overhead Costs		
Average Cost per Case	**Activity-Based Costing**	**Plantwide Overhead Rate**	**Departmental Overhead Rates**
Litigation cases	$9,044	$6,475	$6,768
Mediation cases	3,524	4,625	4,499

The departmental and plantwide overhead rate methods assign overhead on the basis of volume-related measures (billable hours and document filings). Litigation costs *appear* profitable under these methods, because the average costs are below the average revenue of $7,500. ABC, however, focuses attention on activities that drive costs. A large part of overhead costs was for consultants and contract services, which were unrelated to the number of cases, but related to the type of cases consuming those resources. Using ABC, the costs shift from the high-volume cases (mediation) to the low-volume cases (litigation). When the firm considers the consumption of resources for these cases using ABC, it finds that the fees charged to litigate cases is insufficient (average revenue of $7,500 versus average cost of $9,044). The law firm is charging too little for the complex cases that require litigation.

Summary

C1 Distinguish between the plantwide overhead rate method, the departmental overhead rate method, and the activity-based costing method. Overhead costs can be assigned to cost objects using a plantwide rate that combines all overhead costs into a single rate, usually based on direct labor hours, machine hours, or direct labor cost. Multiple departmental overhead rates that include overhead costs traceable to departments are used to allocate overhead based on departmental functions. ABC links overhead costs to activities and assigns overhead based on how much of each activity is required for a product.

C2 Explain cost flows for activity-based costing. With ABC, overhead costs are first traced to the activities that cause them, and then cost pools are formed combining costs caused by the same activity. Overhead rates based on these activities are then used to assign overhead to products in proportion to the amount of activity required to produce them.

C3 Describe the four types of activities that cause overhead costs. The four types of activities that cause overhead costs are: (1) unit level activities, (2) batch level activities, (3) product level activities, and (4) facility level activities. Unit level activities are performed on each unit, batch level activities are performed only on each group of units, and product level activities are performed only on each product line. Facility level activities are performed to sustain facility capacity and are not caused by any specific product. Understanding these types of activities can help in applying activity-based costing.

A1 Identify and assess advantages and disadvantages of the plantwide overhead and departmental overhead rate methods. A single plantwide overhead rate is a simple way to assign overhead cost. A disadvantage is that it can inaccurately assign costs when costs are caused by multiple factors and when different products consume different amounts of inputs. Overhead costing accuracy is improved by use of multiple departmental rates because differences across departmental functions can be linked to costs incurred in departments. Yet, accuracy of cost assignment with departmental rates suffers from the same problems associated with plantwide rates because activities required for each product are not identified with costs of providing those activities.

A2 Identify and assess advantages and disadvantages of activity-based costing. ABC improves product costing accuracy and draws management attention to relevant factors to control. The cost of constructing and maintaining an ABC system can sometimes outweigh its value.

P1 Allocate overhead costs to products using the plantwide overhead rate method. The plantwide overhead rate equals total budgeted overhead divided by budgeted plant volume, the latter often measured in direct labor hours or machine hours. This rate multiplied by the number of direct labor hours (or machine hours) required for each product provides the overhead assigned to each product.

P2 Allocate overhead costs to products using the departmental overhead rate method. When using multiple departmental rates, overhead cost must first be traced to each department and then divided by the measure of output for that department to yield the departmental overhead rate. Overhead is applied to products using this rate as products pass through each department.

P3 Allocate overhead costs to products using activity-based costing. With ABC, overhead costs are matched to activities that cause them. If there is more than one cost with the same activity, these costs are combined into pools. An overhead rate for each pool is determined by dividing total cost for that pool by its activity measure. Overhead costs are assigned to products by multiplying the ABC pool rate by the amount of the activity required for each product.

Guidance Answers to Decision Maker and Decision Ethics

Department Manager When dividing a bill, common sense suggests fairness. That is, if one department consumes more services than another, we attempt to share the bill in proportion to consumption. Equally dividing the bill among the number of departments is fair if each consumed equal services. This same notion applies in assigning costs to products and services. For example, dividing overhead costs by the number of units is fair if all products consumed overhead in equal proportion.

Cost Analyst Before the accounting system can report information, relevant and accurate data must be collected. One step is to ask questions—it is a good way to leverage others' experience and knowledge to quickly learn operations. A cost analyst must also understand the manufacturing operation to itemize activities for ABC. Thus, step two might be to tour the manufacturing facility, observing manufacturing operations, asking probing questions, and requesting recommendations from the people who work in those operations. We must remember that these employees are the experts who can provide the data we need to implement an activity-based costing system.

Entrepreneur Cleaning and sterilizing costs are not directly related to the volume of product manufactured. Thus, changing the number of units produced does not necessarily reduce these costs. Further, expressing costs of cleaning and sterilizing on a per unit basis is often misleading for the person responsible for controlling costs. Costs of cleaning and sterilizing are related to changing from one product line to another. Consequently, the way to control those costs is to control the number of times the packing system has to be changed for a different product line. Thus, efficient product scheduling would help reduce those overhead costs and improve profitability.

Guidance Answers to Quick Checks

1. d
2. a
3. b
4. A cost driver is an activity that causes costs to be incurred. Setup costs, design modifications, and plant services such as maintenance and utilities are examples of typical cost drivers.
5. An activity driver is the measurement used for cost drivers. An example is machine hours.
6. b
7. Three advantages of ABC over traditional methods are: (a) more accurate product costing; (b) more effective cost control; and (c) focus on relevant factors for decision making.
8. Traditional volume-based methods are easier and less costly to implement and maintain. The choice of accounting method should be made by comparing the costs of alternatives with their benefits.

Key Terms

Activity (p. 743)
Activity-based costing (ABC) (p. 743)
Activity-based management (p. 749)
Activity cost driver (p. 746)
Activity cost pool (p. 743)
Activity overhead (pool) rate (p. 743)
Batch level activities (p. 750)
Cost object (p. 739)
Costs of quality (p. 750)
Facility level activities (p. 750)
Lean accounting (p. 752)
Product level activities (p. 750)
Unit level activities (p. 750)
Value-added activities (p. 749)

Multiple Choice Quiz

Answers on p. 775

mhhe.com/wildFINMAN5e

Additional Quiz Questions are available at the book's Website.

1. In comparison to a traditional cost system, and when there are batch level or product level costs, an activity-based costing system usually:
a. Shifts costs from low-volume to high-volume products.
b. Shifts costs from high-volume to low-volume products.
c. Shifts costs from standardized to specialized products.
d. Shifts costs from specialized to standardized products.

2. Which of the following statements is (are) true?
a. An activity-based costing system is generally easier to implement and maintain than a traditional costing system.
b. One of the goals of activity-based management is the elimination of waste by allocating costs to products that waste resources.
c. Activity-based costing uses a number of activity cost pools, each of which is allocated to products on the basis of direct labor hours.
d. Activity rates in activity-based costing are computed by dividing costs from the first-stage allocations by the activity measure for each activity cost pool.

3. All of the following are examples of batch level activities except:
a. Purchase order processing.
b. Setting up equipment.
c. Clerical activity associated with processing purchase orders to produce an order for a standard product.
d. Employee recreational facilities.

4. A company has two products: A and B. It uses activity-based costing and prepares the following analysis showing budgeted cost and activity for each of its three activity cost pools.

Activity Cost Pool	Budgeted Overhead Cost	Budgeted Activity		
		Product A	Product B	Total
Activity 1	$ 80,000	200	800	1,000
Activity 2	58,400	1,000	500	1,500
Activity 3	360,000	600	5,400	6,000

Annual production and sales level of Product A is 18,188 units, and the annual production and sales level of Product B is 31,652 units. The approximate overhead cost per unit of Product B under activity-based costing is:
a. $2.02
b. $5.00
c. $12.87
d. $22.40

5. A company uses activity-based costing to determine the costs of its two products: A and B. The budgeted cost and activity for each of the company's three activity cost pools follow.

Activity Cost Pool	Budgeted Cost	Budgeted Activity		
		Product A	Product B	Total
Activity 1	$19,800	800	300	1,100
Activity 2	16,000	2,200	1,800	4,000
Activity 3	14,000	400	300	700

The activity rate under the activity-based costing method for Activity 3 is approximately:

a. $4.00
b. $8.59
c. $18.00
d. $20.00

Icon denotes assignments that involve decision making.

Discussion Questions

1. Why are overhead costs allocated to products and not traced to products as direct materials and direct labor are?

2. What are three common methods of assigning overhead costs to a product?

3. Why are direct labor hours and machine hours commonly used as the bases for overhead allocation?

4. What are the advantages of using a single plantwide overhead rate?

5. The usefulness of a single plantwide overhead rate is based on two assumptions. What are those assumptions?

6. What is a cost object?

7. Explain why a single plantwide overhead rate can distort the cost of a particular product.

8. Why are multiple departmental overhead rates more accurate for product costing than a single plantwide overhead rate?

9. In what way are departmental overhead rates similar to a single plantwide overhead rate? How are they different?

10. **KTM** reports costs in financial statements. If plantwide overhead rates are allowed for reporting costs to external users, why might a company choose to use a more complicated and more expensive method for assigning overhead costs to products?

11. What is the first step in applying activity-based costing?

12. What is an activity cost driver?

13. **Arctic Cat**'s production requires activities. What are value-added activities?

14. What are the four activity levels associated with activity-based costing? Define each.

15. **Piaggio** is a manufacturer. "Activity-based costing is only useful for manufacturing companies." Is this a true statement? Explain.

16. **Polaris** must assign overhead costs to its products. Activity-based costing is generally considered more accurate than other methods of assigning overhead. If this is so, why do all manufacturing companies not use it?

connect

QUICK STUDY

QS 17-1
Costing terminology
C2

In the blank next to the following terms, place the letter *A* through *D* corresponding to the best description of that term.

1. ______ Activity
2. ______ Activity driver
3. ______ Cost object
4. ______ Cost pool

A. Measurement associated with an activity.
B. A group of costs that have the same activity drivers.
C. Anything to which costs will be assigned.
D. A task that causes a cost to be incurred.

QS 17-2
Overhead cost allocation methods
C1

In the blank next to each of the following terms, place the letter *A* through *D* that corresponds to the description of that term. Some letters are used more than once.

1. ______ Activity-based costing
2. ______ Plantwide overhead rate method
3. ______ Departmental overhead rate method

A. Uses more than one rate to allocate overhead costs to products.
B. Uses only volume-based measures such as direct labor hours to allocate overhead costs to products.
C. Typically uses the most overhead allocation rates.
D. Focuses on the costs of carrying out activities.

QS 17-3
Advantages of plantwide and departmental rate methods A1

List the three main advantages of the plantwide and departmental overhead rate methods.

QS 17-4
Identify activity levels
C3

Identify each of the following activities as unit level (U), batch level (B), product level (P), or facility level (F) to indicate the way each is incurred with respect to production.

1. ______ Paying real estate taxes on the factory building.
2. ______ Attaching labels to collars of shirts.
3. ______ Redesigning a bicycle seat in response to customer feedback.
4. ______ Cleaning the assembly department.
5. ______ Polishing of gold wedding rings.
6. ______ Mixing of bread dough in a commercial bakery.
7. ______ Sampling cookies to determine quality.

QS 17-5
Compute plantwide overhead rates
P1

Rafner Manufacturing identified the following data in its two production departments.

	Assembly	Finishing
Manufacturing overhead costs	$1,200,000	$600,000
Direct labor hours worked	12,000 DLH	20,000 DLH
Machine hours used	6,000 MH	16,000 MH

Required

1. What is the company's single plantwide overhead rate based on direct labor hours?
2. What is the company's single plantwide overhead rate based on machine hours?

QS 17-6
Compute departmental overhead rates P2

Refer to the information in QS 17-5. What are the company's departmental overhead rates if the assembly department assigns overhead based on direct labor hours and the finishing department assigns overhead based on machine hours?

QS 17-7
Compute plantwide overhead rates
P1

Xie Company identified the following activities, costs, and activity drivers. The company manufactures two types of go-karts: Deluxe and Basic. Production volume is 10,000 units of the Deluxe model and 30,000 units of the Basic model.

Activity	Expected Costs	Expected Activity
Handling materials	$625,000	100,000 parts in stock
Inspecting product	900,000	1,500 batches
Processing purchase orders	105,000	700 orders
Paying suppliers	175,000	500 invoices
Insuring the factory	300,000	40,000 square feet
Designing packaging	375,000	10 models

Required

1. Compute a single plantwide overhead rate assuming that the company assigns overhead based on 125,000 budgeted direct labor hours.
2. Assign overhead costs to each model assuming the Deluxe model requires 25,000 direct labor hours and the Basic model requires 60,000 direct labor hours. What is the overhead cost per unit for each model?

QS 17-8
Compute overhead rates under ABC P3

Refer to the information in QS 17-7. Compute the activity rate for each activity, assuming the company uses activity-based costing.

QS 17-9
Assigning costs using ABC
P3

Refer to the data in QS 17-7. Assume that the following information is available for the company's two products.

	Deluxe Model	Basic Model
Production volume.	10,000 units	30,000 units
Parts required	20,000 parts	30,000 parts
Batches made.	250 batches	100 batches
Purchase orders	50 orders	20 orders
Invoices	50 invoices	10 invoices
Space occupied	10,000 sq. ft.	7,000 sq. ft.
Models	1 model	1 model

Required

Assign overhead costs to each product model using activity-based costing (ABC). What is the overhead cost per unit of each model?

QS 17-10
Multiple choice overhead questions
A2

1. If management wants the most accurate product cost, which of the following costing methods should be used?
   a. Volume-based costing using departmental overhead rates
   b. Volume-based costing using a plantwide overhead rate
   c. Normal costing using a plantwide overhead rate
   d. Activity-based costing
2. Which costing method tends to overstate the cost of high-volume products?
   a. Traditional volume-based costing
   b. Activity-based costing
   c. Job order costing
   d. Differential costing
3. Disadvantages of activity-based costing include
   a. It is not acceptable under GAAP for external reporting.
   b. It can be costly to implement.
   c. It can be used in an activity-based management.
   d. Both a. and b.

QS 17-11
Assigning costs using ABC
P3

Aziz Company sells two types of products, Basic and Deluxe. The company provides technical support for users of its products, at an expected cost of $250,000 per year. The company expects to process 10,000 customer service calls per year.

Required

1. Determine the company's cost of technical support per customer service call.
2. During the month of January, Aziz received 550 calls for customer service on its Deluxe model, and 250 calls for customer service on its Basic model. Assign technical support costs to each model using activity-based costing (ABC).

QS 17-12
Computing activity rates
P3

A company uses activity-based costing to determine the costs of its three products: A, B, and C. The budgeted cost and cost driver activity for each of the company's three activity cost pools follow.

		Budgeted Activity of Cost Driver		
Activity Cost Pool	Budgeted Cost	Product A	Product B	Product C
Activity 1	$140,000	20,000	9,000	6,000
Activity 2	$ 90,000	8,000	15,000	7,000
Activity 3	$ 82,000	1,625	1,000	2,500

Compute the activity rates for each of the company's three activities.

QS 17-13
Activity-based costing and overhead cost allocation P3

The following is taken from Ronda Co.'s internal records of its factory with two operating departments. The cost driver for indirect labor and supplies is direct labor costs, and the cost driver for the remaining overhead items is number of hours of machine use. Compute the total amount of overhead cost allocated to Operating Department 1 using activity-based costing.

	Direct Labor	Machine Use Hours
Operating department 1	$18,800	2,000
Operating department 2	13,200	1,200
Totals	$32,000	3,200
Factory overhead costs		
Rent and utilities		$12,200
Indirect labor		5,400
General office expense		4,000
Depreciation—Equipment		3,000
Supplies		2,600
Total factory overhead		$27,200

Check Dept. 1 allocation, $16,700

QS 17-14
Activity-based costing rates and allocations
P3

A company has two products: standard and deluxe. The company expects to produce 36,375 standard units and 62,240 deluxe units. It uses activity-based costing and has prepared the following analysis showing budgeted cost and cost driver activity for each of its three activity cost pools.

		Budgeted Activity of Cost Driver	
Activity Cost Pool	Budgeted Cost	Standard	Deluxe
Activity 1	$93,000	2,500	5,250
Activity 2	$92,000	4,500	5,500
Activity 3	$87,000	3,000	2,800

Required

1. What is the overhead cost per unit for the standard units?
2. What is the overhead cost per unit for the deluxe units?

QS 17-15
Costs of quality
A2

A list of activities that generate quality costs is provided below. For each activity, indicate whether it relates to a prevention activity (P), appraisal activity (A), internal failure activity (I), or external failure activity (E).

a. Inspecting raw materials
b. Training workers in quality techniques
c. Collecting data on a manufacturing process
d. Overtime labor to rework products
e. Cost of additional materials to rework a product
f. Inspecting finished goods inventory
g. Scrapping defective goods
h. Lost sales due to customer dissatisfaction

QS 17-16
Lean accounting and ABC
A2

Toyota embraces lean techniques, including lean accounting. What are the two key components of lean accounting?

connect

EXERCISES

Exercise 17-1
Cost allocation methods
C1

1. When using departmental overhead rates, which of the following cost objects is the first in the cost allocation process?
a. Activities
b. Units of product
c. Product lines
d. Departments

2. Which costing method assumes all products use overhead costs in the same proportions?
a. Activity-based costing
b. Plantwide overhead rate method
c. Departmental overhead rate method
d. All cost allocation methods

3. Which of the following would usually *not* be used in computing plantwide overhead rates?
a. Direct labor hours
b. Number of quality inspections
c. Direct labor dollars
d. Machine hours

4. With ABC, overhead costs should be traced to which cost object first?
a. Units of product
b. Departments
c. Activities
d. Product batches

Exercise 17-2
Cost flows under activity-based costing C2

Explain the two basic stages of cost flows for activity-based costing.

Exercise 17-3
Comparing overhead allocation methods A2

Why is overhead allocation under ABC usually more accurate than either the plantwide overhead allocation method or the departmental overhead allocation method?

Exercise 17-4
Activity classification
C3

Following are activities in providing medical services at Healthsmart Clinic.

A. Registering patients
B. Cleaning beds
C. Stocking examination rooms
D. Washing linens
E. Ordering medical equipment
F. Heating the clinic
G. Providing security services
H. Filling prescriptions

Required

1. Classify each activity as unit level (U), batch level (B), product level (P), or facility level (F).
2. Identify an activity driver that might be used to measure these activities at the clinic.

Exercise 17-5
Comparing costs under ABC to traditional plantwide overhead rate
P1 P3 A1 A2

Smythe Crystal makes fine tableware in its Ireland factory. The following data are taken from its production plans for the year.

Direct labor costs	€5,870,000
Setup costs	630,000

	Wine Glasses	Commemorative Vases
Expected production	211,000 units	17,000 units
Direct labor hours required	254,000 DLH	16,400 DLH
Machine setups required	200 setups	800 setups

Required

1. Determine the setup cost per unit for the wine glasses and for the commemorative vases if setup costs are assigned using a single plantwide overhead rate based on direct labor hours.
2. Determine setup costs per unit for the wine glasses and for the commemorative vases if the setup costs are assigned based on the number of setups.
3. Which method is better for assigning costs to each product? Explain.

Check (2) Vases, €29.65 per unit

Exercise 17-6
Using the plantwide overhead rate to assess prices P1

Way Cool produces two different models of air conditioners. The company produces the mechanical systems in their components department. The mechanical systems are combined with the housing assembly in its finishing department. The activities, costs, and drivers associated with these two manufacturing processes and the production support process follow.

Process	Activity	Overhead Cost	Driver	Quantity
Components	Changeover	$ 500,000	Number of batches	800
	Machining	279,000	Machine hours	6,000
	Setups	225,000	Number of setups	120
		$1,004,000		
Finishing	Welding	$ 180,300	Welding hours	3,000
	Inspecting	210,000	Number of inspections	700
	Rework	75,000	Rework orders	300
		$ 465,300		
Support	Purchasing	$ 135,000	Purchase orders	450
	Providing space	32,000	Number of units	5,000
	Providing utilities	65,000	Number of units	5,000
		$ 232,000		

Additional production information concerning its two product lines follows.

	Model 145	Model 212
Units produced	1,500	3,500
Welding hours	800	2,200
Batches	400	400
Number of inspections	400	300
Machine hours	1,800	4,200
Setups	60	60
Rework orders	160	140
Purchase orders	300	150

Required

1. Using a plantwide overhead rate based on machine hours, compute the overhead cost per unit for each product line.
2. Determine the total cost per unit for each product line if the direct labor and direct materials costs per unit are $250 for Model 145 and $180 for Model 212.
3. If the market price for Model 145 is $820 and the market price for Model 212 is $480, determine the profit or loss per unit for each model. Comment on the results.

Check (3) Model 212, $(40.26) per unit loss

Exercise 17-7
Using departmental overhead rates to assess prices
P2

Refer to the information in Exercise 17-6 to answer the following requirements.

Required

1. Determine departmental overhead rates and compute the overhead cost per unit for each product line. Base your overhead assignment for the components department on machine hours. Use welding hours to assign overhead costs to the finishing department. Assign costs to the support department based on number of purchase orders.
2. Determine the total cost per unit for each product line if the direct labor and direct materials costs per unit are $250 for Model 145 and $180 for Model 212.
3. If the market price for Model 145 is $820 and the market price for Model 212 is $480, determine the profit or loss per unit for each model. Comment on the results.

Check (3) Model 212, $(20.38) per unit loss

Exercise 17-8
Using ABC to assess prices
P3

Refer to the information in Exercise 17-6 to answer the following requirements.

Required

1. Using ABC, compute the overhead cost per unit for each product line.
2. Determine the total cost per unit for each product line if the direct labor and direct materials costs per unit are $250 for Model 145 and $180 for Model 212.
3. If the market price for Model 145 is $820 and the market price for Model 212 is $480, determine the profit or loss per unit for each model. Comment on the results.

Check (3) Model 212, $34.88 per unit profit

Exercise 17-9
Plantwide overhead rate
P1

Textra Plastics produces parts for a variety of small machine manufacturers. Most products go through two operations, molding and trimming, before they are ready for packaging. Expected costs and activities for the molding department and for the trimming department for 2013 follow.

	Molding	Trimming
Direct labor hours	52,000 DLH	48,000 DLH
Machine hours	30,500 MH	3,600 MH
Overhead costs	$730,000	$590,000

Data for two special order parts to be manufactured by the company in 2013 follow:

	Part A27C	Part X82B
Number of units	9,800 units	54,500 units
Machine hours		
Molding	5,100 MH	1,020 MH
Trimming	2,600 MH	650 MH
Direct labor hours		
Molding	5,500 DLH	2,150 DLH
Trimming	700 DLH	3,500 DLH

Required

1. Compute the plantwide overhead rate using direct labor hours as the base.
2. Determine the overhead cost assigned to each product line using the plantwide rate computed in requirement 1.

Exercise 17-10
Departmental overhead rates
P2

Refer to the information in Exercise 17-9.

Required

1. Compute a departmental overhead rate for the molding department based on machine hours and a department overhead rate for the trimming department based on direct labor hours.
2. Determine the total overhead cost assigned to each product line using the departmental overhead rates from requirement 2.
3. Determine the overhead cost per unit for each product line using the departmental rate.

Exercise 17-11
Assigning overhead costs using the plantwide rate and departmental rate methods
P1 P2

Laval produces lamps and home lighting fixtures. Its most popular product is a brushed aluminum desk lamp. This lamp is made from components shaped in the fabricating department and assembled in its assembly department. Information related to the 35,000 desk lamps produced annually follow.

Direct materials	$280,000
Direct labor	
Fabricating department (7,000 DLH × $20 per DLH)	$140,000
Assembly department (16,000 DLH × $29 per DLH)	$464,000
Machine hours	
Fabricating department	15,040 MH
Assembly department	21,000 MH

Expected overhead cost and related data for the two production departments follow.

	Fabricating	Assembly
Direct labor hours	75,000 DLH	125,000 DLH
Machine hours	80,000 MH	62,500 MH
Overhead cost	$300,000	$200,000

Required

1. Determine the plantwide overhead rate for Laval using direct labor hours as a base.
2. Determine the total manufacturing cost per unit for the aluminum desk lamp using the plantwide overhead rate.
3. Compute departmental overhead rates based on machine hours in the fabricating department and direct labor hours in the assembly department.
4. Use departmental overhead rates from requirement 3 to determine the total manufacturing cost per unit for the aluminum desk lamps.

Check (2) $26.90 per unit

Check (4) $27.60 per unit

Exercise 17-12
Using ABC for strategic decisions
P1 P3

Consider the following data for two products of Gitano Manufacturing.

	Overhead Cost	Product A	Product B
Number of units produced		10,000 units	2,000 units
Direct labor cost (@$24 per DLH)		0.20 DLH per unit	0.25 DLH per unit
Direct materials cost		$2 per unit	$3 per unit
Activity			
Machine setup	$121,000		
Materials handling	48,000		
Quality control	80,000		
	$249,000		

Required

1. Using direct labor hours as the basis for assigning overhead costs, determine the total production cost per unit for each product line.
2. If the market price for Product A is $20 and the market price for Product B is $60, determine the profit or loss per unit for each product. Comment on the results.
3. Consider the following additional information about these two product lines. If ABC is used for assigning overhead costs to products, what is the cost per unit for Product A and for Product B?

Check (2) Product B, $26.10 per unit profit

	Product A	Product B
Number of setups required for production	10 setups	12 setups
Number of parts required.	1 part/unit	3 parts/unit
Inspection hours required	40 hours	210 hours

4. Determine the profit or loss per unit for each product. Should this information influence company strategy? Explain.

(4) Product B, ($24.60) per unit loss

Exercise 17-13
Using ABC in a service company
P3

Cardiff and Delp is an architectural firm that provides services for residential construction projects. The following data pertain to a recent reporting period.

	Activities	Costs
Design department		
Client consultation	1,500 contact hours	$270,000
Drawings	2,000 design hours	115,000
Modeling	40,000 square feet	30,000
Project management department		
Supervision	600 days	$120,000
Billings	8 jobs	10,000
Collections	8 jobs	12,000

Required

1. Using ABC, compute the firm's activity overhead rates. Form activity cost pools where appropriate.
2. Assign costs to a 9,200 square foot job that requires 450 contact hours, 340 design hours, and 200 days to complete.

Check (2) $150,200

Exercise 17-14
Activity-based costing
P3 A2

Glassworks Inc. produces two types of glass shelving, rounded edge and squared edge, on the same production line. For the current period, the company reports the following data.

	Rounded Edge	Squared Edge	Total
Direct materials	$19,000	$ 43,200	$ 62,200
Direct labor	12,200	23,800	36,000
Overhead (300% of direct labor cost)	36,600	71,400	108,000
Total cost	$67,800	$138,400	$206,200
Quantity produced	10,500 ft.	14,100 ft.	
Average cost per ft. (rounded)	$ 6.46	$ 9.82	

Glassworks's controller wishes to apply activity-based costing (ABC) to allocate the $108,000 of overhead costs incurred by the two product lines to see whether cost per foot would change markedly from that reported above. She has collected the following information.

Overhead Cost Category (Activity Cost Pool)	Cost
Supervision	$ 5,400
Depreciation of machinery	56,600
Assembly line preparation.	46,000
Total overhead	$108,000

She has also collected the following information about the cost drivers for each category (cost pool) and the amount of each driver used by the two product lines.

Overhead Cost Category (Activity Cost Pool)	Driver	Usage: Rounded Edge	Squared Edge	Total
Supervision	Direct labor cost($)	$12,200	$23,800	$36,000
Depreciation of machinery	Machine hours	500 hours	1,500 hours	2,000 hours
Assembly line preparation	Setups (number)	40 times	210 times	250 times

Check (2) Rounded edge, $5.19; Squared edge, $10.76

Required

1. Assign these three overhead cost pools to each of the two products using ABC.
2. Determine average cost per foot for each of the two products using ABC.
3. Compare the average cost per foot under ABC with the average cost per foot under the current method for each product. Explain why a difference between the two cost allocation methods exists.

Exercise 17-15
Activity-based costing
P3

Surgery Center is an outpatient surgical clinic that was profitable for many years, but Medicare has cut its reimbursements by as much as 40%. As a result, the clinic wants to better understand its costs. It decides to prepare an activity-based cost analysis, including an estimate of the average cost of both general surgery and orthopedic surgery. The clinic's three cost centers and their cost drivers follow.

Cost Center	Cost	Cost Driver	Driver Quantity
Professional salaries	$1,600,000	Professional hours	10,000
Patient services and supplies	27,000	Number of patients	600
Building cost	150,000	Square feet	1,500

The two main surgical units and their related data follow.

Service	Hours	Square Feet*	Patients
General surgery	2,500	600	400
Orthopedic surgery	7,500	900	200

* Orthopedic surgery requires more space for patients, supplies, and equipment.

Check (2) Average cost of general (orthopedic) surgery, $1,195 ($6,495) per patient

Required

1. Compute the cost per cost driver for each of the three cost centers.
2. Use the results from part 1 to allocate costs from each of the three cost centers to both the general surgery and the orthopedic surgery units. Compute total cost and average cost per patient for both the general surgery and the orthopedic surgery units.

connect

PROBLEM SET A

Problem 17-1A
Comparing costs using ABC with the plantwide overhead rate
P1 P3 A1 A2

The following data are for the two products produced by Tadros Company.

	Product A	Product B
Direct materials	$15 per unit	$24 per unit
Direct labor hours	0.3 DLH per unit	1.6 DLH per unit
Machine hours	0.1 MH per unit	1.2 MH per unit
Batches	125 batches	225 batches
Volume	10,000 units	2,000 units
Engineering modifications	12 modifications	58 modifications
Number of customers	500 customers	400 customers
Market price	$30 per unit	$120 per unit

The company's direct labor rate is $20 per direct labor hour (DLH). Additional information follows.

	Costs	Driver
Indirect manufacturing		
Engineering support	$24,500	Engineering modifications
Electricity	34,000	Machine hours
Setup costs	52,500	Batches
Nonmanufacturing		
Customer service	81,000	Number of customers

Required

1. Compute the manufacturing cost per unit using the plantwide overhead rate based on direct labor hours. What is the gross profit per unit?
2. How much gross profit is generated by each customer of Product A using the plantwide overhead rate? How much gross profit is generated by each customer of Product B using the plantwide overhead rate? What is the cost of providing customer service to each customer? What information is provided by this comparison?
3. Determine the manufacturing cost per unit of each product line using ABC. What is the gross profit per unit?
4. How much gross profit is generated by each customer of Product A using ABC? How much gross profit is generated by each customer of Product B using ABC? Is the gross profit per customer adequate?
5. Which method of product costing gives better information to managers of this company? Explain why.

Check (1) Product A, $26.37 per unit cost

(3) Product A, $24.30 per unit cost

Problem 17-2A
Assessing impacts of using a plantwide overhead rate versus ABC
A1 A2

Xylon Company manufactures custom-made furniture for its local market and produces a line of home furnishings sold in retail stores across the country. The company uses traditional volume-based methods of assigning direct materials and direct labor to its product lines. Overhead has always been assigned by using a plantwide overhead rate based on direct labor hours. In the past few years, management has seen its line of retail products continue to sell at high volumes, but competition has forced it to lower prices on these items. The prices are declining to a level close to its cost of production.

Meanwhile, its custom-made furniture is in high demand and customers have commented on its favorable (lower) prices compared to its competitors. Management is considering dropping its line of retail products and devoting all of its resources to custom-made furniture.

Required

1. What reasons could explain why competitors are forcing the company to lower prices on its high-volume retail products?
2. Why do you believe the company charges less for custom-order products than its competitors?
3. Does a company's costing method have any effect on its pricing decisions? Explain.
4. Aside from the differences in volume of output, what production differences do you believe exist between making custom-order furniture and mass-market furnishings?
5. What information might the company obtain from using ABC that it might not obtain using volume-based costing methods?

Problem 17-3A
Applying activity-based costing
P1 P3 A1 A2 C3

Craft Pro Machining produces machine tools for the construction industry. The following details about overhead costs were taken from its company records.

Production Activity	Indirect Labor	Indirect Materials	Other Overhead
Grinding	$320,000		
Polishing		$135,000	
Product modification	600,000		
Providing power..............			$255,000
System calibration	500,000		

Additional information on the drivers for its production activities follows.

Grinding	13,000 machine hours
Polishing	13,000 machine hours
Product modification	1,500 engineering hours
Providing power	17,000 direct labor hours
System calibration	400 batches

Required

1. Classify each activity as unit level, batch level, product level, or facility level.
2. Compute the activity overhead rates using ABC. Form cost pools as appropriate.
3. Determine overhead costs to assign to the following jobs using ABC.

	Job 3175	Job 4286
Number of units	200 units	2,500 units
Machine hours	550 MH	5,500 MH
Engineering hours	26 eng. hours	32 eng. hours
Batches	30 batches	90 batches
Direct labor hours	500 DLH	4,375 DLH

192,500
12,800
65,625
112,300

Check (4) Job 3175, $373.25 per unit

4. What is the overhead cost per unit for Job 3175? What is the overhead cost per unit for Job 4286?
5. If the company used a plantwide overhead rate based on direct labor hours, what is the overhead cost for each unit of Job 3175? Of Job 4286?
6. Compare the overhead costs per unit computed in requirements 4 and 5 for each job. Which method more accurately assigns overhead costs?

Problem 17-4A
Evaluating product line costs and prices using ABC
P3

Bright Day Company produces two beverages, Hi-Voltage and EasySlim. Data about these products follow.

	Hi-Voltage	EasySlim
Production volume	12,500 bottles	180,000 bottles
Liquid materials	1,400 gallons	37,000 gallons
Dry materials	620 pounds	12,000 pounds
Bottles	12,500 bottles	180,000 bottles
Labels	3 labels per bottle	1 label per bottle
Machine setups	500 setups	300 setups
Machine hours	200 MH	3,750 MH

Additional data from its two production departments follow.

Department	Driver	Cost
Mixing department		
Liquid materials	Gallons	$ 2,304
Dry materials	Pounds	6,941
Utilities	Machine hours	1,422
Bottling department		
Bottles	Units	$77,000
Labeling	Labels per bottle	6,525
Machine setup	Setups	20,000

Required

1. Determine the cost of each product line using ABC.
2. What is the cost per bottle for Hi-Voltage? What is the cost per bottle of EasySlim? (*Hint:* Your answer should draw on the total cost for each product line computed in requirement 1.)

Check (3) $2.22 profit per bottle

3. If Hi-Voltage sells for $3.75 per bottle, how much profit does the company earn per bottle of Hi-Voltage that it sells?
4. What is the minimum price that the company should set per bottle of EasySlim? Explain.

Problem 17-5A
Pricing analysis with ABC and a plantwide overhead rate
A1 A2 P1 P3

Sara's Salsa Company produces its condiments in two types: Extra Fine for restaurant customers and Family Style for home use. Salsa is prepared in department 1 and packaged in department 2. The activities, overhead costs, and drivers associated with these two manufacturing processes and its production support activities follow.

Process	Activity	Overhead Cost	Driver	Quantity
Department 1	Mixing	$ 4,500	Machine hours	1,500
	Cooking	11,250	Machine hours	1,500
	Product testing	112,500	Batches	600
		$128,250		
Department 2	Machine calibration	$250,000	Production runs	400
	Labeling	12,000	Cases of output	120,000
	Defects	6,000	Cases of output	120,000
		$268,000		
Support	Recipe formulation	$ 90,000	Focus groups	45
	Heat, lights, and water	27,000	Machine hours	1,500
	Materials handling	65,000	Container types	8
		$182,000		

Additional production information about its two product lines follows.

	Extra Fine	Family Style
Units produced	20,000 cases	100,000 cases
Batches	200 batches	400 batches
Machine hours	500 MH	1,000 MH
Focus groups	30 groups	15 groups
Container types	5 containers	3 containers
Production runs	200 runs	200 runs

Required

1. Using a plantwide overhead rate based on cases, compute the overhead cost that is assigned to each case of Extra Fine Salsa and each case of Family Style Salsa.
2. Using the plantwide overhead rate, determine the total cost per unit for the two products if the direct materials and direct labor cost is $6 per case of Extra Fine and $5 per case of Family Style.
3. If the market price of Extra Fine Salsa is $18 per case and the market price of Family Style Salsa is $9 per case, determine the gross profit per case for each product. What might management conclude about each product line?
4. Using ABC, compute the total cost per case for each product type if the direct labor and direct materials cost is $6 per case of Extra Fine and $5 per case of Family Style.
5. If the market price is $18 per case of Extra Fine and $9 per case of Family Style, determine the gross profit per case for each product. How should management interpret the market prices given your computations?
6. Would your pricing analysis be improved if the company used departmental rates based on machine hours in department 1 and number of cases in department 2, instead of ABC? Explain.

Check (2) Cost per case: Extra Fine, $10.82; Family Style, $9.82

(4) Cost per case: Extra Fine, $20.02; Family Style, $7.98

PROBLEM SET B

Problem 17-1B
Comparing costs using ABC with the plantwide overhead rate
A1 A2 P1 P3

Wade Company makes two distinct products with the following information available for each.

	Standard	Deluxe
Direct materials	$4 per unit	$8 per unit
Direct labor hours	4 DLH per unit	5 DLH per unit
Machine hours	3 MH per unit	3 MH per unit
Batches	175 batches	75 batches
Volume	40,000 units	10,000 units
Engineering modifications	50 modifications	25 modifications
Number of customers	1,000 customers	1,000 customers
Market price	$92 per unit	$125 per unit

The company's direct labor rate is $20 per direct labor hour (DLH). Additional information follows.

	Costs	Driver
Indirect manufacturing		
Engineering support	$ 56,250	Engineering modifications
Electricity	112,500	Machine hours
Setup costs	41,250	Batches
Nonmanufacturing		
Customer service	250,000	Number of customers

Required

Check (1) Gross profit per unit: Standard, $3.80; Deluxe, $12.80

1. Compute the manufacturing cost per unit using the plantwide overhead rate based on machine hours. What is the gross profit per unit?

2. How much gross profit is generated by each customer of the standard product using the plantwide overhead rate? How much gross profit is generated by each customer of the deluxe product using the plantwide overhead rate? What is the cost of providing customer service to each customer? What information is provided by this comparison?

(3) Gross profit per unit: Standard, $4.09; Deluxe, $11.64

3. Determine the manufacturing cost per unit of each product line using ABC. What is the gross profit per unit?

4. How much gross profit is generated by each customer of the standard product using ABC? How much gross profit is generated by each customer of the deluxe product using ABC? Is the gross profit per customer adequate?

5. Which method of product costing gives better information to managers of this company? Explain.

Problem 17-2B
Assessing impacts of using a plantwide overhead rate versus ABC
A1 A2

Midwest Paper produces cardboard boxes. The boxes require designing, cutting, and printing. (The boxes are shipped flat and customers fold them as necessary.) Midwest has a reputation for providing high-quality products and excellent service to customers, who are major U.S. manufacturers. Costs are assigned to products based on the number of machine hours required to produce them.

Three years ago, a new marketing executive was hired. She suggested the company offer custom design and manufacturing services to small specialty manufacturers. These customers required boxes for their products and were eager to have Midwest as a supplier. Within one year Midwest found that it was so busy with orders from small customers, that it had trouble supplying boxes to all its customers on a timely basis. Large, long-time customers began to complain about slow service and several took their business elsewhere. Within another 18 months, Midwest was in financial distress with a backlog of orders to be filled.

Required

1. What do you believe are the major costs of making its boxes? How are those costs related to the volume of boxes produced?

2. How did Midwest's new customers differ from its previous customers?

3. Would the unit cost to produce a box for new customers be different from the unit cost to produce a box for its previous customers? Explain.

4. Could Midwest's fate have been different if it had used ABC for determining the cost of its boxes?

5. What information would have been available with ABC that might have been overlooked using a traditional volume-based costing method?

Problem 17-3B
Applying activity-based costing
P1 P3 A1 A2 C3

Ryan Foods produces gourmet gift baskets that it distributes online as well as from its small retail store. The following details about overhead costs are taken from its records.

Production Activity	Indirect Labor	Indirect Materials	Other Overhead
Wrapping	$300,000	$200,000	
Assembling	400,000		
Product design	180,000		
Obtaining business licenses			$100,000
Cooking	150,000	120,000	

Additional information on the drivers for its production activities follows.

Wrapping	100,000 units
Assembling	20,000 direct labor hours
Product design	3,000 design hours
Obtaining business licenses	20,000 direct labor hours
Cooking	1,000 batches

Required

1. Classify each activity as unit level, batch level, product level, or facility level.
2. Compute the activity overhead rates using ABC. Form cost pools as appropriate.
3. Determine the overhead cost to assign to the following jobs using ABC.

	Holiday Basket	Executive Basket
Number of units	8,000 units	1,000 units
Direct labor hours	2,000 DLH	500 DLH
Design hours	40 design hours	40 design hours
Batches	80 batches	200 batches

4. What is the overhead cost per unit for the Holiday Basket? What is the overhead cost per unit for the Executive Basket?
5. If the company used a plantwide overhead rate based on direct labor hours, what is the overhead cost for each Holiday Basket unit? What would be the overhead cost for each Executive Basket unit if a single plantwide overhead rate is used?
6. Compare the costs per unit computed in requirements 4 and 5 for each job. Which cost assignment method provides the most accurate cost? Explain.

Check (4) Holiday Basket, $14.25 per unit

(5) Holiday Basket, $18.13 per unit

Problem 17-4B
Evaluating product line costs and prices using ABC
P3

Mathwerks produces two electronic, handheld educational games: *Fun with Fractions* and *Count Calculus*. Data on these products follow.

	Fun with Fractions	Count Calculus
Production volume	150,000 units	10,000 units
Components	450,000 parts	100,000 parts
Direct labor hours	15,000 DLH	2,000 DLH
Packaging materials	150,000 boxes	10,000 boxes
Shipping cartons	100 units per carton	25 units per carton
Machine setups	52 setups	52 setups
Machine hours	5,000 MH	2,000 MH

Additional data from its two production departments follow.

Department	Driver	Cost
Assembly department		
Component cost	Parts	$495,000
Assembly labor	Direct labor hours	244,800
Maintenance	Machine hours	100,800
Wrapping department		
Packaging materials	Boxes	$460,800
Shipping	Cartons	27,360
Machine setup	Setups	187,200

Required

1. Using ABC, determine the cost of each product line.
2. What is the cost per unit for Fun with Fractions? What is the cost per unit of Count Calculus?
3. If Count Calculus sells for $59.95 per unit, how much profit does the company earn per unit of Count Calculus sold?
4. What is the minimum price that the company should set per unit of Fun with Fractions? Explain.

Check (3) $32.37 profit per unit

Problem 17-5B
Pricing analysis with ABC and a plantwide overhead rate
A1 A2 P1 P3

Tent Pro produces two lines of tents sold to outdoor enthusiasts. The tents are cut to specifications in department A. In department B the tents are sewn and folded. The activities, costs, and drivers associated with these two manufacturing processes and its production support activities follow.

Process	Activity	Overhead Cost	Driver	Quantity
Department A	Pattern alignment	$ 64,400	Batches	560
	Cutting	50,430	Machine hours	12,300
	Moving product	100,800	Moves	2,400
		$215,630		
Department B	Sewing	$327,600	Direct labor hours	4,200
	Inspecting	24,000	Inspections	600
	Folding	47,880	Units	22,800
		$399,480		
Support	Design	$280,000	Modification orders	280
	Providing space	51,600	Square feet	8,600
	Materials handling	184,000	Square yards	920,000
		$515,600		

Additional production information on the two lines of tents follows.

	Pup Tent	Pop-Up Tent
Units produced	15,200 units	7,600 units
Moves	800 moves	1,600 moves
Batches	140 batches	420 batches
Number of inspections	240 inspections	360 inspections
Machine hours	7,000 MH	5,300 MH
Direct labor hours	2,600 DLH	1,600 DLH
Modification orders	70 modification orders	210 modification orders
Space occupied	4,300 square feet	4,300 square feet
Material required	450,000 square yards	470,000 square yards

Required

1. Using a plantwide overhead rate based on direct labor hours, compute the overhead cost that is assigned to each pup tent and each pop-up tent.
2. Using the plantwide overhead rate, determine the total cost per unit for the two products if the direct materials and direct labor cost is $25 per pup tent and $32 per pop-up tent.
3. If the market price of the pup tent is $65 and the market price of the pop-up tent is $200, determine the gross profit per unit for each tent. What might management conclude about the pup tent?
4. Using ABC, compute the total cost per unit for each tent if the direct labor and direct materials cost is $25 per pup tent and $32 per pop-up tent.
5. If the market price is $65 per pup tent and $200 per pop-up tent, determine the gross profit per unit for each tent. Comment on the results.
6. Would your pricing analysis be improved if the company used, instead of ABC, departmental rates determined using machine hours in Department A and direct labor hours in Department B? Explain.

Check (4) Pup tent, $58.46 per unit cost

SERIAL PROBLEM
Success Systems
P3
Sage 50

(This serial problem began in Chapter 1 and continues through most of the book. If previous chapter segments were not completed, the serial problem can begin at this point. It is helpful, but not necessary, to use the Working Papers that accompany the book.)

SP 17 After reading an article about activity-based costing in a trade journal for the furniture industry, Adria Lopez wondered if it was time to critically analyze overhead costs at Success Systems. In a recent month, Adria found that setup costs, inspection costs, and utility costs made up most of its overhead. Additional information about overhead follows.

Activity	Cost	Driver
Setting up machines	$20,000	25 batches
Inspecting components	$ 7,500	5,000 parts
Providing utilities	$10,000	5,000 machine hours

Overhead has been applied to output at a rate of 50% of direct labor costs. The following data pertain to Job 6.15.

Direct materials	$2,500
Direct labor	$3,500
Batches	2 batches
Number of parts	400 parts
Machine hours	600 machine hours

Required

1. Classify each of its three overhead activities as unit level, batch level, product level, or facility level.
2. What is the total cost of Job 6.15 if Success Systems applies overhead at 50% of direct labor cost?
3. What is the total cost of Job 6.15 if Success Systems uses activity-based costing?
4. Which approach to assigning overhead gives a better representation of the costs incurred to produce Job 6.15? Explain.

Beyond the Numbers

REPORTING IN ACTION
C3 A2
Polaris
Arctic Cat

BTN 17-1 Refer to financial statements of Polaris (Polaris.com) and Arctic Cat (arcticcat.com) to answer the following.

Required

1. Identify at least two activities at Polaris and at Arctic Cat that cause costs to be incurred. Do you believe these companies should be concerned about controlling costs of the activities you identified? Explain.
2. Would you classify Polaris and Arctic Cat as service, merchandising, or manufacturing companies? Explain.
3. Is activity-based costing useful for companies such as Polaris and Arctic Cat? Explain.

COMPARATIVE ANALYSIS
C2 A2
Polaris
Arctic Cat

BTN 17-2 Polaris and Arctic Cat are competitors in the sales of recreational and off-road vehicles. Compare these companies' income statements and answer the following.

Required

1. Which company has a higher ratio of costs, defined as cost of goods sold plus total operating expenses, to revenues? Use the two most recent years' income statements from Appendix A. Show your analysis.
2. How might the use of activity-based costing help the less competitive company become *more* competitive?
3. Polaris sells its vehicles directly to dealers. Assume a dealer is considering opening a new retail store. What are the activities associated with opening a new retail store?

ETHICS CHALLENGE

A2 C3

BTN 17-3 In conducting interviews and observing factory operations to implement an activity-based costing system, you determine that several activities are unnecessary or redundant. For example, warehouse personnel were inspecting purchased components as they were received at the loading dock. Later that day, the components were inspected again on the shop floor before being installed in the final product. Both of these activities caused costs to be incurred but were not adding value to the product. If you include this observation in your report, one or more employees who perform inspections will likely lose their jobs.

Required

1. As a plant employee, what is your responsibility to report your findings to superiors?
2. Should you attempt to determine if the redundancy is justified? Explain.
3. What is your responsibility to the employees whose jobs will likely be lost by your report?
4. What facts should you consider before making your decision to report or not?

COMMUNICATING IN PRACTICE

A2

BTN 17-4 The chief executive officer (CEO) of your company recently returned from a luncheon meeting where activity-based costing was presented and discussed. Though her background is not in accounting, she has worked for the company for 15 years and is thoroughly familiar with its operations. Her impression of the presentation about ABC was that it was just another way of dividing up total overhead cost and that the total would still be the same "no matter how you sliced it."

Required

Write a memorandum to the CEO, no more than one page, explaining how ABC is different from traditional volume-based costing methods. Also, identify its advantages and disadvantages vis-à-vis traditional methods. Be sure it is written to be understandable to someone who is not an accountant.

TAKING IT TO THE NET

A2

BTN 17-5 Accounting professionals that work for private companies often obtain the Certified Management Accountant (CMA) designation to indicate their proficiency in several business areas in addition to managerial accounting. The CMA examination is administered by the Institute of Management Accountants (IMA).

Required

Go to the IMA Website (IMAnet.org) and determine which parts of the CMA exam likely cover activity-based costing. A person planning to become a CMA should take what college course work?

TEAMWORK IN ACTION

C2 C3

BTN 17-6 Observe the operations at your favorite fast-food restaurant.

Required

1. How many people does it take to fill a typical order of sandwich, beverage, and one side-order?
2. Describe the activities involved in its food service process.
3. What costs are related to each activity identified in requirement 2?

ENTREPRENEURIAL DECISION

C3

BTN 17-7 **New Belgium Brewing Company** has expanded its product offerings to include many varieties of specialty and seasonal brews. Kim Jordan, CEO of New Belgium Brewing Company, realizes that financial success depends on cost control as well as revenue generation.

Required

1. If New Belgium Brewing Company wanted to expand its product line to include malted energy drinks, what activities would it need to perform that are not required for its current product lines?
2. Related to part 1, should the additional overhead costs related to new product lines be shared by existing product lines? Explain your reasoning.

BTN 17-8 Visit and observe the processes of three different fast-food restaurants—these visits can be done as individuals or as teams. The objective of activity-based costing is to accurately assign costs to products and to improve operational efficiency.

HITTING THE ROAD
C2 C3

Required

1. Individuals (or teams) can be assigned to each of three different fast-food establishments. Make a list of the activities required to process an order of a sandwich, beverage, and one side-order at each restaurant. Record the time required for each process, from placing the order to receiving the completed order.
2. What activities do the three establishments have in common? What activities are different across the establishments?
3. Is the number of activities related to the time required to process an order? Is the number of activities related to the price charged to customers? Explain both.
4. Make recommendations for improving the processes you observe. Would your recommendations increase or decrease the cost of operations?

BTN 17-9 Visit the Websites and review the financial statements for **KTM** (KTM.com) and **Piaggio** (piaggio.com). Each of these companies sells street vehicles like motorcycles or scooters in global markets.

GLOBAL DECISION
C3

KTM
PIAGGIO

Required

1. For KTM in 2011, what are the largest three geographic markets in which it sells products? What is the amount (in millions of euros) of sales in each market?
2. For Piaggio in 2011, what are the largest three geographic markets in which it sells products? What is the amount (in millions of euros) of sales in each market? *Hint:* EMEA refers to Europe, the Middle East, and Africa. SEA refers to Southeast Asia.
3. How would customer service activities differ across different geographic markets?

ANSWERS TO MULTIPLE CHOICE QUIZ

1. b; Under traditional costing methods, overhead costs are allocated to products on the basis of some measure of volume such as direct labor hours or machine hours. This results in much of the overhead cost being allocated to high-volume products. In contrast, under activity-based costing, some overhead costs are allocated on the basis of batch level or product level activities. This change in allocation bases results in shifting overhead costs from high-volume products to low-volume products.
2. d; Generally, an activity-based costing system is more difficult to implement and maintain than a traditional costing system (thus answer **a** is false). Instead of eliminating waste by allocating costs to products that waste resources, activity-based management is a management approach that focuses on managing activities as a means of eliminating waste and reducing delays and defects (thus answer **b** is false). Instead of using a single allocation base (such as direct labor hours), activity-based costing uses a number of allocation bases for assigning costs to products (thus answer **c** is false). Answer **d** is true.
3. d; Batch level activities are activities that are performed each time a batch of goods is handled or processed, regardless of how many units are in a batch. Further, the amount of resources consumed depends on the number of batches rather than on the number of units in the batch. Worker recreational facilities relate to the organization as a whole rather than to specific batches and, as such, are not considered to be batch level. On the other hand, purchase order processing, setting up equipment, and the clerical activities described are activities that are performed each time a batch of goods is handled or processed, and, as such, are batch level activities.
4. c;

	(A) Activity Rate (Budgeted overhead cost ÷ Budgeted activity)	(B) Actual Activity	(A × B) Overhead Cost Applied to Production
Activity 1	($80,000 ÷ 1,000) = $80.00	800	$ 64,000
Activity 2	($58,400 ÷ 1,500) = $38.93*	500	19,465
Activity 3	($360,000 ÷ 6,000) = $60.00	5,400	324,000
Total overhead cost per unit for Product B			$407,465
Divided by number of units produced			÷ 31,652
Overhead cost per unit of Product B			$ 12.87

* rounded

5. d; The activity rate for Activity 3 is determined as follows:

Budgeted cost	÷	Budgeted activity	=	Activity rate
$14,000	÷	700	=	$20

18

Cost Behavior and Cost-Volume-Profit Analysis

A Look Back

Chapter 17 introduced the activity-based costing (ABC) system, which has the potential for greater accuracy of cost allocations and for providing managers with better cost information for strategic decisions.

A Look at This Chapter

This chapter shows how information on both costs and sales behavior is useful to managers in performing cost-volume-profit analysis. This analysis is an important part of successful management and sound business decisions.

A Look Ahead

Chapter 19 compares reports prepared under variable costing with those under absorption costing, and it explains how variable costing can improve managerial decisions.

Learning Objectives

CONCEPTUAL

C1 Describe different types of cost behavior in relation to production and sales volume. (p. 778)

C2 Describe several applications of cost-volume-profit analysis. (p. 789)

ANALYTICAL

A1 Compute the contribution margin and describe what it reveals about a company's cost structure. (p. 785)

A2 Analyze changes in sales using the degree of operating leverage. (p. 795)

PROCEDURAL

P1 Determine cost estimates using the scatter diagram, high-low, and regression methods of estimating costs. (p. 781)

P2 Compute the break-even point for a single product company. (p. 785)

P3 Graph costs and sales for a single product company. (p. 787)

P4 Compute the break-even point for a multiproduct company. (p. 793)

Decision Insight

Sporting Success

"Put passion into your work"

—PAUL CUNNINGHAM

GLEN ROCK, NJ—Most quarterbacks in backyard football games have a glaring weakness: They can't throw good passes. Paul Cunningham, lifelong sports fan and master craftsman, set out to make "an exceptional quality football, slightly smaller than an NFL ball, so that the average person can throw it." As a result, what started as a side project in his home workshop turned into a full-fledged business, **Leather Head Sports (Leatherheadsports.com)**. As Paul notes, "I've been able to leave the corporate world and do this full-time."

Paul's forays began when he crafted leather baseballs for the Major League Baseball Hall of Fame to use in recreating 19th century baseball games. Now, Paul makes leather baseballs, which he sells as Lemon Balls™, along with a line of Leather Head™ footballs and medicine balls. Paul makes every Leather Head™ ball himself. "I want someone to look at my football and see the passion that went into it," says Paul.

Paul stresses that he, like many entrepreneurs, had to learn through a process of trial and error. "Every hide is different, and I tried many different approaches to making a football." Now, upon receiving an order, Paul begins his production process by grabbing a side of top-quality leather. Using custom-made cutting dies, he hand cuts the leather panels. He then sews the leather panels together, inserts a rubber bladder, and laces the ball with rawhide lace. The result is what Paul calls the "official football of collegiate tailgating."

Operating at a small scale and using expensive, top-quality materials require Paul to understand and control his costs. Successful entrepreneurs must understand cost behavior to succeed. Identifying fixed and variable costs is key to understanding break-even points and maintaining the right product mix. Paul's small but diverse product line has considerably different selling prices and costs. Contribution margin income statements, which separate fixed and variable costs, enable entrepreneurs like Paul to quickly see how changes in selling prices, variable costs, or fixed costs impact profit. Understanding contribution margins and cost-volume-profit analyses enables small businesses to profit and grow.

Paul encourages young entrepreneurs to get out and make it happen. His sights are set on growing his company, possibly by bringing in additional craftsmen. Scaling his business in this way would make understanding how costs relate to volume and profit even more important. "I work hard," says Paul, "but I love working with my hands and creating things." Sounds like a perfect pass.

[Sources: *Leather Head Sports Website,* January 2013; http://www.youtube.com/watch?v=GaL3qxV4UzQ; http://video.foxbusiness.com/v/1404850982001/investors-consider-adding-fine-art-to-portfoliomix/?playlist_id=87185; http://video.foxbusiness.com/v/3972553/]

Chapter Preview

This chapter describes different types of costs and shows how changes in a company's operating volume affect these costs. The chapter also analyzes a company's costs and sales to explain how different operating strategies affect profit or loss. Managers use this type of analysis to forecast what will happen if changes are made to costs, sales volume, selling prices, or product mix. They then use these forecasts to select the best business strategy for the company.

Cost Behavior and Cost-Volume-Profit Analysis

Identifying Cost Behavior
- Fixed costs
- Variable costs
- Mixed costs
- Step-wise costs
- Curvilinear costs

Measuring Cost Behavior
- Scatter diagrams
- High-low method
- Least-squares regression
- Comparison of cost estimation methods

Using Break-Even Analysis
- Computing contribution margin
- Computing break-even
- Computing margin of safety
- Preparing a cost-volume-profit chart
- Assumptions in cost-volume-profit analysis

Applying Cost-Volume-Profit Analysis
- Computing income from sales and costs
- Computing sales for target income
- Using sensitivity analysis
- Computing multiproduct break-even

IDENTIFYING COST BEHAVIOR

Planning a company's future activities and events is crucial to successful management. One of the first steps in planning is to predict the volume of activity, the costs to be incurred, sales to be made, and profit to be received. An important tool to help managers carry out this step is **cost-volume-profit (CVP) analysis,** which helps them predict how changes in costs and sales levels affect income. In its basic form, CVP analysis involves computing the sales level at which a company neither earns an income nor incurs a loss, called the *break-even point.* For this reason, this basic form of cost-volume-profit analysis is often called *break-even analysis.* Managers use variations of CVP analysis to answer questions like:

Point: *Profit* is another term for *income.*

- What sales volume is needed to earn a target income?
- What is the change in income if selling prices decline and sales volume increases?
- How much does income increase if we install a new machine to reduce labor costs?
- How will income change if we change the sales mix of our products or services?

Consequently, cost-volume-profit analysis is useful in a wide range of business decisions.

Conventional cost-volume-profit analysis requires management to classify all costs as either *fixed* or *variable* with respect to production or sales volume. The remainder of this section discusses the concepts of fixed and variable cost behavior as they relate to CVP analysis.

Decision Insight

No Free Lunch Hardly a week goes by without a company advertising a free product with the purchase of another. Examples are a free printer with a digital camera purchase or a free monitor with a computer purchase. Can these companies break even, let alone earn profits? We are reminded of the *no-free-lunch* adage, meaning that companies expect profits from the companion or add-on purchase to make up for the free product. ■

C1 Describe different types of cost behavior in relation to production and sales volume.

Fixed Costs

A *fixed cost* remains unchanged in amount when the volume of activity varies from period to period within a relevant range. For example, $32,000 in monthly rent paid for a factory building remains the same whether the factory operates with a single eight-hour shift or around the clock with three shifts. This means that rent cost is the same each month at any level of output from zero to the plant's full productive capacity. Notice that while *total* fixed cost does not change as the level of production changes, the fixed cost *per unit* of output decreases as volume increases. For instance, if 200 units are produced when monthly rent is $32,000, the average rent cost per unit is $160 (computed as $32,000/200 units); and when 100 units are produced, the average rent cost per unit is $320 (computed as $32,000/100 units). When production increases to 1,000 units per month, the average rent cost per unit decreases to $32 (computed as $32,000/1,000 units). The average rent cost decreases to $16 per unit if production increases to 2,000 units per month. Common examples of fixed costs include depreciation, property taxes, office salaries, and many service department costs.

When production volume and costs are graphed, units of product are usually plotted on the *horizontal axis* and dollars of cost are plotted on the *vertical axis.* Fixed costs then are represented as a horizontal line because they remain constant at all levels of production. To illustrate, the top graph in Exhibit 18.1 shows that fixed costs remain at $32,000 at all production levels up to the company's monthly capacity of 2,000 units of output. The bottom graph in Exhibit 18.1 shows that fixed costs per unit fall as production levels increase. This drop in costs per unit as production levels increase is known as *economies of scale.* The *relevant range* for fixed costs in Exhibit 18.1 is 0 to 2,000 units. If the relevant range changes (that is, production capacity extends beyond this range), the amount of fixed costs will likely change.

Example: If the fixed cost line in Exhibit 18.1 is shifted upward, does the total cost line shift up, down, or remain in the same place? *Answer:* It shifts up by the same amount.

EXHIBIT 18.1

Relations of Total and Per-Unit Costs to Volume

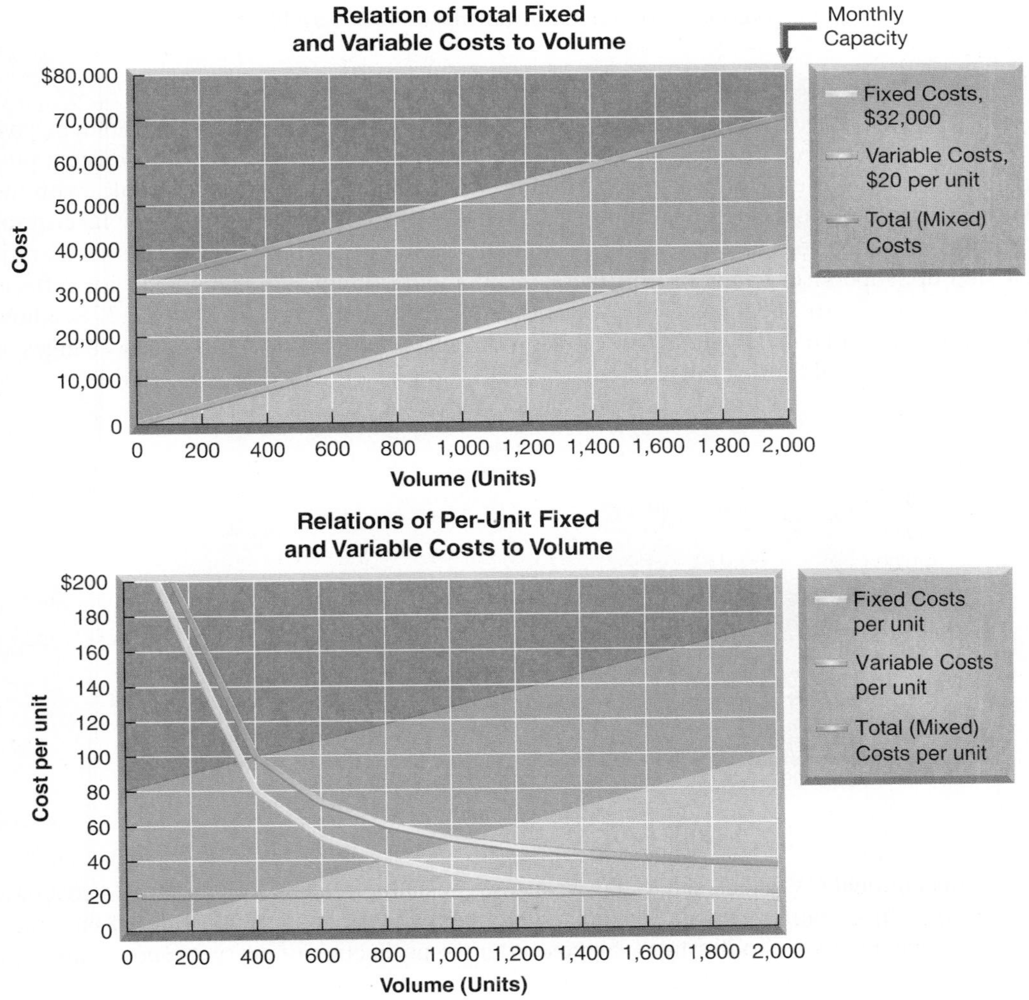

Example: If the level of fixed costs in Exhibit 18.1 changes, does the slope of the total cost line change? *Answer:* No, the slope doesn't change. The total cost line is simply shifted upward or downward.

Variable Costs

Point: Fixed costs are constant in total but vary (decline) per unit as more units are produced. Variable costs vary in total but are fixed per unit.

A *variable cost* changes in proportion to changes in volume of activity. The direct materials cost of a product is one example of a variable cost. If one unit of product requires materials costing $20, total materials costs are $200 when 10 units of product are manufactured, $400 for 20 units, $600 for 30 units, and so on. Notice that variable cost *per unit* remains constant but the *total* amount of variable cost changes with the level of production. In addition to direct materials, common variable costs include direct labor (if employees are paid per unit), sales commissions, shipping costs, and some overhead costs.

When variable costs are plotted on a graph of cost and volume, they appear as a straight line starting at the zero cost level. This straight line is upward (positive) sloping. The line rises as volume of activity increases. A variable cost line using a $20 per unit cost is graphed in Exhibit 18.1. The bottom graph in Exhibit 18.1 shows that variable cost per unit is constant as production levels change.

Mixed Costs

A **mixed cost** includes both fixed and variable cost components. For example, compensation for sales representatives often includes a fixed monthly salary and a variable commission based on sales. Like a fixed cost, a mixed cost is greater than zero when volume is zero; but unlike a fixed cost, it increases steadily in proportion to increases in volume. The mixed cost line in the top graph Exhibit 18.1 starts on the vertical axis at the $32,000 fixed cost point. Thus, at the zero volume level, total (mixed) cost equals the fixed costs. As the activity level increases, the mixed cost line increases at an amount equal to the variable cost per unit. This line is highest when the volume of activity is at 2,000 units (the end point of the relevant range). In CVP analysis, mixed costs are often separated into fixed and variable components. The fixed component is added to other fixed costs, and the variable component is added to other variable costs.

Step-Wise Costs

A **step-wise cost** reflects a step pattern in costs. Salaries of production supervisors often behave in a step-wise manner in that their salaries are fixed within a *relevant range* of the current production volume. However, if production volume expands significantly (for example, with the addition of another shift), additional supervisors must be hired. This means that the total cost for supervisory salaries goes up by a lump-sum amount. Similarly, if volume takes another significant step up, supervisory salaries will increase by another lump sum. This behavior reflects a step-wise cost, also known as a *stair-step cost,* which is graphed in Exhibit 18.2. See how the step-wise cost line is flat within ranges (steps). Then, when volume significantly changes, it shifts to another level for that range (step).

EXHIBIT 18.2

Step-Wise and Curvilinear Costs

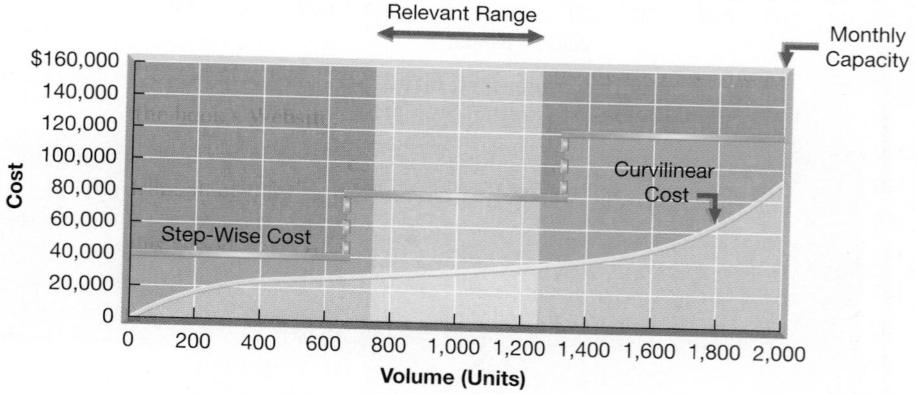

In a conventional CVP analysis, a step-wise cost is usually treated as either a fixed cost or a variable cost. This treatment involves manager judgment and depends on the width of the range and the expected volume. To illustrate, suppose after the production of every 25 snowboards, an operator lubricates the finishing machine. The cost of this lubricant reflects a step-wise pattern. Also, suppose that after the production of every 1,000 units, the snowboard cutting tool is replaced. Again, this is a step-wise cost. Note that the range of 25 snowboards is much narrower than the range of 1,000 snowboards. Some managers might treat the lubricant cost as a variable cost and the cutting tool cost as a fixed cost.

Point: Computer spreadsheets are important and effective tools for CVP analysis and for analyzing alternative "what-if" strategies.

Curvilinear Costs

A variable cost, as explained, is a *linear* cost; that is, it increases at a constant rate as volume of activity increases. A **curvilinear cost,** also called a *nonlinear cost,* increases at a nonconstant rate as volume increases. When graphed, curvilinear costs appear as a curved line. Exhibit 18.2 shows a curvilinear cost beginning at zero when production is zero and then increasing at different rates.

An example of a curvilinear cost is total direct labor cost when workers are paid by the hour. At low to medium levels of production, adding more employees allows each of them to specialize by doing certain tasks repeatedly instead of doing several different tasks. This often yields additional units of output at lower costs. A point is eventually reached at which adding more employees creates inefficiencies. For instance, a large crew demands more time and effort in communicating and coordinating their efforts. While adding employees in this case increases output, the labor cost per unit increases, and the total labor cost goes up at a steeper slope. This pattern is seen in Exhibit 18.2 where the curvilinear cost curve starts at zero, rises, flattens out, and then increases at a faster rate as output nears the maximum.

Point: Cost-volume-profit analysis helped Rod Canion, Jim Harris, and Bill Murto raise start-up capital of $20 million to launch **Compaq Computer.** They showed that break-even volumes were attainable within the first year.

Quick Check

Answers — p. 799

1. Which of the following statements is typically true? (*a*) Variable cost per unit increases as volume increases, (*b*) fixed cost per unit decreases as volume increases, or (*c*) a curvilinear cost includes both fixed and variable elements.
2. Describe the behavior of a fixed cost.
3. If cost per unit of activity remains constant (fixed), why is it called a variable cost?

MEASURING COST BEHAVIOR

P1 Determine cost estimates using the scatter diagram, high-low, and regression methods of estimating costs.

Identifying and measuring cost behavior requires careful analysis and judgment. An important part of this process is to identify costs that can be classified as either fixed or variable, which often requires analysis of past cost behavior. Three methods are commonly used to analyze past costs: scatter diagrams, the high-low method, and least-squares regression. Each method is discussed in this section using the unit and cost data shown in Exhibit 18.3, which

EXHIBIT 18.3

Data for Estimating Cost Behavior

Month	Units Produced	Total Cost
January	27,500	$21,500
February.	17,500	20,500
March	25,000	25,000
April	35,000	21,500
May.	47,500	25,500
June	22,500	18,500
July	30,000	23,500
August	52,500	28,500
September	37,500	26,000
October	67,500	29,000
November	62,500	31,000
December	57,500	26,000

are taken from a start-up company that uses units produced as the activity base in estimating cost behavior.

Scatter Diagrams

Scatter diagrams display past cost and unit data in graphical form. In preparing a scatter diagram, units are plotted on the horizontal axis and cost is plotted on the vertical axis. Each individual point on a scatter diagram reflects the cost and number of units for a prior period. In Exhibit 18.4, the prior 12 months' costs and numbers of units are graphed. Each point reflects total costs incurred and units produced for one of those months. For instance, the point labeled March had units produced of 25,000 and costs of $25,000.

EXHIBIT 18.4

Scatter Diagram

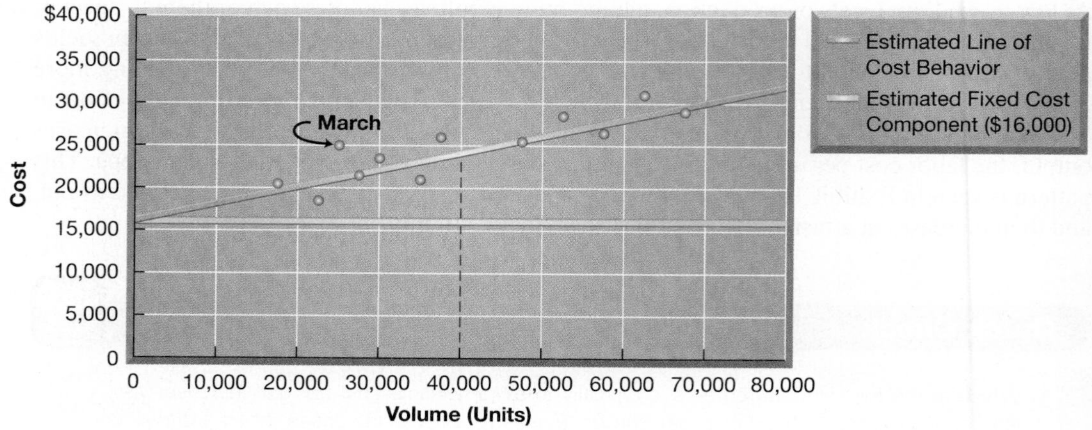

The **estimated line of cost behavior** is drawn on a scatter diagram to reflect the relation between cost and unit volume. This line best visually "fits" the points in a scatter diagram. Fitting this line demands judgment. The line drawn in Exhibit 18.4 intersects the vertical axis at approximately $16,000, which reflects fixed cost. To compute variable cost per unit, or the slope, we perform three steps. First, we select any two points on the horizontal axis (units), say 0 and 40,000. Second, we draw a vertical line from each of these points to intersect the estimated line of cost behavior. The point on the vertical axis (cost) corresponding to the 40,000 units point that intersects the estimated line is roughly $24,000. Similarly, the cost corresponding to zero units is $16,000 (the fixed cost point). Third, we compute the slope of the line, or variable cost, as the change in cost divided by the change in units. Exhibit 18.5 shows this computation.

EXHIBIT 18.5

Variable Cost per Unit (Scatter Diagram)

$$\frac{\textbf{Change in cost}}{\textbf{Change in units}} = \frac{\$24{,}000 - \$16{,}000}{40{,}000 - 0} = \frac{\$8{,}000}{40{,}000} = \$0.20 \text{ per unit}$$

Example: In Exhibits 18.4 and 18.5, if units are projected at 30,000, what is the predicted cost? *Answer:* Approximately $22,000.

Variable cost is $0.20 per unit. Thus, the cost equation that management will use to estimate costs for different unit levels is **$16,000 plus $0.20 per unit**.

High-Low Method

The **high-low method** is a way to estimate the cost equation by graphically connecting the two cost amounts at the highest and lowest unit volumes. In our case, the lowest number of units is 17,500, and the highest is 67,500. The costs corresponding to these unit volumes are $20,500 and $29,000, respectively (see the data in Exhibit 18.3). The estimated line of cost behavior for the high-low method is then drawn by connecting these two points on the scatter diagram corresponding to the lowest and highest unit volumes as follows.

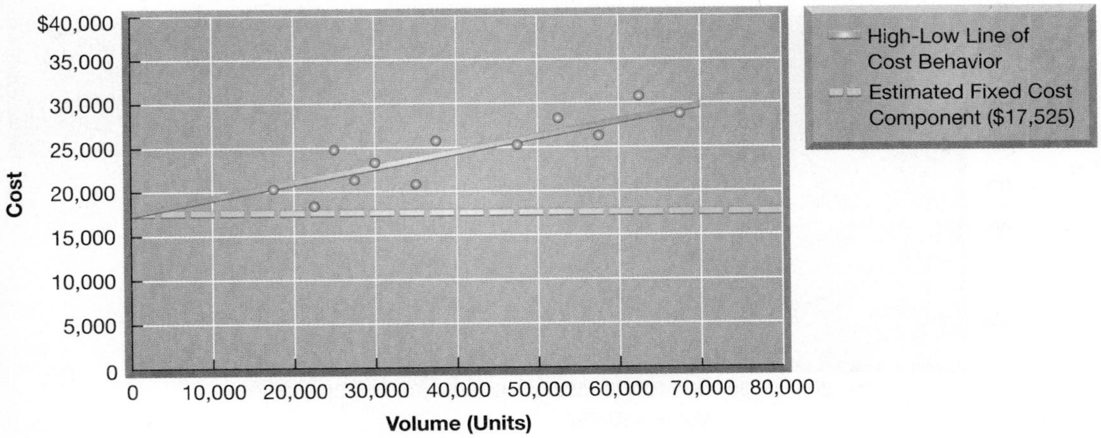

Point: Note that the high-low method identifies the high and low points of the volume (activity) base, and the costs linked with those extremes—which may not be the highest and lowest costs.

The variable cost per unit is determined as the change in cost divided by the change in units and uses the data from the high and low unit volumes. This results in a slope, or variable cost per unit, of $0.17 as computed in Exhibit 18.6.

EXHIBIT 18.6

Variable Cost per Unit (High-Low Method)

$$\frac{\textbf{Change in cost}}{\textbf{Change in units}} = \frac{\$29{,}000 - \$20{,}500}{67{,}500 - 17{,}500} = \frac{\$8{,}500}{50{,}000} = \$0.17 \text{ per unit}$$

To estimate the fixed cost for the high-low method, we use the knowledge that total cost equals fixed cost plus variable cost per unit times the number of units. Then we pick either the high or low point to determine the fixed cost. This computation is shown in Exhibit 18.7—where we use the high point (67,500 units) in determining the fixed cost of $17,525. Use of the low point (17,500 units) yields the same fixed cost estimate: $20,500 = Fixed cost + ($0.17 per unit × 17,500), or Fixed cost = $17,525.

EXHIBIT 18.7

Fixed Cost (High-Low Method)

Total cost = Fixed cost + (Variable cost × Units)

$29,000 = Fixed cost + ($0.17 per unit × 67,500 units)

Then, Fixed cost = $17,525

Thus, the cost equation used to estimate costs at different units is **$17,525 plus $0.17 per unit**. This cost equation differs slightly from that determined from the scatter diagram method. A deficiency of the high-low method is that it ignores all cost points except the highest and lowest. The result is less precision because the high-low method uses the most extreme points rather than the more usual conditions likely to recur.

Least-Squares Regression

Least-squares regression is a statistical method for identifying cost behavior. For our purposes, we use the cost equation estimated from this method but leave the computational details for more advanced courses. Such computations for least-squares regression are readily done using most spreadsheet programs or calculators. We illustrate this using Excel® in Appendix 18A.

The regression cost equation for the data presented in Exhibit 18.3 is **$16,947 plus $0.19 per unit**; that is, the fixed cost is estimated as $16,947 and the variable cost at $0.19 per unit. Both costs are reflected in the following graph.

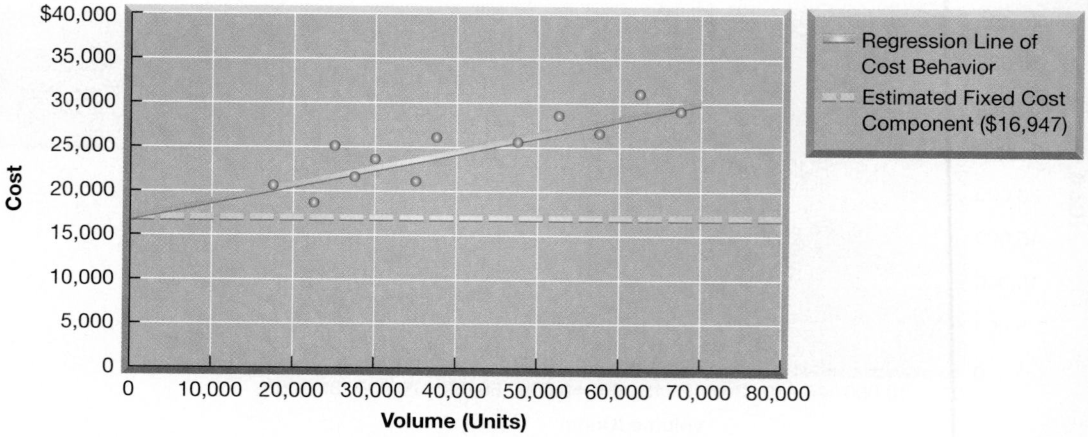

Comparison of Cost Estimation Methods

The three cost estimation methods result in slightly different estimates of fixed and variable costs as summarized in Exhibit 18.8. Estimates from the scatter diagram are based on a visual fit of the cost line and are subject to interpretation. Estimates from the high-low method use only two sets of values corresponding to the lowest and highest unit volumes. Estimates from least-squares regression use a statistical technique and all available data points.

EXHIBIT 18.8
Comparison of Cost Estimation Methods

Estimation Method	Fixed Cost	Variable Cost
Scatter diagram	$16,000	$0.20 per unit
High-low method	17,525	0.17 per unit
Least-squares regression	16,947	0.19 per unit

We must remember that all three methods use *past data.* Thus, cost estimates resulting from these methods are only as good as the data used for estimation. Managers must establish that the data are reliable in deriving cost estimates for the future. If the data are reliable, the use of more data points, as in the regression or scatter diagram methods, should yield more accurate estimates than the high-low method. However, the high-low method is easier to apply than the regression method and less subject to interpretation than the scatter diagram approach.

Quick Check Answers — p. 799

4. Which of the following methods is likely to yield the most precise estimated line of cost behavior? (*a*) High-low, (*b*) least-squares regression, or (*c*) scatter diagram.
5. What is the primary weakness of the high-low method?
6. Using conventional CVP analysis, a mixed cost should be (*a*) disregarded, (*b*) treated as a fixed cost, or (*c*) separated into fixed and variable components.

USING BREAK-EVEN ANALYSIS

Break-even analysis is a special case of cost-volume-profit analysis. This section describes break-even analysis by computing the break-even point and preparing a CVP (or break-even) chart.

Contribution Margin and Its Measures

We explained how managers classify costs by behavior. This often refers to classifying costs as being fixed or variable with respect to volume of activity. In manufacturing companies, volume of activity usually refers to the number of units produced. We then classify a cost as either fixed or variable, depending on whether total cost changes as the number of units produced changes. Once we separate costs by behavior, we can then compute a product's contribution margin. **Contribution margin per unit,** or *unit contribution margin,* is the amount by which a product's unit selling price exceeds its total variable cost per unit. This excess amount contributes to covering fixed costs and generating profits on a per unit basis. Exhibit 18.9 shows the contribution margin per unit formula.

A1 Compute the contribution margin and describe what it reveals about a company's cost structure.

Contribution margin per unit = Sales price per unit − Total variable cost per unit

EXHIBIT 18.9
Contribution Margin per Unit

The **contribution margin ratio,** which is the percent of a unit's selling price that exceeds total unit variable cost, is also useful for business decisions. It can be interpreted as the percent of each sales dollar that remains after deducting the total unit variable cost. Exhibit 18.10 shows the formula for the contribution margin ratio.

$$\textbf{Contribution margin ratio} = \frac{\textbf{Contribution margin per unit}}{\textbf{Sales price per unit}}$$

EXHIBIT 18.10
Contribution Margin Ratio

To illustrate the use of contribution margin, let's consider **Rydell,** which sells footballs for $100 each and incurs variable costs of $70 per football sold. Its fixed costs are $24,000 per month with monthly capacity of 1,800 units (footballs). Rydell's contribution margin per unit is $30, which is computed as follows.

Selling price per unit	$100
Variable cost per unit	70
Contribution margin per unit	$ 30

Its contribution margin ratio is 30%, computed as $30/$100. This reveals that for each unit sold, Rydell has $30 that contributes to covering fixed cost and profit. If we consider sales in dollars, a contribution margin of 30% implies that for each $1 in sales, Rydell has $0.30 that contributes to fixed cost and profit.

Decision Maker

Sales Manager You are evaluating orders from two customers but can accept only one of the orders because of your company's limited capacity. The first order is for 100 units of a product with a contribution margin ratio of 60% and a selling price of $1,000. The second order is for 500 units of a product with a contribution margin ratio of 20% and a selling price of $800. The incremental fixed costs are the same for both orders. Which order do you accept? ■ [Answer—p. 798]

Computing the Break-Even Point

P2 Compute the break-even point for a single product company.

The **break-even point** is the sales level at which a company neither earns a profit nor incurs a loss. The concept of break-even is applicable to nearly all organizations, activities, and events. One of the most important items of information when launching a project is whether it will break even—that is, whether sales will at least cover total costs. The break-even point can be expressed in either units or dollars of sales.

To illustrate break-even analysis, let's again look at Rydell, which sells footballs for $100 per unit and incurs $70 of variable costs per unit sold. Its fixed costs are $24,000 per month. Rydell breaks even for the month when it sells 800 footballs (sales volume of $80,000). We compute this break-even point using the formula in Exhibit 18.11. This formula uses the contribution margin per unit, which for Rydell is $30 ($100 − $70). From this we can compute the break-even sales volume as $24,000/$30, or 800 units per month.

EXHIBIT 18.11

Formula for Computing Break-Even Sales (in Units)

$$\textbf{Break-even point in units} = \frac{\textbf{Fixed costs}}{\textbf{Contribution margin per unit}}$$

At a price of $100 per unit, monthly sales of 800 units yield sales dollars of $80,000 (called *break-even sales dollars*). This $80,000 break-even sales can be computed directly using the formula in Exhibit 18.12.

EXHIBIT 18.12

Formula for Computing Break-Even Sales (in Dollars)

$$\textbf{Break-even point in dollars} = \frac{\textbf{Fixed costs}}{\textbf{Contribution margin ratio}}$$

Point: Even if a company operates at a level in excess of its break-even point, management may decide to stop operating because it is not earning a reasonable return on investment.

Rydell's break-even point in dollars is computed as $24,000/0.30, or $80,000 of monthly sales. To verify that Rydell's break-even point equals $80,000 (or 800 units), we prepare a simplified income statement in Exhibit 18.13. It shows that the $80,000 revenue from sales of 800 units exactly equals the sum of variable and fixed costs.

EXHIBIT 18.13

Contribution Margin Income Statement for Break-Even Sales

RYDELL COMPANY
Contribution Margin Income Statement (at Break-Even)
For Month Ended January 31, 2013

Sales (800 units at $100 each)	$80,000
Variable costs (800 units at $70 each)	56,000
Contribution margin	24,000
Fixed costs	24,000
Net income	$ 0

Point: A contribution margin income statement is also referred to as a ***variable costing income statement.*** This differs from the traditional ***absorption costing*** approach where all product costs are assigned to units sold and to units in ending inventory. Recall that variable costing expenses all fixed product costs. Thus, income for the two approaches differs depending on the level of finished goods inventory; the lower inventory is, the more similar the two approaches are.

The statement in Exhibit 18.13 is called a *contribution margin income statement.* It differs in format from a conventional income statement in two ways. First, it separately classifies costs and expenses as variable or fixed. Second, it reports contribution margin (Sales − Variable costs). The contribution margin income statement format is used in this chapter's assignment materials because of its usefulness in CVP analysis.

Computing the Margin of Safety

All companies wish to sell more than the break-even number of units. The excess of expected sales over the break-even sales level is called a company's **margin of safety,** the amount that sales can drop before the company incurs a loss. It can be expressed in units, dollars, or even as a percent of the predicted level of sales. To illustrate, if Rydell's expected sales are $100,000, the margin of safety is $20,000 above break-even sales of $80,000. As a percent, the margin of safety is 20% of expected sales as shown in Exhibit 18.14.

EXHIBIT 18.14

Computing Margin of Safety (in Percent)

$$\textbf{Margin of safety (in percent)} = \frac{\textbf{Expected sales} - \textbf{Break-even sales}}{\textbf{Expected sales}}$$

$$= \frac{\$100{,}000 - \$80{,}000}{\$100{,}000} = 20\%$$

Management must assess whether the margin of safety is adequate in light of factors such as sales variability, competition, consumer tastes, and economic conditions.

Preparing a Cost-Volume-Profit Chart

Exhibit 18.15 is a graph of Rydell's cost-volume-profit relations. This graph is called a **cost-volume-profit (CVP) chart,** or a *break-even chart* or *break-even graph.* The horizontal axis is the number of units produced and sold and the vertical axis is dollars of sales and costs. The lines in the chart depict both sales and costs at different output levels.

P3 Graph costs and sales for a single product company.

EXHIBIT 18.15

Cost-Volume-Profit Chart

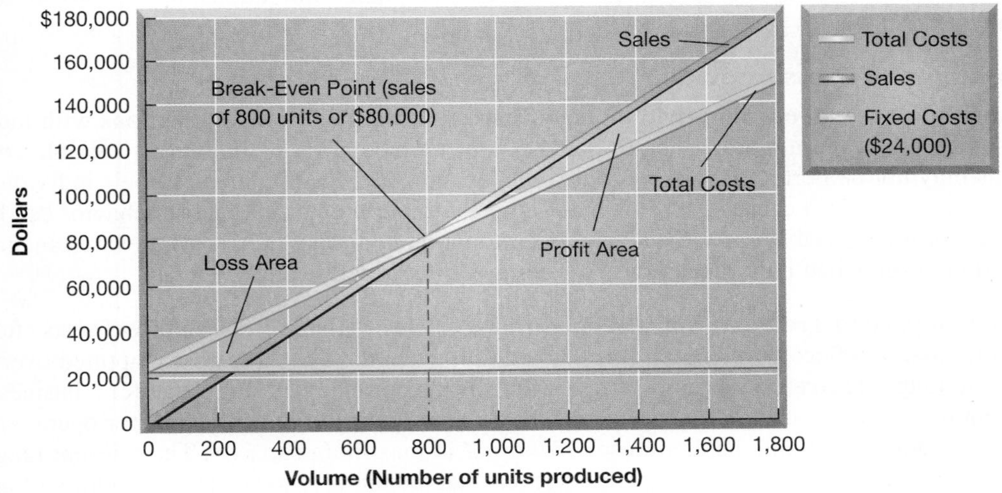

We follow three steps to prepare a CVP chart, which can also be drawn with computer programs that convert numeric data to graphs:

1. Plot fixed costs on the vertical axis ($24,000 for Rydell). Draw a horizontal line at this level to show that fixed costs remain unchanged regardless of output volume (drawing this fixed cost line is not essential to the chart).
2. Draw the total (variable plus fixed) cost line for a relevant range of volume levels. This line starts at the fixed costs level on the vertical axis because total costs equal fixed costs at zero volume. The slope of the total cost line equals the variable cost per unit ($70). To draw the line, compute the total costs for any volume level, and connect this point with the vertical axis intercept ($24,000). Do not draw this line beyond the productive capacity for the planning period (1,800 units for Rydell).
3. Draw the sales line. Start at the origin (zero units and zero dollars of sales) and make the slope of this line equal to the selling price per unit ($100). To sketch the line, compute dollar sales for any volume level and connect this point with the origin. Do not extend this line beyond the productive capacity. Total sales will be at the highest level at maximum capacity.

Point: CVP analysis is often based on *sales volume*, using either units sold or dollar sales. Other output measures, such as the number of units produced, can also be used.

The total cost line and the sales line intersect at 800 units in Exhibit 18.15, which is the break-even point—the point where total dollar sales of $80,000 equals the sum of both fixed and variable costs ($80,000).

On either side of the break-even point, the vertical distance between the sales line and the total cost line at any specific volume reflects the profit or loss expected at that point. At volume levels to the left of the break-even point, this vertical distance is the amount of the expected loss because the total costs line is above the total sales line. At volume levels to the right of the break-even point, the vertical distance represents the expected profit because the total sales line is above the total cost line.

Example: In Exhibit 18.15, the sales line intersects the total cost line at 800 units. At what point would the two lines intersect if selling price is increased by 20% to $120 per unit? *Answer:* $24,000/($120 − $70) = 480 units

Decision Maker

Operations Manager As a start-up manufacturer, you wish to identify the behavior of manufacturing costs to develop a production cost budget. You know three methods can be used to identify cost behavior from past data, but past data are unavailable because this is a start-up. What do you do? ■ [Answer—p. 799]

Making Assumptions in Cost-Volume-Profit Analysis

Cost-volume-profit analysis assumes that relations can normally be expressed as simple lines similar to those in Exhibits 18.4 and 18.15. CVP analysis assumes that selling prices per unit, variable costs per unit, and total fixed costs are all held constant. If the expected costs and sales behavior differ from the assumptions, the results of CVP analysis can be limited. While the behavior of individual costs and sales may not be perfectly consistent with CVP assumptions, we can still perform useful analyses in spite of these assumptions' limitations, for reasons we describe next.

Working with Assumptions

Summing costs can offset individual deviations. Deviations from assumptions with individual costs are often minor when these costs are summed. That is, individual variable cost items may not be perfectly variable, but when we sum these variable costs, their individual deviations can offset each other. This means the assumption of variable cost behavior can be proper for total variable costs. Similarly, an assumption that total fixed costs are constant can be proper even when individual fixed cost items are not exactly constant.

CVP is applied to a relevant range of operations. Sales, variable costs, and fixed costs often are reasonably reflected in straight lines on a graph when the assumptions are applied over a relevant range. The **relevant range of operations** is the normal operating range for a business. Except for unusually difficult or prosperous times, management typically plans for operations within a range of volume neither close to zero nor at maximum capacity. The relevant range excludes extremely high and low operating levels that are unlikely to occur. The validity of assuming that a specific cost is fixed or variable is more acceptable when operations are within the relevant range. As shown in Exhibit 18.2, a curvilinear cost can be treated as variable and linear if the relevant range covers volumes where it has a nearly constant slope. If the normal range of activity changes, some costs might need reclassification.

Example: If the selling price declines, what happens to the break-even point? *Answer:* It increases.

CVP analysis yields estimates. CVP analysis yields approximate answers to questions about costs, volumes, and profits. These answers do not have to be precise because the analysis makes rough estimates about the future. For example, to simplify analysis, we sometimes assume that the production level is the same as the sales level. That is, inventory levels do not change. This often is justified by arguing that CVP analysis provides only approximations. With just-in-time inventory systems, production levels should approximate sales levels, thus CVP estimates should be more accurate. As long as managers understand that CVP analysis gives estimates, it can be a useful tool for starting the planning process. Other qualitative factors also must be considered.

Quick Check Answers — p. 799

7. Fixed cost divided by the contribution margin ratio yields the (*a*) break-even point in dollars, (*b*) contribution margin per unit, or (*c*) break-even point in units.
8. A company sells a product for $90 per unit with variable costs of $54 per unit. What is the contribution margin ratio?
9. Refer to Quick Check (8). If fixed costs for the period are $90,000, what is the break-even point in dollars?
10. What is a company's margin of safety?
11. What three basic assumptions are used in CVP analysis?

Working with Changes in Estimates Because CVP analysis uses estimates, knowing how changes in those estimates impact break-even is useful. For example, a manager might form three estimates for each of the components of break-even: optimistic, most likely, and pessimistic. Then ranges of break-even points in units can be computed using the formula in Exhibit 18.11.

To illustrate, assume Rydell's managers provide the set of estimates in Exhibit 18.16.

EXHIBIT 18.16

Alternative Estimates for Break-Even Analysis

	Selling Price per Unit	Variable Cost per Unit	Total Fixed Costs
Optimistic	$105	$68	$21,000
Most likely	100	70	24,000
Pessimistic	95	72	27,000

If, for example, Rydell's managers believe they can raise the selling price of a football to $105, without any change in unit variable or total fixed costs, then the revised contribution margin per football is $35, and the revised break-even in units follows in Exhibit 18.17.

EXHIBIT 18.17

Revised Break-Even in Units

$$\text{Revised break-even point in units} = \frac{\$24{,}000}{\$35} = 686 \text{ units (rounded)}$$

Repeating this calculation using each of the other eight separate estimates above, and graphing the results, yields the three scatter diagrams in Exhibit 18.18.

EXHIBIT 18.18

Scatter Diagrams—Break-Even Points for Alternative Estimates

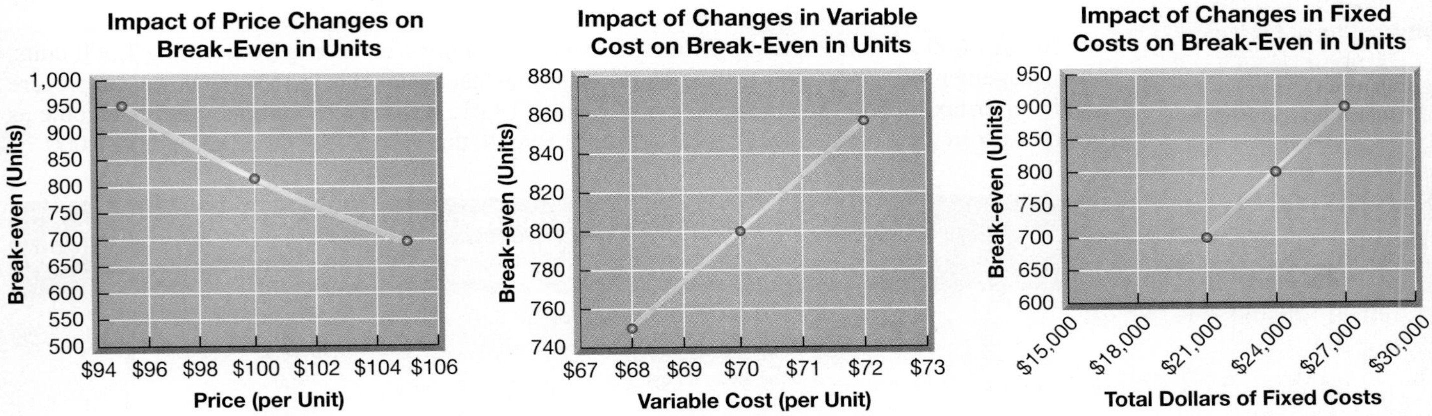

These scatter diagrams show how changes in selling prices, variable costs, and fixed costs impact break-even. When selling prices can be increased without impacting unit variable costs or total fixed costs, break-even decreases. When competition drives selling prices down, and the company cannot reduce costs, break-even increases. Increases in either variable or fixed costs, if they cannot be passed on to customers via higher selling prices, will increase break-even. If costs can be reduced and selling prices held constant, the break-even decreases.

Point: This analysis changed only one estimate at a time; managers can examine how combinations of changes in estimates will impact break-even.

APPLYING COST-VOLUME-PROFIT ANALYSIS

Managers consider a variety of strategies in planning business operations. Cost-volume-profit analysis is useful in helping managers evaluate the likely effects of these strategies, which is the focus of this section.

Computing Income from Sales and Costs

C2 Describe several applications of cost-volume-profit analysis.

An important question managers often ask is "What is the predicted income from a predicted level of sales?" To answer this, we look at four variables in CVP analysis. These variables and their relations to income (pretax) are shown in Exhibit 18.19. We use these relations to compute expected income from predicted sales and cost levels.

EXHIBIT 18.19

Income Relations in CVP Analysis

Sales
− Variable costs
Contribution margin
− Fixed costs
Income (pretax)

To illustrate, let's assume that Rydell's management expects to sell 1,500 units in January 2013. What is the amount of income if this sales level is achieved? Following Exhibit 18.19, we compute Rydell's expected income in Exhibit 18.20.

EXHIBIT 18.20

Computing Expected Pretax Income from Expected Sales

RYDELL COMPANY
Contribution Margin Income Statement
For Month Ended January 31, 2013

Sales (1,500 units at $100 each)	$150,000
Variable costs (1,500 units at $70 each)	105,000
Contribution margin	45,000
Fixed costs	24,000
Income (pretax)	$ 21,000

The $21,000 income is pretax. To find the amount of *after-tax* income from selling 1,500 units, management must apply the proper tax rate. Assume that the tax rate is 25%. Then we can prepare the after-tax income statement shown in Exhibit 18.21. We can also compute pretax income as after-tax income divided by (1 − tax rate); for Rydell, this is $15,750/(1 − 0.25), or $21,000.

EXHIBIT 18.21

Computing Expected After-Tax Income from Expected Sales

RYDELL COMPANY
Contribution Margin Income Statement
For Month Ended January 31, 2013

Sales (1,500 units at $100 each)	$150,000
Variable costs (1,500 units at $70 each)	105,000
Contribution margin	45,000
Fixed costs	24,000
Pretax income	21,000
Income taxes (25%)	5,250
Net income (after tax)	$ 15,750

Management then assesses whether this income is an adequate return on assets invested. Management should also consider whether sales and income can be increased by raising or lowering prices. CVP analysis is a good tool for addressing these kinds of "what-if" questions.

Computing Sales for a Target Income

Many companies' annual plans are based on certain income targets (sometimes called *budgets*). Rydell's income target for this year is to increase income by 10% over the prior year. When prior year income is known, Rydell easily computes its target income. CVP analysis helps to determine the sales level needed to achieve the target income. Planning for the year is then based on this level.

We use the formula shown in Exhibit 18.22 to compute sales for a target *after-tax* income. To illustrate, Rydell has monthly fixed costs of $24,000 and a 30% contribution margin ratio. Assume that it sets a target monthly after-tax income of $9,000 when the tax rate is 25%. This means the pretax income is targeted at $12,000 [$9,000/(1 − 0.25)] with a tax expense of $3,000. Using the formula in Exhibit 18.22, we find that $120,000 of sales are needed to produce a $9,000 after-tax income.

$$\textbf{Dollar sales at target after-tax income} = \frac{\textbf{Fixed costs} + \textbf{Target pretax income}}{\textbf{Contribution margin ratio}}$$

$$= \frac{\$24{,}000 + \$12{,}000}{30\%} = \$120{,}000$$

EXHIBIT 18.22

Computing Sales (Dollars) for a Target After-Tax Income

We can alternatively compute *unit sales* instead of dollar sales. To do this, we substitute *contribution margin per unit* for the contribution margin ratio in the denominator. This gives the number of units to sell to reach the target after-tax income. Exhibit 18.23 illustrates this for Rydell. The two computations in Exhibits 18.22 and 18.23 are equivalent because sales of 1,200 units at $100 per unit equal $120,000 of sales.

Point: Break-even is a special case of the formulas in Exhibits 18.22 and 18.23; simply set target pretax income to $0 and the formulas reduce to those in Exhibits 18.11 and 18.12.

$$\textbf{Unit sales at target after-tax income} = \frac{\textbf{Fixed costs} + \textbf{Target pretax income}}{\textbf{Contribution margin per unit}}$$

$$= \frac{\$24{,}000 + \$12{,}000}{\$30} = 1{,}200 \text{ units}$$

EXHIBIT 18.23

Computing Sales (Units) for a Target After-Tax Income

Decision Ethics

Supervisor Your team is conducting a cost-volume-profit analysis for a new product. Different sales projections have different incomes. One member suggests picking numbers yielding favorable income because any estimate is "as good as any other." Another member points to a scatter diagram of 20 months' production on a comparable product and suggests dropping unfavorable data points for cost estimation. What do you do? ■ [Answer—p. 799]

We can also use the contribution margin income statement approach to compute sales for a target income. In step 1, we insert the fixed costs ($24,000) and the desired after tax profit level ($9,000) into a contribution margin income statement, as shown in Exhibit 18.24. To achieve an after tax profit of $9,000, Rydell's pretax income must be $12,000, computed as $9,000/(1 − 0.25). We insert this as step 2 in the pretax income row in the contribution margin income statement and solve for Rydell's income taxes ($12,000 − $9,000), or $3,000. To cover its fixed costs of $24,000 and yield a pretax income of $12,000, Rydell must generate a contribution margin of $36,000 (computed as $24,000 plus $12,000). We enter this in the contribution margin row as step 3. With a contribution margin ratio of 30%, sales must be $120,000, computed as $36,000/0.30, to yield a contribution margin of $36,000. We enter this in the sales row of the contribution margin income statement as step 3 and solve for variable costs of $84,000 (computed as $120,000 − $36,000). At a selling price of $100 per unit, Rydell must sell 1,200 units ($120,000/$100) to earn after tax net income of $9,000.

RYDELL COMPANY
Contribution Margin Income Statement
For Month Ended January 31, 2013

	Step 1	Step 2	Step 3
Sales	?	?	$120,000
Variable costs	?	?	84,000
Contribution margin	?	?	36,000
Fixed costs	24,000	24,000	24,000
Income (pretax)	?	12,000	12,000
Incomes taxes (25%)	?	3,000	3,000
Net income (after tax)	$ 9,000	$ 9,000	$ 9,000
	$9,000/(1 − 0.25)	$24,000 + $12,000	$36,000/0.30

EXHIBIT 18.24

Using the Contribution Margin Income Statement to Find Target Sales

Using Sensitivity Analysis

Earlier we showed how changing one of the estimates in a CVP analysis impacts break-even. We can also examine strategies that impact several estimates in the CVP analysis. For instance, we might want to know what happens to income if we automate a currently manual process. We can use CVP analysis to predict income if we can describe how these changes affect a company's fixed costs, variable costs, selling price, and volume.

To illustrate, assume that Rydell Company is looking into buying a new machine that would increase monthly fixed costs from $24,000 to $30,000 but decrease variable costs from $70 per unit to $60 per unit. The machine is used to produce output whose selling price will remain unchanged at $100. This results in increases in both the unit contribution margin and the contribution margin ratio. The revised contribution margin per unit is $40 ($100 − $60), and the revised contribution margin ratio is 40% of selling price ($40/$100). Using CVP analysis, Rydell's revised break-even point in dollars would be $75,000 as computed in Exhibit 18.25.

Example: If fixed costs decline, what happens to the break-even point? *Answer:* It decreases.

EXHIBIT 18.25

Revising Break-even When Changes Occur

$$\textbf{Revised break-even point in dollars} = \frac{\textbf{Revised fixed costs}}{\textbf{Revised contribution margin ratio}} = \frac{\$30{,}000}{40\%} = \$75{,}000$$

We can also use the contribution margin income statement approach in sensitivity analysis, as we show in Exhibit 18.26. The revised fixed costs and the revised contribution margin ratio can be used to address other issues including computation of (1) expected income for a given sales level and (2) the sales level needed to earn a target income. Once again, we can use sensitivity analysis to generate different sets of revenue and cost estimates that are *optimistic, pessimistic,* and *most likely.* Different CVP analyses based on these estimates provide different scenarios that management can analyze and use in planning business strategy.

EXHIBIT 18.26

Using the Contribution Margin Income Statement in Sensitivity Analysis

RYDELL COMPANY
Contribution Margin Income Statement
For Month Ended January 31, 2013

	Step 1	Step 2	Step 3
Sales	?	?	$75,000
Variable costs	?	?	45,000
Contribution margin	?	30,000	30,000
Fixed costs	30,000	30,000	30,000
Income (pretax)	$ 0	$ 0	$ 0
		$30,000 + $0	$30,000/0.40

Decision Insight

RFID-CVP Companies are increasingly using radio-frequency identification (RFID) tags to control inventory. Affixed to products, RFID tags enable companies to reduce costs of inventory theft and scanning errors. Are RFID systems economically feasible? Railroad companies have long used RFID tags on rail cars. While expensive, these tags can be reused thousands of times, thus the cost per tag falls as railroad traffic increases. Such economies of scale and other cost savings make RFID a better-than break-even investment for railroad companies. ■

Quick Check

Answers — p. 799

12. A company has fixed costs of $50,000 and a 25% contribution margin ratio. What dollar sales are necessary to achieve an after-tax net income of $120,000 if the tax rate is 20%? (*a*) $800,000, (*b*) $680,000, or (*c*) $600,000.
13. If a company's contribution margin ratio decreases from 50% to 25%, what can be said about the unit sales needed to achieve the same target income level?

Computing a Multiproduct Break-Even Point

P4 Compute the break-even point for a multiproduct company.

To this point, we have looked only at cases where the company sells a single product or service. This was to keep the basic CVP analysis simple. However, many companies sell multiple products or services, and we can modify the CVP analysis for use in these cases. An important assumption in a multiproduct setting is that the sales mix of different products is known and remains constant during the planning period. **Sales mix** is the ratio (proportion) of the sales volumes for the various products. For instance, if a company normally sells 10,000 footballs, 5,000 softballs, and 4,000 basketballs per month, its sales mix can be expressed as 10:5:4 for footballs, softballs, and basketballs.

To apply multiproduct CVP analysis, we can estimate the break-even point by using a **composite unit,** which consists of a specific number of units of each product in proportion to their expected sales mix. Multiproduct CVP analysis treats this composite unit as a single product. To illustrate, let's look at Hair-Today, a styling salon that offers three cuts: basic, ultra, and budget in the ratio of 4 basic units to 2 ultra units to 1 budget unit (expressed as 4:2:1). Management wants to estimate its break-even point for next year. Unit selling prices for these three cuts are basic, \$20; ultra, \$32; and budget, \$16. Using the 4:2:1 sales mix, the selling price of a composite unit of the three products is computed as follows.

4 units of basic @ \$20 per unit	\$ 80
2 units of ultra @ \$32 per unit	64
1 unit of budget @ \$16 per unit	16
Selling price of a composite unit	**\$160**

Hair-Today's fixed costs are \$192,000 per year, and its variable costs of the three products are basic, \$13; ultra, \$18.00; and budget, \$8.00. Variable costs for a composite unit of these products follow.

Point: Selling prices and variable costs are usually expressed in per unit amounts. Fixed costs are usually expressed in total amounts.

4 units of basic @ \$13 per unit	\$52
2 units of ultra @ \$18 per unit	36
1 unit of budget @ \$8 per unit	8
Variable costs of a composite unit	**\$96**

Hair-Today's \$64 contribution margin for a composite unit is computed by subtracting the variable costs of a composite unit (\$96) from its selling price (\$160). We then use the contribution margin to determine Hair-Today's break-even point in composite units in Exhibit 18.27.

EXHIBIT 18.27

Break-Even Point in Composite Units

$$\textbf{Break-even point in composite units} = \frac{\textbf{Fixed costs}}{\textbf{Contribution margin per composite unit}}$$

$$= \frac{\$192{,}000}{\$64} = 3{,}000 \text{ composite units}$$

This computation implies that Hair-Today breaks even when it sells 3,000 composite units. To determine how many units of each product it must sell to break even, we multiply the number of units of each product in the composite by 3,000 as follows.

Point: The break-even point in dollars for Exhibit 18.27 is \$192,000/(\$64/\$160) = \$480,000.

Basic:	4 × 3,000	12,000 units
Ultra:	2 × 3,000	6,000 units
Budget:	1 × 3,000	3,000 units

Instead of computing contribution margin per composite unit, a company can compute a **weighted-average contribution margin.** Given the 4:2:1 product mix, basic cuts comprise 57.14% (computed as 4/7) of the company's haircuts, ultra makes up 28.57% of its business, and budget cuts comprise 14.29%. The weighted-average contribution margin follows in Exhibit 18.28.

EXHIBIT 18.28

Weighted-Average Contribution Margin

	Unit contribution margin	×	Percentage of sales mix	=	Weighted unit contribution margin
Basic	$ 7		57.14%		$4.000
Ultra	14		28.57		4.000
Budget	8		14.29		1.143
Weighted-average contribution margin					$9.143

The company's break-even point in units is computed in Exhibit 18.29 as follows:

EXHIBIT 18.29

Break-Even in Units using Weighted-Average Contribution Margin

$$\textbf{Break-even point in units} = \frac{\textbf{Fixed costs}}{\textbf{Weighted-average contribution margin}}$$

$$= \frac{\$192{,}000}{\$9.143} = 21{,}000 \text{ units}$$

We see that the weighted-average contribution margin method yields 21,000 whole units as the break-even amount, the same total as the composite unit approach.

Exhibit 18.30 verifies the results for composite units by showing Hair-Today's sales and costs at this break-even point using a contribution margin income statement.

EXHIBIT 18.30

Multiproduct Break-Even Income Statement

HAIR-TODAY
Forecasted Contribution Margin Income Statement (at Break-Even)

	Basic	Ultra	Budget	Totals
Sales				
Basic (12,000 @ $20)	$240,000			
Ultra (6,000 @ $32)		$192,000		
Budget (3,000 @ $16)			$48,000	
Total sales				$480,000
Variable costs				
Basic (12,000 @ $13)	156,000			
Ultra (6,000 @ $18)		108,000		
Budget (3,000 @ $8)			24,000	
Total variable costs				288,000
Contribution margin	$ 84,000	$ 84,000	$24,000	192,000
Fixed costs				192,000
Net income				$ 0

A CVP analysis using composite units can be used to answer a variety of planning questions. Once a product mix is set, all answers are based on the assumption that the mix remains constant at all relevant sales levels as other factors in the analysis do. We also can vary the sales mix to see what happens under alternative strategies.

Point: Enterprise resource planning (ERP) systems can quickly generate multiproduct break-even analyses.

Decision Maker

Entrepreneur A CVP analysis indicates that your start-up, which markets electronic products, will break even with the current sales mix and price levels. You have a target income in mind. What analysis might you perform to assess the likelihood of achieving this income? ■ [Answer—p. 799]

Quick Check

Answers – p. 799

14. The sales mix of a company's two products, X and Y, is 2:1. Unit variable costs for both products are $2, and unit sales prices are $5 for X and $4 for Y. What is the contribution margin per composite unit? (*a*) $5, (*b*) $10, or (*c*) $8.
15. What additional assumption about sales mix must be made in doing a conventional CVP analysis for a company that produces and sells more than one product?

GLOBAL VIEW

Survey evidence shows that many German companies have elaborate and detailed cost accounting systems. Over 90 percent of companies surveyed report their systems focus on *contribution margin*. This focus helps German companies like **Volkswagen** control costs and plan their production levels. Recently, Volkswagen announced it expects its Spanish brand *Seat* to break even within five years. For 2010, the *Seat* brand lost €311 million on revenue of €5.038 billion (349,000 units).

Degree of Operating Leverage — Decision Analysis

A2 Analyze changes in sales using the degree of operating leverage.

CVP analysis is especially useful when management begins the planning process and wishes to predict outcomes of alternative strategies. These strategies can involve changes in selling prices, fixed costs, variable costs, sales volume, and product mix. Managers are interested in seeing the effects of changes in some or all of these factors.

One goal of all managers is to get maximum benefits from their fixed costs. Managers would like to use 100% of their output capacity so that fixed costs are spread over the largest number of units. This would decrease fixed cost per unit and increase income. The extent, or relative size, of fixed costs in the total cost structure is known as **operating leverage.** Companies having a higher proportion of fixed costs in their total cost structure are said to have higher operating leverage. An example of this is a company that chooses to automate its processes instead of using direct labor, increasing its fixed costs and lowering its variable costs. A useful managerial measure to help assess the effect of changes in the level of sales on income is the **degree of operating leverage (DOL)** defined in Exhibit 18.31.

EXHIBIT 18.31

Degree of Operating Leverage

DOL = Total contribution margin (in dollars)/Pretax income

To illustrate, let's return to Rydell Company. At a sales level of 1,200 units, Rydell's total contribution margin is \$36,000 (1,200 units × \$30 contribution margin per unit). Its pretax income, after subtracting fixed costs of \$24,000, is \$12,000 (\$36,000 − \$24,000). Rydell's degree of operating leverage at this sales level is 3.0, computed as contribution margin divided by pretax income (\$36,000/\$12,000). We then use DOL to measure the effect of changes in the level of sales on pretax income. For instance, suppose Rydell expects sales to increase by 10%. If this increase is within the relevant range of operations, we can expect this 10% increase in sales to result in a 30% increase in pretax income computed as DOL multiplied by the increase in sales (3.0 × 10%). Similar analyses can be done for expected decreases in sales.

DEMONSTRATION PROBLEM

Sport Caps Co. manufactures and sells caps for different sporting events. The fixed costs of operating the company are \$150,000 per month, and the variable costs for caps are \$5 per unit. The caps are sold for \$8 per unit. The fixed costs provide a production capacity of up to 100,000 caps per month.

Required

1. Use the formulas in the chapter to compute the following:

a. Contribution margin per cap.

b. Break-even point in terms of the number of caps produced and sold.

c. Amount of net income at 30,000 caps sold per month (ignore taxes).

d. Amount of net income at 85,000 caps sold per month (ignore taxes).

e. Number of caps to be produced and sold to provide \$45,000 of after-tax income, assuming an income tax rate of 25%.

2. Draw a CVP chart for the company, showing cap output on the horizontal axis. Identify (*a*) the break-even point and (*b*) the amount of pretax income when the level of cap production is 70,000. (Omit the fixed cost line.)

3. Use the formulas in the chapter to compute the

a. Contribution margin ratio.

b. Break-even point in terms of sales dollars.

c. Amount of net income at $250,000 of sales per month (ignore taxes).

d. Amount of net income at $600,000 of sales per month (ignore taxes).

e. Dollars of sales needed to provide $45,000 of after-tax income, assuming an income tax rate of 25%.

PLANNING THE SOLUTION

- Identify the formulas in the chapter for the required items expressed in units and solve them using the data given in the problem.
- Draw a CVP chart that reflects the facts in the problem. The horizontal axis should plot the volume in units up to 100,000, and the vertical axis should plot the total dollars up to $800,000. Plot the total cost line as upward sloping, starting at the fixed cost level ($150,000) on the vertical axis and increasing until it reaches $650,000 at the maximum volume of 100,000 units. Verify that the break-even point (where the two lines cross) equals the amount you computed in part 1.
- Identify the formulas in the chapter for the required items expressed in dollars and solve them using the data given in the problem.

SOLUTION TO DEMONSTRATION PROBLEM

1. a. Contribution margin per cap = Selling price per unit − Variable cost per unit = $8 − $5 = $3

b. Break-even point in caps

$$= \frac{\text{Fixed costs}}{\text{Contribution margin per cap}} = \frac{\$150{,}000}{\$3} = \underline{\underline{50{,}000 \text{ caps}}}$$

c. Net income at 30,000 caps sold = (Units × Contribution margin per unit) − Fixed costs = (30,000 × $3) − $150,000 = $(60,000) loss

d. Net income at 85,000 caps sold = (Units × Contribution margin per unit) − Fixed costs = (85,000 × $3) − $150,000 = $105,000 profit

e. Pretax income = $45,000/(1 − 0.25) = $60,000

Income taxes = $60,000 × 25% = $15,000

Units needed for $45,000 income

$$= \frac{\text{Fixed costs} + \text{Target pretax income}}{\text{Contribution margin per cap}}$$

$$= \frac{\$150{,}000 + \$60{,}000}{\$3} = \underline{\underline{70{,}000 \text{ caps}}}$$

2. CVP chart.

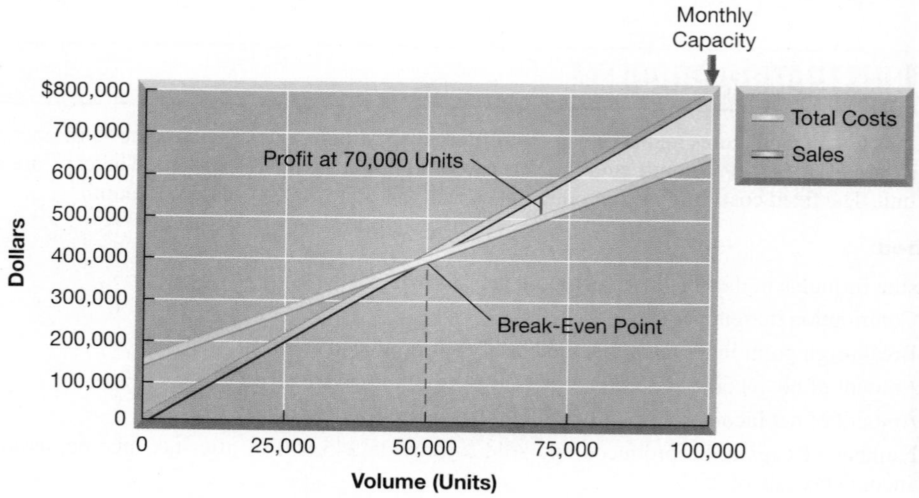

3. a. Contribution margin ratio
$$= \frac{\text{Contribution margin per unit}}{\text{Selling price per unit}} = \frac{\$3}{\$8} = \underline{\underline{0.375}}, \text{ or } \underline{\underline{37.5\%}}$$

b. Break-even point in dollars
$$= \frac{\text{Fixed costs}}{\text{Contribution margin ratio}} = \frac{\$150{,}000}{37.5\%} = \underline{\underline{\$400{,}000}}$$

c. Net income at sales of \$250,000
$$= (\text{Sales} \times \text{Contribution margin ratio}) - \text{Fixed costs}$$
$$= (\$250{,}000 \times 37.5\%) - \$150{,}000 = \underline{\underline{\$(56{,}250)\text{ loss}}}$$

d. Net income at sales of \$600,000
$$= (\text{Sales} \times \text{Contribution margin ratio}) - \text{Fixed costs}$$
$$= (\$600{,}000 \times 37.5\%) - \$150{,}000 = \underline{\underline{\$75{,}000\text{ income}}}$$

e. Dollars of sales to yield \$45,000 after-tax income
$$= \frac{\text{Fixed costs} + \text{Target pretax income}}{\text{Contribution margin ratio}}$$
$$= \frac{\$150{,}000 + \$60{,}000}{37.5\%} = \underline{\underline{\$560{,}000}}$$

APPENDIX

Using Excel to Estimate Least-Squares Regression 18A

Microsoft Excel® and other spreadsheet software can be used to perform least-squares regressions to identify cost behavior. In Excel®, the INTERCEPT and SLOPE functions are used. The following screen shot reports the data from Exhibit 18.3 in cells Al through C13 and shows the cell contents to find the intercept (cell B15) and slope (cell B16). Cell B15 uses Excel® to find the intercept from a least-squares regression of total cost (shown as C2:C13 in cell B15) on units produced (shown as B2:B13 in cell B15). Spreadsheet software is useful in understanding cost behavior when many data points (such as monthly total costs and units produced) are available.

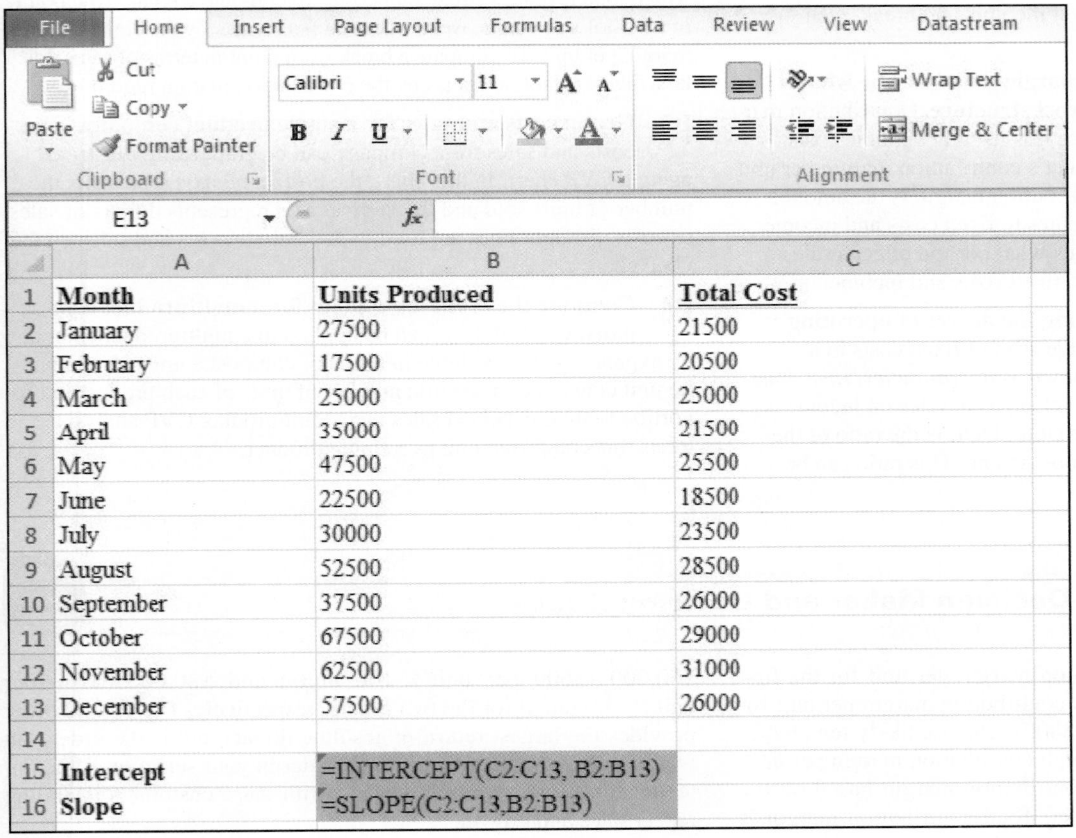

	A	B	C
1	**Month**	**Units Produced**	**Total Cost**
2	January	27500	21500
3	February	17500	20500
4	March	25000	25000
5	April	35000	21500
6	May	47500	25500
7	June	22500	18500
8	July	30000	23500
9	August	52500	28500
10	September	37500	26000
11	October	67500	29000
12	November	62500	31000
13	December	57500	26000
14			
15	**Intercept**	=INTERCEPT(C2:C13, B2:B13)	
16	**Slope**	=SLOPE(C2:C13,B2:B13)	

Excel® can also be used to create scatter diagrams such as that in Exhibit 18.4. In contrast to visually drawing a line that "fits" the data, Excel® more precisely fits the regression line. To draw a scatter diagram with a line of fit, follow these steps:

1. Highlight the data cells you wish to diagram; in this example, start from cell C13 and highlight through cell B2.
2. Then select "Insert" and "Scatter" from the drop-down menus. Selecting the chart type in the upper left corner of the choices under Scatter will produce a diagram that looks like that in Exhibit 18.4, without a line of fit.
3. To add a line of fit (also called trend line), select "Layout" and "Trendline" from the drop-down menus. Selecting "Linear Trendline" will produce a diagram that looks like that in Exhibit 18.4, including the line of fit.

Summary

C1 **Describe different types of cost behavior in relation to production and sales volume.** Cost behavior is described in terms of how its amount changes in relation to changes in volume of activity within a relevant range. Fixed costs remain constant to changes in volume. Total variable costs change in direct proportion to volume changes. Mixed costs display the effects of both fixed and variable components. Step-wise costs remain constant over a small volume range, then change by a lump sum and remain constant over another volume range, and so on. Curvilinear costs change in a nonlinear relation to volume changes.

C2 **Describe several applications of cost-volume-profit analysis.** Cost-volume-profit analysis can be used to predict what can happen under alternative strategies concerning sales volume, selling prices, variable costs, or fixed costs. Applications include "what-if" analysis, computing sales for a target income, and break-even analysis.

A1 **Compute the contribution margin and describe what it reveals about a company's cost structure.** Contribution margin per unit is a product's sales price less its total variable costs. Contribution margin ratio is a product's contribution margin per unit divided by its sales price. Unit contribution margin is the amount received from each sale that contributes to fixed costs and income. The contribution margin ratio reveals what portion of each sales dollar is available as contribution to fixed costs and income.

A2 **Analyze changes in sales using the degree of operating leverage.** The extent, or relative size, of fixed costs in a company's total cost structure is known as *operating leverage.* One tool useful in assessing the effect of changes in sales on income is the degree of operating leverage, or DOL. DOL is the ratio of the contribution margin divided by pretax income. This ratio can be used to determine the expected percent change in income given a percent change in sales.

P1 **Determine cost estimates using the scatter diagram, high-low, and regression methods of estimating costs.** Three different methods used to estimate costs are the scatter diagram, the high-low method, and least-squares regression. All three methods use past data to estimate costs. Cost estimates from a scatter diagram are based on a visual fit of the cost line. Estimates from the high-low method are based only on costs corresponding to the lowest and highest sales. The least-squares regression method is a statistical technique and uses all data points.

P2 **Compute the break-even point for a single product company.** A company's break-even point for a period is the sales volume at which total revenues equal total costs. To compute a break-even point in terms of sales units, we divide total fixed costs by the contribution margin per unit. To compute a break-even point in terms of sales dollars, divide total fixed costs by the contribution margin ratio.

P3 **Graph costs and sales for a single product company.** The costs and sales for a company can be graphically illustrated using a CVP chart. In this chart, the horizontal axis represents the number of units sold and the vertical axis represents dollars of sales or costs. Straight lines are used to depict both costs and sales on the CVP chart.

P4 **Compute the break-even point for a multiproduct company.** CVP analysis can be applied to a multiproduct company by expressing sales volume in terms of composite units. A composite unit consists of a specific number of units of each product in proportion to their expected sales mix. Multiproduct CVP analysis treats this composite unit as a single product.

Guidance Answers to Decision Maker and Decision Ethics

Sales Manager The contribution margin per unit for the first order is $600 (60% of $1,000); the contribution margin per unit for the second order is $160 (20% of $800). You are likely tempted to accept the first order based on its high contribution margin per unit, but you must compute the total contribution margin based on the number of units sold for each order. Total contribution margin is $60,000 ($600 per unit × 100 units) and $80,000 ($160 per unit × 500 units) for the two orders, respectively. The second order provides the largest return in absolute dollars and is the order you would accept. Another factor to consider in your selection is the potential for a long-term relationship with these customers including repeat sales and growth.

Operations Manager Without the availability of past data, none of the three methods described in the chapter can be used to measure cost behavior. Instead, the manager must investigate whether data from similar manufacturers can be accessed. This is likely difficult due to the sensitive nature of such data. In the absence of data, the manager should develop a list of the different production inputs and identify input-output relations. This provides guidance to the manager in measuring cost behavior. After several months, actual cost data will be available for analysis.

Supervisor Your dilemma is whether to go along with the suggestions to "manage" the numbers to make the project look like it will achieve sufficient profits. You should not succumb to these suggestions. Many people will likely be affected negatively if you manage the predicted numbers and the project eventually is unprofitable. Moreover, if it does fail, an investigation would likely reveal that data in the proposal were "fixed" to make it look good. Probably the only benefit from managing the numbers is the short-term payoff of pleasing those who proposed the product. One way to deal with this dilemma is to prepare several analyses showing results under different assumptions and then let senior management make the decision.

Entrepreneur You must first compute the level of sales required to achieve the desired net income. Then you must conduct sensitivity analysis by varying the price, sales mix, and cost estimates. Results from the sensitivity analysis provide information you can use to assess the possibility of reaching the target sales level. For instance, you might have to pursue aggressive marketing strategies to push the high-margin products, or you might have to cut prices to increase sales and profits, or another strategy might emerge.

Guidance Answers to Quick Checks

1. *b*

2. A fixed cost remains unchanged in total amount regardless of output levels. However, fixed *cost per unit* declines with increased output.

3. Such a cost is considered variable because the *total* cost changes in proportion to volume changes.

4. *b*

5. The high-low method ignores all costs and sales (activity base) volume data points except the costs corresponding to the highest and lowest (most extreme) sales (activity base) volume.

6. *c*

7. *a*

8. ($90 − $54)/$90 = 40%

9. $90,000/40% = $225,000

10. A company's margin of safety is the excess of the predicted sales level over its break-even sales level.

11. Three basic CVP assumptions are that (1) selling price per unit is constant, (2) variable costs per unit are constant, and (3) total fixed costs are constant.

12. a; Two steps are required for explanation:
(1) Pretax income = $120,000/(1 − 0.20) = $150,000

(2) $\frac{\$50{,}000 + \$150{,}000}{25\%} = \$800{,}000$

13. If the contribution margin ratio decreases from 50% to 25%, unit sales would have to double.

14. *c*; Selling price of a composite unit:

2 units of X @ $5 per unit	$10
1 unit of Y @ $4 per unit	4
Selling price of a composite unit	$14

Variable costs of a composite unit:

2 units of X @ $2 per unit	$4
1 unit of Y @ $2 per unit	2
Variable costs of a composite unit	$6

Therefore, the contribution margin per composite unit is $8.

15. It must be assumed that the sales mix remains unchanged at all sales levels in the relevant range.

Key Terms

Absorption costing (p. 786)
Break-even point (p. 785)
Composite unit (p. 793)
Contribution margin per unit (p. 785)
Contribution margin ratio (p. 785)
Cost-volume-profit (CVP) analysis (p. 778)
Cost-volume-profit (CVP) chart (p. 787)
Curvilinear cost (p. 781)
Degree of operating leverage (DOL) (p. 795)
Estimated line of cost behavior (p. 782)
High-low method (p. 782)
Least-squares regression (p. 783)
Margin of safety (p. 786)
Mixed cost (p. 780)
Operating leverage (p. 795)
Relevant range of operations (p. 788)
Sales mix (p. 793)
Scatter diagram (p. 782)
Step-wise cost (p. 780)
Variable costing income statement (p. 786)
Weighted-average contribution margin (p. 793)

Multiple Choice Quiz

Answers on p. 813 mhhe.com/wildFINMAN5e

Additional Quiz Questions are available at the book's Website.

1. A company's only product sells for $150 per unit. Its variable costs per unit are $100, and its fixed costs total $75,000. What is its contribution margin per unit?
   a. $50
   b. $250
   c. $100
   d. $150
   e. $25
2. Using information from question 1, what is the company's contribution margin ratio?
   a. 66⅔%
   b. 100%
   c. 50%
   d. 0%
   e. 33⅓%
3. Using information from question 1, what is the company's break-even point in units?
   a. 500 units
   b. 750 units
   c. 1,500 units
   d. 3,000 units
   e. 1,000 units
4. A company's forecasted sales are $300,000 and its sales at break-even are $180,000. Its margin of safety in dollars is
   a. $180,000.
   b. $120,000.
   c. $480,000.
   d. $60,000.
   e. $300,000.
5. A product sells for $400 per unit and its variable costs per unit are $260. The company's fixed costs are $840,000. If the company desires $70,000 pretax income, what is the required dollar sales?
   a. $2,400,000
   b. $200,000
   c. $2,600,000
   d. $2,275,000
   e. $1,400,000

A Superscript letter A denotes assignments based on Appendix 18A

Icon denotes assignments that involve decision making.

Discussion Questions

1. What is a variable cost? Identify two variable costs.
2. When output volume increases, do variable costs per unit increase, decrease, or stay the same within the relevant range of activity? Explain.
3. When output volume increases, do fixed costs per unit increase, decrease, or stay the same within the relevant range of activity? Explain.
4. How is cost-volume-profit analysis useful?
5. How do step-wise costs and curvilinear costs differ?
6. Describe the contribution margin ratio in layperson's terms.
7. Define and explain the *contribution margin ratio.*
8. Define and describe *contribution margin* per unit.
9. In performing CVP analysis for a manufacturing company, what simplifying assumption is usually made about the volume of production and the volume of sales?
10. What two arguments tend to justify classifying all costs as either fixed or variable even though individual costs might not behave exactly as classified?
11. How does assuming that operating activity occurs within a relevant range affect cost-volume-profit analysis?
12. List three methods to measure cost behavior.
13. How is a scatter diagram used to identify and measure the behavior of a company's costs?
14. In cost-volume-profit analysis, what is the estimated profit at the break-even point?
15. Assume that a straight line on a CVP chart intersects the vertical axis at the level of fixed costs and has a positive slope that rises with each additional unit of volume by the amount of the variable costs per unit. What does this line represent?
16. KTM has both fixed and variable costs. Why are fixed costs depicted as a horizontal line on a CVP chart?
17. Each of two similar companies has sales of $20,000 and total costs of $15,000 for a month. Company A's total costs include $10,000 of variable costs and $5,000 of fixed costs. If Company B's total costs include $4,000 of variable costs and $11,000 of fixed costs, which company will enjoy more profit if sales double?
18. _______ of _______ reflects expected sales in excess of the level of break-even sales.
19. Arctic Cat produces snowmobiles for sale. Identify some of the variable and fixed product costs associated with that production. [*Hint:* Limit costs to product costs.]
20. Should Polaris use single product or multiproduct break-even analysis? Explain.
21. Piaggio is thinking of expanding sales of its most popular scooter model by 65%. Should we expect its variable and fixed costs for this model to stay within the relevant range? Explain.

connect

QUICK STUDY

QS 18-1
Cost behavior identification
C1

Listed here are four series of separate costs measured at various volume levels. Examine each series and identify whether it is best described as a fixed, variable, step-wise, or curvilinear cost. (It can help to graph the cost series.)

Volume (Units)	Series 1	Series 2	Series 3	Series 4
0	$ 0	$450	$ 800	$100
100	800	450	800	105
200	1,600	450	800	120
300	2,400	450	1,600	145
400	3,200	450	1,600	190
500	4,000	450	2,400	250
600	4,800	450	2,400	320

QS 18-2
Cost behavior identification
C1

Determine whether each of the following is best described as a fixed, variable, or mixed cost with respect to product units.

1. Rubber used to manufacture athletic shoes.
2. Maintenance of factory machinery.
3. Packaging expense.
4. Wages of an assembly-line worker paid on the basis of acceptable units produced.
5. Factory supervisor's salary.
6. Taxes on factory building.
7. Depreciation expense of warehouse.

QS 18-3
Cost behavior estimation—high-low method
P1

The following information is available for a company's maintenance cost over the last seven months. Using the high-low method, estimate both the fixed and variable components of its maintenance cost.

Month	Maintenance Hours	Maintenance Cost
June	9	$5,450
July	18	6,900
August	12	5,100
September	15	6,000
October	21	6,900
November	24	8,100
December	6	3,600

QS 18-4
Cost behavior estimation—scatter diagram
P1

This scatter diagram reflects past maintenance hours and their corresponding maintenance costs.

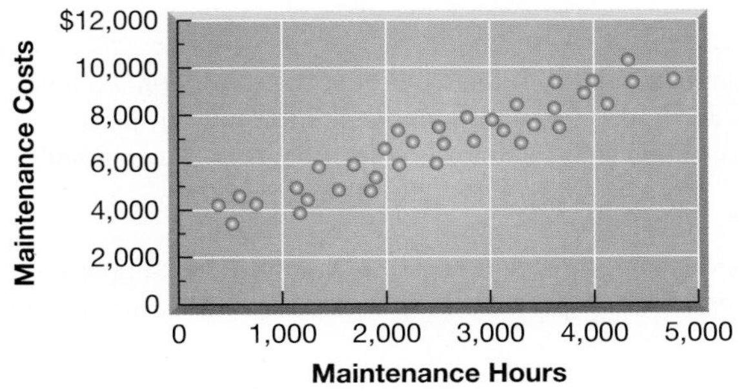

1. Draw an estimated line of cost behavior.
2. Estimate the fixed and variable components of maintenance costs.

QS 18-5
Contribution margin ratio
A1

Compute and interpret the contribution margin ratio using the following data: sales, $5,000; total variable cost, $3,000.

QS 18-6
Contribution margin per unit and break-even units P2

SBD Phone Company sells its cordless phone for $90 per unit. Fixed costs total $162,000, and variable costs are $36 per unit. Determine the (1) contribution margin per unit and (2) break-even point in units.

QS 18-7
Assumptions in CVP analysis C2

Refer to the information from QS 18-6. How will the break-even point in units change in response to each of the following independent changes in selling price per unit, variable cost per unit, or total fixed costs? Use I for increase and D for decrease. (It is not necessary to compute new break-even points.)

Change	Break-even in Units Will
1. Total fixed cost to $190,000	________
2. Variable cost to $34 per unit	________
3. Selling price per unit to $80	________
4. Variable cost to $67 per unit	________
5. Total fixed cost to $150,000	________
6. Selling price per unit to $120	________

QS 18-8
Contribution margin ratio and break-even dollars P2

Refer to QS 18-6. Determine the (1) contribution margin ratio and (2) break-even point in dollars.

QS 18-9
CVP analysis and target income P2

Refer to QS 18-6. Assume that SBD Phone Co. is subject to a 30% income tax rate. Compute the units of product that must be sold to earn after-tax income of $140,000. (Round to the nearest whole unit.)

QS 18-10
CVP assumptions C2

Which one of the following is an assumption that underlies cost-volume-profit analysis?

1. The selling price per unit must change in proportion to the number of units sold.
2. All costs have approximately the same relevant range.
3. For costs classified as variable, the costs per unit of output must change constantly.
4. For costs classified as fixed, the costs per unit of output must remain constant.

QS 18-11
Operating leverage analysis A2

A high proportion of Company A's total costs are variable with respect to units sold; a high proportion of Company B's total costs are fixed with respect to units sold. Which company is likely to have a higher degree of operating leverage (DOL)? Explain.

QS 18-12
Multiproduct break-even P4

US-Mobile Company manufactures and sells two products, conventional phones and smart phones, in the ratio of 5:3. Fixed costs are $105,000, and the contribution margin per composite unit is $125. What number of both conventional and smart phones is sold at the break-even point?

QS 18-13
CVP graph P3

Corme Company expects sales of $34 million (400,000 units). The company's total fixed costs are $17.5 million and its variable costs are $35 per unit. Prepare a CVP chart from this information.

QS 18-14
Contribution margin A1

A recent income statement for **Volkswagen** reports the following (in € millions). Assume 75 percent of the cost of sales and 75 percent of the selling and administrative costs are variable costs, and the remaining 25 percent of each is fixed. Compute the contribution margin (in € millions). (Round computations using percentages to the nearest whole euro.)

Sales	€126,875
Cost of sales	105,431
Selling and administrative expenses	15,500

connect

EXERCISES

Exercise 18-1
Measurement of cost behavior using a scatter diagram
P1

A company reports the following information about its sales and its cost of sales. Each unit of its product sells for $500. Use these data to prepare a scatter diagram. Draw an estimated line of cost behavior and determine whether the cost appears to be variable, fixed, or mixed.

Period	Sales	Cost of Sales	Period	Sales	Cost of Sales
1	$22,500	$15,150	4	11,250	8,250
2	17,250	11,250	5	13,500	9,000
3	15,750	10,500	6	18,750	14,250

Exercise 18-2
Cost behavior in graphs
C1

Following are five graphs representing various cost behaviors. (1) Identify whether the cost behavior in each graph is mixed, step-wise, fixed, variable, or curvilinear. (2) Identify the graph (by number) that best illustrates each cost behavior: (a) Factory policy requires one supervisor for every 30 factory workers; (b) real estate taxes on factory; (c) electricity charge that includes the standard monthly charge plus a charge for each kilowatt hour; (d) commissions to salespersons; and (e) costs of hourly paid workers that provide substantial gains in efficiency when a few workers are added but gradually smaller gains in efficiency when more workers are added.

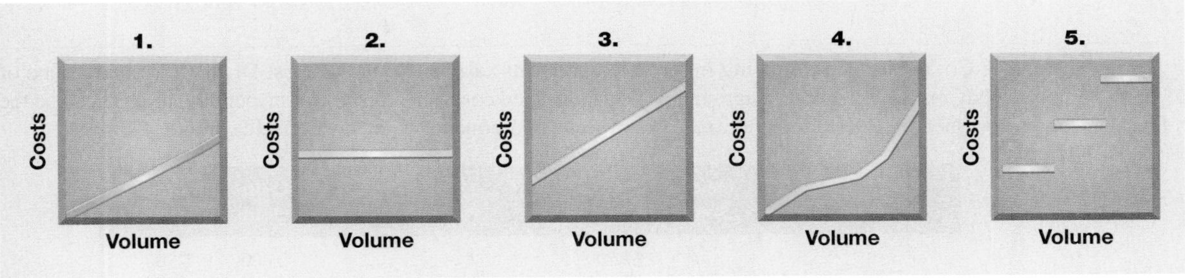

Exercise 18-3
Cost behavior defined
C1

The left column lists several cost classifications. The right column presents short definitions of those costs. In the blank space beside each of the numbers in the right column, write the letter of the cost best described by the definition.

A. Total cost
B. Mixed cost
C. Variable cost
D. Curvilinear cost
E. Step-wise cost
F. Fixed cost

_______ **1.** This cost is the combined amount of all the other costs.

_______ **2.** This cost remains constant over a limited range of volume; when it reaches the end of its limited range, it changes by a lump sum and remains at that level until it exceeds another limited range.

_______ **3.** This cost has a component that remains the same over all volume levels and another component that increases in direct proportion to increases in volume.

_______ **4.** This cost increases when volume increases, but the increase is not constant for each unit produced.

_______ **5.** This cost remains constant over all volume levels within the productive capacity for the planning period.

_______ **6.** This cost increases in direct proportion to increases in volume; its amount is constant for each unit produced.

Exercise 18-4
Cost behavior identification
C1

Following are five series of costs *A* through *E* measured at various volume levels. Examine each series and identify which is fixed, variable, mixed, step-wise, or curvilinear.

	Volume (Units)	Series A	Series B	Series C	Series D	Series E
1	0	$ 0	$2,500	$ 0	$1,000	$5,000
2	400	3,600	3,100	6,000	1,000	5,000
3	800	7,200	3,700	6,600	2,000	5,000
4	1,200	10,800	4,300	7,200	2,000	5,000
5	1,600	14,400	4,900	8,200	3,000	5,000
6	2,000	18,000	5,500	9,600	3,000	5,000
7	2,400	21,600	6,100	13,500	4,000	5,000

Exercise 18-5
Predicting sales and variable costs using contribution margin C2

Bloom Company management predicts that it will incur fixed costs of $160,000 and earn pretax income of $164,000 in the next period. Its expected contribution margin ratio is 25%. Use this information to compute the amounts of (1) total dollar sales and (2) total variable costs.

Exercise 18-6
Scatter diagram and measurement of cost behavior
P1

Use the following information about sales and costs to prepare a scatter diagram. Draw a cost line that reflects the behavior displayed by this cost. Determine whether the cost is variable, step-wise, fixed, mixed, or curvilinear.

Period	Sales	Costs	Period	Sales	Costs
1	$760	$590	9	$580	$390
2	800	560	10	320	240
3	200	230	11	240	230
4	400	400	12	720	550
5	480	390	13	280	260
6	620	550	14	440	410
7	680	590	15	380	260
8	540	430			

Exercise 18-7
Cost behavior estimation—scatter diagram and high-low
P1

Felix & Co. reports the following information about its sales and cost of sales. Draw an estimated line of cost behavior using a scatter diagram, and compute fixed costs and variable costs per unit sold. Then use the high-low method to estimate the fixed and variable components of the cost of sales.

Period	Units Sold	Cost of Sales	Period	Units Sold	Cost of Sales
1	0	$2,500	6	2,000	5,500
2	400	3,100	7	2,400	6,100
3	800	3,700	8	2,800	6,700
4	1,200	4,300	9	3,200	7,300
5	1,600	4,900	10	3,600	7,900

Exercise 18-8^{A}
Measurement of cost behavior using regression P1

Refer to the information from Exercise 18-7. Use spreadsheet software to use ordinary least-squares regression to estimate the cost equation, including fixed and variable cost amounts.

Exercise 18-9
Contribution margin
A2

A jeans maker is designing a new line of jeans called the Slims. The jeans will sell for $205 per pair and cost $164 per pair in variable costs to make. (1) Compute the contribution margin per pair. (2) Compute the contribution margin ratio. (3) Describe what the contribution margin ratio reveals about this new jeans line.

Exercise 18-10
Contribution margin and break-even P2

Blanchard Company manufactures a single product that sells for $180 per unit and whose total variable costs are $135 per unit. The company's annual fixed costs are $562,500. (1) Use this information to compute the company's (a) contribution margin, (b) contribution margin ratio, (c) break-even point in units, and (d) break-even point in dollars of sales.

Exercise 18-11
CVP chart P3

Refer to the information in Exercise 18-10. Prepare a CVP chart for the company.

Exercise 18-12
Income reporting and break-even analysis C2

Refer to Exercise 18-10. (1) Prepare a contribution margin income statement for Blanchard Company showing sales, variable costs, and fixed costs at the break-even point. (2) If the company's fixed costs increase by $135,000, what amount of sales (in dollars) is needed to break even? Explain.

Exercise 18-13
Computing sales to achieve target income C2

Blanchard Company management (in Exercise 18-10) targets an annual after-tax income of $810,000. The company is subject to a 20% income tax rate. Assume that fixed costs remain at $562,500. Compute the (1) unit sales to earn the target after-tax net income and (2) dollar sales to earn the target after-tax net income.

Exercise 18-14
Forecasted income statement
C2

Blanchard Company's sales manager (in Exercise 18-10) predicts that annual sales of the company's product will soon reach 40,000 units and its price will increase to $200 per unit. According to the production manager, the variable costs are expected to increase to $140 per unit but fixed costs will remain at $562,500. The income tax rate is 20%. What amounts of pretax and after-tax income can the company expect to earn from these predicted changes? (*Hint:* Prepare a forecasted contribution margin income statement as in Exhibit 18.21.)

Check Forecasted income, $1,470,000

Exercise 18-15
Predicting unit and dollar sales
C2

Nombre Company management predicts $390,000 of variable costs, $430,000 of fixed costs, and a pretax income of $155,000 in the next period. Management also predicts that the contribution margin per unit will be $9. Use this information to compute the (1) total expected dollar sales for next period and (2) number of units expected to be sold next period.

Exercise 18-16
Computation of variable and fixed costs
C2

Cooper Company expects to sell 200,000 units of its product next year, which would generate total sales of $17 million. Management predicts that pretax net income for next year will be $1,250,000 and that the contribution margin per unit will be $25. Use this information to compute next year's total expected (a) variable costs and (b) fixed costs.

Exercise 18-17
CVP analysis using composite units P4

Handy Home sells windows and doors in the ratio of 8:2 (windows:doors). The selling price of each window is $200 and of each door is $500. The variable cost of a window is $125 and of a door is $350. Fixed costs are $900,000. Use this information to determine the (1) selling price per composite unit, (2) variable costs per composite unit, (3) break-even point in composite units, and (4) number of units of each product that will be sold at the break-even point.

Check (3) 1,000 composite units

Exercise 18-18
CVP analysis using weighted-average contribution margin
P4

Refer to the information from Exercise 18-17. Use the information to determine the (1) weighted-average contribution margin, (2) break-even point in units, and (3) number of units of each product that will be sold at the break-even point.

Exercise 18-19
CVP analysis using composite units
P4

R&R Tax Service offers tax and consulting services to individuals and small businesses. Data for fees and costs of three types of tax returns follow. R&R provides services in the ratio of 5:3:2 (easy, moderate, business). Fixed costs total $18,000 for the tax season. Use this information to determine the (1) selling price per composite unit, (2) variable costs per composite unit, (3) break-even point in composite units, and (4) number of units of each product that will be sold at the break-even point.

Type of Return	Fee Charged	Variable Cost per Return
Easy (form 1040EZ)	$ 50	$ 30
Moderate (form 1040)	125	75
Business	275	100

Exercise 18-20
CVP analysis using weighted-average contribution margin
P4

Refer to the information from Exercise 18-19. Use the information to determine the (1) weighted-average contribution margin, (2) break-even point in units, and (3) number of units of each product that will be sold at the break-even point.

Exercise 18-21
Operating leverage computed and applied
A2

Company A is a manufacturer with current sales of $6,000,000 and a 60% contribution margin. Its fixed costs equal $2,600,000. Company B is a consulting firm with current service revenues of $4,500,000 and a 25% contribution margin. Its fixed costs equal $375,000. Compute the degree of operating leverage (DOL) for each company. Identify which company benefits more from a 20% increase in sales and explain why.

connect

PROBLEM SET A

Problem 18-1A
Contribution margin income statement and contribution margin ratio
A1

The following costs result from the production and sale of 1,000 drum sets manufactured by Tom Thompson Company for the year ended December 31, 2013. The drum sets sell for $500 each. The company has a 25% income tax rate.

Variable production costs	
Plastic for casing	$ 17,000
Wages of assembly workers	82,000
Drum stands	26,000
Variable selling costs	
Sales commissions	15,000
Fixed manufacturing costs	
Taxes on factory	5,000
Factory maintenance	10,000
Factory machinery depreciation	40,000
Fixed selling and administrative costs	
Lease of equipment for sales staff	10,000
Accounting staff salaries	35,000
Administrative management salaries	125,000

Required

Check (1) Net income, $101,250

1. Prepare a contribution margin income statement for the company.

2. Compute its contribution margin per unit and its contribution margin ratio.

Analysis Component

3. Interpret the contribution margin and contribution margin ratio from part 2.

Problem 18-2A
CVP analysis and charting
P2 P3

mhhe.com/wildFINMAN5e

Xcite Equipment Co. manufactures and markets a number of rope products. Management is considering the future of Product XT, a special rope for hang gliding, that has not been as profitable as planned. Since Product XT is manufactured and marketed independently of the other products, its total costs can be precisely measured. Next year's plans call for a $200 selling price per 100 yards of XT rope. Its fixed costs for the year are expected to be $270,000, up to a maximum capacity of 700,000 yards of rope. Forecasted variable costs are $140 per 100 yards of XT rope.

Required

Check (1) Break-even sales, 4,500 units

1. Estimate Product XT's break-even point in terms of (a) sales units and (b) sales dollars.

2. Prepare a CVP chart for Product XT like that in Exhibit 18.15. Use 7,000 units (700,000 yards/100 yards) as the maximum number of sales units on the horizontal axis of the graph, and $1,400,000 as the maximum dollar amount on the vertical axis.

3. Prepare a contribution margin income statement showing sales, variable costs, and fixed costs for Product XT at the break-even point.

Problem 18-3A
Scatter diagram and cost behavior estimation
P1

Alden Co.'s monthly sales and cost data for its operating activities of the past year follow. Management wants to use these data to predict future fixed and variable costs.

Month	Sales	Total Cost	Month	Sales	Total Cost
1	$320,000	$160,000	7	$340,000	$220,000
2	160,000	100,000	8	280,000	160,000
3	280,000	220,000	9	80,000	64,000
4	200,000	100,000	10	160,000	140,000
5	300,000	230,000	11	100,000	100,000
6	200,000	120,000	12	110,000	80,000

Required

1. Prepare a scatter diagram for these data with sales volume (in $) plotted on the horizontal axis and total cost plotted on the vertical axis.
2. Estimate both the variable costs per sales dollar and the total monthly fixed costs using the high-low method. Draw the total costs line on the scatter diagram in part 1.
3. Use the estimated line of cost behavior and results from part 2 to predict future total costs when sales volume is (a) $200,000 and (b) $300,000.

Check (2) Variable costs, $0.60 per sales dollar; fixed costs, $16,000

Problem 18-4A
Break-even analysis; income targeting and forecasting
C2 P2 A1

Astro Co. sold 20,000 units of its only product and incurred a $50,000 loss (ignoring taxes) for the current year as shown here. During a planning session for year 2014's activities, the production manager notes that variable costs can be reduced 50% by installing a machine that automates several operations. To obtain these savings, the company must increase its annual fixed costs by $200,000. The maximum output capacity of the company is 40,000 units per year.

ASTRO COMPANY Contribution Margin Income Statement For Year Ended December 31, 2013	
Sales	$1,000,000
Variable costs	800,000
Contribution margin	200,000
Fixed costs	250,000
Net loss	$ (50,000)

Required

1. Compute the break-even point in dollar sales for year 2013.
2. Compute the predicted break-even point in dollar sales for year 2014 assuming the machine is installed and there is no change in the unit sales price.
3. Prepare a forecasted contribution margin income statement for 2014 that shows the expected results with the machine installed. Assume that the unit sales price and the number of units sold will not change, and no income taxes will be due.
4. Compute the sales level required in both dollars and units to earn $140,000 of after-tax income in 2014 with the machine installed and no change in the unit sales price. Assume that the income tax rate is 30%. (*Hint:* Use the procedures in Exhibits 18.22 and 18.23.) (Round answers to whole dollars or units.)
5. Prepare a forecasted contribution margin income statement that shows the results at the sales level computed in part 4. Assume an income tax rate of 30%.

Check (3) Net income, $150,000

(4) Required sales, $1,083,333 or 21,667 units

Problem 18-5A
Break-even analysis, different cost structures, and income calculations
C2 A1 P4

Vanna Co. produces and sells two products, T and O. It manufactures these products in separate factories and markets them through different channels. They have no shared costs. This year, the company sold 50,000 units of each product. Sales and costs for each product follow.

	Product T	Product O
Sales	$2,000,000	$2,000,000
Variable costs	1,600,000	250,000
Contribution margin	400,000	1,750,000
Fixed costs	125,000	1,475,000
Income before taxes	275,000	275,000
Income taxes (32% rate)	88,000	88,000
Net income	$ 187,000	$ 187,000

Required

1. Compute the break-even point in dollar sales for each product. (Round the answer to whole dollars.)
2. Assume that the company expects sales of each product to decline to 30,000 units next year with no change in unit sales price. Prepare forecasted financial results for next year following the format of the contribution margin income statement as just shown with columns for each of the two products (assume a 32% tax rate). Also, assume that any loss before taxes yields a 32% tax savings.
3. Assume that the company expects sales of each product to increase to 60,000 units next year with no change in unit sales price. Prepare forecasted financial results for next year following the format of the contribution margin income statement shown with columns for each of the two products (assume a 32% tax rate).

Check (2) After-tax income: T, $78,200; O, $(289,000)

(3) After-tax income: T, $241,400; O, $425,000

Analysis Component

4. If sales greatly decrease, which product would experience a greater loss? Explain.
5. Describe some factors that might have created the different cost structures for these two products.

Problem 18-6A
Analysis of price, cost, and volume changes for contribution margin and net income
P2 A1

mhhe.com/wildFINMAN5e

This year Bertrand Company sold 40,000 units of its only product for $25 per unit. Manufacturing and selling the product required $200,000 of fixed manufacturing costs and $325,000 of fixed selling and administrative costs. Its per unit variable costs follow.

Material	$8.00
Direct labor (paid on the basis of completed units)	5.00
Variable overhead costs	1.00
Variable selling and administrative costs	0.50

Next year the company will use new material, which will reduce material costs by 50% and direct labor costs by 60% and will not affect product quality or marketability. Management is considering an increase in the unit sales price to reduce the number of units sold because the factory's output is nearing its annual output capacity of 45,000 units. Two plans are being considered. Under plan 1, the company will keep the price at the current level and sell the same volume as last year. This plan will increase income because of the reduced costs from using the new material. Under plan 2, the company will increase price by 20%. This plan will decrease unit sales volume by 10%. Under both plans 1 and 2, the total fixed costs and the variable costs per unit for overhead and for selling and administrative costs will remain the same.

Required

1. Compute the break-even point in dollar sales for both (a) plan 1 and (b) plan 2.
2. Prepare a forecasted contribution margin income statement with two columns showing the expected results of plan 1 and plan 2. The statements should report sales, total variable costs, contribution margin, total fixed costs, income before taxes, income taxes (30% rate), and net income.

Check (1) Break-even: Plan 1, $750,000; Plan 2, $700,000

(2) Net income: Plan 1, $122,500; Plan 2, $199,500

Problem 18-7A
Break-even analysis with composite units
P4

Patriot Co. manufactures and sells three products: red, white, and blue. Their unit sales prices are red, $20; white, $35; and blue, $65. The per unit variable costs to manufacture and sell these products are red, $12; white, $22; and blue, $50. Their sales mix is reflected in a ratio of 5:4:2 (red:white:blue). Annual fixed costs shared by all three products are $250,000. One type of raw material has been used to manufacture all three products. The company has developed a new material of equal quality for less cost. The new material would reduce variable costs per unit as follows: red, by $6; white, by $12; and blue, by $10. However, the new material requires new equipment, which will increase annual fixed costs by $50,000. (Round answers to whole composite units.)

Required

1. If the company continues to use the old material, determine its break-even point in both sales units and sales dollars of each individual product.
2. If the company uses the new material, determine its new break-even point in both sales units and sales dollars of each individual product.

Check (1) Old plan break-even, 2,050 composite units (rounded)

(2) New plan break-even, 1,364 composite units (rounded)

Analysis Component

3. What insight does this analysis offer management for long-term planning?

PROBLEM SET B

Problem 18-1B
Contribution margin income statement and contribution margin ratio
A1

The following costs result from the production and sale of 12,000 CD sets manufactured by Gilmore Company for the year ended December 31, 2013. The CD sets sell for $18 each. The company has a 25% income tax rate.

Variable manufacturing costs	
Plastic for CD sets	$ 1,500
Wages of assembly workers	30,000
Labeling	3,000
Variable selling costs	
Sales commissions	6,000
Fixed manufacturing costs	
Rent on factory	6,750
Factory cleaning service	4,520
Factory machinery depreciation	20,000
Fixed selling and administrative costs	
Lease of office equipment	1,050
Systems staff salaries	15,000
Administrative management salaries	120,000

Required

1. Prepare a contribution margin income statement for the company.
2. Compute its contribution margin per unit and its contribution margin ratio.

Check (1) Net income, $6,135

Analysis Component

3. Interpret the contribution margin and contribution margin ratio from part 2.

Problem 18-2B
CVP analysis and charting
P2 P3

Hip-Hop Co. manufactures and markets several products. Management is considering the future of one product, electronic keyboards, that has not been as profitable as planned. Since this product is manufactured and marketed independently of the other products, its total costs can be precisely measured. Next year's plans call for a $350 selling price per unit. The fixed costs for the year are expected to be $42,000, up to a maximum capacity of 700 units. Forecasted variable costs are $210 per unit.

Required

1. Estimate the keyboards' break-even point in terms of (a) sales units and (b) sales dollars.
2. Prepare a CVP chart for keyboards like that in Exhibit 18.15. Use 700 keyboards as the maximum number of sales units on the horizontal axis of the graph, and $250,000 as the maximum dollar amount on the vertical axis.
3. Prepare a contribution margin income statement showing sales, variable costs, and fixed costs for keyboards at the break-even point.

Check (1) Break-even sales, 300 units

Problem 18-3B
Scatter diagram and cost behavior estimation
P1

Kyo Co.'s monthly sales and costs data for its operating activities of the past year follow. Management wants to use these data to predict future fixed and variable costs. (Dollar amounts are in thousands.)

Month	Sales	Total Cost	Month	Sales	Total Cost
1	$195	$ 97	7	$145	$ 93
2	125	87	8	185	105
3	105	73	9	135	85
4	155	89	10	85	58
5	95	81	11	175	95
6	215	110	12	115	79

Required

1. Prepare a scatter diagram for these data with sales volume (in $) plotted on the horizontal axis and total costs plotted on the vertical axis.

Check (2) Variable costs, $0.40 per sales dollar; fixed costs, $24

2. Estimate both the variable costs per sales dollar and the total monthly fixed costs using the high-low method. Draw the total costs line on the scatter diagram in part 1.
3. Use the estimated line of cost behavior and results from part 2 to predict future total costs when sales volume is (a) $100 and (b) $170.

Problem 18-4B
Break-even analysis; income targeting and forecasting
C2 P2 A1

Rivera Co. sold 20,000 units of its only product and incurred a $50,000 loss (ignoring taxes) for the current year as shown here. During a planning session for year 2014's activities, the production manager notes that variable costs can be reduced 50% by installing a machine that automates several operations. To obtain these savings, the company must increase its annual fixed costs by $150,000. The maximum output capacity of the company is 40,000 units per year.

RIVERA COMPANY Contribution Margin Income Statement For Year Ended December 31, 2013	
Sales	$750,000
Variable costs	600,000
Contribution margin	150,000
Fixed costs	200,000
Net loss	$ (50,000)

Required

1. Compute the break-even point in dollar sales for year 2013.
2. Compute the predicted break-even point in dollar sales for year 2014 assuming the machine is installed and no change occurs in the unit sales price. (Round the change in variable costs to a whole number.)
3. Prepare a forecasted contribution margin income statement for 2014 that shows the expected results with the machine installed. Assume that the unit sales price and the number of units sold will not change, and no income taxes will be due.
4. Compute the sales level required in both dollars and units to earn $140,000 of after-tax income in 2014 with the machine installed and no change in the unit sales price. Assume that the income tax rate is 30%. (*Hint:* Use the procedures in Exhibits 18.22 and 18.23.) (Round sales in dollars to whole dollars and round sales in units to the next whole unit.)
5. Prepare a forecasted contribution margin income statement that shows the results at the sales level computed in part 4. Assume an income tax rate of 30%.

Check (3) Net income, $100,000

(4) Required sales, $916,667 or 24,445 units

Problem 18-5B
Break-even analysis, different cost structures, and income calculations
C2 P4 A1

Mingei Co. produces and sells two products, BB and TT. It manufactures these products in separate factories and markets them through different channels. They have no shared costs. This year, the company sold 50,000 units of each product. Sales and costs for each product follow.

	Product BB	Product TT
Sales	$800,000	$800,000
Variable costs	560,000	100,000
Contribution margin	240,000	700,000
Fixed costs	100,000	560,000
Income before taxes	140,000	140,000
Income taxes (32% rate)	44,800	44,800
Net income	$ 95,200	$ 95,200

Required

1. Compute the break-even point in dollar sales for each product. (Round the answer to the next whole dollar.)
2. Assume that the company expects sales of each product to decline to 33,000 units next year with no change in the unit sales price. Prepare forecasted financial results for next year following the format of the contribution margin income statement as shown here with columns for each of the two products (assume a 32% tax rate, and that any loss before taxes yields a 32% tax savings).
3. Assume that the company expects sales of each product to increase to 64,000 units next year with no change in the unit sales prices. Prepare forecasted financial results for next year following the format of the contribution margin income statement as shown here with columns for each of the two products (assume a 32% tax rate).

Check (2) After-tax income: BB, $39,712; TT, $(66,640)

(3) After-tax income: BB, $140,896; TT, $228,480

Analysis Component

4. If sales greatly increase, which product would experience a greater increase in profit? Explain.

5. Describe some factors that might have created the different cost structures for these two products.

Problem 18-6B
Analysis of price, cost, and volume changes for contribution margin and net income
A1 P2

This year Best Company earned a disappointing 5.6% after-tax return on sales (net income/sales) from marketing 100,000 units of its only product. The company buys its product in bulk and repackages it for resale at the price of $20 per unit. Best incurred the following costs this year.

Total variable unit costs	$800,000
Total variable packaging costs	$100,000
Fixed costs	$950,000
Income tax rate	25%

The marketing manager claims that next year's results will be the same as this year's unless some changes are made. The manager predicts the company can increase the number of units sold by 80% if it reduces the selling price by 20% and upgrades the packaging. This change would increase variable packaging costs by 20%. Increased sales would allow the company to take advantage of a 25% quantity purchase discount on the cost of the bulk product. Neither the packaging change nor the volume discount would affect fixed costs, which provide an annual output capacity of 200,000 units.

Required

1. Compute the break-even point in dollar sales under the (a) existing business strategy and (b) new strategy that alters both unit sales price and variable costs. (Round answers to the next whole dollar.)

2. Prepare a forecasted contribution margin income statement with two columns showing the expected results of (a) the existing strategy and (b) changing to the new strategy. The statements should report sales, total variable costs (unit and packaging), contribution margin, fixed costs, income before taxes, income taxes, and net income. Also determine the after-tax return on sales for these two strategies.

Check (1) Break-even sales for new strategy, $1,727,273

(2) Net income: Existing strategy, $112,500; new strategy, $475,500

Problem 18-7B
Break-even analysis with composite units
P4

Milano Co. manufactures and sells three products: product 1, product 2, and product 3. Their unit sales prices are product 1, $40; product 2, $30; and product 3, $20. The per unit variable costs to manufacture and sell these products are product 1, $30; product 2, $15; and product 3, $8. Their sales mix is reflected in a ratio of 6:4:2. Annual fixed costs shared by all three products are $270,000. One type of raw material has been used to manufacture products 1 and 2. The company has developed a new material of equal quality for less cost. The new material would reduce variable costs per unit as follows: product 1 by $10, and product 2, by $5. However, the new material requires new equipment, which will increase annual fixed costs by $50,000.

Required

1. If the company continues to use the old material, determine its break-even point in both sales units and sales dollars of each individual product.

2. If the company uses the new material, determine its new break-even point in both sales units and sales dollars of each individual product.

Check (1) Old plan break-even, 1,875 composite units (rounded)

(2) New plan break-even, 1,429 composite units (rounded)

Analysis Component

3. What insight does this analysis offer management for long-term planning?

SERIAL PROBLEM
Success Systems
P4

(This serial problem began in Chapter 1 and continues through most of the book. If previous chapter segments were not completed, the serial problem can begin at this point. It is helpful, but not necessary, to use the working papers that accompany the book.)

SP 18 Success Systems sells upscale modular desk units and office chairs in the ratio of 3:2 (desk unit:chair). The selling prices are $1,250 per desk unit and $500 per chair. The variable costs are $750 per desk unit and $250 per chair. Fixed costs are $120,000.

Required

1. Compute the selling price per composite unit.

2. Compute the variable costs per composite unit.

3. Compute the break-even point in composite units.

4. Compute the number of units of each product that would be sold at the break-even point.

Check (3) 60 composite units

Beyond the Numbers

REPORTING IN ACTION

C1

Polaris

BTN 18-1 Polaris offers extended service contracts that provide repair and maintenance coverage over its products. As you complete the following requirements, assume that the Polaris services department uses many of Polaris's existing resources such as its facilities, repair machinery, and computer systems.

Required

1. Identify several of the variable, mixed, and fixed costs that the Polaris services department is likely to incur in carrying out its services.
2. Assume that Polaris's services revenues are expected to grow by 25% in the next year. How would we expect the costs identified in part 1 to change, if at all?
3. Based on the answer to part 2, can Polaris use the contribution margin ratio to predict how income will change in response to increases in Polaris's services revenues?

COMPARATIVE ANALYSIS

P2 A2

Polaris

Arctic Cat

BTN 18-2 Both Polaris and Arctic Cat sell motorized vehicles, and each of these companies has a different product mix.

Required

1. Assume the following data are available for both companies. Compute each company's break-even point in unit sales. (Each company sells many motorized vehicles at many different selling prices, and each has its own variable costs. This assignment assumes an *average* selling price per unit and an *average* cost per item.)

	Polaris	Arctic Cat
Average selling price per item sold	$10,500	$11,200
Average variable cost per item sold	$4,200	$5,100
Total fixed costs ($ in thousands)	$146,570	$133,570

2. If unit sales were to decline, which company would experience the larger decline in operating profit? Explain.

ETHICS CHALLENGE

C1

BTN 18-3 Labor costs of an auto repair mechanic are seldom based on actual hours worked. Instead, the amount paid a mechanic is based on an industry average of time estimated to complete a repair job. The repair shop bills the customer for the industry average amount of time at the repair center's billable cost per hour. This means a customer can pay, for example, $120 for two hours of work on a car when the actual time worked was only one hour. Many experienced mechanics can complete repair jobs faster than the industry average. The average data are compiled by engineering studies and surveys conducted in the auto repair business. Assume that you are asked to complete such a survey for a repair center. The survey calls for objective input, and many questions require detailed cost data and analysis. The mechanics and owners know you have the survey and encourage you to complete it in a way that increases the average billable hours for repair work.

Required

Write a one-page memorandum to the mechanics and owners that describes the direct labor analysis you will undertake in completing this survey.

COMMUNICATING IN PRACTICE

C2

BTN 18-4 Several important assumptions underlie CVP analysis. Assumptions often help simplify and focus our analysis of sales and costs. A common application of CVP analysis is as a tool to forecast sales, costs, and income.

Required

Assume that you are actively searching for a job. Prepare a one-half page report identifying (1) three assumptions relating to your expected revenue (salary) and (2) three assumptions relating to your expected costs for the first year of your new job. Be prepared to discuss your assumptions in class.

BTN 18-5 Access and review the entrepreneurial information at Business Owner's Toolkit [Toolkit.com]. Access and review its *New Business Cash Needs Checklist* under the Start Up menu bar or similar worksheets related to controls of cash and costs.

TAKING IT TO THE NET
C1

Required

Write a one-half page report that describes the information and resources available at the Business Owner's Toolkit to help the owner of a start-up business to control and monitor its cash flows and costs.

BTN 18-6 A local movie theater owner explains to you that ticket sales on weekends and evenings are strong, but attendance during the weekdays, Monday through Thursday, is poor. The owner proposes to offer a contract to the local grade school to show educational materials at the theater for a set charge per student during school hours. The owner asks your help to prepare a CVP analysis listing the cost and sales projections for the proposal. The owner must propose to the school's administration a charge per child. At a minimum, the charge per child needs to be sufficient for the theater to break even.

TEAMWORK IN ACTION
C2

Required

Your team is to prepare two separate lists of questions that enable you to complete a reliable CVP analysis of this situation. One list is to be answered by the school's administration, the other by the owner of the movie theater.

BTN 18-7 Leather Head Sports, launched by entrepreneur Paul Cunningham, produces balls for various sports. Selling prices typically range from $40 per ball to $295 per ball.

ENTREPRENEURIAL DECISION
C1 A1

Required

1. Identify at least two fixed costs that will not change regardless of how many footballs Leather Head Sports produces.
2. How could overly optimistic sales estimates potentially hurt Paul Cunningham's business?
3. Explain how cost-volume-profit analysis can help Paul Cunningham manage Leather Head Sports.

BTN 18-8 Multiproduct break-even analysis is often viewed differently when actually applied in practice. You are to visit a local fast-food restaurant and count the number of items on the menu. To apply multiproduct break-even analysis to the restaurant, similar menu items must often be fit into groups. A reasonable approach is to classify menu items into approximately five groups. We then estimate average selling price and average variable cost to compute average contribution margin. (*Hint:* For fast-food restaurants, the highest contribution margin is with its beverages, at about 90%.)

HITTING THE ROAD
P4

Required

1. Prepare a one-year multiproduct break-even analysis for the restaurant you visit. Begin by establishing groups. Next, estimate each group's volume and contribution margin. These estimates are necessary to compute each group's contribution margin. Assume that annual fixed costs in total are $500,000 per year. (*Hint:* You must develop your own estimates on volume and contribution margin for each group to obtain the break-even point and sales.)
2. Prepare a one-page report on the results of your analysis. Comment on the volume of sales necessary to break even at a fast-food restaurant.

BTN 18-9 Access and review Piaggio's Website (www.piaggio.com) to answer the following questions.

GLOBAL DECISION
P4

PIAGGIO

Required

1. Do you believe that Piaggio's managers use single product CVP analysis or multiproduct break-even analysis? Explain.
2. How does the addition of a new product line affect Piaggio's CVP analysis?

ANSWERS TO MULTIPLE CHOICE QUIZ

1. a; $150 − $100 = $50
2. e; ($150 − $100)/$150 = 33⅓%
3. c; $75,000/$50 CM per unit = 1,500 units
4. b; $300,000 − $180,000 = $120,000
5. c; Contribution margin ratio = ($400 − $260)/$400 = 0.35
   Targeted sales = ($840,000 + $70,000)/0.35 = $2,600,000

19

Variable Costing and Performance Reporting

A Look Back

Chapter 18 looked at cost behavior and its use by managers in performing cost-volume-profit analysis. It also illustrated the application of cost-volume-profit analysis.

A Look at This Chapter

This chapter describes managerial accounting reports that reflect variable costing. It also compares reports prepared under variable costing with those under absorption costing, and it explains how variable costing can improve business decisions.

A Look Ahead

Chapter 20 introduces and describes the budgeting process and its importance to management. It also explains the master budget and its usefulness to the planning of future company activities.

Learning Objectives

CONCEPTUAL

C1 Describe how absorption costing can result in over-production. (p. 823)

C2 Explain the role of variable costing in pricing special orders. (p. 825)

ANALYTICAL

A1 Compute and interpret break-even volume in units. (p. 827)

PROCEDURAL

P1 Compute unit cost under both absorption and variable costing. (p. 817)

P2 Prepare and analyze an income statement using absorption costing and using variable costing. (p. 818)

P3 Prepare a contribution margin report. (p. 819)

P4 Convert income under variable costing to the absorption cost basis. (p. 823)

Decision Insight

Shoe Biz

"Be your best, make a difference, and live with passion."
—SAMANTA AND KELVIN JOSEPH

NEW YORK—Business recipe: Take one information systems graduate, mix a bit of international flair, add an accountant, and stir. The result is **Samanta Shoes** **(SamantaShoes.com),** a start-up shoe manufacturer. Founded by Samanta and Kelvin Joseph, their company is aimed at providing "stylish, comfortable, and affordable" shoes, explains Samanta. "I design every shoe, and nothing less than the best material is used."

In the beginning, Kelvin focused on the accounting and financial side of Samanta Shoes. "The knowledge gained from my years at Ernst & Young LLP [a major accounting firm]," explains Kelvin, "enabled me to be more helpful." Knowledge of cost accounting and the importance of controlling costs remains crucial to Samanta's success. Both partners stress the importance of attending to variable manufacturing costs, overhead, and product contribution margins to stay afloat.

With gross annual sales around $1 million, success is causing their company to evolve, but the partners adhere to a quality-first mentality. "It's all in the design," insists Samanta. "[A quality design] allows for more comfort and support." But quality also extends to style and uniqueness. "Women don't like other women having their shoe," explains Samanta. "We don't want to dilute our brand by being too mass market." Kelvin explains that the smallest manufacturing run they can have is 18 pairs of a special line. With small production runs, variable production costs drive decisions regarding product lines and product pricing. Accordingly, a variable costing system, with reports on variable costs, contribution margins, and break-even points, is key.

The partners also continue to apply managerial accounting fundamentals. "Our business cannot survive," says Kelvin, "unless it is profitable." They regularly review the accounting results and assess contribution margins, although Kelvin adds, "money does not equal happiness." Samanta explains, "Live your dreams . . . make a difference . . . give back to your community"—advice that we can all live by. "If you're not enjoying it," continues Samanta, "there's no point to doing it."

[Sources: *Samanta Shoes Website,* January 2013; *Jet,* August 2010; *New York Resident,* August 2004; *Caribbean Vibe,* August 2004; *Black Enterprise,* February 2012; *Regine Magazine,* Spring 2004; *Inc.com,* July 2007]

Chapter Preview

Product-costing information is crucial for most business decisions. This chapter explains and illustrates the concept of variable costing. We then compare variable costing to that of absorption costing commonly used for financial reporting. We show that income is different when computed under variable or absorption costing whenever the number of units produced is different from units sold. We also show how absorption costing can be misleading (though not wrong) and how variable costing can result in better production and pricing decisions.

Variable Costing and Performance Reporting

Variable Costing and Absorption Costing
- Absorption costing
- Variable costing
- Computing unit costs

Performance Reporting (Income) Implications
- When production equals sales
- When production exceeds sales
- When production is less than sales
- Income reporting
- Converting variable cost income to absorption cost

Comparing Variable Costing and Absorption Costing
- Planning production
- Setting prices
- Controlling costs
- Limitations of variable costing
- Variable costing for service firms

INTRODUCING VARIABLE COSTING AND ABSORPTION COSTING

Product costs consist of direct materials, direct labor, and overhead. Direct materials and direct labor costs are those that can be identified and traced to the product(s). Overhead, which consists of costs such as electricity, equipment depreciation, and supervisor salaries, is not traceable to the product. Overhead costs must be allocated to products.

There are a variety of costing methods for identifying and allocating overhead costs to products. A prior chapter focused on *how* to allocate overhead costs to products. This chapter focuses on *what* overhead costs are included in product costs.

Under the traditional costing approach, *all* manufacturing costs are assigned to products. Those costs consist of direct materials, direct labor, variable overhead, and fixed overhead. This traditional approach is referred to as **absorption costing** (also called *full costing*), which assumes that products *absorb* all costs incurred to produce them. While widely used for external financial reporting (GAAP), this costing method can result in misleading product cost information for managers' business decisions.

Under **variable costing,** only costs that change in total with changes in production level are included in product costs. Those consist of direct materials, direct labor, and variable overhead. Fixed overhead does not change with changes in production and, thus, it is excluded from product costs. Instead, fixed overhead is treated as a period cost, meaning it is expensed in the period when it is incurred.

The following diagram compares the absorption and variable costing methods. Under both methods, direct materials, direct labor, and variable overhead are included in product costs. The key difference between the methods lies in their treatment of *fixed* overhead costs—such costs are included in product costs under absorption costing but included in period expenses under variable costing. Recall that product costs are included in inventory until the goods are sold, at which time they are included in cost of goods sold. Period expenses are reported as expenses immediately in the period in which they are incurred.

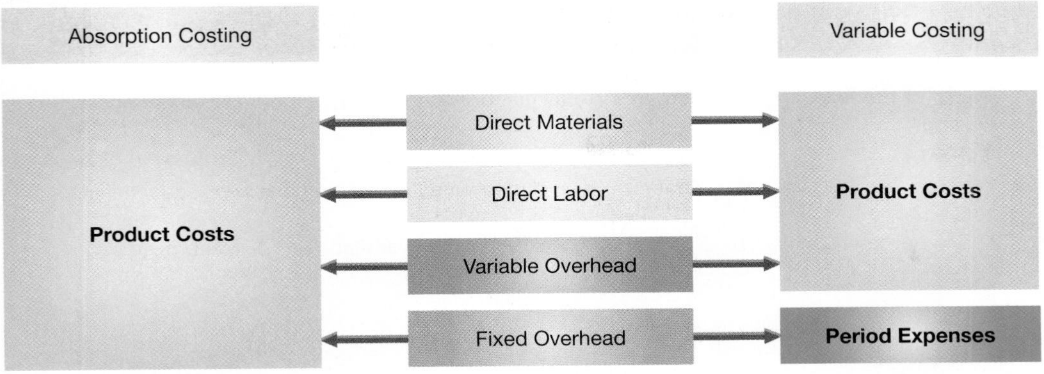

The diagram above helps us understand when the absorption and variable costing methods will yield different income amounts over a period. In particular, differences in income resulting from the alternative methods will be *small* when:

- Fixed overhead is small as a percentage of total manufacturing costs.
- Inventory levels are low. As more companies adopt lean techniques, including just-in-time manufacturing, inventory levels fall. Lower inventory levels reduce differences between absorption and variable costing.
- Inventory turnover is rapid. The more quickly inventory turns over, the more product costs are included in cost of goods sold, relative to the product costs that remain in inventory.
- Period of analysis is long. For example, different costing methods might yield very different income numbers over a quarter or year, but these differences will decrease as income is compared over longer periods.

P1 Compute unit cost under both absorption and variable costing.

Computing Unit Cost

To illustrate the difference between absorption costing and variable costing, let's consider the product cost data in Exhibit 19.1 from IceAge, a skate manufacturer.

EXHIBIT 19.1

Summary Product Cost Data

Direct materials cost	$4 per unit
Direct labor cost	8 per unit
Overhead cost	
Variable overhead cost	$ 180,000
Fixed overhead cost	600,000
Total overhead cost	$ 780,000
Expected units produced	60,000 units

Drawing on the product cost data, Exhibit 19.2 shows the product unit cost computations for both absorption and variable costing. For absorption costing, the product unit cost is $25, which consists of $4 in direct materials, $8 in direct labor, $3 in variable overhead ($180,000/60,000 units), and $10 in fixed overhead ($600,000/60,000 units).

For variable costing, the product unit cost is $15, which consists of $4 in direct materials, $8 in direct labor, and $3 in variable overhead. Fixed overhead costs of $600,000 are treated as a period cost and are recorded as expense in the period incurred. The difference between the two costing methods is the exclusion of fixed overhead from product costs for variable costing.

EXHIBIT 19.2

Unit Cost Computation

	Absorption Costing	Variable Costing
Direct materials cost per unit	$ 4	$ 4
Direct labor cost per unit	8	8
Overhead cost		
Variable overhead cost per unit	3	3
Fixed overhead cost per unit	10	—
Total product cost per unit	$25	$15

Quick Check Answers — p. 831

1. Which of the following cost elements are included when computing unit cost under absorption costing?
   a. Direct materials b. Direct labor c. Variable overhead d. Fixed overhead
2. Which of the following cost elements are included when computing unit cost under variable costing?
   a. Direct materials b. Direct labor c. Variable overhead d. Fixed overhead

PERFORMANCE REPORTING (INCOME) IMPLICATIONS

The prior section illustrated the differences between absorption costing and variable costing in computing unit cost. This section shows the implications of those differences for performance (income) reporting.

To illustrate the reporting implications, we return to IceAge Company. Exhibit 19.3 summarizes the production cost data for IceAge as well as additional data on nonproduction costs. Assume that IceAge's variable costs per unit are constant and that its annual fixed costs remain unchanged during the three-year period 2011 through 2013.

EXHIBIT 19.3

Summary Cost Information for 2011–2013

Production Costs		Nonproduction Costs	
Direct materials cost . .	$4 per unit	Variable selling and administrative expenses . .	$2 per unit
Direct labor cost	$8 per unit	Fixed selling and administrative expenses	$200,000 per year
Variable overhead cost.	$3 per unit		
Fixed overhead cost . . .	$600,000 per year		

The reported sales and production information for IceAge follows. Its sales price was a constant $40 per unit over this time period. We see that the units produced equal those sold for 2011, exceed those sold for 2012, and are less than those sold for 2013.

	Units Produced	Units Sold	Units in Ending Inventory
2011	60,000	60,000	0
2012	60,000	40,000	20,000
2013	60,000	80,000	0

Drawing on the information above, we next prepare the income statement for IceAge both under absorption costing and under variable costing. Our purpose is to highlight differences between these two costing methods under three different cases: when units produced are equal to, exceed, or are less than units sold.

Units Produced Equal Units Sold

P2 Prepare and analyze an income statement using absorption costing and using variable costing.

Exhibit 19.4 presents the 2011 income statement for both costing methods (2012 and 2013 statements will follow). The income statement under variable costing (on the right) is referred to as the **contribution margin income statement.** Contribution margin is the excess of sales over variable costs. This margin contributes to covering all fixed costs and earning income. Under variable costing, the expenses are grouped according to cost behavior—variable or fixed, and production or nonproduction. Under the traditional format of absorption costing, expenses are grouped according to function.

EXHIBIT 19.4

Income for 2011—Quantity Produced Equals Quantity Sold*

ICEAGE COMPANY
Income Statement (Absorption Costing)
For Year Ended December 31, 2011

Sales† (60,000 × $40)	$2,400,000
Cost of goods sold (60,000 × $25*)	1,500,000
Gross margin	900,000
Selling and administrative expenses [$200,000 + (60,000 × $2)]	320,000
Net income	$ 580,000

* See Exhibit 19.2 for unit cost computation under absorption and under variable costing.

† Units produced equal 60,000; units sold equal 60,000.

ICEAGE COMPANY
Income Statement (Variable Costing)
For Year Ended December 31, 2011

Sales† (60,000 × $40)		$2,400,000
Variable expenses		
Variable production costs (60,000 × $15*)	$900,000	
Variable selling and administrative expenses (60,000 × $2)	120,000	1,020,000
Contribution margin		1,380,000
Fixed expenses		
Fixed overhead	600,000	
Fixed selling and administrative expense	200,000	800,000
Net income		$ 580,000

A performance report that excludes fixed expenses and net income is a contribution margin report. Its bottom line is contribution margin.

Point: Contribution margin income statements prepared under variable costing are useful in performing cost-volume-profit analyses.

Exhibit 19.4 reveals that *reported income is identical under absorption costing and variable costing when the number of units produced equals number of the units sold.*

P3 Prepare a contribution margin report.

Contribution Margin Report A performance report that excludes fixed expenses and net income is known as a **contribution margin report.** Looking at the variable costing income statement in Exhibit 19.4, a contribution margin report would end with the contribution margin of $1,380,000. However, a *contribution margin income statement* includes fixed expenses and net income as shown in Exhibit 19.4.

Point: Contribution margin (Sales − Variable expenses) is different from gross margin (Sales − Cost of sales).

Exhibit 19.5 reorganizes the information from Exhibit 19.4 to show the assignment of costs to different expenses and assets under both absorption costing and variable costing. When quantity produced equals quantity sold there is no difference in total costs assigned. Yet, there is a difference in what categories receive those costs. Absorption costing assigns $1,500,000 to cost of goods sold compared to $900,000 for variable costing. The $600,000 difference is a period cost for variable costing.

EXHIBIT 19.5

Production Cost Assignment for 2011

	Cost of Goods Sold (Expense)		Ending Inventory (Asset)		Period Cost (Expense)	2011 Expense
Absorption Costing						
Direct materials	60,000 × $4	$ 240,000	0 × $4	$ 0		$ 240,000
Direct labor	60,000 × $8	480,000	0 × $8	0		480,000
Variable overhead	60,000 × $3	180,000	0 × $3	0		180,000
Fixed overhead	60,000 × $10	600,000	0 × $10	0		600,000
Total costs		$1,500,000		$ 0		**$1,500,000**
Variable Costing						
Direct materials	60,000 × $4	$ 240,000	0 × $4	$ 0		$ 240,000
Direct labor	60,000 × $8	480,000	0 × $8	0		480,000
Variable overhead	60,000 × $3	180,000	0 × $3	0		180,000
Fixed overhead					$600,000	600,000
Total costs		$ 900,000		$ 0	$600,000	**$1,500,000**
Cost difference						**$ 0**

Decision Insight

Manufacturing Margin Some managers compute *manufacturing margin* (also called *production margin*), which is sales less variable production costs. Some managers also require that internal income statements show this amount to highlight variable product costs on income. The contribution margin section of IceAge's variable costing income statement would appear as follows (compare this to Exhibit 19.4).

Sales	$2,400,000
Variable production costs	900,000
Manufacturing margin	1,500,000
Variable selling & admin. exp.	120,000
Contribution margin	$1,380,000

Units Produced Exceed Units Sold

Exhibit 19.6 shows absorption costing and variable costing income statements for 2012. In 2012, 60,000 units were produced, which is the same as in 2011. However, only 40,000 units were sold, which means 20,000 units remain in ending inventory.

The income statements reveal that for 2012, income is $320,000 under absorption costing. Under variable costing, income is $120,000, which is $200,000 less than under absorption costing. The cause of this $200,000 difference rests with the different treatment of fixed overhead under the two costing methods.

EXHIBIT 19.6

Income for 2012—Quantity Produced Exceeds Quantity Sold*

ICEAGE COMPANY
Income Statement (Absorption Costing)
For Year Ended December 31, 2012

Sales† (40,000 × $40)	$1,600,000
Cost of goods sold (40,000 × $25*)	1,000,000
Gross margin	600,000
Selling and administrative expenses [$200,000 + (40,000 × $2)]	280,000
Net income	$ 320,000

* See Exhibit 19.2 for unit cost computation under absorption and under variable costing.

† Units produced equal 60,000; units sold equal 40,000.

ICEAGE COMPANY
Income Statement (Variable Costing)
For Year Ended December 31, 2012

Sales† (40,000 × $40)		$1,600,000
Variable expenses		
Variable production costs (40,000 × $15*)	$600,000	
Variable selling and administrative expenses (40,000 × $2)	80,000	680,000
Contribution margin		920,000
Fixed expenses		
Fixed overhead	600,000	
Fixed selling and administrative expense	200,000	800,000
Net income		$ 120,000

Under variable costing, the entire $600,000 fixed overhead cost is treated as an expense in computing 2012 income. Under absorption costing, the fixed overhead cost is allocated to each unit of product at the rate of $10 per unit (from Exhibit 19.2). When production exceeds sales by 20,000 units (60,000 versus 40,000), the $200,000 ($10 × 20,000 units) of fixed overhead cost allocated to these 20,000 units is carried as part of the cost of ending inventory (see Exhibit 19.7). This means that $200,000 of fixed overhead cost incurred in 2012 is not expensed until future periods when it is reported in cost of goods sold as those products are sold. Consequently, income for 2012 under absorption costing is $200,000 higher than income under variable costing. Even though sales (of 40,000 units) and the number of units produced (totaling 60,000) are the same under both costing methods, net income differs greatly due to the treatment of fixed overhead.

Exhibit 19.7 reorganizes the information from Exhibit 19.6 to show the assignment of costs to different expenses and assets under both absorption costing and variable costing. When quantity produced exceeds quantity sold there is a difference in total costs assigned. As a result, income under absorption costing is greater than under variable costing because of the greater fixed overhead cost allocated to ending inventory (asset) under absorption costing. Those cost differences extend to cost of goods sold, ending inventory, and period costs.

EXHIBIT 19.7

Production Cost Assignment for 2012

	Cost of Goods Sold (Expense)		Ending Inventory (Asset)		Period Cost (Expense)	2012 Expense
Absorption Costing						
Direct materials....	40,000 × $4	$ 160,000	20,000 × $4	$ 80,000		$ 160,000
Direct labor.......	40,000 × $8	320,000	20,000 × $8	160,000		320,000
Variable overhead ..	40,000 × $3	120,000	20,000 × $3	60,000		120,000
Fixed overhead.....	40,000 × $10	400,000	20,000 × $10	200,000		400,000
Total costs		$1,000,000		$500,000		**$1,000,000**
Variable Costing						
Direct materials....	40,000 × $4	$ 160,000	20,000 × $4	$ 80,000		$ 160,000
Direct labor.......	40,000 × $8	320,000	20,000 × $8	160,000		320,000
Variable overhead ..	40,000 × $3	120,000	20,000 × $3	60,000		120,000
Fixed overhead.....					$600,000	600,000
Total costs		$ 600,000		$300,000	$600,000	**$1,200,000**
Cost difference ...						**$ (200,000)**

Units Produced Are Less Than Units Sold

Exhibit 19.8 shows absorption costing and variable costing income statements for 2013. In 2013, IceAge produced 20,000 fewer units than it sold. Production equaled 60,000 units, but units sold were 80,000. This means IceAge sold all that it produced during the period, and it sold all of its beginning finished goods inventory. IceAge's income statements reveal that income is $840,000 under absorption costing, but it is $1,040,000 under variable costing.

Point: IceAge can sell more units than it produced in 2013 because of inventory carried over from 2012.

The cause of this $200,000 difference lies with the treatment of fixed overhead. Beginning inventory in 2013 under absorption costing included $200,000 of fixed overhead cost incurred in 2012, which is assigned to cost of goods sold in 2013 under absorption costing.

EXHIBIT 19.8

Income for 2013—Quantity Produced Is Less Than Quantity Sold*

ICEAGE COMPANY
Income Statement (Absorption Costing)
For Year Ended December 31, 2013

Sales† (80,000 × $40)...............	$3,200,000
Cost of goods sold (80,000 × $25*)...	2,000,000
Gross margin	1,200,000
Selling and administrative expenses [$200,000 + (80,000 × $2)]	360,000
Net income.....................	$ 840,000

* See Exhibit 19.2 for unit cost computation under absorption and under variable costing.

† Units produced equal 60,000; units sold equal 80,000.

ICEAGE COMPANY
Income Statement (Variable Costing)
For Year Ended December 31, 2013

Sales† (80,000 × $40).....		$3,200,000
Variable expenses		
Variable production costs (80,000 × $15*).....	$1,200,000	
Variable selling and administrative expenses (80,000 × $2)	160,000	1,360,000
Contribution margin......		1,840,000
Fixed expenses		
Fixed overhead	600,000	
Fixed selling and administrative expense.....	200,000	800,000
Net income............		$1,040,000

Exhibit 19.9 reorganizes the information from Exhibit 19.8 to show the assignment of costs to different expenses and assets under both absorption costing and variable costing. When quantity produced is less than quantity sold there is a difference in total costs assigned.

Specifically, ending inventory in 2012 under absorption costing was $500,000 (20,000 units × $25) whereas it was only $300,000 (20,000 units × $15) under variable costing—see Exhibit 19.7. Consequently, when that inventory is sold in 2013, the 2013 income under absorption costing is $200,000 less than the income under variable costing. That inventory cost difference flows through cost of goods sold and then to income.

EXHIBIT 19.9

Production Cost Assignment for 2013

		Cost of Goods Sold (Expense)		Ending Inventory (Asset)	Period Cost (Expense)	2013 Expense
Absorption Costing						
Direct materials	80,000 × $4	$ 320,000	0 × $4	$ 0		$ 320,000
Direct labor	80,000 × $8	640,000	0 × $8	0		640,000
Variable overhead	80,000 × $3	240,000	0 × $3	0		240,000
Fixed overhead	80,000 × $10	800,000	0 × $10	0		800,000
Total costs		$2,000,000		$ 0		**$2,000,000**
Variable Costing						
Direct materials	80,000 × $4	$ 320,000	0 × $4	$ 0		$ 320,000
Direct labor	80,000 × $8	640,000	0 × $8	0		640,000
Variable overhead	80,000 × $3	240,000	0 × $3	0		240,000
Fixed overhead					$600,000	600,000
Total costs		$1,200,000		$ 0	$600,000	**$1,800,000**
Cost difference						**$ 200,000**

Summarizing Income Reporting

Income reported under both variable costing and absorption costing for the years 2011 through 2013 for IceAge is summarized in Exhibit 19.10. We see that the differences in income are due to timing, as total income is $1,740,000 for this time period for *both* methods. Further, income under absorption costing and that under variable costing will be different whenever the quantity produced and the quantity sold are different. Specifically, *income under absorption costing is higher when more units are produced relative to units sold and is lower when fewer units are produced than are sold.*

EXHIBIT 19.10

Summary of Income Reporting

	Units Produced	Units Sold	Income under Absorption Costing	Income under Variable Costing	Differences
2011	60,000	60,000	$ 580,000	$ 580,000	$ 0
2012	60,000	40,000	320,000	120,000	200,000
2013	60,000	80,000	840,000	1,040,000	(200,000)
Totals	180,000	180,000	$1,740,000	$1,740,000	$ 0

Our illustration using IceAge had the total number of units produced over 2011–2013 exactly equal to the number of units sold over that period. This meant that the difference between absorption costing income and variable costing income for the *total* three-year period is zero. In reality, it is unusual for production and sales quantities to exactly equal each other over such a short period of time. This means that we normally continue to see differences in income for these two methods extending over several years.

Quick Check Answers – p. 831

3. Which of the following statements is true when units produced exceed units sold?
   a. Variable costing income exceeds absorption costing income.
   b. Variable costing income equals absorption costing income.
   c. Variable costing income is less than absorption costing income.
4. Which of the following statements is true when units produced are less than units sold?
   a. Variable costing income exceeds absorption costing income.
   b. Variable costing income equals absorption costing income.
   c. Variable costing income is less than absorption costing income.

Converting Income under Variable Costing to Absorption Costing

Companies commonly use variable costing for internal reporting and business decisions, and use absorption costing for external reporting and tax reporting. For companies concerned about the cost of maintaining two costing systems, it is comforting to know that we can readily convert reports under variable costing to that using absorption costing.

P4 Convert income under variable costing to the absorption cost basis.

Income under variable costing is restated to that under absorption costing by adding the fixed production cost in ending inventory and subtracting the fixed production cost in beginning inventory, as follows.

$$\text{Income under absorption costing} = \text{Income under variable costing} + \text{Fixed production cost in ending inventory} - \text{Fixed production cost in beginning inventory}$$

Using IceAge's data, in 2012, absorption costing income was $200,000 higher than variable costing income. The $200,000 difference was because the fixed overhead cost incurred in 2012 was allocated to the 20,000 units of ending inventory under absorption costing (and not expensed in 2012 under absorption costing). On the other hand, the $200,000 fixed overhead costs (along with all other fixed costs) were expensed in 2012 under variable costing.

Exhibit 19.11 shows the computations for restating income under the two costing methods. To restate variable costing income to absorption costing income for 2012, we must add back the **fixed overhead cost deferred in** (ending) **inventory.** Similarly, to restate variable costing income to absorption costing income for 2013, we must deduct the **fixed overhead cost recognized from** (beginning) **inventory,** which was incurred in 2012, but expensed in the 2013 cost of goods sold when the inventory was sold.

EXHIBIT 19.11

Converting Variable Costing Income to Absorption Costing Income

	2011	2012	2013
Variable costing income (Exhibit 19.10)	$580,000	$120,000	$1,040,000
Add: Fixed overhead cost deferred in ending inventory (20,000 × $10)	0	200,000	0
Less: Fixed overhead cost recognized from beginning inventory (20,000 × $10)	0	0	(200,000)
Absorption costing income	$580,000	$320,000	$ 840,000

COMPARING VARIABLE COSTING AND ABSORPTION COSTING

This section discusses how absorption costing can lead to undesirable production and pricing decisions and how variable costing can result in better business decisions.

Planning Production

Production planning is an important managerial function. Producing too much leads to excess inventory, which in turn leads to higher storage and financing costs, and to greater risk of product obsolescence. On the other hand, producing too little can lead to lost sales and customer dissatisfaction.

C1 Describe how absorption costing can result in overproduction.

Production levels should be based on reliable sales forecasts. However, overproduction and inventory buildup can occur because of how managers are evaluated and rewarded. For instance, many companies link manager bonuses to income computed under absorption costing because this is how income is reported to shareholders (per GAAP).

To illustrate how a reward system can lead to overproduction under absorption costing, let's use IceAge's 2011 data with one change: assume that its manager decides to produce 100,000 units instead of 60,000. Since only 60,000 units are sold, the 40,000 units of excess production will be stored in ending finished goods inventory.

The left side of Exhibit 19.12 shows the unit cost when 60,000 units are produced (same as Exhibit 19.2). The right side shows unit cost when 100,000 units are produced. The exhibit is prepared under absorption costing for 2011.

EXHIBIT 19.12

Unit Cost under Absorption Costing for Different Production Levels

Absorption Costing When 60,000 Units Are Produced		Absorption Costing When 100,000 Units Are Produced	
Direct materials cost	$ 4 per unit	Direct materials cost	$ 4 per unit
Direct labor cost	8 per unit	Direct labor cost	8 per unit
Variable overhead cost	3 per unit	Variable overhead cost	3 per unit
Total variable cost	15 per unit	Total variable cost	15 per unit
Fixed overhead ($600,000/60,000 units)	10 per unit	Fixed overhead ($600,000/100,000 units)	6 per unit
Total product cost	$25 per unit	Total product cost	$21 per unit

Total production cost *per unit* is $4 less when 100,000 units are produced. Specifically, cost per unit is $21 when 100,000 units are produced versus $25 per unit at 60,000 units. The reason for this difference is because the company is spreading the $600,000 fixed overhead cost over more units when 100,000 units are produced than when 60,000 are produced.

The difference in cost per unit impacts performance reporting. Exhibit 19.13 presents the 2011 income statement under absorption costing for the two alternative production levels.

EXHIBIT 19.13

Income under Absorption Costing for Different Production Levels

ICEAGE COMPANY
Income Statement (Absorption Costing)
For Year Ended December 31, 2011
[60,000 Units Produced; 60,000 Units Sold]

Sales (60,000 × $40)		$2,400,000
Cost of goods sold (60,000 × $25)		1,500,000
Gross margin		900,000
Selling and administrative expenses		
Variable (60,000 × $2)	$120,000	
Fixed	200,000	320,000
Net income		$ 580,000

ICEAGE COMPANY
Income Statement (Absorption Costing)
For Year Ended December 31, 2011
[100,000 Units Produced; 60,000 Units Sold]

Sales (60,000 × $40)		$2,400,000
Cost of goods sold (60,000 × $21)		1,260,000
Gross margin		1,140,000
Selling and administrative expenses		
Variable (60,000 × $2)	$120,000	
Fixed	200,000	320,000
Net income		$ 820,000

Point: The 41% income increase is computed as:

$$\frac{\$820{,}000 - \$580{,}000}{\$580{,}000} = 0.41$$

Common sense suggests that because the company's variable cost per unit, total fixed costs, and sales are identical in both cases, merely producing more units and creating excess ending inventory should not increase income. Yet, as we see in Exhibit 19.13, income under absorption costing is 41% greater if management produces 40,000 more units than necessary and builds up ending inventory. The reason is that $240,000 of fixed overhead (40,000 units × $6) is assigned to ending inventory instead of being expensed as cost of goods sold in 2011. This shows that under absorption costing, a manager can report increased income merely by producing more and disregarding whether the excess units can be sold or not.

Manager bonuses are tied to income computed under absorption costing for many companies. Accordingly, these managers may be enticed to increase production that increases income and their bonuses. This incentive problem encourages inventory buildup, which leads to increased costs in storage, financing, and obsolescence. If the excess inventory is never sold, it will be disposed of at a loss.

The manager incentive problem can be avoided when income is measured using variable costing. To illustrate, Exhibit 19.14 reports income under variable costing for the same production levels used in Exhibit 19.13. This demonstrates that managers cannot increase income under variable costing by merely increasing production without increasing sales.

Why is income under absorption costing affected by the production level when that for variable costing is not? The answer lies in the different treatment of fixed overhead costs for the two methods. Under absorption costing, fixed overhead *per unit* is lower when 100,000 units are produced than when 60,000 units are produced, and then fixed overhead cost is allocated to more units—recall Exhibit 19.12. If those excess units produced are not sold, the fixed overhead cost allocated to those units is not expensed until a future period when those units are sold.

EXHIBIT 19.14

Income under Variable Costing for Different Production Levels

ICEAGE COMPANY
Income Statement (Variable Costing)
For Year Ended December 31, 2011
[60,000 Units Produced; 60,000 Units Sold]

Sales (60,000 × $40)		$2,400,000
Variable expenses		
Variable production costs (60,000 × $15)	$900,000	
Variable selling and administrative expenses (60,000 × $2)	120,000	1,020,000
Contribution margin		1,380,000
Fixed expenses		
Fixed overhead	600,000	
Fixed selling and administrative expense	200,000	800,000
Net income		$ 580,000

ICEAGE COMPANY
Income Statement (Variable Costing)
For Year Ended December 31, 2011
[100,000 Units Produced; 60,000 Units Sold]

Sales (60,000 × $40)		$2,400,000
Variable expenses		
Variable production costs (60,000 × $15)	$900,000	
Variable selling and administrative expenses (60,000 × $2)	120,000	1,020,000
Contribution margin		1,380,000
Fixed expenses		
Fixed overhead	600,000	
Fixed selling and administrative expense	200,000	800,000
Net income		$ 580,000

Reported income under variable costing, on the other hand, is not affected by production level changes because *all* fixed production costs are expensed in the year when incurred. Under variable costing, companies increase reported income by selling more units—it is not possible to increase income just by producing more units and creating excess inventory.

Point: A per unit cost that is constant at all production levels is a *variable cost per unit.*

Decision Ethics

Production Manager Your company produces and sells MP3 players. Due to competition, your company projects sales to be 35% less than last year. In a recent meeting, the CEO expressed concern that top executives may not receive bonuses because of the expected sales decrease. The controller suggests that if the company continues to produce as many units as last year, reported income might achieve the level for bonuses to be paid. Should your company produce excess inventory to maintain income? What ethical issues arise? ■ [Answer—p. 831]

Setting Prices

C2 Explain the role of variable costing in pricing special orders.

Setting prices for products and services is one of the more complex and important managerial decisions. Although many factors impact pricing, cost is a crucial factor. Cost information from both absorption costing and variable costing can aid managers in pricing.

Over the long run, price must be high enough to cover all costs, including variable costs and fixed costs, and still provide an acceptable return to owners. For this purpose, absorption cost information is useful because it reflects the full costs that sales must exceed for the company to be profitable.

Over the short run, however, fixed production costs such as the cost to maintain plant capacity do not change with changes in production levels. With excess capacity, increases in production level would increase variable production costs, but not fixed costs. This implies that while managers try to maintain the long-run price on existing orders, which covers all production costs, managers should accept special orders *provided the special order price exceeds variable cost.*

To illustrate, let's return to the data of IceAge Company. Recall that its variable production cost per unit is $15 and its total production cost per unit is $25 (at production level of 60,000 units). Assume that it receives a special order for 1,000 pairs of skates at an offer price of $22 per pair from a foreign skating school. This special order will not affect IceAge's regular sales and its plant has excess capacity to fill the order.

Drawing on absorption costing information, we observe that cost is $25 per unit and that the special order price is $22 per unit. These data would suggest that management reject the order as it would lose $3,000, computed as 1,000 units at $3 loss per pair ($22 − $25).

However, closer analysis suggests that this order should be accepted. This is because the $22 order price exceeds the $15 variable cost of the product. Specifically, Exhibit 19.15 reveals that the incremental revenue from accepting the order is $22,000 (1,000 units at $22 per unit), whereas the incremental production cost of the order is $15,000 (1,000 units at $15 per unit) and the incremental variable selling and administrative cost is $2,000 (1,000 units at $2 per unit). Thus, both its contribution margin and net income would increase by $5,000 from accepting the order. Variable costing reveals this profitable opportunity while absorption costing hides it.

Point: Use of relevant costs in special order and other managerial decisions is covered more extensively in a later chapter.

EXHIBIT 19.15

Computing Incremental Income for a Special Order

Rejecting Special Order		Accepting Special Order	
Incremental sales	$ 0	Incremental sales (1,000 × $22)	$22,000
Incremental costs	0	Incremental costs	
		Variable production cost (1,000 × $15)	15,000
		Variable selling and admin. expense (1,000 × $2)	2,000
Incremental income	$ 0	Incremental income..................................	$ 5,000

The reason for increased income from accepting the special order lies in the different behavior of variable and fixed production costs. We see that if the order is rejected, only variable costs are saved. Fixed costs, on the other hand, do not change in the short run regardless of rejecting or accepting this order. Since incremental revenue from the order exceeds incremental costs (only variable cost in this case), accepting the special order increases company income.

Point: Fixed overhead costs won't increase when these additional units are sold because the company already has the capacity.

Controlling Costs

Every company strives to control costs to be competitive. An effective cost control practice is to hold managers responsible only for their **controllable costs.** A cost is controllable if a manager has the power to determine or at least markedly affect the amount incurred. **Uncontrollable costs** are not within the manager's control or influence. For example, direct materials cost is controllable by a production supervisor. On the other hand, costs related to production capacity are not controllable by that supervisor as that supervisor does not have authority to change factory size or add new machinery. Generally, variable production costs and fixed production costs are controlled at different levels of management. Similarly, variable selling and administrative costs are usually controlled at a level of management different from that which controls fixed selling and administrative costs.

Under absorption costing, both variable production costs and fixed production costs are included in product cost. This makes it difficult to evaluate the effectiveness of cost control by different levels of managers. Variable costing separates the variable costs from fixed costs and, therefore, makes it easier to identify and assign control over costs.

Decisions to change a company's fixed costs are usually assigned to higher-level managers. This is different from most variable costs that are assigned to lower-level managers and supervisors. When we separately report variable and fixed cost elements, as is done with an income statement in the **contribution format,** it highlights the impact of each cost element for income. This makes it easier for us to identify problem areas and to take cost control measures by appropriate levels of management. This approach is also useful in evaluating the performance of managers of different segments within a company.

Decision Maker

Internal Auditor Your company uses absorption costing for preparing its GAAP-based income statement and balance sheet. Management is disappointed because its external auditors are requiring it to write off an inventory amount because it exceeds what the company could reasonably sell in the foreseeable future. Why would management produce more than it sells? Why would management be disappointed about the write-off? ■ [Answer—p. 831]

Limitations of Reports Using Variable Costing

An important generally accepted accounting principle is that of matching. Most managers interpret the matching principle as expensing all manufacturing costs, both variable and fixed, in the period when the related product is sold rather than when costs are incurred. Thus, and despite the many useful applications and insights provided by variable cost reports, *absorption costing is the only acceptable basis for external reporting under both U.S. GAAP and IFRS*. Also, as we discussed, top executives are often awarded bonuses based on income computed using absorption costing. For income tax purposes, absorption costing is the only acceptable basis for filings with the Internal Revenue Service (IRS) under the Tax Reform Act of 1986. These realities contribute to the widespread use of absorption costing by companies.

Variable Costing for Service Firms

Although most of this chapter's examples used data for a manufacturer, variable costing also applies to service companies. Since service companies do not produce inventory, the differences in income from absorption and variable costing shown for a manufacturer do not apply. Still, a focus on variable costs can be useful in managerial decisions for service firms. One example is "special order" pricing for airlines when they sell tickets a day or so before a flight at deeply discounted prices. Provided the discounted price exceeds variable costs, such sales increase contribution margin and net income.

Quick Check

Answers — p. 831

5. Why is information under variable costing useful in making short-run pricing decisions when idle capacity exits?
6. Discuss the usefulness of absorption costing versus variable costing in controlling costs.
7. What are the limitations of variable costing?

GLOBAL VIEW

U.S. multinational companies must change their business processes when moving their operations to international locations. These changes can impact the company's cost structure. For example, both **McDonald's** and **Yum Brands** offer delivery services in major international cities like Beijing (China) and Seoul (South Korea). Cities like these are heavily populated and real estate costs are high. These factors discourage the building of drive-through facilities, which would increase fixed overhead costs. Fixed overhead costs also fall as these companies process more orders over the Internet and thus build fewer call centers. As fixed overhead costs decrease, the difference in net income that would result from applying variable costing versus absorption costing also decreases.

Source: "Asia Delivers for McDonald's," *The Wall Street Journal*, December 13, 2011.

Break-Even Analysis

Decision Analysis

A1 Compute and interpret break-even volume in units.

The previous chapter discussed cost-volume-profit (CVP) analysis for making managerial decisions. However, if the income statement is prepared under absorption costing, the data needed for CVP analysis are not readily available. Accordingly, substantial effort is required to go back to the accounting records and reclassify the cost data to obtain information necessary for conducting CVP analysis.

On the other hand, if the income statement is prepared using the contribution format, the data needed for CVP analysis are readily available. To illustrate, we can draw on IceAge's contribution margin income statement from Exhibit 19.4 (reproduced below) to readily compute its contribution margin per unit and its break-even volume in units.

ICEAGE COMPANY
Income Statement (Variable Costing)
For Year Ended December 31, 2011

		Dollars		Per Unit
Sales (60,000 × \$40)		\$2,400,000		\$40
Variable expenses				
Variable production costs (60,000 × \$15)	\$900,000		\$15	
Variable selling and administrative expenses (60,000 × \$2)	120,000	1,020,000	2	17
Contribution margin		1,380,000		\$23
Fixed expenses				
Fixed overhead	600,000			
Fixed selling and administrative expense	200,000	800,000		
Net income		\$ 580,000		

We compute and report the company's contribution margin per unit and its components in the far right columns of the exhibit above. Recall that contribution margin per unit is defined as follows.

$$\text{Contribution margin per unit} = \text{Sales price per unit} - \text{Variable cost per unit}$$
$$= \$40 - \$17 = \$23$$

The above report shows that its variable cost per unit consists of \$15 in variable production costs and \$2 in variable selling and administrative costs.

We also see that the company's total fixed costs of \$800,000 is the sum of \$600,000 in fixed overhead cost and \$200,000 in fixed selling and administrative cost. From this information we can compute the company's break-even volume in units as follows.

$$\text{Break-even volume in units} = \frac{\text{Total fixed costs}}{\text{Contribution margin per unit}} = \frac{\$800{,}000}{\$23} = 34{,}783 \text{ units (rounded)}$$

This finding implies that the company must produce and sell 34,783 units to break even (zero income). Sales less than that amount would yield a net loss and sales above that amount would yield net income.

DEMONSTRATION PROBLEM

Navaroli Company began operations on January 5, 2012. Cost and sales information for its first two calendar years of operations are summarized below.

Manufacturing costs	
Direct materials	\$80 per unit
Direct labor	\$120 per unit
Factory overhead costs for the year	
Variable overhead	\$30 per unit
Fixed overhead	\$14,000,000
Nonmanufacturing costs	
Variable selling and administrative	\$10 per unit
Fixed selling and administrative	\$ 8,000,000
Production and sales data	
Units produced, 2012	200,000 units
Units sold, 2012	140,000 units
Units in ending inventory, 2012	60,000 units
Units produced, 2013	80,000 units
Units sold, 2013	140,000 units
Units in ending inventory, 2013	0 units
Sales price per unit	\$600 per unit

Required

1. Prepare an income statement for the company for 2012 under absorption costing.

2. Prepare an income statement for the company for 2012 under variable costing.

3. Explain the source(s) of the difference in reported income for 2012 under the two costing methods.

4. Prepare an income statement for the company for 2013 under absorption costing.

5. Prepare an income statement for the company for 2013 under variable costing.

6. Prepare a schedule to convert variable costing income to absorption costing income for the years 2012 and 2013. Use the format in Exhibit 19.11.

PLANNING THE SOLUTION

- Set up a table to compute the unit cost under the two costing methods (refer to Exhibit 19.2).
- Prepare an income statement under both of the two costing methods (refer to Exhibit 19.6).
- Consider differences in the treatment of fixed production costs for the income statement to answer requirements 3 and 6.

SOLUTION TO DEMONSTRATION PROBLEM

Before the income statement for 2012 is prepared, unit costs for 2012 are computed under the two costing methods as follows.

	Absorption Costing	Variable Costing
Direct materials per unit	$ 80	$ 80
Direct labor per unit	120	120
Overhead per unit		
Variable overhead per unit	30	30
Fixed overhead per unit*	70	—
Total production cost per unit	$300	$230

* Fixed overhead per unit = $14,000,000 ÷ 200,000 units = $70 per unit.

1. Absorption costing income statement for 2012.

NAVAROLI COMPANY Income Statement For Year Ended December 31, 2012	
Sales (140,000 × $600)	$84,000,000
Cost of goods sold (140,000 × $300)	42,000,000
Gross margin	42,000,000
Selling and administrative expenses ($1,400,000 + $8,000,000)	9,400,000
Net income	$32,600,000

2. Variable costing income statement for 2012.

NAVAROLI COMPANY Income Statement (Contribution Format) For Year Ended December 31, 2012		
Sales (140,000 × $600)		$84,000,000
Variable expenses		
Variable production costs (140,000 × $230)	$32,200,000	
Variable selling and administrative costs	1,400,000	33,600,000
Contribution margin		50,400,000
Fixed expenses		
Fixed overhead	14,000,000	
Fixed selling and administrative	8,000,000	22,000,000
Net income		$28,400,000

3. Income under absorption costing is $4,200,000 more than that under variable costing even though sales are identical for each. This difference is due to the different treatment of fixed overhead cost. Under variable costing, the entire $14,000,000 of fixed overhead is expensed on the 2012 income statement. However, under absorption costing, $70 of fixed overhead cost is allocated to each of the 200,000 units produced. Since there were 60,000 units unsold at year-end, $4,200,000 (60,000 units × $70 per unit) of fixed overhead cost allocated to these units will be carried on its balance sheet in ending inventory. Consequently, reported income under absorption costing is $4,200,000 higher than variable costing income for the current period.

Before the income statement for 2013 is prepared, unit costs are computed under the two costing methods as follows.

	Absorption Costing	Variable Costing
Direct materials per unit	$ 80	$ 80
Direct labor per unit	120	120
Overhead per unit		
Variable overhead per unit	30	30
Fixed overhead per unit*	175	—
Total production cost per unit	$405	$230

* Fixed overhead per unit = $14,000,000/80,000 units = $175 per unit.

4. Absorption costing income statement for 2013.

NAVAROLI COMPANY Income Statement For Year Ended December 31, 2013		
Sales (140,000 × $600)		$84,000,000
Cost of goods sold		
From beginning inventory (60,000 × $300)	$18,000,000	
Produced during the year (80,000 × $405)	32,400,000	50,400,000
Gross margin		33,600,000
Selling and administrative expenses ($1,400,000 + $8,000,000)		9,400,000
Net income		$24,200,000

5. Variable costing income statement for 2013.

NAVAROLI COMPANY Income Statement (Contribution Format) For Year Ended December 31, 2013		
Sales (140,000 × $600)		$84,000,000
Variable expenses		
Variable production costs (140,000 × $230)	$32,200,000	
Variable selling and administrative costs	1,400,000	33,600,000
Contribution margin		50,400,000
Fixed expenses		
Fixed overhead	14,000,000	
Fixed selling and administrative	8,000,000	22,000,000
Net income		$28,400,000

6. Conversion of variable costing income to absorption costing income.

	2012	2013
Variable costing income	$28,400,000	$28,400,000
Add: Fixed overhead cost deferred in ending inventory (60,000 × $70)	4,200,000	0
Less: Fixed overhead cost recognized from beginning inventory (60,000 × $70)	0	(4,200,000)
Absorption costing income	$32,600,000	$24,200,000

Summary

C1 Describe how absorption costing can result in over-production. Under absorption costing, fixed overhead costs are allocated to all units including both units sold and units in ending inventory. Consequently, expenses associated with the fixed overhead allocated to ending inventory are deferred to a future period. As a result, the larger ending inventory is, the more overhead cost is deferred to the future, and the greater current period income is.

C2 Explain the role of variable costing in pricing special orders. Over the short run, fixed production costs such as cost of maintaining plant capacity do not change with changes in production levels. When there is excess capacity, increases in production levels would only increase variable costs. Thus, managers should accept special orders as long as the order price is greater than the variable cost. This is because accepting the special order would increase only variable costs.

A1 Compute and interpret break-even volume in units. Break-even volume in units is defined as total fixed costs divided by contribution margin per unit. The result gives managers a unit goal to achieve breakeven; if the goal is surpassed, the company earns income.

P1 Compute unit cost under both absorption and variable costing. Absorption cost per unit includes direct materials, direct labor, and *all* overhead, whereas variable cost per unit includes direct materials, direct labor, and only *variable* overhead.

P2 Prepare and analyze an income statement using absorption costing and using variable costing. The variable costing income statement differs from the absorption costing income statement in that it classifies expenses based on cost behavior rather than function. Instead of gross margin, the variable costing income statement shows contribution margin. This contribution margin format focuses attention on the relation between costs and sales that is not evident from the absorption costing format. Under absorption costing, some fixed overhead cost is allocated to ending inventory and is carried on the balance sheet to the next period. However, all fixed costs are expensed in the period incurred under variable costing. Consequently, absorption costing income is generally greater than variable costing income if units produced exceed units sold, and conversely.

P3 Prepare a contribution margin report. Under variable costing, the total variable costs are first deducted from sales to arrive at contribution margin. Variable costs and contribution margin are also shown as ratios (after dividing by dollar sales).

P4 Convert income under variable costing to the absorption cost basis. Variable costing income can be adjusted to absorption costing income by adding the fixed cost allocated to ending inventory and subtracting the fixed cost previously allocated to beginning inventory.

Guidance Answers to Decision Maker and Decision Ethics

Production Manager Under absorption costing, fixed production costs are spread over all units produced. Thus, fixed cost for each unit would be lower if more units are produced because the fixed cost is spread over more units. This means the company can increase income by producing excess units even if sales remain constant. With sales lagging, producing excess inventory leads to increased financing cost and inventory obsolescence. Also, producing excess inventory to meet income levels for bonuses harms company owners and is unethical. You must discuss this with the appropriate managers.

Internal Auditor If manager bonuses are tied to income, they would have incentives to increase income for personal gain. If absorption costing is used to determine income, management can reduce current period expenses (and raise income) with over-production, which shifts fixed production costs to future periods. This decision fails to consider whether there is a viable market for all units that are produced. If there is not, an auditor can conclude that the inventory does not have "future economic value" and pressure management to write it off. Such a write-off reduces income by the cost of the excess inventory.

Guidance Answers to Quick Checks

1. a, b, c, and d; Direct materials, direct labor, variable overhead, and fixed overhead.
2. a, b, and c; Direct materials, direct labor, and variable overhead.
3. c; see Exhibit 19.6
4. a; see Exhibit 19.8
5. This is because only the variable cost will be avoided if a special order is rejected, as fixed cost does not change with changes to short-run sales. This means a company is better off taking an order provided the order price exceeds variable cost.
6. Variable costs and fixed costs are typically influenced by decisions at different managerial levels. Since reports under variable costing separate variable costs from fixed costs, variable costing makes it easier to identify and control these cost elements.
7. Variable costing is not accepted for external reporting and income tax purposes—only absorption costing is acceptable for those purposes.

Key Terms

Absorption costing (also called **full costing**) (p. 816)
Contribution format (p. 826)
Contribution margin income statement (p. 818)
Contribution margin report (p. 819)
Controllable costs (p. 826)
Fixed overhead cost deferred in inventory (p. 823)
Fixed overhead cost recognized from inventory (p. 823)
Uncontrollable costs (p. 826)
Variable costing (also called **direct or marginal costing**) (p. 816)

Multiple Choice Quiz

Answers on p. 845 mhhe.com/wildFINMAN5e

Additional Quiz Questions are available at the book's Website.

Answer questions 1 and 2 using the following company data.

Units produced	1,000
Variable costs	
Direct materials	$3 per unit
Direct labor	$5 per unit
Variable overhead	$3 per unit
Variable selling and administrative	$1 per unit
Fixed overhead	$3,000
Fixed selling and administrative	$1,000

1. Product cost per unit under absorption costing is:
a. $11
b. $12
c. $14
d. $15
e. $16

2. Product cost per unit under variable costing is:
a. $11
b. $12
c. $14
d. $15
e. $16

3. Under variable costing, which costs are included in product cost?
a. All variable product costs, including direct materials, direct labor, and variable overhead.
b. All variable and fixed allocations of product costs, including direct materials, direct labor, and both variable and fixed overhead.
c. All variable product costs except for variable overhead.
d. All variable and fixed allocations of product costs, except for both variable and fixed overhead.

4. The difference between unit product cost under absorption costing as compared to that under variable costing is:
a. Direct materials and direct labor.
b. Fixed and variable portions of overhead.
c. Fixed overhead only.
d. Variable overhead only.

5. When production exceeds sales, which of the following is true?
a. No change occurs to inventories for either absorption costing or variable costing methods.
b. Use of absorption costing produces a higher net income than the use of variable costing.
c. Use of absorption costing produces a lower net income than the use of variable costing.
d. Use of absorption costing causes inventory value to decrease more than it would through the use of variable costing.

Icon denotes assignments that involve decision making.

Discussion Questions

1. What costs are normally included as part of product costs under the method of variable costing?

2. What costs are normally included as part of product costs under the method of absorption costing?

3. When units produced exceed units sold for a reporting period, would income under variable costing be greater than, equal to, or less than income under absorption costing? Explain.

4. Describe how the following items are computed: *a.* Gross margin, and *b.* Contribution margin

5. How can absorption costing lead to incorrect short-run pricing decisions?

6. What conditions must exist to achieve accurate short-run pricing decisions using variable costing?

7. Describe the usefulness of variable costing for controlling company costs.

8. Describe how use of absorption costing in determining income can lead to over-production and a buildup of inventory. Explain how variable costing can avoid this same problem.

9. What are the major limitations of variable costing?

10. Polaris uses variable costing for several business decisions. How can variable costing income statements be converted to absorption costing?

Polaris

11. Explain how contribution margin analysis is useful for managerial decisions and performance evaluations.

12. KTM's managers rely on reports of variable costs. How can variable costing reports prepared using the contribution margin format help managers in computing break-even volume in units? **KTM**

13. Assume that Arctic Cat has received a special order from a retailer for 100 specially outfitted snowmobiles. This is a one-time order, which will not require any additional capacity or fixed costs. What should Arctic Cat consider when determining a selling price for these snowmobiles? Arctic Cat

14. How can Piaggio use variable costing to help better understand its operations and to make better pricing decisions? **PIAGGIO**

connect

QUICK STUDY

QS 19-1
Absorption costing and over-production
C1

Under absorption costing a company had the following per unit costs when 10,000 units were produced.

Direct labor	$ 2
Direct material	3
Variable overhead	4
Total variable cost	9
Fixed overhead ($50,000/10,000 units)	5
Total production cost per unit	$14

Required

1. Compute the company's total production cost per unit if 12,500 units had been produced.
2. Why might a manager of a company using absorption costing produce more units than can currently be sold?

QS 19-2
Computing manufacturing margin P3

D'Souza Company sold 10,000 units of its product at a price of $80 per unit. Total variable cost is $50 per unit, consisting of $40 in variable production cost and $10 in variable selling and administrative cost. Compute the manufacturing (production) margin for the company under variable costing.

QS 19-3
Computing contribution margin
P3

Refer to the information for D'Souza Company in QS 19-2. Compute the contribution margin.

QS 19-4
Computing unit cost under absorption costing
P1

Vijay Company reports the following information regarding its production costs. Compute its production cost per unit under absorption costing.

Direct materials	$10 per unit
Direct labor	$20 per unit
Overhead costs for the year	
Variable overhead	$10 per unit
Fixed overhead	$160,000
Units produced	20,000 units

QS 19-5
Computing unit cost under variable costing P1

Refer to Vijay Company's data in QS 19-4. Compute its production cost per unit under variable costing.

QS 19-6
Variable costing income statement
P2

Aces Inc., a manufacturer of tennis rackets, began operations this year. The company produced 6,000 rackets and sold 4,900. Each racket was sold at a price of $90. Fixed overhead costs are $78,000 and fixed selling and administrative costs are $65,200. The company also reports the following per unit costs for the year:

Variable production costs	$25.00
Variable selling and administrative expenses	2.00

Prepare an income statement under variable costing.

QS 19-7
Absorption costing income statement P2

Refer to information in QS 19-6. Prepare an income statement under absorption costing.

QS 19-8
Production level, absorption costing, and gross margin
P3

Ramort Company reports the following cost data for its single product. The company regularly sells 20,000 units of its product at a price of $60 per unit. If Ramort doubles its production to 40,000 units while sales remain at the current 20,000 unit level, by how much would the company's gross margin increase or decrease under absorption costing?

Direct materials	$10 per unit
Direct labor	$12 per unit
Overhead costs for the year	
Variable overhead	$3 per unit
Fixed overhead per year	$40,000
Normal production level (in units)	20,000 units

QS 19-9
Production level, variable costing, and gross margin P2 P3

Refer to the information about Ramort Company in QS 19-8. Would the answer to the question in QS 19-8 change if the company uses variable costing? Explain.

QS 19-10
Special order pricing
C2

Li Company produces a product that sells for $84 per unit. A customer contacts Li and offers to purchase 2,000 units of its product at a price of $68 per unit. Variable production costs with this order would be $30 per unit, and variable selling expenses would be $18 per unit. Assuming that this special order would not require any additional fixed costs, and that Li has sufficient capacity to produce the product without affecting regular sales, explain to Li's management why it might be a good decision to accept this special order.

QS 19-11
Break-even volume in units A1

Assume a company sells a given product for $85 per unit. How many units must be sold to break even if variable selling costs are $27 per unit, variable production costs are $23 per unit, and total fixed costs are $700,000?

QS 19-12
Converting variable costing income to absorption costing
P4

Diaz Company reports the following variable costing income statement for its single product. This company's sales totaled 50,000 units, but its production was 80,000 units. It had no beginning finished goods inventory for the current period.

DIAZ COMPANY
Income Statement (Variable Costing)

Sales (50,000 units × $60 per unit)	$3,000,000
Variable expenses	
Variable manufacturing expense (50,000 units × $28 per unit)	1,400,000
Variable selling and admin. expense (50,000 units × $5 per unit)	250,000
Total variable expenses	1,650,000
Contribution margin	1,350,000
Fixed expenses	
Fixed overhead	320,000
Fixed selling and administrative expense	160,000
Total fixed expenses	480,000
Net income	$ 870,000

1. Convert this company's variable costing income statement to an absorption costing income statement.
2. Explain the difference in income between the variable costing and absorption costing income statement.

QS 19-13
Converting variable costing income to absorption costing income P4

Ming Company had net income of $772,200 based on variable costing. Beginning and ending inventories were 7,800 units and 5,200 units, respectively. Assume the fixed overhead per unit was $3.00 for both the beginning and ending inventory. What is net income under absorption costing?

QS 19-14
Converting variable costing income to absorption costing income P4

Mortech had net income of $250,000 based on variable costing. Beginning and ending inventories were 50,000 units and 48,000 units, respectively. Assume the fixed overhead per unit was $0.75 for both the beginning and ending inventory. What is net income under absorption costing?

connect

EXERCISES

Exercise 19-1
Computing unit and inventory costs under absorption costing and variable costing

P1

Trio Company reports the following information for the current year, which is its first year of operations.

Direct materials	$15 per unit
Direct labor	$16 per unit
Overhead costs for the year	
Variable overhead	$ 80,000 per year
Fixed overhead	$160,000 per year
Units produced this year	20,000 units
Units sold this year	14,000 units
Ending finished goods inventory in units	6,000 units

1. Compute the cost per unit of finished goods using absorption costing.
2. Compute the cost per unit of finished goods using variable costing.
3. Determine the cost of ending finished goods inventory using absorption costing.
4. Determine the cost of ending finished goods inventory using variable costing.

Check (1) Absorption cost per unit, $43; (2) Variable cost per unit, $35

Exercise 19-2
Income reporting under absorption costing and variable costing

P2

Sims Company, a manufacturer of in-home decorative fountains, began operations on September 1 of the current year. Its cost and sales information for this year follows.

Production costs	
Direct materials	$40 per unit
Direct labor	$60 per unit
Overhead costs for the year	
Variable overhead	$3,000,000
Fixed overhead	$7,000,000
Nonproduction costs for the year	
Variable selling and administrative	$ 770,000
Fixed selling and administrative	$4,250,000
Production and sales for the year	
Units produced	100,000 units
Units sold	70,000 units
Sales price per unit	$350 per unit

1. Prepare an income statement for the company using variable costing.
2. Prepare an income statement for the company using absorption costing.
3. Under what circumstance(s) is reported income identical under both absorption costing and variable costing?

Check (1) Variable costing income, $3,380,000; (2) Absorption costing income, $5,480,000

Exercise 19-3
Converting absorption costing income to variable costing income

P2 P4

Kenzi Kayaking, a manufacturer of kayaks, began operations this year. During this first year, the company produced 1,050 kayaks and sold 800 at a price of $1,050 each. At the current year-end, the company reported the following income statement information using absorption costing.

Sales (800 × $1,050)	$840,000
Cost of goods sold (800 × $500)	400,000
Gross margin	440,000
Selling and administrative expenses	230,000
Net income	$210,000

Additional Information

a. Production cost per kayak totals $500, which consists of $400 in variable production cost and $100 in fixed production cost—the latter amount is based on $105,000 of fixed production costs allocated to the 1,050 kayaks produced.

b. The $230,000 in selling and administrative expense consists of $75,000 that is variable and $155,000 that is fixed.

Required

Check (1) Variable costing income, $185,000

1. Prepare an income statement for the current year under variable costing.
2. Explain the difference in income between the variable costing and absorption costing income statement.

Exercise 19-4
Break-even volume in units
A1

Rey Company's single product sells at a price of $216 per unit. Cost data for its single product follows. Compute this company's break-even volume in units.

Direct materials	$20 per unit
Direct labor	$28 per unit
Overhead costs	
Variable overhead	$ 6 per unit
Fixed overhead per year	$160,000 per year
Selling and administrative expenses	
Variable	$ 18 per unit
Fixed	$200,000 per year

Exercise 19-5
Converting variable costing income to absorption costing income P2 P4

Hayek Furnaces prepares the income statement under variable costing for its managerial reports, and it prepares the income statement under absorption costing for external reporting. For its first month of operations, 375 furnaces were produced and 225 were sold; this left 150 furnaces in ending inventory. The income statement information under variable costing follows.

Sales (225 × $1,600)	$360,000
Variable production cost (225 × $625)	140,625
Variable selling and administrative expenses (225 × $65)	14,625
Contribution margin	204,750
Fixed overhead cost	56,250
Fixed selling and administrative expense	75,000
Net income	$ 73,500

Check (1) Absorption costing income, $96,000

1. Prepare this company's income statement for its first month of operations under absorption costing.
2. Explain the difference in income between the variable costing and absorption costing income statement.

Exercise 19-6
Income reporting under absorption costing and variable costing
P2 P4

Oak Mart, a producer of solid oak tables, reports the following data from its current year operations, which is its second year of business.

Sales price per unit	$320 per unit
Units produced this year	115,000 units
Units sold this year	118,000 units
Units in beginning-year inventory	3,000 units
Beginning inventory costs	
Variable (3,000 units × $135)	$405,000
Fixed (3,000 units × $80)	240,000
Total	$645,000
Production costs this year	
Direct materials	$40 per unit
Direct labor	$62 per unit
Overhead costs this year	
Variable overhead	$3,220,000
Fixed overhead	$7,400,000
Nonproduction costs this year	
Variable selling and administrative	$1,416,000
Fixed selling and administrative	4,600,000

Check (1) Variable costing income, $8,989,000; (2) Absorption costing income, $8,749,000

1. Prepare the current year income statement for the company using variable costing.
2. Prepare the current year income statement for the company using absorption costing.
3. Explain any difference between the two income numbers under the two costing methods in parts 1 and 2.

Exercise 19-7
Variable costing for services
C2

MidCoast Airlines provides charter airplane services. In October this year, the company was operating at 60% of its capacity when it received a bid from the local community college. The college was organizing a Washington, D.C., trip for its international student group. The college only budgeted $30,000 for roundtrip airfare. MidCoast Airlines normally charges between $50,000 and $60,000 for such service given the number of travelers. MidCoast determined its cost for the roundtrip flight to Washington to be $44,000, which consists of the following:

Variable cost	$15,000
Fixed cost	29,000
Total cost	$44,000

Although the manager at MidCoast supports the college's educational efforts, she could not justify accepting the $30,000 bid for the trip given the projected $14,000 loss. Still, she decides to consult with you, an independent financial consultant. Do you believe the airline should accept the bid from the college? Prepare a memorandum, with supporting computations, explaining why or why not.

Exercise 19-8
Contribution margin format income statement P3

Polarix is a retailer of ATVs (all terrain vehicles) and accessories. An income statement for its Consumer ATV Department for the current year follows. ATVs sell, on average, for $3,800. Variable selling expenses are $270 each. The remaining selling expenses are fixed. Administrative expenses are 40% variable and 60% fixed. The company does not manufacture its own ATVs; it purchases them from a supplier for $1,830 each.

POLARIX
Income Statement—Consumer ATV Department
For Year Ended December 31, 2013

Sales		$646,000
Cost of goods sold		311,100
Gross margin		334,900
Operating expenses		
Selling expenses	$135,000	
Administrative expenses	59,500	194,500
Net income		$140,400

Required

1. Prepare an income statement for this current year using the contribution margin format.
2. For each ATV sold during this year, what is the contribution toward covering fixed expenses and earning income?

Check (2) $1,560

Exercise 19-9
Unit costs and income statement under absorption costing and variable costing
P1 P2

Cool Sky Company reports the following costing data on its product for its first year of operations. During this first year, the company produced 44,000 units and sold 36,000 units at a price of $140 per unit.

Production costs	
Direct materials per unit	$60
Direct labor per unit	$22
Variable overhead per unit	$8
Fixed overhead for the year	$528,000
Selling and administrative cost	
Variable selling and administrative cost per unit	$11
Fixed selling and administrative cost per year	$105,000

1. Assume that this company uses absorption costing.
   a. Determine its unit product cost.
   b. Prepare its income statement for the year under absorption costing.
2. Assume that this company uses variable costing.
   a. Determine its unit product cost.
   b. Prepare its income statement for the year under variable costing.

Check (1a) Absorption cost per unit, $102

(2a) Variable cost per unit, $90

Exercise 19-10
Absorption costing and over-production
C1

Jacquie Inc. reports the following annual cost data for its single product.

Normal production and sales level	60,000 units
Sales price	$56.00 per unit
Direct materials	$9.00 per unit
Direct labor	$6.50 per unit
Variable overhead	$11.00 per unit
Fixed overhead	$720,000 in total

If Jacquie increases its production to 80,000 units, while sales remain at the current 60,000 unit level, by how much would the company's gross margin increase or decrease under absorption costing? Assume the company has idle capacity to double current production.

Exercise 19-11
Variable costing and contribution margin statement
P3

Tee-Pro has three types of costs: t-shirt cost, factory rent cost, and utilities cost. This company sells its shirts for $16.50 each. Management has prepared the following estimated cost information for next month under two different sales levels.

	At 10,000 Shirts	At 12,000 Shirts
T-shirt cost	$80,000	$96,000
Rent cost	6,000	6,000
Utilities cost	8,400	9,900

Required

1. Compute what the company should expect for total variable cost if 11,000 shirts are sold next month. (*Hint:* Use the high-low method to separate shirt and utilities costs into their variable and fixed components.)

2. Prepare its contribution margin statement for a monthly sales volume of 12,000 jackets.

Check (2) Contribution margin, $93,000

Exercise 19-12
Analyzing income growth
P2

A recent annual report for **McDonald**'s reports the following operating income for its United States and APMEA (Asia-Pacific, Middle East, and Africa) geographic segments:

In $ millions	2011	2010	2009
United States	$3,666	$3,446	$3,232
APMEA	1,526	1,200	989

Required

1. Is operating income growing faster in the United States or in the APMEA segment? Explain.

2. Is the difference in operating income growth due to the use of different costing methods (absorption or variable costing) in the U.S. and APMEA segments? Explain.

connect

PROBLEM SET A

Problem 19-1A
Variable costing income statement and conversion to absorption costing income (two consecutive years)
P2 P4

Dowell Company produces a single product. Its income statement under absorption costing for its first two years of operation follow.

	2012	2013
Sales ($46 per unit)	$920,000	$1,840,000
Cost of goods sold ($31 per unit)	620,000	1,240,000
Gross margin	300,000	600,000
Selling and administrative expenses	290,000	340,000
Net income	$ 10,000	$ 260,000

Additional Information

a. Sales and production data for these first two years follow.

	2012	2013
Units produced	30,000	30,000
Units sold	20,000	40,000

b. Variable cost per unit and total fixed costs are unchanged during 2012 and 2013. The company's $31 per unit product cost consists of the following.

Direct materials	$ 5
Direct labor	9
Variable overhead	7
Fixed overhead ($300,000/30,000 units)	10
Total product cost per unit	$31

c. Selling and administrative expenses consist of the following.

	2012	2013
Variable selling and administrative ($2.50 per unit)	$ 50,000	$100,000
Fixed selling and administrative	240,000	240,000
Total selling and administrative	$290,000	$340,000

Required

1. Prepare income statements for the company for each of its first two years under variable costing.
2. Explain any difference between the absorption costing income and the variable costing income for these two years.

Check (1) 2012 net loss, $(90,000)

Problem 19-2A
CVP analysis, absorption costing, and variable costing
A1

Refer to information about Dowell Company in Problem 19-1A. In the company's planning documents, Kyra Dowell, the company's president, reports that the break-even volume (in units) for the company is 24,000 units. This break-even point is computed as follows.

$$\text{Break-even volume} = \frac{\text{Total fixed cost}}{\text{Contribution margin per unit}} = \frac{\$540{,}000}{\$22.50} = 24{,}000 \text{ units}$$

Total fixed cost consists of $300,000 in fixed production cost and $240,000 in fixed selling and administrative expenses. The contribution margin per unit of $22.50 is computed by deducting the $23.50 variable cost per unit (which consists of $21 in variable production cost and $2.50 in variable selling and administrative cost) from the $46 sales price per unit. In 2012, the company sold 20,000 units, which was below break-even, and Kyra was concerned that the company's income statement would show a net loss. To her surprise, the company's 2012 income statement revealed a net income of $10,000 as shown in Problem 19-1A.

Required

Prepare a one-half-page memorandum to the president explaining how the company could report net income when it sold less than its break-even volume in units.

Problem 19-3A
Variable costing income statement and conversion to absorption costing income
P2 P4

Trez Company began operations this year. During this first year, the company produced 100,000 units and sold 80,000 units. The absorption costing income statement for its first year of operations follows.

Sales (80,000 units × $50 per unit)		$4,000,000
Cost of goods sold		
Beginning inventory	$ 0	
Cost of goods manufactured (100,000 units × $30 per unit)	3,000,000	
Cost of goods available for sale	3,000,000	
Ending inventory (20,000 × $30)	600,000	
Cost of goods sold		2,400,000
Gross margin		1,600,000
Selling and administrative expenses		530,000
Net income		$1,070,000

Additional Information

a. Selling and administrative expenses consist of $350,000 in annual fixed expenses and $2.25 per unit in variable selling and administrative expenses.

b. The company's product cost of $30 per unit is computed as follows.

Direct materials	$5 per unit
Direct labor	$14 per unit
Variable overhead	$2 per unit
Fixed overhead ($900,000/100,000 units)	$9 per unit

Required

Check (1) Variable costing income, $890,000

1. Prepare an income statement for the company under variable costing.

2. Explain any difference between the income under variable costing (from part 1) and the income reported above.

Problem 19-4A
Variable cost analysis for a services company
C2

Grand Garden is a luxury hotel with 150 suites. Its regular suite rate is $250 per night per suite. The hotel's cost per night is $140 per suite and consists of the following.

Variable direct labor and materials cost	$ 30
Fixed cost [($6,022,500/150 suites) ÷ 365 days]	110
Total cost per night per suite	$140

The hotel manager received an offer to hold the local Bikers' Club annual meeting at the hotel in March, which is the hotel's low season with an occupancy rate of under 50%. The Bikers' Club would reserve 50 suites for three nights if the hotel could offer a 50% discount, or a rate of $125 per night. The hotel manager is inclined to reject the offer because the cost per suite per night is $140. The manager believes that if 50 suites are offered at the rate of $125 per night for three nights, the hotel would lose $2,250, computed as ($125 − $140) × 50 suites × 3 nights.

Required

Check $14,250 contribution margin

Prepare an analysis of this offer for the hotel manager. Explain (with supporting computations) whether the offer from the Bikers' Club should be accepted or rejected.

Problem 19-5A
Income reporting, absorption costing, and managerial ethics
C1 P2

Blazer Chemical produces and sells an ice-melting granular used on roadways and sidewalks in winter. It annually produces and sells about 100 tons of its granular. In its nine-year history, the company has never reported a net loss. However, because of this year's unusually mild winter, projected demand for its product is only 60 tons. Based on its predicted production and sales of 60 tons, the company projects the following income statement (under absorption costing).

Sales (60 tons at $21,000 per ton)	$1,260,000
Cost of goods sold (60 tons at $16,000 per ton)	960,000
Gross margin	300,000
Selling and administrative expenses	318,600
Net loss	$ (18,600)

Its product cost information follows and consists mainly of fixed cost because of its automated production process requiring expensive equipment.

Variable direct labor and material costs per ton	$ 3,500
Fixed cost per ton ($750,000 ÷ 60 tons)	12,500
Total product cost per ton	$16,000

Selling and administrative expenses consist of variable selling and administrative expenses of $310 per ton and fixed selling and administrative expenses of $300,000 per year. The company's president is concerned about the adverse reaction from its creditors and shareholders if the projected net loss is reported. The operations manager mentions that since the company has large storage capacity, it can report a net income by keeping its production at the usual 100-ton level even though it expects to sell only 60 tons. The president was puzzled by the suggestion that the company can report income by producing more without increasing sales.

Required

1. Can the company report a net income by increasing production to 100 tons and storing the excess production in inventory? Your explanation should include an income statement (using absorption costing) based on production of 100 tons and sales of 60 tons.
2. Should the company produce 100 tons given that projected demand is 60 tons? Explain, and also refer to any ethical implications of such a managerial decision.

Check (1) $281,400 absorption costing income

PROBLEM SET B

Problem 19-1B
Variable costing income statement and conversion to absorption costing income (two consecutive years)
P2 P4

Azule Company produces a single product. Its income statement under absorption costing for its first two years of operation follow.

	2012	2013
Sales ($35 per unit)	$1,925,000	$2,275,000
Cost of goods sold ($26 per unit)	1,430,000	1,690,000
Gross margin	495,000	585,000
Selling and administrative expenses	465,000	495,000
Net income	$ 30,000	$ 90,000

Additional Information

a. Sales and production data for these first two years follow:

	2012	2013
Units produced	60,000	60,000
Units sold	55,000	65,000

b. Its variable cost per unit and total fixed costs are unchanged during 2012 and 2013. Its $26 per unit product cost consists of the following.

Direct materials	$ 4
Direct labor	6
Variable overhead	8
Fixed overhead ($480,000/60,000 units)	8
Total product cost per unit	$26

c. Its selling and administrative expenses consist of the following.

	2012	2013
Variable selling and administrative ($3 per unit)	$165,000	$195,000
Fixed selling and administrative	300,000	300,000
Total selling and administrative	$465,000	$495,000

Required

1. Prepare this company's income statements under variable costing for each of its first two years.
2. Explain any difference between the absorption costing income and the variable costing income for these two years.

Check (1) 2012 net loss, $(10,000)

Problem 19-2B
CVP analysis, absorption costing, and variable costing
A1

Refer to information about Azule Company in Problem 19-1B. In the company's planning documents, Roberta Azule, the company president, reports that the company's break-even volume in unit sales is 55,715 units. This break-even point is computed as follows.

$$\text{Break-even volume} = \frac{\text{Total fixed cost}}{\text{Contribution margin per unit}} = \frac{\$780,000}{\$14} = 55,715 \text{ units (rounded)}$$

Total fixed cost consists of $480,000 in fixed production cost and $300,000 in fixed selling and administrative expenses. The contribution margin per unit of $14 is computed by deducting the $21 variable cost per unit (which consists of $18 in variable production cost and $3 in variable selling and administrative cost) from the $35 sales price per unit. In 2012, it sold 55,000 units, which was below break-even, and Roberta was concerned that the company's income statement would show a net loss. To her surprise, the company's 2012 income statement revealed a net income of $30,000 as shown in Problem 19-1B.

Required

Prepare a one-half-page memorandum to the president explaining how the company could report net income when it sold less than its break-even volume in units.

Problem 19-3B
Variable costing income statement and conversion to absorption costing income
P2 P4

E'Lonte Company began operations this year. During this first year, the company produced 300,000 units and sold 250,000 units. Its income statement under absorption costing for its first year of operations follows.

Sales (250,000 units × $18 per unit)		$4,500,000
Cost of goods sold		
Beginning inventory	$ 0	
Cost of goods manufactured (300,000 units × $7.50 per unit)	2,250,000	
Cost of goods available for sale	2,250,000	
Ending inventory (50,000 × $7.50)	375,000	
Cost of goods sold		1,875,000
Gross margin		2,625,000
Selling and administrative expenses		2,200,000
Net income		$ 425,000

Additional Information

a. Selling and administrative expenses consist of $1,200,000 in annual fixed expenses and $4 per unit in variable selling and administrative expenses.

b. The company's product cost of $7.50 per unit is computed as follows.

Direct materials	$2.00 per unit
Direct labor	$2.40 per unit
Variable overhead	$1.60 per unit
Fixed overhead ($450,000/300,000 units)	$1.50 per unit

Required

Check (1) Variable costing income, $350,000

1. Prepare the company's income statement under variable costing.

2. Explain any difference between the company's income under variable costing (from part 1) and the income reported above.

Problem 19-4B
Variable cost analysis for a services company
C2

Empire Plaza Hotel is a luxury hotel with 400 rooms. Its regular room rate is $300 per night per room. The hotel's cost is $165 per night per room and consists of the following.

Variable direct labor and materials cost	$ 40
Fixed cost [($18,250,000/400 rooms) ÷ 365 days]	125
Total cost per night per room	$165

The hotel manager received an offer to hold the Junior States of America (JSA) convention at the hotel in February, which is the hotel's low season with an occupancy rate of under 45%. JSA would reserve 100 rooms for four nights if the hotel could offer a 50% discount, or a rate of $150 per night. The hotel manager is inclined to reject the offer because the cost per room per night is $165. The manager believes that if 100 rooms are offered at the rate of $150 per night for four nights, the hotel would lose $6,000, computed as ($150 − $165) × 100 rooms × 4 nights.

Required

Check Contribution margin, $44,000

Prepare an analysis of this offer for the hotel manager. Explain (with supporting computations) whether the offer from JSA should be accepted or rejected.

Problem 19-5B
Income reporting, absorption costing, and managerial ethics
C1 P2

Chem-Melt produces and sells an ice-melting granular used on roadways and sidewalks in winter. The company annually produces and sells about 300,000 lbs of its granular. In its ten-year history, the company has never reported a net loss. Because of this year's unusually mild winter, projected demand for its product is only 250,000 lbs. Based on its predicted production and sales of 250,000 lbs, the company projects the following income statement under absorption costing.

Sales (250,000 lbs at $8 per lb.)	$2,000,000
Cost of goods sold (250,000 lbs at $6.80 per lb.)	1,700,000
Gross margin	300,000
Selling and administrative expenses	450,000
Net loss	$ (150,000)

Its product cost information follows and consists mainly of fixed production cost because of its automated production process requiring expensive equipment.

Variable direct labor and materials costs per lb.	$2.00
Fixed production cost per lb ($1,200,000/250,000 lbs.)	4.80
Total product cost per lb.	$6.80

The company's selling and administrative expenses are all fixed. The president is concerned about the adverse reaction from its creditors and shareholders if the projected net loss is reported. The controller suggests that since the company has large storage capacity, it can report a net income by keeping its production at the usual 300,000 lbs level even though it expects to sell only 250,000 lbs. The president was puzzled by the suggestion that the company can report a profit by producing more without increasing sales.

Required

1. Can the company report a net income by increasing production to 300,000 lbs and storing the excess production in inventory? Your explanation should include an income statement (using absorption costing) based on production of 300,000 lbs and sales of 250,000 lbs.
2. Should the company produce 300,000 lbs given that projected demand is 250,000 lbs? Explain, and also refer to any ethical implications of such a managerial decision.

Check (1) $50,000 absorption income

SERIAL PROBLEM
Success Systems
P2 P4

(This serial problem began in Chapter 1 and continues through most of the book. If previous chapter segments were not completed, the serial problem can begin at this point. It is helpful, but not necessary, to use the Working Papers that accompany the book.)

SP 19 Adria Lopez expects sales of her line of computer workstation furniture to equal 300 workstations (at a sales price of $3,000) for 2014. The workstations' manufacturing costs include the following.

Direct materials	$800 per unit
Direct labor	$400 per unit
Variable overhead	$100 per unit
Fixed overhead	$24,000 per year

The selling expenses related to these workstations follow.

Variable selling expenses	$50 per unit
Fixed selling expenses	$4,000 per year

Adria is considering how many workstations to produce in 2014. She is confident that she will be able to sell any workstations in her 2014 ending inventory during 2015. However, Adria does not want to overproduce as she does not have sufficient storage space for many more workstations.

Required

1. Compute Success Systems' absorption costing income assuming
   a. 300 workstations are produced.
   b. 320 workstations are produced.

[continued on next page]

2. Compute Success Systems' variable costing income assuming
   a. 300 workstations are produced.
   b. 320 workstations are produced.
3. Explain to Adria any differences in the income figures determined in parts 1 and 2. How should Adria use the information from parts 1 and 2 to help make production decisions?

Beyond the Numbers

REPORTING IN ACTION
P2
Polaris

BTN 19-1 **Polaris**'s ending inventory amounts (in $ millions) are shown below:

2011	2010	2009
$298.04	$235.93	$179.32

Required

1. Assume Polaris uses variable costing for some of its internal reports. For each of the years 2011 and 2010, would net income based on variable costing be higher, lower, or no different from net income based on absorption costing? Explain.
2. Assume Polaris is considering implementing a just-in-time (JIT) inventory system. Would a JIT system increase, decrease, or have no effect on differences in net income between absorption costing and variable costing? Explain.

COMPARATIVE ANALYSIS
P2
Polaris
Arctic Cat

BTN 19-2 **Polaris** offers its dealers financing plans while **Arctic Cat** currently relies on outside companies to provide its dealers' financing. Assume Arctic Cat is considering starting its own finance unit to provide financing directly to its dealers.

Required

1. What are some of the costs that Arctic Cat should consider when deciding whether to offer financing services to its dealers? Are these costs different from what Polaris must consider when offering additional new financing services? Explain.
2. Would variable or absorption costing be more useful to Arctic Cat in analyzing whether its new financing service is profitable? Explain.

ETHICS CHALLENGE
P2

BTN 19-3 FDP Company produces a variety of home security products. Gary Price, the company's president, is concerned with the fourth quarter market demand for the company's products. Unless something is done in the last two months of the year, the company is likely to miss its earnings expectation of Wall Street analysts. Price still remembers when FDP's earnings were below analysts' expectation by two cents a share three years ago, and the company's share price fell 19% the day earnings were announced. In a recent meeting, Price told his top management that something must be done quickly. One proposal by the marketing vice president was to give a deep discount to the company's major customers to increase the company's sales in the fourth quarter. The company controller pointed out that while the discount could increase sales, it may not help the bottom line; to the contrary, it could lower income. The controller said, "Since we have enough storage capacity, we might simply increase our production in the fourth quarter to increase our reported profit."

Required

1. Gary Price is not sure how the increase in production without a corresponding increase in sales could help boost the company's income. Explain to Price how reported income varies with respect to production level.
2. Is there an ethical concern in this situation? If so, which parties are affected? Explain.

COMMUNICATING IN PRACTICE
A1

BTN 19-4 Mertz Chemical has three divisions. Its consumer product division faces strong competition from companies overseas. During its recent teleconference, Ryan Peterson, the consumer product division manager, reported that his division's sales for the current year were below its break-even point. However, when the division's annual reports were received, Billie Mertz, the company president, was surprised that the consumer product division actually reported a profit of $264,000. How could this be possible?

Required

Assume that you work in the corporate controller's office. Write a one-half-page memorandum to the president explaining how the division can report income even if its sales are below the break-even point.

TAKING IT TO THE NET
P2

BTN 19-5 This chapter discussed the variable costing method and how to use variable costing information to make various business decisions. We also can find several Websites on variable costing and its business applications.

Required

1. Review the Website of Value Based Management at ValueBasedManagement.net. Identify and print the site page on the topic of variable costing (valuebasedmanagement.net/methods_variable_costing.html).
2. What other phrases are used in practice for *variable costing?*
3. According to this Website, what are the consequences of variable costing for profit calculation?

TEAMWORK IN ACTION
P4

BTN 19-6 This chapter identified many decision contexts in which variable costing information is more relevant than absorption costing. However, absorption costing is still used by many companies and remains the only acceptable basis for external (and tax) reporting.

Required

Break into teams and identify at least one specific decision context in which absorption costing information is more relevant than variable costing. Be prepared to discuss your answers in class.

ENTREPRENEURIAL DECISION
P4

BTN 19-7 Samanta Shoes, which was launched by entrepreneurs Samanta and Kelvin Joseph, produces high-quality shoes in unique styles and limited quantities. Selling prices for a pair of Samanta shoes can range from $100 per pair to $350 per pair.

Required

1. Based on information in this chapter's opener, identify at least four examples of the types of costs that likely explain the wide range of shoe selling prices.
2. The founders of Samanta Shoes use variable costing in their business decisions. If Samanta Shoes used absorption costing, would you expect the company's income to be more, less than, or about the same as its income measured under variable costing? Explain.

HITTING THE ROAD
C2

BTN 19-8 Visit a local hotel and observe its daily operating activities. The costs associated with some of its activities are variable while others are fixed with respect to occupancy levels.

Required

1. List cost items that are likely variable for the hotel.
2. List cost items that are likely fixed for the hotel.
3. Compare the fixed cost items with variable cost items. Rank costs within each category based on your perception of which ones you believe are the larger.
4. Based on your observations and the answers to parts 1 through 3, explain why many hotels offer discounts as high as 50% or more during their low occupancy season.

GLOBAL DECISION
P2

KTM
Polaris

BTN 19-9 Assume that KTM (KTM.com) is considering offering financing services for its dealers. However, instead of developing the division internally, KTM is considering buying a company that already offers such services.

Required

Would absorption or variable costing be most useful to KTM in evaluating whether to acquire an existing business that provides dealer financing services similar to those offered by Polaris? Explain.

ANSWERS TO MULTIPLE CHOICE QUIZ

1. c; $14, computed as $3 + $5 + $3 + ($3,000/1,000 units).
2. a; $11, computed as $3 + $5 + $3 (consisting of all variable product costs).
3. a
4. c
5. b

20

Master Budgets and Performance Planning

A Look Back

Chapter 19 compared reports prepared under variable costing with those under absorption costing, and it explained how variable costing can improve managerial decisions.

A Look at This Chapter

This chapter explains the importance of budgeting and describes the master budget and its preparation. It also discusses the value of the master budget to the planning of future business activities.

A Look Ahead

Chapter 21 focuses on flexible budgets, standard costs, and variance reporting. It explains the usefulness of these procedures and reports for business decisions.

Learning Objectives

CONCEPTUAL

C1 Describe the importance and benefits of budgeting and the process of budget administration. (p. 848)

C2 Describe a master budget and the process of preparing it. (p. 852)

ANALYTICAL

A1 Analyze expense planning using activity-based budgeting. (p. 862)

PROCEDURAL

P1 Prepare each component of a master budget and link each to the budgeting process. (p. 854)

P2 Link both operating and capital expenditures budgets to budgeted financial statements. (p. 858)

P3 *Appendix 20A*—Prepare production and manufacturing budgets. (p. 868)

Decision Insight

Fresh Profits

"Talk is cheap . . . execution sets you apart"
—**MATTHEW CORRIN**

CHICAGO, IL—Matthew Corrin was tired of eating typical lunch fare. Stuck in a greasy deli, Matthew realized "the service and food was lackluster. I needed an alternative." The then 22-year-old budding entrepreneur set off to build a restaurant based on fresh, healthy foods served in an environmentally sustaining environment. Today, Matthew's company, **Freshii** (**Freshii.com**), has over 60 stores across several countries.

Matthew admits he was "totally naïve. Restaurants are one of the hardest businesses. A thousand things have to go right every day." Unfortunately, many things did go wrong at the beginning. "The first day we ran out of food at lunch. We ordered more but ran out again on the second day," recalls Matt. Making accurate sales forecasts is one of the most important, but most difficult, parts of preparing business budgets. Sales forecasts are especially challenging for new businesses. Through hard work and help from his girlfriend (now wife), Matthew's business broke sales records every day for its first six months. "Those first days were a turning point for me. I realized if I could get through that, I could survive anything" says Matthew.

Matthew learned his business by doing "whatever needed to be done." "This isn't rocket science," he says, "just hard work." In addition to learning the nuances of the restaurant business, Matthew had to learn budgeting and cost concepts. As Matthew explains, the perishability of food items is a key variable. Food costs can vary due to weather, supply disruptions, and other factors. Matthew updates his budgets frequently to factor in changing costs and customer tastes.

Matthew advises young entrepreneurs to "go for it." "Some might say starting a restaurant with no previous food or retail experience wasn't the smartest move. But, isn't that the entrepreneurial spirit, to just jump in and figure it out on the fly?" As his company continues to grow, the budgeting process and master budgets become even more important. Budgets help formalize plans and goals, and help direct and monitor employees. Matthew also uses budgeted income statements to determine how changes in the cost of food, labor, and overhead will impact his bottom line.

While linking budgeted data to budgeted financial statements and using that information to control costs is important, Matthew stresses "you have to execute every day and generate a buzz." From humble beginnings, Freshii has over 400 new locations in development, forecasted sales of $50 million, and, in Matthew's words, "a vision to be the Starbucks of the fresh food business." Bold and fresh.

[Sources: *Freshii Website,* January 2013; *Inc.com,* March 16, 2011, and June 27, 2011; *Canada Restaurant News,* January 31, 2011; *Under30ceo.com,* October 25, 2010.]

Chapter Preview

Management seeks to turn its strategies into action plans. These action plans include financial details that are compiled in a master budget. The budgeting process serves several purposes, including motivating employees and communicating with them. The budget process also helps coordinate a company's activities toward common goals and is useful in evaluating results and management performance. This chapter explains how to prepare a master budget and use it as a formal plan of a company's future activities. The ability to prepare this type of plan is of enormous help in starting and operating a company. Such planning gives managers a glimpse into the future, and it can help translate ideas into actions.

Master Budgets and Performance Planning

Budget Process
- Strategic budgeting
- Benchmarking budgets
- Budgeting and human behavior
- Budgeting as a management tool
- Budgeting communication

Budget Administration
- Budget committee
- Budget reporting
- Budget timing

Master Budget
- Master budget components
- Operating budgets
- Capital expenditures budget
- Financial budgets

BUDGET PROCESS

Strategic Budgeting

C1 Describe the importance and benefits of budgeting and the process of budget administration.

Most companies prepare long-term strategic plans spanning 5 to 10 years. They then fine-tune them in preparing medium-term and short-term plans. Strategic plans usually set a company's long-term direction. They provide a road map for the future about potential opportunities such as new products, markets, and investments. The strategic plan can be inexact, given its long-term focus. Medium- and short-term plans are more operational and translate strategic plans into actions. These action plans are fairly concrete and consist of defined objectives and goals.

Short-term financial plans are called *budgets* and typically cover a one-year period. A **budget** is a formal statement of a company's future plans. It is usually expressed in monetary terms because the economic or financial aspects of the business are the primary factors driving management's decisions. All managers should be involved in **budgeting,** the process of planning future business actions and expressing them as formal plans. Managers who plan carefully and formalize plans in a budgeting process increase the likelihood of both personal and company success. (Although most firms prepare annual budgets, it is not unusual for organizations to prepare three-year and five-year budgets that are revised at least annually.)

Companies Performing Annual Budgeting

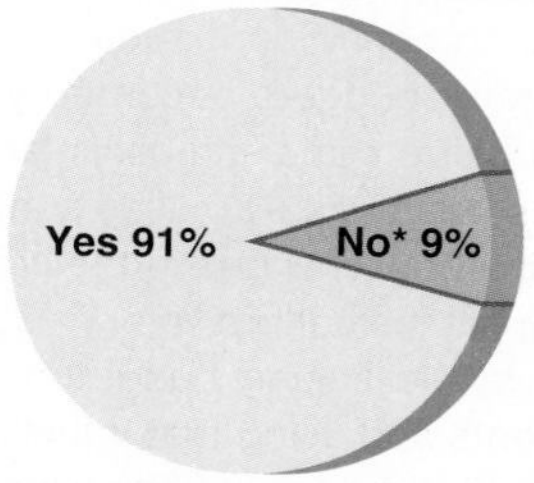

*Most of the 9% have eliminated annual budgeting in favor of rolling or continual budgeting.

The relevant focus of a budgetary analysis is the future. Management must focus on future transactions and events and the opportunities available. A focus on the future is important because the pressures of daily operating problems often divert management's attention and take precedence over planning. A good budgeting system counteracts this tendency by formalizing the planning process and demanding relevant input. Budgeting makes planning an explicit management responsibility.

Benchmarking Budgets

The control function requires management to evaluate (benchmark) business operations against some norm. Evaluation involves comparing actual results against one of two usual alternatives: (1) past performance or (2) expected performance.

An evaluation assists management in identifying problems and taking corrective actions if necessary. Evaluation using expected, or budgeted, performance is potentially superior to using past performance to decide whether actual results trigger a need for corrective actions. This is so because past performance fails to consider several changes that can affect current and future activities. Changes in economic conditions, shifts in competitive advantages within the industry, new product developments, increased or decreased advertising, and other factors reduce the usefulness of comparisons with past results. In hi-tech industries, for instance, increasing competition, technological advances, and other innovations often reduce the usefulness of performance comparisons across years.

Budgeted performance is computed after careful analysis and research that attempts to anticipate and adjust for changes in important company, industry, and economic factors. Therefore, budgets usually provide management an effective control and monitoring system.

Budgeting and Human Behavior

Budgeting provides standards for evaluating performance and can affect the attitudes of employees evaluated by them. It can be used to create a positive effect on employees' attitudes, but it can also create negative effects if not properly applied. Budgeted levels of performance, for instance, must be realistic to avoid discouraging employees. Personnel who will be evaluated should be consulted and involved in preparing the budget to increase their commitment to meeting it. Performance evaluations must allow the affected employees to explain the reasons for apparent performance deficiencies.

The budgeting process has three important guidelines: (1) Employees affected by a budget should be consulted when it is prepared (*participatory budgeting*), (2) goals reflected in a budget should be attainable, and (3) evaluations should be made carefully with opportunities to explain any failures. Budgeting can be a positive motivating force when these guidelines are followed. Budgeted performance levels can provide goals for employees to attain or even exceed as they carry out their responsibilities. This is especially important in organizations that consider the annual budget a "sacred" document.

Point: The practice of involving employees in the budgeting process is known as *participatory budgeting*.

Managers must also be aware of potential negative outcomes of budgeting. Under participatory budgeting, some employees might understate sales budgets and overstate expense budgets to allow them a cushion, or *budgetary slack,* to aid in meeting targets. For some businesses, pressure to meet budgeted results might lead employees to engage in unethical behavior or commit fraud. Finally, some employees might always spend their budgeted amounts, even on unnecessary items, to ensure their budgets aren't reduced for the next period.

Example: Assume a company's sales force receives a bonus when sales exceed the budgeted amount. How would this arrangement affect the participatory sales forecasts?
Answer: Sales reps may understate their budgeted sales.

Decision Ethics

Budget Staffer Your company's earnings for the current period will be far below the budgeted amount reported in the press. One of your superiors, who is aware of the upcoming earnings shortfall, has accepted a management position with a competitor. This superior is selling her shares of the company. What are your ethical concerns, if any? ■ [Answer—p. 870]

Budgeting as a Management Tool

An important management objective in large companies is to ensure that activities of all departments contribute to meeting the company's overall goals. This requires coordination. Budgeting helps to achieve this coordination.

We describe later in this chapter that a company's budget, or operating plan, is based on its objectives. This operating plan starts with the sales budget, which drives all other budgets including production, materials, labor, and overhead. The budgeting process coordinates the activities of these various departments to meet the company's overall goals.

Budgeting Communication

Managers of small companies can adequately explain business plans directly to employees through conversations and other informal communications. However, conversations can create uncertainty and confusion if not supported by clear documentation of the plans. A written budget is preferred and can inform employees in all types of organizations about management's plans. The budget can also communicate management's specific action plans for the employees in the budget period.

Decision Insight

Budgets Exposed When companies go public and their securities trade on an organized stock exchange, management usually develops specific future plans and budgets. For this purpose, companies often develop detailed six- to twelve-month budgets and less-detailed budgets spanning two to five years. ■

BUDGET ADMINISTRATION

Budget Committee

The task of preparing a budget should not be the sole responsibility of any one department. Similarly, the budget should not be simply handed down as top management's final word. Instead, budget figures and budget estimates developed through a *bottom-up* process usually are more useful. This includes, for instance, involving the sales department in preparing sales estimates. Likewise, the production department should have initial responsibility for preparing its own expense budget. Without active employee involvement in preparing budget figures, there is a risk these employees will feel that the numbers fail to reflect their special problems and needs.

Most budgets should be developed by a bottom-up process, but the budgeting system requires central guidance. This guidance is supplied by a budget committee of department heads and other executives responsible for seeing that budgeted amounts are realistic and coordinated. If a department submits initial budget figures not reflecting efficient performance, the budget committee should return them with explanatory comments on how to improve them. Then the originating department must either adjust its proposals or explain why they are acceptable. Communication between the originating department and the budget committee should continue as needed to ensure that both parties accept the budget as reasonable, attainable, and desirable.

Point: In a large company, developing a budget through a bottom-up process can involve hundreds of employees and take several weeks to finalize.

The concept of continuous improvement applies to budgeting as well as production. For example, one of the world's largest energy companies streamlined its monthly budget report from a one-inch-thick stack of monthly control reports to a tidy, two-page flash report on monthly earnings and key production statistics. The key to this efficiency gain was the integration of new budgeting and cost allocation processes with its strategic planning process. Its controller explained the new role of the finance department with respect to the budgetary control process as follows: "there's less of an attitude that finance's job is to control. People really have come to see that our job is to help attain business objectives."

Budget Reporting

The budget period usually coincides with the accounting period. Most companies prepare at least an annual budget, which reflects the objectives for the next year. To provide specific guidance, the annual budget usually is separated into quarterly or monthly budgets. These short-term budgets allow management to periodically evaluate performance and take needed corrective action.

Managers can compare actual results to budgeted amounts in a report such as that shown in Exhibit 20.1. This report shows actual amounts, budgeted amounts, and their differences. A difference is called a *variance*. Management examines variances, particularly large ones, to identify areas for improvement and corrective action.

EXHIBIT 20.1

Comparing Actual Performance with Budgeted Performance

ECCENTRIC MUSIC Income Statement with Variances from Budget For Month Ended April 30, 2013	Actual	Budget	Variance
Net sales	$60,500	$57,150	$+3,350
Cost of goods sold	41,350	39,100	+2,250
Gross profit	19,150	18,050	+1,100
Operating expenses			
Selling expenses			
Sales salaries	6,250	6,000	+250
Advertising	900	800	+100
Store supplies	550	500	+50
Depreciation—Store equipment	1,600	1,600	
Total selling expenses	9,300	8,900	+400
General and administrative expenses			
Office salaries	2,000	2,000	
Office supplies used	165	150	+15
Rent	1,100	1,100	
Insurance	200	200	
Depreciation—Office equipment	100	100	
Total general and administrative expenses	3,565	3,550	+15
Total operating expenses	12,865	12,450	+415
Net income	$ 6,285	$ 5,600	$ +685

Example: Assume that you must explain variances to top management. Which variances in Exhibit 20.1 would you research and why? *Answer:* Sales and cost of goods sold—due to their large variances.

Budget Timing

The time period required for the annual budgeting process can vary considerably. For example, budgeting for 2014 can begin as early as January 2013 or as late as December 2013. Large, complex organizations usually require a longer time to prepare their budgets than do smaller organizations. This is so because considerable effort is required to coordinate the different units (departments) within large organizations.

Companies Using Rolling Budgets

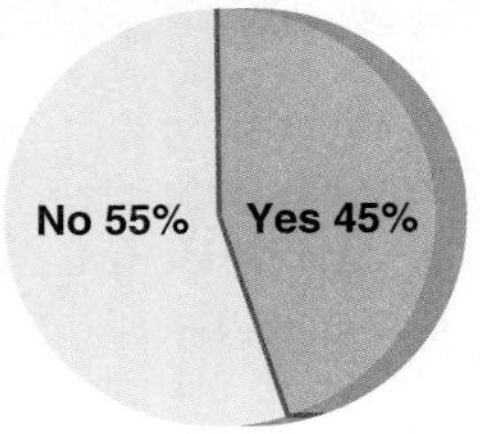

Many companies apply **continuous budgeting** by preparing **rolling budgets.** As each monthly or quarterly budget period goes by, these companies revise their entire set of budgets for the months or quarters remaining and add new monthly or quarterly budgets to replace the ones that have lapsed. At any point in time, monthly or quarterly budgets are available for the next 12 months or four quarters. Exhibit 20.2 shows rolling budgets prepared at the end of five consecutive

EXHIBIT 20.2

Rolling Budgets

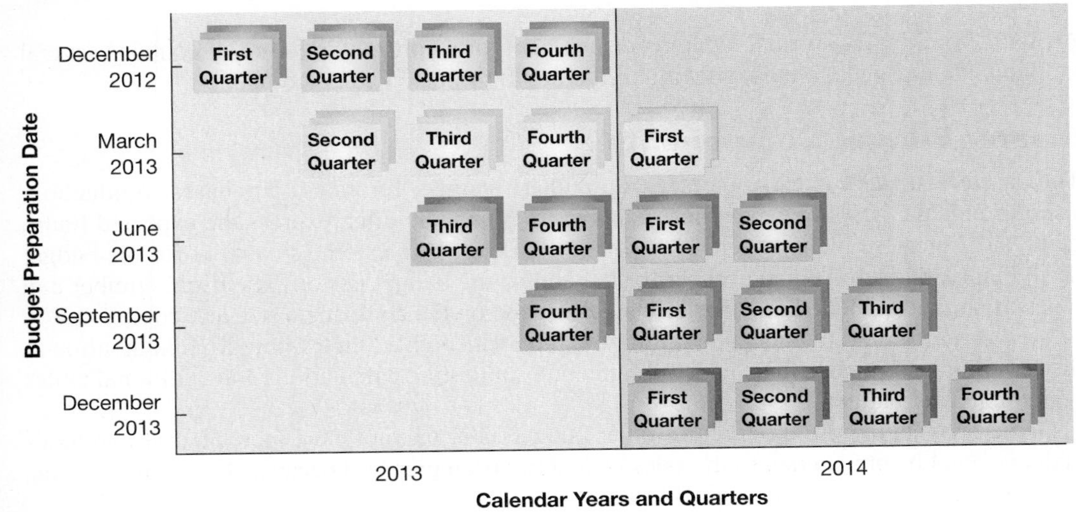

periods. The first set (at top) is prepared in December 2012 and covers the four calendar quarters of 2013. In March 2013, the company prepares another rolling budget for the next four quarters through March 2014. This same process is repeated every three months. As a result, management is continuously planning ahead.

Exhibit 20.2 reflects an annual budget composed of four quarters prepared four times per year using the most recent information available. For example, the budget for the fourth quarter of 2013 is prepared in December 2012 and revised in March, June, and September of 2013. When continuous budgeting is not used, the fourth-quarter budget is nine months old and perhaps out of date when applied.

Decision Insight

Budget Calendar Many companies use long-range operating budgets. For large companies, three groups usually determine or influence the budgets: creditors, directors, and management. All three are interested in the companies' future cash flows and earnings. The annual budget process often begins six months or more before the budget is due to the board of directors. A typical budget calendar, shown here, provides insight into the budget process during a typical calendar year. ■

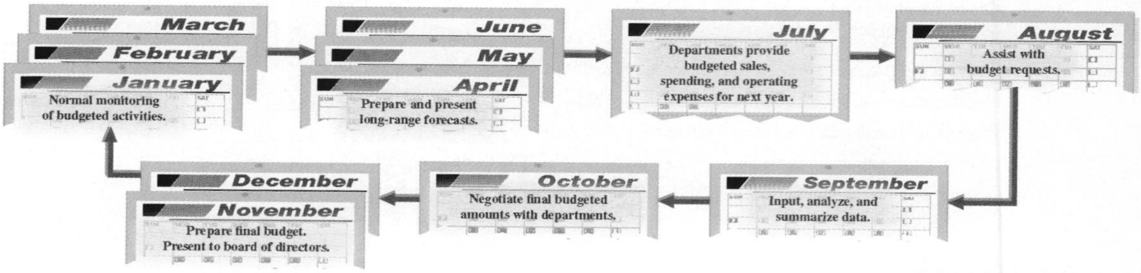

Quick Check

Answers — p. 870

1. What are the major benefits of budgeting?
2. What is the main responsibility of the budget committee?
3. What is the usual time period covered by a budget?
4. What are rolling budgets?

MASTER BUDGET

C2 Describe a master budget and the process of preparing it.

A **master budget** is a formal, comprehensive plan for a company's future. It contains several individual budgets that are linked with each other to form a coordinated plan.

Master Budget Components

The master budget typically includes individual budgets for sales, purchases, production, various expenses, capital expenditures, and cash. Managers often express the expected financial results of these planned activities with both a budgeted income statement for the budget period and a budgeted balance sheet for the end of the budget period. The usual number and types of budgets included in a master budget depend on the company's size and complexity. A master budget should include, at a minimum, the budgets listed in Exhibit 20.3. In addition to these individual budgets, managers often include supporting calculations and additional tables with the master budget.

Some budgets require the input of other budgets. For example, the merchandise purchases budget cannot be prepared until the sales budget has been prepared because the number of units

EXHIBIT 20.3

Basic Components of a Master Budget

Operating budgets
- *Sales budget*
- For merchandisers add: *Merchandise purchases budget* (units to be purchased)
- For manufacturers add: *Production budget* (units to be produced)
  Manufacturing budget (manufacturing costs)
- *Selling expense budget*
- *General and administrative expense budget*

Capital expenditures budget (expenditures for plant assets)

Financial budgets
- *Cash budget* (cash receipts and disbursements)
- *Budgeted income statement*
- *Budgeted balance sheet*

to be purchased depends on how many units are expected to be sold. As a result, we often must sequentially prepare budgets within the master budget.

A typical sequence for a master budget consists of the five steps in Exhibit 20.4. Any stage in this budgeting process might reveal undesirable outcomes, so changes often must be made to prior budgets by repeating the previous steps. For instance, an early version of the cash budget could show an insufficient amount of cash unless cash outlays are reduced. This could yield a reduction in planned equipment purchases. A preliminary budgeted balance sheet could also reveal too much debt from an ambitious capital expenditures budget. Findings such as these often result in revised plans and budgets.

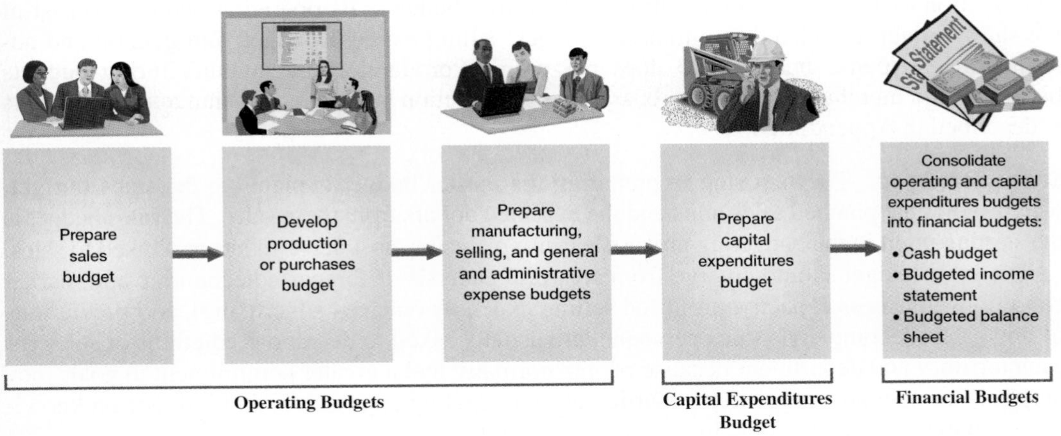

EXHIBIT 20.4

Master Budget Sequence

The remainder of this section explains how Hockey Den (HD), a retailer of youth hockey sticks, prepares its master budget. Its master budget includes operating, capital expenditures, and cash budgets for each month in each quarter. It also includes a budgeted income statement for each quarter and a budgeted balance sheet as of the last day of each quarter. We show how HD prepares budgets for October, November, and December 2013. Exhibit 20.5 presents HD's balance sheet at the start of this budgeting period, which we often refer to as we prepare the component budgets.

Decision Insight

Incentive Pay Budgets are important in determining managers' pay. A recent survey shows that 82% of large companies tie managers' bonus payments to beating budget goals. For these companies, bonus payments are frequently more than 20% of total manager pay. ■

EXHIBIT 20.5

Balance Sheet Prior to the Budgeting Periods

HOCKEY DEN Balance Sheet September 30, 2013		
Assets		
Cash		$ 20,000
Accounts receivable		42,000
Inventory (900 units @ $60)		54,000
Equipment*	$200,000	
Less accumulated depreciation	36,000	164,000
Total assets		$280,000
Liabilities and Equity		
Liabilities		
Accounts payable	$ 58,200	
Income taxes payable (due 10/31/2013)	20,000	
Note payable to bank	10,000	$ 88,200
Stockholders' equity		
Common stock	150,000	
Retained earnings	41,800	191,800
Total liabilities and equity		$280,000

* Equipment is depreciated on a straight-line basis over 10 years (salvage value is $20,000).

Operating Budgets

P1 Prepare each component of a master budget and link each to the budgeting process.

This section explains HD's preparation of operating budgets. Its operating budgets consist of the sales budget, merchandise purchases budget, selling expense budget, and general and administrative expense budget. HD does not prepare production and manufacturing budgets because it is a merchandiser. (The preparation of production budgets and manufacturing budgets is described in Appendix 20A.)

Sales Budget The first step in preparing the master budget is planning the **sales budget,** which shows the planned sales units and the expected dollars from these sales. The sales budget is the starting point in the budgeting process because plans for most departments are linked to sales.

The sales budget should emerge from a careful analysis of forecasted economic and market conditions, business capacity, proposed selling expenses (such as advertising), and predictions of unit sales. A company's sales personnel are usually asked to develop predictions of sales for each territory and department because people normally feel a greater commitment to goals they help set. Another advantage to this participatory budgeting approach is that it draws on knowledge and experience of people involved in the activity.

To illustrate, in September 2013, HD sold 700 hockey sticks at $100 per unit. After considering sales predictions and market conditions, HD prepares its sales budget for the next quarter (three months) plus one extra month (see Exhibit 20.6). The sales budget includes

EXHIBIT 20.6

Sales Budget for Planned Unit and Dollar Sales

HOCKEY DEN Monthly Sales Budget October 2013–January 2014	Budgeted Unit Sales	Budgeted Unit Price	Budgeted Total Sales
September 2013 (actual)	700	$100	$ 70,000
October 2013	1,000	$100	$100,000
November 2013	800	100	80,000
December 2013	1,400	100	140,000
Totals for the quarter	3,200	100	$320,000
January 2014	900	100	$ 90,000

January 2014 because the purchasing department relies on estimated January sales to decide on December 2013 inventory purchases. The sales budget in Exhibit 20.6 includes forecasts of both unit sales and unit prices. Some sales budgets are expressed only in total sales dollars, but most are more detailed. Management finds it useful to know budgeted units and unit prices for many different products, regions, departments, and sales representatives.

Decision Maker

Entrepreneur You run a start-up that manufactures designer clothes. Business is seasonal, and fashions and designs quickly change. How do you prepare reliable annual sales budgets? ■ [Answer—p. 870]

Merchandise Purchases Budget Companies use various methods to help managers make inventory purchasing decisions. These methods recognize that the number of units added to inventory depends on budgeted sales volume. Whether a company manufactures or purchases the product it sells, budgeted future sales volume is the primary factor in most inventory management decisions. A company must also consider its inventory system and other factors that we discuss next.

Just-in-time inventory systems. Managers of *just-in-time* (JIT) inventory systems use sales budgets for short periods (often as few as one or two days) to order just enough merchandise or materials to satisfy the immediate sales demand. This keeps the amount of inventory to a minimum (or zero in an ideal situation). A JIT system minimizes the costs of maintaining inventory, but it is practical only if customers are content to order in advance or if managers can accurately determine short-term sales demand. Suppliers also must be able and willing to ship small quantities regularly and promptly.

Point: Accurate estimates of future sales are crucial in a JIT system.

Safety stock inventory systems. Market conditions and manufacturing processes for some products do not allow use of a just-in-time system. Companies in these cases maintain sufficient inventory to reduce the risk and cost of running short. This practice requires enough purchases to satisfy the budgeted sales amounts and to maintain a **safety stock,** a quantity of inventory that provides protection against lost sales caused by unfulfilled demands from customers or delays in shipments from suppliers.

Merchandise purchases budget preparation. A merchandiser usually expresses a **merchandise purchases budget** in both units and dollars. Exhibit 20.7 shows the general layout for this budget in equation form. If this formula is expressed in units and only one product is involved, we can compute the number of dollars of inventory to be purchased for the budget by multiplying the units to be purchased by the cost per unit.

EXHIBIT 20.7

General Formula for a Merchandise Purchases Budget

Inventory to be purchased = Budgeted ending inventory + Budgeted cost of sales for the period − Budgeted beginning inventory

To illustrate, after assessing the cost of keeping inventory along with the risk and cost of inventory shortages, HD decided that the number of units in its inventory at each month-end should equal 90% of next month's predicted sales. For example, inventory at the end of October should equal 90% of budgeted November sales, and the November ending inventory should equal 90% of budgeted December sales, and so on. Also, HD's suppliers expect the September 2013 per unit cost of $60 to remain unchanged through January 2014. This information along with knowledge of 900 units in inventory at September 30 (see Exhibit 20.5) allows the company to prepare the merchandise purchases budget shown in Exhibit 20.8.

Example: Assume Hockey Den adopts a JIT system in purchasing merchandise. How will its sales budget differ from its merchandise purchases budget? *Answer:* The two budgets will be similar because future inventory should be near zero.

The first three lines of HD's merchandise purchases budget determine the required ending inventories (in units). Budgeted unit sales are then added to the desired ending inventory to give the required units of available merchandise. We then subtract beginning inventory to

EXHIBIT 20.8

Merchandise Purchases Budget

HOCKEY DEN
Merchandise Purchases Budget
October 2013–December 2013

	October	November	December
Next month's budgeted sales (units)	800	1,400	900
Ratio of inventory to future sales	× 90%	× 90%	× 90%
Budgeted ending inventory (units)	720	1,260	810
Add budgeted sales (units)	1,000	800	1,400
Required units of available merchandise	1,720	2,060	2,210
Deduct beginning inventory (units)	900	720	1,260
Units to be purchased	820	1,340	950
Budgeted cost per unit	$ 60	$ 60	$ 60
Budgeted cost of merchandise purchases	$49,200	$80,400	$57,000

Example: If ending inventory in Exhibit 20.8 is required to equal 80% of next month's predicted sales, how many units must be purchased each month? *Answer:* Budgeted ending inventory: Oct. = 640 units; Nov. = 1,120 units; Dec. = 720 units. Required purchases: Oct. = 740 units; Nov. = 1,280 units; Dec. = 1,000 units.

determine the budgeted number of units to be purchased. The last line is the budgeted cost of the purchases, computed by multiplying the number of units to be purchased by the predicted cost per unit.

We already indicated that some budgeting systems describe only the total dollars of budgeted sales. Likewise, a system can express a merchandise purchases budget only in terms of the total cost of merchandise to be purchased, omitting the number of units to be purchased. This method assumes a constant relation between sales and cost of goods sold. HD, for instance, might assume the expected cost of goods sold to be 60% of sales, computed from the budgeted unit cost of $60 and the budgeted sales price of $100. However, it still must consider the effects of changes in beginning and ending inventories in determining the amounts to be purchased.

Selling Expense Budget The **selling expense budget** is a plan listing the types and amounts of selling expenses expected during the budget period. Its initial responsibility usually rests with the vice president of marketing or an equivalent sales manager. The selling expense budget is normally created to provide sufficient selling expenses to meet sales goals reflected in the sales budget. Predicted selling expenses are based on both the sales budget and the experience of previous periods. After some or all of the master budget is prepared, management might decide that projected sales volume is inadequate. If so, subsequent adjustments in the sales budget can require corresponding adjustments in the selling expense budget.

To illustrate, HD's selling expense budget is in Exhibit 20.9. The firm's selling expenses consist of commissions paid to sales personnel and a $2,000 monthly salary paid to the sales manager. Sales commissions equal 10% of total sales and are paid in the month sales occur. Sales commissions are variable with respect to sales volume, but the sales manager's salary is fixed. No advertising expenses are budgeted for this particular quarter.

EXHIBIT 20.9

Selling Expense Budget

HOCKEY DEN
Selling Expense Budget
October 2013–December 2013

	October	November	December	Totals
Budgeted sales	$100,000	$80,000	$140,000	$320,000
Sales commission percent	× 10%	× 10%	× 10%	× 10%
Sales commissions	10,000	8,000	14,000	32,000
Salary for sales manager	2,000	2,000	2,000	6,000
Total selling expenses	$ 12,000	$10,000	$ 16,000	$ 38,000

Example: If sales commissions in Exhibit 20.9 are increased, which budgets are affected? *Answer:* Selling expenses budget, cash budget, and budgeted income statement.

General and Administrative Expense Budget The **general and administrative expense budget** plans the predicted operating expenses not included in the selling expenses budget. General and administrative expenses can be either variable or fixed with respect to sales volume. The office manager responsible for general administration often is responsible for preparing the initial general and administrative expense budget.

Exhibit 20.10 shows HD's general and administrative expense budget. It includes salaries of $54,000 per year, or $4,500 per month (paid each month when they are earned). Using information in Exhibit 20.5, the depreciation on equipment is computed as $18,000 per year [($200,000 − $20,000)/10 years], or $1,500 per month ($18,000/12 months).

EXHIBIT 20.10

General and Administrative Expense Budget

HOCKEY DEN General and Administrative Expense Budget October 2013–December 2013	October	November	December	Totals
Administrative salaries	$4,500	$4,500	$4,500	$13,500
Depreciation of equipment	1,500	1,500	1,500	4,500
Total general and administrative expenses	$6,000	$6,000	$6,000	$18,000

Example: In Exhibit 20.10, how would a rental agreement of $5,000 per month plus 1% of sales affect the general and administrative expense budget? (Budgeted sales are in Exhibit 20.6.)
Answer: Rent expense: Oct. = $6,000; Nov. = $5,800; Dec. = $6,400; Total = $18,200; *Revised total general and administrative expenses:* Oct. = $12,000; Nov. = $11,800; Dec. = $12,400; Total = $36,200.

Interest expense and income tax expense are often classified as general and administrative expenses in published income statements but normally cannot be planned at this stage of the budgeting process. The prediction of interest expense follows the preparation of the cash budget and the decisions regarding debt. The predicted income tax expense depends on the budgeted amount of pretax income. Both interest and income taxes are usually beyond the control of the office manager. As a result, they are not used in comparison to the budget to evaluate that person's performance.

Decision Insight

No Biz Like Snow Biz Ski resorts' costs of making snow are in the millions of dollars for equipment alone. Snowmaking involves spraying droplets of water into the air, causing them to freeze and come down as snow. Making snow can cost more than $2,000 an hour. Snowmaking accounts for 40 to 50 percent of the operating budgets for many ski resorts. ■

Quick Check

Answers — p. 870

5. What is a master budget?
6. A master budget (*a*) always includes a manufacturing budget specifying the units to be produced; (*b*) is prepared with a process starting with the operating budgets and continues with the capital expenditures budget and then financial budgets; or (*c*) is prepared with a process ending with the sales budget.
7. What are the three primary categories of budgets in the master budget?
8. In preparing monthly budgets for the third quarter, a company budgeted sales of 120 units for July and 140 units for August. Management wants each month's ending inventory to be 60% of next month's sales. The June 30 inventory consists of 50 units. How many units of product for July acquisition should the merchandise purchases budget specify for the third quarter? (*a*) 84, (*b*) 120, (*c*) 154, or (*d*) 204.
9. How do the operating budgets for merchandisers and manufacturers differ?
10. How does a just-in-time inventory system differ from a safety stock system?

Capital Expenditures Budget

The **capital expenditures budget** lists dollar amounts to be both received from plant asset disposals and spent to purchase additional plant assets to carry out the budgeted business activities. It is usually prepared after the operating budgets. Since a company's plant assets determine its productive capacity, this budget is usually affected by long-range plans for the business. Yet the process of preparing a sales or purchases budget can reveal that the company requires more (or less) capacity, which implies more (or less) plant assets.

Capital budgeting is the process of evaluating and planning for capital (plant asset) expenditures. This is an important management task because these expenditures often involve long-run commitments of large amounts, affect predicted cash flows, and impact future debt and equity financing. This means that the capital expenditures budget is often linked with management's evaluation of the company's ability to take on more debt. We describe capital budgeting in Chapter 24.

Hockey Den does not anticipate disposal of any plant assets through December 2013, but it does plan to acquire additional equipment for $25,000 cash near the end of December 2013. This is the only budgeted capital expenditure from October 2013 through January 2014. Thus, no separate budget is shown. Hockey Den's cash budget will reflect this $25,000 planned expenditure.

Financial Budgets

After preparing its operating and capital expenditures budgets, a company uses information from these budgets to prepare at least three financial budgets: the cash budget, budgeted income statement, and budgeted balance sheet.

P2 Link both operating and capital expenditures budgets to budgeted financial statements.

Cash Budget After developing budgets for sales, merchandise purchases, expenses, and capital expenditures, the next step is to prepare the **cash budget,** which shows expected cash inflows and outflows during the budget period. It is especially important to maintain a cash balance necessary to meet ongoing obligations. By preparing a cash budget, management can prearrange loans to cover anticipated cash shortages before they are needed. A cash budget also helps management avoid a cash balance that is too large. Too much cash is undesirable because it earns a relatively low (if any) return. Exhibit 20.11 shows the general formula for the cash budget.

EXHIBIT 20.11

General Formula for Cash Budget

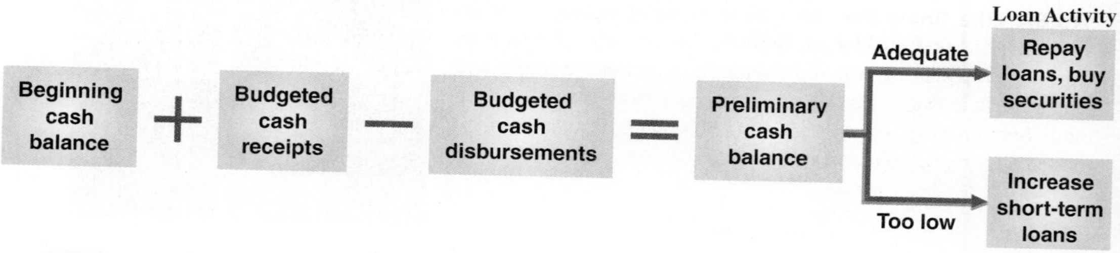

When preparing a cash budget, we add expected cash receipts to the beginning cash balance and deduct expected cash disbursements. If the expected (preliminary) ending cash balance is too low, additional cash requirements appear in the budget as planned increases from short-term loans. If the expected ending cash balance exceeds the desired balance, the excess is used to repay loans or to acquire short-term investments. Information for preparing the cash budget is mainly taken from the operating and capital expenditures budgets.

Cash Receipts from Sales To illustrate, Exhibit 20.12 presents HD's budgeted cash receipts.

EXHIBIT 20.12

Computing Budgeted Cash Receipts

	September	October	November	December
Sales	$70,000	$100,000	$80,000	$140,000
Less ending accounts receivable (60%)	42,000	60,000	48,000	84,000
Cash receipts from				
Cash sales (40% of sales)		40,000	32,000	56,000
Collections of prior month's receivables		42,000	60,000	48,000
Total cash receipts		$ 82,000	$92,000	$104,000

We begin with reference to HD's budgeted sales (Exhibit 20.6). Analysis of past sales indicates that 40% of the firm's sales are for cash. The remaining 60% are credit sales; these customers are expected to pay in full in the month following the sales. We now can compute the budgeted cash receipts from customers as shown in Exhibit 20.12. October's budgeted cash receipts consist of $40,000 from expected cash sales ($100,000 × 40%) plus the anticipated collection of $42,000 of accounts receivable from the end of September.

Cash Disbursements for Merchandise Next, we see that HD's merchandise purchases are entirely on account. It makes full payment during the month following its purchases. Therefore, cash disbursements for purchases can be computed from the September 30, 2013, balance sheet (Exhibit 20.5), for October disbursements, and the merchandise purchases budget (Exhibit 20.8), for November and December disbursements. This is shown in Exhibit 20.13.

EXHIBIT 20.13

Computing Cash Disbursements for Purchases

	October	November	December
Purchases (from Exhibit 20.8)	$49,200	$80,400	$57,000
Cash disbursements for			
Current month purchases (0%)	0	0	0
Prior month purchases (100%)	58,200*	49,200	80,400
Total cash disbursements for purchases	$58,200	$49,200	$80,400

*From September 30 balance sheet (Exhibit 20.5)

The schedule above can be modified for alternative payment timing. For example, if Hockey Den paid for 20% of its purchases in the month of purchase, and paid the remaining 80% of a month's purchases in the following month, its cash disbursements in December would equal $75,720, computed as (20% × $57,000) plus (80% × $80,400).

Exhibit 20.14 shows the full cash budget for Hockey Den, beginning with information on budgeted cash receipts from Exhibit 20.13 and budgeted cash purchases for merchandise from Exhibit 20.13. Next we discuss HD's other cash disbursements and loan activity on its cash budget.

EXHIBIT 20.14

Cash Budget

HOCKEY DEN
Cash Budget
October 2013–December 2013

	October	November	December
Beginning cash balance	$ 20,000	$ 20,000	$ 22,272
Cash receipts from customers (Exhibit 20.12)	82,000	92,000	104,000
Total cash available	102,000	112,000	126,272
Cash disbursements			
Payments for merchandise (Exhibit 20.13)	58,200	49,200	80,400
Sales commissions (Exhibit 20.9)	10,000	8,000	14,000
Salaries			
Sales (Exhibit 20.9)	2,000	2,000	2,000
Administrative (Exhibit 20.10)	4,500	4,500	4,500
Income taxes payable (Exhibit 20.5)	20,000		
Dividends ($150,000 × 2%)		3,000	
Interest on bank loan			
October ($10,000 × 1%)*	100		
November ($22,800 × 1%)		228	
Purchase of equipment			25,000
Total cash disbursements	94,800	66,928	125,900
Preliminary cash balance	$ 7,200	$ 45,072	$ 372
Loan activity			
Additional loan from bank	12,800		19,628
Repayment of loan to bank		22,800	
Ending cash balance	$ 20,000	$ 22,272	$ 20,000
Loan balance, end of month	$ 22,800	$ 0	$ 19,628

* Beginning loan balance from Exhibit 20.5

Example: If the minimum ending cash balance in Exhibit 20.14 is changed to $25,000 for each month, what is the projected loan balance at Dec. 31, 2013?

Answer:

Loan balance, Oct. 31	$27,800
November interest	278
November payment	25,022
Loan balance, Nov. 30	2,778
December interest	28
Additional loan in Dec.	21,928
Loan balance, Dec. 31	$24,706

The monthly budgeted cash disbursements for sales commissions and salaries are taken from the selling expense budget (Exhibit 20.9) and the general and administrative expense budget (Exhibit 20.10). The cash budget is unaffected by depreciation as reported in the general and administrative expenses budget.

Cash Disbursements for Other Items Income taxes are due and payable in October as shown in the September 30, 2013, balance sheet (Exhibit 20.5). The cash budget in Exhibit 20.14 shows this $20,000 expected payment in October. Predicted income tax expense for the quarter ending December 31 is 40% of net income and is due in January 2014. It is therefore not reported in the October–December 2013 cash budget but in the budgeted income statement as income tax expense and on the budgeted balance sheet as income tax liability.

Hockey Den also pays a cash dividend equal to 2% of the par value of common stock in the second month of each quarter. The cash budget in Exhibit 20.14 shows a November payment of $3,000 for this purpose (2% of $150,000; see Exhibit 20.5).

Loan Activity Analyzing Hockey Den's loan activity is necessary in computing its budgeted cash disbursements for interest. Hockey Den has an agreement with its bank that promises additional loans at each month-end, if necessary, to keep a minimum cash balance of $20,000. If the cash balance exceeds $20,000 at a month-end, HD uses the excess to repay loans. Interest is paid at each month-end at the rate of 1% of the beginning balance of these loans. For October, this payment is 1% of the $10,000 amount reported in the balance sheet of Exhibit 20.5. For November, HD expects to pay interest of $228, computed as 1% of the $22,800 expected loan balance at October 31. No interest is budgeted for December because the company expects to repay the loans in full at the end of November. Exhibit 20.14 shows that the October 31 cash balance declines to $7,200 (before any loan-related activity). This amount is less than the $20,000 minimum. Hockey Den will bring this balance up to the minimum by borrowing $12,800 with a short-term note. At the end of November, the budget shows an expected cash balance of $45,072 before any loan activity. This means that HD expects to repay $22,800 of debt. The equipment purchase budgeted for December reduces the expected cash balance to $372, far below the $20,000 minimum. The company expects to borrow $19,628 in that month to reach the minimum desired ending balance.

Decision Insight

Cash Cushion Why do some companies maintain a minimum cash balance when the budget shows extra cash is not needed? For example, iPhone sales have pushed Apple's cash and investments balance to over $97 billion. For Apple's CEO Tim Cook the cushion provides "flexibility and security," important in navigating uncertain economic times. ■

Budgeted Income Statement One of the final steps in preparing the master budget is to summarize the income effects. The **budgeted income statement** is a managerial accounting report showing predicted amounts of sales and expenses for the budget period. Information needed for preparing a budgeted income statement is primarily taken from already prepared budgets. The volume of information summarized in the budgeted income statement is so large for some companies that they often use spreadsheets to accumulate the budgeted transactions and classify them by their effects on income. We condense HD's budgeted income statement and show it in Exhibit 20.15. All information in this exhibit is taken from earlier budgets. Also, we now can predict the amount of income tax expense for the quarter, computed as 40% of the budgeted pretax income. This amount is included in the cash budget and/or the budgeted balance sheet as necessary.

Point: Lenders often require potential borrowers to provide cash budgets, budgeted income statements, and budgeted balance sheets, as well as data on past performance.

Budgeted Balance Sheet The final step in preparing the master budget is summarizing the company's financial position. The **budgeted balance sheet** shows predicted amounts for the

EXHIBIT 20.15

Budgeted Income Statement

HOCKEY DEN Budgeted Income Statement For Three Months Ended December 31, 2013		
Sales (Exhibit 20.6, 3,200 units @ $100)		$320,000
Cost of goods sold (3,200 units @ $60)		192,000
Gross profit		128,000
Operating expenses		
Sales commissions (Exhibit 20.9)	$32,000	
Sales salaries (Exhibit 20.9)	6,000	
Administrative salaries (Exhibit 20.10)	13,500	
Depreciation on equipment (Exhibit 20.10)	4,500	
Interest expense (Exhibit 20.14)	328	56,328
Income before income taxes		71,672
Income tax expense ($71,672 × 40%)		28,669
Net income		$ 43,003

company's assets, liabilities, and equity as of the end of the budget period. HD's budgeted balance sheet in Exhibit 20.16 is prepared using information from the other budgets. The sources of amounts are reported in the notes to the budgeted balance sheet.[1]

EXHIBIT 20.16

Budgeted Balance Sheet

HOCKEY DEN Budgeted Balance Sheet December 31, 2013		
Assets		
Cash[a]		$ 20,000
Accounts receivable[b]		84,000
Inventory[c]		48,600
Equipment[d]	$225,000	
Less accumulated depreciation[e]	40,500	184,500
Total assets		$337,100
Liabilities and Equity		
Liabilities		
Accounts payable[f]	$ 57,000	
Income taxes payable[g]	28,669	
Bank loan payable[h]	19,628	$105,297
Stockholders' equity		
Common stock[i]	150,000	
Retained earnings[j]	81,803	231,803
Total liabilities and equity		$337,100

[a] Ending balance for December from the cash budget in Exhibit 20.14.
[b] 60% of $140,000 sales budgeted for December from the sales budget in Exhibit 20.6.
[c] 810 units in budgeted December ending inventory at the budgeted cost of $60 per unit (from the purchases budget in Exhibit 20.8).
[d] September 30 balance of $200,000 from the beginning balance sheet in Exhibit 20.5 plus $25,000 cost of new equipment from the cash budget in Exhibit 20.14.
[e] September 30 balance of $36,000 from the beginning balance sheet in Exhibit 20.5 plus $4,500 expense from the general and administrative expense budget in Exhibit 20.10.
[f] Budgeted cost of purchases for December from the purchases budget in Exhibit 20.8.
[g] Income tax expense from the budgeted income statement for the fourth quarter in Exhibit 20.15.
[h] Budgeted December 31 balance from the cash budget in Exhibit 20.14.
[i] Unchanged from the beginning balance sheet in Exhibit 20.5.
[j] September 30 balance of $41,800 from the beginning balance sheet in Exhibit 20.5 plus budgeted net income of $43,003 from the budgeted income statement in Exhibit 20.15 minus budgeted cash dividends of $3,000 from the cash budget in Exhibit 20.14.

---

[1] An eight-column spreadsheet, or work sheet, can be used to prepare a budgeted balance sheet (and income statement). The first two columns show the ending balance sheet amounts from the period prior to the budget period. The budgeted transactions and adjustments are entered in the third and fourth columns in the same manner as adjustments are entered on an ordinary work sheet. After all budgeted transactions and adjustments have been entered, the amounts in the first two columns are combined with the budget amounts in the third and fourth columns and sorted to the proper Income Statement (fifth and sixth columns) and Balance Sheet columns (seventh and eighth columns). Amounts in these columns are used to prepare the budgeted income statement and balance sheet.

Decision Insight

Strategic Planning Most companies allocate dollars based on budgets submitted by department managers. These managers verify the numbers and monitor the budget. Managers must remember, however, that a budget is judged by its success in helping achieve the company's mission. One analogy is that a hiker must know the route to properly plan a hike and monitor hiking progress. ■

Quick Check

Answers — p. 870

11. In preparing a budgeted balance sheet, (*a*) plant assets are determined by analyzing the capital expenditures budget and the balance sheet from the beginning of the budget period, (*b*) liabilities are determined by analyzing the general and administrative expense budget, or (*c*) retained earnings are determined from information contained in the cash budget and the balance sheet from the beginning of the budget period.
12. What sequence is followed in preparing the budgets that constitute the master budget?

GLOBAL VIEW

Royal Phillips Electronics of the Netherlands is a diversified company. Preparing budgets and evaluating progress helps the company achieve its goals. In a recent annual report the company reports that it budgets sales to grow at a faster pace than overall economic growth. Based on this sales target, company managers prepare detailed operating, capital expenditure, and financial budgets.

Budgeted and actual results of companies that do global business are impacted by changes in foreign currency exchange rates. While most of Royal Phillips' cash disbursements are in euros, the company's sales are in euros, U.S. dollars, Chinese yuan, Brazilian real, and other currencies. Forecasting future exchange rates and their impact on sales budgets is difficult. In addition, global economic and political uncertainties add to budgeting challenges.

Decision Analysis Activity-Based Budgeting

A1 Analyze expense planning using activity-based budgeting.

Activity-based budgeting (ABB) is a budget system based on expected activities. Knowledge of expected activities and their levels for the budget period enables management to plan for resources required to perform the activities. To illustrate, we consider the budget of a company's accounting department. Traditional budgeting systems list items such as salaries, supplies, equipment, and utilities. Such an itemized budget informs management of the use of the funds budgeted (for example, salaries), but management cannot assess the basis for increases or decreases in budgeted amounts as compared to prior periods. Accordingly, management often makes across-the-board cuts or increases. In contrast, ABB requires management to list activities performed by, say, the accounting department such as auditing, tax reporting, financial reporting, and cost accounting. Exhibit 20.17 contrasts a traditional budget with an activity-based

EXHIBIT 20.17

Activity-Based Budgeting versus Traditional Budgeting (for an accounting department)

Activity-Based Budget		Traditional Budget	
Auditing	$ 58,000	Salaries	$152,000
Tax reporting	71,000	Supplies	22,000
Financial reporting	63,000	Depreciation	36,000
Cost accounting	32,000	Utilities	14,000
Total	$224,000	Total	$224,000

budget for a company's accounting department. An understanding of the resources required to perform the activities, the costs associated with these resources, and the way resource use changes with changes in activity levels allows management to better assess how expenses will change to accommodate changes in activity levels. Moreover, by knowing the relation between activities and costs, management can attempt to reduce costs by eliminating nonvalue-added activities.

Decision Maker

Environmental Manager You hold the new position of environmental control manager for a chemical company. You are asked to develop a budget for your job and identify job responsibilities. How do you proceed? ■ [Answer—p. 870]

DEMONSTRATION PROBLEM

Wild Wood Company's management asks you to prepare its master budget using the following information. The budget is to cover the months of April, May, and June of 2013.

WILD WOOD COMPANY
Balance Sheet
March 31, 2013

Assets		**Liabilities and Equity**	
Cash	$ 50,000	Accounts payable	$156,000
Accounts receivable	175,000	Short-term notes payable	12,000
Inventory	126,000	Total current liabilities	168,000
Total current assets	351,000	Long-term note payable	200,000
Equipment, gross	480,000	Total liabilities	368,000
Accumulated depreciation	(90,000)	Common stock	235,000
Equipment, net	390,000	Retained earnings	138,000
		Total stockholders' equity	373,000
Total assets	$741,000	Total liabilities and equity	$741,000

Additional Information

a. Sales for March total 10,000 units. Each month's sales are expected to exceed the prior month's results by 5%. The product's selling price is $25 per unit.

b. Company policy calls for a given month's ending inventory to equal 80% of the next month's expected unit sales. The March 31 inventory is 8,400 units, which complies with the policy. The purchase price is $15 per unit.

c. Sales representatives' commissions are 12.5% of sales and are paid in the month of the sales. The sales manager's monthly salary will be $3,500 in April and $4,000 per month thereafter.

d. Monthly general and administrative expenses include $8,000 administrative salaries, $5,000 depreciation, and 0.9% monthly interest on the long-term note payable.

e. The company expects 30% of sales to be for cash and the remaining 70% on credit. Receivables are collected in full in the month following the sale (none is collected in the month of the sale).

f. All merchandise purchases are on credit, and no payables arise from any other transactions. One month's purchases are fully paid in the next month.

g. The minimum ending cash balance for all months is $50,000. If necessary, the company borrows enough cash using a short-term note to reach the minimum. Short-term notes require an interest payment of 1% at each month-end (before any repayment). If the ending cash balance exceeds the minimum, the excess will be applied to repaying the short-term notes payable balance.

h. Dividends of $100,000 are to be declared and paid in May.

i. No cash payments for income taxes are to be made during the second calendar quarter. Income taxes will be assessed at 35% in the quarter.

j. Equipment purchases of $55,000 are scheduled for June.

Required

Prepare the following budgets and other financial information as required:

1. Sales budget, including budgeted sales for July.
2. Purchases budget, the budgeted cost of goods sold for each month and quarter, and the cost of the June 30 budgeted inventory.
3. Selling expense budget.
4. General and administrative expense budget.
5. Expected cash receipts from customers and the expected June 30 balance of accounts receivable.
6. Expected cash payments for purchases and the expected June 30 balance of accounts payable.
7. Cash budget.
8. Budgeted income statement.
9. Budgeted statement of retained earnings.
10. Budgeted balance sheet.

PLANNING THE SOLUTION

- The sales budget shows expected sales for each month in the quarter. Start by multiplying March sales by 105% and then do the same for the remaining months. July's sales are needed for the purchases budget. To complete the budget, multiply the expected unit sales by the selling price of $25 per unit.
- Use these results and the 80% inventory policy to budget the size of ending inventory for April, May, and June. Add the budgeted sales to these numbers and subtract the actual or expected beginning inventory for each month. The result is the number of units to be purchased each month. Multiply these numbers by the per unit cost of $15. Find the budgeted cost of goods sold by multiplying the unit sales in each month by the $15 cost per unit. Compute the cost of the June 30 ending inventory by multiplying the expected units available at that date by the $15 cost per unit.
- The selling expense budget has only two items. Find the amount of the sales representatives' commissions by multiplying the expected dollar sales in each month by the 12.5% commission rate. Then include the sales manager's salary of $3,500 in April and $4,000 in May and June.
- The general and administrative expense budget should show three items. Administrative salaries are fixed at $8,000 per month, and depreciation is $5,000 per month. Budget the monthly interest expense on the long-term note by multiplying its $200,000 balance by the 0.9% monthly interest rate.
- Determine the amounts of cash sales in each month by multiplying the budgeted sales by 30%. Add to this amount the credit sales of the prior month (computed as 70% of prior month's sales). April's cash receipts from collecting receivables equals the March 31 balance of $175,000. The expected June 30 accounts receivable balance equals 70% of June's total budgeted sales.
- Determine expected cash payments on accounts payable for each month by making them equal to the merchandise purchases in the prior month. The payments for April equal the March 31 balance of accounts payable shown on the beginning balance sheet. The June 30 balance of accounts payable equals merchandise purchases for June.
- Prepare the cash budget by combining the given information and the amounts of cash receipts and cash payments on account that you computed. Complete the cash budget for each month by either borrowing enough to raise the preliminary balance to the minimum or paying off short-term debt as much as the balance allows without falling below the minimum. Show the ending balance of the short-term note in the budget.
- Prepare the budgeted income statement by combining the budgeted items for all three months. Determine the income before income taxes and multiply it by the 35% rate to find the quarter's income tax expense.
- The budgeted statement of retained earnings should show the March 31 balance plus the quarter's net income minus the quarter's dividends.
- The budgeted balance sheet includes updated balances for all items that appear in the beginning balance sheet and an additional liability for unpaid income taxes. Amounts for all asset, liability, and equity accounts can be found either in the budgets, other calculations, or by adding amounts found there to the beginning balances.

SOLUTION TO DEMONSTRATION PROBLEM

1. Sales budget

	April	May	June	July
Prior period's unit sales	10,000	10,500	11,025	11,576
Plus 5% growth	500	525	551	579
Projected unit sales	10,500	11,025	11,576	12,155

	April	May	June	Quarter
Projected unit sales	10,500	11,025	11,576	
Selling price per unit	× $25	× $25	× $25	
Projected sales	$262,500	$275,625	$289,400	$827,525

2. Purchases budget

	April	May	June	Quarter
Next period's unit sales (part 1)	11,025	11,576	12,155	
Ending inventory percent	× 80%	× 80%	× 80%	
Desired ending inventory	8,820	9,261	9,724	
Current period's unit sales (part 1)	10,500	11,025	11,576	
Units to be available	19,320	20,286	21,300	
Less beginning inventory	8,400	8,820	9,261	
Units to be purchased	10,920	11,466	12,039	
Budgeted cost per unit	× $15	× $15	× $15	
Projected purchases	$163,800	$171,990	$180,585	$516,375

Budgeted cost of goods sold

	April	May	June	Quarter
This period's unit sales (part 1)	10,500	11,025	11,576	
Budgeted cost per unit	× $15	× $15	× $15	
Projected cost of goods sold	$157,500	$165,375	$173,640	$496,515

Budgeted inventory for June 30

Units (part 2)	9,724
Cost per unit	× $15
Total	$145,860

3. Selling expense budget

	April	May	June	Quarter
Budgeted sales (part 1)	$262,500	$275,625	$289,400	$827,525
Commission percent	× 12.5%	× 12.5%	× 12.5%	× 12.5%
Sales commissions	32,813	34,453	36,175	103,441
Manager's salary	3,500	4,000	4,000	11,500
Projected selling expenses	$ 36,313	$ 38,453	$ 40,175	$114,941

4. General and administrative expense budget

	April	May	June	Quarter
Administrative salaries	$ 8,000	$ 8,000	$ 8,000	$24,000
Depreciation	5,000	5,000	5,000	15,000
Interest on long-term note payable (0.9% × $200,000)	1,800	1,800	1,800	5,400
Projected expenses	$14,800	$14,800	$14,800	$44,400

5. Expected cash receipts from customers

	April	May	June	Quarter
Budgeted sales (part 1)	$262,500	$275,625	$289,400	
Ending accounts receivable (70%)	$183,750	$192,938	$202,580	
Cash receipts				
Cash sales (30% of budgeted sales)	$ 78,750	$ 82,687	$ 86,820	$248,257
Collections of prior month's receivables	175,000	183,750	192,938	551,688
Total cash to be collected	$253,750	$266,437	$279,758	$799,945

6. Expected cash payments to suppliers

	April	May	June	Quarter
Cash payments (equal to prior month's purchases)	$156,000	$163,800	$171,990	$491,790
Expected June 30 balance of accounts payable (June purchases)			$180,585	

7. Cash budget

	April	May	June
Beginning cash balance	$ 50,000	$ 89,517	$ 50,000
Cash receipts (part 5)	253,750	266,437	279,758
Total cash available	303,750	355,954	329,758
Cash payments			
Payments for merchandise (part 6)	156,000	163,800	171,990
Sales commissions (part 3)	32,813	34,453	36,175
Salaries			
Sales (part 3)	3,500	4,000	4,000
Administrative (part 4)	8,000	8,000	8,000
Interest on long-term note (part 4)	1,800	1,800	1,800
Dividends		100,000	
Equipment purchase			55,000
Interest on short-term notes			
April ($12,000 × 1.0%)	120		
June ($6,099 × 1.0%)			61
Total cash payments	202,233	312,053	277,026
Preliminary balance	101,517	43,901	52,732
Loan activity			
Additional loan		6,099	
Loan repayment	(12,000)		(2,732)
Ending cash balance	$ 89,517	$ 50,000	$ 50,000
Ending short-term notes	$ 0	$ 6,099	$ 3,367

8.

WILD WOOD COMPANY
Budgeted Income Statement
For Quarter Ended June 30, 2013

Sales (part 1)		$827,525
Cost of goods sold (part 2)		496,515
Gross profit		331,010
Operating expenses		
Sales commissions (part 3)	$103,441	
Sales salaries (part 3)	11,500	
Administrative salaries (part 4)	24,000	
Depreciation (part 4)	15,000	
Interest on long-term note (part 4)	5,400	
Interest on short-term notes (part 7)	181	
Total operating expenses		159,522
Income before income taxes		171,488
Income taxes (35%)		60,021
Net income		$111,467

9.

WILD WOOD COMPANY
Budgeted Statement of Retained Earnings
For Quarter Ended June 30, 2013

Beginning retained earnings (given)	$138,000
Net income (part 8)	111,467
	249,467
Less cash dividends (given)	100,000
Ending retained earnings	$149,467

10.

WILD WOOD COMPANY
Budgeted Balance Sheet
June 30, 2013

Assets		
Cash (part 7)		$ 50,000
Accounts receivable (part 5)		202,580
Inventory (part 2)		145,860
Total current assets		398,440
Equipment (given plus purchase)	$535,000	
Less accumulated depreciation (given plus expense)	105,000	430,000
Total assets		$828,440
Liabilities and Equity		
Accounts payable (part 6)		$180,585
Short-term notes payable (part 7)		3,367
Income taxes payable (part 8)		60,021
Total current liabilities		243,973
Long-term note payable (given)		200,000
Total liabilities		443,973
Common stock (given)		235,000
Retained earnings (part 9)		149,467
Total stockholders' equity		384,467
Total liabilities and equity		$828,440

APPENDIX

20A Production and Manufacturing Budgets

P3 Prepare production and manufacturing budgets.

Unlike a merchandising company, a manufacturer must prepare a **production budget** instead of a merchandise purchases budget. A production budget, which shows the number of units to be produced each month, is similar to merchandise purchases budgets except that the number of units to be purchased each month (as shown in Exhibit 20.8) is replaced by the number of units to be manufactured each month. A production budget does not show costs; it is *always expressed in units of product.* Exhibit 20A.1 shows the production budget for **Toronto Sticks Company (TSC),** a manufacturer of hockey sticks. TSC is an exclusive supplier of hockey sticks to Hockey Den, meaning that TSC uses HD's budgeted sales figures (Exhibit 20.6) to determine its production and manufacturing budgets.

EXHIBIT 20A.1

Production Budget

TSC
Production Budget
October 2013–December 2013

	October	November	December
Next period's budgeted sales (units)	800	1,400	900
Ratio of inventory to future sales	× 90%	× 90%	× 90%
Budgeted ending inventory (units)	720	1,260	810
Add budgeted sales for the period (units)	1,000	800	1,400
Required units of available production	1,720	2,060	2,210
Deduct beginning inventory (units)	(900)	(720)	(1,260)
Units to be produced	820	1,340	950

A **manufacturing budget** shows the budgeted costs for direct materials, direct labor, and overhead. It is based on the budgeted production volume from the production budget. The manufacturing budget for most companies consists of three individual budgets: direct materials budget, direct labor budget, and overhead budget. Exhibits 20A.2–20A.4 show these three manufacturing budgets for TSC. These budgets yield the total expected cost of goods to be manufactured in the budget period.

The *direct materials budget* is driven by the budgeted materials needed to satisfy each month's production requirement. To this we must add the desired ending inventory requirements. The desired ending inventory of direct materials as shown in Exhibit 20A.2 is 50% of next month's budgeted materials requirements of wood. For instance, in October 2013, an ending inventory of 335 units of material is desired (50% of November's 670 units). The desired ending inventory for December 2013 is 225 units, computed from the direct material requirement of 450 units for a production level of 900 units in January 2014. The total materials requirements are computed by adding the desired ending inventory figures to that month's budgeted production material requirements. For October 2013, the total materials requirement is 745 units (335 + 410). From the total materials requirement, we then subtract the units of

EXHIBIT 20A.2

Direct Materials Budget

TSC
Direct Materials Budget
October 2013–December 2013

	October	November	December
Budget production (units)	820	1,340	950
Materials requirements per unit	× 0.5	× 0.5	× 0.5
Materials needed for production (units)	410	670	475
Add budgeted ending inventory (units)	335	237.5	225
Total materials requirements (units)	745	907.5	700
Deduct beginning inventory (units)	(205)	(335)	(237.5)
Materials to be purchased (units)	540	572.5	462.5
Material price per unit	$ 20	$ 20	$ 20
Total cost of direct materials purchases	$10,800	$11,450	$9,250

materials available in beginning inventory. For October 2013, the materials available from September 2013 are computed as 50% of October's materials requirements to satisfy production, or 205 units (50% of 410). Therefore, direct materials purchases in October 2013 are budgeted at 540 units (745 − 205). See Exhibit 20A.2.

TSC's *direct labor budget* is shown in Exhibit 20A.3. About 15 minutes of labor time is required to produce one unit. Labor is paid at the rate of $12 per hour. Budgeted labor hours are computed by multiplying the budgeted production level for each month by one-quarter (0.25) of an hour. Direct labor cost is then computed by multiplying budgeted labor hours by the labor rate of $12 per hour.

EXHIBIT 20A.3

Direct Labor Budget

TSC
Direct Labor Budget
October 2013–December 2013

	October	November	December
Budgeted production (units)	820	1,340	950
Labor requirements per unit (hours)	× 0.25	× 0.25	× 0.25
Total labor hours needed	205	335	237.5
Labor rate (per hour)	$ 12	$ 12	$ 12
Labor dollars	$2,460	$4,020	$2,850

TSC's *factory overhead budget* is shown in Exhibit 20A.4. The variable portion of overhead is assigned at the rate of $2.50 per unit of production. The fixed portion stays constant at $1,500 per month. The budget in Exhibit 20A.4 is in condensed form; most overhead budgets are more detailed, listing each overhead cost item. We explain these more detailed overhead budgets in the next chapter.

EXHIBIT 20A.4

Factory Overhead Budget

TSC
Factory Overhead Budget
October 2013–December 2013

	October	November	December
Budgeted production (units)	820	1,340	950
Variable factory overhead rate	× $2.50	× $2.50	× $2.50
Budgeted variable overhead	2,050	3,350	2,375
Budgeted fixed overhead	1,500	1,500	1,500
Budgeted total overhead	$3,550	$4,850	$3,875

Summary

C1 Describe the importance and benefits of budgeting and the process of budget administration. Planning is a management responsibility of critical importance to business success. Budgeting is the process management uses to formalize its plans. Budgeting promotes management analysis and focuses its attention on the future. Budgeting also provides a basis for evaluating performance, serves as a source of motivation, is a means of coordinating activities, and communicates management's plans and instructions to employees. Budgeting is a detailed activity that requires administration. At least three aspects are important: budget committee, budget reporting, and budget timing. A budget committee oversees the budget preparation. The budget period pertains to the time period for which the budget is prepared such as a year or month.

C2 Describe a master budget and the process of preparing it. A master budget is a formal overall plan for a company. It consists of plans for business operations and capital expenditures, plus the financial results of those activities. The budgeting process begins with a sales budget. Based on expected sales volume, companies can budget purchases, selling expenses, and administrative expenses. Next, the capital expenditures budget is prepared, followed by the cash budget and budgeted financial statements. Manufacturers also must budget production quantities, materials purchases, labor costs, and overhead.

A1 Analyze expense planning using activity-based budgeting. Activity-based budgeting requires management to identify activities performed by departments, plan necessary activity levels, identify resources required to perform these activities, and budget the resources.

P1 Prepare each component of a master budget and link each to the budgeting process. The term *master budget* refers to a collection of individual component budgets. Each component budget is designed to guide persons responsible for activities covered by that component. A master budget must reflect the components of a company and their interaction in pursuit of company goals.

P2 Link both operating and capital expenditures budgets to budgeted financial statements. The operating budgets, capital expenditures budget, and cash budget contain much of the information to prepare a budgeted income statement for the budget period and a budgeted balance sheet at the end of the budget period. Budgeted financial statements show the expected financial consequences of the planned activities described in the budgets.

P3 Prepare production and manufacturing budgets. A manufacturer must prepare a *production budget* instead of a purchases budget. A *manufacturing budget* shows the budgeted production costs for direct materials, direct labor, and overhead.

Guidance Answers to Decision Maker and Decision Ethics

Budget Staffer Your superior's actions appear unethical because she is using private information for personal gain. As a budget staffer, you are low in the company's hierarchical structure and probably unable to confront this superior directly. You should inform an individual with a position of authority within the organization about your concerns.

Entrepreneur You must deal with two issues. First, because fashions and designs frequently change, you cannot heavily rely on previous budgets. As a result, you must carefully analyze the market to understand what designs are in vogue. This will help you plan the product mix and estimate demand. The second issue is the budgeting period. An annual sales budget may be unreliable because tastes can quickly change. Your best bet might be to prepare monthly and quarterly sales budgets that you continuously monitor and revise.

Environmental Manager You are unlikely to have data on this new position to use in preparing your budget. In this situation, you can use activity-based budgeting. This requires developing a list of activities to conduct, the resources required to perform these activities, and the expenses associated with these resources. You should challenge yourself to be absolutely certain that the listed activities are necessary and that the listed resources are required.

Guidance Answers to Quick Checks

1. Major benefits include promoting a focus on the future; providing a basis for evaluating performance; providing a source of motivation; coordinating the departments of a business; and communicating plans and instructions.
2. The budget committee's responsibility is to provide guidance to ensure that budget figures are realistic and coordinated.
3. Budget periods usually coincide with accounting periods and therefore cover a month, quarter, or a year. Budgets can also be prepared for longer time periods, such as five years.
4. Rolling budgets are budgets that are periodically revised in the ongoing process of continuous budgeting.
5. A master budget is a comprehensive or overall plan for the company that is generally expressed in monetary terms.
6. *b*
7. The master budget includes operating budgets, the capital expenditures budget, and financial budgets.
8. *c*; Computed as $(60\% \times 140) + 120 - 50 = 154$.
9. Merchandisers prepare merchandise purchases budgets; manufacturers prepare production and manufacturing budgets.
10. A just-in-time system keeps the level of inventory to a minimum and orders merchandise or materials to meet immediate sales demand. A safety stock system maintains an inventory that is large enough to meet sales demands plus an amount to satisfy unexpected sales demands and an amount to cover delayed shipments from suppliers.
11. *a*
12. (a) Operating budgets (such as sales, selling expense, and administrative budgets), (b) capital expenditures budget, (c) financial budgets: cash budget, budgeted income statement, and budgeted balance sheet.

Key Terms

Activity-based budgeting (ABB) (p. 862)
Budget (p. 848)
Budgeted balance sheet (p. 860)
Budgeted income statement (p. 860)
Budgeting (p. 848)
Capital expenditures budget (p. 858)
Cash budget (p. 858)
Continuous budgeting (p. 851)
General and administrative expense budget (p. 857)
Manufacturing budget (p. 868)
Master budget (p. 852)
Merchandise purchases budget (p. 855)
Production budget (p. 868)
Rolling budgets (p. 851)
Safety stock (p. 855)
Sales budget (p. 854)
Selling expense budget (p. 856)

Multiple Choice Quiz

Answers on p. 893 mhhe.com/wildFINMAN5e

Additional Quiz Questions are available at the book's Website.

1. A plan that reports the units or costs of merchandise to be purchased by a merchandising company during the budget period is called a
   a. Capital expenditures budget.
   b. Cash budget.
   c. Merchandise purchases budget.
   d. Selling expenses budget.
   e. Sales budget.
2. A hardware store has budgeted sales of $36,000 for its power tool department in July. Management wants to have $7,000 in power tool inventory at the end of July. Its beginning inventory of power tools is expected to be $6,000. What is the budgeted dollar amount of merchandise purchases?
   a. $36,000
   b. $43,000
   c. $42,000
   d. $35,000
   e. $37,000
3. A store has the following budgeted sales for the next five months.

May	$210,000
June	186,000
July	180,000
August	220,000
September	240,000

Cash sales are 25% of total sales and all credit sales are expected to be collected in the month following the sale. The total amount of cash expected to be received from customers in September is
   a. $240,000
   b. $225,000
   c. $ 60,000
   d. $165,000
   e. $220,000
4. A plan that shows the expected cash inflows and cash outflows during the budget period, including receipts from loans needed to maintain a minimum cash balance and repayments of such loans, is called
   a. A rolling budget.
   b. An income statement.
   c. A balance sheet.
   d. A cash budget.
   e. An operating budget.
5.[A] The following sales are predicted for a company's next four months.

	September	October	November	December
Unit sales	480	560	600	480

Each month's ending inventory of finished goods should be 30% of the next month's sales. At September 1, the finished goods inventory is 140 units. The budgeted production of units for October is
   a. 572 units.
   b. 560 units.
   c. 548 units.
   d. 600 units.
   e. 180 units.

[A] *Superscript letter A denotes assignments based on Appendix 20A, relating to production, direct materials, direct labor, and factory overhead budgets.*
Icon denotes assignments that involve decision making.

Discussion Questions

1. Identify at least three roles that budgeting plays in helping managers control and monitor a business.
2. What two common benchmarks can be used to evaluate actual performance? Which of the two is generally more useful?
3. What is the benefit of continuous budgeting?
4. Identify three usual time horizons for short-term planning and budgets.
5. Why should each department participate in preparing its own budget?
6. How does budgeting help management coordinate and plan business activities?
7. Why is the sales budget so important to the budgeting process?
8. What is a selling expense budget? What is a capital expenditures budget?
9. Budgeting promotes good decision making by requiring managers to conduct ______ and by focusing their attention on the ______.
10. **Piaggio** prepares a cash budget. What is a cash budget? Why must operating budgets and the capital expenditures budget be prepared before the cash budget? PIAGGIO
11. **KTM** regularly uses budgets. What is the difference between a production budget and a manufacturing budget? KTM
12. Would a manager of an **Apple** retail store participate more in budgeting than a manager at the corporate offices? Explain. Apple
13. Does the manager of a **Arctic Cat** distribution center participate in long-term budgeting? Explain. Arctic Cat
14. Assume that **Polaris'** snowmobile division is charged with preparing a master budget. Identify the participants—for example, the sales manager for the sales budget—and describe the information each person provides in preparing the master budget. Polaris

connect

QUICK STUDY

QS 20-1
Components of a master budget
C2

Which one of the following sets of items are all necessary components of the master budget?

1. Operating budgets, historical income statement, and budgeted balance sheet.
2. Prior sales reports, capital expenditures budget, and financial budgets.
3. Sales budget, operating budgets, and historical financial budgets.
4. Operating budgets, financial budgets, and capital expenditures budget.

QS 20-2
Budget motivation C1

The motivation of employees is one goal of budgeting. Identify three guidelines that organizations should follow if budgeting is to serve effectively as a source of motivation for employees.

QS 20-3
Merchandising: Purchases budget P1

Montel Company's July sales budget calls for sales of $600,000. The store expects to begin July with $50,000 of inventory and to end the month with $40,000 of inventory. Gross margin is typically 40% of sales. Determine the budgeted cost of merchandise purchases for July.

QS 20-4
Budgeting process C1

Good management includes good budgeting. (1) Explain why the bottom-up approach to budgeting is considered a more successful management technique than a top-down approach. (2) Provide an example of implementation of the bottom-up approach to budgeting.

QS 20-5
Computing budgeted accounts receivable
P2

Lighthouse Company anticipates total sales for June and July of $420,000 and $398,000, respectively. Cash sales are normally 60% of total sales. Of the credit sales, 20% are collected in the same month as the sale, 70% are collected during the first month after the sale, and the remaining 10% are collected in the second month. Determine the amount of accounts receivable reported on the company's budgeted balance sheet as of July 31.

QS 20-6
Cash budget
P1

Use the following information to prepare a cash budget for the month ended on March 31 for Gado Merchandising Company. The budget should show expected cash receipts and cash disbursements for the month of March and the balance expected on March 31.

a. Beginning cash balance on March 1, $72,000.
b. Cash receipts from sales, $300,000.
c. Budgeted cash disbursements for purchases, $140,000.
d. Budgeted cash disbursements for salaries, $80,000.
e. Other budgeted cash expenses, $45,000.
f. Cash repayment of bank loan, $20,000.

QS 20-7
Activity-based budgeting
A1

Activity-based budgeting is a budget system based on *expected activities.* (1) Describe activity-based budgeting, and explain its preparation of budgets. (2) How does activity-based budgeting differ from traditional budgeting?

QS 20-8[A]
Manufacturing: Production budget
P3

Forrest Company manufactures watches and has a JIT policy that ending inventory must equal 10% of the next month's sales. It estimates that October's actual ending inventory will consist of 40,000 watches. November and December sales are estimated to be 400,000 and 350,000 watches, respectively. Compute the number of watches to be produced that would appear on the company's production budget for the month of November.

QS 20-9[A]
Manufacturing: Factory overhead budget P3

Refer to information from QS 20-8. Forrest Company assigns variable overhead at the rate of $1.50 per unit of production. Fixed overhead equals $4,600,000 per month. Prepare a factory overhead budget for November.

QS 20-10
Sales budget P1

Grace sells miniature digital cameras for $250 each. 1,000 units were sold in May, and it forecasts 4% growth in unit sales each month. Determine (a) the number of camera sales and (b) the dollar amount of camera sales for the month of June.

QS 20-11
Selling expense budget P1

Refer to information from QS 20-10. Grace pays a sales manager a monthly salary of $6,000 and a commission of 8% of camera sales (in dollars). Prepare a selling expense budget for the month of June.

QS 20-12
Cash budget P1

Refer to information from QS 20-10. Assume 60% of Grace's sales are for cash. The remaining 40% are credit sales; these customers pay in the month following the sale. Compute the budgeted cash receipts for June.

QS 20-13
Budgeted financial statements P2

Following are selected accounts for a company. For each account, indicate whether it will appear on a budgeted income statement (BIS) or a budgeted balance sheet (BBS). If an item will not appear on either budgeted financial statement, label it NA.

Sales	______	Interest paid on note payable	______
Office salaries paid	______	Cash dividends paid	______
Accumulated depreciation	______	Bank loan owed	______
Amortization expense	______	Cost of goods sold	______

QS 20-14
Cash receipts P1

The Candle Shoppe reports the following sales forecast: August, $150,000; September, $170,000. Cash sales are normally 40% of total sales and all credit sales are expected to be collected in the month following the date of sale. Prepare a schedule of cash receipts for September.

QS 20-15
Cash receipts P1

Wells Company reports the following sales forecast: September, $55,000; October, $66,000; and November, $80,000. All sales are on account. Collections of credit sales are received as follows: 20% in the month of sale, 70% in the first month after sale, and 10% in the second month after sale. Prepare a schedule of cash receipts for November.

QS 20-16
Merchandising: Cash disbursements for merchandise P1

Gordands purchased $600,000 of merchandise in August and expects to purchase $720,000 in September. Merchandise purchases are paid as follows: 25% in the month of purchase and 75% in the following month. Compute cash disbursements for merchandise for September.

QS 20-17
Merchandising: Cash disbursements for merchandise P1

Meyer Co. forecasts merchandise purchases of $15,800 in January, $18,600 in February, and $20,200 in March; 40% of purchases are paid in the month of purchase and 60% are paid in the following month. At December 31 of the prior year, the balance of Accounts Payable (for December purchases) is $22,000. Prepare a schedule of cash disbursements for merchandise for each of the months of January, February, and March.

QS 20-18
Merchandising: Computing purchases P1

Raider-X Company forecasts sales of 18,000 units for April. Beginning inventory is 3,000 units. The desired ending inventory is 30% higher than the beginning inventory. How many units should Raider-X purchase in April?

QS 20-19
Merchandising: Computing purchases P1

Lexi Company forecasts unit sales of 1,040,000 in April, 1,220,000 in May, 980,000 in June, and 1,020,000 in July. Beginning inventory on April 1 is 280,000 units, and the company wants to have 30% of next month's sales in inventory at the end of each month. Prepare a merchandise purchases budget for the months of April, May, and June.

QS 20-20[A]
Manufacturing: Production budget P3

Champ, Inc. predicts the following sales in units for the coming three months:

	May	June	July
Sales in units	180	200	240

Each month's ending inventory of finished units should be 60% of the next month's sales. The April 30 finished goods inventory is 50 units. Compute Champ's budgeted production (in units) for May.

QS 20-21[A]
Manufacturing: Direct materials budget P3

Zortek Corp. budgets production of 400 units in January and 200 units in February. Each finished unit requires five pounds of raw material Z, which costs $2 per pound. Each month's ending inventory of raw materials should be 40% of the following month's budgeted production. The January 1 raw materials inventory has 130 pounds of Z. Prepare a direct materials budget for January.

QS 20-22A
Manufacturing: Direct labor budget P3

Tora Co. plans to produce 1,020 units in July. Each unit requires two hours of direct labor. The direct labor rate is $20 per hour. Prepare a direct labor budget for July.

QS 20-23
Sales budget P1

Scora, Inc., is preparing its master budget for the quarter ending March 31. It sells a single product for $50 per unit. Budgeted sales for the next four months follow. Prepare a sales budget for the months of January, February, and March.

	January	February	March	April
Sales in units	1,200	2,000	1,600	1,400

QS 20-24
Cash receipts budget P1

Refer to information in QS 20-23. In addition, sales are 40% cash and 60% on credit. All credit sales are collected in the month following the sale. The January 1 balance in accounts receivable is $15,000. Prepare a schedule of budgeted cash receipts for January, February, and March.

QS 20-25
Selling expense budget P1

Refer to information in QS 20-23. In addition, sales commissions are 10% of sales and the company pays a sales manager a salary of $6,000 per month. Sales commissions and salaries are paid in the month incurred. Prepare a selling expense budget for January, February, and March.

QS 20-26
Budgeted loan activity P1

Messers Company is preparing a cash budget for February. The company has $20,000 cash at the beginning of February and anticipates $75,000 in cash receipts and $100,250 in cash disbursements during February. What amount, if any, must the company borrow during February to maintain a $5,000 cash balance? The company has no loans outstanding on February 1.

QS 20-27
Operating budgets P1

Royal Phillips Electronics of the Netherlands reports sales of €25,400 million for a recent year. Assume that the company expects sales growth of 3 percent for the next year. Also assume that selling expenses are typically 20 percent of sales, while general and administrative expenses are 4 percent of sales.

Required

1. Compute budgeted sales for the next year.
2. Assume budgeted sales for next year is €26,000 million, and then compute budgeted selling expenses and budgeted general and administrative expenses for the next year.

EXERCISES

Exercise 20-1
Preparation of cash budgets (for three periods) P1

Kayak Co. budgeted the following cash receipts (excluding cash receipts from loans received) and cash disbursements (excluding cash disbursements for loan and interest payments) for the first three months of next year.

	Cash Receipts	Cash Disbursements
January	$525,000	$475,000
February.........	400,000	350,000
March...........	450,000	525,000

According to a credit agreement with the company's bank, Kayak promises to have a minimum cash balance of $30,000 at each month-end. In return, the bank has agreed that the company can borrow up to $150,000 at an annual interest rate of 12%, paid on the last day of each month. The interest is computed based on the beginning balance of the loan for the month. The company has a cash balance of $30,000 and a loan balance of $60,000 at January 1. Prepare monthly cash budgets for each of the first three months of next year.

Check January ending cash balance, $30,000

Exercise 20-2
Merchandising: Preparation of purchases budgets (for three periods) P1

Walker Company prepares monthly budgets. The current budget plans for a September ending inventory of 30,000 units. Company policy is to end each month with merchandise inventory equal to a specified percent of budgeted sales for the following month. Budgeted sales and merchandise purchases for the three most recent months follow. (1) Prepare the merchandise purchases budget for the months of July, August, and September. (2) Compute the ratio of ending inventory to the next month's sales for each budget prepared in part 1. (3) How many units are budgeted for sale in October?

	Sales (Units)	Purchases (Units)
July	180,000	200,250
August	315,000	308,250
September	270,000	259,500

Exercise 20-3
Merchandising: Preparation of a cash budget
P1

Use the following information to prepare the July cash budget for Acco Co. It should show expected cash receipts and cash disbursements for the month and the cash balance expected on July 31.

a. Beginning cash balance on July 1: $50,000.

b. Cash receipts from sales: 30% is collected in the month of sale, 50% in the next month, and 20% in the second month after sale (uncollectible accounts are negligible and can be ignored). Sales amounts are: May (actual), $1,720,000; June (actual), $1,200,000; and July (budgeted), $1,400,000.

c. Payments on merchandise purchases: 60% in the month of purchase and 40% in the month following purchase. Purchases amounts are: June (actual), $700,000; and July (budgeted), $750,000.

d. Budgeted cash disbursements for salaries in July: $275,000.

e. Budgeted depreciation expense for July: $36,000.

f. Other cash expenses budgeted for July: $200,000.

g. Accrued income taxes due in July: $80,000.

h. Bank loan interest due in July: $6,600.

Check Ending cash balance, $122,400

Exercise 20-4
Merchandising: Preparing a budgeted income statement and balance sheet
P2

Use the information in Exercise 20-3 and the following additional information to prepare a budgeted income statement for the month of July and a budgeted balance sheet for July 31.

a. Cost of goods sold is 55% of sales.

b. Inventory at the end of June is $80,000 and at the end of July is $60,000.

c. Salaries payable on June 30 are $50,000 and are expected to be $60,000 on July 31.

d. The equipment account balance is $1,600,000 on July 31. On June 30, the accumulated depreciation on equipment is $280,000.

e. The $6,600 cash payment of interest represents the 1% monthly expense on a bank loan of $660,000.

f. Income taxes payable on July 31 are $30,720, and the income tax rate applicable to the company is 30%.

g. The only other balance sheet accounts are: Common Stock, with a balance of $600,000 on June 30; and Retained Earnings, with a balance of $964,000 on June 30.

Check Net income, $71,680; Total assets, $2,686,400

Exercise 20-5
Merchandising: Computing budgeted cash payments for purchases
P1

Hardy Company's cost of goods sold is consistently 60% of sales. The company plans to carry ending merchandise inventory for each month equal to 20% of the next month's budgeted cost of good sold. All merchandise is purchased on credit, and 50% of the purchases made during a month is paid for in that month. Another 35% is paid for during the first month after purchase, and the remaining 15% is paid for during the second month after purchase. Expected sales are: August (actual), $325,000; September (actual), $320,000; October (estimated), $250,000; November (estimated), $310,000. Use this information to determine October's expected cash payments for purchases. (*Hint:* Use the layout of Exhibit 20.8, but revised for the facts given here.)

Check Budgeted purchases: August, $194,400; October, $157,200

Exercise 20-6
Merchandising: Computing budgeted purchases and costs of goods sold
P1

Quick Dollar Company purchases all merchandise on credit. It recently budgeted the following month-end accounts payable balances and merchandise inventory balances. Cash payments on accounts payable during each month are expected to be: May, $1,600,000; June, $1,490,000; July, $1,425,000; and August, $1,495,000. Use the available information to compute the budgeted amounts of (1) merchandise purchases for June, July, and August and (2) cost of goods sold for June, July, and August.

	Accounts Payable	Merchandise Inventory
May 31	$150,000	$250,000
June 30	200,000	400,000
July 31.	235,000	300,000
August 31.	195,000	330,000

Check June purchases, $1,540,000; June cost of goods sold, $1,390,000

Exercise 20-7
Merchandising: Computing budgeted accounts payable and purchases—sales forecast in dollars
P1 P2

Check July purchases, $236,600; Sept. payments on accts. pay., $214,235

Big Sound, a merchandising company specializing in home computer speakers, budgets its monthly cost of goods sold to equal 70% of sales. Its inventory policy calls for ending inventory in each month to equal 20% of the next month's budgeted cost of goods sold. All purchases are on credit, and 25% of the purchases in a month is paid for in the same month. Another 60% is paid for during the first month after purchase, and the remaining 15% is paid for in the second month after purchase. The following sales budgets are set: July, $350,000; August, $290,000; September, $320,000; October, $275,000; and November, $265,000. Compute the following: (1) budgeted merchandise purchases for July, August, September, and October; (2) budgeted payments on accounts payable for September and October; and (3) budgeted ending balances of accounts payable for September and October. (*Hint:* For part 1, refer to Exhibits 20.7 and 20.8 for guidance, but note that budgeted sales are in dollars for this assignment.)

Exercise 20-8A
Manufacturing: Preparing production budgets (for two periods) P3

Check Second quarter production, 480,000 units

Electro Company manufactures an innovative automobile transmission for electric cars. Management predicts that ending inventory for the first quarter will be 75,000 units. The following unit sales of the transmissions are expected during the rest of the year: second quarter, 450,000 units; third quarter, 525,000 units; and fourth quarter, 475,000 units. Company policy calls for the ending inventory of a quarter to equal 20% of the next quarter's budgeted sales. Prepare a production budget for both the second and third quarters that shows the number of transmissions to manufacture.

Exercise 20-9A
Manufacturing: Direct materials budget
P3

Refer to information from Exercise 20-8. Each transmission requires 0.80 pounds of a key raw material. Electro Company aims to end each quarter with an ending inventory of direct materials equal to 50% of next quarter's budgeted materials requirements. Direct materials cost $170 per unit. Prepare a direct materials budget for the second quarter.

Exercise 20-10A
Manufacturing: Direct labor budget P3

Refer to information from Exercise 20-8. Each transmission requires 4 direct labor hours, at a cost of $12 per hour. Prepare a direct labor budget for the second quarter.

Exercise 20-11
Merchandising: Budgeted cash disbursements
P1

Hector Company reports the following:

	July	August	September
Sales	$50,000	$72,000	$66,000
Purchases	14,400	19,200	21,600

Payments for purchases are made in the month after purchase. Selling expenses are 10% of sales, administrative expenses are 8% of sales, and both are paid in the month of sale. Rent expense of $7,400 is paid monthly. Depreciation expense is $2,300 per month. Prepare a schedule of budgeted cash disbursements for August and September.

Exercise 20-12
Budgeted cash receipts
P1

Jasper Company has sales on account and sales for cash. Specifically, 70% of its sales are on account and 30% are for cash. Credit sales are collected in full in the month following the sale. The company forecasts sales of $525,000 for April, $535,000 for May, and $560,000 for June. The beginning balance of Accounts Receivable is $400,000 on April 1. Prepare a schedule of budgeted cash receipts for April, May, and June.

Exercise 20-13
Cash budget
P1

Karim Corp. requires a minimum $8,000 cash balance. If necessary, loans are taken to meet this requirement at a cost of 1% interest per month (paid monthly). Any excess cash is used to repay loans at month-end. The cash balance on July 1 is $8,400 and the company has no outstanding loans. Forecasted cash receipts (other than for loans received) and forecasted cash payments (other than for loan or interest payments) are:

	July	August	September
Cash receipts	$20,000	$26,000	$40,000
Cash disbursements	28,000	30,000	22,000

Prepare a cash budget for July, August, and September. Round interest payments to the nearest whole dollar.

Exercise 20-14
Cash budget
P1

Foyert Corp. requires a minimum $30,000 cash balance. If necessary, loans are taken to meet this requirement at a cost of 1% interest per month (paid monthly). Any excess cash is used to repay loans at month-end. The cash balance on October 1 is $30,000 and the company has an outstanding loan of $10,000. Forecasted cash receipts (other than for loans received) and forecasted cash payments (other than for loan or interest payments) follow. Prepare a cash budget for October, November, and December. Round interest payments to the nearest whole dollar.

	October	November	December
Cash receipts	$110,000	$80,000	$100,000
Cash disbursements	120,000	75,000	80,000

Exercise 20-15
Merchandising: Cash budget
P1

Castor, Inc. is preparing its master budget for the quarter ended June 30. Budgeted sales and cash payments for merchandise for the next three months follow:

	April	May	June
Budgeted sales	$32,000	$40,000	$24,000
Budgeted cash payments for merchandise	20,200	16,800	17,200

Sales are 50% cash and 50% on credit. All credit sales are collected in the month following the sale. The March 30 balance sheet includes balances of $12,000 in cash, $12,000 in accounts receivable, $11,000 in accounts payable, and a $2,000 balance in loans payable. A minimum cash balance of $12,000 is required. Loans are obtained at the end of any month when a cash shortage occurs. Interest is 1% per month based on the beginning of the month loan balance and is paid at each month-end. If an excess balance of cash exists, loans are repaid at the end of the month. Operating expenses are paid in the month incurred and consist of sales commissions (10% of sales), shipping (2% of sales), office salaries ($5,000 per month) and rent ($3,000 per month). Prepare a cash budget for each of the months of April, May, and June (round all dollar amounts to the nearest whole dollar).

Exercise 20-16
Merchandising: Cash budget
P1

Kelsey is preparing its master budget for the quarter ended September 30. Budgeted sales and cash payments for merchandise for the next three months follow:

	July	August	September
Budgeted sales	$64,000	$80,000	$48,000
Budgeted cash payments for merchandise	40,400	33,600	34,400

Sales are 20% cash and 80% on credit. All credit sales are collected in the month following the sale. The June 30 balance sheet includes balances of $15,000 in cash; $45,000 in accounts receivable; $4,500 in accounts payable; and a $5,000 balance in loans payable. A minimum cash balance of $15,000 is required. Loans are obtained at the end of any month when a cash shortage occurs. Interest is 1% per month based on the beginning of the month loan balance and is paid at each month-end. If an excess balance of cash exists, loans are repaid at the end of the month. Operating expenses are paid in the month incurred and consist of sales commissions (10% of sales), office salaries ($4,000 per month), and rent ($6,500 per month). (1) Prepare a cash receipts budget for July, August, and September. (2) Prepare a cash budget for each of the months of July, August, and September. (Round all dollar amounts to the nearest whole dollar.)

Exercise 20-17
Merchandising: Budgeted balance sheet
P2

The following information is available for Zetrov Company:

a. The cash budget for March shows an ending bank loan of $10,000 and an ending cash balance of $50,000.

b. The sales budget for March indicates sales of $140,000. Accounts receivable are expected to be 70% of the current-month sales.

c. The merchandise purchases budget indicates that $89,000 in merchandise will be purchased on account in March. Purchases on account are paid 100% in the month following the purchase. Ending inventory for March is predicted to be 600 units at a cost of $35 each.

d. The budgeted income statement for March shows net income of $48,000. Depreciation expense of $1,000 and $26,000 in income tax expense were used in computing net income for March. Accrued taxes will be paid in April.

e. The balance sheet for February shows equipment of $84,000 with accumulated depreciation of $46,000, common stock of $25,000, and ending retained earnings of $8,000. There are no changes budgeted in the equipment or common stock accounts.

Prepare a budgeted balance sheet for March.

Exercise 20-18
Merchandising: Budgeted income statement
P2

Fortune, Inc., is preparing its master budget for the first quarter. The company sells a single product at a price of $25 per unit. Sales (in units) are forecasted at 45,000 for January, 55,000 for February, and 50,000 for March. Cost of goods sold is $14 per unit. Other expense information for the first quarter follows. Prepare a budgeted income statement for this first quarter.

Commissions	8% of sales
Rent	$14,000 per month
Advertising	15% of sales
Office salaries	$75,000 per month
Depreciation	$40,000 per month
Interest	15% annually on a $250,000 note payable
Tax rate.	30%

Exercise 20-19^A
Manufacturing: Direct labor budget
P3

The production budget for Manner Company shows units to be produced as follows: July, 620; August, 680; September, 540. Each unit produced requires two hours of direct labor. The direct labor rate is currently $20 per hour but is predicted to be $21 per hour in September. Prepare a direct labor budget for the months July, August, and September.

Exercise 20-20^A
Manufacturing: Production budget
P3

Hospitable Co. provides the following sales forecast for the next four months:

	April	May	June	July
Sales (units)	500	580	540	620

The company wants to end each month with ending finished goods inventory equal to 25% of next month's sales. Finished goods inventory on April 1 is 190 units. Assume July's budgeted production is 540 units. Prepare a production budget for the months of April, May, and June.

Exercise 20-21^A
Manufacturing: Direct materials budget P3

Refer to the information in Exercise 20-20. In addition, assume each finished unit requires five pounds of raw materials and the company wants to end each month with raw materials inventory equal to 30% of next month's production needs. Beginning raw materials inventory for April was 663 pounds.

Prepare a direct materials budget for April, May, and June.

Exercise 20-22
Master budget definitions
C2

Match the definitions 1 through 9 with the term or phrase a through i.

A. Budget
B. Merchandise purchases budget
C. Cash budget
D. Safety stock
E. Budgeted income statement
F. General and administrative expense budget
G. Sales budget
H. Master budget
I. Budgeted balance sheet

_____ **1.** A comprehensive business plan that includes specific plans for expected sales, the units of product to be produced, the merchandise or materials to be purchased, the expenses to be incurred, the long-term assets to be purchased, and the amounts of cash to be borrowed or loans to be repaid, as well as a budgeted income statement and balance sheet.

_____ **2.** A quantity of inventory or materials over the minimum to reduce the risk of running short.

_____ **3.** A plan showing the units of goods to be sold and the sales to be derived; the usual starting point in the budgeting process.

_____ **4.** An accounting report that presents predicted amounts of the company's revenues and expenses for the budgeting period.

_____ **5.** An accounting report that presents predicted amounts of the company's assets, liabilities, and equity balances at the end of the budget period.

_____ **6.** A plan that shows the units or costs of merchandise to be purchased by a merchandising company during the budget period.

_____ **7.** A formal statement of a company's future plans, usually expressed in monetary terms.

_____ **8.** A plan that shows predicted operating expenses not included in the selling expenses budget.

_____ **9.** A plan that shows the expected cash inflows and cash outflows during the budget period, including receipts from any loans needed to maintain a minimum cash balance and repayments of such loans.

Exercise 20-23
Budget consequences C1

Participatory budgeting can sometimes lead to negative consequences. Identify three potential negative outcomes that can arise from participatory budgeting.

Exercise 20-24
Activity-based budgeting
A1

Render Co. CPA is preparing activity-based budgets for 2013. The partners expect the firm to generate billable hours for the year as follows:

Data entry	2,200 hours
Auditing	4,800 hours
Tax	4,300 hours
Consulting	750 hours

The company pays $10 per hour to data-entry clerks, $40 per hour to audit personnel, $50 per hour to tax personnel, and $50 per hour to consulting personnel. Prepare a schedule of budgeted labor costs for 2013 using activity-based budgeting.

Exercise 20-25
Manufacturing: Direct materials budget
P3

Rida, Inc., a manufacturer in a seasonal industry, is preparing its direct materials budget for the second quarter. It forecasts sales of 225,000 units in the second quarter and 262,500 units in the third quarter. It also plans production of 52,500 units for the third quarter. Based on this information, the company plans to produce 240,000 units in the second quarter. Other information is as follows:

Direct materials	Each unit requires 0.60 pounds of a key raw material, priced at $175 per pound. The company plans to end each quarter with an ending inventory of materials equal to 50% of next quarter's budgeted materials requirements.
Direct labor	Each finished unit requires 4 direct labor hours, at a cost of $9 per hour.
Variable overhead	Applied at the rate of $11 per direct labor hour.
Fixed overhead	Budgeted at $450,000 per quarter

Prepare a direct materials budget for the second quarter.

Exercise 20-26
Manufacturing: Direct labor and factory overhead budgets
P3

Refer to Exercise 20-25. For the second quarter, prepare (1) a direct labor budget and (2) a factory overhead budget.

Exercise 20-27
Manufacturing: Direct materials budget
P3

Rad Co. provides the following sales forecast and production budget for the next four months:

	April	May	June	July
Sales (units)	500	580	530	600
Budgeted production (units)	442	570	544	540

The company plans for finished goods inventory of 120 units at the end of June. In addition, each finished unit requires five pounds of raw materials and the company wants to end each month with raw materials inventory equal to 30% of next month's production needs. Beginning raw materials inventory for April was 663 pounds. Each finished unit requires 0.50 hours of direct labor at the rate of $16 per hour. The company budgets variable overhead at the rate of $20 per direct labor hour and budgets fixed overhead of $8,000 per month. Prepare a raw materials budget for April, May, and June.

Exercise 20-28
Manufacturing: Direct labor and factory overhead budgets
P3

Refer to Exercise 20-27. For April, May, and June, prepare (1) a direct labor budget and (2) a factory overhead budget.

connect

PROBLEM SET A

Problem 20-1A
Merchandising: Preparation and analysis of purchases budgets
C2 P1

mhhe.com/wildFINMAN5e

Keggler's Supply is a merchandiser of three different products. The company's February 28 inventories are footwear, 20,000 units; sports equipment, 80,000 units; and apparel, 50,000 units. Management believes that excessive inventories have accumulated for all three products. As a result, a new policy dictates that ending inventory in any month should equal 30% of the expected unit sales for the following month. Expected sales in units for March, April, May, and June follow.

	Budgeted Sales in Units			
	March	April	May	June
Footwear	15,000	25,000	32,000	35,000
Sports equipment	70,000	90,000	95,000	90,000
Apparel	40,000	38,000	37,000	25,000

Required

1. Prepare a merchandise purchases budget (in units) for each product for each of the months of March, April, and May.

Check (1) March budgeted purchases Footwear, 2,500; Sports equip., 17,000; Apparel, 1,400

Analysis Component

2. The purchases budgets in part 1 should reflect fewer purchases of all three products in March compared to those in April and May. What factor caused fewer purchases to be planned? Suggest business conditions that would cause this factor to both occur and impact the company in this way.

Problem 20-2A
Merchandising: Preparation of cash budgets (for three periods)
C2 P2

mhhe.com/wildFINMAN5e

During the last week of August, Oneida Company's owner approaches the bank for an $100,000 loan to be made on September 2 and repaid on November 30 with annual interest of 12%, for an interest cost of $3,000. The owner plans to increase the store's inventory by $80,000 during September and needs the loan to pay for inventory acquisitions. The bank's loan officer needs more information about Oneida's ability to repay the loan and asks the owner to forecast the store's November 30 cash position. On September 1, Oneida is expected to have a $5,000 cash balance, $159,100 of accounts receivable, and $125,000 of accounts payable. Its budgeted sales, merchandise purchases, and various cash disbursements for the next three months follow.

	Budgeted Figures*	September	October	November
1	Budgeted Figures*	September	October	November
2	Sales	$250,000	$375,000	$400,000
3	Merchandise purchases	240,000	225,000	200,000
4	Cash disbursements			
5	Payroll	20,000	22,000	24,000
6	Rent	10,000	10,000	10,000
7	Other cash expenses	35,000	30,000	20,000
8	Repayment of bank loan			100,000
9	Interest on the bank loan			3,000

* Operations began in August; August sales were $215,000 and purchases were $125,000.

The budgeted September merchandise purchases include the inventory increase. All sales are on account. The company predicts that 25% of credit sales is collected in the month of the sale, 45% in the month following the sale, 20% in the second month, 9% in the third, and the remainder is uncollectible. Applying these percents to the August credit sales, for example, shows that $96,750 of the $215,000 will be collected in September, $43,000 in October, and $19,350 in November. All merchandise is purchased on credit; 80% of the balance is paid in the month following a purchase, and the remaining 20% is paid in the second month. For example, of the $125,000 August purchases, $100,000 will be paid in September and $25,000 in October.

Required

Prepare a cash budget for September, October, and November for Oneida Company. Show supporting calculations as needed.

Check Budgeted cash balance: September, $99,250; October, $69,500; November, $22,600

Problem 20-3A
Merchandising: Preparation and analysis of cash budgets with supporting inventory and purchases budgets
C2 P2

Aztec Company sells its product for $180 per unit. Its actual and projected sales follow.

	Units	Dollars
April (actual)	4,000	$ 720,000
May (actual)	2,000	360,000
June (budgeted)	6,000	1,080,000
July (budgeted)	5,000	900,000
August (budgeted)	3,800	684,000

All sales are on credit. Recent experience shows that 20% of credit sales is collected in the month of the sale, 50% in the month after the sale, 28% in the second month after the sale, and 2% proves to be uncollectible. The product's purchase price is $110 per unit. All purchases are payable within 12 days. Thus, 60% of purchases made in a month is paid in that month and the other 40% is paid in the next month. The company has a policy to maintain an ending monthly inventory of 20% of the next month's unit sales plus a safety stock of 100 units. The April 30 and May 31 actual inventory levels are consistent with this policy. Selling and administrative expenses for the year are $1,320,000 and are paid evenly throughout the year in cash. The company's minimum cash balance at month-end is $100,000. This minimum is maintained, if necessary, by borrowing cash from the bank. If the balance exceeds $100,000, the company repays as much of the loan as it can without going below the minimum. This type of loan carries an annual 12% interest rate. On May 31, the loan balance is $25,000, and the company's cash balance is $100,000. (Round amounts to the nearest dollar.)

Required

1. Prepare a table that shows the computation of cash collections of its credit sales (accounts receivable) in each of the months of June and July.
2. Prepare a table that shows the computation of budgeted ending inventories (in units) for April, May, June, and July.
3. Prepare the merchandise purchases budget for May, June, and July. Report calculations in units and then show the dollar amount of purchases for each month.
4. Prepare a table showing the computation of cash payments on product purchases for June and July.
5. Prepare a cash budget for June and July, including any loan activity and interest expense. Compute the loan balance at the end of each month.

Check (1) Cash collections: June, $597,600; July, $820,800

(3) Budgeted purchases: May, $308,000; June, $638,000

(5) Budgeted ending loan balance: June, $43,650; July, $0

Analysis Component

6. Refer to your answer to part 5. Aztec's cash budget indicates the company will need to borrow more than $18,000 in June. Suggest some reasons that knowing this information in May would be helpful to management.

Problem 20-4A
Merchandising: Preparation and analysis of budgeted income statements
C2 P2

Merline, a one-product mail-order firm, buys its product for $75 per unit and sells it for $150 per unit. The sales staff receives a 10% commission on the sale of each unit. Its December income statement follows.

MERLINE COMPANY
Income Statement
For Month Ended December 31, 2013

Sales	$2,250,000
Cost of goods sold	1,125,000
Gross profit	1,125,000
Expenses	
Sales commissions (10%)	225,000
Advertising	250,000
Store rent	30,000
Administrative salaries	45,000
Depreciation	50,000
Other expenses	10,000
Total expenses	610,000
Net income	$ 515,000

Management expects December's results to be repeated in January, February, and March of 2014 without any changes in strategy. Management, however, has an alternative plan. It believes that unit sales will increase at a rate of 10% *each* month for the next three months (beginning with January) if the item's selling price is reduced to $125 per unit and advertising expenses are increased by 15% and remain at that level for all three months. The cost of its product will remain at $75 per unit, the sales staff will continue to earn a 10% commission, and the remaining expenses will stay the same.

Required

Check (1) Budgeted net income: January, $196,250; February, $258,125; March, $326,187

1. Prepare budgeted income statements for each of the months of January, February, and March that show the expected results from implementing the proposed changes. Use a three-column format, with one column for each month.

Analysis Component

2. Use the budgeted income statements from part 1 to recommend whether management should implement the proposed changes. Explain.

Problem 20-5A
Merchandising: Preparation of a complete master budget
C2 P1 P2

Near the end of 2013, the management of Dimsdale Sports Co., a merchandising company, prepared the following estimated balance sheet for December 31, 2013.

DIMSDALE SPORTS COMPANY
Estimated Balance Sheet
December 31, 2013

Assets			Liabilities and Equity		
Cash	$ 36,000		Accounts payable	$360,000	
Accounts receivable	525,000		Bank loan payable	15,000	
Inventory	150,000		Taxes payable (due 3/15/2014)	90,000	
Total current assets		$ 711,000	Total liabilities		$465,000
Equipment	540,000		Common stock	472,500	
Less accumulated depreciation	67,500		Retained earnings	246,000	
Equipment, net		472,500	Total stockholders' equity		718,500
Total assets		$1,183,500	Total liabilities and equity		$1,183,500

To prepare a master budget for January, February, and March of 2014, management gathers the following information.

a. Dimsdale Sports' single product is purchased for $30 per unit and resold for $55 per unit. The expected inventory level of 5,000 units on December 31, 2013, is more than management's desired level for 2014, which is 20% of the next month's expected sales (in units). Expected sales are: January, 7,000 units; February, 9,000 units; March, 11,000 units; and April, 10,000 units.

b. Cash sales and credit sales represent 25% and 75%, respectively, of total sales. Of the credit sales, 60% is collected in the first month after the month of sale and 40% in the second month after the month of sale. For the December 31, 2013, accounts receivable balance, $125,000 is collected in January and the remaining $400,000 is collected in February.

c. Merchandise purchases are paid for as follows: 20% in the first month after the month of purchase and 80% in the second month after the month of purchase. For the December 31, 2013, accounts payable balance, $80,000 is paid in January and the remaining $280,000 is paid in February.

d. Sales commissions equal to 20% of sales are paid each month. Sales salaries (excluding commissions) are $60,000 per year.

e. General and administrative salaries are $144,000 per year. Maintenance expense equals $2,000 per month and is paid in cash.

f. Equipment reported in the December 31, 2013, balance sheet was purchased in January 2013. It is being depreciated over eight years under the straight-line method with no salvage value. The following amounts for new equipment purchases are planned in the coming quarter: January, $36,000; February, $96,000; and March, $28,800. This equipment will be depreciated under the straight-line method over eight years with no salvage value. A full month's depreciation is taken for the month in which equipment is purchased.

g. The company plans to acquire land at the end of March at a cost of $150,000, which will be paid with cash on the last day of the month.

h. Dimsdale Sports has a working arrangement with its bank to obtain additional loans as needed. The interest rate is 12% per year, and interest is paid at each month-end based on the beginning balance. Partial or full payments on these loans can be made on the last day of the month. The company has agreed to maintain a minimum ending cash balance of $25,000 in each month.

i. The income tax rate for the company is 40%. Income taxes on the first quarter's income will not be paid until April 15.

Required

Prepare a master budget for each of the first three months of 2014; include the following component budgets (show supporting calculations as needed, and round amounts to the nearest dollar):

1. Monthly sales budgets (showing both budgeted unit sales and dollar sales).

2. Monthly merchandise purchases budgets.

3. Monthly selling expense budgets.

4. Monthly general and administrative expense budgets.

5. Monthly capital expenditures budgets.

6. Monthly cash budgets.

7. Budgeted income statement for the entire first quarter (not for each month).

8. Budgeted balance sheet as of March 31, 2014.

Check (2) Budgeted purchases: January, $114,000; February, $282,000
(3) Budgeted selling expenses: January, $82,000; February, $104,000
(6) Ending cash bal.: January, $30,100; February, $210,300
(8) Budgeted total assets at March 31, $1,568,650

Problem 20-6A[A]
Manufacturing: Preparing production and manufacturing budgets
C2 P3

Black Diamond Company produces snow skis. Each ski requires 2 pounds of carbon fiber. The company's management predicts that 5,000 skis and 6,000 pounds of carbon fiber will be in inventory on June 30 of the current year and that 150,000 skis will be sold during the next (third) quarter. A set of two skis sells for $300. Management wants to end the third quarter with 3,500 skis and 4,000 pounds of carbon fiber in inventory. Carbon fiber can be purchased for $15 per pound. Each ski requires 0.5 hours of direct labor at $20 per hour. Variable overhead is applied at the rate of $8 per direct labor hour. The company budgets fixed overhead of $1,782,000 for the quarter.

Required

1. Prepare the third-quarter production budget for skis.

2. Prepare the third-quarter direct materials (carbon fiber) budget; include the dollar cost of purchases.

Check (1) Units manuf., 148,500; (2) Cost of carbon fiber purchases, $4,425,000

[continued on next page]

3. Prepare the direct labor budget for the third quarter.
4. Prepare the factory overhead budget for the third quarter.

Problem 20-7A
Manufacturing: Preparation of a complete master budget
C2 P1 P2 P3

The management of Zigby Manufacturing prepared the following estimated balance sheet for March, 2013:

ZIGBY MANUFACTURING
Estimated Balance Sheet
March 31, 2013

Assets		Liabilities and Equity	
Cash	$ 40,000	Accounts payable	$ 200,500
Accounts receivable	342,248	Short-term notes payable	12,000
Raw materials inventory	98,500	Total current liabilities	212,500
Finished goods inventory	325,540	Long-term note payable	500,000
Total current assets	806,288	Total liabilities	712,500
Equipment, gross	600,000	Common stock	335,000
Accumulated depreciation	(150,000)	Retained earnings	208,788
Equipment, net	450,000	Total stockholders' equity	543,788
Total assets	$1,256,288	Total liabilities and equity	$1,256,288

To prepare a master budget for April, May, and June of 2013, management gathers the following information:

a. Sales for March total 20,500 units. Forecasted sales in units are as follows: April, 20,500; May, 19,500; June, 20,000; July, 20,500. Sales of 240,000 units are forecasted for the entire year. The product's selling price is $23.85 per unit and its total product cost is $19.85 per unit.

b. Company policy calls for a given month's ending raw materials inventory to equal 50% of the next month's materials requirements. The March 31 raw materials inventory is 4,925 units, which complies with the policy. The expected June 30 ending raw materials inventory is 4,000 units. Raw materials cost $20 per unit. Each finished unit requires 0.50 units of raw materials.

c. Company policy calls for a given month's ending finished goods inventory to equal 80% of the next month's expected unit sales. The March 31 finished goods inventory is 16,400 units, which complies with the policy.

d. Each finished unit requires 0.50 hours of direct labor at a rate of $15 per hour.

e. Overhead is allocated based on direct labor hours. The predetermined variable overhead rate is $2.70 per direct labor hour. Depreciation of $20,000 per month is treated as fixed factory overhead.

f. Sales representatives' commissions are 8% of sales and are paid in the month of the sales. The sales manager's monthly salary is $3,000 per month.

g. Monthly general and administrative expenses include $12,000 administrative salaries and 0.9% monthly interest on the long-term note payable.

h. The company expects 30% of sales to be for cash and the remaining 70% on credit. Receivables are collected in full in the month following the sale (none is collected in the month of the sale).

i. All raw materials purchases are on credit, and no payables arise from any other transactions. One month's raw materials purchases are fully paid in the next month.

j. The minimum ending cash balance for all months is $40,000. If necessary, the company borrows enough cash using a short-term note to reach the minimum. Short-term notes require an interest payment of 1% at each month-end (before any repayment). If the ending cash balance exceeds the minimum, the excess will be applied to repaying the short-term notes payable balance.

k. Dividends of $10,000 are to be declared and paid in May.

l. No cash payments for income taxes are to be made during the second calendar quarter. Income tax will be assessed at 35% in the quarter and paid in the third calendar quarter.

m. Equipment purchases of $130,000 are budgeted for the last day of June.

Required

Prepare the following budgets and other financial information as required. All budgets and other financial information should be prepared for the second calendar quarter, except as otherwise noted below. Round calculations up to the nearest whole dollar, except for the amount of cash sales, which should be rounded down to the nearest whole dollar.

1. Sales budget.
2. Production budget.
3. Raw materials budget.
4. Direct labor budget.
5. Factory overhead budget.
6. Selling expense budget.
7. General and administrative expense budget.
8. Cash budget.
9. Budgeted income statement for the entire first quarter (not for each month separately).
10. Budgeted statement of retained earnings.
11. Budgeted balance sheet as of the end of the second calendar quarter.

Check (2) Units to produce: April, 19,700; May, 19,900
(3) Cost of raw materials purchases, April, $198,000
(5) Total overhead cost, May, $46,865
(8) Ending cash balance: April, $83,346; May, $124,295
(10) Budgeted total assets, June 30: $1,299,440

PROBLEM SET B

Problem 20-1B
Merchandising: Preparation and analysis of purchases budgets
C2 P1

H20 Sports Company is a merchandiser of three different products. The company's March 31 inventories are water skis, 40,000 units; tow ropes, 90,000 units; and life jackets, 150,000 units. Management believes that excessive inventories have accumulated for all three products. As a result, a new policy dictates that ending inventory in any month should equal 10% of the expected unit sales for the following month. Expected sales in units for April, May, June, and July follow.

	Budgeted Sales in Units			
	April	May	June	July
Water skis	70,000	90,000	130,000	100,000
Tow ropes	100,000	90,000	110,000	100,000
Life jackets	160,000	190,000	200,000	120,000

Required

1. Prepare a merchandise purchases budget (in units) for each product for each of the months of April, May, and June.

Check (1) April budgeted purchases: Water skis, 39,000; Tow ropes, 19,000; Life jackets, 29,000

Analysis Component

2. The purchases budgets in part 1 should reflect fewer purchases of all three products in April compared to those in May and June. What factor caused fewer purchases to be planned? Suggest business conditions that would cause this factor to both occur and affect the company as it has.

Problem 20-2B
Merchandising: Preparation of cash budgets (for three periods)
C2 P2

During the last week of March, Sony Stereo's owner approaches the bank for a $80,000 loan to be made on April 1 and repaid on June 30 with annual interest of 12%, for an interest cost of $2,400. The owner plans to increase the store's inventory by $60,000 in April and needs the loan to pay for inventory acquisitions. The bank's loan officer needs more information about Sony Stereo's ability to repay the loan and asks the owner to forecast the store's June 30 cash position. On April 1, Sony Stereo is expected to have a $3,000 cash balance, $135,000 of accounts receivable, and $100,000 of accounts payable. Its budgeted sales, merchandise purchases, and various cash disbursements for the next three months follow.

	Budgeted Figures*	April	May	June
2	Sales	$220,000	$300,000	$380,000
3	Merchandise purchases	210,000	180,000	220,000
4	Cash disbursements			
5	Payroll	16,000	17,000	18,000
6	Rent	6,000	6,000	6,000
7	Other cash expenses	64,000	8,000	7,000
8	Repayment of bank loan			80,000
9	Interest on the bank loan.........			2,400

*Operations began in March; March sales were $180,000 and purchases were $100,000.

The budgeted April merchandise purchases include the inventory increase. All sales are on account. The company predicts that 25% of credit sales is collected in the month of the sale, 45% in the month following the sale, 20% in the second month, 9% in the third, and the remainder is uncollectible. Applying these percents to the March credit sales, for example, shows that $81,000 of the $180,000 will be collected in April, $36,000 in May, and $16,200 in June. All merchandise is purchased on credit; 80% of the balance is paid in the month following a purchase and the remaining 20% is paid in the second month. For example, of the $100,000 March purchases, $80,000 will be paid in April and $20,000 in May.

Check Budgeted cash balance: April, $53,000; May, $44,000; June, $34,800

Required

Prepare a cash budget for April, May, and June for Sony Stereo. Show supporting calculations as needed.

Problem 20-3B
Merchandising: Preparation and analysis of cash budgets with supporting inventory and purchases budgets
C2 P2

Connick Company sells its product for $22 per unit. Its actual and projected sales follow.

	Units	Dollars
January (actual)	18,000	$396,000
February (actual)	22,500	495,000
March (budgeted)	19,000	418,000
April (budgeted)	18,750	412,500
May (budgeted)	21,000	462,000

All sales are on credit. Recent experience shows that 40% of credit sales is collected in the month of the sale, 35% in the month after the sale, 23% in the second month after the sale, and 2% proves to be uncollectible. The product's purchase price is $12 per unit. All purchases are payable within 21 days. Thus, 30% of purchases made in a month is paid in that month and the other 70% is paid in the next month. The company has a policy to maintain an ending monthly inventory of 20% of the next month's unit sales plus a safety stock of 100 units. The January 31 and February 28 actual inventory levels are consistent with this policy. Selling and administrative expenses for the year are $1,920,000 and are paid evenly throughout the year in cash. The company's minimum cash balance for month-end is $50,000. This minimum is maintained, if necessary, by borrowing cash from the bank. If the balance exceeds $50,000, the company repays as much of the loan as it can without going below the minimum. This type of loan carries an annual 12% interest rate. At February 28, the loan balance is $12,000, and the company's cash balance is $50,000.

Required

Check (1) Cash collections: March, $431,530; April, $425,150

(3) Budgeted purchases: February, $261,600; March, $227,400

(5) Ending cash balance: March, $58,070, April, $94,920

1. Prepare a table that shows the computation of cash collections of its credit sales (accounts receivable) in each of the months of March and April.
2. Prepare a table showing the computations of budgeted ending inventories (units) for January, February, March, and April.
3. Prepare the merchandise purchases budget for February, March, and April. Report calculations in units and then show the dollar amount of purchases for each month.
4. Prepare a table showing the computation of cash payments on product purchases for March and April.
5. Prepare a cash budget for March and April, including any loan activity and interest expense. Compute the loan balance at the end of each month.

Analysis Component

6. Refer to your answer to part 5. Connick's cash budget indicates whether the company must borrow additional funds at the end of March. Suggest some reasons that knowing the loan needs in advance would be helpful to management.

Problem 20-4B
Merchandising: Preparation and analysis of budgeted income statements
C2 P2

Comp-Media buys its product for $60 and sells it for $130 per unit. The sales staff receives a 10% commission on the sale of each unit. Its June income statement follows.

COMP-MEDIA COMPANY Income Statement For Month Ended June 30, 2013	
Sales	$1,300,000
Cost of goods sold	600,000
Gross profit	700,000
Expenses	
Sales commissions (10%)	130,000
Advertising	200,000
Store rent	24,000
Administrative salaries	40,000
Depreciation	50,000
Other expenses	12,000
Total expenses	456,000
Net income	$ 244,000

Management expects June's results to be repeated in July, August, and September without any changes in strategy. Management, however, has another plan. It believes that unit sales will increase at a rate of 10% *each* month for the next three months (beginning with July) if the item's selling price is reduced to $115 per unit and advertising expenses are increased by 25% and remain at that level for all three months. The cost of its product will remain at $60 per unit, the sales staff will continue to earn a 10% commission, and the remaining expenses will stay the same.

Required

1. Prepare budgeted income statements for each of the months of July, August, and September that show the expected results from implementing the proposed changes. Use a three-column format, with one column for each month.

Check Budgeted net income: July, $102,500; August, $150,350; September, $202,985

Analysis Component

2. Use the budgeted income statements from part 1 to recommend whether management should implement the proposed plan. Explain.

Problem 20-5B
Merchandising: Preparation of a complete master budget
C2 P1 P2

Near the end of 2013, the management of Isle Corp., a merchandising company, prepared the following estimated balance sheet for December 31, 2013.

ISLE CORPORATION Estimated Balance Sheet December 31, 2013					
Assets			**Liabilities and Equity**		
Cash	$ 36,000		Accounts payable	$360,000	
Accounts receivable	525,000		Bank loan payable	15,000	
Inventory	150,000		Taxes payable (due 3/15/2014)	90,000	
Total current assets		$ 711,000	Total liabilities		$ 465,000
Equipment	540,000		Common stock	472,500	
Less accumulated depreciation	67,500		Retained earnings	246,000	
Equipment, net		472,500	Total stockholders' equity		718,500
Total assets		$1,183,500	Total liabilities and equity		$1,183,500

To prepare a master budget for January, February, and March of 2014, management gathers the following information.

a. Isle Corp.'s single product is purchased for $30 per unit and resold for $45 per unit. The expected inventory level of 5,000 units on December 31, 2013, is more than management's desired level for 2014, which is 25% of the next month's expected sales (in units). Expected sales are: January, 6,000 units; February, 8,000 units; March, 10,000 units; and April, 9,000 units.

b. Cash sales and credit sales represent 25% and 75%, respectively, of total sales. Of the credit sales, 60% is collected in the first month after the month of sale and 40% in the second month after the month of sale. For the $525,000 accounts receivable balance at December 31, 2013, $315,000 is collected in January 2014 and the remaining $210,000 is collected in February 2014.

c. Merchandise purchases are paid for as follows: 20% in the first month after the month of purchase and 80% in the second month after the month of purchase. For the $360,000 accounts payable balance at December 31, 2013, $72,000 is paid in January 2014 and the remaining $288,000 is paid in February 2014.

d. Sales commissions equal to 20% of sales are paid each month. Sales salaries (excluding commissions) are $90,000 per year.

e. General and administrative salaries are $144,000 per year. Maintenance expense equals $3,000 per month and is paid in cash.

f. Equipment reported in the December 31, 2013, balance sheet was purchased in January 2013. It is being depreciated over 8 years under the straight-line method with no salvage value. The following amounts for new equipment purchases are planned in the coming quarter: January, $72,000; February, $96,000; and March, $28,800. This equipment will be depreciated using the straight-line method over 8 years with no salvage value. A full month's depreciation is taken for the month in which equipment is purchased.

g. The company plans to acquire land at the end of March at a cost of $150,000, which will be paid with cash on the last day of the month.

h. Isle Corp. has a working arrangement with its bank to obtain additional loans as needed. The interest rate is 12% per year, and interest is paid at each month-end based on the beginning balance. Partial or full payments on these loans can be made on the last day of the month. Isle has agreed to maintain a minimum ending cash balance of $36,000 in each month.

i. The income tax rate for the company is 40%. Income taxes on the first quarter's income will not be paid until April 15.

Required

Prepare a master budget for each of the first three months of 2014; include the following component budgets (show supporting calculations as needed, and round amounts to the nearest dollar):

1. Monthly sales budgets (showing both budgeted unit sales and dollar sales).
2. Monthly merchandise purchases budgets.
3. Monthly selling expense budgets.
4. Monthly general and administrative expense budgets.
5. Monthly capital expenditures budgets.
6. Monthly cash budgets.
7. Budgeted income statement for the entire first quarter (not for each month).
8. Budgeted balance sheet as of March 31, 2014.

Check (2) Budgeted purchases: January, $90,000; February, $255,000; (3) Budgeted selling expenses: January, $61,500; February, $79,500

(6) Ending cash bal.: January, $182,500; February, $107,850

(8) Budgeted total assets at March 31, $1,346,875

Problem 20-6B^A
Manufacturing: Preparing production and manufacturing budgets
C2 P3

NSA Company produces baseball bats. Each bat requires 3 pounds of aluminum alloy. Management predicts that 8,000 bats and 15,000 pounds of aluminum alloy will be in inventory on March 31 of the current year and that 250,000 bats will be sold during this year's second quarter. Bats sell for $80 each. Management wants to end the second quarter with 6,000 finished bats and 12,000 pounds of aluminum alloy in inventory. Aluminum alloy can be purchased for $4 per pound. Each bat requires 0.5 hours of direct labor at $18 per hour. Variable overhead is applied at the rate of $12 per direct labor hour. The company budgets fixed overhead of $1,776,000 for the quarter.

Required

1. Prepare the second-quarter production budget for bats.

2. Prepare the second-quarter direct materials (aluminum alloy) budget; include the dollar cost of purchases.

3. Prepare the direct labor budget for the second quarter.

4. Prepare the factory overhead budget for the second quarter.

Check (1) Units manuf., 248,000; (2) Cost of materials purchases, $2,964,000

Problem 20-7B
Manufacturing: Preparation of a complete master budget
C2 P1 P2 P3

The management of Nabar Manufacturing prepared the following estimated balance sheet for June, 2013:

NABAR MANUFACTURING
Estimated Balance Sheet
June 30, 2013

Assets		Liabilities and Equity	
Cash	$ 40,000	Accounts payable	$ 51,400
Accounts receivable	249,900	Income taxes payable	10,000
Raw materials inventory	35,000	Short-term notes payable	24,000
Finished goods inventory	241,080	Total current liabilities	85,400
Total current assets	565,980	Long-term note payable	300,000
Equipment, gross	720,000	Total liabilities	385,400
Accumulated depreciation	(240,000)	Common stock	600,000
Equipment, net	480,000	Retained earnings	60,580
		Total stockholders' equity	660,580
Total assets	$1,045,980	Total liabilities and equity	$1,045,980

To prepare a master budget for July, August, and September of 2013, management gathers the following information:

a. Sales were 20,000 units in June. Forecasted sales in units are as follows: July, 21,000; August, 19,000; September, 20,000; October, 24,000. The product's selling price is $17 per unit and its total product cost is $14.35 per unit.

b. Company policy calls for a given month's ending finished goods inventory to equal 70% of the next month's expected unit sales. The June 30 finished goods inventory is 16,800 units, which does not comply with the policy.

c. Company policy calls for a given month's ending raw materials inventory to equal 20% of the next month's materials requirements. The June 30 raw materials inventory is 4,375 units (which also fails to meet the policy). The budgeted September 30 raw materials inventory is 1,980 units. Raw materials cost $8 per unit. Each finished unit requires 0.50 units of raw materials.

d. Each finished unit requires 0.50 hours of direct labor at a rate of $16 per hour.

e. Overhead is allocated based on direct labor hours. The predetermined variable overhead rate is $2.70 per direct labor hour. Depreciation of $20,000 per month is treated as fixed factory overhead.

f. Monthly general and administrative expenses include $9,000 administrative salaries and 0.9% monthly interest on the long-term note payable.

g. Sales representatives' commissions are 10% of sales and are paid in the month of the sales. The sales manager's monthly salary is $3,500 per month.

h. The company expects 30% of sales to be for cash and the remaining 70% on credit. Receivables are collected in full in the month following the sale (none is collected in the month of the sale).

i. All raw materials purchases are on credit, and no payables arise from any other transactions. One month's raw materials purchases are fully paid in the next month.

j. Dividends of $20,000 are to be declared and paid in August.

k. Income taxes payable at June 30 will be paid in July. Income tax expense will be assessed at 35% in the quarter and paid in October.

l. Equipment purchases of $100,000 are budgeted for the last day of September.

m. The minimum ending cash balance for all months is $40,000. If necessary, the company borrows enough cash using a short-term note to reach the minimum. Short-term notes require an interest payment of 1% at each month-end (before any repayment). If the ending cash balance exceeds the minimum, the excess will be applied to repaying the short-term notes payable balance.

Required

Prepare the following budgets and other financial information as required. All budgets and other financial information should be prepared for the third calendar quarter, except as otherwise noted below. Round calculations to the nearest whole dollar:

1. Sales budget.
2. Production budget.
3. Raw materials budget.
4. Direct labor budget.
5. Factory overhead budget.
6. Selling expense budget.
7. General and administrative expense budget.
8. Cash budget.
9. Budgeted income statement for the entire quarter (not for each month separately).
10. Budgeted statement of retained earnings for the quarter.
11. Budgeted balance sheet as of September 30, 2013.

Check (2) Units to produce: July, 17,500; August, 19,700
(3) Cost of raw materials purchases, July, $50,760
(5) Total overhead cost, August, $46,595
(8) Ending cash balance: July, $96,835; August, $141,180
(10) Budgeted total assets, Sept. 30: $1,054,920

SERIAL PROBLEM

Success Systems

P2

(This serial problem began in Chapter 1 and continues through most of the book. If previous chapter segments were not completed, the serial problem can begin at this point. It is helpful, but not necessary, to use the Working Papers that accompany the book.)

SP 20 Adria Lopez expects second quarter 2014 sales of her new line of computer furniture to be the same as the first quarter's sales (reported below) without any changes in strategy. Monthly sales averaged 40 desk units (sales price of $1,250) and 20 chairs (sales price of $500).

SUCCESS SYSTEMS
Segment Income Statement*
For Quarter Ended March 31, 2014

Sales†	$180,000
Cost of goods sold‡	115,000
Gross profit	65,000
Expenses	
Sales commissions (10%)	18,000
Advertising expenses	9,000
Other fixed expenses	18,000
Total expenses	45,000
Net income	$ 20,000

* Reflects revenue and expense activity only related to the computer furniture segment.

† Revenue: (120 desks × $1,250) + (60 chairs × $500) = $150,000 + $30,000 = $180,000

‡ Cost of goods sold: (120 desks × $750) + (60 chairs × $250) + $10,000 = $115,000

Adria Lopez believes that sales will increase each month for the next three months (April, 48 desks, 32 chairs; May, 52 desks, 35 chairs; June, 56 desks, 38 chairs) *if* selling prices are reduced to $1,150 for desks and $450 for chairs, and advertising expenses are increased by 10% and remain at that level for all three months. The products' variable cost will remain at $750 for desks and $250 for chairs. The sales staff will continue to earn a 10% commission, the fixed manufacturing costs per month will remain at $10,000 and other fixed expenses will remain at $6,000 per month.

Required

1. Prepare budgeted income statements for each of the months of April, May, and June that show the expected results from implementing the proposed changes. Use a three-column format, with one column for each month.
2. Use the budgeted income statements from part 1 to recommend whether Adria Lopez should implement the proposed changes. Explain.

Check (1) Budgeted income (loss): April, $(660); May, $945

Beyond the Numbers

REPORTING IN ACTION
P2
Polaris

BTN 20-1 Financial statements often serve as a starting point in formulating budgets. Review **Polaris'** financial statements to determine its cash paid for acquisitions of property and equipment in the current year and the budgeted cash needed for such acquisitions in the next year.

Required

1. Which financial statement reports the amount of cash paid for acquisitions of property and equipment? Explain where on the statement this information is reported.
2. Indicate the amount of cash (a) paid for acquisitions of property and equipment in the year ended December 31, 2011, and (b) to be paid (budgeted for) next year under the assumption that annual acquisitions of property and equipment equal 40% of the prior year's net income.

Fast Forward

3. Access Polaris' financial statements for a year ending after December 31, 2011, from either its Website [Polaris.com] or the SEC's EDGAR database [www.SEC.gov]. Compare your answer for part 2 with actual cash paid for acquisitions of property and equipment for that fiscal year. Compute the error, if any, in your estimate. Speculate as to why cash paid for acquisitions of property and equipment was higher or lower than your estimate.

COMPARATIVE ANALYSIS
P2
Polaris
Arctic Cat

BTN 20-2 One source of cash savings for a company is improved management of inventory. To illustrate, assume that **Polaris** and **Arctic Cat** both have $1,000,000 per month in sales of one model of snowmobiles in Canada, and both forecast this level of sales per month for the next 24 months. Also assume that both Polaris and Arctic Cat have a 20% contribution margin, their fixed costs are equal, and that cost of goods sold is the only variable cost. Assume that the main difference between Polaris and Arctic Cat is the distribution system. Polaris uses a just-in-time system and requires ending inventory of only 10% of next month's sales in inventory at each month-end. However, Arctic Cat is building an improved distribution system and currently requires 30% of next month's sales in inventory at each month-end.

Required

1. Compute the amount by which Arctic Cat can reduce its inventory level if it can match Polaris' system of maintaining an inventory equal to 10% of next month's sales. (*Hint:* Focus on the facts given and only on the Canadian market.)
2. Explain how the analysis in part 1 that shows ending inventory levels for both the 30% and 10% required inventory policies can help justify a just-in-time inventory system. Assume a 15% interest cost for resources that are tied up in ending inventory.

ETHICS CHALLENGE

C1

BTN 20-3 Both the budget process and budgets themselves can impact management actions, both positively and negatively. For instance, a common practice among not-for-profit organizations and government agencies is for management to spend any amounts remaining in a budget at the end of the budget period, a practice often called "use it or lose it." The view is that if a department manager does not spend the budgeted amount, top management will reduce next year's budget by the amount not spent. To avoid losing budget dollars, department managers often spend all budgeted amounts regardless of the value added to products or services. All of us pay for the costs associated with this budget system.

Required

Write a one-half page report to a local not-for-profit organization or government agency offering a solution to the "use it or lose it" budgeting problem.

COMMUNICATING IN PRACTICE

C2

BTN 20-4 The sales budget is usually the first and most crucial of the component budgets in a master budget because all other budgets usually rely on it for planning purposes.

Required

Assume that your company's sales staff provides information on expected sales and selling prices for items making up the sales budget. Prepare a one-page memorandum to your supervisor outlining concerns with the sales staff's input in the sales budget when its compensation is at least partly tied to these budgets. More generally, explain the importance of assessing any potential bias in information provided to the budget process.

TAKING IT TO THE NET

C1

BTN 20-5 Access information on e-budgets through The Manage Mentor:
http://www.themanagementor.com/kuniverse/kmailers_universe/finance_kmailers/cfa/budgeting2.htm
Read the information provided.

Required

1. Assume the role of a senior manager in a large, multidivision company. What are the benefits of using e-budgets?
2. As a senior manager, what concerns do you have with the concept and application of e-budgets?

TEAMWORK IN ACTION

A1

BTN 20-6 Your team is to prepare a budget report outlining the costs of attending college (full-time) for the next two semesters (30 hours) or three quarters (45 hours). This budget's focus is solely on attending college; do not include personal items in the team's budget. Your budget must include tuition, books, supplies, club fees, food, housing, and all costs associated with travel to and from college. This budgeting exercise is similar to the initial phase in activity-based budgeting. Include a list of any assumptions you use in completing the budget. Be prepared to present your budget in class.

ENTREPRENEURIAL DECISION

C1

BTN 20-7 **Freshii** sells fresh foods with a focus on healthy fare. Company founder Matthew Corrin stresses the importance of planning and budgeting for business success.

Required

1. How can budgeting help Matthew Corrin efficiently develop and operate his business?
2. Why would sales forecasts and purchases budgets be particularly important for a business like Freshii?

BTN 20-8 To help understand the factors impacting a sales budget, you are to visit three businesses with the same ownership or franchise membership. Record the selling prices of two identical products at each location, such as regular and premium gas sold at **Chevron** stations. You are likely to find a difference in prices for at least one of the three locations you visit.

HITTING THE ROAD

C2 P1

Required

1. Identify at least three external factors that must be considered when setting the sales budget. (*Note:* There is a difference between internal and external factors that impact the sales budget.)
2. What factors might explain any differences identified in the prices of the businesses you visited?

BTN 20-9 Access **KTM**'s income statement (in Appendix A) for the business year 2011.

GLOBAL DECISION

P1

KTM

Required

1. Is KTM's infrastructure and administration expense budget likely to be an important budget in its master budgeting process? Explain.
2. Identify three types of expenses that would be reported as infrastructure and administration expenses on KTM's income statement.
3. Who likely has the initial responsibility for KTM's infrastructure and administration expense budget? Explain.

ANSWERS TO MULTIPLE CHOICE QUIZ

1. c
2. e; Budgeted purchases = $36,000 + $7,000 − $6,000 = $37,000
3. b; Cash collected = 25% of September sales + 75% of August sales = (0.25 × $240,000) + (0.75 × $220,000) = $225,000
4. d
5. a; 560 units + (0.30 × 600 units) − (0.30 × 560 units) = 572 units

21

Flexible Budgets and Standard Costs

A Look Back

Chapter 20 explained the master budget and its component budgets as well as their usefulness for planning and monitoring company activities.

A Look at This Chapter

This chapter describes flexible budgets, variance analysis, and standard costs. It explains how each is used for purposes of better controlling and monitoring of business activities.

A Look Ahead

Chapter 22 describes managerial reports useful in measuring performance and directing a company's activities. It describes responsibility accounting, measuring departmental performance, allocating common costs across departments, and transfer pricing. It also explains financial and nonfinancial performance measures used to evaluate investment center performance.

Learning Objectives

CONCEPTUAL

C1 Define *standard costs* and explain how standard cost information is useful for management by exception. (p. 901)

C2 Describe variances and what they reveal about performance. (p. 903)

ANALYTICAL

A1 Analyze changes in sales from expected amounts. (p. 911)

PROCEDURAL

P1 Prepare a flexible budget and interpret a flexible budget performance report. (p. 898)

P2 Compute materials and labor variances. (p. 904)

P3 Compute overhead variances. (p. 908)

P4 *Appendix 21A*—Prepare journal entries for standard costs and account for price and quantity variances. (p. 918)

Decision Insight

Whoosh!

"Skiing is not just a sport, it's a life-long choice."
—MIKE McCABE

BOULDER, CO—Self-described "ski bum" Jordan Grano wanted a pair of skis that could handle more than one ski season. Frustrated by the quality and performance of "off-the-rack" skis, Jordan began researching how to build better skis. The result is **Folsom Custom Skis** **(folsomskis.com),** the company he founded in 2007. In addition to building custom skis to precise customer specifications, the company also builds "semi-custom" skis which allow customers fewer choices.

Master Builder and current company President Mike McCabe says customers can "take their favorite skis and alter them to suit their needs and wants. We come up with a finished ski built exactly to customer specifications." The company's manufacturing process demands precision. "Design elements like ski turn radius, camber, and taper interact in complex ways and require careful measurement," says Mike. The result is a better-quality and more durable ski as Mike, a professional skier, can attest to. "I was hired to break a set of skis. I failed."

Manufacturers like Folsom Custom Skis must control materials, labor, and overhead costs. Determining standard costs helps. For example, Mike estimates it takes 12 hours to go from design to a complete ski. "We make them as fast as we can but we don't cut corners; we make sure we put an equal amount of time into every one of our skis," explains Mike. Putting too much time into a ski could waste the company's productive capacity, but putting too little time into a ski could result in an inferior product. Attention to variances from standards can keep the manufacturing process on track.

The company uses only the highest quality poplar and bamboo in their skis. Here too, Mike analyzes materials price and quantity variances to control costs. Mike stresses the importance of "having precise specifications and controls to detect problems; we don't use any material that does not meet our requirements." Unfavorable materials price variances could result from rising raw materials prices, which could cause the company to consider alternative suppliers or raising prices.

At an average price of about $1,300 per pair, the company reports revenue of about $300,000 per year. While currently operating at about a break-even level, Mike hopes to double the company's output and ultimately make profits. The use of flexible budgets, reflecting cost estimates at different production levels, can be useful in making business decisions. While attention to budgeting, standards, and variances is important, Mike encourages entrepreneurs to "build a business on something you feel passionate about."

[Sources: *Folsom Custom Skis website,* January 2013; *Boulder County Business Report,* November 13, 2009; *Skiing mag* (*www.skinet.com*), July 2009.]

Chapter Preview

Budgeting helps organize and formalize management's planning activities. This chapter extends the study of budgeting to look more closely at the use of budgets to evaluate performance. Evaluations are important for controlling and monitoring business activities. This chapter also describes and illustrates the use of standard costs and variance analyses. These managerial tools are useful for both evaluating and controlling organizations and for the planning of future activities.

Flexible Budgets

- **Budgetary Process**
  - Control and reporting
  - Fixed budget performance report
  - Budget reports for evaluation
- **Flexible Budget Reports**
  - Purpose
  - Preparation
  - Flexible budget performance report

Standard Costs

- **Materials and Labor Standards**
  - Identifying standard costs
  - Setting standard costs
- **Cost Variances**
  - Analysis
  - Computation
  - Computing materials and labor variances
- **Overhead Standards and Variances**
  - Setting overhead standards
  - Predicting activity levels
  - Computing overhead variances

Section 1—Flexible Budgets

This section introduces fixed budgets and fixed budget performance reports. It then introduces flexible budgets and flexible budget performance reports and illustrates their advantages.

BUDGETARY PROCESS

A master budget reflects management's planned objectives for a future period. The preparation of a master budget is based on a predicted level of activity such as sales volume for the budget period. This section discusses the effects on the usefulness of budget reports when the actual level of activity differs from the predicted level.

Budgetary Control and Reporting

Budgetary control refers to management's use of budgets to monitor and control a company's operations. This includes using budgets to see that planned objectives are met. **Budget reports** contain relevant information that compares actual results to planned activities. This comparison is motivated by a need to both monitor performance and control activities. Budget reports are sometimes viewed as progress reports, or *report cards,* on management's performance in achieving planned objectives. These reports can be prepared at any time and for any period. Three common periods for a budget report are a month, quarter, and year.

Point: Budget reports are often used to determine bonuses of managers.

The budgetary control process involves at least four steps: (1) develop the budget from planned objectives, (2) compare actual results to budgeted amounts and analyze any differences, (3) take corrective and strategic actions, and (4) establish new planned objectives and prepare a new budget. Exhibit 21.1 shows this continual process of budgetary control. Budget reports and

EXHIBIT 21.1

Process of Budgetary Control

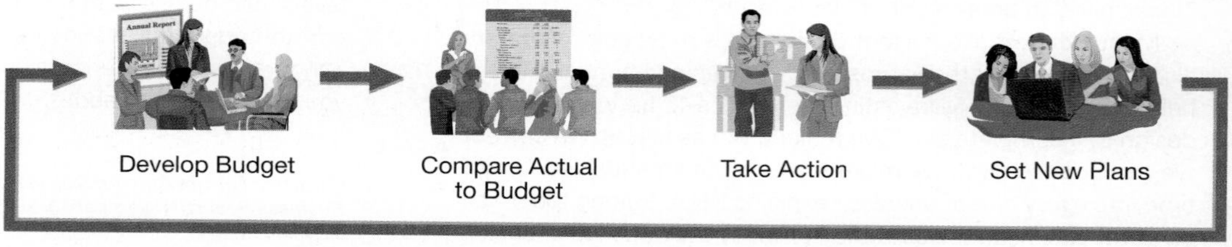

related documents are effective tools for managers to obtain the greatest benefits from this budgetary process.

Fixed Budget Performance Report

In a fixed budgetary control system, the master budget is based on a single prediction for sales volume or other activity level. The budgeted amount for each cost essentially assumes that a specific (or *fixed*) amount of sales will occur. A **fixed budget,** also called a *static budget,* is based on a single predicted amount of sales or other measure of activity.

One benefit of a budget is its usefulness in comparing actual results with planned activities. Information useful for analysis is often presented for comparison in a performance report. As shown in Exhibit 21.2, a **fixed budget performance report** for **Optel** compares actual results for January 2013 with the results expected under its fixed budget that predicted 10,000 (composite) units of sales. Optel manufactures inexpensive eyeglasses, frames, contact lens, and related supplies. For this report, its production volume equals sales volume (its inventory level did not change).

EXHIBIT 21.2

Fixed Budget Performance Report

OPTEL
Fixed Budget Performance Report
For Month Ended January 31, 2013

	Fixed Budget	Actual Results	Variances*
Sales (in units)	10,000	12,000	
Sales (in dollars)	$100,000	$125,000	$25,000 F
Cost of goods sold			
Direct materials	10,000	13,000	3,000 U
Direct labor	15,000	20,000	5,000 U
Overhead			
Factory supplies	2,000	2,100	100 U
Utilities	3,000	4,000	1,000 U
Depreciation—machinery	8,000	8,000	0
Supervisory salaries	11,000	11,000	0
Selling expenses			
Sales commissions	9,000	10,800	1,800 U
Shipping expenses	4,000	4,300	300 U
General and administrative expenses			
Office supplies	5,000	5,200	200 U
Insurance expenses	1,000	1,200	200 U
Depreciation—office equipment	7,000	7,000	0
Administrative salaries	13,000	13,000	0
Total expenses	88,000	99,600	11,600 U
Income from operations	$ 12,000	$ 25,400	$13,400 F

* F = Favorable variance; U = Unfavorable variance.

This type of performance report designates differences between budgeted and actual results as variances. We see the letters *F* and *U* located beside the numbers in the third number column of this report. Their meanings are as follows:

F = **Favorable variance** When compared to budget, the actual cost or revenue contributes to a *higher* income. That is, actual revenue is higher than budgeted revenue, or actual cost is lower than budgeted cost.

U = **Unfavorable variance** When compared to budget, the actual cost or revenue contributes to a *lower* income; actual revenue is lower than budgeted revenue, or actual cost is higher than budgeted cost.

This convention is common in practice and is used throughout this chapter.

Example: How is it that the favorable sales variance in Exhibit 21.2 is linked with so many unfavorable cost and expense variances? *Answer:* Costs have increased with the increase in sales.

Budget Reports for Evaluation

A primary use of budget reports is as a tool for management to monitor and control operations. Evaluation by Optel management is likely to focus on a variety of questions that might include these:

- Why is actual income from operations $13,400 higher than budgeted?
- Are amounts paid for each expense item too high?
- Is manufacturing using too much direct material?
- Is manufacturing using too much direct labor?

The performance report in Exhibit 21.2 provides little help in answering these questions because actual sales volume is 2,000 units higher than budgeted. A manager does not know if this higher level of sales activity is the cause of variations in total dollar sales and expenses or if other factors have influenced these amounts. This inability of fixed budget reports to adjust for changes in activity levels is a major limitation of a fixed budget performance report. That is, it fails to show whether actual costs are out of line due to a change in actual sales volume or some other factor.

Decision Insight

Cruise Control Budget reporting and evaluation are used at service providers such as **Royal Carribbean Cruises Ltd.** It regularly prepares performance plans and budget requests for its fleet of cruise ships, which describe performance goals, measure outcomes, and analyze variances. ■

FLEXIBLE BUDGET REPORTS

Purpose of Flexible Budgets

To help address limitations with the fixed budget performance report, particularly from the effects of changes in sales volume, management can use a flexible budget. A **flexible budget,** also called a *variable budget,* is a report based on predicted amounts of revenues and expenses corresponding to the actual level of output. Flexible budgets are useful both before and after the period's activities are complete.

A flexible budget prepared before the period is often based on several levels of activity. Budgets for those different levels can provide a "what-if" look at operations. The different levels often include both a best case and worst case scenario. This allows management to make adjustments to avoid or lessen the effects of the worst case scenario.

Point: A flexible budget yields an "apples to apples" comparison because budgeted activity levels are the same as the actual.

A flexible budget prepared after the period helps management evaluate past performance. It is especially useful for such an evaluation because it reflects budgeted revenues and costs based on the actual level of activity. Thus, comparisons of actual results with budgeted performance are more likely to identify the causes of any differences. This can help managers focus attention on real problem areas and implement corrective actions. This is in contrast to a fixed budget, whose primary purpose is to assist managers in planning future activities and whose numbers are based on a single predicted amount of budgeted sales or production.

Preparation of Flexible Budgets

P1 Prepare a flexible budget and interpret a flexible budget performance report.

A flexible budget is designed to reveal the effects of volume of activity on revenues and costs. To prepare a flexible budget, management relies on the distinctions between fixed and variable costs. Recall that the cost per unit of activity remains constant for variable costs so that the total amount of a variable cost changes in direct proportion to a change in activity level. The total amount of fixed cost remains unchanged regardless of changes in the level of activity within a relevant (normal) operating range. (Assume that costs can be reasonably classified as variable or fixed within a relevant range.)

When we create the numbers constituting a flexible budget, we express each variable cost as either a constant amount per unit of sales or as a percent of a sales dollar. In the case of a fixed cost, we express its budgeted amount as the total amount expected to occur at any sales volume within the relevant range.

Exhibit 21.3 shows a set of flexible budgets for Optel for January 2013. Seven of its expenses are classified as variable costs. Its remaining five expenses are fixed costs. These classifications result from management's investigation of each expense. Variable and fixed expense categories are *not* the same for every company, and we must avoid drawing conclusions from specific cases. For example, depending on the nature of a company's operations, office supplies expense can be either fixed or variable with respect to sales.

Point: The usefulness of a flexible budget depends on valid classification of variable and fixed costs. Some costs are mixed and must be analyzed to determine their variable and fixed portions.

EXHIBIT 21.3

Flexible Budgets

OPTEL
Flexible Budgets
For Month Ended January 31, 2013

	Flexible Budget		Flexible Budget for Unit Sales of		
	Variable Amount per Unit	Total Fixed Cost	10,000	12,000	14,000
Sales	$10.00		$100,000	$120,000	$140,000
Variable costs					
Direct materials	1.00		10,000	12,000	14,000
Direct labor	1.50		15,000	18,000	21,000
Factory supplies	0.20		2,000	2,400	2,800
Utilities	0.30		3,000	3,600	4,200
Sales commissions	0.90		9,000	10,800	12,600
Shipping expenses	0.40		4,000	4,800	5,600
Office supplies	0.50		5,000	6,000	7,000
Total variable costs	4.80		48,000	57,600	67,200
Contribution margin	$ 5.20		$ 52,000	$ 62,400	$ 72,800
Fixed costs					
Depreciation—machinery		$ 8,000	8,000	8,000	8,000
Supervisory salaries		11,000	11,000	11,000	11,000
Insurance expense		1,000	1,000	1,000	1,000
Depreciation—office equipment		7,000	7,000	7,000	7,000
Administrative salaries		13,000	13,000	13,000	13,000
Total fixed costs		$40,000	40,000	40,000	40,000
Income from operations			$ 12,000	$ 22,400	$ 32,800

The layout for the flexible budgets in Exhibit 21.3 follows a *contribution margin format*—beginning with sales followed by variable costs and then fixed costs. Both the expected individual and total variable costs are reported and then subtracted from sales. The difference between sales and variable costs equals contribution margin. The expected amounts of fixed costs are listed next, followed by the expected income from operations before taxes.

Example: Using Exhibit 21.3, what is the budgeted income from operations for unit sales of (a) 11,000 and (b) 13,000? *Answers:* $17,200 for unit sales of 11,000; $27,600 for unit sales of 13,000.

The first and second number columns of Exhibit 21.3 show the flexible budget amounts for variable costs per unit and each fixed cost for any volume of sales in the relevant range. The third, fourth, and fifth columns show the flexible budget amounts computed for three different sales volumes. For instance, the third column's flexible budget is based on 10,000 units. These numbers are the same as those in the fixed budget of Exhibit 21.2 because the expected volumes are the same for these two budgets.

Recall that Optel's actual sales volume for January is 12,000 units. This sales volume is 2,000 units more than the 10,000 units originally predicted in the master budget. When differences between actual and predicted volume arise, the usefulness of a flexible budget is apparent. For instance, compare the flexible budget for 10,000 units in the third column (which is the same as the fixed budget in Exhibit 21.2) with the flexible budget for 12,000 units in the fourth

Point: Flexible budgeting allows a budget to be prepared at the *actual* output level. Performance reports are then prepared comparing the flexible budget to actual revenues and costs.

column. The higher levels for both sales and variable costs reflect nothing more than the increase in sales activity. Any budget analysis comparing actual with planned results that ignores this information is less useful to management.

To illustrate, when we evaluate Optel's performance, we need to prepare a flexible budget showing actual and budgeted values at 12,000 units. As part of a complete profitability analysis, managers could compare the actual income of $25,400 (from Exhibit 21.2) with the $22,400 income expected at the actual sales volume of 12,000 units (from Exhibit 21.3). This results in a total favorable income variance of $3,000 to be explained and interpreted. This variance is markedly lower from the $13,400 favorable variance identified in Exhibit 21.2 using a fixed budget, but still suggests good performance. After receiving the flexible budget based on January's actual volume, management must determine what caused this $3,000 difference. The next section describes a flexible budget performance report that provides guidance in this analysis.

Decision Maker

Entrepreneur The heads of both the strategic consulting and tax consulting divisions of your financial services firm complain to you about the unfavorable variances on their performance reports. "We worked on more consulting assignments than planned. It's not surprising our costs are higher than expected. To top it off, this report characterizes our work as *poor!*" How do you respond? ■ [Answer—p. 920]

Flexible Budget Performance Report

A **flexible budget performance report** lists differences between actual performance and budgeted performance based on actual sales volume or other activity level. This report helps direct management's attention to those costs or revenues that differ substantially from budgeted amounts. Exhibit 21.4 shows Optel's flexible budget performance report for January. We prepare this report after the actual volume is known to be 12,000 units. This report shows a $5,000 favorable variance in total dollar sales. Because actual and budgeted volumes are both 12,000 units, the $5,000 sales variance must have resulted from a higher than expected selling price.

EXHIBIT 21.4

Flexible Budget Performance Report

OPTEL
Flexible Budget Performance Report
For Month Ended January 31, 2013

	Flexible Budget	Actual Results	Variances*
Sales (12,000 units)	$120,000	$125,000	$5,000 F
Variable costs			
Direct materials	12,000	13,000	1,000 U
Direct labor	18,000	20,000	2,000 U
Factory supplies	2,400	2,100	300 F
Utilities	3,600	4,000	400 U
Sales commissions	10,800	10,800	0
Shipping expenses	4,800	4,300	500 F
Office supplies	6,000	5,200	800 F
Total variable costs	57,600	59,400	1,800 U
Contribution margin	62,400	65,600	3,200 F
Fixed costs			
Depreciation—machinery	8,000	8,000	0
Supervisory salaries	11,000	11,000	0
Insurance expense	1,000	1,200	200 U
Depreciation—office equipment	7,000	7,000	0
Administrative salaries	13,000	13,000	0
Total fixed costs	40,000	40,200	200 U
Income from operations	$ 22,400	$ 25,400	$3,000 F

* F = Favorable variance; U = Unfavorable variance.

Further analysis of the facts surrounding this $5,000 sales variance reveals a favorable sales variance per unit of nearly $0.42 as shown here:

Actual average price per unit (rounded to cents)	$125,000/12,000 = $10.42
Budgeted price per unit	$120,000/12,000 = 10.00
Favorable sales variance per unit	$5,000/12,000 = $ 0.42

The other variances in Exhibit 21.4 also direct management's attention to areas where corrective actions can help control Optel's operations. Each expense variance is analyzed as the sales variance was. We can think of each expense as the joint result of using a given number of units of input and paying a specific price per unit of input. Optel's expense variances total $2,000 unfavorable, suggesting poor control of some costs, particularly direct materials and direct labor.

Each variance in Exhibit 21.4 is due in part to a difference between *actual price* per unit of input and *budgeted price* per unit of input. This is a **price variance.** Each variance also can be due in part to a difference between *actual quantity* of input used and *budgeted quantity* of input. This is a **quantity variance.** We explain more about this breakdown, known as **variance analysis,** next in the standard costs section of this chapter.

Quick Check Answers — p. 921

1. A flexible budget (*a*) shows fixed costs as constant amounts of cost per unit of activity, (*b*) shows variable costs as constant amounts of cost per unit of activity, or (*c*) is prepared based on one expected amount of budgeted sales or production.
2. What is the initial step in preparing a flexible budget?
3. What is the main difference between a fixed and a flexible budget?
4. What is the contribution margin?

Section 2—Standard Costs

C1 Define *standard costs* and explain how standard cost information is useful for management by exception.

Standard costs are preset costs for delivering a product or service under normal conditions. These costs are established by personnel, engineering, and accounting studies using past experiences and data. Management uses these costs to assess the reasonableness of actual costs incurred for producing the product or providing the service. When actual costs vary from standard costs, management follows up to identify potential problems and take corrective actions. **Management by exception** means that managers focus attention on the most significant differences between actual costs and standard costs and give less attention to areas where performance is reasonably close to standard. Management by exception is especially useful when directed at controllable items, enabling top management to affect the actions of lower-level managers responsible for the company's revenues and costs.

Standard costs are often used in preparing budgets because they are the anticipated costs incurred under normal conditions. Terms such as *standard materials cost, standard labor cost,* and *standard overhead cost* are often used to refer to amounts budgeted for direct materials, direct labor, and overhead.

Point: Business practice often uses the word *budget* when speaking of total amounts and *standard* when discussing per unit amounts.

While many managers use standard costs to investigate manufacturing costs, standard costs can also help control *nonmanufacturing* costs. Companies providing services instead of products can also benefit from the use of standard costs. For example, while quality medical service is paramount, efficiency in providing that service is also important to medical professionals. The use of budgeting and standard costing is touted as an effective means to control and monitor medical costs, especially overhead.

Decision Ethics

Internal Auditor You discover a manager who always spends exactly what is budgeted. About 30% of her budget is spent just before the period-end. She admits to spending what is budgeted, whether or not it is needed. She offers three reasons: (1) she doesn't want her budget cut, (2) "management by exception" focuses on budget deviations; and (3) she believes the money is budgeted to be spent. What action do you take? ■ [Answer—p. 920]

MATERIALS AND LABOR STANDARDS

This section explains how to set materials and labor standards and how to prepare a standard cost card.

Identifying Standard Costs

Managerial accountants, engineers, personnel administrators, and other managers combine their efforts to set standard costs. To identify standards for direct labor costs, we can conduct time and motion studies for each labor operation in the process of providing a product or service. From these studies, management can learn the best way to perform the operation and then set the standard labor time required for the operation under normal conditions. Similarly, standards for materials are set by studying the quantity, grade, and cost of each material used. Standards for overhead costs are explained later in the chapter.

Example: What factors might be considered when deciding whether to revise standard costs? *Answer:* Changes in the processes and/or resources needed to carry out the processes.

Regardless of the care used in setting standard costs and in revising them as conditions change, actual costs frequently differ from standard costs, often as a result of one or more factors. For instance, the actual quantity of material used can differ from the standard, or the price paid per unit of material can differ from the standard. Quantity and price differences from standard amounts can also occur for labor. That is, the actual labor time and actual labor rate can vary from what was expected. The same analysis applies to overhead costs.

Decision Insight

Cruis'n Standards The **Corvette** consists of hundreds of parts for which engineers set standards. Various types of labor are also involved in its production, including machining, assembly, painting, and welding, and standards are set for each. Actual results are periodically compared with standards to assess performance. ■

Setting Standard Costs

To illustrate the setting of a standard cost, we consider a professional league baseball bat manufactured by **ProBat.** Its engineers have determined that manufacturing one bat requires 0.90 kg. of high-grade wood. They also expect some loss of material as part of the process because of inefficiencies and waste. This results in adding an *allowance* of 0.10 kg., making the standard requirement 1.0 kg. of wood for each bat.

Point: Companies promoting continuous improvement strive to achieve ideal standards by eliminating inefficiencies and waste.

The 0.90 kg. portion is called an *ideal standard;* it is the quantity of material required if the process is 100% efficient without any loss or waste. Reality suggests that some loss of material usually occurs with any process. The standard of 1.0 kg. is known as the *practical standard,* the quantity of material required under normal application of the process.

High-grade wood can be purchased at a standard price of $25 per kg. The purchasing department sets this price as the expected price for the budget period. To determine this price, the purchasing department considers factors such as the quality of materials, future economic conditions, supply factors (shortages and excesses), and any available discounts. The engineers also decide that two hours of labor time (after including allowances) are required to manufacture a bat. The wage rate is $20 per hour (better than average skilled labor is required). ProBat assigns all overhead at the rate of $10 per labor hour. The standard costs of direct materials, direct labor, and overhead for one bat are shown in Exhibit 21.5 in what is called a *standard cost card.* These cost amounts are then used to prepare manufacturing budgets for a budgeted level of production.

EXHIBIT 21.5
Standard Cost Card

STANDARD COST CARD

Production factor	Cost factor	Total
Direct materials (wood)	1 kg. @ $25 per kg.	$25
Direct labor	2 hours @ $20 per hour	40
Overhead	2 labor hours @ $10 per hour	20
	Total	$85

REMARKS:
Based on standard costs of direct materials, direct labor, and overhead for a single ProBat

SUMMARY:	
Materials	$25
Labor	40
Overhead	20
Total cost	$85

COST VARIANCES

C2 Describe variances and what they reveal about performance.

A **cost variance,** also simply called a *variance,* is the difference between actual and standard costs. A cost variance can be favorable or unfavorable. A variance from standard cost is considered favorable if actual cost is less than standard cost. It is considered unfavorable if actual cost is more than standard cost.[1] This section discusses variance analysis.

Cost Variance Analysis

Variances are usually identified in performance reports. When a variance occurs, management wants to determine the factors causing it. This often involves analysis, evaluation, and explanation. The results of these efforts should enable management to assign responsibility for the variance and then to take actions to correct the situation.

To illustrate, ProBat's standard materials cost for producing 500 bats is $12,500. Assume that its actual materials cost for those 500 bats is $13,000. The $500 unfavorable variance raises questions that call for answers that, in turn, can lead to changes to correct the situation and eliminate this variance in the next period. A performance report often identifies the existence of a problem, but we must follow up with further investigation to see what can be done to improve future performance.

Exhibit 21.6 shows the flow of events in the effective management of variance analysis. It shows four steps: (1) preparing a standard cost performance report, (2) computing and analyzing variances, (3) identifying questions and their explanations, and (4) taking corrective and strategic actions. These variance analysis steps are interrelated and are frequently applied in good organizations.

EXHIBIT 21.6
Variance Analysis

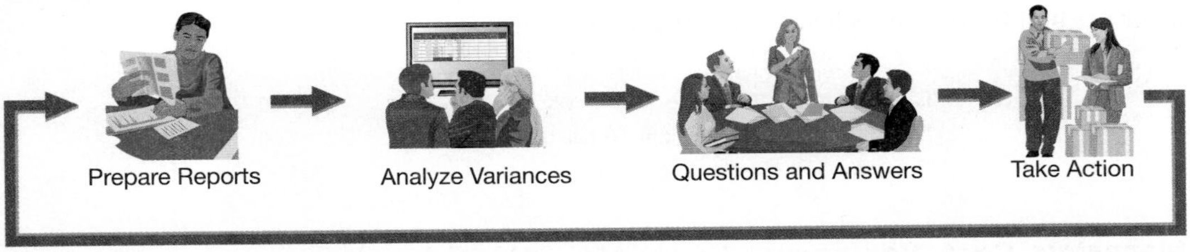

Cost Variance Computation

Management needs information about the factors causing a cost variance, but first it must properly compute the variance. In its most simple form, a cost variance (CV) is computed as the difference between actual cost (AC) and standard cost (SC) as shown in Exhibit 21.7.

[1] Short-term favorable variances can sometimes lead to long-term unfavorable variances. For instance, if management spends less than the budgeted amount on maintenance or insurance, the performance report would show a favorable variance. Cutting these expenses can lead to major losses in the long run if machinery wears out prematurely or insurance coverage proves inadequate.

EXHIBIT 21.7

Cost Variance Formulas

Cost Variance (CV) = **Actual Cost** (AC) − **Standard Cost** (SC)

where:

Actual Cost (AC) = **Actual Quantity** (AQ) × **Actual Price** (AP)

Standard Cost (SC) = **Standard Quantity** (SQ) × **Standard Price** (SP)

A cost variance is further defined by its components. Actual quantity (AQ) is the input (material or labor) used to manufacture the quantity of output. Standard quantity (SQ) is the expected input for the quantity of output. Actual price (AP) is the amount paid to acquire the input (material or labor), and standard price (SP) is the expected price.

Point: Price and quantity variances for direct labor are nearly always referred to as *rate* and *efficiency variances*, respectively.

Two main factors cause a cost variance: (1) the difference between actual price and standard price results in a *price* (or rate) *variance* and (2) the difference between actual quantity and standard quantity results in a *quantity* (or usage or efficiency) *variance*. To assess the impacts of these two factors in a cost variance, we use the formulas in Exhibit 21.8.

EXHIBIT 21.8

Price Variance and Quantity Variance Formulas

Actual Cost
AQ × AP

AQ × SP

Standard Cost
SQ × SP

Price Variance
(AQ × AP) − (AQ × SP)

Quantity Variance
(AQ × SP) − (SQ × SP)

Cost Variance

In computing a price variance, the quantity (actual) is held constant. In computing a quantity variance, the price (standard) is held constant. The cost variance, or total variance, is the sum of the price and quantity variances. These formulas identify the sources of the cost variance. Managers sometimes find it useful to apply an alternative (but equivalent) computation for the price and quantity variances as shown in Exhibit 21.9.

EXHIBIT 21.9

Alternative Price Variance and Quantity Variance Formulas

Price Variance (PV) = [**Actual Price** (AP) − **Standard Price** (SP)] × **Actual Quantity** (AQ)

Quantity Variance (QV) = [**Actual Quantity** (AQ) − **Standard Quantity** (SQ)] × **Standard Price** (SP)

The results from applying the formulas in Exhibits 21.8 and 21.9 are identical.

Computing Materials and Labor Variances

P2 Compute materials and labor variances.

We illustrate the computation of the materials and labor cost variances using data from **G-Max,** a company that makes specialty golf equipment and accessories for individual customers. This company has set the following standard quantities and costs for materials and labor per unit for one of its hand-crafted golf clubheads:

Direct materials (0.5 lb. per unit at $20 per lb.)	$10.00
Direct labor (1 hr. per unit at $8 per hr.)	8.00
Total standard direct cost per unit	$18.00

Materials Cost Variances During May 2013, G-Max budgeted to produce 4,000 clubheads (units). It actually produced only 3,500 units. It used 1,800 pounds of direct materials (titanium) costing $21.00 per pound, meaning its total materials cost was $37,800. This information allows us to compute both actual and standard direct materials costs for G-Max's 3,500 units and its direct materials cost variance as follows:

Actual cost	1,800 lbs. @ $21.00 per lb.	= $37,800
Standard cost	1,750 lbs. @ $20.00 per lb.	= 35,000
Direct materials cost variance (unfavorable)		= $ 2,800

To better isolate the causes of this $2,800 unfavorable total direct materials cost variance, the materials price and quantity variances for these G-Max clubheads are computed and shown in Exhibit 21.10.

EXHIBIT 21.10

Materials Price and Quantity Variances*

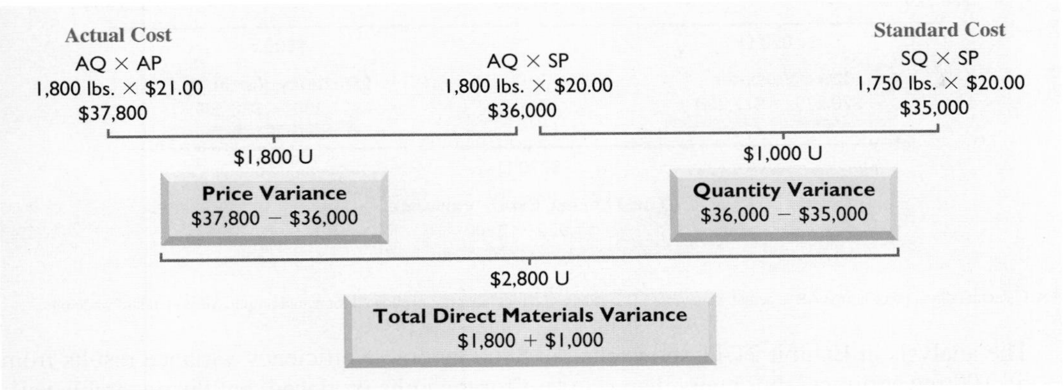

*AQ is actual quantity; AP is actual price; SP is standard price; SQ is standard quantity allowed for actual output.

The $1,800 unfavorable price variance results from paying $1 more per unit than the standard price, computed as 1,800 lbs. × $1. The $1,000 unfavorable quantity variance is due to using 50 lbs. more materials than the standard quantity, computed as 50 lbs. × $20. The total direct materials variance is $2,800 and it is unfavorable. This information allows management to ask the responsible individuals for explanations and corrective actions.

The purchasing department is usually responsible for the price paid for materials. Responsibility for explaining the price variance in this case rests with the purchasing manager if a price higher than standard caused the variance. The production department is usually responsible for the amount of material used and in this case is responsible for explaining why the process used more than the standard amount of materials.

Example: Identify at least two factors that might have caused the unfavorable quantity variance and the unfavorable price variance in Exhibit 21.10. *Answer:* Poor quality materials or untrained workers for the former; poor price negotiation or higher-quality materials for the latter.

Variance analysis presents challenges. For instance, the production department could have used more than the standard amount of material because its quality did not meet specifications and led to excessive waste. In this case, the purchasing manager is responsible for explaining why inferior materials were acquired. However, the production manager is responsible for explaining what happened if analysis shows that waste was due to inefficiencies, not poor quality material.

In evaluating price variances, managers must recognize that a favorable price variance can indicate a problem with poor product quality. **Redhook Ale**, a micro brewery in the Pacific Northwest, can probably save 10% to 15% in material prices by buying six-row barley malt instead of the better two-row from Washington's Yakima valley. Attention to quality, however, has helped Redhook Ale increase its sales. Redhook's purchasing activities are judged on both the quality of the materials and the purchase price variance.

Labor Cost Variances Labor cost for a specific product or service depends on the number of hours worked (quantity) and the wage rate paid to employees (price). When actual amounts for a task differ from standard, the labor cost variance can be divided into a rate (price) variance and an efficiency (quantity) variance.

To illustrate, G-Max's direct labor standard for 3,500 units of its hand-crafted clubheads is one hour per unit, or 3,500 hours at $8 per hour. Since only 3,400 hours at $8.30 per hour were actually used to complete the units, the actual and standard labor costs are

Actual cost	3,400 hrs. @ $8.30 per hr.	= $28,220
Standard cost	3,500 hrs. @ $8.00 per hr.	= 28,000
Direct labor cost variance (unfavorable)		= $ 220

This analysis shows that actual cost is merely $220 over the standard and suggests no immediate concern. Computing both the labor rate and efficiency variances reveals a different picture, however, as shown in Exhibit 21.11.

EXHIBIT 21.11

Labor Rate and Efficiency Variances*

Actual Cost		Standard Cost
AH × AR	AH × SR	SH × SR
3,400 hrs. × $8.30	3,400 hrs. × $8.00	3,500 hrs. × $8.00
$28,220	$27,200	$28,000

$1,020 U — **Rate Variance** $28,220 − $27,200

$800 F — **Efficiency Variance** $27,200 − $28,000

$220 U — **Total Direct Labor Variance** $1,020 − $800

* AH is actual direct labor hours: AR is actual wage rate; SH is standard direct labor hours allowed for actual output; SR is standard wage rate.

Example: Compute the rate variance and the efficiency variance for Exhibit 21.11 if 3,700 actual hours are used at an actual price of $7.50 per hour. *Answer:* $1,850 favorable labor rate variance and $1,600 unfavorable labor efficiency variance.

The analysis in Exhibit 21.11 shows that an $800 favorable efficiency variance results from using 100 fewer direct labor hours than standard for the units produced, but this favorable variance is more than offset by a wage rate that is $0.30 per hour higher than standard. The personnel administrator or the production manager needs to explain why the wage rate is higher than expected. The production manager should also explain how the labor hours were reduced. If this experience can be repeated and transferred to other departments, more savings are possible.

One possible explanation of these labor rate and efficiency variances is the use of workers with different skill levels. If this is the reason, senior management must discuss the implications with the production manager who has the responsibility to assign workers to tasks with the appropriate skill level. In this case, an investigation might show that higher-skilled workers were used to produce 3,500 units of hand-crafted clubheads. As a result, fewer labor hours might be required for the work, but the wage rate paid these workers is higher than standard because of their greater skills. The effect of this strategy is a higher than standard total cost, which would require actions to remedy the situation or adjust the standard.

Decision Maker

Production Manager You receive the manufacturing variance report for June and discover a large unfavorable labor efficiency (quantity) variance. What factors do you investigate to identify its possible causes? ■ [Answer—p. 920]

Quick Check

Answers — p. 921

5. A standard cost (*a*) changes in direct proportion to changes in the level of activity, (*b*) is an amount incurred at the actual level of production for the period, or (*c*) is an amount incurred under normal conditions to provide a product or service.

6. What is a cost variance?

7. The following information is available for York Company.

Actual direct labor hours per unit	2.5 hours
Standard direct labor hours per unit	2.0 hours
Actual production (units)	2,500 units
Budgeted production (units)	3,000 units
Actual rate per hour	$3.10
Standard rate per hour	$3.00

The labor efficiency variance is (*a*) $3,750 U, (*b*) $3,750 F, or (*c*) $3,875 U.

8. Refer to Quick Check 7; the labor rate variance is (*a*) $625 F or (*b*) $625 U.

9. If a materials quantity variance is favorable and a materials price variance is unfavorable, can the total materials cost variance be favorable?

OVERHEAD STANDARDS AND VARIANCES

When standard costs are used, a predetermined overhead rate is used to assign standard overhead costs to products or services produced. This predetermined rate is often based on some overhead allocation base (such as standard labor cost, standard labor hours, or standard machine hours).

Setting Overhead Standards

Standard overhead costs are the amounts expected to occur at a certain activity level. Unlike direct materials and direct labor, overhead includes fixed costs and variable costs. This results in the average overhead cost per unit changing as the predicted volume changes. Since standard costs are also budgeted costs, they must be established before the reporting period begins. Standard overhead costs are therefore average per unit costs based on the predicted activity level.

To establish the standard overhead cost rate, management uses the same cost structure it used to construct a flexible budget at the end of a period. This cost structure identifies the different overhead cost components and classifies them as variable or fixed. To get the standard overhead rate, management selects a level of activity (volume) and predicts total overhead cost. It then divides this total by the allocation base to get the standard rate. Standard direct labor hours expected to be used to produce the predicted volume is a common allocation base and is used in this section.

Point: With increased automation, machine hours are frequently used in applying overhead instead of labor hours.

To illustrate, Exhibit 21.12 shows the overhead cost structure used to develop G-Max's flexible overhead budgets for May 2013. The predetermined standard overhead rate for May is set before the month begins. The first two number columns list the per unit amounts of variable costs and the monthly amounts of fixed costs. The four right-most columns show the costs expected to occur at four different levels of production activity. The predetermined overhead rate per labor hour is smaller as volume of activity increases because total fixed costs remain constant.

EXHIBIT 21.12

Flexible Overhead Budgets

G-MAX
Flexible Overhead Budgets
For Month Ended May 31, 2013

	Flexible Budget		Flexible Budget at Capacity Level of			
	Variable Amount per Unit	Total Fixed Cost	70%	80%	90%	100%
Production (in units)	1 unit		3,500	4,000	4,500	5,000
Factory overhead						
Variable costs						
Indirect labor	$0.40/unit		$1,400	$1,600	$1,800	$2,000
Indirect materials	0.30/unit		1,050	1,200	1,350	1,500
Power and lights	0.20/unit		700	800	900	1,000
Maintenance	0.10/unit		350	400	450	500
Total variable overhead costs	$1.00/unit		3,500	4,000	4,500	5,000
Fixed costs (per month)						
Building rent		$1,000	1,000	1,000	1,000	1,000
Depreciation—machinery		1,200	1,200	1,200	1,200	1,200
Supervisory salaries		1,800	1,800	1,800	1,800	1,800
Total fixed overhead costs		$4,000	4,000	4,000	4,000	4,000
Total factory overhead			$7,500	$8,000	$8,500	$9,000
Standard direct labor hours 1 hr./unit			3,500 hrs.	4,000 hrs.	4,500 hrs.	5,000 hrs.
Predetermined overhead rate per standard direct labor hour			$ 2.14	$ 2.00	$ 1.89	$ 1.80

Predicting Activity Levels

When choosing the predicted activity level, management considers many factors. The level can be set as high as 100% of capacity, but this is rare. Factors causing the activity level to be less than full capacity include difficulties in scheduling work, equipment under repair or maintenance, and insufficient product demand. Good long-run management practices often call for some plant capacity in excess of current operating needs to allow for special opportunities and demand changes.

G-Max managers predicted an 80% activity level for May, or a production volume of 4,000 clubheads. At this volume, they budget \$8,000 as the May total overhead. This choice implies a \$2 per unit (labor hour) average overhead cost (\$8,000/4,000 units). Since G-Max has a standard of one direct labor hour per unit, the predetermined standard overhead rate for May is \$2 per standard direct labor hour. The variable overhead rate remains constant at \$1 per direct labor hour regardless of the budgeted production level. The fixed overhead rate changes according to the budgeted production volume. For instance, for the predicted level of 4,000 units of production, the fixed rate is \$1 per hour (\$4,000 fixed costs/4,000 units). For a production level of 5,000 units, however, the fixed rate is \$0.80 per hour (\$4,000 fixed costs/5,000 units).

Point: Variable costs per unit remain constant, but fixed costs per unit decline with increases in volume. This means the average total overhead cost per unit declines with increases in volume.

Decision Insight

Measuring Up In the spirit of continuous improvement, competitors compare their processes and performance standards against benchmarks established by industry leaders. Those that use **benchmarking** include Jiffy Lube, All Tune and Lube, and Speedee Oil Change and Tune-Up. ■

P3 Compute overhead variances.

Computing Overhead Cost Variances

When standard costs are used, the cost accounting system applies overhead to the good units produced using the predetermined standard overhead rate. At period-end, the difference between the total overhead cost applied to products and the total overhead cost actually incurred is called an **overhead cost variance** (total overhead variance), which is defined in Exhibit 21.13.

EXHIBIT 21.13

Overhead Cost Variance

Overhead cost variance (OCV) = Actual overhead incurred (AOI) − Standard overhead applied (SOA)

The standard overhead applied is based on the predetermined overhead rate (at the predicted activity level) and the standard number of hours that should have been used, based on the actual production. To illustrate, G-Max produced 3,500 units during the month, which should have used 3,500 direct labor hours. From Exhibit 21.12, G-Max's predetermined overhead rate at the predicted capacity level of 4,000 units was \$2.00 per direct labor hour, so the standard overhead applied is \$7,000 (computed as 3,500 direct labor hours × \$2.00). Additional data from cost reports show that the actual overhead cost incurred in the month is \$7,650. G-Max's total overhead variance is thus \$650, computed as:

Actual total overhead (given)	\$7,650
Standard overhead applied (3,500 DLH × \$2.00)	7,000
Total overhead variance (unfavorable).	\$ 650

This variance is unfavorable, as G-Max's actual overhead was higher than it should have been based on budgeted amounts.

Controllable and Volume Variances To help identify factors causing the overhead cost variance, managers analyze this variance separately for controllable and volume variances, as illustrated in Exhibit 21.14. The results provide information useful for taking strategic actions to improve company performance.

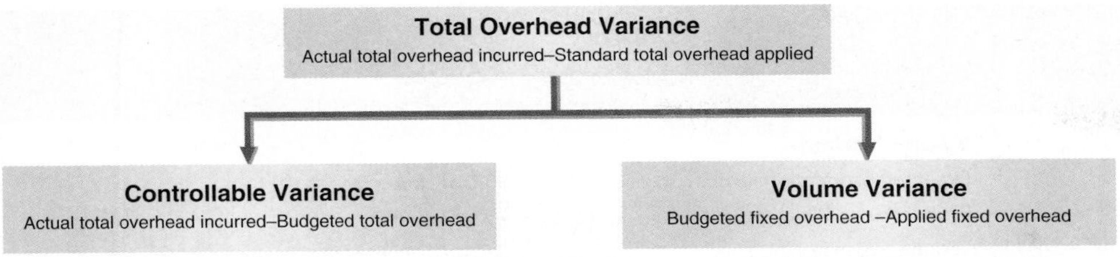

EXHIBIT 21.14

Framework for Understanding Total Overhead Variance

The **controllable variance** is the difference between actual overhead costs incurred and the budgeted overhead costs based on a flexible budget. The controllable variance is so named because it refers to activities usually under management control. A **volume variance** occurs when there is a difference between the actual volume of production and the standard volume of production. The volume variance is based solely on *fixed* overhead. The budgeted fixed overhead amount is the same regardless of the volume of production (within the relevant range). The applied fixed overhead is based, however, on the standard direct labor hours allowed for the actual volume of production, using the flexible budget. When a company operates at a capacity level different from what it expected, the volume variance will differ from zero. We next compute the controllable and volume variances for G-Max.

Returning to the G-Max data, the flexible budget in Exhibit 21.12 shows budgeted factory overhead of $7,500 at the production volume of 3,500 units during the month. The controllable variance is then computed as:

Controllable Variance	
Actual total overhead (given)	$7,650
Applied total overhead (from flexible budget)	7,500
Controllable variance (unfavorable)	$ 150

We then compute the volume variance. G-Max's budgeted fixed overhead at the predicted capacity level for the month was $4,000. Recall from Exhibit 21.12 that G-Max's predetermined fixed overhead at the predicted capacity level of 4,000 units was $1 per hour. Thus, G-Max's applied fixed overhead was $3,500, computed as 3,500 direct labor hours × $1.00 per unit. G-Max's volume variance is then computed as:

Volume Variance	
Budgeted fixed overhead (at predicted capacity)	$4,000
Applied fixed overhead (3,500 DLH × $1.00)	3,500
Volume variance (unfavorable)	$ 500

Analyzing Controllable and Volume Variances How should the top management of G-Max interpret the unfavorable controllable and volume variances? An unfavorable volume variance means that the company did not reach its predicted operating level. In this case, 80% of manufacturing capacity was budgeted but only 70% was used. Management needs to know why the actual level of production differs from the expected level. The main purpose of the volume variance is to identify what portion of the total overhead variance is caused by failing to meet the expected production level. Often the reasons for failing to meet this expected production level are due to factors, for example customer demand, that are beyond employees' control. This information permits management to focus on explanations for the controllable variance, as we discuss next.

Overhead Variance Reports To help management isolate the reasons for the $150 unfavorable controllable variance, an *overhead variance report* can be prepared. A complete overhead variance report provides managers information about specific overhead costs and how they differ from budgeted amounts. Exhibit 21.15 shows G-Max's overhead variance report for May. It reveals that (1) fixed costs and maintenance costs were incurred as expected, (2) costs for indirect labor and power and lights were higher than expected, and (3) indirect materials cost was less than expected.

EXHIBIT 21.15

Overhead Variance Report

G-MAX
Overhead Variance Report
For Month Ended May 31, 2013

Volume Variance

Expected production level	80% of capacity
Production level achieved	70% of capacity
Volume variance	**$500 (unfavorable)**

Controllable Variance	**Flexible Budget**	**Actual Results**	**Variances***
Variable overhead costs			
Indirect labor	$1,400	$1,525	$125 U
Indirect materials	1,050	1,025	25 F
Power and lights	700	750	50 U
Maintenance	350	350	0
Total variable overhead costs	3,500	3,650	150 U
Fixed overhead costs			
Building rent	1,000	1,000	0
Depreciation—machinery	1,200	1,200	0
Supervisory salaries	1,800	1,800	0
Total fixed overhead costs	4,000	4,000	0
Total overhead costs	$7,500	$7,650	$150 U

* F = Favorable variance; U = Unfavorable variance.

The total controllable variance amount ($150 unfavorable) is also readily available from Exhibit 21.15. The overhead variance report shows the total volume variance as $500 unfavorable (shown at the top) and the $150 unfavorable controllable variance (reported at the bottom right). The sum of the controllable variance and the volume variance equals the total overhead variance of $650 unfavorable.

Appendix 21A describes an expanded analysis of overhead variances.

Quick Check

Answers — p. 921

10. Under what conditions is an overhead volume variance considered favorable?
11. To use management by exception, a company (*a*) need not study fixed overhead variances, (*b*) should compute variances from flexible budget amounts to allow management to focus its attention on significant differences between actual and budgeted results, or (*c*) should analyze only variances for direct materials and direct labor.

GLOBAL VIEW

BMW, a German automobile manufacturer, uses concepts of standard costing and variance analysis. Production begins with huge rolls of steel and aluminum, which are then cut and pressed by large machines. Material must meet high quality standards, and the company sets standards for each of its machine operations. In the Assembly department, highly-trained employees complete the assembly of the painted car chassis, often to customer specifications. Again, BMW sets standards for how much labor should be used and monitors its employee performance. The company then computes and analyzes materials price and quantity variances and labor rate and efficiency variances and takes action as needed.

Sales Variances — Decision Analysis

A1 Analyze changes in sales from expected amounts.

This chapter explained the computation and analysis of cost variances. A similar variance analysis can be applied to sales. To illustrate, consider the following sales data from G-Max for two of its golf products, Excel golf balls and Big Bert® drivers.

	Budgeted	Actual
Sales of Excel golf balls (units)	1,000 units	1,100 units
Sales price per Excel golf ball...........	$10	$10.50
Sales of Big Bert® drivers (units)	150 units	140 units
Sales price per Big Bert® driver.........	$200	$190

Using this information, we compute both the *sales price variance* and the *sales volume variance* as shown in Exhibit 21.16. The total sales price variance is $850 unfavorable, and the total sales volume variance is $1,000 unfavorable. Neither total variance implies anything positive about these two products. However, further analysis of these total sales variances reveals that both the sales price and sales volume variances for Excel golf balls are favorable, meaning that both the unfavorable total sales price variance and the unfavorable total sales volume variance are due to the Big Bert driver.

EXHIBIT 21.16

Computing Sales Variances*

Excel Golf Balls	Actual Results AS × AP	Flexible Budget AS × BP	Fixed Budget BS × BP
Sales dollars (balls)	(1,100 × $10.50) **$11,550**	(1,100 × $10) **$11,000**	(1,000 × $10) **$10,000**
	$550 F **Sales Price Variance**		$1,000 F **Sales Volume Variance**
Big Bert® Drivers			
Sales dollars (drivers)	(140 × $190) **$26,600**	(140 × $200) **$28,000**	(150 × $200) **$30,000**
	$1,400 U **Sales Price Variance**		$2,000 U **Sales Volume Variance**
Total	**$850 U**		**$1,000 U**

* AS = actual sales units; AP = actual sales price; BP = budgeted sales price; BS = budgeted sales units (fixed budget).

Managers use sales variances for planning and control purposes. The sales variance information is used to plan future actions to avoid unfavorable variances. G-Max sold 90 total combined units (both balls and drivers) more than planned, but these 90 units were not sold in the proportion budgeted. G-Max sold fewer than the budgeted quantity of the higher-priced driver, which contributed to the unfavorable total sales variances. Managers use such detail to question what caused the company to sell more golf balls and fewer drivers. Managers also use this information to evaluate and even reward their salespeople. Extra compensation is paid to salespeople who contribute to a higher profit margin. Finally, with multiple products, the sales volume variance can be separated into a *sales mix variance* and a *sales quantity variance*. The sales mix variance is the difference between the actual and budgeted sales mix of the products. The sales quantity variance is the difference between the total actual and total budgeted quantity of units sold.

Decision Maker

Sales Manager The current performance report reveals a large favorable sales volume variance but an unfavorable sales price variance. You did not expect to see a large increase in sales volume. What steps do you take to analyze this situation? ■ [Answer—p. 920]

DEMONSTRATION PROBLEM

Pacific Company provides the following information about its budgeted and actual results for June 2013. Although the expected June volume was 25,000 units produced and sold, the company actually produced and sold 27,000 units as detailed here:

	Budget (25,000 units)	Actual (27,000 units)
Selling price	$5.00 per unit	$5.23 per unit
Variable costs (per unit)		
Direct materials	1.24 per unit	1.12 per unit
Direct labor	1.50 per unit	1.40 per unit
Factory supplies*	0.25 per unit	0.37 per unit
Utilities*	0.50 per unit	0.60 per unit
Selling costs	0.40 per unit	0.34 per unit
Fixed costs (per month)		
Depreciation—machinery*	$3,750	$3,710
Depreciation—building*	2,500	2,500
General liability insurance	1,200	1,250
Property taxes on office equipment	500	485
Other administrative expense	750	900

* Indicates factory overhead item; $0.75 per unit or $3 per direct labor hour for variable overhead, and $0.25 per unit or $1 per direct labor hour for fixed overhead.

Standard costs based on expected output of 25,000 units

	Per Unit of Output	Quantity to Be Used	Total Cost
Direct materials, 4 oz. @ $0.31/oz.	$1.24/unit	100,000 oz.	$31,000
Direct labor, 0.25 hrs. @ $6.00/hr.	1.50/unit	6,250 hrs.	37,500
Overhead	1.00/unit		25,000

Actual costs incurred to produce 27,000 units

	Per Unit of Output	Quantity Used	Total Cost
Direct materials, 4 oz. @ $0.28/oz.	$1.12/unit	108,000 oz.	$30,240
Direct labor, 0.20 hrs. @ $7.00/hr.	1.40/unit	5,400 hrs.	37,800
Overhead	1.20/unit		32,400

Standard costs based on expected output of 27,000 units

	Per Unit of Output	Quantity to Be Used	Total Cost
Direct materials, 4 oz. @ $0.31/oz.	$1.24/unit	108,000 oz.	$33,480
Direct labor, 0.25 hrs. @ $6.00/hr.	1.50/unit	6,750 hrs.	40,500
Overhead			26,500

Required

1. Prepare June flexible budgets showing expected sales, costs, and net income assuming 20,000, 25,000, and 30,000 units of output produced and sold.
2. Prepare a flexible budget performance report that compares actual results with the amounts budgeted if the actual volume had been expected.
3. Apply variance analysis for direct materials and direct labor.
4. Compute the total overhead variance, and the controllable and volume variances.
5. Compute spending and efficiency variances for overhead. (Refer to Appendix 21A.)
6. Prepare journal entries to record standard costs, and price and quantity variances, for direct materials, direct labor, and factory overhead. (Refer to Appendix 21A.)

PLANNING THE SOLUTION

- Prepare a table showing the expected results at the three specified levels of output. Compute the variable costs by multiplying the per unit variable costs by the expected volumes. Include fixed costs at the given amounts. Combine the amounts in the table to show total variable costs, contribution margin, total fixed costs, and income from operations.
- Prepare a table showing the actual results and the amounts that should be incurred at 27,000 units. Show any differences in the third column and label them with an *F* for favorable if they increase income or a *U* for unfavorable if they decrease income.
- Using the chapter's format, compute these total variances and the individual variances requested:
  - Total materials variance (including the direct materials quantity variance and the direct materials price variance).
  - Total direct labor variance (including the direct labor efficiency variance and rate variance).
  - Total overhead variance (including both controllable and volume overhead variances and their component variances).

SOLUTION TO DEMONSTRATION PROBLEM

1.

PACIFIC COMPANY
Flexible Budgets
For Month Ended June 30, 2013

	Flexible Budget				
	Variable Amount per Unit	Total Fixed Cost	Flexible Budget for Unit Sales of 20,000	Flexible Budget for Unit Sales of 25,000	Flexible Budget for Unit Sales of 30,000
Sales	$5.00		$100,000	$125,000	$150,000
Variable costs					
Direct materials	1.24		24,800	31,000	37,200
Direct labor	1.50		30,000	37,500	45,000
Factory supplies	0.25		5,000	6,250	7,500
Utilities	0.50		10,000	12,500	15,000
Selling costs	0.40		8,000	10,000	12,000
Total variable costs	3.89		77,800	97,250	116,700
Contribution margin	$1.11		22,200	27,750	33,300
Fixed costs					
Depreciation—machinery		$3,750	3,750	3,750	3,750
Depreciation—building		2,500	2,500	2,500	2,500
General liability insurance		1,200	1,200	1,200	1,200
Property taxes on office equipment		500	500	500	500
Other administrative expense		750	750	750	750
Total fixed costs		$8,700	8,700	8,700	8,700
Income from operations			$ 13,500	$ 19,050	$ 24,600

2.

PACIFIC COMPANY
Flexible Budget Performance Report
For Month Ended June 30, 2013

	Flexible Budget	Actual Results	Variance*
Sales (27,000 units)	$135,000	$141,210	$6,210 F
Variable costs			
Direct materials	33,480	30,240	3,240 F
Direct labor	40,500	37,800	2,700 F
Factory supplies	6,750	9,990	3,240 U
Utilities	13,500	16,200	2,700 U
Selling costs	10,800	9,180	1,620 F
Total variable costs	105,030	103,410	1,620 F
Contribution margin	29,970	37,800	7,830 F
Fixed costs			
Depreciation—machinery	3,750	3,710	40 F
Depreciation—building	2,500	2,500	0
General liability insurance	1,200	1,250	50 U
Property taxes on office equipment	500	485	15 F
Other administrative expense	750	900	150 U
Total fixed costs	8,700	8,845	145 U
Income from operations	$ 21,270	$ 28,955	$7,685 F

* F = Favorable variance; U = Unfavorable variance.

3. Variance analysis of materials and labor costs.

Materials cost variances

Actual cost	108,000 oz. @ $0.28	$30,240
Standard cost	108,000 oz. @ $0.31	33,480
Direct materials cost variance (favorable)		$ 3,240

Price and quantity variances (based on formulas in Exhibit 21.10):

Actual Cost		Standard Cost
AQ × AP	AQ × SP	SQ × SP
108,000 oz. × $0.28	108,000 oz. × $0.31	108,000 oz. × $0.31
$30,240	$33,480	$33,480

$3,240 F **Price Variance**

$0 **Quantity Variance**

$3,240 F **Total Direct Materials Variance**

Labor cost variances

Actual cost	5,400 hrs. @ $7.00	$37,800
Standard cost	6,750 hrs. @ $6.00	40,500
Direct labor cost variance (favorable)		$ 2,700

Rate and efficiency variances (based on formulas in Exhibit 21.11):

Actual Cost		Standard Cost
AH × AR	AH × SR	SH × SR
5,400 hrs. × $7	5,400 hrs. × $6	6,750 hrs. × $6
$37,800	$32,400	$40,500

$5,400 U **Rate Variance**

$8,100 F **Efficiency Variance**

$2,700 F **Total Direct Labor Variance**

4. Total, controllable, and volume variances for overhead.

Overhead cost variances		
Total overhead cost incurred	27,000 units @ $1.20	$32,400
Total overhead applied	27,000 units @ $1.00	27,000
Overhead cost variance (unfavorable)		$ 5,400
Controllable variance		
Actual overhead (given)		$32,400
Applied overhead (from flexible budget for 27,000 units)		26,500
Controllable variance (unfavorable)		$ 5,900
Volume variance		
Budgeted fixed overhead (at predicted capacity)		$ 6,250
Applied fixed overhead (6,750 × $1.00)		6,750
Volume variance (favorable)		$ 500

5. Variable and fixed overhead spending and efficiency variances.

Variable overhead variance *(factory supplies and utilities)*

Variable overhead cost incurred	($9,990 + $16,200)	$26,190
Variable overhead cost applied	6,750 hrs. @ $3/hr.	20,250
Variable overhead cost variance (unfavorable)		$ 5,940

Spending and efficiency variances (based on formulas in Exhibit 21A.2):

Actual Overhead		**Applied Overhead**
AH × AVR	AH × SVR	SH × SVR
	5,400 × $3	6,750 × $3
$26,190	$16,200	$20,250

$9,990 U — **Spending Variance**

$4,050 F — **Efficiency Variance**

$5,940 U — **Total Variable Overhead Variance**

Fixed overhead (depreciation on machinery and building)

Fixed overhead cost incurred	($3,710 + $2,500)	$ 6,210
Fixed overhead cost applied	6,750 hrs. @ $1/hr.	6,750
Fixed overhead cost variance (favorable)		$ 540

Spending and volume variances (based on formulas in Exhibit 21A.2):

Actual Overhead	**Budgeted Overhead**	**Applied Overhead**
		6,750 × $1
$6,210	$6,250	$6,750

$40 F — **Spending Variance**

$500 F — **Volume Variance**

$540 F — **Total Fixed Overhead Variance**

We can also compute

Controllable variance: $5,900 U (both spending variances plus efficiency variance)

Volume variance: 500 F (identified as above)

6.

Goods in Process Inventory	33,480	
Direct Materials Price Variance		3,240
Raw Materials Inventory		30,240
Goods in Process Inventory	40,500	
Direct Labor Rate Variance	5,400	
Direct Labor Efficiency Variance		8,100
Factory Payroll		37,800
Goods in Process Inventory*	27,000	
Variable Overhead Spending Variance	9,990	
Variable Overhead Efficiency Variance		4,050
Fixed Overhead Spending Variance		40
Fixed Overhead Volume Variance		500
Factory Overhead†		32,400

* $20,250 + $6,750 †$26,190 + $6,210

APPENDIX

21A Expanded Overhead Variances and Standard Cost Accounting System

Expanded Overhead Variances Similar to analysis of direct materials and direct labor, overhead variances can be more completely analyzed. Exhibit 21A.1 shows an expanded framework for understanding these component overhead variances. This framework uses classifications of overhead costs as either variable or fixed. A **spending variance** occurs when management pays an amount different than the standard price to acquire an item. For instance, the actual wage rate paid to indirect labor might be higher than the standard rate. Similarly, actual supervisory salaries might be different than expected. Spending variances such as these cause management to investigate the reasons that the amount paid differs from the standard. Both variable and fixed overhead costs can yield their own spending variances. Analyzing variable overhead includes computing an **efficiency variance,** which occurs when standard direct labor hours (the allocation base) expected for actual production differ from the actual direct labor hours used. This efficiency variance reflects on the cost-effectiveness in using the overhead allocation base (such as direct labor).

EXHIBIT 21A.1

Expanded Framework for Total Overhead Variance

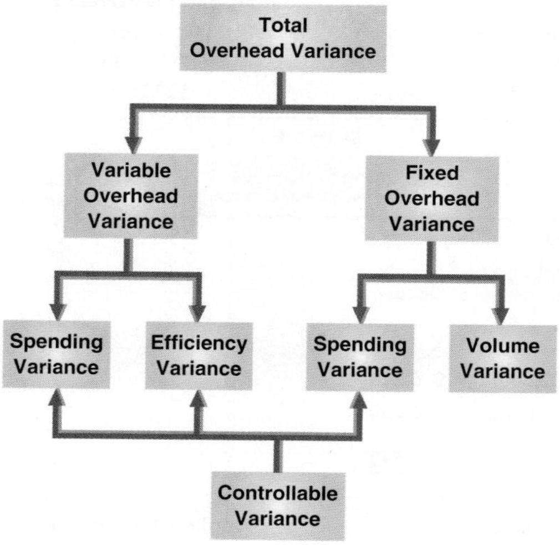

Exhibit 21A.1 shows that we can combine the variable overhead spending variance, the fixed overhead spending variance, and the variable overhead efficiency variance to get the controllable variance.

Computing Variable and Fixed Overhead Cost Variances To illustrate the computation of more detailed overhead cost variances, we return to the G-Max data. We know that G-Max produced 3,500 units when 4,000 units were budgeted. Additional data from cost reports show that the actual overhead cost incurred is $7,650 (the variable portion of $3,650 and the fixed portion of $4,000). Recall from Exhibit 21.12 that each unit requires 1 hour of direct labor, that variable overhead is applied at a rate of $1.00 per direct labor hour, and that the predetermined fixed overhead rate is $1.00 per direct labor hour. Using this information, we can compute overhead variances for both variable and fixed overhead as follows:

Actual variable overhead (given)	$3,650
Applied variable overhead (3,500 × $1.00)	3,500
Variable overhead variance (unfavorable)	$ 150

Actual fixed overhead (given)	$4,000
Applied fixed overhead (3,500 × $1.00)	3,500
Fixed overhead variance (unfavorable)	$ 500

Management should seek to determine the causes of these unfavorable variances and take corrective action. To help better isolate the causes of these variances, more detailed overhead variances can be used, as shown in the next section.

Expanded Overhead Variance Formulas Exhibit 21A.2 shows formulas to use in computing detailed overhead variances that can better identify reasons for variable and fixed overhead variances.

EXHIBIT 21A.2

Variable and Fixed Overhead Variances

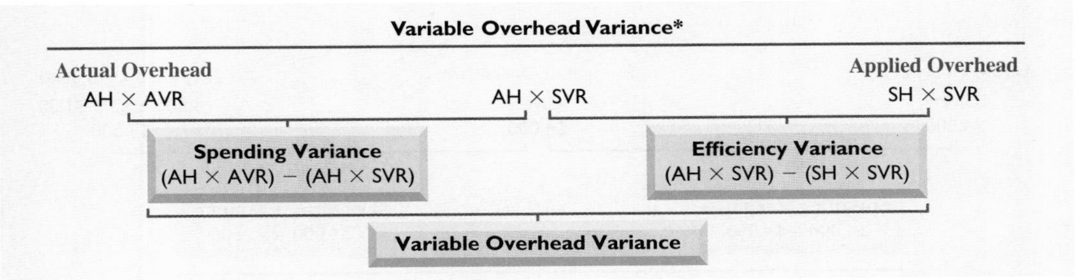

* AH = actual direct labor hours; AVR = actual variable overhead rate; SH = standard direct labor hours; SVR = standard variable overhead rate.

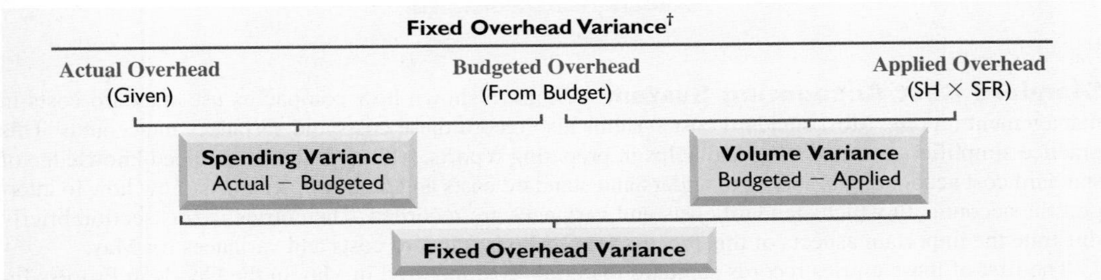

†SH = standard direct labor hours; SFR = standard fixed overhead rate.

Variable Overhead Cost Variances Using these formulas, Exhibit 21A.3 offers insight into the causes of G-Max's $150 unfavorable variable overhead cost variance. Recall that G-Max applies overhead based on direct labor hours as the allocation base. We know that it used 3,400 direct labor hours to produce 3,500 units. This compares favorably to the standard requirement of 3,500 direct labor hours at one labor hour per unit. At a standard variable overhead rate of $1.00 per direct labor hour, this should have resulted in variable overhead costs of $3,400 (middle column of Exhibit 21A.3).

EXHIBIT 21A.3

Computing Variable Overhead Cost Variances

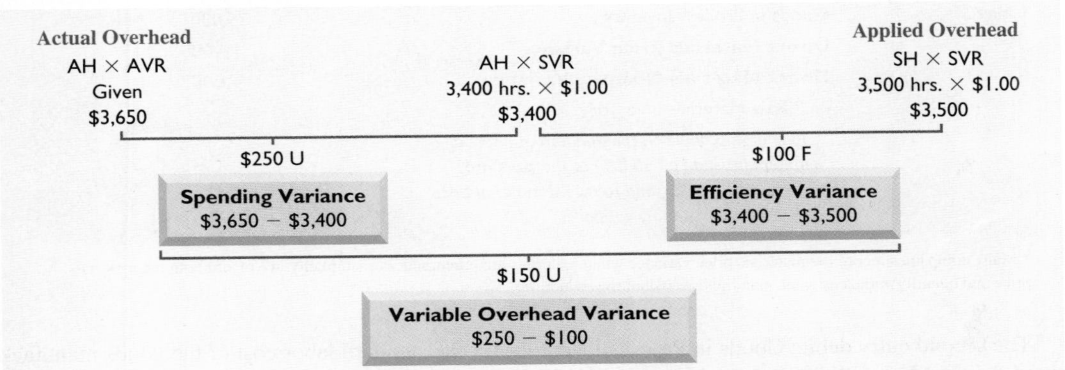

G-Max's cost records, however, report actual variable overhead of $3,650, or $250 higher than expected. This means G-Max has an unfavorable variable overhead spending variance of $250 ($3,650 − $3,400). On the other hand, G-Max used 100 fewer labor hours than expected to make 3,500 units, and its actual variable overhead is lower than its applied variable overhead. Thus, G-Max has a favorable variable overhead efficiency variance of $100 ($3,400 − $3,500).

Fixed Overhead Cost Variances Exhibit 21A.4 provides insight into the causes of G-Max's $500 unfavorable fixed overhead variance. G-Max reports that it incurred $4,000 in actual fixed overhead; this amount equals the budgeted fixed overhead for May at the expected production level of 4,000 units (see Exhibit 21.12). Thus, the fixed overhead spending variance is zero, suggesting good control of fixed overhead costs. G-Max's budgeted fixed overhead application rate is $1 per hour ($4,000/4,000 direct labor hours), but the actual production level is only 3,500 units. Using this information, we can compute the fixed overhead volume variance shown in Exhibit 21A.4. The applied fixed overhead is computed by multiplying 3,500 standard hours allowed for the actual production by the $1 fixed overhead allocation rate. The volume variance of $500 occurs because 500 fewer units are produced than budgeted; namely, 80% of the manufacturing capacity is budgeted but only 70% is used.

EXHIBIT 21A.4

Computing Fixed Overhead Cost Variances

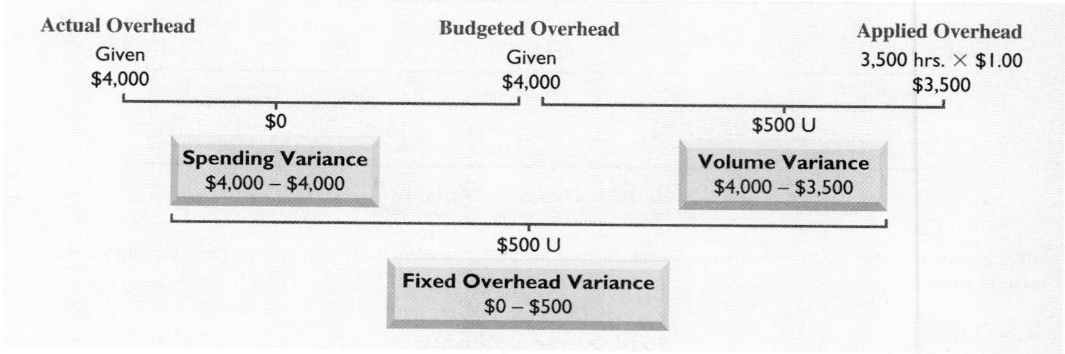

P4 Prepare journal entries for standard costs and account for price and quantity variances.

Standard Cost Accounting System We have shown how companies use standard costs in management reports. Most standard cost systems also record these costs and variances in accounts. This practice simplifies recordkeeping and helps in preparing reports. Although we do not need knowledge of standard cost accounting practices to understand standard costs and their use, we must know how to interpret the accounts in which standard costs and variances are recorded. The entries in this section briefly illustrate the important aspects of this process for G-Max's standard costs and variances for May.

The first of these entries records standard materials cost incurred in May in the Goods in Process Inventory account. This part of the entry is similar to the usual accounting entry, but the amount of the debit equals the standard cost ($35,000) instead of the actual cost ($37,800). This entry credits Raw Materials Inventory for actual cost. The difference between standard and actual direct materials costs is recorded with debits to two separate materials variance accounts (recall Exhibit 21.10). Both the materials price and quantity variances are recorded as debits because they reflect additional costs higher than the standard cost (if actual costs were less than the standard, they are recorded as credits). This treatment (debit) reflects their unfavorable effect because they represent higher costs and lower income.

Assets	= Liabilities +	Equity
+35,000		−1,000
−37,800		−1,800

May 31	Goods in Process Inventory	35,000	
	Direct Materials Price Variance*	**1,800**	
	Direct Materials Quantity Variance	**1,000**	
	Raw Materials Inventory		37,800
	To charge production for standard quantity of materials used (1,750 lbs.) at the standard price ($20 per lb.), and to record material price and material quantity variances.		

* Many companies record the materials price variance when materials are purchased. For simplicity, we record both the materials price and quantity variances when materials are issued to production.

The second entry debits Goods in Process Inventory for the standard labor cost of the goods manufactured during May ($28,000). Actual labor cost ($28,220) is recorded with a credit to the Factory Payroll account. The difference between standard and actual labor costs is explained by two variances (see Exhibit 21.11). The direct labor rate variance is unfavorable and is debited to that account. The direct labor efficiency variance is favorable and that account is credited. The direct labor efficiency variance is favorable because it represents a lower cost and a higher net income.

May 31	Goods in Process Inventory	28,000	
	Direct Labor Rate Variance	**1,020**	
	Direct Labor Efficiency Variance		**800**
	Factory Payroll		28,220
	To charge production with 3,500 standard hours of direct labor at the standard $8 per hour rate, and to record the labor rate and efficiency variances.		

Assets	=	Liabilities	+	Equity
+28,000				+28,220
				− 1,020
				+ 800

The entry to assign standard predetermined overhead to the cost of goods manufactured must debit the $7,000 predetermined amount to the Goods in Process Inventory account. Actual overhead costs of $7,650 were debited to Factory Overhead during the period (entries not shown here). Thus, when Factory Overhead is applied to Goods in Process Inventory, the actual amount is credited to the Factory Overhead account. To account for the difference between actual and standard overhead costs, the entry includes a $250 debit to the Variable Overhead Spending Variance, a $100 credit to the Variable Overhead Efficiency Variance, and a $500 debit to the Volume Variance (recall Exhibits 21A.3 and 21A.4). An alternative (simpler) approach is to record the difference with a $150 debit to the Controllable Variance account and a $500 debit to the Volume Variance account (recall from Exhibit 21A.1 that controllable variance is the sum of both variable overhead variances and the fixed overhead spending variance).

May 31	Goods in Process Inventory	7,000	
	Volume Variance	**500**	
	Variable Overhead Spending Variance	**250**	
	Variable Overhead Efficiency Variance		**100**
	Factory Overhead		7,650
	To apply overhead at the standard rate of $2 per standard direct labor hour (3,500 hours), and to record overhead variances.		

Assets	=	Liabilities	+	Equity
+7,000				+7,650
				− 250
				− 500
				+ 100

The balances of these different variance accounts accumulate until the end of the accounting period. As a result, the unfavorable variances of some months can offset the favorable variances of other months.

These ending variance account balances, which reflect results of the period's various transactions and events, are closed at period-end. If the amounts are *immaterial,* they are added to or subtracted from the balance of the Cost of Goods Sold account. This process is similar to that shown in the job order costing chapter for eliminating an underapplied or overapplied balance in the Factory Overhead account. (*Note:* These variance balances, which represent differences between actual and standard costs, must be added to or subtracted from the materials, labor, and overhead costs recorded. In this way, the recorded costs equal the actual costs incurred in the period; a company must use actual costs in external financial statements prepared in accordance with generally accepted accounting principles.)

Point: If variances are material they can be allocated between Goods in Process Inventory, Finished Goods Inventory, and Cost of Goods Sold. This closing process is explained in advanced courses.

Quick Check

Answers – p. 921

12. A company uses a standard cost accounting system. Prepare the journal entry to record these direct materials variances:

Direct materials cost actually incurred	$73,200
Direct materials quantity variance (favorable)	3,800
Direct materials price variance (unfavorable)	1,300

13. If standard costs are recorded in the manufacturing accounts, how are recorded variances treated at the end of an accounting period?

Summary

C1 Define *standard costs* and explain how standard cost information is useful for management by exception. Standard costs are the normal costs that should be incurred to produce a product or perform a service. They should be based on a careful examination of the processes used to produce a product or perform a service as well as the quantities and prices that should be incurred in carrying out those processes. On a performance report, standard costs (which are flexible budget amounts) are compared to actual costs, and the differences are presented as variances. Standard cost accounting provides management information about costs that differ from budgeted (expected) amounts. Performance reports disclose the costs or areas of operations that have significant variances from budgeted amounts. This allows managers to focus attention on the exceptions and less attention on areas proceeding normally.

C2 Describe variances and what they reveal about performance. Management can use variances to monitor and control activities. Total cost variances can be broken into price and quantity variances to direct management's attention to those responsible for quantities used and prices paid.

A1 Analyze changes in sales from expected amounts. Actual sales can differ from budgeted sales, and managers can investigate this difference by computing both the sales price and sales volume variances. The *sales price variance* refers to that portion of total variance resulting from a difference between actual and budgeted selling prices. The *sales volume variance* refers to that portion of total variance resulting from a difference between actual and budgeted sales quantities.

P1 Prepare a flexible budget and interpret a flexible budget performance report. A flexible budget expresses variable costs in per unit terms so that it can be used to develop budgeted amounts for any volume level within the relevant range. Thus, managers compute budgeted amounts for evaluation after a period for the volume that actually occurred. To prepare a flexible budget, we express each variable cost as a constant amount per unit of sales (or as a percent of sales dollars). In contrast, the budgeted amount of each fixed cost is expressed as a total amount expected to occur at any sales volume within the relevant range. The flexible budget is then determined using these computations and amounts for fixed and variable costs at the expected sales volume.

P2 Compute materials and labor variances. Materials and labor variances are due to differences between the actual costs incurred and the budgeted costs. The price (or rate) variance is computed by comparing the actual cost with the flexible budget amount that should have been incurred to acquire the actual quantity of resources. The quantity (or efficiency) variance is computed by comparing the flexible budget amount that should have been incurred to acquire the actual quantity of resources with the flexible budget amount that should have been incurred to acquire the standard quantity of resources.

P3 Compute overhead variances. Overhead variances are due to differences between the actual overhead costs incurred and the overhead applied to production. An overhead spending variance arises when the actual amount incurred differs from the budgeted amount of overhead. An overhead efficiency (or volume) variance arises when the flexible overhead budget amount differs from the overhead applied to production. It is important to realize that overhead is assigned using an overhead allocation base, meaning that an efficiency variance (in the case of variable overhead) is a result of the overhead application base being used more or less efficiently than planned.

P4^A Prepare journal entries for standard costs and account for price and quantity variances. When a company records standard costs in its accounts, the standard costs of materials, labor, and overhead are debited to the Goods in Process Inventory account. Based on an analysis of the material, labor, and overhead costs, each quantity variance, price variance, volume variance, and controllable variance is recorded in a separate account. At period-end, if the variances are material, they are allocated among the balances of the Goods in Process Inventory, Finished Goods Inventory, and Cost of Goods Sold accounts. If they are not material, they are simply debited or credited to the Cost of Goods Sold account.

Guidance Answers to Decision Maker and Decision Ethics

Entrepreneur From the complaints, this performance report appears to compare actual results with a fixed budget. This comparison is useful in determining whether the amount of work actually performed was more or less than planned, but it is not useful in determining whether the divisions were more or less efficient than planned. If the two consulting divisions worked on more assignments than expected, some costs will certainly increase. Therefore, you should prepare a flexible budget using the actual number of consulting assignments and then compare actual performance to the flexible budget.

Internal Auditor Although the manager's actions might not be unethical, this action is undesirable. The internal auditor should report this behavior, possibly recommending that for the purchase of such discretionary items, the manager must provide budgetary requests using an activity-based budgeting process. The internal auditor would then be given full authority to verify this budget request.

Production Manager As production manager, you should investigate the causes for any labor-related variances although you may not be responsible for them. An unfavorable labor efficiency variance occurs because more labor hours than standard were used during the period. There are at least three possible reasons for this: (1) materials quality could be poor, resulting in more labor consumption due to rework; (2) unplanned interruptions (strike, breakdowns, accidents) could have occurred during the period; and (3) a different labor mix might have occurred for a strategic reason such as to expedite orders. This new labor mix could have consisted of a larger proportion of untrained labor, which resulted in more labor hours.

Sales Manager The unfavorable sales price variance suggests that actual prices were lower than budgeted prices. As the sales manager, you want to know the reasons for a lower than expected price. Perhaps your salespeople lowered the price of certain products by offering quantity discounts. You then might want to know what prompted them to offer the quantity dis counts (perhaps competitors were offering discounts). You want to break the sales volume variance into both the sales mix and sales quantity variances. You could find that although the sales quantity variance is favorable, the sales mix variance is not. Then you need to investigate why the actual sales mix differs from the budgeted sales mix.

Guidance Answers to Quick Checks

1. *b*
2. The first step is classifying each cost as variable or fixed.
3. A fixed budget is prepared using an expected volume of sales or production. A flexible budget is prepared using the actual volume of activity.
4. The contribution margin equals sales less variable costs.
5. *c*
6. It is the difference between actual cost and standard cost.
7. *a*; Total actual hours: 2,500 × 2.5 = 6,250
   Total standard hours: 2,500 × 2.0 = 5,000
   Efficiency variance = (6,250 − 5,000) × $3.00
   = $3,750 U
8. *b*; Rate variance = ($3.10 − $3.00) × 6,250 = $625 U
9. Yes, this will occur when the materials quantity variance is more than the materials price variance.
10. The overhead volume variance is favorable when the actual operating level is higher than the expected level.
11. *b*
12.

Goods in Process Inventory	75,700	
Direct Materials Price Variance	1,300	
Direct Materials Quantity Variance		3,800
Raw Materials Inventory		73,200

13. If the variances are material, they should be prorated among the Goods in Process Inventory, Finished Goods Inventory, and Cost of Goods Sold accounts. If they are not material, they can be closed to Cost of Goods Sold.

Key Terms

Benchmarking (p. 908)
Budget report (p. 896)
Budgetary control (p. 896)
Controllable variance (p. 909)
Cost variance (p. 903)
Efficiency variance (p. 916)
Favorable variance (p. 897)
Fixed budget (p. 897)
Fixed budget performance report (p. 897)
Flexible budget (p. 898)
Flexible budget performance report (p. 900)
Management by exception (p. 901)
Overhead cost variance (p. 908)
Price variance (p. 901)
Quantity variance (p. 901)
Spending variance (p. 916)
Standard costs (p. 901)
Unfavorable variance (p. 897)
Variance analysis (p. 901)
Volume variance (p. 909)

Multiple Choice Quiz

Answers on p. 939 mhhe.com/wildFINMAN5e

Additional Quiz Questions are available at the book's Website.

1. A company predicts its production and sales will be 24,000 units. At that level of activity, its fixed costs are budgeted at $300,000, and its variable costs are budgeted at $246,000. If its activity level declines to 20,000 units, what will be its fixed costs and its variable costs?
   a. Fixed, $300,000; variable, $246,000
   b. Fixed, $250,000; variable, $205,000
   c. Fixed, $300,000; variable, $205,000
   d. Fixed, $250,000; variable, $246,000
   e. Fixed, $300,000; variable, $300,000
2. Using the following information about a single product company, compute its total actual cost of direct materials used.
   - Direct materials standard cost: 5 lbs. × $2 per lb. = $10.
   - Total direct materials cost variance: $15,000 unfavorable.
   - Actual direct materials used: 300,000 lbs.
   - Actual units produced: 60,000 units.

   a. $585,000
   b. $600,000
   c. $300,000
   d. $315,000
   e. $615,000
3. A company uses four hours of direct labor to produce a product unit. The standard direct labor cost is $20 per hour. This period the company produced 20,000 units and used 84,160 hours of direct labor at a total cost of $1,599,040. What is its labor rate variance for the period?
   a. $83,200 F
   b. $84,160 U
   c. $84,160 F
   d. $83,200 U
   e. $ 960 F

4. A company's standard for a unit of its single product is $6 per unit in variable overhead (4 hours × $1.50 per hour). Actual data for the period show variable overhead costs of $150,000 and production of 24,000 units. Its total variable overhead cost variance is
a. $ 6,000 F.
b. $ 6,000 U.
c. $114,000 U.
d. $114,000 F.
e. $ 0.

5. A company's standard for a unit of its single product is $4 per unit in fixed overhead ($24,000 total/6,000 units budgeted). Actual data for the period show total actual fixed overhead of $24,100 and production of 4,800 units. Its volume variance is
a. $4,800 U.
b. $4,800 F.
c. $ 100 U.
d. $ 100 F.
e. $4,900 U.

A Superscript letter A denotes assignments based on Appendix 21A.
Icon denotes assignments that involve decision making.

Discussion Questions

1. What limits the usefulness to managers of fixed budget performance reports?
2. Identify the main purpose of a flexible budget for managers.
3. Prepare a flexible budget performance report title (in proper form) for Spalding Company for the calendar year 2013. Why is a proper title important for this or any report?
4. What type of analysis does a flexible budget performance report help management perform?
5. In what sense can a variable cost be considered constant?
6. What department is usually responsible for a direct labor rate variance? What department is usually responsible for a direct labor efficiency variance? Explain.
7. What is a price variance? What is a quantity variance?
8. What is the purpose of using standard costs?
9. KTM monitors its fixed overhead. In an analysis of fixed overhead cost variances, what is the volume variance? **KTM**
10. What is the predetermined standard overhead rate? How is it computed?
11. In general, variance analysis is said to provide information about ________ and ________ variances.
12. **Polaris** monitors its overhead. In an analysis of overhead cost variances, what is the controllable variance and what causes it? **Polaris**
13. What are the relations among standard costs, flexible budgets, variance analysis, and management by exception?
14. How can the manager of snowmobile sales at **Arctic Cat** use flexible budgets to enhance performance? Arctic Cat
15. Is it possible for a retail store such as **Apple** to use variances in analyzing its operating performance? Explain. Apple
16. Assume that **Piaggio** is budgeted to operate at 80% of capacity but actually operates at 75% of capacity. What effect will the 5% deviation have on its controllable variance? Its volume variance? **PIAGGIO**

connect

QUICK STUDY

QS 21-1
Flexible budget performance report
P1

Beech Company sold 105,000 units of its product in May. For the level of production achieved in May, the budgeted amounts were: sales, $1,300,000; variable costs, $750,000; and fixed costs, $300,000. The following actual financial results are available for May. Prepare a flexible budget performance report for May.

Sales (105,000 units)	$1,275,000
Variable costs	712,500
Fixed costs	300,000

QS 21-2
Standard cost card C1

BatCo makes metal baseball bats. Each bat requires 1 kg. of aluminum at $18 per kg. and 0.25 direct labor hours at $20 per hour. Overhead is assigned at the rate of $40 per labor hour. What amounts would appear on a standard cost card for BatCo?

QS 21-3
Cost variances C2

Refer to information in QS 21-2. Assume the actual cost to manufacture one metal bat was $40. Compute the cost variance and classify it as favorable or unfavorable.

QS 21-4
Management by exception
C1

Managers use *management by exception* for control purposes. (1) Describe the concept of management by exception. (2) Explain how standard costs help managers apply this concept to monitor and control costs.

QS 21-5 Materials cost variances P2

Juan Company's output for the current period was assigned a $150,000 standard direct materials cost. The direct materials variances included a $12,000 favorable price variance and a $2,000 favorable quantity variance. What is the actual total direct materials cost for the current period?

QS 21-6 Labor cost variances P2

Frontera Company's output for the current period results in a $20,000 unfavorable direct labor rate variance and a $10,000 unfavorable direct labor efficiency variance. Production for the current period was assigned an $400,000 standard direct labor cost. What is the actual total direct labor cost for the current period?

QS 21-7 Materials cost variances P2

For the current period, Kayenta Company's manufacturing operations yield a $4,000 unfavorable price variance on its direct materials usage. The actual price per pound of material is $78; the standard price is $77.50. How many pounds of material are used in the current period?

QS 21-8 Overhead cost variances P3

Alvarez Company's output for the current period yields a $20,000 favorable overhead volume variance and a $60,400 unfavorable overhead controllable variance. Standard overhead charged to production for the period is $225,000. What is the actual total overhead cost incurred for the period?

QS 21-9[A] Preparing overhead entries P4

Refer to the information in QS 21-8. Alvarez records standard costs in its accounts. Prepare the journal entry to charge overhead costs to the Goods in Process Inventory account and to record any variances.

QS 21-10 Total overhead cost variance P3

Mosaic Company applies overhead using machine hours and reports the following information. Compute the total variable overhead cost variance.

Actual machine hours used	4,700 hours
Standard machine hours	5,000 hours
Actual variable overhead rate per hour	$4.15
Standard variable overhead rate per hour	$4.00

QS 21-11[A] Overhead spending and efficiency variances P3

Refer to the information from QS 21-10. Compute the variable overhead spending variance and the variable overhead efficiency variance.

QS 21-12 Computing sales price and volume variances A1

Farad, Inc. specializes in selling used SUVs. During the first six months of 2013, the dealership sold 50 trucks at an average price of $9,000 each. The budget for the first six months of 2013 was to sell 45 trucks at an average price of $9,500 each. Compute the dealership's sales price variance and sales volume variance for the first six months of 2013.

QS 21-13 Flexible budget P1

Based on predicted production of 24,000 units, a company anticipates $300,000 of fixed costs and $246,000 of variable costs. If the company actually produces 20,000 units, what are the flexible budget amounts of fixed and variable costs?

QS 21-14 Flexible budget P1

Brodrick Company expects to produce 20,000 units for the year ending December 31. A flexible budget for 20,000 units of production reflects sales of $400,000; variable costs of $80,000; and fixed costs of $150,000. If the company instead produces and sells 26,000 units for the year, calculate the expected level of income from operations.

QS 21-15 Flexible budget performance report P1

Refer to information in QS 21-14. Assume that actual sales are $480,000, actual variable costs for the year are $112,000, and actual fixed costs for the year are $145,000. Prepare a flexible budget performance report for the year.

QS 21-16 Materials variances P2

Tercer reports the following on one of its products. Compute the direct materials price and quantity variances.

Direct materials standard (4 lbs. @ $2/lb.)	$8 per finished unit
Actual direct materials used	300,000 lbs.
Actual finished units produced	60,000 units
Actual cost of direct materials used	$535,000

QS 21-17
Direct labor variances
P2

The following information describes a company's usage of direct labor in a recent period. Compute the direct labor rate and efficiency variances for the period.

Actual direct labor hours used	65,000
Actual direct labor rate per hour	$15
Standard direct labor rate per hour	$14
Standard direct labor hours for units produced	67,000

QS 21-18
Controllable overhead variance
P3

Fogel Co. expects to produce 116,000 units for the year. The company's flexible budget for 116,000 units of production shows variable overhead costs of $162,400 and fixed overhead costs of $124,000. For the year, the company incurred actual overhead costs of $262,800 while producing 110,000 units. Compute the controllable overhead variance.

QS 21-19
Controllable overhead variance
P3

AirPro Corp. reports the following for November. Compute the controllable overhead variance for November.

Actual total factory overhead incurred	$28,175
Standard factory overhead:	
Variable overhead	$3.10 per unit produced
Fixed overhead	
($12,000/12,000 predicted units to be produced)	$1 per unit
Predicted units produced	12,000 units
Actual units produced	9,800 units

QS 21-20
Volume variance P3

Refer to information in QS 21-19. Compute the overhead volume variance for November.

QS 21-21
Sales variances A1

In a recent year, **BMW** sold 216,944 of its 1 Series cars. Assume the company expected to sell 225,944 of these cars during the year. Also assume the budgeted sales price for each car was $30,000, and the actual sales price for each car was $30,200. Compute the sales price variance and the sales volume variance.

EXERCISES

Exercise 21-1
Classification of costs as fixed or variable
P1

JPAK Company manufactures and sells mountain bikes. It normally operates eight hours a day, five days a week. Using this information, classify each of the following costs as fixed or variable. If additional information would affect your decision, describe the information.

a. Bike frames
b. Screws for assembly
c. Repair expense for tools
d. Direct labor
e. Bike tires
f. Gas used for heating
g. Incoming shipping expenses
h. Taxes on property
i. Office supplies
j. Depreciation on tools
k. Management salaries

Exercise 21-2
Preparation of flexible budgets
P1

Tempo Company's fixed budget for the first quarter of calendar year 2013 reveals the following. Prepare flexible budgets following the format of Exhibit 21.3 that show variable costs per unit, fixed costs, and three different flexible budgets for sales volumes of 6,000, 7,000, and 8,000 units.

Sales (7,000 units)		$2,800,000
Cost of goods sold		
Direct materials	$280,000	
Direct labor	490,000	
Production supplies	175,000	
Plant manager salary	65,000	1,010,000
Gross profit		1,790,000
Selling expenses		
Sales commissions	140,000	
Packaging	154,000	
Advertising	125,000	419,000
Administrative expenses		
Administrative salaries	85,000	
Depreciation—office equip.	35,000	
Insurance	20,000	
Office rent	36,000	176,000
Income from operations		$1,195,000

Check Income (at 6,000 units), $972,000

Exercise 21-3
Preparation of a flexible budget performance report
P1

Solitaire Company's fixed budget performance report for June follows. The $315,000 budgeted expenses include $294,000 variable expenses and $21,000 fixed expenses. Actual expenses include $27,000 fixed expenses. Prepare a flexible budget performance report showing any variances between budgeted and actual results. List fixed and variable expenses separately.

	Fixed Budget	Actual Results	Variances
Sales (in units)	8,400	10,800	
Sales (in dollars)	$420,000	$540,000	$120,000 F
Total expenses	315,000	378,000	63,000 U
Income from operations	$105,000	$162,000	$ 57,000 F

Check Income variance, $21,000 F

Exercise 21-4
Preparation of a flexible budget performance report
P1

Bay City Company's fixed budget performance report for July follows. The $647,500 budgeted expenses include $487,500 variable expenses and $160,000 fixed expenses. Actual expenses include $158,000 fixed expenses. Prepare a flexible budget performance report that shows any variances between budgeted results and actual results. List fixed and variable expenses separately.

	Fixed Budget	Actual Results	Variances
Sales (in units)	7,500	7,200	
Sales (in dollars)	$750,000	$737,000	$13,000 U
Total expenses	647,500	641,000	6,500 F
Income from operations	$102,500	$ 96,000	$ 6,500 U

Check Income variance, $4,000 F

Exercise 21-5
Computation and interpretation of labor variances P2

After evaluating Null Company's manufacturing process, management decides to establish standards of 3 hours of direct labor per unit of product and $15 per hour for the labor rate. During October, the company uses 16,250 hours of direct labor at a $247,000 total cost to produce 5,600 units of product. In November, the company uses 22,000 hours of direct labor at a $335,500 total cost to produce 6,000 units of product. (1) Compute the rate variance, the efficiency variance, and the total direct labor cost variance for each of these two months. (2) Interpret the October direct labor variances.

Check (1) October rate variance, $3,250 U

Exercise 21-6
Computation of total variable and fixed overhead variances
P3

Sedona Company set the following standard costs for one unit of its product for 2013.

Direct material (20 lbs. @ $2.50 per lb.)	$ 50.00
Direct labor (10 hrs. @ $8.00 per hr.)	80.00
Factory variable overhead (10 hrs. @ $4.00 per hr.)	40.00
Factory fixed overhead (10 hrs. @ $1.60 per hr.)	16.00
Standard cost	$186.00

The $5.60 ($4.00 + $1.60) total overhead rate per direct labor hour is based on an expected operating level equal to 75% of the factory's capacity of 50,000 units per month. The following monthly flexible budget information is also available.

	Operating Levels (% of capacity)		
	70%	75%	80%
Budgeted output (units)	35,000	37,500	40,000
Budgeted labor (standard hours)	350,000	375,000	400,000
Budgeted overhead (dollars)			
Variable overhead	$1,400,000	$1,500,000	$1,600,000
Fixed overhead	600,000	600,000	600,000
Total overhead	$2,000,000	$2,100,000	$2,200,000

During the current month, the company operated at 70% of capacity, employees worked 340,000 hours, and the following actual overhead costs were incurred.

Variable overhead costs	$1,375,000
Fixed overhead costs	628,600
Total overhead costs	$2,003,600

Check (2) Variable overhead cost variance, $25,000 F

(1) Show how the company computed its predetermined overhead application rate per hour for total overhead, variable overhead, and fixed overhead. (2) Compute the total variable and total fixed overhead variances.

Exercise 21-7[A]
Computation and interpretation of overhead spending, efficiency, and volume variances P3

Check (1) Variable overhead: Spending, $15,000 U; Efficiency, $40,000 F

Refer to the information from Exercise 21-6. Compute and interpret the following.

1. Variable overhead spending and efficiency variances.
2. Fixed overhead spending and volume variances.
3. Controllable variance.

Exercise 21-8
Computation and interpretation of materials variances P2

Check Price variance, $2,200 U

Hart Company made 3,000 bookshelves using 22,000 board feet of wood costing $266,200. The company's direct materials standards for one bookshelf are 8 board feet of wood at $12 per board foot. (1) Compute the direct materials variances incurred in manufacturing these bookshelves. (2) Interpret the direct materials variances.

Exercise 21-9[A]
Materials variances recorded and closed
P4

Check (2) Cr. to Cost of Goods Sold, $21,800

Refer to Exercise 21-8. Hart Company records standard costs in its accounts and its material variances in separate accounts when it assigns materials costs to the Goods in Process Inventory account. (1) Show the journal entry that both charges the direct materials costs to the Goods in Process Inventory account and records the materials variances in their proper accounts. (2) Assume that Hart's material variances are the only variances accumulated in the accounting period and that they are immaterial. Prepare the adjusting journal entry to close the variance accounts at period-end. (3) Identify the variance that should be investigated according to the management by exception concept. Explain.

Exercise 21-10
Computation of total overhead rate and total overhead variance
P3

Check (1) Variable overhead rate, $11.00 per hour

World Company expects to operate at 80% of its productive capacity of 50,000 units per month. At this planned level, the company expects to use 25,000 standard hours of direct labor. Overhead is allocated to products using a predetermined standard rate based on direct labor hours. At the 80% capacity level, the total budgeted cost includes $50,000 fixed overhead cost and $275,000 variable overhead cost. In the current month, the company incurred $305,000 actual overhead and 22,000 actual labor hours while producing 35,000 units. (1) Compute the overhead application rate for total overhead. (2) Compute the total overhead variance.

Exercise 21-11
Computation of volume and controllable overhead variances
P3

Check (2) $14,375 U

Refer to the information from Exercise 21-10. Compute the (1) overhead volume variance and (2) overhead controllable variance.

Exercise 21-12
Computing and interpreting sales variances
A1

Comp Wiz sells computers. During May 2013, it sold 350 computers at a $1,200 average price each. The May 2013 fixed budget included sales of 365 computers at an average price of $1,100 each. (1) Compute the sales price variance and the sales volume variance for May 2013. (2) Interpret the findings.

Exercise 21-13
Standard costs
C1

Match the terms labeled a through e with their correct definition labeled 1 through 5.

a. Standard cost card
b. Management by exception
c. Standard cost
d. Ideal standard
e. Practical standard

1. Quantity of input required under normal conditions.
2. Quantity of input required if a production process is 100% efficient.
3. Managing by focusing on large differences from standard costs.
4. Record that accumulates standard cost information.
5. Preset cost for delivering a product or service under normal conditions.

Exercise 21-14
Cost variances
C2

Presented below are terms preceded by letters a through j and a list of definitions 1 through 10. Enter the letter of the term with the definition, using the space preceding the definition.

a. Fixed budget
b. Standard costs
c. Price variance
d. Quantity variance
e. Volume variance
f. Controllable variance
g. Cost variance
h. Flexible budget
i. Variance analysis
j. Management by exception

_______ **1.** The difference between actual and budgeted sales or cost caused by the difference between the actual price per unit and the budgeted price per unit.
_______ **2.** A planning budget based on a single predicted amount of sales or production volume; unsuitable for evaluations if the actual volume differs from the predicted volume.
_______ **3.** Preset costs for delivering a product, component, or service under normal conditions.
_______ **4.** A process of examining the differences between actual and budgeted sales or costs and describing them in terms of the amounts that resulted from price and quantity differences.
_______ **5.** The difference between the total budgeted overhead cost and the overhead cost that was allocated to products using the predetermined fixed overhead rate.
_______ **6.** A budget prepared based on predicted amounts of revenues and expenses corresponding to the actual level of output.
_______ **7.** The difference between actual and budgeted cost caused by the difference between the actual quantity and the budgeted quantity.
_______ **8.** The combination of both overhead spending variances (variable and fixed) and the variable overhead efficiency variance.
_______ **9.** A management process to focus on significant variances and give less attention to areas where performance is close to the standard.
_______ **10.** The difference between actual cost and standard cost, made up of a price variance and a quantity variance.

Exercise 21-15
Analyzing variances
C1

Resset Co. provides the following results of April's operations: F indicates favorable and U indicates unfavorable. Applying the management by exception approach, which of the variances are of greatest concern? Why?

Direct materials price variance	$ 300 F
Direct materials quantity variance	3,000 U
Direct labor rate variance	100 U
Direct labor efficiency variance	2,200 F
Controllable overhead variance	400 U
Fixed overhead volume variance	500 F

Exercise 21-16
Direct materials and direct labor variances
P2

The following information describes production activities of Mercer Manufacturing for the year:

Actual raw materials used	16,000 lbs. at $4.05 per lb.
Actual factory payroll	5,545 hours for a total of $105,355
Actual units produced	30,000

Budgeted standards for each unit produced are 0.50 pounds of raw material at $4.00 per pound and 10 minutes of direct labor at $20 per hour. (1) Compute the direct materials price and quantity variances. (2) Compute the direct labor rate and efficiency variances. Indicate whether each variance is favorable or unfavorable.

PROBLEM SET A

connect

Problem 21-1A
Computation of materials, labor, and overhead variances
P2 P3

mhhe.com/wildFINMAN5e

Trico Company set the following standard unit costs for its single product.

Direct materials (30 lbs. @ $4 per lb.)	$120.00
Direct labor (5 hrs. @ $14 per hr.)	70.00
Factory overhead—variable (5 hrs. @ $8 per hr.)	40.00
Factory overhead—fixed (5 hrs. @ $10 per hr.)	50.00
Total standard cost	$280.00

The predetermined overhead rate is based on a planned operating volume of 80% of the productive capacity of 60,000 units per quarter. The following flexible budget information is available.

	Operating Levels		
	70%	80%	90%
Production in units	42,000	48,000	54,000
Standard direct labor hours	210,000	240,000	270,000
Budgeted overhead			
Fixed factory overhead	$2,400,000	$2,400,000	$2,400,000
Variable factory overhead	$1,680,000	$1,920,000	$2,160,000

During the current quarter, the company operated at 90% of capacity and produced 54,000 units of product; actual direct labor totaled 265,000 hours. Units produced were assigned the following standard costs:

Direct materials (1,620,000 lbs. @ $4 per lb.)	$ 6,480,000
Direct labor (270,000 hrs. @ $14 per hr.)	3,780,000
Factory overhead (270,000 hrs. @ $18 per hr.)	4,860,000
Total standard cost	$15,120,000

Actual costs incurred during the current quarter follow:

Direct materials (1,615,000 lbs. @ $4.10)	$ 6,621,500
Direct labor (265,000 hrs. @ $13.75)	3,643,750
Fixed factory overhead costs	2,350,000
Variable factory overhead costs	2,200,000
Total actual costs	$14,815,250

Required

1. Compute the direct materials cost variance, including its price and quantity variances.
2. Compute the direct labor variance, including its rate and efficiency variances.
3. Compute the overhead controllable and volume variances.

Check (1) Materials variances: Price, $161,500 U; Quantity, $20,000 F.
(2) Labor variances: Rate, $66,250 F; Efficiency, $70,000 F

Problem 21-2A[A]
Expanded overhead variances
P3

Refer to information in Problem 21-1A.

Required

Compute these variances: (a) variable overhead spending and efficiency, (b) fixed overhead spending and volume, and (c) total overhead controllable.

Problem 21-3A
Preparation and analysis of a flexible budget P1

Phoenix Company's 2013 master budget included the following fixed budget report. It is based on an expected production and sales volume of 15,000 units.

PHOENIX COMPANY
Fixed Budget Report
For Year Ended December 31, 2013

Sales		$3,000,000
Cost of goods sold		
Direct materials	$975,000	
Direct labor	225,000	
Machinery repairs (variable cost)	60,000	
Depreciation—plant equipment	300,000	
Utilities ($45,000 is variable)	195,000	
Plant management salaries	200,000	1,955,000
Gross profit		1,045,000
Selling expenses		
Packaging	75,000	
Shipping	105,000	
Sales salary (fixed annual amount)	250,000	430,000
General and administrative expenses		
Advertising expense	125,000	
Salaries	241,000	
Entertainment expense	90,000	456,000
Income from operations		$ 159,000

Required

1. Classify all items listed in the fixed budget as variable or fixed. Also determine their amounts per unit or their amounts for the year, as appropriate.
2. Prepare flexible budgets (see Exhibit 21.3) for the company at sales volumes of 14,000 and 16,000 units.
3. The company's business conditions are improving. One possible result is a sales volume of approximately 18,000 units. The company president is confident that this volume is within the relevant range of existing capacity. How much would operating income increase over the 2013 budgeted amount of $159,000 if this level is reached without increasing capacity?
4. An unfavorable change in business is remotely possible; in this case, production and sales volume for 2013 could fall to 12,000 units. How much income (or loss) from operations would occur if sales volume falls to this level?

Check (2) Budgeted income at 16,000 units, $260,000

(4) Potential operating loss, $(144,000)

Problem 21-4A
Preparation and analysis of a flexible budget performance report
P1 P2 A1

mhhe.com/wildFINMAN5e

Refer to the information in Problem 21-3A. Phoenix Company's actual income statement for 2013 follows.

PHOENIX COMPANY
Statement of Income from Operations
For Year Ended December 31, 2013

Sales (18,000 units)		$3,648,000
Cost of goods sold		
Direct materials	$1,185,000	
Direct labor	278,000	
Machinery repairs (variable cost)	63,000	
Depreciation—plant equipment	300,000	
Utilities (fixed cost is $147,500)	200,500	
Plant management salaries	210,000	2,236,500
Gross profit		1,411,500
Selling expenses		
Packaging	87,500	
Shipping	118,500	
Sales salary (annual)	268,000	474,000
General and administrative expenses		
Advertising expense	132,000	
Salaries	241,000	
Entertainment expense	93,500	466,500
Income from operations		$ 471,000

Check (1) Variances: Fixed costs, $36,000 U; Income, $9,000 F

Required

1. Prepare a flexible budget performance report for 2013.

Analysis Component

2. Analyze and interpret both the (a) sales variance and (b) direct materials variance.

Problem 21-5A
Flexible budget preparation; computation of materials, labor, and overhead variances; and overhead variance report
P1 P2 P3 C2

Antuan Company set the following standard costs for one unit of its product.

Direct materials (6 lbs. @ $5 per lb.)	$ 30
Direct labor (2 hrs. @ $17 per hr.)	34
Overhead (2 hrs. @ $18.50 per hr.)	37
Total standard cost	$101

The predetermined overhead rate ($18.50 per direct labor hour) is based on an expected volume of 75% of the factory's capacity of 20,000 units per month. Following are the company's budgeted overhead costs per month at the 75% level.

Overhead Budget (75% Capacity)		
Variable overhead costs		
Indirect materials	$ 45,000	
Indirect labor	180,000	
Power	45,000	
Repairs and maintenance	90,000	
Total variable overhead costs		$360,000
Fixed overhead costs		
Depreciation—building	24,000	
Depreciation—machinery	80,000	
Taxes and insurance	12,000	
Supervision	79,000	
Total fixed overhead costs		195,000
Total overhead costs		$555,000

The company incurred the following actual costs when it operated at 75% of capacity in October.

Direct materials (91,000 lbs. @ $5.10 per lb.)		$ 464,100
Direct labor (30,500 hrs. @ $17.25 per hr.)		526,125
Overhead costs		
Indirect materials	$ 44,250	
Indirect labor	177,750	
Power	43,000	
Repairs and maintenance	96,000	
Depreciation—building	24,000	
Depreciation—machinery	75,000	
Taxes and insurance	11,500	
Supervision	89,000	560,500
Total costs		$1,550,725

Check (2) Budgeted total overhead at 13,000 units, $507,000.

(3) Materials variances: Price, $9,100 U; Quantity, $5,000 U

Required

1. Examine the monthly overhead budget to (a) determine the costs per unit for each variable overhead item and its total per unit costs, and (b) identify the total fixed costs per month.

2. Prepare flexible overhead budgets (as in Exhibit 21.12) for October showing the amounts of each variable and fixed cost at the 65%, 75%, and 85% capacity levels.

3. Compute the direct materials cost variance, including its price and quantity variances.

4. Compute the direct labor cost variance, including its rate and efficiency variances.

5. Prepare a detailed overhead variance report (as in Exhibit 21.15) that shows the variances for individual items of overhead.

(4) Labor variances: Rate, $7,625 U; Efficiency, $8,500 U

Problem 21-6A[A]
Materials, labor, and overhead variances; overhead variance report
C2 P2 P3

Kegler Company has set the following standard costs per unit for the product it manufactures.

Direct materials (15 lbs. @ $4 per lb.)	$ 60.00
Direct labor (3 hrs. @ $15 per hr.)	45.00
Overhead (3 hrs. @ $3.85 per hr.)	11.55
Total standard cost	$116.55

The predetermined overhead rate is based on a planned operating volume of 80% of the productive capacity of 10,000 units per month. The following flexible budget information is available.

	Operating Levels		
	70%	80%	90%
Production in units	7,000	8,000	9,000
Standard direct labor hours	21,000	24,000	27,000
Budgeted overhead			
Variable overhead costs			
Indirect materials	$13,125	$15,000	$16,875
Indirect labor	21,000	24,000	27,000
Power	5,250	6,000	6,750
Maintenance	2,625	3,000	3,375
Total variable costs	42,000	48,000	54,000
Fixed overhead costs			
Rent of factory building	15,000	15,000	15,000
Depreciation—machinery	10,000	10,000	10,000
Supervisory salaries	19,400	19,400	19,400
Total fixed costs	44,400	44,400	44,400
Total overhead costs	$86,400	$92,400	$98,400

During May, the company operated at 90% of capacity and produced 9,000 units, incurring the following actual costs.

Direct materials (138,000 lbs. @ $3.75 per lb.)		$ 517,500
Direct labor (31,000 hrs. @ $15.10 per hr.)		468,100
Overhead costs		
Indirect materials	$15,000	
Indirect labor	26,500	
Power	6,750	
Maintenance	4,000	
Rent of factory building	15,000	
Depreciation—machinery	10,000	
Supervisory salaries	22,000	99,250
Total costs		$1,084,850

Required

1. Compute the direct materials variance, including its price and quantity variances.

2. Compute the direct labor variance, including its rate and efficiency variances.

[continued on next page]

Check (1) Materials variances: Price, $34,500 F; Quantity, $12,000 U
(2) Labor variances: Rate, $3,100 U; Efficiency, $60,000 U

3. Compute these variances: (a) variable overhead spending and efficiency, (b) fixed overhead spending and volume, and (c) total overhead controllable.
4. Prepare a detailed overhead variance report (as in Exhibit 21.15) that shows the variances for individual items of overhead.

Problem 21-7A[A]
Materials, labor, and overhead variances recorded and analyzed
C1 P4

Boss Company's standard cost accounting system recorded this information from its December operations.

Standard direct materials cost	$100,000
Direct materials quantity variance (unfavorable)	3,000
Direct materials price variance (favorable)	500
Actual direct labor cost	90,000
Direct labor efficiency variance (favorable)	7,000
Direct labor rate variance (unfavorable)	1,200
Actual overhead cost	375,000
Volume variance (unfavorable)	12,000
Controllable variance (unfavorable)	9,000

Required

Check (1) Dr. Goods in Process Inventory (for overhead), $354,000

1. Prepare December 31 journal entries to record the company's costs and variances for the month. (Do not prepare the journal entry to close the variances.)

Analysis Component

2. Identify the areas that would attract the attention of a manager who uses management by exception. Explain what action(s) the manager should consider.

PROBLEM SET B

Problem 21-1B
Computation of materials, labor, and overhead variances
P2 P3

Kryll Company set the following standard unit costs for its single product.

Direct materials (25 lbs. @ $4 per lb.)	$100.00
Direct labor (6 hrs. @ $8 per hr.)	48.00
Factory overhead—variable (6 hrs. @ $5 per hr.)	30.00
Factory overhead—fixed (6 hrs. @ $7 per hr.)	42.00
Total standard cost	$220.00

The predetermined overhead rate is based on a planned operating volume of 80% of the productive capacity of 60,000 units per quarter. The following flexible budget information is available.

	Operating Levels		
	70%	80%	90%
Production in units	42,000	48,000	54,000
Standard direct labor hours	252,000	288,000	324,000
Budgeted overhead			
Fixed factory overhead	$2,016,000	$2,016,000	$2,016,000
Variable factory overhead	1,260,000	1,440,000	1,620,000

During the current quarter, the company operated at 70% of capacity and produced 42,000 units of product; direct labor hours worked were 250,000. Units produced were assigned the following standard costs:

Direct materials (1,050,000 lbs. @ $4 per lb.)	$4,200,000
Direct labor (252,000 hrs. @ $8 per hr.)	2,016,000
Factory overhead (252,000 hrs. @ $12 per hr.)	3,024,000
Total standard cost	$9,240,000

Actual costs incurred during the current quarter follow:

Direct materials (1,000,000 lbs. @ $4.25)	$4,250,000
Direct labor (250,000 hrs. @ $7.75)	1,937,500
Fixed factory overhead costs	1,960,000
Variable factory overhead costs	1,200,000
Total actual costs	$9,347,500

Required

1. Compute the direct materials cost variance, including its price and quantity variances.
2. Compute the direct labor variance, including its rate and efficiency variances.
3. Compute the total overhead controllable and volume variances.

Check (1) Materials variances: Price, $250,000 U; Quantity, $200,000 F (2) Labor variances: Rate, $62,500 F; Efficiency, $16,000 F

Problem 21-2B[A]
Expanded overhead variances
P3

Refer to information in Problem 21-1B.

Required

Compute these variances: (a) variable overhead spending and efficiency, (b) fixed overhead spending and volume, and (c) total overhead controllable.

Problem 21-3B
Preparation and analysis of a flexible budget P1 A1

Tohono Company's 2013 master budget included the following fixed budget report. It is based on an expected production and sales volume of 20,000 units.

TOHONO COMPANY
Fixed Budget Report
For Year Ended December 31, 2013

Sales		$3,000,000
Cost of goods sold		
Direct materials	$1,200,000	
Direct labor	260,000	
Machinery repairs (variable cost)	57,000	
Depreciation—machinery	250,000	
Utilities (25% is variable cost)	200,000	
Plant manager salaries	140,000	2,107,000
Gross profit		893,000
Selling expenses		
Packaging	80,000	
Shipping	116,000	
Sales salary (fixed annual amount)	160,000	356,000
General and administrative expenses		
Advertising	81,000	
Salaries	241,000	
Entertainment expense	90,000	412,000
Income from operations		$ 125,000

Required

1. Classify all items listed in the fixed budget as variable or fixed. Also determine their amounts per unit or their amounts for the year, as appropriate.
2. Prepare flexible budgets (see Exhibit 21.3) for the company at sales volumes of 18,000 and 24,000 units.
3. The company's business conditions are improving. One possible result is a sales volume of approximately 28,000 units. The company president is confident that this volume is within the relevant range of existing capacity. How much would operating income increase over the 2013 budgeted amount of $125,000 if this level is reached without increasing capacity?
4. An unfavorable change in business is remotely possible; in this case, production and sales volume for 2013 could fall to 14,000 units. How much income (or loss) from operations would occur if sales volume falls to this level?

Check (2) Budgeted income at 24,000 units, $372,400

(4) Potential operating loss, $(246,100)

Problem 21-4B
Preparation and analysis of a flexible budget performance report
P1 A1

Refer to the information in Problem 21-3B. Tohono Company's actual income statement for 2013 follows.

TOHONO COMPANY Statement of Income from Operations For Year Ended December 31, 2013		
Sales (24,000 units)		$3,648,000
Cost of goods sold		
Direct materials	$1,400,000	
Direct labor	360,000	
Machinery repairs (variable cost)	60,000	
Depreciation—machinery	250,000	
Utilities (variable cost, $64,000)	218,000	
Plant manager salaries	155,000	2,443,000
Gross profit		1,205,000
Selling expenses		
Packaging	90,000	
Shipping	124,000	
Sales salary (annual)	162,000	376,000
General and administrative expenses		
Advertising expense	104,000	
Salaries	232,000	
Entertainment expense	100,000	436,000
Income from operations		$ 393,000

Required

Check (1) Variances: Fixed costs, $45,000 U; Income, $20,600 F

1. Prepare a flexible budget performance report for 2013.

Analysis Component

2. Analyze and interpret both the (a) sales variance and (b) direct materials variance.

Problem 21-5B
Flexible budget preparation; computation of materials, labor, and overhead variances; and overhead variance report
P1 P2 P3 C2

Suncoast Company set the following standard costs for one unit of its product.

Direct materials (4.5 lb. @ $6 per kg.)	$27
Direct labor (1.5 hrs. @ $12 per hr.)	18
Overhead (1.5 hrs. @ $16 per hr.)	24
Total standard cost	$69

The predetermined overhead rate ($16.00 per direct labor hour) is based on an expected volume of 75% of the factory's capacity of 20,000 units per month. Following are the company's budgeted overhead costs per month at the 75% level.

Overhead Budget (75% Capacity)		
Variable overhead costs		
Indirect materials	$22,500	
Indirect labor	90,000	
Power	22,500	
Repairs and maintenance	45,000	
Total variable overhead costs		$180,000
Fixed overhead costs		
Depreciation—building	24,000	
Depreciation—machinery	72,000	
Taxes and insurance	18,000	
Supervision	66,000	
Total fixed overhead costs		180,000
Total overhead costs		$360,000

The company incurred the following actual costs when it operated at 75% of capacity in December.

Direct materials (69,000 lbs. @ $6.10)		$ 420,900
Direct labor (22,800 hrs. @ $12.30)		280,440
Overhead costs		
Indirect materials	$21,600	
Indirect labor	82,260	
Power	23,100	
Repairs and maintenance	46,800	
Depreciation—building	24,000	
Depreciation—machinery	75,000	
Taxes and insurance	16,500	
Supervision	66,000	355,260
Total costs		$1,056,600

Required

1. Examine the monthly overhead budget to (a) determine the costs per unit for each variable overhead item and its total per unit costs, and (b) identify the total fixed costs per month.
2. Prepare flexible overhead budgets (as in Exhibit 21.12) for December showing the amounts of each variable and fixed cost at the 65%, 75%, and 85% capacity levels.
3. Compute the direct materials cost variance, including its price and quantity variances.
4. Compute the direct labor cost variance, including its rate and efficiency variances.
5. Prepare a detailed overhead variance report (as in Exhibit 21.15) that shows the variances for individual items of overhead.

Check (2) Budgeted total overhead at 17,000 units, $384,000

(3) Materials variances: Price, $6,900 U; Quantity, $9,000 U

(4) Labor variances: Rate, $6,840 U; Efficiency, $3,600 U

Problem 21-6B^A
Materials, labor, and overhead variances; overhead variance report
C2 P2 P3

Guadelupe Company has set the following standard costs per unit for the product it manufactures.

Direct materials (10 lbs. @ $3.00 per lb.)	$30.00
Direct labor (4 hr. @ $6 per hr.)	24.00
Overhead (4 hr. @ $2.50 per hr.)	10.00
Total standard cost	$64.00

The predetermined overhead rate is based on a planned operating volume of 80% of the productive capacity of 10,000 units per month. The following flexible budget information is available.

	Operating Levels		
	70%	80%	90%
Production in units	7,000	8,000	9,000
Standard direct labor hours	28,000	32,000	36,000
Budgeted overhead			
Variable overhead costs			
Indirect materials	$ 8,750	$10,000	$11,250
Indirect labor	14,000	16,000	18,000
Power	3,500	4,000	4,500
Maintenance	1,750	2,000	2,250
Total variable costs	28,000	32,000	36,000
Fixed overhead costs			
Rent of factory building	12,000	12,000	12,000
Depreciation—machinery	20,000	20,000	20,000
Taxes and insurance	2,400	2,400	2,400
Supervisory salaries	13,600	13,600	13,600
Total fixed costs	48,000	48,000	48,000
Total overhead costs	$76,000	$80,000	$84,000

During March, the company operated at 90% of capacity and produced 9,000 units, incurring the following actual costs.

Direct materials (92,000 lbs. @ 2.95 per lb.)		$271,400
Direct labor (37,600 hrs. @ $6.05 per hr.)		227,480
Overhead costs		
Indirect materials	$10,000	
Indirect labor	16,000	
Power	4,500	
Maintenance	3,000	
Rent of factory building	12,000	
Depreciation—machinery	19,200	
Taxes and insurance	3,000	
Supervisory salaries	14,000	81,700
Total costs		$580,580

Check (1) Materials variances: Price, $4,600 F; Quantity, $6,000 U
(2) Labor variances: Rate, $1,880 U; Efficiency, $9,600 U

Required

1. Compute the direct materials cost variance, including its price and quantity variances.
2. Compute the direct labor variance, including its rate and efficiency variances.
3. Compute these variances: (a) variable overhead spending and efficiency, (b) fixed overhead spending and volume, and (c) total overhead controllable.
4. Prepare a detailed overhead variance report (as in Exhibit 21.15) that shows the variances for individual items of overhead.

Problem 21-7B[A]
Materials, labor, and overhead variances recorded and analyzed
C1 P4

Kenya Company's standard cost accounting system recorded this information from its June operations.

Standard direct materials cost	$130,000
Direct materials quantity variance (favorable)	5,000
Direct materials price variance (favorable)	1,500
Actual direct labor cost	65,000
Direct labor efficiency variance (favorable)	3,000
Direct labor rate variance (unfavorable)	500
Actual overhead cost	250,000
Volume variance (unfavorable)	12,000
Controllable variance (unfavorable)	8,000

Check (1) Dr. Goods in Process Inventory (for overhead), $230,000

Required

1. Prepare journal entries dated June 30 to record the company's costs and variances for the month. (Do not prepare the journal entry to close the variances.)

Analysis Component

2. Identify the areas that would attract the attention of a manager who uses management by exception. Describe what action(s) the manager should consider.

SERIAL PROBLEM

Success Systems
P1

(This serial problem began in Chapter 1 and continues through most of the book. If previous chapter segments were not completed, the serial problem can begin at this point. It is helpful, but not necessary, to use the working papers that accompany the book.)

SP 21 Success Systems' second quarter 2014 fixed budget performance report for its computer furniture operations follows. The $156,000 budgeted expenses include $108,000 in variable expenses for desks and $18,000 in variable expenses for chairs, as well as $30,000 fixed expenses. The actual expenses include

$31,000 fixed expenses. Prepare a flexible budget performance report that shows any variances between budgeted results and actual results. List fixed and variable expenses separately.

	Fixed Budget	Actual Results	Variances
Desk sales (in units)	144	150	
Chair sales (in units)	72	80	
Desk sales (in dollars)	$180,000	$186,000	$6,000 F
Chair sales (in dollars)	$ 36,000	$ 41,200	$5,200 F
Total expenses	$156,000	$163,880	$7,880 U
Income from operations	$ 60,000	$ 63,320	$3,320 F

Check Variances: Fixed expenses, $1,000 U

Beyond the Numbers

REPORTING IN ACTION
C1
Polaris

BTN 21-1 Analysis of flexible budgets and standard costs emphasizes the importance of a similar unit of measure for meaningful comparisons and evaluations. When **Polaris** compiles its financial reports in compliance with GAAP, it applies the same unit of measurement, U.S. dollars, for most measures of business operations. One issue for Polaris is how best to adjust account values for its subsidiaries that compile financial reports in currencies other than the U.S. dollar.

Required

1. Read Polaris's Note 1 in Appendix A and identify the financial statement where it reports the annual adjustment (remeasurement) for foreign currency translation.
2. Translating financial statements requires the use of a currency exchange rate. For each of the following three financial statement items, explain the exchange rate the company would apply to translate into U.S. dollars.
   a. Cash
   b. Sales revenue
   c. Property, plant and equipment

COMPARATIVE ANALYSIS
A1
Polaris
Arctic Cat

BTN 21-2 The usefulness of budgets, variances, and related analyses often depends on the accuracy of management's estimates of future sales activity.

Required

1. Identify and record the prior three years' sales (in dollars) for **Polaris** and for **Arctic Cat** using their financial statements in Appendix A.
2. Using the data in part *1*, predict both companies' sales activity for the next two to three years. (If possible, compare your predictions to actual sales figures for those years.)

ETHICS CHALLENGE
C1

BTN 21-3 Setting materials, labor, and overhead standards is challenging. If standards are set too low, companies might purchase inferior products and employees might not work to their full potential. If standards are set too high, companies could be unable to offer a quality product at a profitable rate and employees could be overworked. The ethical challenge is to set a high but reasonable standard. Assume that as a manager, you are asked to set the standard materials price and quantity for the new 1,000 CKB Mega-Max chip, a technically advanced product. To properly set the price and quantity standards, you assemble a team of specialists to provide input.

Required

Identify four types of specialists that you would assemble to provide information to help set the materials price and quantity standards. Briefly explain why you chose each individual.

COMMUNICATING IN PRACTICE

P4 C2

BTN 21-4 The reason we use the words *favorable* and *unfavorable* when evaluating variances is made clear when we look at the closing of accounts. To see this, consider that (1) all variance accounts are closed at the end of each period (temporary accounts), (2) a favorable variance is always a credit balance, and (3) an unfavorable variance is always a debit balance. Write a one-half page memorandum to your instructor with three parts that answer the three following requirements. (Assume that variance accounts are closed to Cost of Goods Sold.)

Required

1. Does Cost of Goods Sold increase or decrease when closing a favorable variance? Does gross margin increase or decrease when a favorable variance is closed to Cost of Goods Sold? Explain.
2. Does Cost of Goods Sold increase or decrease when closing an unfavorable variance? Does gross margin increase or decrease when an unfavorable variance is closed to Cost of Goods Sold? Explain.
3. Explain the meaning of a favorable variance and an unfavorable variance.

TAKING IT TO THE NET

C1

BTN 21-5 Access **iSixSigma**'s Website (**iSixSigma.com**) to search for and read information about *benchmarking* to complete the following requirements. (*Hint:* Look in the "dictionary" link.)

Required

1. Write a one-paragraph explanation (in layperson's terms) of benchmarking.
2. How does standard costing relate to benchmarking?

TEAMWORK IN ACTION

C2

BTN 21-6 Many service industries link labor rate and time (quantity) standards with their processes. One example is the standard time to board an aircraft. The reason time plays such an important role in the service industry is that it is viewed as a competitive advantage: best service in the shortest amount of time. Although the labor rate component is difficult to observe, the time component of a service delivery standard is often readily apparent—for example, "Lunch will be served in less than five minutes, or it is free."

Required

Break into teams and select two service industries for your analysis. Identify and describe all the time elements each industry uses to create a competitive advantage.

ENTREPRENEURIAL DECISION

C1 C2

BTN 21-7 **Folsom Custom Skis**, as discussed in the chapter opener, uses a costing system with standard costs for direct materials, direct labor, and overhead costs. Two comments frequently are mentioned in relation to standard costing and variance analysis: "Variances are not explanations" and "Management's goal is not to minimize variances."

Required

Write a short memo to Mike McCabe, Folsom Custom Skis' President, (no more than 1 page) interpreting these two comments in the context of his business.

HITTING THE ROAD

C1

BTN 21-8 Training employees to use standard amounts of materials in production is common. Typically large companies invest in this training but small organizations do not. One can observe these different practices in a trip to two different pizza businesses. Visit both a local pizza business and a national pizza chain business and then complete the following.

Required

1. Observe and record the number of raw material items used to make a typical cheese pizza. Also observe how the person making the pizza applies each item when preparing the pizza.
2. Record any differences in how items are applied between the two businesses.
3. Estimate which business is more profitable from your observations. Explain.

GLOBAL DECISION

A1

PIAGGIO

BTN 21-9 Access the annual report of Piaggio (at www.piaggio.com) for the year ended December 31, 2011. The usefulness of its budgets, variances, and related analyses depends on the accuracy of management's estimates of future sales activity.

Required

1. Identify and record the prior two years' sales (in € thousands) for Piaggio from its income statement.
2. Using the data in part *1,* predict sales activity for Piaggio for the next two years. Explain your prediction process.

ANSWERS TO MULTIPLE CHOICE QUIZ

1. c; Fixed costs remain at $300,000; Variable costs = ($246,000/24,000 units) × 20,000 units = $205,000.
2. e; Budgeted direct materials + Unfavorable variance = Actual cost of direct materials used; or, 60,000 units × $10 per unit = $600,000 + $15,000 U = $615,000.
3. c; (AH × AR) − (AH × SR) = $1,599,040 – (84,160 hours × $20 per hour) = $84,160 F.
4. b; Actual variable overhead − Variable overhead applied to production = Variable overhead cost variance; or $150,000 − (96,000 hours × $1.50 per hour) = $6,000 U.
5. a; Budgeted fixed overhead − Fixed overhead applied to production = Volume variance; or $24,000 − (4,800 units × $4 per unit) = $4,800 U.

Performance Measurement and Responsibility Accounting

22

A Look Back

Chapter 21 discussed flexible budgets, variance analysis, and standard costs. It explained how management uses each to control and monitor business activities.

A Look at This Chapter

This chapter describes responsibility accounting, measuring departmental performance, allocating common costs across departments, and transfer pricing. It also explains financial and nonfinancial performance measures used to evaluate investment center performance.

A Look Ahead

Chapter 23 explains several tools and procedures used in making and evaluating short-term managerial decisions.

Learning Objectives

CONCEPTUAL

C1 Distinguish between direct and indirect expenses and identify bases for allocating indirect expenses to departments. (p. 945)

C2 *Appendix 22A*—Explain transfer pricing and methods to set transfer prices. (p. 961)

C3 *Appendix 22B*—Describe allocation of joint costs across products. (p. 962)

ANALYTICAL

A1 Analyze investment centers using return on assets and residual income. (p. 953)

A2 Analyze investment centers using profit margin and investment turnover. (p. 954)

A3 Analyze investment centers using the balanced scorecard. (p. 955)

A4 Compute cycle time and cycle efficiency, and explain their importance to production management. (p. 957)

PROCEDURAL

P1 Prepare a responsibility report for a cost center. (p. 944)

P2 Allocate indirect expenses to departments (p. 946)

P3 Prepare departmental income statements and contribution reports. (p. 947)

Decision Insight

Go Blue!

"Do the dirty work yourself."

—BRIAN LINTON

PHILADELPHIA, PA—Brian Linton has a passion for oceans. Growing up in Singapore, Brian spent time scuba diving and tending to his 30 fish tanks. Traveling the world enabled Brian to see the "good, the bad, and the ugly of oceans and waterways." Combining his love of the water with an entrepreneurial spirit, Brian started his company **United By Blue (UnitedByBlue.com),** an apparel and jewelry company that removes one pound of trash in oceans and waterways for every product sold. As Brian notes, the company's unique business model was driven by "a quest for concrete ways to contribute to real and significant conservation efforts."

Building off Brian's college experiences selling jewelry he imported from Thailand, United By Blue sells men's and women's clothing, bags, and jewelry. The company uses organic cotton and creative designs to make products that elicit a fun vibe associated with oceans and harbor villages. Offering a diverse product line requires Brian to pay attention to cost management and departmental profits. The Sand Shack, a product in the company's jewelry department, "is a line of jewelry with chunky turquoise stones that generates much of the profits the company runs on," says Brian. His managers monitor direct, indirect, and controllable costs; allocate indirect costs to departments; and "measure return on investment (ROI)," explains Brian.

While focusing on controlling costs, United By Blue also strives to remove plastic from its packaging. "The number one material we collect during cleanups is plastic debris. We try to eliminate as much plastic as we can from our supply chain," says Brian. Apparel tags are made from biodegradable substances, infused with flower seeds. T-shirts are packaged in banana fiber paper. "We use things that go back to the earth in a very natural way and actually grow life." While these materials are more costly than plastic, they better fit the company's philosophy and, Brian believes, help generate new business. "We have customers that double their orders the next season because of the cleanups," Brian notes.

As United By Blue continues to grow, Brian focuses on financial *and* nonfinancial performance measures. Revenues were $330,000 in 2010, and were projected to exceed $800,000 in 2011. A focus on departmental contribution margins enables the company to operate efficiently to finance future growth. Likewise, more revenues mean the company collects more trash, over 80,000 pounds by the end of 2011 and a goal of over a million pounds by the end of 2012. As company founder and chief trash collector, this nonfinancial indicator measures progress toward Brian's vision of "doing the most good possible."

Brian encourages young entrepreneurs to "leave a positive impact on this world" by focusing on what you love. "My heart is in the ocean, so whatever I am doing is going to be in that realm. Whatever your passion is, leave that positive impact."

[Sources: *United By Blue* Website, January 2013; *Bloomberg Businessweek,* January 9, 2012; *MO.com* interview, *http://www.mo.com/brian-linton-united-by-blue; Philadelphia Magazine,* July 2011; *PRweb.com,* January 2012.]

Chapter Preview

This chapter describes how to measure performance when organizations are split into separate departments. It discusses responsibility accounting and how to allocate indirect costs of shared items such as utilities, advertising, and rent. This knowledge helps managers better measure and evaluate departmental performance. The chapter also introduces additional managerial accounting reports useful in managing a company's activities and explains how and why management divides companies into departments.

Performance Measurement and Responsibility Accounting

Responsibility Accounting

- Motivation for departmentalization
- Departmental evaluation
- Controllable versus uncontrollable costs

Cost Centers

- Responsibility accounting system
- Evaluating cost center performance

Profit Centers

- Direct and indirect expenses
- Allocation of indirect expenses
- Departmental income statements
- Departmental contribution to overhead

Investment Centers

- Financial performance measures
- Nonfinancial performance measures
- Transfer pricing

RESPONSIBILITY ACCOUNTING

Companies are divided into *departments,* also called *subunits,* when they are too large to be managed effectively as a single unit. The use of departments creates a need for performance measures to evaluate department performance. A **responsibility accounting system** can be set up to control costs and expenses and evaluate department managers' performance by assigning costs and expenses to the managers responsible for controlling them. This chapter introduces responsibility accounting and departmental performance measures.

Point: Responsibility accounting is sometimes referred to as *departmental accounting.*

Motivation for Departmentalization

Many companies are so large and complex that they are broken into separate divisions for efficiency and/or effectiveness purposes. Divisions then are usually organized into separate departments. When a company is departmentalized, each department is often placed under the direction of a manager. As a company grows, management often divides departments into new departments so that responsibilities for a department's activities do not overwhelm the manager's ability to oversee and control them. A company also creates departments to take advantage of the skills of individual managers. Departments are broadly classified as either operating or service departments.

Operating departments perform an organization's main functions. For example, an accounting firm's main functions usually include auditing, tax, and advisory services. Similarly, the production and selling departments of a manufacturing firm perform its main functions and serve as operating departments. *Service departments* provide support to an organization's operating departments. Examples of service departments are payroll, human resource management, accounting, and executive management. Service departments do not engage in activities that generate revenues, yet their support is crucial for the operating departments' success.

Departmental Evaluation

When a company is divided into departments, managers need to know how each department is performing. The accounting system must supply information about resources used and outputs achieved by each department. This requires a system to measure and accumulate revenue and expense information for each department whenever possible.

Departmental information is rarely distributed publicly because of its potential usefulness to competitors. Information about departments is prepared for internal managers to help control operations, appraise performance, allocate resources, and plan strategy. If a department is highly profitable, management may decide to expand its operations, or if a department is performing poorly, information about revenues or expenses can suggest useful changes.

More companies are emphasizing customer satisfaction as a main responsibility of many departments. This has led to changes in the measures reported. Increasingly, financial measurements are being supplemented with quality and customer satisfaction indexes. **Motorola**, for instance, uses two key measures: the number of defective parts per million parts produced and the percent of orders delivered on time to customers. (Note that some departments have only "internal customers.")

Financial information used to evaluate a department depends on whether it is evaluated as a profit center, cost center, or investment center. A **profit center** incurs costs and generates revenues; selling departments are often evaluated as profit centers. A **cost center** incurs costs without directly generating revenues. An **investment center** incurs costs and generates revenues, and is responsible for effectively using center assets. The manufacturing departments of a manufacturer and its service departments such as accounting, advertising, and purchasing, are all cost centers.

Evaluating managers' performance depends on whether they are responsible for profit centers, cost centers, or investment centers. Profit center managers are judged on their abilities to generate revenues in excess of the department's costs. They are assumed to influence both revenue generation and cost incurrence. Cost center managers are judged on their abilities to control costs by keeping them within a satisfactory range under an assumption that only they influence costs. Investment center managers are evaluated on their use of center assets to generate income.

Point: Selling departments are often treated as *revenue centers;* their managers are responsible for maximizing sales revenues.

Controllable versus Uncontrollable Costs

We often evaluate a manager's performance using responsibility accounting reports that describe a department's activities in terms of **controllable costs.**[1] A cost is controllable if a manager has the power to determine or at least significantly affect the amount incurred. **Uncontrollable costs** are not within the manager's control or influence. For example, department managers often have little or no control over depreciation expense because they cannot affect the amount of equipment assigned to their departments. Also, department managers rarely control their own salaries. However, they can control or influence items such as the cost of supplies used in their department. When evaluating managers' performances, we should use data reflecting their departments' outputs along with their controllable costs and expenses.

Distinguishing between controllable and uncontrollable costs depends on the particular manager and time period under analysis. For example, the cost of property insurance is usually not controllable at the department manager's level but by the executive responsible for obtaining the company's insurance coverage. Likewise, this executive might not control costs resulting from insurance policies already in force. However, when a policy expires, this executive can renegotiate a replacement policy and then controls these costs. Therefore, all costs are controllable at some management level if the time period is sufficiently long. We must use good judgment in identifying controllable costs.

Quick Check

Answers — p. 965

1. Service departments (*a*) manufacture products, (*b*) make sales directly to customers, (*c*) produce revenues, (*d*) assist operating departments.
2. Explain the difference between a cost center and a profit center. Cite an example of each.
3. Performance reports to evaluate managers should [select *a*, *b* or *c*] (*a*) include data about controllable expenses, (*b*) compare actual results with budgeted levels, or (*c*) both (*a*) and (*b*).

[1] The terms *cost* and *expense* are often used interchangeably in managerial accounting, but they are not necessarily the same. *Cost* often refers to the monetary outlay to acquire some resource that can have present and future benefit. *Expense* usually refers to an expired cost. That is, as the benefit of a resource expires, a portion of its cost is written off as an expense.

COST CENTERS

Responsibility Accounting System

P1 Prepare a responsibility accounting report for a cost center

A *responsibility accounting system* uses the concept of controllable costs to assign managers the responsibility for costs and expenses under their control. Prior to each reporting period, a company prepares plans that identify costs and expenses under each manager's control. These **responsibility accounting budgets** are typically based on the flexible budgeting approach we showed in Chapter 21. To ensure the cooperation of managers and the reasonableness of budgets, managers should be involved in preparing their budgets.

EXHIBIT 22.1

Organizational Responsibility Chart

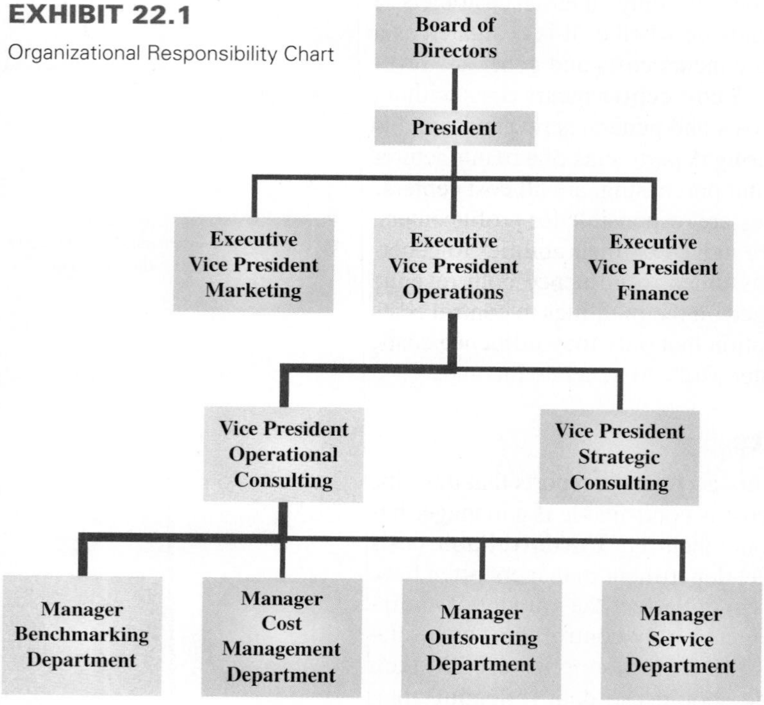

A responsibility accounting system also involves performance reports. A **responsibility accounting performance report** accumulates and reports costs and expenses that a manager is responsible for and their budgeted amounts. Management's analysis of differences between budgeted amounts and actual costs and expenses often results in corrective or strategic managerial actions. Upper-level management uses performance reports to evaluate the effectiveness of lower-level managers in controlling costs and expenses and keeping them within budgeted amounts.

A responsibility accounting system recognizes that control over costs and expenses belongs to several levels of management. We illustrate this by considering the organization chart in Exhibit 22.1. The lines in this chart connecting the managerial positions reflect channels of authority. For example, the four department managers of this consulting firm (benchmarking, cost management, outsourcing, and service) are responsible for controllable costs and expenses incurred in their departments, but these same costs are subject to the overall control of the vice president (VP) for operational consulting. Similarly, this VP's costs are subject to the control of the executive vice president (EVP) for operations, the president, and, ultimately, the board of directors.

Point: Responsibility accounting does not place blame. Instead, responsibility accounting is used to identify opportunities for improving performance.

At lower levels, managers have limited responsibility and relatively little control over costs and expenses. Performance reports for low-level management typically cover few controllable costs. Responsibility and control broaden for higher-level managers; therefore, their reports span a wider range of costs. However, reports to higher-level managers seldom contain the details reported to their subordinates but are summarized for two reasons: (1) lower-level managers are often responsible for these detailed costs and (2) detailed reports can obscure broader, more important issues facing a company.

Evaluating Cost Center Performance

Exhibit 22.2 shows summarized performance reports for the three management levels identified in Exhibit 22.1. Exhibit 22.2 shows that costs under the control of the benchmarking department manager are totaled and included among controllable costs of the VP for operational consulting. Also, costs under the control of the VP are totaled and included among controllable costs of the EVP for operations. In this way, a responsibility accounting system provides relevant information for each management level.

Point: Responsibility accounting usually divides a company into subunits, or *responsibility centers*. A center manager is evaluated on how well the center performs, as reported in responsibility accounting reports.

Technological advances increase our ability to produce vast amounts of information that often exceed our ability to use it. Good managers select relevant data for planning and controlling the areas under their responsibility. A good responsibility accounting system makes every effort to provide relevant information to the right person (the one who controls the cost) at the right time (before a cost is out of control).

EXHIBIT 22.2

Responsibility Accounting Performance Reports for Cost Centers

Executive Vice President, Operations — For July

Controllable Costs	Budgeted Amount	Actual Amount	Over (Under) Budget
Salaries, VPs	$ 80,000	$ 80,000	$ 0
Quality control costs	21,000	22,400	1,400
Office costs	29,500	28,800	(700)
Operational consulting	**276,700**	**279,500**	**2,800**
Strategic consulting	390,000	380,600	(9,400)
Totals	$ 797,200	$ 791,300	$ (5,900)

Vice President, Operational Consulting — For July

Controllable Costs	Budgeted Amount	Actual Amount	Over (Under) Budget
Salaries, department managers	$ 75,000	$ 78,000	$ 3,000
Depreciation	10,600	10,600	0
Insurance	6,800	6,300	(500)
Benchmarking department	**79,600**	**79,900**	**300**
Cost management department	61,500	60,200	(1,300)
Outsourcing department	24,300	24,700	400
Service department	18,900	19,800	900
Totals	**$276,700**	**$279,500**	**$2,800**

Manager, Benchmarking Department — For July

Controllable Costs	Budgeted Amount	Actual Amount	Over (Under) Budget
Salaries	$ 51,600	$ 52,500	$ 900
Supplies	8,000	7,800	(200)
Other controllable costs	20,000	19,600	(400)
Totals	**$ 79,600**	**$ 79,900**	**$ 300**

PROFIT CENTERS

C1 Distinguish between direct and indirect expenses and identify bases for allocating indirect expenses to departments.

When departments are organized as profit centers, responsibility accounting focuses on how well each department controlled costs and generated revenues. This leads to **departmental income statements** as a common way to report profit center performance. When a company computes departmental profits, it confronts some accounting challenges that involve allocating expenses across its operating departments. We next illustrate these allocations and departmental income statement reporting.

Direct and Indirect Expenses

Direct expenses are costs readily traced to a department because they are incurred for that department's sole benefit. They require no allocation across departments. For example, the salary of an employee who works in only one department is a direct expense of that one department. Direct expenses are often, but not always, controllable costs.

Indirect expenses are costs that are incurred for the joint benefit of more than one department and cannot be readily traced to only one department. For example, if two or more departments share a single building, all enjoy the benefits of the expenses for rent, heat, and light. Indirect expenses are allocated across departments benefiting from them when we need information about departmental profits. Ideally, we allocate indirect expenses by using a cause-effect relation. When we cannot identify cause-effect relations, we allocate each indirect expense on a

Point: Utility expense has elements of both direct and indirect expenses.

basis approximating the relative benefit each department receives. Measuring the benefit for each department from an indirect expense can be difficult. Indirect expenses are typically considered uncontrollable costs when evaluating a department manager's performance.

Illustration of Indirect Expense Allocation To illustrate how to allocate an indirect expense, we consider a retail store that purchases janitorial services from an outside company. Management allocates this cost across the store's three departments according to the floor space each occupies. Costs of janitorial services for a recent month are $300. Exhibit 22.3 shows the square feet of floor space each department occupies. The store computes the percent of total square feet allotted to each department and uses it to allocate the $300 cost.

EXHIBIT 22.3

Indirect Expense Allocation

Department	Square Feet	Percent of Total	Allocated Cost
Jewelry	2,400	60%	$180
Watch repair	600	15	45
China and silver	1,000	25	75
Totals	4,000	100%	$300

Specifically, because the jewelry department occupies 60% of the floor space, 60% of the total $300 cost is assigned to it. The same procedure is applied to the other departments. When the allocation process is complete, these and other allocated costs are deducted from the gross profit for each department to determine net income for each. One consideration in allocating costs is to motivate managers and employees to behave as desired. As a result, a cost incurred in one department might be best allocated to other departments when one of the other departments caused the cost.

Allocation of Indirect Expenses

P2 Allocate indirect expenses to departments.

This section describes how to identify the bases used to allocate indirect expenses across departments. No standard rule identifies the best basis because expense allocation involves several factors, and the relative importance of these factors varies across departments and organizations. Judgment is required, and people do not always agree. Employee morale suffers when allocations are perceived as unfair. Thus, it is important to carefully design and explain the allocation of service department costs. In our discussion, note the parallels between activity-based costing and the departmental expense allocation procedures described here.

Wages and Salaries Employee wages and salaries can be either direct or indirect expenses. If their time is spent entirely in one department, their wages are direct expenses of that department. However, if employees work for the benefit of more than one department, their wages are indirect expenses and must be allocated across the departments benefited. An employee's contribution to a department usually depends on the number of hours worked in contributing to that department. Thus, a reasonable basis for allocating employee wages and salaries is the *relative amount of time spent in each department.* In the case of a supervisor who manages more than one department, recording the time spent in each department may not always be practical. Instead, a company can allocate the supervisor's salary to departments on the basis of the number of employees in each department—a reasonable basis if a supervisor's main task is managing people. Another basis of allocation is on sales across departments, also a reasonable basis if a supervisor's job reflects on departmental sales.

Point: Some companies ask supervisors to estimate time spent supervising specific departments for purposes of expense allocation.

Rent and Related Expenses Rent expense for a building is reasonably allocated to a department on the basis of floor space it occupies. Location can often make some floor space more valuable than other space. Thus, the allocation method can charge departments that occupy more valuable space a higher expense per square foot. Ground floor retail space, for instance, is often more valuable than basement or upper-floor space because all customers pass departments near the entrance but fewer go beyond the first floor. When no precise measures of floor space values exist, basing allocations on data such as customer traffic and real estate assessments is helpful. When a company owns its building, its expenses for depreciation, taxes, insurance, and other related building expenses are allocated like rent expense.

Advertising Expenses Effective advertising of a department's products increases its sales and customer traffic. Moreover, advertising products for some departments usually helps other departments' sales because customers also often buy unadvertised products. Thus, many stores treat advertising as an indirect expense allocated on the basis of each department's proportion of total sales. For example, a department with 10% of a store's total sales is assigned 10% of advertising expense. Another method is to analyze each advertisement to compute the Web/newspaper space or TV/radio time devoted to the products of a department and charge that department for the proportional costs of advertisements. Management must consider whether this more detailed and costly method is justified.

Equipment and Machinery Depreciation Depreciation on equipment and machinery used only in one department is a direct expense of that department. Depreciation on equipment and machinery used by more than one department is an indirect expense to be allocated across departments. Accounting for each department's depreciation expense requires a company to keep records showing which departments use specific assets. The number of hours that a department uses equipment and machinery is a reasonable basis for allocating depreciation.

Utilities Expenses Utilities expenses such as heating and lighting are usually allocated on the basis of floor space occupied by departments. This practice assumes their use is uniform across departments. When this is not so, a more involved allocation can be necessary, although there is often a trade-off between the usefulness of more precise allocations and the effort to compute them. Manufacturers often allocate electricity cost to departments on the basis of the horsepower of equipment located in each department.

Service Department Expenses To generate revenues, operating departments require support services provided by departments such as personnel, payroll, advertising, and purchasing. Such service departments are typically evaluated as cost centers because they do not produce revenues. (Evaluating them as profit centers requires the use of a system that "charges" user departments a price that then serves as the "revenue" generated by service departments.) A departmental accounting system can accumulate and report costs incurred directly by each service department for this purpose. The system then allocates a service department's expenses to operating departments benefiting from them. Exhibit 22.4 shows some commonly used bases for allocating service department expenses to operating departments.

Point: When a service department "charges" its user departments within a company, a *transfer pricing system* must be set up to determine the "revenue" from its services provided.

EXHIBIT 22.4

Bases for Allocating Service Department Expenses

Service Department	Common Allocation Bases
Office expenses	Number of employees or sales in each department
Personnel expenses	Number of employees in each department
Payroll expenses	Number of employees in each department
Advertising expenses	Sales or amount of advertising charged directly to each department
Purchasing costs	Dollar amounts of purchases or number of purchase orders processed
Cleaning expenses	Square feet of floor space occupied
Maintenance expenses	Square feet of floor space occupied

Departmental Income Statements

P3 Prepare departmental income statements and contribution reports.

An income statement can be prepared for each operating department once expenses have been assigned to it. Its expenses include both direct expenses and its share of indirect expenses. For this purpose, compiling all expenses incurred in service departments before assigning them to operating departments is useful. We illustrate the steps to prepare departmental income statements using **A-1 Hardware** and its five departments. Two of them (office and purchasing) are service departments and the other three (hardware, housewares, and appliances) are operating (selling) departments. Allocating costs to operating departments and preparing departmental income statements involves four steps.

Step 1: Accumulating revenues and direct expenses by department.

Step 2: Allocating indirect expenses across departments.

Step 3: Allocating service department expenses to operating departments.

Step 4: Preparing departmental income statements.

Exhibit 22.5 summarizes the steps in preparing departmental performance reports for cost centers and profit centers. A-1 Hardware's service departments (general office and purchasing) are cost centers, so their performance will be based on how well they controlled total service department expenses. The company's operating departments (hardware, housewares, and appliances) are profit centers, and their performance will be based on how well they generated departmental net income.

EXHIBIT 22.5

Departmental Performance Reporting

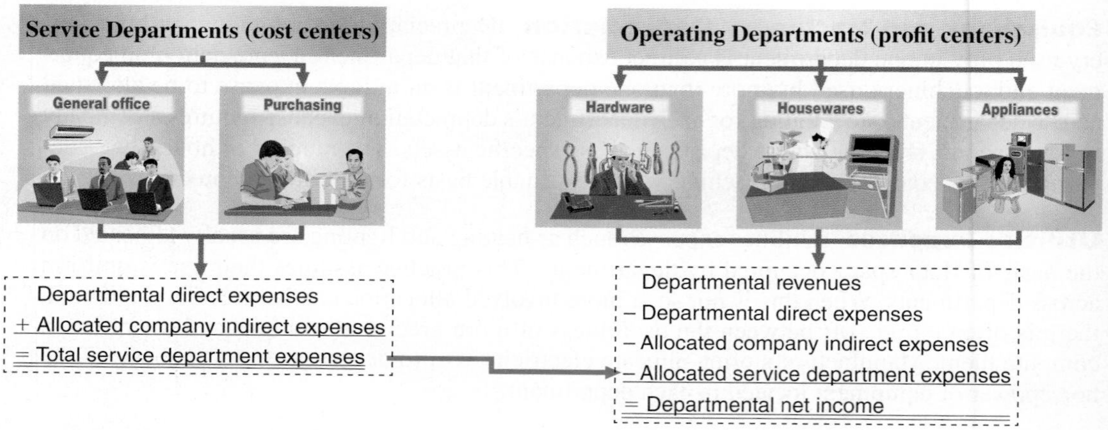

Step 1: Step 1 accumulates revenues and direct expenses in departmental accounts for each department. As cost centers, the service departments do not generate revenues. Direct expenses include salaries, wages, and other expenses that each department incurs but does not share with any other department.

Step 2: Step 2 allocates indirect company expenses across all service and operating departments. Indirect expenses can include items such as depreciation, rent, advertising, and any other expenses that cannot be directly assigned to a department. Indirect expenses are recorded in *company* accounts, an allocation base is identified for each expense, and costs are allocated using a *departmental expense allocation spreadsheet* described next.

Point: We sometimes allocate service department costs across other service departments before allocating them to operating departments. This "step-wise" process is in advanced courses.

Step 3: Step 3 allocates service department expenses to operating departments. Service department expenses are not allocated to other service departments.[2] Exhibit 22.6 reflects the allocation of service department expenses using the allocation base(s). All of the direct and indirect expenses of service departments are allocated to operating departments.

Computations for both steps 2 and 3 are commonly made using a departmental expense allocation spreadsheet as shown in Exhibit 22.6. The first two sections of this spreadsheet list direct expenses and indirect expenses by department. The third section lists the service department expenses and their allocations to operating departments. The allocation bases are identified in the second column, and total expense amounts are reported in the third column.

[2] In some cases we allocate a service department's expenses to other service departments when they use its services. For example, expenses of a payroll office benefit all service and operating departments and can be assigned to all departments. Nearly all examples and assignment materials in this book allocate service expenses only to operating departments for simplicity.

EXHIBIT 22.6

Departmental Expense Allocation Spreadsheet

A-1 HARDWARE
Departmental Expense Allocations
For Year Ended December 31, 2013

	Allocation Base	Expense Account Balance	General Office Dept.	Purchasing Dept.	Hardware Dept.	Housewares Dept.	Appliances Dept.
			Allocation of Expenses to Departments				
Direct expenses							
Salaries expense	Payroll records	$51,900	$13,300	$8,200	$15,600	$ 7,000	$ 7,800
Depreciation—Equipment	Depreciation records	1,500	500	300	400	100	200
Supplies expense	Requisitions	900	200	100	300	200	100
Indirect expenses							
Rent expense	Amount and value of space	12,000	600	600	4,860	3,240	2,700
Utilities expense	Floor space	2,400	300	300	810	540	450
Advertising expense	Sales	1,000			500	300	200
Insurance expense	Value of insured assets	2,500	400	200	900	600	400
Total department expenses		72,200	15,300	9,700	23,370	11,980	11,850
Service department expenses							
General office department	Sales		(15,300)		7,650	4,590	3,060
Purchasing department	Purchase orders			(9,700)	3,880	2,630	3,190
Total expenses allocated to operating departments		$72,200	$ 0	$ 0	$34,900	$19,200	$18,100

Second (step 2), the four indirect expenses of rent, utilities, advertising, and insurance are allocated to all departments using the allocation bases identified. For example, consider rent allocation. Exhibit 22.7 lists the five departments' square footage of space occupied.

EXHIBIT 22.7

Departments' Allocation Bases

Department	Floor Space (Square Feet)	Value of Insured Assets ($)	Sales ($)	Number of Purchase Orders
General office	1,500	$ 38,000		—
Purchasing	1,500	19,000		—*
Hardware	4,050	85,500	$119,500	394
Housewares	2,700	57,000	71,700	267
Appliances	2,250	38,000	47,800	324
Total	12,000	$237,500	$239,000	985

* Purchasing department tracks purchase orders by department.

The two service departments (office and purchasing) occupy 25% of the total space (3,000 sq. feet/12,000 sq. feet). However, they are located near the back of the building, which is of lower value than space near the front that is occupied by operating departments. Management estimates that space near the back accounts for $1,200 of the total rent expense of $12,000. Exhibit 22.8 shows how we allocate the $1,200 rent expense between these two service departments in proportion to their square footage. Exhibit 22.8 shows a simple rule for cost

EXHIBIT 22.8

Allocating Indirect (Rent) Expense to Service Departments

Department	Square Feet	Percent of Total	Allocated Cost
General office	1,500	50.0%	$ 600
Purchasing	1,500	50.0	600
Totals	3,000	100.0%	$1,200

allocations: Allocated cost = Percentage of allocation base × Total cost. We then allocate the remaining $10,800 of rent expense to the three operating departments as shown in Exhibit 22.9.

EXHIBIT 22.9

Allocating Indirect (Rent) Expense to Operating Departments

Department	Square Feet	Percent of Total	Allocated Cost
Hardware	4,050	45.0%	$ 4,860
Housewares	2,700	30.0	3,240
Appliances	2,250	25.0	2,700
Totals	9,000	100.0%	$10,800

We continue step 2 by allocating the $2,400 of utilities expense to all departments based on the square footage occupied as shown in Exhibit 22.10.

EXHIBIT 22.10

Allocating Indirect (Utilities) Expense to All Departments

Department	Square Feet	Percent of Total	Allocated Cost
General office	1,500	12.50%	$ 300
Purchasing	1,500	12.50	300
Hardware	4,050	33.75	810
Housewares	2,700	22.50	540
Appliances	2,250	18.75	450
Totals	12,000	100.00%	$2,400

Exhibit 22.11 shows the allocation of $1,000 of advertising expense to the three operating departments on the basis of sales dollars. We exclude service departments from this allocation because they do not generate sales.

EXHIBIT 22.11

Allocating Indirect (Advertising) Expense to Operating Departments

Department	Sales	Percent of Total	Allocated Cost
Hardware	$119,500	50.0%	$ 500
Housewares	71,700	30.0	300
Appliances	47,800	20.0	200
Totals	$239,000	100.0%	$1,000

To complete step 2 we allocate insurance expense to each service and operating department as shown in Exhibit 22.12.

EXHIBIT 22.12

Allocating Indirect (Insurance) Expense to All Departments

Department	Value of Insured Assets	Percent of Total	Allocated Cost
General office	$ 38,000	16.0%	$ 400
Purchasing	19,000	8.0	200
Hardware	85,500	36.0	900
Housewares	57,000	24.0	600
Appliances	38,000	16.0	400
Total	$237,500	100.0%	$2,500

Third (step 3), total expenses of the two service departments are allocated to the three operating departments as shown in Exhibits 22.13 and 22.14.

EXHIBIT 22.13

Allocating Service Department (General Office) Expenses to Operating Departments

Department	Sales	Percent of Total	Allocated Cost
Hardware	$119,500	50.0%	$ 7,650
Housewares	71,700	30.0	4,590
Appliances	47,800	20.0	3,060
Total	$239,000	100.0%	$15,300

EXHIBIT 22.14

Allocating Service Department (Purchasing) Expenses to Operating Departments

Department	Number of Purchase Orders	Percent of Total	Allocated Cost
Hardware	394	40.00%	$3,880
Housewares	267	27.11	2,630
Appliances	324	32.89	3,190
Total	985	100.00%	$9,700

Step 4: The departmental expense allocation spreadsheet can now be used to prepare performance reports for the company's service and operating departments. The general office and purchasing departments are cost centers, and their managers will be evaluated on their control of costs. Actual amounts of service department expenses can be compared to budgeted amounts to help assess cost center manager performance.

Amounts in the operating department columns are used to prepare departmental income statements as shown in Exhibit 22.15. This exhibit uses the spreadsheet for its operating expenses; information on sales and cost of goods sold comes from departmental records.

Example: If the $15,300 general office expenses in Exhibit 22.6 are allocated equally across departments, what is net income for the hardware department and for the combined company? *Answer:* Hardware income, $13,350; combined income, $19,000.

EXHIBIT 22.15

Departmental Income Statements (Operating Departments)

A-1 HARDWARE
Departmental Income Statements
For Year Ended December 31, 2013

	Hardware Department	Housewares Department	Appliances Department	Combined	
Sales	$119,500	$71,700	$47,800	$239,000	
Cost of goods sold	73,800	43,800	30,200	147,800	
Gross profit	45,700	27,900	17,600	91,200	
Operating expenses					
Salaries expense	15,600	7,000	7,800	30,400	Direct expenses
Depreciation expense—Equipment	400	100	200	700	Direct expenses
Supplies expense	300	200	100	600	Direct expenses
Rent expense	4,860	3,240	2,700	10,800	Allocated indirect expenses
Utilities expense	810	540	450	1,800	Allocated indirect expenses
Advertising expense	500	300	200	1,000	Allocated indirect expenses
Insurance expense	900	600	400	1,900	Allocated indirect expenses
Share of general office expenses	7,650	4,590	3,060	15,300	Allocated service department expenses
Share of purchasing expenses	3,880	2,630	3,190	9,700	Allocated service department expenses
Total operating expenses	34,900	19,200	18,100	72,200	
Net income (loss)	**$10,800**	**$8,700**	**$ (500)**	**$19,000**	

Departmental Contribution to Overhead

Data from departmental income statements are not always best for evaluating each profit center's performance, especially when indirect expenses are a large portion of total expenses and when weaknesses in assumptions and decisions in allocating indirect expenses can markedly affect net income. Also, operating department managers might have no control over the level of service department services they use. In these and other cases, we might better evaluate profit center performance using the **departmental contribution to overhead,** which is a report of the amount of sales less *direct* expenses.[3] (We can also examine cost center performance by focusing on control of direct expenses.)

[3] A department's contribution is said to be "to overhead" because of the practice of considering all indirect expenses as overhead. Thus, the excess of a department's sales over direct expenses is a contribution toward at least a portion of its total overhead.

EXHIBIT 22.16

Departmental Contribution to Overhead

A-1 HARDWARE
Income Statement Showing Departmental Contribution to Overhead
For Year Ended December 31, 2013

	Hardware Department	Housewares Department	Appliances Department	Combined
Sales	$119,500	$ 71,700	$47,800	$239,000
Cost of goods sold	73,800	43,800	30,200	147,800
Gross profit	45,700	27,900	17,600	91,200
Direct expenses				
Salaries expense	15,600	7,000	7,800	30,400
Depreciation expense—Equipment	400	100	200	700
Supplies expense	300	200	100	600
Total direct expenses	16,300	7,300	8,100	31,700
Departmental contributions to overhead	**$29,400**	**$20,600**	**$ 9,500**	**$59,500**
Indirect expenses				
Rent expense				10,800
Utilities expense				1,800
Advertising expense				1,000
Insurance expense				1,900
General office department expense				15,300
Purchasing department expense				9,700
Total indirect expenses				40,500
Net income				$ 19,000
Contribution as percent of sales	24.6%	28.7%	19.9%	24.9%

Point: Net income is the same in Exhibits 22.15 and 22.16. The method of reporting indirect expenses in Exhibit 22.16 does not change total net income but does identify each operating department's contribution to overhead and net income.

The upper half of Exhibit 22.16 shows a departmental (profit center) contribution to overhead as part of an expanded income statement. This format is common when reporting departmental contributions to overhead. Using the information in Exhibits 22.15 and 22.16, we can evaluate the profitability of the three profit centers. For instance, let's compare the performance of the appliances department as described in these two exhibits. Exhibit 22.15 shows a $500 net loss resulting from this department's operations, but Exhibit 22.16 shows a $9,500 positive contribution to overhead, which is 19.9% of the appliance department's sales. The contribution of the appliances department is not as large as that of the other selling departments, but a $9,500 contribution to overhead is better than a $500 loss. This tells us that the appliances department is not a money loser. On the contrary, it is contributing $9,500 toward defraying total indirect expenses of $40,500.

Quick Check

Answers — p. 965

4. If a company has two operating (selling) departments (shoes and hats) and two service departments (payroll and advertising), which of the following statements is correct? (*a*) Wages incurred in the payroll department are direct expenses of the shoe department, (*b*) Wages incurred in the payroll department are indirect expenses of the operating departments, or (*c*) Advertising department expenses are allocated to the other three departments.
5. Which of the following bases can be used to allocate supervisors' salaries across operating departments? (*a*) Hours spent in each department, (*b*) number of employees in each department, (*c*) sales achieved in each department, or (*d*) any of the above, depending on which information is most relevant and accessible.
6. What three steps are used to allocate expenses to operating departments?
7. An income statement showing departmental contribution to overhead, (*a*) subtracts indirect expenses from each department's revenues, (*b*) subtracts only direct expenses from each department's revenues, or (*c*) shows net income for each department.

EVALUATING INVESTMENT CENTER PERFORMANCE

This section introduces both financial and nonfinancial measures of investment center performance.

Financial Performance Evaluation Measures

A1 Analyze investment centers using return on assets and residual income.

Investment center managers are typically evaluated using performance measures that combine income and assets. Consider the following data for ZTel, a company which operates two divisions: LCD and S-Phone. The LCD division manufactures liquid crystal display (LCD) touch-screen monitors and sells them for use in computers, cellular phones, and other products. The S-Phone division sells smartphones, mobile phones that also function as personal computers, MP3 players, cameras, and global positioning satellite (GPS) systems. Exhibit 22.17 shows current year income and assets for those divisions.

EXHIBIT 22.17

Investment Center Income and Assets

	LCD	S-Phone
Net income	$ 526,500	$ 417,600
Average invested assets	2,500,000	1,850,000

Investment Center Return on (Assets) Investment One measure to evaluate division performance is the **investment center return on total assets,** commonly called *return on investment* (ROI) or *return on assets* (ROA). This measure is computed as follows:

$$\textbf{Return on investment} = \frac{\textbf{Investment center net income}}{\textbf{Investment center average invested assets}}$$

The return on investment for the LCD division is 21% (rounded), computed as $526,500/ $2,500,000. The S-Phone division's return on investment is 23% (rounded), computed as $417,600/$1,850,000. Though the LCD division earned more dollars of net income, it was less efficient in using its assets to generate income compared to the S-Phone division.

Investment Center Residual Income Another way to evaluate division performance is to compute **investment center residual income,** which is computed as follows:

$$\textbf{Residual income} = \textbf{Investment center net income} - \textbf{Target investment center net income}$$

Assume ZTel's top management sets target net income at 8% of divisional assets. For an investment center, this **hurdle rate** is typically the cost of obtaining financing. Applying this hurdle rate using the data from Exhibit 22.17 yields the residual income for ZTel's divisions in Exhibit 22.18.

EXHIBIT 22.18

Investment Center Residual Income

	LCD	S-Phone
Net income	$526,500	$417,600
Less: Target net income		
$2,500,000 × 8%	200,000	
$1,850,000 × 8%		148,000
Investment center residual income	$326,500	$269,600

Unlike return on assets, residual income is expressed in dollars. The LCD division outperformed the S-Phone division on the basis of residual income. However, this result is due in part to the LCD division having a larger asset base than the S-Phone division.

Using residual income to evaluate division performance encourages division managers to accept all opportunities that return more than the target net income, thus increasing company value. For example, the S-Phone division might not want to accept a new customer that will provide a 15% return on investment, since that will reduce the S-Phone division's overall return on investment (23% as shown above). However, the S-Phone division should accept this opportunity because the new customer would increase residual income by providing net income above the target net income.

Issues in Computing Return on (Assets) Investment and Residual Income

Evaluations of investment center performance using return on assets and residual income can be impacted by how a company answers the questions below:

1. How do you compute average invested assets? It is common to compute the average by adding the year's beginning amount of invested assets to the year's ending amount of invested assets, and dividing that sum by 2. Averages based on monthly or quarterly asset amounts are also acceptable.
2. How do you measure invested assets? It is common to measure invested assets using their *net* book values. For example, depreciable assets would be measured at their cost minus accumulated depreciation. As net book value declines over a depreciable asset's useful life, the result is that return on assets and residual income would increase over that asset's life. This might cause managers not to invest in new assets. In addition, in measuring invested assets, companies commonly exclude assets that are not used in generating investment center net income such as land held for resale.
3. How do you measure investment center income? It is common to exclude both interest expense and tax expense from investment center income. Interest expense reflects a company's financing decisions, and tax expense is typically considered outside the control of an investment center manager. Excluding interest and taxes in these calculations enables more meaningful comparisons of return on assets and residual income across investment centers and companies.

Point: *Economic Value Added* (EVA®), developed and trademarked by Stern, Stewart, and Co., is an approach to address issues in computing residual income. This method uses a variety of adjustments to compute income, assets, and the hurdle rate.

Decision Insight

In-the-Money Executive pay is often linked to performance measures. Bonus payments are often based on exceeding a target return on investment or certain balanced scorecard indicators. Stock awards, such as stock options and restricted stock, reward executives when their company's stock price rises. The goal of bonus plans and stock awards is to encourage executives to make decisions that increase company performance and value. ■

A2 Analyze investment centers using profit margin and investment turnover.

Investment Center Profit Margin and Investment Turnover We can further examine investment center (division) performance by splitting return on investment into **profit margin** and **investment turnover** as follows

Return on investment = Profit margin × Investment turnover

$$\frac{\textbf{Investment center net income}}{\textbf{Investment center average assets}} = \frac{\textbf{Investment center net income}}{\textbf{Investment center sales}} \times \frac{\textbf{Investment center sales}}{\textbf{Investment center average assets}}$$

Profit margin measures the income earned per dollar of sales. **Investment turnover** measures how efficiently an investment center generates sales from its invested assets. Profit margin is expressed as a percent, while investment turnover is interpreted as the number of times assets were converted into sales. Higher profit margin and higher investment turnover indicate better performance. To illustrate, consider **Best Buy** which reports in Exhibit 22.19 results for two divisions (segments): Domestic and International.

EXHIBIT 22.19

Best Buy Division Sales, Income, and Assets

($ millions)	Domestic	International
Sales	$37,186	$13,086
Net income	2,031	83
Average invested assets	10,021	8,055

Profit margin and investment turnover for its Domestic and International divisions are computed and shown in Exhibit 22.20:

EXHIBIT 22.20

Best Buy Division Profit Margin and Investment Turnover

($ millions)	Domestic	International
Profit Margin		
$2,031/$37,186	5.55%	
$83/$13,086		0.6%
Investment Turnover		
$37,186/$10,021	3.71	
$13,086/$8,055		1.62
Return on Investment		
5.55% × 3.71	20.59%	
0.6% × 1.62		1.01%

Best Buy's Domestic division generates 5.55 cents of profit per $1 of sales, while its International division generates less than 1 cent of profit per dollar of sales. Its Domestic division also uses its assets more efficiently; its investment turnover of 3.71 is over twice that of its International division's 1.62. Alternatively, if Best Buy's Domestic division instead had sales of $40 billion, net income of $3 billion, and average invested assets of $4 billion, its profit margin, investment turnover, and return on assets would be 7.5%, 4%, and 30%, respectively. Top management can use profit margin and investment turnover to evaluate the performance of division managers. The measures can also aid management when considering further investment in its divisions. As a result of both a much higher profit margin and a more rapid investment turnover, the Domestic division's return on investment (20.59%) is much greater than that of the International division (0.97%).

Decision Maker

Division Manager You manage a division in a highly competitive industry. You will receive a cash bonus if your division achieves an ROI above 12%. Your division's profit margin is 7%, equal to the industry average, and your division's investment turnover is 1.5. What actions can you take to increase your chance of receiving the bonus? ■ [Answer—p. 965]

Quick Check

Answers – p. 965

8. A division reports sales of $50,000, income of $2,000, and average invested assets of $10,000. Compute the division's (*a*) profit margin, (*b*) investment turnover, and (*c*) return on investment.

Nonfinancial Performance Evaluation Measures

A3 Analyze investment centers using the balanced scorecard.

Evaluating performance solely on financial measures such as return on investment or residual income has limitations. For example, some investment center managers might forgo profitable opportunities to keep their return on investment high. Also, residual income is less useful when comparing investment centers of different size. And, both return on investment and residual income can encourage managers to focus too heavily on short-term financial goals.

In response to these limitations, companies consider nonfinancial measures. For example, a delivery company such as **FedEx** might track the percentage of on-time deliveries. The percentage of defective tennis balls manufactured can be used to assess performance of **Penn**'s production managers. **Walmart**'s credit card screens commonly ask customers at check-out whether the cashier was friendly or the store was clean. This kind of information can help division managers run their divisions and help top management evaluate division manager performance.

Balanced Scorecard The **balanced scorecard** is a system of performance measures, including nonfinancial measures, used to assess company and division manager performance. The balanced scorecard requires managers to think of their company from four perspectives:

1. **Customer:** What do customers think of us?
2. **Internal processes:** Which of our operations are critical to meeting customer needs?
3. **Innovation and learning:** How can we improve?
4. **Financial:** What do our owners think of us?

Point: One survey indicates that nearly 60% of global companies use some form of a balanced scorecard.

The balanced scorecard collects information on several key performance indicators within each of the four perspectives. These key indicators vary across companies. Exhibit 22.21 lists common performance measures.

EXHIBIT 22.21

Balanced Scorecard Performance Indicators

Customer	Internal Process	Innovation/Learning	Financial
• Customer satisfaction rating	• Defect rates	• Employee satisfaction	• Net income
• # of new customers acquired	• Cycle time	• Employee turnover	• ROI
• % of on-time deliveries	• Product costs	• $ spent on training	• Sales growth
• % of sales from new products	• Labor hours per order	• # of new products	• Cash flow
• Time to fill orders	• Production days without an accident	• # of patents	• Residual income
• % of sales returned		• $ spent on research	• Stock price

After selecting key performance indicators, companies collect data on each indicator and compare actual amounts to expected amounts to assess performance. For example, a company might have a goal of filling 98% of customer orders within two hours. Balanced scorecard reports are often presented in graphs or tables that can be updated frequently. Such timely information aids division managers in their decisions, and can be used by top management to evaluate division manager performance.

Exhibit 22.22 is an example of balanced scorecard reporting on the customer perspective for an Internet retailer. This scorecard reports for example that the retailer is getting 62% of its potential customers successfully through the checkout process, and that 2.2% of all orders are returned. The *color* of the arrows in the right-most column reveals whether the company is exceeding its goal (green), barely meeting the goal (yellow), or not meeting the goal (red). The *direction* of the arrows reveals any trend in performance: an upward arrow indicates improvement, a downward arrow indicates declining performance, and an arrow pointing sideways indicates no change. A

EXHIBIT 22.22

Balanced Scorecard Reporting: Internet Retailer

Customer Perspective	Actual	Goal
Checkout success	62%	↑
Orders returned	2.2%	↔
Customer satisfaction rating	9.5	↑
Number of customer complaints	142	↓

review of these arrows' color and direction suggests the retailer is meeting or exceeding its goals on checkout success, orders returned, and customer satisfaction. Further, checkout success and customer satisfaction are improving. The red arrow shows the company has received more customer complaints than was hoped for; however, the number of customer complaints is declining. A manager would combine this information with similar information on the internal process, innovation and learning, and financial perspectives to get an overall view of division performance.

Decision Maker

Center Manager Your center's usual return on total assets is 19%. You are considering two new investments for your center. The first requires a $250,000 average investment and is expected to yield annual net income of $50,000. The second requires a $1 million average investment with an expected annual net income of $175,000. Do you pursue either? ■ [Answer—p. 965]

GLOBAL VIEW

L'Oreal is an international cosmetics company incorporated in France. With multiple brands and operations in over 100 countries, the company uses concepts of departmental accounting and controllable costs to evaluate performance. For example, its 2010 annual report shows the following for the major divisions in its Cosmetics branch:

Division	Operating Profit (€ millions)	
Consumer products	€1,765	
Professional products	552	
Luxury products	791	
Active cosmetics	277	€3,385 ← Similar to "Departmental contributions to overhead" in Exhibit 22.16
Nonallocated costs		(513)
Cosmetics branch total		€2,872 ← Similar to "Net income" in Exhibit 22.16

For L'Oreal, nonallocated costs include costs that are not controllable by division managers, including fundamental research and development and costs of service operations like insurance and banking. Excluding noncontrollable costs enables L'Oreal to prepare more meaningful division performance evaluations.

Cycle Time and Cycle Efficiency — Decision Analysis

A4 Compute cycle time and cycle efficiency, and explain their importance to production management.

Manufacturing companies commonly use nonfinancial measures to evaluate the performance of their production processes. For example, as lean manufacturing practices help companies move toward just-in-time manufacturing, it is important for these companies to reduce the time to manufacture their products and to improve manufacturing efficiency. One metric that measures that time element is **cycle time (CT).** A definition of cycle time is in Exhibit 22.23.

EXHIBIT 22.23
Cycle Time

Cycle time = Process time + Inspection time + Move time + Wait time

Process time is the time spent producing the product. *Inspection time* is the time spent inspecting (1) raw materials when received, (2) goods in process while in production, and (3) finished goods prior to shipment. *Move time* is the time spent moving (1) raw materials from storage to production and (2) goods in process from one factory location to another factory location. *Wait time* is the time that an order or job sits with no production applied to it; this can be due to order delays, bottlenecks in production, and poor scheduling.

Process time is considered **value-added time** because it is the only activity in cycle time that adds value to the product from the customer's perspective. The other three time activities are considered **non-value-added time** because they add no value to the customer.

Companies strive to reduce non-value-added time to improve **cycle efficiency (CE).** Cycle efficiency is the ratio of value-added time to total cycle time—see Exhibit 22.24.

EXHIBIT 22.24
Cycle Efficiency

$$\textbf{Cycle efficiency} = \frac{\textbf{Value-added time}}{\textbf{Cycle time}}$$

To illustrate, assume that Rocky Mountain Bikes receives and produces an order for 500 Tracker® mountain bikes. Assume that the following times were measured during production of this order.

Process time... 1.8 days **Inspection time... 0.5 days** **Move time... 0.7 days** **Wait time... 3.0 days**

In this case, cycle time is 6.0 days, computed as 1.8 days + 0.5 days + 0.7 days + 3.0 days. Also, cycle efficiency is 0.3, or 30%, computed as 1.8 days divided by 6.0 days. This means that Rocky Mountain Bikes spends 30% of its time working on the product (value-added time). The other 70% is spent on non-value-added activities.

If a company has a CE of 1, it means that its time is spent entirely on value-added activities. If the CE is low, the company should evaluate its production process to see if it can identify ways to reduce non-value-added activities. The 30% CE for Rocky Mountain Bikes is low and its management should look for ways to reduce non-value-added activities.

DEMONSTRATION PROBLEM

Management requests departmental income statements for Hacker's Haven, a computer store that has five departments. Three are operating departments (hardware, software, and repairs) and two are service departments (general office and purchasing).

	General Office	Purchasing	Hardware	Software	Repairs
Sales	—	—	$960,000	$600,000	$840,000
Cost of goods sold	—	—	500,000	300,000	200,000
Direct expenses					
Payroll	$60,000	$45,000	80,000	25,000	325,000
Depreciation	6,000	7,200	33,000	4,200	9,600
Supplies	15,000	10,000	10,000	2,000	25,000

The departments incur several indirect expenses. To prepare departmental income statements, the indirect expenses must be allocated across the five departments. Then the expenses of the two service departments must be allocated to the three operating departments. Total cost amounts and the allocation bases for each indirect expense follow.

Indirect Expense	Total Cost	Allocation Basis
Rent	$150,000	Square footage occupied
Utilities	50,000	Square footage occupied
Advertising	125,000	Dollars of sales
Insurance	30,000	Value of assets insured
Service departments		
General office	?	Number of employees
Purchasing	?	Dollars of cost of goods sold

The following additional information is needed for indirect expense allocations.

Department	Square Feet	Sales	Insured Assets	Employees	Cost of Goods Sold
General office	500		$ 60,000		
Purchasing	500		72,000		
Hardware	4,000	$ 960,000	330,000	5	$ 500,000
Software	3,000	600,000	42,000	5	300,000
Repairs	2,000	840,000	96,000	10	200,000
Totals	10,000	$2,400,000	$600,000	20	$1,000,000

Required

1. Prepare a departmental expense allocation spreadsheet for Hacker's Haven.
2. Prepare a departmental income statement reporting net income for each operating department and for all operating departments combined.

PLANNING THE SOLUTION

- Set up and complete four tables to allocate the indirect expenses—one each for rent, utilities, advertising, and insurance.
- Allocate the departments' indirect expenses using a spreadsheet like the one in Exhibit 22.6. Enter the given amounts of the direct expenses for each department. Then enter the allocated amounts of the indirect expenses that you computed.
- Complete two tables for allocating the general office and purchasing department costs to the three operating departments. Enter these amounts on the spreadsheet and determine the total expenses allocated to the three operating departments.
- Prepare departmental income statements like the one in Exhibit 22.15. Show sales, cost of goods sold, gross profit, individual expenses, and net income for each of the three operating departments and for the combined company.

SOLUTION TO DEMONSTRATION PROBLEM

Allocations of the four indirect expenses across the five departments.

Rent	Square Feet	Percent of Total	Allocated Cost
General office	500	5.0%	$ 7,500
Purchasing	500	5.0	7,500
Hardware	4,000	40.0	60,000
Software	3,000	30.0	45,000
Repairs	2,000	20.0	30,000
Totals	10,000	100.0%	$150,000

Utilities	Square Feet	Percent of Total	Allocated Cost
General office	500	5.0%	$ 2,500
Purchasing	500	5.0	2,500
Hardware	4,000	40.0	20,000
Software	3,000	30.0	15,000
Repairs	2,000	20.0	10,000
Totals	10,000	100.0%	$50,000

Advertising	Sales Dollars	Percent of Total	Allocated Cost
Hardware	$ 960,000	40.0%	$ 50,000
Software	600,000	25.0	31,250
Repairs	840,000	35.0	43,750
Totals	$2,400,000	100.0%	$125,000

Insurance	Assets Insured	Percent of Total	Allocated Cost
General office	$ 60,000	10.0%	$ 3,000
Purchasing	72,000	12.0	3,600
Hardware	330,000	55.0	16,500
Software	42,000	7.0	2,100
Repairs	96,000	16.0	4,800
Totals	$600,000	100.0%	$30,000

1. Allocations of service department expenses to the three operating departments.

General Office Allocations to	Employees	Percent of Total	Allocated Cost
Hardware	5	25.0%	$23,500
Software	5	25.0	23,500
Repairs	10	50.0	47,000
Totals	20	100.0%	$94,000

Purchasing Allocations to	Cost of Goods Sold	Percent of Total	Allocated Cost
Hardware	$ 500,000	50.0%	$37,900
Software	300,000	30.0	22,740
Repairs	200,000	20.0	15,160
Totals	$1,000,000	100.0%	$75,800

HACKER'S HAVEN
Departmental Expense Allocations
For Year Ended December 31, 2013

	Allocation Base	Expense Account Balance	General Office Dept.	Purchasing Dept.	Hardware Dept.	Software Dept.	Repairs Dept.
Direct Expenses							
Payroll		$ 535,000	$ 60,000	$ 45,000	$ 80,000	$ 25,000	$ 325,000
Depreciation		60,000	6,000	7,200	33,000	4,200	9,600
Supplies		62,000	15,000	10,000	10,000	2,000	25,000
Indirect Expenses							
Rent	Square ft.	150,000	7,500	7,500	60,000	45,000	30,000
Utilities	Square ft.	50,000	2,500	2,500	20,000	15,000	10,000
Advertising	Sales	125,000	—	—	50,000	31,250	43,750
Insurance	Assets	30,000	3,000	3,600	16,500	2,100	4,800
Total expenses		1,012,000	94,000	75,800	269,500	124,550	448,150
Service Department Expenses							
General office	Employees		(94,000)		23,500	23,500	47,000
Purchasing	Goods sold			(75,800)	37,900	22,740	15,160
Total expenses allocated to operating departments		$1,012,000	$ 0	$ 0	$330,900	$170,790	$510,310

2. Departmental income statements for Hacker's Haven.

HACKER'S HAVEN
Departmental Income Statements
For Year Ended December 31, 2013

	Hardware	Software	Repairs	Combined
Sales	$ 960,000	$ 600,000	$ 840,000	$2,400,000
Cost of goods sold	500,000	300,000	200,000	1,000,000
Gross profit	460,000	300,000	640,000	1,400,000
Expenses				
Payroll	80,000	25,000	325,000	430,000
Depreciation	33,000	4,200	9,600	46,800
Supplies	10,000	2,000	25,000	37,000
Rent	60,000	45,000	30,000	135,000
Utilities	20,000	15,000	10,000	45,000
Advertising	50,000	31,250	43,750	125,000
Insurance	16,500	2,100	4,800	23,400
Share of general office	23,500	23,500	47,000	94,000
Share of purchasing	37,900	22,740	15,160	75,800
Total expenses	330,900	170,790	510,310	1,012,000
Net income	$129,100	$129,210	$129,690	$ 388,000

APPENDIX

Transfer Pricing 22A

C2 Explain transfer pricing and methods to set transfer prices.

Divisions in decentralized companies sometimes do business with one another. For example, a separate division of **Harley-Davidson** manufactures its plastic and fiberglass parts used in the company's motorcycles. **Anheuser-Busch**'s metal container division makes cans and lids used in its brewing operations, and also sells cans and lids to soft-drink companies. A division of **Prince** produces strings used in tennis rackets made by Prince and other manufacturers.

Determining the price that should be used to record transfers between divisions in the same company is the focus of this appendix. Because these transactions are transfers within the same company, the price to record them is called the **transfer price.** In decentralized organizations, division managers have input on or decide those prices. Transfer prices can be used in cost, profit, and investment centers. Since these transfers are not with customers outside the company, the transfer price has no direct impact on the company's overall profits. However, transfer prices can impact performance evaluations and, if set incorrectly, lead to bad decisions.

Point: Transfer pricing can impact company profits when divisions are located in countries with different tax rates; this is covered in advanced courses.

Alternative Transfer Prices Exhibit 22A.1 reports data on the LCD division of ZTel. LCD manufactures liquid crystal display (LCD) touch-screen monitors for use in ZTel's S-Phone division's smartphones, which sell for $400 each. The monitors can also be used in other products. So, LCD can sell its monitors to buyers other than S-Phone. Likewise, the S-Phone division can purchase monitors from suppliers other than LCD.

EXHIBIT 22A.1

LCD Division Manufacturing Information—Monitors

Production capacity	100,000 units
Selling price per unit to outside customers	$80
Variable manufacturing costs per unit	$40
Fixed manufacturing costs	$2,000,000

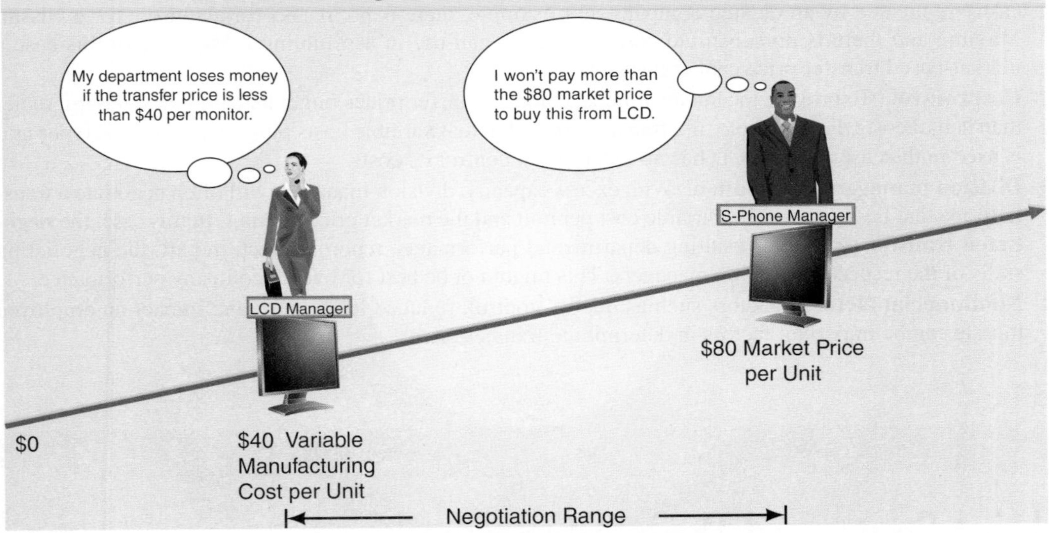

Exhibit 22A.1 reveals the range of transfer prices for transfers of monitors from LCD to S-Phone. The manager of LCD wants to report a division profit; thus, this manager will not accept a transfer price less than $40 (variable manufacturing cost per unit) because doing so would cause the division to lose money on each monitor transferred. The LCD manager will only consider transfer prices of $40 or more. On the other hand, the S-Phone division manager also wants to report a division profit. Thus, this manager will not pay more than $80 per monitor because similar monitors can be bought from outside suppliers at that price. The S-Phone manager will only consider transfer prices of $80 or less. As any transfer price between $40 and $80 per monitor is possible, how does ZTel determine the transfer price? The answer depends in part on whether the LCD division has excess capacity to manufacture monitors.

No Excess Capacity Assume the LCD division can sell every monitor it produces, and thus is producing 100,000 units. In that case, a **market-based transfer price** of $80 per monitor is preferred. At that price, the LCD division manager is willing to either transfer monitors to S-Phone or sell to outside customers. The S-Phone manager cannot buy monitors for less than $80 from outside suppliers, so the $80 price is acceptable. Further, with a transfer price of $80 per monitor, top management of ZTel is indifferent to S-Phone buying from LCD or buying similar-quality monitors from outside suppliers.

With no excess capacity, the LCD manager will not accept a transfer price less than $80 per monitor. For example, suppose the S-Phone manager suggests a transfer price of $70 per monitor. At that price the LCD manager incurs an unnecessary *opportunity cost* of $10 per monitor (computed as $80 market price minus $70 transfer price). This would lower the LCD division's income and hurt its performance evaluation.

Excess Capacity Assume that the LCD division has excess capacity. For example, the LCD division might currently be producing only 80,000 units. Because LCD has $2,000,000 of fixed manufacturing costs, both LCD and the top management of ZTel prefer that S-Phone purchases its monitors from LCD. For example, if S-Phone purchases its monitors from an outside supplier at the market price of $80 each, LCD manufactures no units. Then, LCD reports a division loss equal to its fixed costs, and ZTel overall reports a lower net income as its costs are higher. Consequently, with excess capacity, LCD should accept any transfer price of $40 per unit or greater and S-Phone should purchase monitors from LCD. This will allow LCD to recover some (or all) of its fixed costs and increase ZTel's overall profits. For example, if a transfer price of $50 per monitor is used, the S-Phone manager is pleased to buy from LCD, since that price is below the market price of $80. For each monitor transferred from LCD to S-Phone at $50, the LCD division receives a *contribution margin* of $10 (computed as $50 transfer price less $40 variable cost) to contribute towards recovering its fixed costs. This form of transfer pricing is called **cost-based transfer pricing.** Under this approach the transfer price might be based on variable costs, total costs, or variable costs plus a markup. Determining the transfer price under excess capacity is complex and is covered in advanced courses.

Transfer Pricing Approaches Used by Companies

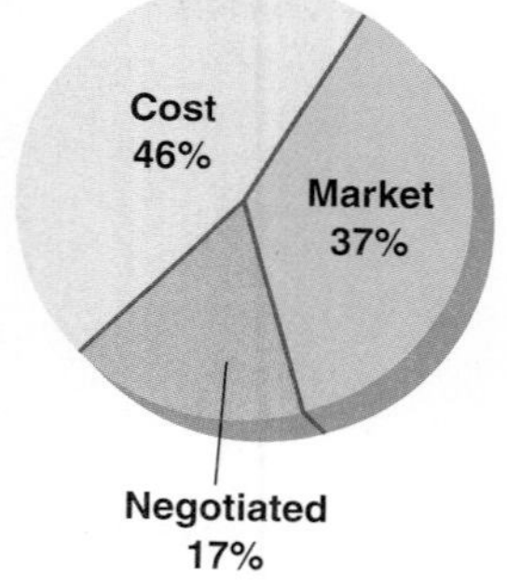

Additional Issues in Transfer Pricing Several additional issues arise in determining transfer prices which include the following:

- **No market price exists.** Sometimes there is no market price for the product being transferred. The product might be a key component that requires additional conversion costs at the next stage and is not easily replicated by an outside company. For example, there is no market for a console for a **Nissan** Maxima and there is no substitute console **Nissan** can use in assembling a Maxima. In this case a market-based transfer price cannot be used.
- **Cost control.** To provide incentives for cost control, transfer prices might be based on standard, rather than actual costs. For example, if a transfer price of actual variable costs plus a markup of $20 per unit is used in the case above, LCD has no incentive to control its costs.
- **Division managers' negotiation.** With excess capacity, division managers will often negotiate a transfer price that lies between the variable cost per unit and the market price per unit. In this case, the **negotiated transfer price** and resulting departmental performance reports reflect, in part, the negotiating skills of the respective division managers. This might not be best for overall company performance.
- **Nonfinancial factors.** Factors such as quality control, reduced lead times, and impact on employee morale can be important factors in determining transfer prices.

APPENDIX

22B Joint Costs and Their Allocation

C3 Describe allocation of joint costs across products.

Most manufacturing processes involve **joint costs,** which refer to costs incurred to produce or purchase two or more products at the same time. A joint cost is like an indirect expense in the sense that more than one cost object share it. For example, a sawmill company incurs a joint cost when it buys logs that it cuts into lumber as shown in Exhibit 22B.1. The joint cost includes the logs (raw material) and its cutting (conversion) into boards classified as Clear, Select, No. 1 Common, No. 2 Common, No. 3 Common, and other types of lumber and by-products.

When a joint cost is incurred, a question arises as to whether to allocate it to different products resulting from it. The answer is that when management wishes to estimate the costs of individual products, joint costs are included and must be allocated to these joint products. However, when management needs information to help decide whether to sell a product at a certain point in the production process or to process it further, the joint costs are ignored.

Financial statements prepared according to GAAP must assign joint costs to products. To do this, management must decide how to allocate joint costs across products benefiting from these costs. If some products are sold and others remain in inventory, allocating joint costs involves assigning costs to both cost of goods sold and ending inventory.

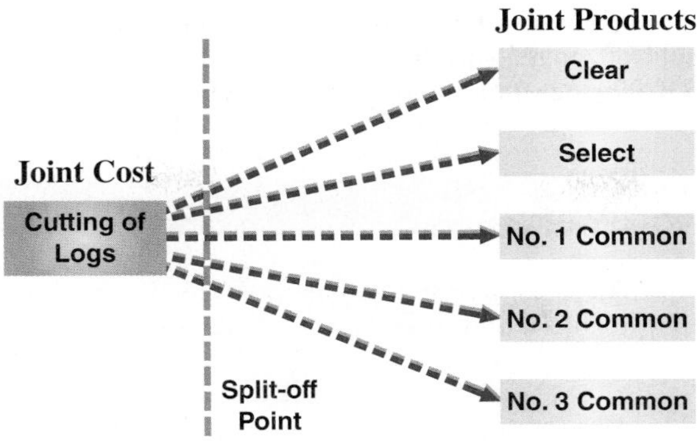

EXHIBIT 22B.1

Joint Products from Logs

The two usual methods to allocate joint costs are the (1) *physical basis* and (2) the *value basis.* The physical basis typically involves allocating joint cost using physical characteristics such as the ratio of pounds, cubic feet, or gallons of each joint product to the total pounds, cubic feet, or gallons of all joint products flowing from the cost. This method is not preferred because the resulting cost allocations do not reflect the relative market values the joint cost generates. The preferred approach is the value basis, which allocates joint cost in proportion to the sales value of the output produced by the process at the "split-off point"; see Exhibit 22B.1.

Physical Basis Allocation of Joint Cost To illustrate the physical basis of allocating a joint cost, we consider a sawmill that bought logs for $30,000. When cut, these logs produce 100,000 board feet of lumber in the grades and amounts shown in Exhibit 22B.2. The logs produce 20,000 board feet of No. 3 Common lumber, which is 20% of the total. With physical allocation, the No. 3 Common lumber is assigned 20% of the $30,000 cost of the logs, or $6,000 ($30,000 × 20%). Because this low-grade lumber sells for $4,000, this allocation gives a $2,000 loss from its production and sale. The physical basis for allocating joint costs does not reflect the extra value flowing into some products or the inferior value flowing into others. That is, the portion of a log that produces Clear and Select grade lumber is worth more than the portion used to produce the three grades of common lumber, but the physical basis fails to reflect this.

EXHIBIT 22B.2

Allocating Joint Costs on a Physical Basis

Grade of Lumber	Board Feet Produced	Percent of Total	Allocated Cost	Sales Value	Gross Profit
Clear and Select	10,000	10.0%	$ 3,000	$12,000	$ 9,000
No. 1 Common	30,000	30.0	9,000	18,000	9,000
No. 2 Common	40,000	40.0	12,000	16,000	4,000
No. 3 Common	20,000	20.0	6,000	4,000	(2,000)
Totals	100,000	100.0%	$30,000	$50,000	$20,000

Value Basis Allocation of Joint Cost Exhibit 22B.3 illustrates the value basis method of allocation. It determines the percents of the total costs allocated to each grade by the ratio of each grade's sales value to the total sales value of $50,000 (sales value is the unit selling price multiplied by the number of units produced). The Clear and Select lumber grades receive 24% of the total cost ($12,000/$50,000) instead of the 10% portion using a physical basis. The No. 3 Common lumber receives only 8% of the total cost, or $2,400, which is much less than the $6,000 assigned to it using the physical basis.

EXHIBIT 22B.3

Allocating Joint Costs on a Value Basis

Grade of Lumber	Sales Value	Percent of Total	Allocated Cost	Gross Profit
Clear and Select	$12,000	24.0%	$ 7,200	$ 4,800
No. 1 Common	18,000	36.0	10,800	7,200
No. 2 Common	16,000	32.0	9,600	6,400
No. 3 Common	4,000	8.0	2,400	1,600
Totals	$50,000	100.0%	$30,000	$20,000

Example: Refer to Exhibit 22B.3. If the sales value of Clear and Select lumber is changed to $10,000, what is the revised ratio of the market value of No. 1 Common to the total?
Answer: $18,000/$48,000 = 37.5%

An outcome of value basis allocation is that *each* grade produces exactly the same 40% gross profit at the split-off point. This 40% rate equals the gross profit rate from selling all the lumber made from the $30,000 logs for a combined price of $50,000.

Quick Check Answers — p. 965

9. A company produces three products, B1, B2, and B3. The joint cost incurred for the current month for these products is $180,000. The following data relate to this month's production:

Product	Units Produced	Unit Sales Value
B1	96,000	$3.00
B2	64,000	6.00
B3	32,000	9.00

The amount of joint cost allocated to product B3 using the value basis allocation is (*a*) $30,000, (*b*) $54,000, or (*c*) $90,000.

Summary

C1 Distinguish between direct and indirect expenses and identify bases for allocating indirect expenses to departments. Direct expenses are traced to a specific department and are incurred for the sole benefit of that department. Indirect expenses benefit more than one department. Indirect expenses are allocated to departments when computing departmental net income. Ideally, we allocate indirect expenses by using a cause-effect relation for the allocation base. When a cause-effect relation is not identifiable, each indirect expense is allocated on a basis reflecting the relative benefit received by each department.

C2 Explain transfer pricing and methods to set transfer prices. Transfer prices are used to record transfers of items between divisions of the same company. Transfer prices can be based on costs or market prices, or can be negotiated by division managers.

C3 Describe allocation of joint costs across products. A joint cost refers to costs incurred to produce or purchase two or more products at the same time. When income statements are prepared, joint costs are usually allocated to the resulting joint products using either a physical or value basis.

A1 Analyze investment centers using return on assets and residual income. A financial measure often used to evaluate an investment center manager is the *investment center return on total assets,* also called *return on investment.* This measure is computed as the center's net income divided by the center's average total assets. Residual income, computed as investment center net income minus a target net income is an alternative financial measure of investment center performance.

A2 Analyze investment centers using profit margin and investment turnover. Return on investment can also be computed as profit margin times investment turnover. Profit margin (equal to net income/sales) measures the income earned per dollar of sales and investment turnover (equal to sales/assets) measures how efficiently a division uses its assets.

A3 A balanced scorecard uses a combination of financial and nonfinancial measures to evaluate performance. Customer, internal process, and innovation and learning are the three primary perspectives of nonfinancial measures used in balanced scorecards.

A4 Compute cycle time and cycle efficiency, and explain their importance to production management. It is important for companies to reduce the time to produce their products and to improve manufacturing efficiency. One measure of that time is cycle time (CT), defined as Process time + Inspection time + Move time + Wait time. Process time is value-added time; the others are non-value-added time. Cycle efficiency (CE) is the ratio of value-added time to total cycle time. If CE is low, management should evaluate its production process to see if it can reduce non-value-added activities.

P1 Prepare a responsibility report for a cost center. Responsibility accounting systems provide information for evaluating the performance of department managers. A responsibility accounting system's performance reports for evaluating department managers should include only the expenses (and revenues) that each manager controls.

P2 Allocate indirect expenses to departments. Indirect expenses include items like depreciation, rent, advertising, and other expenses that cannot be assigned directly to departments. Indirect expenses are recorded in company accounts, an allocation base is identified for each expense, and costs are allocated to departments. Departmental expense allocation spreadsheets are often used in allocating indirect expenses to departments.

P3 Prepare departmental income statements and contribution reports. Each profit center (department) is assigned its expenses to yield its own income statement. These costs include its direct expenses and its share of indirect expenses. The departmental income statement lists its revenues and costs of goods sold to determine gross profit. Its operating expenses (direct expenses and its indirect expenses allocated to the department) are deducted from gross profit to yield departmental net income. The departmental contribution report is similar to the departmental income statement in terms of computing the gross profit for each department. Then the direct operating expenses for each department are deducted from gross profit to determine the contribution generated by each department. Indirect operating expenses are deducted *in total* from the company's combined contribution.

Guidance Answers to Decision Maker and Decision Ethics

Division Manager Your division's ROI without further action is 10.5% (equal to 7% × 1.5). In a highly competitive industry, it is difficult to increase profit margins by raising prices. Your division might be better able to control its costs to increase its profit margin. In addition, you might engage in a marketing program to increase sales without increasing your division's invested assets. Investment turnover and thus ROI will increase if the marketing campaign attracts customers.

Center Manager We must first realize that the two investment opportunities are not comparable on the basis of absolute dollars of income or on assets. For instance, the second investment provides a higher income in absolute dollars but requires a higher investment. Accordingly, we need to compute return on total assets for each alternative: (1) $50,000 ÷ $250,000 = 20%, and (2) $175,000 ÷ $1 million = 17.5%. Alternative 1 has the higher return and is preferred over alternative 2. Do you pursue one, both, or neither? Because alternative 1's return is higher than the center's usual return of 19%, it should be pursued, assuming its risks are acceptable. Also, since alternative 1 requires a small investment, top management is likely to be more agreeable to pursuing it. Alternative 2's return is lower than the usual 19% and is not likely to be acceptable.

Guidance Answers to Quick Checks

1. *d*
2. A cost center, such as a service department, incurs costs without directly generating revenues. A profit center, such as a product division, incurs costs but also generates revenues.
3. *c*
4. *b*
5. *d*
6. (1) Assign the direct expenses to each department. (2) Allocate indirect expenses to all departments. (3) Allocate the service department expenses to the operating departments.
7. *b*
8. a) $2,000/50,000 = 4%; b) $50,000/10,000 = 5; $2,000/10,000 = 20%.
9. *b*; $180,000 × ([32,000 × $9]/[96,000 × $3 + 64,000 × $6 + 32,000 × $9]) = $54,000.

Key Terms

Balanced scorecard (p. 956)
Controllable costs (p. 943)
Cost-based transfer pricing (p. 962)
Cost center (p. 943)
Cycle efficiency (p. 958)
Cycle Time (CT) (p. 957)
Departmental contribution to overhead (p. 951)
Departmental income statements (p. 945)
Direct expenses (p. 945)
Hurdle rate (p. 953)
Indirect expenses (p. 945)
Investment center (p. 943)
Investment center residual income (p. 953)
Investment center return on total assets (p. 953)
Investment turnover (p. 954)
Joint cost (p. 962)
Market-based transfer price (p. 962)
Negotiated transfer price (p. 962)
Non-value-added time (p. 958)
Profit center (p. 943)
Profit margin (p. 954)
Responsibility accounting budget (p. 944)
Responsibility accounting performance report (p. 944)
Responsibility accounting system (p. 942)
Transfer price (p. 961)
Uncontrollable costs (p. 943)
Value-added time (p. 958)

Multiple Choice Quiz

Answers on p. 983

mhhe.com/wildFINMAN5e

Additional Quiz Questions are available at the book's Website.

1. A retailer has three departments—housewares, appliances, and clothing—and buys advertising that benefits all departments. Advertising expense is $150,000 for the year, and departmental sales for the year follow: housewares, $356,250; appliances, $641,250; clothing, $427,500. How much advertising expense is allocated to appliances if allocation is based on departmental sales?
   a. $37,500
   b. $67,500
   c. $45,000
   d. $150,000
   e. $641,250

2. Indirect expenses
   a. Cannot be readily traced to one department.
   b. Are allocated to departments based on the relative benefit each department receives.
   c. Are the same as uncontrollable expenses.
   d. a, b, and c above are all true.
   e. a and b above are true.
3. A division reports the information below. What is the division's investment (asset) turnover?

Sales	$500,000
Income	75,000
Average assets	200,000

   a. 37.5%
   b. 15.0
   c. 2.5
   d. 2.67
   e. 4.0
4. A company operates three retail departments as profit centers, and the following information is available for each. Which department has the largest dollar amount of departmental contribution to overhead and what is the dollar amount contributed?

Department	Sales	Cost of Goods Sold	Direct Expenses	Allocated Indirect Expenses
X	$500,000	$350,000	$50,000	$40,000
Y	200,000	75,000	20,000	50,000
Z	350,000	150,000	75,000	10,000

   a. Department Y, $ 55,000
   b. Department Z, $125,000
   c. Department X, $500,000
   d. Department Z, $200,000
   e. Department X, $ 60,000
5. Using the data in question 4, Department X's contribution to overhead as a percentage of sales is
   a. 20%
   b. 30%
   c. 12%
   d. 48%
   e. 32%

A(B) Superscript letter A (B) denotes assignments based on Appendix 22A (22B).
Icon denotes assignments that involve decision making.

Discussion Questions

1. Why are many companies divided into departments?
2. What is the difference between operating departments and service departments?
3. What are controllable costs?
4. Controllable and uncontrollable costs must be identified with a particular _____ and a definite _____ period.
5. Why should managers be closely involved in preparing their responsibility accounting budgets?
6. What are two main goals in managerial accounting for reporting on and analyzing departments?
7. Is it possible to evaluate a cost center's profitability? Explain.
8. What is the difference between direct and indirect expenses?
9. Suggest a reasonable basis for allocating each of the following indirect expenses to departments: (a) salary of a supervisor who manages several departments, (b) rent, (c) heat, (d) electricity for lighting, (e) janitorial services, (f) advertising, (g) expired insurance on equipment, and (h) property taxes on equipment.
10. **Piaggio** has many departments. How is a department's contribution to overhead measured? PIAGGIO
11. **KTM** aims to give its managers timely cost reports. In responsibility accounting, who receives timely cost reports and specific cost information? Explain. KTM
12.[A] What is a transfer price? Under what conditions is a market-based transfer price most likely to be used?
13.[B] What is a joint cost? How are joint costs usually allocated among the products produced from them?
14.[B] Give two examples of products with joint costs.
15. Each retail store of **Apple** has several departments. Why is it useful for its management to (a) collect accounting information about each department and (b) treat each department as a profit center? Apple
16. **Polaris** delivers its products to locations around the world. List three controllable and three uncontrollable costs for its delivery department. Polaris
17. Define and describe *cycle time* and identify the components of cycle time.
18. Explain the difference between value-added time and non-value-added time.
19. Define and describe *cycle efficiency*.
20. Can management of a company such as **Arctic Cat** use cycle time and cycle efficiency as useful measures of performance? Explain. Arctic Cat

connect

QUICK STUDY

QS 22-1
Allocation and measurement terms
C1

In each blank next to the following terms, place the identifying letter of its best description.

1. ______ Cost center
2. ______ Investment center
3. ______ Departmental accounting system
4. ______ Operating department
5. ______ Profit center
6. ______ Responsibility accounting system
7. ______ Service department

A. Incurs costs without directly yielding revenues.
B. Provides information used to evaluate the performance of a department.
C. Holds manager responsible for revenues, costs, and investments.
D. Engages directly in manufacturing or in making sales directly to customers.
E. Does not directly manufacture products but contributes to profitability of the entire company.
F. Incurs costs and also generates revenues.
G. Provides information used to evaluate the performance of a department manager.

QS 22-2
Basis for cost allocation
C1

For each of the following types of indirect expenses and service department expenses, identify one allocation basis that could be used to distribute it to the departments indicated.

1. Computer service expenses of production scheduling for operating departments.
2. General office department expenses of the operating departments.
3. Maintenance department expenses of the operating departments.
4. Electric utility expenses of all departments.

QS 22-3
Responsibility accounting terms
C1

In each blank next to the following terms, place the identifying letter of its best description.

1. ______ Indirect expenses
2. ______ Controllable costs
3. ______ Direct expenses
4. ______ Uncontrollable costs

A. Costs not within a manager's control or influence
B. Costs that can be readily traced to a department
C. Cost that a manager has the ability to affect
D. Costs incurred for the joint benefit of more than one department

QS 22-4
Departmental contribution to overhead
P3

Use the information in the following table to compute each department's contribution to overhead (both in dollars and as a percent). Which department contributes the largest dollar amount to total overhead? Which contributes the highest percent (as a percent of sales)? Round percents to one decimal.

	Dept. A	Dept. B	Dept. C
Sales	$53,000	$180,000	$84,000
Cost of goods sold	34,185	103,700	49,560
Gross profit	18,815	76,300	34,440
Total direct expenses	3,660	37,060	7,386
Contribution to overhead	$ ______	$ ______	$ ______
Contribution percent	______ %	______ %	______ %

QS 22-5
Computing investment center return on assets
A1

Compute return on assets for each of the divisions below (each is an investment center). Comment on the relative performance of each investment center.

Investment Center	Net Income	Average Assets	Return on Assets
Cameras and camcorders	$4,500,000	$20,000,000	______
Phones and communications	1,500,000	12,500,000	______
Computers and accessories	800,000	10,000,000	______

QS 22-6
Computing residual income A1

Refer to information in QS 22-5. Assume a target income of 12% of average invested assets. Compute residual income for each division.

QS 22-7
Computing profit margin and investment turnover A2

A company's shipping division (an investment center) has sales of $2,420,000, net income of $516,000, and average invested assets of $2,250,000. Compute the division's profit margin and investment turnover.

QS 22-8
Performance measures
A1 A2

Fill in the blanks in the schedule below for two separate investment centers A and B. Round answers to the nearest whole percent.

	Investment Center A	Investment Center B
Sales	$______	$10,400,000
Net income	$ 352,000	$______
Average invested assets	$1,400,000	$______
Profit margin	8%	______%
Investment turnover	______	1.5
Return on (assets) investment	______%	12%

QS 22-9
Performance measures—balanced scorecard
A3

Classify each of the performance measures below into the most likely balanced scorecard perspective it relates to. Label your answers using C (customer), P (internal process), I (innovation and growth), or F (financial).

1. Customer wait time ______
2. Number of days of employee absences ______
3. Profit margin ______
4. Number of new products introduced ______
5. Change in market share ______
6. Employee training sessions attended ______
7. Length of time raw materials are in inventory ______
8. Customer satisfaction index ______

QS 22-10
Performance measures—balanced scorecard
A3

Walt Disney reports the following information for its two Parks and Resorts divisions.

	East Coast		West Coast	
	Current year	Prior year	Current year	Prior year
Hotel occupancy rates	89%	86%	92%	93%

Assume Walt Disney uses a balanced scorecard and sets a target of 90% occupancy in its resorts. Using Exhibit 22.22 as a guide, show how the company's performance on hotel occupancy would appear on a balanced scorecard report.

QS 22-11A
Determining transfer prices without excess capacity
C2

The Windshield division of Fast Car Co. makes windshields for use in Fast Car's Assembly division. The Windshield division incurs variable costs of $200 per windshield and has capacity to make 500,000 windshields per year. The market price is $450 per windshield. The Windshield division incurs total fixed costs of $3,000,000 per year. If the Windshield division is operating at full capacity, what transfer price should be used on transfers between the Windshield and Assembly divisions? Explain.

QS 22-12A
Determining transfer prices with excess capacity C2

Refer to information in QS 22-11. If the Windshield division has excess capacity, what is the range of possible transfer prices that could be used on transfers between the Windshield and Assembly divisions? Explain.

QS 22-13B
Joint cost allocation
C3

A company purchases a 10,020 square foot commercial building for $325,000 and spends an additional $50,000 to divide the space into two separate rental units and prepare it for rent. Unit A, which has the desirable location on the corner and contains 3,340 square feet, will be rented for $1.00 per square foot. Unit B contains 6,680 square feet and will be rented for $0.75 per square foot. How much of the joint cost should be assigned to Unit B using the value basis of allocation?

QS 22-14
Rent expense allocated to departments
P2

Car Mart pays $130,000 rent each year for its two-story building. The space in this building is occupied by five departments as specified here.

Paint department	1,440 square feet of first-floor space
Engine department	3,360 square feet of first-floor space
Window department	2,016 square feet of second-floor space
Electrical department	960 square feet of second-floor space
Accessory department	1,824 square feet of second-floor space

The company allocates 65% of total rent expense to the first floor and 35% to the second floor, and then allocates rent expense for each floor to the departments occupying that floor on the basis of space occupied. Determine the rent expense to be allocated to each department. (Round percents to the nearest one-tenth and dollar amounts to the nearest whole dollar.)

Check Allocated to Paint Dept., $25,350

QS 22-15
Return on investment A1

For a recent year **L'Oreal** reported operating profit of €3,385 (in millions) for its Cosmetics division. Total assets were €12,888 at the beginning of the year and €13,099 (in millions) at the end of the year. Compute return on investment for the year. State your answer as a percent, rounded to one decimal.

QS 22-16
Manufacturing cycle time and efficiency
A4

Compute and interpret (*a*) manufacturing cycle time and (*b*) manufacturing cycle efficiency using the following information from a manufacturing company.

Process time	15 minutes
Inspection time	2 minutes
Move time	6.4 minutes
Wait time	36.6 minutes

QS 22-17
Allocating costs to departments
P1

Macee Department Store has three departments, and it conducts advertising campaigns that benefit all departments. Advertising costs are $100,000 this year, and departmental sales for this year follows. How much advertising cost is allocated to each department if the allocation is based on departmental sales?

Department	Sales
Department 1	$220,000
Department 2	400,000
Department 3	180,000

QS 22-18
Allocating costs to departments
P1

Mervon Company has two operating departments: Mixing and Bottling. Mixing has 300 employees and occupies 22,000 square feet. Bottling has 200 employees and occupies 18,000 square feet. Indirect factory costs for the current period follow: Administrative, $160,000; and Maintenance, $200,000. Administrative costs are allocated to operating departments based on the number of workers. Determine the administrative cost allocated to each operating department.

QS 22-19
Allocating costs to departments
P1

Refer to the information in QS 22-18. If the maintenance costs are allocated to operating departments based on square footage, determine the amount of maintenance costs allocated to each operating department.

connect

EXERCISES

Exercise 22-1
Departmental expense allocations
P2

Woh Che Co. has four departments: materials, personnel, manufacturing, and packaging. In a recent month, the four departments incurred three shared indirect expenses. The amounts of these indirect expenses and the bases used to allocate them follow.

Indirect Expense	Cost	Allocation Base
Supervision	$ 82,500	Number of employees
Utilities	50,000	Square feet occupied
Insurance	22,500	Value of assets in use
Total	$155,000	

Departmental data for the company's recent reporting period follow.

Department	Employees	Square Feet	Asset Values
Materials	27	25,000	$ 6,000
Personnel	9	5,000	1,200
Manufacturing	63	55,000	37,800
Packaging	51	15,000	15,000
Total	150	100,000	$60,000

(1) Use this information to allocate each of the three indirect expenses across the four departments.
(2) Prepare a summary table that reports the indirect expenses assigned to each of the four departments.

Check (2) Total of $29,600 assigned to Materials Dept.

Exercise 22-2
Managerial performance evaluation
P1

Maryanne Dinardo manages an auto dealership's service department. The recent month's income statement for his department follows. (1) Analyze the items on the income statement and identify those that definitely should be included on a performance report used to evaluate Dinardo's performance. List them and explain why you chose them. (2) List and explain the items that should definitely be excluded. (3) List the items that are not definitely included or excluded and explain why they fall into that category.

Revenues		
Sales of parts	$ 72,000	
Sales of services	105,000	$177,000
Costs and expenses		
Cost of parts sold	30,000	
Building depreciation	9,300	
Income taxes allocated to department	8,700	
Interest on long-term debt	7,500	
Manager's salary	12,000	
Payroll taxes	8,100	
Supplies	15,900	
Utilities	4,400	
Wages (hourly)	16,000	
Total costs and expenses		111,900
Departmental net income		$ 65,100

Exercise 22-3
Departmental contribution report
P3

Below are departmental income statements for a guitar manufacturer. The manufacturer is considering dropping its electric guitar department since it has a net loss. The company classifies advertising, rent, and utilities expenses as indirect. (1) Prepare a departmental contribution report that shows each department's contribution to overhead. (2) Based on contribution to overhead, should the electric guitar department be eliminated?

WHOLESALE GUITARS
Departmental Income Statements
For Year Ended December 31, 2013

	Acoustic	Electric
Sales	$112,500	$105,500
Cost of goods sold	55,675	66,750
Gross profit	56,825	38,750
Operating expenses		
Advertising expense	8,075	6,250
Depreciation expense-equipment	10,150	9,000
Salaries expense	17,300	13,500
Supplies expense	2,030	1,700
Rent expense	6,105	5,950
Utilities expense	3,045	2,550
Total operating expenses	46,705	38,950
Net income (loss)	**$ 10,120**	**($200)**

Exercise 22-4
Departmental expense allocation spreadsheet
P2

Marathon Running Shop has two service departments (advertising and administration) and two operating departments (shoes and clothing). During 2013, the departments had the following direct expenses and occupied the following amount of floor space.

Department	Direct Expenses	Square Feet
Advertising	$ 18,000	1,120
Administrative	25,000	1,400
Shoes	103,000	7,140
Clothing	15,000	4,340

The advertising department developed and distributed 120 advertisements during the year. Of these, 90 promoted shoes and 30 promoted clothing. The store sold $350,000 of merchandise during the year. Of this amount, $273,000 is from the shoes department, and $77,000 is from the clothing department. The utilities expense of $64,000 is an indirect expense to all departments. Prepare a departmental expense allocation spreadsheet for Marathon Running Shop. The spreadsheet should assign (1) direct expenses to each of the four departments, (2) the $64,000 of utilities expense to the four departments on the basis of floor space occupied, (3) the advertising department's expenses to the two operating departments on the basis of the number of ads placed that promoted a department's products, and (4) the administrative department's expenses to the two operating departments based on the amount of sales. Provide supporting computations for the expense allocations.

Check Total expenses allocated to Shoes Dept., $177,472

Exercise 22-5
Service department expenses allocated to operating departments P2

The following is a partially completed lower section of a departmental expense allocation spreadsheet for Cozy Bookstore. It reports the total amounts of direct and indirect expenses allocated to its five departments. Complete the spreadsheet by allocating the expenses of the two service departments (advertising and purchasing) to the three operating departments.

			Allocation of Expenses to Departments				
	Allocation Base	Expense Account Balance	Advertising Dept.	Purchasing Dept.	Books Dept.	Magazines Dept.	Newspapers Dept.
Total department expenses..........		$698,000	$24,000	$34,000	$425,000	$90,000	$125,000
Service department expenses							
Advertising department.............	Sales		?		?	?	?
Purchasing department.............	Purch. orders			?	?	?	?
Total expenses allocated to operating departments.............		?	$ 0	$ 0	?	?	?

Advertising and purchasing department expenses are allocated to operating departments on the basis of dollar sales and purchase orders, respectively. Information about the allocation bases for the three operating departments follows.

Department	Sales	Purchase Orders
Books...............	$495,000	516
Magazines............	198,000	360
Newspapers..........	207,000	324
Total................	$900,000	1,200

Check Total expenses allocated to Books Dept., $452,820

Exercise 22-6
Indirect payroll expense allocated to departments
P2

Jessica Porter works in both the jewelry department and the hosiery department of a retail store. Porter assists customers in both departments and arranges and stocks merchandise in both departments. The store allocates Porter's $30,000 annual wages between the two departments based on a sample of the time worked in the two departments. The sample is obtained from a diary of hours worked that Porter kept in a randomly chosen two-week period. The diary showed the following hours and activities spent in the two departments. Allocate Porter's annual wages between the two departments.

Selling in jewelry department..	51 hours
Arranging and stocking merchandise in jewelry department........................	6 hours
Selling in hosiery department	12 hours
Arranging and stocking merchandise in hosiery department	7 hours
Idle time spent waiting for a customer to enter one of the selling departments	4 hours

Check Assign $7,500 to Hosiery

Exercise 22-7
Investment center analysis
A1

You must prepare a return on investment analysis for the regional manager of Fast & Great Burgers. This growing chain is trying to decide which outlet of two alternatives to open. The first location (A) requires a $1,000,000 investment and is expected to yield annual net income of $160,000. The second location (B) requires a $600,000 investment and is expected to yield annual net income of $108,000. Compute the return on investment for each Fast & Great Burgers alternative and then make your recommendation in a one-half page memorandum to the regional manager. (The chain currently generates an 18% return on total assets.)

Exercise 22-8
Computing return on assets and residual income; investing decision
A1

Megamart, a retailer of consumer goods, provides the following information on two of its departments (each considered an investment center).

Investment Center	Sales	Net Income	Average Invested Assets
Electronics	$40,000,000	$2,880,000	$16,000,000
Sporting goods.	20,000,000	2,040,000	12,000,000

(1) Compute return on investment for each department. Using return on investment, which department is most efficient at using assets to generate returns for the company? (2) Assume a target income level of 12% of average invested assets. Compute residual income for each department. Which department generated the most residual income for the company? (3) Assume the Electronics department is presented with a new investment opportunity that will yield a 15% return on assets. Should the new investment opportunity be accepted? Explain.

Exercise 22-9
Computing margin and turnover; department efficiency A2

Refer to information in Exercise 22-8. Compute profit margin and investment turnover for each department. Which department generates the most net income per dollar of sales? Which department is most efficient at generating sales from average invested assets?

Exercise 22-10
Performance measures—balanced scorecard
A3

USA Airlines uses the following performance measures. Classify each of the performance measures below into the most likely balanced scorecard perspective it relates to. Label your answers using C (customer), P (internal process), I (innovation and growth), or F (financial).

1. Cash flow from operations ______
2. Number of reports of mishandled or lost baggage ______
3. Percentage of on-time departures ______
4. On-time flight percentage ______
5. Percentage of ground crew trained ______
6. Return on investment ______
7. Market value ______
8. Accidents or safety incidents per mile flown ______
9. Customer complaints ______
10. Flight attendant training sessions attended ______
11. Time airplane is on ground between flights ______
12. Airplane miles per gallon of fuel ______
13. Revenue per seat ______
14. Cost of leasing airplanes ______

Exercise 22-11A
Determining transfer prices
C2

The Trailer department of Baxter Bicycles makes bike trailers that attach to bicycles and can carry children or cargo. The trailers have a retail price of $200 each. Each trailer incurs $80 of variable manufacturing costs. The Trailer department has capacity for 40,000 trailers per year, and incurs fixed costs of $1,000,000 per year.

Required

1. Assume the Assembly division of Baxter Bicycles wants to buy 15,000 trailers per year from the Trailer division. If the Trailer division can sell all of the trailers it manufactures to outside customers, what price should be used on transfers between Baxter Bicycle's divisions? Explain.
2. Assume the Trailer division currently only sells 20,000 trailers to outside customers, and the Assembly division wants to buy 15,000 trailers per year from the Trailer division. What is the range of acceptable prices that could be used on transfers between Baxter Bicycle's divisions? Explain.
3. Assume transfer prices of either $80 per trailer or $140 per trailer are being considered. Comment on the preferred transfer prices from the perspectives of the Trailer division manager, the Assembly division manager, and the top management of Baxter Bicycles.

Exercise 22-12B
Joint real estate costs assigned
C3

Heart & Home Properties is developing a subdivision that includes 600 home lots. The 450 lots in the Canyon section are below a ridge and do not have views of the neighboring canyons and hills; the 150 lots in the Hilltop section offer unobstructed views. The expected selling price for each Canyon lot is $55,000 and for each Hilltop lot is $110,000. The developer acquired the land for $4,000,000 and spent another $3,500,000 on street and utilities improvements. Assign the joint land and improvement costs to the lots using the value basis of allocation and determine the average cost per lot.

Check Total Hilltop cost, $3,000,000

Exercise 22-13B
Joint product costs assigned
C3

Pirate Seafood Company purchases lobsters and processes them into tails and flakes. It sells the lobster tails for $21 per pound and the flakes for $14 per pound. On average, 100 pounds of lobster are processed into 52 pounds of tails and 22 pounds of flakes, with 26 pounds of waste. Assume that the company purchased 2,400 pounds of lobster for $4.50 per pound and processed the lobsters with an additional labor cost of $1,800. No materials or labor costs are assigned to the waste. If 1,096 pounds of tails and 324 pounds of flakes are sold, what is (1) the allocated cost of the sold items and (2) the allocated cost of the ending inventory? The company allocates joint costs on a value basis. (Round the dollar cost per pound to the nearest thousandth.)

Check (2) Inventory cost, $2,268

Exercise 22-14
Profit margin and investment turnover
A2

L'Oreal reports the following for a recent year for the major divisions in its Cosmetics branch.

(€ millions)	Sales	Income	Total Assets End of Year	Total Assets Beginning of Year
Professional products	€ 2,717	€ 552	€ 2,624	€ 2,516
Consumer products	9,530	1,765	5,994	5,496
Luxury products	4,507	791	3,651	4,059
Active cosmetics	1,386	278	830	817
Total	€18,140	€3,386	€13,099	€12,888

1. Compute profit margin for each division. State your answers as percents, rounded to two decimal places. Which L'Oreal division has the highest profit margin?
2. Compute investment turnover for each division. Round your answers to two decimal places. Which L'Oreal division has the best investment turnover?

connect

PROBLEM SET A

Problem 22-1A
Allocation of building occupancy costs to departments
P2

mhhe.com/wildFINMAN5e

National Bank has several departments that occupy both floors of a two-story building. The departmental accounting system has a single account, Building Occupancy Cost, in its ledger. The types and amounts of occupancy costs recorded in this account for the current period follow.

Depreciation—Building	$18,000
Interest—Building mortgage	27,000
Taxes—Building and land	9,000
Gas (heating) expense	3,000
Lighting expense	3,000
Maintenance expense	6,000
Total occupancy cost	$66,000

The building has 4,000 square feet on each floor. In prior periods, the accounting manager merely divided the $66,000 occupancy cost by 8,000 square feet to find an average cost of $8.25 per square foot and then charged each department a building occupancy cost equal to this rate times the number of square feet that it occupied.

Diane Linder manages a first-floor department that occupies 1,000 square feet, and Juan Chiro manages a second-floor department that occupies 1,800 square feet of floor space. In discussing the departmental reports, the second-floor manager questions whether using the same rate per square foot for all departments makes sense because the first-floor space is more valuable. This manager also references a recent real estate study of average local rental costs for similar space that shows first-floor space worth $30 per square foot and second-floor space worth $20 per square foot (excluding costs for heating, lighting, and maintenance).

Required

Check (1) Total allocated to Linder and Chiro, $23,100 (2) Total occupancy cost to Linder, $9,600

1. Allocate occupancy costs to the Linder and Chiro departments using the current allocation method.

2. Allocate the depreciation, interest, and taxes occupancy costs to the Linder and Chiro departments in proportion to the relative market values of the floor space. Allocate the heating, lighting, and maintenance costs to the Linder and Chiro departments in proportion to the square feet occupied (ignoring floor space market values).

Analysis Component

3. Which allocation method would you prefer if you were a manager of a second-floor department? Explain.

Problem 22-2A
Departmental income statements; forecasts
P3

mhhe.com/wildFINMAN5e

Williams Company began operations in January 2013 with two operating (selling) departments and one service (office) department. Its departmental income statements follow.

WILLIAMS COMPANY
Departmental Income Statements
For Year Ended December 31, 2013

	Clock	Mirror	Combined
Sales	$130,000	$55,000	$185,000
Cost of goods sold	63,700	34,100	97,800
Gross profit	66,300	20,900	87,200
Direct expenses			
Sales salaries	20,000	7,000	27,000
Advertising	1,200	500	1,700
Store supplies used	900	400	1,300
Depreciation—Equipment	1,500	300	1,800
Total direct expenses	23,600	8,200	31,800
Allocated expenses			
Rent expense	7,020	3,780	10,800
Utilities expense	2,600	1,400	4,000
Share of office department expenses	10,500	4,500	15,000
Total allocated expenses	20,120	9,680	29,800
Total expenses	43,720	17,880	61,600
Net income	$ 22,580	$ 3,020	$ 25,600

Williams plans to open a third department in January 2014 that will sell paintings. Management predicts that the new department will generate $50,000 in sales with a 55% gross profit margin and will require the following direct expenses: sales salaries, $8,000; advertising, $800; store supplies, $500; and equipment depreciation, $200. It will fit the new department into the current rented space by taking some square footage from the other two departments. When opened the new painting department will fill one-fifth of the space presently used by the clock department and one-fourth used by the mirror department. Management does not predict any increase in utilities costs, which are allocated to the departments in proportion to occupied space (or rent expense). The company allocates office department expenses to the operating departments in proportion to their sales. It expects the painting department to increase total office department expenses by $7,000. Since the painting department will bring new customers into the store, management expects sales in both the clock and mirror departments to increase by 8%. No changes for those departments' gross profit percents or their direct expenses are expected except for store supplies used, which will increase in proportion to sales.

Required

Check 2014 forecasted combined net income (sales), $43,472 ($249,800)

Prepare departmental income statements that show the company's predicted results of operations for calendar year 2014 for the three operating (selling) departments and their combined totals. (Round percents to the nearest one-tenth and dollar amounts to the nearest whole dollar.)

Problem 22-3A
Responsibility accounting performance reports; controllable and budgeted costs P1

Billie Whitehorse, the plant manager of Travel Free's Indiana plant, is responsible for all of that plant's costs other than her own salary. The plant has two operating departments and one service department. The camper and trailer operating departments manufacture different products and have their own managers. The office department, which Whitehorse also manages, provides services equally to the two operating departments. A budget is prepared for each operating department and the office department. The company's responsibility accounting system must assemble information to present budgeted and actual costs in performance reports for each operating department manager and the plant manager. Each performance report includes only those costs that a particular operating department manager can control: raw materials, wages, supplies used, and equipment depreciation. The plant manager is responsible for the department managers' salaries, utilities, building rent, office salaries other than her own, and other office costs plus all costs controlled by the two operating department managers. The annual departmental budgets and actual costs for the two operating departments follow.

	Budget			Actual		
	Campers	Trailers	Combined	Campers	Trailers	Combined
Raw materials	$195,000	$275,000	$ 470,000	$194,200	$273,200	$ 467,400
Employee wages	104,000	205,000	309,000	106,600	206,400	313,000
Dept. manager salary	43,000	52,000	95,000	44,000	53,500	97,500
Supplies used	33,000	90,000	123,000	31,700	91,600	123,300
Depreciation—Equip.	60,000	125,000	185,000	60,000	125,000	185,000
Utilities	3,600	5,400	9,000	3,300	5,000	8,300
Building rent	5,700	9,300	15,000	5,300	8,700	14,000
Office department costs	68,750	68,750	137,500	67,550	67,550	135,100
Totals	$513,050	$830,450	$1,343,500	$512,650	$830,950	$1,343,600

The office department's annual budget and its actual costs follow.

	Budget	Actual
Plant manager salary	$ 80,000	$ 82,000
Other office salaries	32,500	30,100
Other office costs	25,000	23,000
Totals	$137,500	$135,100

Required

1. Prepare responsibility accounting performance reports like those in Exhibit 22.2 that list costs controlled by the following:

a. Manager of the camper department.

b. Manager of the trailer department.

c. Manager of the Indiana plant.

In each report, include the budgeted and actual costs and show the amount that each actual cost is over or under the budgeted amount.

Check (1a) $500 total over budget

(1c) Indiana plant controllable costs, $1,900 total under budget

Analysis Component

2. Did the plant manager or the operating department managers better manage costs? Explain.

Problem 22-4A[B]
Allocation of joint costs
C3

Georgia Orchards produced a good crop of peaches this year. After preparing the following income statement, the company believes it should have given its No. 3 peaches to charity and saved its efforts.

GEORGIA ORCHARDS
Income Statement
For Year Ended December 31, 2013

	No. 1	No. 2	No. 3	Combined
Sales (by grade)				
No. 1: 300,000 lbs. @ $1.50/lb	$450,000			
No. 2: 300,000 lbs. @ $1.00/lb		$300,000		
No. 3: 750,000 lbs. @ $0.25/lb			$ 187,500	
Total sales				$937,500
Costs				
Tree pruning and care @ $0.30/lb	90,000	90,000	225,000	405,000
Picking, sorting, and grading @ $0.15/lb	45,000	45,000	112,500	202,500
Delivery costs	15,000	15,000	37,500	67,500
Total costs	150,000	150,000	375,000	675,000
Net income (loss)	$300,000	$150,000	$(187,500)	$262,500

In preparing this statement, the company allocated joint costs among the grades on a physical basis as an equal amount per pound. The company's delivery cost records show that $30,000 of the $67,500 relates to crating the No. 1 and No. 2 peaches and hauling them to the buyer. The remaining $37,500 of delivery costs is for crating the No. 3 peaches and hauling them to the cannery.

Required

Check (1) $129,600 tree pruning and care costs allocated to No. 2

(2) Net income from No. 1 & No. 2 peaches, $140,400 & $93,600

1. Prepare reports showing cost allocations on a sales value basis to the three grades of peaches. Separate the delivery costs into the amounts directly identifiable with each grade. Then allocate any shared delivery costs on the basis of the relative sales value of each grade.

2. Using your answers to part 1, prepare an income statement using the joint costs allocated on a sales value basis.

Analysis Component

3. Do you think delivery costs fit the definition of a joint cost? Explain.

Problem 22-5A
Manufacturing cycle time and efficiency
A4

Oakwood Company produces maple bookcases to customer order. It received an order from a customer to produce 5,000 bookcases. The following information is available for the production of the bookcases.

Process time	6.0 days
Inspection time	0.8 days
Move time	3.2 days
Wait time	5.0 days

Required

1. Compute the company's manufacturing cycle time.

Check (2) Manufacturing cycle efficiency, 0.40

2. Compute the company's manufacturing cycle efficiency. Interpret your answer.

Analysis Component

3. Assume that Oakwood wishes to increase its manufacturing cycle efficiency to 0.75. What are some ways that it can accomplish this?

Problem 22-6A
Departmental contribution to income
P1

Vortex Company operates a retail store with two departments. Information about those departments follows.

	Department A	Department B
Sales	$800,000	$450,000
Cost of goods sold	497,000	291,000
Direct expenses		
Salaries	125,000	88,000
Insurance	20,000	10,000
Utilities	24,000	14,000
Depreciation	21,000	12,000
Maintenance	7,000	5,000

The company also incurred the following indirect costs.

Salaries	$36,000
Insurance	6,000
Depreciation	15,000
Office expenses	50,000

Indirect costs are allocated as follows: salaries on the basis of sales; insurance and depreciation on the basis of square footage; and office expenses on the basis of number of employees. Additional information about the departments follows.

Department	Square footage	Number of employees
A	28,000	75
B	12,000	50

Required

1. For each department, determine the departmental contribution to overhead and the departmental net income.
2. Should Department B be eliminated? Explain.

Check (1) Dept. A net income, $38,260

PROBLEM SET B

Problem 22-1B
Allocation of building occupancy costs to departments
P2

Harmon's has several departments that occupy all floors of a two-story building that includes a basement floor. Harmon rented this building under a long-term lease negotiated when rental rates were low. The departmental accounting system has a single account, Building Occupancy Cost, in its ledger. The types and amounts of occupancy costs recorded in this account for the current period follow.

Building rent	$400,000
Lighting expense	25,000
Cleaning expense	40,000
Total occupancy cost	$465,000

The building has 7,500 square feet on each of the upper two floors but only 5,000 square feet in the basement. In prior periods, the accounting manager merely divided the $465,000 occupancy cost by 20,000 square feet to find an average cost of $23.25 per square foot and then charged each department a building occupancy cost equal to this rate times the number of square feet that it occupies.

Jordan Style manages a department that occupies 2,000 square feet of basement floor space. In discussing the departmental reports with other managers, she questions whether using the same rate per square foot for all departments makes sense because different floor space has different values. Style checked a recent real estate report of average local rental costs for similar space that shows first-floor space worth $40 per square foot, second-floor space worth $20 per square foot, and basement space worth $10 per square foot (excluding costs for lighting and cleaning).

Required

1. Allocate occupancy costs to Style's department using the current allocation method.
2. Allocate the building rent cost to Style's department in proportion to the relative market value of the floor space. Allocate to Style's department the lighting and cleaning costs in proportion to the square feet occupied (ignoring floor space market values). Then, compute the total occupancy cost allocated to Style's department.

Check Total costs allocated to Style's Dept., (1) $46,500; (2) Total occupancy cost to Style $22,500

Analysis Component

3. Which allocation method would you prefer if you were a manager of a basement department?

Problem 22-2B
Departmental income statements; forecasts P3

Bonanza Entertainment began operations in January 2013 with two operating (selling) departments and one service (office) department. Its departmental income statements follow.

BONANZA ENTERTAINMENT
Departmental Income Statements
For Year Ended December 31, 2013

	Movies	Video Games	Combined
Sales	$600,000	$200,000	$800,000
Cost of goods sold	420,000	154,000	574,000
Gross profit	180,000	46,000	226,000
Direct expenses			
Sales salaries	37,000	15,000	52,000
Advertising	12,500	6,000	18,500
Store supplies used	4,000	1,000	5,000
Depreciation—Equipment	4,500	3,000	7,500
Total direct expenses	58,000	25,000	83,000
Allocated expenses			
Rent expense	41,000	9,000	50,000
Utilities expense	7,380	1,620	9,000
Share of office department expenses	56,250	18,750	75,000
Total allocated expenses	104,630	29,370	134,000
Total expenses	162,630	54,370	217,000
Net income (loss)	$ 17,370	$ (8,370)	$ 9,000

The company plans to open a third department in January 2014 that will sell compact discs. Management predicts that the new department will generate $300,000 in sales with a 35% gross profit margin and will require the following direct expenses: sales salaries, $18,000; advertising, $10,000; store supplies, $2,000; and equipment depreciation, $1,200. The company will fit the new department into the current rented space by taking some square footage from the other two departments. When opened, the new compact disc department will fill one-fourth of the space presently used by the movie department and one-third of the space used by the video game department. Management does not predict any increase in utilities costs, which are allocated to the departments in proportion to occupied space (or rent expense). The company allocates office department expenses to the operating departments in proportion to their sales. It expects the compact disc department to increase total office department expenses by $10,000. Since the compact disc department will bring new customers into the store, management expects sales in both the movie and video game departments to increase by 8%. No changes for those departments' gross profit percents or for their direct expenses are expected, except for store supplies used, which will increase in proportion to sales.

Required

Check 2014 forecasted movies net income (sales), $52,450 ($648,000)

Prepare departmental income statements that show the company's predicted results of operations for calendar year 2014 for the three operating (selling) departments and their combined totals. (Round percents to the nearest one-tenth and dollar amounts to the nearest whole dollar.)

Problem 22-3B
Responsibility accounting performance reports; controllable and budgeted costs
P1

Britney Brown, the plant manager of LMN Co.'s Chicago plant, is responsible for all of that plant's costs other than her own salary. The plant has two operating departments and one service department. The refrigerator and dishwasher operating departments manufacture different products and have their own managers. The office department, which Brown also manages, provides services equally to the two operating departments. A monthly budget is prepared for each operating department and the office department. The company's responsibility accounting system must assemble information to present budgeted and actual costs in performance reports for each operating department manager and the plant manager. Each performance report includes only those costs that a particular operating department manager can control: raw materials, wages, supplies used, and equipment depreciation. The plant manager is responsible for the department managers' salaries, utilities, building rent, office salaries other than her own, and other office costs plus all costs controlled by the two operating department managers. The April departmental budgets and actual costs for the two operating departments follow.

	Budget			Actual		
	Refrigerators	Dishwashers	Combined	Refrigerators	Dishwashers	Combined
Raw materials	$400,000	$200,000	$ 600,000	$385,000	$202,000	$ 587,000
Employee wages	170,000	80,000	250,000	174,700	81,500	256,200
Dept. manager salary	55,000	49,000	104,000	55,000	46,500	101,500
Supplies used	15,000	9,000	24,000	14,000	9,700	23,700
Depreciation—Equip.	53,000	37,000	90,000	53,000	37,000	90,000
Utilities	30,000	18,000	48,000	34,500	20,700	55,200
Building rent	63,000	17,000	80,000	65,800	16,500	82,300
Office department costs	70,500	70,500	141,000	75,000	75,000	150,000
Totals	$856,500	$480,500	$1,337,000	$857,000	$488,900	$1,345,900

The office department's budget and its actual costs for April follow.

	Budget	Actual
Plant manager salary	$ 80,000	$ 85,000
Other office salaries	40,000	35,200
Other office costs	21,000	29,800
Totals	$141,000	$150,000

Required

1. Prepare responsibility accounting performance reports like those in Exhibit 22.2 that list costs controlled by the following:

a. Manager of the refrigerator department.

b. Manager of the dishwasher department.

c. Manager of the Chicago plant.

In each report, include the budgeted and actual costs for the month and show the amount by which each actual cost is over or under the budgeted amount.

Check (1a) $11,300 total under budget

(1c) Chicago plant controllable costs, $3,900 total over budget

Analysis Component

2. Did the plant manager or the operating department managers better manage costs? Explain.

Problem 22-4B[B]
Allocation of joint costs
C3

Rita and Rick Redding own and operate a tomato grove. After preparing the following income statement, Rita believes they should have offered the No. 3 tomatoes to the public for free and saved themselves time and money.

RITA AND RICK REDDING
Income Statement
For Year Ended December 31, 2013

	No. 1	No. 2	No. 3	Combined
Sales (by grade)				
No. 1: 500,000 lbs. @ $1.80/lb	$900,000			
No. 2: 400,000 lbs. @ $1.25/lb		$500,000		
No. 3: 100,000 lbs. @ $0.40/lb			$ 40,000	
Total sales				$1,440,000
Costs				
Land preparation, seeding, and cultivating @ $0.70/lb	350,000	280,000	70,000	700,000
Harvesting, sorting, and grading @ $0.04/lb	20,000	16,000	4,000	40,000
Delivery costs	10,000	7,000	3,000	20,000
Total costs	380,000	303,000	77,000	760,000
Net income (loss)	$520,000	$197,000	$(37,000)	$ 680,000

In preparing this statement, Rita and Rick allocated joint costs among the grades on a physical basis as an equal amount per pound. Also, their delivery cost records show that $17,000 of the $20,000 relates to crating the No. 1 and No. 2 tomatoes and hauling them to the buyer. The remaining $3,000 of delivery costs is for crating the No. 3 tomatoes and hauling them to the cannery.

Required

1. Prepare reports showing cost allocations on a sales value basis to the three grades of tomatoes. Separate the delivery costs into the amounts directly identifiable with each grade. Then allocate any shared delivery costs on the basis of the relative sales value of each grade. (Round percents to the nearest one-tenth and dollar amounts to the nearest whole dollar.)

Check (1) $1,120 harvesting, sorting and grading costs allocated to No. 3

2. Using your answers to part 1, prepare an income statement using the joint costs allocated on a sales value basis.

(2) Net income from No. 1 & No. 2 tomatoes, $426,569 & $237,151

Analysis Component

3. Do you think delivery costs fit the definition of a joint cost? Explain.

Problem 22-5B
Manufacturing cycle time and efficiency
A4

Best Ink produces ink-jet printers for personal computers. It received an order for 500 printers from a customer. The following information is available for this order.

Process time	16.0 hours
Inspection time	3.5 hours
Move time	9.0 hours
Wait time	21.5 hours

Required

1. Compute the company's manufacturing cycle time.
2. Compute the company's manufacturing cycle efficiency. Interpret your answer.

Analysis Component

3. Assume that Best Ink wishes to increase its manufacturing cycle efficiency to 0.80. What are some ways that it can accomplish this?

Problem 22-6B
Departmental contribution to income
P1

Sadar Company operates a store with two departments: videos and music. Information about those departments follows.

	Videos Department	Music Department
Sales	$370,500	$279,500
Cost of goods sold	320,000	175,000
Direct expenses		
Salaries	35,000	25,000
Maintenance	12,000	10,000
Utilities	5,000	4,500
Insurance	4,200	3,700

The company also incurred the following indirect costs.

Advertising	$15,000
Salaries	27,000
Office expenses	3,200

Indirect costs are allocated as follows: advertising on the basis of sales; salaries on the basis of number of employees; and office expenses on the basis of square footage. Additional information about the departments follows.

Department	Square footage	Number of employees
Videos	5,000	3
Music	3,000	2

Required

Check (1) Music dept. net income, $42,850

1. For each department, determine the departmental contribution to overhead and the departmental net income.
2. Should the video department be eliminated? Explain.

SERIAL PROBLEM

Success Systems
A3

(This serial problem began in Chapter 1 and continues through most of the book. If previous chapter segments were not completed, the serial problem can begin at this point. It is helpful, but not necessary, to use the Working Papers that accompany the book.)

SP 22 Adria Lopez's two departments, computer consulting services and computer workstation furniture manufacturing, have each been profitable. Adria has heard of the balanced scorecard and wants you to provide details on how it could be used to measure performance of her departments.

Required

1. Explain the four performance perspectives included in a balanced scorecard.
2. For each of the four performance perspectives included in a balanced scorecard, provide examples of measures Adria could use to measure performance of her departments.

Beyond the Numbers

REPORTING IN ACTION
C1
Polaris

BTN 22-1 Review Polaris's income statement in Appendix A and identify its revenues for the years ended December 31, 2011, December 31, 2010, and December 31, 2009. For the year ended December 31, 2011, Polaris reports the following product revenue mix. (Assume that its product revenue mix is the same for each of the three years reported when answering the requirements.)

Off-Road Vehicles	Snowmobiles	On-Road Vehicles	Parts, Garments, & Accessories
69%	11%	5%	15%

Required

1. Compute the amount of revenue from each of its product lines for the years ended December 31, 2011, December 31, 2010, and December 31, 2009.
2. If Polaris wishes to evaluate each of its product lines, how can it allocate its operating expenses to each of them to determine each product line's profitability?

Fast Forward

3. Access Polaris's annual report for a fiscal year ending after December 31, 2011, from its Website (Polaris.com) or the SEC's EDGAR database (sec.gov). Compute its revenues for its product lines for the most recent year(s). Compare those results to those from part 1. How has its product mix changed?

COMPARATIVE ANALYSIS
A2
Polaris
Arctic Cat

BTN 22-2 Polaris and Arctic Cat compete in several on-road and off-road motorized vehicle categories. Sales, income, and asset information is provided for each company below.

(in thousands)	Polaris	Arctic Cat
Sales	$2,656,949	$464,651
Net income	227,575	13,007
Invested assets, beginning of year	1,061,647	246,084
Invested assets, end of year	1,228,024	272,906

Required

1. Compute profit margin for each company.
2. Compute investment turnover for each company.

Analysis Component

3. Using your answers to the questions above, compare the companies' performance during the most recent year.

ETHICS CHALLENGE
P3

BTN 22-3 Senior Security Co. offers a range of security services for senior citizens. Each type of service is considered within a separate department. Mary Pincus, the overall manager, is compensated partly on the basis of departmental performance by staying within the quarterly cost budget. She often revises operations to make sure departments stay within budget. Says Pincus, "I will not go over budget even if it means slightly compromising the level and quality of service. These are minor compromises that don't significantly affect my clients, at least in the short term."

Required

1. Is there an ethical concern in this situation? If so, which parties are affected? Explain.
2. Can Mary Pincus take action to eliminate or reduce any ethical concerns? Explain.
3. What is Senior Security's ethical responsibility in offering professional services?

COMMUNICATING IN PRACTICE

P2

BTN 22-4 Improvement Station is a national home improvement chain with more than 100 stores throughout the country. The manager of each store receives a salary plus a bonus equal to a percent of the store's net income for the reporting period. The following net income calculation is on the Denver store manager's performance report for the recent monthly period.

Sales	$2,500,000
Cost of goods sold	800,000
Wages expense	500,000
Utilities expense	200,000
Home office expense	75,000
Net income	$ 925,000
Manager's bonus (0.5%)	$ 4,625

In previous periods, the bonus had also been 0.5%, but the performance report had not included any charges for the home office expense, which is now assigned to each store as a percent of its sales.

Required

Assume that you are the national office manager. Write a one-half page memorandum to your store managers explaining why home office expense is in the new performance report.

TAKING IT TO THE NET

P2

BTN 22-5 This chapter described and used spreadsheets to prepare various managerial reports (see Exhibit 22-6). You can download from Websites various tutorials showing how spreadsheets are used in managerial accounting and other business applications.

Required

1. Link to the Website Lacher.com. Select "Excel Examples." Identify and list three tutorials for review.
2. Describe in a one-half page memorandum to your instructor how the applications described in each tutorial are helpful in business and managerial decision making.

TEAMWORK IN ACTION

P1

Polaris

Arctic Cat

BTN 22-6 **Polaris**, and **Arctic Cat** compete across the world in several markets.

Required

1. Design a three-tier responsibility accounting organizational chart assuming that you have available internal information for both companies. Use Exhibit 22.1 as an example. The goal of this assignment is to design a reporting framework for the companies; numbers are not required. Limit your reporting framework to sales activity only.
2. Explain why it is important to have similar performance reports when comparing performance within a company (and across different companies). Be specific in your response.

ENTREPRENEURIAL DECISION

P3

BTN 22-7 Brian Linton's company, **United By Blue**, sells jewelry and apparel. His company's plans call for continued expansion into other types of products.

Required

1. How can United By Blue use departmental income statements to assist in understanding and controlling operations?
2. Are departmental income statements always the best measure of a department's performance? Explain.
3. Provide examples of nonfinancial performace indicators United By Blue might use as part of a balanced scorecard system of performance evaluation.

BTN 22-8 Visit a local movie theater and check out both its concession area and its showing areas. The manager of a theater must confront questions such as:

HITTING THE ROAD
C1 P1

- How much return do we earn on concessions?
- What types of movies generate the greatest sales?
- What types of movies generate the greatest net income?

Required

Assume that you are the new accounting manager for a 16-screen movie theater. You are to set up a responsibility accounting reporting framework for the theater.

1. Recommend how to segment the different departments of a movie theater for responsibility reporting.
2. Propose an expense allocation system for heat, rent, insurance, and maintenance costs of the theater.

BTN 22-9 Selected product data from Piaggio (www.piaggio.com) follow.

GLOBAL DECISION
P3

PIAGGIO

Product Segment for Year Ended (millions)	Net Sales		Gross Margin	
	December 31, 2011	December 31, 2010	December 31, 2011	December 31, 2010
Two-wheeler vehicles.	€1,025.3	€988.1	€337.1	€330.7
Commercial vehicles	491.1	497.3	117.5	131.6

Required

1. Compute the percentage growth in net sales for each product line from fiscal year 2010 to 2011. Round percents to one decimal.
2. Which product line's net sales grew the fastest?
3. Which segment was the most profitable?
4. How can Piaggio's managers use this information?

ANSWERS TO MULTIPLE CHOICE QUIZ

1. b; [$641,250/($356,250 + $641,250 + $427,500)] × $150,000 = $67,500
2. d;
3. c; $500,000/200,000 = 2.5
4. b;

	Department X	Department Y	Department Z
Sales	$500,000	$200,000	$350,000
Cost of goods sold	350,000	75,000	150,000
Gross profit	150,000	125,000	200,000
Direct expenses	50,000	20,000	75,000
Departmental contribution	$100,000	$105,000	$125,000

5. a; $100,000/$500,000 = 20%

23 Relevant Costing for Managerial Decisions

A Look Back

Chapter 22 focused on responsibility accounting and performance measurement. We identified several reports useful in measuring and analyzing the activities of a company, its departments, and its managers.

A Look at This Chapter

This chapter explains several tools and procedures useful for making and evaluating short-term managerial decisions. It also describes how to assess the consequences of such decisions.

A Look Ahead

Chapter 24 focuses on capital budgeting decisions. It explains and illustrates several methods that help identify projects with the higher return on investment.

Learning Objectives

CONCEPTUAL

C1 Describe the importance of relevant costs for short-term decisions. (p. 986)

ANALYTICAL

A1 Evaluate short-term managerial decisions using relevant costs. (p. 987)

A2 Determine product selling price based on total costs. (p. 994)

PROCEDURAL

P1 Identify relevant costs and apply them to managerial decisions. (p. 988)

Decision Insight

Sweet Success

"Put all of your love into your product."
—CHARLIE FYFFE

LOS ANGELES—Noticing long lines and an inadequate supply of sweets to satisfy his high school friends' cravings, Charlie Fyffe began making brownies and selling them at school. His brownies were an instant hit, and as his clientele and passion for baking grew, so did his desire to start his own business. "I started **Charlie's Brownies (CharliesBrownies.com)** because sweets make people happy and baking is a fun industry," explains Charlie. "I developed a quality original recipe and started selling brownies in simple cake boxes. Staying simple and consistent opened the door to a viable business."

After six months of professional baking classes to sharpen his skills, Charlie turned to the business side. "I had a lot to learn," admits Charlie. "I read entrepreneurial books and did internships to learn how to run a business. Becoming an entrepreneur was hard work, but it allows me a life of freedom outside the cubicle and the opportunity to pursue my dreams and visions." Charlie had to learn how to use accounting information to make important business decisions. For example, attention to contribution margins enables Charlie to decide if adding new product lines, like vegan and gluten-free brownies, would increase profits. Focusing on contribution margins, his own and his competition's, also helps Charlie decide whether to eliminate certain products because they are not profitable.

Charlie applies high standards to his production process. Unlike some companies that can rework substandard materials into a viable product, Charlie explains that "raw materials that don't meet our standards never enter the baking process." Further, although expensive, exotic ingredients like "Chardonnay-infused sea salts create a pop and that undeniable urge to eat another brownie. It isn't heavy, and you want another one." Charlie has also managed to control overhead costs by doing much of the baking, marketing, and delivery himself. "I do whatever it takes to get the job done" he says. "There is never a dull moment!"

Much of Charlie's Brownies business is done online. To meet Charlie's goal of developing the company into a "nationwide and global Brownie Experience," he must focus on relevant costs to help him make good decisions. Determining the optimal sales mix requires Charlie to understand product contribution margins. Charlie also explains that "we need to upgrade our space and add to our capacity." The decision to keep or replace equipment is common in growing businesses, and assessing relevant costs helps Charlie with this and other key managerial decisions.

Charlie advises young entrepreneurs to follow their passion. "Hang out with other overachievers and young entrepreneurs to stay one step ahead," he says. "Stay focused, work hard, and seek guidance from other successful business people." Sounds like a recipe for success.

[Sources: *Charlie's Brownies* Website, January 2013; *JaredSurnamer.com,* August 2011; *PopularFinesse.tumblr.com,* October 2011; *Twentity.com,* February 2011.]

Chapter Preview

Making business decisions involves choosing between alternative courses of action. Many factors affect business decisions, yet analysis typically focuses on finding the alternative that offers the highest return on investment or the greatest reduction in costs. In all situations, managers can reach a sounder decision if they identify the consequences of alternative choices in financial terms. This chapter explains several methods of analysis that can help managers make short-term business decisions.

Relevant Costing for Managerial Decisions

Decisions and Information
- Decision making
- Relevant costs

Decision Scenarios
- Additional business
- Make or buy
- Scrap or rework
- Sell or process
- Sales mix selection
- Segment elimination
- Keep or replace

This chapter focuses on methods that use accounting information to make important managerial decisions. Most of these cases involve short-term decisions. This differs from methods used for longer-term managerial decisions that are described in the next chapter.

DECISIONS AND INFORMATION

This section explains how managers make decisions and the information relevant to those decisions.

Decision Making

Managerial decision making involves five steps: (1) define the decision task, (2) identify alternative courses of action, (3) collect relevant information and evaluate each alternative, (4) select the preferred course of action, and (5) analyze and assess decisions made. These five steps are illustrated in Exhibit 23.1.

EXHIBIT 23.1

Managerial Decision Making

Both managerial and financial accounting information play an important role in most management decisions. The accounting system is expected to provide primarily *financial* information such as performance reports and budget analyses for decision making. *Nonfinancial* information is also relevant, however; it includes information on environmental effects, political sensitivities, and social responsibility.

Relevant Costs

C1 Describe the importance of relevant costs for short-term decisions.

Most financial measures of revenues and costs from accounting systems are based on historical costs. Although historical costs are important and useful for many tasks such as product pricing and the control and monitoring of business activities, we sometimes find that an analysis of *relevant costs,* or *avoidable costs,* is especially useful. Three types of costs are pertinent to our discussion of relevant costs: sunk costs, out-of-pocket costs, and opportunity costs.

A *sunk cost* arises from a past decision and cannot be avoided or changed; it is irrelevant to future decisions. An example is the cost of computer equipment previously purchased by a company. Most of a company's allocated costs, including fixed overhead items such as depreciation and administrative expenses, are sunk costs.

An *out-of-pocket cost* requires a future outlay of cash and is relevant for current and future decision making. These costs are usually the direct result of management's decisions. For instance, future purchases of computer equipment involve out-of-pocket costs. Depreciation and amortization are allocations of the original cost of plant and intangible assets. They are sunk costs, not out-of-pocket costs.

An *opportunity cost* is the potential benefit lost by taking a specific action when two or more alternative choices are available. An example is a student giving up wages from a job to attend summer school. Companies continually must choose from alternative courses of action. For instance, a company making standardized products might be approached by a customer to supply a special (nonstandard) product. A decision to accept or reject the special order must consider not only the profit to be made from the special order but also the profit given up by devoting time and resources to this order instead of pursuing an alternative project. The profit given up is an opportunity cost. Consideration of opportunity costs is important. The implications extend to internal resource allocation decisions. For instance, a computer manufacturer must decide between internally manufacturing a chip versus buying it externally. In another case, management of a multidivisional company must decide whether to continue operating or close a particular division.

Point: Opportunity costs are not entered in accounting records. This does not reduce their relevance for managerial decisions.

Besides relevant costs, management must also consider the relevant benefits associated with a decision. **Relevant benefits** refer to the additional or *incremental* revenue generated by selecting a particular course of action over another. For instance, a student must decide the relevant benefits of taking one course over another. In sum, both relevant costs and relevant benefits are crucial to managerial decision making.

MANAGERIAL DECISION SCENARIOS

A1 Evaluate short-term managerial decisions using relevant costs.

Managers experience many different scenarios that require analyzing alternative actions and making a decision. We describe several different types of decision scenarios in this section. We set these tasks in the context of FasTrac, an exercise supplies and equipment manufacturer introduced earlier. *We treat each of these decision tasks as separate from each other.*

Additional Business

FasTrac is operating at its normal level of 80% of full capacity. At this level, it produces and sells approximately 100,000 units of product annually. Its per unit and annual total sales and costs are shown in Exhibit 23.2.

EXHIBIT 23.2

Selected Operating Income Data

	Per Unit	Annual Total
Sales (100,000 units)	$10.00	$1,000,000
Direct materials	(3.50)	(350,000)
Direct labor	(2.20)	(220,000)
Overhead	(1.10)	(110,000)
Selling expenses	(1.40)	(140,000)
Administrative expenses	(0.80)	(80,000)
Total costs and expenses	(9.00)	(900,000)
Operating income	$ 1.00	$ 100,000

A current buyer of FasTrac's products wants to purchase additional units of its product and export them to another country. This buyer offers to buy 10,000 units of the product at $8.50 per unit, or $1.50 less than the current price. The offer price is low, but FasTrac is considering the proposal because this sale would be several times larger than any single previous sale and it would use idle capacity. Also, the units will be exported, so this new business will not affect current sales.

To determine whether to accept or reject this order, management needs to know whether accepting the offer will increase net income. The analysis in Exhibit 23.3 shows that if management relies incorrectly on per unit historical costs, it would reject the sale because the selling price ($8.50) per unit is less than the total costs per unit ($9.00), and it thus yields a loss. However, historical costs are *not* relevant to this decision. Instead, the relevant costs are the additional costs, called **incremental costs.** These costs, also called *differential costs,* are the additional costs incurred if a company pursues a certain course of action. FasTrac's incremental costs are those related to the added volume that this new order would bring.

EXHIBIT 23.3

Analysis of Additional Business Using Historical Costs

	Per Unit	Total
Sales (10,000 additional units)	$ 8.50	$ 85,000
Total costs and expenses	(9.00)	(90,000)
Operating loss	$(0.50)	**$(5,000)**

P1 Identify relevant costs and apply them to managerial decisions.

To correctly make its decision, FasTrac must analyze the costs of this new business in a different manner. The following information regarding the order is available:

- Manufacturing 10,000 additional units requires direct materials of $3.50 per unit and direct labor of $2.20 per unit (same as for all other units).
- Manufacturing 10,000 additional units adds $5,000 of incremental overhead costs for power, packaging, and indirect labor (all variable costs).
- Incremental commissions and selling expenses from this sale of 10,000 additional units would be $2,000 (all variable costs).
- Incremental administrative expenses of $1,000 for clerical efforts are needed (all fixed costs) with the sale of 10,000 additional units.

We use this information, as shown in Exhibit 23.4 to assess how accepting this new business will affect FasTrac's income.

EXHIBIT 23.4

Analysis of Additional Business Using Relevant Costs

	Additional Business	Current Business	Combined
Sales	**$ 85,000**	$1,000,000	$1,085,000
Direct materials	**(35,000)**	(350,000)	(385,000)
Direct labor	**(22,000)**	(220,000)	(242,000)
Overhead	**(5,000)**	(110,000)	(115,000)
Selling expenses	**(2,000)**	(140,000)	(142,000)
Administrative expense	**(1,000)**	(80,000)	(81,000)
Total costs and expenses	**(65,000)**	(900,000)	(965,000)
Operating income	**$ 20,000**	$ 100,000	$ 120,000

The analysis of relevant costs in Exhibit 23.4 suggests that the additional business be accepted. It would provide $85,000 of added revenue while incurring only $65,000 of added costs. This would yield $20,000 of additional pretax income, or a pretax profit margin of 23.5%. More generally, FasTrac would increase its income with any price that exceeded $6.50 per unit ($65,000 incremental cost/10,000 additional units). The key point is that *management must not blindly use historical costs, especially allocated overhead costs.* Instead, the accounting system needs to provide information about the incremental costs to be incurred if the additional business is accepted.

Example: Exhibit 23.4 uses quantitative information. Suggest some qualitative factors to be considered when deciding whether to accept this project. *Answer:* (1) Impact on relationships with other customers and (2) Improved relationship with customer buying additional units.

Other Factors An analysis of the incremental costs pertaining to the additional volume is always relevant for this type of decision. We must proceed cautiously, however, when the additional volume approaches or exceeds the factory's existing available capacity. If the additional volume requires the company to expand its capacity by obtaining more equipment, more space, or more personnel, the incremental costs could quickly exceed the incremental revenue. Another cautionary note is the effect on existing sales. All new units of the extra business will be sold outside FasTrac's normal domestic sales channels. If accepting additional business would cause existing sales to decline, this information must be included in our analysis. The contribution margin lost from a decline in sales is an opportunity cost.

Decision Maker

Partner You are a partner in a small accounting firm that specializes in keeping the books and preparing taxes for clients. A local restaurant is interested in obtaining these services from your firm. Identify factors that are relevant in deciding whether to accept the engagement. ■ [Answer—p. 998]

Make or Buy

The managerial decision to make or buy a component for one of its current products is common and depends on incremental costs. To illustrate, FasTrac has excess productive capacity it can use to manufacture Part 417, a component of the main product it sells. The part is currently purchased and delivered to the plant at a cost of $1.20 per unit. FasTrac estimates that making Part 417 would cost $0.45 for direct materials, $0.50 for direct labor, and an undetermined amount for overhead. The task is to determine how much overhead to add to these costs so we can decide whether to make or buy Part 417. If FasTrac's normal predetermined overhead application rate is 100% of direct labor cost, we might be tempted to conclude that overhead cost is $0.50 per unit, computed as 100% of the $0.50 direct labor cost. We would then mistakenly conclude that total cost is $1.45 per unit ($0.45 of materials + $0.50 of labor + $0.50 of overhead). A wrong decision in this case would be to conclude that the company is better off buying the part at $1.20 each than making it for $1.45 each.

Instead, as we explained earlier, only incremental overhead costs are relevant in this situation. Thus, we must compute an *incremental overhead rate.* Incremental overhead costs might include, for example, additional power for operating machines, extra supplies, added cleanup costs, materials handling, and quality control. We can prepare a per unit analysis in this case as shown in Exhibit 23.5.

EXHIBIT 23.5

Make or Buy Analysis

	Make	Buy
Direct materials	$0.45	—
Direct labor	0.50	—
Overhead costs	[?]	—
Purchase price	—	$1.20
Total incremental costs	**$0.95 + [?]**	**$1.20**

We can see that if incremental overhead costs are less than $0.25 per unit, ($1.20 − $0.95) the total cost of making the component is less than the purchase price of $1.20 and FasTrac should make the part. FasTrac's decision rule in this case is that any amount of overhead less than $0.25 per unit yields a total cost for Part 417 that is less than the $1.20 purchase price. FasTrac must consider several nonfinancial factors in the make or buy decision, including product quality, timeliness of delivery (especially in a just-in-time setting), reactions of customers and suppliers, and other intangibles such as employee morale and workload. It must also consider whether making the part requires incremental fixed costs to expand plant capacity. When these added factors are considered, small cost differences may not matter.

Decision Insight

Make or Buy IT Companies apply make or buy decisions to their services. Many now outsource their information technology activities. Information technology companies provide infrastructure and services to enable businesses to focus on their key activities. It is argued that outsourcing saves money and streamlines operations, and without the headaches. ■

Scrap or Rework

Managers often must make a decision on whether to scrap or rework products in process. Remember that costs already incurred in manufacturing the units of a product that do not meet quality standards are sunk costs that have been incurred and cannot be changed. Sunk costs are irrelevant in any decision on whether to sell the substandard units as scrap or to rework them to meet quality standards.

To illustrate, assume that FasTrac has 10,000 defective units of a product that have already cost $1 per unit to manufacture. These units can be sold as is (as scrap) for $0.40 each, or they can be reworked for $0.80 per unit and then sold for their full price of $1.50 each. Should FasTrac sell the units as scrap or rework them?

To make this decision, management must recognize that the already incurred manufacturing costs of $1 per unit are sunk (unavoidable). These costs are *entirely irrelevant* to the decision. In addition, we must be certain that all costs of reworking defects, including interfering with normal operations, are accounted for in our analysis. For instance, reworking the defects means that FasTrac is unable to manufacture 10,000 *new* units with an incremental cost of $1 per unit and a selling price of $1.50 per unit, meaning it incurs an *opportunity cost* equal to the lost $5,000 net return from making and selling 10,000 new units. This opportunity cost is the difference between the $15,000 revenue (10,000 units × $1.50) from selling these new units and their $10,000 manufacturing costs (10,000 units × $1). Our analysis is reflected in Exhibit 23.6.

EXHIBIT 23.6

Scrap or Rework Analysis

	Scrap	Rework
Sale of scrapped/reworked units (10,000 units)	$ 4,000	$15,000
Less out-of-pocket costs to rework defects ($0.80 per unit)		(8,000)
Less opportunity cost of not making new units		**(5,000)**
Incremental net income	**$4,000**	**$ 2,000**

The analysis yields a $2,000 difference in favor of scrapping the defects, yielding a total incremental net income of $4,000. If we had failed to include the opportunity costs of $5,000, the rework option would have shown an income of $7,000 instead of $2,000, mistakenly making reworking appear more favorable than scrapping.

Quick Check

Answers — p. 998

1. A company receives a special order for 200 units that requires stamping the buyer's name on each unit, yielding an additional fixed cost of $400 to its normal costs. Without the order, the company is operating at 75% of capacity and produces 7,500 units of product at the following costs:

Direct materials	$37,500
Direct labor	60,000
Overhead (30% variable)	20,000
Selling expenses (60% variable)	25,000

The special order will not affect normal unit sales and will not increase fixed overhead and selling expenses. Variable selling expenses on the special order are reduced to one-half the normal amount. The price per unit necessary to earn $1,000 on this order is (*a*) $14.80, (*b*) $15.80, (*c*) $19.80, (*d*) $20.80, or (*e*) $21.80.

2. What are the incremental costs of accepting additional business?

Sell or Process

The managerial decision to sell partially completed products as is or to process them further for sale depends significantly on relevant costs. To illustrate, suppose that FasTrac has 40,000 units of partially finished Product Q. It has already spent $0.75 per unit to manufacture these 40,000 units at a $30,000 total cost. FasTrac can sell the 40,000 units to another manufacturer as raw material for $50,000. Alternatively, it can process them further and produce finished products X, Y, and Z at an incremental cost of $2 per unit. The added processing yields the products and revenues shown in Exhibit 23.7. FasTrac must decide whether the added revenues from selling finished products X, Y, and Z exceed the costs of finishing them.

EXHIBIT 23.7

Revenues from Processing Further

Product	Price	Units	Revenues
Product X	$4.00	10,000	$ 40,000
Product Y..........	6.00	22,000	132,000
Product Z	8.00	6,000	48,000
Spoilage	—	2,000	0
Totals		40,000	$220,000

Exhibit 23.8 shows the two-step analysis for this decision. First, FasTrac computes its incremental revenue from further processing Q into products X, Y, and Z. This amount is the difference between the $220,000 revenue from the further processed products and the $50,000 FasTrac will give up by not selling Q as is (a $50,000 opportunity cost). Second, FasTrac computes its incremental costs from further processing Q into X, Y, and Z. This amount is $80,000 (40,000 units × $2 incremental cost). The analysis shows that FasTrac can earn incremental net income of $90,000 from a decision to further process Q. (Notice that the earlier incurred $30,000 manufacturing cost for the 40,000 units of Product Q does not appear in Exhibit 23.8 because it is a sunk cost and as such is irrelevant to the decision.)

Example: Does the decision change if incremental costs in Exhibit 23.8 increase to $4 per unit and the opportunity cost increases to $95,000? *Answer:* Yes. There is now an incremental net loss of $35,000.

EXHIBIT 23.8

Sell or Process Analysis

Revenue if processed...............	$220,000
Revenue if sold as is...............	(50,000)
Incremental revenue	170,000
Incremental cost to process	(80,000)
Incremental net income	**$ 90,000**

Quick Check

Answers — p. 998

3. A company has already incurred a $1,000 cost in partially producing its four products. Their selling prices when partially and fully processed follow with additional costs necessary to finish these partially processed units:

Product	Unfinished Selling Price	Finished Selling Price	Further Processing Costs
Alpha	$300	$600	$150
Beta	450	900	300
Gamma.............	275	425	125
Delta	150	210	75

Which product(s) should *not* be processed further, (*a*) Alpha, (*b*) Beta, (*c*) Gamma, or (*d*) Delta?

4. Under what conditions is a sunk cost relevant to decision making?

Sales Mix Selection

When a company sells a mix of products, some are likely to be more profitable than others. Management is often wise to concentrate sales efforts on more profitable products. If production facilities or other factors are limited, an increase in the production and sale of one product usually requires reducing the production and sale of others. In this case, management must identify the most profitable combination, or *sales mix* of products. To identify the best sales mix, management must know the contribution margin of each product, the facilities required to produce each product, any constraints on these facilities, and its markets.

Point: A method called *linear programming* is useful for finding the optimal sales mix for several products subject to many market and production constraints. This method is described in advanced courses.

To illustrate, assume that FasTrac makes and sells two products, A and B. The same machines are used to produce both products. A and B have the following selling prices and variable costs per unit:

	Product A	Product B
Selling price per unit	$5.00	$7.50
Variable costs per unit	3.50	5.50
Contribution margin per unit	$1.50	$2.00

The variable costs are included in the analysis because they are the incremental costs of producing these products within the existing capacity of 100,000 machine hours per month. We consider three separate cases.

Demand Is Unlimited and Products Use Same Inputs Assume that (1) each product requires 1 machine hour per unit for production and (2) the demand for these products is unlimited. Under these conditions, FasTrac should produce as much of Product B as it can because of its larger contribution margin of $2 per unit. At full capacity, FasTrac would produce $200,000 of total contribution margin per month, computed as $2 per unit times 100,000 machine hours.

Demand Is Unlimited and Products Use Different Inputs Assume that (1) Product A requires 1 machine hour per unit, (2) Product B requires 2 machine hours per unit, and (3) the demand for these products is unlimited. Under these conditions, FasTrac should produce as much of Product A as it can because it has a contribution margin of $1.50 per machine hour compared with only $1 per machine hour for Product B. Exhibit 23.9 shows the relevant analysis.

EXHIBIT 23.9

Sales Mix Analysis

	Product A	Product B
Selling price per unit	$5.00	$7.50
Variable costs per unit	3.50	5.50
Contribution margin per unit	$1.50	$2.00
Machine hours per unit	1.0	2.0
Contribution margin per machine hour	**$1.50**	**$1.00**

At its full capacity of 100,000 machine hours, FasTrac would produce 100,000 units of Product A, yielding $150,000 of total contribution margin per month. In contrast, if it uses all 100,000 hours to produce Product B, only 50,000 units would be produced yielding a contribution margin of $100,000. These results suggest that when a company faces unlimited demand and limited capacity, only the most profitable product per input should be manufactured.

Example: If Product B's variable costs per unit increase to $6, Product A's variable costs per unit decrease to $3, and the same machine hours per unit are used, which product should FasTrac produce? *Answer:* Product A. Its contribution margin of $2 per machine hour is higher than B's $.75 per machine hour.

Demand Is Limited and Products Use Different Inputs The need for a mix of different products arises when market demand is not sufficient to allow a company to sell all that it produces. For instance, assume that (1) Product A requires 1 machine hour per unit, (2) Product B requires 2 machine hours per unit, and (3) the market for Product A is limited to 80,000 units. Under these conditions, FasTrac should produce no more than 80,000 units of Product A. This would leave another 20,000 machine hours of capacity for making Product B. FasTrac should use this spare capacity to produce 10,000 units of Product B. This sales mix would maximize FasTrac's total contribution margin per month at an amount of $140,000. In this case, the company first produces its most profitable product, up to the point of total demand (or its capacity constraint). It then uses remaining capacity to produce its next most profitable product.

Point: FasTrac might consider buying another machine to reduce the constraint on production. A strategy designed to reduce the impact of constraints or bottlenecks, on production, is called the *theory of constraints.*

Decision Insight

Companies such as **Gap**, **Abercrombie & Fitch**, and **American Eagle** must continuously monitor and manage the sales mix of their product lists. Selling their products in hundreds of countries and territories further complicates their decision process. The contribution margin of each product is crucial to their product mix strategies. ■

Segment Elimination

When a segment such as a department or division is performing poorly, management must consider eliminating it. Segment information on either net income (loss) or its contribution to overhead is not sufficient for this decision. Instead, we must look at the segment's avoidable expenses and unavoidable expenses. **Avoidable expenses,** also called *escapable expenses,* are amounts the company would not incur if it eliminated the segment. **Unavoidable expenses,** also called *inescapable expenses,* are amounts that would continue even if the segment is eliminated.

To illustrate, FasTrac considers eliminating its treadmill division because its $48,300 total expenses are higher than its $47,800 sales. Classification of this division's operating expenses into avoidable or unavoidable expenses is shown in Exhibit 23.10.

EXHIBIT 23.10

Classification of Segment Operating Expenses for Analysis

	Total	Avoidable Expenses	Unavoidable Expenses
Cost of goods sold	$ 30,000	$ 30,000	—
Direct expenses			
Salaries expense	7,900	7,900	—
Depreciation expense—Equipment	200	—	$ 200
Indirect expenses			
Rent and utilities expense	3,150	—	3,150
Advertising expense	400	400	—
Insurance expense	400	300	100
Service department costs			
Share of office department expenses	3,060	2,200	860
Share of purchasing expenses	3,190	1,000	2,190
Total	**$48,300**	**$41,800**	**$6,500**

FasTrac's analysis shows that it can avoid $41,800 expenses if it eliminates the treadmill division. Because this division's sales are $47,800, eliminating it will cause FasTrac to lose $6,000 of income. *Our decision rule is that a segment is a candidate for elimination if its revenues are less than its avoidable expenses.* Avoidable expenses can be viewed as the costs to generate this segment's revenues.

When considering elimination of a segment, we must assess its impact on other segments. A segment could be unprofitable on its own, but it might still contribute to other segments' revenues and profits. It is possible then to continue a segment even when its revenues are less than its avoidable expenses. Similarly, a profitable segment might be discontinued if its space, assets, or staff can be more profitably used by expanding existing segments or by creating new ones. Our decision to keep or eliminate a segment requires a more complex analysis than simply looking at a segment's performance report. Such reports provide useful information, but they do not provide all the information necessary for this decision.

Example: How can insurance be classified as either avoidable or unavoidable? *Answer:* Depends on whether the assets insured can be removed and the premiums canceled.

Example: Give an example of a segment that a company might profitably use to attract customers even though it might incur a loss. *Answer:* Warranty and post-sales services.

Keep or Replace Equipment

Businesses periodically must decide whether to keep using equipment or replace it. Advances in technology typically mean newer equipment can operate more efficiently and at lower cost than older equipment. In making the decision to keep or replace equipment, managers must decide whether the reduction in *variable* manufacturing costs with the new equipment over its useful life is greater than the net purchase price of the equipment. In this setting, the net purchase price of the equipment is its total cost minus any trade-in allowance or cash receipt for the old equipment.

For example, FasTrac has a piece of manufacturing equipment with a book value (cost minus accumulated depreciation) of $20,000 and a remaining useful life of four years. At the end of four years the equipment will have a salvage value of zero. The market value of the equipment is currently $25,000.

FasTrac can purchase a new machine for $100,000 and receive $25,000 in return for trading in its old machine. The new machine will reduce FasTrac's variable manufacturing costs by $18,000 per year over the four-year life of the new machine. FasTrac's incremental analysis is shown in Exhibit 23.11.

EXHIBIT 23.11

Keep or Replace Analysis

	Increase or (Decrease) in Net Income
Cost to buy new machine	$(100,000)
Cash received to trade in old machine	25,000
Reduction in variable manufacturing costs*	72,000
Total increase (decrease) in net income	$ (3,000)

*18,000 × 4 years

The analysis in Exhibit 23.11 shows that FasTrac should not replace the old equipment with this newer version as it will decrease income by $3,000. Note, the book value of the old equipment ($20,000) is not relevant to this analysis. Book value is a sunk cost, and it cannot be changed regardless of whether FasTrac keeps or replaces this equipment.

Qualitative Decision Factors

Managers must consider qualitative factors in making managerial decisions. Consider a decision on whether to buy a component from an outside supplier or continue to make it. Several qualitative decision factors must be considered. For example, the quality, delivery, and reputation of the proposed supplier are important. The effects from deciding not to make the component can include potential layoffs and impaired worker morale. Consider another situation in which a company is considering a one-time sale to a new customer at a special low price. Qualitative factors to consider in this situation include the effects of a low price on the company's image and the threat that regular customers might demand a similar price. The company must also consider whether this customer is really a one-time customer. If not, can it continue to offer this low price in the long run? Clearly, management cannot rely solely on financial data to make such decisions.

Quick Check Answers — p. 998

5. What is the difference between avoidable and unavoidable expenses?
6. A segment is a candidate for elimination if (*a*) its revenues are less than its avoidable expenses, (*b*) it has a net loss, (*c*) its unavoidable expenses are higher than its revenues.

Decision Analysis — Setting Product Price

A2 Determine product selling price based on total costs.

Relevant costs are useful to management in determining prices for special short-term decisions. But longer run pricing decisions of management need to cover both variable and fixed costs, and yield a profit.

There are several methods to help management in setting prices. The *cost-plus* methods are probably the most common, where management adds a markup to cost to reach a target price. We will describe the **total cost method,** where management sets price equal to the product's total costs plus a desired profit on the product. This is a four-step process:

1. Determine total costs.

Total costs = Production (direct materials, direct labor, and overhead) + Nonproduction (selling and administrative) costs

2. Determine total cost per unit.

Total cost per unit = Total costs ÷ Total units expected to be produced and sold

3. Determine the dollar markup per unit.

Markup per unit = Total cost per unit × Markup percentage

where Markup percentage = Desired profit/Total costs

4. Determine selling price per unit.

Selling price per unit = Total cost per unit + Markup per unit

To illustrate, consider a company that produces MP3 players. The company desires a 20% return on its assets of $1,000,000, and it expects to produce and sell 10,000 players. The following additional company information is available:

Variable costs (per unit)	
Production costs	$44
Nonproduction costs	6
Fixed costs (in dollars)	
Overhead	$140,000
Nonproduction	60,000

We apply our four-step process to determine price.

1. Total costs = Production costs + Nonproduction costs
   = [($44 × 10,000 units) + $140,000] + [($6 × 10,000 units) + $60,000]
   = $700,000
2. Total cost per unit = Total costs/Total units expected to be produced and sold
   = $700,000/10,000
   = $70
3. Markup per unit = Total cost per unit × (Desired profit/Total costs)
   = $70 × [(20% × $1,000,000)/$700,000]
   = $20
4. Selling price per unit = Total cost per unit + Markup per unit
   = $70 + $20
   = $90

To verify that our price yields the $200,000 desired profit (20% × $1,000,000), we compute the following simplified income statement using the information above.

Sales ($90 × 10,000)	$900,000
Expenses	
Variable ($50 × 10,000)	500,000
Fixed ($140,000 + $60,000)	200,000
Income	$200,000

Companies use cost-plus pricing as a starting point for determining selling prices. Many factors determine price, including consumer preferences and competition.

DEMONSTRATION PROBLEM

Determine the appropriate action in each of the following managerial decision situations.

1. Packer Company is operating at 80% of its manufacturing capacity of 100,000 product units per year. A chain store has offered to buy an additional 10,000 units at $22 each and sell them to customers so as not to compete with Packer Company. The following data are available.

Costs at 80% Capacity	Per Unit	Total
Direct materials	$ 8.00	$ 640,000
Direct labor	7.00	560,000
Overhead (fixed and variable)	12.50	1,000,000
Totals	$27.50	$2,200,000

In producing 10,000 additional units, fixed overhead costs would remain at their current level but incremental variable overhead costs of $3 per unit would be incurred. Should the company accept or reject this order?

2. Green Company uses Part JR3 in manufacturing its products. It has always purchased this part from a supplier for $40 each. It recently upgraded its own manufacturing capabilities and has enough excess capacity (including trained workers) to begin manufacturing Part JR3 instead of buying it. The company prepares the following cost projections of making the part, assuming that overhead is allocated to the part at the normal predetermined rate of 200% of direct labor cost.

Direct materials	$11
Direct labor	15
Overhead (fixed and variable) (200% of direct labor)	30
Total	$56

The required volume of output to produce the part will not require any incremental fixed overhead. Incremental variable overhead cost will be $17 per unit. Should the company make or buy this part?

3. Gold Company's manufacturing process causes a relatively large number of defective parts to be produced. The defective parts can be (a) sold for scrap, (b) melted to recover the recycled metal for reuse, or (c) reworked to be good units. Reworking defective parts reduces the output of other good units because no excess capacity exists. Each unit reworked means that one new unit cannot be produced. The following information reflects 500 defective parts currently available.

Proceeds of selling as scrap	$2,500
Additional cost of melting down defective parts	400
Cost of purchases avoided by using recycled metal from defects	4,800
Cost to rework 500 defective parts	
Direct materials	0
Direct labor	1,500
Incremental overhead	1,750
Cost to produce 500 new parts	
Direct materials	6,000
Direct labor	5,000
Incremental overhead	3,200
Selling price per good unit	40

Should the company melt the parts, sell them as scrap, or rework them?

PLANNING THE SOLUTION

- Determine whether Packer Company should accept the additional business by finding the incremental costs of materials, labor, and overhead that will be incurred if the order is accepted. Omit fixed costs that the order will not increase. If the incremental revenue exceeds the incremental cost, accept the order.
- Determine whether Green Company should make or buy the component by finding the incremental cost of making each unit. If the incremental cost exceeds the purchase price, the component should be purchased. If the incremental cost is less than the purchase price, make the component.
- Determine whether Gold Company should sell the defective parts, melt them down and recycle the metal, or rework them. To compare the three choices, examine all costs incurred and benefits received

from the alternatives in working with the 500 defective units versus the production of 500 new units. For the scrapping alternative, include the costs of producing 500 new units and subtract the $2,500 proceeds from selling the old ones. For the melting alternative, include the costs of melting the defective units, add the net cost of new materials in excess over those obtained from recycling, and add the direct labor and overhead costs. For the reworking alternative, add the costs of direct labor and incremental overhead. Select the alternative that has the lowest cost. The cost assigned to the 500 defective units is sunk and not relevant in choosing among the three alternatives.

SOLUTION TO DEMONSTRATION PROBLEM

1. This decision involves accepting additional business. Since current unit costs are $27.50, it appears initially as if the offer to sell for $22 should be rejected, but the $27.50 cost includes fixed costs. When the analysis includes only *incremental* costs, the per unit cost is as shown in the following table. The offer should be accepted because it will produce $4 of additional profit per unit (computed as $22 price less $18 incremental cost), which yields a total profit of $40,000 for the 10,000 additional units.

Direct materials	$ 8.00
Direct labor	7.00
Variable overhead (given)	3.00
Total incremental cost	$18.00

2. For this make or buy decision, the analysis must not include the $13 nonincremental overhead per unit ($30 − $17). When only the $17 incremental overhead is included, the relevant unit cost of manufacturing the part is shown in the following table. It would be better to continue buying the part for $40 instead of making it for $43.

Direct materials	$11.00
Direct labor	15.00
Variable overhead	17.00
Total incremental cost	$43.00

3. The goal of this scrap or rework decision is to identify the alternative that produces the greatest net benefit to the company. To compare the alternatives, we determine the net cost of obtaining 500 marketable units as follows:

Incremental Cost to Produce 500 Marketable Units	Sell as Is	Melt and Recycle	Rework Units
Direct materials			
New materials	$ 6,000	$6,000	
Recycled metal materials		(4,800)	
Net materials cost		1,200	
Melting costs		400	
Total direct materials cost	6,000	1,600	
Direct labor	5,000	5,000	$1,500
Incremental overhead	3,200	3,200	1,750
Cost to produce 500 marketable units	14,200	9,800	3,250
Less proceeds of selling defects as scrap	(2,500)		
Opportunity costs*			5,800
Net cost	$11,700	$9,800	$9,050

* The $5,800 opportunity cost is the lost contribution margin from not being able to produce and sell 500 units because of reworking, computed as ($40 − [$14,200/500 units]) × 500 units.

The incremental cost of 500 marketable parts is smallest if the defects are reworked.

Summary

C1 Describe the importance of relevant costs for short-term decisions. A company must rely on relevant costs pertaining to alternative courses of action rather than historical costs. Out-of-pocket expenses and opportunity costs are relevant because these are avoidable; sunk costs are irrelevant because they result from past decisions and are therefore unavoidable. Managers must also consider the relevant benefits associated with alternative decisions.

A1 Evaluate short-term managerial decisions using relevant costs. Relevant costs are useful in making decisions such as to accept additional business, make or buy, and sell as is or process further. For example, the relevant factors in deciding whether to produce and sell additional units of product are incremental costs and incremental revenues from the additional volume.

A2 Determine product selling price based on total costs. Product selling price is estimated using total production and nonproduction costs plus a markup. Price is set to yield management's desired profit for the company.

P1 Identify relevant costs and apply them to managerial decisions. Several illustrations apply relevant costs to managerial decisions, such as whether to accept additional business; make or buy; scrap or rework products; sell products or process them further; or eliminate a segment and how to select the best sales mix.

Guidance Answer to Decision Maker

Partner You should identify the differences between existing clients and this potential client. A key difference is that the restaurant business has additional inventory components (groceries, vegetables, meats, etc.) and is likely to have a higher proportion of depreciable assets. These differences imply that the partner must spend more hours auditing the records and understanding the business, regulations, and standards that pertain to the restaurant business. Such differences suggest that the partner must use a different "formula" for quoting a price to this potential client vis-à-vis current clients.

Guidance Answers to Quick Checks

1. *e*; Variable costs per unit for this order of 200 units follow:

Direct materials ($37,500/7,500)	$ 5.00
Direct labor ($60,000/7,500)	8.00
Variable overhead [(0.30 × $20,000)/7,500]	0.80
Variable selling expenses [(0.60 × $25,000 × 0.5)/7,500]	1.00
Total variable costs per unit	$14.80

Cost to produce special order: (200 × $14.80) + $400 = $3,360.

Price per unit to earn $1,000: ($3,360 + $1,000)/200 = $21.80.

2. They are the additional (new) costs of accepting new business.

3. *d*;

	Incremental benefits		Incremental costs
Alpha	$300 ($600 − $300)	>	$150 (given)
Beta	$450 ($900 − $450)	>	$300 (given)
Gamma	$150 ($425 − $275)	>	$125 (given)
Delta	$ 60 ($210 − $150)	<	$ 75 (given)

4. A sunk cost is *never* relevant because it results from a past decision and is already incurred.

5. Avoidable expenses are ones a company will not incur by eliminating a segment; unavoidable expenses will continue even after a segment is eliminated.

6. *a*

Key Terms

Avoidable expense (p. 993)
Incremental cost (p. 988)
Markup (p. 994)
Relevant benefits (p. 987)
Total cost method (p. 994)
Unavoidable expense (p. 993)

Multiple Choice Quiz

Answers on p. 1013

mhhe.com/wildFINMAN5e

Additional Quiz Questions are available at the book's Website.

1. A company inadvertently produced 3,000 defective MP3 players. The players cost $12 each to produce. A recycler offers to purchase the defective players as they are for $8 each. The production manager reports that the defects can be corrected for $10 each, enabling them to be sold at their regular market price of $19 each. The company should:
   - **a.** Correct the defect and sell them at the regular price.
   - **b.** Sell the players to the recycler for $8 each.
   - **c.** Sell 2,000 to the recycler and repair the rest.
   - **d.** Sell 1,000 to the recycler and repair the rest.
   - **e.** Throw the players away.
2. A company's productive capacity is limited to 480,000 machine hours. Product X requires 10 machine hours to produce; and Product Y requires 2 machine hours to produce. Product X sells for $32 per unit and has variable costs of $12 per unit; Product Y sells for $24 per unit and has variable costs of $10 per unit. Assuming that the company can sell as many of either product as it produces, it should:
   - **a.** Produce X and Y in the ratio of 57% and 43%.
   - **b.** Produce X and Y in the ratio of 83% X and 17% Y.
   - **c.** Produce equal amounts of Product X and Product Y.
   - **d.** Produce only Product X.
   - **e.** Produce only Product Y.
3. A company receives a special one-time order for 3,000 units of its product at $15 per unit. The company has excess capacity and it currently produces and sells the units at $20 each to its regular customers. Production costs are $13.50 per unit, which includes $9 of variable costs. To produce the special order, the company must incur additional fixed costs of $5,000. Should the company accept the special order?
   - **a.** Yes, because incremental revenue exceeds incremental costs.
   - **b.** No, because incremental costs exceed incremental revenue.
   - **c.** No, because the units are being sold for $5 less than the regular price.
   - **d.** Yes, because incremental costs exceed incremental revenue.
   - **e.** No, because incremental cost exceeds $15 per unit when total costs are considered.
4. A cost that cannot be changed because it arises from a past decision and is irrelevant to future decisions is
   - **a.** An uncontrollable cost.
   - **b.** An out-of-pocket cost.
   - **c.** A sunk cost.
   - **d.** An opportunity cost.
   - **e.** An incremental cost.
5. The potential benefit of one alternative that is lost by choosing another is known as
   - **a.** An alternative cost.
   - **b.** A sunk cost.
   - **c.** A differential cost.
   - **d.** An opportunity cost.
   - **e.** An out-of-pocket cost.

Icon denotes assignments that involve decision making.

Discussion Questions

1. Identify the five steps involved in the managerial decision-making process.
2. Is nonfinancial information ever useful in managerial decision making?
3. What is a relevant cost? Identify the two types of relevant costs.
4. Why are sunk costs irrelevant in deciding whether to sell a product in its present condition or to make it into a new product through additional processing?
5. **Arctic Cat** has many types of costs. What is an out-of-pocket cost? What is an opportunity cost? Are opportunity costs recorded in the accounting records?
6. **Piaggio** must confront sunk costs. Why are sunk costs irrelevant in deciding whether to sell a product in its present condition or to make it into a new product through additional processing?
7. Identify some qualitative factors that should be considered when making managerial decisions.
8. Identify the incremental costs incurred by **Apple** for shipping one additional iPod from a warehouse to a retail store along with the store's normal order of 75 iPods.
9. **KTM** is considering eliminating one of its stores in a large U.S. city. What are some factors that it should consider in making this decision?
10. Assume that **Polaris** manufactures and sells 60,000 units of a product at $11,000 per unit in domestic markets. It costs $6,000 per unit to manufacture ($4,000 variable cost per unit, $2,000 fixed cost per unit). Can you describe a situation under which the company is willing to sell an additional 8,000 units of the product in an international market at $5,000 per unit?

connect

QUICK STUDY

QS 23-1
Identification of relevant costs
P1

Helix Company has been approached by a new customer to provide 2,000 units of its regular product at a special price of $6 per unit. The regular selling price of the product is $8 per unit. Helix is operating at 75% of its capacity of 10,000 units. Identify whether the following costs are relevant to Helix's decision as to whether to accept the order at the special selling price. No additional fixed manufacturing overhead will be incurred because of this order. The only additional selling expense on this order will be a $0.50 per unit shipping cost. There will be no additional administrative expenses because of this order. Place an X in the appropriate column to identify whether the cost is relevant or irrelevant to accepting this order.

Item	Relevant	Not relevant
a. Selling price of $6.00 per unit	_____	_____
b. Direct materials cost of $1.00 per unit	_____	_____
c. Direct labor of $2.00 per unit	_____	_____
d. Variable manufacturing overhead of $1.50 per unit	_____	_____
e. Fixed manufacturing overhead of $0.75 per unit	_____	_____
f. Regular selling expenses of $1.25 per unit	_____	_____
g. Additional selling expenses of $0.50 per unit	_____	_____
h. Administrative expenses of $0.60 per unit	_____	_____

QS 23-2
Analysis of relevant costs A1

Refer to the data in QS 23-1. Based on financial considerations alone, should Helix accept this order at the special price? Explain.

QS 23-3
Identification of relevant nonfinancial factors P1

Refer to QS 23-1 and QS 23-2. What nonfinancial factors should Helix consider before accepting this order? Explain.

QS 23-4
Sell or process
P1 A1

Garcia Company has 10,000 units of its product that were produced last year at a total cost of $150,000. The units were damaged in a rain storm because the warehouse where they were stored developed a leak in the roof. Garcia can sell the units as is for $2 each or it can repair the units at a total cost of $18,000 and then sell them for $5 each. Should Garcia sell the units as is or repair them and then sell them? Explain.

QS 23-5
Relevant costs
C1

Label each of the following statements as either true ("T") or false ("F").

1. Relevant costs are also known as unavoidable costs.
2. Incremental costs are also known as differential costs.
3. An out-of-pocket cost requires a current and/or future outlay of cash.
4. An opportunity cost is the potential benefit that is lost by taking a specific action when two or more alternative choices are available.
5. A sunk cost will change with a future course of action.

QS 23-6
Analysis of incremental costs
A1 P1

Kando Company incurs a $9 per unit cost for Product A, which it currently manufactures and sells for $13.50 per unit. Instead of manufacturing and selling this product, the company can purchase Product B for $5 per unit and sell it for $12 per unit. If it does so, unit sales would remain unchanged and $5 of the $9 per unit costs assigned to Product A would be eliminated. Should the company continue to manufacture Product A or purchase Product B for resale?

QS 23-7
Selection of sales mix
A1

Excel Memory Company can sell all units of computer memory X and Y that it can produce, but it has limited production capacity. It can produce two units of X per hour *or* three units of Y per hour, and it has 4,000 production hours available. Contribution margin is $5 for product X and $4 for product Y. What is the most profitable sales mix for this company?

QS 23-8
Sell or process decision
A1 P1

Holmes Company produces a product that can either be sold as is or processed further. Holmes has already spent $50,000 to produce 1,250 units that can be sold now for $67,500 to another manufacturer. Alternatively, Holmes can process the units further at an incremental cost of $250 per unit. If Holmes processes further, the units can be sold for $375 each. Compute the incremental income if Holmes processes further.

QS 23-9
Scrap or rework
A1 P1

Signal mistakenly produced 10,000 defective cell phones. The phones cost $60 each to produce. A salvage company will buy the defective phones as they are for $30 each. It would cost Signal $80 per phone to rework the phones. If the phones are reworked, Signal could sell them for $110 each. Compute the incremental net income from reworking the phones.

QS 23-10
Decision to accept additional business
A1 P1

Radar Company sells bikes for $300 each. The company currently sells 3,750 bikes per year and could make as many as 5,000 bikes per year. The bikes cost $225 each to make; $150 in variable costs per bike and $75 of fixed costs per bike. Radar received an offer from a potential customer who wants to buy 750 bikes for $250 each. Incremental fixed costs to make this order are $50,000. No other costs will change if this order is accepted. Compute Radar's additional income (ignore taxes) if it accepts this order.

QS 23-11
Segment elimination
A1 P1

A guitar manufacturer is considering eliminating its electric guitar division because its $76,000 expenses are higher than its $72,000 sales. The company reports the following expenses for this division. Should the division be eliminated?

	Avoidable Expenses	Unavoidable Expenses
Cost of goods sold	$56,000	
Direct expenses	9,250	$1,250
Indirect expenses	470	1,600
Service department costs	6,000	1,430

QS 23-12
Keep or replace decision
A1 P1

Rory Company has a machine with a book value of $75,000 and a remaining five-year useful life. A new machine is available at a cost of $112,500, and Rory can also receive $60,000 for trading in its old machine. The new machine will reduce variable manufacturing costs by $12,000 per year over its five-year useful life. Should the machine be replaced?

connect

EXERCISES

Exercise 23-1
Relevant costs
C1

Fill in each of the blanks below with the correct term.

1. A ______ arises from a past decision and cannot be avoided or changed; it is irrelevant to future decisions.
2. ______ refer to the incremental revenue generated from taking one particular action over another.
3. Relevant costs are also known as ______.
4. An ______ requires a future outlay of cash and is relevant for current and future decision making.
5. An ______ is the potential benefit lost by taking a specific action when two or more alternative choices are available.

Exercise 23-2
Keep or replace
A1 P1

Xinhong Company is considering replacing one of its manufacturing machines. The machine has a book value of $45,000 and a remaining useful life of 5 years, at which time its salvage value will be zero. It has a current market value of $52,000. Variable manufacturing costs are $36,000 per year for this machine. Information on two alternative replacement machines follows. Should Xinhong keep or replace its manufacturing machine? If the machine should be replaced, which alternative new machine should Xinhong purchase?

	Alternative A	Alternative B
Cost	$115,000	$125,000
Variable manufacturing costs per year.........	19,000	15,000

Exercise 23-3
Scrap or rework
A1 P1

A company must decide between scrapping or reworking units that do not pass inspection. The company has 22,000 defective units that cost $6 per unit to manufacture. The units can be sold as is for $2.50 each, or they can be reworked for $4.50 each and then sold for the full price of $8.50 each. If the units are sold as is, the company will have to build 22,000 replacement units at a cost of $6 each, and sell them at the full price of $8.50 each. (1) What is the incremental income from selling the units as scrap? (2) What is the incremental income from reworking and selling the units? (3) Should the company sell the units as scrap or rework them?

Exercise 23-4
Decision to accept additional business or not
A1 P1

Farrow Co. expects to sell 150,000 units of its product in the next period with the following results.

Sales (150,000 units)	$2,250,000
Costs and expenses	
Direct materials	300,000
Direct labor	600,000
Overhead	150,000
Selling expenses	225,000
Administrative expenses	385,500
Total costs and expenses	1,660,500
Net income	$ 589,500

The company has an opportunity to sell 15,000 additional units at $12 per unit. The additional sales would not affect its current expected sales. Direct materials and labor costs per unit would be the same for the additional units as they are for the regular units. However, the additional volume would create the following incremental costs: (1) total overhead would increase by 15% and (2) administrative expenses would increase by $64,500. Prepare an analysis to determine whether the company should accept or reject the offer to sell additional units at the reduced price of $12 per unit.

Check Income increase, $3,000

Exercise 23-5
Decision to accept new business or not
P1 A1

Goshford Company produces a single product and has capacity to produce 100,000 units per month. Costs to produce its current sales of 80,000 units follow. The regular selling price of the product is $100 per unit. Management is approached by a new customer who wants to purchase 20,000 units of the product for $75 per unit. If the order is accepted, there will be no additional fixed manufacturing overhead, and no additional fixed selling and administrative expenses. The customer is not in the company's regular selling territory, so there will be a $5 per unit shipping expense in addition to the regular variable selling and administrative expenses.

	Per Unit	Costs at 80,000 Units
Direct materials	$12.50	$1,000,000
Direct labor	15.00	1,200,000
Variable manufacturing overhead	10.00	800,000
Fixed manufacturing overhead	17.50	1,400,000
Variable selling and administrative expenses	14.00	1,120,000
Fixed selling and administrative expenses	13.00	1,040,000
Totals	$82.00	$6,560,000

Required

1. Determine whether management should accept or reject the new business.
2. What nonfinancial factors should management consider when deciding whether to take this order?

Check (1) Additional volume effect on net income, $370,000

Exercise 23-6
Make or buy decision
A1

Gilberto Company currently manufactures one of its crucial parts at a cost of $4.45 per unit. This cost is based on a normal production rate of 65,000 units per year. Variable costs are $1.95 per unit, fixed costs related to making this part are $65,000 per year, and allocated fixed costs are $58,500 per year. Allocated fixed costs are unavoidable whether the company makes or buys the part. Gilberto is considering buying the part from a supplier for a quoted price of $3.50 per unit guaranteed for a three-year period. Should the company continue to manufacture the part, or should it buy the part from the outside supplier? Support your answer with analyses.

Check $35,750 increased costs to buy

Exercise 23-7
Make or buy decision P1 A1

Gelb Company currently manufactures 40,000 units of a key component for its manufacturing process at a cost of $4.45 per unit. Variable costs are $1.95 per unit, fixed costs related to making this component are $65,000 per year, and allocated fixed costs are $58,500 per year. The allocated fixed costs are unavoidable whether the company makes or buys this component. The company is considering buying this component from a supplier for $3.50 per unit. Should it continue to manufacture the component, or should it buy this component from the outside supplier? Support your decision with analysis of the data provided.

Check Increased cost to make, $3,000

Exercise 23-8
Sell or process decision
A1

Cobe Company has already manufactured 28,000 units of Product A at a cost of $28 per unit. The 28,000 units can be sold at this stage for $700,000. Alternatively, the units can be further processed at a $420,000 total additional cost and be converted into 5,600 units of Product B and 11,200 units of Product C. Per unit selling price for Product B is $105 and for Product C is $70. Prepare an analysis that shows whether the 28,000 units of Product A should be processed further or not.

Exercise 23-9
Sell or rework decision
P1 A1

Varto Company has 7,000 units of its sole product in inventory that it produced last year at a cost of $22 each. This year's model is superior to last year's and the 7,000 units cannot be sold at last year's regular selling price of $35 each. Varto has two alternatives for these items: (1) they can be sold to a wholesaler for $8 each, or (2) they can be reworked at a cost of $125,000 and then sold for $25 each. Prepare an analysis to determine whether Varto should sell the products as is or rework them and then sell them.

Check Incremental net income of reworking, $(6,000)

Exercise 23-10
Analysis of income effects from eliminating departments
A1

Suresh Co. expects its five departments to yield the following income for next year.

		Dept. M	Dept. N	Dept. O	Dept. P	Dept. T
1		Dept. M	Dept. N	Dept. O	Dept. P	Dept. T
2	Sales	$63,000	$35,000	$56,000	$42,000	$ 28,000
3	Expenses					
4	Avoidable	9,800	36,400	22,400	14,000	37,800
5	Unavoidable	51,800	12,600	4,200	29,400	9,800
6	Total expenses	61,600	49,000	26,600	43,400	47,600
7	Net income (loss)	$ 1,400	$(14,000)	$29,400	$(1,400)	$ (19,600)

Recompute and prepare the departmental income statements (including a combined total column) for the company under each of the following separate scenarios: Management (1) does not eliminate any department, (2) eliminates departments with expected net losses, and (3) eliminates departments with sales dollars that are less than avoidable expenses. Explain your answers to parts 2 and 3.

Check Total income (loss) (2) $(21,000), (3) $7,000

Exercise 23-11
Income analysis of eliminating departments
A1

Marinette Company makes several products, including canoes. The company has been experiencing losses from its canoe segment and is considering dropping that product line. The following information is available regarding its canoe segment. Should management discontinue the manufacturing of canoes? Support your decision.

MARINETTE COMPANY
Income Statement—Canoe Segment

Sales		$2,000,000
Variable costs		
Direct materials	$450,000	
Direct labor	500,000	
Variable overhead	300,000	
Variable selling and administrative	200,000	
Total variable costs		1,450,000
Contribution margin		550,000
Fixed costs		
Direct	375,000	
Indirect	300,000	
Total fixed costs		675,000
Net income		$ (125,000)

Check Income impact if canoe segment dropped, $(175,000)

Exercise 23-12
Sales mix determination and analysis
A1

Colt Company owns a machine that can produce two specialized products. Production time for Product TLX is two units per hour and for Product MTV is five units per hour. The machine's capacity is 2,750 hours per year. Both products are sold to a single customer who has agreed to buy all of the company's output up to a maximum of 4,700 units of Product TLX and 2,500 units of Product MTV. Selling prices and variable costs per unit to produce the products follow. Determine (1) the company's most profitable sales mix and (2) the contribution margin that results from that sales mix.

	Product TLX	Product MTV
Selling price per unit	$15.00	$9.50
Variable costs per unit	4.80	5.50

Check (2) $55,940

Exercise 23-13
Sales mix
A1

Childress Company produces three products, K1, S5, and G9. Each product uses the same type of direct material. K1 uses 4 pounds of the material, S5 uses 3 pounds of the material, and G9 uses 6 pounds of the material. Demand for all products is strong, but only 50,000 pounds of material are available. Information about the selling price per unit and variable cost per unit of each product follows. Orders for which product should be produced and filled first, then second, and then third? Support your answer.

	K1	S5	G9
Selling price	$160	$112	$210
Variable costs	96	85	144

Check K1 contribution margin per pound, $16

connect

PROBLEM SET A

Problem 23-1A
Analysis of income effects of additional business
A1 P1

mhhe.com/wildFINMAN5e

Jones Products manufactures and sells to wholesalers approximately 400,000 packages per year of underwater markers at $6 per package. Annual costs for the production and sale of this quantity are shown in the table.

Direct materials	$576,000
Direct labor	144,000
Overhead	320,000
Selling expenses	150,000
Administrative expenses	100,000
Total costs and expenses	$1,290,000

A new wholesaler has offered to buy 50,000 packages for $5.20 each. These markers would be marketed under the wholesaler's name and would not affect Jones Products' sales through its normal channels. A study of the costs of this additional business reveals the following:

- Direct materials costs are 100% variable.
- Per unit direct labor costs for the additional units would be 50% higher than normal because their production would require overtime pay at one-and-one-half times the usual labor rate.
- 25% of the normal annual overhead costs are fixed at any production level from 350,000 to 500,000 units. The remaining 75% of the annual overhead cost is variable with volume.
- Accepting the new business would involve no additional selling expenses.
- Accepting the new business would increase administrative expenses by a $5,000 fixed amount.

Required

Prepare a three-column comparative income statement that shows the following:

1. Annual operating income without the special order (column 1).
2. Annual operating income received from the new business only (column 2).
3. Combined annual operating income from normal business and the new business (column 3).

Check Operating income:
(1) $1,110,000
(2) $126,000

Problem 23-2A
Analysis of income effects of additional business
P1 A1

Calla Company produces skateboards that sell for $50 per unit. The company currently has the capacity to produce 90,000 skateboards per year, but is selling 80,000 skateboards per year. Annual costs for 80,000 skateboards follow.

Direct materials	$ 800,000
Direct labor	640,000
Overhead	960,000
Selling expenses	560,000
Administrative expenses	480,000
Total costs and expenses	$3,440,000

A new retail store has offered to buy 10,000 of its skateboards for $45 per unit. The store is in a different market from Calla's regular customers and it would not affect regular sales. A study of its costs in anticipation of this additional business reveals the following:

- Direct materials and direct labor are 100% variable.
- Thirty percent of overhead is fixed at any production level from 80,000 units to 90,000 units; the remaining 70% of annual overhead costs are variable with respect to volume.
- Selling expenses are 60% variable with respect to number of units sold, and the other 40% of selling expenses are fixed.
- There will be an additional $2 per unit selling expense for this order.
- Administrative expenses would increase by a $1,000 fixed amount.

Required

1. Prepare a three-column comparative income statement that reports the following:
   a. Annual income without the special order.
   b. Annual income from the special order.
   c. Combined annual income from normal business and the new business.
2. Should Calla accept this order? What nonfinancial factors should Calla consider? Explain.

Check (1b) Added income from order, $123,000

Analysis Component

3. Assume that the new customer wants to buy 15,000 units instead of 10,000 units—it will only buy 15,000 units or none and will not take a partial order. Without any computations, how does this change your answer for part 2?

Problem 23-3A
Make or buy
P1 A1

Haver Company currently produces component RX5 for its sole product. The current cost per unit to manufacture the required 50,000 units of RX5 follows.

Direct materials	$ 5.00
Direct labor	8.00
Overhead	9.00
Total cost per unit	$22.00

Direct materials and direct labor are 100% variable. Overhead is 80% fixed. An outside supplier has offered to supply the 50,000 units of RX5 for $18.00 per unit.

Required

1. Determine whether the company should make or buy the RX5.
2. What factors beside cost must management consider when deciding whether to make or buy RX5?

Check (1) Incremental cost to make RX5, $740,000

Problem 23-4A
Sell or process
P1 A1

Harold Manufacturing produces denim clothing. This year, it produced 5,000 denim jackets at a manufacturing cost of $45 each. These jackets were damaged in the warehouse during storage. Management investigated the matter and identified three alternatives for these jackets.

1. Jackets can be sold to a second-hand clothing shop for $6 each.
2. Jackets can be disassembled at a cost of $32,000 and sold to a recycler for $12 each.

3. Jackets can be reworked and turned into good jackets. However, with the damage, management estimates it will be able to assemble the good parts of the 5,000 jackets into only 3,000 jackets. The remaining pieces of fabric will be discarded. The cost of reworking the jackets will be $102,000, but the jackets can then be sold for their regular price of $45 each.

Check Incremental income for alternative 2, $28,000

Required

Which alternative should Harold choose? Show analysis for each alternative.

Problem 23-5A
Analysis of sales mix strategies
A1

Edgerron Company is able to produce two products, G and B, with the same machine in its factory. The following information is available.

	Product G	Product B
Selling price per unit	$120	$160
Variable costs per unit	40	90
Contribution margin per unit	$ 80	$ 70
Machine hours to produce 1 unit	0.4 hours	1.0 hours
Maximum unit sales per month	600 units	200 units

The company presently operates the machine for a single eight-hour shift for 22 working days each month. Management is thinking about operating the machine for two shifts, which will increase its productivity by another eight hours per day for 22 days per month. This change would require $15,000 additional fixed costs per month.

Required

Check Units of Product G: (2) 440 (3) 600 (4) 700

1. Determine the contribution margin per machine hour that each product generates.
2. How many units of Product G and Product B should the company produce if it continues to operate with only one shift? How much total contribution margin does this mix produce each month?
3. If the company adds another shift, how many units of Product G and Product B should it produce? How much total contribution margin would this mix produce each month? Should the company add the new shift? Explain.
4. Suppose that the company determines that it can increase Product G's maximum sales to 700 units per month by spending $12,000 per month in marketing efforts. Should the company pursue this strategy and the double shift? Explain.

Problem 23-6A
Analysis of possible elimination of a department
A1

Elegant Decor Company's management is trying to decide whether to eliminate Department 200, which has produced losses or low profits for several years. The company's 2013 departmental income statement shows the following.

ELEGANT DECOR COMPANY
Departmental Income Statements
For Year Ended December 31, 2013

	Dept. 100	Dept. 200	Combined
Sales	$436,000	$290,000	$726,000
Cost of goods sold	262,000	207,000	469,000
Gross profit	174,000	83,000	257,000
Operating expenses			
Direct expenses			
Advertising	17,000	12,000	29,000
Store supplies used	4,000	3,800	7,800
Depreciation—Store equipment	5,000	3,300	8,300
Total direct expenses	26,000	19,100	45,100

[continued on next page]

[continued from previous page]

Allocated expenses			
Sales salaries	65,000	39,000	104,000
Rent expense	9,440	4,720	14,160
Bad debts expense	9,900	8,100	18,000
Office salary	18,720	12,480	31,200
Insurance expense	2,000	1,100	3,100
Miscellaneous office expenses	2,400	1,600	4,000
Total allocated expenses	107,460	67,000	174,460
Total expenses	133,460	86,100	219,560
Net income (loss)	$ 40,540	$ (3,100)	$ 37,440

In analyzing whether to eliminate Department 200, management considers the following:

a. The company has one office worker who earns $600 per week, or $31,200 per year, and four salesclerks who each earn $500 per week, or $26,000 per year for each salesclerk.

b. The full salaries of two salesclerks are charged to Department 100. The full salary of one salesclerk is charged to Department 200. The salary of the fourth clerk, who works half-time in both departments, is divided evenly between the two departments.

c. Eliminating Department 200 would avoid the sales salaries and the office salary currently allocated to it. However, management prefers another plan. Two salesclerks have indicated that they will be quitting soon. Management believes that their work can be done by the other two clerks if the one office worker works in sales half-time. Eliminating Department 200 will allow this shift of duties. If this change is implemented, half the office worker's salary would be reported as sales salaries and half would be reported as office salary.

d. The store building is rented under a long-term lease that cannot be changed. Therefore, Department 100 will use the space and equipment currently used by Department 200.

e. Closing Department 200 will eliminate its expenses for advertising, bad debts, and store supplies; 70% of the insurance expense allocated to it to cover its merchandise inventory; and 25% of the miscellaneous office expenses presently allocated to it.

Required

1. Prepare a three-column report that lists items and amounts for (a) the company's total expenses (including cost of goods sold)—in column 1, (b) the expenses that would be eliminated by closing Department 200—in column 2, and (c) the expenses that will continue—in column 3.

Check (1) Total expenses: (a) $688,560, (b) $284,070

2. Prepare a forecasted annual income statement for the company reflecting the elimination of Department 200 assuming that it will not affect Department 100's sales and gross profit. The statement should reflect the reassignment of the office worker to one-half time as a salesclerk.

(2) Forecasted net income without Department 200, $31,510

Analysis Component

3. Reconcile the company's combined net income with the forecasted net income assuming that Department 200 is eliminated (list both items and amounts). Analyze the reconciliation and explain why you think the department should or should not be eliminated.

PROBLEM SET B

Problem 23-1B
Analysis of income effects of additional business
A1 P1

Windmire Company manufactures and sells to local wholesalers approximately 300,000 units per month at a sales price of $4 per unit. Monthly costs for the production and sale of this quantity follow.

Direct materials	$384,000
Direct labor	96,000
Overhead	288,000
Selling expenses	120,000
Administrative expenses	80,000
Total costs and expenses	$968,000

A new out-of-state distributor has offered to buy 50,000 units next month for $3.44 each. These units would be marketed in other states and would not affect Windtrax's sales through its normal channels. A study of the costs of this new business reveals the following:

- Direct materials costs are 100% variable.
- Per unit direct labor costs for the additional units would be 50% higher than normal because their production would require overtime pay at one and one half times their normal rate to meet the distributor's deadline.
- Twenty-five percent of the normal annual overhead costs are fixed at any production level from 250,000 to 400,000 units. The remaining 75% is variable with volume.
- Accepting the new business would involve no additional selling expenses.
- Accepting the new business would increase administrative expenses by a $4,000 fixed amount.

Required

Prepare a three-column comparative income statement that shows the following:

Check Operating income: (1) $232,000, (2) $44,000

1. Monthly operating income without the special order (column 1).
2. Monthly operating income received from the new business only (column 2).
3. Combined monthly operating income from normal business and the new business (column 3).

Problem 23-2B
Analysis of income effects of additional business
P1 A1

Mervin Company produces circuit boards that sell for $8 per unit. It currently has capacity to produce 600,000 circuit boards per year, but is selling 550,000 boards per year. Annual costs for the 550,000 circuit boards follow.

Direct materials	$ 825,000
Direct labor	1,100,000
Overhead	1,375,000
Selling expenses	275,000
Administrative expenses	550,000
Total costs and expenses	$4,125,000

An overseas customer has offered to buy 50,000 circuit boards for $6 per unit. The customer is in a different market from its regular customers and would not affect regular sales. A study of its costs in anticipation of this additional business reveals the following:

- Direct materials and direct labor are 100% variable.
- Twenty percent of overhead is fixed at any production level from 550,000 units to 600,000 units; the remaining 80% of annual overhead costs are variable with respect to volume.
- Selling expenses are 40% variable with respect to number of units sold, and the other 60% of selling expenses are fixed.
- There will be an additional $0.20 per unit selling expense for this order.
- Administrative expenses would increase by a $700 fixed amount.

Required

1. Prepare a three-column comparative income statement that reports the following:

Check (1b) Additional income from order, $4,300

a. Annual income without the special order.
b. Annual income from the special order.
c. Combined annual income from normal business and the new business.

2. Should management accept the order? What nonfinancial factors should Mervin consider? Explain.

Analysis Component

3. Assume that the new customer wants to buy 100,000 units instead of 50,000 units—it will only buy 100,000 units or none and will not take a partial order. Without any computations, how does this change your answer in part 2?

Problem 23-3B
Make or buy
P1 A1

Alto Company currently produces component TH1 for its sole product. The current cost per unit to manufacture its required 400,000 units of TH1 follows.

Direct materials	$1.20
Direct labor	1.50
Overhead	6.00
Total cost per unit	$8.70

Direct materials and direct labor are 100% variable. Overhead is 75% fixed. An outside supplier has offered to supply the 400,000 units of TH1 for $4 per unit.

Required

1. Determine whether management should make or buy the TH1.
2. What factors besides cost must management consider when deciding whether to make or buy TH1?

Check (1) Incremental cost to make TH1, $1,680,000

Problem 23-4B
Sell or process
P1 A1

Micron Manufacturing produces electronic equipment. This year, it produced 7,500 oscilloscopes at a manufacturing cost of $300 each. These oscilloscopes were damaged in the warehouse during storage and, while usable, cannot be sold at their regular selling price of $500 each. Management has investigated the matter and has identified three alternatives for these oscilloscopes.

1. They can be sold to a wholesaler for $75 each.
2. They can be disassembled at a cost of $400,000 and the parts sold to a recycler for $130 each.
3. They can be reworked and turned into good units. The cost of reworking the units will be $3,200,000, after which the units can be sold at their regular price of $500 each.

Required

Which alternative should management pursue? Show analysis for each alternative.

Check Incremental income for alternative 2, $575,000

Problem 23-5B
Analysis of sales mix strategies
A1

Sung Company is able to produce two products, R and T, with the same machine in its factory. The following information is available.

	Product R	Product T
Selling price per unit	$60	$80
Variable costs per unit	20	45
Contribution margin per unit	$40	$35
Machine hours to produce 1 unit	0.4 hours	1.0 hours
Maximum unit sales per month	550 units	175 units

The company presently operates the machine for a single eight-hour shift for 22 working days each month. Management is thinking about operating the machine for two shifts, which will increase its productivity by another eight hours per day for 22 days per month. This change would require $3,250 additional fixed costs per month.

Required

1. Determine the contribution margin per machine hour that each product generates.
2. How many units of Product R and Product T should the company produce if it continues to operate with only one shift? How much total contribution margin does this mix produce each month?
3. If the company adds another shift, how many units of Product R and Product T should it produce? How much total contribution margin would this mix produce each month? Should the company add the new shift? Explain.
4. Suppose that the company determines that it can increase Product R's maximum sales to 675 units per month by spending $4,500 per month in marketing efforts. Should the company pursue this strategy and the double shift? Explain.

Check Units of Product R: (2) 440

(3) 550

(4) 675

Problem 23-6B
Analysis of possible elimination of a department
A1

Esme Company's management is trying to decide whether to eliminate Department Z, which has produced low profits or losses for several years. The company's 2013 departmental income statement shows the following.

ESME COMPANY
Departmental Income Statements
For Year Ended December 31, 2013

	Dept. A	Dept. Z	Combined
Sales	$700,000	$175,000	$875,000
Cost of goods sold	461,300	125,100	586,400
Gross profit	238,700	49,900	288,600
Operating expenses			
Direct expenses			
Advertising	27,000	3,000	30,000
Store supplies used	5,600	1,400	7,000
Depreciation—Store equipment	14,000	7,000	21,000
Total direct expenses	46,600	11,400	58,000
Allocated expenses			
Sales salaries	70,200	23,400	93,600
Rent expense	22,080	5,520	27,600
Bad debts expense	21,000	4,000	25,000
Office salary	20,800	5,200	26,000
Insurance expense	4,200	1,400	5,600
Miscellaneous office expenses	1,700	2,500	4,200
Total allocated expenses	139,980	42,020	182,000
Total expenses	186,580	53,420	240,000
Net income (loss)	$ 52,120	$ (3,520)	$ 48,600

In analyzing whether to eliminate Department Z, management considers the following items:

a. The company has one office worker who earns $500 per week or $26,000 per year and four salesclerks who each earn $450 per week or $23,400 per year for each salesclerk.

b. The full salaries of three salesclerks are charged to Department A. The full salary of one salesclerk is charged to Department Z.

c. Eliminating Department Z would avoid the sales salaries and the office salary currently allocated to it. However, management prefers another plan. Two salesclerks have indicated that they will be quitting soon. Management believes that their work can be done by the two remaining clerks if the one office worker works in sales half-time. Eliminating Department Z will allow this shift of duties. If this change is implemented, half the office worker's salary would be reported as sales salaries and half would be reported as office salary.

d. The store building is rented under a long-term lease that cannot be changed. Therefore, Department A will use the space and equipment currently used by Department Z.

e. Closing Department Z will eliminate its expenses for advertising, bad debts, and store supplies; 65% of the insurance expense allocated to it to cover its merchandise inventory; and 30% of the miscellaneous office expenses presently allocated to it.

Required

Check (1) Total expenses: (a) $826,400, (b) $181,960

1. Prepare a three-column report that lists items and amounts for (a) the company's total expenses (including cost of goods sold)—in column 1, (b) the expenses that would be eliminated by closing Department Z—in column 2, and (c) the expenses that will continue—in column 3.

(2) Forecasted net income without Department Z, $55,560

2. Prepare a forecasted annual income statement for the company reflecting the elimination of Department Z assuming that it will not affect Department A's sales and gross profit. The statement should reflect the reassignment of the office worker to one-half time as a salesclerk.

Analysis Component

3. Reconcile the company's combined net income with the forecasted net income assuming that Department Z is eliminated (list both items and amounts). Analyze the reconciliation and explain why you think the department should or should not be eliminated.

SERIAL PROBLEM

Success Systems

P1 A1

(This serial problem began in Chapter 1 and continues through most of the book. If previous chapter segments were not completed, the serial problem can begin at this point. It is helpful, but not necessary, to use the Working Papers that accompany the book.)

SP 23 Adria Lopez has found that her line of computer desks and chairs has become very popular and she is finding it hard to keep up with demand. She knows that she cannot fill all of her orders for both items, so she decides she must determine the optimal sales mix given the resources she has available. Information about the desks and chairs follows.

	Desks	Chairs
Selling price per unit	$1,125	$375
Variable costs per unit	500	200
Contribution margin per unit	$ 625	$175
Direct labor hours per unit	5 hours	4 hours
Expected demand for next quarter	175 desks	50 chairs

Adria has determined that she only has 1,015 direct labor hours available for the next quarter and wants to optimize her contribution margin given the limited number of direct labor hours available.

Required

Determine the optimal sales mix and the contribution margin the business will earn at that sales mix.

Beyond the Numbers

REPORTING IN ACTION

A1

Polaris

BTN 23-1 Revenues for three of **Polaris**' four segments for the year ending December 31, 2011 are reported below. Assume that Polaris reports operating expenses for each of its segments for that same year below.

$ millions	Off-road	Snow	On-road
Revenues	$1,823	$280	$146
Operating expenses	1,586	294	140

Required

1. Compute operating income for each segment.

2. If the results in part 1 are typical, what segments, if any, might Polaris decide to eliminate?

COMPARATIVE ANALYSIS

A1

Polaris

Arctic Cat

BTN 23-2 **Polaris** and **Arctic Cat** sell several different products; most are profitable but some are not. Teams of employees in each company make advertising, investment, and product mix decisions. A certain portion of advertising for both companies is on a local basis to a target audience.

Required

1. Contact the local newspaper and ask the approximate cost of ad space (for example, cost of one page or one-half page of advertising) for a company's product or group of products (such as Polaris ATVs).

2. Estimate how many products this advertisement must sell to justify its cost. Begin by taking the product's sales price advertised for each company and assume a 20% contribution margin.

3. Prepare a one-half page memorandum explaining the importance of effective advertising when making a product mix decision. Be prepared to present your ideas in class.

ETHICS CHALLENGE

P1 A1

BTN 23-3 Bert Asiago, a salesperson for Convertco, received an order from a potential new customer for 50,000 units of Convertco's single product at a price $25 below its regular selling price of $65. Asiago knows that Convertco has the capacity to produce this order without affecting regular sales. He has spoken to Convertco's controller, Bia Morgan, who has informed Asiago that at the $40 selling price, Convertco will not be covering its variable costs of $42 for the product, and she recommends the order not be accepted. Asiago knows that variable costs include his sales commission of $4 per unit. If he accepts a $2 per unit commission, the sale will produce a contribution margin of zero. Asiago is eager to get the new customer because he believes that this could lead to the new customer becoming a regular customer.

Required

1. Determine the contribution margin per unit on the order as determined by the controller.
2. Determine the contribution margin per unit on the order as determined by Asiago if he takes the lower commission.
3. Do you recommend Convertco accept the special order? What factors must management consider?

COMMUNICATING IN PRACTICE

P1

BTN 23-4 Assume that you work for Greeble's Department Store, and your manager requests that you outline the pros and cons of discontinuing its hardware department. That department appears to be generating losses, and your manager believes that discontinuing it will increase overall store profits.

Required

Prepare a memorandum to your manager outlining what Greeble's management should consider when trying to decide whether to discontinue its hardware department.

TAKING IT TO THE NET

A1

BTN 23-5 Many companies must determine whether to internally produce their component parts or to outsource them. Further, some companies now outsource key components or business processes to international providers. Access the Website BizBrim.com and review the available information on business process outsourcing.

Required

1. What types of processes are commonly outsourced, according to Bizbrim?
2. What are some of the benefits listed for business process outsourcing?

TEAMWORK IN ACTION

P1

BTN 23-6 Break into teams and identify costs that an airline such as **Delta Airlines** would incur on a flight from Green Bay to Minneapolis. (1) Identify the individual costs as variable or fixed. (2) Assume that Delta is trying to decide whether to drop this flight because it seems to be unprofitable. Determine which costs are likely to be saved if the flight is dropped. Set up your answer in the following format.

Cost	Variable or Fixed	Cost Saved if Flight Is Dropped	Rationale

ENTREPRENEURIAL DECISION

A1

BTN 23-7 Charlie Fyffe of **Charlie's Brownies** makes brownies and other sweets. Charlie must decide on the best sales mix for his products. Assume that his company has a capacity of 400 hours of processing time available each month and it makes two types of brownies, Deluxe and Premium. Information on these foods follows.

	Deluxe	Premium
Selling price per carton	$70	$90
Variable costs per carton	$40	$50
Processing minutes per carton	60 minutes	120 minutes

Required

1. Assume the markets for both cartons of brownies are unlimited. How many Deluxe cartons and how many Premium cartons should the company make each month? Explain. How much total contribution margin does this mix produce each month?
2. Assume the market for the Deluxe carton is limited to 60 cartons per month, with no market limit for the Premium cartons. How many Deluxe cartons and how many Premium cartons should the company make each month? Explain. How much total contribution margin does this mix produce each month?

HITTING THE ROAD

P3

BTN 23-8 Restaurants are often adding and removing menu items. Visit a restaurant and identify a new food item. Make a list of costs that the restaurant must consider when deciding whether to add that new item. Also, make a list of nonfinancial factors that the restaurant must consider when adding that item.

GLOBAL DECISION

C1

KTM

BTN 23-9 Access KTM's 2011 annual report dated December 31, 2011, from its Website www.KTM.com. Identify and read the section in the Group Status Report—2011, section 12, regarding Sustainability.

Required

KTM reports that they developed a special KTM motorcyle logistics system on reusable metal plates. This special system eliminates additional packaging materials. These sustainability efforts are costly. Why would a company like KTM pursue these costly efforts?

ANSWERS TO MULTIPLE CHOICE QUIZ

1. a; Reworking provides incremental revenue of $11 per unit ($19 − $8); and, it costs $10 to rework them. The company is better off by $1 per unit when it reworks these products and sells them at the regular price.
2. e; Product X has a $2 contribution margin per machine hour [($32 − $12)/10 MH]; Product Y has a $7 contribution margin per machine hour [($24 − $10)/2 MH]. It should produce as much of Product Y as possible.
3. a; Total revenue from the special order = 3,000 units × $15 per unit = $45,000; and, Total costs for the special order = (3,000 units × $9 per unit) + $5,000 = $32,000. Net income from the special order = $45,000 − $32,000 = $13,000. Thus, yes, it should accept the order.
4. c
5. d

24

Capital Budgeting and Investment Analysis

A Look Back

Chapter 23 described several procedures useful for making and evaluating short-term managerial decisions. It also assessed the consequences of such decisions.

A Look at This Chapter

This chapter focuses on evaluating capital budgeting decisions. Several methods are described and illustrated that help managers identify projects with the greater return on investment.

Learning Objectives

CONCEPTUAL

C1 Describe the selection of a hurdle rate for an investment. (p. 1020)

ANALYTICAL

A1 Analyze a capital investment project using break-even time. (p. 1026)

PROCEDURAL

P1 Compute payback period and describe its use. (p. 1017)

P2 Compute accounting rate of return and explain its use. (p. 1019)

P3 Compute net present value and describe its use. (p. 1021)

P4 Compute internal rate of return and explain its use. (p. 1023)

Decision Insight

Wow Factor

"Be in front of your customer . . . [and] have a little bit of an edge."
—**KEITH MULLIN** (far left)

SAN DIEGO—"I have been battling greasy fingers and keyboard crumbs," complained gamer Keith Mullin. "I thought '*there has to be a better way*!'" So, Keith-the-gamer morphed into Keith-the-entrepreneur. In 2008, Keith set up what he calls his "garage startup" and introduced **Gamer Grub®** **(GamerGrub.com),** which is performance snack food for gamers. "I got tired of wiping my hands on my jeans," laughs Keith. "And, I like to multi-task."

Success, however, requires Keith to monitor and minimize costs. "I made the first Gamer Grub prototypes in my mom's kitchen," explains Keith. He eventually set up an accounting system to track costs and match them with revenues. But, Keith says, it is a constant struggle as his business has been tripling in revenues each month. He explains that properly applying capital budgeting methods and acting on that information has helped in his success. However, admits Keith, "it is more of a collaborative effort."

To date, Keith has successfully controlled his costs while monitoring both revenues and customer needs. "You need to be in front of your customer, watch them taste it, watch them understand what you're doing," says Keith. "You have to be out there . . . we have given out at least 16,000 samples!" Keith adds that he applies capital budgeting methods such as net present value and internal rate of return. These methods enable Keith to expand his capacity and enter new markets that deliver high returns. He also relies on analyses from these methods to assess which snacks have positive returns and which investments in production operations to make. But, what keeps him going, admits Keith, is knowing that he offers "different ways to snack while you're computer gaming or multi-tasking."

Keith is on a mission. What motivates him, explains Keith, is the "Wow! If you get that 'Wow' reaction, that's a really good thing." To make that happen, he tracks the accounting numbers to be sure his "Wow food" is a money-making venture. "Gamer Grub allows gamers to consume healthy, game-enhancing snacks," insists Keith. "Without greasy fingers or keyboard crumbs!"

[Sources: *GamerGrub* Website, January 2013; *Entrepreneur,* October 2009; *Business Wire,* September 2008; *MGC* Website, January 2010]

Chapter Preview

Management must assess alternative long-term strategies and investments, and then decide which assets to acquire or sell to achieve company objectives. This analysis process is called capital budgeting, which is one of the more challenging, risky, and important tasks that management undertakes. This task requires predictions and estimates, and management's capital budgeting decisions impact the company for years. This chapter explains and illustrates several methods to aid management in the capital budgeting decisions.

Capital Budgeting and Investment Analysis

Non-present Value Methods
- Payback period
- Accounting rate of return

Present Value Methods
- Net present value
- Internal rate of return
- Comparison of methods

INTRODUCTION TO CAPITAL BUDGETING

The capital expenditures budget is management's plan for acquiring and selling plant assets. **Capital budgeting** is the process of analyzing alternative long-term investments and deciding which assets to acquire or sell. These decisions can involve developing a new product or process, buying a new machine or a new building, or acquiring an entire company. An objective for these decisions is to earn a satisfactory return on investment.

Capital budgeting decisions require careful analysis because they are usually the most difficult and risky decisions that managers make. These decisions are difficult because they require predicting events that will not occur until well into the future. Many of these predictions are tentative and potentially unreliable. Specifically, a capital budgeting decision is risky because (1) the outcome is uncertain, (2) large amounts of money are usually involved, (3) the investment involves a long-term commitment, and (4) the decision could be difficult or impossible to reverse, no matter how poor it turns out to be. Risk is especially high for investments in technology due to innovations and uncertainty.

Point: The nature of capital spending has changed with the business environment. Budgets for information technology have increased from about 25% of corporate capital spending 20 years ago to an estimated 35% today.

Managers use several methods to evaluate capital budgeting decisions. Nearly all of these methods involve predicting cash inflows and cash outflows of proposed investments, assessing the risk of and returns on those flows, and then choosing the investments to make. Management often restates future cash flows in terms of their present value. This approach applies the time value of money: A dollar today is worth more than a dollar tomorrow. Similarly, a dollar tomorrow is worth less than a dollar today. The process of restating future cash flows in terms of their present value is called *discounting*. The time value of money is important when evaluating capital investments, but managers sometimes apply evaluation methods that ignore present value. This section describes four methods for comparing alternative investments.

METHODS NOT USING TIME VALUE OF MONEY

All investments, whether they involve the purchase of a machine or another long-term asset, are expected to produce net cash flows. *Net cash flow* is cash inflows minus cash outflows. Sometimes managers perform simple analyses of the financial feasibility of an investment's net cash flow without using the time value of money. This section explains two of the most common methods in this category: (1) payback period and (2) accounting rate of return.

Payback Period

An investment's **payback period (PBP)** is the expected time period to recover the initial investment amount. Managers prefer investing in assets with shorter payback periods to reduce the risk of an unprofitable investment over the long run. Acquiring assets with short payback periods reduces a company's risk from potentially inaccurate long-term predictions of future cash flows.

P1 Compute payback period and describe its use.

Computing Payback Period with Even Cash Flows To illustrate use of the payback period for an investment with even cash flows, we look at data from FasTrac, a manufacturer of exercise equipment and supplies. (*Even cash flows* are cash flows that are the same each and every year; *uneven cash flows* are cash flows that are not all equal in amount.) FasTrac is considering several different capital investments, one of which is to purchase a machine to use in manufacturing a new product. This machine costs $16,000 and is expected to have an eight-year life with no salvage value. Management predicts this machine will produce 1,000 units of product each year and that the new product will be sold for $30 per unit. Exhibit 24.1 shows the expected annual net cash flows for this asset over its life as well as the expected annual revenues and expenses (including depreciation and income taxes) from investing in the machine.

EXHIBIT 24.1
Cash Flow Analysis

FASTRAC
Cash Flow Analysis—Machinery Investment
January 15, 2013

	Expected Accrual Income	Expected Net Cash Flow
Annual sales of new product	$30,000	$30,000
Deduct annual expenses		
Cost of materials, labor, and overhead (except depreciation)	15,500	15,500
Depreciation—Machinery	2,000	
Additional selling and administrative expenses	9,500	9,500
Annual pretax accrual income	3,000	
Income taxes (30%)	900	900
Annual net income	$ 2,100	
Annual net cash flow		**$ 4,100**

The amount of net cash flow from the machinery is computed by subtracting expected cash outflows from expected cash inflows. The cash flows column of Exhibit 24.1 excludes all noncash revenues and expenses. Depreciation is FasTrac's only noncash item. Alternatively, managers can adjust the projected net income for revenue and expense items that do not affect cash flows. For FasTrac, this means taking the $2,100 net income and adding back the $2,000 depreciation.

Point: Annual net cash flow in Exhibit 24.1 equals net income plus depreciation (a noncash expense).

The formula for computing the payback period of an investment that yields even net cash flows is in Exhibit 24.2.

EXHIBIT 24.2
Payback Period Formula with Even Cash Flows

$$\textbf{Payback period} = \frac{\textbf{Cost of investment}}{\textbf{Annual net cash flow}}$$

The payback period reflects the amount of time for the investment to generate enough net cash flow to return (or pay back) the cash initially invested to purchase it. FasTrac's payback period for this machine is just under four years:

$$\text{Payback period} = \frac{\$16{,}000}{\$4{,}100} = 3.9 \text{ years}$$

The initial investment is fully recovered in 3.9 years, or just before reaching the halfway point of this machine's useful life of eight years.

Example: If an alternative machine (with different technology) yields a payback period of 3.5 years, which one does a manager choose? Answer: The alternative (3.5 is less than 3.9).

Decision Insight

e-Payback Health-care providers are increasingly using electronic systems to improve their operations. With *e-charting,* doctor's orders and notes are saved electronically. Such systems allow for more personalized care plans, more efficient staffing, and reduced costs. Investments in such systems must be evaluated on the basis of payback periods and other financial measures. ■

Computing Payback Period with Uneven Cash Flows Computing the payback period in the prior section assumed even net cash flows. What happens if the net cash flows are uneven? In this case, the payback period is computed using the *cumulative total of net cash flows.* The word *cumulative* refers to the addition of each period's net cash flows as we progress through time. To illustrate, consider data for another investment that FasTrac is considering. This machine is predicted to generate uneven net cash flows over the next eight years. The relevant data and payback period computation are shown in Exhibit 24.3.

EXHIBIT 24.3

Payback Period Calculation with Uneven Cash Flows

Period*	Expected Net Cash Flows	Cumulative Net Cash Flows
Year 0	$(16,000)	$(16,000)
Year 1	3,000	(13,000)
Year 2	4,000	(9,000)
Year 3..........	4,000	(5,000)
Year 4	4,000	(1,000)
Year 5	5,000	4,000
Year 6	3,000	7,000
Year 7	2,000	9,000
Year 8	2,000	11,000
		Payback period = 4.2 years

* All cash inflows and outflows occur uniformly during the year.

Example: Find the payback period in Exhibit 24.3 if net cash flows for the first 4 years are:
Year 1 = $6,000; Year 2 = $5,000;
Year 3 = $4,000; Year 4 = $3,000.
Answer: 3.33 years

Year 0 refers to the period of initial investment in which the $16,000 cash outflow occurs at the end of year 0 to acquire the machinery. By the end of year 1, the cumulative net cash flow is reduced to $(13,000), computed as the $(16,000) initial cash outflow plus year 1's $3,000 cash inflow. This process continues throughout the asset's life. The cumulative net cash flow amount changes from negative to positive in year 5. Specifically, at the end of year 4, the cumulative net cash flow is $(1,000). As soon as FasTrac receives net cash inflow of $1,000 during the fifth year, it has fully recovered the investment. If we assume that cash flows are received uniformly *within* each year, receipt of the $1,000 occurs about one-fifth of the way through the year. This is computed as $1,000 divided by year 5's total net cash flow of $5,000, or 0.20. This yields a payback period of 4.2 years, computed as 4 years plus 0.20 of year 5.

Using the Payback Period Companies desire a short payback period to increase return and reduce risk. The more quickly a company receives cash, the sooner it is available for other uses and the less time it is at risk of loss. A shorter payback period also improves the company's ability to respond to unanticipated changes and lowers its risk of having to keep an unprofitable investment.

Payback period should never be the only consideration in evaluating investments. This is so because it ignores at least two important factors. First, it fails to reflect differences in the timing of net cash flows within the payback period. In Exhibit 24.3, FasTrac's net cash flows in the first five years were $3,000, $4,000, $4,000, $4,000, and $5,000. If another investment had predicted cash flows of $9,000, $3,000, $2,000, $1,800, and $1,000 in these five years, its payback period would also be 4.2 years, but this second alternative could be more desirable because it provides cash more quickly. The second important factor is that the payback period ignores *all* cash flows after the point where its costs are fully recovered. For example, one investment might pay back its cost in 3 years but stop producing cash after 4 years. A second investment might require 5 years to pay back its cost yet continue to produce net cash flows for another 15 years. A focus on only the payback period would mistakenly lead management to choose the first investment over the second.

Quick Check Answers — p. 1030

1. Capital budgeting is (*a*) concerned with analyzing alternative sources of capital, including debt and equity, (*b*) an important activity for companies when considering what assets to acquire or sell, or (*c*) best done by intuitive assessments of the value of assets and their usefulness.
2. Why are capital budgeting decisions often difficult?
3. A company is considering purchasing equipment costing $75,000. Future annual net cash flows from this equipment are $30,000, $25,000, $15,000, $10,000, and $5,000. The payback period is (*a*) 4 years, (*b*) 3.5 years, or (*c*) 3 years.
4. If depreciation is an expense, why is it added back to an investment's net income to compute the net cash flow from that investment?
5. If two investments have the same payback period, are they equally desirable? Explain.

Accounting Rate of Return

P2 Compute accounting rate of return and explain its use.

The **accounting rate of return,** also called *return on average investment,* is computed by dividing a project's after-tax net income by the average amount invested in it. To illustrate, we return to FasTrac's $16,000 machinery investment described in Exhibit 24.1. We first compute (1) the after-tax net income and (2) the average amount invested. The $2,100 after-tax net income is already available from Exhibit 24.1.

If a company uses straight-line depreciation, we can find the average amount invested by using the formula in Exhibit 24.4. Because FasTrac uses straight-line depreciation, its average amount invested for the eight years equals the sum of the book value at the beginning of the asset's investment period and the book value at the end of its investment period, divided by 2, as shown in Exhibit 24.4.

Point: Amount invested includes all costs that must be incurred to get the asset in its location and ready for use.

EXHIBIT 24.4

Computing Average Amount Invested under Straight-Line Depreciation

$$\underset{\text{(straight-line case only)}}{\textbf{Annual average investment}} = \frac{\textbf{Beginning book value + Ending book value}}{\textbf{2}}$$

$$= \frac{\$16{,}000 + \$0}{2} = \$8{,}000$$

If an investment has a salvage value, the average amount invested when using straight-line depreciation is computed as (Beginning book value + Salvage value)/2.

If a company uses a depreciation method other than straight-line, the calculation of average book value is more complicated. In this case, the book value of the asset is computed for *each year* of its life. The general formula for the annual average investment is shown in Exhibit 24.5.

EXHIBIT 24.5

General Formula for Average Amount Invested

$$\underset{\text{(general case)}}{\textbf{Annual average investment}} = \frac{\textbf{Sum of individual years' average book values}}{\textbf{Number of years of the planned investment}}$$

Once we determine the after-tax net income and the average amount invested, the accounting rate of return on the investment can be computed from the annual after-tax net income divided by the average amount invested, as shown in Exhibit 24.6.

EXHIBIT 24.6

Accounting Rate of Return Formula

$$\textbf{Accounting rate of return} = \frac{\textbf{Annual after-tax net income}}{\textbf{Annual average investment}}$$

This yields an accounting rate of return of 26.25% (\$2,100/\$8,000). FasTrac management must decide whether a 26.25% accounting rate of return is satisfactory. To make this decision, we must factor in the investment's risk. For instance, we cannot say an investment with a 26.25% return is preferred over one with a lower return unless we consider any differences in risk. Thus, an investment's return is satisfactory or unsatisfactory only when it is related to returns from other investments with similar lives and risk.

When accounting rate of return is used to choose among capital investments, the one with the least risk, the shortest payback period, and the highest return for the longest time period is often identified as the best. However, use of accounting rate of return to evaluate investment opportunities is limited because it bases the amount invested on book values (not predicted market values) in future periods. Accounting rate of return is also limited when an asset's net incomes are expected to vary from year to year. This requires computing the rate using *average* annual net incomes, yet this accounting rate of return fails to distinguish between two investments with the same average annual net income but different amounts of income in early years versus later years or different levels of income variability.

Quick Check Answers — p. 1030

6. The following data relate to a company's decision on whether to purchase a machine:

Cost	\$180,000
Salvage value	15,000
Annual after-tax net income	40,000

The machine's accounting rate of return, assuming the even receipt of its net cash flows during the year and use of straight-line depreciation, is *(a)* 22%, *(b)* 41%, or *(c)* 21%.

7. Is a 15% accounting rate of return for a machine a good rate?

METHODS USING TIME VALUE OF MONEY

Methods using Time Value of Money

This section describes two methods that help managers with capital budgeting decisions and that use the time value of money: (1) net present value and (2) internal rate of return. *(To apply these methods, you need a basic understanding of the concept of present value. An expanded explanation of present value concepts is in Appendix B near the end of the book. You can use the present value tables at the end of Appendix B to solve many of this chapter's assignments that use the time value of money.)*

Net Present Value

Net present value analysis applies the time value of money to future cash inflows and cash outflows so management can evaluate a project's benefits and costs at one point in time. Specifically, **net present value (NPV)** is computed by discounting the future net cash flows from the investment at the project's required rate of return and then subtracting the initial amount invested. A company's required return, often called its hurdle rate, is typically its **cost of capital,** which is the rate the company must pay to its long-term creditors and shareholders.

C1 Describe the selection of a hurdle rate for an investment.

To illustrate, let's return to FasTrac's proposed machinery purchase described in Exhibit 24.1. Does this machine provide a satisfactory return while recovering the amount invested? Recall that the machine requires a \$16,000 investment and is expected to provide \$4,100 annual net cash inflows for the next eight years. If we assume that net cash flows from this machine are received at each year-end and that FasTrac requires a 12% annual return, net present value can be computed as in Exhibit 24.7.

EXHIBIT 24.7

Net Present Value Calculation with Equal Cash Flows

	Net Cash Flows*	Present Value of 1 at 12%†	Present Value of Net Cash Flows
Year 1	$ 4,100	0.8929	$ 3,661
Year 2	4,100	0.7972	3,269
Year 3	4,100	0.7118	2,918
Year 4	4,100	0.6355	2,606
Year 5	4,100	0.5674	2,326
Year 6	4,100	0.5066	2,077
Year 7	4,100	0.4523	1,854
Year 8	4,100	0.4039	1,656
Totals	$32,800		20,367
Amount invested			**(16,000)**
Net present value			**$ 4,367**

* Cash flows occur at the end of each year.

† Present value of 1 factors are taken from Table B.1 in Appendix B.

P3 Compute net present value and describe its use.

The first number column of Exhibit 24.7 shows the annual net cash flows. Present value of 1 factors, also called *discount factors,* are shown in the second column. Taken from Table B.1 in Appendix B, they assume that net cash flows are received at each year-end. *(To simplify present value computations and for assignment material at the end of this chapter, we assume that net cash flows are received at each year-end.)* Annual net cash flows from the first column of Exhibit 24.7 are multiplied by the discount factors in the second column to give present values shown in the third column. The last three lines of this exhibit show the final NPV computations. The asset's $16,000 initial cost is deducted from the $20,367 total present value of all future net cash flows to give this asset's NPV of $4,367. The machine is thus expected to (1) recover its cost, (2) provide a 12% compounded return, and (3) generate $4,367 above cost. We summarize this analysis by saying the present value of this machine's future net cash flows to FasTrac exceeds the $16,000 investment by $4,367.

Point: The assumption of end-of-year cash flows simplifies computations and is common in practice.

Example: What is the net present value in Exhibit 24.7 if a 10% return is required? *Answer:* $5,873

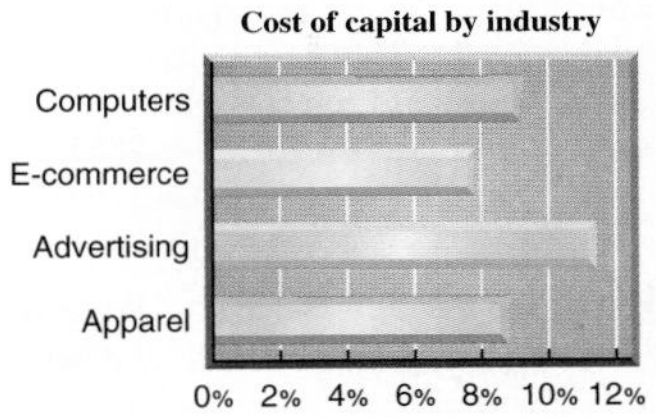

Net Present Value Decision Rule The decision rule in applying NPV is as follows: When an asset's expected cash flows are discounted at the required rate and yield a *positive* net present value, the asset should be acquired. This decision rule is reflected in the graphic below. When comparing several investment opportunities of about the same cost and same risk, we prefer the one with the highest positive net present value.

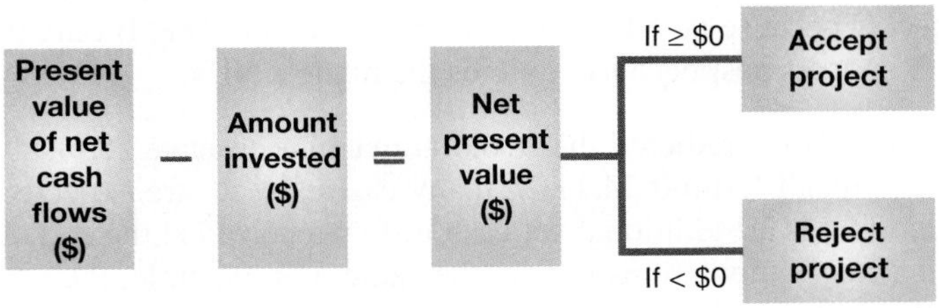

Simplifying Computations The computations in Exhibit 24.7 use separate present value of 1 factors for each of the eight years. Each year's net cash flow is multiplied by its present value of 1 factor to determine its present value. The individual present values for each of the eight net cash flows are added to give the asset's total present value. This computation can be simplified in two ways if annual net cash flows are equal in amount. A series of cash flows of equal dollar amount is called an **annuity.** One way is to add the eight annual present value of 1 factors for a total of 4.9676 and multiply this amount by the annual $4,100 net cash flow to get the $20,367 total present value of net cash flows.[1] A second simplification is to use a calculator

Example: Why does the net present value of an investment increase when a lower discount rate is used? *Answer:* The present value of net cash flows increases.

[1] We can simplify this computation using Table B.3, which gives the present value of 1 to be received periodically for a number of periods. To determine the present value of these eight annual receipts discounted at 12%, go down the 12% column of Table B.3 to the factor on the eighth line. This cumulative discount factor, also known as an *annuity* factor, is 4.9676. We then compute the $20,367 present value for these eight annual $4,100 receipts, computed as 4.9676 × $4,100.

with compound interest functions or a spreadsheet program. We show how to use Excel functions to compute net present value in this chapter's Appendix. Whatever procedure you use, it is important to understand the concepts behind these computations.

Decision Ethics

Systems Manager Top management adopts a policy requiring purchases in excess of $5,000 to be submitted with cash flow projections to the cost analyst for capital budget approval. As systems manager, you want to upgrade your computers at a $25,000 cost. You consider submitting several orders all under $5,000 to avoid the approval process. You believe the computers will increase profits and wish to avoid a delay. What do you do? ■ [Answer—p. 1030]

Uneven Cash Flows Net present value analysis can also be applied when net cash flows are uneven (unequal). To illustrate, assume that FasTrac can choose only one capital investment from among projects A, B, and C. Each project requires the same $12,000 initial investment. Future net cash flows for each project are shown in the first three number columns of Exhibit 24.8.

EXHIBIT 24.8

Net Present Value Calculation with Uneven Cash Flows

	Net Cash Flows			Present Value of 1 at 10%	Present Value of Net Cash Flows		
	A	B	C		A	B	C
Year 1	$ 5,000	$ 8,000	$ 1,000	0.9091	$ 4,546	$ 7,273	$ 909
Year 2	5,000	5,000	5,000	0.8264	4,132	4,132	4,132
Year 3	5,000	2,000	9,000	0.7513	3,757	1,503	6,762
Totals	$15,000	$15,000	$15,000		12,435	12,908	11,803
Amount invested					(12,000)	(12,000)	(12,000)
Net present value					**$ 435**	**$ 908**	**$ (197)**

Example: If 12% is the required return in Exhibit 24.8, which project is preferred? *Answer:* Project B. Net present values are: A = $10; B = $553; C = $(715).

Example: Will the rankings of Projects A, B, and C change with the use of different discount rates, assuming the same rate is used for all projects? *Answer:* No; only the NPV amounts will change.

The three projects in Exhibit 24.8 have the same expected total net cash flows of $15,000. Project A is expected to produce equal amounts of $5,000 each year. Project B is expected to produce a larger amount in the first year. Project C is expected to produce a larger amount in the third year. The fourth column of Exhibit 24.8 shows the present value of 1 factors from Table B.1 assuming 10% required return.

Computations in the right-most columns show that Project A has a $435 positive NPV. Project B has the largest NPV of $908 because it brings in cash more quickly. Project C has a $(197) *negative* NPV because its larger cash inflows are delayed. If FasTrac requires a 10% return, it should reject Project C because its NPV implies a return *under* 10%. If only one project can be accepted, project B appears best because it yields the highest NPV.

Point: Projects with higher cash flows in earlier years generally yield higher net present values.

Salvage Value FasTrac predicted the $16,000 machine to have zero salvage value at the end of its useful life (recall Exhibit 24.1). In many cases, assets are expected to have salvage values. If so, this amount is an additional net cash inflow received at the end of the final year of the asset's life. All other computations remain the same. For example, the net present value of the $16,000 investment that yields $4,100 of net cash flows for eight years is $4,367, as shown in Exhibit 24.7. If that machine is expected to have a $1,500 salvage value at the end of its eight-year life, the present value of this salvage amount is $606 (computed as $1,500 × 0.4039). The net present value of the machine, including the present value of its expected salvage amount, is $4,973 (computed as $4,367 + $606).

Accelerated Depreciation Depreciation computations also affect net present value analysis. FasTrac computes depreciation using the straight-line method. Accelerated depreciation is also commonly used, especially for income tax reports. Accelerated depreciation produces larger depreciation deductions in the early years of an asset's life and smaller deductions in later years. This pattern results in smaller income tax payments in early years and larger payments in later years. Accelerated depreciation does not change the basics of a present value analysis, but it can change the result. Using accelerated depreciation for tax reporting affects the NPV of an asset's cash flows because it produces larger net cash inflows in the early years

Point: Tax savings from depreciation is called: **depreciation tax shield.**

of the asset's life and smaller ones in later years. Being able to use accelerated depreciation for tax reporting always makes an investment more desirable because early cash flows are more valuable than later ones.

Use of Net Present Value In deciding whether to proceed with a capital investment project, we approve the proposal if the NPV is positive but reject it if the NPV is negative. When considering several projects of similar investment amounts and risk levels, we can compare the different projects' NPVs and rank them on the basis of their NPVs. However, if the amount invested differs substantially across projects, the NPV is of limited value for comparison purposes. One means to compare projects, especially when a company cannot fund all positive net present value projects, is to use the **profitability index,** which is computed as:

Example: When is it appropriate to use different discount rates for different projects? *Answer:* When risk levels are different.

$$\textbf{Profitability index} = \frac{\textbf{Net present value of cash flows}}{\textbf{Investment}}$$

A higher profitability index suggests a more desirable project. To illustrate, suppose that Project X requires a $1 million investment and provides a $100,000 NPV. Project Y requires an investment of only $100,000 and returns a $75,000 NPV. Ranking on the basis of NPV puts Project X ahead of Y, yet X's profitability index is only 0.10 ($100,000/$1,000,000) whereas Y's profitability index is 0.75. We must also remember that when reviewing projects with different risks, we computed the NPV of individual projects using different discount rates. The higher the risk, the higher the discount rate.

Inflation Large price-level increases should be considered in NPV analyses. Hurdle rates should already include inflation forecasts. Net cash flows can be adjusted for inflation by using *future value* computations. For example, if the expected net cash inflow in year 1 is $4,100 and 5% inflation is expected, then the expected net cash inflow in year 2 is $4,305, computed as $4,100 × 1.05 (1.05 is the future value of $1 (Table B.2) for 1 period with a 5% rate).

Internal Rate of Return

P4 Compute internal rate of return and explain its use.

Another means to evaluate capital investments is to use the **internal rate of return (IRR),** which equals the rate that yields an NPV of zero for an investment. This means that if we compute the total present value of a project's net cash flows using the IRR as the discount rate and then subtract the initial investment from this total present value, we get a zero NPV.

To illustrate, we use the data for FasTrac's Project A from Exhibit 24.8 to compute its IRR. Exhibit 24.9 shows the two-step process in computing IRR.

EXHIBIT 24.9

Computing Internal Rate of Return (with even cash flows)

Step 1: Compute the present value factor for the investment project.

$$\textbf{Present value factor} = \frac{\textbf{Amount invested}}{\textbf{Net cash flows}} = \frac{\$12{,}000}{\$5{,}000} = 2.4000$$

Step 2: Identify the discount rate (IRR) yielding the present value factor

Search Table B.3 for a present value factor of 2.4000 in the three-year row (equaling the 3-year project duration). The 12% discount rate yields a present value factor of 2.4018. This implies that the IRR is approximately 12%.*

* Since the present value factor of 2.4000 is not exactly equal to the 12% factor of 2.4018, we can more precisely estimate the IRR as follows:

Discount rate	Present Value Factor from Table B.3
12%	2.4018
15%	2.2832
	0.1186 = difference

$$\text{Then, IRR} = 12\% + \left[(15\% - 12\%) \times \frac{2.4018 - 2.4000}{0.1186}\right] = \underline{\underline{12.05\%}}$$

When cash flows are equal, as with Project A, we compute the present value factor (as shown in Exhibit 24.9) by dividing the initial investment by its annual net cash flows. We then use an annuity table to determine the discount rate equal to this present value factor. For FasTrac's Project A, we look across the three-period row of Table B.3 and find that the discount rate corresponding to the present value factor of 2.4000 roughly equals the 2.4018 value for the 12% rate. This row is reproduced here:

Present Value of an Annuity of 1 for Three Periods					
	Discount Rate				
Periods	1%	5%	10%	12%	15%
3	2.9410	2.7232	2.4869	2.4018	2.2832

The 12% rate is the Project's IRR. A more precise IRR estimate can be computed following the procedure shown in the note to Exhibit 24.9. Spreadsheet software and calculators can also compute this IRR. We show how to use an Excel function to compute IRR in this chapter's appendix.

Uneven Cash Flows If net cash flows are uneven, we must use trial and error to compute the IRR. We do this by selecting any reasonable discount rate and computing the NPV. If the amount is positive (negative), we recompute the NPV using a higher (lower) discount rate. We continue these steps until we reach a point where two consecutive computations result in NPVs having different signs (positive and negative). Because the NPV is zero using IRR, we know that the IRR lies between these two discount rates. We can then estimate its value. Spreadsheet programs and calculators can also do these computations.

Decision Insight

CEO-IRR A survey reported that 41% of top managers would reject a project with an internal rate of return *above* the cost of capital if the project would cause the firm to miss its earnings forecast. The roles of benchmarks and manager compensation plans must be considered in capital budgeting decisions. ■

Use of Internal Rate of Return When we use the IRR to evaluate a project, we compare it to a predetermined **hurdle rate,** which is a minimum acceptable rate of return and is applied as follows:

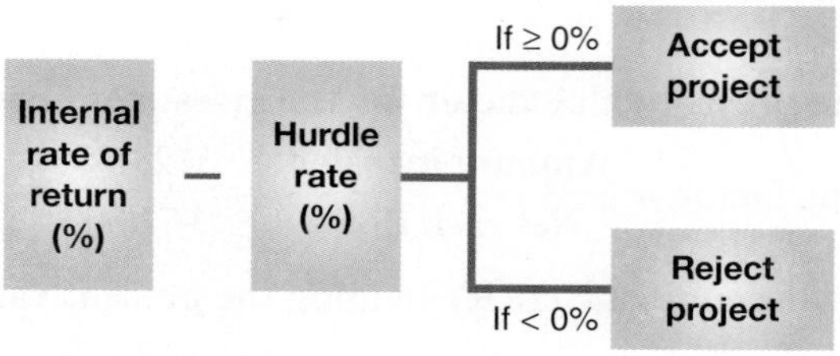

Example: How does management evaluate the risk of an investment? *Answer:* It must assess the uncertainty of future cash flows.

Top management selects the hurdle rate to use in evaluating capital investments. Financial formulas aid in this selection, but the choice of a minimum rate is subjective and left to management. For projects financed from borrowed funds, the hurdle rate must exceed the interest rate paid on these funds. The return on an investment must cover its interest and provide an additional profit to reward the company for its risk. For instance, if money is borrowed at 10%, an average risk investment often requires an after-tax return of 15% (or 5% above the borrowing rate). Remember that lower-risk investments require a lower rate of return compared with higher-risk investments.

If the project is internally financed, the hurdle rate is often based on actual returns from comparable projects. If the IRR is higher than the hurdle rate, the project is accepted. Multiple projects are often ranked by the extent to which their IRR exceeds the hurdle rate. The hurdle rate for individual projects is often different, depending on the risk involved. IRR is not subject to the limitations of NPV when comparing projects with different amounts invested because the IRR is expressed as a percent rather than as an absolute dollar value in NPV.

Decision Maker

Entrepreneur You are developing a new product and you use a 12% discount rate to compute its NPV. Your banker, from whom you hope to obtain a loan, expresses concern that your discount rate is too low. How do you respond? ■ [Answer—p. 1030]

Comparison of Capital Budgeting Methods

We explained four methods that managers use to evaluate capital investment projects. How do these methods compare with each other? Exhibit 24.10 addresses that question. Neither the payback period nor the accounting rate of return considers the time value of money. On the other hand, both the net present value and the internal rate of return do.

EXHIBIT 24.10

Comparing Capital Budgeting Methods

	Payback Period	Accounting Rate of Return	Net Present Value	Internal Rate of Return
Measurement basis	• Cash flows	• Accrual income	• Cash flows • Profitability	• Cash flows • Profitability
Measurement unit	• Years	• Percent	• Dollars	• Percent
Strengths	• Easy to understand • Allows comparison of projects	• Easy to understand • Allows comparison of projects	• Reflects time value of money • Reflects varying risks over project's life	• Reflects time value of money • Allows comparisons of dissimilar projects
Limitations	• Ignores time value of money • Ignores cash flows after payback period	• Ignores time value of money • Ignores annual rates over life of project	• Difficult to compare dissimilar projects	• Ignores varying risks over life of project

The payback period is probably the simplest method. It gives managers an estimate of how soon they will recover their initial investment. Managers sometimes use this method when they have limited cash to invest and a number of projects to choose from. The accounting rate of return yields a percent measure computed using accrual income instead of cash flows. The accounting rate of return is an average rate for the entire investment period. Net present value considers all estimated net cash flows for the project's expected life. It can be applied to even and uneven cash flows and can reflect changes in the level of risk over a project's life. Since it yields a dollar measure, comparing projects of unequal sizes is more difficult. The profitability index, based on each project's net present value, can be used in this case. The internal rate of return considers all cash flows from a project. It is readily computed when the cash flows are even but requires some trial and error or use of a computer estimation when cash flows are uneven. Because the IRR is a percent measure, it is readily used to compare projects with different investment amounts. However, IRR does not reflect changes in risk over a project's life.

Decision Insight

And the Winner Is . . . How do we choose among the methods for evaluating capital investments? Management surveys consistently show the internal rate of return (IRR) as the most popular method followed by the payback period and net present value (NPV). Few companies use the accounting rate of return (ARR), but nearly all use more than one method. ■

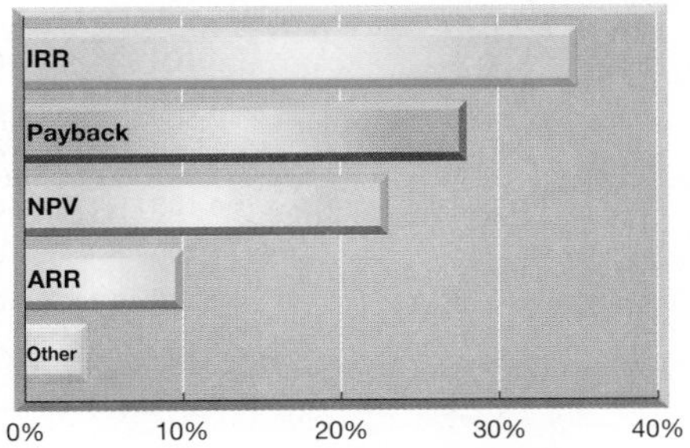

Company Usage of Capital Budgeting Methods

Quick Check

Answers — p. 1031

8. A company can invest in only one of two projects, A or B. Each project requires a $20,000 investment and is expected to generate end-of-period, annual cash flows as follows:

	Year 1	Year 2	Year 3	Total
Project A	$12,000	$8,500	$4,000	$24,500
Project B	4,500	8,500	13,000	26,000

Assuming a discount rate of 10%, which project has the higher net present value?

9. Two investment alternatives are expected to generate annual cash flows with the same net present value (assuming the same discount rate applied to each). Using this information, can you conclude that the two alternatives are equally desirable?

10. When two investment alternatives have the same total expected cash flows but differ in the timing of those flows, which method of evaluating those investments is superior, (*a*) accounting rate of return or (*b*) net present value?

GLOBAL VIEW

Siemens AG is a global electrical engineering and electronics company headquartered in Germany. Recently, the company announced plans to invest £80 million to build a wind turbine plant in the United Kingdom. Net present value analyses support such decisions. In this case, Siemens foresees strong future cash flows based on increased demand for clean sources of energy, like wind power.

Decision Analysis — Break-Even Time

A1 Analyze a capital investment project using break-even time.

The first section of this chapter explained several methods to evaluate capital investments. Break-even time of an investment project is a variation of the payback period method that overcomes the limitation of not using the time value of money. **Break-even time (BET)** is a time-based measure used to evaluate a capital investment's acceptability. Its computation yields a measure of expected time, reflecting the time period until the *present value* of the net cash flows from an investment equals the initial cost of the investment. In basic terms, break-even time is computed by restating future cash flows in terms of present values and then determining the payback period using these present values.

To illustrate, we return to the FasTrac case described in Exhibit 24.1 involving a $16,000 investment in machinery. The annual net cash flows from this investment are projected at $4,100 for eight years. Exhibit 24.11 shows the computation of break-even time for this investment decision.

EXHIBIT 24.11

Break-Even Time Analysis*

Year	Cash Flows	Present Value of 1 at 10%	Present Value of Cash Flows	Cumulative Present Value of Cash Flows
0	$(16,000)	1.0000	$(16,000)	$(16,000)
1	4,100	0.9091	3,727	(12,273)
2	4,100	0.8264	3,388	(8,885)
3	4,100	0.7513	3,080	(5,805)
4	4,100	0.6830	2,800	(3,005)
5	4,100	0.6209	2,546	**(459)**
6	4,100	0.5645	2,314	**1,855**
7	4,100	0.5132	2,104	3,959
8	4,100	0.4665	1,913	5,872

* The time of analysis is the start of year 1 (same as end of year 0). All cash flows occur at the end of each year.

The right-most column of this exhibit shows that break-even time is between 5 and 6 years, or about 5.2 years—also see margin graph (where the line crosses the zero point). This is the time the project takes to break even after considering the time value of money (recall that the payback period computed without considering the time value of money was 3.9 years). We interpret this as cash flows earned after 5.2 years contribute to a positive net present value that, in this case, eventually amounts to $5,872.

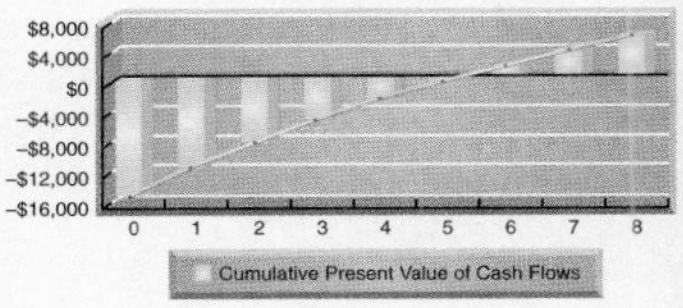

Break-even time is a useful measure for managers because it identifies the point in time when they can expect the cash flows to begin to yield net positive returns. Managers expect a positive net present value from an investment if break-even time is less than the investment's estimated life. The method allows managers to compare and rank alternative investments, giving the project with the shortest break-even time the highest rank.

Decision Maker

Investment Manager Management asks you, the investment manager, to evaluate three alternative investments. Investment recovery time is crucial because cash is scarce. The time value of money is also important. Which capital budgeting method(s) do you use to assess the investments? ■ [Answer—p. 1030]

DEMONSTRATION PROBLEM

White Company can invest in one of two projects, TD1 or TD2. Each project requires an initial investment of $101,250 and produces the year-end cash inflows shown in the following table.

	Net Cash Flows	
	TD1	TD2
Year 1	$ 20,000	$ 40,000
Year 2	30,000	40,000
Year 3	70,000	40,000
Totals	$120,000	$120,000

Required

1. Compute the payback period for both projects. Which project has the shortest payback period?
2. Assume that the company requires a 10% return from its investments. Compute the net present value of each project.
3. Drawing on your answers to parts 1 and 2, determine which project, if any, should be chosen.
4. Compute the internal rate of return for project TD2. Based on its internal rate of return, should project TD2 be chosen?

PLANNING THE SOLUTION

- Compute the payback period for the series of unequal cash flows (Project TD1) and for the series of equal cash flows (Project TD2).
- Compute White Company's net present value of each investment using a 10% discount rate.
- Use the payback and net present value rules to determine which project, if any, should be selected.
- Compute the internal rate of return for the series of equal cash flows (Project TD2) and determine whether that internal rate of return is greater than the company's 10% discount rate.

SOLUTION TO DEMONSTRATION PROBLEM

1. The payback period for a project with a series of equal cash flows is computed as follows:

$$\text{Payback period} = \frac{\text{Cost of investment}}{\text{Annual net cash flow}}$$

For project TD2, the payback period equals 2.53 (rounded), computed as $101,250/$40,000. This means that the company expects to recover its investment in Project TD2 after approximately two and one-half years of its three-year life.

Next, determining the payback period for a series of unequal cash flows (as in Project TD1) requires us to compute the cumulative net cash flows from the project at the end of each year. Assuming the cash outflow for Project TD1 occurs at the end of year 0, and cash inflows occur continuously over years 1, 2, and 3, the payback period calculation follows.

TD1:

Period	Expected Net Cash Flows	Cumulative Net Cash Flows
0	$(101,250)	$(101,250)
1	20,000	(81,250)
2	30,000	(51,250)
3	70,000	18,750

The cumulative net cash flow for Project TD1 changes from negative to positive in year 3. As cash flows are received continuously, the point at which the company has recovered its investment into year 3 is 0.27 (rounded), computed as $18,750/$70,000. This means that the payback period for TD1 is 2.27 years, computed as 2 years plus 0.27 of year 3.

2. TD1:

	Net Cash Flows	Present Value of 1 at 10%	Present Value of Net Cash Flows
Year 1	$ 20,000	0.9091	$ 18,182
Year 2	30,000	0.8264	24,792
Year 3	70,000	0.7513	52,591
Totals	$120,000		95,565
Amount invested			(101,250)
Net present value			**$ (5,685)**

TD2:

	Net Cash Flows	Present Value of 1 at 10%	Present Value of Net Cash Flows
Year 1	$ 40,000	0.9091	$ 36,364
Year 2	40,000	0.8264	33,056
Year 3	40,000	0.7513	30,052
Totals	$120,000		99,472
Amount invested			(101,250)
Net present value			**$ (1,778)**

3. White Company should not invest in either project. Both are expected to yield a negative net present value, and it should invest only in positive net present value projects. Although the company expects to recover its investment from both projects before the end of these projects' useful lives, the projects are not acceptable after considering the time value of money.

4. To compute Project TD2's internal rate of return, we first compute a present value factor as follows:

$$\text{Present value factor} = \frac{\text{Amount invested}}{\text{Net cash flow}} = \$101{,}250/\$40{,}000 = 2.5313 \text{ (rounded)}$$

Then, we search Table B.3 for the discount rate that corresponds to the present value factor of 2.5313 for three periods. From Table B.3, this discount rate is 9%. Project TD2's internal rate of return of 9% is below this company's hurdle rate of 10%. Thus, Project TD2 should *not* be chosen.

APPENDIX

Using Excel to Compute Net Present Value and Internal Rate of Return

24A

Computing present values and internal rates of return for projects with uneven cash flows is tedious and error prone. These calculations can be performed simply and accurately by using functions built into Excel. Many calculators and other types of spreadsheet software can perform them too. To illustrate, consider FasTrac, a company that is considering investing in a new machine with the expected cash flows shown in the following spreadsheet. Cash outflows are entered as negative numbers, and cash inflows are entered as positive numbers. Assume FasTrac requires a 12% annual return, entered as 0.12 in cell C1.

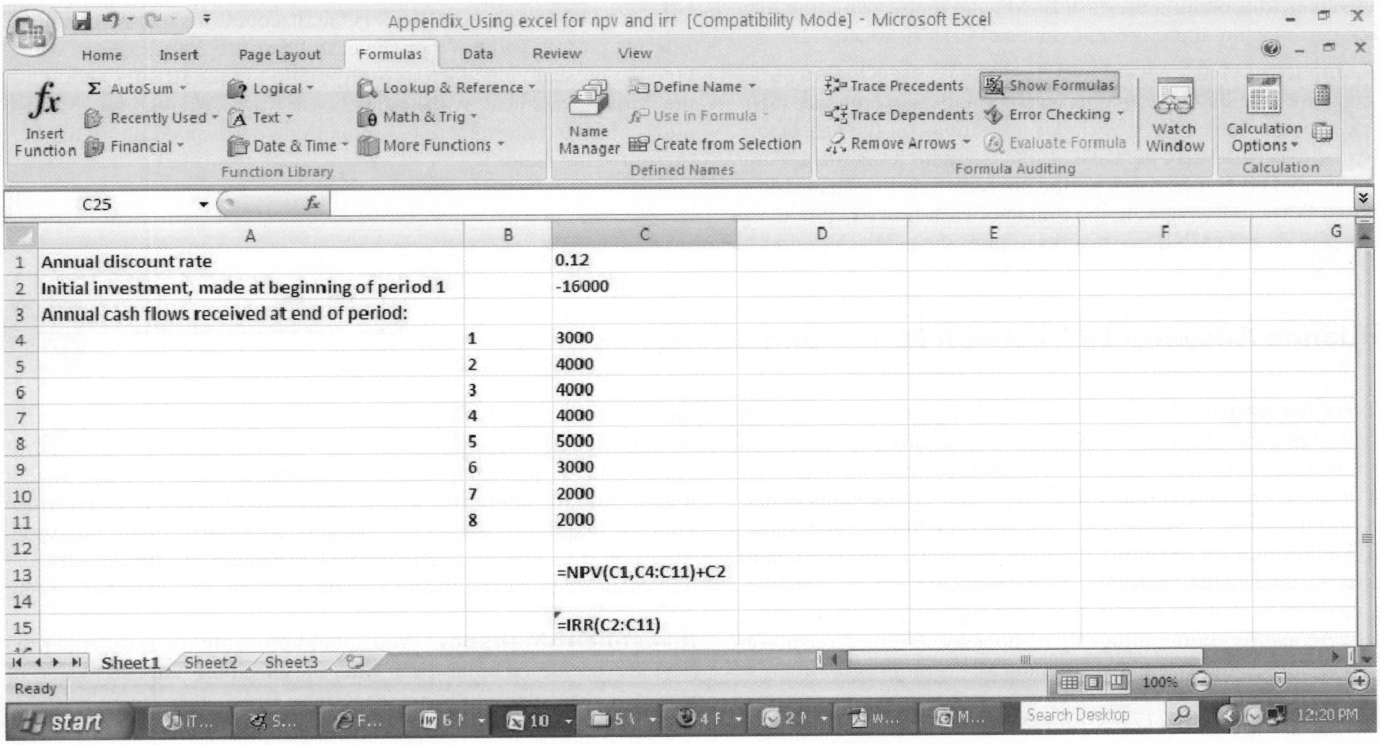

To compute the net present value of this project, the following is entered into cell C13:

=NPV(C1,C4:C11)+C2.

This instructs Excel to use its NPV function to compute the present value of the cash flows in cells C4 through C11, using the discount rate in cell C1, and then add the amount of the (negative) initial investment. For this stream of cash flows and a discount rate of 12%, the net present value is $1,326.03.

To compute the internal rate of return for this project, the following is entered into cell C15:

=IRR(C2:C11).

This instructs Excel to use its IRR function to compute the internal rate of return of the cash flows in cells C2 through C11. By default, Excel starts with a guess of 10%, and then uses trial and error to find the IRR. The IRR equals 14% for this project.

Summary

C1 Describe the selection of a hurdle rate for an investment. Top management should select the hurdle (discount) rate to use in evaluating capital investments. The required hurdle rate should be at least higher than the interest rate on money borrowed because the return on investment must cover the interest and provide an additional profit to reward the company for risk. A company must rely on relevant costs pertaining to alternative courses of action rather than historical costs. Out-of-pocket expenses and opportunity costs are relevant because these are avoidable; sunk costs are irrelevant because they result from past decisions and are therefore unavoidable. Managers must also consider the relevant benefits associated with alternative decisions.

A1 Analyze a capital investment project using break-even time. Break-even time (BET) is a method for evaluating capital investments by restating future cash flows in terms of their present values (discounting the cash flows) and then calculating the payback period using these present values of cash flows.

P1 Compute payback period and describe its use. One way to compare potential investments is to compute and compare their payback periods. The payback period is an estimate of the expected time before the cumulative net cash inflow from the investment equals its initial cost. A payback period analysis fails to reflect risk of the cash flows, differences in the timing of cash flows within the payback period, and cash flows that occur after the payback period.

P2 Compute accounting rate of return and explain its use. A project's accounting rate of return is computed by dividing the expected annual after-tax net income by the average amount of investment in the project. When the net cash flows are received evenly throughout each period and straight-line depreciation is used, the average investment is computed as the average of the investment's initial book value and its salvage value.

P3 Compute net present value and describe its use. An investment's net present value is determined by predicting the future cash flows it is expected to generate, discounting them at a rate that represents an acceptable return, and then by subtracting the investment's initial cost from the sum of the present values. This technique can deal with any pattern of expected cash flows and applies a superior concept of return on investment.

P4 Compute internal rate of return and explain its use. The internal rate of return (IRR) is the discount rate that results in a zero net present value. When the cash flows are equal, we can compute the present value factor corresponding to the IRR by dividing the initial investment by the annual cash flows. We then use the annuity tables to determine the discount rate corresponding to this present value factor.

Guidance Answers to Decision Maker and Decision Ethics

Systems Manager Your dilemma is whether to abide by rules designed to prevent abuse or to bend them to acquire an investment that you believe will benefit the firm. You should not pursue the latter action because breaking up the order into small components is dishonest and there are consequences of being caught at a later stage. Develop a proposal for the entire package and then do all you can to expedite its processing, particularly by pointing out its benefits. When faced with controls that are not working, there is rarely a reason to overcome its shortcomings by dishonesty. A direct assault on those limitations is more sensible and ethical.

Entrepreneur The banker is probably concerned because new products are risky and should therefore be evaluated using a higher rate of return. You should conduct a thorough technical analysis and obtain detailed market data and information about any similar products available in the market. These factors might provide sufficient information to support the use of a lower return. You must convince yourself that the risk level is consistent with the discount rate used. You should also be confident that your company has the capacity and the resources to handle the new product.

Investment Manager You should probably focus on either the payback period or break-even time because both the time value of money and recovery time are important. Break-even time method is superior because it accounts for the time value of money, which is an important consideration in this decision.

Guidance Answers to Quick Checks

1. *b*
2. A capital budgeting decision is difficult because (1) the outcome is uncertain, (2) large amounts of money are usually involved, (3) a long-term commitment is required, and (4) the decision could be difficult or impossible to reverse.
3. *b*
4. Depreciation expense is subtracted from revenues in computing net income but does not use cash and should be added back to net income to compute net cash flows.
5. Not necessarily. One investment can continue to generate cash flows beyond the payback period for a longer time period than the other. The timing of their cash flows within the payback period also can differ.
6. *b*; Annual average investment = ($180,000 + $15,000)/2 = $97,500
   Accounting rate of return = $40,000/$97,500 = 41%
7. For this determination, we need to compare it to the returns expected from alternative investments with similar risk.

8. Project A has the higher net present value as follows:

		Project A		Project B	
Year	Present Value of I at 10%	Net Cash Flows	Present Value of Net Cash Flows	Net Cash Flows	Present Value of Net Cash Flows
1	0.9091	$12,000	$10,909	$ 4,500	$ 4,091
2	0.8264	8,500	7,024	8,500	7,024
3	0.7513	4,000	3,005	13,000	9,767
Totals		$24,500	$20,938	$26,000	$20,882
Amount invested			(20,000)		(20,000)
Net present value			**$ 938**		**$ 882**

9. No, the information is too limited to draw that conclusion. For example, one investment could be riskier than the other, or one could require a substantially larger initial investment.

10. *b*

Key Terms

Accounting rate of return (p. 1019)
Annuity (p. 1021)
Break-even time (BET) (p. 1026)
Capital budgeting (p. 1016)
Cost of capital (p. 1020)
Hurdle rate (p. 1024)
Internal rate of return (IRR) (p. 1023)
Net present value (NPV) (p. 1020)
Payback period (PBP) (p. 1016)
Profitability index (p. 1023)

Multiple Choice Quiz

Answers on p. 1042 mhhe.com/wildFINMAN5e

Additional Quiz Questions are available at the book's Website.

1. The minimum acceptable rate of return for an investment decision is called the
a. Hurdle rate of return.
b. Payback rate of return.
c. Internal rate of return.
d. Average rate of return.
e. Maximum rate of return.

2. A corporation is considering the purchase of new equipment costing $90,000. The projected after-tax annual net income from the equipment is $3,600, after deducting $30,000 depreciation. Assume that revenue is to be received at each year-end, and the machine has a useful life of three years with zero salvage value. Management requires a 12% return on its investments. What is the net present value of this machine?
a. $ 60,444
b. $ 80,700
c. $(88,560)
d. $ 90,000
e. $ (9,300)

3. A disadvantage of using the payback period to compare investment alternatives is that it
a. Ignores cash flows beyond the payback period.
b. Cannot be used to compare alternatives with different initial investments.
c. Cannot be used when cash flows are not uniform.
d. Involves the time value of money.
e. Cannot be used if a company records depreciation.

4. A company is considering the purchase of equipment for $270,000. Projected annual cash inflow from this equipment is $61,200 per year. The payback period is:
a. 0.2 years
b. 5.0 years

5. A company buys a machine for $180,000 that has an expected life of nine years and no salvage value. The company expects an annual net income (after taxes of 30%) of $8,550. What is the accounting rate of return?
a. 4.75%
b. 42.75%
c. 2.85%
d. 9.50%
e. 6.65%

Icon denotes assignments that involve decision making.

Discussion Questions

1. Capital budgeting decisions require careful analysis because they are generally the ________ ________ and ________ decisions that management faces.
2. What is capital budgeting?
3. Identify four reasons that capital budgeting decisions by managers are risky.
4. Identify two disadvantages of using the payback period for comparing investments.
5. Why is an investment more attractive to management if it has a shorter payback period?
6. What is the average amount invested in a machine during its predicted five-year life if it costs $200,000 and has a $20,000 salvage value? Assume that net income is received evenly throughout each year and straight-line depreciation is used.
7. If the present value of the expected net cash flows from a machine, discounted at 10%, exceeds the amount to be invested, what can you say about the investment's expected rate of return? What can you say about the expected rate of return if the present value of the net cash flows, discounted at 10%, is less than the investment amount?
8. Why is the present value of $100 that you expect to receive one year from today worth less than $100 received today? What is the present value of $100 that you expect to receive one year from today, discounted at 12%?
9. Why should managers set the required rate of return higher than the rate at which money can be borrowed when making a typical capital budgeting decision?
10. Polaris managers must select depreciation methods. Why does the use of the accelerated depreciation method (instead of straight line) for income tax reporting increase an investment's value?
11. The management of Piaggio is planning to invest in a new companywide computerized inventory tracking system. What makes this potential investment risky?
12. The management of Arctic Cat is planning to acquire new equipment to manufacture snowmobiles. What are some of the costs and benefits that would be included in Arctic Cat's analysis?
13. KTM is considering expanding a store. Identify three methods management can use to evaluate whether to expand.

Polaris

PIAGGIO

Arctic Cat

KTM

connect

QUICK STUDY

QS 24-1
Payback period P1

Freeman Brothers Co. is considering an investment that requires immediate payment of $27,000 and provides expected cash inflows of $9,000 annually for four years. What is the investment's payback period?

QS 24-2
Analyzing payback periods P1

Park Company is considering two alternative investments. The payback period is 3.5 years for investment A and 4 years for investment B. (1) If management relies on the payback period, which investment is preferred? (2) Why might Park's analysis of these two alternatives lead to the selection of B over A?

QS 24-3
Computation of accounting rate of return P2

Peng Company is considering an investment expected to generate an average net income after taxes of $1,950 for three years. The investment costs $45,000 and has an estimated $6,000 salvage value. Compute the accounting rate of return for this investment; assume the company uses straight-line depreciation. Hint: Use the formula in Exhibit 24.5 when computing the average annual investment.

QS 24-4
Computation of net present value P3

If Quail Company invests $50,000 today, it can expect to receive $10,000 at the end of each year for the next seven years, plus an extra $6,000 at the end of the seventh year. What is the net present value of this investment assuming a required 10% return on investments?

QS 24-5
Profitability index P3

Yokam Company is considering two alternative projects. Project 1 requires an initial investment of $400,000 and has a net present value of cash flows of $1,100,000. Project 2 requires an initial investment of $3,500,000 and has a net present value of cash flows of $2,500,000. Compute the profitability index for each project. Based on the profitability index, which project should the company prefer? Explain.

QS 24-6
Internal rate of return P4

A company is considering investing in a new machine that requires a cash payment of $47,946 today. The machine will generate annual cash flows of $21,000 for the next three years. What is the internal rate of return if the company buys this machine?

QS 24-7
Net present value analysis P3

Tinto Company is planning to invest in a project at a cost of $135,000. This project has the following expected cash flows over its three-year life: Year 1, $45,000; Year 2, $52,000; and Year 3, $78,000. Management requires a 10% rate of return on its investments. Compute the net present value of this investment.

QS 24-8
Computation of break-even time
A1

Heels, a shoe manufacturer, is evaluating the costs and benefits of new equipment that would custom fit each pair of athletic shoes. The customer would have his or her foot scanned by digital computer equipment; this information would be used to cut the raw materials to provide the customer a perfect fit. The new equipment costs $90,000 and is expected to generate an additional $35,000 in cash flows for five years. A bank will make a $90,000 loan to the company at a 10% interest rate for this equipment's purchase. Use the following table to determine the break-even time for this equipment. (Round the present value of cash flows to the nearest dollar.)

Year	Cash Flows*	Present Value of 1 at 10%	Present Value of Cash Flows	Cumulative Present Value of Cash Flows
0	$(90,000)	1.0000		
1	35,000	0.9091		
2	35,000	0.8264		
3	35,000	0.7513		
4	35,000	0.6830		
5	35,000	0.6209		

* All cash flows occur at year-end.

QS 24-9
Capital budgeting methods
P1 P3

Siemens AG invests €80 million to build a manufacturing plant to build wind turbines. The company predicts net cash flows of €16 million per year for the next 8 years. Assume the company requires an 8% rate of return from its investments. (1) What is the payback period of this investment? (2) What is the net present value of this investment?

connect

EXERCISES

Exercise 24-1
Payback period computation; uneven cash flows P1

Beyer Company is considering the purchase of an asset for $180,000. It is expected to produce the following net cash flows. The cash flows occur evenly throughout each year. Compute the payback period for this investment (round years to two decimals).

	Year 1	Year 2	Year 3	Year 4	Year 5	Total
Net cash flows	$60,000	$40,000	$70,000	$125,000	$35,000	$330,000

Check 3.08 years

Exercise 24-2
Payback period computation; declining-balance depreciation
P1

A machine can be purchased for $150,000 and used for 5 years, yielding the following net incomes. In projecting net incomes, double-declining balance depreciation is applied, using a 5-year life and a zero salvage value. Compute the machine's payback period (ignore taxes). (Round the payback period to three decimals.)

	Year 1	Year 2	Year 3	Year 4	Year 5
Net incomes	$10,000	$25,000	$50,000	$37,500	$100,000

Check 2.265 years

Exercise 24-3
Payback period computation; even cash flows
P1

Compute the payback period for each of these two separate investments (round the payback period to two decimals):

a. A new operating system for an existing machine is expected to cost $520,000 and have a useful life of six years. The system yields an incremental after-tax income of $150,000 each year after deducting its straight-line depreciation. The predicted salvage value of the system is $10,000.

b. A machine costs $380,000, has a $20,000 salvage value, is expected to last eight years, and will generate an after-tax income of $60,000 per year after straight-line depreciation.

Exercise 24-4
Accounting rate of return P2

A machine costs $700,000 and is expected to yield an after-tax net income of $52,000 each year. Management predicts this machine has a 10-year service life and a $100,000 salvage value, and it uses straight-line depreciation. Compute this machine's accounting rate of return.

Exercise 24-5
Payback period and accounting rate of return on investment
P1 P2

B2B Co. is considering the purchase of equipment that would allow the company to add a new product to its line. The equipment is expected to cost $360,000 with a 6-year life and no salvage value. It will be depreciated on a straight-line basis. The company expects to sell 144,000 units of the equipment's product each year. The expected annual income related to this equipment follows. Compute the (1) payback period and (2) accounting rate of return for this equipment.

Sales	$225,000
Costs	
Materials, labor, and overhead (except depreciation)	120,000
Depreciation on new equipment	30,000
Selling and administrative expenses	22,500
Total costs and expenses	172,500
Pretax income	52,500
Income taxes (30%)	15,750
Net income	$ 36,750

Check (1) 5.39 years (2) 20.42%

Exercise 24-6
Computing net present value P3

After evaluating the risk of the investment described in Exercise 24-5, B2B Co. concludes that it must earn at least a 8% return on this investment. Compute the net present value of this investment. (Round the net present value to the nearest dollar.)

Exercise 24-7
Computation and interpretation of net present value and internal rate of return
P3 P4

Phoenix Company can invest in each of three cheese-making projects: C1, C2, and C3. Each project requires an initial investment of $228,000 and would yield the following annual cash flows.

	C1	C2	C3
Year 1	$ 12,000	$ 96,000	$180,000
Year 2	108,000	96,000	60,000
Year 3	168,000	96,000	48,000
Totals	$288,000	$288,000	$288,000

(1) Assuming that the company requires a 12% return from its investments, use net present value to determine which projects, if any, should be acquired. (2) Using the answer from part 1, explain whether the internal rate of return is higher or lower than 12% for project C2. (3) Compute the internal rate of return for project C2.

Check (3) IRR = 13%

Exercise 24-8
NPV and profitability index P3

Following is information on two alternative investments being considered by Jolee Company. The company requires a 10% return from its investments.

	Project A	Project B
Initial investment	$(160,000)	$(105,000)
Expected net cash flows in year:		
1	40,000	32,000
2	56,000	50,000
3	80,295	66,000
4	90,400	72,000
5	65,000	24,000

For each alternative project compute the (a) net present value, and (b) profitability index. If the company can only select one project, which should it choose? Explain.

Exercise 24-9[A]
Using Excel to compute IRR P4

Refer to the information in Exercise 24-8. Create an Excel spreadsheet to compute the internal rate of return for each of the projects. Round the percentage return to two decimals.

Exercise 24-10
Comparison of payback and BET
P1 A1

This chapter explained two methods to evaluate investments using recovery time, the payback period and break-even time (BET). Refer to QS 24-8 and (1) compute the recovery time for both the payback period and break-even time, (2) discuss the advantage(s) of break-even time over the payback period, and (3) list two conditions under which payback period and break-even time are similar.

connect

PROBLEM SET A

Problem 24-1A
Computation of payback period, accounting rate of return, and net present value
P1 P2 P3

mhhe.com/wildFINMAN5e

Factor Company is planning to add a new product to its line. To manufacture this product, the company needs to buy a new machine at a $480,000 cost with an expected four-year life and a $20,000 salvage value. All sales are for cash, and all costs are out of pocket except for depreciation on the new machine. Additional information includes the following.

Expected annual sales of new product	$1,840,000
Expected annual costs of new product	
Direct materials	480,000
Direct labor	672,000
Overhead excluding straight-line depreciation on new machine	336,000
Selling and administrative expenses	160,000
Income taxes	30%

Required

1. Compute straight-line depreciation for each year of this new machine's life. (Round depreciation amounts to the nearest dollar.)
2. Determine expected net income and net cash flow for each year of this machine's life. (Round answers to the nearest dollar.)
3. Compute this machine's payback period, assuming that cash flows occur evenly throughout each year. (Round the payback period to two decimals.)
4. Compute this machine's accounting rate of return, assuming that income is earned evenly throughout each year. (Round the percentage return to two decimals.)
5. Compute the net present value for this machine using a discount rate of 7% and assuming that cash flows occur at each year-end. (*Hint:* Salvage value is a cash inflow at the end of the asset's life. Round the net present value to the nearest dollar.)

Check (4) 21.56%

(5) $107,356

Problem 24-2A
Analysis and computation of payback period, accounting rate of return, and net present value
P1 P2 P3

Most Company has an opportunity to invest in one of two new projects. Project Y requires a $350,000 investment for new machinery with a four-year life and no salvage value. Project Z requires a $350,000 investment for new machinery with a three-year life and no salvage value. The two projects yield the following predicted annual results. The company uses straight-line depreciation, and cash flows occur evenly throughout each year.

	Project Y	Project Z
Sales	$350,000	$280,000
Expenses		
Direct materials	49,000	35,000
Direct labor	70,000	42,000
Overhead including depreciation	126,000	126,000
Selling and administrative expenses	25,000	25,000
Total expenses	270,000	228,000
Pretax income	80,000	52,000
Income taxes (30%)	24,000	15,600
Net income	$ 56,000	$ 36,400

Required

1. Compute each project's annual expected net cash flows. (Round the net cash flows to the nearest dollar.)
2. Determine each project's payback period. (Round the payback period to two decimals.)
3. Compute each project's accounting rate of return. (Round the percentage return to one decimal.)
4. Determine each project's net present value using 8% as the discount rate. For part 4 only, assume that cash flows occur at each year-end. (Round the net present value to the nearest dollar.)

Check For Project Y: (2) 2.44 years, (3) 32% (4) $125,286

Analysis Component

5. Identify the project you would recommend to management and explain your choice.

Problem 24-3A
Computation of cash flows and net present values with alternative depreciation methods
P3

Manning Corporation is considering a new project requiring a $90,000 investment in test equipment with no salvage value. The project would produce $66,000 of pretax income before depreciation at the end of each of the next six years. The company's income tax rate is 40%. In compiling its tax return and computing its income tax payments, the company can choose between the two alternative depreciation schedules shown in the table.

	Straight-Line Depreciation	MACRS Depreciation*
Year 1	$ 9,000	$18,000
Year 2	18,000	28,800
Year 3	18,000	17,280
Year 4	18,000	10,368
Year 5	18,000	10,368
Year 6	9,000	5,184
Totals	$90,000	$90,000

* The modified accelerated cost recovery system (MACRS) for depreciation is discussed in Chapter 8.

Required

1. Prepare a five-column table that reports amounts (assuming use of straight-line depreciation) for each of the following for each of the six years: (a) pretax income before depreciation, (b) straight-line depreciation expense, (c) taxable income, (d) income taxes, and (e) net cash flow. Net cash flow equals the amount of income before depreciation minus the income taxes. (Round answers to the nearest dollar.)
2. Prepare a five-column table that reports amounts (assuming use of MACRS depreciation) for each of the following for each of the six years: (a) pretax income before depreciation, (b) MACRS depreciation expense, (c) taxable income, (d) income taxes, and (e) net cash flow. Net cash flow equals the income amount before depreciation minus the income taxes. (Round answers to the nearest dollar.)
3. Compute the net present value of the investment if straight-line depreciation is used. Use 10% as the discount rate. (Round the net present value to the nearest dollar.)
4. Compute the net present value of the investment if MACRS depreciation is used. Use 10% as the discount rate. (Round the net present value to the nearest dollar.)

Check Net present value: (3) $108,518 (4) $110,303

Analysis Component

5. Explain why the MACRS depreciation method increases this project's net present value.

Problem 24-4A
Computing net present value of alternate investments
P3

Interstate Manufacturing is considering either replacing one of its old machines with a new machine or having the old machine overhauled. Information about the two alternatives follows. Management requires a 10% rate of return on its investments.

Alternative 1: Keep the old machine and have it overhauled. If the old machine is overhauled, it will be kept for another five years and then sold for its salvage value.

Cost of old machine	$112,000
Cost of overhaul	150,000
Annual expected revenues generated	95,000
Annual cash operating costs after overhaul	42,000
Salvage value of old machine in 5 years	15,000

Alternative 2: Sell the old machine and buy a new one. The new machine is more efficient and will yield substantial operating cost savings with more product being produced and sold.

Cost of new machine	$300,000
Salvage value of old machine now	29,000
Annual expected revenues generated	100,000
Annual cash operating costs	32,000
Salvage value of new machine in 5 years	20,000

Required

1. Determine the net present value of alternative 1.
2. Determine the net present value of alternative 2.
3. Which alternative do you recommend that management select? Explain.

Check (1) Net present value of Alternative 1, $60,226

Problem 24-5A
Payback period, break-even time, and net present value
P1 A1

Sentinel Company is considering an investment in technology to improve its operations. The investment will require an initial outlay of $250,000 and will yield the following expected cash flows. Management requires investments to have a payback period of three years, and it requires a 10% return on investments.

Period	Cash Flow
1	$ 47,000
2	52,000
3	75,000
4	94,000
5	125,000

Required

1. Determine the payback period for this investment. (Round the answer to one decimal.)
2. Determine the break-even time for this investment. (Round the answer to one decimal.)
3. Determine the net present value for this investment.

Check (1) Payback period, 3.8 years

Analysis Component

4. Should management invest in this project? Explain.

Problem 24-6A
Payback period, break-even time, and net present value
P1 A1

Lenitnes Company is considering an investment in technology to improve its operations. The investment will require an initial outlay of $250,000 and will yield the following expected cash flows. Management requires investments to have a payback period of three years, and it requires a 10% return on its investments.

Period	Cash Flow
1	$125,000
2	94,000
3	75,000
4	52,000
5	47,000

Required

1. Determine the payback period for this investment. (Round the answer to one decimal.)
2. Determine the break-even time for this investment. (Round the answer to one decimal.)
3. Determine the net present value for this investment.

Check (1) Payback period, 2.4 years

Analysis component

4. Should management invest in this project? Explain.
5. Compare your answers for parts 1 through 4 with those for Problem 24-5A. What are the causes of the differences in results and your conclusions?

PROBLEM SET B

Problem 24-1B
Computation of payback period, accounting rate of return, and net present value
P1 P2 P3

Cortino Company is planning to add a new product to its line. To manufacture this product, the company needs to buy a new machine at a $300,000 cost with an expected four-year life and a $20,000 salvage value. All sales are for cash and all costs are out of pocket, except for depreciation on the new machine. Additional information includes the following.

Expected annual sales of new product	$1,150,000
Expected annual costs of new product	
Direct materials	300,000
Direct labor	420,000
Overhead excluding straight-line depreciation on new machine	210,000
Selling and administrative expenses	100,000
Income taxes	30%

Required

1. Compute straight-line depreciation for each year of this new machine's life. (Round depreciation amounts to the nearest dollar.)

2. Determine expected net income and net cash flow for each year of this machine's life. (Round answers to the nearest dollar.)

3. Compute this machine's payback period, assuming that cash flows occur evenly throughout each year. (Round the payback period to two decimals.)

Check (4) 21.88%

4. Compute this machine's accounting rate of return, assuming that income is earned evenly throughout each year. (Round the percentage return to two decimals.)

(5) $70,915

5. Compute the net present value for this machine using a discount rate of 7% and assuming that cash flows occur at each year-end. (*Hint:* Salvage value is a cash inflow at the end of the asset's life.)

Problem 24-2B
Analysis and computation of payback period, accounting rate of return, and net present value
P1 P2 P3

Aikman Company has an opportunity to invest in one of two projects. Project A requires a $240,000 investment for new machinery with a four-year life and no salvage value. Project B also requires a $240,000 investment for new machinery with a three-year life and no salvage value. The two projects yield the following predicted annual results. The company uses straight-line depreciation, and cash flows occur evenly throughout each year.

	Project A	Project B
Sales	$250,000	$200,000
Expenses		
Direct materials	35,000	25,000
Direct labor	50,000	30,000
Overhead including depreciation	90,000	90,000
Selling and administrative expenses	18,000	18,000
Total expenses	193,000	163,000
Pretax income	57,000	37,000
Income taxes (30%)	17,100	11,100
Net income	$ 39,900	$ 25,900

Required

1. Compute each project's annual expected net cash flows. (Round net cash flows to the nearest dollar.)

Check For Project A: (2) 2.4 years
(3) 33.3%
(4) $90,879

2. Determine each project's payback period. (Round the payback period to two decimals.)

3. Compute each project's accounting rate of return. (Round the percentage return to one decimal.)

4. Determine each project's net present value using 8% as the discount rate. For part 4 only, assume that cash flows occur at each year-end. (Round net present values to the nearest dollar.)

Analysis Component

5. Identify the project you would recommend to management and explain your choice.

Problem 24-3B
Computation of cash flows and net present values with alternative depreciation methods
P3

Grossman Corporation is considering a new project requiring a $30,000 investment in an asset having no salvage value. The project would produce $12,000 of pretax income before depreciation at the end of each of the next six years. The company's income tax rate is 40%. In compiling its tax return and computing its income tax payments, the company can choose between two alternative depreciation schedules as shown in the table.

	Straight-Line Depreciation	MACRS Depreciation*
Year 1	$ 3,000	$ 6,000
Year 2	6,000	9,600
Year 3	6,000	5,760
Year 4	6,000	3,456
Year 5	6,000	3,456
Year 6	3,000	1,728
Totals	$30,000	$30,000

* The modified accelerated cost recovery system (MACRS) for depreciation is discussed in Chapter 8.

Required

1. Prepare a five-column table that reports amounts (assuming use of straight-line depreciation) for each of the following items for each of the six years: (a) pretax income before depreciation, (b) straight-line depreciation expense, (c) taxable income, (d) income taxes, and (e) net cash flow. Net cash flow equals the amount of income before depreciation minus the income taxes. (Round answers to the nearest dollar.)

2. Prepare a five-column table that reports amounts (assuming use of MACRS depreciation) for each of the following items for each of the six years: (a) income before depreciation, (b) MACRS depreciation expense, (c) taxable income, (d) income taxes, and (e) net cash flow. Net cash flow equals the amount of income before depreciation minus the income taxes. (Round answers to the nearest dollar.)

3. Compute the net present value of the investment if straight-line depreciation is used. Use 10% as the discount rate. (Round the net present value to the nearest dollar.)

4. Compute the net present value of the investment if MACRS depreciation is used. Use 10% as the discount rate. (Round the net present value to the nearest dollar.)

Check Net present value: (3) $10,041 (4) $10,635

Analysis Component

5. Explain why the MACRS depreciation method increases the net present value of this project.

Problem 24-4B
Computing net present value of alternate investments
P3

Archer Foods has a freezer that is in need of repair and is considering whether to replace the old freezer with a new freezer or have the old freezer extensively repaired. Information about the two alternatives follows. Management requires a 10% rate of return on its investments.

Alternative 1: Keep the old freezer and have it repaired. If the old freezer is repaired, it will be kept for another 8 years and then sold for its salvage value.

Cost of old freezer	$75,000
Cost of repair	50,000
Annual expected revenues generated	63,000
Annual cash operating costs after repair	55,000
Salvage value of old freezer in 8 years	3,000

Alternative 2: Sell the old freezer and buy a new one. The new freezer is larger than the old one and will allow the company to expand its product offerings, thereby generating more revenues. Also, it is more energy efficient and will yield substantial operating cost savings.

Cost of new freezer	$150,000
Salvage value of old freezer now	5,000
Annual expected revenues generated	68,000
Annual cash operating costs	30,000
Salvage value of new freezer in 8 years	8,000

Required

1. Determine the net present value of alternative 1.

2. Determine the net present value of alternative 2.

3. Which alternative do you recommend that management select? Explain.

Check (1) Net present value of Alternative 1, $(5,921)

Problem 24-5B
Payback period, break-even time, and net present value
P1 A1

Aster Company is considering an investment in technology to improve its operations. The investment will require an initial outlay of $800,000 and yield the following expected cash flows. Management requires investments to have a payback period of two years, and it requires a 10% return on its investments.

Period	Cash Flow
1	$300,000
2	350,000
3	400,000
4	450,000

Required

Check (1) Payback period, 2.4 years

1. Determine the payback period for this investment.
2. Determine the break-even time for this investment.
3. Determine the net present value for this investment.

Analysis Component

4. Should management invest in this project? Explain.

Problem 24-6B

Payback period, break-even time, and net present value

P1 A1

Retsa Company is considering an investment in technology to improve its operations. The investment will require an initial outlay of $800,000 and will yield the following expected cash flows. Management requires investments to have a payback period of two years, and it requires a 10% return on its investments.

Period	Cash Flow
1	$450,000
2	400,000
3	350,000
4	300,000

Required

Check (1) Payback period, 1.9 years

1. Determine the payback period for this investment. (Round the answer to one decimal.)
2. Determine the break-even time for this investment. (Round the answer to one decimal.)
3. Determine the net present value for this investment.

Analysis Component

4. Should management invest in this project? Explain.
5. Compare your answers for parts 1 through 4 with those for Problem 24-5B. What are the causes of the differences in results and your conclusions?

SERIAL PROBLEM

Success Systems

P1 P2

(This serial problem began in Chapter 1 and continues through most of the book. If previous chapter segments were not completed, the serial problem can begin at this point. It is helpful, but not necessary, to use the Working Papers that accompany the book.)

SP 24 Adria Lopez is considering the purchase of equipment for Success Systems that would allow the company to add a new product to its computer furniture line. The equipment is expected to cost $300,000 and to have a six-year life and no salvage value. It will be depreciated on a straight-line basis. Success Systems expects to sell 100 units of the equipment's product each year. The expected annual income related to this equipment follows.

Sales	$375,000
Costs	
Materials, labor, and overhead (except depreciation)	200,000
Depreciation on new equipment	50,000
Selling and administrative expenses	37,500
Total costs and expenses	287,500
Pretax income	87,500
Income taxes (30%)	26,250
Net income	$ 61,250

Required

Compute the (1) payback period and (2) accounting rate of return for this equipment. (Record answers as percents, rounded to one decimal.)

Beyond the Numbers

REPORTING IN ACTION
P3
Polaris

BTN 24-1 Assume **Polaris** invested $2.12 million to expand its manufacturing capacity. Assume that these assets have a ten-year life, and that Polaris requires a 10% internal rate of return on these assets.

Required

1. What is the amount of annual cash flows that Polaris must earn from these projects to have a 10% internal rate of return? (*Hint:* Identify the 10-period, 10% factor from the present value of an annuity table, and then divide $2.12 million by this factor to get the annual cash flows necessary.)

Fast Forward

2. Access Polaris's financial statements for fiscal years ended after December 31, 2011, from its Website (Polaris.com) or the SEC's Website (SEC.gov).
   a. Determine the amount that Polaris invested in capital assets for the most recent year. (*Hint:* Refer to the statement of cash flows.)
   b. Assume a 10-year life and a 10% internal rate of return. What is the amount of cash flows that Polaris must earn on these new projects?

COMPARATIVE ANALYSIS
P3 P4
Polaris
Arctic Cat

BTN 24-2 Assume that **Arctic Cat** invests $2.42 million in capital expenditures, including $1.08 million related to manufacturing capacity. Assume that these projects have a seven-year life and that management requires a 15% internal rate of return on those projects.

Required

1. What is the amount of annual cash flows that Arctic Cat must earn from those expenditures to achieve a 15% internal rate of return? (*Hint:* Identify the 7-period, 15% factor from the present value of an annuity table and then divide $1.08 million by the factor to get the annual cash flows required.)
2. BTN 24-1 must be completed to answer part 2. How does your answer to part 1 compare to **Polaris**'s required cash flows determined in BTN 24-1? What does this imply about each company's cash flow requirements for these types of projects?

ETHICS CHALLENGE
P3

BTN 24-3 A consultant commented that "too often the numbers look good but feel bad." This comment often stems from estimation error common to capital budgeting proposals that relate to future cash flows. Three reasons for this error often exist. First, reliably predicting cash flows several years into the future is very difficult. Second, the present value of cash flows many years into the future (say, beyond 10 years) is often very small. Third, it is difficult for personal biases and expectations not to unduly influence present value computations.

Required

1. Compute the present value of $100 to be received in 10 years assuming a 12% discount rate.
2. Why is understanding the three reasons mentioned for estimation errors important when evaluating investment projects? Link this response to your answer for part 1.

COMMUNICATING IN PRACTICE
P1 P2 P3 P4

BTN 24-4 Payback period, accounting rate of return, net present value, and internal rate of return are common methods to evaluate capital investment opportunities. Assume that your manager asks you to identify the type of measurement basis and unit that each method offers and to list the advantages and disadvantages of each. Present your response in memorandum format of less than one page.

TAKING IT TO THE NET
P1 P3

BTN 24-5 Capital budgeting is an important topic and there are Websites designed to help people understand the methods available. Access TeachMeFinance.com's capital budgeting web page (teachmefinance.com/capitalbudgeting.html). This web page contains an example of a capital budgeting case involving a $15,000 initial cash outflow.

Required

Compute the payback period and the net present value (assuming a 10% required rate of return) of the following investment—assume that its cash flows occur at year-end. Compared to the example case at the

Website, the larger cash inflows in the example below occur in the later years of the project's life. Is this investment acceptable based on the application of these two capital budgeting methods? Explain.

Year	Cash Flow
0	$(15,000)
1	1,000
2	2,000
3	3,000
4	6,000
5	7,000

TEAMWORK IN ACTION
P1 P3

BTN 24-6 Break into teams and identify four reasons that an international airline such as **Southwest** or **Delta** would invest in a project when its direct analysis using both payback period and net present value indicate it to be a poor investment. (*Hint:* Think about qualitative factors.) Provide an example of an investment project supporting your answer.

ENTREPRENEURIAL DECISION
P1 P2 P3 P4

BTN 24-7 Read the chapter opener about Keith Mullin and his company, **Gamer Grub**. Keith is considering building a new, larger warehousing center to make his business more efficient and reduce costs. He expects that an efficient warehouse could reduce his costs by 20%.

Required

1. What are some of the management tools that Keith can use to evaluate whether the new warehousing center will be a good investment?
2. What information does he need to use the tools that are identified in your answer to part 1?
3. What are some of the advantages and disadvantages of each tool identified in your answer to part 1?

HITTING THE ROAD
P3

BTN 24-8 Visit or call a local auto dealership and inquire about leasing a car. Ask about the down payment and the required monthly payments. You will likely find the salesperson does not discuss the cost to purchase this car but focuses on the affordability of the monthly payments. This chapter gives you the tools to compute the cost of this car using the lease payment schedule in present dollars and to estimate the profit from leasing for an auto dealership.

Required

1. Compare the cost of leasing the car to buying it in present dollars using the information from the dealership you contact. (Assume you will make a final payment at the end of the lease and then own the car.)
2. Is it more costly to lease or buy the car? Support your answer with computations.

GLOBAL DECISION
C1

PIAGGIO

BTN 24-9 **Piaggio**'s annual report includes information about its debt and interest rates. One statement in its annual report reveals that Piaggio recently issued 10-year bonds with a market return of about 6.5%.

Required

Explain how Piaggio would use that 6.5% rate to evaluate its investments in capital projects.

ANSWERS TO MULTIPLE CHOICE QUIZ

1. a

2. e;

	Net Cash Flow	Present Value of an Annuity of 1 at 12%	Present Value of Cash Flows
Years 1–3	$3,600 + $30,000	2.4018	$ 80,700
Amount invested			(90,000)
Net present value			$ (9,300)

3. a

4. c; Payback = $270,000/$61,200 per year = 4.4 years.

5. d; Accounting rate of return = $8,550/[($180,000 + $0)/2] = 9.5%.

Appendix

A

Financial Statement Information

This appendix includes financial information for (1) **Polaris**, (2) **Arctic Cat**, (3) **KTM**, and (4) **Piaggio**. Polaris is a manufacturer of ATVs, snowmobiles, motorcycles and electric vehicles; it competes with Arctic Cat in the United States and globally. KTM and Piaggio also compete with Polaris and Arctic Cat, and are two of Europe's leading manufacturers of two-, three-, and four-wheel vehicles. The information in this Appendix is taken from their annual 10-K reports (or annual reports for KTM and Piaggio) filed with the SEC or other regulatory agency. An **annual report** is a summary of a company's financial results for the year along with its current financial condition and future plans. This report is directed to external users of financial information, but it also affects the actions and decisions of internal users.

A company often uses an annual report to showcase itself and its products. Many annual reports include photos, diagrams, and illustrations related to the company. The primary objective of annual reports, however, is the *financial section,* which communicates much information about a company, with most data drawn from the accounting information system. The layout of an annual report's financial section is fairly established and typically includes the following:

- Letter to Shareholders
- Financial History and Highlights
- Management Discussion and Analysis
- Management's Report on Financial Statements and on Internal Controls
- Report of Independent Accountants (Auditor's Report) and on Internal Controls
- Financial Statements
- Notes to Financial Statements
- List of Directors and Officers

This appendix provides the financial statements for Polaris (plus selected notes), Arctic Cat, KTM, and Piaggio. The appendix is organized as follows:

Polaris
Arctic Cat
KTM
PIAGGIO

Many assignments at the end of each chapter refer to information in this appendix. We encourage readers to spend time with these assignments; they are especially useful in showing the relevance and diversity of financial accounting and reporting.

> *Special note:* The SEC maintains the EDGAR (**E**lectronic **D**ata **G**athering, **A**nalysis, and **R**etrieval) database at www.SEC.gov for U.S. filers. The **Form 10-K** is the annual report form for most companies. It provides electronically accessible information. The **Form 10-KSB** is the annual report form filed by small businesses. It requires slightly less information than the Form 10-K. One of these forms must be filed within 90 days after the company's fiscal year-end. (Forms 10-K405, 10-KT, 10-KT405, and 10-KSB405 are slight variations of the usual form due to certain regulations or rules.)

POLARIS INDUSTRIES INC.
CONSOLIDATED BALANCE SHEETS

December 31 (In thousands, except per share data)	2011	2010
ASSETS		
Current Assets		
Cash and cash equivalents	$ 325,336	$ 393,927
Trade receivables, net	115,302	89,294
Inventories, net	298,042	235,927
Prepaid expenses and other	37,608	21,628
Income taxes receivable	24,723	—
Deferred tax assets	77,665	67,369
Total current assets	878,676	808,145
Property and Equipment		
Land, buildings and improvements	123,771	118,831
Equipment and tooling	524,382	488,562
	648,153	607,393
Less accumulated depreciation	(434,375)	(423,382)
Property and equipment, net	213,778	184,011
Investments in finance affiliate	42,251	37,169
Investments in other affiliates	5,000	1,009
Deferred tax assets	10,601	—
Goodwill and other intangible assets, net	77,718	31,313
Total Assets	$1,228,024	$1,061,647
LIABILITIES AND SHAREHOLDERS' EQUITY		
Current Liabilities		
Current portion of long-term borrowings under credit agreement	—	$ 100,000
Current portion of capital lease obligations	$ 2,653	—
Accounts payable	146,743	113,248
Accrued expenses		
Compensation	187,671	126,781
Warranties	44,355	32,651
Sales promotions and incentives	81,228	75,494
Dealer holdback	76,512	79,688
Other	75,730	53,744
Income taxes payable	639	2,604
Total current liabilities	615,531	584,210
Long term income taxes payable	7,837	5,509
Deferred income taxes	—	937
Capital lease obligations	4,600	—
Long-term debt	100,000	100,000
Total liabilities	727,968	690,656
Shareholders' Equity		
Preferred stock $0.01 par value, 20,000 shares authorized, no shares issued and outstanding	—	—
Common stock $0.01 par value, 160,000 shares authorized, 68,430 and 68,468 shares issued and outstanding	684	685
Additional paid-in capital	165,518	79,239
Retained earnings	321,831	285,169
Accumulated other comprehensive income, net	12,023	5,898
Total shareholders' equity	500,056	370,991
Total Liabilities and Shareholders' Equity	$1,228,024	$1,061,647

Shares outstanding, common stock, additional paid-in-capital, retained earnings and per share data have been adjusted to give effect to the two-for-one stock split declared on July 20, 2011, paid on September 12, 2011 to shareholders of record on September 2, 2011.

POLARIS INDUSTRIES INC.
CONSOLIDATED STATEMENTS OF INCOME

For the Years Ended December 31 (In thousands, except per share data)	2011	2010	2009
Sales	$2,656,949	$1,991,139	$1,565,887
Cost of sales	1,916,366	1,460,926	1,172,668
Gross profit	740,583	530,213	393,219
Operating expenses			
Selling and marketing	178,725	142,353	111,137
Research and development	105,631	84,940	62,999
General and administrative	130,395	99,055	71,184
Total operating expenses	414,751	326,348	245,320
Income from financial services	24,092	16,856	17,071
Operating income	349,924	220,721	164,970
Non-operating expense (income)			
Interest expense	3,987	2,680	4,111
(Gain) loss on securities available for sale	—	(825)	8,952
Other expense (income), net	(689)	325	733
Income before income taxes	346,626	218,541	151,174
Provision for income taxes	119,051	71,403	50,157
Net income	$ 227,575	$ 147,138	$ 101,017
Basic net income per share	$ 3.31	$ 2.20	$ 1.56
Diluted net income per share	$ 3.20	$ 2.14	$ 1.53
Weighted average shares outstanding:			
Basic	68,792	66,900	64,798
Diluted	71,057	68,765	66,148

Shares outstanding and per share data have been adjusted to give effect to the two-for-one stock split declared on July 20, 2011, paid on September 12, 2011 to shareholders of record on September 2, 2011.

POLARIS

POLARIS INDUSTRIES INC.
CONSOLIDATED STATEMENTS OF SHAREHOLDERS' EQUITY AND COMPREHENSIVE INCOME

(In thousands, except per share data)	Number of Shares	Common Stock	Additional Paid-In Capital	Retained Earnings	Accumulated Other Comprehensive Income (Loss)	Total
Balance, December 31, 2008	64,984	$650	—	$ 140,234	$ (3,857)	$ 137,027
Employee stock compensation	62	1	10,225			10,226
Proceeds from stock issuances under employee plans	472	4	4,729			4,733
Tax effect of exercise of stock options			(410)			(410)
Cash dividends declared ($0.78 per share)				(50,177)		(50,177)
Repurchase and retirement of common shares	(222)	(2)	(4,554)			(4,556)
Comprehensive income:						
Net Income				101,017		
Foreign currency translation adjustments, net of tax of $69					115	
Reclassification of unrealized loss on available for sale securities to the income statement, net of tax of $2,277					6,675	
Unrealized loss on available for sale securities, net of tax benefit of $230					(382)	
Unrealized gain on derivative instruments, net of tax of $165					273	
Total comprehensive income						107,698
Balance, December 31, 2009	65,296	653	9,990	191,074	2,824	204,541
Employee stock compensation	308	3	18,049			18,052
Proceeds from stock issuances under employee plans	4,066	41	68,064			68,105
Tax effect of exercise of stock options			10,610			10,610
Cash dividends declared ($0.80 per share)				(53,043)		(53,043)
Repurchase and retirement of common shares	(1,202)	(12)	(27,474)			(27,486)
Comprehensive income:						
Net Income				147,138		
Foreign currency translation adjustments, net of tax of $222					3,131	
Unrealized gain on available for sale securities, net of tax benefit of $230					382	
Unrealized loss on derivative instruments, net of tax benefit of $256					(439)	
Total comprehensive income						150,212
Balance, December 31, 2010	68,468	685	79,239	285,169	5,898	370,991
Employee stock compensation	290	3	20,545			20,548
Proceeds from stock issuances under employee plans	2,280	22	45,632			45,654
Tax effect of exercise of stock options			23,120			23,120
Cash dividends declared ($0.90 per share)				(61,585)		(61,585)
Repurchase and retirement of common shares	(2,608)	(26)	(3,018)	(129,328)		(132,372)
Comprehensive income:						
Net Income				227,575		
Foreign currency translation adjustments, net of tax benefit of $6,782					2,554	
Unrealized gain/(loss) on derivative instruments, net of tax of $2,125					3,571	
Total comprehensive income						233,700
Balance, December 31, 2011	68,430	$684	$165,518	$ 321,831	$12,023	$ 500,056

Shares outstanding, common stock, additional paid-in-capital, retained earnings and per share data have been adjusted to give effect to the two-for-one stock split declared on July 20, 2011, paid on September 12, 2011 to shareholders of record on September 2, 2011.

POLARIS INDUSTRIES INC.
CONSOLIDATED STATEMENTS OF CASH FLOWS

For the Year Ended December 31 (In thousands)	2011	2010	2009
Operating Activities			
Net income	$ 227,575	$147,138	$ 101,017
Adjustments to reconcile net income to net cash provided by operating activities:			
(Gain) loss on securities available for sale	—	(825)	8,952
Depreciation and amortization	66,390	66,519	64,593
Noncash compensation	20,548	18,052	10,226
Noncash income from financial services	(4,444)	(4,574)	(4,021)
Noncash expense from other affiliates	133	1,376	382
Deferred income taxes	(16,946)	(16,888)	13,573
Tax effect of share-based compensation exercises	(23,120)	(10,610)	410
Changes in current operating items:			
Trade receivables	(23,115)	1,111	8,192
Inventories	(49,973)	(56,612)	42,997
Accounts payable	27,232	37,580	(40,329)
Accrued expenses	80,668	107,363	(24,759)
Income taxes payable/receivable	(1,343)	7,033	7,325
Prepaid expenses and others, net	(1,075)	956	4,643
Net cash provided by operating activities	302,530	297,619	193,201
Investing Activities			
Purchase of property and equipment	(84,484)	(55,718)	(43,932)
Investments in finance affiliate	(12,588)	(9,173)	(3,007)
Distributions from finance affiliate	11,950	17,910	17,261
Investment in other affiliates	(5,000)	—	—
Proceeds from sale of investments	876	9,061	—
Acquisition of businesses, net of cash acquired	(51,899)	(4,738)	—
Net cash used for investment activities	(141,145)	(42,118)	(29,678)
Financing Activities			
Borrowings under credit agreement / senior notes	100,000	—	364,000
Repayments under credit agreement	(202,333)	—	(364,000)
Repurchase and retirement of common shares	(132,372)	(27,486)	(4,556)
Cash dividends to shareholders	(61,585)	(53,043)	(50,177)
Tax effect of proceeds from share-based compensation exercises	23,120	10,610	(410)
Proceeds from stock issuances under employee plans	45,654	68,105	4,733
Net cash used for financing activities	(227,516)	(1,814)	(50,410)
Impact of currency exchange rates on cash balances	(2,460)	—	—
Net increase (decrease) in cash and cash equivalents	(68,591)	253,687	113,113
Cash and cash equivalents at beginning of period	393,927	140,240	27,127
Cash and cash equivalents at end of period	$ 325,336	$393,927	$ 140,240

Supplemental Cash Flow Information:			
Interest paid on debt borrowings	$ 3,350	$ 2,813	$ 3,966
Income taxes paid	$ 132,088	$ 81,142	$ 29,039

POLARIS INDUSTRIES INC.
SELECTED NOTES TO CONSOLIDATED FINANCIAL STATEMENTS

Note 1. Organization and Significant Accounting Policies

Polaris Industries Inc. ("Polaris" or the "Company") a Minnesota corporation, and its subsidiaries, are engaged in the design, engineering, manufacturing and marketing of innovative, high-quality, high-performance Off-Road Vehicles ("ORV"), Snowmobiles, and On-Road Vehicles, including motorcycles and Small Electric Vehicles. Polaris products, together with related parts, garments and accessories are sold worldwide through a network of dealers, distributors and its subsidiaries located in the United States, Canada, France, the United Kingdom, Australia, Norway, Sweden, Germany, Spain, China, India and Brazil.

Basis of presentation: The accompanying consolidated financial statements include the accounts of Polaris and its wholly-owned subsidiaries. All inter-company transactions and balances have been eliminated in consolidation. Income from financial services is reported as a component of operating income to better reflect income from ongoing operations, of which financial services has a significant impact.

During the 2011 third quarter, the Board of Directors declared a two-for-one split of the Company's outstanding shares of Common Stock. On September 12, 2011, Polaris shareholders received one additional share of Common Stock for each share they held of record at the close of business on September 2, 2011. All amounts, including shares and per share information, have been adjusted to give effect to the two-for-one stock split.

Investment in finance affiliate: The caption Investment in finance affiliate in the consolidated balance sheets represents Polaris' 50 percent equity interest in Polaris Acceptance, a partnership agreement between GE Commercial Distribution Finance Corporation ("GECDF") and one of Polaris' wholly-owned subsidiaries. Polaris Acceptance provides floor plan financing to Polaris dealers in the United States. Polaris' investment in Polaris Acceptance is accounted for under the equity method, and is recorded as investments in finance affiliate in the consolidated balance sheets.

Investment in other affiliates: The caption Investments in other affiliates in the consolidated balance sheets for the period ended December 31, 2011 represents the Company's October 2011 investment in Brammo, Inc., a privately held manufacturer of electric motorcycles. This investment represents a minority interest in Brammo and is accounted for under the cost method.

(Gain) Loss on Securities Available for Sale: The net gain of $825,000 in 2010 on securities available for sale resulted from a $1,594,000 gain on the sale of our remaining investment in KTM during the 2010 third quarter offset by a related non-cash impairment charge of $769,000 during the 2010 second quarter. In the first quarter 2009, we recorded a non-cash impairment charge on securities held for sales of $8,952,000 from the decline in the fair value of the KTM shares owned by Polaris as of March 31, 2009, when it was determined that the decline in the fair value of the KTM shares owned by the Company was other than temporary.

Use of estimates: The preparation of financial statements in conformity with accounting principles generally accepted in the United States requires management to make estimates and assumptions that affect the reported amounts of assets and liabilities and disclosure of contingent assets and liabilities at the date of the financial statements and the reported amounts of revenues and expenses during the reporting period. Ultimate results could differ from those estimates.

Cash equivalents: Polaris considers all highly liquid investments purchased with an original maturity of 90 days or less to be cash equivalents. Cash equivalents are stated at cost, which approximates fair value. Such investments consist principally of money market mutual funds.

Allowance for doubtful accounts: Polaris' financial exposure to collection of accounts receivable is limited due to its agreements with certain finance companies. For receivables not serviced through these finance companies, the Company provides a reserve for doubtful accounts based on historical rates and trends. This reserve is adjusted periodically as information about specific accounts becomes available.

Inventories: Inventories are stated at the lower of cost (first-in, first-out method) or market. The major components of inventories are as follows (in thousands):

December 31	2011	2010
Raw materials and purchased components	**$ 61,296**	$ 35,580
Service parts, garments and accessories	**77,437**	60,813
Finished goods	**175,252**	155,744
Less: reserves	**(15,943)**	(16,210)
Inventories	**$298,042**	$235,927

Property and equipment: Property and equipment is stated at cost. Depreciation is provided using the straight-line method over the estimated useful life of the respective assets, ranging from 10–40 years for buildings and improvements and from 1–7 years for equipment and tooling. Fully depreciated tooling is eliminated from the accounting records annually.

Research and Development Expenses: Polaris records research and development expenses in the period in which they are incurred as a component of operating expenses. In the years ended December 31, 2011, 2010, and 2009, Polaris incurred $105,631,000, $84,940,000, and $62,999,000, respectively.

Advertising Expenses: Polaris records advertising expenses as a component of selling and marketing expenses in the period in which they are incurred. In the years ended December 31, 2011, 2010, and 2009, Polaris incurred $48,877,000, $40,833,000 and $37,433,000, respectively.

Shipping and Handling Costs: Polaris records shipping and handling costs as a component of cost of sales at the time the product is shipped.

Product warranties: Polaris provides a limited warranty for its ORVs for a period of six months and for a period of one year for its snowmobiles and motorcycles and a two year period for SEVs. Polaris provides longer warranties in certain geographical markets as determined by local regulations and market conditions and may provide longer warranties related to certain promotional programs.

Polaris' standard warranties require the Company or its dealers to repair or replace defective products during such warranty periods at no cost to the consumer. The warranty reserve is established at the time of sale to the dealer or distributor based on management's best estimate using historical rates and trends. Adjustments to the warranty reserve are made from time to time as actual claims become known in order to properly estimate the amounts necessary to settle future and existing claims on products sold as of the balance sheet date. Factors that could have an impact on the warranty accrual in any given year include the following: improved manufacturing quality, shifts in product mix, changes in warranty coverage periods, snowfall and its impact on snowmobile usage, product recalls and any significant changes in sales volume. The activity in the warranty reserve during the years presented is as follows (in thousands):

For the Year Ended December 31	2011	2010	2009
Balance at beginning of year	**$ 32,651**	$ 25,520	$ 28,631
Additions to warranty reserve through acquisitions	**2,727**	—	—
Additions charged to expense	**46,217**	43,721	40,977
Warranty claims paid	**(37,240)**	(36,590)	(44,088)
Balance at end of year	**$ 44,355**	$ 32,651	$ 25,520

Sales promotions and incentives: Polaris provides for estimated sales promotion and incentive expenses, which are recognized as a reduction to sales, at the time of sale to the dealer or distributor. Polaris recorded accrued liabilities of $81,228,000 and $75,494,000 related to various sales promotions and incentive programs as of December 31, 2011 and 2010, respectively.

Dealer holdback programs: Dealer holdback represents a portion of the invoiced sales price that is expected to be subsequently returned to the dealer or distributor as a sales incentive upon the ultimate retail sale of the product. Polaris recorded accrued liabilities of $76,512,000 and $79,688,000, for dealer holdback programs in the consolidated balance sheets as of December 31, 2011 and 2010, respectively.

Foreign currency translation: The functional currency for each of the Polaris foreign subsidiaries is their respective local currencies. The assets and liabilities in all Polaris foreign entities are translated at the foreign exchange rate in effect at the balance sheet date. Translation gains and losses are reflected as a component of Accumulated other comprehensive income in the shareholders' equity section of the accompanying consolidated balance sheets. Revenues and expenses in all of Polaris' foreign entities are translated at the average foreign exchange rate in effect for each month of the quarter. Transaction gains and losses including intercompany transactions denominated in a currency other than the functional currency of the entity involved are included in "Other income (expense), net" on our Consolidated statements of income. The net Accumulated other comprehensive income related to translation gains and losses was a net gain of $9,545,000 and $6,991,000 at December 31, 2011 and 2010, respectively.

Revenue recognition: Revenues are recognized at the time of shipment to the dealer or distributor or other customers. Product returns, whether in the normal course of business or resulting from repossession under its customer financing program, have not been material. Polaris sponsors certain sales incentive programs and accrues liabilities for estimated sales promotion expenses and estimated holdback amounts that are recognized as reductions to sales when products are sold to the dealer or distributor customer.

Comprehensive income: Components of comprehensive income include net income, foreign currency translation adjustments, unrealized gains or losses on derivative instruments, and unrealized gains or losses on securities held for sale, net of tax. The Company has chosen to disclose comprehensive income in the accompanying consolidated statements of shareholders' equity and comprehensive income.

Note 3. Financing

The following summarizes activity under Polaris' credit arrangements (dollars in thousands):

	2011	2010	2009
Total borrowings at December 31,	**$100,000**	$200,000	$200,000
Average outstanding borrowings during year	**$133,800**	$200,000	$268,100
Maximum outstanding borrowings during year	**$200,000**	$200,000	$345,000
Interest rate at December 31	**4.40%**	0.65%	0.79%

The carrying amounts of the Company's long-term debt approximates its fair vale as December 31, 2011 and 2010.

Note 4. Goodwill and Other Intangible Assets

Goodwill and other intangible assets: ASC Topic 350 prohibits the amortization of goodwill and intangible assets with indefinite useful lives. Topic 350 requires that these assets be reviewed for impairment at least annually. An impairment charge for goodwill is recognized only when the estimated fair value of a reporting unit, including goodwill, is less than its carrying amount. The results of the analyses indicated that no goodwill or intangible impairment existed. In accordance with Topic 350, the Company will continue to complete an impairment analysis on an annual basis. Goodwill and other intangible assets, net, consist of $44,668,000 and $28,354,000 of goodwill and $33,050,000 and $2,959,000 of intangible assets, net of accumulated amortization, for the periods ended December 31, 2011 and December 31, 2010, respectively. Amortization expense for intangible assets during 2011 and 2010 was $1,018,000 and $188,000, respectively.

Note 9. Commitments and Contingencies

Product liability: Polaris is subject to product liability claims in the normal course of business. Polaris is currently self-insured for all product liability claims. The estimated costs resulting from any losses are charged to operating expenses when it is probable a loss has been incurred and the amount of the loss is reasonably determinable. The Company utilizes historical trends and actuarial analysis tools, along with an analysis of current claims, to assist in determining the appropriate loss reserve levels. At December 31, 2011, the Company had an accrual of $16,861,000 for the probable payment of pending claims related to product liability litigation associated with Polaris products. This accrual is included as a component of Other Accrued expenses in the accompanying consolidated balance sheets.

Leases: Polaris leases buildings and equipment under non-cancelable operating leases. Total rent expense under all operating lease agreements was $9,184,000, $5,553,000 and $4,999,000 for 2011, 2010 and 2009, respectively. Future minimum annual lease payments under capital and operating leases with non-cancelable terms in excess of one year as of December 31, 2011, including payments for the Monterrey, Mexico facility operating lease were as follows (in thousands):

Lease Obligations	Capital Leases	Operating Leases
2012	**$2,653**	$ 7,184
2013	**2,190**	5,845
2014	**1,444**	4,857
2015	**701**	3,899
2016	**222**	3,460
Thereafter	**43**	11,644
Total future minimum lease obligation	**$7,253**	$36,889

Note 12. Segment Reporting

Polaris has reviewed ASC Topic 280 and determined that the Company meets the aggregation criteria outlined since the Company's segments have similar (1) economic characteristics, (2) product and services, (3) production processes, (4) customers, (5) distribution channels, and (6) regulatory environments. Therefore, the Company reports as a single reportable business segment. The following data relates to Polaris' foreign operations:

For the Year Ended December 31 (In thousands)	2011	2010	2009
Canadian subsidiary:			
Sales	**$368,487**	$279,309	$239,240
Identifiable assets	**18,008**	42,936	35,462
Other foreign countries:			
Sales	**$424,363**	$305,864	$252,419
Identifiable assets	**252,519**	145,528	97,771

POLARIS INDUSTRIES INC.
SCHEDULE II—VALUATION AND QUALIFYING ACCOUNTS

(In thousands) Allowance for Doubtful Accounts	Balance at Beginning of Period	Additions Charged to Costs and Expenses	Additions Through Acquisition	Other Changes Add (Deduct)	Balance at End of Period
2009: Deducted from asset accounts—Allowance for doubtful accounts receivable	$6,098	$5,741	—	$(2,246)[1]	$9,593
2010: Deducted from asset accounts—Allowance for doubtful accounts receivable	$9,593	$1,599	—	$(4,823)[1]	$6,369
2011: Deducted from asset accounts—Allowance for doubtful accounts receivable	$6,369	$ 25	$532	$(2,453)[1]	$4,473
Inventory Reserve					
2009: Deducted from asset accounts—Allowance for obsolete inventory	$17,216	$6,400	—	$(8,023)[2]	$15,593
2010: Deducted from asset accounts—Allowance for obsolete inventory	$15,593	$5,840	—	$(5,223)[2]	$16,210
2011: Deducted from asset accounts—Allowance for obsolete inventory	$16,210	$4,611	$725	$(5,603)[2]	$15,943

1 Uncollectible accounts receivable written off, net of recoveries.

2 Inventory disposals, net of recoveries

POLARIS INDUSTRIES INC.

Selected Financial Data

(Dollars in millions, except per-share data)	For the Years Ended December 31 2011	2010	2009	2008	2007	2006
Statement of Operations Data						
Sales Data:						
Total sales	$2,656.9	$1,991.1	$1,565.9	$1,948.3	$1,780.0	$1,656.5
Percent change from prior year	33%	27%	-20%	9%	7%	-11%
Sales mix by product:						
Off-Road Vehicles	69%	69%	65%	67%	67%	67%
Snowmobiles	11%	10%	12%	10%	10%	10%
On-Road Vehicles	5%	4%	3%	5%	6%	7%
Parts, Garments and Accessories	15%	17%	20%	18%	17%	16%
Gross Profit Data:						
Total gross profit	$ 740.6	$ 530.2	$ 393.2	$ 445.7	$ 393.0	$ 359.4
Percent of sales	27.9%	26.6%	25.1%	22.9%	22.1%	21.7%
Operating Expense Data:						
Total operating expenses	$ 414.7	$ 326.3	$ 245.3	$ 284.1	$ 262.3	$ 238.4
Percent of sales	15.6%	16.4%	15.7%	14.6%	14.7%	14.4%
Operating Income Data:						
Total operating income	$ 349.9	$ 220.7	$ 165.0	$ 182.8	$ 176.0	$ 168.1
Percent of sales	13.2%	11.1%	10.5%	9.4%	9.9%	10.1%
Net Income Data:						
Net income from continuing operations	$ 227.6	$ 147.1	$ 101.0	$ 117.4	$ 112.6	$ 112.8
Percent of sales	8.6%	7.4%	6.5%	6.0%	6.3%	6.8%
Diluted net income per share from continuing operations	$ 3.20	$ 2.14	$ 1.53	$ 1.75	$ 1.55	$ 1.36
Net income	$ 227.6	$ 147.1	$ 101.0	$ 117.4	$ 111.7	$ 107.0
Diluted net income per share	$ 3.20	$ 2.14	$ 1.53	$ 1.75	$ 1.54	$ 1.29
Cash Flow Data:						
Cash flow provided by continuing operations	$ 302.5	$ 297.9	$ 193.2	$ 176.2	$ 213.2	$ 152.8
Purchase of property and equipment for continuing operations	84.5	55.7	43.9	76.6	63.7	52.6
Repurchase and retirement of common stock	132.4	27.5	4.6	107.2	103.1	307.6
Cash dividends to shareholders	61.6	53.0	50.2	49.6	47.7	50.2
Cash dividends per share	$ 0.90	$ 0.80	$ 0.78	$ 0.76	$ 0.68	$ 0.62
Balance Sheet Data (at end of year):						
Cash and cash equivalents	$ 325.3	$ 393.9	$ 140.2	$ 27.2	$ 63.3	$ 19.6
Current assets	878.7	808.1	491.5	443.6	447.6	393.0
Total assets	1,228.0	1,061.6	763.7	751.1	769.9	778.8
Current liabilities	615.5	584.2	343.1	404.8	388.2	361.4
Long-term debt	104.6	100.0	200.0	200.0	200.0	250.0
Shareholders' equity	500.1	371.0	204.5	137.0	173.0	167.4

ARCTIC CAT

ARCTIC CAT INC.

CONSOLIDATED BALANCE SHEETS

March 31	2011	2010
ASSETS		
Current Assets		
Cash and cash equivalents	$ 14,700,000	$ 31,811,000
Short term investments	110,413,000	39,251,000
Accounts receivable, less allowances	23,732,000	29,227,000
Inventories	61,478,000	81,361,000
Prepaid expenses	4,048,000	4,384,000
Deferred income taxes	17,669,000	14,981,000
Total current assets	232,040,000	201,015,000
Property and Equipment		
Machinery, equipment and tooling	195,189,000	185,023,000
Land, building and improvements	28,924,000	28,937,000
	224,113,000	213,960,000
Less accumulated depreciation	184,883,000	170,644,000
	39,230,000	43,316,000
Other Assets	1,636,000	1,753,000
	$272,906,000	$246,084,000
LIABILITIES AND SHAREHOLDERS' EQUITY		
Current Liabilities		
Accounts payable	$ 41,666,000	$ 37,303,000
Accrued expenses	44,398,000	35,042,000
Income taxes payable	1,380,000	2,975,000
Total current liabilities	87,444,000	75,320,000
Deferred Income Taxes	2,426,000	3,425,000
Commitments and Contingencies	—	—
Shareholders' Equity		
Preferred stock, par value $1.00; 2,050,000 shares authorized; none issued	—	—
Preferred stock—Series A Junior Participating, par value $1.00; 450,000 shares authorized; none issued	—	—
Common stock, par value $.01; 37,440,000 shares authorized; shares issued and outstanding: 12,199,271 in 2011 and 12,125,985 in 2010	122,000	121,000
Class B common stock, par value $.01; 7,560,000 shares authorized; shares issued and outstanding: 6,102,000 in 2011 and 2010	61,000	61,000
Additional paid-in-capital	7,280,000	5,053,000
Accumulated other comprehensive loss	(1,920,000)	(2,382,000)
Retained earnings	177,493,000	164,486,000
Total shareholders' equity	183,036,000	167,339,000
	$272,906,000	$246,084,000

ARCTIC CAT INC.
CONSOLIDATED STATEMENTS OF OPERATIONS

Years ended March 31	2011	2010	2009
Net sales			
Snowmobile & ATV units	$363,015,000	$350,871,000	$454,589,000
Parts, garments, & accessories	101,636,000	99,857,000	109,024,000
Total net sales	464,651,000	450,728,000	563,613,000
Cost of goods sold			
Snowmobile & ATV units	302,783,000	309,217,000	411,776,000
Parts, garments, & accessories	60,359,000	58,275,000	68,665,000
Total cost of goods sold	363,142,000	367,492,000	480,441,000
Gross profit	101,509,000	83,236,000	83,172,000
Operating expenses			
Selling & marketing	33,540,000	33,929,000	43,971,000
Research & development	15,029,000	12,926,000	18,404,000
General & administrative	34,805,000	35,045,000	33,904,000
Goodwill impairment charge	—	—	1,750,000
Total operating expenses	83,374,000	81,900,000	98,029,000
Operating profit (loss)	18,135,000	1,336,000	(14,857,000)
Other income (expense)			
Interest income	107,000	12,000	117,000
Interest expense	(11,000)	(250,000)	(1,015,000)
Total other income (expense)	96,000	(238,000)	(898,000)
Earnings (loss) before incomes taxes	18,231,000	1,098,000	(15,755,000)
Income tax expense (benefit)	5,224,000	(777,000)	(6,247,000)
Net earnings (loss)	$ 13,007,000	$ 1,875,000	$ (9,508,000)
Net earnings (loss) per share			
Basic	$ 0.71	$ 0.10	$ (0.53)
Diluted	$ 0.70	$ 0.10	$ (0.53)
Weighted average share outstanding			
Basic	18,232,000	18,220,000	18,070,000
Diluted	18,539,000	18,291,000	18,070,000

ARCTIC CAT INC.

CONSOLIDATED STATEMENTS OF SHAREHOLDERS' EQUITY

Years ended March 31	Common Stock		Class B Common Stock		Additional Paid-in Capital	Accumulated Other Comprehensive Income (Loss)	Retained Earnings	Total
	Shares	Amount	Shares	Amount				
Balances at March 31, 2008 . . .	11,833,485	$118,000	6,102,000	$61,000	$ —	$ 4,768,000	$175,915,000	$180,862,000
Restricted stock awards	163,500	2,000	—	—	(2,000)	—	—	—
Restricted stock forfeited	(9,500)	—	—	—	—	—	—	—
Stock based compensation expense	—	—	—	—	2,570,000	—	—	2,570,000
Comprehensive loss:								
Net loss	—	—	—	—	—	—	(9,508,000)	(9,508,000)
Unrealized loss on derivative instruments, net of tax	—	—	—	—	—	(133,000)	—	(133,000)
Foreign currency adjustment	—	—	—	—	—	(5,147,000)	—	(5,147,000)
Total comprehensive loss . . .								(14,788,000)
Dividends ($.21 per share) . .	—	—	—	—	—	—	(3,796,000)	(3,796,000)
Balances at March 31, 2009 . . .	11,987,485	120,000	6,102,000	61,000	2,568,000	(512,000)	162,611,000	164,848,000
Restricted stock awards	140,500	1,000	—	—	(1,000)	—	—	—
Restricted stock forfeited	(2,000)	—	—	—	—	—	—	—
Stock based compensation expense	—	—	—	—	2,486,000	—	—	2,486,000
Comprehensive income:								
Net earnings	—	—	—	—	—	—	1,875,000	1,875,000
Unrealized gain on derivative instruments, net of tax	—	—	—	—	—	244,000	—	244,000
Foreign currency adjustment	—	—	—	—	—	(2,114,000)	—	(2,114,000)
Total comprehensive income								5,000
Balances at March 31, 2010 . . .	12,125,985	121,000	6,102,000	61,000	5,053,000	(2,382,000)	164,486,000	167,339,000
Exercise of stock options	184,869	2,000	—	—	726,000	—	—	728,000
Tax benefits from stock options exercised	—	—	—	—	745,000	—	—	745,000
Repurchase of common stock	(183,953)	(2,000)	—	—	(2,417,000)	—	—	(2,419,000)
Restricted stock awards	78,500	1,000	—	—	(1,000)	—	—	—
Restricted stock forfeited	(6,130)	—	—	—	—	—	—	—
Stock based compensation expense	—	—	—	—	3,174,000	—	—	3,174,000
Comprehensive income:								
Net earnings	—	—	—	—	—	—	13,007,000	13,007,000
Unrealized loss on derivative instruments, net of tax	—	—	—	—	—	(1,147,000)	—	(1,147,000)
Foreign currency adjustment	—	—	—	—	—	1,609,000	—	1,609,000
Total comprehensive income								13,469,000
Balances at March 31, 2011 . .	**12,199,271**	**$122,000**	**6,102,000**	**$61,000**	**$ 7,280,000**	**$(1,920,000)**	**$177,493,000**	**$183,036,000**

ARCTIC CAT INC.

CONSOLIDATED STATEMENTS OF CASH FLOWS

Years ended March 31	2011	2010	2009
Cash flows from operating activities			
Net earnings (loss)	**$ 13,007,000**	$ 1,875,000	$ (9,508,000)
Adjustments to reconcile net earnings to net cash provided by (used in) operating activities			
Depreciation and amortization	**15,816,000**	22,779,000	28,981,000
Loss on the disposal of assets	**105,000**	144,000	252,000
Impairment of goodwill	**—**	—	1,750,000
Deferred income taxes benefit	**(3,194,000)**	(3,577,000)	(6,379,000)
Stock based compensation expense	**3,174,000**	2,486,000	2,570,000
Changes in operating assets and liabilities			
Trading securities	**(71,162,000)**	(39,082,000)	24,837,000
Accounts receivable, less allowances	**5,543,000**	9,400,000	(437,000)
Inventories	**20,587,000**	40,003,000	2,798,000
Prepaid expenses	**345,000**	205,000	(1,246,000)
Accounts payable	**2,879,000**	(7,668,000)	(29,615,000)
Accrued expenses	**9,238,000**	(585,000)	(3,392,000)
Income taxes	**(1,461,000)**	3,335,000	8,980,000
Net cash provided by (used in) operating activities	**(5,123,000)**	29,315,000	19,591,000
Cash flows from investing activities			
Purchases of property and equipment	**(11,761,000)**	(6,540,000)	(14,226,000)
Proceeds from the sale of assets	**87,000**	—	—
Net cash used in investing activities	**(11,674,000)**	(6,540,000)	(14,226,000)
Cash flows from financing activities			
Checks written in excess of bank balance	**—**	221,000	—
Proceeds from short-term borrowings	**1,012,000**	73,429,000	227,230,000
Payments on short-term borrowings	**(1,012,000)**	(73,429,000)	(227,230,000)
Proceeds from issuance of common stock	**728,000**	—	—
Tax benefit from stock option exercises	**745,000**	—	—
Repurchase of common stock	**(2,419,000)**	—	—
Dividends paid	**—**	—	(3,796,000)
Net cash provided by (used in) financing activities	**(946,000)**	221,000	(3,796,000)
Effect of exchange rate changes on cash and cash equivalents	**632,000**	(2,429,000)	(382,000)
Net increase (decrease) in cash and cash equivalents	**(17,111,000)**	20,567,000	1,187,000
Cash and cash equivalents at beginning of year	**31,811,000**	11,244,000	10,057,000
Cash and cash equivalents at end of year	**$ 14,700,000**	$ 31,811,000	$ 11,244,000
Supplemental disclosure of cash payments for:			
Income taxes	**$ 9,179,000**	$ 1,935,000	$ 409,000
Interest	**$ 11,000**	$ 250,000	$ 987,000

Supplemental disclosure of non-cash investing and financing activities:

As of March 31, 2011 and 2010, the unrealized gain (loss) on derivative instruments, net of tax was ($1,147,000) and $244,000.

KTM POWER SPORTS AG
CONSOLIDATED INCOME STATEMENT
FOR BUSINESS YEAR 2011

(In thousands of Euro)	2011
Net sales	**526,801**
Cost of goods sold	(371,752)
Gross margin	**155,049**
Selling and sport-activity expenses	(71,952)
R&D expenses	(23,099)
Infrastructure and administration expenses	(20,870)
Other operating expenses	(9,206)
Other operating Income	1,088
Operating result	**31,009**
Interest income	768
Interest expenses	(9,693)
Other financial and participation result	(2,975)
Pre-tax result	**19,109**
Tax on income and earnings	1,709
NET RESULT	**20,818**
Thereof net result to owners	*20,719*
Thereof net result to non-controlling shareholders	*99*
EARNINGS PER SHARE (EUR)	
Basic	2.003
Diluted	1.968

KTM POWER SPORTS AG
CONSOLIDATED STATEMENT OF COMPREHENSIVE INCOME
FOR BUSINESS YEAR 2011

(In thousands of Euro)	2011
Net result of the business year	**20,818**
Currency conversion	107
Valuation of cash flow hedges	11,393
Deferred tax on the valuation of cash flow hedges	(2,848)
Other income	**8,652**
TOTAL INCOME	**29,470**
Thereof net result to owners	*29,371*
Thereof net result to non-controlling shareholders	*99*

KTM POWER SPORTS AG
CONSOLIDATED BALANCE SHEET

AS AT DECEMBER 31

ASSETS

(In thousands of Euro)	12/31/2011	12/31/2010
SHORT-TERM ASSETS		
Liquid assets	14,962	8,946
Accounts receivable – trade to third parties	49,924	53,087
Accounts receivable – trade to affiliated companies	1,443	1,040
Accounts receivable – trade to associated companies	2,227	3,130
Inventory	113,979	108,910
Prepayments	1,649	1,169
Other short-term assets	9,701	7,231
	193,885	**183,513**
LONG-TERM ASSETS		
Financial fixed assets	7,458	6,222
Tangible fixed assets	84,256	63,204
Goodwill	78,793	78,492
Intangible fixed assets	118,202	110,118
Deferred taxes	3,132	3,725
Other long-term assets	49	51
	291,890	**261,812**
ASSETS	**485,775**	**445,325**

EQUITY AND LIABILITIES

(In thousands of Euro)	12/31/2011	12/31/2010
SHORT-TERM LIABILITIES		
Bank loans	5,415	14,061
Accounts payable – trade to third parties	54,578	37,725
Accounts payable – trade to affiliated companies	11,062	7,979
Accounts payable – trade to associated companies	2,600	2,895
Provisions	4,238	3,993
Liabilities – corporate tax	1,470	33
Prepayments	735	1,614
Other short-term liabilities	29,256	33,926
	109,353	**102,226**
LONG-TERM LIABILITIES		
Interest-bearing loans	132,898	129,957
Liabilities for personnel	7,699	6,479
Liabilities from deferred taxes	14,560	15,851
Liabilities to affiliated companies	0	13,021
Other long-term liabilities	1,490	1,005
	156,648	**166,313**
SHAREHOLDER'S EQUITY		
Share capital	10,509	10,109
Reserves including retained earnings	208,987	166,593
Non-controlling shares	279	84
	219,775	**176,786**
EQUITY AND LIABILITIES	**485,775**	**445,325**

KTM POWER SPORTS AG
CONSOLIDATED CASH FLOW STATEMENT
FOR BUSINESS YEAR 2011

(In thousands of Euro)	2011
CONSOLIDATED CASH FLOW FROM OPERATING ACTIVITIES	
+(−) Profit (loss) of the business year	20,818
+(−) Profit (loss) of non-controlling shareholders	(99)
+(−) Depreciation (write-up) of fixed assets	33,368
+(−) Depreciation (write-up) to financial assets	118
+(−) Deferred taxes	(3,352)
− Results from consolidation not affecting income	(649)
− Results from companies validated at-equity not affecting income	(657)
+(−) Addition (disposal) of liabilities for personnel	1,432
−(+) Profit (loss) from the sale of fixed assets	(59)
Consolidated cash flow from earnings	**50,919**
−(+) Increase (decrease) in inventories including prepayments	(5,069)
−(+) Increase (decrease) in accounts receiveable − trade, prepayments, other short- and longterm assets	831
−(+) Increase (decrease) in accounts receivable − trade from affiliated companies	430
−(+) Increase (decrease) in accounts receivable − trade from associated companies	903
(+)− Increase (decrease) in accounts payable − trade, prepayments and other short-term and long-term liabilities	16,346
(+)− Increase (decrease) in accounts payable − trade from affiliated companies	3,083
(+)− Increase (decrease) in accounts payable − trade from associated companies	(295)
(+)− Increase (decrease) from corporate taxes, deferred taxes and other provisions	3,201
	19,429
Cash flow from operating activities	**70,348**
CONSOLIDATED CASH FLOW FROM INVESTMENT ACTIVITIES	
− Investments in fixed assets (outflow of funds for investments)	(37,705)
− Investments in financial assets	(697)
(+)− Changes from first/final consolidation	273
+ Disposal of fixed assets (inflow of funds from sales: book value + profit (− loss) from the disposal of fixed assets)	871
(+)− Currency rate differences from fixed assets	(13)
Consolidated cash flow from investment activities	**(37,271)**
CONSOLIDATED CASH FLOW FROM FINANCING ACTIVITIES	
(+)− Currency rate differences	33
+ Capital increase	1,095
(+)− Increase (decrease) of short-term bank loans	(8,646)
(+)− Change in liabilities to affiliated and associated companies	(259)
(+)− Increase (decrease) in long-term interest bearing loans	(19,479)
+(−) Changes in non-controlling interests	196
+(−) Change deconsolidation Cost Plus subsidiaries	0
Consolidated cash flow from financing activities	**(27,060)**
CONSOLIDATED CASH FLOW	
+(−) Consolidated cash flow from operating activities	70,348
+(−) Consolidated cash flow from investment activities	(37,271)
+(−) Consolidated cash flow from financing activities	(27,060)
Change in the liquidity of the group	**6,017**
+ Starting cash and cash equivalents of the group	8,946
CASH AND CASH EQUIVALENTS OF THE GROUP AS AT DECEMBER 31	**14,962**
Consisting of cash in hand. cheques, cash at bank and term deposits	*14,962*
Interest paid	10,052
Taxes paid	547

KTM

KTM POWER SPORTS AG
DEVELOPMENT OF THE GROUP'S EQUITY CAPITAL

FOR BUSINESS YEAR 2011

(In thousands of Euro)	Nominal capital	Reserves incl. net result for the business year	Revaluation reserve	Cash flow hedge reserve	Currency translation adjustments	Total	Shares of non-controlling Interests	Total share capital
As at December 31, 2010	**10,109**	**163,106**	**17,235**	**(13,648)**	**(100)**	**176,702**	**84**	**176,786**
Currency conversion	0	0	0	0	105	**105**	0	**105**
Financial instruments	0	0	0	8,545	0	**8,545**	0	**8,545**
Profit and loss directly recognized in equity	**0**	**0**	**0**	**8,545**	**105**	**8,650**	**0**	**8,650**
Result of the business year	0	20,719	0	0	0	**20,719**	99	**20,819**
Total profit and loss recognized in equity	**0**	**20,719**	**0**	**8,545**	**105**	**29,369**	**99**	**29,469**
Capital increase	400	13,600	0	0	0	**14,000**	0	**14,000**
Cost of capital increase	0	(480)	0	0	0	**(480)**	0	**(480)**
Change in non-controlling interests	0	(96)	0	0	0	**(96)**	96	**0**
AS AT DECEMBER 31, 2011	**10,509**	**196,849**	**17,235**	**(5,103)**	**5**	**219,495**	**279**	**219,775**

Piaggio Group
Consolidated Income Statement

For Year Ended December 31 (In thousands of Euro)	2011	2010
Net revenues	**1,516,463**	**1,485,351**
Cost for materials	904,060	881,075
Cost for services and leases and rentals	266,484	258,358
Employee costs	247,600	240,115
Depreciation of property, plant and equipment	35,219	35,879
Amortisation of intangible assets	59,794	50,127
Other operating income	122,562	121,128
Other operating costs	20,323	29,821
Operating income	**105,545**	**111,104**
Income/(loss) from investments	2,481	5,252
Financial income	4,087	2,891
Borrowing Costs	31,853	33,905
Net exchange gains/(losses)	(932)	(1,518)
Earnings before tax	**79,328**	**83,824**
Taxation for the period	32,305	40,983
Earnings from continuing activities	**47,023**	**42,841**
Assets held for disposal:		
Profits or losses arising from assets held for disposal		
Net Income (Loss) for the period	**47,023**	**42,841**
Attributable to:		
Shareholders of the Parent Company	**47,053**	**42,811**
Non-controlling interests	**(30)**	**30**
Earnings per share (figures in €)	**0.126**	**0.113**
Diluted earnings per share (figures in €)	**0.126**	**0.112**

Piaggio Group
Consolidated Statement of Comprehensive Income

For Year Ended December 31 (In thousands of Euro)	2011	2010
Profit (loss) for the period (A)	**47,023**	**42,841**
Effective portion of profits (losses) on cash flow hedges	(1,283)	(354)
Profit (loss) deriving from the translation of financial statements of foreign companies denominated in foreign currency	(11,262)	3,060
Total Other Profits (and losses) for the period (B)	**(12,545)**	**2,706**
Total Profit (loss) for the period (A + B)	**34,478**	**45,547**
Attributable to:		
Shareholders of the Parent Company	**34,533**	**45,531**
Non-controlling interests	**(55)**	**16**

Piaggio Group
Consolidated Statement of Financial Position

As of December 31 (In thousands of Euro)	2011	2010
Assets		
Non-current assets		
Intangible assets	649,420	652,622
Property, plant and equipment	274,871	256,759
Investment property		
Investments	2,482	194
Other financial assets	11,836	334
Long-term tax receivables	976	967
Deferred tax assets	55,726	46,294
Trade receivables		
Other receivables	15,165	12,655
Total non-current assets	**1,010,476**	**969,825**
Assets held for sale		
Current assets		
Trade receivables	65,560	90,421
Other receivables	28,028	23,300
Short-term tax receivables	27,245	44,200
Inventories	236,988	240,066
Other financial assets	0	23,051
Cash and cash equivalents	151,887	154,859
Total current assets	**509,708**	**575,897**
Total assets	**1,520,184**	**1,545,722**
Shareholders' equity and liabilities		
Shareholders' equity		
Share capital and reserves attributable to the shareholders of the Parent Company	445,036	441,277
Share capital and reserves attributable to non-controlling interests	1,182	1,613
Total shareholders' equity	**446,218**	**442,890**
Non-current liabilities		
Financial liabilities falling due after one year	329,200	371,048
Trade payables	235	88
Other long-term provisions	12,429	16,993
Deferred tax liabilities	32,735	32,338
Retirement funds and employee benefits	46,603	58,636
Tax payables	2,539	3,361
Other long-term payables	5,948	4,202
Total non-current liabilities	**429,689**	**486,666**
Current liabilities		
Financial liabilities falling due within one year	170,261	156,800
Trade payables	375,263	352,627
Tax payables	20,920	19,290
Other short-term payables	64,718	69,503
Current portion of other long-term provisions	13,115	17,946
Total current liabilities	**644,277**	**616,166**
Total shareholders' equity and liabilities	**1,520,184**	**1,545,722**

Piaggio Group
Consolidated Cash Flow Statement

For Year Ended December 31 (In thousands of Euro)	2011	2010
Operating activities		
Consolidated net income	47,053	42,811
Allocation of profit to non-controlling interests	(30)	30
Taxation for the period	32,305	40,983
Depreciation of property, plant and equipment	35,219	35,879
Amortisation of intangible assets	59,794	50,127
Non-monetary costs for stock options	771	2,650
Allocations for risks and retirement funds and employee benefits	21,134	29,243
Write-downs / (Reversals)	(1,192)	1,755
Losses / (Gains) on the disposal of property, plants and equipment	(6,012)	(2,240)
Losses / (Gains) on the disposal of intangible assets	0	0
Financial income	(3,910)	(2,891)
Dividend income	(193)	(12)
Borrowing Costs	25,558	29,744
Income from public grants	(3,492)	(4,164)
Portion of earnings of affiliated companies	0	45
Change in working capital:		
(Increase)/Decrease in trade receivables	24,861	12,743
(Increase)/Decrease in other receivables	(18,740)	(1,157)
(Increase)/Decrease in inventories	3,078	12,430
Increase/(Decrease) in trade payables	22,783	6,640
Increase/(Decrease) in other payables	8,636	(12,347)
Increase/(Decrease) in provisions for risks	(21,782)	(26,974)
Increase/(Decrease) in retirement funds and employee benefits	(20,795)	(13,028)
Other changes	5,265	(43,774)
Cash generated from operating activities	**210,311**	**158,493**
Interest paid	(22,825)	(23,178)
Taxes paid	(31,862)	(12,774)
Cash flow from operating activities (A)	**155,624**	**122,541**
Investment activities		
Investment in property, plant and equipment	(61,790)	(37,132)
Sale price, or repayment value, of property, plant and equipment	6,542	3,823
Investment in intangible assets	(64,300)	(59,063)
Sale price, or repayment value, of intangible assets	122	261
Purchase of financial assets	0	(23,051)
Sale price of financial assets	23,051	4,127
Collected interests	11,666	2,360
Cash flow from investment activities (B)	**(84,709)**	**(108,675)**
Financing activities		
Exercise of stock options	2,843	
Purchase of treasury shares	(9,080)	(3,344)
Outflow for dividends paid	(25,684)	(25,765)
Loans received	71,400	37,652
Outflow for repayment of loans	(112,727)	(65,174)
Financing received for leases	227	0
Repayment of finance leases	(850)	(758)
Cash flow from funding activities (C)	**(73,871)**	**(57,389)**
Increase / (Decrease) in cash and cash equivalents (A+B+C)	(2,956)	(43,523)
Opening balance	**154,758**	**198,281**
Exchange differences		
Closing balance	**151,802**	**154,758**

Piaggio Group

Changes in Consolidated Shareholders' Equity

Movements from 1 January 2011 / 31 December 2011

In thousands of Euro	Share capital	Share premium reserve	Legal reserve	Reserve for measurement of financial instruments	IAS transition reserve	Group consolidation reserve	Group conversion reserve	Stock option reserve	Performance reserve	Consolidated Group shareholders' equity	Non-controlling interests capital and reserves	Total shareholders' equity
As of 1 January 2011	**203,348**	**3,493**	**11,299**	**(227)**	**(5,859)**	**993**	**(1,850)**	**11,929**	**218,151**	**441,277**	**1,613**	**442,890**
Charges for the period for stock option plans								771		**771**		**771**
Allocation of profits			942						(942)	**0**		**0**
Distribution of dividends									(25,684)	**(25,684)**		**(25,684)**
Purchase of treasury shares	(2,382)								(6,698)	**(9,080)**		**(9,080)**
Exercise of stock options	1,243								1,600	**2,843**		**2,843**
Reacquisiton of the Simest investment									376	**376**	**(376)**	**0**
Total overall profit (loss)				(1,283)			(11,237)		47,053	**34,533**	**(55)**	**34,478**
As of 31 December 2011	**202,209**	**3,493**	**12,241**	**(1,510)**	**(5,859)**	**993**	**(13,087)**	**12,700**	**233,856**	**445,036**	**1,182**	**446,218**

Movements from 1 January 2010 / 31 December 2010

In thousands of Euro	Share capital	Share premium reserve	Legal reserve	Reserve for measurement of financial instruments	IAS transition reserve	Group consolidation reserve	Group conversion reserve	Stock option reserve	Performance reserve	Consolidated Group shareholders' equity	Non-controlling interests capital and reserves	Total shareholders' equity
As of 1 January 2010	**191,616**	**3,493**	**8,996**	**127**	**(5,859)**	**993**	**(5,468)**	**9,279**	**218,484**	**421,661**	**2,141**	**423,802**
Charges for the period for stock option plans								2,650		**2,650**		**2,650**
Allocation of profits			2,303						(2,303)	**0**		**0**
Distribution of dividends									(25,765)	**(25,765)**		**(25,765)**
Cancellation of treasury shares	12,608								(12,608)	**0**		**0**
Purchase of treasury shares	(876)								(2,468)	**(3,344)**		**(3,344)**
Total overall profit (loss)				(354)			3,618		42,811	**46,075**	**(528)**	**45,547**
As of 31 December 2010	**203,348**	**3,493**	**11,299**	**(227)**	**(5,859)**	**993**	**(1,850)**	**11,929**	**218,151**	**441,277**	**1,613**	**442,890**

Appendix

B

Time Value of Money

Learning Objectives

CONCEPTUAL

C1 Describe the earning of interest and the concepts of present and future values. (p. B-1)

PROCEDURAL

P1 Apply present value concepts to a single amount by using interest tables. (p. B-3)

P2 Apply future value concepts to a single amount by using interest tables. (p. B-4)

P3 Apply present value concepts to an annuity by using interest tables. (p. B-5)

P4 Apply future value concepts to an annuity by using interest tables. (p. B-6)

Appendix Preview

The concepts of present and future values are important to modern business, including the preparation and analysis of financial statements. The purpose of this appendix is to explain, illustrate, and compute present and future values. This appendix applies these concepts with reference to both business and everyday activities.

Time Value of Money

Present and Future Value Concepts
- Time is money
- Concept of interest

Value of a Single Amount
- Present value of a single amount
- Future value of a single amount

Value of an Annuity
- Present value of an annuity
- Future value of an annuity

PRESENT AND FUTURE VALUE CONCEPTS

C1 Describe the earning of interest and the concepts of present and future values.

The old saying "Time is money" reflects the notion that as time passes, the values of our assets and liabilities change. This change is due to *interest,* which is a borrower's payment to the owner of an asset for its use. The most common example of interest is a savings account asset. As we keep a balance of cash in the account, it earns interest that the financial institution pays us. An example of a liability is a car loan. As we carry the balance of the loan, we accumulate interest costs on it. We must ultimately repay this loan with interest.

Present and future value computations enable us to measure or estimate the interest component of holding assets or liabilities over time. The present value computation is important when we want to know the value of future-day assets *today.* The future value computation is important when we want to know the value of present-day assets *at a future date.* The first section focuses on the present value of a single amount. The second section focuses on the future value of a single amount. Then both the present and future values of a series of amounts (called an *annuity*) are defined and explained.

Decision Insight

Working for Lotto Winnings Lottery winners often never work again. Kenny Dukes, a recent Georgia lottery winner, doesn't have that option. He is serving parole for burglary charges, and Georgia requires its parolees to be employed (or in school). For his lottery winnings, Dukes had to choose between $31 million in 30 annual payments or $16 million in one lump sum ($10.6 million after-tax); he chose the latter. ■

PRESENT VALUE OF A SINGLE AMOUNT

We graphically express the present value, called p, of a single future amount, called f, that is received or paid at a future date in Exhibit B.1.

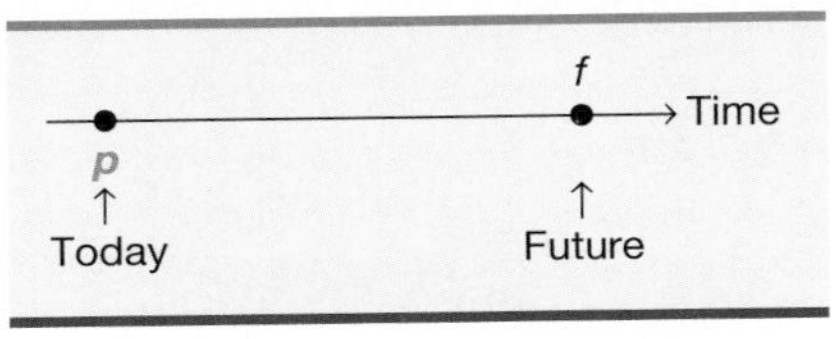

EXHIBIT B.1

Present Value of a Single Amount Diagram

The formula to compute the present value of a single amount is shown in Exhibit B.2, where p = present value; f = future value; i = rate of interest per period; and n = number of periods. (Interest is also called the *discount,* and an interest rate is also called the *discount rate.*)

EXHIBIT B.2

Present Value of a Single Amount Formula

$$p = \frac{f}{(1 + i)^n}$$

To illustrate present value concepts, assume that we need $220 one period from today. We want to know how much we must invest now, for one period, at an interest rate of 10% to provide for this $220. For this illustration, the p, or present value, is the unknown amount—the specifics are shown graphically as follows:

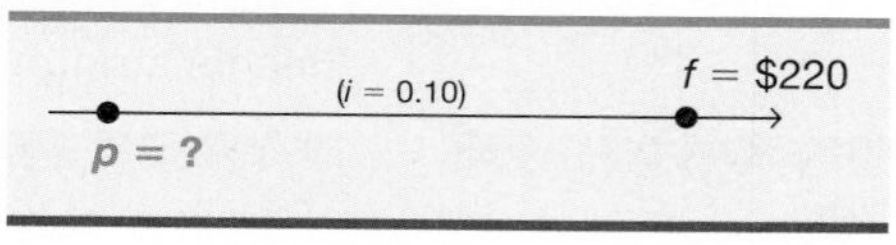

Conceptually, we know p must be less than $220. This is obvious from the answer to this question: Would we rather have $220 today or $220 at some future date? If we had $220 today, we could invest it and see it grow to something more than $220 in the future. Therefore, we would prefer the $220 today. This means that if we were promised $220 in the future, we would take less than $220 today. But how much less? To answer that question, we compute an estimate of the present value of the $220 to be received one period from now using the formula in Exhibit B.2 as follows:

$$p = \frac{f}{(1 + i)^n} = \frac{\$220}{(1 + 0.10)^1} = \$200$$

We interpret this result to say that given an interest rate of 10%, we are indifferent between $200 today or $220 at the end of one period.

We can also use this formula to compute the present value for *any number of periods.* To illustrate, consider a payment of $242 at the end of two periods at 10% interest. The present value of this $242 to be received two periods from now is computed as follows:

$$p = \frac{f}{(1 + i)^n} = \frac{\$242}{(1 + 0.10)^2} = \$200$$

Together, these results tell us we are indifferent between $200 today, or $220 one period from today, or $242 two periods from today given a 10% interest rate per period.

The number of periods (n) in the present value formula does not have to be expressed in years. Any period of time such as a day, a month, a quarter, or a year can be used. Whatever period is used, the interest rate (i) must be compounded for the same period. This means that if a situation expresses n in months and i equals 12% per year, then i is transformed into interest earned per month (or 1%). In this case, interest is said to be *compounded monthly.*

A present value table helps us with present value computations. It gives us present values (factors) for a variety of both interest rates (i) and periods (n). Each present value in a present value table assumes that the future value (f) equals 1. When the future value (f) is different from 1, we simply multiply the present value (p) from the table by that future value to give us the estimate. The formula used to construct a table of present values for a single future amount of 1 is shown in Exhibit B.3.

EXHIBIT B.3

Present Value of 1 Formula

$$p = \frac{1}{(1 + i)^n}$$

This formula is identical to that in Exhibit B.2 except that f equals 1. Table B.1 at the end of this appendix is such a present value table. It is often called a **present value of 1 table**. A present value table involves three factors: p, i, and n. Knowing two of these three factors allows us to compute the third. (A fourth is f, but as already explained, we need only multiply the 1 used in the formula by f.) To illustrate the use of a present value table, consider three cases.

P1 Apply present value concepts to a single amount by using interest tables.

Case 1 (solve for p when knowing i and n). To show how we use a present value table, let's look again at how we estimate the present value of \$220 (the f value) at the end of one period ($n = 1$) where the interest rate (i) is 10%. To solve this case, we go to the present value table (Table B.1) and look in the row for 1 period and in the column for 10% interest. Here we find a present value (p) of 0.9091 based on a future value of 1. This means, for instance, that \$1 to be received one period from today at 10% interest is worth \$0.9091 today. Since the future value in this case is not \$1 but \$220, we multiply the 0.9091 by \$220 to get an answer of \$200.

Case 2 (solve for n when knowing p and i). To illustrate, assume a \$100,000 future value (f) that is worth \$13,000 today (p) using an interest rate of 12% (i) but where n is unknown. In particular, we want to know how many periods (n) there are between the present value and the future value. To put this in context, it would fit a situation in which we want to retire with \$100,000 but currently have only \$13,000 that is earning a 12% return and we will be unable to save any additional money. How long will it be before we can retire? To answer this, we go to Table B.1 and look in the 12% interest column. Here we find a column of present values (p) based on a future value of 1. To use the present value table for this solution, we must divide \$13,000 (p) by \$100,000 (f), which equals 0.1300. This is necessary because *a present value table defines* f *equal to 1, and* p *as a fraction of 1.* We look for a value nearest to 0.1300 (p), which we find in the row for 18 periods (n). This means that the present value of \$100,000 at the end of 18 periods at 12% interest is \$13,000; alternatively stated, we must work 18 more years.

Case 3 (solve for i when knowing p and n). In this case, we have, say, a \$120,000 future value (f) worth \$60,000 today (p) when there are nine periods (n) between the present and future values, but the interest rate is unknown. As an example, suppose we want to retire with \$120,000, but we have only \$60,000 and we will be unable to save any additional money, yet we hope to retire in nine years. What interest rate must we earn to retire with \$120,000 in nine years? To answer this, we go to the present value table (Table B.1) and look in the row for nine periods. To use the present value table, we must divide \$60,000 (p) by \$120,000 (f), which equals 0.5000. Recall that this step is necessary because a present value table defines f equal to 1 and p as a fraction of 1. We look for a value in the row for nine periods that is nearest to 0.5000 (p), which we find in the column for 8% interest (i). This means that the present value of \$120,000 at the end of nine periods at 8% interest is \$60,000 or, in our example, we must earn 8% annual interest to retire in nine years.

Quick Check Answer — p. B-7

1. A company is considering an investment expected to yield \$70,000 after six years. If this company demands an 8% return, how much is it willing to pay for this investment?

FUTURE VALUE OF A SINGLE AMOUNT

We must modify the formula for the present value of a single amount to obtain the formula for the future value of a single amount. In particular, we multiply both sides of the equation in Exhibit B.2 by $(1 + i)^n$ to get the result shown in Exhibit B.4.

EXHIBIT B.4

Future Value of a Single Amount Formula

$$f = p \times (1 + i)^n$$

The future value (f) is defined in terms of p, i, and n. We can use this formula to determine that \$200 (p) invested for 1 (n) period at an interest rate of 10% (i) yields a future value of \$220 as follows:

$$f = p \times (1 + i)^n$$
$$= \$200 \times (1 + 0.10)^1$$
$$= \$220$$

P2 Apply future value concepts to a single amount by using interest tables.

This formula can also be used to compute the future value of an amount for *any number of periods* into the future. To illustrate, assume that \$200 is invested for three periods at 10%. The future value of this \$200 is \$266.20, computed as follows:

$$f = p \times (1 + i)^n$$
$$= \$200 \times (1 + 0.10)^3$$
$$= \$266.20$$

A future value table makes it easier for us to compute future values (f) for many different combinations of interest rates (i) and time periods (n). Each future value in a future value table assumes the present value (p) is 1. As with a present value table, if the future amount is something other than 1, we simply multiply our answer by that amount. The formula used to construct a table of future values (factors) for a single amount of 1 is in Exhibit B.5.

EXHIBIT B.5

Future Value of 1 Formula

$$f = (1 + i)^n$$

Table B.2 at the end of this appendix shows a table of future values for a current amount of 1. This type of table is called a **future value of 1 table**.

There are some important relations between Tables B.1 and B.2. In Table B.2, for the row where $n = 0$, the future value is 1 for each interest rate. This is so because no interest is earned when time does not pass. We also see that Tables B.1 and B.2 report the same information but in a different manner. In particular, one table is simply the *inverse* of the other. To illustrate this inverse relation, let's say we invest \$100 for a period of five years at 12% per year. How much do we expect to have after five years? We can answer this question using Table B.2 by finding the future value (f) of 1, for five periods from now, compounded at 12%. From that table we find $f = 1.7623$. If we start with \$100, the amount it accumulates to after five years is \$176.23 (\$100 × 1.7623). We can alternatively use Table B.1. Here we find that the present value (p) of 1, discounted five periods at 12%, is 0.5674. Recall the inverse relation between present value and future value. This means that $p = 1/f$ (or equivalently, $f = 1/p$). We can compute the future value of \$100 invested for five periods at 12% as follows: $f = \$100 \times (1/0.5674) = \$176.24$ (which equals the \$176.23 just computed, except for a 1 cent rounding difference).

A future value table involves three factors: f, i, and n. Knowing two of these three factors allows us to compute the third. To illustrate, consider these three possible cases.

Case 1 (solve for f when knowing i and n). Our preceding example fits this case. We found that \$100 invested for five periods at 12% interest accumulates to \$176.24.

Case 2 (solve for n when knowing f and i). In this case, we have, say, \$2,000 (p) and we want to know how many periods (n) it will take to accumulate to \$3,000 (f) at 7% (i) interest. To answer this, we go to the future value table (Table B.2) and look in the 7% interest column. Here we find a column of future values (f) based on a present value of 1. To use a future value table, we must divide \$3,000 (f) by \$2,000 (p), which equals 1.500. This is necessary because *a future value table defines* p *equal to 1, and* f *as a multiple of 1.* We look for a value nearest to 1.50 (f), which we find in the row for six periods (n). This means that \$2,000 invested for six periods at 7% interest accumulates to \$3,000.

Case 3 (solve for i when knowing f and n). In this case, we have, say, \$2,001 (p), and in nine years (n) we want to have \$4,000 (f). What rate of interest must we earn to accomplish this? To answer that, we go to Table B.2 and search in the row for nine periods. To use a future value table, we must divide \$4,000 (f) by \$2,001 (p), which equals 1.9990. Recall that this is necessary because a future value table defines p equal to 1 and f as a multiple of 1. We look for a value nearest to 1.9990 (f), which we find in the column for 8% interest (i). This means that $2,001 invested for nine periods at 8% interest accumulates to $4,000.

Quick Check Answer — p. B-7

2. Assume that you win a $150,000 cash sweepstakes. You decide to deposit this cash in an account earning 8% annual interest, and you plan to quit your job when the account equals $555,000. How many years will it be before you can quit working?

PRESENT VALUE OF AN ANNUITY

An *annuity* is a series of equal payments occurring at equal intervals. One example is a series of three annual payments of $100 each. An *ordinary annuity* is defined as equal end-of-period payments at equal intervals. An ordinary annuity of $100 for three periods and its present value (p) are illustrated in Exhibit B.6.

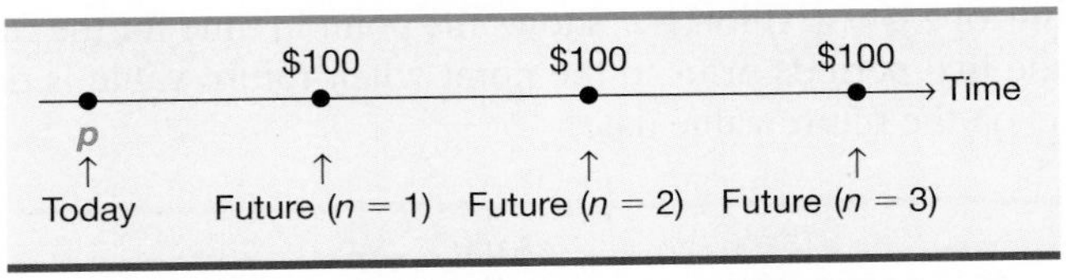

EXHIBIT B.6

Present Value of an Ordinary Annuity Diagram

P3 Apply present value concepts to an annuity by using interest tables.

One way to compute the present value of an ordinary annuity is to find the present value of each payment using our present value formula from Exhibit B.3. We then add each of the three present values. To illustrate, let's look at three $100 payments at the end of each of the next three periods with an interest rate of 15%. Our present value computations are

$$p = \frac{\$100}{(1 + 0.15)^1} + \frac{\$100}{(1 + 0.15)^2} + \frac{\$100}{(1 + 0.15)^3} = \$228.32$$

This computation is identical to computing the present value of each payment (from Table B.1) and taking their sum or, alternatively, adding the values from Table B.1 for each of the three payments and multiplying their sum by the $100 annuity payment.

A more direct way is to use a present value of annuity table. Table B.3 at the end of this appendix is one such table. This table is called a **present value of an annuity of 1 table.** If we look at Table B.3 where $n = 3$ and $i = 15\%$, we see the present value is 2.2832. This means that the present value of an annuity of 1 for three periods, with a 15% interest rate, equals 2.2832.

A present value of an annuity formula is used to construct Table B.3. It can also be constructed by adding the amounts in a present value of 1 table. To illustrate, we use Tables B.1 and B.3 to confirm this relation for the prior example:

From Table B.1		From Table B.3	
i = 15%, n = 1	0.8696		
i = 15%, n = 2	0.7561		
i = 15%, n = 3	0.6575		
Total	2.2832	i = 15%, n = 3	2.2832

We can also use business calculators or spreadsheet programs to find the present value of an annuity.

Decision Insight

Blessed Winnings "I don't have good luck—I'm blessed," proclaimed Andrew "Jack" Whittaker, 55, a sewage treatment contractor, after winning the largest ever undivided jackpot in a U.S. lottery. Whittaker had to choose between $315 million in 30 annual installments or $170 million in one lump sum ($112 million after-tax). ■

Quick Check

Answer — p. B-7

3. A company is considering an investment paying $10,000 every six months for three years. The first payment would be received in six months. If this company requires an 8% annual return, what is the maximum amount it is willing to pay for this investment?

FUTURE VALUE OF AN ANNUITY

The future value of an *ordinary annuity* is the accumulated value of each annuity payment with interest as of the date of the final payment. To illustrate, let's consider the earlier annuity of three annual payments of $100. Exhibit B.7 shows the point in time for the future value (f). The first payment is made two periods prior to the point when future value is determined, and the final payment occurs on the future value date.

EXHIBIT B.7

Future Value of an Ordinary Annuity Diagram

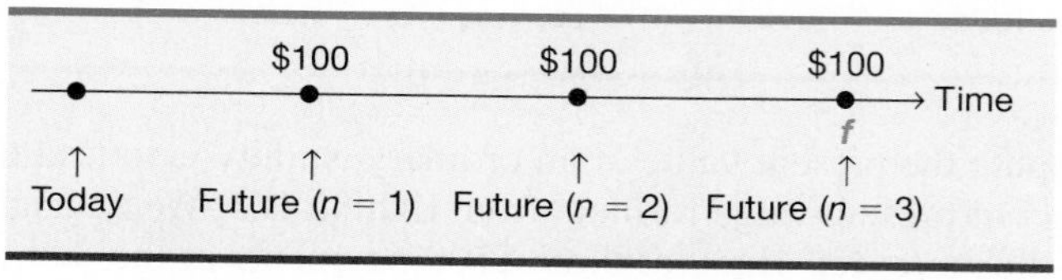

One way to compute the future value of an annuity is to use the formula to find the future value of *each* payment and add them. If we assume an interest rate of 15%, our calculation is

$$f = \$100 \times (1 + 0.15)^2 + \$100 \times (1 + 0.15)^1 + \$100 \times (1 + 0.15)^0 = \$347.25$$

This is identical to using Table B.2 and summing the future values of each payment, or adding the future values of the three payments of 1 and multiplying the sum by $100.

P4 Apply future value concepts to an annuity by using interest tables.

A more direct way is to use a table showing future values of annuities. Such a table is called a **future value of an annuity of 1 table**. Table B.4 at the end of this appendix is one such table. Note that in Table B.4 when $n = 1$, the future values equal 1 ($f = 1$) for all rates of interest. This is so because such an annuity consists of only one payment and the future value is determined on the date of that payment—no time passes between the payment and its future value. The future value of an annuity formula is used to construct Table B.4. We can also construct it by adding the amounts from a future value of 1 table. To illustrate, we use Tables B.2 and B.4 to confirm this relation for the prior example:

From Table B.2		From Table B.4	
$i = 15\%, n = 0$	1.0000		
$i = 15\%, n = 1$	1.1500		
$i = 15\%, n = 2$	1.3225		
Total	3.4725	$i = 15\%, n = 3$	3.4725

Note that the future value in Table B.2 is 1.0000 when $n = 0$, but the future value in Table B.4 is 1.0000 when $n = 1$. Is this a contradiction? No. When $n = 0$ in Table B.2, the future value is determined on the date when a single payment occurs. This means that no interest is earned because no time has passed, and the future value equals the payment. Table B.4 describes annuities with equal payments occurring at the end of each period. When $n = 1$, the annuity has one payment, and its future value equals 1 on the date of its final and only payment. Again, no time passes between the payment and its future value date.

Quick Check Answer — p. B-7

4. A company invests $45,000 per year for five years at 12% annual interest. Compute the value of this annuity investment at the end of five years.

Summary

C1 Describe the earning of interest and the concepts of present and future values. Interest is payment by a borrower to the owner of an asset for its use. Present and future value computations are a way for us to estimate the interest component of holding assets or liabilities over a period of time.

P1 Apply present value concepts to a single amount by using interest tables. The present value of a single amount received at a future date is the amount that can be invested now at the specified interest rate to yield that future value.

P2 Apply future value concepts to a single amount by using interest tables. The future value of a single amount invested at a specified rate of interest is the amount that would accumulate by the future date.

P3 Apply present value concepts to an annuity by using interest tables. The present value of an annuity is the amount that can be invested now at the specified interest rate to yield that series of equal periodic payments.

P4 Apply future value concepts to an annuity by using interest tables. The future value of an annuity invested at a specific rate of interest is the amount that would accumulate by the date of the final payment.

Guidance Answers to Quick Checks

1. $70,000 × 0.6302 = $44,114 (use Table B.1, $i = 8\%$, $n = 6$).

2. $555,000/$150,000 = 3.7000; Table B.2 shows this value is not achieved until after 17 years at 8% interest.

3. $10,000 × 5.2421 = $52,421 (use Table B.3, $i = 4\%$, $n = 6$).

4. $45,000 × 6.3528 = $285,876 (use Table B.4, $i = 12\%$, $n = 5$).

connect

QUICK STUDY

QS B-1 Identifying interest rates in tables C1

Assume that you must make future value estimates using the *future value of 1 table* (Table B.2). Which interest rate column do you use when working with the following rates?

1. 8% annual rate, compounded quarterly

2. 12% annual rate, compounded annually

3. 6% annual rate, compounded semiannually

4. 12% annual rate, compounded monthly

QS B-2 Interest rate on an investment P1

Ken Francis is offered the possibility of investing $2,745 today and in return to receive $10,000 after 15 years. What is the annual rate of interest for this investment? (Use Table B.1.)

QS B-3 Number of periods of an investment P1

Megan Brink is offered the possibility of investing $6,651 today at 6% interest per year in a desire to accumulate $10,000. How many years must Brink wait to accumulate $10,000? (Use Table B.1.)

QS B-4 Present value of an amount P1

Flaherty is considering an investment that, if paid for immediately, is expected to return $140,000 five years from now. If Flaherty demands a 9% return, how much is she willing to pay for this investment?

QS B-5 Future value of an amount P2

CII, Inc., invests $630,000 in a project expected to earn a 12% annual rate of return. The earnings will be reinvested in the project each year until the entire investment is liquidated 10 years later. What will the cash proceeds be when the project is liquidated?

QS B-6 Present value of an annuity P3

Beene Distributing is considering a project that will return $150,000 annually at the end of each year for the next six years. If Beene demands an annual return of 7% and pays for the project immediately, how much is it willing to pay for the project?

QS B-7
Future value of an annuity P4

Claire Fitch is planning to begin an individual retirement program in which she will invest $1,500 at the end of each year. Fitch plans to retire after making 30 annual investments in the program earning a return of 10%. What is the value of the program on the date of the last payment (30 years from the present)?

EXERCISES

Exercise B-1
Number of periods of an investment P2

Bill Thompson expects to invest $10,000 at 12% and, at the end of a certain period, receive $96,463. How many years will it be before Thompson receives the payment? (Use Table B.2.)

Exercise B-2
Interest rate on an investment P2

Ed Summers expects to invest $10,000 for 25 years, after which he wants to receive $108,347. What rate of interest must Summers earn? (Use Table B.2.)

Exercise B-3
Interest rate on an investment P3

Jones expects an immediate investment of $57,466 to return $10,000 annually for eight years, with the first payment to be received one year from now. What rate of interest must Jones earn? (Use Table B.3.)

Exercise B-4
Number of periods of an investment P3

Keith Riggins expects an investment of $82,014 to return $10,000 annually for several years. If Riggins earns a return of 10%, how many annual payments will he receive? (Use Table B.3.)

Exercise B-5
Interest rate on an investment P4

Algoe expects to invest $1,000 annually for 40 years to yield an accumulated value of $154,762 on the date of the last investment. For this to occur, what rate of interest must Algoe earn? (Use Table B.4.)

Exercise B-6
Number of periods of an investment P4

Kate Beckwith expects to invest $10,000 annually that will earn 8%. How many annual investments must Beckwith make to accumulate $303,243 on the date of the last investment? (Use Table B.4.)

Exercise B-7
Present value of an annuity P3

Sam Weber finances a new automobile by paying $6,500 cash and agreeing to make 40 monthly payments of $500 each, the first payment to be made one month after the purchase. The loan bears interest at an annual rate of 12%. What is the cost of the automobile?

Exercise B-8
Present value of bonds
P1 P3

Spiller Corp. plans to issue 10%, 15-year, $500,000 par value bonds payable that pay interest semiannually on June 30 and December 31. The bonds are dated December 31, 2013, and are issued on that date. If the market rate of interest for the bonds is 8% on the date of issue, what will be the total cash proceeds from the bond issue?

Exercise B-9
Present value of an amount P1

McAdams Company expects to earn 10% per year on an investment that will pay $606,773 six years from now. Use Table B.1 to compute the present value of this investment. (Round the amount to the nearest dollar.)

Exercise B-10
Present value of an amount and of an annuity P1 P3

Compute the amount that can be borrowed under each of the following circumstances:

1. A promise to repay $90,000 seven years from now at an interest rate of 6%.
2. An agreement made on February 1, 2013, to make three separate payments of $20,000 on February 1 of 2014, 2015, and 2016. The annual interest rate is 10%.

Exercise B-11
Present value of an amount P1

On January 1, 2013, a company agrees to pay $20,000 in three years. If the annual interest rate is 10%, determine how much cash the company can borrow with this agreement.

Exercise B-12
Practical applications of the time value of money
P1 P2 P3 P4

a. How much would you have to deposit today if you wanted to have $60,000 in 4 years? Annual interest rate is 9%.

b. Assume that you are saving up for a trip around the world when you graduate in 2 years. If you can earn 8% on your investments, how much would you have to deposit today to have $15,000 when you graduate?

c. Would you rather have \$463 now or \$1,000 ten years from now? Assume that you can earn 9% on your investments.

d. Assume that a college parking sticker today costs \$90. If the cost of parking is increasing at the rate of 5% per year, how much will the college parking sticker cost in 8 years?

e. Assume that the average price of a new home is \$158,500. If new homes are increasing at a rate of 10% per year, how much will a new home cost in 8 years?

f. An investment will pay you \$10,000 in 10 years, and it will also pay you \$400 at the end of *each* of the next 10 years (years 1 thru 10). If the annual interest rate is 6%, how much would you be willing to pay today for this type of investment?

g. A college student is reported in the newspaper as having won \$10,000,000 in the Kansas State Lottery. However, as is often the custom with lotteries, she does *not* actually receive the entire \$10 million now. Instead she will receive \$500,000 at the end of the year for *each* of the next 20 years. If the annual interest rate is 6%, what is the present value (today's amount) that she won? (Ignore taxes.)

Exercise B-13
Present values of annuities
P3

C&H Ski Club recently borrowed money and agrees to pay it back with a series of six annual payments of \$5,000 each. C&H subsequently borrows more money and agrees to pay it back with a series of four annual payments of \$7,500 each. The annual interest rate for both loans is 6%.

1. Use Table B.1 to find the present value of these two separate annuities. (Round amounts to the nearest dollar.)

2. Use Table B.3 to find the present value of these two separate annuities. (Round amounts to the nearest dollar.)

Exercise B-14
Present value with semiannual compounding
C1 P3

Otto Co. borrows money on April 30, 2013, by promising to make four payments of \$13,000 each on November 1, 2013; May 1, 2014; November 1, 2014; and May 1, 2015.

1. How much money is Otto able to borrow if the interest rate is 8%, compounded semiannually?

2. How much money is Otto able to borrow if the interest rate is 12%, compounded semiannually?

3. How much money is Otto able to borrow if the interest rate is 16%, compounded semiannually?

Exercise B-15
Future value of an amount P2

Mark Welsch deposits \$7,200 in an account that earns interest at an annual rate of 8%, compounded quarterly. The \$7,200 plus earned interest must remain in the account 10 years before it can be withdrawn. How much money will be in the account at the end of 10 years?

Exercise B-16
Future value of an annuity P4

Kelly Malone plans to have \$50 withheld from her monthly paycheck and deposited in a savings account that earns 12% annually, compounded monthly. If Malone continues with her plan for two and one-half years, how much will be accumulated in the account on the date of the last deposit?

Exercise B-17
Future value of an amount plus an annuity P2 P4

Starr Company decides to establish a fund that it will use 10 years from now to replace an aging production facility. The company will make a \$100,000 initial contribution to the fund and plans to make quarterly contributions of \$50,000 beginning in three months. The fund earns 12%, compounded quarterly. What will be the value of the fund 10 years from now?

Exercise B-18
Future value of an amount P2

Catten, Inc., invests \$163,170 today earning 7% per year for nine years. Use Table B.2 to compute the future value of the investment nine years from now. (Round the amount to the nearest dollar.)

Exercise B-19
Using present and future value tables
C1 P1 P2 P3 P4

For each of the following situations, identify (1) the case as either (*a*) a present or a future value and (*b*) a single amount or an annuity, (2) the table you would use in your computations (but do not solve the problem), and (3) the interest rate and time periods you would use.

a. You need to accumulate \$10,000 for a trip you wish to take in four years. You are able to earn 8% compounded semiannually on your savings. You plan to make only one deposit and let the money accumulate for four years. How would you determine the amount of the one-time deposit?

b. Assume the same facts as in part (*a*) except that you will make semiannual deposits to your savings account.

c. You want to retire after working 40 years with savings in excess of \$1,000,000. You expect to save \$4,000 a year for 40 years and earn an annual rate of interest of 8%. Will you be able to retire with more than \$1,000,000 in 40 years? Explain.

d. A sweepstakes agency names you a grand prize winner. You can take \$225,000 immediately or elect to receive annual installments of \$30,000 for 20 years. You can earn 10% annually on any investments you make. Which prize do you choose to receive?

TABLE B.1

Present Value of 1

$p = 1/(1 + i)^n$

Periods	Rate 1%	2%	3%	4%	5%	6%	7%	8%	9%	10%	12%	15%
1	0.9901	0.9804	0.9709	0.9615	0.9524	0.9434	0.9346	0.9259	0.9174	0.9091	0.8929	0.8696
2	0.9803	0.9612	0.9426	0.9246	0.9070	0.8900	0.8734	0.8573	0.8417	0.8264	0.7972	0.7561
3	0.9706	0.9423	0.9151	0.8890	0.8638	0.8396	0.8163	0.7938	0.7722	0.7513	0.7118	0.6575
4	0.9610	0.9238	0.8885	0.8548	0.8227	0.7921	0.7629	0.7350	0.7084	0.6830	0.6355	0.5718
5	0.9515	0.9057	0.8626	0.8219	0.7835	0.7473	0.7130	0.6806	0.6499	0.6209	0.5674	0.4972
6	0.9420	0.8880	0.8375	0.7903	0.7462	0.7050	0.6663	0.6302	0.5963	0.5645	0.5066	0.4323
7	0.9327	0.8706	0.8131	0.7599	0.7107	0.6651	0.6227	0.5835	0.5470	0.5132	0.4523	0.3759
8	0.9235	0.8535	0.7894	0.7307	0.6768	0.6274	0.5820	0.5403	0.5019	0.4665	0.4039	0.3269
9	0.9143	0.8368	0.7664	0.7026	0.6446	0.5919	0.5439	0.5002	0.4604	0.4241	0.3606	0.2843
10	0.9053	0.8203	0.7441	0.6756	0.6139	0.5584	0.5083	0.4632	0.4224	0.3855	0.3220	0.2472
11	0.8963	0.8043	0.7224	0.6496	0.5847	0.5268	0.4751	0.4289	0.3875	0.3505	0.2875	0.2149
12	0.8874	0.7885	0.7014	0.6246	0.5568	0.4970	0.4440	0.3971	0.3555	0.3186	0.2567	0.1869
13	0.8787	0.7730	0.6810	0.6006	0.5303	0.4688	0.4150	0.3677	0.3262	0.2897	0.2292	0.1625
14	0.8700	0.7579	0.6611	0.5775	0.5051	0.4423	0.3878	0.3405	0.2992	0.2633	0.2046	0.1413
15	0.8613	0.7430	0.6419	0.5553	0.4810	0.4173	0.3624	0.3152	0.2745	0.2394	0.1827	0.1229
16	0.8528	0.7284	0.6232	0.5339	0.4581	0.3936	0.3387	0.2919	0.2519	0.2176	0.1631	0.1069
17	0.8444	0.7142	0.6050	0.5134	0.4363	0.3714	0.3166	0.2703	0.2311	0.1978	0.1456	0.0929
18	0.8360	0.7002	0.5874	0.4936	0.4155	0.3503	0.2959	0.2502	0.2120	0.1799	0.1300	0.0808
19	0.8277	0.6864	0.5703	0.4746	0.3957	0.3305	0.2765	0.2317	0.1945	0.1635	0.1161	0.0703
20	0.8195	0.6730	0.5537	0.4564	0.3769	0.3118	0.2584	0.2145	0.1784	0.1486	0.1037	0.0611
25	0.7798	0.6095	0.4776	0.3751	0.2953	0.2330	0.1842	0.1460	0.1160	0.0923	0.0588	0.0304
30	0.7419	0.5521	0.4120	0.3083	0.2314	0.1741	0.1314	0.0994	0.0754	0.0573	0.0334	0.0151
35	0.7059	0.5000	0.3554	0.2534	0.1813	0.1301	0.0937	0.0676	0.0490	0.0356	0.0189	0.0075
40	0.6717	0.4529	0.3066	0.2083	0.1420	0.0972	0.0668	0.0460	0.0318	0.0221	0.0107	0.0037

TABLE B.2

Future Value of 1

$f = (1 + i)^n$

Periods	Rate 1%	2%	3%	4%	5%	6%	7%	8%	9%	10%	12%	15%
0	1.0000	1.0000	1.0000	1.0000	1.0000	1.0000	1.0000	1.0000	1.0000	1.0000	1.0000	1.0000
1	1.0100	1.0200	1.0300	1.0400	1.0500	1.0600	1.0700	1.0800	1.0900	1.1000	1.1200	1.1500
2	1.0201	1.0404	1.0609	1.0816	1.1025	1.1236	1.1449	1.1664	1.1881	1.2100	1.2544	1.3225
3	1.0303	1.0612	1.0927	1.1249	1.1576	1.1910	1.2250	1.2597	1.2950	1.3310	1.4049	1.5209
4	1.0406	1.0824	1.1255	1.1699	1.2155	1.2625	1.3108	1.3605	1.4116	1.4641	1.5735	1.7490
5	1.0510	1.1041	1.1593	1.2167	1.2763	1.3382	1.4026	1.4693	1.5386	1.6105	1.7623	2.0114
6	1.0615	1.1262	1.1941	1.2653	1.3401	1.4185	1.5007	1.5869	1.6771	1.7716	1.9738	2.3131
7	1.0721	1.1487	1.2299	1.3159	1.4071	1.5036	1.6058	1.7138	1.8280	1.9487	2.2107	2.6600
8	1.0829	1.1717	1.2668	1.3686	1.4775	1.5938	1.7182	1.8509	1.9926	2.1436	2.4760	3.0590
9	1.0937	1.1951	1.3048	1.4233	1.5513	1.6895	1.8385	1.9990	2.1719	2.3579	2.7731	3.5179
10	1.1046	1.2190	1.3439	1.4802	1.6289	1.7908	1.9672	2.1589	2.3674	2.5937	3.1058	4.0456
11	1.1157	1.2434	1.3842	1.5395	1.7103	1.8983	2.1049	2.3316	2.5804	2.8531	3.4785	4.6524
12	1.1268	1.2682	1.4258	1.6010	1.7959	2.0122	2.2522	2.5182	2.8127	3.1384	3.8960	5.3503
13	1.1381	1.2936	1.4685	1.6651	1.8856	2.1329	2.4098	2.7196	3.0658	3.4523	4.3635	6.1528
14	1.1495	1.3195	1.5126	1.7317	1.9799	2.2609	2.5785	2.9372	3.3417	3.7975	4.8871	7.0757
15	1.1610	1.3459	1.5580	1.8009	2.0789	2.3966	2.7590	3.1722	3.6425	4.1772	5.4736	8.1371
16	1.1726	1.3728	1.6047	1.8730	2.1829	2.5404	2.9522	3.4259	3.9703	4.5950	6.1304	9.3576
17	1.1843	1.4002	1.6528	1.9479	2.2920	2.6928	3.1588	3.7000	4.3276	5.0545	6.8660	10.7613
18	1.1961	1.4282	1.7024	2.0258	2.4066	2.8543	3.3799	3.9960	4.7171	5.5599	7.6900	12.3755
19	1.2081	1.4568	1.7535	2.1068	2.5270	3.0256	3.6165	4.3157	5.1417	6.1159	8.6128	14.2318
20	1.2202	1.4859	1.8061	2.1911	2.6533	3.2071	3.8697	4.6610	5.6044	6.7275	9.6463	16.3665
25	1.2824	1.6406	2.0938	2.6658	3.3864	4.2919	5.4274	6.8485	8.6231	10.8347	17.0001	32.9190
30	1.3478	1.8114	2.4273	3.2434	4.3219	5.7435	7.6123	10.0627	13.2677	17.4494	29.9599	66.2118
35	1.4166	1.9999	2.8139	3.9461	5.5160	7.6861	10.6766	14.7853	20.4140	28.1024	52.7996	133.1755
40	1.4889	2.2080	3.2620	4.8010	7.0400	10.2857	14.9745	21.7245	31.4094	45.2593	93.0510	267.8635

$$p = \left[1 - \frac{1}{(1+i)^n}\right] / i$$

TABLE B.3

Present Value of an Annuity of 1

Periods	1%	2%	3%	4%	5%	6%	7%	8%	9%	10%	12%	15%
	Rate											
1	0.9901	0.9804	0.9709	0.9615	0.9524	0.9434	0.9346	0.9259	0.9174	0.9091	0.8929	0.8696
2	1.9704	1.9416	1.9135	1.8861	1.8594	1.8334	1.8080	1.7833	1.7591	1.7355	1.6901	1.6257
3	2.9410	2.8839	2.8286	2.7751	2.7232	2.6730	2.6243	2.5771	2.5313	2.4869	2.4018	2.2832
4	3.9020	3.8077	3.7171	3.6299	3.5460	3.4651	3.3872	3.3121	3.2397	3.1699	3.0373	2.8550
5	4.8534	4.7135	4.5797	4.4518	4.3295	4.2124	4.1002	3.9927	3.8897	3.7908	3.6048	3.3522
6	5.7955	5.6014	5.4172	5.2421	5.0757	4.9173	4.7665	4.6229	4.4859	4.3553	4.1114	3.7845
7	6.7282	6.4720	6.2303	6.0021	5.7864	5.5824	5.3893	5.2064	5.0330	4.8684	4.5638	4.1604
8	7.6517	7.3255	7.0197	6.7327	6.4632	6.2098	5.9713	5.7466	5.5348	5.3349	4.9676	4.4873
9	8.5660	8.1622	7.7861	7.4353	7.1078	6.8017	6.5152	6.2469	5.9952	5.7590	5.3282	4.7716
10	9.4713	8.9826	8.5302	8.1109	7.7217	7.3601	7.0236	6.7101	6.4177	6.1446	5.6502	5.0188
11	10.3676	9.7868	9.2526	8.7605	8.3064	7.8869	7.4987	7.1390	6.8052	6.4951	5.9377	5.2337
12	11.2551	10.5753	9.9540	9.3851	8.8633	8.3838	7.9427	7.5361	7.1607	6.8137	6.1944	5.4206
13	12.1337	11.3484	10.6350	9.9856	9.3936	8.8527	8.3577	7.9038	7.4869	7.1034	6.4235	5.5831
14	13.0037	12.1062	11.2961	10.5631	9.8986	9.2950	8.7455	8.2442	7.7862	7.3667	6.6282	5.7245
15	13.8651	12.8493	11.9379	11.1184	10.3797	9.7122	9.1079	8.5595	8.0607	7.6061	6.8109	5.8474
16	14.7179	13.5777	12.5611	11.6523	10.8378	10.1059	9.4466	8.8514	8.3126	7.8237	6.9740	5.9542
17	15.5623	14.2919	13.1661	12.1657	11.2741	10.4773	9.7632	9.1216	8.5436	8.0216	7.1196	6.0472
18	16.3983	14.9920	13.7535	12.6593	11.6896	10.8276	10.0591	9.3719	8.7556	8.2014	7.2497	6.1280
19	17.2260	15.6785	14.3238	13.1339	12.0853	11.1581	10.3356	9.6036	8.9501	8.3649	7.3658	6.1982
20	18.0456	16.3514	14.8775	13.5903	12.4622	11.4699	10.5940	9.8181	9.1285	8.5136	7.4694	6.2593
25	22.0232	19.5235	17.4131	15.6221	14.0939	12.7834	11.6536	10.6748	9.8226	9.0770	7.8431	6.4641
30	25.8077	22.3965	19.6004	17.2920	15.3725	13.7648	12.4090	11.2578	10.2737	9.4269	8.0552	6.5660
35	29.4086	24.9986	21.4872	18.6646	16.3742	14.4982	12.9477	11.6546	10.5668	9.6442	8.1755	6.6166
40	32.8347	27.3555	23.1148	19.7928	17.1591	15.0463	13.3317	11.9246	10.7574	9.7791	8.2438	6.6418

$$f = [(1+i)^n - 1]/i$$

TABLE B.4

Future Value of an Annuity of 1

Periods	1%	2%	3%	4%	5%	6%	7%	8%	9%	10%	12%	15%
	Rate											
1	1.0000	1.0000	1.0000	1.0000	1.0000	1.0000	1.0000	1.0000	1.0000	1.0000	1.0000	1.0000
2	2.0100	2.0200	2.0300	2.0400	2.0500	2.0600	2.0700	2.0800	2.0900	2.1000	2.1200	2.1500
3	3.0301	3.0604	3.0909	3.1216	3.1525	3.1836	3.2149	3.2464	3.2781	3.3100	3.3744	3.4725
4	4.0604	4.1216	4.1836	4.2465	4.3101	4.3746	4.4399	4.5061	4.5731	4.6410	4.7793	4.9934
5	5.1010	5.2040	5.3091	5.4163	5.5256	5.6371	5.7507	5.8666	5.9847	6.1051	6.3528	6.7424
6	6.1520	6.3081	6.4684	6.6330	6.8019	6.9753	7.1533	7.3359	7.5233	7.7156	8.1152	8.7537
7	7.2135	7.4343	7.6625	7.8983	8.1420	8.3938	8.6540	8.9228	9.2004	9.4872	10.0890	11.0668
8	8.2857	8.5830	8.8923	9.2142	9.5491	9.8975	10.2598	10.6366	11.0285	11.4359	12.2997	13.7268
9	9.3685	9.7546	10.1591	10.5828	11.0266	11.4913	11.9780	12.4876	13.0210	13.5795	14.7757	16.7858
10	10.4622	10.9497	11.4639	12.0061	12.5779	13.1808	13.8164	14.4866	15.1929	15.9374	17.5487	20.3037
11	11.5668	12.1687	12.8078	13.4864	14.2068	14.9716	15.7836	16.6455	17.5603	18.5312	20.6546	24.3493
12	12.6825	13.4121	14.1920	15.0258	15.9171	16.8699	17.8885	18.9771	20.1407	21.3843	24.1331	29.0017
13	13.8093	14.6803	15.6178	16.6268	17.7130	18.8821	20.1406	21.4953	22.9534	24.5227	28.0291	34.3519
14	14.9474	15.9739	17.0863	18.2919	19.5986	21.0151	22.5505	24.2149	26.0192	27.9750	32.3926	40.5047
15	16.0969	17.2934	18.5989	20.0236	21.5786	23.2760	25.1290	27.1521	29.3609	31.7725	37.2797	47.5804
16	17.2579	18.6393	20.1569	21.8245	23.6575	25.6725	27.8881	30.3243	33.0034	35.9497	42.7533	55.7175
17	18.4304	20.0121	21.7616	23.6975	25.8404	28.2129	30.8402	33.7502	36.9737	40.5447	48.8837	65.0751
18	19.6147	21.4123	23.4144	25.6454	28.1324	30.9057	33.9990	37.4502	41.3013	45.5992	55.7497	75.8364
19	20.8109	22.8406	25.1169	27.6712	30.5390	33.7600	37.3790	41.4463	46.0185	51.1591	63.4397	88.2118
20	22.0190	24.2974	26.8704	29.7781	33.0660	36.7856	40.9955	45.7620	51.1601	57.2750	72.0524	102.4436
25	28.2432	32.0303	36.4593	41.6459	47.7271	54.8645	63.2490	73.1059	84.7009	98.3471	133.3339	212.7930
30	34.7849	40.5681	47.5754	56.0849	66.4388	79.0582	94.4608	113.2832	136.3075	164.4940	241.3327	434.7451
35	41.6603	49.9945	60.4621	73.6522	90.3203	111.4348	138.2369	172.3168	215.7108	271.0244	431.6635	881.1702
40	48.8864	60.4020	75.4013	95.0255	120.7998	154.7620	199.6351	259.0565	337.8824	442.5926	767.0914	1,779.0903

Appendix

C

Investments and International Operations

A Look at This Appendix

This appendix focuses on investments in securities. We explain how to identify, account for, and report investments in both debt and equity securities. We also explain accounting for transactions listed in a foreign currency.

Learning Objectives

CONCEPTUAL

C1 Distinguish between debt and equity securities and between short-term and long-term investments. (p. C-2)

C2 Describe how to report equity securities with controlling influence. (p. C-9)

C3 *Appendix C-A*—Explain foreign exchange rates and record transactions listed in a foreign currency. (p. C-16)

ANALYTICAL

A1 Compute and analyze the components of return on total assets. (p. C-11)

PROCEDURAL

P1 Account for trading securities. (p. C-5)

P2 Account for held-to-maturity securities. (p. C-6)

P3 Account for available-for-sale securities. (p. C-6)

P4 Account for equity securities with significant influence. (p. C-8)

Decision Insight

100 Million Dollar Investment

"Never be scared of asking for advice."
—CATHERINE COOK

NEW YORK—"We were relatively new in our high school and we just wanted a better way to get to know our classmates," admits Catherine Cook. "We started brainstorming a general idea of what we wanted: superlatives, profiles, classes, groups . . . and **myYearbook** was born!" Catherine, along with her brother Dave, launched myYearbook aimed at teenagers and young adults. "If you think about Facebook as where you go to connect with people you know," explains Catherine, "myYearbook is where you go to connect with people you want to know."

In 2011, myYearbook was the top site for teenagers, according to the online tracking company comScore, with over 33 million users. Catherine says myYearbook employed more than 100 workers at offices in New York and New Hope, Pennsylvania. She admits, however, that "it is really hard to keep up with the site along with my school work."

The next big step according to Catherine was to take myYearbook to a global audience. "The dream we've had for some time now," she says, "is to become a global brand." This step required Catherine to extend her business into international operations and to deal with intercorporate investments. "I am committed to focus on what we do best," she says, "to make myYearbook the number one site to meet new people."

This broad goal has led to business challenges, involving both investments and international operations. "I want to grow myYearbook as far as I can," insists Catherine. That drive led her into discussions with Quepasa.com, a social network whose users are based mainly in Latin America. Explains Catherine, "With Quepasa, we could end up the leader in social discovery!" However, to make this happen, she had to study their international operations, including their financials and accounting disclosures. Catherine explored various investment deals that she could set up with Quepasa, which required her to learn about accounting for investments.

Catherine recently finalized her investment in Quepasa, which involved a merger of their two operations, whereby she and her brother received $18 million in cash and $82 million in stock. Combined, myYearbook.com and Quepasa.com, now rebranded under the name **Meet Me Inc. (MeetMe.com),** have more than 70 million registered users. Catherine aims to launch translated versions of games, social applications, and mobile platform. "I'm working hard at coming up with interesting and fun features for our members," she said. "I'll be in the office every day working on a full pipeline of new features."

[Sources: *MeetMe Website,* January 2013; *The Star-Ledger,* July 2011; *New Jersey Monthly Magazine,* August 2011; *Smart Business Network,* February 2012]

Appendix Preview

This appendix's main focus is investments in securities. Many companies have investments, and many of these are in the form of debt and equity securities issued by other companies. We describe investments in these securities and how to account for them. An increasing number of companies also invest in international operations. We explain how to account for and report international transactions listed in foreign currencies.

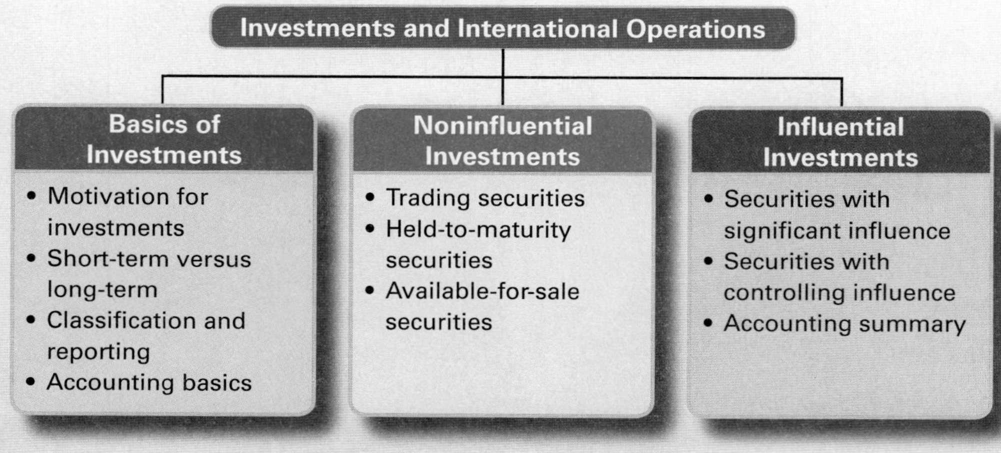

BASICS OF INVESTMENTS

C1 Distinguish between debt and equity securities and between short-term and long-term investments.

This section describes the motivation for investments, the distinction between short- and long-term investments, and the different classes of investments.

Motivation for Investments

Companies make investments for at least three reasons. First, companies transfer *excess cash* into investments to produce higher income. Second, some entities, such as mutual funds and pension funds, are set up to produce income from investments. Third, companies make investments for strategic reasons. Examples are investments in competitors, suppliers, and even customers. Exhibit C.1 shows short-term (S-T) and long-term (L-T) investments as a percent of total assets for several companies.

EXHIBIT C.1

Investments of Selected Companies

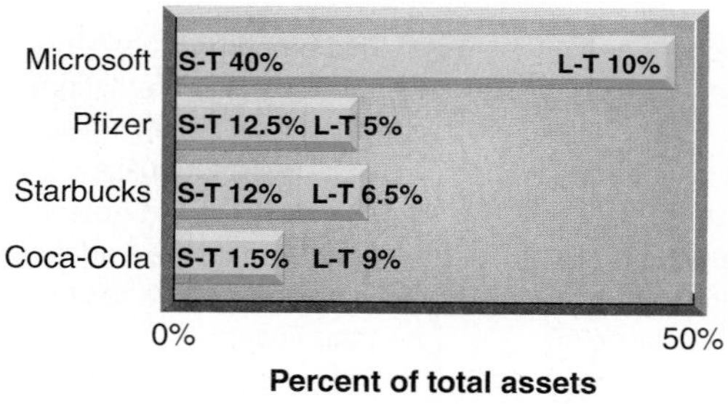

Short-Term Investments Cash equivalents are investments that are both readily converted to known amounts of cash and mature within three months. Many investments, however, mature between 3 and 12 months. These investments are **short-term investments,** also called *temporary investments* and *marketable securities*. Specifically, short-term investments are securities that (1) management intends to convert to cash within one year or the operating cycle, whichever is longer, and (2) are readily convertible to cash. Short-term investments are reported under current assets and serve a purpose similar to cash equivalents.

Long-Term Investments **Long-term investments** in securities are defined as those securities that are not readily convertible to cash or are not intended to be converted into cash in the short term. Long-term investments can also include funds earmarked for a special purpose, such as bond sinking funds and investments in land or other assets not used in the company's operations. Long-term investments are reported in the noncurrent section of the balance sheet, often in its own separate line titled *Long-Term Investments.*

Debt Securities versus Equity Securities Investments in securities can include both debt and equity securities. *Debt securities* reflect a creditor relationship such as investments in notes, bonds, and certificates of deposit; they are issued by governments, companies, and individuals. *Equity securities* reflect an owner relationship such as shares of stock issued by companies.

Classification and Reporting

Accounting for investments in securities depends on three factors: (1) security type, either debt or equity, (2) the company's intent to hold the security either short term or long term, and (3) the company's (investor's) percent ownership in the other company's (investee's) equity securities. Exhibit C.2 identifies five classes of securities using these three factors. It describes each of these five classes of securities and the standard reporting required under each class.

EXHIBIT C.2

Investments in Securities

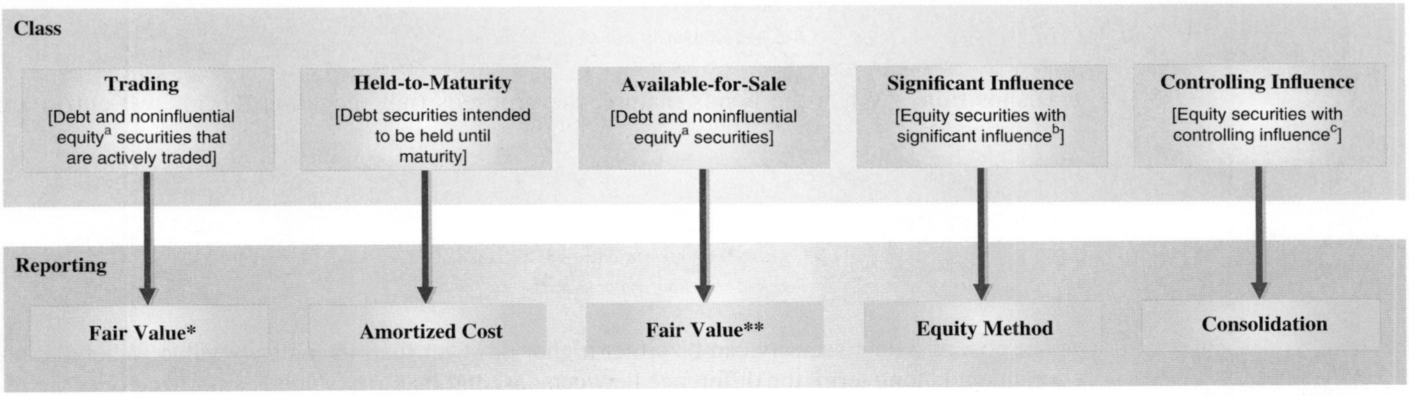

[a] Holding less than 20% of voting stock (equity securities only). [b] Holding 20% or more, but not more than 50%, of voting stock. [c] Holding more than 50% of voting stock.
* Unrealized gains and losses reported on the income statement.
** Unrealized gains and losses reported in the equity section of the balance sheet and in comprehensive income.

Debt Securities: Accounting Basics

This section explains the accounting basics for *debt securities,* including that for acquisition, disposition, and any interest.

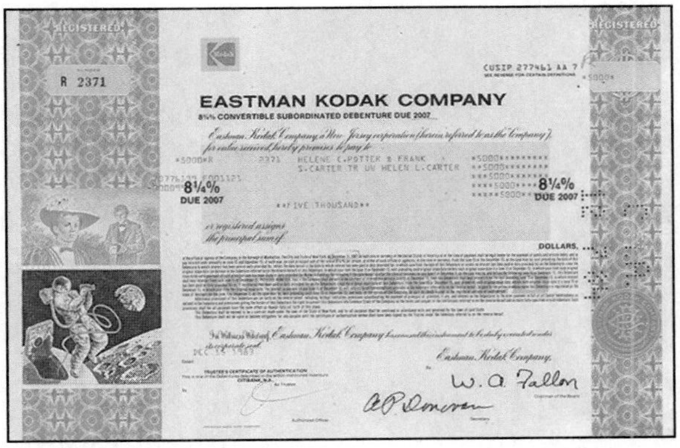

Acquisition. Debt securities are recorded at cost when purchased. To illustrate, assume that Music City paid $29,500 plus a $500 brokerage fee on September 1, 2012, to buy Dell's 7%, two-year bonds payable with a $30,000 par value. The bonds pay interest semiannually on August 31 and February 28. Music City intends to hold the bonds until they mature on August 31, 2014; consequently, they are classified as held-to-maturity (HTM) securities. The entry to record this purchase follows. (If the maturity of the securities was short term, and management's intent was to hold them until they mature, then they would be classified as Short-Term Investments—HTM.)

2012			
Sept. 1	Long-Term Investments—HTM (Dell)	30,000	
	Cash		30,000
	Purchased bonds to be held to maturity.		

Assets = Liabilities + Equity
+30,000
−30,000

Interest earned. Interest revenue for investments in debt securities is recorded when earned. To illustrate, on December 31, 2012, at the end of its accounting period, Music City accrues interest receivable as follows.

Dec. 31	Interest Receivable	700	
	Interest Revenue		700
	Accrued interest earned ($30,000 × 7% × 4/12).		

Assets = Liabilities + Equity
+700 +700

The $700 reflects 4/6 of the semiannual cash receipt of interest—the portion Music City earned as of December 31. Relevant sections of Music City's financial statements at December 31, 2012, are shown in Exhibit C.3.

EXHIBIT C.3

Financial Statement Presentation of Debt Securities

On the income statement for year 2012:	
Interest revenue	**$ 700**
On the December 31, 2012, balance sheet:	
Long-term investments—Held-to-maturity securities (at amortized cost)	**$30,000**

On February 28, 2013, Music City records receipt of semiannual interest.

Assets = Liabilities + Equity
+1,050 +350
−700

Feb. 28	Cash	1,050	
	Interest Receivable		700
	Interest Revenue		350
	Received six months' interest on Dell bonds.		

Disposition. When the bonds mature, the proceeds (not including the interest entry) are recorded as:

Assets = Liabilities + Equity
+30,000
−30,000

2014			
Aug. 31	Cash	30,000	
	Long-Term Investments—HTM (Dell).		30,000
	Received cash from matured bonds.		

Example: What is cost per share?
Answer: Cost per share is the total cost of acquisition, including broker fees, divided by number of shares acquired.

The cost of a debt security can be either higher or lower than its maturity value. When the investment is long term, the difference between cost and maturity value is amortized over the remaining life of the security. We assume for ease of computations that the cost of a long-term debt security equals its maturity value.

Equity Securities: Accounting Basics

This section explains the accounting basics for *equity securities,* including that for acquisition, dividends, and disposition.

Acquisition. Equity securities are recorded at cost when acquired, including commissions or brokerage fees paid. To illustrate, assume that Music City purchases 1,000 shares of Intex common stock at par value for $86,000 on October 10, 2012. It records this purchase of available-for-sale (AFS) securities as follows.

Assets = Liabilities + Equity
+86,000
−86,000

Oct. 10	Long-Term Investments—AFS (Intex)	86,000	
	Cash		86,000
	Purchased 1,000 shares of Intex.		

Dividend earned. Any cash dividends received are credited to Dividend Revenue and reported in the income statement. To illustrate, on November 2, Music City receives a $1,720 quarterly cash dividend on the Intex shares, which it records as:

Assets = Liabilities + Equity
+1,720 +1,720

Nov. 2	Cash	1,720	
	Dividend Revenue		1,720
	Received dividend of $1.72 per share.		

Disposition. When the securities are sold, sale proceeds are compared with the cost, and any gain or loss is recorded. To illustrate, on December 20, Music City sells 500 of the Intex shares for $45,000 cash and records this sale as:

Assets = Liabilities + Equity
+45,000 +2,000
−43,000

Dec. 20	Cash	45,000	
	Long-Term Investments—AFS (Intex)		43,000
	Gain on Sale of Long-Term Investments		2,000
	Sold 500 Intex shares ($86,000 × 500/1,000).		

REPORTING OF NONINFLUENTIAL INVESTMENTS

Companies must value and report most noninfluential investments at *fair value.* The exact reporting requirements depend on whether the investments are classified as (1) trading, (2) held-to-maturity, or (3) available-for-sale.

Trading Securities

P1 Account for trading securities.

Trading securities are *debt and equity securities* that the company intends to actively manage and trade for profit. Frequent purchases and sales are expected and are made to earn profits on short-term price changes. Trading securities are *always* reported as current assets.

Valuing and reporting trading securities. The entire portfolio of trading securities is reported at its fair value; this requires a "fair value adjustment" from the cost of the portfolio. The term *portfolio* refers to a group of securities. Any unrealized gain (or loss) from a change in the fair value of the portfolio of trading securities is reported on the income statement. Most users believe accounting reports are more useful when changes in fair value for trading securities are reported in income.

To illustrate, TechCom's portfolio of trading securities had a total cost of $11,500 and a fair value of $13,000 on December 31, 2012, the first year it held trading securities. The difference between the $11,500 cost and the $13,000 fair value reflects a $1,500 gain. It is an unrealized gain because it is not yet confirmed by actual sales. The fair value adjustment for trading securities is recorded with an adjusting entry at the end of each period to equal the difference between the portfolio's cost and its fair value. TechCom records this gain as follows.

Point: *'Unrealized gain (or loss)'* refers to a change in fair value that is not yet realized through actual sale.

Point: 'Fair Value Adjustment—Trading' is a *permanent account*, shown as a deduction or addition to 'Short-Term Investments—Trading.'

Dec. 31	Fair Value Adjustment—Trading	1,500	
	Unrealized Gain—Income		1,500
	To reflect an unrealized gain in fair values of trading securities.		

Assets	=	Liabilities	+	Equity
+1,500				+1,500

The **Unrealized Gain (or Loss)** is reported in the Other Revenues and Gains (or Expenses and Losses) section on the income statement. Unrealized Gain (or Loss)—Income is a *temporary* account that is closed to Income Summary at the end of each period. Fair Value Adjustment—Trading is a *permanent* account, which adjusts the reported value of the trading securities portfolio from its prior period fair value to the current period fair value. The total cost of the trading securities portfolio is maintained in one account, and the fair value adjustment is recorded in a separate account. For example, TechCom's investment in trading securities is reported in the current assets section of its balance sheet as follows.

Example: If TechCom's trading securities have a cost of $14,800 and a fair value of $16,100 at Dec. 31, 2013, its adjusting entry is

Unrealized Loss—Income	200	
Fair Value Adj.—Trading		200

This is computed as: $1,500 Beg. Dr. bal. + $200 Cr. = $1,300 End. Dr. bal.

Current Assets		
Short-term investments—Trading (at cost)	$11,500	
Fair Value adjustment—Trading	1,500	
Short-term investments—Trading (at fair value)		$13,000
or simply		
Short-term investments—Trading (at fair value; cost is $11,500)		$13,000

Selling trading securities. When individual trading securities are sold, the difference between the net proceeds (sale price less fees) and the cost of the individual trading securities that are sold is recognized as a gain or a loss. Any prior period fair value adjustment to the portfolio is *not* used to compute the gain or loss from sale of individual trading securities. For example, if TechCom sold some of its trading securities that had cost $1,000 for $1,200 cash on January 9, 2013, it would record the following.

Point: Reporting securities at fair value is referred to as *mark-to-market* accounting.

Assets = Liabilities + Equity
+1,200 +200
−1,000

Jan. 9	Cash	1,200	
	Short-Term Investments—Trading		1,000
	Gain on Sale of Short-Term Investments		200
	Sold trading securities costing $1,000 for $1,200 cash.		

A gain is reported in the Other Revenues and Gains section on the income statement, whereas a loss is shown in Other Expenses and Losses. When the period-end fair value adjustment for the portfolio of trading securities is computed, it excludes the cost and fair value of any securities sold.

Held-to-Maturity Securities

P2 Account for held-to-maturity securities.

Held-to-maturity (HTM) securities are *debt* securities a company intends and is able to hold until maturity. They are reported in current assets if their maturity dates are within one year or the operating cycle, whichever is longer. HTM securities are reported in long-term assets when the maturity dates extend beyond one year or the operating cycle, whichever is longer. All HTM securities are recorded at cost when purchased, and interest revenue is recorded when earned.

The portfolio of HTM securities is usually reported at (amortized) cost, which is explained in advanced courses. There is no fair value adjustment to the portfolio of HTM securities—neither to the short-term nor long-term portfolios. The basics of accounting for HTM securities were described earlier in this appendix.

Point: Only debt securities can be classified as *held-to-maturity;* equity securities have no maturity date.

Decision Maker

Money Manager You expect interest rates to sharply fall within a few weeks and remain at this lower rate. What is your strategy for holding investments in fixed-rate bonds and notes? ■ [Answer—p. C-19]

Available-for-Sale Securities

P3 Account for available-for-sale securities.

Available-for-sale (AFS) securities are *debt and equity securities* not classified as trading or held-to-maturity securities. AFS securities are purchased to yield interest, dividends, or increases in fair value. They are not actively managed like trading securities. If the intent is to sell AFS securities within the longer of one year or operating cycle, they are classified as short-term investments. Otherwise, they are classified as long-term.

Valuing and reporting available-for-sale securities. As with trading securities, companies adjust the cost of the portfolio of AFS securities to reflect changes in fair value. This is done with a fair value adjustment to its total portfolio cost. However, any unrealized gain or loss for the portfolio of AFS securities is *not* reported on the income statement. Instead, it is reported in the equity section of the balance sheet (and is part of *comprehensive income,* explained later). To illustrate, assume that Music City had no prior period investments in available-for-sale securities other than those purchased in the current period. Exhibit C.4 shows both the cost and fair value of those investments on December 31, 2012, the end of its reporting period.

Example: If fair value in Exhibit C.4 is $70,000 (instead of $74,550), what entry is made? *Answer:*
Unreal. Loss—Equity 3,000
Fair Value Adj.—AFS. . . 3,000

EXHIBIT C.4
Cost and Fair Value of Available-for-Sale Securities

	Cost	Fair Value	Unrealized Gain (Loss)
Improv bonds	$30,000	$29,050	$ (950)
Intex common stock, 500 shares	43,000	45,500	2,500
Total	$73,000	$74,550	$1,550

The year-end adjusting entry to record the fair value of these investments follows.

Assets = Liabilities + Equity
+1,550 +1,550

Dec. 31	Fair Value Adjustment—Available-for-Sale (LT)	1,550	
	Unrealized Gain—Equity		1,550
	To record adjustment to fair value of available-for-sale securities.		

Exhibit C.5 shows the December 31, 2012, balance sheet presentation—it assumes these investments are long term, but they can also be short term. It is also common to combine the cost of investments with the balance in the Fair Value Adjustment account and report the net as a single amount.

Point: 'Unrealized Loss—Equity' and 'Unrealized Gain—Equity' are *permanent* (balance sheet) equity *accounts.*

EXHIBIT C.5

Balance Sheet Presentation of Available-for-Sale Securities

Assets		
Long-term investments—Available-for-sale (at cost)	$73,000	
Fair value adjustment—Available-for-sale	1,550	
Long-term investments—Available-for-sale (at fair value)		$74,550
or simply		
Long-term investments—Available-for-sale (at fair value; cost is $73,000)		$74,550
Equity		
... consists of usual equity accounts ...		
Add unrealized gain on available-for-sale securities*		$ 1,550

(Reconciled: Fair value adjustment ↔ unrealized gain)

* Often included under the caption Accumulated Other Comprehensive Income.

Let's extend this illustration and assume that at the end of its next calendar year (December 31, 2013), Music City's portfolio of long-term AFS securities has an $81,000 cost and an $82,000 fair value. It records the adjustment to fair value as follows.

Point: Income can be window-dressed upward by selling AFS securities with unrealized gains; income is reduced by selling those with unrealized losses.

Dec. 31	Unrealized Gain—Equity	550	
	Fair Value Adjustment—Available-for-Sale (LT)		550
	To record adjustment to fair value of available-for-sale securities.		

Assets = Liabilities + Equity
−550 −550

The effects of the 2012 and 2013 securities transactions are reflected in the following T-accounts.

Unrealized Gain—Equity

Debit		Credit	
Adj. 12/31/13	550	Bal. 12/31/12	1,550
		Bal. 12/31/13	**1,000**

Fair Value Adjustment—Available-for-Sale (LT)

Debit		Credit	
Bal. 12/31/12	1,550	Adj. 12/31/13	550
Bal. 12/31/13	**1,000**		

Amounts reconcile.

Example: If cost is $83,000 and fair value is $82,000 at Dec. 31, 2013, it records the following adjustment:

Unreal. Gain—Equity	1,550	
Unreal. Loss—Equity	1,000	
Fair Value Adj.—AFS		2,550

Selling available-for-sale securities. Accounting for the sale of individual AFS securities is identical to that described for the sale of trading securities. When individual AFS securities are sold, the difference between the cost of the individual securities sold and the net proceeds (sale price less fees) is recognized as a gain or loss.

Point: 'Fair Value Adjustment—Available-for-Sale' is a permanent account, shown as a deduction or addition to the Investment account.

Quick Check

Answers — p. C-19

1. How are short-term held-to-maturity securities reported (valued) on the balance sheet?
2. How are trading securities reported (valued) on the balance sheet?
3. Where are unrealized gains and losses on available-for-sale securities reported?
4. Where are unrealized gains and losses on trading securities reported?
5. Does the Fair Value Adjustment account have a normal balance?

Alert *Both U.S. GAAP (and IFRS) permit companies to use fair value in reporting financial assets (referred to as the fair value option). This option allows companies to report any financial asset at fair value and recognize value changes in income. This method was previously reserved only for trading securities, but is now an option for available-for-sale and held-to-maturity securities (and other 'financial assets and liabilities' such as accounts and notes receivable, accounts and notes payable, and bonds). U.S. standards also set a 3-level system to determine fair value:*
—Level 1: Use quoted market values
—Level 2: Use observable values from related assets or liabilities
—Level 3: Use unobservable values from estimates or assumptions
To date, a fairly small set of companies has chosen to broadly apply the fair value option—but, we continue to monitor its use ...

REPORTING OF INFLUENTIAL INVESTMENTS

Investment in Securities with Significant Influence

P4 Account for equity securities with significant influence.

A long-term investment classified as **equity securities with significant influence** implies that the investor can exert significant influence over the investee. An investor that owns 20% or more (but not more than 50%) of a company's voting stock is usually presumed to have a significant influence over the investee. In some cases, however, the 20% test of significant influence is overruled by other, more persuasive, evidence. This evidence can either lower the 20% requirement or increase it. The **equity method** of accounting and reporting is used for long-term investments in equity securities with significant influence, which is explained in this section.

Long-term investments in equity securities with significant influence are recorded at cost when acquired. To illustrate, Micron Co. records the purchase of 3,000 shares (30%) of Star Co. common stock at a total cost of $70,650 on January 1, 2012, as follows.

Assets = Liabilities + Equity
+70,650
−70,650

Jan. 1	Long-Term Investments—Star	70,650	
	Cash		70,650
	To record purchase of 3,000 Star shares.		

The investee's (Star) earnings increase both its net assets and the claim of the investor (Micron) on the investee's net assets. Thus, when the investee reports its earnings, the investor records its share of those earnings in its investment account. To illustrate, assume that Star reports net income of $20,000 for 2012. Micron then records its 30% share of those earnings as follows.

Assets = Liabilities + Equity
+6,000 +6,000

Dec. 31	Long-Term Investments—Star	6,000	
	Earnings from Long-Term Investment		6,000
	To record 30% equity in investee earnings.		

The debit reflects the increase in Micron's equity in Star. The credit reflects 30% of Star's net income. Earnings from Long-Term Investment is a *temporary* account (closed to Income Summary at each period-end) and is reported on the investor's (Micron's) income statement. If the investee incurs a net loss instead of a net income, the investor records its share of the loss and reduces (credits) its investment account. The investor closes this earnings or loss account to Income Summary.

The receipt of cash dividends is not revenue under the equity method because the investor has already recorded its share of the investee's earnings. Instead, cash dividends received by an investor from an investee are viewed as a conversion of one asset to another; that is, dividends reduce the balance of the investment account. To illustrate, Star declares and pays $10,000 in cash dividends on its common stock. Micron records its 30% share of these dividends received on January 9, 2013, as:

Assets = Liabilities + Equity
+3,000
−3,000

Jan. 9	Cash	3,000	
	Long-Term Investments—Star		3,000
	To record share of dividend paid by Star.		

The book value of an investment under the equity method equals the cost of the investment plus (minus) the investor's equity in the *undistributed* (*distributed*) earnings of the investee. Once Micron records these transactions, its Long-Term Investments account appears as in Exhibit C.6.

EXHIBIT C.6

Investment in Star Common Stock (Ledger Account)

Long-Term Investment—Star			
1/ 1/2012 Investment acquisition	70,650		
12/31/2012 Share of earnings	6,000		
12/31/2012 Balance	76,650		
		1/ 9/2013 Share of dividend	3,000
1/ 9/2013 Balance	73,650		

Micron's account balance on January 9, 2013, for its investment in Star is $73,650. This is the investment's cost *plus* Micron's equity in Star's earnings since its purchase *less* Micron's equity in Star's cash dividends since its purchase. When an investment in equity securities is sold, the gain or loss is computed by comparing proceeds from the sale with the book value of the investment on the date of sale. If Micron sells its Star stock for $80,000 on January 10, 2013, it records the sale as:

Point: Security prices are sometimes listed in fractions. For example, a debt security with a price of $22\frac{1}{4}$ is the same as $22.25.

Jan. 10	Cash	80,000	
	Long-Term Investments—Star		73,650
	Gain on Sale of Investment		6,350
	Sold 3,000 shares of stock for $80,000.		

Assets	=	Liabilities	+	Equity
+80,000				+6,350
−73,650				

Investment in Securities with Controlling Influence

C2 Describe how to report equity securities with controlling influence.

A long-term investment classified as **equity securities with controlling influence** implies that the investor can exert a controlling influence over the investee. An investor who owns more than 50% of a company's voting stock has control over the investee. This investor can dominate all other shareholders in electing the corporation's board of directors and has control over the investee's management. In some cases, controlling influence can extend to situations of less than 50% ownership. Exhibit C.7 summarizes the accounting for investments in equity securities based on an investor's ownership in the stock.

EXHIBIT C.7

Accounting for Equity Investments by Percent of Ownership

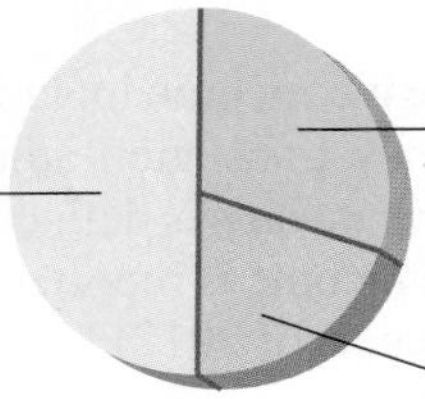

The *equity method with consolidation* is used to account for long-term investments in equity securities with controlling influence. The investor reports *consolidated financial statements* when owning such securities. The controlling investor is called the **parent,** and the investee is called the **subsidiary.** Many companies are parents with subsidiaries. Examples are (1) **Gap, Inc.**, the parent of Gap, Old Navy, and Banana Republic; and (2) **Brunswick**, the parent of Mercury Marine, Sea Ray, and U.S. Marine. A company owning all the outstanding stock of a subsidiary can, if it desires, take over the subsidiary's assets, retire the subsidiary's stock, and merge the subsidiary into the parent. However, there often are financial, legal, and tax advantages if a business operates as a parent controlling one or more subsidiaries. When a company operates as a parent with subsidiaries, each entity maintains separate accounting records. From a legal viewpoint, the parent and each subsidiary are separate entities with all rights, duties, and responsibilities of individual companies.

Consolidated financial statements show the financial position, results of operations, and cash flows of all entities under the parent's control, including all subsidiaries. These statements are prepared as if the business were organized as one entity. The parent uses the equity method in its accounts, but the investment account is *not* reported on the parent's financial statements. Instead, the individual assets and liabilities of the parent and its subsidiaries are combined on one balance sheet. Their revenues and expenses also are combined on one income statement, and their cash flows are combined on one statement of cash flows. The procedures for preparing consolidated financial statements are in advanced courses.

IFRS

Unlike U.S. GAAP, IFRS requires uniform accounting policies be used throughout the group of consolidated subsidiaries. Also, unlike U.S. GAAP, IFRS offers no detailed guidance on valuation procedures. ■

Accounting Summary for Investments in Securities

Exhibit C.8 summarizes the standard accounting for investments in securities. Recall that many investment securities are classified as either short term or long term depending on management's intent and ability to convert them in the future. Understanding the accounting for these investments enables us to draw better conclusions from financial statements in making business decisions.

EXHIBIT C.8

Accounting for Investments in Securities

Classification	Accounting
Short-Term Investment in Securities	
Held-to-maturity (debt) securities	**Cost** (without any discount or premium amortization)
Trading (debt and equity) securities	**Fair value** (with fair value adjustment to income)
Available-for-sale (debt and equity) securities	**Fair value** (with fair value adjustment to equity)
Long-Term Investment in Securities	
Held-to-maturity (debt) securities	**Cost** (with any discount or premium amortization)
Available-for-sale (debt and equity) securities	**Fair value** (with fair value adjustment to equity)
Equity securities with significant influence	Equity method
Equity securities with controlling influence	Equity method (with consolidation)

Comprehensive Income **Comprehensive income** is defined as all changes in equity during a period except those from owners' investments and dividends. Specifically, comprehensive income is computed by adding or subtracting *other comprehensive income* to net income:

Net income	$ #
Other comprehensive income	#
Comprehensive income	$ #

Point: Some users believe that since AFS securities are not actively traded, reporting fair value changes in income would unnecessarily increase income variability and decrease usefulness.

Other comprehensive income includes unrealized gains and losses on available-for-sale securities, foreign currency translation adjustments, and certain pension adjustments. (*Accumulated other comprehensive income* is defined as the cumulative impact of *other comprehensive income.*)

Comprehensive income is reported in financial statements in one of two ways (which reflects new FASB guidance as of 2012):

1. On a separate *statement of comprehensive income* that immediately follows the income statement.
2. On the lower section of the income statement (as a single continuous *statement of income and comprehensive income*).

Option 1 is the most common. **KTM**, for example, reports a statement of comprehensive income following its income statement in Appendix A near the end of the book (Piaggio also applies this same presentation in Appendix A). Following is an abbreviated version of the KTM statement using language more common for U.S. GAAP:

KTM

Net income	**20,818**	
Foreign currency conversion	107	← Other comprehensive income
Valuation of cash flow hedges, net of tax	8,545	← Other comprehensive income
Other comprehensive income	8,652	
Total comprehensive income	**29,470**	

Option 2 adds the components of other comprehensive income to net income on the bottom of the income statement to compute a continuous statement of income and comprehensive income. There is no difference in the numbers; it is simply a matter of how those numbers are presented. A third option, which is no longer acceptable, was to include the components of other comprehensive income and its total along with the total of comprehensive income in the statement of equity. Polaris and Arctic Cat show examples of this presentation, which is no longer acceptable for future years.

Quick Check

Answers — p. C-19

6. Give at least two examples of assets classified as long-term investments.
7. What are the requirements for an equity security to be listed as a long-term investment?
8. Identify similarities and differences in accounting for long-term investments in debt securities that are held-to-maturity versus those available-for-sale.
9. What are the three possible classifications of long-term equity investments? Describe the criteria for each class and the method used to account for each.

GLOBAL VIEW

This section discusses similarities and differences for the accounting and reporting of investments when financial statements are prepared under U.S. GAAP vis-à-vis IFRS.

Accounting for Noninfluential Securities The accounting for noninfluential securities is broadly similar between U.S. GAAP and IFRS. *Trading securities* are accounted for using fair values with unrealized gains and losses reported in net income as fair values change. *Available-for-sale securities* are accounted for using fair values with unrealized gains and losses reported in other comprehensive income as fair values change (and later in net income when realized). *Held-to-maturity securities* are accounted for using amortized cost. Similarly, companies have the option under both systems to apply the fair value option for available-for-sale and held-to-maturity securities. Also, both systems review held-to-maturity securities for impairment. There are some differences in terminology under IFRS: (1) trading securities are commonly referred to as *financial assets at fair value through profit and loss,* and (2) available-for-sale securities are commonly referred to as *available-for-sale financial assets.* NOKIA reports the following categories for noninfluential securities: (1) ***Financial assets at fair value through profit or loss,*** consisting of financial assets held for trading and financial assets designated upon initial recognition as at fair value through profit or loss, (2) ***Available-for-sale financial assets,*** which are measured at fair value.

NOKIA

Accounting for Influential Securities The accounting for influential securities is broadly similar across U.S. GAAP and IFRS. Specifically, under the *equity method,* the share of investee's net income is reported in the investor's income in the same period the investee earns that income; also, the investment account equals the acquisition cost plus the share of investee income less the share of investee dividends (minus amortization of excess on purchase price above fair value of identifiable, limited-life assets). Under the *consolidation method,* investee and investor revenues and expenses are combined, absent intercompany transactions, and subtracting noncontrolling interests. Also, nonintercompany assets and liabilities are similarly combined (eliminating the need for an investment account), and noncontrolling interests are subtracted from equity. There are some differences in terminology: (1) U.S. GAAP companies commonly refer to earnings from long-term investments as *equity in earnings of affiliates* whereas IFRS companies commonly use *equity in earnings of associated (or associate) companies,* (2) U.S. GAAP companies commonly refer to noncontrolling interests in consolidated subsidiaries as *minority interests* whereas IFRS companies commonly use *noncontrolling interests.*

Components of Return on Total Assets — Decision Analysis

A company's **return on total assets** (or simply *return on assets*) is important in assessing financial performance. The return on total assets can be separated into two components, profit margin and total asset turnover, for additional analyses. Exhibit C.9 shows how these two components determine return on total assets.

A1 Compute and analyze the components of return on total assets.

EXHIBIT C.9

Components of Return on Total Assets

Return on total assets = Profit margin × Total asset turnover

$$\frac{\text{Net income}}{\text{Average total assets}} = \frac{\text{Net income}}{\text{Net sales}} \times \frac{\text{Net sales}}{\text{Average total assets}}$$

Profit margin reflects the percent of net income in each dollar of net sales. Total asset turnover reflects a company's ability to produce net sales from total assets. All companies desire a high return on total assets. By considering these two components, we can often discover strengths and weaknesses not revealed by return on total assets alone. This improves our ability to assess future performance and company strategy.

To illustrate, consider return on total assets and its components for **Gap Inc.** in Exhibit C.10.

EXHIBIT C.10

Gap's Components of Return on Total Assets

Fiscal Year	Return on Total Assets	=	Profit Margin	×	Total Asset Turnover
2012	11.5%	=	5.7%	×	2.01
2011	16.0*	=	8.2	×	1.95
2010	14.1*	=	7.7	×	1.83
2009	12.6	=	6.66	×	1.89
2008	10.2*	=	5.28	×	1.92

* Differences due to rounding.

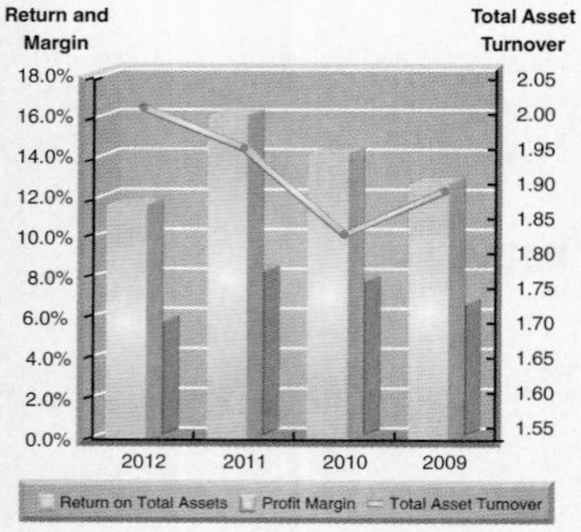

At least three findings emerge. First, Gap's return on total assets improved from 10.2% in 2008 to 11.5% in 2012. Second, total asset turnover has slightly improved over this period, from 1.92 to 2.01. Third, Gap's profit margin steadily increased over this period, from 2008's level of 5.28%. These components reveal the dual role of profit margin and total asset turnover in determining return on total assets. They also reveal that the driver of Gap's recent improvement in return on total assets is not total asset turnover but profit margin.

Generally, if a company is to maintain or improve its return on total assets, it must meet any decline in either profit margin or total asset turnover with an increase in the other. If not, return on assets will decline. Companies consider these components in planning strategies. A component analysis can also reveal where a company is weak and where changes are needed, especially in a competitor analysis. If asset turnover is lower than the industry norm, for instance, a company should focus on raising asset turnover at least to the norm. The same applies to profit margin.

Decision Maker

Retailer You are an entrepreneur and owner of a retail sporting goods store. The store's recent annual performance reveals (industry norms in parentheses): return on total assets = 11% (11.2%); profit margin = 4.4% (3.5%); and total asset turnover = 2.5 (3.2). What does your analysis of these figures reveal? ■ [Answer—p. C-19]

DEMONSTRATION PROBLEM—1

Garden Company completes the following selected transactions related to its short-term investments during 2013.

May 8 Purchased 300 shares of FedEx stock as a short-term investment in available-for-sale securities at $40 per share plus $975 in broker fees.

Sept. 2 Sold 100 shares of its investment in FedEx stock at $47 per share and held the remaining 200 shares; broker's commission was $225.

Oct. 2 Purchased 400 shares of Ajay stock for $60 per share plus $1,600 in commissions. The stock is held as a short-term investment in available-for-sale securities.

Required

1. Prepare journal entries for the above transactions of Garden Company for 2013.

2. Prepare an adjusting journal entry as of December 31, 2013, if the fair values of the equity securities held by Garden Company are $48 per share for FedEx and $55 per share for Ajay. (Year 2013 is the first year Garden Company acquired short-term investments.)

SOLUTION TO DEMONSTRATION PROBLEM—1

1.

May 8	Short-Term Investments—AFS (FedEx)	12,975	
	Cash		12,975
	Purchased 300 shares of FedEx stock (300 × $40) + $975.		

[continued on next page]

[continued from previous page]

Sept. 2	Cash	4,475	
	Gain on Sale of Short-Term Investment		150
	Short-Term Investments—AFS (FedEx)		4,325
	Sold 100 shares of FedEx for $47 per share less a $225 commission. The original cost is ($12,975 × 100/300).		
Oct. 2	Short-Term Investments—AFS (Ajay)	25,600	
	Cash		25,600
	Purchased 400 shares of Ajay for $60 per share plus $1,600 in commissions.		

2. Computation of unrealized gain or loss follows.

Short-Term Investments in Available-for-Sale Securities	Shares	Cost per Share	Total Cost	Fair Value per Share	Total Fair Value	Unrealized Gain (Loss)
FedEx	200	$43.25	$ 8,650	$48.00	$ 9,600	
Ajay	400	64.00	25,600	55.00	22,000	
Totals			$34,250		$31,600	$(2,650)

The adjusting entry follows:

Dec. 31	Unrealized Loss—Equity	2,650	
	Fair Value Adjustment—Available-for-Sale (ST)		2,650
	To reflect an unrealized loss in fair values of available-for-sale securities.		

DEMONSTRATION PROBLEM—2

The following transactions relate to Brown Company's long-term investments during 2012 and 2013. Brown did not own any long-term investments prior to 2012. Show (1) the appropriate journal entries and (2) the relevant portions of each year's balance sheet and income statement that reflect these transactions for both 2012 and 2013.

2012

Sept. 9 Purchased 1,000 shares of Packard, Inc., common stock for $80,000 cash. These shares represent 30% of Packard's outstanding shares.

Oct. 2 Purchased 2,000 shares of AT&T common stock for $60,000 cash as a long-term investment. These shares represent less than a 1% ownership in AT&T.

17 Purchased as a long-term investment 1,000 shares of Apple Computer common stock for $40,000 cash. These shares are less than 1% of Apple's outstanding shares.

Nov. 1 Received $5,000 cash dividend from Packard.

30 Received $3,000 cash dividend from AT&T.

Dec. 15 Received $1,400 cash dividend from Apple.

31 Packard's net income for this year is $70,000.

31 Fair values for the investments in equity securities are Packard, $84,000; AT&T, $48,000; and Apple Computer, $45,000.

31 For preparing financial statements, note the following post-closing account balances: Common Stock, $500,000, and Retained Earnings, $350,000.

2013

Jan. 1 Sold Packard, Inc., shares for $108,000 cash.

May 30 Received $3,100 cash dividend from AT&T.

June 15 Received $1,600 cash dividend from Apple.

Aug. 17 Sold the AT&T stock for $52,000 cash.
19 Purchased 2,000 shares of Coca-Cola common stock for $50,000 cash as a long-term investment. The stock represents less than a 5% ownership in Coca-Cola.
Dec. 15 Received $1,800 cash dividend from Apple.
31 Fair values of the investments in equity securities are Apple, $39,000, and Coca-Cola, $48,000.
31 For preparing financial statements, note the following post-closing account balances: Common Stock, $500,000, and Retained Earnings, $410,000.

PLANNING THE SOLUTION

- Account for the investment in Packard under the equity method.
- Account for the investments in AT&T, Apple, and Coca-Cola as long-term investments in available-for-sale securities.
- Prepare the information for the two years' balance sheets by including the relevant asset and equity accounts, and the two years' income statements by identifying the relevant revenues, earnings, gains, and losses.

SOLUTION TO DEMONSTRATION PROBLEM—2

1. Journal entries for 2012.

Sept. 9	Long-Term Investments—Packard	80,000	
	Cash		80,000
	Acquired 1,000 shares, representing a 30% equity in Packard.		
Oct. 2	Long-Term Investments—AFS (AT&T)	60,000	
	Cash		60,000
	Acquired 2,000 shares as a long-term investment in available-for-sale securities.		
Oct. 17	Long-Term Investments—AFS (Apple)	40,000	
	Cash		40,000
	Acquired 1,000 shares as a long-term investment in available-for-sale securities.		
Nov. 1	Cash	5,000	
	Long-Term Investments—Packard		5,000
	Received dividend from Packard.		
Nov. 30	Cash	3,000	
	Dividend Revenue		3,000
	Received dividend from AT&T.		
Dec. 15	Cash	1,400	
	Dividend Revenue		1,400
	Received dividend from Apple.		
Dec. 31	Long-Term Investments—Packard	21,000	
	Earnings from Investment (Packard)		21,000
	To record 30% share of Packard's annual earnings of $70,000.		
Dec. 31	Unrealized Loss—Equity	7,000	
	Fair Value Adjustment—Available-for-Sale (LT)*		7,000
	To record change in fair value of long-term available-for-sale securities.		

* Fair value adjustment computations:

	Cost	Fair Value	Unrealized Gain (Loss)
AT&T	$ 60,000	$48,000	$(12,000)
Apple	40,000	45,000	5,000
Total	$100,000	$93,000	$ (7,000)

Required balance of the Fair Value Adjustment—Available-for-Sale (LT) account (credit)	$(7,000)
Existing balance	0
Necessary adjustment (credit)	$(7,000)

2. The December 31, 2012, selected balance sheet items appear as follows.

Assets	
Long-term investments	
Available-for-sale securities (at fair value; cost is $100,000)	$ 93,000
Investment in equity securities	96,000
Total long-term investments	189,000
Stockholders' Equity	
Common stock	500,000
Retained earnings	350,000
Unrealized loss—Equity	(7,000)

The relevant income statement items for the year ended December 31, 2012, follow.

Dividend revenue	$ 4,400
Earnings from investment	21,000

1. Journal entries for 2013.

Jan. 1	Cash	108,000	
	Long-Term Investments—Packard		96,000
	Gain on Sale of Long-Term Investments		12,000
	Sold 1,000 shares for cash.		
May 30	Cash	3,100	
	Dividend Revenue		3,100
	Received dividend from AT&T.		
June 15	Cash	1,600	
	Dividend Revenue		1,600
	Received dividend from Apple.		
Aug. 17	Cash	52,000	
	Loss on Sale of Long-Term Investments	8,000	
	Long-Term Investments—AFS (AT&T)		60,000
	Sold 2,000 shares for cash.		
Aug. 19	Long-Term Investments—AFS (Coca-Cola)	50,000	
	Cash		50,000
	Acquired 2,000 shares as a long-term investment in available-for-sale securities.		
Dec. 15	Cash	1,800	
	Dividend Revenue		1,800
	Received dividend from Apple.		
Dec. 31	Fair Value Adjustment—Available-for-Sale (LT)*	4,000	
	Unrealized Loss—Equity		4,000
	To record change in fair value of long-term available-for-sale securities.		

* Fair value adjustment computations:

	Cost	Fair Value	Unrealized Gain (Loss)
Apple	$40,000	$39,000	$(1,000)
Coca-Cola	50,000	48,000	(2,000)
Total	$90,000	$87,000	$(3,000)

Required balance of the Fair Value Adjustment—Available-for-Sale (LT) account (credit)	$(3,000)
Existing balance (credit)	(7,000)
Necessary adjustment (debit)	$ 4,000

2. The December 31, 2013, balance sheet items appear as follows.

Assets	
Long-term investments	
Available-for-sale securities (at fair value; cost is $90,000)	$ 87,000
Stockholders' Equity	
Common stock	500,000
Retained earnings	410,000
Unrealized loss—Equity	(3,000)

The relevant income statement items for the year ended December 31, 2013, follow.

Dividend revenue	$ 6,500
Gain on sale of long-term investments..........	12,000
Loss on sale of long-term investments..........	(8,000)

APPENDIX

C-A Investments in International Operations

Many entities from small entrepreneurs to large corporations conduct business internationally. Some entities' operations occur in so many different countries that the companies are called **multinationals.** Many of us think of **Coca-Cola** and **McDonald's**, for example, as primarily U.S. companies, but most of their sales occur outside the United States. Exhibit C-A.1 shows the percent of international sales and income for selected U.S. companies. Managing and accounting for multinationals present challenges. This section describes some of these challenges and how to account for and report these activities.

EXHIBIT C-A.1

International Sales and Income as a Percent of Their Totals

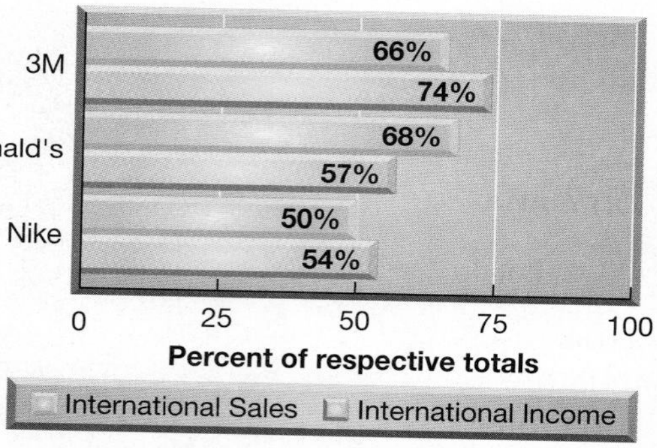

Two major accounting challenges that arise when companies have international operations relate to transactions that involve more than one currency. The first is to account for sales and purchases listed in a foreign currency. The second is to prepare consolidated financial statements with international subsidiaries. For ease in this discussion, we use companies with a U.S. base of operations and assume the need to prepare financial statements in U.S. dollars. This means the *reporting currency* of these companies is the U.S. dollar.

Point: Transactions *listed* or *stated* in a foreign currency are said to be *denominated* in that currency.

C3 Explain foreign exchange rates and record transactions listed in a foreign currency.

Exchange Rates between Currencies Markets for the purchase and sale of foreign currencies exist all over the world. In these markets, U.S. dollars can be exchanged for Canadian dollars, British pounds, Japanese yen, Euros, or any other legal currencies. The price of one currency stated in terms of another currency is called a **foreign exchange rate.** Exhibit C-A.2 lists recent exchange rates for selected currencies. The exchange rate for British pounds and U.S. dollars is $1.8980, meaning 1 British pound could be purchased for $1.8980. On that same day, the exchange rate between Mexican pesos and U.S. dollars is $0.0925, or 1 Mexican peso can be purchased for $0.0925. Exchange rates fluctuate due to changing economic and political conditions, including the supply and demand for currencies and expectations about future events.

Point: To convert currency, see XE.com

Decision Insight

Greek Haircut Investors in government debt securities in the Eurozone must be careful of the heightened default risk associated with securities issued by certain Eurozone member nations. For example, in 2012, buyers of certain Greek bonds were repaid only 30% of principal because of the government's inability to honor its full obligation on the bonds. ■

Source (unit)	Price in $U.S.	Source (unit)	Price in $U.S.
Britain (pound)	$1.8980	Canada (dollar)	$0.9793
Mexico (peso)	0.0925	Japan (yen)	0.0090
Taiwan (dollar)	0.0305	Europe (Euro)	1.2920

* Rates will vary over time based on economic, political, and other changes.

EXHIBIT C-A.2

Foreign Exchange Rates for Selected Currencies*

Sales and Purchases Listed in a Foreign Currency When a U.S. company makes a credit sale to an international customer, accounting for the sale and the account receivable is straightforward if sales terms require the international customer's payment in U.S. dollars. If sale terms require (or allow) payment in a foreign currency, however, the U.S. company must account for the sale and the account receivable in a different manner.

Sales in a Foreign Currency To illustrate, consider the case of the U.S.-based manufacturer Boston Company, which makes credit sales to London Outfitters, a British retail company. A sale occurs on December 12, 2012, for a price of £10,000 with payment due on February 10, 2013. Boston Company keeps its accounting records in U.S. dollars. To record the sale, Boston Company must translate the sales price from pounds to dollars. This is done using the exchange rate on the date of the sale. Assuming the exchange rate on December 12, 2012, is $1.80, Boston records this sale as follows.

Dec. 12	Accounts Receivable—London Outfitters	18,000	
	Sales*		18,000
	To record a sale at £10,000, when the exchange rate equals $1.80. * (£10,000 × $1.80/£)		

Assets = Liabilities + Equity
+18,000 +18,000

When Boston Company prepares its annual financial statements on December 31, 2012, the current exchange rate is $1.84. Thus, the current dollar value of Boston Company's receivable is $18,400 (£10,000 × $1.84/£). This amount is $400 higher than the amount recorded on December 12. Accounting principles require a receivable to be reported in the balance sheet at its current dollar value. Thus, Boston Company must make the following entry to record the increase in the dollar value of this receivable at year-end.

Dec. 31	Accounts Receivable—London Outfitters	400	
	Foreign Exchange Gain		400
	To record the increased value of the British pound for the receivable.		

Assets = Liabilities + Equity
+400 +400

On February 10, 2013, Boston Company receives London Outfitters' payment of £10,000. It immediately exchanges the pounds for U.S. dollars. On this date, the exchange rate for pounds is $1.78. Thus, Boston Company receives only $17,800 (£10,000 × $1.78/£). It records the cash receipt and the loss associated with the decline in the exchange rate as follows.

Point: Foreign exchange gains are credits, and foreign exchange losses are debits.

Feb. 10	Cash	17,800	
	Foreign Exchange Loss	600	
	Accounts Receivable—London Outfitters		18,400
	Received foreign currency payment of an account and converted it into dollars.		

Assets = Liabilities + Equity
+17,800 −600
−18,400

Gains and losses from foreign exchange transactions are accumulated in the Foreign Exchange Gain (or Loss) account. After year-end adjustments, the balance in the Foreign Exchange Gain (or Loss) account is reported on the income statement and closed to the Income Summary account.

Purchases in a Foreign Currency Accounting for credit purchases from an international seller is similar to the case of a credit sale to an international customer. In particular, if the U.S. company is required to make payment in a foreign currency, the account payable must be translated into dollars before the U.S. company can record it. If the exchange rate is different when preparing financial statements and when paying for the purchase, the U.S. company must recognize a foreign exchange gain or loss at those dates. To illustrate, assume NC Imports, a U.S. company, purchases products costing €20,000 (euros) from

Example: Assume that a U.S. company makes a credit purchase from a British company for £10,000 when the exchange rate is $1.62. At the balance sheet date, this rate is $1.72. Does this imply a gain or loss for the U.S. company? *Answer:* A loss.

Hamburg Brewing on January 15, when the exchange rate is $1.20 per euro. NC records this transaction as follows.

Assets	=	Liabilities	+	Equity
+24,000		+24,000		

Jan. 15	Inventory	24,000	
	Accounts Payable—Hamburg Brewing		24,000
	To record a €20,000 purchase when exchange rate is $1.20 (€20,000 × $1.20/€)		

NC Imports makes payment in full on February 14 when the exchange rate is $1.25 per euro, which is recorded as follows.

Assets	=	Liabilities	+	Equity
−25,000		−24,000		−1,000

Feb. 14	Accounts Payable—Hamburg Brewing	24,000	
	Foreign Exchange Loss	1,000	
	Cash		25,000
	To record cash payment towards €20,000 account when exchange rate is $1.25 (€20,000 × $1.25/€).		

Decision Insight

Global Greenback What do changes in foreign exchange rates mean? A decline in the price of the U.S. dollar against other currencies usually yields increased international sales for U.S. companies, without hiking prices or cutting costs, and puts them on a stronger competitive footing abroad. At home, they can raise prices without fear that foreign rivals will undercut them. ■

Consolidated Statements with International Subsidiaries A second challenge in accounting for international operations involves preparing consolidated financial statements when the parent company has one or more international subsidiaries. Consider a U.S.-based company that owns a controlling interest in a French subsidiary. The reporting currency of the U.S. parent is the dollar. The French subsidiary maintains its financial records in euros. Before preparing consolidated statements, the parent must translate financial statements of the French company into U.S. dollars. After this translation is complete (including that for accounting differences), it prepares consolidated statements the same as for domestic subsidiaries. Procedures for translating an international subsidiary's account balances depend on the nature of the subsidiary's operations. The process requires the parent company to select appropriate foreign exchange rates and to apply those rates to the foreign subsidiary's account balances. This is described in advanced courses.

Global: A weaker U.S. dollar often increases global sales for U.S. companies.

Decision Maker

Entrepreneur Assume that Ben and Jerry's purchases milk from dairies in both the U.S. and Canada. The price of the Canadian dollar in terms of the U.S. dollar jumps from US$0.70 to US$0.80. Is the ice cream maker now more or less likely to buy milk from Canadian or U.S. suppliers? ■ [Answer—p. C-19]

Summary

C1 Distinguish between debt and equity securities and between short-term and long-term investments. *Debt securities* reflect a creditor relationship and include investments in notes, bonds, and certificates of deposit. *Equity securities* reflect an owner relationship and include shares of stock issued by other companies. Short-term investments in securities are current assets that meet two criteria: (1) They are expected to be converted into cash within one year or the current operating cycle of the business, whichever is longer and (2) they are readily convertible to cash, or *marketable*. All other investments in securities are long-term. Long-term investments also include assets not used in operations and those held for special purposes, such as land for expansion. Investments in securities are classified into one of five groups: (1) trading securities, which are always short-term, (2) debt securities held-to-maturity, (3) debt and equity securities available-for-sale, (4) equity securities in which an investor has a significant influence over the investee, and (5) equity securities in which an investor has a controlling influence over the investee.

C2 Describe how to report equity securities with controlling influence. If an investor owns more than 50% of another company's voting stock and controls the investee, the investor's financial reports are prepared on a consolidated basis. These reports are prepared as if the company were organized as one entity.

C3A Explain foreign exchange rates and record transactions listed in a foreign currency. A foreign exchange rate is the price of one currency stated in terms of another. An entity with transactions in a foreign currency when the exchange rate changes between the transaction dates and their settlement will experience exchange gains or losses. When a company makes a credit sale to a foreign customer and sales terms call for payment in a foreign currency, the company must translate the foreign currency into dollars to record the receivable. If the exchange rate changes before payment is received, exchange gains or losses are recognized in the year they occur. The same treatment is used when a company makes a credit purchase from a foreign supplier and is required to make payment in a foreign currency.

A1 **Compute and analyze the components of return on total assets.** Return on total assets has two components: profit margin and total asset turnover. A decline in one component must be met with an increase in another if return on assets is to be maintained. Component analysis is helpful in assessing company performance compared to that of competitors and its own past.

P1 **Account for trading securities.** Investments are initially recorded at cost, and any dividend or interest from these investments is recorded in the income statement. Investments classified as trading securities are reported at fair value. Unrealized gains and losses on trading securities are reported in income. When investments are sold, the difference between the net proceeds from the sale and the cost of the securities is recognized as a gain or loss.

P2 **Account for held-to-maturity securities.** Debt securities held-to-maturity are reported at cost when purchased. Interest revenue is recorded as it accrues. The cost of long-term held-to-maturity securities is adjusted for the amortization of any difference between cost and maturity value.

P3 **Account for available-for-sale securities.** Debt and equity securities available-for-sale are recorded at cost when purchased. Available-for-sale securities are reported at their fair values on the balance sheet with unrealized gains or losses shown in the equity section. Gains and losses realized on the sale of these investments are reported in the income statement.

P4 **Account for equity securities with significant influence.** The equity method is used when an investor has a significant influence over an investee. This usually exists when an investor owns 20% or more of the investee's voting stock but not more than 50%. The equity method means an investor records its share of investee earnings with a debit to the investment account and a credit to a revenue account. Dividends received reduce the investment account balance.

Guidance Answers to Decision Maker

Money Manager If you have investments in fixed-rate bonds and notes when interest rates fall, the value of your investments increases. This is so because the bonds and notes you hold continue to pay the same (high) rate while the market is demanding a new lower interest rate. Your strategy is to continue holding your investments in bonds and notes, and, potentially, to increase these holdings through additional purchases.

Retailer Your store's return on assets is 11%, which is similar to the industry norm of 11.2%. However, disaggregation of return on assets reveals that your store's profit margin of 4.4% is much higher than the norm of 3.5%, but your total asset turnover of 2.5 is much lower than the norm of 3.2. These results suggest that, as compared with competitors, you are less efficient in using assets. You need to focus on increasing sales or reducing assets. You might consider reducing prices to increase sales, provided such a strategy does not reduce your return on assets. For instance, you could reduce your profit margin to 4% to increase sales. If total asset turnover increases to more than 2.75 when profit margin is lowered to 4%, your overall return on assets is improved.

Entrepreneur You are now less likely to buy Canadian milk products because it takes more U.S. money to buy a Canadian dollar (and milk). For instance, the purchase of milk from a Canadian dairy with a $1,000 (Canadian dollars) price would have cost the U.S. company $700 (U.S. dollars, computed as C$1,000 × US$0.70) before the rate change, and $800 (US dollars, computed as C$1,000 × US$0.80) after the rate change.

Guidance Answers to Quick Checks

1. Short-term held-to-maturity securities are reported at cost.
2. Trading securities are reported at fair value.
3. The equity section of the balance sheet (and in comprehensive income).
4. The income statement.
5. The Fair Value Adjustment account does not have a normal balance. Its balance is a function of market values for securities which move up or down. The balance of this valuation account is determined by market conditions.
6. Long-term investments include (1) long-term funds earmarked for a special purpose, (2) debt and equity securities that do not meet current asset requirements, and (3) long-term assets not used in the regular operations of the business.
7. An equity investment is classified as long term if it is not marketable or, if marketable, it is not held as an available source of cash to meet the needs of current operations.
8. Debt securities held-to-maturity and debt securities available-for-sale are both recorded at cost. Also, interest on both is accrued as earned. However, only long-term securities held-to-maturity require amortization of the difference between cost and maturity value. In addition, only securities available-for-sale require a period-end adjustment to fair value.
9. Long-term equity investments are placed in one of three categories and accounted for as follows: (a) **available-for-sale** (noninfluential, less than 20% of outstanding stock)—fair value; (b) **significant influence** (20% to 50% of outstanding stock)—equity method; and (c) **controlling influence** (holding more than 50% of outstanding stock)—equity method with consolidation.

Key Terms

Available-for-sale (AFS) securities (p. C-6)
Comprehensive income (p. C-10)
Consolidated financial statements (p. C-9)
Equity method (p. C-8)
Equity securities with controlling influence (p. C-9)
Equity securities with significant influence (p. C-8)
Foreign exchange rate (p. C-16)
Held-to-maturity (HTM) securities (p. C-6)
Long-term investments (p. C-2)
Multinational (p. C-16)
Other comprehensive income (p. C-10)
Parent (p. C-9)
Return on total assets (p. C-11)
Short-term investments (p. C-2)
Subsidiary (p. C-9)
Trading securities (p. C-5)
Unrealized gain (loss) (p. C-5)

Multiple Choice Quiz

Answers on p. C-35

mhhe.com/wildFINMAN5e

1. A company purchased $30,000 of 5% bonds for investment purposes on May 1. The bonds pay interest on February 1 and August 1. The amount of interest revenue accrued at December 31 (the company's year-end) is:
a. $1,500
b. $1,375
c. $1,000
d. $625
e. $300

2. Earlier this period, Amadeus Co. purchased its only available-for-sale investment in the stock of Bach Co. for $83,000. The period-end fair value of this stock is $84,500. Amadeus records a:
a. Credit to Unrealized Gain—Equity for $1,500.
b. Debit to Unrealized Loss—Equity for $1,500.
c. Debit to Investment Revenue for $1,500.
d. Credit to Fair Value Adjustment—Available-for-Sale for $3,500.
e. Credit to Cash for $1,500.

3. Mozart Co. owns 35% of Melody Inc. Melody pays $50,000 in cash dividends to its shareholders for the period. Mozart's entry to record the Melody dividend includes a:
a. Credit to Investment Revenue for $50,000.
b. Credit to Long-Term Investments for $17,500.
c. Credit to Cash for $17,500.
d. Debit to Long-Term Investments for $17,500.
e. Debit to Cash for $50,000.

4. A company has net income of $300,000, net sales of $2,500,000, and total assets of $2,000,000. Its return on total assets equals:
a. 6.7%
b. 12.0%
c. 8.3%
d. 80.0%
e. 15.0%

5. A company had net income of $80,000, net sales of $600,000, and total assets of $400,000. Its profit margin and total asset turnover are:

	Profit Margin	Total Asset Turnover
a.	1.5%	13.3
b.	13.3%	1.5
c.	13.3%	0.7
d.	7.0%	13.3
e.	10.0%	26.7

A Superscript A denotes assignments based on Appendix C-A.
Icon denotes assignments that involve decision making.

Discussion Questions

1. Under what two conditions should investments be classified as current assets?

2. On a balance sheet, what valuation must be reported for short-term investments in trading securities?

3. If a short-term investment in available-for-sale securities costs $10,000 and is sold for $12,000, how should the difference between these two amounts be recorded?

4. Identify the three classes of noninfluential and two classes of influential investments in securities.

5. Under what conditions should investments be classified as current assets? As long-term assets?

6. For investments in available-for-sale securities, how are unrealized (holding) gains and losses reported?

7. If a company purchases its only long-term investments in available-for-sale debt securities this period and their fair value is below cost at the balance sheet date, what entry is required to recognize this unrealized loss?

8. On a balance sheet, what valuation must be reported for debt securities classified as available-for-sale?

9. Under what circumstances are long-term investments in debt securities reported at cost and adjusted for amortization of any difference between cost and maturity value?

10. In accounting for investments in equity securities, when should the equity method be used?

11. Under what circumstances does a company prepare consolidated financial statements?

12.[A] What are two major challenges in accounting for international operations?

13.[A] Assume a U.S. company makes a credit sale to a foreign customer that is required to make payment in its foreign currency. In the current period, the exchange rate is $1.40 on the date of the sale and is $1.30 on the date the customer pays the receivable. Will the U.S. company record an exchange gain or loss?

14.[A] If a U.S. company makes a credit sale to a foreign customer required to make payment in U.S. dollars, can the U.S. company have an exchange gain or loss on this sale?

15. Refer to **Polaris**' statement of changes in shareholders' equity in Appendix A. What is the amount of foreign currency translation adjustment for the year ended December 31, 2011? Is this adjustment an unrealized gain or an unrealized loss?

Polaris

16. Refer to **Arctic Cat**'s statement of stockholders' equity. What was the amount of its fiscal 2011 unrealized gain or loss on derivative instruments?

Arctic Cat

17. Refer to the balance sheet of **KTM** in Appendix A. How can you tell that KTM uses the consolidated method of accounting?

KTM

18. Refer to the financial statements of **Piaggio** in Appendix A. Compute its return on total assets for the year ended December 31, 2011.

PIAGGIO

connect

QUICK STUDY

QS C-1
Short-term equity investments
P1

On April 18, Riley Co. made a short-term investment in 300 common shares of XLT Co. The purchase price is $42 per share and the broker's fee is $250. The intent is to actively manage these shares for profit. On May 30, Riley Co. receives $1 per share from XLT in dividends. Prepare the April 18 and May 30 journal entries to record these transactions.

QS C-2
Available-for-sale securities
P3

Journ Co. purchased short-term investments in available-for-sale securities at a cost of $50,000 on November 25, 2013. At December 31, 2013, these securities had a fair value of $47,000. This is the first and only time the company has purchased such securities.

1. Prepare the December 31, 2013, year-end adjusting entry for the securities' portfolio.

2. For each account in the entry for part 1, explain how it is reported in financial statements.

3. Prepare the April 6, 2014, entry when Journ sells one-half of these securities for $26,000.

QS C-3
Available-for-sale securities
P3

Prepare Hertog Company's journal entries to reflect the following transactions for the current year.

May 7 Purchases 200 shares of Kraft stock as a short-term investment in available-for-sale securities at a cost of $50 per share plus $300 in broker fees.

June 6 Sells 200 shares of its investment in Kraft stock at $56 per share. The broker's commission on this sale is $150.

QS C-4
Available-for-sale securities
P3

Hiker Company completes the following transactions during the current year.

May 9 Purchases 200 shares of Higo stock as a short-term investment in available-for-sale securities at a cost of $25 per share plus $150 in broker fees.

June 2 Sells 100 shares of its investment in Higo stock at $28 per share. The broker's commission on this sale is $90.

Dec. 31 The closing market price (fair value) of the Higo stock is $23 per share.

Prepare the May 9 and June 2 journal entries and the December 31 adjusting entry. This is the first and only time the company purchased such securities.

QS C-5
Identifying long-term investments
C1

Which of the following statements are true of long-term investments?

a. They are held as an investment of cash available for current operations.

b. They can include funds earmarked for a special purpose, such as bond sinking funds.

c. They can include investments in trading securities.

[continued on next page]

d. They can include debt securities held-to-maturity.
e. They are always easily sold and therefore qualify as being marketable.
f. They can include debt and equity securities available-for-sale.
g. They can include bonds and stocks not intended to serve as a ready source of cash.

QS C-6
Describing investments in securities
C1 C2

Complete the following descriptions by filling in the blanks.

1. Equity securities giving an investor significant influence are accounted for using the ______ ______.
2. Available-for-sale debt securities are reported on the balance sheet at ______ ______.
3. Trading securities are classified as ______ assets.
4. Accrual of interest on bonds held as long-term investments requires a credit to ______ ______.
5. The controlling investor (more than 50% ownership) is called the ______, and the investee company is called the ______.

QS C-7
Debt securities transactions
P2

On February 1, 2013, Garzon purchased 6% bonds issued by PBS Utilities at a cost of $40,000, which is their par value. The bonds pay interest semiannually on July 31 and January 31. For 2013, prepare entries to record Garzon's July 31 receipt of interest and its December 31 year-end interest accrual.

QS C-8
Recording equity securities
P3

On May 20, 2013, Montero Co. paid $1,000,000 to acquire 25,000 common shares (10%) of ORD Corp. as a long-term investment. On August 5, 2014, Montero sold one-half of these shares for $625,000. What valuation method should be used to account for this stock investment? Prepare entries to record both the acquisition and the sale of these shares.

QS C-9
Equity method transactions
P4

Assume the same facts as in QS C-8 except that the stock acquired represents 40% of ORD Corp.'s outstanding stock. Also assume that ORD Corp. paid a $100,000 dividend on November 1, 2013, and reported a net income of $700,000 for 2013. Prepare the entries to record (*a*) the receipt of the dividend and (*b*) the December 31, 2013, year-end adjustment required for the investment account.

QS C-10
Recording fair value adjustment for securities
P3

During the current year, Reed Consulting Group acquired long-term available-for-sale securities at a $70,000 cost. At its December 31 year-end, these securities had a fair value of $58,000. This is the first and only time the company purchased such securities.

1. Prepare the necessary year-end adjusting entry related to these securities.
2. Explain how each account used in part 1 is reported in the financial statements.

QS C-11
Equity securities with controlling influence
C2

Complete the following descriptions by filling in the blanks.

1. The controlling investor is called the ______, and the investee is called the ______.
2. A long-term investment classified as equity securities with controlling influence implies that the investor can exert a ______ influence over the investee.

QS C-12
Return on total assets A1

The return on total assets is the focus of analysts, creditors, and other users of financial statements.

1. How is the return on total assets computed?
2. What does this important ratio reflect?

QS C-13
Component return on total assets A1

Return on total assets can be separated into two important components.

1. Write the formula to separate the return on total assets into its two basic components.
2. Explain how these components of the return on total assets are helpful to financial statement users for business decisions.

QS C-14[A]
Foreign currency transactions
C3

A U.S. company sells a product to a British company with the transaction listed in British pounds. On the date of the sale, the transaction total of $14,500 is billed as £10,000, reflecting an exchange rate of 1.45 (that is, $1.45 per pound). Prepare the entry to record (1) the sale and (2) the receipt of payment in pounds when the exchange rate is 1.35.

QS C-15[A]
Foreign currency transactions
C3

On March 1, 2013, a U.S. company made a credit sale requiring payment in 30 days from a Malaysian company, Hamac Sdn. Bhd., in 20,000 Malaysian ringgits. Assuming the exchange rate between Malaysian ringgits and U.S. dollars is $0.4538 on March 1 and $0.4899 on March 31, prepare the entries to record the sale on March 1 and the cash receipt on March 31.

QS C-16
International accounting for investments
P1

The **Carrefour Group** reports the following description of its trading securities (titled "financial assets reported at fair value in the income statement").

> These are financial assets held by the Group in order to make a short-term profit on the sale. These assets are valued at their fair value with variations in value recognized in the income statement.

Note 10 to Carrefour's 2010 financial statements reports €7 million in unrealized gains for 2010 and €26 million in unrealized losses for 2010, both included in the fair value of those financial assets held for trading. What amount of these unrealized gains and unrealized losses, if any, are reported in its 2010 income statement? Explain.

connect

EXERCISES

Exercise C-1
Accounting for short-term trading securities
P1

Prepare journal entries to record the following transactions involving the short-term securities investments of Duke Co., all of which occurred during year 2013.

a. On March 22, purchased 1,000 shares of RIP Company stock at $10 per share plus a $80 brokerage fee. These shares are categorized as trading securities.

b. On September 1, received a $1.00 per share cash dividend on the RIP Company stock purchased in transaction *a*.

c. On October 8, sold 500 shares of RIP Co. stock for $15 per share, less a $50 brokerage fee.

(*c*) Dr. Cash $7,450

Exercise C-2
Accounting for short-term held-to-maturity securities P2

Prepare journal entries to record the following transactions involving the short-term securities investments of Natura Co., all of which occurred during year 2013.

a. On June 15, paid $1,000,000 cash to purchase Remedy's 90-day short-term debt securities ($1,000,000 principal), dated June 15, that pay 10% interest (categorized as held-to-maturity securities).

b. On September 16, received a check from Remedy in payment of the principal and 90 days' interest on the debt securities purchased in transaction *a*.

Exercise C-3
Accounting for short-term available-for-sale securities
P3

Prepare journal entries to record the following transactions involving the short-term securities investments of Krum Co., all of which occurred during year 2013.

a. On August 1, paid $450,000 cash to purchase Houtte's 9% debt securities ($450,000 principal), dated July 30, 2013, and maturing January 30, 2014 (categorized as available-for-sale securities).

b. On October 30, received a check from Houtte for 90 days' interest on the debt securities purchased in transaction *a*.

Exercise C-4
Debt and equity securities and short- and long-term investments
C1

Complete the following descriptions by filling in the blanks.

1. Debt securities reflect a ______ relationship such as investments in notes, bonds, and certificates of deposit.

2. Equity securities reflect an ______ relationship such as shares of stock issued by companies.

3. Short-term investments are securities that (1) management intends to convert to cash within ___ ___ or the ___ ___ whichever is longer, and (2) are readily convertible to ______.

4. Long-term investments in securities are defined as those securities that are ___ ___ convertible to cash or are ___ ___ to be converted into cash in the short term.

Exercise C-5
Equity securities with controlling influence
C2

Complete the following descriptions by filling in the blanks.

1. Consolidated ______ ______ show the financial position, results of operations, and cash flows of all entities under the parent's control, including all subsidiaries.

2. The equity method with ______ is used to account for long-term investments in equity securities with controlling influence.

Exercise C-6
Accounting for trading securities
P1

Brooks Co. purchases various investments in trading securities at a cost of $66,000 on December 27, 2013. (This is its first and only purchase of such securities.) At December 31, 2013, these securities had a fair value of $72,000.

1. Prepare the December 31, 2013, year-end adjusting entry for the trading securities' portfolio.

2. Explain how each account in the entry of part 1 is reported in financial statements.

3. Prepare the January 3, 2014, entry when Brooks sells a portion of its trading securities (that had originally cost $33,000) for $35,000.

Check (3) Gain, $2,000

Exercise C-7
Adjusting available-for-sale securities to fair value
P3

On December 31, 2013, Reggit Company held the following short-term investments in its portfolio of available-for-sale securities. Reggit had no short-term investments in its prior accounting periods. Prepare the December 31, 2013, adjusting entry to report these investments at fair value.

	Cost	Fair Value
Verrizano Corporation bonds payable	$89,600	$91,600
Preble Corporation notes payable	70,600	62,900
Lucerne Company common stock	86,500	83,100

Check Unrealized loss, $9,100

Exercise C-8
Transactions in short-term and long-term investments
P1 P2 P3

Prepare journal entries to record the following transactions involving both the short-term and long-term investments of Cancun Corp., all of which occurred during calendar year 2013. Use the account Short-Term Investments for any transactions that you determine are short term.

a. On February 15, paid $160,000 cash to purchase American General's 90-day short-term notes at par, which are dated February 15 and pay 10% interest (classified as held-to-maturity).

b. On March 22, bought 700 shares of Fran Industries common stock at $51 cash per share plus a $150 brokerage fee (classified as long-term available-for-sale securities).

c. On May 15, received a check from American General in payment of the principal and 90 days' interest on the notes purchased in transaction *a*.

d. On July 30, paid $100,000 cash to purchase MP3 Electronics' 8% notes at par, dated July 30, 2013, and maturing on January 30, 2014 (classified as trading securities).

e. On September 1, received a $1.00 per share cash dividend on the Fran Industries common stock purchased in transaction *b*.

f. On October 8, sold 350 shares of Fran Industries common stock for $64 cash per share, less a $125 brokerage fee.

g. On October 30, received a check from MP3 Electronics for three months' interest on the notes purchased in transaction *d*.

Exercise C-9
Fair value adjustment to available-for-sale securities
P3

On December 31, 2013, Lujack Co. held the following short-term available-for-sale securities.

	Cost	Fair Value
Nintendo Co. common stock	$44,450	$48,900
Atlantic bonds payable	49,000	47,000
Kellogg Co. notes payable	25,000	23,200
McDonald's Corp. common stock	46,300	44,800

Lujack had no short-term investments prior to the current period. Prepare the December 31, 2013, year-end adjusting entry to record the fair value adjustment for these securities.

Exercise C-10
Fair value adjustment to available-for-sale securities
P3

Prescrip Co. began operations in 2012. The cost and fair values for its long-term investments portfolio in available-for-sale securities are shown below. Prepare Prescrip's December 31, 2013, adjusting entry to reflect any necessary fair value adjustment for these investments.

	Cost	Fair Value
December 31, 2012	$120,483	$118,556
December 31, 2013	60,120	90,271

Exercise C-11
Multiyear fair value adjustments to available-for-sale securities
P3

Ticker Services began operations in 2011 and maintains long-term investments in available-for-sale securities. The year-end cost and fair values for its portfolio of these investments follow. Prepare journal entries to record each year-end fair value adjustment for these securities.

	Cost	Fair Value
December 31, 2011	$372,000	$360,860
December 31, 2012	428,500	455,800
December 31, 2013	600,200	700,500
December 31, 2014	876,900	780,200

Exercise C-12
Classifying investments in securities; recording fair values

C1 P2 P3 P4

Information regarding Carperk Company's individual investments in securities during its calendar-year 2013, along with the December 31, 2013, fair values, follows.

a. Investment in Brava Company bonds: $420,500 cost, $457,000 fair value. Carperk intends to hold these bonds until they mature in 2018.

b. Investment in Baybridge common stock: 29,500 shares; $362,450 cost; $391,375 fair value. Carperk owns 32% of Baybridge's voting stock and has a significant influence over Baybridge.

c. Investment in Buffa common stock: 12,000 shares; $165,500 cost; $178,000 fair value. This investment amounts to 3% of Buffa's outstanding shares, and Carperk's goal with this investment is to earn dividends over the next few years.

d. Investment in Newton common stock: 3,500 shares; $90,300 cost; $88,625 fair value. Carperk's goal with this investment is to reap an increase in fair value of the stock over the next three to five years. Newton has 30,000 common shares outstanding.

e. Investment in Farmers common stock: 16,300 shares; $100,860 cost; $111,210 fair value. This stock is marketable and is held as an investment of cash available for operations.

Required

1. Identify whether each investment should be classified as a short-term or long-term investment. For each long-term investment, indicate in which of the long-term investment classifications it should be placed.

2. Prepare a journal entry dated December 31, 2013, to record the fair value adjustment of the long-term investments in available-for-sale securities. Carperk had no long-term investments prior to year 2013.

Check (2) Unrealized gain, $10,825

Exercise C-13
Securities transactions; equity method

P4

Prepare journal entries to record the following transactions and events of Kodax Company.

2013

Jan. 2	Purchased 30,000 shares of Grecco Co. common stock for $408,000 cash plus a broker's fee of $3,000 cash. Bushtex has 90,000 shares of common stock outstanding and its policies will be significantly influenced by Kodax.
Sept. 1	Grecco declared and paid a cash dividend of $1.50 per share.
Dec. 31	Grecco announced that net income for the year is $486,900.

2014

June 1	Grecco declared and paid a cash dividend of $2.10 per share.
Dec. 31	Grecco announced that net income for the year is $702,750.
Dec. 31	Kodax sold 10,000 shares of Grecco for $320,000 cash.

Exercise C-14
Return on total assets

A1

The following information is available from the financial statements of Regae Industries. Compute Regae's return on total assets for 2013 and 2014. (Round returns to one-tenth of a percent.) Comment on the company's efficiency in using its assets in 2013 and 2014.

	2012	2013	2014
Total assets, December 31	$210,000	$340,000	$770,000
Net income	30,200	38,400	60,300

Exercise C-15A
Foreign currency transactions

C3

Leigh of New York sells its products to customers in the United States and the United Kingdom. On December 16, 2013, Leigh sold merchandise on credit to Bronson Ltd. of London at a price of 17,000 pounds. The exchange rate on that day for £1 was $1.4583. On December 31, 2013, when Leigh prepared its financial statements, the rate was £1 for $1.4382. Bronson paid its bill in full on January 15, 2014, at which time the exchange rate was £1 for $1.4482. Leigh immediately exchanged the 17,000 pounds for U.S. dollars. Prepare Leigh's journal entries on December 16, December 31, and January 15 (round to the nearest dollar).

Exercise C-16^A
Computing foreign exchange gains and losses on receivables
C3

On May 8, 2013, Jett Company (a U.S. company) made a credit sale to Lopez (a Mexican company). The terms of the sale required Lopez to pay 800,000 pesos on February 10, 2014. Jett prepares quarterly financial statements on March 31, June 30, September 30, and December 31. The exchange rates for pesos during the time the receivable is outstanding follow.

May 8, 2013	$0.1323
June 30, 2013	0.1352
September 30, 2013	0.1368
December 31, 2013	0.1335
February 10, 2014	0.1386

Compute the foreign exchange gain or loss that Jett should report on each of its quarterly income statements for the last three quarters of 2013 and the first quarter of 2014. Also compute the amount reported on Jett's balance sheets at the end of each of its last three quarters of 2013.

Exercise C-17
International accounting for investments
P3

The **Carrefour Group** reports the following description of its financial assets available-for-sale.

> Assets available for sale are . . . valued at fair value. Unrealized . . . gains or losses are recorded as shareholders' equity until they are sold.

Note 10 to Carrefour's 2010 financial statements reports €18 million in *net* unrealized losses (net of unrealized gains) for 2010, which is included in the fair value of its available-for-sale securities reported on the balance sheet.

1. What amount of the €18 million net unrealized losses, if any, is reported in its 2010 income statement? Explain.
2. If the €18 million net unrealized losses are not reported in the income statement, in which statement are they reported, if any? Explain.

connect

PROBLEM SET A

Problem C-1A
Recording transactions and fair value adjustments for trading securities
P1

Sage 50 QB

Carlsville Company, which began operations in 2013, invests its idle cash in trading securities. The following transactions are from its short-term investments in its trading securities.

2013

Jan. 20	Purchased 800 shares of Ford Motor Co. at $26 per share plus a $125 commission.
Feb. 9	Purchased 2,200 shares of Lucent at $44.25 per share plus a $578 commission.
Oct. 12	Purchased 750 shares of Z-Seven at $7.50 per share plus a $200 commission.

2014

Apr. 15	Sold 800 shares of Ford Motor Co. at $29 per share less a $285 commission.
July 5	Sold 750 shares of Z-Seven at $10.25 per share less a $102.50 commission.
July 22	Purchased 1,600 shares of Hunt Corp. at $30 per share plus a $444 commission.
Aug. 19	Purchased 1,800 shares of Donna Karan at $18.25 per share plus a $290 commission.

2015

Feb. 27	Purchased 3,400 shares of HCA at $34 per share plus a $420 commission.
Mar. 3	Sold 1,600 shares of Hunt at $25 per share less a $250 commission.
June 21	Sold 2,200 shares of Lucent at $42 per share less a $420 commission.
June 30	Purchased 1,200 shares of Black & Decker at $47.50 per share plus a $595 commission.
Nov. 1	Sold 1,800 shares of Donna Karan at $18.25 per share less a $309 commission.

Required

1. Prepare journal entries to record these short-term investment activities for the years shown. (Ignore any year-end adjusting entries.)
2. On December 31, 2015, prepare the adjusting entry to record any necessary fair value adjustment for the portfolio of trading securities when HCA's share price is $36 and Black & Decker's share price is $43.50. (Assume the Fair Value Adjustment—Trading account had an unadjusted balance of zero.)

Check (2) Dr. Fair Value Adjustment—Trading $985

Problem C-2A
Recording, adjusting, and reporting short-term available-for-sale securities
P3

Rose Company had no short-term investments prior to year 2013. It had the following transactions involving short-term investments in available-for-sale securities during 2013.

Apr.	16	Purchased 4,000 shares of Gem Co. stock at $24.25 per share plus a $180 brokerage fee.
May	1	Paid $100,000 to buy 90-day U.S. Treasury bills (debt securities): $100,000 principal amount, 6% interest, securities dated May 1.
July	7	Purchased 2,000 shares of PepsiCo stock at $49.25 per share plus a $175 brokerage fee.
	20	Purchased 1,000 shares of Xerox stock at $16.75 per share plus a $205 brokerage fee.
Aug.	3	Received a check for principal and accrued interest on the U.S. Treasury bills that matured on July 29.
	15	Received an $0.85 per share cash dividend on the Gem Co. stock.
	28	Sold 2,000 shares of Gem Co. stock at $30 per share less a $225 brokerage fee.
Oct.	1	Received a $1.90 per share cash dividend on the PepsiCo shares.
Dec.	15	Received a $1.05 per share cash dividend on the remaining Gem Co. shares.
	31	Received a $1.30 per share cash dividend on the PepsiCo shares.

Required

1. Prepare journal entries to record the preceding transactions and events.
2. Prepare a table to compare the year-end cost and fair values of Rose's short-term investments in available-for-sale securities. The year-end fair values per share are: Gem Co., $26.50; PepsiCo, $46.50; and Xerox, $13.75.
3. Prepare an adjusting entry, if necessary, to record the year-end fair value adjustment for the portfolio of short-term investments in available-for-sale securities.

Check (2) Cost = $164,220

(3) Dr. Unrealized Loss—Equity $4,470

Analysis Component

4. Explain the balance sheet presentation of the fair value adjustment for Rose's short-term investments.
5. How do these short-term investments affect Rose's (*a*) income statement for year 2013 and (*b*) the equity section of its balance sheet at year-end 2013?

Problem C-3A
Recording, adjusting, and reporting long-term available-for-sale securities
P3

Sage 50 QB

Grass Security, which began operations in 2013, invests in long-term available-for-sale securities. Following is a series of transactions and events determining its long-term investment activity.

2013

Jan.	20	Purchased 1,000 shares of Johnson & Johnson at $20.50 per share plus a $240 commission.
Feb.	9	Purchased 1,200 shares of Sony at $46.20 per share plus a $225 commission.
June	12	Purchased 1,500 shares of Mattel at $27.00 per share plus an $195 commission.
Dec.	31	Per share fair values for stocks in the portfolio are Johnson & Johnson, $21.50; Mattel, $30.90; Sony, $38.

2014

Apr.	15	Sold 1,000 shares of Johnson & Johnson at $23.50 per share less a $525 commission.
July	5	Sold 1,500 shares of Mattel at $23.90 per share less a $235 commission.
July	22	Purchased 600 shares of Sara Lee at $22.50 per share plus a $480 commission.
Aug.	19	Purchased 900 shares of Eastman Kodak at $17 per share plus a $198 commission.
Dec.	31	Per share fair values for stocks in the portfolio are: Kodak, $19.25; Sara Lee, $20.00; Sony, $35.00.

2015

Feb.	27	Purchased 2,400 shares of Microsoft at $67.00 per share plus a $525 commission.
June	21	Sold 1,200 shares of Sony at $48.00 per share less a $880 commission.
June	30	Purchased 1,400 shares of Black & Decker at $36.00 per share plus a $435 commission.
Aug.	3	Sold 600 shares of Sara Lee at $16.25 per share less a $435 commission.
Nov.	1	Sold 900 shares of Eastman Kodak at $22.75 per share less a $625 commission.
Dec.	31	Per share fair values for stocks in the portfolio are: Black & Decker, $39.00; Microsoft, $69.00.

Required

1. Prepare journal entries to record these transactions and events and any year-end fair value adjustments to the portfolio of long-term available-for-sale securities.

[continued on next page]

Check (2b) Fair Value Adjustment bal.: 12/31/13, $(3,650); 12/31/14; $(13,818)

(3b) Unrealized Gain at 12/31/2015, $8,040

2. Prepare a table that summarizes the (*a*) total cost, (*b*) total fair value adjustment, and (*c*) total fair value of the portfolio of long-term available-for-sale securities at each year-end.
3. Prepare a table that summarizes (*a*) the realized gains and losses and (*b*) the unrealized gains or losses for the portfolio of long-term available-for-sale securities at each year-end.

Problem C-4A
Long-term investment transactions; unrealized and realized gains and losses
C2 P3 P4

Stoll Co.'s long-term available-for-sale portfolio at December 31, 2012, consists of the following.

Available-for-Sale Securities	Cost	Fair Value
40,000 shares of Company A common stock	$535,300	$490,000
7,000 shares of Company B common stock	159,380	154,000
17,500 shares of Company C common stock	662,750	640,938

Stoll enters into the following long-term investment transactions during year 2013.

Jan. 29 Sold 3,500 shares of Company B common stock for $79,188 less a brokerage fee of $1,500.
Apr. 17 Purchased 10,000 shares of Company W common stock for $197,500 plus a brokerage fee of $2,400. The shares represent a 30% ownership in Company W.
July 6 Purchased 4,500 shares of Company X common stock for $126,562 plus a brokerage fee of $1,750. The shares represent a 10% ownership in Company X.
Aug. 22 Purchased 50,000 shares of Company Y common stock for $375,000 plus a brokerage fee of $1,200. The shares represent a 51% ownership in Company Y.
Nov. 13 Purchased 8,500 shares of Company Z common stock for $267,900 plus a brokerage fee of $2,450. The shares represent a 5% ownership in Company Z.
Dec. 9 Sold 40,000 shares of Company A common stock for $515,000 less a brokerage fee of $4,100.

The fair values of its investments at December 31, 2013, are: B, $81,375; C, $610,312; W, $191,250; X, $118,125; Y, $531,250; and Z, $278,800.

Required

1. Determine the amount Stoll should report on its December 31, 2013, balance sheet for its long-term investments in available-for-sale securities.
2. Prepare any necessary December 31, 2013, adjusting entry to record the fair value adjustment for the long-term investments in available-for-sale securities.
3. What amount of gains or losses on transactions relating to long-term investments in available-for-sale securities should Stoll report on its December 31, 2013, income statement?

Check (2) Cr. Unrealized Loss—Equity, $20,002

Problem C-5A
Accounting for long-term investments in securities; with and without significant influence
P3 P4

Selk Steel Co., which began operations on January 4, 2013, had the following subsequent transactions and events in its long-term investments.

2013

Jan. 5 Selk purchased 60,000 shares (20% of total) of Kildaire's common stock for $1,560,000.
Oct. 23 Kildaire declared and paid a cash dividend of $3.20 per share.
Dec. 31 Kildaire's net income for 2013 is $1,164,000, and the fair value of its stock at December 31 is $30.00 per share.

2014

Oct. 15 Kildaire declared and paid a cash dividend of $2.60 per share.
Dec. 31 Kildaire's net income for 2014 is $1,476,000, and the fair value of its stock at December 31 is $32.00 per share.

2015

Jan. 2 Selk sold all of its investment in Kildaire for $1,894,000 cash.

Part 1

Assume that Selk has a significant influence over Kildaire with its 20% share of stock.

Required

1. Prepare journal entries to record these transactions and events for Selk.
2. Compute the carrying (book) value per share of Selk's investment in Kildaire common stock as reflected in the investment account on January 1, 2015.
3. Compute the net increase or decrease in Selk's equity from January 5, 2013, through January 2, 2015, resulting from its investment in Kildaire.

Check (2) Carrying value per share, $29

Part 2

Assume that although Selk owns 20% of Kildaire's outstanding stock, circumstances indicate that it does not have a significant influence over the investee and that it is classified as an available-for-sale security investment.

Required

1. Prepare journal entries to record the preceding transactions and events for Selk. Also prepare an entry dated January 2, 2015, to remove any balance related to the fair value adjustment.
2. Compute the cost per share of Selk's investment in Kildaire common stock as reflected in the investment account on January 1, 2015.
3. Compute the net increase or decrease in Selk's equity from January 5, 2013, through January 2, 2015, resulting from its investment in Kildaire.

(1) 1/2/2015 Dr. Unrealized Gain—Equity $360,000

(3) Net increase, $682,000

Problem C-6A[A]
Foreign currency transactions
C3

Doering Company, a U.S. corporation with customers in several foreign countries, had the following selected transactions for 2013 and 2014.

2013

Apr. 8 Sold merchandise to Salinas & Sons of Mexico for $5,938 cash. The exchange rate for pesos is $0.1043 on this day.

July 21 Sold merchandise on credit to Sumito Corp. in Japan. The price of 1.5 million yen is to be paid 120 days from the date of sale. The exchange rate for yen is $0.0094 on this day.

Oct. 14 Sold merchandise for 19,000 pounds to Smithers Ltd. of Great Britain, payment in full to be received in 90 days. The exchange rate for pounds is $1.4566 on this day.

Nov. 18 Received Sumito's payment in yen for its July 21 purchase and immediately exchanged the yen for dollars. The exchange rate for yen is $0.0092 on this day.

Dec. 20 Sold merchandise for 17,000 ringgits to Hamid Albar of Malaysia, payment in full to be received in 30 days. On this day, the exchange rate for ringgits is $0.4501.

Dec. 31 Recorded adjusting entries to recognize exchange gains or losses on Doering's annual financial statements. Rates for exchanging foreign currencies on this day follow.

Pesos (Mexico)	$0.1055
Yen (Japan)	0.0093
Pounds (Britain)	1.4620
Ringgits (Malaysia)	0.4456

2014

Jan. 12 Received full payment in pounds from Smithers for the October 14 sale and immediately exchanged the pounds for dollars. The exchange rate for pounds is $1.4699 on this day.

Jan. 19 Received Hamid Albar's full payment in ringgits for the December 20 sale and immediately exchanged the ringgits for dollars. The exchange rate for ringgits is $0.4420 on this day.

Required

1. Prepare journal entries for the Doering transactions and adjusting entries (round amounts to the nearest dollar).
2. Compute the foreign exchange gain or loss to be reported on Doering's 2013 income statement.

Check (2) 2013 total foreign exchange loss, $274

Analysis Component

3. What actions might Doering consider to reduce its risk of foreign exchange gains or losses?

PROBLEM SET B

Problem C-1B
Recording transactions and fair value adjustments for trading securities P1

Harris Company, which began operations in 2013, invests its idle cash in trading securities. The following transactions relate to its short-term investments in its trading securities.

2013

Mar. 10 Purchased 2,400 shares of AOL at $59.15 per share plus a $1,545 commission.
May 7 Purchased 5,000 shares of MTV at $36.25 per share plus a $2,855 commission.
Sept. 1 Purchased 1,200 shares of UPS at $57.25 per share plus a $1,250 commission.

2014

Apr. 26 Sold 5,000 shares of MTV at $34.50 per share less a $2,050 commission.
Apr. 27 Sold 1,200 shares of UPS at $60.50 per share less an $1,788 commission.

June 2 Purchased 3,600 shares of SPW at $172 per share plus a $3,250 commission.
June 14 Purchased 900 shares of Walmart at $50.25 per share plus a $1,082 commission.

2015

Jan. 28 Purchased 2,000 shares of PepsiCo at $43 per share plus a $2,890 commission.
Jan. 31 Sold 3,600 shares of SPW at $168 per share less a $2,040 commission.
Aug. 22 Sold 2,400 shares of AOL at $56.75 per share less a $2,480 commission.
Sept. 3 Purchased 1,500 shares of Vodaphone at $40.50 per share plus an $1,680 commission.
Oct. 9 Sold 900 shares of Walmart at $53.75 per share less a $1,220 commission.

Required

1. Prepare journal entries to record these short-term investment activities for the years shown. (Ignore any year-end adjusting entries.)
2. On December 31, 2015, prepare the adjusting entry to record any necessary fair value adjustment for the portfolio of trading securities when PepsiCo's share price is $41 and Vodaphone's share price is $37. (Assume the Fair Value Adjustment—Trading account had an unadjusted balance of zero.)

Check (2) Cr. Fair Value Adjustment—Trading $13,820

Problem C-2B
Recording, adjusting, and reporting short-term available-for-sale securities
P3

Slip Systems had no short-term investments prior to 2013. It had the following transactions involving short-term investments in available-for-sale securities during 2013.

Feb. 6 Purchased 3,400 shares of Nokia stock at $41.25 per share plus a $3,000 brokerage fee.
15 Paid $20,000 to buy six-month U.S. Treasury bills (debt securities): $20,000 principal amount, 6% interest, securities dated February 15.
Apr. 7 Purchased 1,200 shares of Dell Co. stock at $39.50 per share plus a $1,255 brokerage fee.
June 2 Purchased 2,500 shares of Merck stock at $72.50 per share plus a $2,890 brokerage fee.
30 Received a $0.19 per share cash dividend on the Nokia shares.
Aug. 11 Sold 850 shares of Nokia stock at $46 per share less a $1,050 brokerage fee.
16 Received a check for principal and accrued interest on the U.S. Treasury bills purchased February 15.
24 Received a $0.10 per share cash dividend on the Dell shares.
Nov. 9 Received a $0.20 per share cash dividend on the remaining Nokia shares.
Dec. 18 Received a $0.15 per share cash dividend on the Dell shares.

Required

1. Prepare journal entries to record the preceding transactions and events.
2. Prepare a table to compare the year-end cost and fair values of the short-term investments in available-for-sale securities. The year-end fair values per share are: Nokia, $40.25; Dell, $40.50; and Merck, $59.
3. Prepare an adjusting entry, if necessary, to record the year-end fair value adjustment for the portfolio of short-term investments in available-for-sale securities.

Check (2) Cost = $340,232

(3) Dr. Unrealized Loss—Equity, $41,494

Analysis Component

4. Explain the balance sheet presentation of the fair value adjustment to Slip's short-term investments.
5. How do these short-term investments affect (*a*) its income statement for year 2013 and (*b*) the equity section of its balance sheet at the 2013 year-end?

Problem C-3B
Recording, adjusting, and reporting long-term available-for-sale securities
P3

Paris Enterprises, which began operations in 2013, invests in long-term available-for-sale securities. Following is a series of transactions and events involving its long-term investment activity.

2013

Mar. 10 Purchased 1,200 shares of Apple at $25.50 per share plus $800 commission.
Apr. 7 Purchased 2,500 shares of Ford at $22.50 per share plus $1,033 commission.
Sept. 1 Purchased 600 shares of Polaroid at $47.00 per share plus $890 commission.
Dec. 31 Per share fair values for stocks in the portfolio are: Apple, $27.50; Ford, $21.00; Polaroid, $49.00.

2014

Apr. 26 Sold 2,500 shares of Ford at $20.50 per share less a $1,207 commission.
June 2 Purchased 1,800 shares of Duracell at $19.25 per share plus a $1,050 commission.
June 14 Purchased 1,200 shares of Sears at $21 per share plus a $280 commission.
Nov. 27 Sold 600 shares of Polaroid at $51 per share less a $845 commission.
Dec. 31 Per share fair values for stocks in the portfolio are: Apple, $29.00; Duracell, $18.00; Sears, $23.00.

2015

Jan. 28 Purchased 1,000 shares of Coca-Cola Co. at $40 per share plus a $1,480 commission.
Aug. 22 Sold 1,200 shares of Apple at $21.50 per share less a $1,850 commission.
Sept. 3 Purchased 3,000 shares of Motorola at $28 per share plus a $780 commission.
Oct. 9 Sold 1,200 shares of Sears at $24.00 per share less a $599 commission.
Oct. 31 Sold 1,800 shares of Duracell at $15.00 per share less a $898 commission.
Dec. 31 Per share fair values for stocks in the portfolio are: Coca-Cola, $48.00; Motorola, $24.00.

Required

1. Prepare journal entries to record these transactions and events and any year-end fair value adjustments to the portfolio of long-term available-for-sale securities.
2. Prepare a table that summarizes the (*a*) total cost, (*b*) total fair value adjustment, and (*c*) total fair value for the portfolio of long-term available-for-sale securities at each year-end.
3. Prepare a table that summarizes (*a*) the realized gains and losses and (*b*) the unrealized gains or losses for the portfolio of long-term available-for-sale securities at each year-end.

Check (2b) Fair Value Adjustment bal.: 12/31/13, ($2,873); 12/31/14, $2,220

(3b) Unrealized Loss at 12/31/2015, $6,260

Problem C-4B
Long-term investment transactions; unrealized and realized gains and losses
C2 P3 P4

Troyer's long-term available-for-sale portfolio at December 31, 2012, consists of the following.

Available-for-Sale Securities	Cost	Fair Value
27,500 shares of Company R common stock	$559,125	$599,063
8,500 shares of Company S common stock	308,380	293,250
11,000 shares of Company T common stock	147,295	151,800

Troyer enters into the following long-term investment transactions during year 2013.

Jan. 13 Sold 2,125 shares of Company S stock for $72,250 less a brokerage fee of $1,195.
Mar. 24 Purchased 15,500 shares of Company U common stock for $282,875 plus a brokerage fee of $1,980. The shares represent a 62% ownership interest in Company U.
Apr. 5 Purchased 42,500 shares of Company V common stock for $133,875 plus a brokerage fee of $1,125. The shares represent a 10% ownership in Company V.
Sept. 2 Sold 11,000 shares of Company T common stock for $156,750 less a brokerage fee of $2,700.
Sept. 27 Purchased 2,500 shares of Company W common stock for $50,500 plus a brokerage fee of $1,050. The shares represent a 25% ownership interest in Company W.
Oct. 30 Purchased 5,000 shares of Company X common stock for $48,750 plus a brokerage fee of $1,170. The shares represent a 13% ownership interest in Company X.

The fair values of its investments at December 31, 2013, are: R, $568,125; S, $210,375; U, $272,800; V, $134,938; W, $54,689; and X, $45,625.

Required

1. Determine the amount Troyer should report on its December 31, 2013, balance sheet for its long-term investments in available-for-sale securities.
2. Prepare any necessary December 31, 2013, adjusting entry to record the fair value adjustment of the long-term investments in available-for-sale securities.
3. What amount of gains or losses on transactions relating to long-term investments in available-for-sale securities should Troyer report on its December 31, 2013, income statement?

Check (2) Dr. Unrealized Loss—Equity, $16,267; Cr. Fair Value Adjustment—AFS (LT), $45,580

Problem C-5B
Accounting for long-term investments in securities; with and without significant influence
P3 P4

Brinkley Company, which began operations on January 3, 2013, had the following subsequent transactions and events in its long-term investments.

2013

Jan. 5 Brinkley purchased 20,000 shares (25% of total) of Bloch's common stock for $200,500.
Aug. 1 Bloch declared and paid a cash dividend of $1.05 per share.
Dec. 31 Bloch's net income for 2013 is $82,000, and the fair value of its stock is $11.90 per share.

2014

Aug. 1 Bloch declared and paid a cash dividend of $1.35 per share.
Dec. 31 Bloch's net income for 2014 is $78,000, and the fair value of its stock is $13.65 per share.

2015

Jan. 8 Brinkley sold all of its investment in Bloch for $375,000 cash.

Part 1

Assume that Brinkley has a significant influence over Bloch with its 25% share.

Required

1. Prepare journal entries to record these transactions and events for Brinkley.

2. Compute the carrying (book) value per share of Brinkley's investment in Bloch common stock as reflected in the investment account on January 7, 2015.

Check (2) Carrying value per share, $9.63

3. Compute the net increase or decrease in Brinkley's equity from January 5, 2013, through January 8, 2015, resulting from its investment in Bloch.

Part 2

Assume that although Brinkley owns 25% of Bloch's outstanding stock, circumstances indicate that it does not have a significant influence over the investee and that it is classified as an available-for-sale security investment.

Required

1. Prepare journal entries to record these transactions and events for Brinkley. Also prepare an entry dated January 8, 2015, to remove any balance related to the fair value adjustment.

(1) 1/8/2015 Dr. Unrealized Gain—Equity $72,500

2. Compute the cost per share of Brinkley's investment in Bloch common stock as reflected in the investment account on January 7, 2015.

3. Compute the net increase or decrease in Brinkley's equity from January 5, 2013, through January 8, 2015, resulting from its investment in Bloch.

(3) Net increase, $222,500

Problem C-6B[A]
Foreign currency transactions
C3

Datamix, a U.S. corporation with customers in several foreign countries, had the following selected transactions for 2013 and 2014.

2013

May 26 Sold merchandise for 6.5 million yen to Fuji Company of Japan, payment in full to be received in 60 days. On this day, the exchange rate for yen is $0.0093.

June 1 Sold merchandise to Fordham Ltd. of Great Britain for $64,800 cash. The exchange rate for pounds is $1.4498 on this day.

July 25 Received Fuji's payment in yen for its May 26 purchase and immediately exchanged the yen for dollars. The exchange rate for yen is $0.0092 on this day.

Oct. 15 Sold merchandise on credit to Martinez Brothers of Mexico. The price of 378,000 pesos is to be paid 90 days from the date of sale. On this day, the exchange rate for pesos is $0.1020.

Dec. 6 Sold merchandise for 250,000 yuans to Chi-Ying Company of China, payment in full to be received in 30 days. The exchange rate for yuans is $0.1439 on this day.

Dec. 31 Recorded adjusting entries to recognize exchange gains or losses on Datamix's annual financial statements. Rates of exchanging foreign currencies on this day follow.

Yen (Japan)	$0.0094
Pounds (Britain)	1.4580
Pesos (Mexico)	0.1060
Yuans (China)	0.1450

2014

Jan. 5 Received Chi-Ying's full payment in yuans for the December 6 sale and immediately exchanged the yuans for dollars. The exchange rate for yuans is $0.1580 on this day.

Jan. 13 Received full payment in pesos from Martinez for the October 15 sale and immediately exchanged the pesos for dollars. The exchange rate for pesos is $0.1039 on this day.

Required

1. Prepare journal entries for the Datamix transactions and adjusting entries.

2. Compute the foreign exchange gain or loss to be reported on Datamix's 2013 income statement.

Check (2) 2013 total foreign exchange gain, $1,137

Analysis Component

3. What actions might Datamix consider to reduce its risk of foreign exchange gains or losses?

SERIAL PROBLEM

Success Systems

P1

(This serial problem began in Chapter 1 and continues through most of the book. If previous chapter segments were not completed, the serial problem can begin at this point. It is helpful, but not necessary, to use the Working Papers that accompany the book.)

SP C While reviewing the March 31, 2014, balance sheet of Success Systems, Adria Lopez notes that the business has built a large cash balance of $77,845. Its most recent bank money market statement shows that the funds are earning an annualized return of 0.75%. Adria Lopez decides to make several investments with the desire to earn a higher return on the idle cash balance. Accordingly, in April 2014, Success Systems makes the following investments in trading securities:

April 16 Purchases 400 shares of Johnson & Johnson stock at $50 per share plus $300 commission.
April 30 Purchases 200 shares of Starbucks Corporation at $22 per share plus $250 commission.

On June 30, 2014, the per share market price (fair value) of the Johnson & Johnson shares is $55 and the Starbucks shares is $19.

Required

1. Prepare journal entries to record the April purchases of trading securities by Success Systems.
2. On June 30, 2014, prepare the adjusting entry to record any necessary fair value adjustment to its portfolio of trading securities.

Beyond the Numbers

REPORTING IN ACTION

C3 A1

Polaris

BTN C-1 Refer to **Polaris**' financial statements in Appendix A to answer the following.

1. Are Polaris' financial statements consolidated? How can you tell?
2. What is Polaris' *comprehensive income* for the year ended December 31, 2011?
3. Does Polaris have any foreign operations? How can you tell?
4. Compute Polaris' return on total assets for the year ended December 31, 2011.

Fast Forward

5. Access Polaris' annual report for a fiscal year ending after December 31, 2011, from either its Website (Polaris.com) or the SEC's database (www.SEC.gov). Recompute Polaris' return on total assets for the years subsequent to December 31, 2011.

COMPARATIVE ANALYSIS

A1

Polaris

Arctic Cat

BTN C-2 Key figures for **Polaris** and **Arctic Cat** follow.

	Polaris			Arctic Cat		
($ thousands)	Current Year	1 Year Prior	2 Years Prior	Current Year	1 Year Prior	2 Years Prior
Net income	$ 227,575	$ 147,138	$ 101,017	$ 13,007	$ 1,875	($9,508)
Net sales	2,656,949	1,991,139	1,565,887	464,651	450,728	563,613
Total assets	1,228,024	1,061,647	763,653	272,906	246,084	251,165

Required

1. Compute return on total assets for Polaris and Arctic Cat for the two most recent years.
2. Separate the return on total assets computed in part 1 into its components for both companies and both years according to the formula in Exhibit C.9.
3. Which company has the highest total return on assets? The highest profit margin? The highest total asset turnover? What does this comparative analysis reveal? (Assume an industry average of 10.0% for return on assets.)

ETHICS CHALLENGE

P2 P3

BTN C-3 Kasey Hartman is the controller for Wholemart Company, which has numerous long-term investments in debt securities. Wholemart's investments are mainly in 5-year bonds. Hartman is preparing its year-end financial statements. In accounting for long-term debt securities, she knows that each long-term investment must be designated as a held-to-maturity or an available-for-sale security. Interest rates rose sharply this past year causing the portfolio's fair value to substantially decline. The company does not intend to hold the bonds for the entire 5 years. Hartman also earns a bonus each year, which is computed as a percent of net income.

Required

1. Will Hartman's bonus depend in any way on the classification of the debt securities? Explain.
2. What criteria must Hartman use to classify the securities as held-to-maturity or available-for-sale?
3. Is there likely any company oversight of Hartman's classification of the securities? Explain.

COMMUNICATING IN PRACTICE

P4

BTN C-4 Assume that you are Jolee Company's accountant. Company owner Mary Jolee has reviewed the 2013 financial statements you prepared and questions the $6,000 loss reported on the sale of its investment in Kemper Co. common stock. Jolee acquired 50,000 shares of Kemper's common stock on December 31, 2011, at a cost of $500,000. This stock purchase represented a 40% interest in Kemper. The 2012 income statement reported that earnings from all investments were $126,000. On January 3, 2013, Jolee Company sold the Kemper stock for $575,000. Kemper did not pay any dividends during 2012 but reported a net income of $202,500 for that year. Mary Jolee believes that because the Kemper stock purchase price was $500,000 and was sold for $575,000, the 2013 income statement should report a $75,000 gain on the sale.

Required

Draft a one-half page memorandum to Mary Jolee explaining why the $6,000 loss on sale of Kemper stock is correctly reported.

TAKING IT TO THE NET

C1

BTN C-5 Access the July 28, 2011, 10-K filing (for year-end June 30, 2011) of **Microsoft** (MSFT) at www.SEC.gov. Review its note 4, "Investments."

Required

1. How does the "cost-basis" total amount for its investments as of June 30, 2011, compare to the prior year-end amount?
2. Identify at least eight types of short-term investments held by Microsoft as of June 30, 2011.
3. What were Microsoft's unrealized gains and its unrealized losses from its investments for 2011?
4. Was the cost or fair value ("recorded basis") of the investments higher as of June 30, 2011?

TEAMWORK IN ACTION

C1 C2 P1 P2 P3 P4

BTN C-6 Each team member is to become an expert on a specific classification of long-term investments. This expertise will be used to facilitate other teammates' understanding of the concepts and procedures relevent to the classification chosen.

1. Each team member must select an area for expertise by choosing one of the following classifications of long-term investments.
   - **a.** Held-to-maturity debt securities
   - **b.** Available-for-sale debt and equity securities
   - **c.** Equity securities with significant influence
   - **d.** Equity securities with controlling influence
2. Learning teams are to disburse and expert teams are to be formed. Expert teams are made up of those who select the same area of expertise. The instructor will identify the location where each expert team will meet.
3. Expert teams will collaborate to develop a presentation based on the following requirements. Students must write the presentation in a format they can show to their learning teams in part (4).

Requirements for Expert Presentation

- **a.** Write a transaction for the acquisition of this type of investment security. The transaction description is to include all necessary data to reflect the chosen classification.
- **b.** Prepare the journal entry to record the acquisition.

  [*Note:* The expert team on equity securities with controlling influence will substitute requirements (*d*) and (*e*) with a discussion of the reporting of these investments.]

c. Identify information necessary to complete the end-of-period adjustment for this investment.

d. Assuming that this is the only investment owned, prepare any necessary year-end entries.

e. Present the relevant balance sheet section(s).

4. Re-form learning teams. In rotation, experts are to present to their teams the presentations they developed in part 3. Experts are to encourage and respond to questions.

ENTREPRENEURIAL DECISION

C3

BTN C-7A Refer to the opening feature in this appendix about Catherine and David Cook and their company, myYearbook (now rebranded as MeetMe). Assume that they must acquire the Japanese rights to certain games and social applications that will then be produced for presentation on MeetMe's U.S. site. Assume MeetMe acquires those rights on January 1, 2013, from a Japanese distributor and agrees to pay 12,000,000 yen per year for those rights. Quarterly payments are due March 31, June 30, September 30, and December 31 each year. On January 1, 2013, the yen is worth $0.00891.

Required

1. Prepare the journal entry to record the Internet rights purchased on January 1, 2013.

2. Prepare the journal entries to record the payments on March 31, June 30, September 30, and December 31, 2013. The value of the yen on those dates follows.

March 31	$0.00893
June 30	0.00901
September 30	0.00902
December 31	0.00897

3. How can MeetMe protect itself from unanticipated gains and losses from currency translation if all of the payments are specified to be paid in yen?

HITTING THE ROAD

C3

BTN C-8A Assume that you are planning a spring break trip to Europe. Identify three locations where you can find exchange rates for the dollar relative to the Euro or other currencies.

GLOBAL DECISION

A1

PIAGGIO
Polaris
Arctic Cat

BTN C-9 Piaggio, Polaris, and Arctic Cat are competitors in the global marketplace. Following are selected data from each company.

	Piaggio (Euro thousands)			Polaris		Arctic Cat	
Key Figure	Current Year	One Year Prior	Two Years Prior	Current Year	Prior Year	Current Year	Prior Year
Net income	€ 47,053	€ 42,811	€ 46,031	—	—	—	—
Net sales	1,516,463	1,485,351	1,486,882	—	—	—	—
Total assets	1,520,184	1,545,722	1,564,820	—	—	—	—
Profit margin	?	?	—	8.6%	7.4%	2.8%	0.416%
Total asset turnover	?	?	—	2.31	2.18	1.79	1.81

Required

1. Compute Piaggio's return on total assets, and its components of profit margin and total asset turnover, for the most recent two years using the data provided.

2. Which of these three companies has the highest return on total assets? Highest profit margin? Highest total asset turnover? Interpret these results for the (*a*) current year and (*b*) prior year.

ANSWERS TO MULTIPLE CHOICE QUIZ

1. d; $30,000 × 5% × 5/12 = $625

2. a; Unrealized gain = $84,500 − $83,000 = $1,500

3. b; $50,000 × 35% = $17,500

4. e; $300,000/$2,000,000 = 15%

5. b; Profit margin = $80,000/$600,000 = 13.3%
Total asset turnover = $600,000/$400,000 = 1.5

Glossary

Absorption costing Costing method that assigns both variable and fixed costs to products. *(pp. 786 & 816)*

Accelerated depreciation method Method that produces larger depreciation charges in the early years of an asset's life and smaller charges in its later years. *(p. 342)*

Account Record within an accounting system in which increases and decreases are entered and stored in a specific asset, liability, equity, revenue, or expense. *(p. 53)*

Account balance Difference between total debits and total credits (including the beginning balance) for an account. *(p. 60)*

Account form balance sheet Balance sheet that lists assets on the left side and liabilities and equity on the right. *(p. 68)*

Account payable Liability created by buying goods or services on credit; backed by the buyer's general credit standing.

Accounting Information and measurement system that identifies, records, and communicates relevant information about a company's business activities. *(p. 4)*

Accounting cycle Recurring steps performed each accounting period, starting with analyzing transactions and continuing through the post-closing trial balance (or reversing entries). *(p. 116)*

Accounting equation Equality involving a company's assets, liabilities, and equity; Assets = Liabilities + Equity; also called *balance sheet equation*. *(p. 15)*

Accounting information system People, records, and methods that collect and process data from transactions and events, organize them in useful forms, and communicate results to decision makers. *(p. E-2)*

Accounting period Length of time covered by financial statements; also called *reporting period*. *(p. 98)*

Accounting rate of return Rate used to evaluate the acceptability of an investment; equals the after-tax periodic income from a project divided by the average investment in the asset; also called *rate of return on average investment*. *(p. 1019)*

Accounts payable ledger Subsidiary ledger listing individual creditor (supplier) accounts.

Accounts receivable Amounts due from customers for credit sales; backed by the customer's general credit standing. *(p. 302)*

Accounts receivable ledger Subsidiary ledger listing individual customer accounts. *(p. E-7)*

Accounts receivable turnover Measure of both the quality and liquidity of accounts receivable; indicates how often receivables are received and collected during the period; computed by dividing net sales by average accounts receivable. *(p. 317)*

Accrual basis accounting Accounting system that recognizes revenues when earned and expenses when incurred; the basis for GAAP. *(p. 99)*

Accrued expenses Costs incurred in a period that are both unpaid and unrecorded; adjusting entries for recording accrued expenses involve increasing expenses and increasing liabilities. *(p. 105)*

Accrued revenues Revenues earned in a period that are both unrecorded and not yet received in cash (or other assets); adjusting entries for recording accrued revenues involve increasing assets and increasing revenues. *(p. 107)*

Accumulated depreciation Cumulative sum of all depreciation expense recorded for an asset. *(p. 100)*

Acid-test ratio Ratio used to assess a company's ability to settle its current debts with its most liquid assets; defined as quick assets (cash, short-term investments, and current receivables) divided by current liabilities. *(p. 178)*

Activity An event that causes the consumption of overhead resources in an entity. *(p. 743)*

Activity-based budgeting (ABB) Budget system based on expected activities. *(p. 862)*

Activity-based costing (ABC) Cost allocation method that focuses on activities performed; traces costs to activities and then assigns them to cost objects. *(pp. 9 & 743)*

Activity cost driver Variable that causes an activity's cost to go up or down; a causal factor. *(pp. 12 & 746)*

Activity cost pool Temporary account that accumulates costs a company incurs to support an activity. *(pp. 9 & 743)*

Adjusted trial balance List of accounts and balances prepared after period-end adjustments are recorded and posted. *(p. 110)*

Adjusting entry Journal entry at the end of an accounting period to bring an asset or liability account to its proper amount and update the related expense or revenue account. *(p. 101)*

Aging of accounts receivable Process of classifying accounts receivable by how long they are past due for purposes of estimating uncollectible accounts. *(p. 310)*

Allowance for Doubtful Accounts Contra asset account with a balance approximating uncollectible accounts receivable; also called *Allowance for Uncollectible Accounts*. *(p. 307)*

Allowance method Procedure that (a) estimates and matches bad debts expense with its sales for the period and/or (b) reports accounts receivable at estimated realizable value. *(p. 307)*

Amortization Process of allocating the cost of an intangible asset to expense over its estimated useful life. *(p. 351)*

Annual financial statements Financial statements covering a one-year period; often based on a calendar year, but any consecutive 12-month (or 52-week) period is acceptable. *(p. 98)*

Annual report Summary of a company's financial results for the year with its current financial condition and future plans; directed to external users of financial information. *(p. A-1)*

Annuity Series of equal payments at equal intervals. *(pp. 441 & 1021)*

Appropriated retained earnings Retained earnings separately reported to inform stockholders of funding needs. *(p. 482)*

Asset book value (See *book value*.)

Assets Resources a business owns or controls that are expected to provide current and future benefits to the business. *(p. 15)*

Audit Analysis and report of an organization's accounting system, its records, and its reports using various tests. *(p. 13)*

Auditors Individuals hired to review financial reports and information systems. *Internal auditors* of a company are employed to assess and evaluate its system of internal controls, including the resulting reports. *External auditors* are independent of a company and are hired to assess and evaluate the "fairness" of financial statements (or to perform other contracted financial services). *(p. 13)*

Authorized stock Total amount of stock that a corporation's charter authorizes it to issue. *(p. 469)*

Available-for-sale (AFS) securities Investments in debt and equity securities that are not classified as trading securities or held-to-maturity securities. *(p. C-6)*

Average cost See *weighted average*.

Avoidable expense Expense (or cost) that is relevant for decision making; expense that is not incurred if a department, product, or service is eliminated. *(p. 993)*

Bad debts Accounts of customers who do not pay what they have promised to pay; an expense of selling on credit; also called *uncollectible accounts*. *(p. 306)*

Balance column account Account with debit and credit columns for recording entries and another column for showing the balance of the account after each entry. *(p. 60)*

Balance sheet Financial statement that lists types and dollar amounts of assets, liabilities, and equity at a specific date. *(p. 20)*

Balance sheet equation (See *accounting equation*.)

Balanced scorecard A system of performance measurement that collects information on several key performance indicators within each of four perspectives: customer, internal processes, innovation and learning, and financial. *(p. 956)*

Bank reconciliation Report that explains the difference between the book (company) balance of cash and the cash balance reported on the bank statement. *(p. 273)*

Bank statement Bank report on the depositor's beginning and ending cash balances, and a listing of its changes, for a period. *(p. 272)*

Basic earnings per share Net income less any preferred dividends and then divided by weighted-average common shares outstanding. *(p. 485)*

Batch level activities Activities that are performed each time a batch of goods is handled or processed, regardless of how many units are in a batch; the amount of resources used depends on the number of batches run rather than on the number of units in the batch. *(p. 750)*

Batch processing Accumulating source documents for a period of time and then processing them all at once such as once a day, week, or month. *(p. E-16)*

Bearer bonds Bonds made payable to whoever holds them (the *bearer*); also called *unregistered bonds*. *(p. 436)*

Benchmarking Practice of comparing and analyzing company financial performance or position with other companies or standards. *(p. 908)*

Betterments Expenditures to make a plant asset more efficient or productive; also called *improvements*. *(p. 347)*

Bond Written promise to pay the bond's par (or face) value and interest at a stated contract rate; often issued in denominations of $1,000. *(p. 422)*

Bond certificate Document containing bond specifics such as issuer's name, bond par value, contract interest rate, and maturity date. *(p. 424)*

Bond indenture Contract between the bond issuer and the bondholders; identifies the parties' rights and obligations. *(p. 424)*

Book value Asset's acquisition costs less its accumulated depreciation (or depletion, or amortization); also sometimes used synonymously as the *carrying value* of an account. *(pp. 104 & 341)*

Book value per common share Recorded amount of equity applicable to common shares divided by the number of common shares outstanding. *(p. 486)*

Book value per preferred share Equity applicable to preferred shares (equals its call price [or par value if it is not callable] plus any cumulative dividends in arrears) divided by the number of preferred shares outstanding. *(p. 486)*

Bookkeeping (See *recordkeeping*.)

Break-even point Output level at which sales equals fixed plus variable costs; where income equals zero. *(p. 785)*

Break-even time (BET) Time-based measurement used to evaluate the acceptability of an investment; equals the time expected to pass before the present value of the net cash flows from an investment equals its initial cost. *(p. 1026)*

Budget Formal statement of future plans, usually expressed in monetary terms. *(p. 848)*

Budget report Report comparing actual results to planned objectives; sometimes used as a progress report. *(p. 896)*

Budgetary control Management use of budgets to monitor and control company operations. *(p. 896)*

Budgeted balance sheet Accounting report that presents predicted amounts of the company's assets, liabilities, and equity balances as of the end of the budget period. *(p. 860)*

Budgeted income statement Accounting report that presents predicted amounts of the company's revenues and expenses for the budget period. *(p. 860)*

Budgeting Process of planning future business actions and expressing them as formal plans. *(p. 848)*

Business An organization of one or more individuals selling products and/or services for profit.

Business entity assumption Principle that requires a business to be accounted for separately from its owner(s) and from any other entity. *(p. 12)*

Business segment Part of a company that can be separately identified by the products or services that it provides or by the geographic markets that it serves; also called *segment*. *(p. 588)*

C corporation Corporation that does not qualify for nor elect to be treated as a proprietorship or partnership for income tax purposes and therefore is subject to income taxes; also called *C corp. (p. 12)*

Call price Amount that must be paid to call and retire a callable preferred stock or a callable bond. *(p. 479)*

Callable bonds Bonds that give the issuer the option to retire them at a stated amount prior to maturity. *(p. 436)*

Callable preferred stock Preferred stock that the issuing corporation, at its option, may retire by paying the call price plus any dividends in arrears. *(p. 479)*

Canceled checks Checks that the bank has paid and deducted from the depositor's account. *(p. 272)*

Capital budgeting Process of analyzing alternative investments and deciding which assets to acquire or sell. *(p. 1016)*

Capital expenditures Additional costs of plant assets that provide material benefits extending beyond the current period; also called *balance sheet expenditures. (p. 346)*

Capital expenditures budget Plan that lists dollar amounts to be both received from disposal of plant assets and spent to purchase plant assets. *(p. 858)*

Capital leases Long-term leases in which the lessor transfers substantially all risk and rewards of ownership to the lessee. *(p. 446)*

Capital stock General term referring to a corporation's stock used in obtaining capital (owner financing). *(p. 469)*

Capitalize Record the cost as part of a permanent account and allocate it over later periods.

Carrying (book) value of bonds Net amount at which bonds are reported on the balance sheet; equals the par value of the bonds less any unamortized discount or plus any unamortized premium; also called *carrying amount or book value. (p. 426)*

Cash Includes currency, coins, and amounts on deposit in bank checking or savings accounts. *(p. 263)*

Cash basis accounting Accounting system that recognizes revenues when cash is received and records expenses when cash is paid. *(p. 99)*

Cash budget Plan that shows expected cash inflows and outflows during the budget period, including receipts from loans needed to maintain a minimum cash balance and repayments of such loans. *(p. 266)*

Cash disbursements journal Special journal normally used to record all payments of cash; also called *cash payments journal. (p. E-14)*

Cash discount Reduction in the price of merchandise granted by a seller to a buyer when payment is made within the discount period. *(p. 165)*

Cash equivalents Short-term, investment assets that are readily convertible to a known cash amount or sufficiently close to their maturity date (usually within 90 days) so that market value is not sensitive to interest rate changes. *(p. 264)*

Cash flow on total assets Ratio of operating cash flows to average total assets; not sensitive to income recognition and measurement; partly reflects earnings quality. *(p. 528)*

Cash Over and Short Income statement account used to record cash overages and cash shortages arising from errors in cash receipts or payments. *(p. 265)*

Cash receipts journal Special journal normally used to record all receipts of cash. *(p. E-11)*

Change in an accounting estimate Change in an accounting estimate that results from new information, subsequent developments, or improved judgment that impacts current and future periods. *(pp. 345 & 483)*

Chart of accounts List of accounts used by a company; includes an identification number for each account. *(p. 54)*

Check Document signed by a depositor instructing the bank to pay a specified amount to a designated recipient. *(p. 271)*

Check register Another name for a cash disbursements journal when the journal has a column for check numbers. *(pp. 282 & E-14)*

Classified balance sheet Balance sheet that presents assets and liabilities in relevant subgroups, including current and noncurrent classifications. *(p. 117)*

Clock card Source document used to record the number of hours an employee works and to determine the total labor cost for each pay period. *(p. 660)*

Closing entries Entries recorded at the end of each accounting period to transfer end-of-period balances in revenue, gain, expense, loss, and withdrawal (dividend for a corporation) accounts to the capital account (to retained earnings for a corporation). *(p. 112)*

Closing process Necessary end-of-period steps to prepare the accounts for recording the transactions of the next period. *(p. 112)*

Columnar journal Journal with more than one column. *(p. E-8)*

Committee of Sponsoring Organizations (COSO) Committee of Sponsoring Organizations of the Treadway Commission (or COSO) is a joint initiative of five private sector organizations and is dedicated to providing thought leadership through the development of frameworks and guidance on enterprise risk management, internal control, and fraud deterrence. *(p. 259)*

Common stock Corporation's basic ownership share; also generically called *capital stock. (pp. 13 & 468)*

Common-size financial statement Statement that expresses each amount as a percent of a base amount. In the balance sheet, total assets is usually the base and is expressed as 100%. In the income statement, net sales is usually the base. *(p. 571)*

Comparative financial statement Statement with data for two or more successive periods placed in side-by-side columns, often with changes shown in dollar amounts and percents. *(p. 566)*

Compatibility principle Information system principle that prescribes an accounting system to conform with a company's activities, personnel, and structure. *(p. E-3)*

Complex capital structure Capital structure that includes outstanding rights or options to purchase common stock, or securities that are convertible into common stock. *(p. 485)*

Components of accounting systems Five basic components of accounting systems are source documents, input devices, information processors, information storage, and output devices. *(p. E-3)*

Composite unit Generic unit consisting of a specific number of units of each product; unit comprised in proportion to the expected sales mix of its products. *(p. 793)*

Compound journal entry Journal entry that affects at least three accounts. *(p. 63)*

Comprehensive income Net change in equity for a period, excluding owner investments and distributions. *(p. C-10)*

Computer hardware Physical equipment in a computerized accounting information system.

Computer network Linkage giving different users and different computers access to common databases and programs. *(p. E-16)*

Computer software Programs that direct operations of computer hardware.

Conceptual framework The basic concepts that underlie the preparation and presentation of financial statements for external users; can serve as a guide in developing future standards and to resolve accounting issues that are not addressed directly in current standards using the definitions, recognition criteria, and measurement concepts for assets, liabilities, revenues, and expenses. *(p. 10)*

Conservatism constraint Principle that prescribes the less optimistic estimate when two estimates are about equally likely. *(p. 220)*

Consignee Receiver of goods owned by another who holds them for purposes of selling them for the owner. *(p. 210)*

Consignor Owner of goods who ships them to another party who will sell them for the owner. *(p. 210)*

Consistency concept Principle that prescribes use of the same accounting method(s) over time so that financial statements are comparable across periods. *(p. 219)*

Consolidated financial statements Financial statements that show all (combined) activities under the parent's control, including those of any subsidiaries. *(p. C-9)*

Contingent liability Obligation to make a future payment if, and only if, an uncertain future event occurs. *(p. 390)*

Continuous budgeting Practice of preparing budgets for a selected number of future periods and revising those budgets as each period is completed. *(p. 851)*

Continuous improvement Concept requiring every manager and employee continually to look to improve operations. *(p. 626)*

Contra account Account linked with another account and having an opposite normal balance; reported as a subtraction from the other account's balance. *(p. 103)*

Contract rate Interest rate specified in a bond indenture (or note); multiplied by the par value to determine the interest paid each period; also called *coupon rate, stated rate,* or *nominal rate*. *(p. 425)*

Contributed capital Total amount of cash and other assets received from stockholders in exchange for stock; also called *paid-in capital*. *(p. 15)*

Contributed capital in excess of par value Difference between the par value of stock and its issue price when issued at a price above par.

Contribution format An income statement format that is geared to cost behavior in that costs are separated into variable and fixed categories rather than being separated according to the functions of production, sales, and administration. *(p. 826)*

Contribution margin Sales revenue less total variable costs. *(p. 785)*

Contribution margin income statement Income statement that separates variable and fixed costs; highlights the contribution margin, which is sales less variable expenses. *(p. 818)*

Contribution margin per unit Amount that the sale of one unit contributes toward recovering fixed costs and earning profit; defined as sales price per unit minus variable expense per unit. *(p. 785)*

Contribution margin ratio Product's contribution margin divided by its sale price. *(p. 785)*

Contribution margin report Product's contribution margin divided by its sale price. *(p. 819)*

Control Process of monitoring planning decisions and evaluating the organization's activities and employees. *(p. 611)*

Control principle Information system principle that prescribes an accounting system to aid managers in controlling and monitoring business activities. *(p. E-2)*

Controllable costs Costs that a manager has the power to control or at least strongly influence. *(pp. 615, 826 & 943)*

Controllable variance Combination of both overhead spending variances (variable and fixed) and the variable overhead efficiency variance. *(p. 909)*

Controlling account General ledger account, the balance of which (after posting) equals the sum of the balances in its related subsidiary ledger. *(p. E-7)*

Conversion costs Expenditures incurred in converting raw materials to finished goods; includes direct labor costs and overhead costs. *(p. 619)*

Conversion costs per equivalent unit The combined costs of direct labor and factory overhead per equivalent unit. *(p. 707)*

Convertible bonds Bonds that bondholders can exchange for a set number of the issuer's shares. *(p. 436)*

Convertible preferred stock Preferred stock with an option to exchange it for common stock at a specified rate. *(p. 478)*

Copyright Right giving the owner the exclusive privilege to publish and sell musical, literary, or artistic work during the creator's life plus 70 years. *(p. 352)*

Corporation Business that is a separate legal entity under state or federal laws with owners called *shareholders* or *stockholders*. *(pp. 12 & 466)*

Cost All normal and reasonable expenditures necessary to get an asset in place and ready for its intended use. *(pp. 337 & 339)*

Cost accounting system Accounting system for manufacturing activities based on the perpetual inventory system. *(p. 654)*

Cost-based transfer pricing A transfer pricing system based on the cost of goods or services being transferred across divisions within the same company. *(p. 962)*

Cost-benefit constraint The notion that the benefit of a disclosure exceeds the cost of that disclosure. *(p. 13)*

Cost-benefit principle Information system principle that prescribes the benefits from an activity in an accounting system to outweigh the costs of that activity. *(pp. 262 & E-3)*

Cost center Department that incurs costs but generates no revenues; common example is the accounting or legal department. *(p. 943)*

Cost object Product, process, department, or customer to which costs are assigned. *(pp. 615 & 739)*

Cost of capital Rate the company must pay to its long-term creditors and shareholders. *(p. 1020)*

Cost of goods available for sale Consists of beginning inventory plus net purchases of a period.

Cost of goods manufactured Total manufacturing costs (direct materials, direct labor, and factory overhead) for the period plus beginning goods in process less ending goods in process; also called *net cost of goods manufactured* and *cost of goods completed*. *(p. 705)*

Cost of goods sold Cost of inventory sold to customers during a period; also called *cost of sales*. *(p. 162)*

Costs of quality Costs resulting from manufacturing defective products or providing services that do not meet customer expectations. *(p. 750)*

Cost principle Accounting principle that prescribes financial statement information to be based on actual costs incurred in business transactions. *(p. 11)*

Cost variance Difference between the actual incurred cost and the standard cost. *(p. 903)*

Cost-volume-profit (CVP) analysis Planning method that includes predicting the volume of activity, the costs incurred, sales earned, and profits received. *(p. 778)*

Cost-volume-profit (CVP) chart Graphic representation of cost-volume-profit relations. *(p. 787)*

Coupon bonds Bonds with interest coupons attached to their certificates; bondholders detach coupons when they mature and present them to a bank or broker for collection. *(p. 436)*

Credit Recorded on the right side; an entry that decreases asset and expense accounts, and increases liability, revenue, and most equity accounts; abbreviated Cr. *(p. 57)*

Credit memorandum Notification that the sender has credited the recipient's account in the sender's records. *(p. 171)*

Credit period Time period that can pass before a customer's payment is due. *(p. 165)*

Credit terms Description of the amounts and timing of payments that a buyer (debtor) agrees to make in the future. *(p. 165)*

Creditors Individuals or organizations entitled to receive payments. *(p. 54)*

Cumulative preferred stock Preferred stock on which undeclared dividends accumulate until paid; common stockholders cannot receive dividends until cumulative dividends are paid. *(p. 477)*

Current assets Cash and other assets expected to be sold, collected, or used within one year or the company's operating cycle, whichever is longer. *(p. 118)*

Current liabilities Obligations due to be paid or settled within one year or the company's operating cycle, whichever is longer. *(pp. 119 & 379)*

Current portion of long-term debt Portion of long-term debt due within one year or the operating cycle, whichever is longer; reported under current liabilities. *(p. 387)*

Current ratio Ratio used to evaluate a company's ability to pay its short-term obligations, calculated by dividing current assets by current liabilities. *(p. 121)*

Curvilinear cost Cost that changes with volume but not at a constant rate. *(p. 781)*

Customer orientation Company position that its managers and employees be in tune with the changing wants and needs of consumers. *(p. 626)*

Cycle efficiency (CE) A measure of production efficiency, which is defined as value-added (process) time divided by total cycle time. *(p. 958)*

Cycle time (CT) A measure of the time to produce a product or service, which is the sum of process time, inspection time, move time, and wait time; also called *throughput time*. *(p. 957)*

Date of declaration Date the directors vote to pay a dividend. *(p. 473)*

Date of payment Date the corporation makes the dividend payment. *(p. 473)*

Date of record Date directors specify for identifying stockholders to receive dividends. *(p. 473)*

Days' sales in inventory Estimate of number of days needed to convert inventory into receivables or cash; equals ending inventory divided by cost of goods sold and then multiplied by 365; also called *days' stock on hand*. *(p. 223)*

Days' sales in raw materials inventory Measure of how much raw materials inventory is available in terms of the number of days' sales; defined as Ending raw materials inventory divided by Raw materials used and that quotient multiplied by 365 days. *(p. 628)*

Days' sales uncollected Measure of the liquidity of receivables computed by dividing the current balance of receivables by the annual credit (or net) sales and then multiplying by 365; also called *days' sales in receivables*. *(p. 277)*

Debit Recorded on the left side; an entry that increases asset and expense accounts, and decreases liability, revenue, and most equity accounts; abbreviated Dr. *(p. 57)*

Debit memorandum Notification that the sender has debited the recipient's account in the sender's records. *(p. 166)*

Debt ratio Ratio of total liabilities to total assets; used to reflect risk associated with a company's debts. *(p. 71)*

Debt-to-equity ratio Defined as total liabilities divided by total equity; shows the proportion of a company financed by non-owners (creditors) in comparison with that financed by owners. *(p. 437)*

Debtors Individuals or organizations that owe money. *(p. 51)*

Declining-balance method Method that determines depreciation charge for the period by multiplying a depreciation rate (often twice the straight-line rate) by the asset's beginning-period book value. *(p. 342)*

Deferred income tax liability Corporation income taxes that are deferred until future years because of temporary differences between GAAP and tax rules. *(p. 402)*

Degree of operating leverage (DOL) Ratio of contribution margin divided by pretax income; used to assess the effect on income of changes in sales. *(p. 795)*

Departmental accounting system Accounting system that provides information useful in evaluating the profitability or cost effectiveness of a department.

Departmental contribution to overhead Amount by which a department's revenues exceed its direct expenses. *(p. 951)*

Depletion Process of allocating the cost of natural resources to periods when they are consumed and sold. *(p. 350)*

Departmental income statements Income statements prepared for each operating department within a decentralized organization. *(p. 945)*

Deposit ticket Lists items such as currency, coins, and checks deposited and their corresponding dollar amounts. *(p. 271)*

Deposits in transit Deposits recorded by the company but not yet recorded by its bank. *(p. 274)*

Depreciable cost Cost of a plant asset less its salvage value. *(p. 340)*

Depreciation Expense created by allocating the cost of plant and equipment to periods in which they are used; represents the expense of using the asset. *(pp. 103 & 339)*

Diluted earnings per share Earnings per share calculation that requires dilutive securities be added to the denominator of the basic EPS calculation. *(p. 485)*

Dilutive securities Securities having the potential to increase common shares outstanding; examples are options, rights, convertible bonds, and convertible preferred stock. *(p. 485)*

Direct costs Costs incurred for the benefit of one specific cost object. *(p. 615)*

Direct expenses Expenses traced to a specific department (object) that are incurred for the sole benefit of that department. *(p. 945)*

Direct labor Efforts of employees who physically convert materials to finished product. *(p. 618)*

Direct labor costs Wages and salaries for direct labor that are separately and readily traced through the production process to finished goods. *(p. 618)*

Direct material Raw material that physically becomes part of the product and is clearly identified with specific products or batches of product. *(p. 618)*

Direct material costs Expenditures for direct material that are separately and readily traced through the production process to finished goods. *(p. 618)*

Direct method Presentation of net cash from operating activities for the statement of cash flows that lists major operating cash receipts less major operating cash payments. *(p. 516)*

Direct write-off method Method that records the loss from an uncollectible account receivable at the time it is determined to be uncollectible; no attempt is made to estimate bad debts. *(p. 306)*

Discount on bonds payable Difference between a bond's par value and its lower issue price or carrying value; occurs when the contract rate is less than the market rate. *(p. 425)*

Discount on note payable Difference between the face value of a note payable and the (lesser) amount borrowed; reflects the added interest to be paid on the note over its life.

Discount on stock Difference between the par value of stock and its issue price when issued at a price below par value. *(p. 471)*

Discount period Time period in which a cash discount is available and the buyer can make a reduced payment. *(p. 165)*

Discount rate Expected rate of return on investments; also called *cost of capital, hurdle rate,* or *required rate of return.* *(p. B-2)*

Discounts lost Expenses resulting from not taking advantage of cash discounts on purchases. *(p. 283)*

Dividend in arrears Unpaid dividend on cumulative preferred stock; must be paid before any regular dividends on preferred stock and before any dividends on common stock. *(p. 477)*

Dividend yield Ratio of the annual amount of cash dividends distributed to common shareholders relative to the common stock's market value (price). *(p. 486)*

Dividends Corporation's distributions of assets to its owners. *(p. 15)*

Dodd-Frank Wall Street Reform and Consumer Protection Act *(p. 14)*

Double-declining-balance (DDB) depreciation Depreciation equals beginning book value multiplied by 2 times the straight-line rate. *(p. 342)*

Double-entry accounting Accounting system in which each transaction affects at least two accounts and has at least one debit and one credit. *(p. 57)*

Double taxation Corporate income is taxed and then its later distribution through dividends is normally taxed again for shareholders. *(p. 13)*

Earnings (See *net income.*)

Earnings per share (EPS) Amount of income earned by each share of a company's outstanding common stock; also called *net income per share.* *(p. 485)*

Effective interest method Allocates interest expense over the bond life to yield a constant rate of interest; interest expense for a period is found by multiplying the balance of the liability at the beginning of the period by the bond market rate at issuance; also called *interest method.* *(p. 442)*

Efficiency Company's productivity in using its assets; usually measured relative to how much revenue a certain level of assets generates. *(p. 565)*

Efficiency variance Difference between the actual quantity of an input and the standard quantity of that input. *(p. 916)*

Electronic funds transfer (EFT) Use of electronic communication to transfer cash from one party to another. *(p. 271)*

Employee benefits Additional compensation paid to or on behalf of employees, such as premiums for medical, dental, life, and disability insurance, and contributions to pension plans. *(p. 387)*

Employee earnings report Record of an employee's net pay, gross pay, deductions, and year-to-date payroll information. *(p. 398)*

Enterprise resource planning (ERP) software Programs that manage a company's vital operations, which range from order taking to production to accounting. *(p. E-17)*

Entity Organization that, for accounting purposes, is separate from other organizations and individuals.

EOM Abbreviation for *end of month;* used to describe credit terms for credit transactions. *(p. 165)*

Equity Owner's claim on the assets of a business; equals the residual interest in an entity's assets after deducting liabilities; also called *net assets.* *(p. 15)*

Equity method Accounting method used for long-term investments when the investor has "significant influence" over the investee. *(p. C-8)*

Equity ratio Portion of total assets provided by equity, computed as total equity divided by total assets. *(p. 579)*

Equity securities with controlling influence Long-term investment when the investor is able to exert controlling influence over the investee; investors owning 50% or more of voting stock are presumed to exert controlling influence. *(p. C-9)*

Equity securities with significant influence Long-term investment when the investor is able to exert significant influence over the investee; investors owning 20 percent or more (but less than 50 percent) of voting stock are presumed to exert significant influence. *(p. C-8)*

Equivalent units of production (EUP) Number of units that would be completed if all effort during a period had been applied to units that were started and finished. *(p. 699)*

Estimated liability Obligation of an uncertain amount that can be reasonably estimated. *(p. 387)*

Estimated line of cost behavior Line drawn on a graph to visually fit the relation between cost and sales. *(p. 782)*

Ethics Codes of conduct by which actions are judged as right or wrong, fair or unfair, honest or dishonest. *(pp. 7 & 614)*

Events Happenings that both affect an organization's financial position and can be reliably measured. *(p. 16)*

Expanded accounting equation Assets = Liabilities + Equity; Equity equals [Owner capital − Owner withdrawals + Revenues − Expenses] for a noncorporation; Equity equals [Contributed capital + Retained earnings + Revenues − Expenses] for a corporation where dividends are subtracted from retained earnings. *(p. 15)*

Expense recognition (or **matching**) **principle** (See *matching principle.*)

Expenses Outflows or using up of assets as part of operations of a business to generate sales. *(p. 15)*

External transactions Exchanges of economic value between one entity and another entity. *(p. 16)*

External users Persons using accounting information who are not directly involved in running the organization. *(p. 5)*

Extraordinary gains or losses Gains or losses reported separately from continuing operations because they are both unusual and infrequent. *(p. 588)*

Extraordinary repairs Major repairs that extend the useful life of a plant asset beyond prior expectations; treated as a capital expenditure. *(p. 347)*

Facility level activities Activities that relate to overall production and cannot be traced to specific products; cost associated with these activities pertain to a plant's general manufacturing process. *(p. 750)*

Factory overhead Factory activities supporting the production process that are not direct material or direct labor; also called *overhead* and *manufacturing overhead. (p. 618)*

Factory overhead costs Expenditures for factory overhead that cannot be separately or readily traced to finished goods; also called *overhead costs. (p. 618)*

Fair value option Fair Value Option (FVO) refers to an option to measure eligible items at fair value; eligible items include *financial assets,* such as HTM, AFS, and equity method investments, and *financial liabilities*. FVO is applied "instrument by instrument" and is elected when the eligible item is "first recognized"; once FVO is elected the decision is "irrevocable." When FVO is elected, it is measured at "fair value" and unrealized gains and losses are recognized in earnings. *(p. 435)*

Favorable variance Difference in actual revenues or expenses from the budgeted amount that contributes to a higher income. *(p. 897)*

Federal depository bank Bank authorized to accept deposits of amounts payable to the federal government. *(p. 395)*

Federal Insurance Contributions Act (FICA) Taxes Taxes assessed on both employers and employees; for Social Security and Medicare programs. *(p. 384)*

Federal Unemployment Taxes (FUTA) Payroll taxes on employers assessed by the federal government to support its unemployment insurance program. *(p. 386)*

FIFO method (See *first-in, first-out.*)

Financial accounting Area of accounting aimed mainly at serving external users. *(p. 5)*

Financial Accounting Standards Board (FASB) Independent group of full-time members responsible for setting accounting rules. *(p. 9)*

Financial leverage Earning a higher return on equity by paying dividends on preferred stock or interest on debt at a rate lower than the return earned with the assets from issuing preferred stock or debt; also called *trading on the equity. (p. 479)*

Financial reporting Process of communicating information relevant to investors, creditors, and others in making investment, credit, and business decisions. *(p. 565)*

Financial statement analysis Application of analytical tools to general-purpose financial statements and related data for making business decisions. *(p. 564)*

Financial statements Includes the balance sheet, income statement, statement of owner's (or stockholders') equity, and statement of cash flows. *(p. 5)*

Financing activities Transactions with owners and creditors that include obtaining cash from issuing debt, repaying amounts borrowed, and obtaining cash from or distributing cash to owners. *(p. 512)*

Finished goods inventory Account that controls the finished goods files, which acts as a subsidiary ledger (of the Inventory account) in which the costs of finished goods that are ready for sale are recorded. *(pp. 620 & 657)*

First-in, first-out (FIFO) Method to assign cost to inventory that assumes items are sold in the order acquired; earliest items purchased are the first sold. *(pp. 215 & 711)*

Fiscal year Consecutive 12-month (or 52-week) period chosen as the organization's annual accounting period. *(p. 99)*

Fixed budget Planning budget based on a single predicted amount of volume; unsuitable for evaluations if the actual volume differs from predicted volume. *(p. 897)*

Fixed budget performance report Report that compares actual revenues and costs with fixed budgeted amounts and identifies the differences as favorable or unfavorable variances. *(p. 897)*

Fixed cost Cost that does not change with changes in the volume of activity. *(p. 614)*

Fixed overhead cost deferred in inventory The portion of the fixed manufacturing overhead cost of a period that goes into inventory under the absorption costing method as a result of production exceeding sales. *(p. 823)*

Fixed overhead cost recognized from inventory The portion of the fixed manufacturing overhead cost of a prior period that becomes an expense of the current period under the absorption costing method as a result of sales exceeding production. *(p. 823)*

Flexibility principle Information system principle that prescribes an accounting system be able to adapt to changes in the company, its operations, and needs of decision makers. *(p. E-3)*

Flexible budget Budget prepared (using actual volume) once a period is complete that helps managers evaluate past performance; uses fixed and variable costs in determining total costs. *(p. 898)*

Flexible budget performance report Report that compares actual revenues and costs with their variable budgeted amounts based on actual sales volume (or other level of activity) and identifies the differences as variances. *(p. 900)*

FOB Abbreviation for *free on board;* the point when ownership of goods passes to the buyer; *FOB shipping point* (or *factory*) means the buyer pays shipping costs and accepts ownership of goods when the seller transfers goods to carrier; *FOB destination* means the seller pays shipping costs and buyer accepts ownership of goods at the buyer's place of business. *(p. 167)*

Foreign exchange rate Price of one currency stated in terms of another currency. *(p. C-16)*

Form 940 IRS form used to report an employer's federal unemployment taxes (FUTA) on an annual filing basis. *(p. 395)*

Form 941 IRS form filed to report FICA taxes owed and remitted. *(p. 395)*

Form 10-K (or 10-KSB) Annual report form filed with SEC by businesses (small businesses) with publicly traded securities. *(p. A-1)*

Form W-2 Annual report by an employer to each employee showing the employee's wages subject to FICA and federal income taxes along with amounts withheld. *(p. 397)*

Form W-4 Withholding allowance certificate, filed with the employer, identifying the number of withholding allowances claimed. *(p. 400)*

Franchises Privileges granted by a company or government to sell a product or service under specified conditions. *(p. 353)*

Full disclosure principle Principle that prescribes financial statements (including notes) to report all relevant information about an entity's operations and financial condition. *(p. 11)*

GAAP (See *generally accepted accounting principles.*)

General accounting system Accounting system for manufacturing activities based on the *periodic* inventory system. *(p. 654)*

General and administrative expenses Expenses that support the operating activities of a business. *(p. 175)*

General and administrative expense budget Plan that shows predicted operating expenses not included in the selling expenses budget. *(p. 857)*

General journal All-purpose journal for recording the debits and credits of transactions and events. *(pp. 58 & E-6)*

General ledger (See *ledger.*) *(p. 53)*

General partner Partner who assumes unlimited liability for the debts of the partnership; responsible for partnership management.

General partnership Partnership in which all partners have mutual agency and unlimited liability for partnership debts.

Generally accepted accounting principles (GAAP) Rules that specify acceptable accounting practices. *(p. 9)*

Generally accepted auditing standards (GAAS) Rules that specify acceptable auditing practices.

General-purpose financial statements Statements published periodically for use by a variety of interested parties; includes the income statement, balance sheet, statement of owner's equity (or statement of retained earnings for a corporation), statement of cash flows, and notes to these statements. *(p. 565)*

Going-concern assumption Principle that prescribes financial statements to reflect the assumption that the business will continue operating. *(p. 12)*

Goods in process inventory Account in which costs are accumulated for products that are in the process of being produced but are not yet complete; also called *work in process inventory. (pp. 620 & 656)*

Goodwill Amount by which a company's (or a segment's) value exceeds the value of its individual assets less its liabilities. *(p. 353)*

Gross margin (See *gross profit.*)

Gross margin ratio Gross margin (net sales minus cost of goods sold) divided by net sales; also called *gross profit ratio. (p. 178)*

Gross method Method of recording purchases at the full invoice price without deducting any cash discounts. *(p. 283)*

Gross pay Total compensation earned by an employee. *(p. 383)*

Gross profit Net sales minus cost of goods sold; also called *gross margin. (pp. 162 & 163)*

Gross profit method Procedure to estimate inventory by using the past gross profit rate to estimate cost of goods sold, which is then subtracted from the cost of goods available for sale. *(p. 235)*

Held-to-maturity (HTM) securities Debt securities that a company has the intent and ability to hold until they mature. *(p. C-6)*

High-low method Procedure that yields an estimated line of cost behavior by graphically connecting costs associated with the highest and lowest sales volume. *(p. 782)*

Horizontal analysis Comparison of a company's financial condition and performance across time. *(p. 566)*

Hurdle rate Minimum acceptable rate of return (set by management) for an investment. *(pp. 953 & 1024)*

Impairment Diminishment of an asset value. *(pp. 346 & 352)*

Imprest system Method to account for petty cash; maintains a constant balance in the fund, which equals cash plus petty cash receipts. *(p. 268)*

Inadequacy Condition in which the capacity of plant assets is too small to meet the company's production demands. *(p. 339)*

Income (See *net income.*) *(p. 15)*

Income statement Financial statement that subtracts expenses from revenues to yield a net income or loss over a specified period of time; also includes any gains or losses. *(p. 20)*

Income summary Temporary account used only in the closing process to which the balances of revenue and expense accounts (including any gains or losses) are transferred; its balance is transferred to the capital account (or retained earnings for a corporation). *(p. 113)*

Incremental cost Additional cost incurred only if a company pursues a specific course of action. *(p. 988)*

Indefinite life Asset life that is not limited by legal, regulatory, contractual, competitive, economic, or other factors. *(p. 351)*

Indirect costs Costs incurred for the benefit of more than one cost object. *(p. 615)*

Indirect expenses Expenses incurred for the joint benefit of more than one department (or cost object). *(p. 945)*

Indirect labor Efforts of production employees who do not work specifically on converting direct materials into finished products and who are not clearly identified with specific units or batches of product. *(p. 618)*

Indirect labor costs Labor costs that cannot be physically traced to production of a product or service; included as part of overhead. *(p. 618)*

Indirect material Material used to support the production process but not clearly identified with products or batches of product. *(p. 620)*

Indirect method Presentation that reports net income and then adjusts it by adding and subtracting items to yield net cash from operating activities on the statement of cash flows. *(p. 516)*

Information processor Component of an accounting system that interprets, transforms, and summarizes information for use in analysis and reporting. *(p. E-4)*

Information storage Component of an accounting system that keeps data in a form accessible to information processors.

Infrequent gain or loss Gain or loss not expected to recur given the operating environment of the business. *(p. 588)*

Input device Means of capturing information from source documents that enables its transfer to information processors. *(p. E-4)*

Installment note Liability requiring a series of periodic payments to the lender. *(p. 433)*

Institute of Management Accountants (IMA) A professional association of management accountants. *(p. 614)*

Intangible assets Long-term assets (resources) used to produce or sell products or services; usually lack physical form and have uncertain benefits. *(pp. 119 & 351)*

Interest Charge for using money (or other assets) loaned from one entity to another. *(p. 312)*

Interim financial statements Financial statements covering periods of less than one year; usually based on one-, three-, or six-month periods. *(pp. 98 & 234)*

Interim statements (See *interim financial statements.*)

Internal controls or **Internal control system** All policies and procedures used to protect assets, ensure reliable accounting, promote efficient operations, and urge adherence to company policies. *(pp. 258, 614 & E-2)*

Internal rate of return (IRR) Rate used to evaluate the acceptability of an investment; equals the rate that yields a net present value of zero for an investment. *(p. 1023)*

Internal transactions Activities within an organization that can affect the accounting equation. *(p. 16)*

Internal users Persons using accounting information who are directly involved in managing the organization. *(p. 6)*

International Accounting Standards Board (IASB) Group that identifies preferred accounting practices and encourages global acceptance; issues International Financial Reporting Standards (IFRS). *(p. 9)*

International Financial Reporting Standards (IFRS) Set of international accounting standards explaining how types of transactions and events are reported in financial statements; IFRS are issued by the International Accounting Standards Board *(p. 9)*

Inventory Goods a company owns and expects to sell in its normal operations. *(p. 163)*

Inventory turnover Number of times a company's average inventory is sold during a period; computed by dividing cost of goods sold by average inventory; also called *merchandise turnover*. *(p. 223)*

Investing activities Transactions that involve purchasing and selling of long-term assets, includes making and collecting notes receivable and investments in other than cash equivalents. *(p. 512)*

Investment center Center of which a manager is responsible for revenues, costs, and asset investments. *(p. 943)*

Investment center residual income The net income an investment center earns above a target return on average invested assets. *(p. 953)*

Investment center return on total assets Center net income divided by average total assets for the center. *(p. 953)*

Investment turnover The efficiency with which a company generates sales from its available assets; computed as sales divided by average invested assets. *(p. 954)*

Invoice Itemized record of goods prepared by the vendor that lists the customer's name, items sold, sales prices, and terms of sale. *(p. 281)*

Invoice approval Document containing a checklist of steps necessary for approving the recording and payment of an invoice; also called *check authorization*. *(p. 281)*

Job Production of a customized product or service. *(p. 654)*

Job cost sheet Separate record maintained for each job. *(p. 656)*

Job lot Production of more than one unit of a customized product or service. *(p. 654)*

Job order cost accounting system Cost accounting system to determine the cost of producing each job or job lot. *(pp. 656 & 695)*

Job order production Production of special-order products; also called *customized production*. *(p. 654)*

Joint cost Cost incurred to produce or purchase two or more products at the same time. *(p. 962)*

Journal Record in which transactions are entered before they are posted to ledger accounts; also called *book of original entry*. *(p. 58)*

Journalizing Process of recording transactions in a journal. *(p. 58)*

Just-in-time (JIT) manufacturing Process of acquiring or producing inventory only when needed. *(p. 626)*

Known liabilities Obligations of a company with little uncertainty; set by agreements, contracts, or laws; also called *definitely determinable liabilities*. *(p. 380)*

Land improvements Assets that increase the benefits of land, have a limited useful life, and are depreciated. *(p. 338)*

Large stock dividend Stock dividend that is more than 25% of the previously outstanding shares. *(p. 474)*

Last-in, first-out (LIFO) Method for assigning cost to inventory that assumes costs for the most recent items purchased are sold first and charged to cost of goods sold. *(p. 215)*

Lean accounting System designed to eliminate waste in the accounting process and better reflect the benefits of lean manufacturing techniques. *(p. 752)*

Lean business model Practice of eliminating waste while meeting customer needs and yielding positive company returns. *(p. 626)*

Lease Contract specifying the rental of property. *(pp. 353 & 446)*

Leasehold Rights the lessor grants to the lessee under the terms of a lease. *(p. 353)*

Leasehold improvements Alterations or improvements to leased property such as partitions and storefronts. *(p. 354)*

Least-squares regression Statistical method for deriving an estimated line of cost behavior that is more precise than the high-low method and the scatter diagram. *(p. 783)*

Ledger Record containing all accounts (with amounts) for a business; also called *general ledger*. *(p. 51)*

Lessee Party to a lease who secures the right to possess and use the property from another party (the lessor). *(p. 353)*

Lessor Party to a lease who grants another party (the lessee) the right to possess and use its property. *(p. 353)*

Liabilities Creditors' claims on an organization's assets; involves a probable future payment of assets, products, or services that a company is obligated to make due to past transactions or events. *(p. 15)*

Licenses (See *franchises*.)

Limited liability Owner can lose no more than the amount invested. *(p. 12)*

Limited liability company Organization form that combines select features of a corporation and a limited partnership; provides limited liability to its members (owners), is free of business tax, and allows members to actively participate in management. *(p. D-4)*

Limited liability partnership Partnership in which a partner is not personally liable for malpractice or negligence unless that partner is responsible for providing the service that resulted in the claim. *(p. D-3)*

Limited life (See *useful life*.)

Limited partners Partners who have no personal liability for partnership debts beyond the amounts they invested in the partnership. *(p. 483)*

Limited partnership Partnership that has two classes of partners, limited partners and general partners. *(p. D-3)*

Liquid assets Resources such as cash that are easily converted into other assets or used to pay for goods, services, or liabilities. *(p. 263)*

Liquidating cash dividend Distribution of assets that returns part of the original investment to stockholders; deducted from contributed capital accounts. *(p. 474)*

Liquidation Process of going out of business; involves selling assets, paying liabilities, and distributing remainder to owners.

Liquidity Availability of resources to meet short-term cash requirements. *(pp. 263 & 565)*

List price Catalog (full) price of an item before any trade discount is deducted. *(p. 164)*

Long-term investments Long-term assets not used in operating activities such as notes receivable and investments in stocks and bonds. *(pp. 119, 379 & C-2)*

Long-term liabilities Obligations not due to be paid within one year or the operating cycle, whichever is longer. *(p. 119)*

Lower of cost or market (LCM) Required method to report inventory at market replacement cost when that market cost is lower than recorded cost. *(p. 219)*

Maker of the note Entity who signs a note and promises to pay it at maturity. *(p. 312)*

Management by exception Management process to focus on significant variances and give less attention to areas where performance is close to the standard. *(p. 901)*

Managerial accounting Area of accounting aimed mainly at serving the decision-making needs of internal users; also called *management accounting*. *(pp. 6 & 610)*

Manufacturer Company that uses labor and operating assets to convert raw materials to finished goods. *(p. 16)*

Manufacturing budget Plan that shows the predicted costs for direct materials, direct labor, and overhead to be incurred in manufacturing units in the production budget. *(p. 868)*

Manufacturing statement Report that summarizes the types and amounts of costs incurred in a company's production process for a period; also called *cost of goods manufacturing statement*. *(p. 623)*

Marginal costing *(p. 816)*

Margin of safety Excess of expected sales over the level of break-even sales. *(p. 786)*

Market-based transfer price A transfer pricing system based on the market price of the goods or services being transferred across divisions within the same company. *(p. 962)*

Market prospects Expectations (both good and bad) about a company's future performance as assessed by users and other interested parties. *(p. 565)*

Market rate Interest rate that borrowers are willing to pay and lenders are willing to accept for a specific lending agreement given the borrowers' risk level. *(p. 425)*

Market value per share Price at which stock is bought or sold. *(p. 469)*

Master budget Comprehensive business plan that includes specific plans for expected sales, product units to be produced, merchandise (or materials) to be purchased, expenses to be incurred, plant assets to be purchased, and amounts of cash to be borrowed or loans to be repaid, as well as a budgeted income statement and balance sheet. *(p. 852)*

Matching (or **expense recognition) principle** Prescribes expenses to be reported in the same period as the revenues that were earned as a result of the expenses. *(pp. 11, 100 & 306)*

Materiality constraint Prescribes that accounting for items that significantly impact financial statement and any inferences from them adhere strictly to GAAP. *(pp. 13 & 306)*

Materials consumption report Document that summarizes the materials a department uses during a reporting period; replaces materials requisitions. *(p. 696)*

Materials ledger card Perpetual record updated each time units are purchased or issued for production use. *(p. 658)*

Materials requisition Source document production managers use to request materials for production; used to assign materials costs to specific jobs or overhead. *(p. 659)*

Maturity date of a note Date when a note's principal and interest are due. *(p. 312)*

Measurement principle Principle that prescribes financial statement information, and its underlying transactions and events, be based on relevant measures of valuation; also called the *cost principle*. *(p. 11)*

Merchandise (See *merchandise inventory*.) *(p. 162)*

Merchandise inventory Goods that a company owns and expects to sell to customers; also called *merchandise* or *inventory*. *(p. 163)*

Merchandise purchases budget Plan that shows the units or costs of merchandise to be purchased by a merchandising company during the budget period. *(p. 855)*

Merchandiser Entity that earns net income by buying and selling merchandise. *(p. 162)*

Merit rating Rating assigned to an employer by a state based on the employer's record of employment. *(p. 386)*

Minimum legal capital Amount of assets defined by law that stockholders must (potentially) invest in a corporation; usually defined as par value of the stock; intended to protect creditors. *(p. 469)*

Mixed cost Cost that behaves like a combination of fixed and variable costs. *(p. 780)*

Modified Accelerated Cost Recovery System (MACRS) Depreciation system required by federal income tax law. *(p. 344)*

Monetary unit assumption Principle that assumes transactions and events can be expressed in money units. *(p. 12)*

Mortgage Legal loan agreement that protects a lender by giving the lender the right to be paid from the cash proceeds from the sale of a borrower's assets identified in the mortgage. *(p. 434)*

Multinational Company that operates in several countries. *(p. C-16)*

Multiple-step income statement Income statement format that shows subtotals between sales and net income, categorizes expenses, and often reports the details of net sales and expenses. *(p. 175)*

Mutual agency Legal relationship among partners whereby each partner is an agent of the partnership and is able to bind the partnership to contracts within the scope of the partnership's business. *(p. 466)*

Natural business year Twelve-month period that ends when a company's sales activities are at their lowest point. *(p. 99)*

Natural resources Assets physically consumed when used; examples are timber, mineral deposits, and oil and gas fields; also called *wasting assets*. *(p. 350)*

Negotiated transfer price A system where division managers negotiate to determine the price to use to record transfers of goods or services across divisions within the same company. *(p. 962)*

Net assets (See *equity*.)

Net income Amount earned after subtracting all expenses necessary for and matched with sales for a period; also called *income, profit,* or *earnings*. *(p. 15)*

Net loss Excess of expenses over revenues for a period. *(p. 15)*

Net method Method of recording purchases at the full invoice price less any cash discounts. *(p. 283)*

Net pay Gross pay less all deductions; also called *take-home pay.* *(p. 384)*

Net present value (NPV) Dollar estimate of an asset's value that is used to evaluate the acceptability of an investment; computed by discounting future cash flows from the investment at a satisfactory rate and then subtracting the initial cost of the investment. *(p. 1020)*

Net realizable value Expected selling price (value) of an item minus the cost of making the sale. *(p. 210)*

Noncumulative preferred stock Preferred stock on which the right to receive dividends is lost for any period when dividends are not declared. *(p. 477)*

Noninterest-bearing note Note with no stated (contract) rate of interest; interest is implicitly included in the note's face value.

Nonparticipating preferred stock Preferred stock on which dividends are limited to a maximum amount each year. *(p. 478)*

No-par value stock Stock class that has not been assigned a par (or stated) value by the corporate charter. *(p. 469)*

Nonsufficient funds (NSF) check Maker's bank account has insufficient money to pay the check; also called *hot check.* *(p. 274)*

Non-value-added time The portion of cycle time that is not directed at producing a product or service; equals the sum of inspection time, move time, and wait time. *(p. 958)*

Not controllable costs Costs that a manager does not have the power to control or strongly influence. *(p. 615)*

Note (See *promissory note.*)

Note payable Liability expressed by a written promise to pay a definite sum of money on demand or on a specific future date(s). *(p. 52)*

Note receivable Asset consisting of a written promise to receive a definite sum of money on demand or on a specific future date(s). *(p. 51)*

Objectivity Concept that prescribes independent, unbiased evidence to support financial statement information. *(p. 11)*

Obsolescence Condition in which, because of new inventions and improvements, a plant asset can no longer be used to produce goods or services with a competitive advantage. *(p. 339)*

Off-balance-sheet financing Acquisition of assets by agreeing to liabilities not reported on the balance sheet. *(p. 447)*

Online processing Approach to inputting data from source documents as soon as the information is available. *(p. E-16)*

Operating activities Activities that involve the production or purchase of merchandise and the sale of goods or services to customers, including expenditures related to administering the business. *(p. 511)*

Operating cycle Normal time between paying cash for merchandise or employee services and receiving cash from customers. *(p. 117)*

Operating leases Short-term (or cancelable) leases in which the lessor retains risks and rewards of ownership. *(p. 446)*

Operating leverage Extent, or relative size, of fixed costs in the total cost structure. *(p. 795)*

Opportunity cost Potential benefit lost by choosing a specific action from two or more alternatives. *(p. 616)*

Ordinary repairs Repairs to keep a plant asset in normal, good operating condition; treated as a revenue expenditure and immediately expensed. *(p. 347)*

Organization expenses (costs) Costs such as legal fees and promoter fees to bring an entity into existence. *(p. 467)*

Other comprehensive income (See *comprehensive income.*)

Out-of-pocket cost Cost incurred or avoided as a result of management's decisions. *(p. 616)*

Output devices Means by which information is taken out of the accounting system and made available for use. *(p. E-5)*

Outsourcing Manager decision to buy a product or service from another entity; part of a *make-or-buy* decision; also called *make or buy.*

Outstanding checks Checks written and recorded by the depositor but not yet paid by the bank at the bank statement date. *(p. 274)*

Outstanding stock Corporation's stock held by its shareholders. *(p. 469)*

Overapplied overhead Amount by which the overhead applied to production in a period using the predetermined overhead rate exceeds the actual overhead incurred in a period. *(p. 665)*

Overhead cost variance Difference between the total overhead cost applied to products and the total overhead cost actually incurred. *(p. 908)*

Owner, Capital Account showing the owner's claim on company assets; equals owner investments plus net income (or less net losses) minus owner withdrawals since the company's inception; also referred to as *equity.* *(p. 15)*

Owner investment Assets put into the business by the owner. *(p. 15)*

Owner's equity (See *equity.*)

Owner, Withdrawals Account used to record asset distributions to the owner. (See also *withdrawals.*) *(p. 15)*

Paid-in capital (See *contributed capital.*)

Paid-in capital in excess of par value Amount received from issuance of stock that is in excess of the stock's par value. *(p. 471)*

Par value Value assigned a share of stock by the corporate charter when the stock is authorized. *(p. 469)*

Par value of a bond Amount the bond issuer agrees to pay at maturity and the amount on which cash interest payments are based; also called *face amount* or *face value* of a bond. *(p. 422)*

Par value stock Class of stock assigned a par value by the corporate charter. *(p. 469)*

Parent Company that owns a controlling interest in a corporation (requires more than 50% of voting stock). *(p. C-9)*

Participating preferred stock Preferred stock that shares with common stockholders any dividends paid in excess of the percent stated on preferred stock. *(p. 478)*

Partner return on equity Partner net income divided by average partner equity for the period. *(p. D-4)*

Partnership Unincorporated association of two or more persons to pursue a business for profit as co-owners. *(pp. 12 & D-2)*

Partnership contract Agreement among partners that sets terms under which the affairs of the partnership are conducted; also called *articles of partnership.*

Partnership liquidation Dissolution of a partnership by (1) selling noncash assets and allocating any gain or loss according to partners' income-and-loss ratio, (2) paying liabilities, and (3) distributing any remaining cash according to partners' capital balances. *(p. D-11)*

Patent Exclusive right granted to its owner to produce and sell an item or to use a process for 17 years. *(p. 352)*

Payback period (PBP) Time-based measurement used to evaluate the acceptability of an investment; equals the time expected to pass before an investment's net cash flows equal its initial cost. *(p. 1016)*

Payee of the note Entity to whom a note is made payable. *(p. 312)*

Payroll bank account Bank account used solely for paying employees; each pay period an amount equal to the total employees' net pay is deposited in it and the payroll checks are drawn on it. *(p. 400)*

Payroll deductions Amounts withheld from an employee's gross pay; also called *withholdings*. *(p. 384)*

Payroll register Record for a pay period that shows the pay period dates, regular and overtime hours worked, gross pay, net pay, and deductions. *(p. 397)*

Pension plan Contractual agreement between an employer and its employees for the employer to provide benefits to employees after they retire; expensed when incurred. *(p. 448)*

Period costs Expenditures identified more with a time period than with finished products costs; includes selling and general administrative expenses. *(p. 616)*

Periodic inventory system Method that records the cost of inventory purchased but does not continuously track the quantity available or sold to customers; records are updated at the end of each period to reflect the physical count and costs of goods available. *(p. 164)*

Permanent accounts Accounts that reflect activities related to one or more future periods; balance sheet accounts whose balances are not closed; also called *real accounts*. *(p. 112)*

Perpetual inventory system Method that maintains continuous records of the cost of inventory available and the cost of goods sold. *(p. 164)*

Petty cash Small amount of cash in a fund to pay minor expenses; accounted for using an imprest system. *(p. 268)*

Planning Process of setting goals and preparing to achieve them. *(p. 610)*

Plant asset age Plant asset age is an approximation of the age of plant assets, which is estimated by dividing accumulated depreciation by depreciation expense. *(p. 355)*

Plant assets Tangible long-lived assets used to produce or sell products and services; also called *property, plant and equipment (PP&E)* or *fixed assets*. *(pp. 103 & 336)*

Pledged assets to secured liabilities Ratio of the book value of a company's pledged assets to the book value of its secured liabilities. *(p. 703)*

Post-closing trial balance List of permanent accounts and their balances from the ledger after all closing entries are journalized and posted. *(p. 114)*

Posting Process of transferring journal entry information to the ledger; computerized systems automate this process. *(p. 58)*

Posting reference (PR) column A column in journals in which individual ledger account numbers are entered when entries are posted to those ledger accounts. *(p. 60)*

Predetermined overhead rate Rate established prior to the beginning of a period that relates estimated overhead to another variable, such as estimated direct labor, and is used to assign overhead cost to production. *(p. 662)*

Preemptive right Stockholders' right to maintain their proportionate interest in a corporation with any additional shares issued. *(p. 468)*

Preferred stock Stock with a priority status over common stockholders in one or more ways, such as paying dividends or distributing assets. *(p. 476)*

Premium on bonds Difference between a bond's par value and its higher carrying value; occurs when the contract rate is higher than the market rate; also called *bond premium*. *(p. 428)*

Premium on stock (See *contributed capital in excess of par value*.) *(p. 471)*

Prepaid expenses Items paid for in advance of receiving their benefits; classified as assets. *(p. 101)*

Price-earnings (PE) ratio Ratio of a company's current market value per share to its earnings per share; also called *price-to-earnings*. *(p. 485)*

Price variance Difference between actual and budgeted revenue or cost caused by the difference between the actual price per unit and the budgeted price per unit. *(p. 901)*

Prime costs Expenditures directly identified with the production of finished goods; include direct materials costs and direct labor costs. *(p. 619)*

Principal of a note Amount that the signer of a note agrees to pay back when it matures, not including interest. *(p. 312)*

Principles of internal control Principles prescribing management to establish responsibility, maintain records, insure assets, separate recordkeeping from custody of assets, divide responsibility for related transactions, apply technological controls, and perform reviews. *(p. 259)*

Prior period adjustment Correction of an error in a prior year that is reported in the statement of retained earnings (or statement of stockholders' equity) net of any income tax effects. *(p. 483)*

Pro forma financial statements Statements that show the effects of proposed transactions and events as if they had occurred. *(p. 128)*

Process cost accounting system System of assigning direct materials, direct labor, and overhead to specific processes; total costs associated with each process are then divided by the number of units passing through that process to determine the cost per equivalent unit. *(p. 695)*

Process cost summary Report of costs charged to a department, its equivalent units of production achieved, and the costs assigned to its output. *(p. 704)*

Process operations Processing of products in a continuous (sequential) flow of steps; also called *process manufacturing* or *process production*. *(p. 692)*

Product costs Costs that are capitalized as inventory because they produce benefits expected to have future value; include direct materials, direct labor, and overhead. *(p. 616)*

Product level activities Activities that relate to specific products that must be carried out regardless of how many units are produced and sold or batches run. *(p. 750)*

Production budget Plan that shows the units to be produced each period. *(p. 868)*

Profit (See *net income*.)

Profit center Business unit that incurs costs and generates revenues. *(p. 943)*

Profit margin Ratio of a company's net income to its net sales; the percent of income in each dollar of revenue; also called *net profit margin*. *(pp. 121 & 954)*

Profitability Company's ability to generate an adequate return on invested capital. *(p. 565)*

Profitability index A measure of the relation between the expected benefits of a project and its investment, computed as the present value of expected future cash flows from the investment divided by the cost of the investment; a higher value indicates a more desirable investment, and a value below 1 indicates an unacceptable project. *(p. 1023)*

Promissory note (or **note**) Written promise to pay a specified amount either on demand or at a definite future date; is a *note receivable* for the lender but a *note payable* for the lendee. *(p. 312)*

Proprietorship (See *sole proprietorship.*)

Proxy Legal document giving a stockholder's agent the power to exercise the stockholder's voting rights. *(p. 467)*

Purchase discount Term used by a purchaser to describe a cash discount granted to the purchaser for paying within the discount period. *(p. 165)*

Purchase order Document used by the purchasing department to place an order with a seller (vendor). *(p. 280)*

Purchase requisition Document listing merchandise needed by a department and requesting it be purchased. *(p. 280)*

Purchases journal Journal normally used to record all purchases on credit. *(p. E-13)*

Quantity variance Difference between actual and budgeted revenue or cost caused by the difference between the actual number of units and the budgeted number of units. *(p. 901)*

Ratio analysis Determination of key relations between financial statement items as reflected in numerical measures. *(p. 566)*

Raw materials inventory Goods a company acquires to use in making products. *(p. 620)*

Raw materials inventory turnover ratio Measure of how many times a company turns over (uses in production) its raw materials inventory during a period; defined as Raw materials used divided by Average raw materials inventory. *(p. 628)*

Realizable value Expected proceeds from converting an asset into cash. *(p. 307)*

Receiving report Form used to report that ordered goods are received and to describe their quantity and condition. *(p. 281)*

Recordkeeping Part of accounting that involves recording transactions and events, either manually or electronically; also called *bookkeeping. (p. 4)*

Registered bonds Bonds owned by investors whose names and addresses are recorded by the issuer; interest payments are made to the registered owners. *(p. 436)*

Relevance principle Information system principle prescribing that its reports be useful, understandable, timely, and pertinent for decision making. *(p. E-2)*

Relevant benefits Additional or incremental revenue generated by selecting a particular course of action over another. *(p. 987)*

Relevant range of operations Company's normal operating range; excludes extremely high and low volumes not likely to occur. *(p. 788)*

Report form balance sheet Balance sheet that lists accounts vertically in the order of assets, liabilities, and equity. *(p. 22)*

Responsibility accounting budget Report of expected costs and expenses under a manager's control. *(p. 944)*

Responsibility accounting performance report Responsibility report that compares actual costs and expenses for a department with budgeted amounts. *(p. 944)*

Responsibility accounting system System that provides information that management can use to evaluate the performance of a department's manager. *(p. 942)*

Restricted retained earnings Retained earnings not available for dividends because of legal or contractual limitations. *(p. 482)*

Retail inventory method Method for estimating ending inventory based on the ratio of the amount of goods for sale at cost to the amount of goods for sale at retail. *(p. 234)*

Retailer Intermediary that buys products from manufacturers or wholesalers and sells them to consumers. *(p. 162)*

Retained earnings Cumulative income less cumulative losses and dividends. *(pp. 15 & 470)*

Retained earnings deficit Debit (abnormal) balance in Retained Earnings; occurs when cumulative losses and dividends exceed cumulative income; also called *accumulated deficit. (p. 473)*

Return Monies received from an investment; often in percent form. *(p. 27)*

Return on assets (See *return on total assets.*)

Return on equity Ratio of net income to average equity for the period.

Return on total assets Ratio reflecting operating efficiency; defined as net income divided by average total assets for the period; also called *return on assets* or *return on investment. (pp. 24 & C-11)*

Revenue expenditures Expenditures reported on the current income statement as an expense because they do not provide benefits in future periods. *(p. 346)*

Revenue recognition principle The principle prescribing that revenue is recognized when earned. *(p. 11)*

Revenues Gross increase in equity from a company's business activities that earn income; also called *sales. (p. 15)*

Reverse stock split Occurs when a corporation calls in its stock and replaces each share with less than one new share; increases both market value per share and any par or stated value per share. *(p. 476)*

Reversing entries Optional entries recorded at the beginning of a period that prepare the accounts for the usual journal entries as if adjusting entries had not occurred in the prior period. *(p. 129)*

Risk Uncertainty about an expected return. *(p. 27)*

Rolling budget New set of budgets a firm adds for the next period (with revisions) to replace the ones that have lapsed. *(p. 851)*

S corporation Corporation that meets special tax qualifications so as to be treated like a partnership for income tax purposes. *(p. D-3)*

Safety stock Quantity of inventory or materials over the minimum needed to satisfy budgeted demand. *(p. 855)*

Sales (See *revenues.*)

Sales budget Plan showing the units of goods to be sold or services to be provided; the starting point in the budgeting process for most departments. *(p. 854)*

Sales discount Term used by a seller to describe a cash discount granted to buyers who pay within the discount period. *(p. 165)*

Sales journal Journal normally used to record sales of goods on credit.

Sales mix Ratio of sales volumes for the various products sold by a company. *(p. 793)*

Salvage value Estimate of amount to be recovered at the end of an asset's useful life; also called *residual value* or *scrap value*. *(p. 339)*

Sarbanes-Oxley Act (SOX) Created the *Public Company Accounting Oversight Board,* regulates analyst conflicts, imposes corporate governance requirements, enhances accounting and control disclosures, impacts insider transactions and executive loans, establishes new types of criminal conduct, and expands penalties for violations of federal securities laws. *(pp. 13 & 258)*

Scatter diagram Graph used to display data about past cost behavior and sales as points on a diagram. *(p. 782)*

Schedule of accounts payable List of the balances of all accounts in the accounts payable ledger and their totals. *(p. E-14)*

Schedule of accounts receivable List of the balances of all accounts in the accounts receivable ledger and their totals. *(p. E-9)*

Section 404 (of SOX) Section 404 of SOX requires management and the external auditor to report on the adequacy of the company's internal control on financial reporting, which is the most costly aspect of SOX for companies to implement as documenting and testing important financial manual and automated controls require enormous efforts. Section 404 also requires management to produce an "internal control report" as part of each annual SEC report that affirms "the responsibility of management for establishing and maintaining an adequate internal control structure and procedures for financial reporting." *(p. 259)*

Secured bonds Bonds that have specific assets of the issuer pledged as collateral. *(p. 436)*

Securities and Exchange Commission (SEC) Federal agency Congress has charged to set reporting rules for organizations that sell ownership shares to the public. *(p. 9)*

Segment return on assets Segment operating income divided by segment average (identifiable) assets for the period.

Selling expense budget Plan that lists the types and amounts of selling expenses expected in the budget period. *(p. 856)*

Selling expenses Expenses of promoting sales, such as displaying and advertising merchandise, making sales, and delivering goods to customers. *(p. 175)*

Serial bonds Bonds consisting of separate amounts that mature at different dates. *(p. 436)*

Service company Organization that provides services instead of tangible products.

Shareholders Owners of a corporation; also called *stockholders*. *(p. 13)*

Shares Equity of a corporation divided into ownership units; also called *stock*. *(p. 13)*

Short-term investments Debt and equity securities that management expects to convert to cash within the next 3 to 12 months (or the operating cycle if longer); also called *temporary investments* or *marketable securities*. *(p. C-2)*

Short-term note payable Current obligation in the form of a written promissory note. *(p. 381)*

Shrinkage Inventory losses that occur as a result of theft or deterioration. *(p. 172)*

Signature card Includes the signatures of each person authorized to sign checks on the bank account. *(p. 271)*

Simple capital structure Capital structure that consists of only common stock and nonconvertible preferred stock; consists of no dilutive securities. *(p. 485)*

Single-step income statement Income statement format that includes cost of goods sold as an expense and shows only one subtotal for total expenses. *(p. 176)*

Sinking fund bonds Bonds that require the issuer to make deposits to a separate account; bondholders are repaid at maturity from that account. *(p. 436)*

Small stock dividend Stock dividend that is 25% or less of a corporation's previously outstanding shares. *(p. 474)*

Social responsibility Being accountable for the impact that one's actions might have on society. *(p. 8)*

Sole proprietorship Business owned by one person that is not organized as a corporation; also called *proprietorship*. *(p. 12)*

Solvency Company's long-run financial viability and its ability to cover long-term obligations. *(p. 565)*

Source documents Source of information for accounting entries that can be in either paper or electronic form; also called *business papers*. *(p. 52)*

Special journal Any journal used for recording and posting transactions of a similar type. *(p. E-6)*

Specific identification Method for assigning cost to inventory when the purchase cost of each item in inventory is identified and used to compute cost of inventory. *(pp. 213 & 230)*

Spending variance Difference between the actual price of an item and its standard price. *(p. 916)*

Spreadsheet Computer program that organizes data by means of formulas and format; also called *electronic work sheet*. *(pp. 123 & 532)*

Standard costs Costs that should be incurred under normal conditions to produce a product or component or to perform a service. *(p. 901)*

State Unemployment Taxes (SUTA) State payroll taxes on employers to support its unemployment programs. *(p. 386)*

Stated value stock No-par stock assigned a stated value per share; this amount is recorded in the stock account when the stock is issued. *(p. 470)*

Statement of cash flows A financial statement that lists cash inflows (receipts) and cash outflows (payments) during a period; arranged by operating, investing, and financing. *(pp. 20 & 510)*

Statement of owner's equity Report of changes in equity over a period; adjusted for increases (owner investment and net income) and for decreases (withdrawals and net loss). *(p. 20)*

Statement of partners' equity Financial statement that shows total capital balances at the beginning of the period, any additional investment by partners, the income or loss of the period, the partners' withdrawals, and the partners' ending capital balances; also called *statement of partners' capital*. *(p. D-7)*

Statement of retained earnings Report of changes in retained earnings over a period; adjusted for increases (net income), for decreases (dividends and net loss), and for any prior period adjustment. *(p. 20)*

Statement of stockholders' equity Financial statement that lists the beginning and ending balances of each major equity account and describes all changes in those accounts. *(p. 483)*

Statements of Financial Accounting Standards (SFAS) FASB publications that establish U.S. GAAP.

Step-wise cost Cost that remains fixed over limited ranges of volumes but changes by a lump sum when volume changes occur outside these limited ranges. *(p. 780)*

Stock (See *shares*) *(p. 13)*

Stock dividend Corporation's distribution of its own stock to its stockholders without the receipt of any payment. *(p. 474)*

Stock options Rights to purchase common stock at a fixed price over a specified period of time. *(p. 483)*

Stock split Occurs when a corporation calls in its stock and replaces each share with more than one new share; decreases both the market value per share and any par or stated value per share. *(p. 476)*

Stock subscription Investor's contractual commitment to purchase unissued shares at future dates and prices.

Stockholders (See *shareholders.*) *(p. 13)*

Stockholders' equity A corporation's equity; also called *shareholders' equity* or *corporate capital. (p. 470)*

Straight-line depreciation Method that allocates an equal portion of the depreciable cost of plant asset (cost minus salvage) to each accounting period in its useful life. *(pp. 103 & 341)*

Straight-line bond amortization Method allocating an equal amount of bond interest expense to each period of the bond life. *(p. 426)*

Subsidiary Entity controlled by another entity (parent) in which the parent owns more than 50% of the subsidiary's voting stock. *(p. C-9)*

Subsidiary ledger List of individual subaccounts and amounts with a common characteristic; linked to a controlling account in the general ledger. *(p. E-6)*

Sunk cost Cost already incurred and cannot be avoided or changed. *(p. 616)*

Supplementary records Information outside the usual accounting records; also called *supplemental records. (p. 168)*

Supply chain Linkages of services or goods extending from suppliers, to the company itself, and on to customers.

T-account Tool used to show the effects of transactions and events on individual accounts. *(p. 57)*

Target cost Maximum allowable cost for a product or service; defined as expected selling price less the desired profit. *(p. 655)*

Temporary accounts Accounts used to record revenues, expenses, and withdrawals (dividends for a corporation); they are closed at the end of each period; also called *nominal accounts. (p. 112)*

Term bonds Bonds scheduled for payment (maturity) at a single specified date. *(p. 436)*

Throughput time (See *cycle time.*)

Time period assumption Assumption that an organization's activities can be divided into specific time periods such as months, quarters, or years. *(pp. 12 & 98)*

Time ticket Source document used to report the time an employee spent working on a job or on overhead activities and then to determine the amount of direct labor to charge to the job or the amount of indirect labor to charge to overhead. *(p. 660)*

Times interest earned Ratio of income before interest expense (and any income taxes) divided by interest expense; reflects risk of covering interest commitments when income varies. *(p. 392)*

Total asset turnover Measure of a company's ability to use its assets to generate sales; computed by dividing net sales by average total assets. *(p. 355)*

Total quality management (TQM) Concept calling for all managers and employees at all stages of operations to strive toward higher standards and reduce number of defects. *(p. 626)*

Trade discount Reduction from a list or catalog price that can vary for wholesalers, retailers, and consumers. *(p. 164)*

Trademark or **trade (brand) name** Symbol, name, phrase, or jingle identified with a company, product, or service. *(p. 353)*

Trading on the equity (See *financial leverage.*)

Trading securities Investments in debt and equity securities that the company intends to actively trade for profit. *(p. C-5)*

Transfer price The price used to record transfers of goods or services across divisions within the same company. *(p. 961)*

Transaction Exchange of economic consideration affecting an entity's financial position that can be reliably measured. *(p. 16)*

Treasury stock Corporation's own stock that it reacquired and still holds. *(p. 480)*

Trial balance List of accounts and their balances at a point in time; total debit balances equal total credit balances. *(p. 67)*

Unadjusted trial balance List of accounts and balances prepared before accounting adjustments are recorded and posted. *(p. 110)*

Unavoidable expense Expense (or cost) that is not relevant for business decisions; an expense that would continue even if a department, product, or service is eliminated. *(p. 993)*

Unclassified balance sheet Balance sheet that broadly groups assets, liabilities, and equity accounts. *(p. 117)*

Uncontrollable costs Costs that a manager does not have the power to determine or strongly influence. *(pp. 826 & 943)*

Underapplied overhead Amount by which overhead incurred in a period exceeds the overhead applied to that period's production using the predetermined overhead rate. *(p. 665)*

Unearned revenue Liability created when customers pay in advance for products or services; earned when the products or services are later delivered. *(pp. 55 & 104)*

Unfavorable variance Difference in revenues or costs, when the actual amount is compared to the budgeted amount, that contributes to a lower income. *(p. 897)*

Unit contribution margin Amount a product's unit selling price exceeds its total unit variable cost. *(p. 785)*

Unit level activities Activities that arise as a result of the total volume of goods and services that are produced, and that are performed each time a unit is produced *(p. 750)*

Units-of-production depreciation Method that charges a varying amount to depreciation expense for each period of an asset's useful life depending on its usage. *(p. 341)*

Unlimited liability Legal relationship among general partners that makes each of them responsible for partnership debts if the other partners are unable to pay their shares. *(p. D-3)*

Unrealized gain (loss) Gain (loss) not yet realized by an actual transaction or event such as a sale. *(p. C-5)*

Unsecured bonds Bonds backed only by the issuer's credit standing; almost always riskier than secured bonds; also called *debentures. (p. 436)*

Unusual gain or loss Gain or loss that is abnormal or unrelated to the company's ordinary activities and environment. *(p. 588)*

Useful life Length of time an asset will be productively used in the operations of a business; also called *service life* or *limited life*. *(pp. 339 & 351)*

Value-added activities Activities that add to the value of a product or service *(p. 749)*

Value-added time The portion of cycle time that is directed at producing a product or service; equals process time. *(p. 958)*

Value chain Sequential activities that add value to an entity's products or services; includes design, production, marketing, distribution, and service. *(p. 626)*

Variable cost Cost that changes in proportion to changes in the activity output volume. *(p. 614)*

Variable costing A costing method that includes only variable manufacturing costs—direct materials, direct labor, and variable manufacturing overhead—in unit product costs; also called *direct* or *marginal costing* *(p. 816)*

Variable costing income statement An income statement in which costs are classified as variable or fixed; also called *contribution margin income statement*. *(p. 786)*

Variance analysis Process of examining differences between actual and budgeted revenues or costs and describing them in terms of price and quantity differences. *(p. 901)*

Vendee Buyer of goods or services. *(p. 281)*

Vendor Seller of goods or services. *(p. 280)*

Vertical analysis Evaluation of each financial statement item or group of items in terms of a specific base amount. *(p. 566)*

Volume variance Difference between two dollar amounts of fixed overhead cost; one amount is the total budgeted overhead cost, and the other is the overhead cost allocated to products using the predetermined fixed overhead rate. *(p. 909)*

Voucher Internal file used to store documents and information to control cash disbursements and to ensure that a transaction is properly authorized and recorded. *(p. 267)*

Voucher register Journal (referred to as *book of original entry*) in which all vouchers are recorded after they have been approved. *(p. 282)*

Voucher system Procedures and approvals designed to control cash disbursements and acceptance of obligations. *(p. 266)*

Wage bracket withholding table Table of the amounts of income tax withheld from employees' wages. *(p. 400)*

Warranty Agreement that obligates the seller to correct or replace a product or service when it fails to perform properly within a specified period. *(p. 388)*

Weighted average Method for assigning inventory cost to sales; the cost of available-for-sale units is divided by the number of units available to determine per unit cost prior to each sale that is then multiplied by the units sold to yield the cost of that sale. *(pp. 216, 232 & 702)*

Weighted-average contribution margin The contribution margin per composite unit for a company that provides multiple goods or services; also called *contribution margin per composite unit*. *(p. 793)*

Weighted-average method (See *weighted average*.)

Wholesaler Intermediary that buys products from manufacturers or other wholesalers and sells them to retailers or other wholesalers. *(p. 162)*

Work sheet Spreadsheet used to draft an unadjusted trial balance, adjusting entries, adjusted trial balance, and financial statements. *(p. 123)*

Working capital Current assets minus current liabilities at a point in time. *(p. 575)*

Working papers Analyses and other informal reports prepared by accountants and managers when organizing information for formal reports and financial statements. *(p. 127)*

Credits

Chapter 1
Page 3 © Gabriela Hasbun/Aurora Photos Corbis
Page 9 AP Images/Louis Lanzano
Page 10 Hisham Ibrahim/Getty Images
Page 11 Scott Boehm/Getty Images
Page 16 Ingram Publishing/SuperStock

Chapter 2
Page 49 Courtesy of Nom-Nom Truck
Page 52 Courtesy of Nom-Nom Truck
Page 53 Jamie Squire/Getty Images
Page 54 Andrew D. Bernstein/NBAE/Getty Images

Chapter 3
Page 93 Courtesy of Ash &Dans
Page 95 AP Images/Paul Sakuma
Page 96 © The McGraw-Hill Companies, Inc./Jill Braaten, photographer
Page 100 © Ian Shaw/Alamy
Page 114 Cameron Spencer/Getty Images
Page 115 © STEPHEN D. CANNERELLI/Syracuse Newspapers/ The Image Works

Chapter 4
Page 161 Courtesy of Faithful Fish
Page 167 © Royalty Free/Corbis

Chapter 5
Page 209 Courtesy of Feverish Ice Cream
Page 211 © Andersen Ross/Brand X/Corbis

Chapter 6
Page 257 Boston Globe via Getty Images
Page 258 © Andre Kudyusov/Photodisc/Alamy
Page 259 no credit needed
Page 260 Lawrence Lawry/Getty Images/Photodisc
Page 263 Getty Images

Chapter 7
Page 304 Ken Reid/Getty Images/Photographer's Choice
Page 305 ChinaFotoPress via Getty Images
Page 301 AP Images/Nick Wass

Chapter 8
Page 335 Courtesy of BizChair.com
Page 338 Getty Images
Page 340 Bradley C. Bower/Bloomberg via Getty Images
Page 345 Chris Trotman/Getty Images for NASCAR
Page 347 Purestock/Superstock
Page 350 Digital Vision/Getty Images
Page 352 Hunter Martin/Getty Images
Page 353 AFP/Getty Images

Chapter 9
Page 377 Courtesy of SmartIT Staffing, Inc.
Page 381 Kevin Mazur/WireImage for TIME/Getty Images
Page 383 Adam Gault/Getty Images/OJO Images
Page 388 Jeff Zelevansky/Getty Images
Page 391 John Burcham/National Geographic/Getty Images

Chapter 10
Page 421 Courtesy of Barley & Birch
Page 424 Courtesy of Dow Chemicals

Chapter 11
Page 465 Bloomberg via Getty Images
Page 467 AP Images/Nasdaq via Facebook, Zef Nikolla
Page 468 Courtesy of Green Bay Packers, Inc.

Chapter 12
Page 509 Michael Kovac/Getty Images for TOMS
Page 510 AP Images/Brian Kersey

Chapter 13
Page 563 Getty Images
Page 577 Ingram Publishing/Superstock
Page 582 © Comstock Images/Jupiter Images

Chapter 14
Page 609 Courtesy of Back to the Roots Ventures
Page 613 AP Images/KEYSTONE/Alessandro Della Bella
Page 618 Justin Sullivan/Getty Images
Page 620 Marco Prosch/Getty Images
Page 624 Jin Lee/Bloomberg via Getty Images

Chapter 15
Page 653 Courtesy of Asor and Black
Page 654 Stephen Brashear/Getty Images
Page 662 © Royalty-Free/CORBIS
Page 666T Pixtal/Superstock
Page 666B © culture-images GmbH/Alamy

Chapter 16
Page 691 Courtesy of Three Twins Ice Cream
Page 702 Ken Whitmore/Getty Images/Stone
Page 696 NATALIA KOLESNIKOVA/AFP/Getty Images

Chapter 17
Page 737 Courtesy of New Belgium Brewing Company
Page 740 Getty Images
Page 743 Bloomberg via Getty Images
Page 744 © JoeFox Karting/Alamy
Page 746 AP Images/Christof Stache
Page 749 Getty Images

Chapter 18
Page 777 Courtesy of Leather Head Sports
Page 779 gerenme/Getty Images
Page 785 AP Images/Skip Peterson
Page 792 Getty Images
Page 793 © Lars A. Niki

Chapter 19
Page 815 Courtesy of Samanta Shoes
Page 817 TOSHIFUMI KITAMURA/AFP/Getty Images
Page 820 Steve Mason/Getty Images
Page 825 © David Young-Wolff/PhotoEdit, Inc.
Page 827 Krzysztof Dydynski/Getty Images/Lonely Planet Images

Chapter 20
Page 853 John J. Wild
Page 856 John J. Wild
Page 857 Gail Shotlander/Getty Images
Page 860T John J. Wild
Page 860B Getty Images
Page 862 © Pixland/AGE fotostock
Page 847 Courtesy of Freshii

Chapter 21
Page 895 Courtesy of Folsom Custom Skis
Page 898 2006 The Christian Science Monitor/Getty Images
Page 902 Car Culture/Getty Images
Page 904 KristjanMaack/Getty Images/Nordic Photos
Page 905 © ColorBlind Images/Corbis
Page 907 Halfdark/Getty Images
Page 919 Jordan Grano of Folsom Custom Skis

Chapter 22
Page 941 Photo by Katherine Friedgen, United by Blue ©
Page 946 Rob Melnychuk/Getty Images
Page 953 Alan Bailey/Getty Images

Chapter 23
Page 992 © BananaStock/Punchstock
Page 994 Comstock Images/Jupiter Images
Page 985 Courtesy of Charlie's Brownies

Chapter 24
Page 1024 Robert Kirk/Getty Images
Page 1018 Tetra Images/Getty Images
Page 1015 Courtesy of Gamer Grub

Appendix C
Page C-1 AP Images/Mel Evans
Page C-3 Courtesy of Scripophily.com
Page C-16 Glow Images

Appendix D
Page D.1 Ingram Publishing
Page D.2 Courtesy of College Hunks Hauling Junk LLC
Page D.3 AP Images/Frank Franklin II
Page D.4 Vincent Ricardel/Getty Images

Appendix E
Page E.1 Vstock LLC/Getty Images
Page E.2 REUTERS/SUZANNE PLUNKETT/LANDOV
Page E.3 © Royalty-Free/CORBIS
Page E.4 Jody Dole/Getty Images/The Image Bank
Page E.5 Nick Koudis/Getty Images/PhotoDisc

Index

Note: Page numbers followed by *n* indicate material in footnotes; defined terms and the page number on which the definition appears are shown in **boldface.**

Chart of Accounts

Following is a typical chart of accounts, which is used in several assignments. Every company has its own unique accounts and numbering system.

Assets

Current Assets

101 Cash
102 Petty cash
103 Cash equivalents
104 Short-term investments
105 Fair value adjustment, _______ securities (S-T)
106 Accounts receivable
107 Allowance for doubtful accounts
108 Legal fees receivable
109 Interest receivable
110 Rent receivable
111 Notes receivable
119 Merchandise inventory
120 _________ inventory
121 _________ inventory
124 Office supplies
125 Store supplies
126 _______ supplies
128 Prepaid insurance
129 Prepaid interest
131 Prepaid rent
132 Raw materials inventory
133 Goods in process inventory, _______
134 Goods in process inventory, _______
135 Finished goods inventory

Long-Term Investments

141 Long-term investments
142 Fair value adjustment, _______ securities (L-T)
144 Investment in _______
145 Bond sinking fund

Plant Assets

151 Automobiles
152 Accumulated depreciation—Automobiles
153 Trucks
154 Accumulated depreciation—Trucks
155 Boats
156 Accumulated depreciation—Boats
157 Professional library
158 Accumulated depreciation—Professional library
159 Law library
160 Accumulated depreciation—Law library
161 Furniture
162 Accumulated depreciation—Furniture
163 Office equipment
164 Accumulated depreciation—Office equipment
165 Store equipment
166 Accumulated depreciation—Store equipment
167 _______ equipment
168 Accumulated depreciation—_______ equipment
169 Machinery
170 Accumulated depreciation—Machinery
173 Building _______
174 Accumulated depreciation—Building _______
175 Building _______
176 Accumulated depreciation—Building _______
179 Land improvements _______
180 Accumulated depreciation—Land improvements _______
181 Land improvements _______
182 Accumulated depreciation—Land improvements _______
183 Land

Natural Resources

185 Mineral deposit
186 Accumulated depletion—Mineral deposit

Intangible Assets

191 Patents
192 Leasehold
193 Franchise
194 Copyrights
195 Leasehold improvements
196 Licenses
197 Accumulated amortization—_______

Liabilities

Current Liabilities

201 Accounts payable
202 Insurance payable
203 Interest payable
204 Legal fees payable
207 Office salaries payable
208 Rent payable
209 Salaries payable
210 Wages payable
211 Accrued payroll payable
214 Estimated warranty liability
215 Income taxes payable
216 Common dividend payable
217 Preferred dividend payable
218 State unemployment taxes payable
219 Employee federal income taxes payable
221 Employee medical insurance payable
222 Employee retirement program payable
223 Employee union dues payable
224 Federal unemployment taxes payable
225 FICA taxes payable
226 Estimated vacation pay liability

Unearned Revenues

230 Unearned consulting fees
231 Unearned legal fees
232 Unearned property management fees
233 Unearned _______ fees
234 Unearned _______ fees
235 Unearned janitorial revenue
236 Unearned _______ revenue
238 Unearned rent

Notes Payable

240 Short-term notes payable
241 Discount on short-term notes payable
245 Notes payable
251 Long-term notes payable
252 Discount on long-term notes payable

Long-Term Liabilities

253 Long-term lease liability
255 Bonds payable
256 Discount on bonds payable
257 Premium on bonds payable
258 Deferred income tax liability

Equity

Owner's Equity

301 _____________, Capital
302 _____________, Withdrawals
303 _____________, Capital
304 _____________, Withdrawals
305 _____________, Capital
306 _____________, Withdrawals

Paid-In Capital

307 Common stock, $ _______ par value
308 Common stock, no-par value
309 Common stock, $ _______ stated value
310 Common stock dividend distributable
311 Paid-in capital in excess of par value, Common stock

312 Paid-in capital in excess of stated value, No-par common stock
313 Paid-in capital from retirement of common stock
314 Paid-in capital, Treasury stock
315 Preferred stock
316 Paid-in capital in excess of par value, Preferred stock

Retained Earnings

318 Retained earnings
319 Cash dividends (or Dividends)
320 Stock dividends

Other Equity Accounts

321 Treasury stock, Common
322 Unrealized gain—Equity
323 Unrealized loss—Equity

Revenues

401 ____________ fees earned
402 ____________ fees earned
403 ____________ services revenue
404 ____________ services revenue
405 Commissions earned
406 Rent revenue (or Rent earned)
407 Dividends revenue (or Dividend earned)
408 Earnings from investment in ______
409 Interest revenue (or Interest earned)
410 Sinking fund earnings
413 Sales
414 Sales returns and allowances
415 Sales discounts

Cost of Sales

Cost of Goods Sold

502 Cost of goods sold
505 Purchases
506 Purchases returns and allowances
507 Purchases discounts
508 Transportation-in

Manufacturing

520 Raw materials purchases
521 Freight-in on raw materials
530 Factory payroll
531 Direct labor
540 Factory overhead
541 Indirect materials
542 Indirect labor
543 Factory insurance expired
544 Factory supervision
545 Factory supplies used
546 Factory utilities
547 Miscellaneous production costs
548 Property taxes on factory building
549 Property taxes on factory equipment
550 Rent on factory building
551 Repairs, factory equipment
552 Small tools written off
560 Depreciation of factory equipment
561 Depreciation of factory building

Standard Cost Variance

580 Direct material quantity variance
581 Direct material price variance
582 Direct labor quantity variance
583 Direct labor price variance
584 Factory overhead volume variance
585 Factory overhead controllable variance

Expenses

Amortization, Depletion, and Depreciation

601 Amortization expense—______
602 Amortization expense—______
603 Depletion expense—______
604 Depreciation expense—Boats
605 Depreciation expense—Automobiles
606 Depreciation expense—Building ______
607 Depreciation expense—Building ______
608 Depreciation expense—Land improvements ______
609 Depreciation expense—Land improvements ______
610 Depreciation expense—Law library
611 Depreciation expense—Trucks
612 Depreciation expense—______ equipment
613 Depreciation expense—______ equipment
614 Depreciation expense—______
615 Depreciation expense—______

Employee-Related Expenses

620 Office salaries expense
621 Sales salaries expense
622 Salaries expense
623 ______ wages expense
624 Employees' benefits expense
625 Payroll taxes expense

Financial Expenses

630 Cash over and short
631 Discounts lost
632 Factoring fee expense
633 Interest expense

Insurance Expenses

635 Insurance expense—Delivery equipment
636 Insurance expense—Office equipment
637 Insurance expense—______

Rental Expenses

640 Rent expense
641 Rent expense—Office space
642 Rent expense—Selling space
643 Press rental expense
644 Truck rental expense
645 ______ rental expense

Supplies Expenses

650 Office supplies expense
651 Store supplies expense
652 ______ supplies expense
653 ______ supplies expense

Miscellaneous Expenses

655 Advertising expense
656 Bad debts expense
657 Blueprinting expense
658 Boat expense
659 Collection expense
661 Concessions expense
662 Credit card expense
663 Delivery expense
664 Dumping expense
667 Equipment expense
668 Food and drinks expense
671 Gas and oil expense
672 General and administrative expense
673 Janitorial expense
674 Legal fees expense
676 Mileage expense
677 Miscellaneous expenses
678 Mower and tools expense
679 Operating expense
680 Organization expense
681 Permits expense
682 Postage expense
683 Property taxes expense
684 Repairs expense—______
685 Repairs expense—______
687 Selling expense
688 Telephone expense
689 Travel and entertainment expense
690 Utilities expense
691 Warranty expense
695 Income taxes expense

Gains and Losses

701 Gain on retirement of bonds
702 Gain on sale of machinery
703 Gain on sale of investments
704 Gain on sale of trucks
705 Gain on ______
706 Foreign exchange gain or loss
801 Loss on disposal of machinery
802 Loss on exchange of equipment
803 Loss on exchange of ______
804 Loss on sale of notes
805 Loss on retirement of bonds
806 Loss on sale of investments
807 Loss on sale of machinery
808 Loss on ______
809 Unrealized gain—Income
810 Unrealized loss—Income
811 Impairment gain
812 Impairment loss

Clearing Accounts

901 Income summary
902 Manufacturing summary

MANAGERIAL ANALYSES AND REPORTS

① Cost Types

Variable costs:	Total cost changes in proportion to volume of activity
Fixed costs:	Total cost does not change in proportion to volume of activity
Mixed costs:	Cost consists of both a variable and a fixed element

② Cost Sources

Direct materials:	Raw materials costs directly linked to finished product
Direct labor:	Employee costs directly linked to finished product
Overhead:	Costs indirectly linked to finished product

③ Costing Systems

Job order costing:	Costs assigned to each unique unit or batch of units
Process costing:	Costs assigned to similar products that are mass-produced in a continuous manner

④ Costing Ratios

Contribution margin ratio = (Net sales − Variable costs)/Net sales
Predetermined overhead rate = Estimated overhead costs/Estimated activity base
Break-even point in units = Total fixed costs/Contribution margin per unit

⑤ Planning and Control Metrics

Cost variance = Actual cost − Standard (budgeted) cost
Sales (revenue) variance = Actual sales − Standard (budgeted) sales

⑥ Capital Budgeting

Payback period = Time expected to recover investment cost
Accounting rate of return = Expected annual net income/Average annual investment
Net present value (NPV) = Present value of future cash flows − Investment cost
NPV rule: 1. Compute net present value (NPV in $)
2. If NPV ≥ 0, then accept project; If NPV < 0, then reject project
Internal rate of return rule: 1. Compute internal rate of return (IRR in %)
2. If IRR ≥ hurdle rate, accept project; If IRR < hurdle rate, reject project

⑦ Costing Terminology

Relevant range:	Organization's normal range of operating activity.
Direct cost:	Cost incurred for the benefit of one cost object.
Indirect cost:	Cost incurred for the benefit of more than one cost object.
Product cost:	Cost that is necessary and integral to finished products.
Period cost:	Cost identified more with a time period than with finished products.
Overhead cost:	Cost not separately or directly traceable to a cost object.
Relevant cost:	Cost that is pertinent to a decision.
Opportunity cost:	Benefit lost by choosing an action from two or more alternatives.
Sunk cost:	Cost already incurred that cannot be avoided or changed.
Standard cost:	Cost computed using standard price and standard quantity.
Budget:	Formal statement of an organization's future plans.
Break-even point:	Sales level at which an organization earns zero profit.
Incremental cost:	Cost incurred only if the organization undertakes a certain action.
Transfer price:	Price on transactions between divisions within a company.

⑧ Standard Cost Variances

Total materials variance = Materials price variance + Materials quantity variance

Total labor variance = Labor (rate) variance + Labor efficiency (quantity) variance

Total overhead variance = Overhead controllable variance + Fixed overhead volume variance

Overhead controllable variance = Actual total overhead − Applied total overhead from flexible budget
Fixed overhead volume variance = Budgeted fixed overhead − Applied fixed overhead
Variable overhead variance = Variable overhead spending variance + Variable overhead efficiency variance
Fixed overhead variance = Fixed overhead spending variance + Fixed overhead volume variance
(Variable overhead variance and Fixed overhead variance) = Total overhead variance

Materials price variance = [AQ × AP] − [AQ × SP]
Materials quantity variance = [AQ × SP] − [SQ × SP]
Labor (rate) variance = [AH × AR] − [AH × SR]
Labor efficiency (quantity) variance = [AH × SR] − [SH × SR]

Variable overhead spending variance = [AH × AVR] − [AH × SVR]
Variable overhead efficiency variance = [AH × SVR] − [SH × SVR]
Fixed overhead spending variance = Actual fixed overhead − Budgeted fixed overhead

where AQ is actual quantity of materials; AP is actual price of materials; AH is actual hours of labor; AR is actual rate of wages; AVR is actual variable rate of overhead; SQ is standard quantity of materials; SP is standard price of materials; SH is standard hours of labor; SR is standard rate of wages; SVR is standard variable rate of overhead.

⑨ Sales Variances

Sales price variance = [AS × AP] − [AS × BP]
Sales volume variance = [AS × BP] − [BS × BP]

where AS = actual sales units; AP = actual sales price; BP = budgeted sales price; BS = budgeted sales units (fixed budget)

Manufacturing Statement
For *period* Ended *date*

Direct materials		
Raw materials inventory, Beginning	$	#
Raw materials purchases		#
Raw materials available for use		#
Raw materials inventory, Ending		(#)
Direct materials used		#
Direct labor		#
Overhead costs		
Total overhead costs		#
Total manufacturing costs		#
Add goods in process inventory, Beginning		#
Total cost of goods in process		#
Deduct goods in process inventory, Ending		(#)
Cost of goods manufactured	$	#

Contribution Margin Income Statement
For *period* Ended *date*

Net sales (revenues)	$	#
Total variable costs		#
Contribution margin		#
Total fixed costs		#
Net income	$	#

Flexible Budget
For *period* Ended *date*

	Flexible Budget: Variable Amount per Unit	Flexible Budget: Fixed Cost	Flexible Budget for Unit Sales of #
Sales (revenues)	$ #		$ #
Variable costs			
Examples: Direct materials, Direct labor,			
Other variable costs	#		#
Total variable costs	#		#
Contribution margin	$ #		#
Fixed costs			
Examples: Depreciation, Manager		$ #	#
salaries, Administrative salaries		#	#
Total fixed costs		$ #	#
Income from operations			$ #

Budget Performance Report*
For *period* Ended *date*

	Budget	Actual Performance	Variances†
Sales: In units	#	#	
In dollars	$ #	$ #	$ # F or U
Cost of sales			
Direct costs	#	#	# F or U
Indirect costs	#	#	# F or U
Selling expenses			
Examples: Commissions	#	#	# F or U
Shipping expenses	#	#	# F or U
General and administrative expenses			
Examples: Administrative salaries	#	#	# F or U
Total expenses	$ #	$ #	$ # F or U
Income from operations	$ #	$ #	$ # F or U

† F = Favorable variance; U = Unfavorable variance. * Applies to both flexible and fixed budgets.

Master Budget Sequence

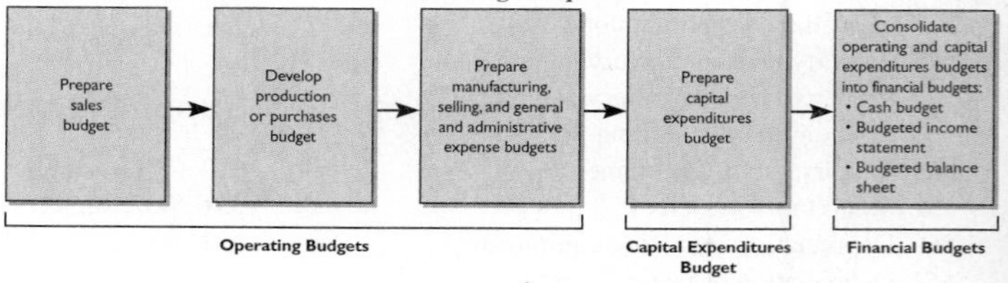

SELECTED TRANSACTIONS AND RELATIONS

① Merchandising Transactions Summary

	Merchandising Transactions	Merchandising Entries	Dr.	Cr.
Purchases	Purchasing merchandise for resale.	• Merchandise Inventory	#	
		Cash or Accounts Payable		#
	Paying freight costs on purchases; FOB shipping point.	• Merchandise Inventory	#	
		Cash		#
	Paying within discount period.	• Accounts Payable	#	
		Merchandise Inventory		#
		Cash		#
	Recording purchase returns or allowances.	• Cash or Accounts Payable	#	
		Merchandise Inventory		#
Sales	Selling merchandise.	• Cash or Accounts Receivable	#	
		Sales		#
		• Cost of Goods Sold..................	#	
		Merchandise Inventory		#
	Receiving payment within discount period.	• Cash	#	
		Sales Discounts	#	
		Accounts Receivable................		#
	Granting sales returns or allowances.	• Sales Returns and Allowances...........	#	
		Cash or Accounts Receivable		#
		• Merchandise Inventory	#	
		Cost of Goods Sold		#
	Paying freight costs on sales; FOB destination.	• Delivery Expense	#	
		Cash		#

	Merchandising Events	Adjusting and Closing Entries		
Adjusting	Adjusting due to shrinkage (occurs when recorded amount larger than physical inventory).	Cost of Goods Sold	#	
		Merchandise Inventory		#
Closing	Closing temporary accounts with credit balances.	Sales	#	
		Income Summary		#
	Closing temporary accounts with debit balances.	Income Summary	#	
		Sales Returns and Allowances		#
		Sales Discounts		#
		Cost of Goods Sold		#
		Delivery Expense		#
		"Other Expenses"		#

② Merchandising Cost Flows

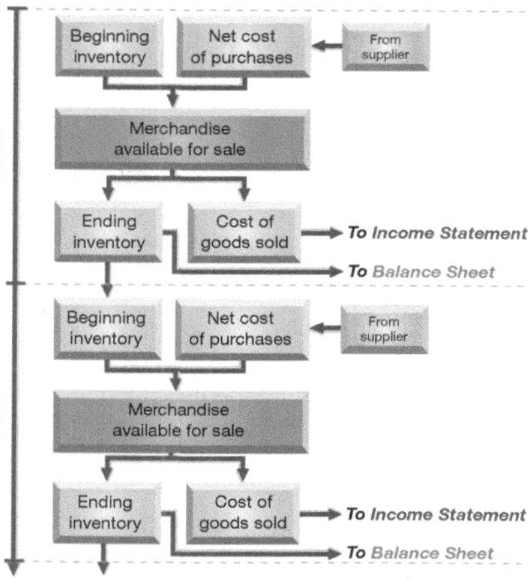

③ Credit Terms and Amounts

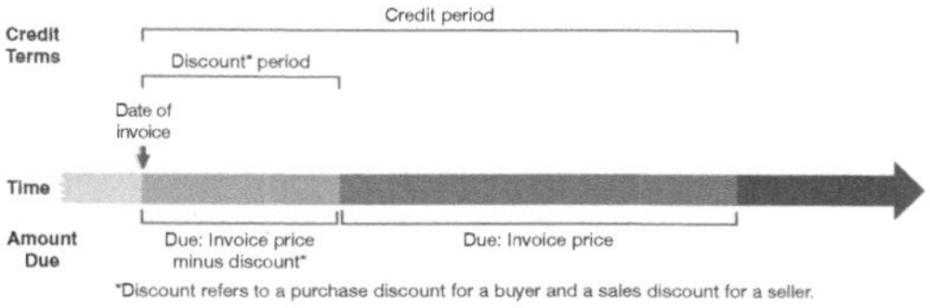

*Discount refers to a purchase discount for a buyer and a sales discount for a seller.

④ Bad Debts Estimation

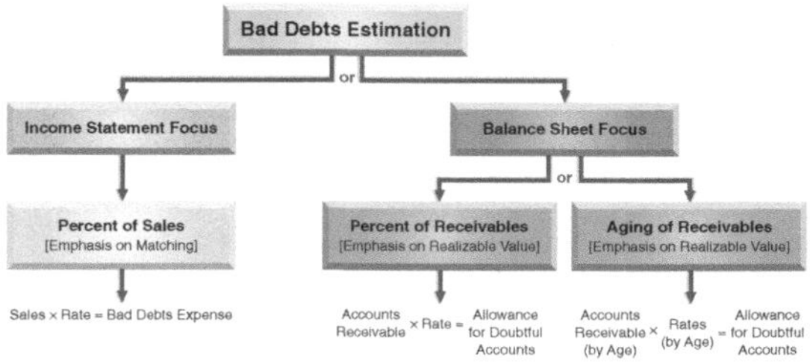

⑤ Bond Valuation

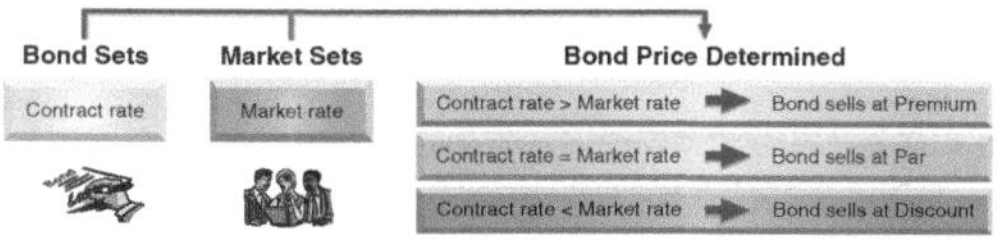

⑥ Stock Transactions Summary

	Stock Transactions	Stock Entries	Dr.	Cr.
Issue Common Stock	Issue par value common stock at par (par stock recorded at par).	Cash	#	
		Common Stock		#
	Issue par value common stock at premium (par stock recorded at par).	Cash	#	
		Common Stock		#
		Paid-In Capital in Excess of Par Value, Common Stock		#
	Issue no-par value common stock (no-par stock recorded at amount received).	Cash	#	
		Common Stock		#
	Issue stated value common stock at stated value (stated stock recorded at stated value).	Cash	#	
		Common stock		#
	Issue stated value common stock at premium (stated stock recorded at stated value).	Cash	#	
		Common stock		#
		Paid-In Capital in Excess of Stated Value, Common Stock		#
Issue Preferred Stock	Issue par value preferred stock at par (par stock recorded at par).	Cash	#	
		Preferred Stock		#
	Issue par value preferred stock at premium (par stock recorded at par).	Cash	#	
		Preferred Stock		#
		Paid-In Capital in Excess of Par Value, Preferred Stock		#
Reacquire Common Stock	Reacquire its own common stock (treasury stock recorded at cost).	Treasury Stock, Common	#	
		Cash		#
Reissue Common Stock	Reissue its treasury stock at cost (treasury stock removed at cost).	Cash	#	
		Treasury Stock, Common		#
	Reissue its treasury stock above cost (treasury stock removed at cost).	Cash	#	
		Treasury Stock, Common		#
		Paid-In Capital, Treasury		#
	Reissue its treasury stock below cost (treasury stock removed at cost; if paid-in capital is insufficient to cover amount below cost, retained earnings is debited for remainder).	Cash	#	
		Paid-In Capital, Treasury............	#	
		Retained Earnings (if necessary)	#	
		Treasury Stock, Common		#

⑦ Dividend Transactions

Account Affected	Type of Dividend: Cash Dividend	Stock Dividend	Stock Split
Cash	Decrease	—	—
Common Stock	—	Increase	—
Retained Earnings ..	Decrease	Decrease	—

⑧ A Rose by Any Other Name

The same financial statement sometimes receives different titles. Following are some of the more common aliases.*

Balance Sheet	Statement of Financial Position Statement of Financial Condition
Income Statement	Statement of Income Operating Statement Statement of Operations Statement of Operating Activity Earnings Statement Statement of Earnings Profit and Loss (P&L) Statement
Statement of Cash Flows	Statement of Cash Flow Cash Flows Statement Statement of Changes in Cash Position Statement of Changes in Financial Position
Statement of Stockholders' Equity	Statement of Shareholders' Equity Statement of Changes in Shareholders' Equity Statement of Stockholders' Equity and Comprehensive Income Statement of Changes in Owner's Equity Statement of Changes in Owner's Capital Statement of Changes in Capital Accounts

*The term **Consolidated** often precedes or follows these statement titles to reflect the combination of different entities, such as a parent company and its subsidiaries.

FUNDAMENTALS

① **Accounting Equation**

Assets		=	Liabilities		+	Equity	
↑ Debit for increases	↓ Credit for decreases		↓ Debit for decreases	↑ Credit for increases		↓ Debit for decreases	↑ Credit for increases

Contributed Capital* + Retained Earnings

Common Stock		−	Dividends		+	Revenues		−	Expenses	
Dr. for decreases	Cr. for increases		Dr. for increases	Cr. for decreases		Dr. for decreases	Cr. for increases		Dr. for increases	Cr. for decreases

Indicates normal balance.

*Includes common stock and any preferred stock.

② **Accounting Cycle**

③ **Adjustments and Entries**

Type	Adjusting Entry	
Prepaid Expenses	Dr. Expense	Cr. Asset*
Unearned Revenues	Dr. Liability	Cr. Revenue
Accrued Expenses	Dr. Expense	Cr. Liability
Accrued Revenues	Dr. Asset	Cr. Revenue

*For depreciation, credit Accumulated Depreciation (contra asset).

④ **4-Step Closing Process**

1. Transfer revenue and gain account balances to Income Summary.
2. Transfer expense and loss account balances to Income Summary.
3. Transfer Income Summary balance to Retained Earnings.
4. Transfer Dividends balance to Retained Earnings.

⑤ **Accounting Concepts**

Characteristics	Assumptions	Principles	Constraints
Relevance	Business entity	Measurement (historical cost)	Cost-benefit
Reliability	Going concern	Revenue recognition	Materiality
Comparability	Monetary unit	Expense recognition	Industry practice
Consistency	Periodicity	Full disclosure	Conservatism

⑥ **Ownership of Inventory**

	Ownership Transfers When Goods Passed To	Transportation Costs Paid By
FOB Shipping Point	Carrier	Buyer
FOB Destination	Buyer	Seller

⑦ **Inventory Costing Methods**

- Specific identification
- First-in, first-out (FIFO)
- Weighted-average
- Last-in, first-out (LIFO)

⑧ **Depreciation and Depletion**

Straight-line: $\frac{\text{Cost} - \text{Salvage value}}{\text{Useful life in periods}} \times \text{Periods expired}$

Units-of-production: $\frac{\text{Cost} - \text{Salvage value}}{\text{Useful life in units}} \times \text{Units produced}$

Declining-balance: Rate* × Beginning-of-period book value

*Rate is often double the straight-line rate, or 2 × (1/Useful life)

Depletion: $\frac{\text{Cost} - \text{Salvage value}}{\text{Total capacity in units}} \times \text{Units extracted}$

⑨ **Interest Computation**

Interest = Principal (face) × Rate × Time

⑩ **Accounting for Investment Securities**

Classification*	Accounting
Short-Term Investment in Securities	
Held-to-maturity (debt) securities	**Cost** (without any discount or premium amortization)
Trading (debt and equity) securities	**Fair value** (with fair value adjustment to income)
Available-for-sale (debt and equity) securities	**Fair value** (with fair value adjustment to equity)
Long-Term Investment in Securities	
Held-to-maturity (debt) securities	**Cost** (with any discount or premium amortization)
Available-for-sale (debt and equity) securities	**Fair value** (with fair value adjustment to equity)
Equity securities with significant influence	Equity method
Equity securities with controlling influence	Equity method (with consolidation)

*A *fair value option* allows companies to report HTM and AFS securities much like trading securities.

ANALYSES

① **Liquidity and Efficiency**

Current ratio $= \frac{\text{Current assets}}{\text{Current liabilities}}$ pp. 117 & 575

Working capital = Current assets − Current liabilities p. 575

Acid-test ratio $= \frac{\text{Cash} + \text{Short-term investments} + \text{Current receivables}}{\text{Current liabilities}}$ pp. 178 & 576

Accounts receivable turnover $= \frac{\text{Net sales}}{\text{Average accounts receivable, net}}$ pp. 317 & 577

Credit risk ratio $= \frac{\text{Allowance for doubtful accounts}}{\text{Accounts receivable, net}}$ p. 317

Inventory turnover $= \frac{\text{Cost of goods sold}}{\text{Average inventory}}$ pp. 223 & 577

Days' sales uncollected $= \frac{\text{Accounts receivable, net}}{\text{Net sales}} \times 365^{*}$ p. 577

Days' sales in inventory $= \frac{\text{Ending inventory}}{\text{Cost of goods sold}} \times 365^{*}$ pp. 223 & 578

Total asset turnover $= \frac{\text{Net sales}}{\text{Average total assets}}$ pp. 355 & 578

Plant asset useful life $= \frac{\text{Plant asset cost}}{\text{Depreciation expense}}$ p. 355

Plant asset age $= \frac{\text{Accumulated depreciation}}{\text{Depreciation expense}}$ p. 355

Days' cash expense coverage $= \frac{\text{Cash and cash equivalents}}{\text{Average daily cash expenses}}$ p. 264

*360 days is also commonly used.

② **Solvency**

Debt ratio $= \frac{\text{Total liabilities}}{\text{Total assets}}$ Equity ratio $= \frac{\text{Total equity}}{\text{Total assets}}$ pp. 69 & 583

Debt-to-equity $= \frac{\text{Total liabilities}}{\text{Total equity}}$ pp. 437 & 579

Times interest earned $= \frac{\text{Income before interest expense and income taxes}}{\text{Interest expense}}$ pp. 392 & 580

Cash coverage of growth $= \frac{\text{Cash flow from operations}}{\text{Cash outflow for plant assets}}$ p. 529

Cash coverage of debt $= \frac{\text{Cash flow from operations}}{\text{Total noncurrent liabilities}}$ p. 529

③ **Profitability**

Profit margin ratio $= \frac{\text{Net income}}{\text{Net sales}}$ p. 117

Gross margin ratio $= \frac{\text{Net sales} - \text{Cost of goods sold}}{\text{Net sales}}$ p. 178

Return on total assets $= \frac{\text{Net income}}{\text{Average total assets}}$ pp. 580 & 953

= Profit margin ratio × Total asset turnover p. 581

Return on common stockholders' equity $= \frac{\text{Net income} - \text{Preferred dividends}}{\text{Average common stockholders' equity}}$ p. 581

Book value per common share $= \frac{\text{Stockholders' equity applicable to common shares}}{\text{Number of common shares outstanding}}$ p. 486

Basic earnings per share $= \frac{\text{Net income} - \text{Preferred dividends}}{\text{Weighted-average common shares outstanding}}$ p. 485

Cash flow on total assets $= \frac{\text{Cash flow from operations}}{\text{Average total assets}}$ p. 528

Payout ratio $= \frac{\text{Cash dividends declared on common stock}}{\text{Net income}}$ p. 486

④ **Market**

Price-earnings ratio $= \frac{\text{Market value (price) per share}}{\text{Earnings per share}}$ p. 485

Dividend yield $= \frac{\text{Annual cash dividends per share}}{\text{Market price per share}}$ pp. 486 & 582

Residual income = Net income − Target net income

Income Statement*
For *period* Ended *date*

Net sales (revenues)		$ #
Cost of goods sold (cost of sales)		#
Gross margin (gross profit)		#
Operating expenses		
Examples: Depreciation, salaries,	$ #	
wages, rent, utilities, interest,	#	
amortization, advertising, taxes	#	
Total operating expenses		#
Nonoperating gains and losses		#
Net income (net profit or earnings)		$ #

* A typical chart of accounts is at the end of the book and classifies all accounts by financial statement categories.

Balance Sheet
Date

ASSETS

Current assets		
Examples: Cash, Cash equivalents, Short-term investments,		
Accounts receivable, Current portion of notes	$ #	
receivable, Inventory, Prepaid expenses	#	
Total current assets		$ #
Long-term investments		
Examples: Investment in stock, Investment in bonds,	#	
Land for expansion	#	
Total long-term investments		#
Plant assets		
Examples: Equipment, Machinery, Buildings, Land	#	
Total plant assets, net of depreciation		#
Intangible assets		
Examples: Patent, Trademark, Copyright, License, Goodwill	#	
Total intangible assets, net of amortization		#
Total assets		$ #

LIABILITIES AND EQUITY

Current liabilities		
Examples: Accounts payable, Wages payable, Salaries	$ #	
payable, Current notes payable, Taxes payable,	#	
Interest payable, Unearned revenues	#	
Total current liabilities		$ #
Long-term liabilities		
Examples: Notes payable, Bonds payable, Lease liability	#	
Total long-term liabilities		#
Total liabilities		#
Equity		
Common stock		#
Paid-in capital in excess of par or stated value		#
Retained earnings		#
Less treasury stock		(#)
Total liabilities and equity		$ #

Statement of Cash Flows
For *period* Ended *date*

Cash flows from operating activities	
[Prepared using the indirect (see below)† or direct method]	
Net cash provided (used) by operating activities	$ #
Cash flows from investing activities	
[List of individual investing inflows and outflows]	
Net cash provided (used) by investing activities	#
Cash flows from financing activities	
[List of individual financing inflows and outflows]	
Net cash provided (used) by financing activities	#
Net increase (decrease) in cash	$ #
Cash (and equivalents) balance at beginning of period	#
Cash (and equivalents) balance at end of period	$ #

Attach separate schedule or note disclosure of "Noncash investing and financing transactions."

†Indirect Method: Cash Flows from Operating Activities

Cash flows from operating activities		
Net income		$ #
Add: Decreases in noncash current assets	$ #	
Increases in current liabilities	#	
Expenses with no cash outflows (examples: depreciation, and amortization of both intangibles and bond discounts)	#	
Nonoperating losses (examples: losses from asset sales and from debt retirements)	#	#
Less: Increases in noncash current assets	#	
Decreases in current liabilities	#	
Revenues with no cash inflows (examples: amortization of bond premiums)	#	
Nonoperating gains (examples: gains from asset sales and from debt retirements)	#	#
Net cash provided (used) by operating activities		$ #

Statement of Retained Earnings
For *period* Ended *date*

Retained earnings, beginning	$ #
Add: Net income	#
	#
Less: Dividends declared	#
Retained earnings, ending	$ #

Statement of Stockholders' Equity†
For *period* Ended *date*

	Common Stock	Capital in Excess of Par	Retained Earnings	Treasury Stock	Total
Balances, beginning	$ #	$ #	$ #	$ #	$ #
Net income	⋮	⋮	⋮	⋮	⋮
Cash dividends	⋮	⋮	⋮	⋮	⋮
Stock issuance	⋮	⋮	⋮	⋮	⋮
Treasury stock purchase	⋮	⋮	⋮	⋮	⋮
Treasury stock reissuance	⋮	⋮	⋮	⋮	⋮
Other	⋮	⋮	⋮	⋮	⋮
Balances, ending	$ #	$ #	$ #	$ #	$ #

† Additional columns and account titles commonly include number of shares, preferred stock, unrealized gains and losses on available-for-sale securities, foreign currency translation, and comprehensive income.

Premium Bond Amortization (Straight-Line) Table†

Semiannual Period-End	Unamortized Bond Premium*	Bond Carrying Value**
Bond life-start	$ #	$ #
....	⋮	⋮
....	⋮	⋮
Bond life-end	0	par

† Bond carrying value is adjusted to par and its amortized premium to zero over the bond life (note: carrying value less unamortized bond premium equals par).
* Equals total bond premium less its accumulated amortization.
** Equals bond par value plus its unamortized bond premium.

Discount Bond Amortization (Straight-Line) Table†

Semiannual Period-End	Unamortized Bond Discount*	Bond Carrying Value**
Bond life-start	$ #	$ #
....	⋮	⋮
....	⋮	⋮
Bond life-end	0	par

† Bond carrying value is adjusted to par and its amortized discount to zero over the bond life (note: unamortized bond discount plus carrying value equals par).
* Equals total bond discount less its accumulated amortization.
** Equals bond par value less its unamortized bond discount.

Effective Interest Amortization Table for Bonds with Semiannual Interest Payment

Semiannual Interest Period-End	Cash Interest Paid[A]	Bond Interest Expense[B]	Discount or Premium Amortization[C]	Unamortized Discount or Premium[D]	Carrying Value[E]
#	#	#	#	#	#
⋮	⋮	⋮	⋮	⋮	⋮

[A] Par value multiplied by the semiannual contract rate.
[B] Prior period's carrying value multiplied by the semiannual market rate.
[C] The difference between interest paid and bond interest expense.
[D] Prior period's unamortized discount or premium less the current period's discount or premium amortization.
[E] Par value less unamortized discount or plus unamortized premium.

Installment Notes Payment Table

Period Ending Date	Beginning Balance	Payments: *Debit* Interest Expense	+	Payments: *Debit* Notes Payable	=	*Credit* Cash	Ending Balance
#	#	#		#		#	#
⋮	⋮	⋮		⋮		⋮	⋮

Bank Reconciliation
Date

Bank statement balance	$#	Book balance	$#
Add: Unrecorded deposits	#	Add: Unrecorded bank credit memoranda	#
Bank errors understating the balance	#	Book errors understating the balance	#
	#		#
Less: Outstanding checks	#	Less: Unrecorded bank debit memoranda	#
Bank errors overstating the balance	#	Book errors overstating the balance	#
Adjusted bank balance	$#	**Adjusted book balance**	$#

Balances are equal (reconciled)